BOOKS BY HENRY KISSINGER

DIPLOMACY

OBSERVATIONS: Selected Speeches and Essays, 1982–1984

YEARS OF UPHEAVAL

FOR THE RECORD: Selected Statements, 1977–1980

WHITE HOUSE YEARS

AMERICAN FOREIGN POLICY: Three Essays

PROBLEMS OF NATIONAL STRATEGY: A Book of Readings (editor)

THE TROUBLED PARTNERSHIP: A Reappraisal of the Atlantic
    Alliance

THE NECESSITY FOR CHOICE: Prospects of American Foreign
    Policy

NUCLEAR WEAPONS AND FOREIGN POLICY

A WORLD RESTORED: Castlereagh, Metternich and the
    Restoration of Peace, 1812–1822

HENRY KISSINGER

DIPLOMACY

SIMON & SCHUSTER
New York   London   Toronto   Sydney   Tokyo   Singapore

SIMON & SCHUSTER
ROCKEFELLER CENTER
1230 AVENUE OF THE AMERICAS
NEW YORK, NEW YORK 10020

SIMON & SCHUSTER AND COLOPHON ARE REGISTERED TRADEMARKS
OF SIMON & SCHUSTER INC.
DESIGNED BY EVE METZ
PHOTO RESEARCH BY NATALIE GOLDSTEIN
MAPS BY ANITA KARL, JAMES KEMP/COMPASS PROJECTIONS
MANUFACTURED IN THE UNITED STATES OF AMERICA

1   3   5   7   9   10   8   6   4   2

LIBRARY OF CONGRESS CATALOGING-IN-PUBLICATION DATA
KISSINGER, HENRY
DIPLOMACY/HENRY KISSINGER.
P.   CM.
INCLUDES BIBLIOGRAPHICAL REFERENCES AND INDEX.
1. DIPLOMACY.   2. UNITED STATES—FOREIGN RELATIONS ADMINISTRATION.
I. TITLE.
JX1662.K57   1994
327.73—DC20   93-44001
CIP
ISBN 0-671-65991-X

The title *Diplomacy* has been used before.
Both the author and the publisher pay tribute to the late
Sir Harold Nicolson's book (Harcourt, Brace & Company, 1939),
which was quite different in scope, intentions, and ideas.

A leatherbound signed first edition of this book
has been published by The Easton Press.

To the men and women of the Foreign Service of the United States of America, whose professionalism and dedication sustain American diplomacy

...As a very important source of strength & security, cherish public credit. One method of preserving it is to use it as sparingly as possible... occasions of expence by cultivating... that... prepare for danger... bursed... The... exertion... Debt... occasion... on... over... Beloved... of... their... tical... next... to have... bases... less inc... bears... selection... ways a choice of... decisive motive... construction of the conduct of the Government in making it, and for a spirit of acquiescence which the public exigencies may at any time dictate.

Observe good faith & justice towards all Nations; cultivate peace & harmony with all. Religion & morality enjoin this conduct; and can it be that good policy does not equally enjoin it? — It will be worthy of a free, enlightened, and, at no distant period, a great Nation, to give to mankind the magnanimous and too novel example of a People always guided by an exalted justice & benevolence. — Who can doubt that in the course of time and things, the fruits of such a plan would richly repay any temporary advantages which might be lost by a steady adherence to it? Can it be, that Providence has not connected the permanent felicity of a Nation with its virtue? — The experiment, at least, is recommended by every sentiment which ennobles human nature. — Alas! is it rendered impossible by its vices?

...per with domestic factions, to practice the arts of seduction, to mislead public opinion, to influence or awe the public councils! — Such an attachment of a smaller or weak, towards a great & powerful Nation, dooms the former to be the satellite of the latter. —

Against the insidious wiles of foreign influence the jealousy of a free people ought to be constantly awake, since history and experience prove that foreign influence is one of the most baneful foes of Republican Government. — But that jealousy to be useful must be impartial; else it becomes the instrument of the very influence to be avoided, instead of a defence against it. — Excessive partiality for one foreign nation and excessive dislike of another, cause those whom they actuate to see danger only on one side, and serve to veil and even second the arts of influence on the other. — Real Patriots, who may resist the intrigues of the favourite, are liable to become suspected and odious; while its tools and dupes usurp the applause & confidence of the people, to surrender their interests. —

The great rule of conduct for us, in regard to foreign Nations is to have with them as little political connection as possible. — So far as we have already formed engagements let them be fulfilled...

In offering to you, my Countrymen these counsels of an old and affectionate friend, I dare not hope they will make the strong and lasting impression, I could wish — that they will control the usual current of the passions, or prevent our Nation from running the course which has hitherto marked the Destiny of Nations: But if I may even flatter myself, that they may be productive of some partial benefit, some occasional good; that they may now & then recur to moderate the fury of party spirit, to warn against the mischiefs of foreign Intrigue, to guard against the Impostures of pretended patriotism — this hope will be a full recompence for the solicitude for your welfare, by which they have been dictated. —

How far in the discharge of my official duties, I have been guided by the principles which have been delineated, the public Records and other evidences of my conduct must witness to You and to the World. — To myself, the assurance of my own conscience is, that I have at least believed myself to be guided by them.

The duty of holding a neutral conduct may be inferred, without any thing more, from the obligation which justice and humanity impose on every Nation, in cases in which it is free to act, to maintain inviolate the relations of Peace and amity towards other Nations. —

The inducements of interest for observing that conduct will best be referred to your own reflections & experience. — With me, a predominant motive has been to endeavour to gain time to our country to settle & mature its yet recent institutions, and to progress without interruption, to that degree of strength & consistency, which is necessary to give it, humanly speaking, the command of its own fortunes. —

Though in reviewing the incidents of my Administration, I am unconscious of intentional error — I am nevertheless too sensible of my defects not to think it probable that I have committed many errors. — Whatever they may be I fervently beseech the Almighty to avert or mitigate the evils to which they may tend. I shall also carry with me the hope that my Country will never cease to view them with indulgence; and that after forty five years of my life dedicated to its service, with an upright zeal, the faults of incompetent abilities will be consigned to oblivion, as myself must soon be to the mansions of rest. — Relying on its kindness in this as in other things, and actuated by that fervent love towards it, which is so natural to a Man, who views in it the native soil of himself and his progenitors for several generations; I anticipate with pleasing expectation that retreat, in which I promise myself to realize, without alloy, the sweet enjoyment of partaking, in the midst of my fellow Citizens, the benign influence of good Laws under a free Government — the ever favourite object of my heart, and the happy reward, as I trust, of our mutual cares, labours and dangers.

United States
19th September 1796

G. Washington

CONTENTS

1   The New World Order   17

2   The Hinge: Theodore Roosevelt or Woodrow Wilson   29

3   From Universality to Equilibrium: Richelieu, William of Orange, and Pitt   56

4   The Concert of Europe: Great Britain, Austria, and Russia   78

5   Two Revolutionaries: Napoleon III and Bismarck   103

6   *Realpolitik* Turns on Itself   137

7   A Political Doomsday Machine: European Diplomacy Before the First World War   168

8   Into the Vortex: The Military Doomsday Machine   201

9   The New Face of Diplomacy: Wilson and the Treaty of Versailles   218

10   The Dilemmas of the Victors   246

11   Stresemann and the Re-emergence of the Vanquished   266

12   The End of Illusion: Hitler and the Destruction of Versailles   288

13   Stalin's Bazaar   332

14   The Nazi-Soviet Pact   350

15   America Re-enters the Arena: Franklin Delano Roosevelt   369

16   Three Approaches to Peace: Roosevelt, Stalin, and Churchill in World War II   394

17   The Beginning of the Cold War   423

18   The Success and the Pain of Containment   446

19   The Dilemma of Containment: The Korean War   473

20   Negotiating with the Communists: Adenauer, Churchill, and Eisenhower   493

21   Leapfrogging Containment: The Suez Crisis   522

22   Hungary: Upheaval in the Empire   550

CONTENTS

23 Khrushchev's Ultimatum: The Berlin Crisis 1958–63   568

24 Concepts of Western Unity: Macmillan, de Gaulle, Eisenhower, and Kennedy   594

25 Vietnam: Entry into the Morass; Truman and Eisenhower   620

26 Vietnam: On the Road to Despair; Kennedy and Johnson   643

27 Vietnam: The Extrication; Nixon   674

28 Foreign Policy as Geopolitics: Nixon's Triangular Diplomacy   703

29 Detente and Its Discontents   733

30 The End of the Cold War: Reagan and Gorbachev   762

31 The New World Order Reconsidered   804

NOTES   837

ACKNOWLEDGMENTS   873

INDEX   877

List of Illustrations

Page 6   Woodrow Wilson addresses the Paris Peace Conference, January 25, 1919.

Page 10   Washington's Farewell Address, manuscript detail. *Inset:* George Washington. Engraving after portrait by Gilbert Stuart.

Page 17   The United Nations General Assembly.

Page 29   *Left:* Theodore Roosevelt, August 1905. *Right:* Woodrow Wilson, July 1919.

Page 56   *Left:* William of Orange. *Right:* Cardinal Richelieu.

Page 78   Congress of Vienna, 1815.

Page 103   *Left:* Otto von Bismarck. *Right:* Napoleon III.

Page 137   Benjamin Disraeli.

Page 168   Emperor William II and Tsar Nicholas II.

Page 201   *Left to right:* Paul von Hindenburg, former Emperor William II, and Erich Ludendorff, 1917.

Page 218   *Left to right:* David Lloyd George, Vittorio Emmanuele Orlando, Georges Clemenceau, and Woodrow Wilson at Versailles, 1919.

Page 246   *Left to right:* Clemenceau, Wilson, Baron Sidney Sonnino, and Lloyd George after signing the Treaty of Versailles, June 28, 1919.

Page 266   Hans Luther, Aristide Briand, and Gustav Stresemann (*right*) with German delegates at the League of Nations.

Page 288   Adolf Hitler and Benito Mussolini in Munich, 1937.

Page 332   Joseph Stalin and aides at first session of Supreme Soviet. Deputies, from left: Nikolai Bulganin, Andrei Zhdanov, Stalin, Kliment Voroshilov and Nikita Khrushchev, January 26, 1938.

Page 350   Vyacheslav Molotov signs Russo-German Nonaggression Pact, August 1939. In background are Joachim von Ribbentrop and Stalin.

Page 369   Franklin Roosevelt and Winston Churchill during Atlantic Charter meeting, August 1941.

Page 394   Churchill, Roosevelt, and Stalin at Yalta, February 1945.

LIST OF ILLUSTRATIONS

Page 423   *Left:* Churchill, Truman, and Stalin at Potsdam, 1945. *Right:* Clement Attlee, Truman, and Stalin at Potsdam, August 1945.

Page 446   John Foster Dulles with dignitaries after signing the Austrian State Treaty, May 1955.

Page 473   Dulles at the Korean front, June 1950.

Page 493   Dwight D. Eisenhower and Churchill in London, 1959.

Page 522   Khrushchev and Gamal Abdel Nasser in Moscow, 1958.

Page 550   Hungarian street fighters during Budapest uprising, October 1956.

Page 568   John F. Kennedy and Khrushchev in Vienna, June 1961.

Page 594   *Left:* Kennedy and Harold Macmillan in Bermuda, December 1961. *Right:* Charles de Gaulle and Konrad Adenauer in Bonn.

Page 620   French infantry at Dien Bien Phu, April 1954.

Page 643   Lyndon B. Johnson, December 1965.

Page 674   Henry Kissinger and Le Duc Tho in Paris, January 1973.

Page 703   Leonid Brezhnev and Richard Nixon, June 1973.

Page 733   Gerald Ford with Anatoly Dobrynin (*left*) and Leonid Brezhnev (*right*) at Vladivostok, November 1974.

Page 762   Mikhail Gorbachev and Ronald Reagan in Geneva, November 1985.

Page 804   Flags of the United States, Great Britain, France, Germany, China, Russia, Japan.

List of Maps

Page 320   French Expansion from 1648 to 1801

Page 321   German Expansion from 1919 to 1939

Page 322   William III's Grand Alliance from 1701 to 1713

Page 323   Alliances in the 1950s

Page 324   Europe After the Congress of Vienna, 1815

Page 326   Europe on the Eve of the First World War, 1914

Page 328   The Cold War World from 1945 to 1989

Page 330   The Post–Cold War World

CHAPTER ONE

The New World Order

Almost as if according to some natural law, in every century there seems to emerge a country with the power, the will, and the intellectual and moral impetus to shape the entire international system in accordance with its own values. In the seventeenth century, France under Cardinal Richelieu introduced the modern approach to international relations, based on the nation-state and motivated by national interest as its ultimate purpose. In the eighteenth century, Great Britain elaborated the concept of the balance of power, which dominated European diplomacy for the next 200 years. In the nineteenth century, Metternich's Austria reconstructed the Concert of Europe and Bismarck's Germany dismantled it, reshaping European diplomacy into a cold-blooded game of power politics.

In the twentieth century, no country has influenced international relations as decisively and at the same time as ambivalently as the United States. No society has more firmly insisted on the inadmissibility of intervention in the domestic affairs of other states, or more passionately asserted that its own values were universally applicable. No nation has been more pragmatic in the day-to-day conduct of its diplomacy, or more ideological in the pursuit of its historic moral convictions. No country has been more reluctant to engage itself abroad even while undertaking alliances and commitments of unprecedented reach and scope.

The singularities that America has ascribed to itself throughout its history have produced two contradictory attitudes toward foreign policy. The first is that America serves its values best by perfecting democracy at home, thereby acting as a beacon for the rest of mankind; the second, that America's values impose on it an obligation to crusade for them around the world. Torn between nostalgia for a pristine past and yearning for a perfect future, American thought has oscillated between isolationism and commitment, though, since the end of the Second World War, the realities of interdependence have predominated.

Both schools of thought—of America as beacon and of America as crusader—envision as normal a global international order based on democracy, free commerce, and international law. Since no such system has ever existed, its evocation often appears to other societies as utopian, if not naïve. Still, foreign skepticism never dimmed the idealism of Woodrow Wilson, Franklin Roosevelt, or Ronald Reagan, or indeed of all other twentieth-century American presidents. If anything, it has spurred America's faith that history can be overcome and that if the world truly wants peace, it needs to apply America's moral prescriptions.

Both schools of thought were products of the American experience. Though other republics have existed, none had been consciously created to vindicate the idea of liberty. No other country's population had chosen to head for a new continent and tame its wilderness in the name of freedom and prosperity for all. Thus the two approaches, the isolationist and the missionary, so contradictory on the surface, reflected a common underlying faith: that the United States possessed the world's best system of government, and that the rest of mankind could attain peace and prosperity by abandoning traditional diplomacy and adopting America's reverence for international law and democracy.

America's journey through international politics has been a triumph of faith over experience. Since the time America entered the arena of world politics in 1917, it has been so preponderant in strength and so convinced of the rightness of its ideals that this century's major international agreements have been embodiments of American values—from the League of Nations and the Kellogg-Briand Pact to the United Nations Charter and the Helsinki Final Act. The collapse of Soviet communism marked the intellectual vindication of American ideals and, ironically, brought America face to face with the kind of world it had been seeking to escape throughout its history. In the emerging international order, nationalism has gained a new lease on life. Nations have pursued self-interest more frequently than high-minded principle, and have competed more than they have cooperated. There is little evidence to suggest that this age-old mode of behavior has changed, or that it is likely to change in the decades ahead.

What *is* new about the emerging world order is that, for the first time, the United States can neither withdraw from the world nor dominate it. America cannot change the way it has perceived its role throughout its history, nor should it want to. When America entered the international arena, it was young and robust and had the power to make the world conform to its vision of international relations. By the end of the Second World War in 1945, the United States was so powerful (at one point about 35 percent of the world's entire economic production was American) that it seemed as if it was destined to shape the world according to its preferences.

John F. Kennedy declared confidently in 1961 that America was strong enough to "pay any price, bear any burden" to ensure the success of liberty. Three decades later, the United States is in less of a position to insist on the immediate realization of all its desires. Other countries have grown into Great Power status. The United States now faces the challenge of reaching its goals in stages, each of which is an amalgam of American values and geopolitical necessities. One of the new necessities is that a world comprising several states of comparable strength must base its order on some concept of equilibrium—an idea with which the United States has never felt comfortable.

When American thinking on foreign policy and European diplomatic traditions encountered each other at the Paris Peace Conference of 1919, the differences in historical experience became dramatically evident. The European leaders sought to refurbish the existing system according to familiar methods; the American peacemakers believed that the Great War had resulted not from intractable geopolitical conflicts but from flawed European practices. In his famous Fourteen Points, Woodrow Wilson told the Europeans that, henceforth, the international system should be based not on the balance of power but on ethnic self-determination, that their security should depend not on military alliances but on collective security, and that their diplomacy should no longer be conducted secretly by experts but on the basis of "open agreements, openly arrived at." Clearly, Wilson had come not so much to discuss the terms for ending a war or

19

for restoring the existing international order, as he had to recast a whole system of international relations as it had been practiced for nearly three centuries.

For as long as Americans have been reflecting on foreign policy, they have ascribed Europe's travails to the balance-of-power system. And since the time Europe first had to concern itself with American foreign policy, its leaders have looked askance at America's self-appointed mission of global reform. Each side has behaved as if the other had freely chosen its mode of diplomatic behavior and could have, were it wiser or less bellicose, selected some other, more agreeable, method.

In fact, both the American and the European approaches to foreign policy were the products of their own unique circumstances. Americans inhabited a nearly empty continent shielded from predatory powers by two vast oceans and with weak countries as neighbors. Since America confronted no power in need of being balanced, it could hardly have occupied itself with the challenges of equilibrium even if its leaders had been seized by the bizarre notion of replicating European conditions amidst a people who had turned their backs on Europe.

The anguishing dilemmas of security that tormented European nations did not touch America for nearly 150 years. When they did, America twice participated in the world wars which had been started by the nations of Europe. In each instance, by the time America got involved, the balance of power had already failed to operate, producing this paradox: that the balance of power, which most Americans disdained, in fact assured American security as long as it functioned as it was designed; and that it was its breakdown that drew America into international politics.

The nations of Europe did not choose the balance of power as the means for regulating their relations out of innate quarrelsomeness or an Old World love of intrigue. If the emphasis on democracy and international law was the product of America's unique sense of security, European diplomacy had been forged in the school of hard knocks.

Europe was thrown into balance-of-power politics when its first choice, the medieval dream of universal empire, collapsed and a host of states of more or less equal strength arose from the ashes of that ancient aspiration. When a group of states so constituted are obliged to deal with one another, there are only two possible outcomes: either one state becomes so strong that it dominates all the others and creates an empire, or no state is ever quite powerful enough to achieve that goal. In the latter case, the pretensions of the most aggressive member of the international community are kept in check by a combination of the others; in other words, by the operation of a balance of power.

The balance-of-power system did not purport to avoid crises or even wars. When working properly, it was meant to limit both the ability of states to dominate others and the scope of conflicts. Its goal was not peace so much as stability and moderation. By definition, a balance-of-power arrangement cannot satisfy every member of the international system completely; it works best when it keeps dissatisfaction below the level at which the aggrieved party will seek to overthrow the international order.

Theorists of the balance of power often leave the impression that it is the natural form of international relations. In fact, balance-of-power systems have existed only rarely in human history. The Western Hemisphere has never known one, nor has the territory of contemporary China since the end of the period of the warring states, over 2,000 years ago. For the greatest part of humanity and the longest periods of history, empire has been the typical mode of government. Empires have no interest in operating within an international system; they aspire to *be* the international system. Empires have no need for a balance of power. That is how the United States has conducted its foreign policy in the Americas, and China through most of its history in Asia.

In the West, the only examples of functioning balance-of-power systems were among the city-states of ancient Greece and Renaissance Italy, and the European state system which arose out of the Peace of Westphalia in 1648. The distinguishing feature of these systems was to elevate a fact of life—the existence of a number of states of substantially equal strength —into a guiding principle of world order.

Intellectually, the concept of the balance of power reflected the convictions of all the major political thinkers of the Enlightenment. In their view, the universe, including the political sphere, operated according to rational principles which balanced each other. Seemingly random acts by reasonable men would, in their totality, tend toward the common good, though the proof of this proposition was elusive in the century of almost constant conflict that followed the Thirty Years' War.

Adam Smith, in *The Wealth of Nations,* maintained that an "invisible hand" would distill general economic well-being out of selfish individual economic actions. In *The Federalist Papers,* Madison argued that, in a large enough republic, the various political "factions" selfishly pursuing their own interests would, by a kind of automatic mechanism, forge a proper domestic harmony. The concepts of the separation of powers and of checks and balances, as conceived by Montesquieu and embodied in the American Constitution, reflected an identical view. The purpose of the separation of powers was to avoid despotism, not to achieve harmonious government; each branch of the government, in the pursuit of its own

21

interests, would restrain excess and thereby serve the common good. The same principles were applied to international affairs. By pursuing its own selfish interests, each state was presumed to contribute to progress, as if some unseen hand were guaranteeing that freedom of choice for each state assured well-being for all.

For over a century, this expectation seemed to be fulfilled. After the dislocations caused by the French Revolution and the Napoleonic Wars, the leaders of Europe restored the balance of power at the Congress of Vienna in 1815 and softened the brutal reliance on power by seeking to moderate international conduct through moral and legal bonds. Yet by the end of the nineteenth century, the European balance-of-power system returned to the principles of power politics and in a far more unforgiving environment. Facing down the adversary became the standard method of diplomacy, leading to one test of strength after another. Finally, in 1914, a crisis arose from which no one shrank. Europe never fully recovered world leadership after the catastrophe of the First World War. The United States emerged as the dominant player but Woodrow Wilson soon made it clear that his country refused to play by European rules.

At no time in its history has America participated in a balance-of-power system. Before the two world wars, America benefited from the operation of the balance of power without being involved in its maneuvers, and while enjoying the luxury of castigating it at will. During the Cold War, America was engaged in an ideological, political, and strategic struggle with the Soviet Union in which a two-power world operated according to principles quite different from those of a balance-of-power system. In a two-power world, there can be no pretense that conflict leads to the common good; any gain for one side is a loss for the other. Victory without war was in fact what America achieved in the Cold War, a victory which has now obliged it to confront the dilemma described by George Bernard Shaw: "There are two tragedies in life. One is to lose your heart's desire. The other is to gain it."

American leaders have taken their values so much for granted that they rarely recognize how revolutionary and unsettling these values can appear to others. No other society has asserted that the principles of ethical conduct apply to international conduct in the same way that they do to the individual—a notion that is the exact opposite of Richelieu's *raison d'état*. America has maintained that the prevention of war is as much a legal as a diplomatic challenge, and that what it resists is not change as such but the method of change, especially the use of force. A Bismarck or a Disraeli would have ridiculed the proposition that foreign policy is about method rather than substance, if indeed he had understood it. No nation has ever imposed the moral demands on itself that America has. And no country has so tormented itself over the gap between its moral values, which are by definition absolute, and the imperfection inherent in the concrete situations to which they must be applied.

During the Cold War, the unique American approach to foreign policy was remarkably appropriate to the challenge at hand. There was a deep ideological conflict, and only one country, the United States, possessed the full panoply of means—political, economic, and military—to organize the defense of the noncommunist world. A nation in such a position is able to insist on its views and can often avoid the problem facing the statesmen of less favored societies: that their means oblige them to pursue goals less ambitious than their hopes, and that their circumstances require them to approach even those goals in stages.

In the Cold War world, the traditional concepts of power had substantially broken down. Most of history has displayed a synthesis of military, political, and economic strength, which in general has proved to be symmetrical. In the Cold War period, the various elements of power became quite distinct. The former Soviet Union was a military superpower and at the same time an economic dwarf. It was also possible for a country to be an economic giant but to be militarily irrelevant, as was the case with Japan.

In the post–Cold War world, the various elements are likely to grow more congruent and more symmetrical. The relative military power of the United States will gradually decline. The absence of a clear-cut adversary will produce domestic pressure to shift resources from defense to other priorities—a process which has already started. When there is no longer a single threat and each country perceives its perils from its own national perspective, those societies which had nestled under American protection will feel compelled to assume greater responsibility for their own security. Thus, the operation of the new international system will move toward equilibrium even in the military field, though it may take some decades to reach that point. These tendencies will be even more pronounced in economics, where American predominance is already declining, and where it has become safer to challenge the United States.

The international system of the twenty-first century will be marked by a seeming contradiction: on the one hand, fragmentation; on the other, growing globalization. On the level of the relations among states, the new order will be more like the European state system of the eighteenth and nineteenth centuries than the rigid patterns of the Cold War. It will contain at least six major powers—the United States, Europe, China, Japan, Russia, and probably India—as well as a multiplicity of medium-sized and smaller countries. At the same time, international relations have become truly global for the first time. Communications are instantaneous; the world economy operates on all continents simultaneously. A whole set of issues has surfaced that can only be dealt with on a worldwide basis, such as nuclear proliferation, the environment, the population explosion, and economic interdependence.

For America, reconciling differing values and very different historical experiences among countries of comparable significance will be a novel experience and a major departure from either the isolation of the last century or the *de facto* hegemony of the Cold War, in ways which this book seeks to illuminate. Equally, the other major players are facing difficulties in adjusting to the emerging world order.

Europe, the only part of the modern world ever to operate a multistate system, invented the concepts of the nation-state, sovereignty, and the balance of power. These ideas dominated international affairs for the better part of three centuries. But none of Europe's erstwhile practitioners of *raison d'état* are now strong enough to act as principals in the emerging international order. They are attempting to compensate for this relative weakness by creating a unified Europe, an effort which absorbs much of their energies. But even if they were to succeed, no automatic guidelines for the conduct of a unified Europe on the global stage would be at hand, since such a political entity has never existed before.

Throughout its history, Russia has been a special case. It arrived late on the European scene—well after France and Great Britain had been consolidated—and none of the traditional principles of European diplomacy seemed to apply to it. Bordering on three different cultural spheres —Europe, Asia, and the Muslim world—Russia contained populations of each, and hence was never a national state in the European sense. Constantly changing shape as its rulers annexed contiguous territories, Russia was an empire out of scale in comparison with any of the European countries. Moreover, with every new conquest, the character of the state changed as it incorporated another brand-new, restive, non-Russian ethnic group. This was one of the reasons Russia felt obliged to maintain huge armies whose size was unrelated to any plausible threat to its external security.

Torn between obsessive insecurity and proselytizing zeal, between the requirements of Europe and the temptations of Asia, the Russian Empire always had a role in the European equilibrium but was never emotionally a part of it. The requirements of conquest and of security became merged in the minds of Russian leaders. Since the Congress of Vienna, the Russian Empire has placed its military forces on foreign soil more often than any other major power. Analysts frequently explain Russian expansionism as stemming from a sense of insecurity. But Russian writers have far more often justified Russia's outward thrust as a messianic vocation. Russia on the march rarely showed a sense of limits; thwarted, it tended to withdraw into sullen resentment. For most of its history, Russia has been a cause looking for opportunity.

Postcommunist Russia finds itself within borders which reflect no historical precedent. Like Europe, it will have to devote much of its energy to redefining its identity. Will it seek to return to its historical rhythm and restore the lost empire? Will it shift its center of gravity eastward and become a more active participant in Asian diplomacy? By what principles and methods will it react to the upheavals around its borders, especially in the volatile Middle East? Russia will always be essential to world order and, in the inevitable turmoil associated with answering these questions, a potential menace to it.

China too faces a world order that is new to it. For 2,000 years, the Chinese Empire had united its world under a single imperial rule. To be sure, that rule had faltered at times. Wars occurred in China no less frequently than they did in Europe. But since they generally took place among contenders for the imperial authority, they were more in the nature of civil rather than international wars, and, sooner or later, invariably led to the emergence of some new central power.

Before the nineteenth century, China never had a neighbor capable of contesting its pre-eminence and never imagined that such a state could arise. Conquerors from abroad overthrew Chinese dynasties, only to be absorbed into Chinese culture to such an extent that they continued the traditions of the Middle Kingdom. The notion of the sovereign equality of states did not exist in China; outsiders were considered barbarians and were relegated to a tributary relationship—that was how the first British envoy to Beijing was received in the eighteenth century. China disdained sending ambassadors abroad but was not above using distant barbarians to overcome the ones nearby. Yet this was a strategy for emergencies, not a day-to-day operational system like the European balance of power, and it failed to produce the sort of permanent diplomatic establishment characteristic of Europe. After China became a humiliated subject of European colonialism in the nineteenth century, it re-emerged only recently —since the Second World War—into a multipolar world unprecedented in its history.

Japan had also cut itself off from all contact with the outside world. For 500 years before it was forcibly opened by Commodore Matthew Perry in 1854, Japan did not even deign to balance the barbarians off against each other or to invent tributary relationships, as the Chinese had. Closed off from the outside world, Japan prided itself on its unique customs, gratified its military tradition by civil war, and rested its internal structure on the conviction that its unique culture was impervious to foreign influence, superior to it, and, in the end, would defeat it rather than absorb it.

In the Cold War, when the Soviet Union was the dominant security threat, Japan was able to identify its foreign policy with America, thousands of miles away. The new world order, with its multiplicity of challenges, will almost certainly oblige a country with so proud a past to re-examine its reliance on a single ally. Japan is bound to become more sensitive to the Asian balance of power than is possible for America, in a different hemisphere and facing in three directions—across the Atlantic, across the Pacific, and toward South America. China, Korea, and Southeast Asia will acquire quite a different significance for Japan than for the United States, and will inaugurate a more autonomous and more self-reliant Japanese foreign policy.

As for India, which is now emerging as the major power in South Asia, its foreign policy is in many ways the last vestige of the heyday of European imperialism, leavened by the traditions of an ancient culture. Before the arrival of the British, the subcontinent had not been ruled as a single political unit for millennia. British colonization was accomplished with small military forces because, at first, the local population saw these as the replacement of one set of conquerors by another. But after it established unified rule, the British Empire was undermined by the very values of popular government and cultural nationalism it had imported into India. Yet, as a nation-state, India is a newcomer. Absorbed by the struggle to feed its vast population, India dabbled in the Nonaligned movement during the Cold War. But it has yet to assume a role commensurate with its size on the international political stage.

Thus, in effect, none of the most important countries which must build a new world order have had any experience with the multistate system that is emerging. Never before has a new world order had to be assembled from so many different perceptions, or on so global a scale. Nor has any previous order had to combine the attributes of the historic balance-of-power systems with global democratic opinion and the exploding technology of the contemporary period.

In retrospect, all international systems appear to have an inevitable symmetry. Once they are established, it is difficult to imagine how history might have evolved had other choices been made, or indeed whether any other choices had been possible. When an international order first comes into being, many choices may be open to it. But each choice constricts

26

the universe of remaining options. Because complexity inhibits flexibility, early choices are especially crucial. Whether an international order is relatively stable, like the one that emerged from the Congress of Vienna, or highly volatile, like those that emerged from the Peace of Westphalia and the Treaty of Versailles, depends on the degree to which they reconcile what makes the constituent societies feel secure with what they consider just.

The two international systems that were the most stable—that of the Congress of Vienna and the one dominated by the United States after the Second World War—had the advantage of uniform perceptions. The statesmen at Vienna were aristocrats who saw intangibles in the same way, and agreed on fundamentals; the American leaders who shaped the postwar world emerged from an intellectual tradition of extraordinary coherence and vitality.

The order that is now emerging will have to be built by statesmen who represent vastly different cultures. They run huge bureaucracies of such complexity that, often, the energy of these statesmen is more consumed by serving the administrative machinery than by defining a purpose. They rise to eminence by means of qualities that are not necessarily those needed to govern, and are even less suited to building an international order. And the only available model of a multistate system was one built by Western societies, which many of the participants may reject.

Yet the rise and fall of previous world orders based on many states—from the Peace of Westphalia to our time—is the only experience on which one can draw in trying to understand the challenges facing contemporary statesmen. The study of history offers no manual of instructions that can be applied automatically; history teaches by analogy, shedding light on the likely consequences of comparable situations. But each generation must determine for itself which circumstances are in fact comparable.

Intellectuals analyze the operations of international systems; statesmen build them. And there is a vast difference between the perspective of an analyst and that of a statesman. The analyst can choose which problem he wishes to study, whereas the statesman's problems are imposed on him. The analyst can allot whatever time is necessary to come to a clear conclusion; the overwhelming challenge to the statesman is the pressure of time. The analyst runs no risk. If his conclusions prove wrong, he can write another treatise. The statesman is permitted only one guess; his mistakes are irretrievable. The analyst has available to him all the facts; he will be judged on his intellectual power. The statesman must act on assessments that cannot be proved at the time that he is making them; he will be judged by history on the basis of how wisely he managed the inevitable change and, above all, by how well he preserves the peace. That is why examining how statesmen have dealt with the problem of world order—what worked or failed and why—is not the end of understanding contemporary diplomacy, though it may be its beginning.

CHAPTER TWO

The Hinge:
Theodore Roosevelt or
Woodrow Wilson

Until early in this century, the isolationist tendency prevailed in American foreign policy. Then, two factors projected America into world affairs: its rapidly expanding power, and the gradual collapse of the international system centered on Europe. Two watershed presidencies marked this progression: Theodore Roosevelt's and Woodrow Wilson's. These men held the reins of government when world affairs were drawing a reluctant nation into their vortex. Both recognized that America had a crucial role to play in world affairs though they justified its emergence from isolation with opposite philosophies.

Roosevelt was a sophisticated analyst of the balance of power. He insisted on an international role for America because its national interest demanded it, and because a global balance of power was inconceivable to him without American participation. For Wilson, the justification of America's international role was messianic: America had an obligation, not to the balance of power, but to spread its principles throughout the world. During the Wilson Administration, America emerged as a key player in world affairs, proclaiming principles which, while reflecting the truisms of American thought, nonetheless marked a revolutionary departure for Old World diplomats. These principles held that peace depends on the spread of democracy, that states should be judged by the same ethical criteria as individuals, and that the national interest consists of adhering to a universal system of law.

To hardened veterans of a European diplomacy based on the balance of power, Wilson's views about the ultimately moral foundations of foreign policy appeared strange, even hypocritical. Yet Wilsonianism has survived while history has bypassed the reservations of his contemporaries. Wilson was the originator of the vision of a universal world organization, the League of Nations, which would keep the peace through collective security rather than alliances. Though Wilson could not convince his own country of its merit, the idea lived on. It is above all to the drumbeat of Wilsonian idealism that American foreign policy has marched since his watershed presidency, and continues to march to this day.

America's singular approach to international affairs did not develop all at once, or as the consequence of a solitary inspiration. In the early years of the Republic, American foreign policy was in fact a sophisticated reflection of the American national interest, which was, simply, to fortify the new nation's independence. Since no European country was capable of posing an actual threat so long as it had to contend with rivals, the Founding Fathers showed themselves quite ready to manipulate the despised balance of power when it suited their needs; indeed, they could be extraordinarily skillful at maneuvering between France and Great Britain not only to preserve America's independence but to enlarge its frontiers. Because they really wanted neither side to win a decisive victory in the wars of the French Revolution, they declared neutrality. Jefferson defined the Napoleonic Wars as a contest between the tyrant on the land (France) and the tyrant of the ocean (England)[1]—in other words, the parties in the European struggle were morally equivalent. Practicing an early form of nonalignment, the new nation discovered the benefit of neutrality as a bargaining tool, just as many an emerging nation has since.

At the same time, the United States did not carry its rejection of Old

World ways to the point of forgoing territorial expansion. On the contrary, from the very beginning, the United States pursued expansion in the Americas with extraordinary singleness of purpose. After 1794, a series of treaties settled the borders with Canada and Florida in America's favor, opened the Mississippi River to American trade, and began to establish an American commercial interest in the British West Indies. This culminated in the Louisiana Purchase of 1803, which brought to the young country a huge, undefined territory west of the Mississippi River from France along with claims to Spanish territory in Florida and Texas—the foundation from which to develop into a great power.

The French Emperor who made the sale, Napoleon Bonaparte, advanced an Old World explanation for such a one-sided transaction: "This accession of territory affirms forever the power of the United States, and I have just given England a maritime rival that sooner or later will lay low her pride."[2] American statesmen did not care what justification France used to sell her possessions. To them, condemnation of Old World power politics did not appear inconsistent with American territorial expansion across North America. For they considered America's westward thrust as America's internal affair rather than as a matter of foreign policy.

In this spirit, James Madison condemned war as the germ of all evils—as the precursor of taxes and armies and all other "instruments for bringing the many under the domination of the few."[3] His successor, James Monroe, saw no contradiction in defending westward expansion on the ground that it was necessary to turn America into a great power:

> It must be obvious to all, that the further the expansion is carried, provided it be not beyond the just limit, the greater will be the freedom of action to both [state and federal] Governments, and the more perfect their security; and, in all other respects, the better the effect will be to the whole American people. Extent of territory, whether it be great or small, gives to a nation many of its characteristics. It marks the extent of its resources, of its population, of its physical force. It marks, in short, the difference between a great and a small power.[4]

Still, while occasionally using the methods of European power politics, the leaders of the new nation remained committed to the principles that had made their country exceptional. The European powers fought innumerable wars to prevent potentially dominant powers from arising. In America, the combination of strength and distance inspired a confidence that any challenge could be overcome *after* it had presented itself. European nations, with much narrower margins of survival, formed coalitions against the *possibility* of change; America was sufficiently remote to gear its policy to resisting the *actuality* of change.

This was the geopolitical basis of George Washington's warning against "entangling" alliances for any cause whatsoever. It would be unwise, he said,

> to implicate ourselves, by artificial ties, in the ordinary vicissitudes of her [European] politics, or the ordinary combinations and collisions of her friendships or enmities. Our detached and distant situation invites and enables us to pursue a different course.[5]

The new nation did not treat Washington's advice as a practical, geopolitical judgment but as a moral maxim. As the repository of the principle of liberty, America found it natural to interpret the security conferred on it by great oceans as a sign of divine providence, and to attribute its actions to superior moral insight instead of to a margin of security not shared by any other nation.

A staple of the early Republic's foreign policy was the conviction that Europe's constant wars were the result of its cynical methods of statecraft. Whereas the European leaders based their international system on the conviction that harmony could be distilled from a competition of selfish interests, their American colleagues envisioned a world in which states would act as cooperative partners, not as distrustful rivals. American leaders rejected the European idea that the morality of states should be judged by different criteria than the morality of individuals. According to Jefferson, there existed

> but one system of ethics for men and for nations—to be grateful, to be faithful to all engagements under all circumstances, to be open and generous, promoting in the long run even the interests of both.[6]

The righteousness of America's tone—at times so grating to foreigners—reflected the reality that America had in fact rebelled not simply against the legal ties that had bound it to the old country but against Europe's system and values. America ascribed the frequency of European wars to the prevalence of governmental institutions which denied the values of freedom and human dignity. "As war is the system of government on the old construction," wrote Thomas Paine, "the animosity which nations reciprocally entertain, is nothing more than what the policy of their governments excites, to keep up the spirit of the system. . . . Man is not the

enemy of man, but through the medium of a false system of government."[7]

The idea that peace depends above all on promoting democratic institutions has remained a staple of American thought to the present day.
Conventional American wisdom has consistently maintained that democracies do not make war against each other. Alexander Hamilton, for one,
challenged the premise that republics were essentially more peaceful
than other forms of government:

> Sparta, Athens, Rome, and Carthage were all republics; two of them,
> Athens and Carthage, of the commercial kind. Yet were they as often
> engaged in wars, offensive and defensive, as the neighboring monar-
> chies of the same times. . . . In the government of Britain the representa-
> tives of the people compose one branch of the national legislature.
> Commerce has been for ages the predominant pursuit of that country.
> Few nations, nevertheless, have been more frequently engaged in
> war. . . .[8]

Hamilton, however, represented a tiny minority. The overwhelming
majority of America's leaders were as convinced then as they are now that
America has a special responsibility to spread its values as its contribution
to world peace. Then, as now, disagreements had to do with method.
Should America actively promote the spread of free institutions as a principal objective of its foreign policy? Or should it rely on the impact of its
example?

The dominant view in the early days of the Republic was that the
nascent American nation could best serve the cause of democracy by
practicing its virtues at home. In the words of Thomas Jefferson, a "just
and solid republican government" in America would be "a standing monument and example" for all the peoples of the world.[9] A year later,
Jefferson returned to the theme that America was, in effect, "acting for all
mankind":

> . . . that circumstances denied to others, but indulged to us, have im-
> posed on us the duty of proving what is the degree of freedom and
> self-government in which a society may venture to leave its individual
> members.[10]

The emphasis American leaders placed on the moral foundations of
America's conduct and on its significance as a symbol of freedom led to
a rejection of the truisms of European diplomacy: that the balance of

power distilled an ultimate harmony out of the competition of selfish interests; and that security considerations overrode the principles of civil law; in other words, that the ends of the state justified the means.

These unprecedented ideas were being put forward by a country which was prospering throughout the nineteenth century, its institutions in good working order and its values vindicated. America was aware of no conflict between high-minded principle and the necessities of survival. In time, the invocation of morality as the means for solving international disputes produced a unique kind of ambivalence and a very American type of anguish. If Americans were obliged to invest their foreign policy with the same degree of rectitude as they did their personal lives, how was security to be analyzed; indeed, in the extreme, did this mean that survival was subordinate to morality? Or did America's devotion to free institutions confer an automatic aura of morality on even the most seemingly self-serving acts? And if this was true, how did it differ from the European concept of *raison d'état,* which asserted that a state's actions can only be judged by their success?

Professors Robert Tucker and David Hendrickson brilliantly analyzed this ambivalence in American thought:

> The great dilemma of Jefferson's statecraft lay in his apparent renunciation of the means on which states had always ultimately relied to ensure their security and to satisfy their ambitions, and his simultaneous unwillingness to renounce the ambitions that normally led to the use of these means. He wished, in other words, that America could have it both ways—that it could enjoy the fruits of power without falling victim to the normal consequences of its exercise.[11]

To this day, the push and pull of these two approaches has been one of the major themes of American foreign policy. By 1820, the United States found a compromise between the two approaches which enabled it to have it both ways until after the Second World War. It continued to castigate what went on across the oceans as the reprehensible result of balance-of-power politics while treating its own expansion across North America as "manifest destiny."

Until the turn of the twentieth century, American foreign policy was basically quite simple: to fulfill the country's manifest destiny, and to remain free of entanglements overseas. America favored democratic governments wherever possible, but abjured action to vindicate its preferences. John Quincy Adams, then Secretary of State, summed up this attitude in 1821:

Wherever the standard of freedom and independence has been or shall be unfurled, there will her [America's] heart, her benedictions and her prayers be. But she goes not abroad, in search of monsters to destroy. She is the well-wisher to the freedom and independence of all. She is the champion and vindicator only of her own.[12]

The reverse side of this policy of American self restraint was the decision to exclude European power politics from the Western Hemisphere, if necessary by using some of the methods of European diplomacy. The Monroe Doctrine, which proclaimed this policy, arose from the attempt of the Holy Alliance—composed of Prussia, Russia, and Austria—to suppress the revolution in Spain in the 1820s. Opposed to intervention in domestic affairs in principle, Great Britain was equally unwilling to countenance the Holy Alliance in the Western Hemisphere.

British Foreign Secretary George Canning proposed joint action to the United States in order to keep Spain's colonies in the Americas out of the grasp of the Holy Alliance. He wanted to make sure that, regardless of what happened in Spain, no European power controlled Latin America. Deprived of its colonies, Spain would not be much of a prize, Canning reasoned, and this would either discourage intervention or make it irrele vant.

John Quincy Adams understood the British theory, but did not trust British motives. It was too soon after the 1812 British occupation of Washington for America to side with the erstwhile mother country. Accordingly, Adams urged President Monroe to exclude European colonial ism from the Americas as a unilateral American decision.

The Monroe Doctrine, proclaimed in 1823, made a moat of the ocean which separated the United States from Europe. Up to that time, the cardinal rule of American foreign policy had been that the United States would not become entangled in European struggles for power. The Monroe Doctrine went the next step by declaring that Europe must not become entangled in American affairs. And Monroe's idea of what constituted American affairs—the whole Western Hemisphere—was expansive indeed.

The Monroe Doctrine, moreover, did not limit itself to declarations of principle. Daringly, it warned the European powers that the new nation would go to war to uphold the inviolability of the Western Hemisphere. It declared that the United States would regard any extension of European power "to any portion of this hemisphere as dangerous to our peace and safety."[13]

Finally, in language less eloquent but more explicit than that of his

Secretary of State two years earlier, President Monroe abjured any intervention in European controversies: "In the wars of the European powers in matters relating to themselves we have never taken any part, nor does it comport with our policy so to do."[14]

America was at one and the same time turning its back on Europe, and freeing its hands to expand in the Western Hemisphere. Under the umbrella of the Monroe Doctrine, America could pursue policies which were not all that different from the dreams of any European king—expanding its commerce and influence, annexing territory—in short, turning itself into a Great Power without being required to practice power politics. America's desire for expansion and its belief that it was a more pure and principled country than any in Europe never clashed. Since it did not regard its expansion as foreign policy, the United States could use its power to prevail—over the Indians, over Mexico, in Texas—and to do so in good conscience. In a nutshell, the foreign policy of the United States was not to have a foreign policy.

Like Napoleon with respect to the Louisiana Purchase, Canning had a right to boast that he had brought the New World into being to redress the balance of the Old, for Great Britain indicated that it would back the Monroe Doctrine with the Royal Navy. America, however, would redress the European balance of power only to the extent of keeping the Holy Alliance out of the Western Hemisphere. For the rest, the European powers would have to maintain their equilibrium without American participation.

For the rest of the century, the principal theme of American foreign policy was to expand the application of the Monroe Doctrine. In 1823, the Monroe Doctrine had warned the European powers to keep out of the Western Hemisphere. By the time of the Monroe Doctrine's centennial, its meaning had been gradually expanded to justify American hegemony in the Western Hemisphere. In 1845, President Polk explained the incorporation of Texas into the United States as necessary to prevent an independent state from becoming "an ally or dependency of some foreign nation more powerful than herself" and hence a threat to American security.[15] In other words, the Monroe Doctrine justified American intervention not only against an existing threat but against any possibility of an overt challenge—much as the European balance of power did.

The Civil War briefly interrupted America's preoccupation with territorial expansion. Washington's primary foreign-policy concern now was to prevent the Confederacy from being recognized by European nations lest a multistate system emerge on the soil of North America and with it the balance-of-power politics of European diplomacy. But by 1868, President

Andrew Johnson was back at the old stand of justifying expansion by the Monroe Doctrine, this time in the purchase of Alaska:

> Foreign possession or control of those communities has hitherto hindered the growth and impaired the influence of the United States. Chronic revolution and anarchy there would be equally injurious.[16]

Something more fundamental than expansion across the American continent was taking place, though it went practically unnoticed by the so-called Great Powers—a new member was joining their club as the United States became the world's most powerful nation. By 1885, the United States had surpassed Great Britain, then considered the world's major industrial power, in manufacturing output. By the turn of the century, it was consuming more energy than Germany, France, Austria-Hungary, Russia, Japan, and Italy combined.[17] Between the Civil War and the turn of the century, American coal production rose by 800 percent, steel rails by 523 percent, railway track mileage by 567 percent, and wheat production by 256 percent. Immigration contributed to the doubling of the American population. And the process of growth was likely to accelerate.

No nation has ever experienced such an increase in its power without seeking to translate it into global influence. America's leaders were tempted. President Andrew Johnson's Secretary of State, Seward, dreamed of an empire including Canada and much of Mexico and extending deep into the Pacific. The Grant Administration wanted to annex the Dominican Republic and toyed with the acquisition of Cuba. These were the kinds of initiatives which contemporary European leaders, Disraeli or Bismarck, would have understood and approved of.

But the American Senate remained focused on domestic priorities and thwarted all expansionist projects. It kept the army small (25,000 men) and the navy weak. Until 1890, the American army ranked fourteenth in the world, after Bulgaria's, and the American navy was smaller than Italy's even though America's industrial strength was thirteen times that of Italy. America did not participate in international conferences and was treated as a second-rank power. In 1880, when Turkey reduced its diplomatic establishment, it eliminated its embassies in Sweden, Belgium, the Netherlands, and the United States. At the same time, a German diplomat in Madrid offered to take a cut in salary rather than be posted to Washington.[18]

But once a country has reached the level of power of post–Civil War America, it will not forever resist the temptation of translating it into a position of importance in the international arena. In the late 1880s,

America began to build up its navy, which, as late as 1880, was smaller than Chile's, Brazil's, or Argentina's. By 1889, Secretary of the Navy Benjamin Tracy was lobbying for a battleship navy and the contemporary naval historian Alfred Thayer Mahan developed a rationale for it.[19]

Though in fact the British Royal Navy protected America from depredations by European powers, American leaders did not perceive Great Britain as their country's protector. Throughout the nineteenth century, Great Britain was considered the greatest challenge to American interests, and the Royal Navy the most serious strategic threat. No wonder that, when America began to flex its muscles, it sought to expel Great Britain's influence from the Western Hemisphere, invoking the Monroe Doctrine which Great Britain had been so instrumental in encouraging.

The United States was none too delicate about the challenge. In 1895, Secretary of State Richard Olney invoked the Monroe Doctrine to warn Great Britain with a pointed reference to the inequalities of power. "To-day," he wrote, "the United States is practically sovereign on this continent, and its fiat is law upon the subjects to which it confines its interposition." America's "infinite resources combined with its isolated position render it master of the situation and practically invulnerable as against any or all other powers."[20] America's renunciation of power politics clearly did not apply to the Western Hemisphere. By 1902, Great Britain had abandoned its claim to a major role in Central America.

Supreme in the Western Hemisphere, the United States began to enter the wider arena of international affairs. America had grown into a world power almost despite itself. Expanding across the continent, it had established its pre-eminence all around its shores while insisting that it had no wish to conduct the foreign policy of a Great Power. At the end of the process, America found itself commanding the sort of power which made it a major international factor, no matter what its preferences. America's leaders might continue to insist that its basic foreign policy was to serve as a "beacon" for the rest of mankind, but there could be no denying that some of them were also becoming aware that America's power entitled it to be heard on the issues of the day, and that it did not need to wait until all of mankind had become democratic to make itself a part of the international system.

No one articulated this reasoning more trenchantly than Theodore Roosevelt. He was the first president to insist that it was America's duty to make its influence felt globally, and to relate America to the world in terms of a concept of national interest. Like his predecessors, Roosevelt was convinced of America's beneficent role in the world. But unlike them, Roosevelt held that America had real foreign policy interests that went far

38

beyond its interest in remaining unentangled. Roosevelt started from the premise that the United States was a power like any other, not a singular incarnation of virtue. If its interests collided with those of other countries, America had the obligation to draw on its strength to prevail.

As a first step, Roosevelt gave the Monroe Doctrine its most interventionist interpretation by identifying it with imperialist doctrines of the period. In what he called a "Corollary" to the Monroe Doctrine, he proclaimed on December 6, 1904, a general right of intervention by "some civilized nation" which, in the Western Hemisphere, the United States alone had a right to exercise: ". . . in the Western Hemisphere the adherence of the United States to the Monroe Doctrine may force the United States, however reluctantly, in flagrant cases of such wrong-doing or impotence, to the exercise of an international police power."[21]

Roosevelt's practice preceded his preaching. In 1902, America had forced Haiti to clear up its debts with European banks. In 1903, it fanned unrest in Panama into a full-scale insurrection. With American help, the local population wrested independence from Colombia, but not before Washington had established the Canal Zone under United States sovereignty on both sides of what was to become the Panama Canal. In 1905, the United States established a financial protectorate over the Dominican Republic. And in 1906, American troops occupied Cuba.

For Roosevelt, muscular diplomacy in the Western Hemisphere was part of America's new global role. The two oceans were no longer wide enough to insulate America from the rest of the world. The United States had to become an actor on the international stage. Roosevelt said as much in a 1902 message to the Congress: "More and more, the increasing interdependence and complexity of international political and economic relations render it incumbent on all civilized and orderly powers to insist on the proper policing of the world."[22]

Roosevelt commands a unique historical position in America's approach to international relations. No other president defined America's world role so completely in terms of national interest, or identified the national interest so comprehensively with the balance of power. Roosevelt shared the view of his countrymen, that America was the best hope for the world. But unlike most of them, he did not believe that it could preserve the peace or fulfill its destiny simply by practicing civic virtues. In his perception of the nature of world order, he was much closer to Palmerston or Disraeli than to Thomas Jefferson.

A great president must be an educator, bridging the gap between his people's future and its experience. Roosevelt taught an especially stern doctrine for a people brought up in the belief that peace is the normal condition among nations, that there is no difference between personal and public morality, and that America was safely insulated from the upheavals affecting the rest of the world. For Roosevelt rebutted each of these propositions. To him, international life meant struggle, and Darwin's theory of the survival of the fittest was a better guide to history than personal morality. In Roosevelt's view, the meek inherited the earth only if they were strong. To Roosevelt, America was not a cause but a great power—potentially the greatest. He hoped to be the president destined to usher his nation onto the world scene so that it might shape the twentieth century in the way Great Britain had dominated the nineteenth —as a country of vast strengths which had enlisted itself, with moderation and wisdom, to work on behalf of stability, peace, and progress.

Roosevelt was impatient with many of the pieties which dominated American thinking on foreign policy. He disavowed the efficacy of international law. What a nation could not protect by its own power could not be safeguarded by the international community. He rejected disarmament, which was just then emerging as an international topic:

> As yet there is no likelihood of establishing any kind of international power . . . which can effectively check wrong-doing, and in these circumstances it would be both foolish and an evil thing for a great and free nation to deprive itself of the power to protect its own rights and even in exceptional cases to stand up for the rights of others. Nothing would more promote iniquity . . . than for the free and enlightened peoples . . . deliberately to render themselves powerless while leaving every despotism and barbarism armed.[23]

Roosevelt was even more scathing when it came to talk about world government:

> I regard the Wilson-Bryan attitude of trusting to fantastic peace treaties, to impossible promises, to all kinds of scraps of paper without any backing in efficient force, as abhorrent. It is infinitely better for a nation and for the world to have the Frederick the Great and Bismarck tradition as regards foreign policy than to have the Bryan or Bryan-Wilson attitude as a permanent national attitude. . . . A milk-and-water righteousness unbacked by force is to the full as wicked as and even more mischievous than force divorced from righteousness.[24]

In a world regulated by power, Roosevelt believed that the natural order of things was reflected in the concept of "spheres of influence," which assigned preponderant influence over large regions to specific powers, for example, to the United States in the Western Hemisphere or to Great Britain on the Indian subcontinent. In 1908, Roosevelt acquiesced to the Japanese occupation of Korea because, to his way of thinking, Japanese-Korean relations had to be determined by the relative power of each country, not by the provisions of a treaty or by international law:

> Korea is absolutely Japan's. To be sure, by treaty it was solemnly cove-nanted that Korea should remain independent. But Korea was itself helpless to enforce the treaty, and it was out of the question to suppose that any other nation . . . would attempt to do for the Koreans what they were utterly unable to do for themselves.[25]

With Roosevelt holding such European-style views, it was not surprising that he approached the global balance of power with a sophistication matched by no other American president and approached only by Richard Nixon. Roosevelt at first saw no need to engage America in the specifics of the European balance of power because he considered it more or less self-regulating. But he left little doubt that, if such a judgment were to prove wrong, he would urge America to engage itself to re-establish the equilibrium. Roosevelt gradually came to see Germany as a threat to the European balance and began to identify America's national interest with those of Great Britain and France.

This was demonstrated in 1906, during the Algeciras Conference, the purpose of which was to settle the future of Morocco. Germany, which insisted on an "open door" to forestall French domination, urged the inclusion of an American representative, because it believed America to have significant trading interests there. In the event, the American consul in Morocco attended, but the role he played disappointed the Germans. Roosevelt subordinated America's commercial interests—which in any event were not large—to his geopolitical view. These were expressed by Henry Cabot Lodge in a letter to Roosevelt at the height of the Moroccan crisis. "France," he said, "ought to be with us and England—in our zone and our combination. It is the sound arrangement economically and politically."[26]

Whereas in Europe, Roosevelt considered Germany the principal threat, in Asia he was concerned with Russian aspirations and thus favored Japan, Russia's principal rival. "There is no nation in the world which, more than Russia, holds in its hands the fate of the coming years," Roosevelt declared.[27] In 1904, Japan, protected by an alliance with Great Britain, attacked Russia. Though Roosevelt proclaimed American neutrality, he leaned toward Japan. A Russian victory, he argued, would be "a blow to

41

civilization."[28] And when Japan destroyed the Russian fleet, he rejoiced: "I was thoroughly pleased with the Japanese victory, for Japan is playing our game."[29]

He wanted Russia to be weakened rather than altogether eliminated from the balance of power—for, according to the maxims of balance-of-power diplomacy, an excessive weakening of Russia would have merely substituted a Japanese for the Russian threat. Roosevelt perceived that the outcome which served America best would be one in which Russia "should be left face to face with Japan so that each may have a moderative action on the other."[30]

On the basis of geopolitical realism rather than high-minded altruism, Roosevelt invited the two belligerents to send representatives to his Oyster Bay home to work out a peace treaty that limited the Japanese victory and preserved equilibrium in the Far East. As a result, Roosevelt became the first American to be awarded the Nobel Peace Prize, for producing a settlement based on maxims like balance of power and spheres of influence which, after his successor, Wilson, would appear quite un-American.

In 1914, Roosevelt initially took a relatively clinical view of Germany's invasion of Belgium and Luxembourg, though it was in flagrant violation of treaties which had established the neutrality of these two countries:

> I am not taking sides one way or the other as concerns the violation or disregard of these treaties. When giants are engaged in a death wrestle, as they reel to and fro they are certain to trample on whoever gets in the way of either of the huge, straining combatants, *unless it is dangerous to do so.*[31]

A few months after the outbreak of war in Europe, Roosevelt reversed his initial judgment about the violation of Belgian neutrality, though, characteristically, it was not the illegality of the German invasion that concerned him but the threat it posed to the balance of power: "... do you not believe that if Germany won in this war, smashed the English Fleet and destroyed the British Empire, within a year or two she would insist upon taking the dominant position in South and Central America...?"[32]

He urged massive rearmament so that America might throw its weight behind the Triple Entente. He regarded a German victory as both possible and dangerous for the United States. A victory for the Central Powers would have forfeited the protection of the British Royal Navy, permitting German imperialism to assert itself in the Western Hemisphere.

That Roosevelt should have considered British naval control of the Atlantic safer than German hegemony was due to such intangible non-power factors as cultural affinity and historical experience. Indeed, there were strong cultural ties between England and America for which there was no counterpart in U.S.-German relations. Moreover, the United States was used to Great Britain ruling the seas and was comfortable with the idea, and no longer suspected Great Britain of expansionist designs in the Americas. Germany, however, was regarded with apprehension. On October 3, 1914, Roosevelt wrote to the British ambassador to Washington (conveniently forgetting his earlier judgment about the inevitability of Germany's disregard of Belgian neutrality) that:

> If I had been President, I should have acted [against Germany] on the thirtieth or thirty-first of July.[33]

In a letter to Rudyard Kipling a month later, Roosevelt admitted to the difficulty of bringing American power to bear on the European war on the basis of his convictions. The American people were unwilling to follow a course of action cast so strictly in terms of power politics:

> If I should advocate all that I myself believe, I would do no good among our people, because they would not follow me. Our people are short-sighted, and they do not understand international matters. Your people have been short-sighted, but they are not as short-sighted as ours in these matters. . . . Thanks to the width of the ocean, our people believe that they have nothing to fear from the present contest, and that they have no responsibility concerning it.[34]

Had American thinking on foreign policy culminated in Theodore Roosevelt, it would have been described as an evolution adapting traditional principles of European statecraft to the American condition. Roosevelt would have been seen as the president who was in office when the United States, having established a dominant position in the Americas, began to make its weight felt as a world power. But American foreign-policy thinking did not end with Roosevelt, nor could it have done so. A leader who confines his role to his people's experience dooms himself to stagnation; a leader who outstrips his people's experience runs the risk of not being understood. Neither its experience nor its values prepared America for the role assigned to it by Roosevelt.

In one of history's ironies, America did in the end fulfill the leading role Roosevelt had envisioned for it, and within Roosevelt's lifetime, but it did so on behalf of principles Roosevelt derided, and under the guidance of a president whom Roosevelt despised. Woodrow Wilson was the embodiment of the tradition of American exceptionalism, and originated what would become the dominant intellectual school of American foreign policy—a school whose precepts Roosevelt considered at best irrelevant and at worst inimical to America's long-range interests.

In terms of all established principles of statecraft, Roosevelt had by far the better of the argument between these two of America's greatest presidents. Nevertheless, it was Wilson who prevailed: a century later, Roosevelt is remembered for his achievements, but it was Wilson who shaped American thought. Roosevelt understood how international politics worked among the nations then conducting world affairs—no American president has had a more acute insight into the operation of international systems. Yet Wilson grasped the mainsprings of American motivation, perhaps the principal one being that America simply did not see itself as a nation like any other. It lacked both the theoretical and the practical basis for the European-style diplomacy of constant adjustment of the nuances of power from a posture of moral neutrality for the sole purpose of preserving an ever-shifting balance. Whatever the realities and the lessons of power, the American people's abiding conviction has been that its exceptional character resides in the practice and propagation of freedom.

Americans could be moved to great deeds only through a vision that coincided with their perception of their country as exceptional. However intellectually attuned to the way the diplomacy of the Great Powers actually operated, Roosevelt's approach failed to persuade his countrymen that they needed to enter the First World War. Wilson, on the other hand, tapped his people's emotions with arguments that were as morally elevated as they were largely incomprehensible to foreign leaders.

Wilson's was an astonishing achievement. Rejecting power politics, he knew how to move the American people. An academic who arrived in politics relatively late, he was elected due to a split in the Republican Party between Taft and Roosevelt. Wilson grasped that America's instinctive isolationism could be overcome only by an appeal to its belief in the exceptional nature of its ideals. Step by step, he took an isolationist country into war, after he had first demonstrated his Administration's devotion to peace by a passionate advocacy of neutrality. And he did so while abjuring any selfish national interests, and by affirming that America sought no other benefit than vindication of its principles.

In Wilson's first State of the Union Address, on December 2, 1913, he laid down the outline of what later came to be known as Wilsonianism.

Universal law and not equilibrium, national trustworthiness and not national self-assertion were, in Wilson's view, the foundations of international order. Recommending the ratification of several treaties of arbitration, Wilson argued that binding arbitration, not force, should become the method for resolving international disputes:

> There is only one possible standard by which to determine controversies between the United States and other nations, and that is compounded of these two elements: Our own honor and our obligations to the peace of the world. A test so compounded ought easily to be made to govern both the establishment of new treaty obligations and the interpretation of those already assumed.[35]

Nothing annoyed Roosevelt as much as high-sounding principles backed by neither the power nor the will to implement them. He wrote to a friend: "If I must choose between a policy of blood and iron and one of milk and water ... why I am for the policy of blood and iron. It is better not only for the nation but in the long run for the world."[36]

By the same token, Roosevelt's proposal to respond to the war in Europe by increasing defense spending made no sense to Wilson. In his second State of the Union address on December 8, 1914, and after the European war had been raging for four months, Wilson rejected an increase in America's armaments, because this would signal that "we had lost our self-possession" as the result of a war "whose causes cannot touch us, whose very existence affords us opportunities for friendship and disinterested service...."[37]

America's influence, in Wilson's view, depended on its unselfishness; it had to preserve itself so that, in the end, it could step forward as a credible arbiter between the warring parties. Roosevelt had asserted that the war in Europe, and especially a German victory, would ultimately threaten American security. Wilson maintained that America was essentially disinterested, hence should emerge as mediator. Because of America's faith in values higher than the balance of power, the war in Europe now afforded it an extraordinary opportunity to proselytize for a new and better approach to international affairs.

Roosevelt ridiculed such ideas and accused Wilson of pandering to isolationist sentiments to help his re-election in 1916. In fact, the thrust of Wilson's policy was quite the opposite of isolationism. What Wilson was proclaiming was not America's withdrawal from the world but the universal applicability of its values and, in time, America's commitment to spreading them. Wilson restated what had become the conventional

American wisdom since Jefferson, but put it in the service of a crusading ideology:

• America's special mission transcends day-to-day diplomacy and obliges it to serve as a beacon of liberty for the rest of mankind.
• The foreign policies of democracies are morally superior because the people are inherently peace-loving.
• Foreign policy should reflect the same moral standards as personal ethics.
• The state has no right to claim a separate morality for itself.

Wilson endowed these assertions of American moral exceptionalism with a universal dimension:

> Dread of the power of any other nation we are incapable of. We are not jealous of rivalry in the fields of commerce or of any other peaceful achievement. We mean to live our own lives as we will; but we mean also to let live. We are, indeed, a true friend to all the nations of the world, because we threaten none, covet the possessions of none, desire the overthrow of none.[38]

No other nation has ever rested its claim to international leadership on its altruism. All other nations have sought to be judged by the compatibility of their national interests with those of other societies. Yet, from Woodrow Wilson through George Bush, American presidents have invoked their country's unselfishness as the crucial attribute of its leadership role. Neither Wilson nor his later disciples, through the present, have been willing to face the fact that, to foreign leaders imbued with less elevated maxims, America's claim to altruism evokes a certain aura of unpredictability; whereas the national interest can be calculated, altruism depends on the definition of its practitioner.

To Wilson, however, the altruistic nature of American society was proof of divine favor:

> It was as if in the Providence of God a continent had been kept unused and waiting for a peaceful people who loved liberty and the rights of men more than they loved anything else, to come and set up an unselfish commonwealth.[39]

The claim that American goals represented providential dispensation implied a global role for America that would prove far more sweeping than

46

any Roosevelt had ever imagined. For he had wanted no more than to improve the balance of power and to invest America's role in it with the importance commensurate with its growing strength. In Roosevelt's conception, America would have been one nation among many—more powerful than most and part of an elite group of great powers—but still subject to the historic ground rules of equilibrium.

Wilson moved America onto a plane entirely remote from such considerations. Disdaining the balance of power, he insisted that America's role was "not to prove . . . our selfishness, but our greatness."[40] If that was true, America had no right to hoard its values for itself. As early as 1915, Wilson put forward the unprecedented doctrine that the security of America was inseparable from the security of *all* the rest of mankind. This implied that it was henceforth America's duty to oppose aggression *everywhere:*

> . . . because we demand unmolested development and the undisturbed government of our own lives upon our own principles of right and liberty, we resent, from whatever quarter it may come, the aggression we ourselves will not practice. We insist upon security in prosecuting our self-chosen lines of national development. We do more than that. We demand it also for others. We do not confine our enthusiasm for individual liberty and free national development to the incidents and movements of affairs which affect only ourselves. We feel it wherever there is a people that tries to walk in these difficult paths of independence and right.[41]

Envisioning America as a beneficent global policeman, this foreshadowed the containment policy, which would be developed after the Second World War.

Even at his most exuberant, Roosevelt would never have dreamt of so sweeping a sentiment portending global interventionism. But, then, he was the warrior-statesman; Wilson was the prophet-priest. Statesmen, even warriors, focus on the world in which they live; to prophets, the "real" world is the one they want to bring into being.

Wilson transformed what had started out as a reaffirmation of American neutrality into a set of propositions laying the foundations for a global crusade. In Wilson's view, there was no essential difference between freedom for America and freedom for the world. Proving that the time spent in faculty meetings, where hairsplitting exegesis reigns supreme, had not been wasted, he developed an extraordinary interpretation of what George Washington had really meant when he warned against foreign entanglements. Wilson redefined "foreign" in a way that would surely have astonished the first president. What Washington meant, according to Wilson, was that America must avoid becoming entangled in the *purposes* of others. But, Wilson argued, nothing that concerns humanity "can be foreign or indifferent to us."[42] Hence America had an unlimited charter to involve itself abroad.

What extraordinary conceit to derive a charter for global intervention from a Founding Father's injunction against foreign entanglements, and to elaborate a philosophy of neutrality that made involvement in war inevitable! As Wilson edged his country ever closer to the world war by articulating his visions of a better world, he evoked a vitality and an idealism that seemed to justify America's hibernation for a century just so it could now enter the international arena with a dynamism and an innocence unknown to its more seasoned partners. European diplomacy had been hardened, and humbled, in the crucible of history; its statesmen saw events through the prism of many dreams proved fragile, of high hopes dashed and ideals lost to the fragility of human foresight. America knew no such limitations, boldly proclaiming, if not the end of history, then surely its irrelevance, as it moved to transform values heretofore considered unique to America into universal principles applicable to all. Wilson was thus able to overcome, at least for a time, the tension in American thinking between America the secure and America the unsullied. America could only approach entry into World War I as an engagement on behalf of peoples everywhere, not just itself, and in the role of the crusader for universal liberties.

Germany's announcement of unrestricted submarine warfare and its sinking of the *Lusitania* became the proximate cause of America's declaration of war. But Wilson did not justify America's entry into the war on the grounds of specific grievances. National interests were irrelevant; Belgium's violation and the balance of power had nothing to do with it. Rather, the war had a moral foundation, whose primary objective was a new and more just international order. "It is a fearful thing," Wilson reflected in the speech asking for a declaration of war,

> to lead this great peaceful people into war, into the most terrible and disastrous of all wars, civilization itself seeming to be in the balance. But right is more precious than peace, and we shall fight for the things which we have always carried nearest our hearts, for democracy, for the right of those who submit to authority to have a voice in their own governments, for the rights and liberties of small nations, for a universal dominion of right by such a concert of free peoples as shall bring peace and safety to all nations and make the world itself at last free.[43]

In a war on behalf of such principles, there could be no compromise. Total victory was the only valid goal. Roosevelt would almost certainly have expressed America's war aims in political and strategic terms; Wilson, flaunting American disinterest, defined America's war aims in entirely moral categories. In Wilson's view, the war was not the consequence of clashing national interests pursued without restraint, but of Germany's unprovoked assault on the international order. More specifically, the true culprit was not the German nation, but the German Emperor himself. In urging a declaration of war, Wilson argued:

> We have no quarrel with the German people. We have no feeling towards them but one of sympathy and friendship. It was not upon their impulse that their government acted in entering this war. It was not with their previous knowledge or approval. It was a war determined upon as wars used to be determined upon in the old, unhappy days when peoples were nowhere consulted by their rulers and wars were provoked and waged in the interest of dynasties.[44]

Though William II had long been regarded as a loose cannon on the European stage, no European statesman had ever advocated deposing him; nobody had viewed the overthrow of the Emperor or of his dynasty as the key to peace in Europe. But once the issue of Germany's domestic structure had been advanced, the war could no longer end in the sort of compromise balancing conflicting interests that Roosevelt had achieved between Japan and Russia ten years earlier. On January 22, 1917, before America had entered the war, Wilson proclaimed its goal to be "peace without victory."[45] What Wilson proposed, however, when America did enter the war was a peace achievable only by total victory.

Wilson's pronouncements soon became conventional wisdom. Even as experienced a figure as Herbert Hoover began to describe the German ruling class as inherently wicked, preying "upon the life blood of other peoples."[46] The mood of the times was aptly expressed by Jacob Schurman, President of Cornell University, who saw the war as a struggle between the "Kingdom of Heaven" and the "Kingdom of Hun-land, which is force and frightfulness."[47]

Yet the overthrow of a single dynasty could not possibly bring about all that Wilson's rhetoric implied. In urging a declaration of war, Wilson extended his moral reach to the entire world; not only Germany but all other nations had to be made safe for democracy; for peace would require "a partnership of democratic nations."[48] In another speech, Wilson went even further by saying that America's power would atrophy unless the United States spread freedom around the globe:

We set this Nation up to make men free, and we did not confine our conception and purpose to America, and now we will make men free. If we did not do that, all the fame of America would be gone, and all her power would be dissipated.[49]

The closest Wilson ever came to stating his war aims in detail was in the Fourteen Points, which will be dealt with in chapter 9. Wilson's historic achievement lies in his recognition that Americans cannot sustain major international engagements that are not justified by their moral faith. His downfall was in treating the tragedies of history as aberrations, or as due to the shortsightedness and the evil of individual leaders, and in his rejection of any objective basis for peace other than the force of public opinion and the worldwide spread of democratic institutions. In the process, he would ask the nations of Europe to undertake something for which they were neither philosophically nor historically prepared, and right after a war which had drained them of substance.

For 300 years, the European nations had based their world order on a balancing of national interests, and their foreign policies on a quest for security, treating every additional benefit as a bonus. Wilson asked the nations of Europe to base their foreign policy on moral convictions, leaving security to result incidentally, if at all. But Europe had no conceptual apparatus for such a disinterested policy, and it still remained to be seen whether America, having just emerged from a century of isolation, could sustain the permanent involvement in international affairs that Wilson's theories implied.

Wilson's appearance on the scene was a watershed for America, one of those rare examples of a leader who fundamentally alters the course of his country's history. Had Roosevelt or his ideas prevailed in 1912, the question of war aims would have been based on an inquiry into the nature of American national interest. Roosevelt would have rested America's entry into the war on the proposition—which he in fact advanced—that, unless America joined the Triple Entente, the Central Powers would win the war and, sooner or later, pose a threat to American security.

The American national interest, so defined, would, over time, have led America to adopt a global policy comparable to Great Britain's toward Continental Europe. For three centuries, British leaders had operated from the assumption that, if Europe's resources were marshaled by a single dominant power, that country would then have the resources to challenge Great Britain's command of the seas, and thus threaten its independence. Geopolitically, the United States, also an island off the shores of Eurasia, should, by the same reasoning, have felt obliged to resist the domination of Europe or Asia by any one power and, even more, the control of *both* continents by the *same* power. In these terms, it should have been the extent of Germany's geopolitical reach and not its moral transgressions that provided the principal *casus belli.*

However, such an Old World approach ran counter to the wellspring of American emotions being tapped by Wilson—as it does to this day. Not even Roosevelt could have managed the power politics he advocated, though he died convinced that he could have. At any rate, Roosevelt was no longer the president, and Wilson had made it clear, even before America entered the war, that he would resist any attempt to base the postwar order on established principles of international politics.

Wilson saw the causes of the war not only in the wickedness of the German leadership but in the European balance-of-power system as well. On January 22, 1917, he attacked the international order which had pre-ceded the war as a system of "organized rivalries":

> The question upon which the whole future peace and policy of the world depends is this: Is the present war a struggle for a just and secure peace, or only for a new balance of power?...There must be, not a balance of power, but a community of power; not organized rivalries, but an organized common peace.[50]

What Wilson meant by "community of power" was an entirely new con-cept that later became known as "collective security" (though William Gladstone in Great Britain had put forward a stillborn variation of it in the course of 1880).[51] Convinced that all the nations of the world had an equal interest in peace and would therefore unite to punish those who disturbed it, Wilson proposed to defend the international order by the moral consensus of the peace-loving:

> ...this age is an age...which rejects the standards of national selfish-ness that once governed the counsels of nations and demands that they shall give way to a new order of things in which the only questions will be: "Is it right?" "Is it just?" "Is it in the interest of mankind?"[52]

To institutionalize this consensus, Wilson put forward the League of Na-tions, a quintessentially American institution. Under the auspices of this world organization, power would yield to morality and the force of arms to the dictates of public opinion. Wilson kept emphasizing that, had the public been adequately informed, the war would never have occurred—ignoring the passionate demonstrations of joy and relief which had greeted the onset of war in *all* capitals, including those of democratic Great Britain and France. If the new theory was to work, in Wilson's view, at least two changes in international governance had to take place: first, the spread of democratic governments throughout the world, and, next, the elaboration of a "new and more wholesome diplomacy" based on "the same high code of honor that we demand of individuals."[53]

In 1918, Wilson stated as a requirement of peace the hitherto unheard-of and breathtakingly ambitious goal of "the destruction of every arbitrary power anywhere that can separately, secretly and of its single choice disturb the peace of the world; or, if it cannot be presently destroyed, at the least its reduction to virtual impotence."[54] A League of Nations so composed and animated by such attitudes would resolve crises without war, Wilson told the Peace Conference on February 14, 1919:

> ... throughout this instrument [the League Covenant] we are depending primarily and chiefly upon one great force, and that is the moral force of the public opinion of the world—the cleansing and clarifying and compelling influences of publicity... so that those things that are destroyed by the light may be properly destroyed by the overwhelming light of the universal expression of the condemnation of the world.[55]

The preservation of peace would no longer spring from the traditional calculus of power but from worldwide consensus backed up by a policing mechanism. A universal grouping of largely democratic nations would act as the "trustee of peace," and replace the old balance-of-power and alliance systems.

Such exalted sentiments had never before been put forward by any nation, let alone been implemented. Nevertheless, in the hands of American idealism they were turned into the common currency of national thinking on foreign policy. Every American president since Wilson has advanced variations of Wilson's theme. Domestic debates have more often dealt with the failure to fulfill Wilson's ideals (soon so commonplace that they were no longer even identified with him) than with whether they were in fact lending adequate guidance in meeting the occasionally brutal challenges of a turbulent world. For three generations, critics have savaged Wilson's analysis and conclusions; and yet, in all this time, Wilson's principles have remained the bedrock of American foreign-policy thinking.

And yet Wilson's intermingling of power and principle also set the stage for decades of ambivalence as the American conscience tried to reconcile its principles with its necessities. The basic premise of collective security was that all nations would view every threat to security in the same way *and* be prepared to run the same risks in resisting it. Not only had nothing like it ever actually occurred, nothing like it was destined to occur in the entire history of both the League of Nations and the United Nations. Only when a threat is truly overwhelming and genuinely affects all, or most, societies is such a consensus possible—as it was during the two world wars and, on a regional basis, in the Cold War. But in the vast majority of cases—and in nearly all of the difficult ones—the nations of the world tend to disagree either about the nature of the threat or about the type of sacrifice they are prepared to make to meet it. This was the case from Italy's aggressions against Abyssinia in 1935 to the Bosnian crisis in 1992. And when it has been a matter of achieving positive objectives or remedying perceived injustices, global consensus has proved even more difficult to achieve. Ironically, in the post–Cold War world, which has no overwhelming ideological or military threat and which pays more lip service to democracy than has any previous era, these difficulties have only increased.

Wilsonianism also accentuated another latent split in American thought on international affairs. Did America have any security interests it needed to defend regardless of the methods by which they were challenged? Or should America resist only changes which could fairly be described as illegal? Was it the fact or the method of international transformation that concerned America? Did America reject the principles of geopolitics altogether? Or did they need to be reinterpreted through the filter of American values? And if these should clash, which would prevail?

The implication of Wilsonianism has been that America resisted, above all, the method of change, and that it had no strategic interests worth defending if they were threatened by apparently legal methods. As late as the Gulf War, President Bush insisted that he was not so much defending vital oil supplies as resisting the principle of aggression. And during the Cold War, some of the domestic American debate concerned the question whether America, with all its failings, had a moral right to organize resistance to the Moscow threat.

Theodore Roosevelt would have had no doubt as to the answer to these questions. To assume that nations would perceive threats identically or be prepared to react to them uniformly represented a denial of everything he had ever stood for. Nor could he envision any world organization to which victim and aggressor could comfortably belong at the same time. In November 1918, he wrote in a letter:

I am for such a League provided we don't expect too much from it. . . .
I am not willing to play the part which even Aesop held up to derision

when he wrote of how the wolves and the sheep agreed to disarm, and how the sheep as a guarantee of good faith sent away the watchdogs, and were then forthwith eaten by the wolves.[56]

The following month, he wrote this to Senator Knox of Pennsylvania:

> The League of Nations may do a little good, but the more pompous it is and the more it pretends to do, the less it will really accomplish. The talk about it has a grimly humorous suggestion of the talk about the Holy Alliance a hundred years ago, which had as its main purpose the perpetual maintenance of peace. The Czar Alexander by the way, was the President Wilson of this particular movement a century ago.[57]

In Roosevelt's estimation, only mystics, dreamers, and intellectuals held the view that peace was man's natural condition and that it could be maintained by disinterested consensus. To him, peace was inherently fragile and could be preserved only by eternal vigilance, by the arms of the strong, and by alliances among the like-minded.

But Roosevelt lived either a century too late or a century too early. His approach to international affairs died with him in 1919; no significant school of American thought on foreign policy has invoked him since. On the other hand, it is surely the measure of Wilson's intellectual triumph that even Richard Nixon, whose foreign policy in fact embodied many of Roosevelt's precepts, considered himself above all a disciple of Wilson's internationalism, and hung a portrait of the wartime president in the Cabinet Room.

The League of Nations failed to take hold in America because the country was not yet ready for so global a role. Nevertheless, Wilson's intellectual victory proved more seminal than any political triumph could have been. For, whenever America has faced the task of constructing a new world order, it has returned in one way or another to Woodrow Wilson's precepts. At the end of World War II, it helped build the United Nations on the same principles as those of the League, hoping to found peace on a concord of the victors. When this hope died, America waged the Cold War not as a conflict between two superpowers but as a moral struggle for democracy. When communism collapsed, the Wilsonian idea that the road to peace lay in collective security, coupled with the world-wide spread of democratic institutions, was adopted by administrations of both major American political parties.

In Wilsonianism was incarnate the central drama of America on the world stage: America's ideology has, in a sense, been revolutionary while, domestically, Americans have considered themselves satisfied with the *status quo*. Tending to turn foreign-policy issues into a struggle between good and evil, Americans have generally felt ill at ease with compromise, as they have with partial or inconclusive outcomes. The fact that America has shied away from seeking vast geopolitical transformations has often associated it with defense of the territorial, and sometimes the political, *status quo*. Trusting in the rule of law, it has found it difficult to reconcile its faith in peaceful change with the historical fact that almost all significant changes in history have involved violence and upheaval.

America found that it would have to implement its ideals in a world less blessed than its own and in concert with states possessed of narrower margins of survival, more limited objectives, and far less self-confidence. And yet America has persevered. The postwar world became largely America's creation, so that, in the end, it did come to play the role Wilson had envisioned for it—as a beacon to follow, and a hope to attain.

CHAPTER THREE

From Universality to Equilibrium: Richelieu, William of Orange, and Pitt

What historians describe today as the European balance-of-power system emerged in the seventeenth century from the final collapse of the medieval aspiration to universality—a concept of world order that represented a blending of the traditions of the Roman Empire and the Catholic Church. The world was conceived as mirroring the Heavens. Just as one God ruled in Heaven, so one emperor would rule over the secular world, and one pope over the Universal Church.

In this spirit, the feudal states of Germany and Northern Italy were grouped under the rule of the Holy Roman Emperor. Into the seventeenth century, this empire had the potential to dominate Europe. France, whose frontier was far west of the Rhine River, and Great Britain were peripheral states with respect to it. Had the Holy Roman Emperor ever succeeded in establishing central control over all the territories technically under his jurisdiction, the relations of the Western European states to it might have been similar to those of China's neighbors to the Middle Kingdom, with France comparable to Vietnam or Korea, and Great Britain to Japan.

For most of the medieval period, however, the Holy Roman Emperor never achieved that degree of central control. One reason was the lack of adequate transportation and communication systems, making it difficult to tie together such extensive territories. But the most important reason was that the Holy Roman Empire had separated control of the church from control of the government. Unlike a pharaoh or a caesar, the Holy Roman Emperor was not deemed to possess divine attributes. Everywhere outside Western Europe, even in the regions governed by the Eastern Church, religion and government were unified in the sense that key appointments to each were subject to the central government; religious authorities had neither the means nor the authority to assert the autonomous position demanded by Western Christianity as a matter of right.

In Western Europe, the potential and, from time to time, actual conflict between pope and emperor established the conditions for eventual constitutionalism and the separation of powers which are the basis of modern democracy. It enabled the various feudal rulers to enhance their autonomy by exacting a price from both contending factions. This, in turn, led to a fractionated Europe—a patchwork of duchies, counties, cities, and bishoprics. Though in theory all the feudal lords owed fealty to the emperor, in practice they did what they pleased. Various dynasties claimed the imperial crown, and central authority almost disappeared. The emperors maintained the old vision of universal rule without any possibility of realizing it. At the fringes of Europe, France, Great Britain, and Spain did not accept the authority of the Holy Roman Empire, though they remained part of the Universal Church.

Not until the Habsburg dynasty had laid near-permanent claim to the imperial crown in the fifteenth century and, through prudent marriages, acquired the Spanish crown and its vast resources, did it become possible for the Holy Roman Emperor to aspire to translate his universal claims into a political system. In the first half of the sixteenth century, Emperor Charles V revived the imperial authority to a point which raised the prospect of a Central European empire, composed of what is today Germany, Austria, Northern Italy, the Czech Republic, Slovakia, Hungary, Eastern France, Belgium, and the Netherlands—a grouping so potentially dominant as to prevent the emergence of anything resembling the European balance of power.

At that very moment, the weakening of the Papacy under the impact of the Reformation thwarted the prospect of a hegemonic European empire. When strong, the Papacy had been a thorn in the side of the Holy Roman Emperor and a formidable rival. When on the decline in the sixteenth century, the Papacy proved equally a bane to the idea of empire. Emperors wanted to see themselves, and wanted others to see them, as the agents of God. But in the sixteenth century, the emperor came to be perceived in Protestant lands less as an agent of God than as a Viennese warlord tied to a decadent pope. The Reformation gave rebellious princes a new freedom of action, in both the religious and the political realms. Their break with Rome was a break with religious universality; their struggle with the Habsburg emperor demonstrated that the princes no longer saw fealty to the empire as a religious duty.

With the concept of unity collapsing, the emerging states of Europe needed some principle to justify their heresy and to regulate their relations. They found it in the concepts of *raison d'état* and the balance of power. Each depended on the other. *Raison d'état* asserted that the well-being of the state justified whatever means were employed to further it; the national interest supplanted the medieval notion of a universal morality. The balance of power replaced the nostalgia for universal monarchy with the consolation that each state, in pursuing its own selfish interests, would somehow contribute to the safety and progress of all the others.

The earliest and most comprehensive formulation of this new approach came from France, which was also one of the first nation-states in Europe. France was the country that stood to lose the most by the reinvigoration of the Holy Roman Empire, because it might well—to use modern terminology—have been "Finlandized" by it. As religious restraints weakened, France began to exploit the rivalries that the Reformation had generated among its neighbors. French rulers recognized that the progressive weakening of the Holy Roman Empire (and even more its disintegration) would enhance France's security and, with good fortune, enable it to expand eastward.

The principal agent for this French policy was an improbable figure, a prince of the Church, Armand Jean du Plessis, Cardinal de Richelieu, First Minister of France from 1624 to 1642. Upon learning of Cardinal Richelieu's death, Pope Urban VIII is alleged to have said, "If there is a God, the Cardinal de Richelieu will have much to answer for. If not . . . well, he had a successful life."[1] This ambivalent epitaph would no doubt have pleased the statesman, who achieved vast successes by ignoring, and indeed transcending, the essential pieties of his age.

Few statesmen can claim a greater impact on history. Richelieu was the father of the modern state system. He promulgated the concept of *raison d'état* and practiced it relentlessly for the benefit of his own country. Under his auspices, *raison d'état* replaced the medieval concept of universal moral values as the operating principle of French policy. Initially, he sought to prevent Habsburg domination of Europe, but ultimately left a legacy that for the next two centuries tempted his successors to establish French primacy in Europe. Out of the failure of these ambitions, a balance of power emerged, first as a fact of life, then as a system for organizing international relations.

Richelieu came into office in 1624, when the Habsburg Holy Roman Emperor Ferdinand II was attempting to revive Catholic universality, stamp out Protestantism, and establish imperial control over the princes of Central Europe. This process, the Counter-Reformation, led to what was later called the Thirty Years' War, which erupted in Central Europe in 1618 and turned into one of the most brutal and destructive wars in the history of mankind.

By 1618, the German-speaking territory of Central Europe, most of which was part of the Holy Roman Empire, was divided into two armed camps—the Protestants and the Catholics. The fuse that set off the war was lit that same year in Prague, and before long all of Germany was drawn into the conflict. As Germany was progressively bled white, its principalities became easy prey for outside invaders. Soon Danish and Swedish armies were cutting their way through Central Europe, and eventually the French army joined the fray. By the time the war ended in 1648, Central Europe had been devastated and Germany had lost almost a third of its population. In the crucible of this tragic conflict, Cardinal Richelieu grafted the principle of *raison d'état* onto French foreign policy, a principle that the other European states adopted in the century that followed.

As a prince of the Church, Richelieu ought to have welcomed Ferdinand's drive to restore Catholic orthodoxy. But Richelieu put the French national interest above any religious goals. His vocation as cardinal did not keep Richelieu from seeing the Habsburg attempt to re-establish the Catholic religion as a geopolitical threat to France's security. To him, it was not a religious act but a political maneuver by Austria to achieve dominance in Central Europe and thereby to reduce France to second-class status.

Richelieu's fear was not without foundation. A glance at the map of Europe shows that France was surrounded by Habsburg lands on all sides: Spain to the south; the Northern Italian city-states, dominated mostly by Spain, in the southeast; Franche-Comté (today the region around Lyon and Savoy), also under Spanish control, in the east, and the Spanish Netherlands in the north. The few frontiers not under the rule of the Spanish Habsburgs were subject to the Austrian branch of the family.

The Duchy of Lorraine owed fealty to the Austrian Holy Roman Emperor, as did strategically important areas along the Rhine in what is present-day Alsace. If Northern Germany were also to fall under Habsburg rule, France would become perilously weak in relation to the Holy Roman Empire.

Richelieu derived little comfort from the fact that Spain and Austria shared France's Catholic faith. Quite to the contrary, a victory for the Counter-Reformation was exactly what Richelieu was determined to prevent. In pursuit of what would today be called a national security interest and was then labeled—for the first time—*raison d'état,* Richelieu was prepared to side with the Protestant princes and exploit the schism within the Universal Church.

Had the Habsburg emperors played according to the same rules or understood the emerging world of *raison d'état,* they would have seen how well placed they were to achieve what Richelieu feared most—the pre-eminence of Austria and the emergence of the Holy Roman Empire as the dominant power on the Continent. Through the centuries, however, the enemies of the Habsburgs benefited from the dynasty's rigidity in adjusting to tactical necessities or understanding future trends. The Habsburg rulers were men of principle. They never compromised their convictions except in defeat. At the start of this political odyssey, therefore, they were quite defenseless against the ruthless Cardinal's machinations.

Emperor Ferdinand II, Richelieu's foil, had almost certainly never heard of *raison d'état.* Even if he had, he would have rejected it as blasphemy, for he saw his secular mission as carrying out the will of God, and always stressed the "holy" in his title as Holy Roman Emperor. Never would he have conceded that divine ends could be achieved by less than moral means. Never would he have thought of concluding treaties with the Protestant Swedes or the Muslim Turks, measures which the Cardinal pursued as a matter of course. Ferdinand's adviser, the Jesuit Lamormaini, thus summarized the Emperor's outlook:

> The false and corrupt policies, which are widespread in these times, he, in his wisdom, condemned from the start. He held that those who followed such policies could not be dealt with, since they practice falsehood and misuse God and religion. It would be a great folly for one to try to strengthen a kingdom, which God alone has granted, with means that God hates.[2]

A ruler committed to such absolute values found it impossible to compromise, let alone to manipulate, his bargaining position. In 1596, while still an archduke, Ferdinand declared, "I would rather die than grant any concessions to the sectarians when it comes to religion."[3] To the detriment of his empire, he certainly lived up to his words. Since he was less concerned with the Empire's welfare than with obeisance to the will of God, he considered himself duty-bound to crush Protestantism even though some accommodation with it clearly would have been in his best interests. In modern terms, he was a fanatic. The words of one of the imperial advisers, Caspar Scioppius, highlight the Emperor's beliefs: "Woe to the king who ignores the voice of God beseeching him to kill the heretics. You should not wage war for yourself, but for God" (*Bellum non tuum, sed Dei esse statuas*).[4] For Ferdinand, the state existed in order to serve religion, not vice versa: "In matters of state, which are so important for our holy confession, one cannot always take into account human considerations; rather, he must hope . . . in God . . . and trust only in Him."[5]

Richelieu treated Ferdinand's faith as a strategic challenge. Though privately religious, he viewed his duties as minister in entirely secular terms. Salvation might be his personal objective, but to Richelieu, the statesman, it was irrelevant. "Man is immortal, his salvation is hereafter," he once said. "The state has no immortality, its salvation is now or never."[6] In other words, states do not receive credit in any world for doing what is right; they are only rewarded for being strong enough to do what is necessary.

Richelieu would never have permitted himself to miss the opportunity which presented itself to Ferdinand in 1629, the eleventh year of the war. The Protestant princes were ready to accept Habsburg political pre-eminence provided they remained free to pursue the religion of their choice and to retain the Church lands they had seized during the Reformation. But Ferdinand would not subordinate his religious vocation to his political needs. Rejecting what would have been a vast triumph and the guarantee of his Empire, determined to stamp out the Protestant heresy, he issued the Edict of Restitution, which demanded that Protestant sovereigns restore all the lands they had seized from the Church since 1555. It was a triumph of zeal over expediency, a classic case in which faith overrode calculations of political self-interest. And it guaranteed a battle to the finish.

Handed this opening, Richelieu was determined to prolong the war until Central Europe had been bled white. He put aside religious scruples with respect to domestic policy as well. In the Grace of Alais of 1629, he granted to French Protestants freedom of worship, the very same freedom the Emperor was fighting to deny the German princes. Having protected his country against the domestic upheavals rending Central Europe, Richelieu set out to exploit Ferdinand's religious fervor in the service of French national ends.

The Habsburg Emperor's inability to understand his national interests —indeed, his refusal to accept the validity of any such concept—gave France's First Minister the opportunity to support and to subsidize the Protestant German princes against the Holy Roman Emperor. The role of defender of the liberties of the Protestant princes against the centralizing goals of the Holy Roman Emperor was an unlikely one for a French prelate and his Catholic French King, Louis XIII. That a prince of the Church was subsidizing the Protestant King of Sweden, Gustavus Adolphus, to make war against the Holy Roman Emperor had revolutionary implications as profound as the upheavals of the French Revolution 150 years later.

In an age still dominated by religious zeal and ideological fanaticism, a dispassionate foreign policy free of moral imperatives stood out like a snow-covered Alp in the desert. Richelieu's objective was to end what he considered the encirclement of France, to exhaust the Habsburgs, and to prevent the emergence of a major power on the borders of France— especially the German border. His only criterion in making alliances was that they served France's interests, and this he did at first with the Protestant states and, later, even with the Muslim Ottoman Empire. In order to exhaust the belligerents and to prolong the war, Richelieu subsidized the enemies of his enemies, bribed, fomented insurrections, and mobilized an extraordinary array of dynastic and legal arguments. He succeeded so well that the war that had begun in 1618 dragged on decade after decade until, finally, history found no more appropriate name for it than its duration—the Thirty Years' War.

France stood on the sidelines while Germany was devastated, until 1635, when sheer exhaustion seemed once again to portend an end to the hostilities and a compromise peace. Richelieu, however, had no interest in compromise until the French King had become as powerful as the Habsburg Emperor, and preferably stronger. In pursuit of this goal, Richelieu convinced his sovereign, in the seventeenth year of the war, of the necessity of entering the fray on the side of the Protestant princes— and with no better justification than the opportunity to exploit France's growing power:

> If it is a sign of singular prudence to have held down the forces opposed to your state for a period of ten years with the forces of your allies, by putting your hand in your pocket and not on your sword, then to engage in open warfare when your allies can no longer exist without

you is a sign of courage and great wisdom; which shows that, in hus-
banding the peace of your kingdom, you have behaved like those economists who, having taken great care to amass money, also know how to
spend it. . . .[7]

The success of a policy of *raison d'état* depends above all on the ability
to assess power relationships. Universal values are defined by their perception and are not in need of constant reinterpretation; indeed they are
inconsistent with it. But determining the limits of power requires a blend
of experience and insight, and constant adjustment to circumstance. In
theory, of course, the balance of power should be quite calculable; in
practice, it has proved extremely difficult to work out realistically. Even
more complicated is harmonizing one's calculations with those of other
states, which is the precondition for the operation of a balance of power.
Consensus on the nature of the equilibrium is usually established by
periodic conflict.

Richelieu had no doubt about his ability to master the challenge, convinced as he was that it was possible to relate means to ends with nearly
mathematical precision. "Logic," he wrote in his *Political Testament,* "requires that the thing that is to be supported and the force that is to
support it should stand in geometrical proportion to each other."[8] Fate
had made him a prince of the Church; conviction put him in the intellectual company of rationalists like Descartes and Spinoza, who thought that
human action could be scientifically charted; opportunity had enabled
him to transform the international order to the vast advantage of his
country. For once, a statesman's estimate of himself was accurate. Richelieu had a penetrating perception of his goals, but he—and his ideas—
would not have prevailed had he not been able to gear his tactics to his
strategy.

So novel and so cold-blooded a doctrine could not possibly pass without challenge. However dominant the doctrine of balance of power was
to become in later years, it was deeply offensive to the universalist tradition founded on the primacy of moral law. One of the most telling cri-
tiques came from the renowned scholar Jansenius, who attacked a policy
cut loose from all moral moorings:

Do they believe that a secular, perishable state should outweigh religion and the Church? . . . Should not the Most Christian King believe
that in the guidance and administration of his realm there is nothing
that obliges him to extend and protect that of Jesus Christ, his Lord? . . .
Would he dare say to God: Let your power and glory and the religion

which teaches men to adore You be lost and destroyed, provided my state is protected and free of risks?[9]

That, of course, was precisely what Richelieu was saying to his contemporaries and, for all we know, to his God. It was the measure of the revolution he had brought about that what his critics thought was a *reductio ad absurdum* (an argument so immoral and dangerous that it refutes itself) was, in fact, a highly accurate summary of Richelieu's thought. As the King's First Minister, he subsumed both religion and morality to *raison d'état,* his guiding light.

Demonstrating how well they had absorbed the cynical methods of the master himself, Richelieu's defenders turned the argument of their critics against them. A policy of national self-interest, they argued, represented the highest moral law; it was Richelieu's critics who were in violation of ethical principle, not he.

It fell to Daniel de Priezac, a scholar close to the royal administration, to make the formal rebuttal, almost certainly with Richelieu's own imprimatur. In classically Machiavellian fashion, Priezac challenged the premise that Richelieu was committing mortal sin by pursuing policies which seemed to favor the spread of heresy. Rather, he argued, it was Richelieu's critics whose souls were at risk. Since France was the most pure and devoted of the European Catholic powers, Richelieu, in serving the interests of France, was serving as well the interests of the Catholic religion.

Priezac did not explain how he had reached the conclusion that France had been endowed with such a unique religious vocation. However, it followed from his premise that strengthening the French state was in the interest of the well-being of the Catholic Church; hence Richelieu's policy was highly moral. Indeed, the Habsburg encirclement posed so great a threat to France's security that it had to be broken, exonerating the French King in whatever methods he chose to pursue that ultimately moral goal.

He seeks peace by means of war, and if in waging it something happens contrary to his desires, it is not a crime of will but of necessity whose laws are most harsh and commands most cruel. . . . A war is just when the intention that causes it to be undertaken is just. . . . The will is therefore the principal element that must be considered, not the means. . . . [He] who intends to kill the guilty sometimes faultlessly sheds the blood of the innocent.[10]

Not to put too fine a point on it, the end justified the means.

Another of Richelieu's critics, Mathieu de Morgues, accused the Cardinal of manipulating religion "as your preceptor Machiavelli showed the ancient Romans doing, shaping it . . . explaining it and applying it as far as it aids the advancement of your designs."[11]

De Morgues's criticism was as telling as that of Jansenius, and as ineffective. Richelieu was indeed the manipulator described, and did use religion precisely in the manner being alleged. He would no doubt have replied that he had merely analyzed the world as it was, much as Machiavelli had. Like Machiavelli, he might well have preferred a world of more refined moral sensibilities, but he was convinced that history would judge his statesmanship by how well he had used the conditions and the factors he was given to work with. Indeed, if, in evaluating a statesman, reaching the goals he sets for himself is a test, Richelieu must be remembered as one of the seminal figures of modern history. For he left behind him a world radically different from the one he had found, and set in motion the policy France would follow for the next three centuries.

In this manner, France became the dominant country in Europe and vastly expanded its territory. In the century following the Peace of Westphalia of 1648, ending the Thirty Years' War, the doctrine of *raison d'état* grew into the guiding principle of European diplomacy. Neither the respect in which statesmen of later centuries would hold Richelieu nor the oblivion which was the fate of his opponent, Ferdinand II, would have surprised the Cardinal, who was utterly without illusions, even about himself. "In matters of state," wrote Richelieu in his *Political Testament,* "he who has the power often has the right, and he who is weak can only with difficulty keep from being wrong in the opinion of the majority of the world"—a maxim rarely contradicted in the intervening centuries.[12]

Richelieu's impact on the history of Central Europe was the reverse of the achievements he garnered on France's behalf. He feared a unified Central Europe and prevented it from coming about. In all likelihood, he delayed German unification by some two centuries. The initial phase of the Thirty Years' War can be viewed as a Habsburg attempt to act as the dynastic unifiers of Germany—much as England had become a nation-state under the tutelage of a Norman dynasty and, a few centuries later, the French had followed suit under the Capets. Richelieu thwarted the Habsburgs and the Holy Roman Empire was divided among more than 300 sovereigns, each free to conduct an independent foreign policy. Germany failed to become a nation-state; absorbed in petty dynastic quarrels, it turned inward. As a result, Germany developed no national political culture and calcified into a provincialism from which it did not emerge until late in the nineteenth century when Bismarck unified it. Germany was turned into the battleground of most European wars, many of which were initiated by France, and missed the early wave of European overseas colonization. When Germany did finally unify, it had so little experience with defining its national interest that it produced many of this century's worst tragedies.

But the gods often punish man by fulfilling his wishes too completely. The Cardinal's analysis that success of the Counter-Reformation would reduce France to an appendage of an increasingly centralized Holy Roman Empire was almost certainly correct, especially if one assumed, as he must have done, that the age of the nation-state had arrived. But whereas the nemesis of Wilsonian idealism is the gap between its professions and reality, the nemesis of *raison d'état* is overextension—except in the hands of a master, and it probably is even then.

For Richelieu's concept of *raison d'état* had no built-in limitations. How far would one go before the interests of the state were deemed satisfied? How many wars were needed to achieve security? Wilsonian idealism, proclaiming a selfless policy, is possessed of the constant danger of neglecting the interests of state; Richelicu's *raison d'état* threatens self-destructive *tours de force*. That is what happened to France after Louis XIV assumed the throne. Richelieu had bequeathed to the French kings a preponderantly strong state with a weak and divided Germany and a decadent Spain on its borders. But Louis XIV gained no peace of mind from security; he saw in it an opportunity for conquest. In his overzealous pursuit of *raison d'état,* Louis XIV alarmed the rest of Europe and brought together an anti-French coalition which, in the end, thwarted his design.

Nevertheless, for 200 years after Richelieu, France was the most influential country in Europe, and has remained a major factor in international politics to this day. Few statesmen of any country can claim an equal achievement. Still, Richelieu's greatest successes occurred when he was the only statesman to jettison the moral and religious restraints of the medieval period. Inevitably, Richelieu's successors inherited the task of managing a system in which most states were operating from his premises. Thereby, France lost the advantage of having adversaries constrained by moral considerations, as Ferdinand had been in the time of Richelieu. Once all states played by the same rules, gains became much more difficult to achieve. For all the glory *raison d'état* brought France, it amounted to a treadmill, a never-ending effort to push France's boundaries outward, to become the arbiter of the conflicts among the German states and thereby to dominate Central Europe until France was drained by the effort and progressively lost the ability to shape Europe according to its design.

Raison d'état provided a rationale for the behavior of individual states, but it supplied no answer to the challenge of world order. *Raison d'état* can lead to a quest for primacy or to establishment of equilibrium. But, rarely does equilibrium emerge from the conscious design. Usually it results from the process of thwarting a particular country's attempt to dominate, as the European balance of power emerged from the effort to contain France.

In the world inaugurated by Richelieu, states were no longer restrained by the pretense of a moral code. If the good of the state was the highest value, the duty of the ruler was the aggrandizement and promotion of his glory. The stronger would seek to dominate, and the weaker would resist by forming coalitions to augment their individual strengths. If the coalition was powerful enough to check the aggressor, a balance of power emerged; if not, some country would achieve hegemony. The outcome was not foreordained and was therefore tested by frequent wars. At its beginning, the outcome could as easily have been empire—French or German—as equilibrium. This is why it took over a hundred years to establish a European order based explicitly on the balance of power. At first, the balance of power was an almost incidental fact of life, not a goal of international politics.

Curiously enough, this is not how it was perceived by the philosophers of the period. Products of the Enlightenment, they mirrored the eighteenth-century faith that out of a clash of competing interests harmony and fairness would emerge. The concept of the balance of power was simply an extension of conventional wisdom. Its primary goal was to prevent domination by one state and to preserve the international order; it was not designed to prevent conflicts, but to limit them. To the hard-headed statesmen of the eighteenth century, the elimination of conflict (or of ambition or of greed) was utopian; the solution was to harness or counterpoise the inherent flaws of human nature to produce the best possible long-term outcome.

The philosophers of the Enlightenment viewed the international system as part of a universe operating like a great clockwork which, never standing still, inexorably advanced toward a better world. In 1751, Voltaire described a "Christian Europe" as "a sort of great republic divided into several states, some monarchical, the others mixed . . . but all in harmony with each other . . . all possessing the same principles of public and political law, unknown in other parts of the world." These states were "above all . . . at one in the wise policy of maintaining among themselves as far as possible an equal balance of power."[13]

Montesquieu took up the same theme. For him, the balance of power distilled unity out of diversity:

> The state of things in Europe is that all the states depend on each other.
> . . . Europe is a single state composed of several provinces.[14]

As these lines were being written, the eighteenth century had already endured two wars over the Spanish succession, a war over the Polish succession, and a series of wars over the Austrian succession.

In the same spirit, the philosopher of history Emmerich de Vattel could write in 1758, the second year of the Seven Years' War, that:

> The continual negotiations that take place, make modern Europe a sort of republic, whose members—each independent, but all bound together by a common interest—unite for the maintenance of order and the preservation of liberty. This is what has given rise to the well-known principle of the balance of power, by which is meant an arrangement of affairs so that no state shall be in a position to have absolute mastery and dominate over the others.[15]

The philosophers were confusing the result with the intent. Throughout the eighteenth century, the princes of Europe fought innumerable wars without there being a shred of evidence that the conscious goal was to implement any general notion of international order. At the precise moment when international relations came to be based on power, so many new factors emerged that calculations became increasingly unmanageable.

The various dynasties henceforth concentrated on enhancing their security by territorial expansion. In the process, the relative power positions of several of them altered drastically. Spain and Sweden were sinking into second-rank status. Poland began its slide toward extinction. Russia (which had been entirely absent from the Peace of Westphalia) and Prussia (which played an insignificant role) were emerging as major powers. The balance of power is difficult enough to analyze when its components are relatively fixed. The task of assessing it and reconciling the assessments of the various powers becomes hopelessly intricate when the relative mights of the powers are in constant flux.

The vacuum created in Central Europe by the Thirty Years' War tempted the surrounding countries to encroach upon it. France kept pressing from the west. Russia was on the march in the east. Prussia expanded in the center of the Continent. None of the key Continental countries felt any special obligation to the balance of power so lauded by the philosophers. Russia thought of itself as too distant. Prussia, as the smallest of the Great Powers, was still too weak to affect the general equilibrium. Every king consoled himself with the thought that strengthening his own rule was the greatest possible contribution to the general peace, and left it to the ubiquitous invisible hand to justify his exertions without limiting his ambitions.

The nature of *raison d'état* as an essentially risk-benefit calculation was shown by the way Frederick the Great justified his seizure of Silesia from Austria, despite Prussia's heretofore amicable relations with that state and despite its being bound by treaty to respect Austria's territorial integrity:

> The superiority of our troops, the promptitude with which we can set them in motion, in a word, the clear advantage we have over our neighbors, gives us in this unexpected emergency an infinite superiority over all other powers of Europe.... England and France are foes. If France should meddle in the affairs of the empire, England could not allow it, so I can always make a good alliance with one or the other. England could not be jealous of my getting Silesia, which would do her no harm, and she needs allies. Holland will not care, all the more since the loans of the Amsterdam business world secured on Silesia will be guaranteed. If we cannot arrange with England and Holland, we can certainly make a deal with France, who cannot frustrate our designs and will welcome the abasement of the imperial house. Russia alone might give us trouble. If the empress lives ... we can bribe the leading counsellors. If she dies, the Russians will be so occupied that they will have no time for foreign affairs....[16]

Frederick the Great treated international affairs as if it were a game of chess. He wanted to seize Silesia in order to expand the power of Prussia. The only obstacle he would recognize to his designs was resistance from superior powers, not moral scruples. His was a risk/reward analysis: if he conquered Silesia, would other states retaliate or seek compensation?

Frederick resolved the calculation in his favor. His conquest of Silesia made Prussia a *bona fide* Great Power, but it also set off a series of wars as other countries tried to adjust to this new player. The first was the War of the Austrian Succession, from 1740 to 1748. In it, Prussia was joined by France, Spain, Bavaria, and Saxony—which in 1743 switched sides— while Great Britain supported Austria. In the second war—the Seven Years' War, from 1756 to 1763—the roles were reversed. Austria was now joined by Russia, France, Saxony, and Sweden, while Great Britain and Hanover supported Prussia. The change of sides was the result of pure calculations of immediate benefit and specific compensations, not of any overriding principle of international order.

Yet a sort of equilibrium gradually emerged out of this seeming anarchy and rapine in which each state sought single-mindedly to augment its own power. It was due not to self-restraint but to the fact that no state, not even France, was strong enough to impose its will on all the others and thus form an empire. When any state threatened to become dominant, its neighbors formed a coalition—not in pursuit of a theory of international relations but out of pure self-interest to block the ambitions of the most powerful.

These constant wars did not lead to the devastations of the religious wars for two reasons. Paradoxically, the absolute rulers of the eighteenth century were in a less strong position to mobilize resources for war than was the case when religion or ideology or popular government could stir the emotions. They were restrained by tradition and perhaps by their own insecurity from imposing income taxes and many other modern exactions, limiting the amount of national wealth potentially devoted to war, and weapons technology was rudimentary.

Above all, the equilibrium on the Continent was reinforced and in fact managed by the appearance of a state whose foreign policy was explicitly dedicated to maintaining the balance. England's policy was based on throwing its weight as the occasion required to the weaker and more threatened side to redress the equilibrium. The original engineer of this policy was King William III of England, a stern and worldly Dutchman by birth. In his native Holland he had suffered from the ambitions of the French Sun King and, when he became King of England, set about forging coalitions to thwart Louis XIV at every turn. England was the one European country whose *raison d'état* did not require it to expand in Europe. Perceiving its national interest to be in the preservation of the European balance, it was the one country which sought no more for itself on the Continent than preventing the domination of Europe by a single power. In pursuit of that objective, it made itself available to any combination of nations opposing such an enterprise.

A balance of power gradually emerged by means of shifting coalitions under British leadership against French attempts to dominate Europe. This dynamic lay at the core of almost every war fought in the eighteenth century and every British-led coalition against French hegemony fought in the name of the selfsame European liberties which Richelieu had first invoked in Germany against the Habsburgs. The balance of power held because the nations resisting French domination were too strong to be overcome, and because a century and a half of expansionism progressively drained France of its wealth.

Great Britain's role as the balancer reflected a geopolitical fact of life. The survival of a relatively small island off the coast of Europe would have been jeopardized had all the resources of the Continent been mobilized under a single ruler. For, in such a case, England (as it was before its union with Scotland in 1707) possessed much smaller resources and population and would have sooner or later been at the mercy of a Continental empire.

England's Glorious Revolution of 1688 forced it into an immediate confrontation with Louis XIV of France. The Glorious Revolution had deposed the Catholic King, James II. Searching for a Protestant replacement on the Continent, England chose William of Orange, ruler *(Stadtbalter)* of the Netherlands, who had a tenuous claim to the British throne through his marriage to Mary, the sister of the deposed King. With William, England imported an ongoing war with Louis XIV over what later became Belgium, a land full of important fortresses and harbors within perilously easy reach of the British coast (though this concern developed only over time). William knew that if Louis XIV succeeded in occupying these fortresses, the Netherlands would lose their independence, the prospects for French domination in Europe would multiply, and England would be directly threatened. William's resolve to send English troops to fight for present day Belgium against France was a precursor of the British decision to fight for Belgium in 1914 when the Germans invaded it.

Henceforth, William would spearhead the fight against Louis XIV. Short, hunchbacked, and asthmatic, William did not at first glance appear to be the man destined to humble the Sun King. But the Prince of Orange possessed an iron will combined with extraordinary mental agility. He convinced himself almost certainly correctly—that if Louis XIV, already the most powerful monarch in Europe, were permitted to conquer the Spanish Netherlands (present-day Belgium), England would be at risk. A coalition capable of reining in the French King had to be forged, not as a matter of the abstract theory of balance of power but for the sake of the independence of both the Netherlands and of England. William recognized that Louis XIV's designs on Spain and its possessions, if realized, would turn France into a superpower that no combination of states would be able to challenge. To forestall that danger, he sought out partners and soon found them. Sweden, Spain, Savoy, the Austrian Emperor, Saxony, the Dutch Republic, and England formed the Grand Alliance—the greatest coalition of forces aligned against a single power that modern Europe had ever seen. For about a quarter of a century (1688–1713), Louis waged almost constant wars against this coalition. In the end, however, France's pursuit of *raison d'état* was reined in by the self-interest of Europe's other states. France would remain the strongest state in Europe, but it would not become dominant. It was a textbook case of the functioning of the balance of power.

71

William's hostility to Louis XIV was neither personal nor based on any anti-French sentiment; it reflected his cold assessment of the Sun King's power and boundless ambition. William once confided to an aide that, had he lived in the 1550s, when the Habsburgs were threatening to become dominant, he would have been "as much a Frenchman as he was now a Spaniard"[17]—a precursor of Winston Churchill's reply in the 1930s to the charge that he was anti-German: "If the circumstances were reversed, we could equally be pro-German and anti-French."[18]

William was perfectly willing to negotiate with Louis XIV when he felt the balance of power could best be served by doing so. For William, the simple calculation was that England would try to maintain a rough balance between the Habsburgs and the Bourbons, so that whoever was weaker would maintain, with British help, the equilibrium of Europe. Ever since Richelieu, the weaker side had been Austria, and therefore Great Britain aligned itself with the Habsburgs against French expansionism.

The idea of acting as the balancer did not commend itself to the British public when it first made its appearance. In the late seventeenth century, British public opinion was isolationist, much like that of America two centuries later. The prevailing argument had it that there would be time enough to resist a threat, when and if the threat presented itself. There was no need to fight conjectural dangers based on what some country *might* do later on.

William played the equivalent of Theodore Roosevelt's later role in America, warning his essentially isolationist people that their safety depended on participation in a balance of power overseas. And his countrymen accepted his views far more quickly than Americans embraced Roosevelt's. Some twenty years after William's death, *The Craftsman,* a newspaper typically representative of the opposition, noted that the balance of power was one of "the original, everlasting principles of British politics," and that peace on the Continent was "so essential a circumstance to the prosperity of a trading island, that . . . it ought to be the constant endeavor of a British ministry to preserve it themselves, and to restore it, when broken or disturbed by others."[19]

Agreeing on the importance of the balance of power did not, however, still British disputes about the best strategy to implement the policy. There were two schools of thought, representing the two major political parties in Parliament, and substantially paralleling a similar disagreement in the United States after the two world wars. The Whigs argued that Great Britain should engage itself only when the balance was actually threatened, and then only long enough to remove the threat. By contrast, the Tories believed that Great Britain's main duty was to *shape* and not simply to protect the balance of power. The Whigs were of the view that there would be plenty of time to resist an assault on the Low Countries after it had actually occurred; the Tories reasoned that a policy of wait-and-see might allow an aggressor to weaken the balance irreparably. Therefore, if Great Britain wished to avoid fighting in Dover, it had to resist aggression along the Rhine or wherever else in Europe the balance of power seemed to be threatened. The Whigs considered alliances as temporary expedients, to be terminated once victory had rendered the common purpose moot, whereas the Tories urged British participation in permanent cooperative arrangements to enable Great Britain to help shape events and to preserve the peace.

Lord Carteret, Tory Foreign Secretary from 1742 to 1744, made an eloquent case for a permanent engagement in Europe. He denounced the Whigs' inclination "to disregard all the troubles and commotions of the continent, not to leave our own island in search of enemies, but to attend our commerce and our pleasures, and, instead of courting danger in foreign countries, to sleep in security, till we are awakened by an alarm upon our coasts." But Great Britain, he said, needed to face the reality of its permanent interest in bolstering the Habsburgs as a counterweight to France, "for if the French monarch once saw himself freed from a rival on that continent, he would sit secure in possession of his conquests, he might then reduce his garrisons, abandon his fortresses, and discharge his troops; but that treasure which now fills the plains with soldiers, would soon be employed in designs more dangerous to our country. . . . We must consequently, my lords, . . . support the House of Austria which is the only power that can be placed in the balance against the princes of the family of Bourbon."[20]

The difference between the foreign-policy strategies of the Whigs and the Tories was practical, not philosophical; tactical, not strategic; and it reflected each party's assessment of Great Britain's vulnerability. The Whigs' policy of wait-and-see reflected the conviction that Great Britain's margin of safety was wide indeed. The Tories found Great Britain's position more precarious. Almost precisely the same distinction would separate American isolationists and American globalists in the twentieth century. Neither Great Britain in the eighteenth and nineteenth centuries nor America in the twentieth found it easy to persuade the citizenry that its safety required permanent commitment rather than isolation.

Periodically, in both countries, a leader would emerge who put before his people the need for permanent engagement. Wilson produced the League of Nations; Carteret flirted with permanent engagements on the

Continent; Castlereagh, Foreign Secretary from 1812 to 1821, advocated a system of European congresses; and Gladstone, Prime Minister in the late nineteenth century, proposed the first version of collective security. In the end, their appeals failed, because, until after the end of the Second World War, neither the English nor the American people could be convinced that they faced a mortal challenge until it was clearly upon them.

In this manner, Great Britain became the balancer of the European equilibrium, first almost by default, later by conscious strategy. Without Great Britain's tenacious commitment to that role, France would almost surely have achieved hegemony over Europe in the eighteenth or nineteenth century, and Germany would have done the same in the modern period. In that sense, Churchill could rightly claim two centuries later that Great Britain had "preserved the liberties of Europe."[21]

Early in the nineteenth century, Great Britain turned its *ad hoc* defense of the balance of power into a conscious design. Until then, it had gone about its policy pragmatically, consistent with the genius of the British people, resisting any country threatening the equilibrium—which, in the eighteenth century, was invariably France. Wars ended with compromise, usually marginally enhancing the position of France but depriving it of the hegemony which was its real goal.

Inevitably, France provided the occasion for the first detailed statement of what Great Britain understood by the balance of power. Having sought pre-eminence for a century and a half in the name of *raison d'état*, France after the Revolution had returned to earlier concepts of universality. No longer did France invoke *raison d'état* for its expansionism, even less the glory of its fallen kings. After the Revolution, France made war on the rest of Europe to preserve its revolution and to spread republican ideals throughout Europe. Once again, a preponderant France was threatening to dominate Europe. Conscript armies and ideological fervor propelled French armies across Europe on behalf of universal principles of liberty, equality, and fraternity. Under Napoleon, they came within a hairsbreadth of establishing a European commonwealth centered on France. By 1807, French armies had set up satellite kingdoms along the Rhine in Italy and Spain, reduced Prussia to a second-rank power, and gravely weakened Austria. Only Russia stood between Napoleon and France's domination of Europe.

Yet Russia already inspired the ambivalent reaction—part hope and part fear—that was to be its lot until the present day. At the beginning of the eighteenth century, the Russian frontier had been on the Dnieper; a century later, it reached the Vistula, 500 miles farther west. At the beginning of the eighteenth century, Russia had been fighting for its existence against Sweden at Poltava, deep in present-day Ukraine. By the middle of the century, it was participating in the Seven Years' War, and its troops were at the outskirts of Berlin. By the end of the century, it would be the principal agent in the partition of Poland.

Russia's raw physical power was made all the more ominous by the merciless autocracy of its domestic institutions. Its absolutism was not mitigated by custom or by an assertive and independent aristocracy, as was the case with the monarchs ruling by divine right in Western Europe. In Russia, everything depended on the whim of the tsar. It was entirely possible for Russian foreign policy to veer from liberalism to conservatism depending on the mood of the incumbent tsar—as indeed it did under the reigning Tsar Alexander I. At home, however, no liberal experiment was ever attempted.

In 1804, the mercurial Alexander I, Tsar of all the Russias, approached British Prime Minister William Pitt the Younger, Napoleon's most implacable enemy, with a proposition. Heavily influenced by the philosophers of the Enlightenment, Alexander I imagined himself as the moral conscience of Europe and was in the last phase of his temporary infatuation with liberal institutions. In that frame of mind, he proposed to Pitt a vague scheme for universal peace, calling for all nations to reform their constitutions with a view to ending feudalism and adopting constitutional rule. The reformed states would thereupon abjure force and submit their disputes with one another to arbitration. The Russian autocrat thus became the unlikely precursor of the Wilsonian idea that liberal institutions were the prerequisite to peace, though he never went so far as to seek to translate these principles into practice among his own people. And within a few years, he would move to the opposite conservative extreme of the political spectrum.

Pitt now found himself in much the same position vis-à-vis Alexander as Churchill would find himself vis-à-vis Stalin nearly 150 years later. He desperately needed Russian support against Napoleon, for it was impossible to imagine how Napoleon could be defeated in any other way. On the other hand, Pitt had no more interest than Churchill would later have in replacing one dominant country with another, or in endorsing Russia as the arbiter of Europe. Above all, British domestic inhibitions did not allow any prime minister to commit his country to basing peace on the political and social reform of Europe. No British war had ever been fought for such a cause, because the British people did not feel threatened by social and political upheavals on the Continent, only by changes in the balance of power.

Pitt's reply to Alexander I captured all of these elements. Ignoring the

Russian's call for the political reform of Europe, he outlined the equilibrium that would need to be constructed if peace was to be preserved. A general European settlement was now being envisaged for the first time since the Peace of Westphalia a century and a half before. And, for the first time ever, a settlement would be explicitly based on the principles of the balance of power.

Pitt saw the principal cause for instability in the weakness of Central Europe, which had repeatedly tempted French incursion and attempts at predominance. (He was too polite and too eager for Russian help to point out that a Central Europe strong enough to withstand French pressures would be equally in a position to thwart Russian expansionist temptations.) A European settlement needed to begin by depriving France of all her postrevolutionary conquests and, in the process, restore the independence of the Low Countries, thereby neatly making the chief British concern a principle of settlement.[22]

Reducing French preponderance would be of no use, however, if the 300-odd smaller German states continued to tempt French pressure and intervention. To thwart such ambitions, Pitt thought it necessary to create "great masses" in the center of Europe by consolidating the German principalities into larger groupings. Some of the states which had joined France or collapsed ignominiously would be annexed by Prussia or Austria. Others would be formed into larger units.

Pitt avoided any reference to a European government. Instead, he proposed that Great Britain, Prussia, Austria, and Russia guarantee the new territorial arrangement in Europe by means of a permanent alliance directed against French aggression—just as Franklin D. Roosevelt later tried to base the post–World War II international order on an alliance against Germany and Japan. Neither Great Britain in the Napoleonic period nor America in World War II could imagine that the biggest threat to peace in the future might prove to be the current ally rather than the yet-to-be-defeated enemy. It was a measure of the fear of Napoleon that a British prime minister should have been willing to agree to what heretofore had been so adamantly rejected by his country—a permanent engagement on the Continent—and that Great Britain should impair its tactical flexibility by basing its policy on the assumption of a permanent enemy.

The emergence of the European balance of power in the eighteenth and nineteenth centuries parallels certain aspects of the post–Cold War world. Then, as now, a collapsing world order spawned a multitude of states pursuing their national interests, unrestrained by any overriding principles. Then, as now, the states making up the international order were groping for some definition of their international role. Then the various states decided to rely entirely on asserting their national interest, putting their trust in the so-called unseen hand. The issue is whether the post–Cold War world can find some principle to restrain the assertion of power and self-interest. Of course, in the end a balance of power always comes about *de facto* when several states interact. The question is whether the maintenance of the international system can turn into a conscious design, or whether it will grow out of a series of tests of strength.

By the time the Napoleonic Wars were ending, Europe was ready to design—for the only time in its history—an international order based on the principles of the balance of power. It had been learned in the crucible of the wars of the eighteenth and early nineteenth centuries that the balance of power could not be left to the residue of the collision of the European states. Pitt's plan had outlined a territorial settlement to rectify the weaknesses of the eighteenth-century world order. But Pitt's Continental allies had learned an additional lesson.

Power is too difficult to assess, and the willingness to vindicate it too various, to permit treating it as a reliable guide to international order. Equilibrium works best if it is buttressed by an agreement on common values. The balance of power inhibits the *capacity* to overthrow the international order; agreement on shared values inhibits the *desire* to overthrow the international order. Power without legitimacy tempts tests of strength; legitimacy without power tempts empty posturing.

Combining both elements was the challenge and the success of the Congress of Vienna, which established a century of international order uninterrupted by a general war.

CHAPTER FOUR

The Concert of Europe: Great Britain, Austria, and Russia

While Napoleon was enduring his first exile, at Elba, the victors of the Napoleonic Wars assembled at Vienna in September 1814 to plan the postwar world. The Congress of Vienna continued to meet all during Napoleon's escape from Elba and his final defeat at Waterloo. In the meantime, the need to rebuild the international order had become even more urgent.

Prince von Metternich served as Austria's negotiator, though, with the Congress meeting in Vienna, the Austrian Emperor was never far from the scene. The King of Prussia sent Prince von Hardenberg, and the newly restored Louis XVIII of France relied on Talleyrand, who thereby maintained his record of having served every French ruler since before the revolution. Tsar Alexander I, refusing to yield the Russian pride of place to anyone, came to speak for himself. The English Foreign Secretary, Lord Castlereagh, negotiated on Great Britain's behalf.

These five men achieved what they had set out to do. After the Congress of Vienna, Europe experienced the longest period of peace it had ever known. No war at all took place among the Great Powers for forty years, and after the Crimean War of 1854, no general war for another sixty. The Vienna settlement corresponded to the Pitt Plan so literally that, when Castlereagh submitted it to Parliament, he attached a draft of the original British design to show how closely it had been followed.

Paradoxically, this international order, which was created more explicitly in the name of the balance of power than any other before or since, relied the least on power to maintain itself. This unique state of affairs occurred partly because the equilibrium was designed so well that it could only be overthrown by an effort of a magnitude too difficult to mount. But the most important reason was that the Continental countries were knit together by a sense of shared values. There was not only a physical equilibrium, but a moral one. Power and justice were in substantial harmony. The balance of power reduces the opportunities for using force; a shared sense of justice reduces the desire to use force. An international order which is not considered just will be challenged sooner or later. But how a people perceives the fairness of a particular world order is determined as much by its domestic institutions as by judgments on tactical foreign-policy issues. For that reason, compatibility between domestic institutions is a reinforcement for peace. Ironic as it may seem, Metternich presaged Wilson, in the sense that he believed that a shared concept of justice was a prerequisite for international order, however diametrically opposed his idea of justice was to what Wilson sought to institutionalize in the twentieth century.

Creating the general balance of power proved relatively simple. The statesmen followed the Pitt Plan like an architect's drawing. Since the idea of national self-determination had not yet been invented, they were not in the least concerned with carving states of ethnic homogeneity out of the territory reconquered from Napoleon. Austria was strengthened in Italy, and Prussia in Germany. The Dutch Republic acquired the Austrian Netherlands (mostly present-day Belgium). France had to give up all conquests and return to the "ancient frontiers" it had possessed before the Revolution. Russia received the heartland of Poland. (In conformity with its policy of not making acquisitions on the Continent, Great Britain confined its territorial gains to the Cape of Good Hope at the southern tip of Africa.)

In Great Britain's concept of world order, the test of the balance of power was how well the various nations could perform the roles assigned to them in the overall design—much as the United States came to regard its alliances in the period after the Second World War. In implementing this approach, Great Britain faced with respect to the Continental countries the same difference in perspective that the United States encountered during the Cold War. For nations simply do not define their purpose as cogs in a security system. Security makes their existence possible; it is never their sole or even principal purpose.

Austria and Prussia no more thought of themselves as "great masses" than France would later see the purpose of NATO in terms of a division of labor. The overall balance of power meant little to Austria and Prussia if it did not at the same time do justice to their own special and complex relationship, or take account of their countries' historic roles.

After the Habsburgs' failure to achieve hegemony in Central Europe in the Thirty Years' War, Austria had abandoned its attempt to dominate all of Germany. In 1806, the vestigial Holy Roman Empire was abolished. But Austria still saw itself as first among equals and was determined to keep every other German state, especially Prussia, from assuming Austria's historic leadership role.

And Austria had every reason to be watchful. Ever since Frederick the Great had seized Silesia, Austria's claim to leadership in Germany had been challenged by Prussia. A ruthless diplomacy, devotion to the military arts, and a highly developed sense of discipline propelled Prussia in the course of a century from a secondary principality on the barren North German plain to a kingdom which, though still the smallest of the Great Powers, was militarily among the most formidable. Its oddly shaped frontiers stretched across Northern Germany from the partly Polish east to the somewhat Latinized Rhineland (which was separated from Prussia's original territory by the Kingdom of Hanover), providing the Prussian state with an overwhelming sense of national mission—if for no higher purpose than to defend its fragmented territories.

Both the relationship between these two largest German states and their relationship to the other German states were central to European stability. Indeed, at least since the Thirty Years' War, Germany's internal arrangements had presented Europe with the same dilemma: whenever Germany was weak and divided, it tempted its neighbors, especially France, into expansionism. At the same time, the prospect of German unity terrified surrounding states, and has continued to do so even in our own time. Richelieu's fear that a united Germany might dominate Europe and overwhelm France had been anticipated by a British observer who wrote in 1609: "... as for Germany, which if it were entirely subject to one Monarchy, would be terrible to all the rest."[1] Historically, Germany has been either too weak or too strong for the peace of Europe.

The architects at the Congress of Vienna recognized that, if Central Europe were to have peace and stability, they would have to undo Richelieu's work of the 1600s. Richelieu had fostered a weak, fragmented Central Europe, providing France with a standing temptation to encroach and to turn it into a virtual playground for the French army. Thus, the statesmen at Vienna set about consolidating, but not unifying, Germany. Austria and Prussia were the leading German states, after which came a number of medium-sized states—Bavaria, Württemberg, and Saxony among them —which had been enlarged and strengthened. The 300-odd pre-Napoleonic states were combined into some thirty and bound together in a new entity called the German Confederation. Providing for common defense against outside aggression, the German Confederation proved to be an ingenious creation. It was too strong to be attacked by France, but too weak and decentralized to threaten its neighbors. The Confederation balanced Prussia's superior military strength against Austria's superior prestige and legitimacy. The purpose of the Confederation was to forestall German unity on a national basis, to preserve the thrones of the various German princes and monarchs, and to forestall French aggression. It succeeded on all these counts.

In dealing with the defeated enemy, the victors designing a peace settlement must navigate the transition from the intransigence vital to victory to the conciliation needed to achieve a lasting peace. A punitive peace mortgages the international order because it saddles the victors, drained by their wartime exertions, with the task of holding down a country determined to undermine the settlement. Any country with a grievance is assured of finding nearly automatic support from the disaffected defeated party. This would be the bane of the Treaty of Versailles.

The victors at the Congress of Vienna, like the victors in the Second World War, avoided making this mistake. It was no easy matter to be generous toward France, which had been trying to dominate Europe for a century and a half and whose armies had camped among its neighbors for a quarter of a century. Nevertheless, the statesmen at Vienna concluded that Europe would be safer if France were relatively satisfied rather than resentful and disaffected. France was deprived of its conquests, but granted its "ancient"—that is, prerevolutionary—frontiers, even though this represented a considerably larger territory than the one Richelieu had ruled. Castlereagh, the Foreign Minister of Napoleon's most implacable foe, made the case that:

The continued excesses of France may, no doubt, yet drive Europe . . .
to a measure of dismemberment . . . [but] let the Allies then take this
further chance of securing that repose which all the Powers of Europe
so much require, with the assurance that if disappointed . . . they will
again take up arms, not only with commanding positions in their hands,
but with that moral force which can alone keep such a confederacy
together. . . .[2]

By 1818, France was admitted to the Congress system at periodic European congresses, which for half a century came close to constituting the
government of Europe.

Convinced that the various nations understood their self-interest sufficiently to defend it if challenged, Great Britain would probably have been
content to leave matters there. The British believed no formal guarantee
was either required or could add much to commonsense analysis. The
countries of Central Europe, however, victims of wars for a century and a
half, insisted on tangible assurances.

Austria in particular faced dangers that were inconceivable to Great
Britain. A vestige of feudal times, Austria was a polyglot empire, grouping
together the multiple nationalities of the Danube basin around its historic
positions in Germany and Northern Italy. Aware of the increasingly disso-
nant currents of liberalism and nationalism which threatened its existence, Austria sought to spin a web of moral restraint to forestall tests of
strength. Metternich's consummate skill was in inducing the key countries
to submit their disagreements to a sense of shared values. Talleyrand
expressed the importance of having some principle of restraint this way:

If . . . the minimum of resisting power . . . were equal to the maximum
of aggressive power . . . there would be a real equilibrium. But . . . the
actual situation admits solely of an equilibrium which is artificial and
precarious and which can only last so long as certain large States are
animated by a spirit of moderation and justice.[3]

After the Congress of Vienna, the relationship between the balance of
power and a shared sense of legitimacy was expressed in two documents:
the Quadruple Alliance, consisting of Great Britain, Prussia, Austria, and
Russia; and the Holy Alliance, which was limited to the three so-called
Eastern Courts—Prussia, Austria, and Russia. In the early nineteenth century, France was regarded with the same fear as Germany has been in the
twentieth century—as a chronically aggressive, inherently destabilizing
power. Therefore, the statesmen at Vienna forged the Quadruple Alliance,

designed to nip any aggressive French tendencies in the bud with over-whelming force. Had the victors convening at Versailles made a similar alliance in 1918, the world might never have suffered a Second World War.

The Holy Alliance was altogether different; Europe had not seen such a document since Ferdinand II had left the throne of the Holy Roman Empire nearly two centuries earlier. It was proposed by the Russian Tsar, who could not bring himself to abandon his self-appointed mission to revamp the international system and reform its participants. In 1804, Pitt had deflated his proposed crusade for liberal institutions; by 1815, Alexander was imbued with too strong a sense of victory to be thus denied—regardless that his current crusade was the exact opposite of what he had advocated eleven years earlier. Now Alexander was in thrall to religion and to conservative values and proposed nothing less than a complete reform of the international system based on the proposition that "the course *formerly* adopted by the Powers in their mutual relations had to be *fundamentally* changed and that it was *urgent* to replace it with an order of things based on the exalted truths of the eternal religion of our Saviour."[4]

The Austrian Emperor joked that he was at a loss as to whether to discuss these ideas in the Council of Ministers or in the confessional. But he also knew that he could neither join the Tsar's crusade nor, in re-buffing it, give Alexander a pretext to go it alone, leaving Austria to face the liberal and national currents of the period without allies. This is why Metternich transformed the Tsar's draft into what came to be known as the Holy Alliance, which interpreted the religious imperative as an obliga-tion by the signatories to preserve the domestic *status quo* in Europe. For the first time in modern history, the European Powers had given them-selves a common mission.

No British statesman could possibly have joined any enterprise estab-lishing a general right—indeed, an obligation—to intervene in the do-mestic affairs of other states. Castlereagh called the Holy Alliance a "piece of sublime mysticism and nonsense."[5] Metternich, however, saw in it an opportunity to commit the Tsar to sustain legitimate rule, and above all to keep him from experimenting with his missionary impulses unilater-ally and without restraint. The Holy Alliance brought the conservative monarchs together in combatting revolution, but it also obliged them to act only in concert, in effect giving Austria a theoretical veto over the adventures of its smothering Russian ally. The so-called Concert of Eu-rope implied that nations which were competitive on one level would settle matters affecting overall stability by consensus.

The Holy Alliance was the most original aspect of the Vienna settlement. Its exalted name has diverted attention from its operational significance, which was to introduce an element of moral restraint into the relationship of the Great Powers. The vested interest which they developed in the survival of their domestic institutions caused the Continental countries to avoid conflicts which they would have pursued as a matter of course in the previous century.

It would be too simple to argue, however, that compatible domestic institutions guarantee a peaceful balance of power by themselves. In the eighteenth century, all the rulers of the Continental countries governed by divine right—their domestic institutions were eminently compatible. Yet these same rulers governed with a feeling of permanence and conducted endless wars with each other precisely because they considered their domestic institutions unassailable.

Woodrow Wilson was not the first to believe that the nature of domestic institutions determined a state's behavior internationally. Metternich believed that too but on the basis of an entirely different set of premises. Whereas Wilson believed the democracies to be peace-loving and reasonable by their very nature, Metternich considered them dangerous and unpredictable. Having witnessed the suffering that a republican France had inflicted on Europe, Metternich identified peace with legitimate rule. He expected the crowned heads of ancient dynasties, if not to preserve the peace, then at least to preserve the basic structure of international relations. In this manner, legitimacy became the cement by which the international order was held together.

The difference between the Wilsonian and the Metternich approaches to domestic justice and international order is fundamental to understanding the contrasting views of America and Europe. Wilson crusaded for principles which he perceived as revolutionary and new. Metternich sought to institutionalize values he considered ancient. Wilson, presiding over a country consciously created to set man free, was persuaded that democratic values could be legislated and then embodied in entirely new worldwide institutions. Metternich, representing an ancient country whose institutions had developed gradually, almost imperceptibly, did not believe that rights could be created by legislation. "Rights," according to Metternich, simply existed in the nature of things. Whether they were affirmed by laws or by constitutions was an essentially technical question which had nothing to do with bringing about freedom. Metternich considered guaranteeing rights to be a paradox: "Things which ought to be taken for granted lose their force when they emerge in the form of arbitrary pronouncements. . . . Objects mistakenly made subject to legislation result only in the limitation, if not the complete annulment, of that which is attempted to be safeguarded."[6]

Some of Metternich's maxims were self-serving rationalizations of the practices of the Austrian Empire, which was incapable of adjusting to the emerging new world. But Metternich also reflected the rationalist conviction that laws and rights existed in nature and not by fiat. His formative experience had been the French Revolution, which started with the proclamation of the Rights of Man and ended with the Reign of Terror. Wilson emerged from a far more benign national experience and, fifteen years before the rise of modern totalitarianism, could not conceive of aberrations in the popular will.

In the post-Vienna period, Metternich played the decisive role in managing the international system and in interpreting the requirements of the Holy Alliance. Metternich was forced to assume this role because Austria was in the direct path of every storm, and its domestic institutions were less and less compatible with the national and liberal trends of the century. Prussia loomed over Austria's position in Germany, and Russia over its Slavic populations in the Balkans. And there was always France, eager to reclaim Richelieu's legacy in Central Europe. Metternich knew that, if these dangers were permitted to turn into tests of strength, Austria would exhaust itself, whatever the outcome of any particular conflict. His policy, therefore, was to avoid crises by building a moral consensus and to deflect those which could not be avoided by discreetly backing whichever nation was willing to bear the brunt of the confrontation—Great Britain vis-à-vis France in the Low Countries, Great Britain and France vis-à-vis Russia in the Balkans, the smaller states vis-à-vis Prussia in Germany.

Metternich's extraordinary diplomatic skill permitted him to translate familiar diplomatic verities into operational foreign policy principles. He managed to convince Austria's two closest allies, each of which represented a geopolitical threat to the Austrian Empire, that the ideological danger posed by revolution outweighed their strategic opportunities. Had Prussia sought to exploit German nationalism, it could have challenged Austrian pre-eminence in Germany a generation before Bismarck. Had Tsars Alexander I and Nicholas I only considered solely Russia's geopolitical opportunities, they would have exploited the disintegration of the Ottoman Empire far more decisively to Austria's peril—as their successors would do later in the century. Both refrained from pushing their advantage because it ran counter to the dominant principle of maintaining the *status quo*. Austria, seemingly on its deathbed after Napoleon's onslaught, was given a new lease on life by the Metternich system, which enabled it to survive for another hundred years.

The man who saved this anachronistic empire and guided its policy for nearly fifty years did not even visit Austria until he was thirteen years old or live there until he was seventeen.[7] Prince Klemens von Metternich's father had been governor general of the Rhineland, then a Habsburg possession. A cosmopolitan figure, Metternich was always more comfortable speaking French than German. "For a long time now," he wrote to Wellington in 1824, "Europe has had for me the quality of a fatherland [*patrie*]."[8] Contemporary opponents sneered at his righteous maxims and polished epigrams. But Voltaire and Kant would have understood his views. A rationalist product of the Enlightenment, he found himself propelled into a revolutionary struggle which was foreign to his temperament, and into becoming the leading minister of a state under siege whose structure he could not modify.

Sobriety of spirit and moderation of objective were the Metternich style: "Little given to abstract ideas, we accept things as they are and we attempt to the maximum of our ability to protect ourselves against delusions about realities."[9] And, "with phrases which on close examination dissolve into thin air, such as the defense of civilization, nothing tangible can be defined."[10]

With such attitudes, Metternich strove to avoid being swept away by the emotion of the moment. As soon as Napoleon was defeated in Russia, and before Russian troops had even reached Central Europe, Metternich had identified Russia as a potential long-term threat. At a time when Austria's neighbors were concentrating on liberation from French rule, he made Austria's participation in the anti-Napoleon coalition dependent on the elaboration of war aims compatible with the survival of his rickety empire. Metternich's attitude was the exact opposite of the position taken by the democracies during the Second World War, when they found themselves in comparable circumstances vis-à-vis the Soviet Union. Like Castlereagh and Pitt, Metternich believed that a strong Central Europe was the prerequisite to European stability. Determined to avoid tests of strength if at all possible, Metternich was as concerned with establishing a moderating style as he was with accumulating raw power:

> The attitude of the [European] powers differs as their geographical situation. France and Russia have but a single frontier and this hardly vulnerable. The Rhine with its triple line of fortresses assures the repose of . . . France; a frightful climate . . . makes the Niemen a no less safe frontier for Russia. Austria and Prussia find themselves exposed on all sides to attack by their neighbouring powers. Continuously menaced by the preponderance of these two powers, Austria and Prussia can find tranquillity only in a wise and measured policy, in relations of goodwill among each other and with their neighbours. . . .[11]

Though Austria needed Russia as a hedge against France, it was wary of its impetuous ally, and especially of the Tsar's crusading bent. Talleyrand said of Tsar Alexander I that he was not for nothing the son of the mad Tsar Paul. Metternich described Alexander as a "strange combination of masculine virtues and feminine weaknesses. Too weak for true ambition, but too strong for pure vanity."[12]

For Metternich, the problem posed by Russia was not so much how to contain its aggressiveness—an endeavor which would have exhausted Austria—as how to temper its ambitions. "Alexander desires the peace of the world," reported an Austrian diplomat, "but not for the sake of peace and its blessings; rather for his own sake; not unconditionally, but with mental reservations: he must remain the arbiter of this peace; from him must emanate the repose and happiness of the world and all of Europe must recognize that this repose is his work, that it is dependent on his goodwill and that it can be disturbed by his whim. . . ."[13]

Castlereagh and Metternich parted company over how to contain a mercurial and meddlesome Russia. As the Foreign Minister of an island power far from the scene of confrontation, Castlereagh was prepared to resist only overt attacks, and even then the attacks had to threaten the equilibrium. Metternich's country, on the other hand, lay in the center of the Continent and could not take such chances. Precisely because Metternich distrusted Alexander, he insisted on staying close to him and concentrated on keeping threats from his direction from ever arising. "If one cannon is fired," he wrote, "Alexander will escape us at the head of his retinue and then there will be no limit any longer to what he will consider his divinely ordained laws."[14]

To dilute Alexander's zealousness, Metternich pursued a two-pronged strategy. Under his leadership, Austria was in the vanguard of the fight against nationalism, though he was adamant about not permitting Austria to be too exposed or to engage in unilateral acts. He was even less inclined to encourage others to act on their own, partly because he feared Russia's missionary zeal could turn into expansionism. For Metternich, moderation was a philosophical virtue and a practical necessity. In his instructions to an Austrian ambassador, he once wrote: "It is more important to eliminate the claims of others than to press our own. . . . We will obtain much in proportion as we ask little."[15] Whenever possible, he tried to temper the Tsar's crusading schemes by involving him in time-consuming consultations and by limiting him to what the European consensus would tolerate.

The second prong of Metternich's strategy was conservative unity. Whenever action became unavoidable, Metternich would resort to a juggling act which he once described as follows: "Austria considers everything with reference to the *substance*. Russia wants above all the *form;* Britain wants the *substance* without the form. . . . It will be our task to combine the *impossibilities* of Britain with the *modes* of Russia."[16] Metternich's dexterity enabled Austria to control the pace of events for a generation by turning Russia, a country he feared, into a partner on the basis of the unity of conservative interests, and Great Britain, which he trusted, into a last resort for resisting challenges to the balance of power. The inevitable outcome, however, would merely be delayed. Even so, to have preserved an ancient state on the basis of values inconsistent with the dominant trends all around it for a full century is not a mean achievement.

Metternich's dilemma was that, the closer he moved toward the Tsar, the more he risked his British connection; and the more he risked that, the closer he *had* to move toward the Tsar to avoid isolation. For Metternich, the ideal combination would have been British support to preserve the territorial balance, and Russian support to quell domestic upheaval— the Quadruple Alliance for geopolitical security, and the Holy Alliance for domestic stability.

But as time passed and the memory of Napoleon faded, that combination became increasingly difficult to sustain. The more the alliances approached a system of collective security and European government, the more Great Britain felt compelled to dissociate itself from it. And the more Great Britain dissociated itself, the more dependent Austria became on Russia, hence the more rigidly it defended conservative values. This was a vicious circle that could not be broken.

However sympathetic Castlereagh might have been to Austria's problems, he was unable to induce Great Britain to address potential, as opposed to actual, dangers. "When the Territorial Balance of Europe is disturbed," avowed Castlereagh, "She [Britain] can interfere with effect, but She is the last Government in Europe which can be expected, or can venture to commit Herself on any question of an abstract character. . . . We shall be found in our Place when actual danger menaces the System of Europe; but this Country cannot, and will not, act upon abstract and speculative Principles of Precaution."[17] Yet the crux of Metternich's problem was that necessity obliged him to treat as practical what Great Britain considered abstract and speculative. Domestic upheaval happened to be the danger Austria found the least manageable.

To soften the disagreement in principle, Castlereagh proposed periodic meetings, or congresses, of the foreign ministers to review the European state of affairs. What became known as the Congress system sought to forge a consensus on the issues confronting Europe and to pave the way for dealing with them on a multilateral basis. Great Britain, however, was not comfortable with a system of European government, because it came too close to the unified Europe that the British had consistently opposed. Traditional British policy apart, no British government had ever undertaken a permanent commitment to review events as they arose without confronting a specific threat. Participating in a European government was no more attractive to British public opinion than the League of Nations would be to Americans a hundred years later, and for much the same reasons.

The British Cabinet made its reserve quite evident as early as the first such conference, the Congress of Aix-la-Chapelle in 1818. Castlereagh was dispatched with these extraordinarily grudging instructions: "We approve [a general declaration] on this occasion, and with difficulty too, by assuring [the secondary powers] that . . . periodic meetings . . . are to be confined to one . . . subject, or even . . . to one power, France, and no engagement to interfere in any manner in which the Law of Nations does not justify interference. . . . Our true policy has always been not to interfere except in great emergencies and then with commanding force."[18] Great Britain wanted France kept in check but, beyond that, the twin fears of "continental entanglements" and a unified Europe prevailed in London.

There was only one occasion when Great Britain found Congress diplomacy compatible with its objectives. During the Greek Revolution of 1821, England interpreted the Tsar's desire to protect the Christian population of the collapsing Ottoman Empire as the first stage of Russia's attempt to conquer Egypt. With British strategic interests at stake, Castlereagh did not hesitate to appeal to the Tsar in the name of the very allied unity he had heretofore sought to restrict to containing France. Characteristically, he elaborated a distinction between theoretical and practical issues: "The question of Turkey is of a totally different character and one which in England we regard not as a theoretical but a practical consideration. . . ."[19]

But Castlereagh's appeal to the Alliance served above all to demonstrate its inherent brittleness. An alliance in which one partner treats his own strategic interests as the sole practical issue confers no additional security on its members. For it provides no obligation beyond what considerations of national interest would have impelled in any event. Metternich undoubtedly drew comfort from Castlereagh's obvious personal sympathy for his objectives, and even for the Congress system itself. Castlereagh, it was said by one of Austria's diplomats, was "like a great lover of music who is at Church; he wishes to applaud but he dare not."[20] But if even the most European-minded of British statesmen dared not applaud what he believed in, Great Britain's role in the Concert of Europe was destined to be transitory and ineffective.

Somewhat like Wilson and his League of Nations a century later, Castlereagh's efforts to persuade Great Britain to participate in a system of European congresses went far beyond what English representative institutions could tolerate on either philosophical or strategic grounds. Castlereagh was convinced, as Wilson would be, that the danger of new aggression could best be avoided if his country joined some permanent European forum that dealt with threats before they developed into crises. He understood Europe better than most of his British contemporaries and knew that the newly created balance would require careful tending. He thought that he had devised a solution Great Britain could support, because it did not go beyond a series of discussion meetings of the foreign ministers of the four victors and had no obligatory features.

But even discussion meetings smacked too much of European government for the British Cabinet. Indeed, the Congress system never even cleared its initial hurdle. When Castlereagh attended the first conference at Aix-la-Chapelle in 1818, France was admitted to the Congress system and Great Britain made its exit from it. The Cabinet refused to let Castlereagh attend any further European congresses, which subsequently took place at Troppau in 1820, at Laibach in 1821, and at Verona in 1822. Great Britain remained aloof from the Congress system, which its own Foreign Secretary had devised, just as, a century later, the United States would distance itself from the League of Nations, which its president had proposed. In each case, the attempt by the leader of the most powerful country to create a general system of collective security failed because of domestic inhibitions and historic traditions.

Both Wilson and Castlereagh believed that the international order established after a catastrophic war could only be protected by the active participation of all of the key members of the international community and especially of their own countries. To Castlereagh and Wilson, security was collective; if any nation was victimized, in the end all would become victims. With security thus perceived as seamless, all states had a common interest in resisting aggression, and an even greater interest in preventing it. In Castlereagh's view, Great Britain, whatever its views on specific issues, had a genuine interest in the preservation of general peace and in the maintenance of the balance of power. Like Wilson, Castlereagh thought that the best way to defend that interest was to have a hand in shaping the decisions affecting international order and in organizing resistance to violations of the peace.

The weakness of collective security is that interests are rarely uniform, and that security is rarely seamless. Members of a general system of collective security are therefore more likely to agree on inaction than on joint action; they either will be held together by glittering generalities, or may witness the defection of the most powerful member, who feels the most secure and therefore least needs the system. Neither Wilson nor Castlereagh was able to bring his country into a system of collective security because their respective societies did not feel threatened by foreseeable dangers and thought that they could deal with them alone or, if need be, find allies at the last moment. To them, participating in the League of Nations or the European Congress system compounded risks without enhancing security.

There was one huge difference between the two Anglo-Saxon states-men, however. Castlereagh was out of tune not only with his contempo-raries but with the entire thrust of modern British foreign policy. He left no legacy; no British statesman has used Castlereagh as a model. Wilson not only responded to the wellsprings of American motivation, but took it to a new and higher level. All his successors have been Wilsonian to some degree, and subsequent American foreign policy has been shaped by his maxims.

Lord Stewart, the British "observer" permitted to attend the various European congresses, who was Castlereagh's half-brother, spent most of his energy defining the limits of Great Britain's involvement rather than contributing to a European consensus. At Troppau, he submitted a memo-randum which affirmed the right to self-defense but insisted that Great Britain would "not charge itself as a member of the Alliance with the moral responsibility of administering a general European Police."[21] At the Congress of Laibach, Lord Stewart was obliged to reiterate that Great Britain would never engage itself against "speculative" dangers. Castle-reagh himself had set forth the British position in a state paper of May 5, 1820. The Quadruple Alliance, he affirmed, was an alliance for the "libera-tion of a great proportion of the Continent of Europe from the military dominion of France. . . . It never was, however, intended as an Union for the Government of the World or for the Superintendence of the Internal Affairs of other States."[22]

In the end, Castlereagh found himself trapped between his convictions and his domestic necessities. From this untenable situation, he could see no exit. "Sir," Castlereagh said at his last interview with the King, "it is necessary to say goodbye to Europe; you and I alone know it and have saved it; no one after me understands the affairs of the Continent."[23] Four days later, he committed suicide.

As Austria grew more and more dependent on Russia, Metternich's most perplexing question became how long his appeals to the Tsar's conservative principles could restrain Russia from exploiting its opportu-nities in the Balkans and at the periphery of Europe. The answer turned out to be nearly three decades, during which time Metternich dealt with revolutions in Naples, Spain, and Greece while effectively maintaining a European consensus and avoiding Russian intervention in the Balkans.

But the Eastern Question would not go away. In essence, it was the result of independence struggles in the Balkans as the various nationalities tried to break loose of Turkish rule. The quandary this posed for the Metternich system was that it clashed with that system's commitment to maintaining the *status quo,* and that the independence movements which today were aimed at Turkey would tomorrow attack Austria. Moreover, the Tsar, who was the most committed to legitimacy, was also the most eager to intervene, but nobody—certainly not in London or Vienna—believed that the Tsar would preserve the *status quo* after his armies had been launched.

For a time, a mutual interest in cushioning the shock of the collapsing Ottoman Empire sustained a warm relationship with Great Britain and Austria. However little the English cared about particular Balkan issues, a Russian advance toward the Straits was perceived as a threat to British interests in the Mediterranean, and encountered tenacious resistance. Metternich never participated directly in these British efforts to oppose Russian expansionism, much as he welcomed them. His careful and, above all, anonymous diplomacy—affirming Europe's unity, flattering the Russians, and cajoling the British—enabled Austria to preserve its Russian option while other states bore the brunt of thwarting Russian expansionism.

Metternich's removal from the scene in 1848 marked the beginning of the end of the high-wire act by which Austria had used the unity of conservative interests to maintain the Vienna settlement. To be sure, legitimacy could not have compensated indefinitely for the steady decline in Austria's geopolitical position or for the growing incompatibility between its domestic institutions and dominant national tendencies. But nuance is the essence of statesmanship. Metternich had finessed the Eastern Question but his successors, unable to adapt Austria's domestic institutions to the times, tried to compensate by bringing Austrian diplomacy into line with the emerging trend of power politics, unrestrained by a concept of legitimacy. It was to be the undoing of the international order.

So it happened that the Concert of Europe was ultimately shattered on the anvil of the Eastern Question. In 1854, the Great Powers were at war for the first time since the days of Napoleon. Ironically, this war, the Crimean War, long condemned by historians as a senseless and utterly avoidable affair, was precipitated not by Russia, Great Britain, or Austria—countries with vast interests in the Eastern Question—but by France.

In 1852, the French Emperor Napoleon III, having just come to power by a coup, persuaded the Turkish Sultan to grant him the sobriquet of Protector of the Christians in the Ottoman Empire, a role the Russian Tsar traditionally reserved for himself. Nicholas I was enraged that Napoleon, whom he considered an illegitimate upstart, should presume to step into Russia's shoes as protector of Balkan Slavs, and demanded equal status with France. When the Sultan rebuffed the Russian emissary, Russia broke off diplomatic relations. Lord Palmerston, who shaped British foreign policy during the mid-nineteenth century, was morbidly suspicious of Russia and urged the dispatch of the Royal Navy to Besika Bay, just outside the Dardanelles. The Tsar still continued in the spirit of the Metternich system: "The four of you," he said, referring to the other Great Powers, "could dictate to me, but this will never happen. I can count on Berlin and Vienna."[24] To show his lack of concern, Nicholas ordered the occupation of the principalities of Moldavia and Wallachia (present-day Romania).

Austria, which had the most to lose from a war, proposed the obvious solution—that France and Russia act as joint protectors of the Ottoman Christians. Palmerston was eager for neither outcome. To strengthen Great Britain's bargaining position, he sent the Royal Navy to the entrance of the Black Sea. This encouraged Turkey to declare war on Russia. Great Britain and France backed Turkey.

The real causes of the war were deeper, however. Religious claims were in fact pretexts for political and strategic designs. Nicholas was pursuing the ancient Russian dream of gaining Constantinople and the Straits. Napoleon III saw an opportunity to end France's isolation and to break up the Holy Alliance by weakening Russia. Palmerston sought some pretext to end Russia's drive toward the Straits once and for all. With the outbreak of war, British warships entered the Black Sea and began to destroy the Russian Black Sea fleet. An Anglo-French force landed in the Crimea to seize the Russian naval base of Sevastopol.

These events spelled nothing but complexity for Austria's leaders. They attached importance to the traditional friendship with Russia while fearing that Russia's advance in the Balkans might increase the restlessness of Austria's Slavic populations. But they feared that siding with their old friend Russia in the Crimea would give France a pretext for attacking Austria's Italian territories.

At first, Austria declared neutrality, which was the sensible course. But the new Austrian Foreign Minister, Count Buol, found inactivity too nerve-racking and the French threat to Austria's possessions in Italy too unsettling. As the British and French armies were besieging Sevastopol, Austria presented an ultimatum to the Tsar, demanding that Russia retreat from Moldavia and Wallachia. That was the decisive factor in ending the Crimean War—at least that is what Russian leaders would think ever after.

Austria had jettisoned Nicholas I and a steadfast friendship with Russia dating back to the Napoleonic Wars. Frivolity compounded by panic caused Metternich's successors to throw away the legacy of conservative unity that had been accumulated so carefully and at times painfully for over a generation. For once Austria cut itself loose from the shackles of shared values, it also freed Russia to conduct its own policy strictly on the basis of geopolitical merit. Pursuing such a course, Russia was bound to clash with Austria over the future of the Balkans and, in time, to seek to undermine the Austrian Empire.

The reason the Vienna settlement had worked for fifty years was that the three Eastern powers—Prussia, Russia, and Austria—had seen their unity as the essential barrier to revolutionary chaos and to French domination of Europe. But in the Crimean War, Austria ("the chamber of peers of Europe," as Talleyrand had called it) maneuvered itself into an uneasy alliance with Napoleon III, who was eager to undermine Austria in Italy, and Great Britain, which was unwilling to engage in European causes. Austria thereby liberated Russia and Prussia, its acquisitive erstwhile partners in the Holy Alliance, to pursue their own undiluted national interests. Prussia exacted its price by forcing Austria to withdraw from Germany, while Russia's growing hostility in the Balkans turned into one of the triggers of the First World War and led to Austria's ultimate collapse.

When faced with the realities of power politics, Austria had failed to realize that its salvation had been the European commitment to legitimacy. The concept of the unity of conservative interests had transcended national borders and thus tended to mitigate the confrontations of power politics. Nationalism had the opposite effect, exalting the national interest, heightening rivalries, and raising the risks for everyone. Austria had thrown itself into a contest which, given all its vulnerabilities, it could not possibly win.

Within five years of the end of the Crimean War, the Italian nationalist leader Camillo Cavour began the process of expelling Austria from Italy by provoking a war with Austria, backed by a French alliance and Russian acquiescence, both of which would previously have seemed inconceivable. Within another five years, Bismarck would defeat Austria in a war for predominance in Germany. Once again, Russia stood aloof and France did the same, albeit reluctantly. In Metternich's day, the Concert of Europe would have consulted and controlled these upheavals. Henceforth diplomacy would rely more on naked power than on shared values. Peace was maintained for another fifty years. But with each decade, tensions multiplied and arms races intensified.

Great Britain fared quite differently in an international system driven by power politics. For one thing, it had never relied on the Congress system for its security; for Great Britain, the new pattern of international relations was more like business as usual. In the course of the nineteenth century, Great Britain became the dominant country in Europe. To be sure, it was strong enough to stand alone and had the advantages of geographic isolation and imperviousness to domestic upheavals on the Continent. But it also had the benefit of steady leaders pursuing an unsentimental commitment to the national interest.

Castlereagh's successors did not understand the Continent nearly as well as he had. But they had a surer grasp of what constituted the essential British national interest, and they pursued it with extraordinary skill and persistence. George Canning, Castlereagh's immediate successor, lost no time in eliminating the last few ties through which Castlereagh had maintained his influence, however remote, on the European Congress system. In 1821, the year before he succeeded Castlereagh, Canning had called for a policy of "neutrality in word and deed."[25] "Let us not," he said, "in the foolish spirit of romance, suppose that we alone could regenerate Europe."[26] Then, after becoming Foreign Secretary, he left no doubt that his guiding principle was the national interest, which, in his view, was incompatible with permanent engagement in Europe:

> ... intimately connected as we are with the system of Europe, it does not follow that we are therefore called upon to mix ourselves on every occasion, with a restless and meddling activity, in the concerns of the nations which surround us.[27]

In other words, Great Britain would reserve the right to steer its own course according to the merits of each case and guided only by its national interest, a policy which made allies either auxiliaries or irrelevant.

Palmerston explained the British definition of national interest as follows in 1856: "When people ask me ... for what is called a policy, the only answer is that we mean to do what may seem to be best, upon each occasion as it arises, making the Interests of Our Country one's guiding principle."[28] Half a century later, the official description of British foreign policy had not gained much in the way of precision, as reflected in this explanation by Foreign Secretary Sir Edward Grey: "British Foreign Ministers have been guided by what seemed to them to be the immediate interest of this country, without making elaborate calculations for the future."[29]

In most other countries, statements such as these would have been ridiculed as tautological—we do what is best because we consider it best. In Great Britain, they were considered illuminating; very rarely was there a call to define that much-used phrase "national interest": "We have no eternal allies and no permanent enemies," said Palmerston. Great Britain required no formal strategy because its leaders understood the British interest so well and so viscerally that they could act spontaneously on each situation as it arose, confident that their public would follow. In the words of Palmerston: "Our interests are eternal, and those interests it is our duty to follow."[30]

British leaders were more likely to be clear about what they were *not* prepared to defend than to identify a *casus belli* in advance. They were even more reluctant to spell out positive aims, perhaps because they liked the *status quo* well enough. Convinced that they would recognize the British national interest when they saw it, British leaders felt no need to elaborate it in advance. They preferred to await actual cases—a position impossible for the Continental countries to adopt, because they *were* those actual cases.

The British view of security was not unlike the view of American isolationists, in that Great Britain felt impervious to all but cataclysmic upheavals. But America and Great Britain differed when it came to the relationship between peace and domestic structure. British leaders did not in any sense consider the spread of representative institutions as a key to peace in the way their American counterparts generally did, nor did they feel concerned about institutions different from their own.

Thus, in 1841, Palmerston spelled out for the British ambassador in St. Petersburg what Great Britain would resist by force of arms, and why it would not resist purely domestic changes:

> One of the general principles which Her Majesty's Government wish to observe as a guide for their conduct in dealing with the relations between England and other States, is, that changes which foreign Nations may chuse to make in their internal Constitution and form of Government, are to be looked upon as matters with which England has no business to interfere by force of arms. . . .
>
> But an attempt of one Nation to seize and to appropriate to itself territory which belongs to another Nation, is a different matter; because such an attempt leads to a derangement of the existing Balance of Power, and by altering the relative strength of States, may tend to create danger to other Powers; and such attempts therefore, the British Government holds itself at full liberty to resist. . . .[31]

Without exception, British ministers were concerned above all with preserving their country's freedom of action. In 1841, Palmerston reiterated Great Britain's abhorrence of abstract cases:

> ... it is not usual for England to enter into engagements with reference to cases which have not actually arisen, or which are not immediately in prospect. ...[32]

Nearly thirty years later, Gladstone brought up the same principle in a letter to Queen Victoria:

> England should keep entire in her own hands the means of estimating her own obligations upon the various states of facts as they arise; she should not foreclose and narrow her own liberty of choice by declarations made to other Powers, in their real or supposed interests, of which they would claim to be at least joint interpreters. ...[33]

Insisting on freedom of action, British statesmen as a rule rejected all variations on the theme of collective security. What later came to be called "splendid isolation" reflected England's conviction that it stood to lose more than it could gain from alliances. So aloof an approach could be entertained only by a country that was sufficiently strong to stand alone, that foresaw no dangers for which it might need the assistance of allies, and that felt certain that any extremity threatening it would threaten its potential allies even more. Great Britain's role as the nation that maintained the European equilibrium gave it all the options its leaders either wanted or needed. This policy was sustainable because it strove for no territorial gains in Europe; England could pick and choose the European quarrels in which to intervene because its only European interest was equilibrium (however voracious the British appetite for colonial acquisitions overseas).

Nonetheless, Great Britain's "splendid isolation" did not keep it from entering into temporary arrangements with other countries to deal with special circumstances. As a sea power without a large standing army, Great Britain occasionally had to cooperate with a continental ally, which it always preferred to choose as the need arose. On such occasions British leaders could show themselves remarkably impervious to past animosities. In the course of Belgium's secession from Holland in 1830, Palmerston first threatened France with war if it sought to dominate the new state, then, a few years later, offered to ally with it to guarantee Belgium's independence: "England alone cannot carry her points on the Continent; she must have allies as instruments to work with."[34]

Of course, Great Britain's various *ad hoc* allies had objectives of their own, which usually involved an extension of influence or territory in Europe. When they went beyond what England considered appropriate, England switched sides or organized new coalitions against erstwhile allies in defense of the equilibrium. Its unsentimental persistence and self-centered determination earned Great Britain the epithet "Perfidious Albion." This type of diplomacy may not have reflected a particularly elevated attitude, but it preserved the peace of Europe, especially after the Metternich system began fraying at the edges.

The nineteenth century marked the apogee of British influence. Great Britain was self-confident and had every right to be. It was the leading industrial nation and the Royal Navy commanded the seas. In an age of domestic upheavals, British internal politics were remarkably serene. When it came to the big issues of the nineteenth century—intervention or nonintervention, defense of the *status quo* or cooperating with change —British leaders refused to be bound by dogma. In the war for Greek independence in the 1820s, Great Britain sympathized with Greece's independence from Ottoman rule as long as doing so did not threaten its strategic position in the Eastern Mediterranean by increasing Russian influence. But by 1840, Great Britain would intervene to contain Russia, thereby supporting the *status quo* in the Ottoman Empire. In the Hungarian Revolution of 1848, Great Britain, formally noninterventionist, in fact welcomed Russia's restoration of the *status quo*. When Italy revolted against Habsburg rule in the 1850s, Great Britain was sympathetic but noninterventionist. To defend the balance of power, Great Britain was neither categorically interventionist nor noninterventionist, neither a bulwark of the Viennese order nor a revisionist power. Its style was relentlessly pragmatic, and the British people took pride in their ability to muddle through.

Yet any pragmatic policy—indeed, especially a pragmatic policy—must be based on some fixed principle in order to prevent tactical skill from dissipating into a random thrashing about. And the fixed principle of British foreign policy, whether acknowledged or not, was its role as protector of the balance of power, which in general meant supporting the weaker against the stronger. By Palmerston's time, the balance of power had grown into such an immutable principle of British policy that it needed no theoretical defense; whatever policy was being pursued at any given moment became inevitably described in terms of protecting the balance of power. Extraordinary flexibility was conjoined to a number of fixed and practical objectives. For instance, the determination to keep the Low Countries out of the hands of a major power did not change between the time of William III and the outbreak of World War I. In 1870, Disraeli reaffirmed that principle:

> It had always been held by the Government of this country that it was for the interest of England that the countries on the European Coast extending from Dunkirk and Ostend to the islands of the North Sea should be possessed by free and flourishing communities, practicing the arts of peace, enjoying the rights of liberty and following those pursuits of commerce which tend to the civilization of man, and should not be in the possession of a great military Power. . . .[35]

It was a measure of how isolated German leaders had become that they were genuinely surprised when, in 1914, Great Britain reacted to the German invasion of Belgium with a declaration of war.

Well into the nineteenth century, the preservation of Austria was considered an important British objective. In the eighteenth century, Marlborough, Carteret, and Pitt had fought several wars to prevent France from weakening Austria. Though Austria had less to fear from French aggression in the nineteenth century, the British still viewed Austria as a useful counterweight to Russian expansion toward the Straits. When the Revolution of 1848 threatened to cause the disintegration of Austria, Palmerston said:

> Austria stands in the centre of Europe, a barrier against encroachment on the one side, and against invasion on the other. The political independence and liberties of Europe are bound up, in my opinion, with the maintenance and integrity of Austria as a great European Power; and therefore anything which tends by direct, or even remote, contingency, to weaken and to cripple Austria, but still more to reduce her from the position of a first-rate Power to that of a secondary State, must be a great calamity to Europe, and one which every Englishman ought to deprecate, and to try to prevent.[36]

After the Revolution of 1848, Austria became progressively weaker and its policy increasingly erratic, diminishing its usefulness as a key element in British policy in the Eastern Mediterranean.

The focus of England's policy was to prevent Russia from occupying the Dardanelles. Austro-Russian rivalries largely involved Russian designs on Austria's Slavic provinces, which did not seriously concern Great Britain, while control of the Dardanelles was not a vital Austrian interest. Great Britain therefore came to judge Austria an unsuitable counterweight to Russia. This was why Great Britain stood by when Austria was defeated by Piedmont in Italy and by Prussia in the contest over primacy in Germany—an indifference which would not have been conceivable a generation before. After the turn of the century, fear of Germany would dominate British policy, and Austria, Germany's ally, for the first time emerged as an opponent in British calculations.

In the nineteenth century, no one would have thought it possible that one day Great Britain would be allied with Russia. In Palmerston's view, Russia was "pursuing a system of universal aggression on all sides, partly from the personal character of the Emperor [Nicholas], partly from the permanent system of the government."[37] Twenty-five years later, this view was echoed by Lord Clarendon, who argued that the Crimean War was "a battle of civilization against barbarism."[38] Great Britain spent the better part of the century attempting to check Russian expansion into Persia and on the approaches to Constantinople and India. It would take decades of German bellicosity and insensitivity to shift the major British security concern to Germany, which did not finally occur until after the turn of the century.

British governments changed more frequently than those of the so-called Eastern Powers; none of Britain's major political figures—Palmerston, Gladstone, and Disraeli—enjoyed uninterrupted tenures, as did Metternich, Nicholas I, and Bismarck. Still, Great Britain maintained an extraordinary consistency of purpose. Once embarked on a particular course, it would pursue it with unrelenting tenacity and dogged reliability, which enabled Great Britain to exert a decisive influence on behalf of tranquillity in Europe.

One cause of Great Britain's single-mindedness in times of crisis was the representative nature of its political institutions. Since 1700, public opinion had played an important role in British foreign policy. No other country in eighteenth-century Europe had an "opposition" point of view with respect to foreign policy; in Great Britain, it was inherent in the system. In the eighteenth century, the Tories as a rule represented the King's foreign policy, which leaned toward intervention in Continental disputes; the Whigs, like Sir Robert Walpole, preferred to retain a measure of aloofness from quarrels on the Continent and sought greater emphasis on overseas expansion. By the nineteenth century, their roles had been reversed. The Whigs, like Palmerston, represented an activist policy, while the Tories, like Derby or Salisbury, were wary of foreign entanglements. Radicals such as Richard Cobden were allied with the Conservatives in advocating a noninterventionist British posture.

Because British foreign policy grew out of open debates, the British people displayed extraordinary unity in times of war. On the other hand, so openly partisan a foreign policy made it possible—though highly unusual—for foreign policy to be reversed when a prime minister was replaced. For instance, Great Britain's support for Turkey in the 1870s ended abruptly when Gladstone, who regarded the Turks as morally reprehensible, defeated Disraeli in the election of 1880.

At all times, Great Britain treated its representative institutions as unique unto itself. Its policies on the Continent were always justified in terms of the British national interest and not ideology. Whenever Great Britain expressed sympathy for a revolution, as it did in Italy in 1848, it did so on eminently practical grounds. Thus, Palmerston approvingly quoted Canning's own pragmatic adage: "That those who have checked improvement because it is innovation, will one day or other be compelled to accept innovation when it has ceased to be improvement."[39] But this was advice based on experience, not a call for the dissemination of British values or institutions. Throughout the nineteenth century, Great Britain judged other countries by their foreign policies and, but for a brief Gladstonian interlude, remained indifferent to their domestic structures.

Though Great Britain and America shared a certain aloofness from day-to-day involvement in international affairs, Great Britain justified its own version of isolationism on dramatically different grounds. America proclaimed its democratic institutions as an example for the rest of the world; Great Britain treated its parliamentary institutions as devoid of relevance to other societies. America came to believe that the spread of democracy would ensure peace; indeed, that a reliable peace could be achieved in no other way. Great Britain might prefer a particular domestic structure but would run no risks on its behalf.

In 1848, Palmerston subordinated Great Britain's historic misgivings about the overthrow of the French monarchy and the emergence of a new Bonaparte by invoking this practical rule of British statecraft: "The invariable principle on which England acts is to acknowledge as the organ of every nation that organ which each nation may deliberately choose to have."[40]

Palmerston was the principal architect of Great Britain's foreign policy for nearly thirty years. In 1841, Metternich analyzed his pragmatic style with cynical admiration:

> . . . what does Lord Palmerston then want? He wants to make France feel the power of England, by proving to her that the Egyptian affair will only finish as he may wish, and without France having any right to take a hand. He wants to prove to the two German powers that he does not need them, that Russia's help suffices for England. He wants to keep Russia in check and drag her in his train by her permanent anxiety of seeing England draw near to France again.[41]

It was not an inaccurate description of what Great Britain understood by the balance of power. In the end, it enabled Great Britain to traverse the century with only one relatively short war with another major power—the Crimean War. Although it was far from anyone's intent when the war started, it was, however, precisely the Crimean War which led to the collapse of the Metternich order, forged so painstakingly at the Congress of Vienna. The disintegration of unity among the three Eastern monarchs removed the moral element of moderation from European diplomacy. Fifteen years of turmoil followed before a new and much more precarious stability emerged.

CHAPTER FIVE

Two Revolutionaries: Napoleon III and Bismarck

The collapse of the Metternich system in the wake of the Crimean War produced nearly two decades of conflict: the war of Piedmont and France against Austria of 1859, the war over Schleswig-Holstein of 1864, the Austro-Prussian War of 1866, and the Franco-Prussian War of 1870. Out of this turmoil, a new balance of power emerged in Europe. France, which had participated in three of the wars and encouraged the others, lost its position of predominance to Germany. Even more importantly, the moral restraints of the Metternich system disappeared. This upheaval became symbolized by the use of a new term for unrestrained balance-of-power policy: the German word *Realpolitik* replaced the French term *raison d'état* without, however, changing its meaning.

The new European order was the handiwork of two rather unlikely collaborators who eventually became arch-adversaries—Emperor Napoleon III and Otto von Bismarck. These two men ignored Metternich's old pieties: that in the interest of stability the legitimate crowned heads of the states of Europe had to be preserved, that national and liberal movements had to be suppressed, and that, above all, relations among states had to be determined by consensus among like-minded rulers. They based their policy on *Realpolitik*—the notion that relations among states are determined by raw power and that the mighty will prevail.

The nephew of the great Bonaparte who had ravaged Europe, Napoleon III had been in his youth a member of Italian secret societies fighting against Austrian dominance in Italy. Elected President in 1848, Napoleon, as a result of a coup, had himself declared Emperor in 1852. Otto von Bismarck was the scion of an eminent Prussian family and a passionate opponent of the liberal Revolution of 1848 in Prussia. Bismarck became *Ministerpräsident* (Prime Minister) in 1862 only because the reluctant King saw no other recourse to overcome a deadlock with a fractious Parliament over military appropriations.

Between them, Napoleon III and Bismarck managed to overturn the Vienna settlement, most significantly the sense of self-restraint which emanated from a shared belief in conservative values. No two more disparate personalities than Bismarck and Napoleon III could be imagined. The Iron Chancellor and the Sphinx of the Tuileries were united in their aversion to the Vienna system. Both felt that the order established by Metternich at Vienna in 1815 was an albatross. Napoleon III hated the Vienna system because it had been expressly designed to contain France. Though Napoleon III did not have the megalomanic ambitions of his uncle, this enigmatic leader felt that France was entitled to an occasional territorial gain and did not want a united Europe standing in his way. He furthermore thought that nationalism and liberalism were values that the world identified with France, and that the Vienna system, by repressing them, put a rein on his ambitions. Bismarck resented Metternich's handiwork because it locked Prussia into being Austria's junior partner in the German Confederation, and he was convinced that the Confederation preserved so many tiny German sovereigns that it shackled Prussia. If Prussia were going to realize its destiny and unify Germany, the Vienna system had to be destroyed.

While sharing a mutual disdain for the established order, the two revolutionaries ended up at diametrically opposite poles in terms of their achievements. Napoleon brought about the reverse of what he set out to accomplish. Fancying himself the destroyer of the Vienna settlement and the inspiration of European nationalism, he threw European diplomacy into a state of turmoil from which France gained nothing in the long run and other nations benefited. Napoleon made possible the unification of

Italy and unintentionally abetted the unification of Germany, two events which weakened France geopolitically and destroyed the historical basis for the dominant French influence in Central Europe. Thwarting either event would have been beyond France's capabilities, yet Napoleon's erratic policy did much to accelerate the process while simultaneously dissipating France's capacity to shape the new international order according to its long-term interests. Napoleon tried to wreck the Vienna system because he thought it isolated France—which to some extent was true—yet by the time his rule had ended in 1870, France was more isolated than it had been during the Metternich period.

Bismarck's legacy was quite the opposite. Few statesmen have so altered the course of history. Before Bismarck took office, German unity was expected to occur through the kind of parliamentary, constitutional government which had been the thrust of the Revolution of 1848. Five years later, Bismarck was well on his way to solving the problem of German unification, which had confounded three generations of Germans, but he did so on the basis of the pre-eminence of Prussian power, not through a process of democratic constitutionalism. Bismarck's solution had never been advocated by any significant constituency. Too democratic for conservatives, too authoritarian for liberals, too power-oriented for legitimists, the new Germany was tailored to a genius who proposed to direct the forces he had unleashed, both foreign and domestic, by manipulating their antagonisms,—a task he mastered but which proved beyond the capacity of his successors.

During his lifetime, Napoleon III was called the "Sphinx of the Tuileries" because he was believed to be hatching vast and brilliant designs, the nature of which no one could discern until they gradually unfolded. He was deemed to be enigmatically clever for having ended France's diplomatic isolation under the Vienna system and for having triggered the disintegration of the Holy Alliance by means of the Crimean War. Only one European leader, Otto von Bismarck, saw through him from the beginning. In the 1850s, his sardonic description of Napoleon had been: "His intelligence is overrated at the expense of his sentimentality."

Like his uncle, Napoleon III was obsessed by his lack of legitimate credentials. Though he considered himself a revolutionary, he yearned to be accepted by the legitimate kings of Europe. Of course, had the Holy Alliance still had its original convictions, it would have tried to overthrow the republican institutions which had replaced French royal rule in 1848. The bloody excesses of the French Revolution were still within living memory but so, too, was the fact that foreign intervention in France had unleashed French revolutionary armies on the nations of Europe in 1792. At the same time, an identical fear of foreign intervention had made republican France loath to export her revolution. Out of this stalemate of inhibitions, the conservative powers reluctantly brought themselves to recognize republican France, which was ruled first by the poet and states-man Alphonse de Lamartine, then by Napoleon as elected President, and, finally, by Napoleon "III" as Emperor, in 1852, after his coup the previous December to overturn the constitutional prohibition against his re-election.

No sooner had Napoleon III proclaimed the Second Empire than the question of recognition arose again. This time it concerned whether to recognize Napoleon as Emperor, since the Vienna settlement had specifically proscribed the Bonaparte family from the French throne. Austria was the first to accept what could not be changed. The Austrian Ambassador to Paris, Baron Hübner, reported a characteristically cynical comment from his chief, Prince Schwarzenberg, dated December 31, 1851, that underlined the end of the Metternich era: " 'The days of principles are gone.' "[1]

Napoleon's next big worry was whether the other monarchs would address him with the appellation "brother," which they used toward each other, or some lesser form of address. In the end, the Austrian and Prussian monarchs yielded to Napoleon's preference, though Tsar Nicholas I remained adamant, refusing to go beyond the address of "friend." Given the Tsar's views of revolutionaries, he no doubt felt he had already rewarded Napoleon beyond his due. Hübner recorded the injured feelings in the Tuileries:

One has the feeling of being snubbed by the old continental courts. This is the worm that eats at the heart of Emperor Napoleon.[2]

Whether these snubs were real or imagined, they revealed the gulf between Napoleon and the other European monarchs, which was one of the psychological roots of Napoleon's reckless and relentless assault on European diplomacy.

The irony of Napoleon's life was that he was much better suited for domestic policy, which basically bored him, than he was for foreign adventures, for which he lacked both the daring and the insight. Whenever he took a breather from his self-appointed revolutionary mission, Napoleon made major contributions to France's development. He brought the Industrial Revolution to France. His encouragement of large credit institutions played a crucial role in France's economic development. And he rebuilt Paris into its grandiose modern appearance. In the early nineteenth century, Paris was still a medieval city with narrow, winding streets. Napoleon provided his close adviser, Baron Haussmann, with the authority and the budget to create the modern city of broad boulevards, great public buildings, and sweeping vistas. That one purpose of the broad avenues was to provide a clear field of fire to discourage revolutions does not detract from the magnificence and the permanence of the achievement.

But foreign policy was Napoleon's passion, and there he found himself torn by conflicting emotions. On the one hand, he realized he would never be able to fulfill his quest for legitimacy, because a monarch's legitimacy is a birthright that cannot be conferred. On the other hand, he did not really want to go down in history as a legitimist. He had been an Italian Carbonari (independence fighter), and considered himself a defender of national self-determination. At the same time, he was averse to running great risks. Napoleon's ultimate goal was to abrogate the territorial clauses of the Vienna settlement and to alter the state system on which it had been based. But he never understood that achieving his goal would also result in a unified Germany, which would forever end French aspirations to dominate Central Europe.

The erratic nature of his policy was therefore a reflection of his personal ambivalence. Distrustful of his "brother" monarchs, Napoleon was driven to dependence on public opinion, and his policy fluctuated with his assessment of what was needed to sustain his popularity. In 1857, the ubiquitous Baron Hübner wrote to the Austrian Emperor:

In his [Napoleon's] eyes foreign policy is only an instrument he uses to secure his rule in France, to legitimize his throne, to found his dynasty. ... [H]e would not shrink from any means, from any combination which suited itself to making him popular at home.[3]

In the process, Napoleon made himself the prisoner of crises he had himself engineered, because he lacked the inner compass to keep him on course. Time and again, he would encourage a crisis—now in Italy, now in Poland, later in Germany—only to recoil before its ultimate consequences. He possessed his uncle's ambition but not his nerve, genius, or, for that matter, raw power. He supported Italian nationalism as long as it was confined to Northern Italy, and advocated Polish independence as long as it involved no risk of war. As for Germany, he simply did not know on which side to place his bet. Having expected a protracted struggle between Austria and Prussia, Napoleon made himself ridiculous by asking Prussia, the victor, to compensate him after the event for his own inability to discern the winner.

What most suited Napoleon's style was a European Congress to redraw the map of Europe, for there he might shine at minimum risk. Nor did Napoleon have any clear idea of just how he wanted the borders altered. In any event, no other Great Power was willing to arrange such a forum to accommodate his domestic needs. No nation agrees to redraw its borders—especially to its own disadvantage—unless there is an overwhelming necessity to do so. As it turned out, the only Congress at which Napoleon presided—the Congress of Paris, which ended the Crimean War—did not redraw the map of Europe; it merely ratified what had been achieved in the war. Russia was forbidden to maintain a navy in the Black Sea and was thus deprived of a defensive capability against another British assault. Russia was also forced to return Bessarabia and the territory of Kars, on the eastern coast of the Black Sea, to Turkey. Additionally, the Tsar was compelled to renounce his claim to be the Protector of the Ottoman Christians, which had been the immediate cause of the war. The Congress of Paris symbolized the splintering of the Holy Alliance, but no participant was prepared to undertake the revision of the map of Europe.

Napoleon never succeeded in assembling another congress to redraw the map of Europe, for one basic reason, which the British ambassador, Lord Clarendon, pointed out to him: a country that seeks great changes and lacks the willingness to run great risks dooms itself to futility.

> I see that the idea of a European Congress is germinating in the Emperor's mind, and with it the *arrondissement* of the French frontier, the abolition of obsolete Treaties, and other *remaniements* as may be necessary. I *improvised* a longish catalogue of dangers and difficulties that such a Congress would entail, unless its decisions were unanimous, which was not probable, or one or two of the strongest Powers were to go to war for what they wanted.[4]

Palmerston once summed up Napoleon's statesmanship by saying: "... ideas proliferated in his head like rabbits in a hutch."[5] The trouble was that these ideas did not relate to any overriding concept. In the disarray of the collapsing Metternich system, France had two strategic options. It could pursue the policy of Richelieu and strive to keep Central Europe divided. This option would have required Napoleon to subordinate his revolutionary convictions, at least within Germany, in favor of the existing legitimate rulers, who were eager to maintain the fragmentation of Central Europe. Or Napoleon could have put himself at the head of a republican crusade, as his uncle had done, in the expectation that France would thereby gain the gratitude of the nationalists and perhaps even the political leadership of Europe.

Unfortunately for France, Napoleon pursued both strategies simultaneously. An advocate of national self-determination, he seemed oblivious to the geopolitical risk this position posed for France in Central Europe. He supported the Polish Revolution but recoiled when confronted by its consequences. He opposed the Vienna settlement as an affront to France without understanding until it was too late that the Vienna world order was the best available security guarantee for France as well.

For the German Confederation was designed to act as a unit only against an overwhelming external danger. Its component states were explicitly forbidden to join together for offensive purposes, and would never have been able to agree on an offensive strategy—as was shown by the fact that the subject had never even been broached in the half-century of the Confederation's existence. France's Rhine frontier, inviolable so long as the Vienna settlement was intact, would not prove to be secure for a century after the collapse of the Confederation, which Napoleon's policy made possible.

Napoleon never grasped this key element of French security. As late as the outbreak of the Austro-Prussian War in 1866—the conflict which ended the Confederation—he wrote to the Austrian Emperor:

> I must confess that it was not without a certain satisfaction that I witnessed the dissolution of the German Confederation organized mainly against France.[6]

The Habsburg responded far more perceptively: ". . . the German Confederation, organized with purely defensive motives, had never, during the half-century of its existence, given its neighbors cause for alarm."[7] The alternative to the German Confederation was not Richelieu's fragmented Central Europe but a unified Germany with a population exceeding that of France and an industrial capacity soon to overshadow it. By attacking the Vienna settlement, Napoleon was transforming a defensive obstacle into a potential offensive threat to French security.

A statesman's test is whether he can discern from the swirl of tactical decisions the true long-term interests of his country and devise an appropriate strategy for achieving them. Napoleon could have basked in the acclaim given to his clever tactics during the Crimean War (which were helped along by Austrian shortsightedness), and in the increased diplomatic options now opening before him. France's interest would have been to stay close to Austria and Great Britain, the two countries most likely to sustain the territorial settlement of Central Europe.

The Emperor's policy, however, was largely idiosyncratic and driven by his mercurial nature. As a Bonaparte, he never felt comfortable cooperating with Austria, whatever *raison d'état* might dictate. In 1858, Napoleon told a Piedmontese diplomat: "Austria is a cabinet for whom I have always felt, and still feel, the most lively repugnance."[8] His penchant for revolutionary projects caused him to go to war with Austria over Italy in 1859. Napoleon alienated Great Britain by annexing Savoy and Nice in the aftermath of the war as well as by his repeated proposals for a European Congress to redraw the frontiers of Europe. To complete his isolation, Napoleon sacrificed his option of allying France with Russia by supporting the Polish Revolution in 1863. Having brought European diplomacy to a state of flux under the banner of national self-determination, Napoleon now suddenly found himself alone when, out of the turmoil he had done so much to cause, a German nation materialized to spell the end of French primacy in Europe.

The Emperor made his first post-Crimea move in Italy in 1859, three years after the Congress of Paris. Nobody had expected Napoleon to return to the vocation of his youth in seeking to liberate Northern Italy from Austrian rule. France would have had little to gain from such an adventure. If it succeeded, it would create a state in a much stronger position to block the traditional French invasion route; if it failed, the humiliation would be compounded by the vagueness of the objective. And whether it succeeded or failed, French armies in Italy would disquiet Europe.

For all these reasons, the British Ambassador, Lord Henry Cowley, was convinced that a French war in Italy was beyond all probability. "It is not in his interests to fight a war," Hübner reported Cowley as saying. "The alliance with England, although shaken for a moment, and still quite dormant, remains the basis of Napoleon III's policy."[9] Some three decades later, Hübner was to offer these reflections:

> We could scarcely comprehend that this man, having reached the pinnacle of honor, unless he was mad, or afflicted with the madness of gamblers, seriously could consider, having no understandable motive, joining in another adventure.[10]

Yet Napoleon surprised all the diplomats with the exception of his ultimate nemesis, Bismarck, who had predicted a French war against Austria and indeed hoped for it as a means of weakening Austria's position in Germany.

In July 1858, Napoleon concluded a secret understanding with Camillo Benso di Cavour, the Prime Minister of Piedmont (Sardinia), the strongest

Italian state, to cooperate in a war against Austria. It was a purely Machiavellian move in which Cavour would unify Northern Italy and Napoleon would receive as his reward Nice and Savoy from Piedmont. By May 1859, a suitable pretext had been found. Austria, always short of steady nerves, permitted itself to be provoked by Piedmontese harassment into declaring war. Napoleon let it be known that this amounted to a declaration of war against France, and launched his armies into Italy.

Oddly enough, in Napoleon's time, when Frenchmen talked of the consolidation of nation-states as the wave of the future, they thought primarily of Italy and not of the much stronger Germany. The French had a sympathy and cultural affinity for Italy that was lacking vis-à-vis their ominous Eastern neighbor. In addition, the mighty economic boom which was to take Germany to the forefront of the European Powers was only just beginning; hence it was not yet obvious that Italy would be any less powerful than Germany. Prussia's cautiousness during the Crimean War strengthened Napoleon's view that Prussia was the weakest of the Great Powers and incapable of strong action without Russian support. Thus, in Napoleon's mind, an Italian war weakening Austria would reduce the power of France's most dangerous German opponent and enhance France's significance in Italy—an egregious misjudgment on both counts.

Napoleon kept open two contradictory options. In the better case, Napoleon could play European statesman: Northern Italy would throw off the Austrian yoke, and the European Powers would gather at a congress under Napoleon's sponsorship and agree to the large-scale territorial revisions he had failed to achieve at the Congress of Paris. In the worse case, the war would reach a stalemate and Napoleon would play the Machiavellian manipulator of *raison d'état,* gaining some advantage from Austria at Piedmont's expense in return for ending the war.

Napoleon pursued the two objectives simultaneously. French armies were victorious at Magenta and Solferino but unleashed such a tide of anti-French sentiment in Germany that, for a time, it appeared as if the smaller German states, fearing a new Napoleonic onslaught, would force Prussia to intervene on Austria's side. Jolted by this first sign of German nationalism and shaken by his visit to the battlefield at Solferino, Napoleon concluded an armistice with Austria at Villafranca on July 11, 1859, without informing his Piedmontese allies.

Not only had Napoleon failed to achieve either of his objectives, he had seriously weakened his country's position in the international arena. Henceforth, the Italian nationalists would carry the principles he had espoused to lengths he had never envisioned. Napoleon's goal of establishing a medium-sized satellite in an Italy divided into perhaps five states annoyed Piedmont, which was not about to abandon its national vocation. Austria remained as adamant about holding on to Venetia as Napoleon was about returning it to Italy, creating yet another insoluble dispute involving no conceivable French interest. Great Britain interpreted the annexation of Savoy and Nice as the beginning of another period of Napoleonic conquests and refused all French initiatives for Napoleon's favorite obsession of holding a European congress. And all the while, German nationalists saw in Europe's turmoil a window of opportunity to advance their own hopes for national unity.

Napoleon's conduct during the Polish revolt of 1863 advanced his journey into isolation. Reviving the Bonaparte tradition of friendship with Poland, Napoleon first tried to convince Russia to make some concessions to its rebellious subjects. But the Tsar would not even discuss such a proposal. Next, Napoleon tried to organize a joint effort with Great Britain, but Palmerston was too wary of the mercurial French Emperor. Finally, Napoleon turned to Austria with the proposition that it give up its own Polish provinces to a not-yet-created Polish state and Venetia to Italy, while seeking compensation in Silesia and the Balkans. The idea held no obvious appeal for Austria, which was being asked to risk war with Prussia and Russia for the privilege of seeing a French satellite emerge on its borders.

Frivolity is a costly indulgence for a statesman, and its price must eventually be paid. Actions geared to the mood of the moment and unrelated to any overall strategy cannot be sustained indefinitely. Under Napoleon, France lost influence over the internal arrangements of Germany, which had been the mainstay of French policy since Richelieu. Whereas Richelieu had understood that a weak Central Europe was the key to French security, Napoleon's policy, driven by his quest for publicity, concentrated on the periphery of Europe, the only place where gains could be made at minimum risk. With the center of gravity of European policy moving toward Germany, France found itself alone.

An ominous event occurred in 1864. For the first time since the Congress of Vienna, Austria and Prussia jointly disrupted the tranquillity of Central Europe, starting a war on behalf of a German cause against a non-German power. The issue at hand was the future of the Elbe duchies of Schleswig and Holstein, which were dynastically linked to the Danish crown but were also members of the German Confederation. The death of the Danish ruler had produced such a complex tangle of political, dynastic, and national issues that Palmerston was prompted to quip that only three people had ever understood it: of these, one was dead, the second was in a lunatic asylum, and he himself was the third but he had forgotten it.

The substance of the dispute was far less important than the coalition of two key German states waging war on tiny Denmark in order to force it to relinquish two ancient German territories linked with the Danish crown. It proved that Germany was capable of offensive action after all and that, should Confederation machinery turn out to be too cumbersome, the two German superpowers might simply ignore it.

According to the traditions of the Vienna system, at this point the Great Powers should have assembled in Congress to restore an approximation of the *status quo ante.* Yet Europe was now in disarray largely due to the actions of the French Emperor. Russia was not prepared to antagonize the two countries which had stood aside while it quelled the Polish revolt. Great Britain was uneasy about the attack on Denmark but would need a Continental ally to intervene, and France, its only feasible partner, inspired little confidence.

History, ideology, and *raison d'état* should have warned Napoleon that events would soon develop a momentum of their own. Yet he wavered between upholding the principles of traditional French foreign policy, which was designed to keep Germany divided, and supporting the principle of nationality, which had been the inspiration of his youth. French Foreign Minister Drouyn de Lhuys wrote to La Tour d'Auvergne, the French Ambassador to London:

> Placed between the rights of a country for which we have long sympathized, and the aspirations of the German population, which we equally have to take into account, we have to act with a greater degree of circumspection than does England.[11]

The responsibility of statesmen, however, is to resolve complexity rather than to contemplate it. For leaders unable to choose among their alternatives, circumspection becomes an alibi for inaction. Napoleon had become convinced of the wisdom of inaction, enabling Prussia and Austria to settle the future of the Elbe duchies. They detached Schleswig-Holstein from Denmark and occupied them jointly while the rest of Europe stood by—a solution which would have been unthinkable under the Metternich system. France's nightmare of German unity was approaching, something Napoleon had been dodging for a decade.

Bismarck was not about to share the leadership of Germany. He turned the joint war for Schleswig-Holstein into another of Austria's seemingly endless series of blunders, which for a decade marked the progressive erosion of its position as a Great Power. The reason these errors occurred was always the same—Austria's appeasing a self-proclaimed opponent by offering to cooperate with it. The strategy of appeasement worked no better with Prussia than it had a decade earlier, during the Crimean War, vis-à-vis France. Far from buying Austria's release from Prussian pressures, the joint victory over Denmark provided a new and highly disadvantageous forum for harassment. Austria was now left to administer the Elbe duchies with a Prussian ally whose Prime Minister, Bismarck, was determined to use the opportunity to bring about a long-desired showdown in a territory hundreds of miles from Austrian soil and adjoining Prussia's principal possessions.

As the tension mounted, Napoleon's ambivalence came into sharper focus. He dreaded German unification but was sympathetic to German nationalism and dithered about solving that insoluble dilemma. He considered Prussia the most genuinely national German state, writing in 1860 that:

> Prussia personifies the German nationality, religious reform, commercial progress, liberal constitutionalism. It is the largest of the truly German monarchies; it has more freedom of conscience, more enlightenment, grants more political rights, than most other German states.[12]

Bismarck would have subscribed to every word. However, for Bismarck, Napoleon's affirmation of Prussia's unique position was the key to Prussia's eventual triumph. In the end, Napoleon's avowed admiration for Prussia amounted to one more alibi for doing nothing. Rationalizing indecision as so much clever maneuvering, Napoleon in fact encouraged an Austro-Prussian war, partly because he was convinced that Prussia would lose. He told Alexandre Walewski, his erstwhile Foreign Minister, in December 1865: "Believe me dear friend, war between Austria and Prussia constitutes one of those unhoped-for eventualities which can bring us more than one advantage."[13] Curiously, in the course of Napoleon's encouragement of the drift toward war, he never seemed to have asked himself why Bismarck was so determined on war if Prussia was so likely to be defeated.

Four months before the Austro-Prussian War started, Napoleon went beyond the tacit to the explicit. In effect urging war, he told the Prussian Ambassador to Paris, Count von der Goltz, in February 1866:

> I ask you to tell the King [of Prussia] that he can always count on my amity. In case of a conflict between Prussia and Austria, I will maintain

the most absolute neutrality. I desire the reunion of the Duchies [Schleswig-Holstein] with Prussia. . . . Should the struggle take on dimensions that one can't yet foresee, I am convinced that I could always reach an understanding with Prussia, whose interests in a great number of questions are identical with those of France, while I see no turf on which I could agree with Austria.[14]

What did Napoleon really want? Was he convinced of the likelihood of a stalemate that would enhance his bargaining position? He was clearly hoping for some Prussian concessions in exchange for his neutrality. Bismarck understood this game. If Napoleon remained neutral, he offered to take a benevolent attitude to French seizure of Belgium, which would have had the additional benefit of embroiling France with Great Britain. Napoleon probably did not take this offer too seriously since he expected Prussia to lose; his moves were designed more to keep Prussia on its course to war than to bargain for benefits. Some years later, Count Armand, the French Foreign Minister's top assistant, admitted:

The only worry that we had at the Foreign Office was that Prussia would be crushed and humiliated to too great an extent, and we were determined to prevent this through timely intervention. The Emperor wanted to let Prussia be defeated, then to intervene and to construct Germany according to his fantasies.[15]

What Napoleon had in mind was an updating of Richelieu's machinations. Prussia was expected to offer France compensation in the West for extrication from its defeat, Venetia would be given to Italy, and a new German arrangement would result in the creation of a North German Confederation under Prussian auspices and a South German grouping supported by France and Austria. The only thing wrong with this scheme was that, whereas the Cardinal knew how to judge the relation of forces and was willing to fight for his judgments, Napoleon was prepared to do neither.

Napoleon procrastinated, hoping for a turn of events that would present him with his deepest desires at no risk. The device he used was his standard ploy of calling for a European congress to avert the threat of war. The reaction by now was equally standard. The other powers, fearful of Napoleon's designs, refused to attend. Wherever he turned, his dilemma awaited him: he could defend the *status quo* by abandoning his support of the nationality principle; or he could encourage revisionism and nationalism and in the process jeopardize the national interests of

France as they had been historically conceived. Napoleon sought refuge in hinting to Prussia about "compensations" without specifying what they were, which convinced Bismarck that French neutrality was a question of price, not principle. Goltz wrote to Bismarck:

> The only difficulty that the Emperor finds in a common stand of Prussia, France and Italy in a congress is the lack of a compensation to be offered to France. One knows what we want; one knows what Italy wants; but the Emperor can't say what France wants, and we can't offer him any suggestion in this regard.[16]

Great Britain made its attendance at the Congress dependent on a prior French agreement to the *status quo*. Instead of seizing upon this consecration of the German arrangements which owed so much to French leadership and to which France owed its security, Napoleon backed off, insisting that, "to maintain the peace, it is necessary to take into account the national passions and requirements."[17] In short, Napoleon was willing to risk an Austro-Prussian war and a unified Germany in order to gain vague spoils in Italy, which affected no real French national interests, and for gains in Western Europe, which he was reluctant to specify. But in Bismarck he was up against a master who insisted on the power of realities, and who exploited for his own ends the cosmetic maneuvers at which Napoleon excelled.

There were French leaders who understood the risks Napoleon was running, and who realized that the so-called compensation he was aiming for involved no basic French interest. In a brilliant speech on May 3, 1866, Adolphe Thiers, a staunch republican opponent of Napoleon and later President of France, predicted correctly that Prussia was likely to emerge as the dominant force in Germany:

> One will see a return of the Empire of Charles V, which formerly resided in Vienna, and now will reside in Berlin which will be close to our border, and will apply pressure to it. . . . You have a right to resist this policy in the name of the interest of France, for France is too important for such a revolution not to menace her gravely. And when she had struggled for two centuries . . . to destroy this colossus, is she prepared to watch as it re-establishes itself before her eyes?![18]

Thiers argued that, in place of Napoleon's vague musings, France should adopt a clear policy of opposition to Prussia and invoke as a pretext the defense of the independence of the German states—the old Richelieu formula. France, he claimed, had the right to resist German unification "first in the name of the independence of the German states . . . second, in the name of her own independence, and, finally in the name of the European balance, which is the interest of all, the interest of universal society. . . . Today one tries to heap ridicule on the term 'European balance' . . . but, what is the European balance? It is the independence of Europe."[19]

It was nearly too late to head off the war between Prussia and Austria that would irrevocably alter the European balance. Analytically, Thiers was correct but the premises for such a policy ought to have been established a decade earlier. Even now, Bismarck might have been brought up short if France had issued a strong warning that it would not permit Austria to be defeated or traditional principalities like the Kingdom of Hanover to be destroyed. But Napoleon rejected such a course because he expected Austria to win, and because he seemed to prize undoing the Vienna settlement and fulfilling the Bonaparte tradition above any analysis of historic French national interests. He replied to Thiers three days later: "I detest those treaties of 1815 which nowadays people want to make the sole basis of our policy."[20]

Little more than a month after Thiers's speech, Prussia and Austria were at war. Against all Napoleon's expectations, Prussia won decisively and quickly. By the rules of Richelieu's diplomacy, Napoleon should have assisted the loser and prevented a clear-cut Prussian victory. But, though he moved an army corps of "observation" to the Rhine, he dithered. Bismarck threw Napoleon the sop of letting him mediate the peace, though this empty gesture could not obscure France's growing irrelevance to German arrangements. At the Treaty of Prague of August 1866, Austria was forced to withdraw from Germany. Two states, Hanover and Hesse-Cassel, which had sided with Austria during the war, were annexed by Prussia along with Schleswig-Holstein and the free city of Frankfurt. By deposing their rulers, Bismarck made it clear that Prussia, once a linchpin of the Holy Alliance, had abandoned legitimacy as the guiding principle of the international order.

The North German states which retained their independence were incorporated into Bismarck's new creation, the North German Confederation, subject to Prussian leadership in everything from trade legislation to foreign policy. The South German states of Bavaria, Baden, and Württemberg were allowed to retain their independence at the price of treaties with Prussia that brought their armies under Prussian military leadership in the event of a war with an outside power. The unification of Germany was now just one crisis away.

Napoleon had maneuvered his country into a dead end from which extrication proved impossible. Too late, he tried for an alliance with Austria, which he had expelled from Italy by military action and from Germany by neutrality. But Austria had lost interest in recovering either position, preferring to concentrate first on rebuilding its empire as a dual monarchy based in Vienna and Budapest, and then on its possessions in the Balkans. Great Britain was put off by France's designs on Luxembourg and Belgium; and Russia never forgave Napoleon his conduct over Poland.

France was now obliged to tend to the collapse of its historic European pre-eminence all by itself. The more hopeless its position, the more Napoleon sought to recoup it by some brilliant move, like a gambler who doubles his bet after each loss. Bismarck had encouraged Napoleon's neutrality in the Austro-Prussian War by dangling before him the prospect of territorial acquisitions—first in Belgium, then in Luxembourg. These prospects vanished whenever Napoleon tried to snatch them because Napoleon wanted his "compensation" handed to him, and because Bismarck saw no reason to run risks when he had already harvested the fruits of Napoleon's indecisiveness.

Humiliated by these demonstrations of impotence, and above all by the increasingly obvious tilt of the European balance against France, Napoleon sought to compensate for his miscalculation that Austria would win the Austro-Prussian War by making an issue of the succession to the Spanish throne, which had become vacant. He demanded an assurance from the Prussian King that no Hohenzollern prince (the Prussian dynasty) would seek the throne. It was another empty gesture capable of producing at best a prestige success without any relevance to the power relationships in Central Europe.

Nobody ever outmaneuvered Bismarck in a fluid diplomacy. In one of his craftier moves, Bismarck used Napoleon's posturing to lure him into declaring war on Prussia in 1870. The French demand that the Prussian King renounce any member of his family ever seeking the Spanish crown was indeed provocative. But the stately old King William, rather than losing his temper, patiently and correctly refused the French ambassador sent to secure the pledge. The King sent his account of the affair to Bismarck, who edited his telegram—taking out any language conveying the patience and propriety with which the King had in fact treated the French ambassador.[21] Bismarck, well ahead of his time, then resorted to a technique which subsequent statesmen developed into an art form: he leaked the so-called Ems Dispatch to the press. The edited version of the King's telegram looked like a royal snub of France. Outraged, the French public demanded war, which Napoleon gave them.

Prussia won quickly and decisively with the assistance of all the other German states. The road now lay clear for completing the unification of Germany, proclaimed rather tactlessly by the Prussian leadership on January 18, 1871, in the Hall of Mirrors of Versailles.

Napoleon had wrought the revolution which he had sought, though its consequences were quite the opposite of what he had intended. The map of Europe had indeed been redrawn, but the new arrangement had irreparably weakened France's influence without bringing Napoleon the renown he craved.

Napoleon had encouraged revolution without understanding its likely outcome. Unable to assess the relationship of forces and to enlist it in fulfilling his long-term goals. Napoleon failed this test. His foreign policy collapsed not because he lacked ideas but because he was unable to establish any order among his multitude of aspirations or any relationship between them and the reality emerging all around him. Questing for publicity, Napoleon never had a single line of policy to guide him. Instead, he was driven by a web of objectives, some of them quite contradictory. When he confronted the crucial crisis of his career, the various impulses canceled each other out.

Napoleon saw the Metternich system as humiliating to France and as a constraint upon its ambitions. He was successful in disrupting the Holy Alliance by driving a wedge between Austria and Russia during the Crimean War. But he did not know what to do with his triumph. From 1853 to 1871 relative chaos prevailed as the European order was reorganized. When this period ended, Germany emerged as the strongest power on the Continent. Legitimacy—the principle of the unity of conservative rulers that had mitigated the harshness of the balance-of-power system during the Metternich years—turned into an empty slogan. Napoleon himself had contributed to all these developments. Overestimating France's strength, he had encouraged every upheaval, convinced that he could turn it to France's benefit.

In the end, international politics came to be based on raw power. And in such a world, there was an inherent gap between France's image of itself as the dominant nation of Europe and its capacity to live up to it—a gap that has blighted French policy to this day. During Napoleon's reign, this was evidenced by the Emperor's inability to implement his endless proposals for holding a European congress to revise the map of Europe. Napoleon called for a congress after the Crimean War in 1856, before the Italian War in 1859, during the Polish revolt in 1863, during the Danish War in 1864, and before the Austro-Prussian War in 1866—always seeking to gain at the conference table the revision of frontiers which he never precisely defined and for which he was not prepared to run the risk of war. Napoleon's problem was that he was not strong enough to insist, and that his schemes were too radical to command consensus.

France's penchant for associating with countries ready to accept its leadership has been a constant factor in French foreign policy since the Crimean War. Unable to dominate an alliance with Great Britain, Germany, Russia, or the United States, and considering junior status incompatible with its notions of national grandeur and its messianic role in the world, France has sought leadership in pacts with lesser powers—with Sardinia, Romania, and the middle German states in the nineteenth century, with Czechoslovakia, Yugoslavia, and Romania in the interwar period.

The same attitude could be found in post–de Gaulle French foreign policy. A century after the Franco-Prussian War, the problem of a more powerful Germany remained France's nightmare. France made the courageous choice of seeking friendship with its feared and admired neighbor. Nevertheless, geopolitical logic would have suggested that France seek close ties with the United States—if only to increase its options. French pride, however, prevented this from happening, leading France to search, sometimes quixotically, for a grouping—occasionally almost *any* grouping—to balance the United States with a European consortium, even at the price of eventual German pre-eminence. In the modern period, France acted at times as a kind of parliamentary opposition to American leadership, trying to build the European Community into an alternative world leader and cultivating ties with nations it could dominate, or thought it could dominate.

Since the end of Napoleon III's reign, France has lacked the power to impose the universalist aspirations it inherited from the French Revolution, or the arena to find an adequate outlet for its missionary zeal. For over a century, France has been finding it difficult to accept the fact that the objective conditions for the pre-eminence Richelieu had brought it disappeared once national consolidation had been achieved in Europe. Much of the prickly style of its diplomacy has been due to attempts by its leaders to perpetuate its role as the center of European policy in an environment increasingly uncongenial to such aspirations. It is ironic that the country that invented *raison d'état* should have had to occupy itself, for the better part of a century, with trying to bring its aspirations in line with its capabilities.

The destruction of the Vienna system, which Napoleon had begun, was completed by Bismarck. Bismarck achieved political prominence as the archconservative opponent of the liberal Revolution of 1848. He was also the first leader to introduce universal male suffrage to Europe, along with the most comprehensive system of social welfare the world would see for sixty years. In 1848, Bismarck strenuously fought the elected Parliament's offer of the German imperial crown to the Prussian King. But a little more than two decades later, he himself would hand that imperial crown to a Prussian king at the end of the process of unifying the German nation on the basis of opposition to liberal principles, and of Prussia's capacity to impose its will by force. This astonishing achievement caused the international order to revert to the unrestrained contests of the eighteenth century, now made all the more dangerous by industrial technology and the capacity to mobilize vast national resources. No longer was there talk of the unity of crowned heads or of harmony among the ancient states of Europe. Under Bismarck's *Realpolitik,* foreign policy became a contest of strength.

Bismarck's accomplishments were as unexpected as his personality. The man of "blood and iron" wrote prose of extraordinary simplicity and beauty, loved poetry, and copied pages of Byron in his diary. The statesman who extolled *Realpolitik* possessed an extraordinary sense of proportion which turned power into an instrument of self-restraint.

What is a revolutionary? If the answer to that question were without ambiguity, few revolutionaries would ever succeed. For revolutionaries almost always start from a position of inferior strength. They prevail because the established order is unable to grasp its own vulnerability. This is especially true when the revolutionary challenge emerges not with a march on the Bastille but in conservative garb. Few institutions have defenses against those who evoke the expectation that they will preserve them.

So it was with Otto von Bismarck. His life began during the flowering of the Metternich system, in a world consisting of three major elements: the European balance of power; an internal German equilibrium between Austria and Prussia; and a system of alliances based on the unity of conservative values. For a generation after the Vienna settlement, international tensions remained low because all the major states perceived a stake in their mutual survival, and because the so-called Eastern Courts of Prussia, Austria, and Russia were committed to each other's values.

Bismarck challenged each of these premises.[22] He was convinced that Prussia had become the strongest German state and did not need the Holy Alliance as a link to Russia. In his view, shared national interests would supply an adequate bond, and Prussian *Realpolitik* could substitute for conservative unity. Bismarck considered Austria an obstacle to Prussia's German mission, not a partner in it. Contrary to the views of nearly all his contemporaries, except perhaps the Piedmontese Prime Minister

Cavour, Bismarck treated Napoleon's restless diplomacy as a strategic opportunity rather than as a threat.

When Bismarck delivered a speech in 1850 attacking the conventional wisdom that German unity required the establishment of parliamentary institutions, his conservative supporters at first did not realize that what they were hearing was above all a challenge to the conservative premises of the Metternich system.

> Prussia's honor does not consist in our playing all over Germany the Don Quixote for vexed parliamentary celebrities, who consider their local constitution threatened. I seek Prussia's honor in keeping Prussia apart from any disgraceful connection with democracy and never admitting that anything occur in Germany without Prussia's permission. . . .[23]

On the surface, Bismarck's attack on liberalism was an application of the Metternich philosophy. Yet it contained a decisive difference in emphasis. The Metternich system had been based on the premise that Prussia and Austria shared a commitment to conservative institutions and needed each other to defeat liberal democratic trends. Bismarck was implying that Prussia could impose its preferences unilaterally; that Prussia could be conservative at home without tying itself to Austria or any other conservative state in foreign policy; and that it needed no alliances to cope with domestic upheaval. In Bismarck, the Habsburgs faced the same challenge with which Richelieu had presented them—a policy divorced from any value system except the glory of the state. And, just as with Richelieu, they did not know how to deal with it or even how to comprehend its nature.

But how was Prussia to sustain *Realpolitik* all alone in the center of the Continent? Since 1815, Prussia's answer had been adherence to the Holy Alliance at almost any price; Bismarck's answer was the exact opposite— to forge alliances and relationships in all directions, so that Prussia would always be closer to each of the contending parties than they were to one another. In this manner, a position of seeming isolation would enable Prussia to manipulate the commitments of the other powers and to sell its support to the highest bidder.

In Bismarck's view, Prussia would be in a strong position to implement such a policy, because it had few foreign-policy interests other than enhancing its own position within Germany. Every other power had more complicated involvements: Great Britain had not only its empire but the overall balance of power to worry about; Russia was simultaneously pressing into Eastern Europe, Asia, and the Ottoman Empire; France had a newfound empire, ambitions in Italy, and an adventure in Mexico on its hands; and Austria was preoccupied with Italy and the Balkans, and with its leadership role in the German Confederation. Because Prussia's policy was so focused on Germany, it really had no major disagreements with any other power except Austria, and at that point the disagreement with Austria was primarily in Bismarck's own mind. Nonalignment, to use a modern term, was the functional equivalent of Bismarck's policy of selling Prussia's cooperation in what he perceived to be a seller's market:

> The present situation forces us not to commit ourselves in advance of the other powers. We are not able to shape the relations of the Great Powers to each other as we wish, but we can maintain freedom of action to utilize to our advantage those relationships which do come about. . . . Our relations to Austria, Britain and Russia do not furnish an obstacle to a rapprochement with any of these powers. Only our relations with France require careful attention so that we keep open the option of going with France as easily as with the other powers. . . .[24]

This hint of rapprochement with Bonaparte France implied a readiness to throw ideology to the wind—in order to free Prussia to ally itself with any country (whatever its domestic institutions) that could advance its interests. Bismarck's policy marked a return to the principles of Richelieu, who, though a Cardinal of the Church, had opposed the Catholic Holy Roman Emperor when it was required by the interests of France. Similarly, Bismarck, though conservative by personal conviction, parted company with his conservative mentors whenever it seemed that their legitimist principles would constrain Prussia's freedom of action.

This implicit disagreement came to a head when, in 1856, Bismarck, then Prussian ambassador to the German Confederation, amplified his view that Prussia be more forthcoming toward Napoleon III, who, in the eyes of Prussia's conservatives, was a usurper of the legitimate king's prerogatives.

Putting Napoleon forward as a potential Prussian interlocutor went beyond what Bismarck's conservative constituency, which had launched and fostered his diplomatic career, could tolerate. It greeted Bismarck's emerging philosophy with the same outraged disbelief among his erstwhile supporters that Richelieu had encountered two centuries earlier when he had advanced the then revolutionary thesis that *raison d'état* should have precedence over religion, and the same which would in our time greet Richard Nixon's policy of détente with the Soviet Union. To conservatives, Napoleon III spelled the threat of a new round of French expansionism and, even more importantly, symbolized a reaffirmation of the hated principles of the French Revolution.

Bismarck did not dispute the conservative analysis of Napoleon any more than Nixon challenged the conservative interpretation of communist motives. Bismarck saw in the restless French ruler, as Nixon did in the decrepit Soviet leadership (see chapter 28), both an opportunity and a danger. He considered Prussia less vulnerable than Austria to either French expansionism or revolution. Nor did Bismarck accept the prevailing opinion of Napoleon's cunning, noting sarcastically that the ability to admire others was not his most highly developed trait. The more Austria feared Napoleon, the more it would have to make concessions to Prussia, and the greater would become Prussia's diplomatic flexibility.

The reasons for Bismarck's break with the Prussian conservatives were much the same as those for Richelieu's debate with his clerical critics, the chief difference being that the Prussian conservatives insisted on universal political principles, rather than universal religious principles. Bismarck asserted that power supplied its own legitimacy; the conservatives argued that legitimacy represented a value beyond calculations of power. Bismarck believed that a correct evaluation of power implied a doctrine of self-limitation; the conservatives insisted that only moral principles could ultimately limit the claims of power.

The conflict evoked a poignant exchange of letters in the late 1850s between Bismarck and his old mentor, Leopold von Gerlach, the Prussian King's military adjutant, to whom Bismarck owed everything—his first diplomatic appointment, his access to the court, his entire career.

The exchange of letters between the two men began when Bismarck sent Gerlach a recommendation that Prussia develop a diplomatic option toward France along with a covering letter in which he placed utility above ideology:

> I cannot escape the mathematical logic of the fact that present-day Austria cannot be our friend. As long as Austria does not agree to a delimitation of spheres of influence in Germany, we must anticipate a contest with it, by means of diplomacy and lies in peace time, with the utilization of every opportunity to give a *coup de grâce*.[25]

Gerlach, however, could not bring himself to accept the proposition that strategic advantage could justify abandoning principle, especially when it involved a Bonaparte. He urged the Metternich remedy—that Prussia bring Austria and Russia closer together and restore the Holy Alliance to enforce the isolation of France.[26]

What Gerlach found even more incomprehensible was another Bismarck proposal to the effect that Napoleon be invited to the maneuvers of a Prussian army corps because "this proof of good relations with France . . . would increase our influence in all diplomatic relations."[27]

The suggestion that a Bonaparte participate in Prussian maneuvers provoked a veritable outburst from Gerlach: "How can a man of your intelligence sacrifice his principles to such an individual as Napoleon. Napoleon is our natural enemy."[28] Had Gerlach seen Bismarck's cynical marginalia —"What of it?"—he might have saved himself the next letter, in which he reiterated his antirevolutionary principles of a lifetime, the same that had led him to support the Holy Alliance and to sponsor Bismarck's early career:

> My political principle is and remains the war against revolution. You will not convince Bonaparte that he is not on the revolutionary side. And he will not stand on any other side because he clearly derives advantage from this. . . . So if my principle of opposing revolution is right . . . it also has to be adhered to in practice.[29]

Yet Bismarck disagreed with Gerlach not because he did not understand him, as Gerlach supposed, but because he understood him only too well. *Realpolitik* for Bismarck depended on flexibility and on the ability to exploit every available option without the constraint of ideology. Just as Richelieu's defenders had done, Bismarck transferred the debate to the one principle he and Gerlach did share, and one that would leave Gerlach at a distinct disadvantage—the overriding importance of Prussian patriotism. Gerlach's insistence on the unity of conservative interests was, according to Bismarck, incompatible with loyalty to their country:

> France interests me only insofar as it affects the situation of my country and we can make policy only with the France which exists. . . . As a romantic I can shed a tear for the fate of Henry V (the Bourbon pretender); as a diplomat I would be his servant if I were French, but as things stand, France, irrespective of the accident who leads it, is for me an unavoidable pawn on the chessboard of diplomacy, where I have no other duty than to serve *my* king and *my* country [Bismarck's emphasis]. I cannot reconcile personal sympathies and antipathies toward foreign powers with my sense of duty in foreign affairs; indeed I see in them the embryo of disloyalty toward the Sovereign and the country I serve.[30]

How was a traditional Prussian to respond to the proposition that Prussian patriotism transcended the principle of legitimacy and that, if circumstances should require it, a generation's faith in the unity of conservative values could verge on disloyalty? Bismarck implacably cut off every intellectual escape route, rejecting in advance Gerlach's argument that legitimacy *was* Prussia's national interest and that therefore Napoleon was Prussia's permanent enemy:

> ... I could deny this—but even if you were right I would not consider it politically wise to let other states know of our fears in peace time. Until the break you predict occurs I would think it useful to encourage the belief ... that the tension with France is not an organic fault of our nature. ...[31]

In other words, *Realpolitik* demanded tactical flexibility, and the Prussian national interest required keeping open the option of making a deal with France. The bargaining position of a country depends on the options it is perceived to have. Closing them off eases the adversary's calculations, and constricts those of the practitioners of *Realpolitik*.

The break between Gerlach and Bismarck became irrevocable in 1860 over the issue of Prussia's attitude toward France's war with Austria over Italy. To Gerlach, the war had eliminated all doubt that Napoleon's true purpose was to set the stage for aggression in the style of the first Bonaparte. Gerlach therefore urged Prussia to support Austria. Bismarck saw instead the opportunity—that if Austria were forced to retreat from Italy, it could serve as the precursor of its eventual expulsion from Germany as well. To Bismarck, the convictions of the generation of Metternich had turned into a dangerous set of inhibitions:

> I stand or fall with my own Sovereign, even if in my opinion he ruins himself stupidly, but for me France will remain France, whether it is governed by Napoleon or by St. Louis and Austria is for me a foreign country. ... I know that you will reply that fact and right cannot be separated, that a properly conceived Prussian policy requires chastity in foreign affairs even from the point of view of utility. I am prepared to discuss the point of utility with you; but if you pose antinomies between right and revolution; Christianity and infidelity; God and the devil; I can argue no longer and can merely say, "I am not of your opinion and you judge in me what is not yours to judge."[32]

This bitter declaration of faith was the functional equivalent of Richelieu's assertion that, since the soul is immortal, man must submit to the judgment of God but that states, being mortal, can only be judged by what works. Like Richelieu, Bismarck did not reject Gerlach's moral views as personal articles of faith—he probably shared most of them; but he denied their relevance to the duties of statesmanship by way of elaborating the distinction between personal belief and *Realpolitik*:

> I did not seek the service of the King.... The God who unexpectedly placed me into it will probably rather show me the way out than let my soul perish. I would overestimate the value of this life strangely... should I not be convinced that after thirty years it will be irrelevant to me what political successes I or my country have achieved in Europe. I can even think out the idea that some day "unbelieving Jesuits" will rule over the Mark Brandenburg [core of Prussia] together with a Bonapartist absolutism.... I am a child of different times than you, but as honest a one of mine as you of yours.[33]

This eerie premonition of Prussia's fate a century later never received an answer from the man to whom Bismarck owed his career.

Bismarck was indeed the child of a different era from that of his erstwhile mentor. Bismarck belonged to the age of *Realpolitik*; Gerlach had been shaped by the period of Metternich. The Metternich system had reflected the eighteenth-century conception of the universe as a great clockwork of intricately meshing parts in which disruption of one part meant upsetting the interaction of the others. Bismarck represented the new age in both science and politics. He perceived the universe not as a mechanical balance, but in its modern version—as consisting of particles in flux whose impact on each other creates what is perceived as reality. Its kindred biological philosophy was Darwin's theory of evolution based on the survival of the fittest.

Driven by such convictions, Bismarck proclaimed the relativity of *all* belief, including even the belief in the permanence of his own country. In the world of *Realpolitik*, it was the statesman's duty to evaluate ideas as forces in relation to all the other forces relevant to making a decision; and the various elements needed to be judged by how well they could serve the national interest, not by preconceived ideologies.

Still, however hard-boiled Bismarck's philosophy might have appeared, it was built on an article of faith as unprovable as Gerlach's premises— namely, that a careful analysis of a given set of circumstances would necessarily lead all statesmen to the same conclusions. Just as Gerlach found it inconceivable that the principle of legitimacy could inspire more than one interpretation, it was beyond Bismarck's comprehension that statesmen might differ in the way they assessed the national interest. Because of his magnificent grasp of the nuances of power and its ramifications, Bismarck was able in his lifetime to replace the philosophical constraints of the Metternich system with a policy of self-restraint. Because these nuances were not as self-evident to Bismarck's successors and imitators, the literal application of *Realpolitik* led to their excessive dependence on military power, and from there to an armament race and two world wars.

Success is often so elusive that statesmen pursuing it rarely bother to consider that it may impose its own penalties. Thus, at the beginning of his career, Bismarck was chiefly preoccupied with applying *Realpolitik* to destroying the world he found, which was still very much dominated by Metternich's principles. This required weaning Prussia from the idea that Austrian leadership in Germany was vital to Prussia's security and to the preservation of conservative values. However true this might have been at the time of the Congress of Vienna, in the middle of the nineteenth century Prussia no longer needed the Austrian alliance to preserve domestic stability or European tranquillity. Indeed, according to Bismarck, the illusion of the need for an Austrian alliance served above all to inhibit Prussia from pursuing its ultimate goal of unifying Germany.

As Bismarck saw it, Prussian history was resplendent with evidence that supported his claim of its primacy within Germany and of its ability to stand alone. For Prussia was not just another German state. Whatever its conservative domestic policies, they could not dim the national luster it had garnered through its tremendous sacrifices in the wars of liberation from Napoleon. It was as if Prussia's very outlines—a series of oddly shaped enclaves stretching across the North German plain from the Vistula to west of the Rhine—had destined it to lead the quest for German unity, even in the eyes of the liberals.

But Bismarck went further. He challenged the conventional wisdom which identified nationalism with liberalism, or at least with the proposition that German unity could only be realized through liberal institutions:

> Prussia has become great not through liberalism and free-thinking but through a succession of powerful, decisive and wise regents who carefully husbanded the military and financial resources of the state and kept them together in their own hands in order to throw them with ruthless courage into the scale of European politics as soon as a favorable opportunity presented itself. . . .[34]

Bismarck relied not on conservative principles but on the unique character of Prussian institutions; he rested Prussia's claim to leadership in Germany on its strength rather than on universal values. In Bismarck's view, Prussian institutions were so impervious to outside influence that

Prussia could exploit the democratic currents of the period as instruments of foreign policy by threatening to encourage greater freedom of expression at home—never mind that no Prussian king had practiced such a policy for four decades, if ever:

> The sense of security that the King remains master in his country even if the whole army is abroad is not shared with Prussia by any other continental state and above all by no other German power. It provides the opportunity to accept a development of public affairs much more in conformity with present requirements. . . . The royal authority in Prussia is so firmly based that the government can without risk encourage a much more lively parliamentary activity and thereby exert pressure on conditions in Germany.[35]

Bismarck rejected the Metternich view that a shared sense of their domestic vulnerability required the close association of the three Eastern Courts. Quite the opposite was the case. Since Prussia was not threatened by domestic upheaval, its very cohesiveness could serve as a weapon to undermine the Vienna settlement by threatening the other powers, especially Austria, with policies fomenting domestic upheavals. For Bismarck, the strength of Prussia's governmental, military, and financial institutions opened the road to Prussian primacy in Germany.

When he was appointed ambassador to the Assembly of the Confederation in 1852 and ambassador to St. Petersburg in 1858, Bismarck ascended to positions which enabled him to advocate his policies. His reports, brilliantly written and remarkably consistent, urged a foreign policy based on neither sentiment nor legitimacy but on the correct assessment of power. In this manner, Bismarck returned to the tradition of such eighteenth-century rulers as Louis XIV and Frederick the Great. Enhancing the influence of the state became the principal, if not the only, objective, restrained solely by the forces massed against it:

> . . . A sentimental policy knows no reciprocity. It is an exclusively Prussian peculiarity.[36]

> . . . For heaven's sake no sentimental alliances in which the consciousness of having performed a good deed furnishes the sole reward for our sacrifice.[37]

> . . . Policy is the art of the possible, the science of the relative.[38]

> Not even the King has the right to subordinate the interests of the state to his personal sympathies or antipathies.[39]

In Bismarck's estimation, foreign policy had a nearly scientific basis, making it possible to analyze the national interest in terms of objective criteria. In such a calculation, Austria emerged as a foreign, not a fraternal, country, and above all as an obstacle to Prussia's rightful place in Germany: "Our policy has no other parade ground than Germany and this is precisely the one which Austria believes it badly requires for itself. . . . We deprive each other of the air we need to breathe. . . . This is a fact which cannot be ignored however unwelcome it may be."[40]

The first Prussian king whom Bismarck served as ambassador, Frederick William IV, was torn between Gerlach's legitimist conservatism and the opportunities inherent in Bismarck's *Realpolitik*. Bismarck insisted that his King's personal regard for the traditionally pre-eminent German state must not inhibit Prussian policy. Since Austria would never accept Prussian hegemony in Germany, Bismarck's strategy was to weaken Austria at every turn. In 1854, during the Crimean War, Bismarck urged that Prussia exploit Austria's break with Russia and attack what was still Prussia's partner in the Holy Alliance without any better justification than the auspiciousness of the occasion:

> Could we succeed in getting Vienna to the point where it does not consider an attack by Prussia on Austria as something outside of all possibility we would soon hear more sensible things from there. . . .[41]

In 1859, during Austria's war with France and Piedmont, Bismarck returned to the same theme:

> The present situation once more presents us with the great prize if we let the war between Austria and France become well established and then move south with our army taking the border posts in our field packs not to impale them again until we reach Lake Constance or at least the regions where the Protestant confession ceases to predominate.[42]

Metternich would have considered this heresy, but Frederick the Great would have applauded a disciple's clever adaptation of his own rationale for conquering Silesia.

Bismarck subjected the European balance of power to the same cold-blooded, relativistic analysis as he did the internal German situation. At the height of the Crimean War, Bismarck outlined the principal options for Prussia:

> We have three threats available: (1) An alliance with Russia; and it is nonsense always to swear at once that we will never go with Russia.

Even if it were true, we should retain the option to use it as a threat. (2) A policy in which we throw ourselves into Austria's arms and compensate ourselves at the expense of perfidious [German] confederates. (3) A change of cabinets to the left whereby we would soon become so "Western" as to outmaneuver Austria completely.[43]

In the same dispatch were listed as equally valid Prussian options: an alliance with Russia against France (presumably on the basis of a community of conservative interests); an arrangement with Austria against the secondary German states (and presumably against Russia); and a shift toward liberalism domestically directed against Austria and Russia (presumably in combination with France). Like Richelieu, Bismarck felt unfettered in his choice of partners, being prepared to ally himself with Russia, Austria, or France; the choice would depend entirely on which could best serve the Prussian national interest. Though a bitter opponent of Austria, Bismarck was prepared to explore an arrangement with Vienna in return for appropriate compensation in Germany. And although he was an arch-conservative in domestic affairs, Bismarck saw no obstacle to shifting Prussia's domestic policy to the left as long as it served a foreign policy purpose. For domestic policy, too, was a tool of *Realpolitik*.

Attempts to tilt the balance of power had, of course, occurred even in the heyday of the Metternich system. But then every effort would have been made to legitimize the change by means of European consensus. The Metternich system sought adjustments through European congresses rather than through a foreign policy of threat and counterthreat. Bismarck would have been the last person to reject the efficacy of moral consensus. But to him, it was only one element of power among many. The stability of the international order depended precisely on this nuance. Pressuring for change without so much as paying lip service to existing treaty relationships, shared values, or the Concert of Europe marked a diplomatic revolution. In time, turning power into the only criterion induced all nations to conduct armament races and foreign policies of confrontation.

Bismarck's views remained academic as long as the key element of the Vienna settlement—the unity of the conservative courts of Prussia, Austria, and Russia—was still intact, and as long as Prussia by itself did not dare to rupture that unity. The Holy Alliance disintegrated unexpectedly and quite rapidly after the Crimean War, when Austria abandoned the deft anonymity by which Metternich had deflected crises from his rickety empire and, after many vacillations, sided with Russia's enemies. Bismarck understood at once that the Crimean War had wrought a diplomatic revolution. "The day of reckoning," he said, "is sure to come even if a few years pass."[44]

Indeed, perhaps the most important document relating to the Crimean War was a dispatch from Bismarck analyzing the situation upon the conclusion of the war in 1856. Characteristically, the dispatch assumed perfect flexibility of diplomatic method and a total absence of scruple in the pursuit of opportunity. German historiography has aptly named Bismarck's dispatch the *"Prachtbericht,"* or the "Master Dispatch." For assembled therein was the essence of *Realpolitik,* though it was still too daring for its addressee, the Prussian Prime Minister, Otto von Manteuffel, whose numerous marginal comments indicate that he was far from persuaded by it.

Bismarck opened with an exposition of Napoleon's extraordinarily favorable position at the end of the Crimean War. Henceforth, he noted, all the states of Europe would be seeking France's friendship, none with a greater prospect of success than Russia:

> An alliance between France and Russia is too natural that it should not come to pass. . . . Up to now the firmness of the Holy Alliance . . . has kept the two states apart; but with the Tsar Nicholas dead and the Holy Alliance dissolved by Austria, nothing remains to arrest the natural rapprochement of two states with nary a conflicting interest.[45]

Bismarck predicted that Austria had maneuvered itself into a trap from which it would not be able to escape by racing the Tsar to Paris. For in order to retain the support of his army, Napoleon would require some issue which could furnish him at a moment's notice with "a not too arbitrary and unjust pretext for intervention. Italy is ideally suited for this role. The ambitions of Sardinia, the memories of Bonaparte and Murat, furnish sufficient excuses and the hatred of Austria will smooth its way."[46] This was, of course, exactly what happened three years later.

How should Prussia position itself in light of the inevitability of tacit Franco-Russian cooperation and the likelihood of a Franco-Austrian conflict? According to the Metternich system, Prussia should have tightened its alliance with conservative Austria, strengthened the German Confederation, established close relations with Great Britain, and sought to wean Russia away from Napoleon.

Bismarck demolished each of these options in turn. Great Britain's land forces were too negligible to be of use against a Franco-Russian alliance. Austria and Prussia would end up having to bear the brunt of the fighting. Nor could the German Confederation add any real strength:

> Aided by Russia, Prussia, and Austria, the German Confederation would probably hold together, because it would believe in victory even without its support; but in the case of a two-front war toward East and West,

those princes who are not under the control of our bayonets would attempt to save themselves through declarations of neutrality, if they did not appear in the field against us. . . .[47]

Although Austria had been Prussia's principal ally for over a generation, it now presented a rather incongruous partner in Bismarck's eyes. It had become the main obstacle to Prussia's growth: "Germany is too small for the two of us . . . , as long as we plough the same furrow, Austria is the only state against which we can make a permanent gain and to which we can suffer a permanent loss."[48]

Whatever aspect of international relations he considered, Bismarck resolved it by the argument that Prussia needed to break its confederate bond to Austria and reverse the policies of the Metternich period in order to weaken its erstwhile ally at every opportunity: "When Austria hitches a horse in front, we hitch one behind."[49]

The bane of stable international systems is their nearly total inability to envision mortal challenge. The blind spot of revolutionaries is their conviction that they can combine all the benefits of their goals with the best of what they are overthrowing. But the forces unleashed by revolution have their own momentum, and the direction in which they are moving cannot necessarily be deduced from the proclamations of their advocates.

So it was with Bismarck. Within five years of coming to power in 1862, he eliminated the Austrian obstacle to German unity by implementing his own advice of the previous decade. Through the three wars described earlier in this chapter, he expelled Austria from Germany and destroyed lingering Richelieuan illusions in France.

The new united Germany did not embody the ideals of the two generations of Germans who had aspired to build a constitutional, democratic state. In fact, it reflected no previous significant strain of German thinking, having come into being as a diplomatic compact among German sovereigns rather than as an expression of popular will. Its legitimacy derived from Prussia's power, not from the principle of national self-determination. Though Bismarck achieved what he had set out to do, the very magnitude of his triumph mortgaged the future of Germany and, indeed, of the European world order. To be sure, he was as moderate in concluding his wars as he had been ruthless in preparing them. As soon as Germany had achieved the borders he considered vital to its security, Bismarck conducted a prudent and stabilizing foreign policy. For two decades, he maneuvered Europe's commitments and interests in masterly fashion on the basis of *Realpolitik* and to the benefit of the peace of Europe.

But, once called forth, the spirits of power refused to be banished by juggling acts, however spectacular or restrained these were. Germany had been unified as the result of a diplomacy presupposing infinite adaptability; yet the very success of that policy removed all flexibility from the international system. There were now fewer participants. And when the number of players declines, the capacity to make adjustments diminishes. The new international system contained both fewer and weightier components, making it difficult to negotiate a generally acceptable balance or to sustain it without constant tests of strength.

These structural problems were magnified by the scope of Prussia's victory in the Franco-Prussian War and by the nature of the peace that concluded it. The German annexation of Alsace-Lorraine produced irreconcilable French antagonism, which eliminated any German diplomatic option toward France.

In the 1850s, Bismarck had considered the French option so essential that he had sacrificed his friendship with Gerlach to promote it. After the annexation of Alsace-Lorraine, French enmity grew into the "organic fault of our nature" against which Bismarck had warned so insistently. And it precluded the policy of his "Master Dispatch" of remaining aloof until other powers were already committed, then selling Prussia's support to whoever offered it the most.

The German Confederation had succeeded in acting as a unit only in the face of threats so overwhelming that they had obliterated the rivalries among the various states; and joint offensive action was structurally impossible. The tenuousness of these arrangements was indeed one of the reasons Bismarck had insisted that German unification be organized under Prussian leadership. But he also paid a price for the new arrangement. Once Germany was transformed from a potential victim of aggression to a threat to the European equilibrium, the remote contingency of the other states of Europe uniting against Germany became a real possibility. And that nightmare in turn drove a German policy that was soon to split Europe into two hostile camps.

The European statesman who grasped the impact of German unification most quickly was Benjamin Disraeli, who was about to become British Prime Minister. In 1871, he said the following about the Franco-Prussian War:

> The war represents the German revolution, a greater political event than the French Revolution of the last century. . . . There is not a diplomatic tradition which has not been swept away. You have a new world. . . . The balance of power has been entirely destroyed.[50]

While Bismarck was at the helm, these dilemmas were obscured by his intricate and subtle diplomacy. Yet in the long term, the very complexity of Bismarck's arrangements doomed them. Disraeli was right on the mark. Bismarck had recast the map of Europe and the pattern of international relations, but in the end he was not able to establish a design his successors could follow. Once the novelty of Bismarck's tactics had worn off, his successors and competitors sought safety in multiplying arms as a way of reducing their reliance on the baffling intangibles of diplomacy. The Iron Chancellor's inability to institutionalize his policies forced Germany onto a diplomatic treadmill it could only escape, first by an arms race, and then by war.

In his domestic policy as well, Bismarck was unable to establish a design his successors could follow. Bismarck, a solitary figure in his lifetime, was even less understood after he passed from the scene and attained mythic proportions. His compatriots remembered the three wars which had achieved German unity but forgot the painstaking preparations that had made them possible, and the moderation required to reap their fruits. They had seen displays of power but without discerning the subtle analysis on which these had been based.

The constitution which Bismarck had designed for Germany compounded these tendencies. Though based on the first universal male suffrage in Europe, the Parliament (the Reichstag) did not control the government, which was appointed by the Emperor and could only be removed by him. The Chancellor was closer to both the Emperor and the Reichstag than each was to the other. Therefore, within limits, Bismarck could play Germany's domestic institutions off against each other, much as he did the other states in his foreign policy. None of Bismarck's successors possessed the skill or the daring to do so. The result was that nationalism unleavened by democracy turned increasingly chauvinistic, while democracy without responsibility grew sterile. The essence of Bismarck's life was perhaps best expressed by the Iron Chancellor himself in a letter he had written to his then still future wife:

> That which is imposing here on earth ... has always something of the quality of the fallen angel who is beautiful but without peace, great in his conceptions and exertions but without success, proud and lonely.[51]

The two revolutionaries who stood at the beginning of the contemporary European state system incarnated many of the dilemmas of the modern period. Napoleon, the reluctant revolutionary, represented the trend of gearing policy to public relations. Bismarck, the conservative revolutionary, reflected the tendency to identify policy with the analysis of power.

Napoleon had revolutionary ideas but recoiled before their implications. Having spent his youth in what the twentieth century would call protest, he never bridged the gap between the formulation of an idea and its implementation. Insecure about his purposes and indeed his legitimacy, he relied on public opinion to bridge that gap. Napoleon conducted his foreign policy in the style of modern political leaders who measure their success by the reaction of the television evening news. Like them, Napoleon made himself a prisoner of the purely tactical, focusing on short-term objectives and immediate results, seeking to impress his public by magnifying the pressures he had set out to create. In the process, he confused foreign policy with the moves of a conjurer. For in the end, it is reality, not publicity, that determines whether a leader has made a difference.

The public does not in the long run respect leaders who mirror its own insecurities or see only the symptoms of crises rather than the long-term trends. The role of the leader is to assume the burden of acting on the basis of a confidence in his own assessment of the direction of events and how they can be influenced. Failing that, crises will multiply, which is another way of saying that a leader has lost control over events. Napoleon turned out to be the precursor of a strange modern phenomenon—the political figure who desperately seeks to determine what the public wants, yet ends up rejected and perhaps even despised by it.

Bismarck did not lack the confidence to act on his own judgments. He brilliantly analyzed the underlying reality and Prussia's opportunity. He built so well that the Germany he created survived defeat in two world wars, two foreign occupations, and two generations as a divided country. Where Bismarck failed was in having doomed his society to a style of policy which could only have been carried on had a great man emerged in every generation. This is rarely the case, and the institutions of imperial Germany militated against it. In this sense, Bismarck sowed the seeds not only of his country's achievements, but of its twentieth-century tragedies. "No one eats with impunity from the tree of immortality,"[52] wrote Bismarck's friend von Roon about him.

Napoleon's tragedy was that his ambitions surpassed his capacities; Bismarck's tragedy was that his capacities exceeded his society's ability to absorb them. The legacy Napoleon left France was strategic paralysis; the legacy Bismarck left Germany was unassimilable greatness.

CHAPTER SIX

Realpolitik Turns on Itself

Realpolitik—foreign policy based on calculations of power and the national interest—brought about the unification of Germany. And the unification of Germany caused *Realpolitik* to turn on itself, accomplishing the opposite of what it was meant to achieve. For the practice of *Realpolitik* avoids armaments races and war only if the major players of an international system are free to adjust their relations in accordance with changing circumstances or are restrained by a system of shared values, or both.

After its unification, Germany became the strongest country on the Continent, and was growing stronger with every decade, thereby revolutionizing European diplomacy. Ever since the emergence of the modern state system in Richelieu's time, the powers at the edge of Europe—Great Britain, France, and Russia—had been exerting pressure on the center. Now, for the first time, the center of Europe was becoming sufficiently powerful to press on the periphery. How would Europe deal with this new giant in its midst?

Geography had created an insoluble dilemma. According to all the traditions of *Realpolitik,* European coalitions were likely to arise to con-

137

tain Germany's growing, potentially dominant, power. Since Germany was located in the center of the Continent, it stood in constant danger of what Bismarck called *"le cauchemar des coalitions"*—the nightmare of hostile, encircling coalitions. But if Germany tried to protect itself against a coalition of all its neighbors—East and West—simultaneously, it was certain to threaten them individually, speeding up the formation of coalitions. Self-fulfilling prophecies became a part of the international system. What was still called the Concert of Europe was in fact riven by two sets of animosities: the enmity between France and Germany, and the growing hostility between the Austro-Hungarian and the Russian Empires.

As for France and Germany, the magnitude of Prussia's victory in the 1870 war had produced a permanent French desire for *revanche,* and German annexation of Alsace-Lorraine gave this resentment a tangible focal point. Resentment soon mixed with fear as French leaders began to sense that the war of 1870–71 had marked the end of the era of French predominance and an irrevocable change in the alignment of forces. The Richelieu system of playing the various German states off against each other in a fragmented Central Europe no longer applied. Torn between memory and ambition, France sublimated its frustrations for nearly fifty years in the single-minded pursuit of regaining Alsace-Lorraine, never considering that success in this effort could do no more than salve French pride without altering the underlying strategic reality. By itself, France was no longer strong enough to contain Germany; henceforth it would always need allies to defend itself. By the same token, France made itself permanently available as the potential ally of any enemy of Germany, thereby restricting the flexibility of German diplomacy and escalating any crisis involving Germany.

The second European schism, between the Austro-Hungarian Empire and Russia, also resulted from German unification. Upon becoming *Ministerpräsident* in 1862, Bismarck had asked the Austrian ambassador to convey to his Emperor the startling proposition that Austria, the capital of the ancient Holy Roman Empire, move its center of gravity from Vienna to Budapest. The ambassador considered the idea so preposterous that, in his report to Vienna, he ascribed it to nervous exhaustion on the part of Bismarck. Yet, once defeated in the struggle for pre-eminence in Germany, Austria had no choice but to act on Bismarck's suggestion. Budapest became an equal, occasionally dominant partner in the newly created Dual Monarchy.

After its expulsion from Germany, the new Austro-Hungarian Empire had no place to expand except into the Balkans. Since Austria had not participated in overseas colonialism, its leaders had come to view the Balkans, with its Slavic population, as the natural arena for Austrian geopolitical ambitions—if only to keep pace with the other Great Powers. Inherent in such a policy was conflict with Russia.

Common sense should have cautioned Austrian leaders against provoking Balkan nationalism, or taking on Russia as a permanent enemy. But common sense was not in abundant supply in Vienna, and even less so in Budapest. Jingoistic nationalism prevailed. The Cabinet in Vienna continued on its course of inertia at home and fits of hysteria in foreign policy, which had progressively isolated it since Metternich's time.

Germany perceived no national interest in the Balkans. But it did perceive a major interest in the preservation of the Austro-Hungarian Empire. For the collapse of the Dual Monarchy would have risked undoing Bismarck's entire German policy. The German-speaking Catholic segment of the empire would seek to join Germany, jeopardizing the pre-eminence of Protestant Prussia, for which Bismarck had struggled so tenaciously. And the disintegration of the Austrian Empire would leave Germany without a single dependable ally. On the other hand, though Bismarck wanted to preserve Austria, he had no desire to challenge Russia. It was a conundrum he could obscure for some decades, but never quite overcome.

To make matters worse, the Ottoman Empire was in the throes of a slow disintegration, creating frequent clashes between the Great Powers over the division of the spoils. Bismarck once said that, in a combination of five players, it is always desirable to be on the side of the three. But since, of the five Great Powers—England, France, Russia, Austria, and Germany—France was hostile, Great Britain unavailable due to its policy of "splendid isolation," and Russia ambivalent because of its conflict with Austria, Germany needed an alliance with both Russia *and* Austria for such a grouping of three. Only a statesman possessed of Bismarck's willpower and skill could even have conceived such a precarious balancing act. Thus, the relationship between Germany and Russia became the key to the peace of Europe.

Once Russia entered the international arena, it established a dominant position with astonishing speed. At the Peace of Westphalia in 1648, Russia had not yet been deemed sufficiently important to be represented. From 1750 onward, however, Russia became an active participant in every significant European war. By the middle of the eighteenth century, Russia was already inspiring a vague uneasiness in Western observers. In 1762, the French *chargé d'affaires* in St. Petersburg reported:

> If Russian ambition is not checked, its effects may be fatal to the neighboring powers. . . . I know that the degree of Russian power should not be measured by its expanse and that its domination of eastern territories is more an imposing phantom than a source of real strength. But I

also suspect that a nation which is capable of braving the intemperance of the seasons better than any other because of the rigor of its native climate, which is accustomed to servile obedience, which needs little to live and is therefore able to wage war at little cost . . . such a nation, I suspect, is likely to conquer. . . .[1]

By the time the Congress of Vienna took place, Russia was arguably the most powerful country on the Continent. By the middle of the twentieth century, it had achieved the rank of one of only two global superpowers before imploding, nearly forty years later, losing many of its vast gains of the previous two centuries in a matter of months.

The absolute nature of the tsar's power enabled Russia's rulers to conduct foreign policy both arbitrarily and idiosyncratically. In the space of six years, between 1756 and 1762, Russia entered the Seven Years' War on the side of Austria and invaded Prussia, switched to Prussia's side at the death of Empress Elizabeth in January 1762, and then withdrew into neutrality when Catherine the Great overthrew her husband in June 1762. Fifty years later, Metternich would point out that Tsar Alexander I had never held a single set of beliefs for longer than five years. Metternich's adviser, Friedrich von Gentz, described the position of the Tsar as follows: "None of the obstacles that restrain and thwart the other sovereigns— divided authority, constitutional forms, public opinion, etc.—exists for the Emperor of Russia. What he dreams of at night he can carry out in the morning."[2]

Paradox was Russia's most distinguishing feature. Constantly at war and expanding in every direction, it nevertheless considered itself permanently threatened. The more polyglot the empire became, the more vulnerable Russia felt, partly because of its need to isolate the various nationalities from their neighbors. To sustain their rule and to surmount the tensions among the empire's various populations, all of Russia's rulers invoked the myth of some vast, foreign threat, which, in time, turned into another of the self-fulfilling prophecies that doomed the stability of Europe.

As Russia expanded from the area around Moscow toward the center of Europe, the shores of the Pacific, and into Central Asia, its quest for security evolved into expansion for its own sake. The Russian historian Vasili Kliuchevsky described the process as follows: ". . . these wars, defensive in their origin, imperceptibly and unintentionally on the part of the Muscovite politicians became wars of aggression—a direct continuation of the unifying policy of the old [pre-Romanov] dynasty, a struggle for Russian territory that had never belonged to the Muscovite state."[3]

Russia gradually turned into as much of a threat to the balance of power in Europe as it did to the sovereignty of neighbors around its vast periphery. No matter how much territory it controlled, Russia inexorably pushed its borders outward. This started out as an essentially defensive motivation, as when Prince Potemkin (best known for placing fake villages along the Tsarina's routes) advocated the conquest of the Crimea from Turkey in 1776 on the reasonable ground that this would improve Russia's capacity to defend its realm.[4] By 1864, however, security had become synonymous with continuous expansion. Chancellor Aleksandr Gorchakov defined Russia's expansion in Central Asia in terms of a permanent obligation to pacify its periphery driven forward by sheer momentum:

> The situation of Russia in Central Asia is similar to that of all civilized states that come into contact with half-savage nomadic tribes without a firm social organization. In such cases, the interests of border security and trade relations always require that the more civilized state have a certain authority over its neighbors. . . .
> The state therefore must make a choice: either to give up this continuous effort and doom its borders to constant unrest . . . or else to advance farther and farther into the heart of the savage lands . . . where the greatest difficulty lies in being able to stop.[5]

Many historians recalled this passage when the Soviet Union invaded Afghanistan in 1979.

Paradoxically, it is also true that for the past 200 years the European balance of power has been preserved on several occasions by Russian efforts and heroism. Without Russia, Napoleon and Hitler would almost certainly have succeeded in establishing universal empires. Janus-like, Russia was at once a threat to the balance of power and one of its key components, essential to the equilibrium but not fully a part of it. For much of its history, Russia accepted only the limits that were imposed on it by the outside world, and even these grudgingly. And yet there were periods, most notably the forty years after the end of the Napoleonic Wars, when Russia did not take advantage of its vast power, and instead put this power in the service of protecting conservative values in Central and Western Europe.

Even when Russia was pursuing legitimacy, its attitudes were far more messianic—and therefore imperialistic—than those of the other conservative courts. Whereas Western European conservatives defined themselves by philosophies of self-restraint, Russian leaders enlisted themselves in the service of crusades. Because the tsars faced virtually no challenge to their legitimacy, they had little understanding of republican movements beyond deeming them to be immoral. Promoters of the unity of conservative values—at least until the Crimean War—they were also prepared to use legitimacy to expand their own influence, earning Nicholas I the sobriquet of "gendarme of Europe." At the height of the Holy Alliance, Friedrich von Gentz wrote this about Alexander I:

> The Emperor Alexander, despite all the zeal and enthusiasm he has consistently shown for the Grand Alliance, is the sovereign who could most easily get along without it. . . . For him the Grand Alliance is only an implement with which he exercises in general affairs the influence that is one of the main objects of his ambition. . . . His interest in the preservation of the system is not, as is true of Austria, Prussia, or England, an interest based on necessity or fear; it is a free and calculated interest, which he is in a position to renounce as soon as a different system should offer him greater advantages.[6]

Like Americans, Russians thought of their society as exceptional. Encountering only nomadic or feudal societies, Russia's expansion into Central Asia had many of the features of America's own westward expansion, and the Russian justification for it, in keeping with the Gorchakov citation above, paralleled the way Americans explained their own "manifest destiny." But the closer Russia approached India, the more it aroused British suspicions, until, in the second half of the nineteenth century, Russian expansion into Central Asia, unlike America's westward march, turned into a foreign policy problem.

The openness of each country's frontiers was among the few common features of American and Russian exceptionalism. America's sense of uniqueness was based on the concept of liberty; Russia's sprang from the experience of common suffering. Everyone was eligible to share in America's values; Russia's were available only to the Russian nation, to the exclusion of most of its non-Russian subjects. America's exceptionalism led it to isolationism alternating with occasional moral crusades; Russia's evoked a sense of mission which often led to military adventures.

The Russian nationalist publicist Mikhail Katkov defined the difference between Western and Russian values as follows:

> . . . everything there is based on contractual relations and everything here on faith; this contrast was originally determined by the position the church adopted in the West and that which it adopted in the East. A basic dual authority exists there; a single authority here.[7]

Nationalist Russian and Pan-Slavic writers and intellectuals invariably ascribed the alleged altruism of the Russian nation to its Orthodox faith. The great novelist and passionate nationalist Fyodor Dostoyevsky interpreted Russian altruism as an obligation to liberate Slavic peoples from foreign rule, if necessary by defying the opposition of the whole of Western Europe. During Russia's 1877 campaign in the Balkans, Dostoyevsky wrote:

> Ask the people; ask the soldier; Why are they arising? Why are they going to war and what do they expect from it? They will tell you, as one man, that they are going to serve Christ and to liberate the oppressed brethren. . . . [W]e shall watch over their mutual harmony and protect their liberty and independence, be it even against all Europe.[8]

Unlike the states of Western Europe, which Russia simultaneously admired, despised, and envied, Russia perceived itself not as a nation but as a cause, beyond geopolitics, impelled by faith, and held together by arms. Dostoyevsky did not confine the role of Russia to liberating fellow Slavs and included watching over their harmony—a social undertaking which easily shaded over into domination. To Katkov, Russia was the Third Rome:

> The Russian tsar is more than the heir of his ancestors; he is the successor of the caesars of Eastern Rome, of the organizers of the church and of its councils which established the very creed of the Christian faith. With the fall of Byzantium, Moscow arose and the greatness of Russia began.[9]

After the Revolution, the passionate sense of mission was transferred to the Communist International.

The paradox of Russian history lies in the continuing ambivalence between messianic drive and a pervasive sense of insecurity. In its ultimate aberration, this ambivalence generated a fear that, unless the empire expanded, it would implode. Thus, when Russia acted as the prime mover in the partitioning of Poland, it did so partly for security reasons and partly for eighteenth-century-style aggrandizement. A century later, that conquest had taken on an autonomous significance. In 1869, Rostislav Andreievich Fadeyev, a Pan-Slavist officer, wrote in his influential essay, "Opinion on the Eastern Question," that Russia had to continue its westward march to protect its existing conquests:

The historical move of Russia from the Dnieper to the Vistula [the partition of Poland] was a declaration of war to Europe, which had broken into a part of the Continent which did not belong to her. Russia now stands in the midst of the enemy's lines—such a condition is only temporary: she must either drive back the enemy or abandon the position . . . must either extend her preeminence to the Adriatic or withdraw again beyond the Dnieper. . . .[10]

Fadeyev's analysis was not very different from George Kennan's, which was made from the opposite side of the dividing line, in his seminal article on the sources of Soviet conduct. In it, he predicted that if the Soviet Union did not succeed in expanding, it would implode and collapse.[11]

Russia's exalted view of itself was rarely shared by the outside world. Despite extraordinary achievements in literature and music, Russia never emerged as the same sort of cultural magnet for its conquered peoples as did the mother countries of some of the other colonial empires. Nor was the Russian Empire ever perceived as a model, either by other societies or by its own subjects. To the outside world, Russia was an elemental force—a mysterious, expansionist presence to be feared and contained, by either co-optation or confrontation.

Metternich had tried the route of co-optation and, for a generation, had been largely successful. But after the unification of Germany and Italy, the great ideological causes of the first half of the nineteenth century had lost their unifying force. Nationalism and revolutionary republicanism were no longer perceived as threats to the European order. As nationalism became the prevailing organizing principle, the crowned heads of Russia, Prussia, and Austria had less and less need to join together in a common defense of legitimacy.

Metternich had been able to establish an approximation of European government because the rulers of Europe considered their ideological unity as the indispensable breakwater against revolution. But by the 1870s, either the fear of revolution had subsided or the various governments thought they could defeat it without outside assistance. By now, two generations had passed since the execution of Louis XVI; the liberal revolutions of 1848 had been mastered; France, though a republic, had lost its proselytizing zeal. No common ideological bond now constrained the ever-sharpening conflict between Russia and Austria over the Balkans, or between Germany and France over Alsace-Lorraine. When the Great Powers viewed each other, they no longer saw partners in a common cause but dangerous, even mortal, rivals. Confrontation emerged as the standard diplomatic method.

In an earlier period, Great Britain had contributed to restraint by acting as the balancer of the European equilibrium. Even now, of all the major European countries, only Great Britain was in a position to conduct a balance-of-power diplomacy unfettered by irreconcilable animosity toward some other power. But Great Britain had grown confused as to what constituted the central threat, and would not regain its bearings for several decades.

The balance of power of the Vienna system, with which Great Britain was familiar, had been radically altered. Unified Germany was achieving the strength to dominate Europe all by itself—an occurrence which Great Britain had always resisted in the past when it came about by conquest. However, most British leaders, Disraeli excepted, saw no reason to oppose a process of national consolidation in Central Europe, which British statesmen had welcomed for decades, especially when its culmination occurred as the result of a war in which France had been technically the aggressor.

Ever since Canning had distanced Great Britain from Metternich's system forty years earlier, Great Britain's policy of splendid isolation had enabled it to play the role of protector of the equilibrium largely because no single country was capable of dominating the Continent by itself. After unification, Germany progressively acquired that capacity. And, confusingly, it did so by means of developing its own national territory and not by conquest. It was Great Britain's style to intervene only when the balance of power was actually under attack and not against the prospect of attack. Since it took decades for the German threat to the European equilibrium to become explicit, Great Britain's foreign policy concerns for the rest of the century were focused on France, whose colonial ambitions clashed with those of Great Britain, especially in Egypt, and on Russia's advance toward the Straits, Persia, India, and later toward China. All of these were colonial issues. In regard to European diplomacy, which produced the crises and wars of the twentieth century, Great Britain continued to practice its policy of splendid isolation.

Bismarck was therefore the dominant figure of European diplomacy until he was dismissed from office in 1890. He wanted peace for the newly created German Empire and sought no confrontation with any other nation. But in the absence of moral bonds among the European states, he faced a Herculean task. He was obliged to keep both Russia and Austria out of the camp of his French enemy. This required preventing Austrian challenges to legitimate Russian objectives and keeping Russia from undermining the Austro-Hungarian Empire. He needed good relations with Russia without antagonizing Great Britain, which was keeping a wary eye on Russian designs on Constantinople and India. Even a genius like Bismarck could not have performed such a precarious balancing act indefinitely; the intensifying strains on the international system were becoming less and less manageable. Nevertheless, for the nearly twenty years that Bismarck led Germany, he practiced the *Realpolitik* he had preached with such moderation and subtlety that the balance of power never broke down.

Bismarck's goal was to give no other power—except irreconcilable France—any cause to join an alliance directed against Germany. Professing the unified Germany to be "satiated" and without further territorial ambitions, Bismarck sought to reassure Russia that Germany had no interest in the Balkans; the Balkans, he said, were not worth the bones of a single Pomeranian grenadier. Keeping Great Britain in mind, Bismarck mounted no challenge on the Continent that might trigger a British concern for the equilibrium, and he kept Germany out of the colonial race. "Here is Russia and here is France and here we are in the middle. That is my map of Africa," was Bismarck's reply to an advocate of German colonialism[12]—a piece of advice domestic politics would later force him to modify.

Reassurance was not enough, however. What Germany needed was an alliance with both Russia and Austria, improbable as that appeared at first glance. Yet Bismarck forged just such an alliance in 1873—the first so-called Three Emperors' League. Proclaiming the unity of the three conservative courts, it looked a great deal like Metternich's Holy Alliance. Had Bismarck suddenly developed an affection for the Metternich system which he had done so much to destroy? The times had changed largely as a result of Bismarck's successes. Though Germany, Russia, and Austria pledged in true Metternich fashion to cooperate in the repression of subversive tendencies in each other's domains, a common aversion to political radicals could no longer hold the Eastern Courts together— above all because each had become confident that domestic upheavals could be repressed without outside aid.

Moreover, Bismarck had lost his solid legitimist credentials. Though his correspondence with Gerlach (see chapter 5) had not been made public, his underlying attitudes were common knowledge. As an advocate of *Realpolitik* throughout his public career, he could not suddenly make dedication to legitimacy credible. The increasingly bitter geopolitical rivalry between Russia and Austria came to transcend the unity of conservative monarchs. Each was in pursuit of the Balkan spoils of the decaying Turkish Empire. Pan-Slavism and old-fashioned expansionism were contributing to an adventurous Russian policy in the Balkans. Plain fear was producing parallel attitudes in the Austro-Hungarian Empire. Thus, while on paper the German Emperor had an alliance with his fellow conservative monarchs in Russia and Austria, these two brethren were in fact at each other's throats. The challenge of how to deal with two partners who perceived each other as mortal threats was destined to torment Bismarck's alliance system for the remainder of his days.

The first Three Emperors' League taught Bismarck that he could no longer control the forces he had unleashed by appealing to Austria's and Russia's domestic principles. Henceforth, he would attempt to manipulate them by emphasizing power and self-interest.

Two events above all demonstrated that *Realpolitik* had become the dominant trend of the period. The first occurred in 1875 in the form of a pseudo-crisis, a contrived war scare triggered by an editorial in a leading German newspaper bearing the provocative headline "Is War Imminent?" The editorial had been placed in reaction to an increase in French military expenditures and the purchase of a large number of horses by the French military. Bismarck may well have inspired the war scare without intending to go any further, for there was no partial German mobilization or threatening troop movements.

Facing down a nonexistent threat is an easy way to enhance a nation's standing. Clever French diplomacy created the impression that Germany was planning a pre-emptive attack. The French Foreign Office put out the story that, in a conversation with the French Ambassador, the Tsar had indicated he would support France in a Franco-German conflict. Great Britain, ever sensitive to the threat of a single power dominating Europe, began to stir. Prime Minister Disraeli instructed his Foreign Secretary, Lord Derby, to approach Russian Chancellor Gorchakov with the idea of intimidating Berlin:

> My own impression is that we should construct some concerted movement to preserve the peace of Europe like Pam [Lord Palmerston] did when he baffled France and expelled the Egyptians from Syria. There might be an alliance between Russia and ourselves for this special purpose; and other powers, as Austria and perhaps Italy might be invited to accede. . . .[13]

That Disraeli, deeply distrustful of Russia's imperial ambitions, could even hint at an Anglo-Russian alliance showed how seriously he took the prospect of German domination of Western Europe. The war scare subsided as quickly as it had blown up, so Disraeli's scheme was never tested. Although Bismarck did not know the details of Disraeli's maneuver, he was too astute not to have sensed Britain's underlying concern.

As George Kennan has demonstrated,[14] there was far less to this crisis than the publicity made it seem. Bismarck had no intention of going to war so soon after humiliating France, though he did not object to leaving France with the impression that he might do so if pushed too far. Tsar Alexander II was not about to guarantee republican France, though he did not mind conveying to Bismarck that that option existed.[15] Thus, Disraeli was reacting to what was still a chimera. Still, the combination of British uneasiness, French maneuvering, and Russian ambivalence convinced Bismarck that only an active policy could stave off the coalition-building which would result a generation later in the Triple Entente, aimed at Germany.

The second crisis was real enough. It came in the form of yet another Balkan crisis, which demonstrated that neither philosophical nor ideological bonds could hold the Three Emperors' League together in the face of the underlying clash of national interests. Because it laid bare the conflict which would ultimately doom Bismarck's European order and plunge Europe into World War I, it will be treated here in some detail.

The Eastern Question, dormant since the Crimean War, again came to dominate the international agenda in the first series of convoluted imbroglios, which, as the century progressed, would become as stereotyped as Japanese Kabuki plays. Some almost accidental event would trigger a crisis; Russia would make threats and Great Britain would dispatch the Royal Navy. Russia would then occupy some part of the Ottoman Balkans to hold as hostage. Great Britain would threaten war. Negotiations would start, during which Russia would reduce its demands, at which precise point the whole thing would blow up.

In 1876, the Bulgarians, who for centuries had lived under Turkish rule, rebelled and were joined by other Balkan peoples. Turkey responded with appalling brutality, and Russia, swept up by Pan-Slavic sentiments, threatened to intervene.

In London, Russia's response raised the all-too-familiar specter of Russian control of the Straits. Ever since Canning, British statesmen had observed the maxim that, if Russia controlled the Straits, it would dominate the Eastern Mediterranean and the Near East, thereby threatening Great Britain's position in Egypt. Therefore, according to British conventional wisdom, the Ottoman Empire, decrepit and inhuman as it was, had to be preserved even at the risk of war with Russia.

This state of affairs presented Bismarck with a grave dilemma. A Russian advance capable of provoking a British military reaction was also likely to rouse Austria to enter the fray. And if Germany was forced to choose between Austria and Russia, Bismarck's foreign policy would be wrecked along with the Three Emperors' League. Whatever happened, Bismarck faced the risk of antagonizing either Austria or Russia, and of quite possibly incurring the wrath of all the parties if he adopted a neutral attitude. "We have always avoided," Bismarck said before the Reichstag in 1878, "in the case of differences of opinion between Austria and Russia, building a majority of two against one by taking the side of one of [the] parties. . . ."[16]

The moderation was classical Bismarck, though it also defined a mounting dilemma as the crisis unfolded. Bismarck's first move was to attempt to tighten the bonds of the Three Emperors' League by seeking to develop a common position. In early 1876, the Three Emperors' League drew up the so-called Berlin Memorandum warning Turkey against continuing its repression. It seemed to imply that, with certain provisos, Russia might intervene in the Balkans on behalf of the Concert of Europe, much as Metternich's Congresses of Verona, Laibach, and Troppau had designated some European power to carry out their decisions.

But there was one enormous difference between taking such action then and doing so now. In Metternich's day, Castlereagh was the British Foreign Secretary and had been sympathetic to intervention by the Holy Alliance, even though Great Britain had refused to participate in it. But now Disraeli was the Prime Minister, and he interpreted the Berlin Memorandum as the first step toward dismantling the Ottoman Empire to the exclusion of Great Britain. This was too close to the European hegemony Great Britain had been opposing for centuries. Complaining to Shuvalov, the Russian Ambassador to London, Disraeli said: "England has been treated as though we were Montenegro or Bosnia."[17] To his frequent correspondent Lady Bradford, he wrote:

> There is no balance and unless we go out of our way to act with the three Northern Powers, they can act without us which is not agreeable for a state like England.[18]

Given the unity being displayed by St. Petersburg, Berlin, and Vienna, it would have been exceedingly difficult for Great Britain to resist whatever they might agree upon. It appeared that Disraeli had no choice but to join the Northern Courts while Russia assaulted Turkey.

However, in the tradition of Palmerston, Disraeli decided to flex British muscles. He moved the Royal Navy to the Eastern Mediterranean and proclaimed his pro-Turkish sentiments—guaranteeing that Turkey would prove obdurate, and forcing whatever latent differences existed in the Three Emperors' League into the open. Never known for excessive modesty, Disraeli declared to Queen Victoria that he had broken the Three Emperors' League. It was, he believed, "virtually extinct, as extinct as the Roman triumvirate."[19]

Benjamin Disraeli was one of the strangest and most extraordinary figures ever to head a British government. Upon learning that he would be named Prime Minister in 1868, he exulted: "Hurray! Hurray! I've climbed to the top of the greasy pole!" By contrast, when Disraeli's permanent adversary, William Ewart Gladstone, was invited to succeed him that same year, the former penned a prolix reflection on the responsibilities of power and his sacred duties to God, which included the prayer that the Almighty imbue him with the fortitude required to carry out the grave responsibilities of the prime minister's office.

The pronouncements of the two great men who dominated British politics in the second half of the nineteenth century capture their antipodal natures: Disraeli—meretricious, brilliant, and mercurial; Gladstone—learned, pious, and grave. It was no small irony that the Victorian Tory Party, composed of country squires and devoutly Anglican aristocratic families, should have produced as its leader this brilliant Jewish adventurer, and that the party of quintessential insiders should have brought to the forefront of the world's stage the quintessential outsider. No Jew had ever risen to such heights in British politics. A century later, it would again be the seemingly hidebound Tories rather than the self-consciously progressive Labour Party that would bring Margaret Thatcher into office —a greengrocer's daughter who proved to be another remarkable leader and Great Britain's first female prime minister.

Disraeli's had been an unlikely career. A novelist as a young man, he was more a member of the *literati* than a policymaker, and was much more likely to have concluded his life as a scintillating writer and conversationalist than as one of the seminal British political figures of the nineteenth century. Like Bismarck, Disraeli believed in expanding the vote to the common man, convinced that the middle classes in England would vote Conservative.

As Tory leader, Disraeli articulated a new form of imperialism different from the essentially commercial expansion Great Britain had practiced since the seventeenth century—by which, it was said, it had built an empire in a fit of absent-mindedness. For Disraeli, the Empire was not an economic necessity but a spiritual one, and a prerequisite to his country's greatness. "The issue is not a mean one," he proclaimed in his famous 1872 Crystal Palace speech. "It is whether you will be content to be a comfortable England, modeled and molded upon Continental principles and meeting in due course an inevitable fate, or whether you will be a great country—an Imperial country—a country where your sons, when they rise, rise to paramount positions, and obtain not merely the esteem of their countrymen, but command the respect of the world."[20]

Adhering to convictions such as these, Disraeli was bound to oppose Russia's threat to the Ottoman Empire. In the name of the European equilibrium, he would not accept the prescriptions of the Three Emperors' League, and in the name of the British Empire, he would oppose Russia as the enforcer of a European consensus on the approaches to Constantinople. For, in the course of the nineteenth century, the notion that Russia was the principal threat to Great Britain's position in the world had taken firm hold. Great Britain perceived its overseas interests menaced by a Russian pincer movement, one prong of which was aimed at Constantinople and the other at India via Central Asia. In the course of its expansion across Central Asia during the second half of the nineteenth century, Russia had elaborated methods of conquest which would become stereotyped. The victim was always so far from the center of world affairs that few Westerners had any precise idea of what was taking place. They could thus fall back on their preconceptions that the tsar was in fact benevolent and his subordinates were bellicose, turning distance and confusion into tools of Russian diplomacy.

Of the European Powers, only Great Britain concerned itself with Central Asia. As Russian expansion pushed ever southward in the direction of India, London's protests were stonewalled by Chancellor Prince Aleksandr Gorchakov, who often did not know what the Russian armies were doing. Lord Augustus Loftus, the British Ambassador in St. Petersburg, speculated that Russia's pressure on India "had not originated with the Sovereign, although he is an absolute monarch, but rather from the dominant part played by the military administration. Where an enormous standing army is maintained, it is absolutely necessary to find employment for it. . . . When a system of conquest sets in, as in Central Asia, one acquisition of territory leads to another, and the difficulty is where to stop."[21] This observation, of course, practically replicated Gorchakov's own words (see page 141, above). On the other hand, the British Cabinet did not much care whether Russia was threatening India by momentum or out of deliberate imperialism.

The same pattern was repeated again and again. Each year, Russian troops would penetrate deeper into the heart of Central Asia. Great Britain would ask for an explanation and receive all kinds of assurances that the Tsar did not intend to annex one square meter of land. At first, such soothing words were able to put matters to rest. But, inevitably, another Russian advance would reopen the issue. For instance, after the Russian army occupied Samarkand (in present-day Uzbekistan) in May 1868, Gorchakov told the British Ambassador, Sir Andrew Buchanan, "that the Russian Government not only did not wish, but that they deeply regretted, the occupation of that city, and he was assured that it would not be permanently retained."[22] Samarkand, of course, remained under Russian sovereignty until the collapse of the Soviet Union more than a century later.

In 1872, the same charade was repeated a few hundred miles to the southeast with respect to the principality of Khiva on the border of present-day Afghanistan. Count Shuvalov, the Tsar's aide-de-camp, was sent to London to reassure the British that Russia had no intention of annexing additional territory in Central Asia:

> Not only was it far from the intention of the Emperor to take possession of Khiva, but positive orders had been prepared to prevent it, and directions given that conditions imposed should be such as could not in any way lead to a prolonged occupation of Khiva.[23]

These assurances had hardly been uttered when word arrived that Russian General Kaufmann had crushed Khiva and imposed a treaty which was the dramatic opposite of Shuvalov's assertions.

In 1875, these methods were applied to Kokand, another principality on the border of Afghanistan. On this occasion, Chancellor Gorchakov felt some need to justify the gap between Russia's assurances and its actions. Ingeniously, he devised an unprecedented distinction between unilateral assurances (which, according to his definition, had no binding force) and formal, bilateral engagements. "The Cabinet in London," he wrote in a note, "appears to derive, from the fact of our having on several occasions spontaneously and amicably communicated to them our views with respect to Central Asia, and particularly our firm resolve not to pursue a policy of conquest or annexation, a conviction that we have contracted definite engagements toward them in regard to this matter."[24] In other words, Russia would insist on a free hand in Central Asia, would set its own limits, and not be bound even by its own assurances.

Disraeli was not about to permit a replay of these methods at the approaches to Constantinople. He encouraged the Ottoman Turks to reject the Berlin Memorandum and to continue their depredations in the Balkans. Despite this show of British firmness, Disraeli was under severe domestic pressure. The Turks' atrocities had turned British public opinion against them, and Gladstone was railing against the amorality of Disraeli's foreign policy. Disraeli thus felt obliged to accede to the London Protocol of 1877, in which he joined the three Northern courts in calling on Turkey to end the slaughter in the Balkans and to reform its administration in the region. The Sultan, however, convinced that Disraeli was on his side no matter what formal demands were made, rejected even this document. Russia's response was a declaration of war.

For a moment, it appeared as if Russia had won the diplomatic game. Not only was it backed by the other two Northern courts, but by France as well, in addition to having a good deal of support in British public opinion. Disraeli's hands were tied; going to war on behalf of Turkey might well bring down his government.

But, as in many previous crises, the Russian leaders overplayed their hand. Led by the brilliant but reckless general and diplomat Nicholas Ignatyev, Russian troops arrived at the gates of Constantinople. Austria began to reconsider its backing of the Russian campaign. Disraeli moved British warships into the Dardanelles. At that point, Ignatyev shocked all of Europe by announcing the terms of the Treaty of San Stefano, which would emasculate Turkey and create a "Big Bulgaria." Extending to the Mediterranean Sea, this enlarged state, it was widely assumed, would be dominated by Russia.

Since 1815, conventional wisdom in Europe had deemed that the fate of the Ottoman Empire could only be resolved by the Concert of Europe as a whole and not by any one power, least of all by Russia. Ignatyev's Treaty of San Stefano raised the possibilities of Russian control of the Straits, which was intolerable to Great Britain, and Russian control of the Balkan Slavs, which was intolerable to Austria. Both Great Britain and Austria-Hungary, therefore, declared that the Treaty was unacceptable.

Suddenly, Disraeli no longer stood alone. To Russia's leaders, his moves signaled the ominous portent of a return of the Crimean War coalition. When Foreign Secretary Lord Salisbury issued his famous Memorandum of April 1878 outlining why the Treaty of San Stefano had to be revised, even Shuvalov, the Russian Ambassador to London and a long-time rival of Ignatyev, agreed. Great Britain threatened war if Russia moved into Constantinople, while Austria threatened war over the division of the spoils in the Balkans.

Bismarck's cherished Three Emperors' League teetered on the verge of collapse. Until this moment, Bismarck had been extraordinarily circumspect. In August 1876, a year before Russian armies moved on Turkey "for the cause of Orthodoxy and Slavdom," Gorchakov had proposed to Bismarck that the Germans host a congress to settle the Balkan crisis. Whereas Metternich or Napoleon III would have jumped at the opportunity to play chief mediator of the Concert of Europe, Bismarck demurred, believing that a congress could only make the differences within the Three Emperors' League explicit. He confided privately that all the participants, including Great Britain, would emerge from such a congress "ill-disposed towards us because not one of them would receive from us the support which he expected."[25] Bismarck also thought it unwise to bring Disraeli and Gorchakov together—"ministers of equally dangerous vanity," was how he described them.

Nevertheless, as it increasingly appeared that the Balkans would become the fuse to set off a general European war, Bismarck reluctantly organized a congress in Berlin, the only capital to which the Russian leaders were willing to come. Yet he preferred to keep his distance from the day-to-day diplomacy, prevailing upon Austro-Hungarian Foreign Minister Andrássy to send out the invitations.

The Congress was scheduled to assemble on June 13, 1878. Before it met, however, Great Britain and Russia had already settled the key issues in an agreement between Lord Salisbury and the new Russian Foreign Minister, Shuvalov, signed on May 30. The "Big Bulgaria" created by the Treaty of San Stefano was replaced by three new entities: a much-reduced, independent state of Bulgaria; the state of Eastern Rumelia, an autonomous entity that was technically under a Turkish governor but whose administration would be overseen by a European Commission (a forerunner of United Nations peacekeeping projects of the twentieth century); the rest of Bulgaria reverted to Turkish rule. Russia's gains in Armenia were reduced. In separate secret agreements, Great Britain promised Austria that it would support Austria's occupation of Bosnia-Herzegovina, and assured the Sultan that it would guarantee Asiatic Turkey. In return, the Sultan gave England the use of Cyprus as a naval base.

By the time the Congress of Berlin met, the danger of war which had induced Bismarck to agree to host the gathering had largely dissipated. The main function of the Congress was to give Europe's blessing to what had already been negotiated. One wonders whether Bismarck would have risked placing himself in the inherently precarious role of mediator had he been able to foresee this outcome. Of course, it is likely that the very imminence of a congress had caused Russia and England to settle separately and rapidly, not wishing to expose to the vagaries of a European congress gains which were far more attainable from each other in direct negotiations.

Working out the details of an already concluded agreement is not exactly heroic work. All the major countries except Great Britain were represented by their foreign ministers. For the first time in British history, both a prime minister and a foreign minister attended an international congress outside the British Isles because Disraeli did not want to delegate the already largely assured prospect of a major diplomatic achievement to Salisbury. The vain and aged Gorchakov, who had negotiated with Metternich at the Congresses of Laibach and Verona more than half a century before, chose the Congress of Berlin for his final appearance on the international stage. "I do not wish to be extinguished like a lamp that is smoking. I want to sink down as though I were a star," he declared upon his arrival in Berlin.[26]

When asked to reflect on the center of gravity at the Congress, Bismarck pointed to Disraeli: *"Der alte Jude, das ist der Mann"* (The old Jew, he is the man).[27] Though their backgrounds could not have been more different, these two men came to admire each other. Both subscribed to *Realpolitik* and hated what they considered moralistic cant. The religious overtones of Gladstone's pronouncements (a man both Disraeli and Bismarck detested) seemed pure humbug to them. Neither Bismarck nor Disraeli had any sympathy for the Balkan Slavs, whom they viewed as chronic and violent troublemakers. Both men were given to biting, cynical quips, broad generalizations, and sarcastic barbs. Bored with nettlesome detail, Bismarck and Disraeli preferred to approach policy in bold, dramatic strokes.

It can be argued that Disraeli was the only statesman who ever got the better of Bismarck. Disraeli arrived at the Congress in the impregnable position of having already achieved his aims—a position which Castlereagh had enjoyed at Vienna, and Stalin after the Second World War. The remaining issues concerned the details of implementing the previous agreement between Great Britain and Russia, and the essentially technical military question of whether Turkey or the new Bulgaria should control the Balkan passes. For Disraeli, the strategic problem at the Congress was to deflect from Great Britain as much as possible Russia's frustration at having to relinquish some of its conquests.

Disraeli succeeded because Bismarck's own position was so complicated. Bismarck perceived no German interest in the Balkans, and basically had no preference with respect to the issues at hand other than that war between Austria and Russia had to be avoided at nearly any cost. He described his role at the Congress as that of the *"ehrlicher Makler"* (honest broker) and introduced almost every statement at the Congress with the words: *"L'Allemagne, qui n'est liée par aucun intérêt direct dans les affaires d'Orient..."* (Germany, which has no direct interest of any kind in Eastern questions...).[28]

Though Bismarck understood the game being played all too well, he nevertheless felt like a person in a nightmare who sees danger approaching but is unable to avoid it. When the German parliament urged Bismarck to take a stronger stand, he retorted that he intended to steer clear. Bismarck pointed out the perils of mediation by referring to an incident in 1851 when Tsar Nicholas I had intervened between Austria and Prussia, in effect on Austria's side:

> Then Tsar Nicholas played the role that [my opponent] now presumes to give Germany; he (Nicholas) came and said: "The first one who shoots, I'll shoot," and as a result peace was maintained. To whose advantage, and to whose disadvantage, that belongs to history, and I don't want to discuss it here. I am simply asking, was this role that Tsar Nicholas played, in which he took one side, ever repaid in gratitude? Certainly not by us in Prussia! . . . Was Tsar Nicholas thanked by Austria? Three years later came the Crimean War, and I don't need to say anything more.[29]

Nor, he might have added, did the Tsar's intervention prevent Prussia from ultimately consolidating Northern Germany—the real issue in 1851.

Bismarck played the hand he had been dealt as well as possible. His approach was generally to back Russia on questions concerning the eastern part of the Balkans (such as the annexation of Bessarabia) and to support Austria on those relating to the western part (such as the occupation of Bosnia-Herzegovina). On only one issue did he come down against Russia. When Disraeli threatened to leave the Congress unless Turkey was left in possession of the mountain passes facing Bulgaria, Bismarck interceded with the Tsar to overrule the Russian negotiator, Shuvalov.

In this manner, Bismarck avoided the estrangement with Russia that had befallen Austria after the Crimean War. But he did not emerge unscathed. Many leading Russians felt cheated of victory. Russia might defer territorial gains for the sake of legitimacy (as Alexander I did in the Greek rebellion in the 1820s, and Nicholas I during the revolutions of 1848), but Russia never relinquished an ultimate objective or accepted compromise as just. Checks to Russian expansionism generally produced sullen resentment.

Thus, after the Congress of Berlin, Russia blamed its failure to achieve all of its aims on the Concert of Europe rather than on its own excessive ambition; not on Disraeli, who had organized the coalition against Russia and threatened war, but on Bismarck, who had managed the Congress in order to avoid a European war. Russia had grown accustomed to British opposition; but that the role of honest broker was being assumed by a traditional ally like Germany was treated by Pan-Slavists as an affront. The Russian nationalist press styled the Congress as a "European coalition against Russia under the leadership of Prince Bismarck,"[30] who was turned into a scapegoat for Russia's failure to achieve its exorbitant goals.

Shuvalov, the principal Russian negotiator at Berlin, who was therefore in a position to know the real state of affairs, summed up Russian jingoistic attitudes in the aftermath of the Congress:

> One prefers to leave people with the mad illusion that Russia's interests have been grievously damaged by the action of certain foreign powers, and in this way one gives sustenance to the most pernicious agitation. Everyone wants peace; the condition of the country urgently demands it, but at the same time one tries to divert to the outside world the effects of the discontents produced, in reality, by the mistakes of one's own policies.[31]

Shuvalov, however, did not reflect Russian public opinion. Though the Tsar himself did not venture as far as his jingoist press or radical Pan-Slavists, neither was he fully reconciled to the outcome of the Congress. In the decades ahead, German perfidy at Berlin would become the staple of many a Russian policy document, including several just prior to the outbreak of World War I. The Three Emperors' League, based on the unity of conservative monarchs, could no longer be maintained. Henceforth, if there was to be any cohesive force in international affairs, it would have to be *Realpolitik* itself.

In the 1850s, Bismarck had advocated a policy which was the Continental equivalent of England's own policy of "splendid isolation." He had urged aloofness from entanglements before throwing Prussia's weight behind whichever side seemed best to serve the Prussian national interest at any given point. This approach avoided alliances, which limited freedom of action, and above all, gave Prussia more options than any potential rival. During the 1870s, Bismarck sought to consolidate the unification of Germany by returning to the traditional alliance with Austria and Russia. But in the 1880s, an unprecedented situation came about. Germany was too strong to stand aloof, for that might unite Europe against it. Nor could it any longer rely on the historic, almost reflexive, support of Russia. Germany was a giant in need of friends.

Bismarck solved this dilemma by completely reversing his previous approach to foreign policy. If he could no longer operate the balance of power by having fewer commitments than any potential adversary, he would arrange more relationships with more countries than any conceivable opponent and thereby be able to choose among many allies, as circumstances required. Abandoning the freedom of maneuver which had characterized his diplomacy for the previous twenty years, Bismarck began to build a system of alliances deftly engineered on the one hand to keep Germany's potential adversaries from coalescing and, on the other, to restrain the actions of Germany's partners. In each of Bismarck's sometimes contradictory coalitions, Germany was always closer to the various partners than any of them was to each other; hence Bismarck always had a veto over common action as well as an option of independent action. For a decade he succeeded in maintaining pacts with his allies' adversaries so that he could restrain tension on all sides.

Bismarck initiated his new policy in 1879 by making a secret alliance with Austria. Aware of Russia's resentment after the Congress of Berlin, he now hoped to build a barrier to further Russian expansion. Unwilling, however, to permit Austria to use German backing to challenge Russia, he also secured a veto over Austrian policy in the Balkans. The warmth with which Salisbury greeted the Austro-German alliance—with the biblical good "tidings of great joy"—assured Bismarck that he was not alone in wanting to check Russian expansionism. Salisbury no doubt hoped that henceforth Austria, backed by Germany, would assume Great Britain's burden of resisting Russian expansion toward the Straits. Fighting battles for other countries' national interest was not Bismarck's specialty. He was especially loath to do so in the Balkans, because he felt such deep disdain for that region's quarrels. "One must give these sheep-stealers plainly to understand," he rumbled about the Balkans on one occasion, "that the European governments have no need to harness themselves to their lusts and their rivalries."[32] Unfortunately for the peace of Europe, his successors would forget these words of caution.

Bismarck proposed to restrain Russia in the Balkans through alliance rather than confrontation. For his part, the Tsar was brought up short at the prospect of isolation. Considering Great Britain to be Russia's chief adversary and France still too weak and, above all, too republican to be a plausible ally, the Tsar agreed to resurrect the Three Emperors' League, this time on the basis of *Realpolitik*.

The benefit of an alliance with his principal opponent was not immediately apparent to the Austrian Emperor. He would have preferred a grouping with Great Britain, with which he shared a common interest in blocking Russia's advance toward the Straits. But Disraeli's defeat in 1880 and Gladstone's advent to power had ended that prospect; Great Britain's participation, even indirectly, in a pro-Turkish, anti-Russian alliance was no longer in the cards.

The second Three Emperors' League made no pretense to any moral concerns. Expressed in the precise conditionality of *Realpolitik,* it committed its signatories to benevolent neutrality in the event that one of them engaged in a war with a fourth country—for instance, should England go to war with Russia, or France with Germany. Germany was thus protected against a two-front war, and Russia was protected against the restoration of the Crimean coalition (of Great Britain, France, and Austria), while Germany's commitment to defend Austria against aggression remained intact. Responsibility for resisting Russian expansionism in the Balkans was shifted onto Great Britain by precluding Austria from joining a coalition aimed at Russia—at least on paper. By balancing partially offsetting alliances, Bismarck was able to achieve almost the same freedom of action he had enjoyed in his previous phase of diplomatic aloofness. Above all, he had removed the incentives that might have turned a local crisis into a general war.

In 1882, the year following the second Three Emperors' League, Bismarck cast his net even more widely by persuading Italy to transform the Dual Alliance between Austria and Germany into a Triple Alliance, including Italy. In general, Italy had stayed aloof from the diplomacy of Central Europe, but it now resented the French conquest of Tunisia, which had pre-empted its own designs in North Africa. Likewise, the shaky Italian monarchy thought that some demonstration of Great Power diplomacy might enable it to resist better the rising tide of republicanism. For its part, Austria sought additional insurance should the Three Emperors' League prove incapable of restraining Russia. In forming the Triple Alliance, Germany and Italy pledged mutual assistance against a French attack, while Italy pledged neutrality to Austria-Hungary in case of a war with Russia, easing Austrian worries about a two-front war. Finally, in 1887, Bismarck encouraged his two allies, Austria and Italy, to conclude the so-called Mediterranean Agreements with Great Britain, by which the parties agreed to preserve jointly the *status quo* in the Mediterranean.

Bismarck's diplomacy had produced a series of interlocking alliances, partially overlapping and partially competitive, which ensured Austria against Russian attack, Russia against Austrian adventurism, and Germany against encirclement, and which drew England into resisting Russian expansion toward the Mediterranean. To reduce challenges to his intricate system, Bismarck did his utmost to satisfy French ambitions everywhere except in Alsace-Lorraine. He encouraged French colonial expansion, in part to deflect French energies from Central Europe, but more to embroil France with colonial rivals, especially Great Britain.

For over a decade, that calculation proved accurate. France and Great Britain nearly clashed over Egypt, France became estranged from Italy over Tunisia, and Great Britain continued to oppose Russia in Central Asia and on the approaches to Constantinople. Eager to avoid conflict with England, Bismarck eschewed colonial expansion until the mid-1880s, limiting Germany's foreign policy to the Continent, where his aims were to preserve the *status quo.*

But, in the end, the requirements of *Realpolitik* became too intricate to sustain. With the passage of time, the conflict between Austria and Russia in the Balkans became unmanageable. Had the balance of power operated in its purest form, the Balkans would have been divided into Russian and Austrian spheres of influence. But public opinion was already too inflamed for such a policy, even in the most autocratic states. Russia could not agree to spheres of influence which left Slavic populations to Austria, and Austria would not agree to strengthening what it considered Russia's Slavic dependencies in the Balkans.

Bismarck's eighteenth-century-style Cabinet Diplomacy was becoming incompatible with an age of mass public opinion. The two representative governments of Great Britain and France responded to their public opinions as a matter of course. In France, this meant mounting pressure for the recovery of Alsace-Lorraine. But the most striking example of the vital new role of public opinion was in Great Britain, when Gladstone defeated Disraeli in 1880 in the only British election fought largely over foreign policy issues, and then reversed Disraeli's Balkan policy.

Gladstone, perhaps the dominant figure of British politics in the nineteenth century, viewed foreign policy in much the same way as Americans did after Wilson. Judging foreign policy by moral instead of geopolitical criteria, he argued that the national aspirations of the Bulgarians were in fact legitimate, and that, as a fellow Christian nation, Great Britain owed support to Bulgaria against the Muslim Turks. The Turks should be made to behave, argued Gladstone, by a coalition of powers which would then assume responsibility for the administration of Bulgaria. Gladstone put forth the same concept that came to be known under President Wilson as "collective security": Europe needed to act jointly, otherwise Great Britain should not act at all.

It must be done, it can only be done with safety, by the united action of the Powers of Europe. Your power is great; but what is above all things essential is, that the mind and heart of Europe in this matter should be one. I need now only speak of the six whom we call great Powers; of Russia, Germany, Austria, France, England, and Italy. The union of them all is not only important, but almost indispensable for entire success and satisfaction.[33]

In 1880, Gladstone, offended by Disraeli's emphasis on geopolitics, launched his landmark Midlothian Campaign, the first whistle-stop campaign in history and the first in which the issues of foreign policy were taken directly to the people. In his old age, Gladstone suddenly came into his own as a public speaker. Asserting that morality was the only basis for a sound foreign policy, Gladstone insisted that Christian decency and respect for human rights ought to be the guiding lights of British foreign policy, not the balance of power and the national interest. At one stop, he declared:

> Remember that the sanctity of life in the hill villages of Afghanistan is as inviolable in the eye of Almighty God as can be your own. Remember that He who has united you as human beings in the same flesh and blood has bound you by the law of mutual love . . . not limited by the boundaries of Christian civilization. . . . [34]

Gladstone blazed a trail which Wilson later followed when he claimed that there could be no distinction between the morality of the individual and the morality of the state. Like Wilson a generation later, he thought that he had detected a global trend toward peaceful change policed by world public opinion:

> Certain it is that a new law of nations is gradually taking hold of the mind, and coming to sway the practice, of the world; a law which recognises independence, which frowns upon aggression, which favours the pacific, not the bloody settlement of disputes, which aims at permanent and not temporary adjustments; above all, which recognises, as a tribunal of paramount authority, the general judgement of civilised mankind.[35]

Every word in this paragraph could have been uttered by Wilson and the implication of it was certainly very similar to Wilson's League of Nations. In drawing a distinction between his policy and Disraeli's in 1879, Gladstone stressed that, rather than practicing a balance of power, he would strive "to keep the Powers of Europe in union together. And why? Because by keeping all in union together you neutralize and fetter and bind up the selfish aims of each. . . . Common action is fatal to selfish aims. . . ."[36] Of course, the inability to keep all of Europe together was the precise cause for mounting tensions. No cause was foreseeable—certainly not the future of Bulgaria—that could heal the breach between France and Germany, or between Austria and Russia.

No British prime minister before Gladstone had used such rhetoric. Castlereagh had treated the Concert of Europe as an instrument for enforcing the Vienna settlement. Palmerston saw it as a tool for preserving the balance of power. Far from viewing the Concert of Europe as an enforcer of the *status quo,* Gladstone assigned it the revolutionary role of bringing about an entirely new world order. These ideas were to remain dormant until Wilson appeared on the scene a generation later.

To Bismarck, such views were pure anathema. It is not surprising that these two titanic figures cordially detested each other. Bismarck's attitude toward Gladstone paralleled that of Theodore Roosevelt toward Wilson: he considered the great Victorian part humbug, part menace. Writing to the German Emperor in 1883, the Iron Chancellor noted:

> Our task would be easier if in England that race of great statesmen of earlier times who had an understanding of European politics, had not completely died out. With such an incapable politician as Gladstone, who is nothing but a great orator, it is impossible to pursue a policy in which England's position can be counted upon.[37]

Gladstone's view of his adversary was far more direct, for instance, when he called Bismarck "the incarnation of evil."[38]

Gladstone's ideas on foreign policy suffered the same fate as Wilson's, in that they stirred his compatriots to withdrawal from global affairs rather than greater participation. On the level of day-to-day diplomacy, Gladstone's coming to power in 1880 made little difference to Great Britain's imperial policy in Egypt and east of Suez. But it did keep England from being a factor in the Balkans and in the European equilibrium in general.

Gladstone's second tenure in office (1880–85) thus had the paradoxical effect of removing the safety net under Bismarck, the most moderate of the Continental statesmen, just as Canning's withdrawal from Europe had driven Metternich toward the Tsar. As long as the Palmerston/Disraeli view dominated British foreign policy, Great Britain could serve as the last resort whenever Russia went too far in the Balkans or on the approaches to Constantinople. With Gladstone, this assurance came to an end, making Bismarck ever more dependent on his increasingly anachronistic triangle with Austria and Russia.

The Eastern Courts—heretofore the bulwark of conservatism—in a way proved even more susceptible to nationalistic public opinion than the representative governments. Germany's domestic structure had been designed by Bismarck to permit him to apply to it the maxims of his balance-of-power diplomacy, yet it also had a strong tendency to invite demagoguery. Despite the fact that the Reichstag was elected by what was the widest suffrage in Europe, German governments were appointed by the emperor and reported to him, not to the Reichstag.

Thus deprived of responsibility, Reichstag members were at liberty to indulge in the most extreme rhetoric. The fact that the military budget was voted for periods of five years at a time tempted governments to create crises during the crucial year in which the defense program would be voted. Given enough time, this arrangement might well have evolved into a constitutional monarchy with a government responsible to Parliament. But during the crucial, formative years of the new Germany, governments were highly susceptible to nationalist propaganda and too prone to inventing foreign dangers to rally their constituencies.

Russian foreign policy, too, suffered from the rabid propaganda of the Pan-Slavs, whose basic themes were a call for an aggressive policy in the Balkans and a showdown with Germany. A Russian official explained to the Austrian ambassador toward the end of the reign of Alexander II, in 1879:

> People here are simply *afraid* of the nationalistic press. . . . It is the flag of nationalism they have pinned upon themselves that protects them and assures them of powerful support. Ever since the nationalistic tendency has come so prominently to the fore, and particularly since it succeeded in prevailing against all better advice, in the question of going to war [against Turkey], the so-called "national" party . . . has become a real power, especially because it embraces the entire army.[39]

Austria, the other polyglot empire, was in a similar position.

In these circumstances, it became increasingly difficult for Bismarck to execute his precarious balancing act. In 1881, a new tsar, Alexander III, came to the throne in St. Petersburg, unrestrained by conservative ideology like his grandfather, Nicholas I, or by personal affection for the aged German Emperor, like his father, Alexander II. Indolent and autocratic, Alexander III distrusted Bismarck, in part because Bismarck's policy was too complicated for him to understand. On one occasion he even said that, whenever he saw any mention of Bismarck in a dispatch, he placed a cross next to his name. The Tsar's suspicions were reinforced by his Danish wife, who could not forgive Bismarck for taking Schleswig-Holstein from her native country.

The Bulgarian crisis of 1885 brought all these impulses to a head. Another revolt produced the greater Bulgaria which Russia had sought so passionately a decade earlier, and which Great Britain and Austria had feared. Demonstrating how history can falsify the most firmly held expectations, the new Bulgaria, far from being dominated by Russia, was unified under a German prince. The court at St. Petersburg blamed Bismarck for what the German chancellor in fact would have far preferred to avoid. The Russian court was outraged and the Pan-Slavs, who saw a conspiracy in every corner west of the Vistula, spread the rumor that Bismarck was behind a diabolical anti-Russian plot. In this atmosphere, Alexander refused to renew the Three Emperors' League in 1887.

Bismarck, however, was not ready to give up on his Russian option. He knew that, left to its own devices, Russia would sooner or later drift into an alliance with France. Yet in the conditions of the 1880s, with Russia and Great Britain permanently on the verge of war, such a course increased Russia's peril vis-à-vis Germany without diminishing British antagonism. Moreover, Germany still had a British option, especially now that Gladstone had left office. Alexander, in any event, had good reason to doubt that France would run the risk of war over the Balkans. In other words, Russo-German ties still reflected a very real, if diminishing, convergence of national interests and not simply Bismarck's predilections —though, without his diplomatic skill, these common interests would not have found formal expression.

Ever ingenious, Bismarck now came up with his last major initiative, the so-called Reinsurance Treaty. Germany and Russia promised each other to stay neutral in a war with a third country unless Germany attacked France, or Russia attacked Austria. Theoretically, Russia and Germany were now guaranteed against a two-front war, provided they stayed on the defensive. However, much depended on how the aggressor was defined, especially since mobilization was becoming increasingly equated with a declaration of war (see chapter 8). Since that question was never posed, there were obvious limits to the Reinsurance Treaty, the utility of which was further impaired by the Tsar's insistence on keeping it secret.

The secrecy of the agreement was the clearest illustration of the conflict between the requirements of cabinet diplomacy and the imperatives of an increasingly democratized foreign policy. Matters had become so complex that two levels of secrecy existed within the secret Reinsurance Treaty. The second level was a particularly confidential codicil in which Bismarck promised not to stand in the way of Russia's attempt to acquire Constantinople, and to help increase Russian influence in Bulgaria. Neither assurance would have gladdened Germany's ally, Austria, not to speak of Great Britain—though Bismarck would hardly have been unhappy had Great Britain and Russia become embroiled over the future of the Straits.

Despite its complexities, the Reinsurance Treaty maintained the indispensable link between St. Petersburg and Berlin. And it reassured St. Petersburg that, though Germany would defend the integrity of the Austro-Hungarian Empire, it would not assist in its expansion at Russia's expense. Germany thus achieved at least a delay in a Franco-Russian alliance.

That Bismarck had put his intricate foreign policy into the service of restraint and the preservation of peace was shown by his reaction to pressure from German military leaders urging a pre-emptive war against Russia when the Three Emperors' League ended in 1887. Bismarck doused all such speculations in a speech to the Reichstag in which he tried to give St. Petersburg a reputation to uphold as a way of discouraging a Franco-Russian alliance:

> Peace with Russia will not be disturbed from our side; and I do not believe Russia will attack us. I also do not believe that the Russians are looking around for alliances in order to attack us in company with others, or that they would be inclined to take advantages of difficulties that we might encounter on another side, in order to attack us with ease.[40]

Nevertheless, for all its dexterity and moderation, Bismarck's balancing act was due to end soon. The maneuvers were becoming too complex to sustain, even for the master. Overlapping alliances designed to ensure restraint led to suspicion instead, while the growing importance of public opinion reduced everyone's flexibility.

However skillful Bismarck's diplomacy, the need for so high a degree of manipulation was proof of the strains which a powerful, unified Germany had placed on the European balance of power. Even while Bismarck was still at the helm, imperial Germany inspired disquiet. Indeed, Bismarck's machinations, which were intended to provide reassurance, over time had an oddly unsettling effect, partly because his contemporaries had such difficulty comprehending their increasingly convoluted nature. Fearful of being outmaneuvered, they tended to hedge their bets. But this course of action also limited flexibility, the mainspring of *Realpolitik* as a substitute for conflict.

Though Bismarck's style of diplomacy was probably doomed by the end of his period in office, it was far from inevitable that it should have been replaced by a mindless armaments race and rigid alliances more comparable to the later Cold War than to a traditional balance of power. For nearly twenty years, Bismarck preserved the peace and eased international tension with his moderation and flexibility. But he paid the price of misunderstood greatness, for his successors and would-be imitators could draw no better lesson from his example than multiplying arms and waging a war which would cause the suicide of European civilization.

By 1890, the concept of the balance of power had reached the end of its potential. It had been made necessary in the first place by the multitude of states emerging from the ashes of medieval aspirations to universal empire. In the eighteenth century, its corollary of *raison d'état* had led to frequent wars whose primary function was to prevent the emergence of a dominant power and the resurrection of a European empire. The balance of power had preserved the liberties of states, not the peace of Europe.

Balance-of-power policy reached its zenith in the forty years after the Napoleonic Wars. It operated smoothly during this period because the equilibrium had been deliberately designed to enhance balance, and, as importantly, because it was buttressed by a sense of shared values, at least among the conservative courts. After the Crimean War, that sense of shared values gradually eroded, and matters reverted to eighteenth-century conditions, now made all the more dangerous by modern technology and the growing role of public opinion. Even the despotic states could appeal to their publics by invoking a foreign danger—and by substituting outside threats for democratic consensus. National consolidation of the states of Europe reduced the number of players and the ability to substitute diplomatic combinations for the deployment of power, while the collapse of a shared sense of legitimacy eroded moral restraint.

Despite America's historic aversion to the balance of power, these lessons are relevant to post–Cold War American foreign policy. For the first time in its history, America is currently part of an international system in which it is the strongest country. Though a military superpower, America can no longer impose its will because neither its power nor its ideology lends itself to imperial ambitions. And nuclear weapons, in which America is preponderant militarily, tend toward an equalization of usable power.

The United States therefore finds itself increasingly in a world with numerous similarities to nineteenth-century Europe, albeit on a global scale. One can hope that something akin to the Metternich system evolves, in which a balance of power is reinforced by a shared sense of values. And in the modern age, these values would have to be democratic.

Yet Metternich had not had to create his legitimate order; it essentially already existed. In the contemporary world, democracy is far from universal, and where it is proclaimed it is not necessarily defined in commensurable terms. It is reasonable for the United States to try to buttress equilibrium with moral consensus. To be true to itself, America must try to forge the widest possible moral consensus around a global commitment to democracy. But it dare not neglect the analysis of the balance of power. For the quest for moral consensus becomes self-defeating when it destroys the equilibrium.

If a Metternich-type system based on legitimacy is not possible, America will have to learn to operate in a balance-of-power system, however uncongenial it may find such a course. In the nineteenth century, there were two models for balance-of-power systems: the British model exemplified by the Palmerston/Disraeli approach; and Bismarck's model. The British approach was to wait for the balance of power to be threatened directly before engaging itself, and then almost always on the weaker side; Bismarck's approach sought to prevent challenges from arising by establishing close relations with as many parties as possible, by building overlapping alliance systems, and by using the resulting influence to moderate the claims of the contenders.

Strange as it may seem in light of America's experiences with Germany in the course of two world wars, the Bismarck style of operating a balance of power is probably more attuned to the traditional American approach to international relations. The Palmerston/Disraeli method would require a disciplined aloofness from disputes and a ruthless commitment to the equilibrium in the face of threats. Both the disputes and the threats would have to be assessed almost entirely in terms of balance of power. America would find it quite difficult to marshal either the aloofness or the ruthlessness, not to mention the willingness to interpret international affairs strictly in terms of power.

Bismarck's later policy sought to restrain power in advance by some consensus on shared objectives with various groups of countries. In an interdependent world, America will find it difficult to practice Great Britain's splendid isolation. But it is also unlikely that it will be able to establish a comprehensive system of security equally applicable to all parts of the world. The most likely—and constructive—solution would be partially overlapping alliance systems, some focusing on security, others on economic relations. The challenge for America will be to generate objectives growing out of American values that can hold together these various groupings (see chapter 31).

In any event, by the end of the nineteenth century, both of these approaches to foreign policy were fading. Great Britain no longer felt predominant enough to risk isolation. And Bismarck was dismissed from office by an impatient new emperor who set himself the immodest task of improving on the policy of the master. In the process, the balance of power turned rigid, and Europe headed toward a catastrophe all the more devastating because nobody believed it was possible.

CHAPTER SEVEN

A Political Doomsday Machine: European Diplomacy Before the First World War

By the end of the twentieth century's first decade, the Concert of Europe, which had maintained peace for a century, had for all practical purposes ceased to exist. The Great Powers had thrown themselves with blind frivolity into a bipolar struggle that led to petrification into two power blocs, anticipating the pattern of the Cold War fifty years later. There was one important difference, however. In the age of nuclear weapons, the avoidance of war would be a major, perhaps the principal, foreign policy goal. At the beginning of the twentieth century, wars could still be started with a touch of frivolity. Indeed, some European thinkers held that periodic bloodletting was cathartic, a naïve hypothesis that was brutally punctured by the First World War.

For decades, historians have been debating who must bear responsibility for the outbreak of the First World War. Yet no one country can be singled out for that mad dash to disaster. Each of the major powers contributed its quota of shortsightedness and irresponsibility, and did so with an insouciance which would never again be possible once the disaster they had wrought entered the collective memory of Europe. They had forgotten Pascal's warning in *Pensées*—if they had ever known it—"We run heedlessly into the abyss after putting something in front of us to stop us seeing it."

There was surely enough blame to go around. The nations of Europe transformed the balance of power into an armaments race without understanding that modern technology and mass conscription had made general war the greatest threat to their security, and to European civilization as a whole. Though all the nations of Europe contributed to the disaster with their policies, it was Germany and Russia which undermined any sense of restraint by their very natures.

Throughout the process of German unification, there had been little concern about its impact on the balance of power. For 200 years, Germany had been the victim, not the instigator, of the wars of Europe. In the Thirty Years' War, the Germans had suffered casualties estimated as high as 30 percent of their entire population, and all the decisive battles of the dynastic wars of the eighteenth century and of the Napoleonic Wars were fought on German soil.

It was therefore nearly inevitable that a united Germany would aim to prevent the recurrence of these tragedies. But it was not inevitable that the new German state should have approached this challenge largely as a military problem, or that German diplomats after Bismarck should have conducted foreign policy with such bullying assertiveness. Whereas Frederick the Great's Prussia had been the weakest of the Great Powers, soon after unification, Germany became the strongest and as such proved disquieting to its neighbors. In order to participate in the Concert of Europe, it therefore needed to show special restraint in its foreign policy.[1] Unfortunately, after Bismarck's departure, moderation was the quality Germany lacked the most.

The reason German statesmen were obsessed with naked power was that, in contrast to other nation-states, Germany did not possess any integrating philosophical framework. None of the ideals which had shaped the modern nation-state in the rest of Europe was present in Bismarck's construction—not Great Britain's emphasis on traditional liberties, the French Revolution's appeal to universal freedom, or even the benign universalist imperialism of Austria. Strictly speaking, Bismarck's Germany did not embody the aspirations of a nation-state at all, because he had deliberately excluded the Austrian Germans. Bismarck's Reich was an artifice, being foremost a greater Prussia whose principal purpose was to increase its own power.

169

The absence of intellectual roots was a principal cause of the aimlessness of German foreign policy. The memory of having served for so long as Europe's main battlefield had produced a deep-seated sense of insecurity in the German people. Though Bismarck's empire was now the strongest power on the Continent, German leaders always felt vaguely threatened, as was evidenced by their obsession with military preparedness compounded by bellicose rhetoric. German military planners always thought in terms of fighting off a combination of *all* of Germany's neighbors simultaneously. In readying themselves for that worst-case scenario, they helped to make it a reality. For a Germany strong enough to defeat a coalition of all its neighbors was obviously also more than capable of overwhelming any of them individually. At the sight of the military colossus on their borders, Germany's neighbors drew together for mutual protection, transforming the German quest for security into an agent of its own insecurity.

A wise and restrained policy might have postponed and perhaps even averted the looming peril. But Bismarck's successors, abandoning his restraint, relied more and more on sheer strength, as expressed in one of their favorite pronouncements—that Germany was to serve as the hammer and not the anvil of European diplomacy. It was as if Germany had expended so much energy on achieving nationhood that it had not had time to think through what purpose the new state should serve. Imperial Germany never managed to develop a concept of its own national interest. Swayed by the emotions of the moment and hampered by an extraordinary lack of sensitivity to foreign psyches, German leaders after Bismarck combined truculence with indecisiveness, hurling their country, first into isolation and then into war.

Bismarck had taken great pains to downplay assertions of German power, using his intricate system of alliances to restrain his many partners and to keep their latent incompatibilities from erupting into war. Bismarck's successors lacked the patience and the subtlety for such complexity. When Emperor William I died in 1888, his son, Frederick (whose liberalism had so worried Bismarck), governed for a mere ninety-eight days before succumbing to throat cancer. He was succeeded by his son, William II, whose histrionic demeanor gave observers the uneasy sense that the ruler of Europe's most powerful nation was both immature and erratic. Psychologists have ascribed William's restless bullying to an attempt to compensate for having been born with a deformed arm—a grave blow to a member of Prussia's royal family with its exalted military traditions. In 1890, the brash young Emperor dismissed Bismarck, refusing to govern in the shadow of so towering a figure. Henceforth, it was the Kaiser's diplomacy which would become so central to the peace of Europe. Winston Churchill captured William's essence in sardonic style:

> Just strut around and pose and rattle the undrawn sword. All he wished was to feel like Napoleon, and be like him without having had to fight his battles. Surely less than this would not pass muster. If you are the summit of a volcano, the least you can do is smoke. So he smoked, a pillar of cloud by day and the gleam of fire by night, to all who gazed from afar; and slowly and surely these perturbed observers gathered and joined themselves together for mutual protection.
>
> ... but underneath all this posing and its trappings, was a very ordinary, vain, but on the whole well-meaning man, hoping to pass himself off as a second Frederick the Great.[2]

What the Kaiser wanted most was international recognition of Germany's importance and, above all, of its power. He attempted to conduct what he and his entourage called *Weltpolitik,* or global policy, without ever defining that term or its relationship to the German national interest. Beyond the slogans lay an intellectual vacuum: truculent language masked an inner hollowness; vast slogans obscured timidity and the lack of any sense of direction. Boastfulness coupled with irresolution in action reflected the legacy of two centuries of German provincialism. Even if German policy had been wise and responsible, integrating the German colossus into the existing international framework would have been a daunting task. But the explosive mix of personalities and domestic institutions prevented any such course, leading instead to a mindless foreign policy which specialized in bringing down on Germany everything it had always feared.

In the twenty years after Bismarck's dismissal, Germany managed to foster an extraordinary reversal of alliances. In 1898, France and Great Britain had been on the verge of war over Egypt. Animosity between Great Britain and Russia had been a constant factor of international relations for most of the nineteenth century. At various times, Great Britain had been looking for allies against Russia, trying Germany before settling on Japan. No one would have thought that Great Britain, France, and Russia could possibly end up on the same side. Yet, ten years later, that was exactly what came to pass under the impact of insistent and threatening German diplomacy.

For all the complexity of his maneuvers, Bismarck had never attempted to go beyond the traditions of the balance of power. His successors, however, were clearly not comfortable with the balance of power, and never seemed to understand that, the more they magnified their own strength, the more they would encourage the compensating coalitions and arms buildups inherent in the system of European equilibrium.

German leaders resented the reluctance of other countries to ally themselves with a nation that was already the strongest in Europe, and whose strength was generating fears of German hegemony. Bullying tactics seemed to Germany's leaders the best way to bring home to their neighbors the limits of their own strength and, presumably, the benefits of Germany's friendship. This taunting approach had quite the opposite effect. Trying to achieve absolute security for their country, German leaders after Bismarck threatened every other European nation with absolute insecurity, triggering countervailing coalitions nearly automatically. There are no diplomatic shortcuts to domination; the only route that leads to it is war, a lesson the provincial leaders of post-Bismarck Germany learned only when it was too late to avoid a global catastrophe.

Ironically, for the greater part of imperial Germany's history, Russia, not Germany, was considered the main threat to peace. First Palmerston and then Disraeli were convinced that Russia intended to penetrate into Egypt and India. By 1913, the corresponding fear among German leaders that they were about to be overrun by the Russian hordes had reached such a pitch that it contributed significantly to their decision to force the fateful showdown a year later.

In fact, there was little hard evidence to substantiate the fear that Russia might seek a European empire. The claims by German military intelligence of having proof that Russia was in fact preparing for such a war were as true as they were irrelevant. All the countries of both alliances, intoxicated with the new technology of railways and mobilization schedules, were constantly engaged in military preparations out of proportion to any of the issues being disputed. But, precisely because these fervid preparations could not be related to any definable objective, they were interpreted as portents of vast, if nebulous, ambitions. Characteristically, Prince von Bülow, German Chancellor from 1900 to 1909, espoused Frederick the Great's view that "of all Prussia's neighbors the Russian Empire is the most dangerous in its strength as well as in its position."[3]

Throughout, Europe found something decidedly eerie about the vastness and persistence of Russia. All the nations of Europe were seeking aggrandizement by means of threats and counterthreats. But Russia seemed impelled to expand by a rhythm all its own, containable only by the deployment of superior force, and usually by war. Throughout numerous crises, a reasonable settlement often seemed well within Russia's reach, much better in fact than what ultimately emerged. Yet Russia always preferred the risk of defeat to compromise. This had been true in the Crimean War of 1854, the Balkan Wars of 1875–78, and prior to the Russo-Japanese War of 1904.

One explanation for these tendencies was that Russia belonged partly to Europe, partly to Asia. In the West, Russia was part of the Concert of Europe and participated in the elaborate rules of the balance of power. But even there, Russian leaders were generally impatient with appeals to the equilibrium and prone to resorting to war if their demands were not met—for example, in the prelude to the Crimean War of 1854, and the Balkan Wars, and again in 1885, when Russia nearly went to war with Bulgaria. In Central Asia, Russia was dealing with weak principalities to which the principle of the balance of power did not apply, and in Siberia —until it ran up against Japan—it was able to expand much as America had across a sparsely populated continent.

In European forums, Russia would listen to the arguments on behalf of the balance of power but did not always abide by its maxims. Whereas the nations of Europe had always maintained that the fate of Turkey and the Balkans had to be settled by the Concert of Europe, Russia, on the other hand, invariably sought to deal with this question unilaterally and by force—in the Treaty of Adrianople in 1829, the Treaty of Unkiar Ske-lessi in 1833, the conflict with Turkey in 1853, and the Balkan Wars of 1875–78 and 1885. Russia expected Europe to look the other way and felt aggrieved when it did not. The same problem would recur after the Second World War, when the Western allies maintained that the fate of Eastern Europe concerned Europe as a whole, while Stalin insisted that Eastern Europe, and especially Poland, were within the Soviet sphere and that therefore their future should be settled without reference to the Western democracies. And, like his tsarist predecessors, Stalin proceeded unilaterally. Inevitably, however, some coalition of Western forces would arise to resist Russia's military thrusts and to undo Russia's impositions on its neighbors. In the post–World War II period, it would take a generation for the historic pattern to reassert itself.

Russia on the march rarely exhibited a sense of limits. Thwarted, it nursed its grievances and bided its time for revenge—against Great Britain through much of the nineteenth century, against Austria after the Crimean War, against Germany after the Congress of Berlin, and against the United States during the Cold War. It remains to be seen how the new post-Soviet Russia will react to the collapse of its historic empire and satellite orbit once it fully absorbs the shock of its disintegration.

In Asia, Russia's sense of mission was even less constrained by political or geographic obstacles. For all of the eighteenth century and most of the nineteenth, Russia found itself alone in the Far East. It was the first European power to deal with Japan, and the first to conclude an agreement with China. This expansion, accomplished by relatively few settlers and military adventurers, produced no conflict with the European powers. Sporadic Russian clashes with China proved no more significant. In return for Russian assistance against warring tribes, China conceded large areas of territory to Russian administration in the eighteenth and nineteenth centuries, giving rise to a series of "unequal treaties" which every Chinese government since then, especially the communist one, has denounced.

Characteristically, Russia's appetite for Asian territory seemed to grow with each new acquisition. In 1903, Serge Witte, the Russian Finance Minister and a confidant of the Tsar, wrote to Nicholas II: "Given our enormous frontier with China and our exceptionally favorable situation, the absorption by Russia of a considerable part of the Chinese Empire is only a question of time."[4] As with the Ottoman Empire, Russia's leaders took the position that the Far East was Russia's own business and that the rest of the world had no right to intervene. Russia's advances on all fronts sometimes occurred simultaneously; more often they shifted back and forth, depending on where expansion seemed least risky.

Imperial Russia's policymaking apparatus reflected the empire's dual nature. Russia's Foreign Office was a department of the Chancery, staffed by independent officials whose orientation was essentially toward the West.[5] Frequently Baltic Germans, these officials considered Russia a European state with policies which should be implemented in the context of the Concert of Europe. The Chancery's role, however, was contested by the Asiatic Department, which was equally independent and responsible for Russian policy toward the Ottoman Empire, the Balkans, and the Far East—in other words, for every front where Russia was actually advancing.

Unlike the Chancery, the Asiatic Department did not consider itself a part of the Concert of Europe. Viewing the European nations as obstacles to its designs, the Asiatic Department treated the European nations as irrelevant and, whenever possible, sought to fulfill Russian goals through unilateral treaties or by wars initiated without any reference to Europe. Since Europe insisted that issues concerning the Balkans and the Ottoman Empire be settled in concert, frequent conflicts were inevitable, while Russia's outrage mounted at being thus thwarted by powers it considered interlopers.

Partly defensive, partly offensive, Russian expansion was always ambiguous, and this ambiguity generated Western debates over Russia's true intentions that lasted through the Soviet period. One reason for the perennial difficulty in understanding Russia's purposes was that the Russian government, even in the communist period, always had more in common with an eighteenth-century autocratic court than with a twentieth-century superpower. Neither imperial nor communist Russia ever produced a great foreign minister. Like Nesselrode, Gorchakov, Giers, Lamsdorff, and even Gromyko, its foreign ministers were all accomplished and able but lacked the authority to design long-range policy. They were little more than servants of a volatile and easily distracted autocrat, for whose favor they had to compete amidst many overriding domestic concerns. Imperial Russia had no Bismarck, no Salisbury, no Roosevelt—in short, no hands-on minister with executive powers over all aspects of foreign affairs.

Even when the ruling tsar was a dominant personality, the autocratic system of Russian policymaking inhibited the evolution of a coherent foreign policy. Once the tsars found a foreign minister with whom they felt comfortable, they tended to retain him into his dotage, as was the case with Nesselrode, Gorchakov, and Giers. Among them, these three foreign ministers served for most of the nineteenth century. Even in their extreme old age, they proved invaluable to foreign statesmen, who considered them the only personalities worth seeing in St. Petersburg because they were the only officials with access to the tsar. Protocol prohibited virtually anybody else from seeking an audience with the tsar.

To complicate decision-making further, the tsar's executive power frequently clashed with his aristocratic notions of princely life-style. For example, immediately after the signing of the Reinsurance Treaty, a key period in Russia's foreign affairs, Alexander III left St. Petersburg for four consecutive months, from July through October 1887, to go yachting, observe maneuvers, and visit his in-laws in Denmark. With the only real decision-maker thus out of reach, Russia's foreign policy floundered. Not only were the tsar's policies often driven by the emotions of the moment, they were greatly influenced by the nationalist agitation fanned by the military. Military adventurers, like General Kaufmann in Central Asia, paid hardly any attention to the foreign ministers. Gorchakov was probably telling the truth about how little he knew of Central Asia in his conversations with the British ambassadors described in the previous chapter.

By the time of Nicholas II, who ruled from 1894 to 1917, Russia was forced to pay the price for its arbitrary institutions. Nicholas first took Russia into a disastrous war with Japan and then permitted his country to become captive to an alliance system which made war with Germany virtually inevitable. While Russia's energies had been geared to expansion and consumed by attendant foreign conflicts, its social and political structure had grown brittle. Defeat in the war with Japan in 1905 should have served as a warning that the time for domestic consolidation—as advocated by the great reformer, Peter Stolypin—was drawing short. What Russia needed was a respite; what it received was another foreign enterprise. Thwarted in Asia, Russia reverted to its dream of Pan-Slavism and a push toward Constantinople, which, this time, ran out of control.

The irony was that, after a certain point, expansionism no longer enhanced Russia's power but brought about its decline. In 1849, Russia was widely considered the strongest nation in Europe. Seventy years later, its dynasty collapsed and it temporarily disappeared from the ranks of the Great Powers. Between 1848 and 1914, Russia was involved in over half a dozen wars (other than colonial wars), far more than any other major power. In each of these conflicts, except for the intervention in Hungary in 1849, the financial and political costs to Russia far exceeded the possible gains. Though each of these conflicts took its toll, Russia continued to identify Great Power status with territorial expansion; it hungered for more land, which it neither needed nor was able to digest. Tsar Nicholas II's close adviser, Serge Witte, promised him that "from the shores of the Pacific and the heights of the Himalayas Russia would dominate not only the affairs of Asia but those of Europe as well."[6] Economic, social, and political development would have been far more advantageous to Great Power status in the Industrial Age than a satellite in Bulgaria or a protectorate in Korea.

A few Russian leaders, such as Gorchakov, were wise enough to realize that, for Russia, "the extension of territory was the extension of weakness,"[7] but their views were never able to moderate the Russian mania for new conquests. In the end, the communist empire collapsed for essentially the same reasons that the tsars' had. The Soviet Union would have been much better off had it stayed within its borders after the Second World War and established relations with what came to be known as the satellite orbit comparable to those it maintained with Finland.

When two colossi—a powerful, impetuous Germany and a huge, relentless Russia—rub up against each other at the center of the Continent, conflict is probable, no matter that Germany had nothing to gain from a war with Russia and that Russia had everything to lose in a war with Germany. The peace of Europe therefore depended on the one country that had played the role of balancer so skillfully and with such moderation throughout the nineteenth century.

In 1890, the term "splendid isolation" still accurately described British foreign policy. British subjects proudly referred to their country as the "balance wheel" of Europe—the weight of which prevented any one of the various coalitions among the Continental powers from becoming dominant. Entanglement in these alliances was traditionally nearly as repugnant to British statesmen as it was to American isolationists. Yet only twenty-five years later, Englishmen would be dying by the hundreds of thousands on the muddy fields of Flanders as they fought at the side of a French ally against a German foe.

A remarkable change occurred in British foreign policy between 1890 and 1914. It was no small irony that the man who led Great Britain through the first part of this transition represented everything traditional about Great Britain and British foreign policy. For the Marquis of Salisbury was the ultimate insider. He was the scion of the ancient Cecil family, whose ancestors had served as top ministers to British monarchs since the time of Queen Elizabeth I. King Edward VII, who reigned from 1901 to 1910 and came from an upstart family compared with the Cecils, was known to complain occasionally at the condescending tone Salisbury used toward him.

Salisbury's rise in politics was as effortless as it was foreordained. After an education at Christ Church, Oxford, the young Salisbury toured Europe, perfected his French, and met heads of state. By the age of forty-eight, after serving as viceroy of India, he became Disraeli's Foreign Minister and played a major role at the Congress of Berlin, where he did most of the detailed day-to-day negotiating. After Disraeli's death, he took over the leadership of the Tory Party and, apart from Gladstone's last government of 1892–94, was the dominant figure in British politics during the last fifteen years of the nineteenth century.

In some respects, Salisbury's position was not unlike that of President George Bush, though he served longer in his nation's highest office. Both men bestrode a world which was receding by the time they came to power, though that fact was not obvious to either of them. Both left an impact by knowing how to operate what they had inherited. Bush's view of the world was shaped by the Cold War, in which he had risen to prominence and over whose end he was obliged to preside while at the pinnacle of his career; Salisbury's formative experiences had been in the Palmerston era of unparalleled British power overseas and of intractable Anglo-Russian rivalry, both of which were clearly coming to an end during his leadership.

Salisbury's government had to grapple with the decline in Great Britain's relative standing. Its vast economic power was now matched by Germany's; Russia and France had expanded their imperial efforts and were challenging the British Empire nearly everywhere. Though Great Britain was still pre-eminent, the dominance it had enjoyed in the middle of the nineteenth century was slipping. Just as Bush adjusted skillfully to what he had not foreseen, by the 1890s Great Britain's leaders recognized the need to relate traditional policy to unexpected realities.

Overweight and rumpled in his physical appearance, Lord Salisbury more adequately embodied Great Britain's contentment with the *status quo* than he did its transformation. As the author of the phrase "splendid isolation," Salisbury, on the face of it, promised to carry on the traditional British policies of holding a firm line overseas against other imperial powers, and of involving Great Britain in Continental alliances only when it was required as a last resort to prevent an aggressor from overturning the balance. For Salisbury, Great Britain's insular position meant that its ideal policy was to be active on the high seas and to remain unentangled in the customary Continental alliances. "We are fish," he bluntly asserted on one occasion.

In the end, Salisbury was obliged to recognize that Great Britain's overextended empire was straining under the pressures of Russia in the Far and Near East, and of France in Africa. Even Germany was entering the colonial race. Though France, Germany, and Russia were frequently in conflict with one another on the Continent, they always clashed with Great Britain overseas. For Great Britain possessed not only India, Canada, and a large portion of Africa, but insisted on dominating vast territories which, for strategic reasons, it wanted to keep from falling into the hands of another power even though it did not seek to control them directly. Salisbury called this claim a "sort of ear-mark upon territory, which, in case of a break-up, England did not want any other power to have."[8] These areas included the Persian Gulf, China, Turkey, and Morocco. During the 1890s, Great Britain felt beleaguered by endless clashes with Russia in Afghanistan, around the Straits, and in Northern China, and with France in Egypt and Morocco.

With the Mediterranean Agreements of 1887, Great Britain became indirectly associated with the Triple Alliance of Germany, Austria-Hungary, and Italy in the hope that Italy and Austria might strengthen its hand in dealing with France in North Africa, and with Russia in the Balkans. Yet the Mediterranean Agreements proved to be only a stopgap.

The new German empire, deprived of its master strategist, did not know what to do with its opportunity. Geopolitical realities were gradually drawing Great Britain out of its splendid isolation, though there was enough handwringing about it by traditionalists. The first move toward greater involvement with the Continent was on behalf of warmer relations with imperial Germany. Convinced that Russia and Great Britain desperately needed Germany, German policymakers thought they could drive a hard bargain with both of them simultaneously without specifying the nature of the bargain they were seeking or ever imagining that they might be pushing Russia and Great Britain closer together. When rebuffed in these all-or-nothing overtures, German leaders would withdraw into sulkiness, which quickly changed to truculence. This approach was in sharp contrast to that of France, which settled for slow, step-by-step progress, waiting twenty years for Russia and another decade and a half for Great Britain to propose an agreement. For all the noise post-Bismarck Germany made, its foreign policy was overwhelmingly amateurish, shortsighted, and even timid when faced with the confrontations it had itself generated.

William II's first diplomatic move along what turned into a fated course came in 1890, shortly after he had dismissed Bismarck, when he rejected the Tsar's offer to renew the Reinsurance Treaty for another three-year term. By rejecting Russia's overture at the very beginning of his rule, the Kaiser and his advisers pulled the perhaps most important thread out of the fabric of Bismarck's system of overlapping alliances. Three considerations motivated them: first, they wanted to make their policy as "simple and transparent" as possible (the new Chancellor, Caprivi, confessed on one occasion that he simply did not possess Bismarck's ability to keep eight balls in the air at once); second, they wanted to reassure Austria that their alliance with it was their top priority; finally, they considered the Reinsurance Treaty an obstacle to their preferred course of forging an alliance with Great Britain.

Each of these considerations demonstrated the lack of geopolitical understanding by which the Germany of William II progressively isolated itself. Complexity was inherent in Germany's location *and* history; no "simple" policy could take account of its many aspects. It had been precisely the ambiguity of a simultaneous treaty with Russia and an alliance with Austria that had enabled Bismarck to act as a balancer between Austrian fears and Russian ambitions for twenty years without having to break with either or to escalate the endemic Balkan crises. Ending the Reinsurance Treaty brought about exactly the opposite situation: limiting Germany's options promoted Austrian adventurism. Nikolai de Giers, the Russian Foreign Minister, understood this immediately, noting: "Through the dissolution of our treaty [the Reinsurance Treaty], Vienna has been liberated from the wise and well-meaning, but also stern control of Prince Bismarck."[9]

Abandoning the Reinsurance Treaty not only caused Germany to lose leverage vis-à-vis Austria, it above all increased Russia's anxieties. Germany's reliance on Austria was interpreted in St. Petersburg as a new predisposition to support Austria in the Balkans. Once Germany had positioned itself as an obstacle to Russian aims in a region that had never before represented a vital German interest, Russia was certain to search for a counterweight, which France was only too eager to supply.

Russia's temptations to move in France's direction were strengthened by a German colonial agreement with Great Britain, which swiftly followed the Kaiser's refusal to renew the Reinsurance Treaty. Great Britain acquired from Germany the sources of the Nile and tracts of land in East Africa, including the island of Zanzibar. As a *quid pro quo,* Germany received a relatively inconsequential strip of land linking South-West Africa to the Zambezi River, the so-called Caprivi Strip, and the island of Helgoland in the North Sea, which was presumed to have some strategic value in safeguarding the German coast from naval attack.

It was not a bad bargain for either side, though it turned into the first of a series of misunderstandings. London undertook the agreement as a means of settling African colonial issues; Germany saw it as a prelude to an Anglo-German alliance; and Russia, going even further, interpreted it as England's first step into the Triple Alliance. Thus Baron Staal, the Russian Ambassador to Berlin, anxiously reported the pact between his country's historic friend, Germany, and its traditional foe, Great Britain, in these terms:

> When one is united by numerous interests and positive engagements on one point of the globe, one is almost certain to proceed in concert in all the great questions that may arise in the international field. . . . Virtually the entente with Germany has been accomplished. It cannot help but react upon the relations of England with the other powers of the Triple Alliance.[10]

Bismarck's nightmare of coalitions was now in train, for the end of the Reinsurance Treaty had paved the way for a Franco-Russian alliance.

Germany had calculated that France and Russia would never form an alliance, because Russia had no interest in fighting for Alsace-Lorraine, and France had no interest in fighting for the Balkan Slavs. It turned out to be one of the many egregious misconceptions of imperial Germany's post-Bismarck leadership. Once Germany was irrevocably committed to Austria's side, France and Russia in fact needed each other, however divergent their goals, because neither could achieve its own strategic objectives without first defeating, or at least weakening, Germany. France needed to do so because Germany would never relinquish Alsace-Lorraine without war, while Russia knew it would not be able to inherit the Slavic parts of the Austrian Empire without defeating Austria—which

Germany had made clear it would resist by its refusal to renew the Reinsurance Treaty. And Russia had no chance against Germany without the assistance of France.

Within a year of Germany's refusal to renew the Reinsurance Treaty, France and Russia had signed their Entente Cordiale, which provided mutual diplomatic support. Giers, the venerable Russian Foreign Minister, warned that the agreement would not solve the fundamental problem that Great Britain, not Germany, was Russia's principal adversary. Desperate to escape the isolation to which Bismarck had consigned it, France agreed to add a clause to the Franco-Russian agreement obliging France to give Russia diplomatic support in any colonial conflict with Great Britain.

To French leaders, this anti-British clause seemed a small entrance fee to establish what was bound to turn into an anti-German coalition. Thereafter, French efforts would be directed at extending the Franco-Russian agreement into a military alliance. Though Russian nationalists favored such a military pact to speed the dismemberment of the Austrian Empire, Russian traditionalists were uneasy. Giers' eventual successor as Foreign Minister, Count Vladimir Lamsdorff, wrote in his diary in early February 1892:

> They (the French) are also preparing to besiege us with proposals for an agreement about joint military actions in case of an attack by a third party. . . . But why overdo a good thing? We need peace and quiet in view of the miseries of the famine, of the unsatisfactory state of our finances, of the uncompleted state of our armaments program, of the desperate state of our transportation system, and finally of the renewed activity in the camp of the nihilists.[11]

In the end, French leaders overcame Lamsdorff's doubts, or else he was overruled by the Tsar. In 1894, a military convention was signed in which France agreed to aid Russia if Russia was attacked by Germany, or by Austria in combination with Germany. Russia would support France in case of an attack by Germany, or by Germany in combination with Italy. Whereas the Franco-Russian Agreement of 1891 had been a diplomatic instrument and could plausibly have been argued to be aimed at Great Britain as well as at Germany, the sole adversary foreseen by this military convention was Germany. What George Kennan would later call "the fateful alliance" (the entente between France and Russia of 1891, followed by the military convention of 1894) marked a watershed in Europe's rush toward war.

It was the beginning of the end for the operation of the balance of power. The balance of power works best if at least one of the following conditions pertains: First, each nation must feel itself free to align with any other state, depending on the circumstances of the moment. Through much of the eighteenth century, the equilibrium was adjusted by constantly shifting alignments; it was also the case in the Bismarck period until 1890. Second, when there are fixed alliances but a balancer sees to it that none of the existing coalitions becomes predominant—the situation after the Franco-Russian treaty, when Great Britain continued to act as balancer and was in fact being wooed by both sides. Third, when there are rigid alliances and no balancer exists, but the cohesion of the alliances is relatively low so that, on any given issue, there are either compromises or changes in alignment.

When none of these conditions prevails, diplomacy turns rigid. A zero sum game develops in which any gain of one side is conceived as a loss for the other. Armaments races and mounting tensions become inevitable. This was the situation during the Cold War, and in Europe tacitly after Great Britain joined the Franco-Russian alliance, thereby forming the Triple Entente starting in 1908.

Unlike during the Cold War, the international order after 1891 did not turn rigid after a single challenge. It took fifteen years before each of the three elements of flexibility was destroyed in sequence. After the formation of the Triple Entente, the balance of power ceased to function. Tests of strength became the rule and not the exception. Diplomacy as the art of compromise ended. It was only a question of time before some crisis would drive events out of control.

But in 1891, as France and Russia lined up against it, Germany still hoped that it could bring about the offsetting alliance with Great Britain for which William II yearned but which his impetuousness made impossible. The colonial agreement of 1890 did not lead to the alliance the Russian Ambassador had feared. Its failure to materialize was partly due to British domestic politics. When the aged Gladstone returned to office in 1892 for the last time, he bruised the Kaiser's tender ego by rejecting any association with autocratic Germany or Austria.

Yet the fundamental reason for the failure of the several attempts to arrange an Anglo-German alliance was the German leadership's persistent incomprehension of traditional British foreign policy as well as of the real requirements of its own security. For a century and a half, Great Britain had refused to commit itself to an open-ended military alliance. It would make only two kinds of engagements: limited military agreements to deal with definable, clearly specified dangers; or entente-type arrangements to cooperate diplomatically on those issues in which interests with another country ran parallel. In a sense, the British definition of entente was, of course, a tautology: Great Britain would cooperate when it chose to cooperate. But an entente also had the effect of creating moral and psychological ties and a presumption—if not a legal obligation—of joint action in crises. And it would have kept Great Britain apart from France and Russia, or at least complicated their rapprochement.

Germany refused such informal procedures. William II insisted on what he called a Continental-type alliance. "If England wants allies or aid," he said in 1895, "she must abandon her non-committal policy and provide continental type guarantees or treaties."[12] But what could the Kaiser have meant by a Continental-type guarantee? After nearly a century of splendid isolation, Great Britain was clearly not ready to undertake the permanent Continental commitment it had so consistently avoided for 150 years, especially on behalf of Germany, which was fast becoming the strongest country on the Continent.

What made this German pressure for a formal guarantee so self-defeating was that Germany did not really need it, because it was strong enough to defeat any prospective Continental adversary or combination of them, so long as Great Britain did not take their side. What Germany should have asked of Great Britain was not an alliance, but benevolent neutrality in a Continental war—and for that an entente-type arrangement would have been sufficient. By asking for what it did not need, and by offering what Great Britain did not want (sweeping commitments to defend the British Empire), Germany led Great Britain to suspect that it was in fact seeking world domination.

German impatience deepened the reserve of the British, who were beginning to entertain grave doubts about the judgment of their suitor. "I do not like to disregard the plain anxiety of my German friends," wrote Salisbury. "But it is not wise to be guided too much by their advice now. Their Achitophel is gone. They are much pleasanter and easier to deal with; but one misses the extraordinary penetration of the old man [Bismarck]."[13]

While the German leadership impetuously pursued alliances, the German public was demanding an ever more assertive foreign policy. Only the Social Democrats held out for a time, though in the end they, too, succumbed to public opinion and supported Germany's declaration of war in 1914. The leading German classes had no experience with European diplomacy, much less with the *Weltpolitik* on which they were so loudly insisting. The Junkers, who had led Prussia to the domination of Germany, would bear the weight of opprobrium after the two world wars, especially in the United States. In fact, they were the social stratum least guilty of overreaching in foreign affairs, being basically geared to Continental policy and having little interest in events outside Europe. Rather, it was the new industrial managerial and the growing professional classes that provided the nucleus of nationalist agitation without encountering in the political system the sort of parliamentary buffer which had evolved in Great Britain and France over several centuries. In the Western democracies, the strong nationalist currents were channeled through parliamentary institutions; in Germany, they had to find expression in extra-parliamentary pressure groups.

As autocratic as Germany was, its leaders were extremely sensitive to public opinion and heavily influenced by nationalistic pressure groups. These groups saw diplomacy and international relations almost as if they were sporting events, always pushing the government to a harder line, more territorial expansion, more colonies, a stronger army, or a larger navy. They treated the normal give-and-take of diplomacy, or the slightest hint of German diplomatic concession, as an egregious humiliation. Kurt Rietzler, the political secretary of the German Chancellor Theobald von Bethmann-Hollweg, who was in office when war was declared, remarked aptly: "The threat of war in our time lies . . . in the internal politics of those countries in which a weak government is confronted by a strong nationalist movement."[14]

This emotional and political climate produced a major German diplomatic gaffe—the so-called Krüger Telegram—by which the Emperor undermined his option for a British alliance for at least the rest of the century. In 1895, a Colonel Jameson, supported by British colonial interests and most notably by Cecil Rhodes, led a raid into the independent Boer states of the South African Transvaal. The raid was a total failure and a great embarrassment to Salisbury's government, which claimed to have had no direct involvement in it. The German nationalist press gloated, urging an even more thorough humiliation of the British.

Friedrich von Holstein, a principal councilor and *éminence grise* in the Foreign Ministry, saw the disastrous raid as an opportunity to teach the British the advantages of a friendly Germany by showing them just how prickly an adversary it could be. For his own part, the Kaiser found the opportunity to swagger irresistible. Shortly after New Year's Day 1896, he dispatched a message to President Paul Krüger of the Transvaal congratulating him for repelling "the attacks from without." It was a direct slap at Great Britain and raised the specter of a German protectorate in the heart of what the British regarded as their own sphere of interest. In reality, the Krüger Telegram represented neither German colonial aspirations nor German foreign policy, for it was purely a public-relations ploy and it achieved that objective: "Nothing that the government has done for years," wrote the liberal *Allgemeine Zeitung* on January 5, "has given as complete satisfaction. . . . It is written from the soul of the German people."[15]

Germany's shortsightedness and insensitivity accelerated this trend. The Kaiser and his entourage convinced themselves that, since courting Great Britain had failed to produce an alliance, perhaps some demonstration of the cost of German displeasure would prove more persuasive. Unfortunately for Germany, that approach belied the historical record, which offered no example of a British susceptibility to being bullied.

What started out as a form of harassment to demonstrate the value of German friendship gradually turned into a genuine strategic challenge. No issue was as likely to turn Great Britain into an implacable adversary as a threat to its command of the seas. Yet this was precisely what Germany undertook, seemingly without realizing that it was embarking on an irrevocable challenge. Starting in the mid-1890s, domestic pressures to build up a large German navy began to mount, spearheaded by the "navalists," one of a growing number of pressure groups which consisted of a mix of industrialists and naval officers. Since they developed a vested interest in tensions with Great Britain to justify naval appropriations, they treated the Krüger Telegram as a godsend, as they did any other issue denoting the possibility of conflict with Great Britain in remote corners of the globe, ranging from the status of Samoa to the boundaries of the Sudan and the future of the Portuguese colonies.

Thus began a vicious cycle which culminated in confrontation. For the privilege of building a navy which, in the subsequent world war, had only one inconclusive encounter with the British fleet in the battle of Jutland, Germany managed to add Great Britain to its growing list of adversaries. For there was no question that England would resist once a Continental country already in possession of the strongest army in Europe began aiming for parity with Great Britain on the seas.

Yet the Kaiser seemed oblivious to the impact of his policies. British irritation with German bluster and the naval buildup did not, at first, change the reality that France was pressing Great Britain in Egypt, and that Russia was challenging it in Central Asia. What if Russia and France decided to cooperate, applying simultaneous pressure in Africa, Afghanistan, and China? What if the Germans joined them in an assault on the Empire in South Africa? British leaders began to doubt whether splendid isolation was still an appropriate foreign policy.

The most important and vocal spokesman of this group was the Colonial Secretary, Joseph Chamberlain. A dashing figure who was Salisbury's

junior by a whole generation, Chamberlain seemed to embody the twentieth century in his call for some alliance—preferably German—while the
older patrician adhered strictly to the isolationist impulse of the previous
century. In a major speech in November 1899, Chamberlain called for a
"Teutonic" alliance, consisting of Great Britain, Germany, and the United
States.[16] Chamberlain felt so strongly about it that he transmitted his
scheme to Germany without Salisbury's approval. But the German leaders
continued to hold out for formal guarantees and remained oblivious to
the reality that the terms were irrelevant and that what should have mattered to them most was British neutrality in a Continental war.

In October 1900, Salisbury's poor health forced him to give up the
office of Foreign Secretary, though he retained the post of Prime Minister.
His successor at the Foreign Office was Lord Lansdowne, who agreed
with Chamberlain that Great Britain could no longer enjoy safety through
splendid isolation. Yet Lansdowne was unable to muster a consensus for
a full-scale formal alliance with Germany, the Cabinet being unwilling to
go further than an entente-style arrangement: ". . . an understanding with
regard to the policy which they (the British and the German governments) might pursue in reference to particular questions or in particular
parts of the world in which they are alike interested."[17] It was substantially
the same formula which would lead to the Entente Cordiale with France
a few years later and which proved quite sufficient to bring Great Britain
into the World War on the side of France.

Once again, however, Germany rejected the attainable in favor of what
was on the face of it unachievable. The new German Chancellor Bülow
refused an entente-style arrangement with Great Britain because he was
more worried about public opinion than he was about geopolitical vistas
—especially given his priority of persuading the Parliament to vote a
large increase in the German navy. He would curtail the naval program
for nothing less than British adherence to a triple alliance consisting
of Germany, Austria, and Italy. Salisbury rejected Bülow's all-or-nothing
gambit, and, for the third time in a decade, an Anglo-German agreement
aborted.

The essential incompatibility between British and German perceptions
of foreign policy could be seen in the way the two leaders explained their
failure to agree. Bülow was all emotion as he accused Great Britain of
provincialism, ignoring the fact that Great Britain had been conducting a
global foreign policy for over a century before Germany was even unified:

> English politicians know little about the Continent. From a continental
> point of view they know as much as we do about ideas in Peru or

Siam. They are naive in their conscious egotism and in a certain blind confidence. They find it difficult to credit really bad intentions in others. They are very quiet, very phlegmatic and very optimistic. . . . [18]

Salisbury's reply took the form of a lesson in sophisticated strategic analysis for his restless and rather vague interlocutor. Citing a tactless comment by the German Ambassador to London, to the effect that Great Britain needed an alliance with Germany in order to escape dangerous isolation, he wrote:

> The liability of having to defend the German and Austrian frontiers against Russia is heavier than that of *having to defend the British Isles against France* . . . Count Hatzfeldt [the German Ambassador] speaks of our *"isolation"* as constituting a serious danger for us. *Have we ever felt that danger practically?* If we had succumbed in the revolutionary war, our fall would not have been due to our isolation. We had many allies, but they would not have saved us if the French Emperor had been able to command the Channel. Except during his [Napoleon's] reign we have never even been in danger; and, therefore, it is impossible for us to judge whether the "isolation" under which we are supposed to suffer, does or does not contain in it any elements of peril. It would hardly be wise to incur novel and most onerous obligations, in order to guard against a *danger in whose existence we have no historical reason for believing.* [19]

Great Britain and Germany simply did not have enough parallel interests to justify the formal global alliance imperial Germany craved. The British feared that further additions to German strength would turn their would-be ally into the sort of dominant power they had historically resisted. At the same time, Germany did not relish assuming the role of a British auxiliary on behalf of issues traditionally considered peripheral to German interests, such as the threat to India, and Germany was too arrogant to understand the benefits of British neutrality.

Foreign Secretary Lansdowne's next move demonstrated that the German leaders' conviction that their country was indispensable to Great Britain was a case of inflated self-appraisal. In 1902, he stunned Europe by forging an alliance with Japan, the first time since Richelieu's dealings with the Ottoman Turks that any European country had gone for help outside the Concert of Europe. Great Britain and Japan agreed that if either of them became involved in a war with *one* other power over China or Korea, the other would observe neutrality. If, however, either signatory was attacked by *two* adversaries, the other signatory was obliged

187

to assist its partner. Because the alliance would operate only if Japan were fighting two adversaries, Great Britain finally had discovered an ally which was willing, indeed eager, to contain Russia without, however, seeking to entangle it in extraneous arrangements—one, moreover, whose Far East location placed it in an area of greater strategic interest to Great Britain than the Russo-German frontier. And Japan was protected against France, which, without the alliance, might have sought to use the war to strengthen its claims on Russian support. From then on, Great Britain would lose interest in Germany as a strategic partner; indeed, in the course of time, it would come to regard Germany as a geopolitical threat.

As late as 1912, there was still a chance of settling Anglo-German difficulties. Lord Haldane, first Lord of the Admiralty, visited Berlin to discuss a relaxation of tensions. Haldane was instructed to seek an accommodation with Germany on the basis of a naval accord along with this pledge of British neutrality: "If either of the high contracting parties (i.e., Britain and Germany) becomes entangled in a war in which it cannot be said to be the aggressor, the other will at least observe towards the Power so entangled a benevolent neutrality."[20] The Kaiser, however, insisted that England pledge neutrality "should war be forced upon Germany,"[21] which sounded to London like a demand that Great Britain stand on the sidelines if Germany decided to launch a pre-emptive war against Russia or France. When the British refused to accept the Kaiser's wording, he in turn rejected theirs; the German Navy Bill went forward, and Haldane returned to London empty-handed.

The Kaiser still had not grasped that Great Britain would not go beyond a tacit bargain, which was really all that Germany needed. "If England only intends to extend her hand to us under the condition that we must limit our fleet," he wrote, "that is an unbounded impudence which contains in it a bad insult to the German people and their Emperor. This offer must be rejected *a limine*. . . ."[22] As convinced as ever that he could intimidate England into a formal alliance, the Kaiser boasted: "I have shown the English that, when they touch our armaments, they bite on granite. Perhaps by this I have increased their hatred but won their respect, which will induce them in due course to resume negotiations, it is to be hoped in a more modest tone and with a more fortunate result."[23]

The Kaiser's impetuous and imperious quest for alliance merely succeeded in magnifying Great Britain's suspicions. The German naval program on top of German harassment of Great Britain during the Boer War of 1899–1902 led to a thorough reassessment of British foreign policy. For a century and a half, Great Britain had considered France as the principal threat to the European equilibrium, to be resisted with the assistance of some German state, usually with Austria, occasionally with Prussia. And it had viewed Russia as the gravest danger to its empire. But once it had the Japanese alliance in hand, Great Britain began to reconsider its historic priorities. In 1903, Great Britain initiated a systematic effort to settle outstanding colonial issues with France, culminating in the so-called Entente Cordiale of 1904—precisely the sort of arrangement for informal cooperation that Germany had consistently rejected. Almost immediately afterward, Great Britain began to explore a similar arrangement with Russia.

Because the Entente was formally a colonial agreement, it did not represent a technical break with the traditional British policy of "splendid isolation." Yet its practical effect was that Great Britain abandoned the position of balancer and attached itself to one of the two opposing alliances. In July 1903, when the Entente was being negotiated, a French representative in London told Lansdowne as a *quid pro quo* that France would do its utmost to relieve Great Britain of Russian pressures elsewhere:

> . . . that the most serious menace to the peace of Europe lay in Germany, that a good understanding between France and England was the only means of holding German designs in check, and that if such an understanding could be arrived at, England would find that France would be able to exercise a salutary influence over Russia and thereby relieve us from many of our troubles with that country.[24]

Within a decade, Russia, previously tied to Germany by the Reinsurance Treaty, had become a military ally of France, while Great Britain, an on-again-off-again suitor of Germany, joined the French diplomatic camp. Germany had achieved the extraordinary feat of isolating itself and of bringing together three erstwhile enemies in a hostile coalition aimed against it.

A statesman aware of approaching danger has to make a basic decision. If he believes that the threat will mount with the passage of time, he must try to nip it in the bud. But if he concludes that the looming danger reflects a fortuitous, if accidental, combination of circumstances, he is usually better off waiting and letting time erode the peril. Two hundred years earlier, Richelieu had recognized the danger in the hostile encirclement of France—indeed, avoiding it was the core of his policy. But he understood as well the various components of that potential danger. He decided that premature action would drive the states surrounding France together. Thus he made time his ally and waited for the latent differences among France's adversaries to emerge. Then, and only after these had become entrenched, did he permit France to enter the fray.

The Kaiser and his advisers had neither the patience nor the acumen for such a policy—even though the countries by which Germany felt threatened were anything but natural allies. Germany's reaction to the looming encirclement was to accelerate the same diplomacy which had brought about the danger in the first place. It tried to split the young Entente Cordiale by finding some pretext to face down France, thereby demonstrating that British support was either illusory or ineffective.

Germany's opportunity to test the strength of the Entente presented itself in Morocco, where French designs were in violation of a treaty affirming Morocco's independence, and where Germany had substantial commercial interests. The Kaiser chose to make his point while on a cruise in March 1905. Landing at Tangier, he declared Germany's resolve to uphold the independence of Morocco. The German leaders were gambling, first, that the United States, Italy, and Austria would support their open-door policy, second, that in the aftermath of the Russo-Japanese War, Russia would not be able to involve itself, and third, that Great Britain would be only too happy to be relieved of its obligation to France at an international conference.

All of these assumptions were proved wrong because fear of Germany overrode every other consideration. In the first challenge to the Entente Cordiale, Great Britain backed France to the hilt and would not go along with Germany's call for a conference until France had accepted it. Austria and Italy were reluctant to venture anywhere near the brink of war. Nevertheless, German leaders invested a huge amount of prestige in this growing dispute, on the reasoning that anything less than a diplomatic victory demonstrating the irrelevance of the Entente would be disastrous.

Throughout his reign, the Kaiser was better at starting crises than he was at concluding them. He found dramatic encounters exciting but lacked the nerve for prolonged confrontation. William II and his advisers were correct in their assessment that France was not prepared to go to war. But, as it turned out, neither were they. All they really achieved was the dismissal of French Foreign Minister Delcassé, a token victory because Delcassé soon returned in another position, retaining a major role in French politics. In terms of the substance of the dispute, the German leaders, lacking the courage of their boastful rhetoric, permitted themselves to be fobbed off with a conference scheduled in six months' time in the Spanish town of Algeciras. When a country threatens war and then backs down in favor of a conference to be held at some later date, it automatically diminishes the credibility of its threat. (This was also the way the Western democracies would defuse Khrushchev's Berlin ultimatum a half century later.)

The extent to which Germany had isolated itself became evident at the opening of the Algeciras Conference in January 1906. Edward Grey, the Foreign Secretary of Great Britain's new Liberal government, warned the German Ambassador to London that, in the event of war, Great Britain would stand alongside France:

> . . . in the event of an attack upon France by Germany arising out of our Morocco Agreement, public feeling in England would be so strong that no British government could remain neutral . . . [25]

The German leaders' emotionalism and inability to define long-range objectives turned Algeciras into a diplomatic debacle for their country. The United States, Italy, Russia, and Great Britain all refused to take Germany's side. The results of this first Moroccan crisis were the exact opposite of what German leaders had sought to achieve. Instead of wrecking the Entente Cordiale, it led to Franco-British military cooperation and lent impetus to the Anglo-Russian Entente of 1907.

After Algeciras, Great Britain agreed to the military cooperation with a Continental power that it had avoided for so long. Consultations began between the leaders of the British and French navies. The Cabinet was not at ease with this new departure. Grey wrote to Paul Cambon, the French Ambassador to London, in an effort to hedge his bets:

> We have agreed that consultation between experts is not, and ought not to be, regarded as an engagement that commits either Government to action in a contingency that has not arisen and may never arise. . . . [26]

It was the traditional British escape clause that London not commit itself legally to specific circumstances in which it would be *obliged* to take military action. France accepted this sop to parliamentary control, convinced that military staff talks would wield their own reality, whatever the legal obligation. For a decade and a half, German leaders had refused to grant Great Britain this sort of leeway. The French had the political acumen to live with British ambiguity, and to rely on the conviction that a moral obligation was developing which, in a time of crisis, might well carry the day.

With the emergence of the Anglo-French-Russian bloc of 1907, only two forces remained in play in European diplomacy: the Triple Entente and the alliance between Germany and Austria. German encirclement became complete. Like the Anglo-French Entente, the British agreement with Russia began as a colonial accord. For some years, Great Britain and Russia had been slowly putting their colonial disputes to rest. Japan's victory over Russia in 1905 effectively ruined Russia's Far Eastern ambitions. By the summer of 1907, it became safe for Great Britain to offer Russia generous terms in Afghanistan and Persia, dividing Persia into three spheres of influence: the Russians were given the northern region; a central region was declared neutral; and Great Britain claimed control of the south. Afghanistan went to the British sphere. Anglo-Russian relations, which ten years earlier had been marred by disputes covering a third of the globe from Constantinople to Korea, were finally serene. The degree of British preoccupation with Germany was shown by the fact that, to secure Russian cooperation, Great Britain was prepared to abandon its determination to keep Russia out of the Dardanelles. As Foreign Secretary Grey remarked: "Good relations with Russia meant that our old policy of closing the Straits against her, and throwing our weight against her at any conference of the Powers must be abandoned."[27]

Some historians[28] have claimed that the real Triple Entente was two colonial agreements gone awry, and that Great Britain had wanted to protect its empire, not to encircle Germany. There is a classic document, however, the so-called Crowe Memorandum, which leaves no reasonable doubt that Great Britain joined the Triple Entente in order to thwart what it feared was a German drive for world domination. On January 1, 1907, Sir Eyre Crowe, a prominent British Foreign Office analyst, explained why, in his view, an accommodation with Germany was impossible and entente with France was the only option. The Crowe Memorandum was at a level of analysis never reached by any document of post-Bismarck Germany. The conflict had become one between strategy and brute power—and unless there is a huge disproportion of strength, which was not the case, the strategist has the upper hand because he can plan his actions while his adversary is obliged to improvise. Admitting to major differences between Great Britain and both France and Russia, Crowe nevertheless assessed these as being subject to compromise because they reflected definable, and therefore limited, objectives. What made German foreign policy so menacing was the lack of any discernible rationale behind its ceaseless global challenges, which extended across regions as far-flung as South Africa, Morocco, and the Near East. In addition, the German drive for maritime power was "incompatible with the survival of the British Empire."

According to Crowe, Germany's unconstrained conduct guaranteed confrontation: "The union of the greatest military with the greatest naval power in one state would compel the world to combine for the riddance of such an incubus."[29]

True to the tenets of *Realpolitik,* Crowe argued that structure, not motive, determined stability: Germany's intentions were essentially irrelevant; what mattered were its capabilities. He put forward two hypotheses:

> Either Germany is definitely aiming at a general political hegemony and maritime ascendancy, threatening the independence of her neighbours and ultimately the existence of England; Or Germany, free from any such clear-cut ambition, and thinking for the present merely of using her legitimate position and influence as one of the leading Powers in the council of nations, is seeking to promote her foreign commerce, spread the benefits of German culture, extend the scope of her national energies, and create fresh German interests all over the world wherever and whenever a peaceful opportunity offers. . . .[30]

Crowe insisted that these distinctions were irrelevant because, in the end, they would be overridden by the temptations inherent in Germany's growing power:

> . . . it is clear that the second scheme (of semi-independent evolution, not entirely unaided by statecraft) may at any stage merge into the first, or conscious-design scheme. Moreover, if ever the evolution scheme should come to be realized, the position thereby accruing to Germany would obviously constitute as formidable a menace to the rest of the world as would be presented by any deliberate conquest of a similar position by 'malice aforethought'.[31]

Though the Crowe Memorandum did not actually go further than to oppose an understanding with Germany, its thrust was clear: if Germany did not abandon its quest for maritime supremacy and moderate its so-called *Weltpolitik,* Great Britain was certain to join Russia and France in opposing it. And it would do so with the implacable tenacity that had brought down French and Spanish pretensions in previous centuries.

Great Britain made it clear that it would not stand for any further accretion of German strength. In 1909, Foreign Secretary Grey made this point in response to a German offer to *slow down* (but not end) its naval buildup if Great Britain agreed to stay neutral in a German war against France and Russia. The proposed agreement, argued Grey,

> . . . would serve to establish German hegemony in Europe and would not last long after it had served that purpose. It is in fact an invitation to

help Germany to make a European combination which could be directed against us when it suited her to use it. . . . If we sacrifice the other Powers to Germany, we shall eventually be attacked.[32]

After the creation of the Triple Entente, the cat-and-mouse game Germany and Great Britain had played in the 1890s grew deadly serious and turned into a struggle between a *status quo* power and a power demanding a change in the equilibrium. With diplomatic flexibility no longer possible, the only way to alter the balance of power was by adding more arms or by victory in war.

The two alliances were facing each other across a gulf of growing mutual distrust. Unlike the period of the Cold War, the two groupings did not fear war; they were in fact more concerned with preserving their cohesiveness than with avoiding a showdown. Confrontation became the standard method of diplomacy.

Nevertheless, there was still a chance to avoid catastrophe because there were actually few issues that justified war dividing the alliances. No other member of the Triple Entente would have gone to war to help France regain Alsace-Lorraine; Germany, even in its exalted frame of mind, was unlikely to support an Austrian war of aggression in the Balkans. A policy of restraint might have delayed the war and caused the unnatural alliances gradually to disintegrate—especially as the Triple Entente had been forged by fear of Germany in the first place.

By the end of the first decade of the twentieth century, the balance of power had degenerated into hostile coalitions whose rigidity was matched by the reckless disregard for consequence with which they had been assembled. Russia was tied to a Serbia teeming with nationalist, even terrorist, factions and which, having nothing to lose, had no concern for the risk of a general war. France had handed a blank check to a Russia eager to restore its self-respect after the Russo-Japanese War. Germany had done the same for an Austria desperate to protect its Slavic provinces against agitation from Serbia, which, in turn, was backed by Russia. The nations of Europe had permitted themselves to become captives of reckless Balkan clients. Far from restraining these nations of unbounded passion and limited sense of global responsibility, they allowed themselves to be dragged along by the paranoia that their restless partners might shift alliances if they were not given their way. For a few years, crises were still being surmounted although each new one brought the inevitable showdown closer. And Germany's reaction to the Triple Entente revealed a dogged determination to repeat the same mistake over and over again; every problem became transformed into a test of manhood to prove that Germany was decisive and powerful while its adversaries lacked resolution and strength. Yet, with each new German challenge, the bonds of the Triple Entente grew tighter.

In 1908, an international crisis occurred over Bosnia-Herzegovina, worth retelling because it illustrates the tendency of history to repeat itself. Bosnia-Herzegovina had been the backwater of Europe, its fate having been left in an ambiguous status at the Congress of Berlin because no one really knew what to do with it. This no-man's-land between the Ottoman and Habsburg Empires, which contained Roman Catholic, Orthodox, and Muslim religions, and Croatian, Serbian, and Muslim populations, had never been a state or even self-governing. It only seemed governable if none of these groups was asked to submit to the others. For thirty years, Bosnia-Herzegovina had been under Turkish suzerainty, Austrian administration, and local autonomy without experiencing a serious challenge to this multinational arrangement which left the issue of ultimate sovereignty unsettled. Austria had waited thirty years to initiate outright annexation because the passions of the polyglot mix were too complex even for the Austrians to sort out, despite their long experience of administering in the midst of chaos. When they finally did annex Bosnia-Herzegovina, they did so more to score a point against Serbia (and indirectly Russia) than to achieve any coherent political objective. As a result, Austria upset the delicate balance of offsetting hatreds.

Three generations later, in 1992, the same elemental passions erupted over comparable issues, confounding all but the zealots directly involved and those familiar with the region's volatile history. Once more, an abrupt change in government turned Bosnia-Herzegovina into a cauldron. As soon as Bosnia was declared an independent state, all the nationalities fell upon each other in a struggle for dominance, with the Serbs settling old scores in a particularly brutal manner.

Taking advantage of Russia's weakness in the wake of the Russo-Japanese War, Austria frivolously implemented a thirty-year-old secret codicil from the Congress of Berlin in which the powers had agreed to let Austria annex Bosnia-Herzegovina. Heretofore, Austria had been satisfied with *de facto* control because it wanted no more Slavic subjects. But in 1908, Austria reversed that decision, fearing its empire was about to dissolve under the impact of Serbian agitation and thinking that it needed some success to demonstrate its continued pre-eminence in the Balkans. In the intervening three decades, Russia had lost its dominant position in Bulgaria and the Three Emperors' League had lapsed. Not unreasonably, Russia was outraged that the all-but-forgotten agreement should now be invoked to permit Austria to acquire a territory which a Russian war had liberated.

But outrage does not guarantee success, especially when its target is already in possession of the prize. For the first time, Germany placed itself squarely behind Austria, signaling that it was prepared to risk a European war if Russia challenged the annexation. Then, making matters even more tense, Germany demanded formal Russian and Serbian recognition of Austria's move. Russia had to swallow this humiliation because Great Britain and France were not yet ready to go to war over a Balkan issue, and because Russia was in no position to go to war all alone so soon after its defeat in the Russo-Japanese War.

Germany thus placed itself as an obstacle in Russia's path and in an area where it had never before asserted a vital interest—indeed, where Russia had heretofore been able to count on Germany to moderate Austria's ambitions. Germany demonstrated not only its recklessness but a severe lapse of historical memory. Only half a century before, Bismarck had accurately predicted that Russia would never forgive Austria for humiliating it in the Crimean War. Now, Germany was making the same mistake, compounding Russia's estrangement, which had started at the Congress of Berlin.

Humiliating a great country without weakening it is always a dangerous game. Though Germany thought it was teaching Russia the importance of German goodwill, Russia resolved never to be caught flat-footed again. The two great Continental powers thus began to play a game called "chicken" in American slang, in which two drivers hurtle their vehicles toward each other, each hoping that the other will veer off at the last moment while counting on his own more steady nerves. Unfortunately, this game was played on several different occasions in pre–World War I Europe. Each time a collision was avoided, the collective confidence in the game's ultimate safety was strengthened, causing everyone to forget that a single failure would produce irrevocable catastrophe.

As if Germany wanted to make perfectly sure that it had not neglected to bully any potential adversary or to give all of them sufficient reason to tighten their bonds to each other in self-defense, it next challenged France. In 1911, France, now effectively the civil administrator of Morocco, responded to local unrest by sending troops to the city of Fez, in clear violation of the Algeciras accord. To the wild applause of the nationalist German press, the Kaiser reacted by dispatching the gunboat *Panther* to the Moroccan port of Agadir. "Hurrah! A Deed!" wrote the *Rheinisch-Westfälische Zeitung* on July 2, 1911. "Action at last, a liberating deed which must dissolve the cloud of pessimism everywhere."[33] The *Münchener Neueste Nachrichten* advised that the government push ahead with every energy, "even if out of such a policy, circumstances arise that we cannot foresee today."[34] In what passed for subtlety in the German press, the journal was basically urging Germany to risk war over Morocco.

The grandiloquently named *"Panther* Leap" had the same ending as Germany's previous efforts to break its self-inflicted encirclement. Once again, Germany and France seemed poised on the brink of a war, with Germany's goals as ill-defined as ever. What sort of compensation was it seeking this time? A Moroccan port? Part of Morocco's Atlantic coast? Colonial gains elsewhere? It wanted to intimidate France but could find no operational expression for that objective.

In keeping with their evolving relationship, Great Britain backed France more firmly than it had at Algeciras in 1906. The shift in British public opinion was demonstrated by the attitude of its then Chancellor of the Exchequer, David Lloyd George, who had a well-deserved reputation for pacifism and as an advocate of good relations with Germany. On this occasion, however, he delivered a major speech which warned that if

> ... a situation were to be forced upon us in which peace could only be preserved by the surrender of the great and beneficent position we had won by centuries of heroism and achievement ... then I say emphatically that peace at that price would be a humiliation intolerable for a great country like ours to endure.[35]

Even Austria turned a cold shoulder on its powerful ally, seeing no point in staking its survival on a North African adventure. Germany backed down, accepting a large but worthless tract of land in Central Africa, a transaction which elicited a groan from Germany's nationalistic press. "We practically risked a world war for a few Congolese swamps," wrote the *Berliner Tageblatt* on November 3, 1911.[36] Yet what ought to have been criticized was not the value of the new acquisitions but the wisdom of threatening a different country with war every few years without being able to define a meaningful objective, each time magnifying the fear which had brought the hostile coalitions into being in the first place.

If German tactics had by now become stereotyped, so had the Anglo-French response. In 1912, Great Britain, France, and Russia started military staff talks, the significance of which was only formally limited by the usual British disclaimer that they constituted no legally binding commitment. Even this constraint was belied to some extent by the Anglo-French Naval Treaty of 1912, according to which the French fleet was moved to the Mediterranean and Great Britain assumed responsibility for defending the French Atlantic coast. Two years later, this agreement would be invoked as a moral obligation for Great Britain to enter the First World War because, so it was claimed, France had left its Channel coast undefended in reliance on British support. (Twenty-eight years later, in 1940, a similar agreement between the United States and Great Britain would enable Great Britain to move its Pacific fleet to the Atlantic, implying a moral obligation on the part of the United States to protect Great Britain's nearby defenseless Asian possessions against Japanese attack.)

In 1913, German leaders culminated the alienation of Russia by another of their fitful and pointless maneuvers. This time, Germany agreed to reorganize the Turkish army and to send a German general to assume command over Constantinople. William II dramatized the challenge by sending off the training mission with a typically grandiloquent flourish, expressing his hope that "the German flags will soon fly over the fortifications of the Bosphorus."[37]

Few events could have enraged Russia more than Germany's laying claim to the position in the Straits that Europe had denied to Russia for a century. Russia had with difficulty reconciled itself to the control of the Straits by a weak country like Ottoman Turkey, but it would never acquiesce to domination of the Dardanelles by another Great Power. The Russian Foreign Minister, Sergei Sazonov, wrote to the Tsar in December 1913: "To abandon the Straits to a powerful state would be synonymous with subordinating the whole economic development of southern Russia to this state."[38] Nicholas II told the British Ambassador that "Germany was aiming at acquiring such a position at Constantinople as would enable it to shut in Russia altogether in the Black Sea. Should she attempt to carry out this policy, he would have to resist it with all his power, even if war should be the only alternative."[39]

Though Germany devised a face-saving formula for removing the German commander from Constantinople (by promoting him to field marshal, which, according to German tradition, meant he could no longer command troops in the field), irreparable damage had been done. Russia understood that Germany's support to Austria over Bosnia-Herzegovina had not been an aberration. The Kaiser, regarding these developments as tests of his manhood, told his chancellor on February 25, 1914: "Russo-Prussian relations are dead once and for all! We have become enemies!"[40] Six months later, World War I broke out.

An international system had evolved whose rigidity and confrontational style paralleled that of the later Cold War. But in fact, the pre–World War I international order was far more volatile than the Cold War world. In the Nuclear Age, only the United States and the Soviet Union had the technical means to start a general war in which the risks were so cataclysmic that neither superpower dared to delegate such awesome power to an ally, however close. By contrast, prior to World War I, each member of the two main coalitions was in a position not only to start a war but to blackmail its allies into supporting it.

For a while, the alliance system itself provided a certain restraint. France held Russia back in conflicts which primarily involved Austria; Germany played a similar role with Austria vis-à-vis Russia. In the Bosnian crisis of 1908, France made it clear that it would not go to war over a Balkan issue. During the Moroccan crisis of 1911, French President Calliaux was told firmly that any French attempt to resolve a colonial crisis by force would not receive Russian support. As late as the Balkan War of 1912, Germany warned Austria that there were limits to German backing, and Great Britain pressured Russia to moderate its acts on behalf of the volatile and unpredictable Balkan League, which was led by Serbia. At the London Conference of 1913, Great Britain helped to thwart Serbian annexation of Albania, which would have been intolerable to Austria.

The London Conference of 1913 would, however, be the last time that the pre–World War I international system could ease conflicts. Serbia was unhappy with Russia's lukewarm support, while Russia resented Great Britain's posture as an impartial arbiter and France's clear reluctance to go to war. Austria, on the verge of disintegrating under Russian and South Slav pressures, was upset that Germany was not backing it more vigorously. Serbia, Russia, and Austria all expected greater support from their allies; France, Great Britain, and Germany feared that they might lose their partners if they did not support them more forcefully in the next crisis.

Afterward, each Great Power was suddenly seized by panic that a conciliatory stance would make it appear weak and unreliable and cause its partners to leave it facing a hostile coalition all alone. Countries began to assume levels of risk unwarranted by their historic national interests or by any rational long-term strategic objective. Richelieu's dictum that means must correspond to ends was violated almost daily. Germany accepted the risk of world war in order to be seen as supportive of Vienna's South Slav policy, in which it had no national interest. Russia was willing to risk a fight to the death with Germany in order to be viewed as Serbia's steadfast ally. Germany and Russia had no major conflict with each other; their confrontation was by proxy.

In 1912, the new French President, Raymond Poincaré, informed the Russian Ambassador with respect to the Balkans that "if Russia goes to war, France will also, as we know that in this question Germany is behind Austria."[41] The gleeful Russian Ambassador reported "a completely new French view" that "the territorial grabs by Austria affect the general European balance and therefore France's interests."[42] That same year, the British Undersecretary in the Foreign Office, Sir Arthur Nicholson, wrote to the British Ambassador in St. Petersburg: "I do not know how much longer we shall be able to follow our present policy of dancing on a tight rope, and not be compelled to take some definite line or other. I am also haunted by the same fear as you—lest Russia should become tired of us and strike a bargain with Germany."[43]

Not to be outdone in recklessness, the Kaiser promised Austria in 1913 that, in the next crisis, Germany would follow it into war if necessary. On July 7, 1914, the German Chancellor explained the policy which, less than four weeks later, would lead to actual war: "If we urge them [the Austrians] ahead, then they will say we pushed them in; if we dissuade them, then it will become a matter of our leaving them in the lurch. Then they will turn to the Western Powers, whose arms are wide open, and we will lose our last ally, such as it is."[44] The precise benefit Austria was to draw from an alliance with the Triple Entente was left undefined. Nor was it likely that Austria could join a grouping containing Russia, which sought to undermine Austria's Balkan position. Historically, alliances had been formed to augment a nation's strength in case of war; as World War I approached, the primary motive for war was to strengthen the alliances.

The leaders of all the major countries simply did not grasp the implications of the technology at their disposal, or of the coalitions they were feverishly constructing. They seemed oblivious to the huge casualties of the still relatively recent American Civil War, and expected a short, decisive conflict. It never occurred to them that the failure to make their alliances correspond to rational political objectives would lead to the destruction of civilization as they knew it. Each alliance had too much at stake to permit the traditional Concert of Europe diplomacy to work. Instead, the Great Powers managed to construct a diplomatic doomsday machine, though they were unaware of what they had done.

CHAPTER EIGHT

Into the Vortex: The Military Doomsday Machine

The astonishing aspect of the outbreak of the First World War is not that a crisis simpler than many already surmounted had finally triggered a global catastrophe, but that it took so long for it to happen. By 1914, the confrontation between Germany and Austria-Hungary on the one side, and the Triple Entente on the other, had turned deadly earnest. The statesmen of all the major countries had helped to construct the diplomatic doomsday mechanism that made each succeeding crisis progressively more difficult to solve. Their military chiefs had vastly compounded the peril by adding strategic plans which compressed the time available for decision-making. Since the military plans depended on speed and the diplomatic machinery was geared to its traditional leisurely pace, it became impossible to disentangle the crisis under intense time pressure. To make matters worse, the military planners had not adequately explained the implications of their handiwork to their political colleagues.

Military planning had, in effect, become autonomous. The first step in this direction occurred during the negotiation for a Franco-Russian military alliance in 1892. Up to that time, alliance negotiations had been about the *casus belli,* or what specific actions by the adversary might oblige allies to go to war. Almost invariably, its definition hinged on who was perceived to have initiated the hostilities.

In May 1892, the Russian negotiator, Adjutant General Nikolai Obruchev, sent a letter to his Foreign Minister, Giers, explaining why the traditional method for defining the *casus belli* had been overtaken by modern technology. Obruchev argued that what mattered was who mobilized first, not who fired the first shot: "The undertaking of mobilization can no longer be considered as a peaceful act; on the contrary, it represents the most decisive act of war."[1]

The side that procrastinated in mobilizing would lose the benefit of its alliances and enable its enemy to defeat each adversary in turn. The need for all the allies to mobilize simultaneously had become so urgent in the minds of European leaders that it turned into the keystone of solemn diplomatic engagements. The purpose of alliances was no longer to guarantee support *after* a war had started, but to guarantee that each ally would mobilize as soon as and, it was hoped, just before, any adversary did. When alliances so constructed confronted each other, threats based on mobilization became irreversible because stopping mobilization in midstream was more disastrous than not having started it at all. If one side stopped while the other proceeded, it would be at a growing disadvantage with every passing day. If both sides tried to stop simultaneously, it would be technically so difficult that almost certainly the mobilization would be completed before the diplomats could agree on how to arrest it.

This doomsday procedure effectively removed the *casus belli* from political control. Every crisis had a built-in escalator to war—the decision to mobilize—and every war was certain to become general.

Far from deploring the prospect of automatic escalation, Obruchev welcomed it enthusiastically. The last thing he wanted was a local conflict. For, if Germany were to stay out of a war between Russia and Austria, it would simply emerge afterward in a position to dictate the terms of the peace. In Obruchev's fantasy, this was what Bismarck had done at the Congress of Berlin:

Less than any other can our diplomacy count on an isolated conflict of Russia, for example, with Germany, or Austria, or Turkey alone. The Congress of Berlin was lesson enough for us in this connection, and it

202

taught us whom we should regard as our most dangerous enemy—the one who fights with us directly or the one who waits for our weakening and then dictates the terms of peace? . . .[2]

According to Obruchev, it was in Russia's interest to make certain that every war would be general. The benefit to Russia of a well-constructed alliance with France would be to prevent the possibility of a localized war:

At the outset of every European war there is always a great temptation for the diplomats to localize the conflict and to limit its effects as far as possible. But in the present armed and agitated condition of continental Europe, Russia must regard any such localization of the war with particular skepticism, because this could unduly strengthen the possibilities not only for those of our enemies who are hesitating and have not come out into the open, but also for vacillating allies.[3]

In other words, a defensive war for limited objectives was *against* Russia's national interest. Any war had to be total, and the military planners could grant no other option to the political leaders:

Once we have been drawn into a war, we cannot conduct that war otherwise than with all our forces, and against both our neighbors. In the face of the readiness of entire armed peoples to go to war, no other sort of war can be envisaged than the most decisive sort—a war that would determine for long into the future the relative political positions of the European powers, and especially of Russia and Germany.[4]

However trivial the cause, war would be total; if its prelude involved only one neighbor, Russia should see to it that the other was drawn in. Almost grotesquely, the Russian general staff *preferred* to fight Germany and Austria-Hungary jointly than just one of them. A military convention carrying out Obruchev's ideas was signed on January 4, 1894. France and Russia agreed to mobilize together should *any* member of the Triple Alliance mobilize for *any* reason whatsoever. The doomsday machine was complete. Should Germany's ally, Italy, mobilize against France over Savoy, for instance, Russia would have to mobilize against Germany; if Austria mobilized against Serbia, France was now obliged to mobilize against Germany. Since it was virtually certain that at some point some nation would mobilize for some cause, it was only a matter of time before a general war broke out, for it required only *one* mobilization by a major power to start the doomsday machinery for all of them.

At least Tsar Alexander III understood that the game now being played was for the highest stakes. When Giers asked him, "... what would we gain by helping the French destroy Germany?" he replied: "What we would gain would be that Germany, as such, would disappear. It would break up into a number of small, weak states, the way it used to be."[5] German war aims were equally sweeping and nebulous. The much-invoked European equilibrium had turned into a battle to the death, though not one of the statesmen involved could have explained what cause justified such nihilism or what political aims would be served by the conflagration.

What Russian planners were putting forward as theory, the German general staff translated into operational planning at almost the exact moment that Obruchev was negotiating the Franco-Russian military alliance. And with German thoroughness, the imperial generals pushed the mobilization concept to its absolute extreme. The chief of the German staff, Alfred von Schlieffen, was as obsessed by mobilization schedules as his Russian and French counterparts. But whereas the Franco-Russian military leaders were concerned with defining the obligation to mobilize, Schlieffen focused on implementing the concept.

Refusing to leave anything to the vagaries of the political environment, Schlieffen tried to devise a foolproof plan for escaping Germany's dreaded encirclement. Just as Bismarck's successors had abandoned his complex diplomacy, so Schlieffen jettisoned the strategic concepts of Helmuth von Moltke, the military architect of Bismarck's three rapid victories between 1864 and 1870.

Moltke had devised a strategy that left open the option of a political solution to Bismarck's nightmare of hostile coalitions. In case of a two-front war, Moltke planned to split the German army more or less evenly between the East and the West, and to go on the defensive on both fronts. Since France's principal objective was to regain Alsace-Lorraine, it was certain to attack. If Germany defeated that offensive, France would be obliged to consider a compromise peace. Moltke specifically warned against extending military operations to Paris, having learned in the Franco-Prussian War how difficult it was to conclude a peace while besieging the enemy's capital.

Moltke proposed the same strategy for the Eastern front—namely, to defeat a Russian attack and to follow it by pushing the Russian army back to a strategically significant distance, and then to offer a compromise peace. Whichever forces first achieved victory would be available to aid the armies on the other front. In this manner, the scale of the war, the sacrifices, and the political solution would be kept in some sort of balance.[6]

But just as Bismarck's successors had been uncomfortable with the ambiguities of his overlapping alliances, so Schlieffen rejected Moltke's plan because it left the military initiative to Germany's enemies. Nor did Schlieffen approve of Moltke's preference for political compromise over total victory. Determined to impose terms which were, in effect, unconditional surrender, Schlieffen elaborated a scheme for a quick and decisive victory on one front and then throwing all of Germany's forces against the other adversary, thereby achieving a clear-cut outcome on both fronts. Because a quick, knockout blow in the East was precluded by the slow pace of Russian mobilization, which was expected to take six weeks, and by Russia's vast territory, Schlieffen decided to destroy the French army first, before the Russian army was fully mobilized. To circumvent the heavy French fortifications at the German border, Schlieffen came up with the idea of violating Belgian neutrality by wheeling the German army through its territory. He would capture Paris and trap the French army from the rear in its fortresses along the border. In the meantime, Germany would stay on the defensive in the East.

The plan was as brilliant as it was reckless. A minimum knowledge of history would have revealed that Great Britain would surely go to war if Belgium was invaded—a fact which seems to have totally eluded the Kaiser and the German general staff. For twenty years after the Schlieffen Plan was devised in 1892, Germany's leaders had made innumerable proposals to Great Britain to gain its support—or at least neutrality—in a European war, all of which were rendered illusory by German military planning. There was no cause for which Great Britain had fought as consistently or implacably as the independence of the Low Countries. And Great Britain's conduct in the wars against Louis XIV and Napoleon testified to its tenacity. Once engaged, it would fight to the end, even if France were defeated. Nor did the Schlieffen Plan allow for the possibility of failure. If Germany did not destroy the French army—which was possible, since the French had interior lines and railways radiating from Paris whereas the German army had to march by foot in an arc through a devastated countryside—Germany would be forced into Moltke's strategy of defense on both fronts after it had destroyed the possibility of a political compromise peace by occupying Belgium. Where the principal goal of Bismarck's foreign policy had been to avoid a two-front war and of Moltke's military strategy to limit it, Schlieffen insisted on a two-front war conducted in an all-out fashion.

With German deployment focused against France while the most likely origin of the conflict would be in Eastern Europe, Bismarck's nightmare question, "what if there is a two-front war?" was transformed into Schlieffen's nightmare question, "what if there is not a two-front war?" If France were to declare neutrality in a Balkan war, Germany might face the danger of a French declaration of war *after* Russian mobilization was complete, as Obruchev had already explained from the other side of the European dividing line. If, on the other hand, Germany ignored France's offer of neutrality, Schlieffen's plan would put Germany in the uncomfortable position of attacking non-belligerent Belgium in order to get to non-belligerent France. Schlieffen therefore had to invent a reason to assault France should France stay on the sidelines. He created an impossible standard for what Germany would accept as French neutrality. Germany would regard France as neutral only if it agreed to cede one of its major fortresses to Germany—in other words, only if France put itself at Germany's mercy and abdicated its position as a Great Power.

The unholy mix of general political alliances and hair-trigger military strategies guaranteed a vast bloodletting. The balance of power had lost any semblance of the flexibility it had had during the eighteenth and nineteenth centuries. Wherever war erupted (and it would almost certainly be in the Balkans), the Schlieffen Plan saw to it that the initial battles would be fought in the West between countries having next to no interest in the immediate crisis. Foreign policy had abdicated to military strategy, which now consisted of gambling on a single throw of the dice. A more mindless and technocratic approach to war would have been difficult to imagine.

Though the military leaders of both sides insisted on the most destructive kind of war, they were ominously silent about its political consequences in light of the military technology they were pursuing. What would Europe look like after a war on the scale they were planning? What changes could justify the carnage they were preparing? There was not a single specific Russian demand on Germany or a single German demand on Russia, which merited a local war, much less a general one.

The diplomats on both sides were silent, too, largely because they did not understand the political implications of their countries' time bomb, and because nationalistic politics in each country made them afraid to challenge their military establishments. This conspiracy of silence prevented the political leaders of all the major countries from requesting military plans which established some correspondence between military and political objectives.

Considering the catastrophe they were brewing, there was something almost eerie about the lightheartedness of European leaders as they embarked on their disastrous course. Surprisingly few warnings were ever uttered, an honorable exception being that of Peter Durnovo, a former Russian Interior Minister who became a member of the State Council.

In February 1914—six months before the war—he wrote a prophetic memorandum for the Tsar:

> The main burden of the war will undoubtedly fall on us, since England is hardly capable of taking a considerable part in a continental war, while France, poor in manpower, will probably adhere to strictly defensive tactics, in view of the enormous losses by which war will be attended under present conditions of military technique. The part of a battering-ram, making a breach in the very thick of the German defense, will be ours. . . .[7]

In Durnovo's judgment, these sacrifices would be wasted because Russia would not be able to make permanent territorial gains by fighting on the side of Great Britain, its traditional geopolitical opponent. Though Great Britain would concede gains to Russia in Central Europe, an additional slice of Poland would only magnify the already strong centrifugal tendencies within the Russian Empire. Adding to the Ukrainian population, said Durnovo, would spur demands for an independent Ukraine. Therefore, victory might have the ironic result of fostering enough ethnic turmoil to reduce the Tsar's empire to Little Russia.

Even if Russia realized its century-old goal of conquering the Dardanelles, Durnovo pointed out that such an achievement would prove strategically empty:

> [It] would not give us an outlet to the open sea, however, since on the other side of them there lies a sea consisting almost wholly of territorial waters, a sea dotted with numerous islands where the British navy, for instance, would have no trouble whatever in closing to us every inlet and outlet, irrespective of the Straits.[8]

Why this simple geopolitical fact should have eluded three generations of Russians desiring the conquest of Constantinople—and of Englishmen determined to thwart them—remains a mystery.

Durnovo went on to argue that a war would bring even fewer economic benefits to Russia. By any calculation, it would cost far more than could possibly be recouped. A German victory would destroy the Russian economy while a Russian victory would drain the German economy, leaving nothing for reparations no matter which side won:

> There can be no doubt that the war will necessitate expenditures which are beyond Russia's limited financial means. We shall have to obtain credit from allied and neutral countries, but this will not be granted

gratuitously. As to what will happen if the war should end disastrously for us, I do not wish to discuss now. The financial and economic consequences of defeat can be neither calculated nor even foreseen, and will undoubtedly spell the total ruin of our entire national economy. But even victory promises us extremely unfavorable financial prospects; a totally ruined Germany will not be in a position to compensate us for the cost involved. Dictated in the interest of England, the peace treaty will not afford Germany opportunity for sufficient economic recuperation to cover our war expenditures, even at a distant time.[9]

Yet Durnovo's strongest reason for opposing the war was his prediction that war would inevitably lead to social revolution—first in the defeated country and then spreading from there to the victor:

It is our firm conviction, based upon a long and careful study of all contemporary subversive tendencies, that there must inevitably break out in the defeated country a social revolution which, by the very nature of things, will spread to the country of the victor.[10]

There is no evidence that the Tsar saw the memorandum that might have saved his dynasty. Nor is there any record of a comparable analysis in other European capitals. The closest anyone came to Durnovo's views were a few epigrammatic comments by Bethmann-Hollweg, the Chancellor who would lead Germany into the war. In 1913, already much too late, he had expressed, quite accurately, why German foreign policy proved so unsettling to the rest of Europe:

Challenge everybody, put yourself in everybody's path and actually weaken no one in this fashion. Reason: aimlessness, the need for little prestige successes and solicitude for every current of public opinion.[11]

That same year, Bethmann-Hollweg laid down another maxim, which might have saved his country had it been put into practice twenty years earlier:

We must keep France in check through a cautious policy towards Russia and England. Naturally this does not please our chauvinists and is unpopular. But I see no alternative for Germany in the near future.[12]

By the time these lines were written, Europe was already headed into the vortex. The locale of the crisis that triggered the First World War was irrelevant to the European balance of power, and the *casus belli* as accidental as the preceding diplomacy had been reckless.

On June 28, 1914, Franz Ferdinand, heir to the Habsburg throne, paid for Austria's rashness in having annexed Bosnia-Herzegovina in 1908 with his life. Not even the manner of his assassination could escape the singular mix of the tragic and the absurd that marked Austria's disintegration. The young Serbian terrorist failed in his first attempt to assassinate Franz Ferdinand, wounding the driver of the Archduke's vehicle instead. After arriving at the governor's residence and chastising the Austrian administrators for their negligence, Franz Ferdinand, accompanied by his wife, decided to visit the victim at the hospital. The royal couple's new driver took a wrong turn and, in backing out of the street, came to a stop in front of the astonished would-be assassin, who had been drowning his frustrations in liquor at a sidewalk café. With his victims so providentially delivered to him by themselves, the assassin did not fail a second time.

What started out as a near-accident turned into a conflagration with the inevitability of a Greek tragedy. Because the Archduke's wife was not of royal blood, none of the kings of Europe attended the funeral. Had the crowned heads of state congregated and had an opportunity to exchange views, they might have proven more reluctant to go to war a few weeks later over what had been, after all, a terrorist plot.

In all likelihood, not even a royal summit could have prevented Austria from lighting the fuse which the Kaiser now rashly handed it. Remembering his promise of the previous year to back Austria in the next crisis, he invited the Austrian Ambassador to lunch on July 5 and urged speedy action against Serbia. On July 6, Bethmann-Hollweg confirmed the Kaiser's pledge: "Austria must judge what is to be done to clear up her relations with Serbia; but whatever Austria's decision, she could count with certainty upon it, that Germany will stand behind her as an ally."[13]

Austria at last had the blank check it had sought for so long, and a real grievance to which it might be applied. Insensitive as ever to the full implications of his bravado, William II vanished on a cruise to the Norwegian fjords (this in the days before radio). Exactly what he had in mind is not clear, but he obviously did not anticipate a European war. The Kaiser and his chancellor apparently calculated that Russia was not yet ready for war and would stand by while Serbia was humiliated, as it had done in 1908. In any event, they believed they were in a better position for a showdown with Russia than they would be a few years later.

Maintaining their unbroken record of misjudging the psychology of potential adversaries, the German leaders were now as convinced of the vastness of their opportunity as when they had tried to force Great Britain into an alliance by building a large navy, or to isolate France by threatening war over Morocco. Operating from the assumption that Austria's success might break their ever-tighter encirclement by disillusioning Russia with the Triple Entente, they ignored France, which they deemed irreconcilable, and evaded mediation by Great Britain lest it spoil their triumph. They had persuaded themselves that if, against all expectations, war did break out, Great Britain would either remain neutral or intervene too late. Yet Serge Sazonov, Russia's Foreign Minister at the outbreak of the war, described why Russia would not back off this time:

> Ever since the Crimean War, we could entertain no illusions on the subject of Austria's feelings toward us. On the day she initiated her predatory policy in the Balkans, hoping thereby to prop up the tottering structure of her dominion, her relations with us became more and more unfriendly. We were able, however, to reconcile ourselves to this inconvenience, until it became clear that her Balkan policy had the sympathy of Germany, and received encouragement from Berlin.[14]

Russia felt it had to resist what it interpreted as a German maneuver to destroy its position among the Slavs by humiliating Serbia, its most reliable ally in the area. "It was clear," wrote Sazonov, "that we had to do not with the rash decision of a short-sighted Minister, undertaken at his own risk and on his own responsibility, but with a carefully prepared plan, elaborated with the aid of the German Government, without whose consent and promise of support Austria-Hungary would never have ventured upon its execution."[15]

Another Russian diplomat later wrote nostalgically of the difference between the Germany of Bismarck and the Germany of the Kaiser:

> The Great War was the inevitable consequence of the encouragement given by Germany to Austria-Hungary in her policy of penetration into the Balkans, which was combined with the grandiose Pan-German idea of a Germanized "Middle-Europe." In Bismarck's day this never would have happened. What did happen was the result of Germany's novel ambition to grapple with a task more stupendous than that of Bismarck —without a Bismarck.[16]*

---

* The Russian memoirs must be taken with a grain of salt because they were trying to shift the total responsibility for the war onto Germany's shoulders. Sazonov in particular must bear part of the blame because he clearly belonged to the war party pushing for full mobilization—even though his overall analysis has much merit.

The Russian diplomats were paying the Germans too great an honor, for the Kaiser and his advisers had no more of a long-range plan in 1914 than they had had during any previous crisis. The crisis over the Archduke's assassination ran out of control because no leader was prepared to back down and every country was concerned above all with living up to formal treaty obligations rather than to an overall concept of long-range common interest. What Europe lacked was some all-encompassing value system to bind the powers together, such as had existed in the Metternich system or the cold-blooded diplomatic flexibility of Bismarck's *Realpolitik*. World War I started not because countries broke their treaties, but because they fulfilled them to the letter.

Of the many curious aspects of the prelude to the First World War, one of the strangest was that nothing happened at first. Austria, true to its operating style, procrastinated, in part because Vienna needed time to overcome the reluctance of Hungarian Prime Minister Stephen Tisza to risk the Empire. When he finally yielded, Vienna issued a forty-eight-hour ultimatum to Serbia on July 23, deliberately putting forward such onerous conditions that they were sure to be rejected. Yet the delay had cost Austria the benefits of the widespread initial feelings of indignation in Europe over the Archduke's assassination.

In Metternich's Europe, with its shared commitment to legitimacy, there can be little doubt that Russia would have sanctioned Austrian retribution against Serbia for the assassination of a prince in direct line of succession to the Austrian throne. But by 1914, legitimacy was no longer a common bond. Russia's sympathy for its ally, Serbia, outweighed its outrage at the assassination of Franz Ferdinand.

For the entire month following the assassination, Austrian diplomacy had been dilatory. Then came the mad rush to cataclysm in the space of less than a week. The Austrian ultimatum drove events out of the control of the political leaders. For once the ultimatum had been issued, any major country was in a position to trigger the irreversible race to mobilization. Ironically, the mobilization juggernaut was set off by the one country for which mobilization schedules were essentially irrelevant. For, alone among all the major powers, Austria's military plans were still old-fashioned in that they did not depend on speed. It mattered little to Austrian war plans which week the war started, as long as its armies were able to fight Serbia sooner or later. Austria had delivered its ultimatum to Serbia in order to forestall mediation, not to speed military operations. Nor did Austrian mobilization threaten any other major power, since it would take a month to be completed.

Thus, the mobilization schedules which made war inevitable were set in motion by the country whose army did not actually start fighting until *after* the major battles in the West were already over. On the other hand and whatever the state of Austria's readiness, if Russia wanted to threaten Austria, it would have to mobilize some troops, an act which would trigger the irreversible in Germany (though none of the political leaders seemed to have grasped this danger). The paradox of July 1914 was that the countries which had political reasons to go to war were not tied to rigid mobilization schedules while nations with rigid schedules, such as Germany and Russia, had no political reason to go to war.

Great Britain, the country in the best position to arrest this chain of events, hesitated. It had next to no interest in the Balkan crisis, though it did have a major interest in preserving the Triple Entente. Dreading war, it feared a German triumph even more. Had Great Britain declared unambiguously its intentions and made Germany understand that it would enter a general war, the Kaiser might well have turned away from confrontation. That is how Sazonov saw it later:

> I cannot refrain from expressing the opinion that if in 1914 Sir Edward Grey had, as I insistently requested him, made a timely and equally unambiguous announcement of the solidarity of Great Britain with France and Russia, he might have saved humanity from that terrible cataclysm, the consequences of which endangered the very existence of European civilization.[17]

The British leaders were reluctant to risk the Triple Entente by indicating any hesitation to support their allies and, somewhat contradictorily, did not want to threaten Germany so as to keep open the option of mediating at the right moment. As a result, Great Britain fell between two stools. It had no legal obligation to go to war on the side of France and Russia, as Grey assured the House of Commons on June 11, 1914, a little more than two weeks before the Archduke's assassination:

> ... if war arose between European Powers, there were no unpublished agreements which would restrict or hamper the freedom of the Government or Parliament to decide whether or not Great Britain should participate in a war....[18]

Legally, this was certainly true. But there was an intangible moral dimension involved as well. The French navy was in the Mediterranean because of France's naval agreement with Great Britain; as a result, the coast of northern France would be wide open to the German navy if Great Britain stayed out of the war. As the crisis developed, Bethmann-Hollweg pledged not to employ the German navy against France if Great Britain promised to remain neutral. But Grey refused this bargain, for the same reason that he had rejected the German offer in 1909 to slow down its naval buildup in return for British neutrality in a European war—he suspected that after France was defeated, Great Britain would be at Germany's mercy.

> You must inform the German Chancellor that his proposal that we should bind ourselves to neutrality on such terms cannot for a moment be entertained.
> ... For us to make this bargain with Germany at the expense of France would be a disgrace from which the good name of this country would never recover.
> The Chancellor also in effect asks us to bargain away whatever obligation or interest we have as regards the neutrality of Belgium. We could not entertain that bargain either.[19]

Grey's dilemma was that his country had become snared between the pressures of public opinion and the traditions of its foreign policy. On the one hand, the lack of public support for going to war over a Balkan issue would have suggested mediation. On the other hand, if France were defeated or lost confidence in the British alliance, Germany would be in the dominant position the British had always resisted. Therefore, it is highly probable that, in the end, Great Britain would have gone to war to prevent a French military collapse even if Germany had not invaded Belgium, although it could have taken some time for the British people's support for the war to crystallize. During that period, Great Britain might have tried to mediate. However, Germany's decision to challenge one of the most established principles of English foreign policy—that the Low Countries must not fall into the hands of a major power—served to resolve British doubts and guaranteed that the war would not end with a compromise.

Grey reasoned that, by not taking sides in the early stages of the crisis, Great Britain would retain its claim to the impartiality which might permit it to broker a solution. And past experience supported this strategy. The outcome of heightened international tensions for twenty years had invariably been a conference. However, in no previous crisis had there been any mobilization. As all the Great Powers were getting ready to mobilize, the margin of time available for traditional diplomatic methods vanished. Thus, in the crucial ninety-six hours during which mobilization schedules destroyed the opportunity for political maneuvering, the British Cabinet in effect assumed the role of bystander.

Austria's ultimatum backed Russia against the wall at a moment when it already believed it had been sorely misused. Bulgaria, whose liberation from Turkish rule had been brought about by Russia through several wars, was leaning toward Germany. Austria, having annexed Bosnia-Herzegovina, seemed to be seeking to turn Serbia, Russia's last significant Balkan ally, into a protectorate. Finally, with Germany establishing itself in Constantinople, Russia could only wonder whether the age of Pan-Slavism might not end in the Teutonic domination of everything it had coveted for a century.

Even so, Tsar Nicholas II was not eager for a showdown with Germany. At a ministerial meeting on July 24, he reviewed Russia's options. The Finance Minister, Peter Bark, reported the Tsar as saying: "War would be disastrous for the world, and once it had broken out it would be difficult to stop." In addition, Bark noted, "The German Emperor had frequently assured him of his sincere desire to safeguard the peace of Europe." And he reminded the ministers of "the German Emperor's loyal attitude during the Russo-Japanese War and during the internal troubles that Russia had experienced afterwards."[20]

The rebuttal came from Aleksandr Krivoshein, the powerful Minister of Agriculture. Demonstrating Russia's endemic refusal to forget a slight, he argued that, despite the Kaiser's kind letters to his cousin, Tsar Nicholas, the German had bullied Russia during the Bosnian crisis of 1908. Therefore, "public and parliamentary opinion would fail to understand why, at the critical moment involving Russia's vital interest, the Imperial Government was reluctant to act boldly. . . . Our exaggeratedly prudent attitudes had unfortunately not succeeded in placating the Central European Powers."[21]

Krivoshein's argument was supported by a dispatch from the Russian Ambassador in Sofia to the effect that, if Russia backed down, "our prestige in the Slav world and in the Balkans would perish never to return."[22] Heads of government are notoriously vulnerable to arguments that question their courage. In the end, the Tsar suppressed his premonitions of disaster and opted for backing Serbia even at the risk of war, though he stopped short of ordering mobilization.

When Serbia responded to Austria's ultimatum on July 25 in an unexpectedly conciliatory fashion—accepting all Austrian demands except one—the Kaiser, just back from his cruise, thought that the crisis was over. But he did not count on Austria's determination to exploit the backing he had proffered so incautiously. Above all, he had forgotten—if indeed he had ever known it—that, with the Great Powers so close to the brink of war, mobilization schedules were likely to outrun diplomacy.

On July 28, Austria declared war against Serbia, even though it would not be ready for military action until August 12. On the same day, the Tsar ordered partial mobilization against Austria and discovered to his surprise that the only plan the general staff had readied was for general mobilization against both Germany and Austria, despite the fact that for the past fifty years Austria had stood in the way of Russia's Balkan ambitions, and that a localized Austro-Russian war had been a staple of military-staff schools during that entire period. Russia's Foreign Minister, unaware that he was living in a fool's paradise, sought to reassure Berlin on July 28: "The military measures taken by us in consequence of the Austria declaration of war . . . not a single one of them was directed against Germany."[23]

The Russian military leaders, without exception disciples of Obruchev's theories, were appalled by the Tsar's restraint. They wanted general mobilization and thus war with Germany, which had taken no military steps so far. One of the leading generals told Sazonov that "war had become inevitable and that we were in danger of losing it before we had time to unsheath our sword."[24]

If the Tsar had been too hesitant for his generals, he was far too decisive for Germany. All German war plans were based on knocking France out of a war within six weeks, and then turning against a presumably still not fully mobilized Russia. Any Russian mobilization—even a partial one—would cut into this timetable and lower the odds of Germany's already risky gamble. Accordingly, on July 29, Germany demanded that Russia stop its mobilization or Germany would follow suit. And everyone knew that German mobilization was tantamount to war.

The Tsar was too weak to yield. Stopping partial mobilization would have unraveled the entire Russian military planning, and the resistance of his generals convinced him that the die was cast. On July 30, Nicholas ordered full mobilization. On July 31, Germany once more demanded an end to Russian mobilization. When that request was ignored, Germany declared war on Russia. This occurred without a single serious political exchange between St. Petersburg and Berlin about the substance of the crisis, and in the absence of any tangible dispute between Germany and Russia.

Germany now faced the problem that its war plans required an immediate attack on France, which had been quiescent throughout the crisis except to encourage Russia not to compromise by pledging France's unconditional support. Understanding at last where twenty years of histrionics had landed him, the Kaiser tried to divert Germany's mobilization away from France and toward Russia. His attempt to rein in the military was as much in vain as the Tsar's previous, similar effort to limit the scope of Russian mobilization. The German general staff was no more willing than its Russian counterpart to scrap twenty years of planning; indeed, no more than the Russian staff did it have an alternate plan. Though both the Tsar and the Emperor had wanted to pull back from the brink, neither knew how to do it—the Tsar because he was prevented from carrying out partial mobilization, the Kaiser because he was kept from mobilizing only against Russia. Both were thwarted by the military machinery which they had helped to construct and which, once set in motion, proved irreversible.

On August 1, Germany inquired of France whether it intended to re-main neutral. Had France replied in the affirmative, Germany would have demanded the fortresses of Verdun and Toulon as tokens of good faith. Instead, France replied rather enigmatically that it would act in accor-dance with its national interest. Germany, of course, had no specific issue with which to justify war with France, which had been a bystander in the Balkan crisis. Again, the mobilization schedules were the driving force. Thus, Germany trumped up some French border violations and, on Au-gust 3, declared war. The same day, German troops, carrying out the Schlieffen Plan, invaded Belgium. On the next day, August 4, to the sur-prise of no one except the German leaders, Great Britain declared war on Germany.

The Great Powers had succeeded in turning a secondary Balkan crisis into a world war. A dispute over Bosnia and Serbia had led to the invasion of Belgium, at the other end of Europe, which had in turn made Great Britain's entry into the war inevitable. Ironically, by the time the decisive battles were being fought on the Western front, Austrian troops had still not taken the offensive against Serbia.

Germany learned too late that there can be no certainty in war and that its obsessive quest for a quick and decisive victory had landed it in a draining war of attrition. In implementing the Schlieffen Plan, Germany dashed all its hopes for British neutrality without succeeding in destroy-ing the French army, which had been the purpose of taking the risks in the first place. Ironically, Germany lost the offensive battle in the West and won the defensive battle in the East, much as the elder Moltke had foreseen. In the end, Germany was obliged to adopt Moltke's defensive strategy in the West as well after having committed itself to a policy which excluded the compromise political peace on which Moltke's strategy had been based.

The Concert of Europe failed miserably because the political leadership had abdicated. As a result, the sort of European Congress which throughout most of the nineteenth century had provided a cooling-off period or led to an actual solution, was not even attempted. European leaders had provided for every contingency except the time needed for diplomatic conciliation. And they had forgotten Bismarck's dictum: "Woe to the leader whose arguments at the end of a war are not as plausible as they were at the beginning."

By the time events had run their course, 20 million lay dead; the Austro-Hungarian Empire had disappeared; three of the four dynasties which entered the war—the German, the Austrian, and the Russian—were overthrown. Only the British royal house remained standing. Afterward, it was hard to recall exactly what had triggered the conflagration. All that anyone knew was that, from the ashes produced by monumental folly, a new European system had to be constructed, though its nature was difficult to discern amidst the passion and the exhaustion deposited by the carnage.

CHAPTER NINE

The New Face of Diplomacy: Wilson and the Treaty of Versailles

On November 11, 1918, British Prime Minister David Lloyd George announced that an armistice between Germany and the Allied Powers had been signed with these words: "I hope that we may say that thus, this fateful morning, come to an end all wars."[1] In reality, Europe was a mere two decades away from an even more cataclysmic war.

Since nothing about the First World War had gone as planned, it was inevitable that the quest for peace would prove as futile as the expectations with which nations had launched themselves into the catastrophe. Every participant had anticipated a brief war and had left the determination of its peace terms to the sort of diplomatic congress which had ended European conflicts for the past century. But as the casualties mounted to horrendous proportions, they obliterated the political disputes of the

218

prelude to the conflict—the competition for influence in the Balkans, the possession of Alsace-Lorraine, and the naval race. The nations of Europe came to blame their suffering on the inherent evil of their adversaries, and convinced themselves that compromise could bring no real peace; the enemy had to be totally defeated or the war fought to utter exhaustion.

Had European leaders continued the practices of the prewar international order, a compromise peace would have been made in the spring of 1915. Offensives by each side had run their bloody course, and stalemate prevailed on all fronts. But just as mobilization schedules had run away with diplomacy in the week prior to the outbreak of the war, so now the scale of the sacrifices stood in the way of a sensible compromise. Instead, the leaders of Europe kept raising their terms, thereby not only compounding the incompetence and the irresponsibility with which they had slid into war, but destroying the world order in which their nations had coexisted for nearly a century.

By the winter of 1914–15, military strategy and foreign policy had lost touch with each other. None of the belligerents dared to explore a compromise peace. France would not settle without regaining Alsace-Lorraine; Germany would not consider a peace in which it would be asked to give up the territory it had conquered. Once plunged into war, the leaders of Europe became so obsessed with fratricide, so maddened by the progressive destruction of an entire generation of their young men, that victory turned into its own reward, regardless of the ruins on which that triumph would have to be erected. Murderous offensives confirmed the military stalemate and produced casualties unimaginable before the advent of modern technology. Efforts to enlist new allies deepened the political deadlock. For each new ally—Italy and Romania on the Allied side, Bulgaria on the side of the Central Powers—demanded its share of the anticipated booty, thereby destroying whatever flexibility might have remained to diplomacy.

Peace terms gradually took on a nihilistic character. The aristocratic, somewhat conspiratorial style of nineteenth-century diplomacy proved irrelevant in the age of mass mobilization. The Allied side specialized in couching the war in moral slogans such as "the war to end all wars" or "making the world safe for Democracy"—especially after America entered the war. The first of these goals was understandable, if not highly promising, for nations that had been fighting each other in various combinations for a thousand years. Its practical interpretation was the complete disarmament of Germany. The second proposition—spreading democracy—required the overthrow of German and Austrian domestic institutions. Both Allied slogans therefore implied a fight to the finish.

Great Britain, which in the Napoleonic Wars had produced a blueprint for European equilibrium via the Pitt Plan, supported the pressures for an all-out victory. In December 1914, a German feeler offering to withdraw from Belgium in exchange for the Belgian Congo was rejected by British Foreign Secretary Grey with the argument that the Allies must be given "security against any future attack from Germany."[2]

Grey's comment marked a transformation in the British attitude. Until shortly before the outbreak of the war, Great Britain had identified its security with the balance of power, which it protected by supporting the weaker side against the stronger. By 1914, Great Britain felt less and less comfortable in this role. Sensing that Germany had become stronger than all the rest of the Continent combined, Great Britain felt it could no longer play its traditional role of trying to remain above the fray in Europe. Because it perceived Germany as a hegemonic threat in Europe, a return to the *status quo ante* would do nothing to alleviate the fundamental problem. Thus, Great Britain, too, would no longer accept compromise and insisted on its own "guarantees," which amounted to the permanent weakening of Germany, especially a sharp reduction of the German High Sea Fleet—something Germany would never accept unless it were totally defeated.

The German terms were both more precise and more geopolitical. Yet with their characteristic lack of a sense of proportion, the German leaders, too, asked for what amounted to unconditional surrender. In the West, they demanded the annexation of the coal fields of northern France and military control over Belgium, including the port of Antwerp, which guaranteed Great Britain's implacable hostility. In the East, Germany only stated formal terms with respect to Poland, where, on November 5, 1916, it promised to create "an independent State with a hereditary and constitutional monarchy"[3]—dashing any prospect for a compromise peace with Russia. (Germany's hope had been that the promise of Polish independence would produce enough Polish volunteers for five divisions; as it turned out, only 3,000 recruits showed up.)[4] After defeating Russia, Germany imposed the Treaty of Brest-Litovsk on March 3, 1918, by which it annexed a third of European Russia and established a protectorate over the Ukraine. In finally defining what it meant by *Weltpolitik,* Germany was opting for the domination of Europe at the very least.

The First World War began as a typical cabinet war, with notes being passed from embassy to embassy, and telegrams being distributed among sovereign monarchs at all the decisive steps on the road to actual combat. But once war had been declared, and as the streets of European capitals filled with cheering throngs, the conflict ceased being a conflict of chancelleries and turned into a struggle of the masses. After the first two years of the war, each side was stating terms incompatible with any notion of equilibrium.

What proved beyond everyone's imagination was that both sides would win and lose at the same time: that Germany would defeat Russia and seriously weaken both France and England; but that, in the end, the Western Allies, with America's indispensable assistance, would emerge as the victors. The aftermath of the Napoleonic Wars had been a century of peace based on equilibrium and sustained by common values. The aftermath of World War I was social upheaval, ideological conflict, and another world war.

The enthusiasm that marked the beginning of the war evaporated once the peoples of Europe came to understand that their governments' ability to produce the carnage was not matched by a commensurate ability to achieve either victory or peace. In the resulting maelstrom, the Eastern Courts, whose unity had sustained the peace of Europe in the days of the Holy Alliance, were overthrown. The Austro-Hungarian Empire disappeared altogether. The Russian Empire was taken over by the Bolsheviks and for two decades receded into the periphery of Europe. Germany was successively racked by defeat, revolution, inflation, economic depression, and dictatorship. France and Great Britain did not benefit from the weakened state of their adversaries. They had sacrificed the best of their young men for a peace which left the enemy geopolitically stronger than it had been before the war.

Before the full dimension of this largely self-inflicted debacle could become evident, a new player appeared on the scene to end once and for all what had up to this time been called the Concert of Europe. Amidst the rubble and the disillusionment of three years of carnage, America stepped into the international arena with a confidence, a power, and an idealism that were unimaginable to its more jaded European allies.

America's entry into the war made total victory technically possible, but it was for goals which bore little relation to the world order Europe had known for some three centuries and for which it had presumably entered the war. America disdained the concept of the balance of power and considered the practice of *Realpolitik* immoral. America's criteria for international order were democracy, collective security, and self-determination—none of which had undergirded any previous European settlement.

To Americans, the dissonance between their philosophy and European thought underlined the merit of their beliefs. Proclaiming a radical departure from the precepts and experiences of the Old World, Wilson's idea of world order derived from Americans' faith in the essentially peaceful nature of man and an underlying harmony of the world. It followed that democratic nations were, by definition, peaceful; people granted self-determination would no longer have reason to go to war or to oppress others. Once all the peoples of the world had tasted of the blessings of peace and democracy, they would surely rise as one to defend their gains.

European leaders had no categories of thought to encompass such views. Neither their domestic institutions nor their international order had been based on political theories postulating man's essential goodness. Rather, they had been designed to place man's demonstrated selfishness in the service of a higher good. European diplomacy was predicated not on the peace-loving nature of states but on their propensity for war, which needed to be either discouraged or balanced. Alliances were formed in the pursuit of specific, definable objectives, not in the defense of peace in the abstract.

Wilson's doctrines of self-determination and collective security put European diplomats on thoroughly unfamiliar terrain. The assumption behind all European settlements had been that borders could be adjusted to promote the balance of power, the requirements of which took precedence over the preferences of the affected populations. This was how Pitt had envisaged the "great masses" to contain France at the end of the Napoleonic Wars.

Throughout the nineteenth century, for example, Great Britain and Austria resisted the breakup of the Ottoman Empire because they were convinced that the smaller nations emerging from it would undermine international order. To their way of thinking, the smaller nations' inexperience would magnify endemic ethnic rivalries, while their relative weakness would tempt Great Power encroachment. In the British and Austrian view, the smaller states had to subordinate their national ambitions to the broader interests of peace. In the name of equilibrium, France had been prevented from annexing the French-speaking Walloon part of Belgium, and Germany was discouraged from uniting with Austria (though Bismarck had his own reasons for not seeking a union with Austria).

Wilson entirely rejected this approach, as the United States has done ever since. In America's view, it was not self-determination which caused wars but the lack of it; not the absence of a balance of power that produced instability but the pursuit of it. Wilson proposed to found peace on the principle of collective security. In his view and that of all his disciples, the security of the world called for, not the defense of the national interest, but of peace as a legal concept. The determination of whether a breach of peace had indeed been committed required an international institution, which Wilson defined as the League of Nations.

Oddly enough, the idea for such an organization first surfaced in London, heretofore the bastion of balance-of-power diplomacy. And the motive for it was not an attempt to invent a new world order but England's search for a good reason why America should enter a war of the old order. In September 1915, in a revolutionary departure from British practice, Foreign Secretary Grey wrote to Wilson's confidant, Colonel House, with a proposal which he believed the idealistic American President would not be able to refuse.

To what extent, asked Grey, might the President be interested in a League of Nations committed to enforcing disarmament and to the pacific settlement of disputes?

> Would the President propose that there should be a League of Nations binding themselves to side against any Power which broke a treaty . . . or which refused, in case of dispute, to adopt some other method of settlement than that of war?[5]

It was unlikely that Great Britain, which for 200 years had steered clear of open-ended alliances, had suddenly developed a taste for open-ended commitments on a global scale. Yet Great Britain's determination to prevail against the immediate threat of Germany was so great that its Foreign Secretary could bring himself to put forward a doctrine of collective security, the most open-ended commitment imaginable. Every member of his proposed world organization would have an obligation to resist aggression anywhere and from whatever quarter, and to penalize nations which rejected the pacific settlement of disputes.

Grey knew his man. From the days of his youth, Wilson had believed that American federal institutions should serve as a model for an eventual "parliament of man"; early in his presidency, he was already exploring a Pan-American pact for the Western Hemisphere. Grey could not have been surprised—though surely he was gratified—to receive a prompt reply falling in with what was, in retrospect, his rather transparent hint.

The exchange was perhaps the earliest demonstration of the "special relationship" between America and Great Britain that would enable Great Britain to maintain a unique influence in Washington long after the decline of its power in the wake of the Second World War. A common language and cultural heritage combined with great tactfulness to enable British leaders to inject their ideas into the American decision-making process in such a manner that they imperceptibly seemed to be a part of Washington's own. Thus, when, in May 1916, Wilson advanced for the first time his scheme for a world organization, he was no doubt convinced that it had been his own idea. And in a way it had been, since Grey had proposed it in full awareness of Wilson's likely convictions.

Regardless of its immediate parentage, the League of Nations was a quintessentially American concept. What Wilson envisaged was a "universal association of the nations to maintain the inviolate security of the highway of the seas for the common and unhindered use of all the nations of the world, and to prevent any war begun either contrary to treaty covenants or without warning and full submission of the causes to the opinion of the world—a virtual guarantee of territorial integrity and political independence."[6]

Initially, however, Wilson refrained from offering American participation in this "universal association." Finally in January 1917, he took the leap and advocated American membership, using, amazingly enough, the Monroe Doctrine as a model:

> I am proposing, as it were, that the nations should with one accord adopt the doctrine of President Monroe as the doctrine of the world: that no nation should seek to extend its polity over any other nation or people, ... that all nations henceforth avoid entangling alliances which would draw them into competitions of power....[7]

Mexico was probably astonished to learn that the president of the country which had seized a third of its territory in the nineteenth century and had sent its troops into Mexico the preceding year was now presenting the Monroe Doctrine as a guarantee for the territorial integrity of sister nations and as a classic example of international cooperation.

Wilson's idealism stopped short of the belief that his views would prevail in Europe on their inherent merits. He showed himself quite prepared to supplement argument with pressure. Shortly after America entered the war in April 1917, he wrote to Colonel House: "When the war is over we can force them to our way of thinking, because by that time they will, among other things, be financially in our hands."[8] For the time being, several of the Allies lingered over their responses to Wilson's idea. Though they could not quite bring themselves to approve views so contrary to their traditions, they also needed America far too much to voice their reservations.

In late October 1917, Wilson dispatched House to ask the Europeans to formulate war aims which would reflect his proclaimed aim for a peace without annexations or indemnities safeguarded by a world authority. For several months, Wilson refrained from putting forward his own views because, as he explained to House, France and Italy might object if

America expressed doubts about the justice of their territorial aspirations.[9]

Finally, on January 8, 1918, Wilson proceeded on his own. With extraordinary eloquence and elevation, he put forward America's war aims before a joint session of Congress, presenting them in the form of Fourteen Points which were divided into two parts. He described eight points as being obligatory in the sense that they "must" be fulfilled. These included open diplomacy, freedom of the seas, general disarmament, the removal of trade barriers, impartial settlement of colonial claims, the restoration of Belgium, the evacuation of Russian territory, and, as the crown jewel, the establishment of a League of Nations.

Wilson introduced the remaining six points, which were more specific, with the statement that they "should" rather than "must" be achieved, presumably because, in his view, they were not absolutely indispensable. Surprisingly, the restoration of Alsace-Lorraine to France was included in the non-obligatory category, even though a determination to regain that region had sustained French policy for half a century and through unprecedented sacrifices in the war. Other "desirable" goals were described as autonomy for the minorities of the Austro-Hungarian and Ottoman Empires, readjustment of Italy's frontiers, evacuation of the Balkans, internationalization of the Dardanelles, and the creation of an independent Poland with access to the sea. Did Wilson mean to imply that these six conditions were subject to compromise? Poland's access to the sea and the modification of Italy's frontiers would surely be difficult to reconcile with the principle of self-determination and were, for this reason, the first flaws in the moral symmetry of Wilson's design.

Wilson concluded his presentation with an appeal to Germany in the name of the spirit of conciliation with which America would approach the building of a new international order—an attitude precluding historical war aims:

> We grudge her no achievement or distinction of learning or of pacific enterprise such as have made her record very bright and very enviable. We do not wish to injure her or to block in any way her legitimate influence or power. We do not wish to fight her either with arms or with hostile arrangements of trade if she is willing to associate herself with us and the other peace-loving nations of the world in covenants of justice and law and fair dealing. We wish her only to accept a place of equality among the peoples of the world....[10]

Never before had such revolutionary goals been put forward with so few guidelines as to how to implement them. The world Wilson envisaged would be based on principle, not power; on law, not interest—for both victor and vanquished; in other words, a complete reversal of the historical experience and method of operation of the Great Powers. Symbolic of this was the way Wilson described his and America's role in the war. America had joined what, due to Wilson's aversion to the word "ally," he preferred to call "one side" of one of the most ferocious wars in history, and Wilson was acting as if he were the principal mediator. For what Wilson seemed to be saying was that the war had been fought not to achieve certain specific conditions but to engender a particular attitude on the part of Germany. Hence the war had been about conversion, not geopolitics.

In an address at London's Guildhall on December 28, 1918, after the Armistice, Wilson explicitly condemned the balance of power as unstable and based on "jealous watchfulness and an antagonism of interests":

> They [the Allied soldiers] fought to do away with an old order and to establish a new one, and the center and characteristic of the old order was that unstable thing which we used to call the "balance of power" —a thing in which the balance was determined by the sword which was thrown in the one side or the other; a balance which was determined by the unstable equilibrium of the competitive interests. . . . The men who have fought in this war have been the men from free nations who were determined that that sort of thing should end now and forever.[11]

Wilson was surely right about the European nations' having made a mess of things. However, it was not so much the balance of power as Europe's abdication of it that had caused the debacle of World War I. The leaders of pre–World War I Europe had neglected the historic balance of power and abandoned the periodic adjustments which had avoided final show-downs. They had substituted a bipolar world much less flexible than even the Cold War world of the future, in that it lacked the cataclysmic inhibitions of the Nuclear Age. While paying lip service to equilibrium, the leaders of Europe had catered to the most nationalistic elements of their public opinion. Neither their political nor their military arrangements allowed for any flexibility; there was no safety valve between the *status quo* and conflagration. This had led to crises that could not be settled and to endless public posturing that, in the end, permitted no retreat.

Wilson accurately identified some of the principal challenges of the twentieth century—most especially how to put power into the service of peace. But his solutions too often compounded the problems he identified. For he ascribed competition among states primarily to the absence of self-determination and to economic motives. Yet history shows many other, more frequent, causes of competition, prominent among which are national aggrandizement and the exaltation of the ruler or the ruling group. Disdainful of such impulses, Wilson was convinced that the spread of democracy would arrest them and self-determination would deprive them of their focal points.

Wilson's remedy of collective security presupposed that the nations of the world would unite against aggression, injustice, and, presumably, excessive selfishness. In an appearance before the Senate early in 1917, Wilson asserted that the establishment of equal rights among states would provide the precondition for maintaining peace through collective security regardless of the power each nation represented.

> Right must be based upon the common strength, not upon the individual strength, of the nations upon whose concert peace will depend. Equality of territory or of resources there of course cannot be; nor any other sort of equality not gained in the ordinary peaceful and legitimate development of the peoples themselves. But no one asks or expects anything more than an equality of rights. Mankind is looking now for freedom of life, not for equipoises of power.[12]

Wilson was proposing a world order in which resistance to aggression would be based on moral rather than geopolitical judgments. Nations would ask themselves whether an act was unjust rather than whether it was threatening. Though America's allies had little faith in this new dispensation, they felt too weak to challenge it. America's allies knew or thought they knew how to calculate equilibrium based on power; they had no confidence that they, or anyone else, knew how to assess equilibrium on the basis of moral precepts.

Before America's entry into the war, the European democracies never dared to express openly their doubts about Wilson's ideas and indeed made every attempt to enlist Wilson by humoring him. By the time America did join the Allies, they were desperate. The combined forces of Great Britain, France, and Russia had not been sufficient to overcome Germany and, in the aftermath of the Russian Revolution, they feared that America's entry into the war might do no more than offset Russia's collapse. The Treaty of Brest-Litovsk with Russia showed what fate Germany had in mind for the losers. Fear of German victory kept Great Britain and France from debating war aims with their idealistic American partner.

After the Armistice, the Allies found themselves in a better position to express their reservations. Nor would it have been the first time that a

European alliance was strained or broken in the aftermath of victory (for example, the Congress of Vienna went through a phase in which the victors threatened each other with war). Yet the victors of the First World War were too drained by their sacrifices and still too dependent on the American giant to risk a testy dialogue with it, or its withdrawal from the peace settlement.

This was especially true of France, which now found itself in a truly tragic position. For two centuries it had struggled to achieve the mastery of Europe, but, in the war's aftermath, it no longer had confidence in its ability to protect even its own frontiers against a defeated enemy. French leaders felt instinctively that containing Germany was beyond the capacity of their ravaged society. War had exhausted France and the peace seemed to induce premonitions of further catastrophe. France, which had fought for its existence, now struggled for its identity. France dared not stand alone, yet its most powerful ally was proposing to found the peace on principles that turned security into a judicial process.

Victory brought home to France the stark realization that revanche had cost it too dearly, and that it had been living off capital for nearly a century. France alone knew just how weak it had become in comparison with Germany, though nobody else, especially not America, was prepared to believe it. Thus, on the eve of victory began a Franco-American dialogue which accelerated the process of French demoralization. Like Israel in the modern period, France masked its vulnerability with prickliness, and incipient panic with intransigence. And, like Israel in the modern period, it stood in constant danger of isolation.

Though France's allies insisted that its fears were exaggerated, French leaders knew better. In 1880, the French had represented 15.7 percent of Europe's population. By 1900, that figure had declined to 9.7 percent. In 1920, France had a population of 41 million and Germany a population of 65 million, causing the French statesman Briand to answer critics of his conciliatory policy toward Germany with the argument that he was conducting the foreign policy of France's birthrate.

France's relative economic decline was even more dramatic. In 1850, France had been the largest industrial nation on the Continent. By 1880, German production of steel, coal, and iron exceeded that of France. In 1913, France produced 41 million tons of coal compared with Germany's 279 million tons; by the late 1930s, the disparity was to widen to 47 million tons produced by France against Germany's total of 351 million tons.[13]

The residual strength of the defeated enemy marked the essential difference between the post-Vienna and post-Versailles international orders, and the reason for it was the disunity of the victors after Versailles. A coalition of powers defeated Napoleon and a coalition of powers was needed to surmount imperial Germany. Even after losing, both of the vanquished—France in 1815 and Germany in 1918—remained strong enough to overcome any one of the coalition members singly and perhaps even a combination of two of them. The difference was that, in 1815, the peacemakers at the Congress of Vienna stayed united and formed the Quadruple Alliance—an overwhelming coalition of four powers that would crush any revisionist dreams. In the post-Versailles period, the victors did not remain allied, America and the Soviet Union withdrew altogether, and Great Britain was highly ambivalent as far as France was concerned.

It was not until the post-Versailles period that France came to the searing realization that its defeat by Germany in 1871 had not been an aberration. The only way France could have maintained equilibrium with Germany by itself would have been to break Germany up into its component states, perhaps by re-establishing the German Confederation of the nineteenth century. Indeed, France fitfully pursued this objective by encouraging separatism in the Rhineland and by occupying the Saar coal mines.

Two obstacles, however, stood in the way of the partitioning of Germany. For one, Bismarck had built too well. The Germany he created retained its sense of unity through defeats in two world wars, through the French occupation of the Ruhr area in 1923, and the Soviet imposition of a satellite state in Eastern Germany for a generation after the Second World War. When the Berlin Wall came down in 1989, French President Mitterrand briefly toyed with the idea of cooperating with Gorbachev to obstruct German unification. But Gorbachev was too preoccupied with domestic problems to undertake such an adventure, and France was not strong enough to attempt it alone. A similar French weakness prevented the partitioning of Germany in 1918. Even if France had been up to the task, its allies, especially America, would not have tolerated so crass a violation of the principle of self-determination. But neither was Wilson prepared to insist on a peace of reconciliation. In the end, he went along with several punitive provisions contradicting the equal treatment promised in the Fourteen Points.

The attempt to reconcile American idealism with France's nightmares turned out to be beyond human ingenuity. Wilson traded modification of the Fourteen Points for the establishment of the League of Nations, to which he looked to remedy any legitimate grievances left over from the peace treaty. France settled for far fewer punitive measures than it thought commensurate with its sacrifices in the hope of evoking a long-term American commitment to French security. Ultimately, no country achieved its objective: Germany was not reconciled, France was not made secure, and the United States withdrew from the settlement.

Wilson was the star of the Peace Conference, which convened in Paris between January and June 1919. In the days when travel to Europe took a week by ship, many of Wilson's advisers had warned that an American president could not afford to be away from Washington for months on end. In fact, in Wilson's absence his strength in the Congress did deteriorate, proving especially costly when the peace treaty came up for ratification. Wilson's absence from Washington aside, it is almost always a mistake for heads of state to undertake the details of a negotiation. They are then obliged to master specifics normally handled by their foreign offices and are deflected onto subjects more appropriate to their subordinates, while being kept from issues only heads of state can resolve. Since no one without a well-developed ego reaches the highest office, compromise is difficult and deadlocks are dangerous. With the domestic positions of the interlocutors so often dependent on at least the semblance of success, negotiations more often concentrate on obscuring differences than they do on dealing with the essence of a problem.

This proved to be Wilson's fate at Paris. With every passing month, he was drawn more deeply into haggling over details which had never concerned him before. The longer he stayed, the more the sense of urgency to bring matters to a conclusion overrode the desire to create an entirely new international order. The final outcome was made inevitable by the procedure used to negotiate the peace treaty. Because a disproportionate amount of time was spent adjusting territorial questions, the League of Nations emerged as a sort of *deus ex machina,* to straighten out later the ever-widening gap between Wilson's moral claims and the actual terms of the settlement.

The mercurial Welshman David Lloyd George, who represented Great Britain, had told his public shortly before the Peace Conference that he would "squeeze Germany until the pips squeak." But, confronted by a volatile Germany and a fretful France, he focused on maneuvering between Clemenceau and Wilson. In the end, he went along with the punitive provisions, invoking the League as the mechanism by which any inequities would later be corrected.

Arguing on behalf of France's point of view was the battle-scarred and aged Georges Clemenceau. Nicknamed "the Tiger," he was a veteran of decades of domestic battles, from the overthrow of Napoleon III to the vindication of Captain Dreyfus. Yet, at the Paris Conference, he set himself a task that was beyond even his ferocious capacities. Striving for a peace which would somehow undo Bismarck's work and reassert Richelieu-style primacy on the Continent, he exceeded the tolerance of the international system and, indeed, the capacities of his own society. The clock simply could not be turned back 150 years. No other nation either shared or fully grasped France's objectives. Frustration would prove to be Clemenceau's lot, and progressive demoralization France's future.

Vittorio Orlando, the Italian Prime Minister, represented the last of the "Big Four." Though he cut a fine figure, he was frequently overshadowed by his energetic Foreign Minister, Sidney Sonnino. The Italian negotiators, it turned out, had come to Paris to collect their booty rather than to design a new world order. The Allies had induced Italy into the war by promising it the South Tirol and the Dalmatian coast in the Treaty of London of 1915. Since the South Tirol was predominantly Austro-German and the Dalmatian coast Slavic, Italy's claims were in direct conflict with the principle of self-determination. Yet Orlando and Sonnino deadlocked the Conference until, in utter exasperation, South Tirol (though not Dalmatia) was turned over to Italy. This "compromise" demonstrated that the Fourteen Points were not etched in stone, and opened the floodgates to various other adjustments which, collectively, ran counter to the prevailing principle of self-determination without either improving the old balance of power or creating a new one.

Unlike the Congress of Vienna, the Paris Peace Conference did not include the defeated powers. As a result, the months of negotiation cast the Germans beneath a pall of uncertainty, which encouraged illusions. They recited Wilson's Fourteen Points as if by heart and, though their own peace program would have been brutal, deluded themselves into believing that the Allies' final settlement would be relatively mild. Therefore, when the peacemakers revealed their handiwork in June 1919, the Germans were shocked and embarked on two decades of systematically undermining it.

Lenin's Russia, which was also not invited, attacked the entire enterprise on the ground that it was a capitalist orgy organized by countries whose ultimate goal was to intervene in the civil war in Russia. Thus it happened that the peace concluding the war to end all wars did not include the two strongest nations of Europe—Germany and Russia—which, between them, contained well over half of Europe's population and by far the largest military potential. That fact alone would have doomed the Versailles settlement.

Nor did its procedures encourage a comprehensive approach. The Big Four—Wilson, Clemenceau, Lloyd George, and Orlando—were the dominant figures, but they could not control the proceedings in the same way that the ministers of the Great Powers had dominated the Congress of Vienna a hundred years earlier. The negotiators at Vienna had concentrated above all on establishing a new balance of power, for which the Pitt Plan had served as a general blueprint. The leaders at Paris were constantly being diverted by an unending series of sideshows.

Twenty-seven states were invited. Envisioned as a forum for all the peoples of the world, the Conference, in the end, turned into a free-for-all. The Supreme Council—composed of the heads of government of Great Britain, France, Italy, and the United States—was the highest-ranking of the innumerable commissions and sections making up the Conference. In addition, there was the Council of Five, composed of the Supreme Council plus the head of government of Japan; and a Council of Ten, which was the Council of Five and their foreign ministers. Delegates from the smaller countries were free to address the more elite groups about their various concerns. It underlined the democratic nature of the Conference, but was also very time-consuming.

Since no agenda had been agreed upon prior to the Conference, delegates arrived not knowing in what particular order the issues would be addressed. Thus, the Paris Conference ended up having fifty-eight different committees. Most of them dealt with territorial questions. A separate committee for each country was established. Additionally, there were committees dealing with war guilt and war criminals, with reparations, ports, waterways and railways, with labor, and, finally, with the League of Nations. All together, the Conference's committee members sat through 1,646 meetings.

Endless discussions about peripheral subjects obscured the central fact that, for the peace to be stable, the settlement had to have some overarching concept—especially a long-term view about the future role of Germany. In theory, the American principles of collective security and self-determination were to play that role. In practice, the real issue at the Conference, and one which would prove irresolvable, was the differences between the American concept of international order and that of the Europeans, particularly the French. Wilson rejected the idea that international conflicts had structural causes. Deeming harmony to be natural, Wilson strove for institutions which would sweep away the illusion of clashing interests and permit the underlying sense of world community to assert itself.

France, the theater of many a European war and itself a participant in many more, was not to be persuaded that clashing national interests were illusory, or that there existed some nebulous, underlying harmony heretofore hidden from mankind. Two German occupations in the course of fifty years had made France obsessively fearful of another round of conquest. It would aspire to tangible guarantees of its security and leave the moral improvement of mankind to others. But tangible guarantees implied either a weakening of Germany or an assurance that, in the event of another war, other countries, especially the United States and Great Britain, would be on the side of France.

Since dismembering Germany was opposed by America, and collective security was too nebulous for France, the only remaining solution to France's problem was an American and British pledge to defend it. And that, precisely, was what both Anglo-Saxon countries were extremely reluctant to give. With no such assurance forthcoming, France was reduced to pleading for expedients. Geography protected America, and the surrender of the German fleet had dispersed British concerns about control of the seas. France alone among the victors was being asked to rest its security on world opinion. André Tardieu, a principal French negotiator, argued that:

> For France, as for Great Britain and the United States, it is necessary to create a zone of safety. . . . This zone the naval Powers create by their fleets, and by the elimination of the German fleet. This zone France, unprotected by the ocean, unable to eliminate the millions of Germans trained to war, must create by the Rhine, by an inter-allied occupation of that river.[14]

Yet France's demand to separate the Rhineland from Germany ran up against the American conviction that "such a peace would then be made as would be contrary to everything we have stood for."[15] The American delegation argued that separating the Rhineland from Germany and stationing Allied troops there would engender a permanent German grievance. Philip Kerr, a British delegate, told Tardieu that Great Britain considered an independent Rhenish state "a source of complication and of weakness. . . . If local conflicts occur, whither will they lead? If war results from these conflicts, neither England nor her Dominions will have that deep feeling of solidarity with France which animated them in the last war."[16]

French leaders were far less worried about later German grievances than about Germany's ultimate power. Tardieu held his ground:

> You say that England does not like English troops to be used away from home. It is a question of fact. England has always had troops in India

233

and Egypt. Why? Because she knows that her frontier is not at Dover.
. . . *To ask us to give up occupation, is like asking England and the
United States to sink their fleet of battleships.*[17]

If France was denied a buffer, it would need some other assurance,
preferably an alliance with Great Britain and the United States. If need
be, France was prepared to accept an interpretation of the concept of
collective security to achieve the same result as a traditional alliance.

Wilson was so eager to establish the League of Nations that he occasionally put forward theories encouraging French hopes. On several occasions, Wilson described the League as an international tribunal to
adjudicate disputes, alter boundaries, and infuse international relations
with much-needed elasticity. One of Wilson's advisers, Dr. Isaiah Bowman, summed up Wilson's ideas in a memorandum drafted aboard the
ship transporting them to the Peace Conference in December 1918. The
League would provide for:

> . . . *territorial integrity plus later alteration of terms and alteration of
> boundaries if it could be shown that injustice had been done or that
> conditions had changed.* And such alteration would be the easier to
> make in time as *passion subsided* and matters could be viewed in the
> light of justice rather than in the light of a peace conference at the close
> of a protracted war. . . . [The] opposite of such a course was to maintain
> the idea of the *Great Powers and of balance of power,* and such an idea
> *had always produced* only *"aggression and selfishness and war."*[18]

After the plenary session of February 14, 1919, at which Wilson unveiled
the League Covenant, he spoke in nearly identical terms to his wife: "This
is our first real step forward, for I now realize, more than ever before,
that once established, the League can arbitrate and correct mistakes which
are inevitable in the treaty we are trying to make at this time."[19]

As Wilson envisaged it, the League of Nations would have the dual
mandate of enforcing the peace and rectifying its inequities. Nevertheless,
Wilson was gripped by a profound ambivalence. It would have been
impossible to find a single historical example of European borders being
changed by appeals to justice or purely legal processes; in almost every
instance, they had been altered—or defended—in the name of the national interest. Yet Wilson was well aware that the American people were
not even remotely ready for a military commitment in defense of the
provisions of the Treaty of Versailles. In essence, Wilson's ideas translated
into institutions tantamount to world government, which the American
people were even less prepared to accept than a global police force.

Wilson sought to sidestep this problem by invoking world public opinion rather than world government or military force as the ultimate sanction against aggression. This is how he described it to the Peace Conference in February 1919:

> ... throughout this instrument [the League of Nations] we are depending primarily and chiefly upon one great force, and that is the moral force of the public opinion of the world. ...[20]

And what public opinion could not resolve, economic pressure would surely accomplish. According to the Bowman Memorandum:

> In cases involving discipline there was the alternative to war, namely, the boycott; trade, including postal and cable facilities, could be denied a state that had been guilty of wrongdoing.[21]

No European state had ever seen such mechanisms at work or could bring itself to believe in their feasibility. In any case, it was too much to expect from France, which had expended so much blood and treasure in order just barely to survive, only to find itself faced with a vacuum in Eastern Europe and a Germany whose actual strength was much greater than its own.

For France, therefore, the League of Nations had only one purpose, and that was to activate military assistance against Germany should that be needed. An ancient and by this time depleted country, France could not bring itself to trust in the basic premise of collective security, that all nations would assess threats in the same way or that, if they did, they would reach identical conclusions about how to resist. If collective security failed, America—and perhaps Great Britain—could always defend themselves, as a last resort, on their own. But for France, there was no last resort; its judgment had to prove right the first time. If the basic assumption of collective security turned out to be wrong, France, unlike America, could not fight another traditional war; it would cease to exist. France was therefore not seeking a general assurance, but a guarantee applicable to its specific circumstances. This the American delegation resolutely refused to give.

Though Wilson's reluctance to commit America to more than a declaration of principles was understandable in light of his domestic pressures, it magnified France's forebodings. The United States had never hesitated to use force to back up the Monroe Doctrine, which Wilson constantly invoked as a model for his new international order. Yet America turned coy when the issue of German threats to the European balance of power arose. Did this not signify that the European equilibrium was a lesser security interest for the United States than conditions in the Western Hemisphere? To remove this distinction, the French representative on the relevant committee, Léon Bourgeois, kept pressing for an international army or any other mechanism that would endow the League of Nations with automatic enforcement machinery in case Germany abrogated the Versailles settlement—the only cause of war that interested France.

For a fleeting moment, Wilson seemed to endorse the concept by referring to the proposed Covenant as a guarantee of the "land titles of the world."[22] But Wilson's entourage was horrified. Its members knew that the Senate would never ratify a standing international army or a permanent military commitment. One of Wilson's advisers even argued that a provision stipulating the use of force to resist aggression would be unconstitutional:

A substantial objection to such a provision is that it would be void if contained in a treaty of the United States, as Congress under the Constitution had the power to declare war. A war automatically arising upon a condition subsequent, pursuant to a treaty provision, is not a war declared by Congress.[23]

Taken literally, this meant that no alliance with the United States could ever have binding force.

Wilson quickly tacked back to the undiluted doctrine of collective security. In rejecting the French proposal, he described standby enforcement machinery as unnecessary because the League itself would serve to inspire overwhelming confidence around the world. He maintained that "the only method . . . lies in our having confidence in the good faith of the nations who belong to the League. . . . When danger comes, we too will come, but you must trust us."[24]

Trust is not a commodity in abundant supply among diplomats. When the survival of nations is at stake, statesmen look for more tangible guarantees—especially if a country is as precariously situated as France. The persuasiveness of the American argument resided in the absence of an alternative; however ambiguous the League obligations, they were still better than nothing. Lord Cecil, one of the British delegates, was saying just that when he scolded Léon Bourgeois for his threats not to join the League unless the Covenant was endowed with enforcement machinery. "America," Cecil told Bourgeois, "had nothing to gain from the League of Nations; . . . she could let European affairs go and take care of her own; the offer that was made by America for support was practically a present to France. . . ."[25]

Though beset by many doubts and premonitions, France finally yielded to the painful logic of the Briton's argument, and acceded to the tautology contained in Article 10 of the League of Nations Charter: "The Council shall advise upon the means by which this obligation [i.e., the preservation of territorial integrity] shall be fulfilled."[26] That is, in case of an emergency, the League of Nations would agree to that on which it could agree. This was, of course, what the nations of the world would have typically done even if there had been no Covenant; and this was precisely the circumstance which traditional alliances sought to remedy by invoking the formal obligation of mutual assistance for specifically defined circumstances.

A French memorandum bluntly stressed the inadequacy of the proposed League security arrangements:

> Suppose that instead of a defensive military understanding—very limited indeed—which was given effect between Great Britain and France in 1914, there had been no other bond between the two countries than the general agreements contained in the Covenant of the League, the British intervention would have been less prompt and Germany's victory thereby assured. So we believe that, under present conditions, the aid provided for by the Covenant of the League would arrive too late.[27]

Once it had become clear that America was refusing to incorporate any concrete security provisions into the Covenant, France resumed its pressure for dismembering Germany. It proposed the establishment of an independent Rhenish republic as a demilitarized buffer zone, and sought to create an incentive for such a state by exempting it from reparations. When the United States and Great Britain balked, France suggested that, at a minimum, the Rhineland be separated from Germany until the League's institutions had had a chance to develop and its enforcement machinery could be tested.

In an effort to placate France, Wilson and the British leaders offered as a substitute for the dismemberment of Germany a treaty guaranteeing the new settlement. America and Great Britain would agree to go to war if Germany violated the settlement. It was very similar to the agreement that the allies at the Congress of Vienna had created to reinsure themselves against France. But there was one important difference: after the Napoleonic Wars, the allies had genuinely believed in a French threat and sought to provide security against it; after World War I, Great Britain and the United States did not really believe in a German threat; they offered their guarantee without being either convinced that it was necessary or particularly determined to implement it.

The principal French negotiator was jubilant, describing the British guarantee as "unprecedented." Great Britain had occasionally entered into temporary agreements, he maintained, but had never previously submitted to a permanent obligation: "She has at times lent her aid; she has never bound herself in advance to give it."[28] Tardieu considered America's proposed commitment an equally momentous departure from its historic pattern of isolationism.[29]

In their eagerness for formal guarantees, French leaders overlooked the crucial fact that the "unprecedented" Anglo-Saxon decisions were primarily a tactic to induce France to abandon its demand that Germany be dismembered. In foreign policy, the term "unprecedented" is always somewhat suspect, because the actual range of innovation is so circumscribed by history, domestic institutions, and geography.

Had Tardieu been privy to the American delegation's reaction, he would have understood how tenuous the guarantee really was. Wilson's advisers were unanimous in opposing their chief. Had not the new diplomacy been explicitly created to do away with this type of national commitment? Had America fought the war only to end up in a traditional alliance? House wrote in his diary:

> I thought I ought to call the President's attention to the perils of such a treaty. Among other things, it would be looked upon as a direct blow at the League of Nations. The League is supposed to do just what this treaty proposed, and if it were necessary for the nations to make such treaties, then why the League of Nations?[30]

It was a fair question. For, if the League performed as advertised, the guarantee was unnecessary; and if the guarantee was necessary, the League was not living up to its design and all postwar concepts would be in doubt. The isolationists in the United States Senate had misgivings of their own. They were not so much worried that the guarantee conflicted with the League as that the devious Europeans were luring America into the web of their corrupt ancient entanglements. The guarantee did not last long. The Senate's refusal to ratify the Treaty of Versailles rendered it moot; and Great Britain jumped at the pretext to release itself from its commitment as well. France's abandonment of its claims turned out to be permanent, and the guarantee ephemeral.

Out of all these crosscurrents finally emerged the Treaty of Versailles, named after the Hall of Mirrors of Versailles Palace in which it was signed. The location seemed to invite unnecessary humiliation. Fifty years earlier, Bismarck had tactlessly proclaimed the unified Germany there; now, the victors inflicted an insult of their own. Nor was their handiwork likely to calm the international environment. Too punitive for conciliation, too lenient to keep Germany from recovering, the treaty of Versailles condemned the exhausted democracies to constant vigilance and to the need for permanent enforcement against an irreconcilable and revisionist Germany.

The Fourteen Points notwithstanding, the Treaty was punitive in territorial, economic, and military areas. Germany had to surrender 13 percent of its prewar territory. Economically important Upper Silesia was handed over to a newly created Poland, which also received an outlet to the Baltic Sea and the area around Posen, thereby creating the "Polish Corridor" separating East Prussia from the rest of Germany. The tiny territory of Eupen-et-Malmédy was given to Belgium, and Alsace-Lorraine was returned to France.

Germany lost its colonies, the legal status of which occasioned a dispute between Wilson on the one side and France, Great Britain, and Japan on the other, all three of which wanted to annex their share of the spoils. Wilson insisted that such a direct transfer would violate the principle of self-determination. The Allies finally arrived at the so-called Mandate Principle, which was as ingenious as it was hypocritical. German colonies as well as former Ottoman territories in the Middle East were assigned to the various victors with a "mandate" under League supervision, to facilitate their independence. What that meant was never specifically defined, nor in the end did the mandates lead to independence any more rapidly than in other colonial areas.

The Treaty's military restrictions reduced the German army to 100,000 volunteers and its navy to six cruisers and a few smaller vessels. Germany was forbidden to possess offensive weapons such as submarines, aircraft, tanks, or heavy artillery, and its general staff was dissolved. To supervise German disarmament, an Allied Military Control Commission was created and given, as it turned out, extremely vague and ineffective authority.

Despite Lloyd George's electioneering promise to "squeeze" Germany, the Allies began to realize that an economically prostrate Germany might produce a world economic crisis affecting their own societies. But the victorious populations showed little interest in the warnings of theoretical economists. The British and the French demanded that Germany indemnify their civilian populations for all damages. Against his better judgment,

Wilson finally agreed to a provision that made Germany pay for the pensions of war victims and some compensation for their families. Such a provision was unheard of; no previous European peace treaty had ever contained such a clause. No figure was set for these claims; it was to be determined at some later date, generating a source of endless controversy.

Other economic penalties included immediate payment of $5 billion in cash or in kind. France was to receive large quantities of coal as compensation for Germany's destruction of its mines during the occupation of eastern France. To make up for ships sunk by German submarines, Great Britain was awarded much of the German merchant fleet. Germany's foreign assets, totaling about $7 billion, were seized, along with many German patents (thanks to the Versailles Treaty, Bayer Aspirin is an American, not a German product). Germany's major rivers were internationalized, and its ability to raise tariffs was restricted.

These terms mortgaged the new international order instead of helping to create it. When the victors assembled in Paris, they proclaimed a new era in history. So eager were they to avoid what they considered the mistakes of the Congress of Vienna that the British delegation commissioned the renowned historian Sir Charles Webster to write a treatise on the subject.[31] Yet what they finally produced was a fragile compromise between American utopianism and European paranoia—too conditional to fulfill the dreams of the former, too tentative to alleviate the fears of the latter. An international order that can be preserved only by force is precarious, all the more so when the countries which must bear the principal burden for enforcement—in this case Great Britain and France —were at odds.

It soon became apparent that, as a practical matter, the principle of self-determination could not be applied in the clear-cut sort of way envisaged by the Fourteen Points, especially among the successor states of the Austro-Hungarian Empire. Czechoslovakia ended up with 3 million Germans, 1 million Hungarians, and half a million Poles out of a population of some 15 million; nearly a third of the total population was neither Czech nor Slovak. And Slovakia was not an enthusiastic part of a Czech-dominated state, as it would demonstrate by seceding in 1939 and again in 1992.

The new Yugoslavia fulfilled the aspirations of South Slavic intellectuals. But to create that state, it was necessary to cross the fault line of European history, which divided the Western and the Eastern Roman empires, the Catholic and the Orthodox religions, the Latin and the Cyrillic scripts—a fault line running roughly between Croatia and Serbia, which had never in their complex histories belonged to the same political unit. The bill for this came due after 1941, in a murderous civil war which started all over again in 1991.

Romania acquired millions of Hungarians, Poland millions of Germans and the guardianship of a corridor separating East Prussia from the rest of Germany. At the end of this process, which was conducted in the name of self-determination, nearly as many people lived under foreign rule as during the days of the Austro-Hungarian Empire, except that now they were distributed across many more, much weaker, nation-states which, to undermine stability even further, were in conflict with each other.

When it was too late, Lloyd George understood the dilemma into which the victorious Allies had maneuvered themselves. In a memorandum to Wilson dated March 25, 1919, he wrote:

> I can not conceive any greater cause of future war than that the German people, who have certainly proved themselves one of the most vigorous and powerful races in the world should be surrounded by a number of small states, many of them consisting of people who have never previously set up a stable government for themselves, but each of them containing large masses of Germans clamouring for reunion with their native land.[32]

But by then, the conference had already progressed too far toward its closing date in June. Nor was any alternative principle for organizing the world order available, now that the balance of power had been discarded.

Later on, many German leaders were to claim that their country had been tricked into the Armistice by Wilson's Fourteen Points, which were then systematically violated. Such propositions were so much self-pitying nonsense. Germany had ignored the Fourteen Points as long as it thought that it had a chance of winning the war, and had, soon after the proclamation of the Fourteen Points, imposed a Carthaginian peace on Russia at Brest-Litovsk, violating every one of Wilson's principles. The only reason Germany finally ended the war had to do with pure power calculations —with the American army involved, its final defeat was only a question of time. When it asked for an armistice, Germany was exhausted, its defenses were breaking, and Allied armies were about to drive into German territory. Wilson's principles in fact spared Germany much more severe retribution.

With better reason, historians have argued that it was the refusal of the United States to join the League that doomed the Treaty of Versailles. America's failure to ratify the Treaty or the guarantee of French borders connected with it certainly contributed to France's demoralization. But, given the isolationist mood of the country, American membership in the League or ratification of the guarantee would not have made a significant difference. Either way, the United States would not have used force to resist aggression, or else it would have defined aggression in terms which did not apply to Eastern Europe—much as Great Britain was to do in the 1930s.

The debacle of the Treaty of Versailles was structural. The century of peace produced by the Congress of Vienna had been buttressed by three pillars, each of which was indispensable: a peace of conciliation with France; a balance of power; and a shared sense of legitimacy. The relatively conciliatory peace with France would not in itself have prevented French revisionism. But France knew that the Quadruple and Holy Alliances could always assemble superior power, making French expansionism far too risky. At the same time, periodic European congresses gave France an opportunity to participate in the Concert of Europe as an equal. Above all, the major countries had shared common values so that existing grievances did not coalesce into an attempt to overthrow the international order.

The Treaty of Versailles fulfilled none of these conditions. Its terms were too onerous for conciliation but not severe enough for permanent subjugation. In truth, it was not easy to strike a balance between satisfying and subjugating Germany. Having considered the prewar world order too confining, Germany was not likely to be satisfied with *any* terms available after defeat.

France had three strategic choices: it could try to form an anti-German coalition; it could seek to partition Germany; or it could try to conciliate Germany. All attempts to form alliances failed because Great Britain and America refused, and Russia was no longer part of the equilibrium. Partitioning Germany was resisted by the same countries which rejected an alliance but on whose support in an emergency France nevertheless had to rely. And it was both too late and too early for the conciliation of Germany—too late because conciliation was incompatible with the Treaty of Versailles, too early because French public opinion was not yet ready for it.

Paradoxically, France's vulnerability and Germany's strategic advantage were both magnified by the Treaty of Versailles despite its punitive provisions. Before the war, Germany had faced strong neighbors in both the East and the West. It could not expand in either direction without encountering a major state—France, the Austro-Hungarian Empire, or Russia. But after the Treaty of Versailles, there was no longer a counterweight to

Germany in the East. With France weakened, the Austro-Hungarian Empire dissolved, and Russia out of the picture for some time, there was simply no way of reconstructing the old balance of power, especially since the Anglo-Saxon powers refused to guarantee the Versailles settlement.

As early as 1916, Lord Balfour, then British Foreign Secretary, foresaw at least a part of the danger that lay ahead for Europe when he warned that an independent Poland might leave France defenseless in another war: if "Poland was made an independent kingdom, becoming a buffer state between Russia and Germany, France would be at the mercy of Germany in the next war, for this reason, that Russia could not come to her aid without violating the neutrality of Poland"[33]—exactly the dilemma in 1939. To contain Germany, France needed an ally in the East that could force Germany to fight a two-front war. Russia was the only country strong enough to fulfill that role. But with Poland separating Germany and Russia, Russia could only pressure Germany by violating Poland. And Poland was too weak to play Russia's role. What the Treaty of Versailles did was to give an incentive to Germany and Russia to partition Poland, precisely what they did twenty years later.

Lacking a Great Power in the East with which to ally itself, France sought to strengthen the new states to create the illusion of a two-front challenge to Germany. It backed the new East European states in their effort to extract more territory from Germany or from what was left of Hungary. Obviously, the new states had an incentive to encourage the French delusion that they might come to serve as a counterweight to Germany. Yet these infant states could not possibly assume the role that, up to this time, Austria and Russia had played. They were too weak and racked by internal conflicts and mutual rivalries. And to their east loomed a reconstituted Russia, seething over its own territorial losses. Once it recovered its strength, Russia would prove as great a threat to the independence of the small states as Germany.

Thus the stability of the Continent came to rest on France. It had taken the combined forces of America, Great Britain, France, and Russia to subdue Germany. Of these countries, America was again isolationist, and Russia was severed from Europe by a revolutionary drama and by the so-called *cordon sanitaire* of small Eastern European states standing in the way of direct Russian assistance to France. To preserve the peace, France would have had to play policeman all over Europe. Not only had it lost the stomach and the strength for so interventionist a policy but, had it attempted one, it would have found itself alone, abandoned by both America and Great Britain.

The most dangerous weakness of the Versailles settlement, however, was psychological. The world order created by the Congress of Vienna had been cemented by the principle of conservative unity that had meshed with the requirements of the balance of power; in effect, the powers that were most needed to maintain the settlement also considered it just. The Versailles settlement was stillborn because the values it extolled clashed with the incentives needed to enforce it: the majority of the states required to defend the agreement considered it unjust in one way or another.

The paradox of the First World War was that it had been fought to curb German power and looming predominance, and that it had aroused public opinion to a pitch which prevented the establishment of a conciliatory peace. Yet, in the end, Wilsonian principles inhibited a peace which curbed Germany's power and there was no shared sense of justice. The price for conducting foreign policy on the basis of abstract principles is the impossibility of distinguishing among individual cases. Since the leaders at Versailles were not willing to reduce German power by either the implicit rights of victory or the calculations of the balance of power, they were obliged to justify German disarmament as the first installment of a general plan of disarmament, and reparations as an expiation of guilt for the war itself.

In justifying German disarmament in this way, the Allies undermined the psychological readiness that was required to sustain their agreement. From the first, Germany could, and did, claim that it was being discriminated against, and demanded that it either be permitted to rearm or that other nations disarm to its level. In the process, the disarmament provisions of the Treaty of Versailles ended up demoralizing the victors. At every disarmament conference, Germany would seize the moral high ground, in which it was usually supported by Great Britain. But if France did grant Germany equality in rearmament, the possibility of safeguarding the independence of the nations of Eastern Europe would vanish. The disarmament clauses were therefore bound to lead to either the disarmament of France or the rearmament of Germany. In neither case would France be strong enough to defend Eastern Europe or, in the long run, even itself.

Similarly, the prohibition against the union of Austria and Germany violated the principle of self-determination, as did the presence of a large German minority in Czechoslovakia and, to a lesser extent, of a German minority in Poland. German irredentism was thus supported by the organizing principle of the Treaty of Versailles, compounding the guilty conscience of the democracies.

The gravest psychological blight on the Treaty was Article 231, the so-called War Guilt clause. It stated that Germany was solely responsible for the outbreak of World War I, and delivered a severe moral censure. Most of the punitive measures against Germany in the Treaty—economic, military, and political—were based on the assertion that the whole conflagration had been entirely Germany's fault.

Eighteenth-century peacemakers would have regarded "war guilt clauses" as absurd. For them, wars were amoral inevitabilities caused by clashing interests. In the treaties that concluded eighteenth-century wars, the losers paid a price without its being justified on moral grounds. But for Wilson and the peacemakers at Versailles, the cause of the war of 1914–18 had to be ascribed to some evil which had to be punished.

When the hatreds had diminished, however, astute observers began to see that responsibility for the outbreak of the war was far more complicated. To be sure, Germany bore a heavy responsibility, but was it fair to single out Germany for punitive measures? Was Article 231 really proper? Once this question began being asked, especially in Great Britain in the 1920s, the will to enforce the punitive measures against Germany contained in the Treaty began to waver. The peacemakers, assailed by their own consciences, wondered if what they had wrought was fair, and this fostered a lack of resolve in maintaining the Treaty. Germany, of course, was irresponsible on this issue. In German public discourse, Article 231 became known as the "War Guilt Lie." The physical difficulty of establishing a balance of power was matched by the psychological difficulty of creating a moral equilibrium.

Thus, the framers of the Versailles settlement achieved the precise opposite of what they had set out to do. They had tried to weaken Germany physically but instead strengthened it geopolitically. From a long-term point of view, Germany was in a far better position to dominate Europe after Versailles than it had been before the war. As soon as Germany threw off the shackles of disarmament, which was just a matter of time, it was bound to emerge more powerful than ever. Harold Nicolson summed it up: "We came to Paris confident that the new order was about to be established; we left it convinced that the new order had merely fouled the old."[34]

CHAPTER TEN

The Dilemmas
of the Victors

The policing of the Versailles agreement was based on two general concepts which canceled each other out. The first failed because it was too sweeping, the second, because it was too grudging. The concept of collective security was so general as to prove inapplicable to circumstances most likely to disturb the peace; the informal Franco-English cooperation which replaced it was far too tenuous and ambivalent to resist major German challenges. And before five years had elapsed, the two powers vanquished in the war came together at Rapallo. The growing cooperation between Germany and the Soviet Union was a crucial blow to the Versailles system, something the democracies were too demoralized to grasp immediately.

At the end of the First World War, the age-old debate about the relative roles of morality and interest in international affairs seemed to have been resolved in favor of the dominance of law and ethics. Under the shock of the cataclysm, many hoped for a better world as free as possible from the kind of *Realpolitik* which, in their view, had decimated the youth of a generation. America emerged as the catalyst of this process even as it was withdrawing into isolationism. Wilson's legacy was that Europe embarked on the Wilsonian course of trying to preserve stability via collective security rather than the traditional European approach of alliances and the balance of power, despite the absence of America.

In subsequent American usage, alliances in which America participated (such as NATO) were generally described as instruments of collective security. This is not, however, how the term was originally conceived, for in their essence, the concepts of collective security and of alliances are diametrically opposed. Traditional alliances were directed against specific threats and defined precise obligations for specific groups of countries linked by shared national interests or mutual security concerns. Collective security defines no particular threat, guarantees no individual nation, and discriminates against none. It is theoretically designed to resist *any* threat to the peace, by whoever might pose it and against whomever it might be directed. Alliances always presume a specific potential adversary; collective security defends international law in the abstract, which it seeks to sustain in much the same way that a judicial system upholds a domestic criminal code. It no more assumes a particular culprit than does domestic law. In an alliance, the *casus belli* is an attack on the interests or the security of its members. The *casus belli* of collective security is the violation of the principle of "peaceful" settlement of disputes in which all peoples of the world are assumed to have a common interest. Therefore, force has to be assembled on a case-by-case basis from a shifting group of nations with a mutual interest in "peacekeeping."

The purpose of an alliance is to produce an obligation more predictable and precise than an analysis of national interest. Collective security works in the exact opposite way. It leaves the application of its principles to the interpretation of particular circumstances when they arise, unintentionally putting a large premium on the mood of the moment and, hence, on national self-will.

Collective security contributes to security only if all nations—or at least all nations relevant to collective defense—share nearly identical views about the nature of the challenge and are prepared to use force or apply sanctions on the "merits" of the case, regardless of the specific national interest they may have in the issues at hand. Only if these conditions are fulfilled can a world organization devise sanctions or act as an arbiter of international affairs. This was how Wilson had perceived the role of collective security as the end of the war approached in September 1918:

> National purposes have fallen more and more into the background and the common purpose of enlightened mankind has taken their place. The counsels of plain men have become on all hands more simple and straightforward and more unified than the counsels of sophisticated men of affairs, who still retain the impression that they are playing a game of power and playing for high stakes.[1]

The fundamental difference between the Wilsonian and the European interpretations of the causes of international conflict is reflected in these words. European-style diplomacy presumes that national interests have a tendency to clash, and views diplomacy as the means for reconciling them; Wilson, on the other hand, considered international discord the result of "clouded thinking," not an expression of a genuine clash of interests. In the practice of *Realpolitik,* statesmen shoulder the task of relating particular interests to general ones through a balance of incentives and penalties. In the Wilsonian view, statesmen are required to apply universal principles to specific cases. Moreover, statesmen are generally treated as the causes of conflict, because they are believed to distort man's natural bent toward harmony with abstruse and selfish calculations.

The conduct of most statesmen at Versailles belied Wilsonian expectations. Without exception, they stressed their national interests, leaving the defense of the common purposes to Wilson, whose country in fact had no national interest (in the European sense) in the territorial issues of the settlement. It is in the nature of prophets to redouble their efforts, not to abandon them, in the face of a recalcitrant reality. The obstacles Wilson encountered at Versailles raised no doubt in his mind about the feasibility of his new dispensation. On the contrary, they fortified his faith in its necessity. And he was confident that the League and the weight of world opinion would correct the many provisions of the Treaty that departed from his principles.

Indeed, the power of Wilson's ideals was demonstrated by their impact on Great Britain, the motherland of the balance-of-power policy. The official British commentary on the League Covenant declared that "the ultimate and most effective sanction must be the public opinion of the civilised world."[2] Or, as Lord Cecil argued before the House of Commons, "what we rely upon is public opinion . . . and if we are wrong about it, then the whole thing is wrong."[3]

It seems improbable that the scions of the policy of Pitt, Canning, Palmerston, and Disraeli would have come to such conclusions on their own. At first they went along with Wilson's policy in order to ensure American support in the war. As time went on, Wilsonian principles succeeded in capturing British public opinion. By the 1920s and 1930s, Great Britain's defense of collective security was no longer tactical. Wilsonianism had made a genuine convert.

In the end, collective security fell prey to the weakness of its central premise—that all nations have the same interest in resisting a particular act of aggression and are prepared to run identical risks in opposing it. Experience has shown these assumptions to be false. No act of aggression involving a major power has ever been defeated by applying the principle of collective security. Either the world community has refused to assess the act as one which constituted aggression, or it has disagreed over the appropriate sanctions. And when sanctions were applied, they inevitably reflected the lowest common denominator, often proving so ineffectual that they did more harm than good.

At the time of the Japanese conquest of Manchuria in 1932, the League had no machinery for sanctions. It remedied this defect, but faced with Italian aggression against Abyssinia, it voted for sanctions while stopping short of imposing a cutoff of oil with the slogan "All sanctions short of war." When Austria was forcibly united with Germany and Czechoslovakia's freedom was extinguished, there was no League reaction at all. The last act of the League of Nations, which no longer contained Germany, Japan, or Italy, was to expel the Soviet Union after it attacked Finland in 1939. It had no effect on Soviet actions.

During the Cold War, the United Nations proved equally ineffective in every case involving Great Power aggression, due to either the communist veto in the Security Council or the reluctance on the part of smaller countries to run risks on behalf of issues they felt did not concern them. The United Nations was ineffective or at the sidelines during the Berlin crises and during the Soviet interventions in Hungary, Czechoslovakia, and Afghanistan. It was irrelevant in the Cuban Missile Crisis until the two superpowers agreed to settle. America was able to invoke the authority of the United Nations against North Korean aggression in 1950 only because the Soviet representative was boycotting the Security Council and the General Assembly was still dominated by countries eager to enlist America against the threat of Soviet aggression in Europe. The United Nations did provide a convenient meeting place for diplomats and a useful forum for the exchange of ideas. It also performed important technical functions. But it failed to fulfill the underlying premise of collective security—the prevention of war and collective resistance to aggression.

This has been true of the United Nations even in the post–Cold War period. In the Gulf War of 1991, it did indeed ratify American actions, but resistance to Iraqi aggression was hardly an application of the doctrine of collective security. Not waiting for an international consensus, the United States had unilaterally dispatched a large expeditionary force. Other nations could gain influence over America's actions only by joining what was in effect an American enterprise; they could not avoid the risks of conflict by vetoing it. Additionally, domestic upheavals in the Soviet Union and China gave the permanent members of the UN Security Council an incentive to maintain America's goodwill. In the Gulf War, collective security was invoked as a justification of American leadership, not as a substitute for it.

Of course, these lessons had not yet been learned in the innocent days when the concept of collective security was first being introduced into diplomacy. The post-Versailles statesmen had half-convinced themselves that armaments were the cause of tensions, not the result of them, and half-believed that if goodwill replaced the suspiciousness of traditional diplomacy, international conflict might be eradicated. Despite having been emotionally drained by the war, the European leaders should have realized that a general doctrine of collective security could never work, even if it overcame all the other hurdles it faced, as long as it excluded three of the most powerful nations of the world: the United States, Germany, and the Soviet Union. For the United States had refused to join the League, Germany was barred from it, and the Soviet Union, which was treated as a pariah, disdained it.

The country suffering most grievously under the postwar order was "victorious" France. French leaders knew that the provisions of the Treaty of Versailles would not keep Germany permanently weak. After the last European war—the Crimean War of 1854–56—the victors, Great Britain and France, had managed to maintain the military provisions for less than twenty years. In the wake of the Napoleonic Wars, France became a full-fledged member of the European Concert after only three years. After Versailles, France's decline vis-à-vis Germany grew progressively more evident, even as it seemed to dominate Europe militarily. France's victorious Commander-in-Chief, Marshal Ferdinand Foch, was right when he said about the Treaty of Versailles: "This is not peace; it is an Armistice for twenty years."[4]

By 1924, the staff of the British ground forces had reached the same conclusion when it predicted that Germany would again be going to war with Great Britain over issues that would be "simply a repetition of the conditions which brought us into the late war."[5] The restraints imposed by the Treaty of Versailles, it argued, would delay German rearmament by at most nine months once Germany felt strong enough politically to throw off the shackles of Versailles—which the general staff presciently assessed as being probable within ten years. Concurring with the analysis of the French, the British general staff also predicted that France would be helpless unless, in the meantime, it made a military alliance with "first-class powers."

Yet the only first-class power available was Great Britain, whose political leaders did not accept the views of their military advisers. Instead, their policy was based on the mistaken belief that France was already too powerful and that the last thing it needed was a British alliance. Great Britain's leaders considered demoralized France to be the potentially dominant power and in need of being balanced, while revisionist Germany was perceived as the aggrieved party in need of conciliation. Both assumptions—that France was militarily dominant and that Germany had been harshly treated—were correct in the short term; but as premises of British policy, they were disastrous in the long term. Statesmen stand or fall on their perceptions of trends. And British postwar leaders failed to perceive the long-range dangers before them.

France desperately wanted a military alliance with Great Britain, to replace the guarantee that had lapsed when the United States Senate refused to ratify the Versailles Treaty. Never having made a military alliance with the country they considered to be the strongest in Europe, British leaders now perceived France as rekindling its historic threat to dominate the Continent. In 1924, the Central Department of the British Foreign Office described the French occupation of the Rhineland as a "jumping-off point for an incursion into Central Europe,"[6] a judgment totally at variance with French psychology of the period. Even more inanely, the Foreign Office memorandum treated the occupation of the Rhineland as an encirclement of Belgium, creating "a direct menace to the Scheldt and Zuider Zee, and therefore an indirect menace to this country."[7] Not to be outdone in generating anti-French suspicions, the Admiralty weighed in with an argument straight from the wars of the Spanish Succession or the Napoleonic Wars: that the Rhineland dominated Dutch and Belgian ports whose control would severely impair the British Royal Navy's planning in the event of war with France.[8]

There was no hope whatsoever of maintaining a balance of power in Europe so long as Great Britain considered the primary threat to be a country whose nearly panicky foreign policy was geared to fending off another German assault. Indeed, in a kind of historic reflex, many in Great Britain began to look to Germany to balance France. For example, the British Ambassador in Berlin, Viscount d'Abernon, reported that it was in England's interest to maintain Germany as a counterweight to France. "As long as Germany is a coherent whole, there is more or less a balance of power in Europe," he wrote in 1923. If Germany disintegrated, France would be "in undisputed military and political control, based upon her army and her military alliances."[9] This was true enough but hardly the likely scenario that British diplomacy would confront in the decades ahead.

Great Britain was right to argue, as it always had, that, after victory, the reconstruction of international order required the return of the erstwhile enemy to the community of nations. But appeasing Germany's grievances would not restore stability as long as the balance of power continued to shift inexorably in Germany's direction. France and Great Britain, whose unity was essential to maintaining the last shred of the European balance of power, were glaring at each other in frustration and incomprehension, while the real threats to the equilibrium—Germany and the Soviet Union —stood at the sidelines in sullen resentment. Great Britain vastly exaggerated France's strength; France vastly overestimated its ability to use the Treaty of Versailles to compensate for its growing inferiority vis-à-vis Germany. Great Britain's fear of possible French hegemony on the Continent was absurd; France's belief that it could conduct foreign policy on the basis of keeping Germany prostrate was delusion tinged by despair.

Perhaps the most important reason for Great Britain's rejection of a French alliance was that its leaders did not in their hearts consider the Versailles Treaty just, least of all the settlement of Eastern Europe, and feared that an alliance with France, which had pacts with the Eastern European countries, might draw them into a conflict over the wrong issues and in defense of the wrong countries. Lloyd George expressed the conventional wisdom of that time:

> The British people ... would not be ready to be involved in quarrels which might arise regarding Poland or Danzig of Upper Silesia. ... The British people felt that the populations of that quarter of Europe were unstable and excitable; they might start fighting at any time and the rights and wrongs of the dispute might be very hard to disentangle.[10]

Holding attitudes such as these, British leaders used discussions about the possibility of a French alliance primarily as a tactical device to ease French pressures on Germany, not as a serious contribution to international security.

France thus continued its hopeless quest of keeping Germany weak; Great Britain sought to devise security arrangements to calm French fears without incurring a British commitment. It was a circle never to be squared, for Great Britain could not bring itself to extend to France the one assurance that might have brought about a calmer and more conciliatory French foreign policy toward Germany—a full military alliance.

Realizing in 1922 that the British Parliament would never countenance a formal military commitment, French Prime Minister Briand reverted to the precedent of the Entente Cordiale of 1904—Anglo-French diplomatic cooperation without military provisions. But in 1904, Great Britain had felt threatened by Germany's naval program and by its constant bullying. By the 1920s, it feared Germany less than France, whose conduct it mistakenly attributed to arrogance rather than to panic. Though Great Britain grudgingly acceded to Briand's proposal, its real motive in doing so was reflected in a cynical Cabinet note which defended the French alliance as a means of strengthening Great Britain's relations with Germany:

> Germany is to us the most important country in Europe not only on account of our trade with her, but also because she is the key to the situation in Russia. By helping Germany we might under existing conditions expose ourselves to the charge of deserting France; but if France was our ally no such charge could be made.[11]

Whether it was because French President Alexandre Millerand sensed the British evasion or simply found the arrangement too amorphous, he rejected Briand's scheme, which led to the Prime Minister's resignation.

Frustrated in its attempt to elicit a traditional British alliance, France next attempted to achieve the same result through the League of Nations by elaborating a precise definition of aggression. This would then be turned into a precise obligation within the framework of the League of Nations—thereby transforming the League into a global alliance. In September 1923, at French and British urging, the League Council devised a universal treaty of mutual assistance. In the event of conflict, the Council would be empowered to designate which country was the aggressor and which the victim. Every League member would then be obliged to assist the victim, by force if necessary, on the continent on which that signatory was situated (this clarification was added to avoid incurring a League obligation to help in colonial conflicts). Since obligations of the doctrine of collective security are meant to derive from general causes rather than from national interests, the treaty stipulated that, to be eligible for assistance, the victim must have previously signed a disarmament agreement approved by the League, and have been reducing its armed forces according to an agreed schedule.

Since the victim is usually the weaker side, the League's Treaty of Mutual Assistance was in fact providing incentives for aggression by asking the more vulnerable side to compound its difficulties. There was something absurd about the proposition that the international order would henceforth be defended on behalf of excellent disarmers rather than of vital national interests. Moreover, since reduction schedules of a general disarmament treaty would take years to negotiate, the universal Treaty of Mutual Assistance was creating a vast vacuum. With the League obligation to resist being placed into a distant and nebulous future, France and any other threatened country would have to face their perils alone.

Despite its escape clauses, the Treaty failed to command support. The United States and the Soviet Union refused to consider it. Germany's opinion was never solicited. Once it became clear that the draft treaty would have obliged Great Britain, with colonies on every continent, to assist any victim of aggression anywhere, Labour Prime Minister Ramsay MacDonald also felt obliged to report that Great Britain could not accept the Treaty, even though it had helped to draft it.

By now, France's quest for security had turned obsessive. Far from accepting the futility of its effort, it refused to abandon its search for criteria compatible with collective security, especially since the British government under Ramsay MacDonald so strongly supported collective security and disarmament—the so-called progressive causes represented by the League. Finally, MacDonald and the new French Prime Minister, Edouard Herriot, came up with a variation of the previous proposal. The Geneva Protocol of 1924 required League arbitration for all international conflicts and established three criteria for a universal obligation to assist victims of aggression: the aggressor's refusal to permit the Council to settle the dispute by conciliation; the aggressor's failure to submit the issue to judicial settlement or arbitration; and, of course, the victim's membership in a scheme for general disarmament. Each signatory was obliged to assist the victim by all available means against the aggressor so defined.[12]

The Geneva Protocol, however, failed as well for the same reason as the Treaty of Mutual Assistance and all the other schemes for collective security in the 1920s had failed. It went too far for Great Britain and not nearly far enough for France. Great Britain had proposed it in order to draw France into disarmament, not to generate an additional defense obligation. France had pursued the Protocol primarily as an obligation of mutual assistance—having only a secondary interest, if that, in disarmament. To underscore the futility of this exercise, the United States announced that it would not honor the Geneva Protocol or tolerate any interference with U.S. trade under its provisions. When the chairman of the British Imperial Defense Staff warned that the Protocol would dangerously overextend British forces, the Cabinet withdrew it in early 1925.

It was a preposterous state of affairs. Resisting aggression had been made dependent on the prior disarmament of the victim. Geopolitical considerations and the strategic importance of the region, reasons for which nations had been going to war for centuries, were being deprived of legitimacy. According to this approach, Great Britain would defend Belgium because it had disarmed, not because it was strategically vital. After months of negotiations, the democracies were advancing neither disarmament nor security. The tendency of collective security to transform aggression into an abstract, legal problem and its refusal to consider any specific threat or commitment had a demoralizing rather than a reassuring effect.

Despite the passionate lip service it paid to the concept, Great Britain clearly considered the obligations of collective security less binding than those of traditional alliances. For the Cabinet proved to be quite fertile in inventing various formulae for collective security while it adamantly rejected a formal alliance with France until the very eve of the war, a decade and a half later. Surely it would not have made such a distinction unless it viewed the obligations of collective security as less likely to have to be implemented or easier to evade than those of alliances.

The wisest course for the Allies would have been to relieve Germany voluntarily of the most onerous provisions of Versailles and to forge a firm Franco-British alliance. This is what Winston Churchill had in mind when he advocated an alliance with France "if (and only if) she entirely alters her treatment of Germany and loyally accepts a British policy of help and friendship towards Germany."[13] Such a policy was never pursued with any consistency, however. French leaders were too afraid of both Germany and their own public opinion, which was deeply hostile to Germany, and British leaders were too suspicious of French designs.

The disarmament provisions of the Treaty of Versailles widened the Anglo-French split. Ironically, they eased Germany's road toward military parity, which, given the weakness of Eastern Europe, would spell geopolitical superiority in the long run. For one thing, the Allies had compounded discrimination with incompetence by neglecting to set up any verification machinery for the disarmament provisions. In a letter to Colonel House in 1919, André Tardieu, a principal French negotiator at Versailles, predicted that the failure to set up verification machinery would cripple the disarmament clauses of the Treaty:

> . . . a weak instrument is being drawn up, dangerous and absurd. . . . Will the League say to Germany, 'Prove that my information is false,' or even, 'We wish to verify.' But then it is claiming a right of supervision, and Germany will reply: 'By what right?'
>
> That is what Germany will reply and she will be justified in so replying, if she is not forced by the Treaty to recognize the right of verification.[14]

In the innocent days before the study of arms control had become an academic subject, no one thought it odd to be asking Germany to verify its own disarmament. To be sure, an Inter-Allied Military Control Commission had been set up. But it had no independent right of inspection; it could only ask the German government for information about German violations—not exactly a foolproof procedure. The Commission was disbanded in 1926, leaving the verification of German compliance to Allied intelligence services. No wonder the disarmament provisions were being grossly violated long before Hitler refused to carry them out.

On the political level, German leaders skillfully insisted on the general disarmament promised in the Versailles Treaty, of which their own disarmament was to have been the first stage. With the passage of time, they managed to obtain British support for this proposition, and used it as well to justify the failure to fulfill other provisions of the Treaty. To put pressure on France, Great Britain announced dramatic reductions of its own ground forces (on which it had never relied for security), though not of its navy (on which, of course, it did). France's security, on the other hand, depended totally on its standing army's being significantly larger than Germany's because the industrial potential of Germany and its population were so superior. The pressure to alter this balance—through either German rearmament or French disarmament—had the practical consequence of reversing the results of the war. By the time Hitler came to power, it was already quite apparent that the disarmament provisions of the Treaty would soon be in tatters, making Germany's geopolitical advantage apparent.

Reparations were another element of the disunity between France and Great Britain. Until the Versailles Treaty, it had been axiomatic that the vanquished paid reparations. After the Franco-Prussian War of 1870, Germany did not feel compelled to invoke any principle other than its victory for the indemnity it imposed on France; nor did it do so in 1918 with respect to the staggering reparations bill it presented to Russia in the Treaty of Brest-Litovsk.

Yet, in the new world order of Versailles, the Allies had come to believe that reparations required a moral justification. They found it in Article 231, or the War Guilt Clause, described in the previous chapter. The clause was furiously attacked in Germany, and eliminated the already low incentive there to cooperate with the peace settlement.

One of the astonishing aspects of the Versailles Treaty was that its drafters included so invidious and precise a clause on war guilt without specifying the total amount to be paid in reparations. The determination of the reparations figure had been left to future expert commissions because the amount which the Allies had led their publics to expect was so exorbitant, it could never have survived Wilson's scrutiny or the analysis of serious financial experts.

In this manner, reparations, like disarmament, became a weapon of the German revisionists; experts increasingly doubted not only the morality but the feasibility of the claims. John Maynard Keynes' *Treatise on the Economic Consequences of the Peace* was a prime example.[15] Finally, the bargaining position of the victor always diminishes with time. Whatever is not exacted during the shock of defeat becomes increasingly difficult to attain later—a lesson America had to learn with respect to Iraq at the end of the 1991 Gulf War.

It was not until 1921—two years after the signing of the Versailles Treaty—that a figure for reparations was finally established. It was absurdly high: 132 billion Goldmarks (some $40 billion, which amounts to approximately $323 billion in present value), a sum which would have necessitated German payments for the rest of the century. Predictably, Germany claimed insolvency; even if the international financial system could have accommodated such a vast transfer of resources, no democratic German government could have survived agreeing to it.

In the summer of 1921, Germany paid the first installment of the reparations bill, transferring 1 billion Marks ($250 million). But it did so by printing paper Marks and selling them for foreign currency on the open market—in other words, by inflating its currency to the point where no significant transfer of resources was taking place. At the end of 1922, Germany proposed a four-year moratorium on reparations.

The demoralization of the Versailles international order and of France, its leading European pillar, was now far advanced. No enforcement machinery existed for reparations, and no verification machinery for disarmament. Since France and Great Britain disagreed on both issues, Germany was disgruntled, and the United States and the Soviet Union were out of the picture, Versailles had in effect led to a kind of international guerrilla war rather than to world order. Four years after the Allied victory, Germany's bargaining position was becoming stronger than that of France. In this atmosphere, British Prime Minister Lloyd George called for an international conference to meet at Genoa in April 1922 in a sensible attempt to discuss reparations, war debts, and European recovery as a package—much as the Marshall Plan would do a generation later. Since it was impossible to conceive of European economic recovery without the two largest Continental countries (which also happened to be the principal debtors), Germany and the Soviet Union, the two pariahs of European diplomacy, were invited to an international conference for the first time in the postwar period. The result was not the contribution to international order of Lloyd George's hopes, but an opportunity for the two outcasts to come together.

Nothing remotely resembling the Soviet Union had appeared on the horizon of European diplomacy since the French Revolution. For the first time in over a century, a country had dedicated itself officially to overthrowing the established order. The French revolutionaries had striven to change the character of the state; the Bolsheviks, going a step further, proposed to abolish the state altogether. Once the state had withered away, in Lenin's phrase, there would be no need for diplomacy or foreign policy.

At first, this attitude unsettled both the Bolsheviks and those with whom they were obliged to deal. The early Bolsheviks had developed theories of class struggle and imperialism as causes of war. However, they never dealt with the question of how to conduct foreign policy among sovereign states. They were certain that world revolution would follow their victory in Russia in a few months' time; extreme pessimists thought it might take as long as a few years. Leon Trotsky, the first Soviet Foreign Minister, viewed his task as little more than that of a clerk who, in order to discredit the capitalists, would make public the various secret treaties by which they had proposed to divide the spoils of the war amongst themselves. He defined his role as being to "issue a few revolutionary proclamations to the peoples of the world and then shut up shop."[16] None of the early communist leaders thought it possible that a communist state could coexist with capitalist countries for decades. Since after a few months or years the state was expected to disappear altogether, the principal task of early Soviet foreign policy was believed to be the encouragement of world revolution, not the management of relations among states.

In such an environment, the exclusion of the Soviet Union from the peacemaking at Versailles was understandable. The Allies had no incentive to involve in their deliberations a country that had already made a separate peace with Germany, and whose agents were trying to overthrow their governments. Nor did Lenin and his colleagues have any desire to participate in the international order they were seeking to destroy.

Nothing in their endless, abstruse internal debates had prepared the early Bolsheviks for the state of war they had in fact inherited. They had no specific peace program because they did not think of their country as a state, only as a cause. They therefore acted as if ending the war and promoting European revolution were the same process. Indeed, their first foreign-policy decree, issued the day after the 1917 Revolution, was the so-called Decree on Peace—an appeal to governments and peoples of the world for what they described as a democratic peace.[17]

Bolshevik illusions crumbled quickly. The German High Command agreed to negotiations for a peace treaty at Brest-Litovsk and to an armistice while talks were taking place. At first, Trotsky imagined that he would be able to use the threat of world revolution as a bargaining weapon, and to act as a kind of attorney for the proletariat. Unfortunately for Trotsky, the German negotiator was a victorious general, not a philosopher. Max Hoffmann, Chief of Staff of the Eastern front, understood the balance of forces and put forward brutal terms in January 1918. He demanded the annexation of the entire Baltic area, a slice of Belorussia, a *de facto* protectorate over an independent Ukraine, and a huge indemnity. Tiring of Trotsky's procrastination, Hoffmann finally produced a map with a broad blue line showing the Germans' demands, and made it clear that Germany would not retire behind that line until Russia had demobilized—in other words, until it was defenseless.

Hoffmann's ultimatum generated the first significant communist debate on foreign policy, which began in January 1918. Supported by Stalin, Lenin urged appeasement; Bukharin advocated revolutionary war. Lenin argued that, if a German revolution did not occur or it failed, Russia would suffer a "smashing defeat," leading to an even more disadvantageous peace, "a peace moreover which would be concluded not by a Socialist government, but by some other.... Such being the state of affairs, it would be absolutely impermissible tactics to stake the fate of the Socialist revolution which has begun in Russia merely on the chance that the German revolution may begin in the immediate future."[18]

Arguing on behalf of an essentially ideological foreign policy, Trotsky advocated the policy of "no war, no peace."[19] Yet the weaker side has the option of playing for time only against an adversary that considers negotiations as operating according to their own internal logic—an illusion to which the United States has been especially subject. The Germans had no such views. When Trotsky returned with instructions proclaiming a policy of neither peace nor war and announced unilaterally that the war was over, the Germans resumed military operations. Faced with total defeat, Lenin and his colleagues accepted Hoffmann's terms and signed the Treaty of Brest-Litovsk, accepting coexistence with imperial Germany.

The principle of coexistence would be invoked time and again over the next sixty years by the Soviets, with the reactions of the protagonists remaining constant: the democracies would each time hail the Soviet proclamation of peaceful coexistence as a sign of conversion to a permanent policy of peace. Yet, for their part, communists always justified periods of peaceful coexistence on the ground that the relation of forces was not conducive to confrontation. The obvious corollary was that, as that relationship changed, so would the Bolsheviks' devotion to peaceful coexistence. According to Lenin, it was reality which dictated coexistence with the capitalist foe:

> By concluding a separate peace, we are freeing ourselves in the largest measure possible *at the present moment* from both warring imperialist groups; by utilizing their mutual enmity we utilize the war, which makes a bargain between them against us difficult.[20]

The high point of that policy was, of course, the Hitler-Stalin Pact of 1939. Potential inconsistencies were easily rationalized. "We are convinced," said a communist statement, "that the most consistent socialist policy can be reconciled with the sternest realism and most level-headed practicality."[21]

In 1920, Soviet policy took the final step in acknowledging the need for a more traditional policy toward the West when Foreign Minister Georgi Chicherin said:

> There may be differences of opinion as to the duration of the capitalist system, but at present the capitalist system exists, so that a *modus vivendi* must be found. . . .[22]

Despite the revolutionary rhetoric, in the end national interest emerged as a dominant Soviet goal, becoming elevated into a socialist verity just as it had stood for so long at the core of the policies of the capitalist states. Survival was now the immediate goal and coexistence the tactic.

Yet the socialist state soon confronted another military threat when, in April 1920, it was attacked by Poland. Polish forces reached the neighborhood of Kiev before they were defeated. When the Red Army, in a counterthrust, approached Warsaw, the Western Allies intervened, demanding an end to the offensive and peace. British Foreign Secretary Lord Curzon proposed a dividing line between Poland and Russia which the Soviets were prepared to accept. Poland, however, refused, so the final settlement was made along the prewar military lines, far to the east of what Curzon had proposed.

Poland thus managed to sharpen the antagonism of its two historic enemies: Germany, from which it had acquired Upper Silesia and the Polish corridor; and the Soviet Union, from which it had seized the territory east of what became known as the Curzon Line. When the smoke cleared, the Soviet Union found itself free at last of wars and revolution, yet having paid for it with the loss of most of the tsars' conquests in the Baltic, Finland, Poland, Bessarabia, and along the Turkish frontier. By 1923, Moscow had reclaimed control of Ukraine and Georgia, which had seceded from the Russian Empire during the turmoil—an event not forgotten by many contemporary Russian leaders.

To restore domestic control, the Soviet Union had to make a pragmatic compromise between revolutionary crusades and *Realpolitik*, between the proclamation of world revolution and the practice of peaceful coexistence. Though it opted to defer world revolution, the Soviet Union was far from a supporter of the existing order. It saw in peace an opportunity to pit the capitalists against each other. Its particular target was Germany, which had always played a major role in Soviet thought and in Russian sentiment. In December 1920, Lenin described the Soviet strategy:

> Our existence depends, first, on the existence of a radical split in the camp of the imperialist powers and, secondly, on the fact that the victory of the Entente and the Versailles peace have thrown the vast majority of the German nation into a position where they cannot live. ... The German bourgeois government madly hates the Bolsheviks, but the interests of the international situation are pushing it towards peace with Soviet Russia against its own will.[23]

Germany was coming to the same conclusion. During the Russo-Polish war, General Hans von Seeckt, the architect of the postwar German army, had written:

261

The present Polish state is a creation of the Entente. It is to replace the pressure formerly exercised by Russia on the eastern frontier of Germany. The fight of Soviet Russia with Poland hits not only the latter, but above all the Entente—France and Britain. If Poland collapses the whole edifice of the Versailles Treaty totters. From this it follows clearly that Germany has no interest in rendering any help to Poland in her struggle with Russia.[24]

Von Seeckt's view confirmed the fears aired by Lord Balfour a few years earlier (and quoted in the last chapter)—that Poland gave Russia and Germany a common enemy and obviated their balancing one another, as they had done throughout the nineteenth century. In the Versailles system, Germany faced not a Triple Entente but a multitude of states in various stages of disagreement with each other, all of them opposed as well by a Soviet Union with territorial grievances very similar to Germany's. It was only a matter of time before the two outcasts pooled their resentments.

The occasion arose in 1922 at Rapallo, an Italian seaside town near Genoa, and the site of Lloyd George's international conference. Ironically, it was made possible by the constant haggling over reparations that had been going on since the Treaty of Versailles, and that had intensified after the presentation of the Allied reparations bill and Germany's claim that it was unable to pay.

A major obstacle to the conference's success was that Lloyd George had neither the power nor the wisdom with which Secretary of State George Marshall would later steer his own reconstruction program to fruition. At the last moment, France refused to permit the subject of reparations to be included in the agenda, fearing, quite correctly, that France would be pressed to reduce the total amount. It seemed that France prized above all its unfulfillable, albeit internationally recognized, claim to some attainable compromise. Germany was looking for a moratorium on reparations. The Soviets were suspicious that the Allies might try to end the impasse by linking tsarist debts to German reparations, whereby the Soviet Union would be asked to acknowledge the tsars' debts and to reimburse itself from German reparations. Article 116 of the Treaty of Versailles had left open precisely this possibility.

The Soviet government had no more intention of acknowledging tsarist debts than it did of recognizing British and French financial claims. Nor was it anxious to add Germany to its already extensive list of adversaries by joining the reparations merry-go-round. In order to prevent the Genoa Conference from resolving this issue to the Soviets' disadvantage, Moscow proposed in advance of the conference that the two pariahs establish diplomatic relations and mutually renounce all claims against each other. Not wanting to be the first European country to establish diplomatic relations with the Soviet Union and thereby possibly jeopardize its chances of obtaining relief from the reparations bill, Germany evaded the proposition. The proposal remained on the table until events at Genoa forced a change of attitude.

Soviet Foreign Minister Georgi Chicherin, an aristocrat by birth who became a passionate believer in the Bolshevik cause, relished the opportunity provided by Genoa to put revolutionary convictions into the service of *Realpolitik*. He proclaimed "peaceful coexistence" in terms which placed practical cooperation above the requirements of ideology:

> . . . the Russian delegation recognize that in the present period of history, which permits the parallel existence of the old social order and of the new order now being born, economic collaboration between the States representing these two systems of property is imperatively necessary for the general economic reconstruction.[25]

At the same time, Chicherin coupled the appeal for cooperation with proposals well designed to compound the confusion of the democracies. He spelled out an agenda so sweeping that it could neither be implemented nor ignored by democratic governments—a tactic that would remain a constant of Soviet diplomacy. This agenda included the abolition of weapons of mass destruction, a world economic conference, and international control of all waterways. The purpose was to mobilize Western public opinion and to give Moscow a reputation for peaceful internationalism which would make it difficult for the democracies to organize the anticommunist crusade which was the Kremlin's nightmare.

Chicherin found himself an outsider at Genoa, though no more so than the members of the German delegation. The Western Allies remained oblivious to the temptations they were creating for both Germany and the Soviet Union by pretending that these two most powerful countries on the Continent could simply be ignored. Three requests by the German Chancellor and his Foreign Minister for a meeting with Lloyd George were rebuffed. Simultaneously, France proposed holding private consultations with Great Britain and the Soviet Union from which Germany would be excluded. The purpose of these meetings was to resurrect the shopworn scheme of trading tsarist debts for German reparations—a proposal which even less suspicious diplomats than the Soviets would have construed as a trap to undermine the prospect of improved German-Soviet relations.

By the end of the first week of the conference, both Germany and the Soviet Union were worried that they would be pitted against each other. When one of Chicherin's aides telephoned the German delegation at the conspiratorial hour of one-fifteen in the morning on April 16, 1922, proposing a meeting later that day at Rapallo, the Germans jumped at the invitation. They were anxious to end their isolation as much as the Soviets wanted to avoid the dubious privilege of becoming German creditors. The two foreign ministers lost little time drafting an agreement in which Germany and the Soviet Union established full diplomatic relations, re-nounced claims against each other, and granted each other Most Favored Nation status. Lloyd George, upon receiving belated intelligence of the meeting, frantically tried to reach the German delegation to invite them to the interview he had repeatedly rejected. The message reached Ra-thenau, the German negotiator, as he was about to leave for the signing of the Soviet-German agreement. He hesitated, then muttered: *"Le vin est tiré; il faut le boire"* (The wine is drawn; it must be drunk).[26]

Within a year, Germany and the Soviet Union were negotiating secret agreements for military and economic cooperation. Though Rapallo later came to be a symbol of the dangers of Soviet-German rapprochement, it was in fact one of those fateful accidents which seem inevitable only in retrospect: accidental in the sense that neither side planned for it to happen when it did; inevitable because the stage for it had been set by the Western Allies' ostracism of the two largest Continental countries, by their creation of a belt of weak states between them hostile to each, and by their dismemberment of both Germany and the Soviet Union. All of this created the maximum incentive for Germany and the Soviet Union to overcome their ideological hostility and to cooperate in undermining Versailles.

Rapallo by itself did not have that consequence; it symbolized, how-ever, a common overriding interest which continued to draw together Soviet and German leaders for the remainder of the interwar period. George Kennan has ascribed this agreement in part to Soviet persistence, in part to Western disunity and complacency.[27] Clearly, the Western de-mocracies were shortsighted and fatuous. But once they had made the error of drafting the Treaty of Versailles, only extremely forbidding choices were left to them. In the long run, Soviet-German cooperation could have been forestalled only by a British and French deal with one or the other of them. But the minimum price of such a deal with Germany would have been the rectification of the Polish border and, almost cer-tainly, the abolition of the Polish Corridor. In such a Europe, France could only have avoided German domination by a firm alliance with Great

Britain, which, of course, the British refused to consider. Similarly, the practical implication of any deal with the Soviet Union would have been the restoration of the Curzon Line, which Poland would have rejected and France would not consider. The democracies were not prepared to pay either price, or even to admit to the dilemma of how to defend the Versailles settlement without allowing either Germany or the Soviet Union a significant role.

This being the case, there was always the possibility that the two Continental giants might opt to partition Eastern Europe between themselves rather than join a coalition directed against the other. Thus it remained to Hitler and Stalin, unfettered by the past and driven by their lusts for power, to blow away the house of cards assembled by the well-meaning, peace-loving, and essentially timid statesmen of the interwar period.

CHAPTER ELEVEN

Stresemann and the Re-emergence of the Vanquished

All the principles of balance-of-power diplomacy as they had been practiced in Europe since William III would have commanded that Great Britain and France form an anti-German alliance to rein in the revisionist impulses of their restless neighbor. Ultimately, Great Britain and France were each weaker than Germany—even a defeated Germany—and could hope to counterbalance it only in coalition. But that coalition was never formed. Great Britain abandoned the single-minded pursuit of equilibrium that had distinguished its policy for three centuries. It oscillated between a superficial application of the balance of power, which it aimed at France, and a growing devotion to the new principle of collective security, which it recoiled from enforcing. France pursued a foreign policy of desperation, alternating between using the Treaty of Versailles to delay German recovery and making halfhearted attempts to reconcile its ominous neighbor. Thus it happened that the statesman destined to do the most to shape the diplomatic landscape of the 1920s—Gustav Stresemann—came not from one of the victorious powers, but from defeated Germany.

But before the emergence of Stresemann, there was to be one more doomed effort by France to assure its security by its own efforts. At the end of 1922, with reparations elusive, disarmament controversial, meaningful British security guarantees unavailable, and German-Soviet rapprochement taking place, France found itself at the end of its emotional tether. Raymond Poincaré, its wartime President, took over as Prime Minister and decided in favor of unilateral enforcement of the Versailles reparations clause. In January 1923, French and Belgian troops occupied the Ruhr, Germany's industrial heartland, without consulting the other Allies.

Lloyd George would remark many years later: "If there had been no Rapallo, there would have been no Ruhr."[1] But it is also true that, had Great Britain been prepared to undertake a security guarantee, France would not have embarked on so desperate a step as occupying Germany's industrial heartland. And if France had been more ready to compromise on reparations (and on the disarmament issue), Great Britain might have been more forthcoming about forging an alliance—though how meaningful this alliance would have been, given the near-pacifist state of British public opinion, is another matter.

Ironically, France's sole unilateral military initiative demonstrated that it had in fact lost the capacity to act alone. France took control of the industries of the Ruhr region in order to exploit its steel and coal as a substitute for the reparations payments refused by the Germans. The German government ordered passive resistance and paid the coal and steel workers not to work. Though the policy bankrupted the German government—and sparked hyperinflation—it also prevented France from achieving its objective, thereby turning the occupation of the Ruhr into a massive French failure.

France was now thoroughly isolated. The United States expressed its displeasure by withdrawing its own army of occupation from the Rhineland. Great Britain glowered. Germany saw in this split between the Allies an opportunity for rapprochement with Great Britain. The heady atmosphere of national resistance to the French occupation even led some German leaders to resurrect the old project of an Anglo-German alliance—another instance of Germany's ingrained tendency to overestimate its options. The British Ambassador to Berlin, Lord d'Abernon, reported a conversation in which a leading German statesman resurrected some of the arguments of imperial Germany for a British alliance, declaring that "the position of 1914 is today reversed. It is quite clear that, as in 1914 England had fought Germany to withstand a military domination of Europe, so in the course of a few years she might fight France on the same grounds. The question is whether England would carry on that fight alone or whether she would have allies."[2]

No responsible British leader thought of going so far as allying his country with Germany. Nevertheless, on August 11, 1923, Foreign Secretary Curzon and Foreign Office official Sir Eyre Crowe (author of the Crowe Memorandum of 1907) demanded that France reconsider its course in the Ruhr at the risk of losing Great Britain's support in a future crisis with Germany. Poincaré was not impressed. He did not consider British support a favor to France but, rather, a requirement of the British national interest: ". . . in case a situation like in 1914 develops . . . England, in its own interest, will have to take the same measure as she took back then."[3]

Poincaré turned out to be right about what Great Britain's ultimate choice would be when faced with a situation similar to that of 1914. But he miscalculated as to the amount of time it would take Great Britain to realize it was indeed facing a similar crisis and that, in the interim, the rickety Versailles system would be in a shambles.

The occupation of the Ruhr ended in the fall of 1923. France did not succeed in generating a significant separatist movement in the Ruhr or even in the Rhineland, which, according to the terms of the Versailles Treaty, the German army was not permitted to enter and therefore could not go into to quell a separatist movement. The coal mined during the occupation barely paid for the costs of administering the territory. In the meantime, Germany was beset by insurrections developing in Saxony (from the political left) and in Bavaria (from the right). Inflation raged, threatening the ability of the German government to carry out any of its obligations. France's insistence on full reparations had become unfulfillable as a result of French actions.

France and Great Britain had managed to checkmate each other: France, by insisting on weakening Germany by unilateral action and thereby forfeiting British support; Great Britain, by insisting on conciliation without considering its impact on the balance of power, thereby forfeiting French security. Even a disarmed Germany proved strong enough to thwart unilateral French actions—an augury of what lay ahead once Germany threw off the shackles of Versailles.

In the 1920s, whenever the democracies came to a dead end, they would invoke the League of Nations rather than face geopolitical realities.

Even the British general staff fell into this trap. The very memorandum quoted in the previous chapter that had identified Germany as the principal threat and deemed France incapable of offering effective resistance, fell in with the prevailing orthodoxies: in its conclusions, the general staff had no better idea than "strengthening" the League (whatever that meant) and making "alliances *ad hoc* in such situations as . . . Germany running amok."[4]

That recommendation was a nearly guaranteed prescription for failure. The League was too divided and, by the time Germany ran amok, it would be too late to organize alliances. Now, all Germany needed to ensure for itself an even more commanding long-term position than it had enjoyed before the war was a statesman sufficiently farsighted and patient to erode the discriminatory provisions of the Treaty of Versailles.

Such a leader emerged in 1923, when Gustav Stresemann became Foreign Minister and then Chancellor. His method for renewing Germany's strength was the so-called policy of "fulfillment," which amounted to a total reversal of previous German policy and the abandonment of the diplomatic guerrilla war his predecessors had waged against the provisions of the Versailles Treaty. "Fulfillment" relied on taking advantage of the obvious discomfort of Great Britain and France with the distance between their principles and the terms of Versailles. In return for a German effort to meet an eased reparations schedule, Stresemann strove to be released from the most onerous political and military provisions of Versailles by the Allies themselves.

A nation defeated in war and partially occupied by foreign troops has basically two choices. It can challenge the victor in the hope of making enforcement of the peace too painful; or it can cooperate with the victor while regaining strength for a later confrontation. Both strategies contain risks. After a military defeat, resistance invites a test of strength at the moment of maximum weakness; collaboration risks demoralization, because policies which appeal to the victor also tend to confuse the public opinion of the vanquished.

Before Stresemann, Germany had pursued the policy of resistance. Confrontational tactics had enabled it to prevail in the Ruhr crisis, but Germany's grievances were hardly allayed by the French withdrawal from the Ruhr. Strangely enough, the return of Alsace-Lorraine to France was not controversial. But the redrawing of Germany's borders, giving Poland large tracts of German territory, faced passionate nationalistic opposition. Finally, there were widespread pressures to throw off the restrictions on German military strength. And there was nearly unanimous consensus in Germany that the Allied reparations demands were outrageous.

Unlike the nationalists, Stresemann understood that no matter how unpopular the Versailles Treaty—indeed, regardless of how much he hated it himself—he needed British and, to some extent, French help to throw off its most onerous provisions. The Rapallo understanding had been a useful tactic to unnerve the Western democracies. But because the Soviet Union was too impoverished to aid German economic recovery and too isolated to lend support in most diplomatic confrontations, its real impact would be felt only after Germany became strong enough to challenge the Versailles settlement openly. Above all, regaining economic strength required foreign loans, something Germany would find difficult in an atmosphere of confrontation. Thus, Stresemann's policy of fulfillment reflected above all his realistic assessment of the requirements of German political and economic recovery: "Germany's basic military weakness," he wrote, "spells out the limits, the nature, and the methods of Germany's foreign policy."[5]

Though the fulfillment policy was grounded in realism, that commodity was in no more abundant supply in postwar Germany (especially in conservative circles) than it had been in the days when the conservatives' policies had so heavily contributed to the outbreak of World War I. Ending the war while German forces still stood on Allied soil had enabled those responsible for Germany's participation in the war to escape the consequences of their folly, and to saddle their more moderate successors with the blame. Lloyd George had foreseen this result when, on October 26, 1918, he commented to the War Cabinet about Germany's first peace overtures:

> The Prime Minister said that industrial France had been devastated and Germany had escaped. At the first moment when we were in a position to put the lash on Germany's back she said "I give up." The question arose whether we ought not to continue lashing her as she had lashed France.[6]

His colleagues, however, thought Great Britain too exhausted to pursue such a course. Foreign Secretary Austen Chamberlain replied wearily that "vengeance was too expensive these days."[7]

As Lloyd George had predicted, the new Weimar Republic was from the outset besieged by nationalist agitators, even though it had been granted peace terms far more generous than what the military high command could have obtained. Germany's new democratic leaders received no credit for preserving their country's substance under the most difficult of circumstances. In politics, however, there are few rewards for mitigating damage because it is rarely possible to prove that worse consequences would in fact have occurred.

270

Just as, two generations later, it took a conservative American president to engineer America's opening to China, only a leader with the impeccable conservative credentials of Stresemann could have even thought of basing German foreign policy on cooperating, however ambivalently, with the hated Versailles settlement. The son of a beer distributor, Stresemann was born in Berlin in 1878 and had built his political career by espousing the views of the conservative, pro-business bourgeois National Liberal Party. He became its leader in 1917. A man of great conviviality, he loved literature and history, and his conversations were frequently sprinkled with allusions to German classics. Nevertheless, his early views on foreign policy reflected the conventional conservative wisdom. For example, he was convinced that Germany had been lured into the war by a jealous Great Britain eager to preserve its own primacy.

As late as 1917, Stresemann had advocated vast conquests in both the East and the West, as well as the annexation of French and British colonial possessions in Asia and Africa. He had also supported unrestricted submarine warfare, the calamitous decision which brought America into the war. That the man who had called the Treaty of Versailles "the greatest swindle in history"[8] should initiate a policy of fulfillment seems a strange turn of events only to those who believe that *Realpolitik* cannot teach the benefits of moderation.

Stresemann was the first postwar German leader—and the only democratic leader—who exploited the geopolitical advantages which the Versailles settlement conferred on Germany. He grasped the essentially brittle nature of the Franco-English relationship, and used it to widen the wedge between the two wartime allies. He cleverly exploited the British fear of a German collapse vis-à-vis both France and the Soviet Union. An official British analyst described Germany as a crucial bulwark against the spread of Bolshevism, using arguments which would show that "fulfillment" was making progress. The German government was "supported by [a] majority of National Assembly, is genuinely democratic, intends to carry out [the] Treaty of Peace to [the] best of its ability, and is deserving [of] frank support from Allies." If British support failed, Germany "will inevitably gravitate toward Bolshevism now and ultimately perhaps to absolute monarchism again."[9]

Great Britain's arguments in favor of assistance to Germany bear a certain resemblance to American propositions regarding aid to Russia in the Yeltsin period. In neither case was there an assessment of the consequences of the "success" of the policy being advocated. If fulfillment succeeded, Germany would become progressively stronger and be in a position to threaten the equilibrium of Europe. Similarly, if a post–Cold War international aid program to Russia achieves its objective, growing Russian strength will produce geopolitical consequences all around the vast periphery of the former Russian Empire.

In both cases, the advocates of conciliation had positive, even far-sighted, goals. The Western democracies were wise to go along with Stresemann's fulfillment policy. But they erred in not tightening the bonds among themselves. The policy of fulfillment was bound to bring closer the day described by General von Seeckt: "We must regain our power, and as soon as we do, we will naturally take back everything we lost."[10] America was farsighted in offering aid to post–Cold War Russia; but once Russia recovers economically, its pressure on neighboring countries is certain to mount. This may be a price worth paying, but it would be a mistake not to recognize that there is a price.

In the early stages of his fulfillment policy, Stresemann's ultimate aims were irrelevant. Whether he was seeking permanent conciliation or an overthrow of the existing order—or, as was most likely, keeping both options open—he first had to free Germany from the controversy over reparations. With the exception of France, the Allies were equally eager to put the issue behind them and to begin receiving some reparations at last. As for France, it hoped to escape from the self-inflicted trap of having occupied the Ruhr.

Stresemann skillfully proposed international arbitration for a new schedule of reparations, expecting an international forum to prove less exacting than France alone was likely to be. In November 1923, France accepted the appointment of an American banker, Charles G. Dawes, as "impartial arbiter" to reduce France's reparation claim—a galling symbol of the disintegration of the wartime alliance. The Dawes Committee's recommendations establishing a reduced schedule of payments for five years were accepted in April 1924.

Over the next five years, Germany paid out about $1 billion in reparations and received loans of about $2 billion, much of it from the United States. In effect, America was paying Germany's reparations, while Germany used the surplus from American loans to modernize its industry. France had insisted on reparations in order to keep Germany weak. Forced to choose between a weak Germany and a Germany capable of paying reparations, France had opted for the latter, but then had to stand by as reparations helped to rebuild Germany's economic and, ultimately, its military power.

By the end of 1923, Stresemann was in a position to claim some success:

All our measures of a political and diplomatic nature, through deliberate co-operation by the two Anglo-Saxon Powers, the estrangement of Italy from her neighbour [France], and the vacillation of Belgium, have combined to create a situation for France that the country will not in the long run be able to sustain.[11]

Stresemann's assessment was accurate. The fulfillment policy produced an insoluble quandary for both France and the entire European order. French security required a certain amount of discrimination against Germany in the military field; otherwise, Germany's superior potential in manpower and resources would prevail. But without equality—the right to build armaments like any other European country—Germany would never accept the Versailles system, and fulfillment would come to a halt.

Fulfillment placed British diplomats in a difficult position as well. If Great Britain did not grant Germany military equality as a *quid pro quo* for Germany's meeting its reparations payments, Germany could well revert to its earlier intransigence. But military equality for Germany would imperil France. Great Britain might have made an alliance with France to counterbalance Germany, but it did not wish to become entangled in France's alliances in Eastern Europe or to find itself at war with Germany over some piece of Polish or Czech territory. "For the Polish Corridor," said Austen Chamberlain in 1925, paraphrasing Bismarck's remark about the Balkans, "no British government ever will or ever can risk the bones of a British grenadier."[12] His prediction, like Bismarck's, was disproved by events. Great Britain did go to war—just as Germany had earlier in the century—and for the very cause it had so consistently disdained.

To avoid this dilemma, Austen Chamberlain in 1925 developed an idea for a limited alliance among Great Britain, France, and Belgium which would guarantee only their borders with Germany—in essence a military alliance to resist German aggression in the West. By this time, however, Stresemann's fulfillment policy had made such headway that he held a near-veto over Allied initiatives. To forestall Germany's being identified as the potential aggressor, he declared that a pact without Germany was a pact against Germany.

Half-convinced that Germany's fear of encirclement had contributed to its bellicose prewar policy, Chamberlain retreated to a curious hybrid agreement in which he sought to blend a traditional alliance with the new principle of collective security. In keeping with the alliance concept originally proposed, the new pact—signed at Locarno, Switzerland— guaranteed the borders between France, Belgium, and Germany against

273

aggression. True to the principle of collective security, the draft presumed neither aggressor nor victim but promised resistance against aggression from whatever quarter in *either* direction. The *casus belli* was no longer an aggressive act by a specific country but the violation of a legal norm by *any* country.

By the mid-1920s, Stresemann, the Minister of defeated Germany, was in the driver's seat much more than Briand and Chamberlain, the representatives of the victors. In return for renouncing revisionism in the West, Stresemann drew from Briand and Chamberlain an implicit recognition that the Versailles Treaty required revision in the East. Germany accepted its *Western* frontier with France and Belgium, and the permanent demilitarization of the Rhineland; Great Britain and Italy guaranteed this arrangement, pledging assistance to repel invasions across the frontiers or into the demilitarized Rhineland from whatever direction. At the same time, Stresemann refused to accept Germany's border with Poland, which the other signatories also refused to guarantee. Germany concluded arbitration agreements with its Eastern neighbors, pledging peaceful settlement of all disputes. Yet Great Britain refused to extend its guarantee even to that pledge. Finally, Germany agreed to enter the League of Nations, thereby assuming a general obligation to settle all disputes by peaceful means, which, in theory, included the unrecognized borders in the East.

The Locarno Pact was greeted with exuberant relief as the dawning of a new world order. The three foreign ministers—Aristide Briand of France, Austen Chamberlain of Great Britain, and Gustav Stresemann of Germany —received the Nobel Peace Prize. But amidst all the jubilation, no one noticed that the statesmen had sidestepped the real issues; Locarno had not so much pacified Europe as it had defined the next battlefield.

The reassurance felt by the democracies at Germany's formal recognition of its Western frontier showed the extent of the demoralization and the confusion that had been caused by the mélange of old and new views on international affairs. For in that recognition was implicit that the Treaty of Versailles, which had ended a victorious war, had been unable to command compliance with the victors' peace terms, and that Germany had acquired the option of observing only those provisions which it chose to reaffirm. In this sense, Stresemann's unwillingness to recognize Germany's Eastern frontiers was ominous; while Great Britain's refusal to guarantee even the arbitration treaties gave international sanction to two classes of frontier in Europe—those accepted by Germany and guaranteed by the other powers, and those neither accepted by Germany nor guaranteed by the other powers.

To confuse matters further, three tiers of commitments now prevailed in Europe. The first consisted of traditional alliances backed by the conventional machinery of staff talks and political consultations. No longer in vogue, these were confined to French arrangements with the weak new states in Eastern Europe—alliances which Great Britain refused to join. In the event of German aggression in Eastern Europe, France would face a choice between undesirable alternatives: abandoning Poland and Czechoslovakia, or fighting alone, which had been its recurring nightmare since 1870 and was not something it was very likely to undertake. The second tier consisted of special guarantees such as Locarno, obviously deemed less binding than formal alliances, which explains why they never encountered obstacles in the House of Commons. Finally, there was the League of Nations' own commitment to collective security, which was in practice devalued by Locarno. For, if collective security was in fact reliable, Locarno was unnecessary; and if Locarno was necessary, the League of Nations was, by definition, inadequate to assure the security of even its principal founding members.

Because neither the Locarno-type guarantee nor the general concept of collective security identified a potential aggressor, both rendered advance military planning impossible. Even if concerted military action had been possible—and there is no example of it during the League period—the bureaucratic machinery guaranteed endless delays for fact-finding and various other League conciliation procedures.

All of these unprecedented diplomatic stipulations compounded the uneasiness of the countries which considered themselves most threatened. Italy ended up guaranteeing frontiers along the Rhine, which it had never in its history identified with national security. Italy's primary interest in Locarno had been to gain recognition as a Great Power. Having achieved that goal, it saw no reason to run any actual risks—as it would amply demonstrate when the Rhine frontier was challenged ten years later. For Great Britain, Locarno signified the first agreement in which a major power simultaneously guaranteed an erstwhile ally *and* a recently defeated enemy while pretending to be impartial between them.

Locarno represented not so much reconciliation between France and Germany as endorsement of the military outcome of the recent war. Germany had been defeated in the West but had overcome Russia in the East. Locarno in effect confirmed both results and laid the basis for Germany's ultimate assault on the Eastern settlement.

Locarno, hailed in 1925 as turning the corner toward permanent peace, in fact marked the beginning of the end of the Versailles international order. From then on, the distinction between victor and vanquished became more and more murky—a situation which could have been beneficial had the victor gained from it a heightened sense of security or the defeated become reconciled to living with a modified settlement. Neither occurred. France's frustration and sense of impotence grew with every passing year. So did nationalist agitation in Germany. The wartime Allies had all abdicated their responsibilities—America shirked its role in designing the peace, Great Britain renounced its historic role as balancer, and France relinquished its responsibility as guardian of the Versailles settlement. Only Stresemann, leader of a defeated Germany, had a long-range policy, and he inexorably moved his country to the center of the international stage.

The sole remaining hope for a peaceful new world order was that the emotional lift of the agreement itself and the expectations it produced, as summed up in the slogan "the spirit of Locarno," might overcome its structural failings. Contrary to Wilson's teachings, it was not the broad masses which promoted this new atmosphere but the foreign ministers —Chamberlain, Briand, and Stresemann—of the countries whose suspicions and rivalries had produced the war and prevented the consolidation of the peace.

Since there was no geopolitical basis for the Versailles order, the statesmen were driven to invoking their personal relationships as a means of maintaining it—a step none of their predecessors had ever taken. The aristocrats who had conducted foreign policy in the nineteenth century belonged to a world in which intangibles were understood in the same way. Most of them were comfortable with each other. Nevertheless, they did not believe that their personal relations could influence their assessments of their countries' national interests. Agreements were never justified by the "atmosphere" they generated, and concessions were never made to sustain individual leaders in office. Nor did leaders address each other by their first names as a way of underlining their good relations with each other for the sake of their publics' opinions.

That style of diplomacy changed after World War I. Since then, the trend toward personalizing relations has accelerated. When Briand welcomed Germany to the League, he stressed Stresemann's human qualities, and Stresemann responded in kind. Similarly, Austen Chamberlain's alleged personal predilection for France caused Stresemann to accelerate his policy of fulfillment and to recognize Germany's Western border when Chamberlain replaced the more pro-German Lord Curzon as foreign secretary in 1924.

Austen Chamberlain was the scion of a distinguished family. The son of the brilliant and mercurial Joseph Chamberlain, advocate of an alliance with Germany early in the century, he was the half-brother of Neville Chamberlain, who was to make the Munich settlement. Like his father, Austen wielded massive power in Great Britain's coalition governments. But, also like his father, he never reached the highest office; indeed, he was the only leader of the Conservative Party in the twentieth century who did not become prime minister. As one quip had it, Austen "always played the game, and always lost it." Harold Macmillan said of Austen Chamberlain: "He spoke well, but never in the grand style. He was clear, but not incisive. . . . He was respected, but never feared."[13]

Chamberlain's major diplomatic accomplishment was his role in forging the Locarno Pact. Because Chamberlain was known to be a Francophile, having once remarked that he "loved France like a woman," Stresemann feared an incipient Franco-English alliance. It was this fear that moved Stresemann to originate the process that led to Locarno.

In retrospect, the weakness of the policy of creating two classes of frontiers in Europe has become obvious. But Chamberlain viewed it as a crucial extension of Great Britain's strategic commitments, which went to the limit of what the British public would support. Until the beginning of the eighteenth century, Great Britain's security frontier had been at the Channel. Throughout the nineteenth century, the security frontier had been at the borders of the Low Countries. Austen Chamberlain tried to extend it to the Rhine, where, in the end, it was not supported when Germany challenged it in 1936. A guarantee to Poland was beyond the ken of British statesmen in 1925.

Aristide Briand was a classic political leader of the Third Republic. Starting his career as a left-wing firebrand, he became a fixture in French Cabinets—occasionally as prime minister but more frequently as foreign minister (he served in fourteen governments in that capacity). He recognized early on that France's relative position vis-à-vis Germany was declining and concluded that reconciliation with Germany represented France's best hope for long-term security. Relying on his convivial personality, he hoped to relieve Germany of the most onerous provisions of the Treaty of Versailles.

Briand's policy could not be popular in a country devastated by German armies. Nor is it at all easy to determine to what extent Briand's was an attempt to end a century-old enmity or whether it represented a reluctant *Realpolitik*. In times of crisis, Frenchmen preferred the tough and austere Poincaré, who insisted on rigid enforcement of Versailles. When crises became too painful to sustain—as after the occupation of the Ruhr —Briand would re-emerge. The trouble with this constant alternation was that France lost the capacity to pursue the policies of either of these two antipodal figures to their logical conclusions: France was no longer strong enough to carry out Poincaré's policy, yet French public opinion gave Briand too little to offer to Germany to achieve permanent reconciliation.

Whatever his ultimate motives, Briand understood that, if France did not pursue conciliation, it would be extorted from it by Anglo-Saxon pressure and by Germany's growing strength. Stresemann, though an ardent opponent of the Treaty of Versailles, believed that a relaxation of tensions with France would speed revision of the disarmament clauses and lay the basis for a revision of Germany's eastern borders.

On September 27, 1926, Briand and Stresemann met in the quaint village of Thoiry, in the French Jura Mountains near Geneva. Germany had just been admitted to the League of Nations and welcomed by a warm, eloquent, and personal speech from Briand. In this heady atmosphere, the two statesmen worked out a package deal designed to settle the war once and for all. France would return the Saar without the plebiscite called for by the Treaty of Versailles. French troops would evacuate the Rhineland within a year, and the Inter-Allied Military Control Commission (IMCC) would be withdrawn from Germany. In return, Germany would pay 300 million Marks for the Saar mines, speed up reparations payments to France, and fulfill the Dawes Plan. Briand was in effect offering to trade the most invidious provisions of Versailles for help with French economic recovery. The agreement demonstrated the unequal bargaining position of the two sides. Germany's gains were permanent and irrevocable; France's benefits were one-time, transitory, financial contributions, some of which repeated what Germany had previously promised.

The agreement ran into problems in both capitals. German nationalists violently opposed any form of cooperation with Versailles, however advantageous the specific terms, and Briand was accused of throwing away the Rhineland buffer. There were further difficulties with the bond issue for financing additional German expenditures. On November 11, Briand abruptly broke off the talks, declaring that "the prompt fulfillment of the Thoiry idea had been crushed by technical obstacles."[14]

This was the last attempt at a general settlement between France and Germany in the interwar period. Nor is it clear whether it would have made all that much difference had it been implemented. For the basic question posed by Locarno diplomacy remained—whether conciliation would cause Germany to accept the Versailles international order or accelerate Germany's capacity to threaten it.

After Locarno, that question became increasingly moot. Great Britain was convinced that conciliation was the only practical course. America believed it was a moral imperative as well. Strategic or geopolitical analysis having become unfashionable, the nations talked about justice even while they strenuously disagreed about its definition. A spate of treaties affirming general principles and appeals to the League followed—partly from conviction, partly from exhaustion, and partly from the desire to avoid painful geopolitical realities.

The post-Locarno period witnessed France's step-by-step retreat from the Versailles settlement—against its better judgment—under constant British (and American) pressures to go even further. After Locarno, capital —mostly American—poured into Germany, accelerating the modernization of its industry. The Inter-Allied Military Control Commission, which had been created to supervise German disarmament, was abolished in 1927, and its functions were turned over to the League of Nations, which had no means of verifying compliance.

Germany's secret rearmament accelerated. As early as 1920, the then minister of industry, Walther Rathenau, had consoled the German military with the argument that the provisions of Versailles leading to the dismantling of heavy German armaments would affect primarily weapons which would in any event soon become obsolete. And nothing, he argued, could prevent research on modern weapons or the creation of the industrial capacity to build them quickly. Attending army maneuvers in 1926, shortly after Locarno was ratified and at the moment that Briand and Stresemann were meeting at Thoiry, Field Marshal von Hindenburg, the Commander of the German army for the last three years of the war and the recently elected President of Germany, said: "I have seen today that the German army's traditional standard of spirit and skill has been preserved."[15] If that was so, France's security would be in jeopardy as soon as the restrictions on the size of the German army were lifted.

As the disarmament issue moved to the forefront of international diplomacy, this threat loomed ever closer. Demanding political equality, Germany was carefully creating the psychological framework for insisting on military parity later. France refused to disarm unless it obtained additional security guarantees; Great Britain, the only country in a position to extend them, refused to guarantee the Eastern settlement and would go no further than Locarno with respect to the Western settlement, thereby underlining the fact that Locarno was less of a commitment than an alliance.

To avoid, or at least to delay, the day of formal German equality, France began to play the game of developing criteria for the reduction of arms as favored by League of Nations disarmament experts. It submitted an analytical paper to the League Preparatory Commission relating actual power to potential power, trained reserves to demographic trends, and weapons-in-being to the rate of technological change. But none of the finely spun theories could get around the key issue, which was that, at equal levels of armaments, however low, French security was in jeopardy because of Germany's superior mobilization potential. The more France seemed to accept the premises of the Preparatory Commission, the more pressure it generated against itself. In the end, all the various French maneuvers served primarily to magnify the Anglo-Saxons' conviction that France was the real obstacle to disarmament and therefore to peace.

The poignancy of the French dilemma was that, after Locarno, France was no longer in a position to pursue its convictions and had to settle for mitigating its fears. French policy grew increasingly reactive and defensive. Symbolic of this state of mind was that France began to construct the Maginot Line within two years of Locarno—at a time when Germany was still disarmed and the independence of the new states of Eastern Europe depended on France's ability to come to their aid. In the event of German aggression, Eastern Europe could only be saved if France adopted an offensive strategy centered on its using the demilitarized Rhineland as a hostage. Yet the Maginot Line indicated that France intended to stay on the defensive inside its own borders, thereby liberating Germany to work its will in the East. French political and military strategies were no longer in step.

Confused leaders have a tendency to substitute public relations maneuvers for a sense of direction. Driven by the desire to be perceived as doing something, Briand used the occasion of the tenth anniversary of America's entry into the war to submit in June 1927 a draft treaty to Washington according to which the two governments would renounce war in their relations with each other and agree to settle all their disputes by peaceful means. The American Secretary of State, Frank B. Kellogg, did not quite know how to respond to a document which renounced what no one feared and offered what everyone took for granted. The approach of the election year of 1928 helped to clear Kellogg's mind; "peace" was popular, and Briand's draft had the advantage of not involving any practical consequence.

In early 1928, Secretary Kellogg ended his silence and accepted the draft treaty. But he went Briand one better, proposing that the renunciation of war include as many other nations as possible. The offer proved as irresistible as it was meaningless. On August 27, 1928, the Pact of Paris (popularly known as the Kellogg-Briand Pact), renouncing war as an instrument of national policy, was signed with great fanfare by fifteen nations. It was quickly ratified by practically all the countries of the world, including Germany, Japan, and Italy, the nations whose aggressions would blight the next decade.

No sooner was the Pact signed than second thoughts began to seize the world's statesmen. France qualified its original proposal by inserting a clause legalizing wars of self-defense and wars to honor obligations arising out of the League Covenant, the Locarno guarantees, and all of France's alliances. This brought matters back to their starting point, for the exceptions encompassed every conceivable practical case. Next, Great Britain insisted on freedom of action in order to defend its empire. America's reservations were the most sweeping of all; it invoked the Monroe Doctrine, the right of self-defense, and the stipulation that each nation be its own judge of the requirements of self-defense. Retaining every possible loophole, the United States rejected participation in any enforcement action as well.

In testifying before the Senate Foreign Relations Committee a few months later, Kellogg presented the extraordinary theory that the United States had no obligation under the Pact to help victims of aggression, since such aggression would already have proved that the Pact had been abrogated. "Supposing some other nation does break this treaty; why should we interest ourselves in it?" asked Senator Walsh from Montana. "There is not a bit of reason," replied the Secretary of State.[16]

Kellogg had reduced the treaty to the tautology that the Pact of Paris would preserve the peace as long as the peace was being preserved. War was banned in all circumstances except those which were foreseeable. No wonder that D. W. Brogan had this to say about the Kellogg-Briand Pact: "The United States, which had abolished the evils of drink by the Eighteenth Amendment, invited the world to abolish war by taking the pledge. The world, not quite daring to believe or doubt, obeyed."[17]

In the event, Briand's original idea was transformed by his erstwhile allies into a new means of putting pressure on France. Henceforth it was widely argued that, with war outlawed, France had an obligation to accelerate its own disarmament. To symbolize the era of goodwill, the Allies ended the occupation of the Rhineland in 1928, five years ahead of schedule.

Concurrently, Austen Chamberlain let it be known that, as far as Great Britain was concerned, the Polish border with Germany could, and indeed should, be modified, if only the Germans were civilized about it:

> If she [Germany] comes into the League and plays her part there in a friendly and conciliatory spirit I myself believe that within a reasonable number of years she will find herself in a position where her economic

281

and commercial support is so necessary and her political friendship so desirable to Poland that, without having recourse to the League machinery, she will be able to make a friendly arrangement on her own account directly with the Poles.... If the German public and press could be restrained from talking so much about the eastern frontiers, they might get more quickly to a solution.[18]

Stresemann skillfully used Germany's entry into the League both to increase his options toward the Soviet Union and to intensify German pressure on France for parity in armaments. For example, Stresemann asked for and was granted an exemption permitting German participation in the enforcement provisions of the League Charter (Article 16) on the ground that a disarmed Germany was in no position to face the risks of sanctions. Next, in Bismarckian fashion, Stresemann notified Moscow that his request for the exemption had been due to Germany's reluctance to join any anti-Soviet coalition.

Moscow took the hint. Within a year of Locarno, in April 1926, a treaty of neutrality between the Soviet Union and Germany was signed in Berlin. Each party agreed to remain neutral if the other was attacked; each agreed not to join any political combination or economic boycott aimed at the other—presumably regardless of the issue. In effect, this meant that the two countries excluded themselves from the application of collective security against each other. And Germany had already exempted itself from sanctions against anyone else. Berlin and Moscow were united in hostility to Poland, as German Chancellor Wirth told his Ambassador to Moscow, Ulrich von Brockdorff-Rantzau: "One thing I tell you frankly; Poland must be eliminated.... I do not conclude any treaty which might strengthen Poland."[19]

Nevertheless, French leaders, especially Briand, concluded that the fulfillment policy remained France's only realistic option. If France's worst fears came to pass and Germany resumed a bellicose policy, the hope of eventually gaining British support and maintaining America's goodwill would surely be jeopardized if France could be blamed for having wrecked conciliation.

Gradually, Europe's center of gravity shifted to Berlin. Amazingly, at least in retrospect, Stresemann's domestic position was disintegrating all this time. The prevailing nationalist attitude could be seen in the reaction to the so-called Young Plan, which the Allies had proposed when the five-year term for the Dawes Plan ran out in 1929. The Young Plan reduced German reparations even further and established a terminal, albeit distant, date for them. In 1924, the Dawes Plan had been adopted with the support of German conservatives; in 1929, the Young Plan, which offered considerably better terms, came under violent attack from German conservatives who were backed by the surging Nazi Party and by the communists. It was finally approved in the Reichstag by just twenty votes.

For a few years, the purported spirit of Locarno had signified the aspiration toward goodwill among the former adversaries of the First World War. But in German, the word "spirit" is also a synonym for "ghost," and by the end of the decade it was becoming fashionable in nationalistic circles to joke about the "ghost" of Locarno. This cynical attitude toward the centerpiece of the Versailles international order existed even in the halcyon days of German economic recovery, before the Depression had radicalized German politics beyond repair.

Stresemann died on October 3, 1929. He proved irreplaccable because Germany had no other leader of comparable talent or subtlety and, above all, because the rehabilitation of Germany and the pacification of Europe had in such large part been due to the confidence the Western powers had placed in his personality. For quite a long time, the prevailing view was that Stresemann had embodied all the qualities of the "good European." In this sense, he was treated as a precursor of the great Konrad Adenauer, who recognized that France and Germany in fact shared a common destiny across the gulf of their historic rivalries.

Yet, when Stresemann's papers became available, they seemed to contradict the benign estimation of him. They revealed a calculating practitioner of *Realpolitik* who pursued the traditional German national interest with ruthless persistence. For Stresemann, these interests were straightforward: to restore Germany to its pre-1914 stature, to dispose of the financial burdens of reparations, to attain military parity with France and Great Britain, to revise Germany's Eastern border, and to achieve the union (*Anschluss*) of Austria and Germany. Edgar Stern-Rubarth, a Stresemann aide, described his chief's objectives as follows:

> Stresemann's ultimate hope, as he once confessed to me, was: To free the Rhineland, to recover Eupen-Malmédy, and the Saar, to perfect Austria's *Anschluss,* and to have, under mandate or otherwise an African colony where essential tropical raw materials could be secured and an outlet created for the surplus energy of the younger generation.[20]

Stresemann was therefore clearly not a "good European" in the post–World War II sense of the phrase, a criterion which did not yet exist, however. Most Western statesmen shared Stresemann's view that Versailles required revision, especially in the East, and that Locarno was but a stage in this process. For France, of course, it was unbearably painful to have to deal with a resurgent Germany after a war in which it had expended its very substance. Yet this was also an accurate reflection of the new distribution of power. Stresemann understood that, even within the limits of Versailles, Germany was potentially the strongest nation in Europe. He drew from this assessment the *Realpolitik* conclusion that he had before him an opportunity to rebuild Germany to at least its pre-1914 level and probably beyond.

Unlike his nationalist critics, however—and quite contrary to the Nazis—Stresemann relied on patience, compromise, and the blessing of European consensus to achieve his goals. Mental agility allowed him to trade paper concessions—especially on the sensitive and symbolic issue of reparations—for an end to the military occupation of Germany and for the prospect of long-term changes which could not fail to place his country in an increasingly pivotal position. Unlike the German nationalists, however, he saw no need for a violent revision of Versailles.

Stresemann's opportunity to pursue his policy was inherent in Germany's resources and potential. The war had not crippled Germany's power, and Versailles had enhanced its geopolitical position. Not even a vastly more catastrophic defeat in World War II would succeed in eliminating Germany's influence in Europe. Rather than seeing Stresemann as a precursor of the Nazi assault on Western values, it would be more accurate to view Nazi excesses as an interruption of Stresemann's gradual and almost certainly peaceful progression to achieving a decisive role for his country in Europe.

Over time, tactic for Stresemann might well have turned into strategy, and expedient into conviction. In our own period, the original motive for President Sadat's rapprochement with Israel was almost certainly to undermine the West's image of Arab bellicosity and to place Israel on the psychological defensive. Like Stresemann, Sadat tried to drive a wedge between his adversary and its friends. By fulfilling reasonable Israeli demands, he hoped to weaken its ultimate refusal to return Arab, and especially Egyptian, land. But as time went on, Sadat actually turned into the apostle of peace and the healer of international rifts, which at first may well have been a pose. In time, the pursuit of peace and conciliation ceased to be for Sadat tools of the national interest and turned into values in and of themselves. Was Stresemann heading along a similar path? His premature death has left us with that possibility as one of history's unsolved riddles.

At the time of Stresemann's death, the reparations issue was on the way to being resolved, and Germany's western border had been settled.

Germany remained revisionist with respect to its eastern borders and to the disarmament provisions of the Versailles Treaty. The attempt to pressure Germany by occupying its territory had failed, and the modified collective security approach of Locarno had not stilled German claims for parity. The statesmen of Europe now took refuge in an all-out commitment to disarmament as their best hope for peace.

The notion that Germany was entitled to parity had by now become fixed in the British mind. As early as in his first term in office, in 1924, Labour Prime Minister Ramsay MacDonald had proclaimed disarmament as his top priority. In his second term, starting in 1929, he stopped construction of a naval base in Singapore and the building of new cruisers and submarines. In 1932, his government announced a moratorium on airplane construction. MacDonald's principal adviser on the subject, Philip Noel-Baker, declared that only disarmament could prevent another war.

The basic inconsistency between parity for Germany and security for France remained unresolved, however, perhaps because it was irresoluble. In 1932, a year before Hitler came to power, French Prime Minister Edouard Herriot predicted: "I have no illusions. I am convinced that Germany wishes to rearm. . . . We are at a turning point in history. Until now Germany has practised a policy of submission. . . . [N]ow she is beginning a positive policy. Tomorrow it will be a policy of territorial demands."[21] The most remarkable aspect of this statement was its passive, resigned tone. Herriot said nothing about the French army, which was still the largest in Europe; about the Rhineland, demilitarized under Locarno; about a still-disarmed Germany; or about French responsibility for the security of Eastern Europe. Unwilling to fight for its convictions, France now simply awaited its fate.

Great Britain saw matters on the Continent from a quite different perspective. Wanting to conciliate Germany, it relentlessly pressed France to accede to German parity in armaments. Disarmament experts are notoriously ingenious in coming up with schemes which meet the formal aspect of security issues without addressing the substance. Thus, the British experts devised a proposal granting Germany parity but without allowing conscription, thereby theoretically putting a premium on France's larger pool of trained reserves (as if Germany, having come this far, could not find a means to evade this last, relatively minor, restriction).

In that same fateful year before Hitler's rise to power, the democratic German government felt confident enough to walk out of the Disarmament Conference in protest against what it called French discrimination. It was wooed back with the promise of "[e]quality of rights in a system which would provide security for all nations,"[22] a weaseling phrase implying the theoretical right to parity with "security" provisions which made it too difficult to achieve. The public mood had gone beyond such subtleties. *The New Statesman,* an organ of the British Labour Party, greeted the formula as "the unqualified recognition of the principle of the equality of states." At the other end of the British political spectrum, the *Times* spoke approvingly of "the timely redress of inequality."[23]

The formula of "equality [within] a system [of] security" was, however, a contradiction in terms. France was no longer strong enough to defend itself against Germany, and Great Britain continued to refuse the military alliance with France that could have established a crude approximation of geopolitical equality (though, based on the experience of the war, even that was questionable). While insisting on defining equality in the purely formalistic terms of ending the discriminatory treatment of Germany, England remained silent about the impact of such equality on the European equilibrium. In 1932, an exasperated Prime Minister MacDonald told French Foreign Minister Paul-Boncour: "French demands always created the difficulty that they required of Great Britain that she should assume further obligations, and this at the moment could not be contemplated."[24] This demoralizing impasse continued until Hitler walked out of disarmament negotiations in October 1933.

After a decade in which diplomacy had focused on Europe, it was— unexpectedly—Japan which demonstrated the hollowness of collective security and of the League itself, ushering in a decade of mounting violence in the 1930s.

In 1931, Japanese forces occupied Manchuria, which legally was a part of China, although the authority of the Chinese central government had not operated there for many years. Intervention on such a scale had not been attempted since the founding of the League. But the League had no enforcement machinery for even the economic sanctions contemplated in its article 16. In its hesitations, the League exemplified the basic dilemma of collective security: no country was prepared to fight a war against Japan (or was in a position to do so without American participation, since the Japanese navy dominated Asian waters). Even if the machinery for economic sanctions had existed, no country was willing to curtail trade with Japan in the midst of the Depression; on the other hand, no country was willing to accept the occupation of Manchuria. None of the League members knew how to overcome these self-inflicted contradictions.

Finally, a mechanism was devised for doing nothing at all. It took the form of a fact-finding mission—the standard device for diplomats signaling that inaction is the desired outcome. Such commissions take time to assemble, to undertake studies, and to reach a consensus—by which point, with luck, the problem might even have gone away. Japan felt so confident of this pattern that it took the lead in recommending such a study. What came to be known as the Lytton Commission reported that Japan had justified grievances but had erred by not first exhausting all peaceful means of redress. This mildest of rebukes for occupying a territory larger than itself proved too much for Japan, which responded by withdrawing from the League of Nations. It was the first step toward the unraveling of the entire institution.

In Europe, the whole incident was treated as a kind of aberration peculiar to distant continents. Disarmament talks continued as if there were no Manchurian crisis, turning the debate over security versus parity into a largely ceremonial act. Then, on January 30, 1933, Hitler came to power in Germany and demonstrated that the Versailles system had indeed been a house of cards.

CHAPTER TWELVE

The End of Illusion:
Hitler and the
Destruction of Versailles

Hitler's advent to power marked one of the greatest calamities in the history of the world. But for him, the collapse of the house of cards which represented the Versailles international order might have proceeded in a peaceful, or at least noncatastrophic, fashion. That Germany would emerge from that process as the strongest nation on the Continent was inevitable; the orgy of killing and devastation that it unleashed was the work of one demonic personality.

Hitler attained eminence through his oratory. Unlike other revolutionary leaders, he was a solitary political adventurer representing no major school of political thought. His philosophy, as expressed in *Mein Kampf,* ranged from the banal to the fantastic and consisted of a popularized repackaging of right-wing, radical, conventional wisdom. Standing alone, it could never have launched an intellectual current that culminated in revolution, as had Marx's *Das Kapital* or the works of the philosophers of the eighteenth century.

Demagogic skill catapulted Hitler to the leadership of Germany and remained his stock in trade throughout his career. With the instincts of an outcast and an unerring eye for psychological weaknesses, he shunted his adversaries from disadvantage to disadvantage, until they were thoroughly demoralized and ready to acquiesce to his domination. Internationally, he ruthlessly exploited the democracies' guilty conscience about the Treaty of Versailles.

As the head of government, Hitler operated by instinct rather than analysis. Fancying himself an artist, he resisted sedentary habits and was constantly and restlessly on the move. He disliked Berlin and found solace in his Bavarian retreat, to which he would repair for months at a time, though he quickly grew bored even there. Since he disdained orderly work procedures and his ministers found it difficult to gain access to him, policymaking occurred in fits and starts. Anything consistent with his flashes of frenetic activity thrived; anything requiring sustained effort tended to languish.

The essence of demagoguery resides in the ability to distill emotion and frustration into a single moment. Gratifying that moment and achieving a mesmeric, nearly sensual relationship with his entourage and the public at large became Hitler's specialties. Abroad, Hitler was most successful when the world perceived him as pursuing normal, limited objectives. All his great foreign policy triumphs occurred in the first five years of his rule, 1933–38, and were based on his victims' assumption that his aim was to reconcile the Versailles system with its purported principles.

Once Hitler abandoned the pretense of rectifying injustice, his credibility vanished. Embarking on naked conquest for its own sake made him lose his touch. There were still occasional flashes of intuition, as in his design of the campaign against France in 1940 and in his refusal to permit a retreat in front of Moscow in 1941, which would almost certainly have caused a collapse of the German army. However, Hitler's seminal experience seems to have been Germany's defeat in World War I. He never ceased to recount how he first learned of it while bedridden in a military hospital, partially blinded by mustard gas. Ascribing Germany's collapse to treachery, a Jewish conspiracy, and lack of will, he would for the rest of his life insist that Germany could be defeated only by itself, not by foreigners. This line of thinking transmuted the defeat of 1918 into treason, while the failure on the part of Germany's leaders to fight to the end became a staple of Hitler's obsessive rhetoric and mind-numbing monologues.

Hitler always seemed strangely unfulfilled by his victories; in the end, he only seemed able to realize his image of himself by overcoming imminent collapse through sheer willpower. Psychologists may find therein one explanation for his conducting the war in a manner that seemed to lack a strategic or political rationale until Germany's resources had been squandered and Hitler could finally, and still unyieldingly, fulfill himself by defying the world in a bomb shelter in the encircled capital of his almost completely occupied country.

Demagogic skill and egomania were two sides of the same coin. Hitler was incapable of normal conversation, and either engaged in long monologues or lapsed into bored silences when some interlocutor managed to seize the floor—and at times even dozed off.[1] Hitler was wont to ascribe his, in truth, nearly miraculous rise from Vienna's netherworld to unchallenged rule over Germany to personal qualities unrivaled by any contemporary. Thus, a recital of his rise to power entered the deadening liturgy of Hitler's "table talks" as transcribed by his disciples.[2]

Hitler's egomania had deadlier consequences as well; he had convinced himself—and, what is more significant, his entourage—that, because his faculties were so unique, all his goals had to be accomplished in his own lifetime. Since, on the basis of his family history, he had estimated that his life would be relatively short, he was never able to permit any of his successes to mature, and pushed forward according to a timetable established by his assessment of his physical powers. History offers no other example of a major war being started on the basis of medical conjecture.

When all was said and done, Hitler's startling early successes amounted to an accelerated harvesting of opportunities which had been created by the policies of the predecessors he despised, especially Stresemann. Like the Peace of Westphalia, the Treaty of Versailles left a powerful country confronting a group of much smaller and unprotected states on its eastern border. The difference, however, was that while this had been intentional at Westphalia, quite the opposite was true of Versailles. Versailles and Locarno had smoothed Germany's road into Eastern Europe, where a patient German leadership would in time have achieved a preponderant position by peaceful means, or perhaps even have had it handed to it by the West. But Hitler's reckless megalomania turned what could have been a peaceful evolution into a world war.

At first, Hitler's true nature was obscured by his seeming ordinariness. Neither the German nor the Western European establishment believed that he really meant to overturn the existing order, even though he announced his intentions to that effect often enough. Tired of harassment by the ever-growing Nazi Party, demoralized by the Depression and political chaos, a conservative German leadership appointed Hitler as Chancellor, and tried to reassure itself by surrounding him with respectable conservatives (there were only three Nazi Party members in Hitler's first Cabinet of January 30, 1933). Hitler, however, had not come all that long way to be contained by parliamentary maneuvers. With a few brusque strokes (and on June 30, 1934, a purge assassinating a number of rivals and opponents), he made himself dictator of Germany within eighteen months of taking office.

The Western democracies' initial reaction to Hitler's ascendancy was to accelerate their commitment to disarmament. Germany's government was now headed by a chancellor who had proclaimed his intention to overthrow the Versailles settlement, to rearm, and then to engage in a policy of expansion. Even so, the democracies saw no need for taking special precautions. If anything, Hitler's accession to power strengthened Great Britain's determination to pursue disarmament. Some British diplomats even thought that Hitler represented a better hope for peace than the less stable governments which had preceded him. "[Hitler's] signature would bind all Germany like no other German's in all her past,"[3] British Ambassador Phipps wrote exuberantly to the Foreign Office. A British guarantee for France was unnecessary, according to Ramsay MacDonald, because, if Germany broke a disarmament agreement, "the strength of world opposition to her cannot be exaggerated."[4]

France, of course, was not reassured by such soothing pronouncements. Its chief problem still remained how to find security if Germany rearmed and Great Britain refused a guarantee. If world public opinion were really all that decisive in dealing with violators, why should Great Britain be so reluctant to give a guarantee? Because "public opinion in England would not support it," replied Sir John Simon, the Foreign Secretary, thus making explicit France's nightmare that Great Britain could not be relied on to defend what it would not guarantee.[5] But why would the British public not support a guarantee? Because it did not consider such an attack likely, replied Stanley Baldwin, head of the Conservative Party and in all but name leader of the British government:

> If it could be proved that Germany was rearming, then a new situation
> would immediately arise, which Europe would have to face. . . . If that
> situation arose, His Majesty's Government would have to consider it
> very seriously, but that situation had not yet arisen.[6]

The argument was endlessly circular and endlessly contradictory: a guarantee was both too risky and unnecessary; after achieving parity, Germany would be satisfied. Yet a guarantee of what Germany presumably was not challenging would be too dangerous even though the condemnation of world opinion would stop a violator in its tracks. Finally, Hitler himself put an end to the evasions and the hypocrisy. On October 14, 1933, Germany left the Disarmament Conference forever—not because Hitler had been rebuffed but because he was afraid that German demands for parity might be met, thereby thwarting his desires for unrestricted rearmament. A week later, Hitler withdrew from the League of Nations. In early 1934, he announced German rearmament. In separating itself from the world community in this way, Germany did not suffer any visible damage.

Hitler had clearly laid down a challenge, yet the democracies were uncertain as to what it really meant. By rearming, was Hitler not in fact implementing what most members of the League had already conceded in principle? Why react before Hitler had in fact committed some definable act of aggression? After all, was that not what collective security was all about? In this manner, the leaders of the Western democracies avoided the pain of being obliged to make ambiguous choices. It was much easier to wait for some clear demonstration of Hitler's bad faith because, in its absence, public backing for strong measures could not be relied on—or so the leaders of the democracies thought. Hitler, of course, had every incentive to obscure his true intentions until it was too late for the Western democracies to mount effective resistance. In any event, the democratic statesmen of the interwar period feared war more than they feared a weakening of the balance of power. Security, argued Ramsay MacDonald, must be sought "not by military but by moral means."

Hitler skillfully exploited such attitudes by periodically launching peace offensives that were deftly geared to the illusions of his potential victims. When he withdrew from the disarmament talks, he offered to limit the German army to 300,000 men and the German air force to half the size of that of France. The offer diverted attention from the fact that Germany had scrapped the limit of 100,000 established at Versailles while seemingly agreeing to new ceilings that could not be reached for several years—at which point those limits, too, would no doubt be jettisoned.

France refused the offer, declaring it would look after its own security. The haughtiness of the French reply could not obscure the reality that France's nightmare—military parity with Germany (or worse)—was now upon it. Great Britain drew the conclusion that disarmament had become more important than ever. The Cabinet announced: "Our policy is still to seek by international cooperation the limitation and reduction of world armaments, as our obligations under the Covenant and as the only means to prevent a race in armaments."[7] Indeed, the Cabinet reached the extraordinary decision that the best option was to bargain from what, by its own estimate, was turning into a position of weakness. On November 29, 1933—six weeks after Hitler had ordered the German delegation to leave the Disarmament Conference—Baldwin told the Cabinet:

> If we had no hope of achieving any limitation of armaments we should have every right to feel disquietude as to the situation not only so far as concerns the Air Force, but also the Army and Navy. [Britain was] using every possible effort to bring about a scheme of disarmament which would include Germany.[8]

Since Germany was rearming and the state of British defenses was, in Baldwin's own words, disquieting, a greater British defense effort might indeed have seemed to be in order. Yet Baldwin took exactly the opposite approach. He continued a freeze in the production of military aircraft, which had been instituted in 1932. The gesture was intended "as a further earnest of His Majesty's Government's desire to promote the work of the Disarmament Conference."[9] Baldwin failed to explain what incentive Hitler would have to negotiate disarmament as long as Great Britain was engaging in unilateral disarmament. (A more charitable explanation for Baldwin's actions is that Great Britain was developing new models of aircraft; having nothing to produce until these were ready, Baldwin was making a virtue out of a necessity.)

As for France, it took refuge in wishful thinking. The British Ambassador to Paris reported: "France has, in fact, fallen back on a policy of extreme caution, she is opposed to any forceful measures which would savour of military adventure."[10] A report to Edouard Daladier, then Minister of War, shows that even France had begun to lean toward League orthodoxy. The French military attaché in Berlin proclaimed disarmament as the most effective way of containing Hitler, having convinced himself that more dangerous fanatics than Hitler were lurking in the wings:

> It seems that there is no other way for us than to reach an understanding which will contain . . . at least for a while, Germany's military devel-

opment.... If Hitler is sincere in proclaiming his desire for peace, we will be able to congratulate ourselves on having reached agreement; if he has other designs or if he has to give way one day to some fanatic we will at least have postponed the outbreak of a war and that is indeed a gain.[11]

Great Britain and France opted to let German rearmament unfold because, quite literally, they did not know what else to do. Great Britain was not yet prepared to give up on collective security and the League, and France had become so dispirited that it could not bring itself to act on its premonitions: France dared not act alone, and Great Britain refused to act in concert.

In retrospect, it is easy to ridicule the fatuousness of the assessment of Hitler's motives by his contemporaries. But his ambitions, not to mention his criminality, were not all that apparent at the outset. In his first two years in office, Hitler was primarily concerned with solidifying his rule. But in the eyes of many British and French leaders, Hitler's truculent foreign policy style was more than counterbalanced by his staunch anticommunism, and by his restoration of the German economy.

Statesmen always face the dilemma that, when their scope for action is greatest, they have a minimum of knowledge. By the time they have garnered sufficient knowledge, the scope for decisive action is likely to have vanished. In the 1930s, British leaders were too unsure about Hitler's objectives and French leaders too unsure about themselves to act on the basis of assessments which they could not prove. The tuition fee for learning about Hitler's true nature was tens of millions of graves stretching from one end of Europe to the other. On the other hand, had the democracies forced a showdown with Hitler early in his rule, historians would still be arguing about whether Hitler had been a misunderstood nationalist or a maniac bent on world domination.

The West's obsession with Hitler's motives was, of course, misguided in the first place. The tenets of the balance of power should have made it clear that a large and strong Germany bordered on the east by small and weak states was a dangerous threat. *Realpolitik* teaches that, regardless of Hitler's motives, Germany's relations with its neighbors would be determined by their relative power. The West should have spent less time assessing Hitler's motives and more time counterbalancing Germany's growing strength.

No one has stated the result of the Western Allies' hesitancy to confront Hitler better than Joseph Goebbels, Hitler's diabolical propaganda chief. In April 1940, on the eve of the Nazi invasion of Norway, he told a secret briefing:

Up to now we have succeeded in leaving the enemy in the dark concerning Germany's real goals, just as before 1932 our domestic foes never saw where we were going or that our oath of legality was just a trick. . . . They could have suppressed us. They could have arrested a couple of us in 1925 and that would have been that, the end. No, they let us through the danger zone. That's exactly how it was in foreign policy too. . . . In 1933 a French premier ought to have said (and if I had been the French premier I would have said it): "The new Reich Chancellor is the man who wrote *Mein Kampf,* which says this and that. This man cannot be tolerated in our vicinity. Either he disappears or we march!" But they didn't do it. They left us alone and let us slip through the risky zone, and we were able to sail around all dangerous reefs. *And when we were done, and well armed, better than they, then they started the war!* [Italics in original.][12]

The leaders of the democracies refused to face the fact that, once Germany attained a given level of armaments, Hitler's real intentions would become irrelevant. The rapid growth of German military strength was bound to overturn the equilibrium unless it was either stopped or balanced.

This in fact was Churchill's lonely message. But in the 1930s, the lead time for recognizing prophets was still quite long. So the British leaders, in a rare show of unanimity extending across the entire political spectrum, rejected Churchill's warnings. Starting from the premise that disarmament, not preparedness, was the key to peace, they treated Hitler as a psychological problem, not a strategic danger.

When, in 1934, Churchill urged that Great Britain respond to German rearmament by a buildup in the Royal Air Force, government and opposition leaders united in scorn. Herbert Samuel spoke on behalf of the Liberal Party: "It would seem as if he were engaged not in giving sound, sane advice . . . but . . . in a reckless game of bridge. . . . All these formulas are dangerous."[13] Sir Stafford Cripps put forward the Labour Party's case with supercilious sarcasm:

One could picture him as some old baron in the Middle Ages who is laughing at the idea of the possibility of disarmament in the baronies of this country and pointing out that the only way in which he and his feudal followers could maintain their safety and their cows was by having as strong an armament as possible.[14]

Conservative Prime Minister Baldwin made the rejection of Churchill unanimous when he informed the House of Commons that he had not "given up hope either for the limitation or for the restriction of some kind of arms." According to Baldwin, accurate information about German air strength was "extraordinarily difficult" to obtain—though he did not reveal why this should be so.[15] Nevertheless, he was confident that "[i]t is not the case that Germany is rapidly approaching equality with us."[16] Baldwin felt "no ground at this moment for undue alarm and still less for panic." Chiding Churchill's figures as "exaggerated," he stressed that "there is no immediate menace confronting us or anyone in Europe at this moment—no actual emergency."[17]

France sought shelter behind an accumulation of halfhearted alliances by transforming the unilateral guarantees of Czechoslovakia, Poland, and Romania of the 1920s into mutual defense treaties. It meant that those countries would now be obliged to come to France's assistance even if Germany chose to settle scores with France before turning east.

It was an empty, indeed a pathetic, gesture. The alliances were logical enough as French guarantees for the weak new states of Eastern Europe. But they were not suited for serving as the sort of mutual assistance treaties which would confront Germany with the risk of a two-front war. They were too weak to rein in Germany in the East; offensive operations against Germany to relieve France were out of the question. Underscoring the irrelevance of these pacts, Poland balanced its commitments to France with a nonaggression treaty with Germany so that, in case of an attack on France, Poland's formal obligations would cancel each other out —or, more precisely, they would leave Poland free to choose that alignment which promised it the greatest benefit at the moment of crisis.

A new Franco-Soviet agreement signed in 1935 demonstrated the magnitude of France's psychological and political demoralization. Before World War I, France had eagerly sought a political alliance with Russia and did not rest until that political understanding had been turned into a military pact. In 1935, France's position was strategically far weaker and its need for Soviet military support nearly desperate. Nevertheless, France grudgingly concluded a political alliance with the Soviet Union while adamantly rejecting military staff talks. As late as 1937, France would not permit Soviet observers to attend its annual maneuvers.

There were three reasons for the aloof behavior of French leaders, all of which surely magnified Stalin's congenital distrust of the Western democracies. The first was their fear that too close an association with the Soviet Union would weaken France's indispensable ties to Great Britain. Second, France's Eastern European allies, situated between the Soviet Union and Germany, were not prepared to permit Soviet troops to enter their territory, rendering it difficult to find a subject for meaningful Franco-Soviet staff talks. Finally, as early as 1938, French leaders felt so intimidated by Germany that they feared staff talks with the Soviet Union might, in the words of then Prime Minister Chautemps, "produce a declaration of war by Germany."[18]

France thus ended up in a military alliance with countries too weak to help it, a political alliance with the Soviet Union with which it dared not cooperate militarily, and strategic dependence on Great Britain, which flatly refused to consider *any* military commitment. This arrangement was a prescription for a nervous breakdown, not a grand strategy.

The only serious moves France made in response to growing German strength were in the direction of Italy. Mussolini was not exactly a devotee of collective security but he had a clear sense of Italy's limitations, especially where Germany was concerned. He feared that German annexation of Austria would lead to a demand for the return of the South Tirol, which was ethnically German. In January 1935, then Foreign Minister Pierre Laval concluded what came close to being a military alliance. Agreeing to consult each other in the event of any threat to the independence of Austria, Italy and France initiated military-staff talks in which they went so far as to discuss stationing Italian troops along the Rhine and French troops along the Austrian frontier.

Three months later, after Hitler had reintroduced conscription, an approximation of an alliance among Great Britain, France, and Italy seemed to be developing. Their heads of government met in the Italian resort of Stresa, where they agreed to resist any German attempt to change the Versailles Treaty by force. It was a minor historical irony that Mussolini should have hosted a conference to defend the Versailles settlement since he had long been a critic of Versailles, arguing that the treaty had shortchanged Italy.

Stresa was to be the last time that the victors of the First World War considered joint action. Two months after the conference, Great Britain signed a naval accord with Germany, which showed that, where its own security was concerned, Great Britain preferred to rely on bilateral deals with the adversary rather than on its Stresa partners. Germany agreed to limit its fleet to thirty-five percent of Great Britain's for the next ten years, though it was granted the right to an equal number of submarines.

The terms of the Naval Treaty were less significant than what they revealed about the state of mind of the democracies. The British Cabinet surely realized that the naval agreement in effect acquiesced to the German abrogation of the naval provisions of the Versailles Treaty and thereby, at a minimum, went against the spirit of the Stresa front. Its practical effect was to establish new ceilings on a bilateral basis—ceilings, moreover, at the outer limit of Germany's capacity to build—a method of arms control that was to become increasingly popular during the Cold War. The naval agreement also signified that Great Britain preferred to conciliate the adversary rather than rely on its partners in the Stresa front —the psychological framework for what later came to be known as the policy of appeasement.

Soon thereafter, the Stresa front collapsed altogether. An adherent of *Realpolitik,* Mussolini took it for granted that he had a free hand for the kind of colonial expansion that had been routine prior to World War I. Consequently, he set about carving out an African empire in 1935 by conquering Abyssinia, Africa's last independent nation, and, in the process, avenging an Italian humiliation by Abyssinian forces dating back to the turn of the century.

But, whereas Mussolini's aggression would have been accepted prior to World War I, it was now being initiated in a world that was in thrall to collective security and the League of Nations. Public opinion, especially in Great Britain, had already castigated the League for "failing" to prevent Japan's conquest of Manchuria; in the interim, a mechanism for economic sanctions had been put in place. By the time Italy invaded Abyssinia in 1935, the League had an official remedy for such aggression. Abyssinia was, moreover, a member of the League of Nations, though only as the result of a rather curious reversal of circumstances. In 1925, Italy had sponsored Abyssinia's admission to the League in order to check presumed British designs. Great Britain had acquiesced reluctantly, after arguing that Abyssinia was too barbaric for full-fledged membership in the international community.

Now both countries were hoist by their own petard: Italy, by engaging in what had, by any standard, been unprovoked aggression against a member of the League; Great Britain, because it faced a challenge to collective security and not just another African colonial problem. To complicate matters, Great Britain and France had already conceded at Stresa that Abyssinia lay within Italy's sphere of interest. Laval was to say later that he had had in mind a role for Italy similar to that of France in Morocco—that is, one of indirect control. But Mussolini could not be expected to understand that France and Great Britain, having conceded this much, would sacrifice a near-alliance against Germany over the distinction between annexation and indirect control over Abyssinia.

France and Great Britain never came to grips with the reality that they faced two mutually exclusive options. If they concluded that Italy was essential to protecting Austria and, indirectly, perhaps even to helping maintain the demilitarized Rhineland it had guaranteed at Locarno, they would have needed to come up with some compromise to save Italy's face in Africa and to keep the Stresa front intact. Alternatively, if the League was indeed the best instrument for both containing Germany and for rallying the Western public against aggression, it was necessary to pursue sanctions until it had been demonstrated that aggression did not pay. There was no middle ground.

Yet the middle ground was exactly what the democracies, no longer having the self-confidence to define their choices, sought. Under British leadership, the League machinery of economic sanctions was activated. At the same time, Laval privately assured Mussolini that Italy's access to oil would not be disrupted. Great Britain pursued essentially the same course by politely inquiring in Rome whether oil sanctions would lead to war. When Mussolini—both predictably and untruthfully—answered in the affirmative, the British Cabinet had the alibi it needed to combine its support for the League with an appeal to the widespread dread of war. This policy came to be expressed in the slogan "all sanctions short of war."

Later, Prime Minister Stanley Baldwin was to say somewhat wistfully that any sanctions that were likely to have worked would also have been likely to lead to war. So much, at any rate, for the notion that economic sanctions provide an alternative to force in resisting aggression—an argument that would be repeated some fifty years later in the United States over the issue of how to deal with Iraq's annexation of Kuwait, albeit with a happier outcome.

Foreign Secretary Samuel Hoare understood that Great Britain had derailed its own strategy. To resist the impending German threat, Great Britain's leaders should have confronted Hitler and conciliated Mussolini. They did just the opposite: they appeased Germany and confronted Italy. Grasping the absurdity of this state of affairs, Hoare and Laval devised a compromise in December 1935: Italy would receive Abyssinia's fertile plains; Haile Selassie would continue to rule in the mountain fastness which was the historical site of his kingdom; Great Britain would contribute to these compromises by giving landlocked Abyssinia access to the sea via British Somalia. Mussolini was fully expected to accept the plan, and Hoare was to present it for League approval.

The Hoare-Laval plan came to naught because it was leaked to the press before it could be placed before the League of Nations—an extraordinarily rare event in those days. The resulting cry of outrage forced Hoare to resign—the victim of seeking a practical compromise in the face of an aroused public opinion. Anthony Eden, his successor, speedily returned to the cocoon of collective security and economic sanctions—without, however, being willing to resort to force.

In a pattern that would be repeated in successive crises, the democracies justified their aversion to using force by vastly overestimating the military prowess of the adversary. London convinced itself that it could not handle the Italian fleet without French assistance. France went along halfheartedly and moved its fleet to the Mediterranean, further jeopardizing its relationship with Italy as a Locarno guarantor and a Stresa partner. Even with this overwhelming accumulation of force, oil sanctions were never invoked. And ordinary sanctions did not work rapidly enough to prevent Abyssinia's defeat—if indeed they could have worked at all.

Italy's conquest of Abyssinia was completed by May 1936, when Mussolini proclaimed the king of Italy, Victor Emmanuel, as emperor of the newly named Ethiopia. Less than two months later, on June 30, the Council of the League of Nations met to consider the *fait accompli*. Haile Selassie sounded the death knell of collective security in a forlorn personal appeal:

> It is not merely a question of a settlement in the matter of Italian aggression. It is a question of collective security; of the very existence of the League; of the trust placed by States in international treaties; of the value of promises made to small states that their integrity and their independence shall be respected and assured. It is a choice between the principle of equality of States and the imposition upon small Powers of the bonds of vassalage.[19]

On July 15, the League lifted all sanctions against Italy. Two years later, in the wake of Munich, Great Britain and France subordinated their moral objections to their fear of Germany by recognizing the Abyssinian conquest. Collective security had condemned Haile Selassie to losing *all* of his country rather than the half he would have lost under the *Realpolitik* of the Hoare-Laval plan.

In terms of military power, Italy was not remotely comparable to Great Britain, France, or Germany. But the void created by the aloofness of the Soviet Union turned Italy into a useful auxiliary in maintaining the independence of Austria and, to a limited extent, of the demilitarized Rhineland. As long as Great Britain and France had appeared to be the strongest nations in Europe, Mussolini had supported the Versailles settlement, especially since he profoundly distrusted Germany and at first disdained Hitler's personality. His resentment over Ethiopia, coupled with his analysis of the actual power relationships, convinced Mussolini that persistence in the Stresa front might end up compelling Italy to bear the full brunt of German aggressiveness. Ethiopia therefore marked the beginning of Italy's inexorable march toward Germany, motivated in equal parts by acquisitiveness and fear.

It was in Germany, however, that the Ethiopian fiasco left the most lasting impression. The British Ambassador in Berlin reported: "Italy's victory opened a new chapter. It was unavoidable that in a land where power is worshipped England's prestige would sink."[20] With Italy out of the Stresa front, Germany's sole remaining obstacle on the road to Austria and Central Europe was the open door provided by the demilitarized Rhineland. And Hitler wasted no time slamming it.

On the morning of Sunday, March 7, 1936, Hitler ordered his army into the demilitarized Rhineland, marking the overthrow of the last remaining safeguard of the Versailles settlement. According to the Versailles Treaty, German military forces were barred from the Rhineland and a zone of fifty kilometers to the east of it. Germany had confirmed this provision at Locarno; the League of Nations had endorsed Locarno, and Great Britain, France, Belgium, and Italy had guaranteed it.

If Hitler could prevail in the Rhineland, Eastern Europe would be at Germany's mercy. None of the new states of Eastern Europe stood a chance of defending themselves against a revisionist Germany, either through their own efforts or in combination with each other. Their only hope was that France could deter German aggression by threatening to march into the Rhineland.

Once again, the Western democracies were torn by uncertainty over Hitler's intentions. Technically, he was merely reoccupying German territory. Simultaneously, he was offering all sorts of reassurances, including the offer of a nonaggression treaty with France. Once again, it was argued that Germany would be satisfied as soon as it had been conceded the right to defend its own national borders, something every other European nation simply took for granted. Did British and French leaders have the moral right to risk their peoples' lives in order to maintain a so blatantly discriminatory state of affairs? On the other hand, was it not their moral duty to confront Hitler while Germany was not yet fully armed, and thereby possibly save untold lives?

History has given the answer; contemporaries, however, were tormented by doubt. For, in 1936, Hitler continued to benefit from his unique combination of psychotic intuition and demonic willpower. The democracies still believed that they were dealing with a normal, if somewhat excessive, national leader who was seeking to restore his country to a position of equality in Europe. Great Britain and France were absorbed in trying to read Hitler's mind. Was he sincere? Did he really want peace? To be sure, these were valid questions, but foreign policy builds on quicksand when it disregards actual power relationships and relies on prophesies of another's intentions.

With his uncanny ability to exploit his adversaries' weaknesses, Hitler chose precisely the right moment to reoccupy the Rhineland. The League of Nations, bogged down in sanctions against Italy, was far from eager to take on a confrontation with another major power. The war in Abyssinia had driven a wedge between the Western Powers and Italy, one of the guarantors of Locarno. Great Britain, another guarantor, having just recoiled from imposing oil sanctions against Italy at sea, where it was dominant, would surely be even less eager to risk ground warfare for a cause which involved no violation of national boundaries.

Though no country had a bigger stake in a demilitarized Rhineland than France, none was more ambivalent about resisting Germany's violation of it. The Maginot Line bespoke France's obsession with the strategic defensive, and the military equipment and training of the French army left little doubt that the First World War had quenched its traditional offensive spirit. France seemed resigned to await its fate behind the Maginot Line and to risk nothing beyond its frontiers—not in Eastern Europe or, for that matter, in the Rhineland.

Nevertheless, the reoccupation of the Rhineland represented a bold gamble on Hitler's part. Conscription had been in effect for less than a year. The German army was far from ready for war. Indeed, the small advance guard entering the demilitarized zone was ordered to conduct a fighting retreat at the first signs of French intervention. Hitler, however, compensated for his lack of military strength with ample psychological daring. He flooded the democracies with proposals hinting at his willingness to discuss troop limitations in the Rhineland and to bring Germany back into the League of Nations. He appealed to widespread distrust of the Soviet Union by claiming his move was a riposte to the Franco-Soviet Pact of 1935. He offered a fifty-kilometer demilitarized zone on both sides of the German frontier and a twenty-five-year nonaggression treaty. The demilitarization proposal had the double virtue of hinting that permanent peace was only the stroke of a pen away, while neatly demolishing the Maginot Line, which backed up against the German frontier.

Hitler's interlocutors did not require a great deal of encouragement to adopt a passive stance. A convenient alibi here and there suited their preference for doing nothing. Ever since Locarno, it had been a cardinal principle of French policy never to risk war with Germany except in alliance with Great Britain, though British assistance was technically unnecessary so long as Germany remained disarmed. In the single-minded pursuit of that goal, French leaders had swallowed countless frustrations and supported many disarmament initiatives which, in their hearts, they knew to be ill-conceived.

302

France's overwhelming psychological dependence on Great Britain may explain why it made no military preparations, not even when the French Ambassador in Berlin, André François-Poncet, warned on November 21, 1935, that a German move on the Rhineland was imminent—a full three and a half months before it actually occurred.[21] Yet France dared neither to mobilize nor to undertake precautionary military measures lest it be accused of provoking what it feared. France also did not raise the issue in negotiations with Germany because it did not know what to do if Germany ignored its warnings or declared its intentions.

What is nearly inexplicable about France's conduct in 1935, however, is why the French general staff made no provisions whatsoever in its own internal planning even after François-Poncet's warning. Did the French general staff not believe its own diplomats? Was it because France could not bring itself to leave the shelter of its fortifications even in defense of the vital buffer zone represented by the demilitarized Rhineland? Or did France already feel so utterly doomed that its primary goal had become to defer war in the hope that some unforeseeable change would occur in its favor—though it would no longer be able to bring such a change about by its own actions?

The towering symbol for this state of mind was, of course, the Maginot Line, which France had constructed at huge cost over a period of ten years. France had thereby committed itself to the strategic defensive in the very year when it had guaranteed the independence of Poland and Czechoslovakia. A sign of equal confusion was the incomprehensible French decision to stop construction of the Maginot Line at the Belgian frontier, which belied all the experiences of the First World War. For, if a Franco-German war was indeed possible, then why not a German assault through Belgium? If France feared that Belgium would collapse if it indicated that the main line of defense excluded that country, Belgium could have been given the choice of agreeing to the extension of the Maginot Line along the Belgian-German frontier, and, if this were rejected, the Maginot Line could have been extended to the sea along the Franco-Belgian frontier. France did neither.

What political leaders decide, intelligence services tend to seek to justify. Popular literature and films often depict the opposite—policymakers as the helpless tools of intelligence experts. In the real world, intelligence assessments more often follow than guide policy decisions. This may explain the wild exaggeration of German strength that blighted French military estimates. At the time of the German reoccupation of the Rhineland, General Maurice Gamelin, the French Commander-in-Chief, told civilian leaders that Germany's trained military manpower already equaled that of France, and that Germany had more equipment than France—an absurd estimate in the second year of German rearmament. Policy recommendations flowed from this flawed premise of German military might. Gamelin concluded that France must not undertake *any* military countermeasures without general mobilization, a step which its political leaders would not risk without British support—not even though the German force entering the Rhineland numbered about 20,000, while the French standing army could count on 500,000 even without mobilization.

Everything now came back to the dilemma which had bedeviled the democracies for twenty years. Great Britain would recognize only one threat to the European balance of power—the violation of France's borders. Determined never to fight for Eastern Europe, it perceived no vital British interest in a demilitarized Rhineland serving as a kind of hostage in the West. Nor would Great Britain go to war to uphold its own Locarno guarantee. Eden had made this clear a month before the occupation of the Rhineland. In February 1936, the French government finally roused itself to inquire of Great Britain what its position would be if Hitler carried out what François-Poncet had reported. Eden's treatment of the potential violation of two international agreements—Versailles and Locarno—sounded like the opening of a commercial bargain:

> . . . as the zone was constituted primarily to give security to France and Belgium, it is for these two Governments, in the first instance, to make up their minds as to what value they attach to, and what price they are prepared to pay for, its maintenance. . . . It would be preferable for Great Britain and France to enter betimes into negotiations with the German Government for the surrender on conditions of our rights in the zone while such surrender still has a bargaining value.[22]

Eden in effect took the position that the best that could be hoped for was a negotiation in which the Allies, in return for giving up established and recognized rights (and in which Great Britain refused to honor its own guarantee), would receive—what exactly? Time? Other assurances? Great Britain left the answer regarding the *quid pro quo* to France, but conveyed by its conduct that fighting on behalf of solemn obligations in the Rhineland was not part of the British strategy.

After Hitler marched into the Rhineland, Great Britain's attitude became even more explicit. The day after the German move, the British Secretary of State for War told the German Ambassador:

> . . . though the British people were prepared to fight for France in the event of a German incursion into French territory, they would not

resort to arms on account of the recent occupation of the Rhineland.
... [M]ost of them [the British people] probably took the view that they
did not care "two hoots" about the Germans reoccupying their own
territory.[23]

Great Britain's doubts were soon extended even to countermeasures
short of war. The Foreign Office told the American chargé d'affaires:
"England would make every endeavour to prevent the imposition of
military and/or economic sanctions against Germany."[24]

Foreign Minister Pierre Flandin pleaded France's case in vain. He presciently told the British that, once Germany had fortified the Rhineland,
Czechoslovakia would be lost and that, soon after, general war would
become unavoidable. Although he was proved right, it was never altogether clear whether Flandin was seeking British support for French
military action or developing a French alibi for inaction. Churchill obviously thought the latter, noting dryly, "These were brave words; but
action would have spoken louder."[25]

Great Britain was deaf to Flandin's entreaties. The vast majority of its
leadership still believed that peace depended on disarmament, and that
the new international order would have to be based on reconciliation
with Germany. The British felt that it was more important to rectify the
mistakes of Versailles than to vindicate the commitments of Locarno. A
Cabinet minute of March 17—ten days after Hitler's move—noted that
"our own attitude had been governed by the desire to utilize Herr Hitler's
offers in order to obtain a permanent settlement."[26]

What the Cabinet had to say *sotto voce*, the Opposition felt quite free
to put forward without restraint. During the course of a debate on defense
matters in the House of Commons that same month, it was declared by
Labour member Arthur Greenwood:

> Herr Hitler made a statement sinning with one hand but holding out
> the olive branch with the other, which ought to be taken at face value.
> They may prove to be the most important gestures yet made.... It is
> idle to say these statements were insincere.... The issue is peace and
> not defence.[27]

In other words, the Opposition clearly advocated the revision of Versailles and the abandonment of Locarno. They wanted Great Britain to sit
back and wait for Hitler's purposes to become clearer. It was a reasonable
policy as long as its advocates understood that every passing year would
increase exponentially the ultimate cost of resistance should the policy
fail.

It is not necessary to retrace step by step the path by which France and Great Britain attempted to transform strategic dross into political gold, or upheaval into an opportunity for the policy of appeasement. What matters is that, at the end of this process, the Rhineland was fortified, Eastern Europe had fallen beyond the reach of French military assistance, and Italy was moving closer to providing Hitler's Germany with its first ally. Just as France had been reconciled to Locarno by an ambiguous British guarantee—whose virtue in British eyes had been that it was *less* than an alliance—so the abrogation of Locarno elicited the even more ambiguous British commitment to send two divisions to defend France should the French border be violated.

Once again, Great Britain had skillfully dodged a full commitment to defend France. But what exactly did it achieve? France, of course, saw through the evasion but accepted it as a halfhearted British step toward the long-sought formal alliance. Great Britain interpreted its pledge of two divisions as a means of restraining France from undertaking a defense of Eastern Europe. For the British commitment would not apply if the French army invaded Germany in defense of Czechoslovakia or Poland. On the other hand, two British divisions were not remotely relevant to the problem of deterring a German attack on France. Great Britain, the mother country of the balance-of-power policy, had totally lost touch with its operating principles.

For Hitler, the reoccupation of the Rhineland opened the road to Central Europe, militarily as well as psychologically. Once the democracies had accepted it as a *fait accompli,* the strategic basis for resisting Hitler in Eastern Europe disappeared. "If on 7 March you could not defend yourself," asked the Romanian Foreign Minister, Nicolae Titulescu, of his French counterpart, "how will you defend us against the aggressor?"[28] The question grew increasingly unanswerable as the Rhineland was being fortified.

Psychologically, the impact of the democracies' passive stance was even more profound. Appeasement now became an official policy, and rectifying the inequities of Versailles the conventional wisdom. In the West, there was no longer anything left to rectify. But it stood to reason that, if France and Great Britain would not defend Locarno, which they had guaranteed, there was not a chance of their upholding the Versailles settlement in Eastern Europe, which Great Britain had questioned from the beginning and had explicitly refused to guarantee on more than one occasion—the last time in the undertaking to send two divisions to France.

By now, France had abandoned the Richelieu traditions. It no longer

relied even on itself, but sought surcease from its dangers through German goodwill. In August 1936, five months after the reoccupation of
the Rhineland, Dr. Hjalmar Schacht, Germany's Economics Minister, was
received in Paris by Léon Blum—Prime Minister of a Popular Front government containing communists and a Jew. "I am a Marxist and a Jew,"
said Blum, but "we cannot achieve anything if we treat ideological barriers as insurmountable."[29] Blum's Foreign Minister, Yvon Delbos, was at a
loss as to how to describe what this meant practically, other than "making
concessions to Germany piecemeal in order to stave off war."[30] Nor did
he explain whether this process had a terminal point. France, the country
which, for 200 years, had fought innumerable wars in Central Europe in
order to control its own fate, had retreated to grasping at whatever security could be wrung out of trading piecemeal concessions for time and to
hoping that, along the way, either German appetites would become satiated or some other *deus ex machina* would remove the danger.

The policy of appeasement which France implemented warily, Great
Britain pursued eagerly. In 1937, the year after the Rhineland was remilitarized, British Foreign Secretary Lord Halifax symbolized the democracies' moral retreat by visiting Hitler's aerie at Berchtesgaden. He praised
Nazi Germany "as the bulwark of Europe against Bolshevism" and listed
a number of issues with respect to which "possible alterations might be
destined to come about with the passage of time." Danzig, Austria, and
Czechoslovakia were specifically mentioned. Halifax's only caveat related
to the method by which the changes would be accomplished: "England
was interested to see that any alterations should come through the course
of peaceful evolution and that methods should be avoided which might
cause far-reaching disturbances."[31]

It would have taxed the comprehension of a less determined leader
than Hitler why, if it was prepared to concede adjustments in Austria,
Czechoslovakia, and the Polish Corridor, Great Britain would balk at the
method Germany used to make those adjustments. Having yielded the
substance, why should Great Britain draw the line at procedure? What
possible peaceful argument did Halifax expect could convince the victims
of the merits of suicide? League orthodoxy and the doctrine of collective
security had it that it was the *method* of change which had to be resisted;
but history teaches that nations go to war in order to resist the *fact* of
change.

By the time of Halifax's visit to Hitler, France's strategic situation had
deteriorated even further. In July 1936, a military coup led by General
Francisco Franco had triggered the Spanish Civil War. Franco was openly
supported by large shipments of equipment from Germany and Italy;

soon thereafter, German and Italian "volunteers" were dispatched, and fascism seemed poised to spread its ideas by force. France now faced the same challenge Richelieu had resisted 300 years earlier—the prospect of hostile governments on all its borders. But unlike their great predecessor, the French governments of the 1930s dithered, unable to decide which they feared more—the dangers they were facing or the means needed to redress them.

Great Britain had participated in the wars of the Spanish succession early in the eighteenth century, and against Napoleon in Spain a century later. In each case, Great Britain had resisted the most aggressive European power's attempt to draw Spain into its orbit. Now it either failed to perceive a threat to the balance of power in a fascist victory in Spain or it perceived fascism as a lesser threat than a radical left-wing Spain tied to the Soviet Union (which seemed to many to be the most likely alternative). But, above all, Great Britain wanted to avoid a war. Its Cabinet warned France that Great Britain reserved the right to remain neutral if a war should result from French arms deliveries to republican Spain— even though, under international law, France had every right to sell arms to the legitimate Spanish government. France waffled, then proclaimed an embargo on arms shipments while periodically acquiescing in its violation. That policy, however, only demoralized France's friends and cost France the respect of its adversaries.

In this atmosphere, French and British leaders met in London on November 29–30, 1937, to chart a common course. Neville Chamberlain, who had replaced Baldwin as prime minister, came straight to the point. He invited discussion of the obligations inherent in France's alliance with Czechoslovakia. This is the sort of query diplomats initiate when they are looking for loopholes in order to escape honoring their commitments. Presumably, the independence of Austria was not even worth talking about.

French Foreign Minister Delbos responded in a manner which conveyed that he had understood the implications of the question very well indeed. Treating the Czech issue in terms of juridical rather than political or strategic considerations, he confined himself to a strictly legal exegesis of France's obligation:

> ... this treaty engaged France in the event of Czechoslovakia being a victim of an aggression. If uprisings among the German population occurred and were supported by armed intervention from Germany, the treaty committed France in a manner to be determined according to the gravity of the facts.[32]

Delbos did not discuss the geopolitical importance of Czechoslovakia or the impact which France's abandonment of an ally would have on his country's credibility in maintaining the independence of other countries in Eastern Europe. Instead, he stressed that France's obligations might or might not apply to the one realistic existing threat—unrest among Czechoslovakia's German minority backed by German military force. Chamberlain grasped at the proffered loophole and turned it into a rationale for appeasement:

> It seemed desirable to try to achieve some agreement with Germany on Central Europe, whatever might be Germany's aims, even if she wished to absorb some of her neighbours; one could in effect hope to delay the execution of German plans, and even to restrain the Reich for such a time that its plans might become impractical in the long run.[33]

But if procrastination did not work, what was Great Britain going to do? Having conceded that Germany would revise its eastern borders, would Great Britain go to war over the timetable? The answer was self-evident —countries do not go to war over the rate of change by which something they have already conceded is being achieved. Czechoslovakia was doomed not at Munich but at London, nearly a year earlier.

As it happened, Hitler had decided at about the same time to sketch his own long-term strategy. The occasion was an assemblage of almost all of Germany's general officers, whom, on November 5, 1937, Hitler treated to a candid exposé of his strategic views. His adjutant, Hossbach, kept a detailed record. No one present had cause to complain afterward that he did not know in which direction his leader was heading. For Hitler made it clear that his aims went far beyond an attempt to restore Germany's pre–World War I position. What Hitler outlined was the program of *Mein Kampf*—the conquest of large tracts of land in Eastern Europe and in the Soviet Union for colonization. Hitler knew very well that such a project would encounter resistance: "German policy [would] have to reckon with the two hateful antagonists England and France."[34] He stressed that Germany had stolen a march on Great Britain and France in its rearmament but that the advantage was transitory and would diminish at an accelerating rate after 1943. War, therefore, had to start before then.

Hitler's generals were disturbed by the vastness of his plans and by the imminence of their execution. But they timidly swallowed Hitler's designs. Some military leaders toyed vaguely with the idea of a coup once Hitler had given the actual order to go to war. But Hitler always moved too fast. His stunning early successes deprived his generals of the moral justification (in their eyes) for such a step—not that making coups against constituted authority had ever been a specialty of German generals.

As for the Western democracies, they did not yet grasp the ideological gulf that separated them from the German dictator. They believed in peace as an end, and were straining their every nerve to avoid war. Hitler, on the other hand, feared peace and craved war. "Mankind has grown strong in eternal struggles," he had written in *Mein Kampf;* "and it will only perish through eternal peace."[35]

By 1938, Hitler felt strong enough to cross the national boundaries established at Versailles. His first target was his native country of Austria, which had been left in an anomalous position by the settlements of St.-Germain in 1919 and Trianon in 1920 (the equivalent of Versailles for the Austro-Hungarian Empire). Until 1806, Austria had been the center of the Holy Roman Empire; until 1866, it had been a leading—for some, *the* leading—German state. Expelled from its historic role in Germany by Bismarck, it had shifted its emphasis to its Balkan and Central European possessions until it lost them as well in the First World War. A one-time empire shrunk to its small German-speaking core, Austria had been prohibited by the Treaty of Versailles from joining Germany—a clause which stood in obvious defiance of the principle of self-determination. Even though *Anschluss* with Germany remained the goal of many on both sides of the Austro-German border (including Stresemann), it was again blocked by the Allies in 1930.

Thus, the union of Germany and Austria had about it that sense of ambiguity so essential to the success of Hitler's early challenges. It fulfilled the principle of self-determination while undermining the balance of power, which statesmen were less and less willing to invoke to justify the use of force. After a month of Nazi threats and Austrian concessions and second thoughts, on March 12, 1938, German troops marched into Austria. There was no resistance, and the Austrian population, much of it deliriously joyful, seemed to feel that, shorn of its empire and left helpless in Central Europe, it preferred a future as a German province to being a minor player on the Central European stage.

The democracies' halfhearted protests against Germany's annexation of Austria hardly registered moral concern while shying away from any concrete measures. As the death knell of collective security was sounded, the League of Nations stood silent while a member country was swallowed by a powerful neighbor. The democracies now turned doubly committed to appeasement in the hope that Hitler would stop his march once he had returned all ethnic Germans to the fatherland.

Destiny chose Czechoslovakia as the subject of that experiment. Like other successor states of Austro-Hungary, it was nearly as multinational as the Empire had been. Out of a population of some 15 million, nearly a third were neither Czech nor Slovak, and the Slovak commitment to the state was shaky. Three and a half million Germans, close to a million Hungarians, and nearly half a million Poles were incorporated into the new state. To exacerbate matters, these minorities dwelled in territories contiguous to their ethnic homelands, which rendered the claim that they should rejoin their mother countries even more weighty in light of the prevailing Versailles orthodoxy of self-determination.

At the same time, Czechoslovakia was politically and economically the most advanced of the successor states. It was genuinely democratic and had a standard of living comparable to Switzerland's. It maintained a large army, much of whose excellent equipment was of domestic Czech design and manufacture; it had military alliances with France and the Soviet Union. In terms of traditional diplomacy, therefore, it was no easy matter to abandon Czechoslovakia; in terms of self-determination, it was equally difficult to defend it. Emboldened by his successful remilitarization of the Rhineland, Hitler began in 1937 to threaten Czechoslovakia on behalf of its ethnic Germans. At first, these threats were ostensibly to pressure the Czechs into granting special rights to the German minority in "Sudeten-land," as the German propaganda dubbed that territory. But in 1938, Hitler turned up the heat of his rhetoric by intimating that he intended to annex Sudetenland into the German Reich by force. France was commit-ted to protecting Czechoslovakia, as was the Soviet Union, though Soviet help for the Czechs had been made conditional on prior French actions. Moreover, whether Poland or Romania would have allowed Soviet troops to traverse their territory in defense of Czechoslovakia remains very doubtful.

From the start, Great Britain opted for appeasement. On March 22, shortly after the annexation of Austria, Halifax reminded the French lead-ers that the Locarno guarantee applied only to the French border and might lapse if France implemented its treaty commitments in Central Europe. A Foreign Office memorandum warned: "Those commitments [the Locarno guarantee] are, in their view, no mean contribution to the maintenance of peace in Europe and, though they have no intention of withdrawing from them, they cannot see their way to add to them."[36] Great Britain's sole security frontier was at the borders of France; if France's security concerns extended any further, specifically, if it tried to defend Czechoslovakia, it would be on its own.

A few months later, the British Cabinet sent a fact-finding mission to Prague under Lord Runciman to explore possible means of conciliation.

The practical consequence of that mission was to advertise Great Britain's reluctance to defend Czechoslovakia. The facts were already well known; any conceivable conciliation would have required some dismemberment of Czechoslovakia. Munich, therefore, was not a surrender but a state of mind and the nearly inevitable outgrowth of the democracies' effort to sustain a geopolitically flawed settlement with rhetoric about collective security and self-determination.

Even America, the country most identified with the creation of Czechoslovakia, dissociated itself from the crisis at an early stage. In September, President Roosevelt suggested holding a negotiation on some neutral ground.[37] Yet, if American embassies abroad were reporting accurately, Roosevelt could have had no illusion about the attitudes which France, and even more so Great Britain, would bring to any such conference. Indeed, Roosevelt reinforced these attitudes by making the statement that "the Government of the United States ... will assume no obligations in the conduct of the present negotiations."[38]

The situation was as if made to order for Hitler's talent in waging psychological warfare. Throughout the summer, he worked to magnify hysteria about an imminent war without, in fact, making any specific threat. Finally, after Hitler had engaged in a vicious personal attack on the Czech leadership at the annual Nazi Party rally in Nuremberg in early September 1938, Chamberlain's nerves snapped. Though no formal demands had been made and no real diplomatic exchanges had taken place, Chamberlain decided to end the tension on September 15 by visiting Hitler. Hitler showed his disdain by choosing Berchtesgaden as the meeting place—the location in Germany farthest from London and the least accessible. In those days, traveling from London to Berchtesgaden required an airplane trip of five hours, in what turned out to be Chamberlain's first flight, at the age of sixty-nine.

After enduring several hours of Hitler's ranting about the alleged mistreatment of the Sudeten Germans, Chamberlain agreed to dismember Czechoslovakia. All Czechoslovak districts with populations that were more than 50-percent German were to be returned to Germany. The details were to be worked out at a second meeting in a few days' time, at Bad Godesberg, in the Rhineland. It was symptomatic of Hitler's negotiating style that he termed this subsequent locale a "concession"; though much closer to London than the first site, it was still well within Germany. In the interval, Chamberlain "persuaded" the Czechoslovak government to accept his proposal—"sadly" so, in the words of the Czech leaders.[39]

At Bad Godesberg on September 22, Hitler raised the ante and made it clear that he sought the abject humiliation of Czechoslovakia. He would not agree to the time-consuming procedure of district-by-district plebiscites and frontier demarcations, demanding instead the immediate evacuation of the entire Sudeten territory, the process to start on September 26—four days later—to be completed in no more than forty-eight hours. Czech military installations were to be left intact for the German armed forces. To weaken the rump state even further, Hitler demanded border rectifications for Hungary and Poland on behalf of their own minorities. When Chamberlain objected to being presented with an ultimatum, Hitler snidely pointed to the word "memorandum" typed on top of his presentation. After hours of acrimonious argument, Hitler made another "concession": he would give Czechoslovakia until 2:00 P.M. on September 28 to reply, and until October 1 to begin withdrawing from the Sudeten territory.

Chamberlain could not bring himself to inflict such a total humiliation on Czechoslovakia, and French Prime Minister Daladier drew the line even more adamantly. For some days, war seemed imminent. Trenches were being dug in British parks. This was the period in which Chamberlain made the melancholy comment that Great Britain was being asked to go to war for a faraway country about which it knew nothing—this from the leader of a country which had fought for centuries on the approaches to India without blinking.

But what was the *casus belli?* Great Britain had already accepted the principle of Czechoslovak dismemberment along with self-determination for the Sudeten Germans. Great Britain and France were approaching the decision to go to war not in order to sustain an ally but over the few weeks' difference in the rate at which it would be dismantled and a few territorial adjustments which were marginal compared to what had already been conceded. Perhaps it was just as well that Mussolini took everybody off the hook right before the deadline by proposing that a conference already being planned between the foreign ministers of Italy and Germany be expanded to include the heads of government of France (Daladier), Great Britain (Chamberlain), Germany (Hitler), and Italy (Mussolini).

The four leaders met on September 29 in Munich, the birthplace of the Nazi Party, the sort of symbolism victors reserve for themselves. Little time was spent on negotiations: Chamberlain and Daladier made a halfhearted attempt to return to their original proposal; Mussolini produced a paper containing Hitler's Bad Godesberg proposal; Hitler defined the issues in the form of a sarcastic ultimatum. Since his deadline of October 1 had caused him to be accused of proceeding in an atmosphere of violence, he said that the task at hand was "to absolve the action of such a character."[40] In other words, the sole purpose of the conference was to accept Hitler's Bad Godesberg program peacefully before he went to war to impose it.

Chamberlain and Daladier's conduct over the previous months gave them no real choice but to accept Mussolini's draft. Czech representatives were left languishing in anterooms while their country was being dismembered. The Soviet Union was not invited at all. Great Britain and France assuaged their guilty consciences by offering to guarantee the remaining fragment of disarmed Czechoslovakia—a preposterous gesture coming from nations which had refused to honor the guarantee of an intact, well-armed fellow democracy. It goes without saying that the guarantee was never implemented.

Munich has entered our vocabulary as a specific aberration—the penalty of yielding to blackmail. Munich, however, was not a single act but the culmination of an attitude which began in the 1920s and accelerated with each new concession. For over a decade, Germany had been throwing off the restrictions of Versailles one by one: the Weimar Republic had rid Germany of reparations, of the Inter-Allied Military Control Commission, and of Allied occupation of the Rhineland. Hitler had denounced the restrictions on German armaments, the prohibition against conscription, and the demilitarization provisions of Locarno. Even in the 1920s, Germany had never accepted the Eastern frontiers, and the Allies had never insisted that it accept them. Finally, as so often happens, decisions cumulatively developed their own momentum.

By conceding that the Versailles settlement was iniquitous, the victors eroded the psychological basis for defending it. The victors of the Napoleonic Wars had made a generous peace, but they had also organized the Quadruple Alliance in order to leave no ambiguity about their determination to defend it. The victors of World War I had made a punitive peace and, after having themselves created the maximum incentive for revisionism, cooperated in dismantling their own settlement.

For two decades, the balance of power had been alternately rejected and ridiculed; the leaders of the democracies told their peoples that, henceforth, the world order would be based on a higher morality. Then, when the challenge to the new world order finally came, the democracies —Great Britain with conviction, France with doubt tinged by despair— had no recourse but to drain the cup of conciliation to demonstrate to their peoples that Hitler could not in fact be appeased.

This explains why the Munich agreement was greeted with such wild acclaim by the vast majority of its contemporaries. Franklin Roosevelt was among those congratulating Chamberlain: "Good man," he said.[41] The leaders of the British Commonwealth were more effusive. The Prime Minister of Canada wrote:

> May I convey to you the warm congratulations of the Canadian people, and with them, an expression of their gratitude, which is felt from one end of the dominion to the other. My colleagues and Government join with me in unbounded admiration at the service you have rendered mankind.[42]

Not to be outdone, the Australian Prime Minister said:

> Colleagues and I desire to express our warmest congratulations at the outcome of the negotiations at Munich. Australians in common with all other peoples of the British empire owe a deep debt of gratitude to you for your unceasing efforts to preserve the peace.[43]

Strangely enough, all of the eyewitnesses to the Munich Conference concurred that, far from triumphant, Hitler was morose. He had wanted war, which he regarded as indispensable to the realization of his ambitions. He probably needed it for psychological reasons as well; nearly all of his public utterances, which he viewed as the most vital aspect of his public life, related in one way or another to his wartime experiences. Even though Hitler's generals strongly opposed war—to the point of fitfully planning to overthrow him should he make a final decision to attack— Hitler left Munich with the sense of having been cheated. And, by his own inverted reasoning, he may well have been right. For had he managed to contrive a war over Czechoslovakia, it is doubtful that the democracies could have sustained the sacrifices necessary to win it. The issue was too incompatible with the principle of self-determination, and public opinion was not sufficiently prepared for the almost certain initial reverses of such a war.

Paradoxically, Munich turned into the psychological end of the line for Hitler's strategy. Until then, he had always been able to appeal to the democracies' sense of guilt about the inequities of Versailles; afterward, his only weapon was brute force, and there was a limit to how much blackmail even those most afraid of war would accept before taking a stand.

This was especially true of Great Britain. By his conduct at Bad Godesberg and at Munich, Hitler used up the last reserves of British goodwill. Despite his fatuous statement of having brought "peace for our time," when he returned to London, Chamberlain was determined never to be blackmailed again, and launched a major rearmament program.

In fact, Chamberlain's conduct in the Munich crisis was more complex than posterity has depicted it. Wildly popular in the wake of Munich, he was ever after associated with surrender. The democratic public is unforgiving in the face of debacles, even when these result from carrying out its own immediate wishes. Chamberlain's reputation collapsed once it became clear that he had not achieved "peace for our time." Hitler soon found another pretext for war, and by then Chamberlain could not even garner credit for having managed the process by which Great Britain was able to weather the storm as a united people and with a restored air force.

In retrospect, it is easy to disparage the often naïve pronouncements of the appeasers. Yet most of them were decent men earnestly seeking to implement the new dispensation contrived by Wilsonian idealism under the cloud of general disillusionment with traditional European diplomacy, and the pervasive sense of spiritual and physical exhaustion. In no previous period could a British prime minister have justified an agreement, in the way Chamberlain had Munich—as a "removal of those suspicions and those animosities which have so long poisoned the air"[44] —as if foreign policy belonged to a branch of psychology. Still, these views had all sprung from an idealistic effort to transcend the legacies of *Realpolitik* and European history by appealing to reason and justice.

It did not take Hitler long to shatter the illusions of the appeasers, thereby hastening his own ultimate downfall. In March 1939, less than six months after Munich, Hitler occupied the rump of Czechoslovakia. The Czech portion became a German protectorate; Slovakia was designated a technically independent state, if a German satellite. Though Great Britain and France had offered to guarantee Czechoslovakia at Munich, that pledge was never formalized, nor could have been.

The destruction of Czechoslovakia made no geopolitical sense whatsoever; it showed that Hitler was beyond rational calculation and bent on war. Deprived of its defenses and of its French and Soviet alliances, Czechoslovakia was bound to slip into the German orbit, and Eastern Europe was certain to adjust to the new power realities. The Soviet Union had just purged its entire political and military leadership and would not be a factor for some time. All Hitler had to do was wait, because, with France in effect neutralized, Germany would eventually emerge as the dominant power in Eastern Europe. Waiting, of course, was what Hitler was emotionally least capable of doing.

The British and French reaction (spearheaded by London) of drawing the line made equally little sense in terms of traditional power politics. The seizure of Prague changed neither the balance of power nor the foreseeable course of events. But in terms of the Versailles principles, the occupation of Czechoslovakia marked a watershed because it demonstrated that Hitler sought the domination of Europe and not self-determination or equality.

Hitler's blunder was not so much to have violated historic principles of equilibrium as to have offended the moral premises of British postwar foreign policy. His transgression was to incorporate *non*-German populations into the Reich, thereby violating the principle of self-determination, on behalf of which all his previous unilateral exactions had been tolerated. Great Britain's patience was neither inexhaustible nor the result of a weak national character; and Hitler had, at last, fulfilled the British public's moral definition of aggression, if not yet the British government's. After a few days of hesitation, Chamberlain moved his policy into line with British public opinion. From that point on, Great Britain would resist Hitler not in order to comply with historic theories of equilibrium, but, quite simply, because Hitler could no longer be trusted.

Ironically, the Wilsonian approach to international relations, which had facilitated Hitler's advances beyond what any previous European system would have considered acceptable, after a certain point also caused Great Britain to draw the line more rigorously than it would have in a world based on *Realpolitik*. If Wilsonianism had prevented earlier resistance to Hitler, it also laid the foundation for implacable opposition to him once its moral criteria had been unambiguously violated.

When Hitler laid claim to Danzig in 1939 and sought modification of the Polish Corridor, the issues at hand were essentially no different from those of the year before. Danzig was a thoroughly German town, and its free-city status flew as much in the face of the principle of self-determination as had adjudication of the Sudeten territory to Czechoslovakia. Though the population of the Polish Corridor was more mixed, some adjustment of borders that was more responsive to the principle of self-determination was quite possible—at least theoretically. Yet what had changed beyond Hitler's comprehension was that, once he had crossed the line of what was morally tolerable, the same moral perfectionism which had formerly generated pliability in the democracies transformed itself into unprecedented intransigence. After Germany occupied Czechoslovakia, British public opinion would tolerate no further concessions; from then on, the outbreak of the Second World War was only a matter of time—unless Hitler remained quiescent, which, for him, proved psychologically impossible.

Before that momentous event could come to pass, however, the international system received one more shock—this time from the other great revisionist power it had ignored throughout most of the turbulent 1930s —Stalin's Soviet Union.

THE MAPS

French Expansion from 1648 to 1801   320

German Expansion from 1919 to 1939   321

William III's Grand Alliance from 1701 to 1713   322

Alliances in the 1950s   323

Europe After the Congress of Vienna, 1815   324

Europe on the Eve of the First World War, 1914   326

The Cold War World from 1945 to 1989   328

The Post–Cold War World   330

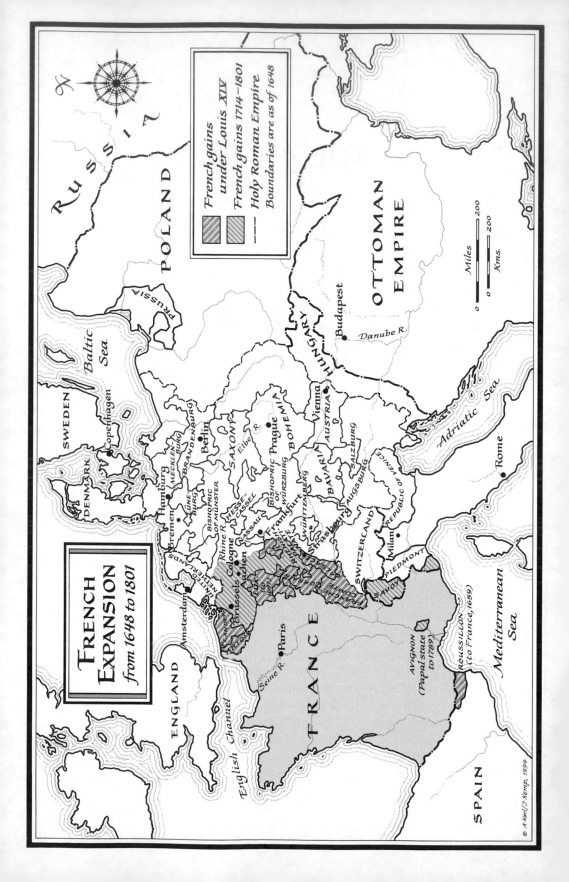

FRENCH EXPANSION from 1648 to 1801

French gains under Louis XIV
French gains 1714–1801
— Holy Roman Empire
Boundaries are as of 1648

Miles 200
Kms. 200

RUSSIA

POLAND

PRUSSIA

SWEDEN

Baltic Sea

DENMARK

Copenhagen

Hamburg

Bremen

MECKLEN-BURG

LÜNE-BURG

BRANDENBURG

Berlin

BISHOPRIC OF MÜNSTER

SAXONY

Elbe R.

Prague

BOHEMIA

Rhine R.

Cologne

HESSE CASSEL

Aachen

NASSAU

BISHOPRIC OF WÜRZBURG

Frankfurt

WÜRTTEMBERG

Vienna

AUSTRIA

HUNGARY

Budapest

Danube R.

OTTOMAN EMPIRE

Salzburg

AUGSBURG

BAVARIA

Strasbourg

SWITZERLAND

REPUBLIC OF VENICE

Adriatic Sea

Rome

Milan

PIEDMONT

SAVOY

Mediterranean Sea

UNITED NETHERLANDS

Amsterdam

Brussels

ENGLAND

English Channel

Seine R.

Paris

FRANCE

AVIGNON (Papal state to 1789)

ROUSSILLON (to France, 1659)

SPAIN

© A Karl/J Kemp, 1994

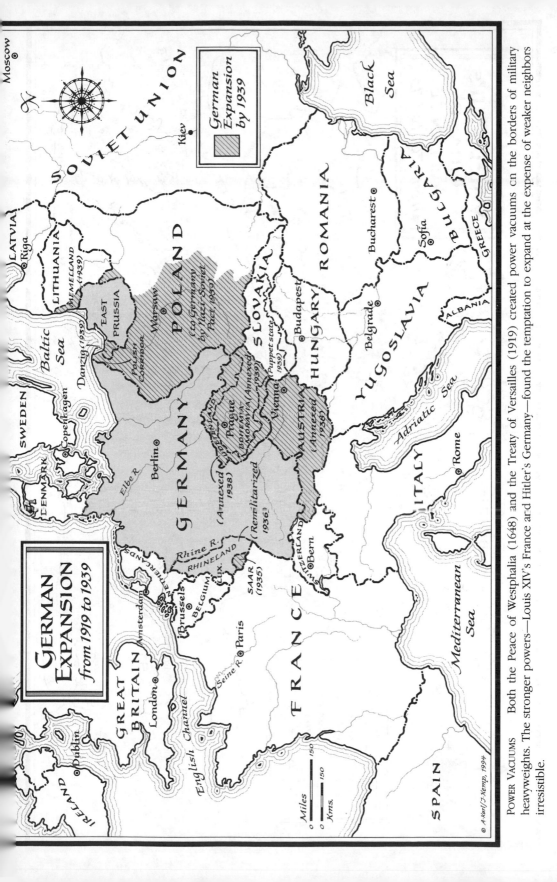

GERMAN EXPANSION
from 1919 to 1939

German Expansion by 1939

Moscow

SOVIET UNION

Kiev

N

LATVIA
Riga

LITHUANIA
MEMELLAND (1939)

EAST PRUSSIA

Danzig (1939)

Baltic Sea

SWEDEN

DENMARK
Copenhagen

POLAND
(to Germany by Nazi-Soviet Pact 1939)

Warsaw

POLISH CORRIDOR

Berlin

Elbe R.

GERMANY

SUDETENLAND
(Annexed 1938)

Prague

BOHEMIA-MORAVIA
(Annexed 1939)

SLOVAKIA
(Puppet state 1939)

Vienna

AUSTRIA
(Annexed 1938)

HUNGARY
Budapest

ROMANIA
Bucharest

Black Sea

BULGARIA
Sofia

GREECE

ALBANIA

YUGOSLAVIA
Belgrade

Adriatic Sea

(Annexed 1938)

RHINELAND
(Remilitarized 1936)

Rhine R.

SWITZERLAND
Bern

SAAR
(1935)

LUX.

BELGIUM
Brussels

NETHERLANDS
Amsterdam

GREAT BRITAIN
London

Dublin

IRELAND

English Channel

Seine R.
Paris

FRANCE

ITALY
Rome

Mediterranean Sea

SPAIN

Miles
0   150
Kms.
0   150

© A.Karl/J.Kemp, 1994

POWER VACUUMS   Both the Peace of Westphalia (1648) and the Treaty of Versailles (1919) created power vacuums on the borders of military heavyweights. The stronger powers—Louis XIV's France and Hitler's Germany—found the temptation to expand at the expense of weaker neighbors irresistible.

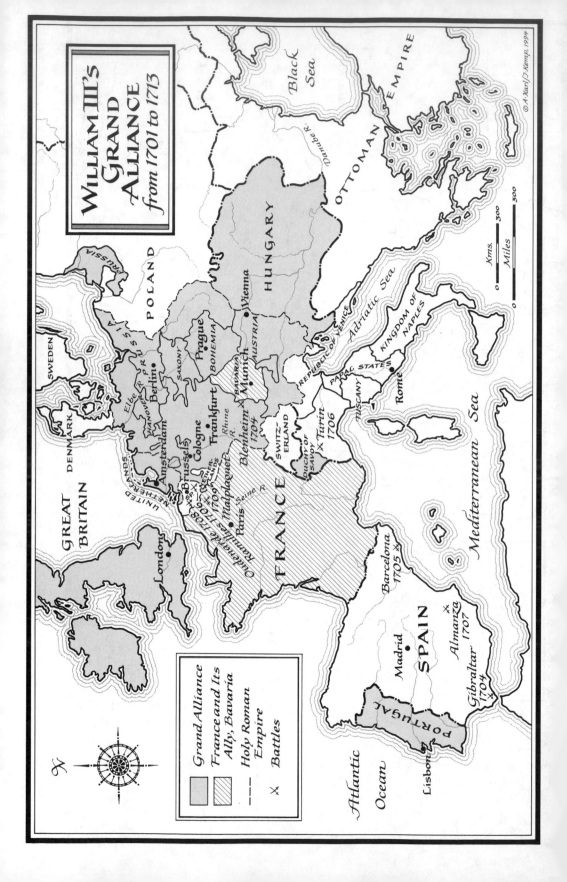

WILLIAM III'S GRAND ALLIANCE *from 1701 to 1713*

© A.Karl/J.Kemp, 1994

Black Sea

OTTOMAN EMPIRE

Danube R.

HUNGARY

SWEDEN

P R U S S I A

POLAND

Elbe R.

HANOVER

Berlin

SAXONY

Prague

BOHEMIA

Vienna

AUSTRIA

Munich

BAVARIA

Blenheim 1704

Adriatic Sea

REPUBLIC OF VENICE

PAPAL STATES

TUSCANY

Rome

KINGDOM OF NAPLES

Kms.
Miles
0   300

DENMARK

GREAT BRITAIN

UNITED NETHERLANDS

Amsterdam

Brussels

Cologne

Frankfurt

Rhine R.

SPAN. NETHER.

Malplaquet 1709

Oudenarde 1708

Ramillies 1706

Paris

Seine R.

FRANCE

SWITZ- ERLAND

DUCHY OF SAVOY

Turin 1706

London

Mediterranean Sea

Barcelona 1705

SPAIN

Madrid

Almanza 1707

Gibraltar 1704

PORTUGAL

Lisbon

Atlantic Ocean

Grand Alliance

France and Its Ally, Bavaria

Holy Roman Empire

Battles

✕

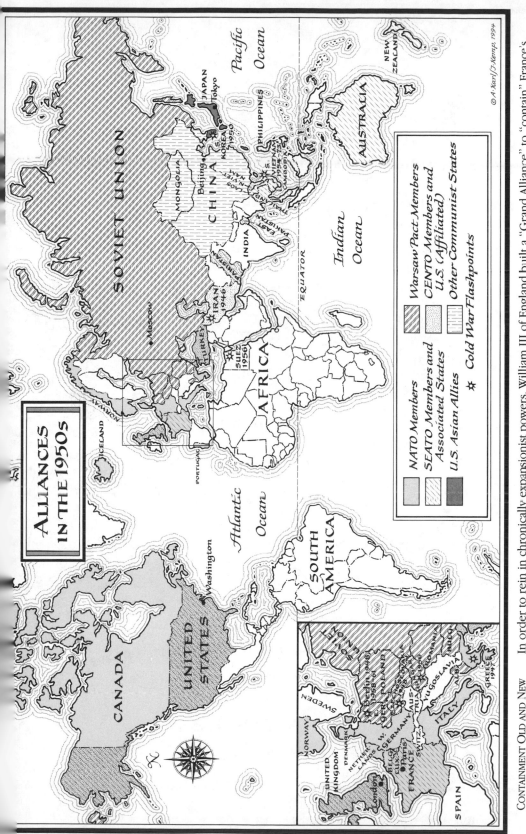

CONTAINMENT OLD AND NEW   In order to rein in chronically expansionist powers, William III of England built a "Grand Alliance" to "contain" France's outward thrusts. The United States similarly built a system of alliances to contain the Soviet Union in the 1950s.

N

UNITED
KINGDOM

North
Sea

DENMARK

Atlantic

Ocean

London

Amsterdam

NETHERLANDS

HANOVER

MECKLEN-
BURG

Elbe R.

BERLIN
1878

PRUSSIA

SAXONY

Brussels

AIX-LA-
CHAPELLE
1818

English Channel

PARIS
1856

Seine R.

LUXEM-
BOURG

Frankfurt

BOHEMIA

Rhine R.

BADEN

WÜRTTEM-
BERG

BAVARIA

Munich

FRANCE

Bern

SWITZERLAND

AUSTRIA

LAIBACH
1821

PIEDMONT

Milan
VERONA
1822

LOMBARDY-VENETIA

PARMA

MODENA

Adria

SPAIN

PORTUGAL

CORSICA

TUSCANY

PAPAL
STATES

Rome

KINGDOM OF THE
TWO SICILIES

Mediterranean Sea

Kms.
0 ————— 300

0 ————— 300
Miles

AFRICA

BALANCE OF POWER AND THE CONGRESS SYSTEM   The peacemakers at Vienna consolidated Central Europe into the German Confederation, ending the power vacuum

EUROPE AFTER
THE CONGRESS OF
VIENNA, 1815

Baltic
Sea

PRUSSIA

•Warsaw

RUSSIA

☆ TROPPAU 1820

AUSTRIAN

☆ VIENNA 1815
Buda••Pest

EMPIRE

HUNGARY

Danube R.

Black Sea

OTTOMAN EMPIRE

☆ Sites of International
   Congresses
   Quadruple Alliance
   Boundary of German
   Confederation

© A·Karl/J·Kemp, 1994

which had tempted French expansionism. The Quadruple Alliance was formed to block French aggression. European congresses, the last of which was held in Berlin in 1878, met periodically to sort out solutions to Europe's major conflicts.

THE BALANCE OF POWER PETRIFIES   When war broke out in 1914, the Franco-Russian
Alliance was already twenty-three years old, and the Austro-German Alliance was
thirty-five years old. A newcomer to Continental alliances, Great Britain joined the

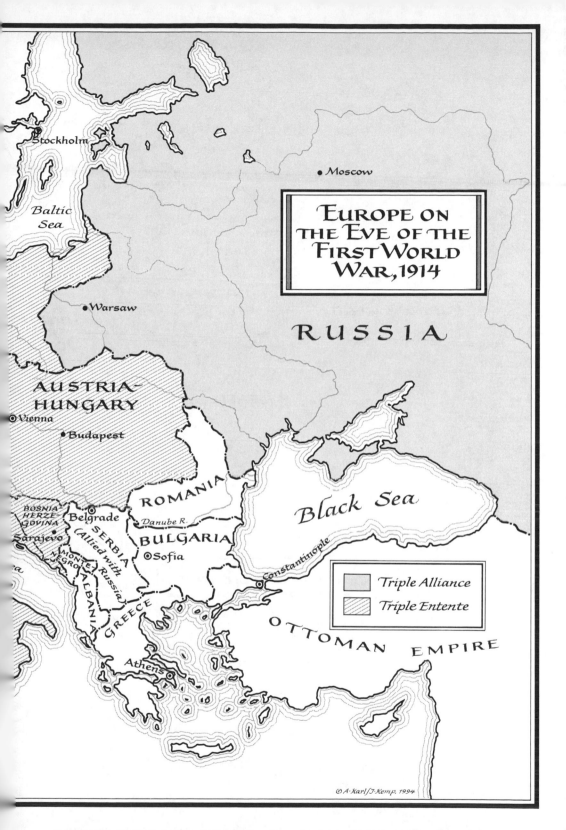

EUROPE ON THE EVE OF THE FIRST WORLD WAR, 1914

Stockholm

Baltic Sea

Moscow

Warsaw

RUSSIA

AUSTRIA-HUNGARY

Vienna

Budapest

ROMANIA

Belgrade

Danube R.

BOSNIA-HERZE-GOVINA

Sarajevo

SERBIA (Allied with Russia)

BULGARIA

Sofia

Black Sea

Constantinople

MONTE-NEGRO

ALBANIA

GREECE

Athens

OTTOMAN EMPIRE

| | Triple Alliance |
| | Triple Entente |

© A·Karl/J·Kemp, 1994

Franco-Russian bloc with agreements in 1904 and 1907. Both alliances were entangled in Europe's trouble spots, most fatefully in the Balkans, so that a minor conflict had the potential to draw all the Great Powers into war.

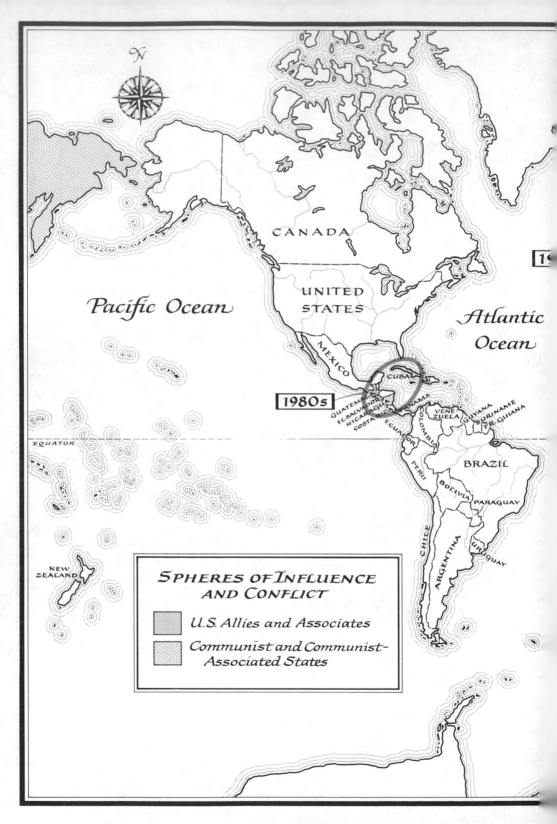

Pacific Ocean

CANADA

UNITED
STATES

*Atlantic
Ocean*

MEXICO

1980s

CUBA

GUATEMALA
EL SALVADOR
NICARAGUA
COSTA RICA
PANAMA

VENE-
ZUELA

GUYANA
SURINAME
FR. GUIANA

COLOMBIA

ECUADOR

EQUATOR

PERU

BRAZIL

BOLIVIA

PARAGUAY

CHILE

ARGENTINA

URUGUAY

NEW
ZEALAND

SPHERES OF INFLUENCE
AND CONFLICT

U.S. Allies and Associates

*Communist and Communist-
Associated States*

COLD WAR SPHERES OF INFLUENCE   In the years following 1945, the United States and
the Soviet Union established spheres of influence in Europe. In the 1950s, spheres
were consolidated in Northeast Asia. In the 1960s, the theater of competition moved

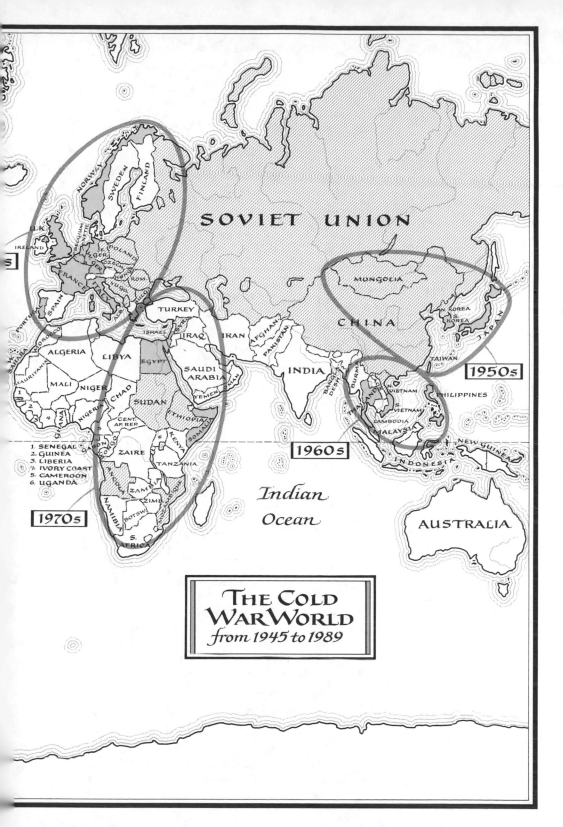

NORWAY SWEDEN FINLAND

SOVIET UNION

U.K.
IRELAND

BELGIUM
NETH.
E. GER.
W. GER.
E. POLAND
FRANCE
CZECH
AUST.
HUNG.
ROM.
SPAIN
PORTUGAL
ITALY
YUGO.
ALB.
GREECE

MONGOLIA

N. KOREA
S. KOREA
JAPAN

CHINA

1950s

MOROCCO
W. SAHARA
MAURITANIA
ALGERIA
LIBYA
MALI
NIGER
CHAD
SUDAN
ETHIOPIA
SOMALIA
EGYPT
ISRAEL
TURKEY
IRAQ
IRAN
AFGHAN.
PAKISTAN
SAUDI ARABIA
YEMEN
OMAN

INDIA
BANGLA DESH
BURMA
THAILAND
VIETNAM
LAOS
S. VIETNAM
CAMBODIA
MALAYSIA
PHILIPPINES

TAIWAN

NIGERIA
CENT. AFR. REP.
GABON
CONGO
ZAIRE
KENYA
TANZANIA
ANGOLA
ZAMBIA
ZIMBABWE
MOZAMBIQUE
NAMIBIA
BOTSW.
S. AFRICA

1960s

1. SENEGAL
2. GUINEA
3. LIBERIA
4. IVORY COAST
5. CAMEROON
6. UGANDA

NEW GUINEA
INDONESIA

Indian Ocean

AUSTRALIA

1970s

THE COLD WAR WORLD
from 1945 to 1989

to Southeast Asia, where spheres were eventually consolidated. In the 1970s, the two
superpowers battled for influence in the Middle East and Africa; in the 1980s, in
Central America.

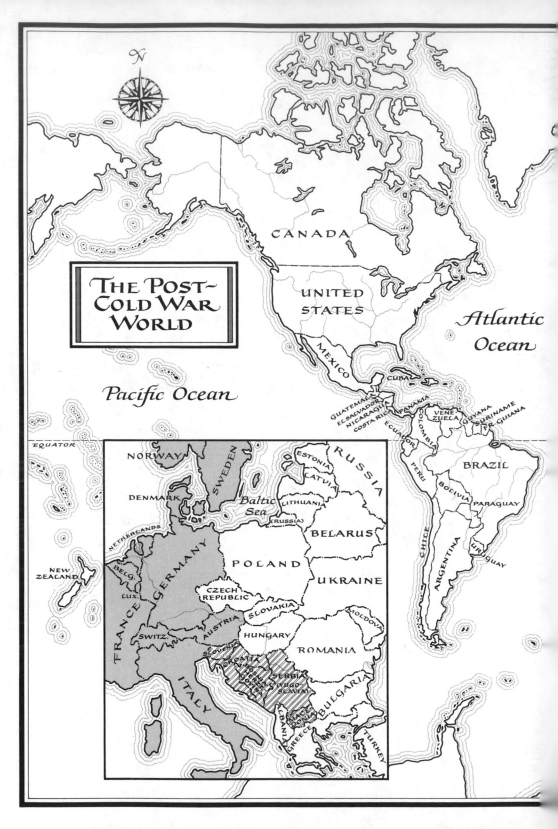

THE POST-COLD WAR WORLD   With the collapse of the Soviet sphere of influence in
1989, new instability has emerged in Central Asia, the Caucasus, the Persian Gulf, the

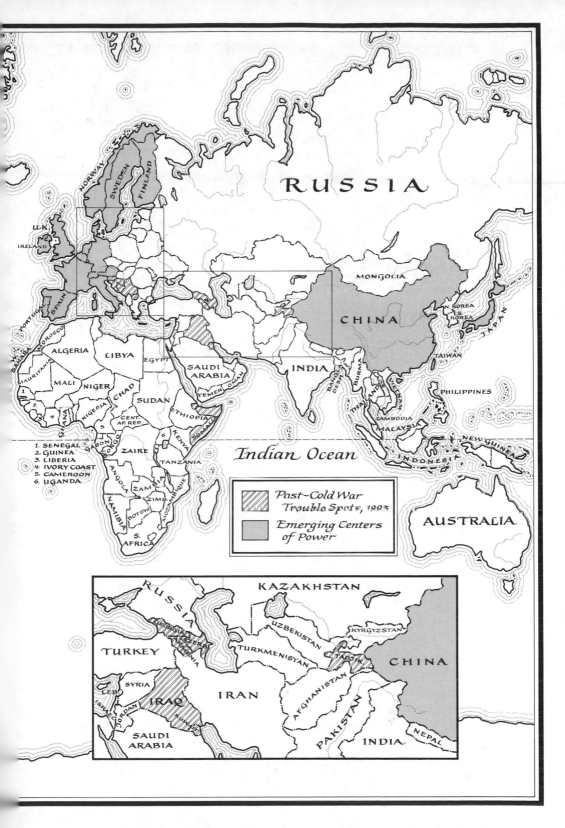

RUSSIA

U.K.

IRELAND

NORWAY   SWEDEN   FINLAND

PORTUGAL   SPAIN

SAHARA   MOROCCO

ALGERIA   LIBYA   EGYPT

MAURITANIA

MALI   NIGER   CHAD   SUDAN

1   NIGERIA   CENT. AF.REP   ETHIOPIA

2   GABON   SOMAL

3   ZAIRE   KENYA

4   TANZANIA

5   ANGOLA   ZAMBI

ZAMBIA   ZIMB

BOTSW   MOZ

S. AFRICA

1. SENEGAL
2. GUINEA
3. LIBERIA
4. IVORY COAST
5. CAMEROON
6. UGANDA

SAUDI ARABIA   YEMEN   OMAN

MONGOLIA

CHINA

N. KOREA

S. KOREA

JAPAN

TAIWAN

INDIA   BANGLA DESH   BURMA   THAILAND   VIETNAM

PHILIPPINES

CAMBODIA   MALAYSIA

INDONESIA   NEW GUINEA

Indian Ocean

AUSTRALIA

| | *Post~Cold War Trouble Spots, 1993* |
| | *Emerging Centers of Power* |

KAZAKHSTAN

RUSSIA

TURKEY   GEORGIA   AZERBAIJAN   ARMENIA

UZBEKISTAN   KYRGYZSTAN

TURKMENISTAN   TAJIK   CHINA

SYRIA   LEB   IRAN   AFGHANISTAN

ISRAEL   IRAQ   JORDAN   KUW   PAKISTAN   NEPAL

SAUDI ARABIA   INDIA

Horn of Africa, and the Balkans. In the meantime, new power centers have developed
in Japan, China, and Western Europe, making for a multipolar world.

CHAPTER THIRTEEN

Stalin's Bazaar

If ideology necessarily determined foreign policy, Hitler and Stalin would never have joined hands any more than Richelieu and the Sultan of Turkey would have three centuries earlier. But common geopolitical interest is a powerful bond, and it was pushing the old enemies, Hitler and Stalin, inexorably together.

When it happened, the democracies were incredulous; their stunned surprise indicated that they had no better understanding of Stalin's mentality than they had of Hitler's. Stalin's career, like Hitler's, had been forged on the fringes of society, though it took him much longer to reach absolute power. Hitler's reliance on demagogic brilliance caused him to stake everything on a single throw of the dice. Stalin prevailed by undermining his rivals from deep within the communist bureaucracy, where the other contenders for power had ignored him because they did not at first view the sinister figure from Georgia as a serious rival. Hitler succeeded by overwhelming his associates with elemental single-mindedness; Stalin accrued power by dint of implacable anonymity.

Hitler transposed his Bohemian work habits and mercurial personality into decision-making, endowing his government with a fitful and occasionally dilettantish quality. Stalin incorporated the rigorous catechisms of his early religious training into the brutal exegeses of the Bolshevik world view, and transformed ideology into an instrument of political control. Hitler thrived on the succor of the adoration of the masses. Stalin was far too paranoid to rely on so personal an approach. He craved ultimate victory far more than immediate approbation, and preferred to achieve it by destroying, one by one, all of his potential rivals.

Hitler's ambitions needed to be fulfilled within his own lifetime; in his statements, he represented only himself. Stalin was equally megalomaniacal but viewed himself as a servant of historical truth. Unlike Hitler, Stalin had incredible patience. Unlike the leaders of the democracies, he was at all times prepared to undertake a meticulous study of power relationships. Precisely because he was so convinced that his ideology embodied historical truth, Stalin ruthlessly pursued the Soviet national interest unencumbered by what he considered hypocritical moral baggage or sentimental attachments.

Stalin was indeed a monster; but in the conduct of international relations, he was the supreme realist—patient, shrewd, and implacable, the Richelieu of his period. Without knowing it, the Western democracies were tempting fate by counting on an irreconcilable ideological conflict between Stalin and Hitler, by teasing Stalin with a French pact that foreswore military cooperation, by excluding the Soviet Union from the Munich Conference, and by rather ambivalently entering into military talks with Stalin only when it was already too late to prevent him from making a pact with Hitler. The leaders of the democracies confused Stalin's ponderous, mildly theological speeches with rigidity of both thought and policy. Yet Stalin's rigidity extended only to communist ideology. His communist convictions enabled him to be extraordinarily flexible in his tactics.

Beyond these psychological aspects, Stalin's character had a philosophical core which made him nearly incomprehensible to Western leaders. As an old Bolshevik, he had suffered imprisonment, exile, and privation on behalf of his convictions for decades before coming to power. Priding themselves on having a superior insight into the dynamics of history, the Bolsheviks saw their role as helping along the objective historical process. In their view, the difference between themselves and noncommunists was akin to the difference between scientists and laymen. In analyzing physical phenomena, the scientist does not actually bring them about; his understanding of why they occur enables him occasionally to manipulate the process, though never according to anything but the phenomena's own inherent laws. In the same spirit, the Bolsheviks thought of themselves as scientists of history—helping to make its dynamics apparent, perhaps even to speed them up, but never to change their immutable direction.

Communist leaders presented themselves as implacable, beyond compassion, and as unswerving from their historical task as they were unswayable by conventional arguments, especially when these came from nonbelievers. The communists felt they had an edge in the conduct of diplomacy because they thought they understood their interlocutors better than they could ever understand themselves. In the communist mind, concessions could only be made, if at all, to "objective reality," never to the persuasiveness of the diplomats with whom they were negotiating. Diplomacy thus belonged to the process by which the existing order would eventually be overturned; whether it would be overthrown by a diplomacy of peaceful coexistence or by military conflict depended on the assessment of the relation of forces.

One principle in Stalin's universe of inhuman and cold-blooded calculation was, however, immutable: nothing could justify fighting hopeless battles for dubious causes. Philosophically, the ideological conflict with Nazi Germany was part of a general conflict with the capitalists that, as far as Stalin was concerned, embraced France and Great Britain. Which country ended up bearing the brunt of Soviet hostility depended entirely on which one Moscow considered the greater threat at any given moment.

Morally, Stalin did not distinguish among the various capitalist states. His true opinion of the countries extolling the virtues of universal peace was evident in his reaction to the signing of the Kellogg-Briand Pact in 1928:

> They talk about pacifism; they speak about peace among European states. Briand and [Austen] Chamberlain are embracing each other.... All this is nonsense. From European history we know that every time that treaties envisaging a new arrangement of forces for new wars have been signed, these treaties have been called treaties of peace ... [although] they were signed for the purpose of depicting new elements of the coming war.[1]

Stalin's ultimate nightmare, of course, was a coalition of all the capitalist countries attacking the Soviet Union simultaneously. In 1927, Stalin described Soviet strategy in the same way Lenin had a decade earlier: "... a great deal ... depends on whether we shall succeed in deferring the inevitable war with the capitalist world ... until the time ... when the capitalists start fighting each other...."[2] To encourage this prospect, the Soviet

334

Union had concluded the Rapallo agreement with Germany in 1922 and the neutrality treaty of Berlin in 1926, which it renewed in 1931, explicitly promising to stay out of a capitalist war.

As far as Stalin was concerned, Hitler's vituperative anticommunism did not constitute an insuperable obstacle to good relations with Germany. When Hitler came to power, Stalin wasted no time making conciliatory gestures. "[W]e are far from being enthusiastic about the fascist regime in Germany," Stalin stated at the Seventeenth Party Congress in January 1934. "[I]t is not a question of fascism here, if only for the reason that fascism in Italy, for example, has not prevented the USSR from establishing the best relations with that country. . . . Our orientation in the past and our orientation at the present time is towards the USSR, and the USSR alone. And if the interests of the USSR demand rapprochement with one country or another which is not interested in disturbing peace, we adopt this course without hesitation."[3]

Stalin, the great ideologue, was in fact putting his ideology in the service of *Realpolitik*. Richelieu or Bismarck would have had no difficulty understanding his strategy. It was the statesmen representing the democracies who were wearing ideological blinkers; having rejected power politics, they thought that the precondition to good relations among nations was a general belief in the premises of collective security, and that ideological hostility would preclude any possibility of practical cooperation between the fascists and the communists.

The democracies were wrong on both counts. In due course, Stalin did move into the anti-Hitler camp, but only very reluctantly and after his overtures to Nazi Germany had been rebuffed. Convinced at last that Hitler's anti-Bolshevik rhetoric might well be serious, Stalin set about constructing the widest possible coalition to contain it. His new strategy emerged at the Seventh (and last) Congress of the Communist International in July and August 1935.[4] Calling for a united front of all peace-loving peoples, it signaled the abandonment of the communist tactics of the 1920s, when, in an effort to paralyze European parliamentary institutions, Communist Parties had consistently voted with antidemocratic groups, including the fascists.

The principal spokesman of the new Soviet foreign policy was Maxim Litvinov, who had been appointed Foreign Minister in order to play just this role. Urbane, fluent in English, and Jewish, he was of bourgeois origin and was married to the daughter of a British historian. His formal credentials were better suited to a class enemy than a man destined for a career in Soviet diplomacy. Under Litvinov's stewardship, the Soviet Union joined the League of Nations, and became one of the most vocal proponents of collective security. Stalin was quite prepared to resort to Wilsonian rhetoric in order to gain insurance against the prospect that Hitler might actually carry out what he had written in *Mein Kampf* and make the Soviet Union his principal target. As the political scientist Robert Legvold has pointed out, Stalin's purpose was to extract maximum assistance from the capitalist world, not to make peace with it.[5]

A deep sense of mutual distrust pervaded the relations between the democracies and the Soviet Union. Stalin signed pacts with France in 1935 and with Czechoslovakia the following year. But the French leaders of the 1930s took the opposite course and refused military staff talks. Inevitably, Stalin interpreted this as an invitation to Hitler to attack the Soviet Union first. To reinsure himself, Stalin made Soviet help to Czechoslovakia dependent on the prior fulfillment of French obligations to Czechoslovakia. This, of course, gave Stalin the option of leaving the imperialists to fight it out among themselves. The Franco-Soviet treaty was hardly a relationship made in heaven.

France's willingness to create political ties with the Soviet Union while simultaneously rejecting a military alliance with it illustrates the never-never land into which the foreign policy of the democracies had drifted between the wars. The democracies valued the rhetoric of collective security but recoiled from giving it an operational content. World War I should have taught Great Britain and France that, even in alliance, fighting Germany by themselves was a precarious enterprise. After all, Germany had nearly prevailed in 1918, despite the fact that America had joined the Allies. To consider fighting Germany without Soviet or American assistance combined the Maginot Line mentality with a gross overestimation of their strength.

Only extremely wishful thinking on the part of the democracies' leaders could have led to the widespread belief that Stalin—the original Bolshevik and a staunch believer in so-called objective, material factors —could have converted to the juridical and moral doctrine of collective security. For Stalin and his colleagues had reasons other than ideology to be unenthusiastic about the established international order. After all, the Soviet frontiers with Poland had been imposed by force and Romania had seized Bessarabia, which the Soviets considered their own.

Nor did the potential German victims in Eastern Europe desire Soviet help. The combination of the Versailles settlement and the Russian Revolution had created an insoluble problem for any system of collective security in Eastern Europe: without the Soviet Union, it could not work militarily; with it, it could not work politically.

Western diplomacy did little to ease Stalin's paranoia about a capitalist anti-Soviet cabal. The Soviet Union was not consulted in the diplomacy surrounding the abrogation of the Locarno Pact, and was excluded altogether from the Munich Conference. It was brought into discussions for a security system in Eastern Europe only grudgingly and quite late, after the occupation of Czechoslovakia in 1939.

Nevertheless, it is a misreading of Stalin's psychology to blame the Hitler-Stalin Pact largely on Western policy. Stalin's paranoia was amply demonstrated by his elimination of all potential domestic rivals and the murder or deportation of millions more who opposed him only in his fantasies. In spite of that, when it came to foreign policy, Stalin proved himself the ultimate cold calculator and took great pride in not letting himself be provoked into any rash moves, especially by capitalist leaders whose understanding of the correlation of forces he rated far below his own.

One can only speculate what Stalin might have intended at the time of Munich. Yet his least likely course at the moment when he was convulsing his country with purge after purge would have been automatic and suicidal implementation of a mutual assistance treaty. Since the treaty with Czechoslovakia committed the Soviet Union only *after* France was at war, it left Stalin with a number of options. For instance, he could demand passage through Romania and Poland and use the nearly certain refusal of those countries as an alibi to await the outcome of battles in Central and Western Europe. Or else, depending on his assessment of the consequences, he could recapture the Russian territories lost to Poland and Romania in the aftermath of the Russian Revolution, much as he did a year later. The most unlikely outcome was one in which the Soviet Union would mount the barricades as the last defender of the Versailles territorial settlement in the name of collective security.

No doubt, Munich confirmed Stalin's suspicions about the democracies. Yet nothing could fundamentally deflect him from seeking to fulfill, at nearly any cost, what he considered his Bolshevik duty—pitting the capitalists against each other and keeping the Soviet Union from becoming a victim of their wars. The effect of Munich, therefore, was primarily to alter Stalin's tactics. For now he opened up a bazaar for bids on a Soviet pact—one which the democracies had no hope of winning if Hitler was prepared to make a serious offer. When, on October 4, 1938, the French Ambassador called on the Soviet Foreign Ministry to explain the Munich agreement, he was greeted by Vladimir Potemkin, the Deputy Commissar for Foreign Affairs, with these menacing words: "My poor friend, what have you done? For us, I see no other outcome than a fourth partition of Poland."[6]

The epigram was a glimpse into Stalin's icy approach to foreign policy. After Munich, Poland was certain to become Germany's next target. Since Stalin wanted neither to confront the German army at the existing Soviet frontier nor to fight Hitler, a fourth partition of Poland was the only alternative (indeed, similar reasoning had led Catherine the Great to promote the first partition of Poland with Prussia and Austria in 1772). The fact that Stalin waited an entire year for Hitler to make the first move attested to the steely nerves with which he conducted his foreign policy.

With his objective firmly in place, Stalin next moved swiftly to withdraw the Soviet Union from the front line. On January 27, 1939, the London *News Chronicle* published an article by its diplomatic correspondent (known to be close to Moscow's ambassador, Ivan Maisky) outlining a possible deal between the Soviet Union and Germany. The author repeated Stalin's standard thesis that there was no significant difference between the Western democracies and the fascist dictators and used it to release the Soviet Union from any automatic commitment to collective security:

> At present, the Soviet government evidently has no intention of giving any help to Great Britain and France if the latter come into conflict with Germany and Italy. . . . From the point of view of the Soviet government, there is no great difference between the positions of the British and French governments on the one hand and the German and Italian on the other, which would justify serious sacrifices in the defence of Western democracy.[7]

Since the Soviet Union saw no need to choose between the various capitalists on the basis of ideology, disagreements between Moscow and Berlin could be solved on a practical basis. Lest the point be missed, Stalin took the unprecedented step of having the article reprinted verbatim in *Pravda,* the official Communist Party newspaper.

On March 10, 1939—five days before Hitler occupied Prague—Stalin stepped forward with his own authoritative statement of Moscow's new strategy. The occasion was the Eighteenth Party Congress, the first such meeting held since Stalin's endorsement of collective security and "united fronts" five years earlier. The delegates' feelings must have been dominated by relief at still being alive, for the purges had decimated their ranks: only thirty-five of the 2,000 delegates from five years before were now in attendance; 1,100 of the remainder had been arrested for counter-revolutionary activities; ninety-eight of the 131 members of the Central Committee had been liquidated, as had been three out of five marshals of the Red Army, all eleven deputy commissars for defense, all military district commanders, and seventy-five out of the eighty members of the Supreme Military Council.[8] The Eighteenth Party Congress was hardly a celebration of continuity. Its attendees were vastly more concerned with the requirements of their own personal survival than with the arcane subtleties of foreign policy.

As had been the case in 1934, Stalin's basic theme before this terrified audience was the peaceful intentions of the Soviet Union in a hostile international environment. His conclusions, however, marked a radical break from the collective security concept of the previous Party Congress. For, in effect, Stalin declared Soviet neutrality in the conflict among the capitalists:

> The foreign policy of the Soviet Union is clear and explicit. We stand for peace and the strengthening of business relations with all countries. That is our position; and we shall adhere to this position as long as these countries maintain like relations with the Soviet Union and as long as they make no attempt to trespass on the interests of our country.[9]

To make certain that the obtuse capitalist leaders did not miss his point, Stalin repeated almost verbatim the central argument of the *News Chronicle* article: that, since the democracies and Germany had similar social structures, the differences between Germany and the Soviet Union were no more insurmountable than the differences between any other capitalist country and the Soviet Union. Summing up, he voiced his determination to retain freedom of action and to sell Moscow's goodwill in any impending war to the highest bidder. In an ominous phrase, Stalin vowed "[t]o be cautious and not allow our country to be drawn into conflicts by warmongers who are accustomed to have others pull the chestnuts out of the fire for them."[10] In effect, Stalin was inviting Nazi Germany to make a bid.

Stalin's new policy differed from the old primarily in terms of emphasis. Even in the heyday of his support for collective security and "united fronts," Stalin had always hedged Soviet commitments in a way that permitted him to retain the option of making a separate deal after the war had begun. But now, in the spring of 1939, when the remaining fragment of Czechoslovakia had not yet been occupied by Germany, Stalin was going one step further. He began maneuvering for the opportunity to make a separate deal *before* the war. No one should have complained that Stalin had kept his intentions secret; the shock of the democracies was due to their inability to understand that Stalin, the passionate revolutionary, was above all a cold-blooded strategist.

After the occupation of Prague, Great Britain abandoned its policy of appeasement toward Germany. The British Cabinet now exaggerated the imminence of a Nazi threat to the same degree to which it had previously underestimated it. It was convinced that Hitler would immediately follow the destruction of Czechoslovakia with another assault—some thought on Belgium, others on Poland. In late March 1939, rumor had it that the target was Romania, which did not even share a border with Germany. Yet it would have been highly uncharacteristic of Hitler to attack a second, unrelated, target quite so soon. More typically, his tactic was to allow the impact of one coup to demoralize his next intended victim before striking again. At any rate, we know in retrospect that Great Britain had far more time to plan its strategy than its leaders believed. Moreover, had the British Cabinet carefully analyzed Stalin's pronouncements at the Eighteenth Party Congress, it would have realized that, the more eagerly Great Britain organized resistance to Hitler, the more aloof Stalin was likely to be in order to magnify his leverage vis-à-vis both sides.

The British Cabinet now faced a fundamental strategic choice, though there is no evidence that it was aware of it. In resisting Hitler, it had to decide whether its approach would be based on constructing a system of collective security or a traditional alliance. If it chose the former, the widest group of nations would be invited to join the anti-Nazi resistance; if it chose the latter, Britain would have to make compromises—to harmonize its interests with those of potential allies, like the Soviet Union.

The Cabinet opted for collective security. On March 17, notes were sent to Greece, Yugoslavia, France, Turkey, Poland, and the Soviet Union inquiring how they would respond to the supposed threat to Romania—the premise being that they must all share the same interests and represent a single attitude. Britain suddenly seemed to be offering what it had withheld since 1918—a territorial guarantee for all of Eastern Europe.

The responses of the various nations once again demonstrated the essential weakness of the doctrine of collective security—the assumption that all nations, and at a minimum all the potential victims, have the same interest in resisting aggression. Every Eastern European nation presented its own problems as a special case and emphasized national, not collective, concerns. Greece made its reaction dependent on Yugoslavia's; Yugoslavia inquired as to Great Britain's intentions—bringing matters back to their starting point. Poland indicated that it was not prepared to take sides between Great Britain and Germany, or to engage itself in the defense of Romania. Poland and Romania would not agree to Soviet participation in the defense of their countries. And the response of the Soviet Union was to propose a conference in Bucharest of all the countries to which the British inquiry had been addressed.

This was a clever maneuver. If the conference took place, it would establish the principle of Soviet participation in the defense of countries that were as afraid of Moscow as they were of Berlin; if its initiative was rejected, the Kremlin would have an excuse to stay aloof while pursuing its preferred option of exploring accommodation with Germany. Moscow was in effect asking the countries of Eastern Europe to identify Germany as the principal threat to their existence, and to challenge it *before* Moscow had clarified its intentions. Since no Eastern European country was prepared to do this, the Bucharest conference never came about.

The unenthusiastic responses caused Neville Chamberlain to pursue other arrangements. On March 20, he suggested a declaration of intent by Great Britain, France, Poland, and the Soviet Union to consult with each other in the event of any threat to the independence of any European state, "with a view to taking common action." A revival of the Triple Entente of pre–World War I, the proposal said nothing about either the military strategy that would be implemented should deterrence fail or the prospects for cooperation between Poland and the Soviet Union, which was simply taken for granted.

For its part, Poland, whose romantic overestimation of its military capacities Great Britain seemed to share, refused joint action with the Soviet Union, facing Great Britain with a choice between Poland and the Soviet Union. If it guaranteed Poland, Stalin's incentive to participate in the common defense would decline. Since Poland was situated between Germany and the Soviet Union, Great Britain would be committed to go to war before Stalin needed to make any decision. On the other hand, if Great Britain concentrated on a Soviet pact, Stalin was sure to demand his pound of flesh for helping the Poles by pushing the Soviet border westward, toward the Curzon Line.

Spurred on by public outrage and convinced that retreat would further weaken Great Britain's position, the British Cabinet refused to sacrifice any more countries, whatever the dictates of geopolitics. At the same time, British leaders suffered from the misapprehension that Poland was somehow militarily stronger than the Soviet Union, and that the Red Army had no offensive value—a plausible enough assessment in light of the massive purges of Soviet military leaders that had just taken place. Above all, the British leaders deeply distrusted the Soviet Union. "I must confess," Chamberlain wrote, "to the very most profound distrust of Russia. I have no belief whatever in her ability to maintain an effective offensive, even if she wanted to. And I distrust her motives, which seem to me to have little connection with our ideas of liberty, and to be concerned only with getting everyone else by the ears."[11]

Believing itself to be under a severe time constraint, Great Britain took the plunge and announced the kind of peacetime Continental guarantee it had consistently rejected since the Treaty of Versailles. Worried about reports of an imminent German attack on Poland, Chamberlain did not even pause to negotiate a bilateral alliance with Poland. Instead, he drafted a unilateral guarantee to Poland with his own hand on March 30, 1939, and presented it to Parliament the next day. The guarantee was meant to be a stopgap to deter Nazi aggression, a threat which turned out to be based on false information. The guarantee was to be followed by a more leisurely attempt to create a broad system of collective security. Soon thereafter, unilateral guarantees based on the same reasoning were extended to Greece and Romania.

Driven by moral outrage and strategic confusion, Great Britain thus slid into guarantees on behalf of countries which all of its postwar prime ministers had insisted it could not, and would not, defend. The post-Versailles realities of Eastern Europe had grown so remote to the British experience that the Cabinet did not even realize it had made a choice which would multiply Stalin's options toward Germany and ease his withdrawal from the proposed common front.

Great Britain's leaders took Stalin's participation in their strategy so much for granted that they believed they could control both its timing and scope. Foreign Secretary Lord Halifax urged that the Soviet Union be held in reserve and "invited to lend a hand in certain circumstances in the most convenient form."[12] What Halifax had specifically in mind was supplying munitions, not moving Soviet troops to beyond their border. He did not explain what incentive the Soviet Union might have to play so subsidiary a role.

In fact the British guarantee to Poland and Romania removed whatever incentive the Soviets might have had to enter into a serious negotiation about an alliance with the Western democracies. For one thing, it guaranteed all the borders of the Soviet Union's European neighbors except for the Baltic States, and, at least on paper, thwarted Soviet ambitions as much as it did Germany's. (The fact that Great Britain could have been oblivious to this reality was a measure of the degree to which the "united front of peace-loving countries" had taken hold in the Western mind.) But, more important, the unilateral British guarantees were a gift to Stalin because they provided him with the maximum he would have asked for in any negotiation which started, as most negotiations do, with an empty slate. If Hitler moved east, Stalin was now assured of Great Britain's commitment to go to war well before the Soviet frontier was reached. Stalin thus garnered the benefit of a *de facto* alliance with Great Britain without any need to reciprocate.

Great Britain's guarantee to Poland was based on four assumptions, each of which turned out to be wrong: that Poland was a significant military power, perhaps more so than the Soviet Union; that France and Great Britain together were strong enough to defeat Germany without the help of other allies; that the Soviet Union had an interest in maintaining the *status quo* in Eastern Europe; and that the ideological gulf between Germany and the Soviet Union was ultimately so unbridgeable that the Soviet Union would join the anti-Hitler coalition sooner or later.

Poland was heroic, but it was not a significant military power. Its task was made all the less manageable because the French general staff misled Poland about its actual intentions, implying that some sort of French offensive was in prospect. The defensive strategy to which France was in fact committed would oblige Poland to face the full fury of the German onslaught alone—a task which Western leaders should have known was far beyond Poland's capacities. At the same time, Poland could not be induced to accept Soviet help, because its leaders were convinced (correctly, as it turned out) that any "liberating" Soviet army would turn into an army of occupation. And the democracies' assessment was that they could win a war against Germany by themselves even if Poland were defeated.

The Soviets' interest in preserving the *status quo* in Eastern Europe ended with the Eighteenth Party Congress—if, indeed, it had ever really existed. Crucially, Stalin did in fact have the option of turning to Hitler and, after the British guarantee to Poland, could play his Nazi card with considerable safety. His task was eased because the Western democracies refused to grasp his strategy—which would have been quite clear to Richelieu, Metternich, Palmerston, or Bismarck. Quite simply, it was to make certain that the Soviet Union was always the last major power to commit itself, thereby achieving the freedom of action for a bazaar in which either Soviet cooperation or Soviet neutrality would be offered to the highest bidder.

Before the British guarantee to Poland, Stalin had had to be wary lest Soviet overtures to Germany cause the democracies to wash their hands of Eastern Europe, leaving him to face Hitler alone. After the guarantee, he had an assurance not only that Great Britain would fight for his Western frontier but that the war would start 600 miles to the west, on the German-Polish frontier.

Stalin had only two remaining concerns. First, he had to make certain that the British guarantee to Poland was solid; second, he would have to find out whether the German option really existed. Paradoxically, the more Great Britain demonstrated its good faith with respect to Poland, which it was required to do in order to deter Hitler, the more maneuvering room Stalin gained with respect to Germany. Great Britain sought to preserve the Eastern European *status quo*. Stalin aimed for the greatest range of choices and to overturn the Versailles settlement. Chamberlain wanted to prevent war. Stalin, who felt war was inevitable, wanted the benefits of war without participating in it.

Stalin decorously pirouetted between the two sides. But in the end, it was no contest. Hitler alone was in a position to offer him the territorial gain in Eastern Europe that he was after, and for this he was quite willing to pay the price of a European war which spared the Soviet Union. On April 14, Great Britain proposed a unilateral declaration by the Soviet Union that "in the event of any act of aggression against any European neighbour of the Soviet Union, which was resisted by the country concerned, the assistance of the Soviet government would be available."[13] Stalin refused to put his head inside a noose and rejected the one-sided and naïve proposal. On April 17, he replied with a counteroffer in three parts: an alliance among the Soviet Union, France, and Great Britain; a military convention to give it effect; and a guarantee for all the countries between the Baltic and the Black seas.

Stalin had to know that such a proposal would never be accepted. First of all, the Eastern European countries did not want it; second, negotiating a detailed military convention would have taken more time than was available; and, finally, Great Britain had not been withholding an alliance from France for the past decade and a half to give one now to a country it had deemed worthy of no more important a role than as a supplier of munitions. "It cannot be pretended," said Chamberlain, "that such an alliance is necessary in order that the smaller countries of Eastern Europe should be furnished with munitions."[14]

Overcoming their reservations, the British leaders inched week by week toward meeting Stalin's terms while he continually raised the ante. In May, Vyacheslav Molotov, Stalin's trusted confidant, had replaced Litvinov as Foreign Minister, signifying that Stalin had personally taken charge of the negotiations and that good personal relations between the negotiators were no longer a Soviet priority. In his abrasively pedantic manner, Molotov demanded that all the countries along the Soviet Union's western border be guaranteed by both sides and that they be specifically enumerated (ensuring a formal refusal from at least some of them). He also insisted that the term "aggression" be expanded to cover "indirect aggression," defined as any concession to German threats, even if force had not actually been used. Since the Soviet Union reserved for itself the definition of what was meant by "yielding," Stalin was also in effect demanding an unlimited right of intervention in the domestic affairs of all the Soviet Union's European neighbors.

By July, Stalin had learned enough. He knew that the British leaders would consent—however reluctantly—to an alliance on close to his terms. On July 23, the Soviet and Western negotiators agreed on a draft treaty that was apparently satisfactory to both sides. Stalin had now acquired a safety net for determining exactly what Hitler had to offer.

Throughout the spring and summer, Stalin carefully signaled that he was ready to entertain a German proposal. Hitler, however, was wary of making the first move lest Stalin use it to extract better terms from Great Britain and France. Stalin had the same fear in reverse. He too was reluctant to make the first move because, if it became public, Great Britain might abandon its Eastern commitments and oblige him to face Hitler alone. Nor was he in any hurry; unlike Hitler, he faced no deadlines, and his nerves were strong. So Stalin waited, raising Hitler's anxieties.

On July 26, Hitler blinked. If he were to attack Poland before the autumn rains, he needed to know by September 1 at the latest what Stalin intended to do. Karl Schnurre, the head of a German team negotiating a new trade agreement with the Soviet Union, was instructed to begin broaching political subjects. Using mutual hostility toward the capitalist West as a bond, he assured his Soviet counterpart that "there was no problem between these two countries from the Baltic to the Black Sea or in the Far East that could not be solved."[15] Schnurre offered to have these discussions continued at a high-level political meeting with the Soviets.

Showing eagerness rarely speeds up negotiations. No experienced statesman settles just because his interlocutor feels a sense of urgency; he is far more likely to use such impatience to try to extract even better terms. In any case, Stalin was not to be stampeded. Thus, it was not until mid-August that Molotov was instructed to receive the German Ambassador, von der Schulenburg, with a list of questions to determine precisely what Schnurre was offering. Pressure on the Japanese not to threaten Siberia? A nonaggression treaty? A pact on the Baltic States? A deal on Poland?

By this time, Hitler was in such a hurry that, although he hated doing so, he was prepared to give way on every point. On August 11, he told the high commissioner of Danzig:

Everything I undertake is directed against Russia. If the West is too stupid and too blind to comprehend that, I will be forced to come to an understanding with the Russians, to smash the West, and then after its defeat, to turn against the Soviet Union with my assembled forces.[16]

It was certainly an accurate statement of Hitler's priorities: from Great Britain, he wanted noninterference in Continental affairs, and from the Soviet Union, he wanted *Lebensraum,* or living space. It was a measure of Stalin's achievement that he was about to reverse Hitler's priorities, however temporarily.

In responding to Molotov's questions, von der Schulenburg informed him that Hitler was prepared to send his Foreign Minister, Joachim von Ribbentrop, to Moscow immediately with full authority to settle all outstanding issues. Stalin could not help noticing that Hitler was prepared to negotiate at a level Great Britain had consistently evaded, for no British minister had seen fit to visit Moscow during all the months of negotiation, even though some had ventured as far east as Warsaw.

Unwilling to show his hand until he knew precisely what was being offered, Stalin turned up the pressure on Hitler another notch. Molotov was instructed to express appreciation for Ribbentrop's enthusiasm but to say that an agreement in principle was needed before the utility of a visit could be determined. Hitler was invited to frame a precise proposal, including a secret protocol to deal with specific territorial questions. Even the obtuse Ribbentrop must have understood the purpose of Molotov's request. Any leak of the proposal would be a German draft; Stalin's hands would remain clean, and failure of the negotiations could be ascribed to a Soviet refusal to go along with German expansionism.

By now, Hitler's nervousness had reached a fever pitch. For a decision to strike at Poland had to be reached in a matter of days. On August 20, he wrote directly to Stalin. The letter itself posed something of a challenge for German protocol officers. Since Stalin's only title was "General Secretary of the Communist Party of the Soviet Union" and he held no governmental position, they could not decide how to address him. Finally, the letter was dispatched simply to "M. Stalin, Moscow." It stated: "I am convinced that the substance of the supplementary protocol desired by the Soviet Union can be cleared in the shortest possible time if a responsible German statesman can come to Moscow himself to negotiate."[17]

Stalin had won his gamble on keeping Soviet options open until the last second. For Hitler was clearly about to offer him for free what, in any alliance with Great Britain and France, he could only have gained after a bloody war with Germany. On August 21, Stalin replied, expressing his hope "that the German-Soviet Nonaggression Pact will mark a decisive turn for the better in the political relations between our two countries. . . ."[18] Ribbentrop was invited to come to Moscow forty-eight hours later, on August 23.

Ribbentrop had been in Moscow no more than an hour before he was ushered into Stalin's presence. The Soviet leader showed little interest in a nonaggression pact and even less in the professions of friendship which Ribbentrop had incorporated into his remarks. The focal point of his concern was the secret protocol dividing up Eastern Europe. Ribbentrop proposed that Poland be divided into spheres of influence along the 1914 border, the principal difference being that Warsaw would remain on the German side. Whether some semblance of Polish independence would be maintained or whether Germany and the Soviet Union would annex all their conquests was left open. With respect to the Baltics, Ribbentrop proposed that Finland and Estonia fall within the Russian sphere (giving Stalin his long-desired buffer zone around Leningrad), that Lithuania go to Germany, and that Latvia be partitioned. When Stalin demanded all of Latvia, Ribbentrop telegraphed Hitler, who gave way—as he would with respect to Stalin's claim to take Bessarabia from Romania. An elated Ribbentrop returned to Berlin, where a euphoric Hitler greeted him as "a second Bismarck."[19] A mere three days had transpired between the time of Hitler's initial message to Stalin and the completion of a diplomatic revolution.

Afterward, there was the usual postmortem about who was responsible for this shocking turn of events. Some blamed Great Britain's grudging negotiating style. The historian A. J. P. Taylor has shown that, in the exchanges between Great Britain and the Soviet Union, the Soviets, rather uncharacteristically, responded to British proposals much more quickly than the British did to Soviet messages. From this fact Taylor concluded, in my view incorrectly, that the Kremlin was more anxious for an alliance than London was.[20] I believe it was much more a case of Stalin's being eager to keep Great Britain in play and not rattle it prematurely—at least until he could determine Hitler's intentions.

The British Cabinet obviously made a number of grave psychological errors. Not only did no minister visit Moscow, but London delayed its agreement to joint military planning until early August. Even then, an admiral was made the head of the British delegation, though ground warfare was the principal, if not the only, subject on Soviet minds. Moreover, the delegation traveled to the Soviet Union by boat, taking five days to reach its destination, which did not exactly denote a sense of urgency.

Finally, however worthy the moral considerations, Great Britain's reluctance to guarantee the Baltic States was bound to be interpreted by the paranoid leader in Moscow as an invitation to Hitler to attack the Soviet Union, bypassing Poland.

Yet it was not Great Britain's clumsy diplomatic conduct that had led to the Nazi-Soviet Pact. The real problem was that Great Britain could not meet Stalin's terms without abandoning every principle it had stood for since the end of the First World War. There was no point in drawing a line against the rape of small countries by Germany if that implied having to grant the same privilege to the Soviet Union. A more cynical British leadership might have drawn the line at the Soviet border instead of Poland's, thereby greatly improving Great Britain's bargaining position with the Soviet Union and giving Stalin a serious incentive to negotiate about protecting Poland. To their moral credit, the democracies could not bring themselves to consecrate another set of aggressions, not even on behalf of their own security. *Realpolitik* would have dictated an analysis of the strategic implications of Great Britain's guarantee to Poland, whereas the Versailles international order required that Great Britain's course be sustained by essentially moral and legal considerations. Stalin had a strategy but no principles; the democracies defended principle without ever developing a strategy.

Poland could not be defended with the French army inert behind the Maginot Line, and the Soviet army waiting inside its own frontiers. In 1914, the nations of Europe had gone to war because military and political planning had lost touch with each other. As the general staffs had polished their plans, the political leaders neither understood them nor had any political objectives commensurate with the magnitude of the military effort being envisaged.

In 1939, military and political planning again lost touch, this time for the exactly opposite reason. The Western powers had an eminently sensible and moral political objective—to stop Hitler. But they were never able to develop a military strategy to attain that goal. In 1914, strategists were too reckless; in 1939, they were too self-effacing. In 1914, the military of every country were spoiling for war; in 1939, they had so many misgivings (even in Germany) that they abdicated their judgment to the political leaders. In 1914, there had been a strategy but no policy; in 1939, there was a policy but no strategy.

Russia played a decisive role in the outbreak of both wars. In 1914, Russia had contributed to the start of the war by rigidly adhering to its alliance with Serbia and to an inflexible mobilization schedule; in 1939, when Stalin relieved Hitler of the fear of a two-front war, he must have known that he was making a general war inevitable. In 1914, Russia had gone to war to preserve its honor; in 1939, it encouraged war to share in the spoils of Hitler's conquests.

Germany, however, conducted itself in exactly the same manner prior to the outbreak of both world wars—with impatience and a lack of perspective. In 1914, it had gone to war to break up an alliance which almost surely would not have held together in the absence of German bullying; in 1939, it was unwilling to wait for its inevitable evolution into the decisive nation of Europe. And that would have required the precise opposite of Hitler's strategy—a period of repose to permit post-Munich geopolitical realities to sink in. In 1914, the German Emperor's emotional imbalance and lack of a clear concept of the national interest had prevented him from waiting; in 1939, an ingenious psychotic determined to wage war while still at the height of his physical powers swept all rational calculations aside. The needlessness of Germany's decision to go to war in both instances has been illustrated by the fact that, despite two major defeats and after being deprived of about a third of its pre–World War I territory, Germany remains Europe's most powerful, and probably most influential, nation.

As for the Soviet Union in 1939, it was ill-equipped for the struggle that was about to take place. Yet, by the end of World War II, it counted as a global superpower. As Richelieu had in the seventeenth century, Stalin in the twentieth century took advantage of the fragmentation in Central Europe. The ascent of the United States to superpower status was foreordained by America's industrial might. The Soviet ascendancy had its origin in the ruthless manipulation of Stalin's bazaar.

CHAPTER FOURTEEN

The Nazi-Soviet Pact

Until 1941, Hitler and Stalin had pursued untraditional goals by using traditional means. Stalin waited for the day when a communist world might be steered from within the Kremlin. Hitler had outlined his mad vision of a racially pure empire governed by the German master race in his book, *Mein Kampf*. Two more revolutionary visions could hardly have been imagined. Yet the means which Hitler and Stalin employed, culminating in their pact of 1939, could have been taken from a treatise on eighteenth-century statecraft. On one level, the Nazi-Soviet Pact was a repetition of the partitions of Poland effected by Frederick the Great, Catherine the Great, and Empress Maria Theresa in 1772. Unlike these three monarchs, however, Hitler and Stalin were ideological adversaries. For a while, their common national interest in seeking the demise of Poland overrode their ideological differences. When their pact finally unraveled in 1941, the largest land war in the history of mankind was unleashed, in effect by the will of one man. It is no small irony that the twentieth century—the age of popular will and of impersonal forces—should have been forged by so few individuals, and that its greatest calamity might have been avoided by the elimination of a single individual.

As the German army smashed Poland in less than a month, the French forces, confronting only under-strength German divisions, watched passively from behind the Maginot Line. A period appropriately nicknamed the "phony war" followed, during which France's demoralization became complete. For hundreds of years, France had been fighting wars for specific political objectives—to keep Central Europe divided or, as in World War I, to regain Alsace-Lorraine. Now it was supposed to be fighting on behalf of a country which had already been conquered and in the defense of which it had not lifted a finger. In effect, France's dispirited population faced another *fait accompli* and a war which lacked an underlying strategy.

For how did Great Britain and France propose to win the war against a country which had nearly prevailed against them when Russia and the United States were on the side of the Allies? They were acting as if it were possible to wait behind the Maginot Line for the British blockade of Germany to squeeze Hitler into submission. But why should Germany hold still for this slow strangulation? And why should it attack the Maginot Line when the road through Belgium lay wide open, this time to be taken by the full German army since there was no longer an Eastern front? And if defense was indeed as dominant in war as the French general staff believed—despite the contrary lesson of the Polish campaign—what other fate could await France than a second war of attrition in a generation and before it had recovered from the first?

While France waited, Stalin seized his strategic opportunity. But before the secret protocol regarding the division of Eastern Europe could be implemented, Stalin wanted it revised. Like an eighteenth-century prince disposing of territory without even a tip of the hat to self-determination, Stalin proposed a new deal to Germany less than a month after completing the Nazi-Soviet Pact: swapping the Polish territory between Warsaw and the Curzon Line, which, under the secret protocol, was to go to the Soviet Union, for Lithuania, which was to go to Germany. Stalin's purpose, of course, was to create an additional buffer for Leningrad. Nor did he seem to feel the need for so much as the pretense of any justification for his geostrategic maneuvers other than the requirements of Soviet security. Hitler accepted Stalin's proposal.

Stalin wasted no time collecting on his end of the secret protocol. With the war in Poland still raging, the Soviet Union proposed a military alliance to the three tiny Baltic States, along with the right to establish military bases on their territory. Denied help from the West, the small republics had no alternative other than to take this first step in losing their independence. On September 17, 1939, less than three weeks after the outbreak of the war, the Red Army occupied the slice of Poland that had been designated to the Soviet sphere.

By November, it was Finland's turn. Stalin demanded Soviet military bases on Finnish soil and the surrender of the Karelian Isthmus, near Leningrad. But Finland proved to be made of sterner stuff. It rejected the Soviet demand and fought when Stalin went to war. Though Finnish forces inflicted severe losses on the Red Army, which was still reeling from Stalin's massive purges, in the end numbers told. After a few months of heroic resistance, Finland succumbed to the Soviet Union's crushing superiority.

In terms of the grand strategy of the Second World War, the Russo-Finnish war was a sideshow. Yet it served to demonstrate the degree to which France and Great Britain had lost their sense for the strategic realities. Blinded by a temporary stalemate imposed by the outnumbered Finns, London and Paris seduced themselves with the suicidal speculation that the Soviet Union might represent the soft underbelly of the Axis (to which, of course, it did not belong). Preparations were made to send 30,000 troops into Finland through Sweden and Northern Norway. On the way, they would cut Germany off from the iron ore in Northern Norway and Sweden, which was being shipped to Germany from the northern Norwegian port of Narvik. The fact that neither of these countries was prepared to grant them transit rights did not dim the enthusiasm of the French and British planners.

The threat of Allied intervention may have helped Finland to obtain a better settlement than the original Soviet demands would have suggested but, in the end, nothing could keep Stalin from pushing the Soviet defense line away from the approaches to Leningrad. For historians, the puzzle remains as to what possessed Great Britain and France to come within a hairsbreadth of fighting both the Soviet Union and Nazi Germany simultaneously three months before the collapse of France proved the whole scheme was nothing but a pipedream.

In May 1940, the "phony war" ended. The German army repeated its maneuver of 1914 by wheeling through Belgium, the principal difference being that the major thrust was now at the center of the front rather than on the right wing. Paying the price for a decade and a half of doubts and evasions, France collapsed. Though the efficiency of the German military machine was by now well established, observers were shocked at the speed with which France was routed. In the First World War, German armies had spent four years pushing toward Paris in vain; every mile was achieved at enormous human expense. In 1940, the German *Blitzkrieg* cut through France; by the end of June, German troops were marching along the Champs-Elysées. Hitler seemed to be master of the Continent.

But, like other conquerors before him, Hitler did not know how to end the war he had so recklessly started. He had three choices: he could try to defeat Great Britain; he could make peace with Great Britain; or he could seek to conquer the Soviet Union and then, using its vast resources, turn back west with all his forces and complete the destruction of Great Britain.

During the summer of 1940, Hitler attempted the first two approaches. In a boastful speech on July 19, he hinted that he was prepared to make a compromise peace with Great Britain. In effect, he asked it to relinquish the prewar German colonies and to renounce interference in affairs on the Continent. In return, he would guarantee the British Empire.[1]

Hitler's proposal was analogous to what imperial Germany had been offering Great Britain for two decades prior to World War I—though then it had been framed in more conciliatory language and England's strategic situation had been much more favorable. Perhaps, if Hitler had been more specific about what a Europe organized by Germany would look like, some of the British leaders—such as Lord Halifax, though never Churchill—toying with the idea of negotiating with Germany might have been tempted. By in effect asking Great Britain to grant Germany complete freedom of action on the Continent, Hitler evoked the traditional British response—one which Sir Edward Grey had made in 1909 in reaction to a similar proposal by far more rational German leaders than Hitler (and while France was still a major power) when he noted that, if Great Britain sacrificed the Continental nations to Germany, it would sooner or later be attacked on the British Isles (see chapter 7). Nor would Great Britain take seriously a "guarantee" for its Empire. No German leader ever grasped the British view that any nation capable of protecting the Empire was also capable of conquering it— as Sir Eyre Crowe had already pointed out in his famous 1907 Memorandum (see chapter 7).

Churchill, of course, was far too sophisticated and had studied too much history to have any illusion that, at the end of the war, Great Britain would still be the premier world power or even in the front rank. Either

Germany or the United States would claim that position. Churchill's intransigence toward Germany in the summer of 1940 can therefore be interpreted as a decision in favor of American over German hegemony. American pre-eminence might prove uncomfortable at times, but at least its culture and language were familiar and there were no ostensibly clashing interests. Finally, there was always the prospect of that "special" relationship between Great Britain and America that would have been inconceivable with Nazi Germany. By the summer of 1940, Hitler had maneuvered himself into the position where he himself had become the *casus belli*.

Hitler now turned to his second option of seeking to destroy the British air force and, if necessary, of invading the British Isles. But he never went further than to toy with the idea. Landing operations had not been a part of German prewar planning, and the plan was abandoned because of a shortage of landing craft and the inability of the Luftwaffe to destroy the Royal Air Force. By the end of the summer, Germany again found itself in a position not so very dissimilar from the one it had been in during the First World War; having achieved major successes, it was unable to translate them into final victory.

Hitler, of course, was in an excellent position to go on the strategic defensive—Great Britain was not strong enough to challenge the German army alone; America would have found it nearly impossible to enter the war; and Stalin, however he might play with the idea of intervention, would in the end always have found some reason to postpone it. But waiting for others to take the initiative was against Hitler's nature. It was therefore inevitable that his mind would turn to an attack on the Soviet Union.

As early as July 1940, Hitler ordered preliminary staff plans for a Soviet campaign. He told his generals that, once the Soviet Union was defeated, Japan would be able to throw all its armed forces against America, diverting Washington's attention to the Pacific. An isolated Great Britain without the prospect of American support would be forced to give up the fight: "Britain's hope lies in Russia and the United States," Hitler noted accurately. "If the hopes pinned on Russia are disappointed then America too will fall by the wayside, because elimination of Russia would tremendously increase Japan's power in the Far East. . . . "[2] Hitler, however, was not quite ready to give the order to attack. First he would explore the possibility of luring the Soviets into a joint attack on the British Empire and of disposing of the British before turning east.

Stalin realized all too well the difficulty of his position. France's collapse wrecked the expectation—which Stalin had shared with all the Western military experts—that the war would be the same sort of lengthy struggle of attrition that World War I had been. Stalin's fondest hope, that Germany and the Western democracies would exhaust themselves, had evaporated. If Great Britain fell as well, the German army would be freed for an attack eastward, and would be able to make use of the full resources of Europe according to the concept Hitler had advertised in *Mein Kampf.*

Stalin reacted in nearly stereotypic fashion. At no point in his career did he react to danger by displaying fear, even when he must have felt it. Convinced that an admission of weakness would tempt an adversary to raise his terms, he always tried to obscure strategic dilemmas with intransigence. If Hitler tried to exploit his victory in the West by applying pressure against the Soviet Union, Stalin would make the prospect of extracting concessions from him as unattractive and painful as possible. An excruciatingly careful calculator, he failed, however, to take into account Hitler's neurotic personality and thus excluded the possibility that Hitler might respond to a challenge with a two-front war, no matter how reckless such a course.

Stalin opted for a two-pronged strategy. He accelerated harvesting the remainder of the booty promised him in the secret protocol. In June 1940, while Hitler was still occupied with France, Stalin issued an ultimatum to Romania to cede Bessarabia and also demanded northern Bukovina. The latter was not part of the secret agreement, and possession of it would place Soviet forces all along the Romanian portion of the Danube River. That same month, he incorporated the Baltic States into the Soviet Union by forcing them to agree to sham elections in which not quite 20 percent of the population participated. When the process was completed, Stalin had regained all the territory Russia had lost at the end of the First World War; and the Allies had paid the last of a series of installments on the cost of having excluded both Germany and the Soviet Union from the 1919 Peace Conference.

Concurrent with strengthening his strategic position, Stalin continued his efforts to placate his ominous neighbor by supplying Hitler's war machine with raw materials. As early as February 1940—before Germany's victory over France—a trade agreement was signed in Stalin's presence committing the Soviet Union to deliver large quantities of raw materials to Germany. Germany, in turn, provided the Soviet Union with coal and manufactured goods. The Soviet Union meticulously observed the provisions of the agreement and generally exceeded them. Indeed, literally up to the very moment when the Germans finally attacked, Soviet railroad cars were still crossing the border checkpoints with their deliveries.

None of Stalin's moves, however, could alter the geopolitical reality that Germany had become the dominant power in Central Europe. Hitler had made it quite plain that he would not tolerate any Soviet expansion beyond the provisions of the secret protocol. In August 1940, Germany and Italy forced Romania, which Stalin by this time considered a part of the Soviet sphere of influence, to return two-thirds of Transylvania to Hungary, a near-ally of the Axis Powers. Determined to protect Romania's oil supplies, Hitler drew the line more explicitly in September by guaranteeing Romania and ordering a motorized division and air forces to Romania to back up the guarantee.

In the same month, tension grew at the other end of Europe. In violation of the secret protocol, which had placed Finland in the Soviet sphere of influence, Finland agreed to permit German troops to cross its territory en route to Northern Norway. Moreover, there were significant German arms deliveries, whose only conceivable objective could be to strengthen Finland against Soviet pressure. When Molotov asked Berlin for more concrete information, he was given evasive replies. Soviet and German troops were beginning to jostle each other across the entire length of Europe.

For Stalin, the most ominous new development, however, occurred on September 27, 1940, when Germany, Italy, and Japan signed a Tripartite Pact obliging each of them to go to war against any additional country that joined the British side. To be sure, the Pact specifically excluded the relations of each of the signatories with the Soviet Union. This meant that Japan undertook no obligation to participate in a German-Soviet war, no matter who struck first, but was required to fight America in case it entered the war against Germany. Though the Tripartite Pact was ostensibly aimed at Washington, Stalin had no cause to feel reassured. Whatever the legal provisions, he had to expect that the three Pact members would at some point turn on him. That he was the odd man out was evident from the fact that he had not even been informed about the negotiations until the Pact had been concluded.

By the fall of 1940, tensions were mounting at such a rate that the two dictators made what would turn out to be their last diplomatic effort to outmaneuver each other. Hitler's goal was to lure Stalin into a joint assault on the British Empire so as to destroy him all the more surely once Germany's rear was secure. Stalin attempted to gain time in the hope that Hitler might overreach somewhere along the way, but also in order to determine what he might be able to scavenge in the process. Nothing came of the efforts to arrange a face-to-face meeting between Hitler and Stalin in the wake of the Tripartite Pact. Each leader did his best to avoid it by claiming he could not leave his own country, and the logical meeting place—Brest-Litovsk, at the frontier—carried too much historical baggage.

On October 13, 1940, Ribbentrop wrote a long letter to Stalin giving his own interpretation of the course of events since his visit to Moscow the year before. It was an unusual breach of protocol for a foreign minister to address not his counterpart but a leader who did not even have a formal governmental office (Stalin's sole position remained General Secretary of the Communist Party).

Ribbentrop's letter compensated in pomposity for its lack of diplomatic finesse. He blamed Soviet-German disagreements over Finland and Romania on British machinations, without explaining how London might have accomplished such a feat. And he insisted that the Tripartite Pact had not been directed against the Soviet Union—indeed, the Soviet Union would be welcome to join in a division of the spoils between the European dictators and Japan after the war. Ribbentrop concluded by inviting Molotov to pay a return visit to Berlin. On that occasion, Ribbentrop averred the possibility that the Soviet Union's joining the Tripartite Pact could be discussed.[3]

Stalin was far too cautious to divide spoils which had not yet been conquered, or to enter the front line of a confrontation designed by others. Still, he would keep open the option of dividing the booty with Hitler in case Great Britain simply collapsed—just as he would do in 1945, when he joined the war against Japan in its final stage for a heavy price. On October 22, Stalin replied to Ribbentrop's letter with alacrity laced with irony. Thanking Ribbentrop for his "instructive analysis of recent events," he refrained from offering his own personal assessment of them. Perhaps to show that two could play at stretching protocol, he accepted the invitation for Molotov to come to Berlin, unilaterally setting a very early date—November 10—less than three weeks away.[4]

Hitler accepted the proposal immediately, which led to another misunderstanding. Stalin interpreted the speed of Hitler's acceptance to mean that the Soviet relationship remained as crucial to Germany as it had been the previous year, hence as proof that his tough tactics were paying off. Hitler's eagerness, however, sprang from his need to get on with his planning if he were indeed to attack the Soviet Union in the spring of 1941.

The depth of distrust between these two would-be partners was evident before the meetings even started. Molotov refused to board a German train sent to the border to escort him to Berlin. The Soviet delegation was obviously concerned that the elegance of the German cars might be matched by the extensiveness of their bugging devices. (In the end, the

German cars were hitched onto the back of the Soviet train, whose under-carriages had been specially constructed so that they could be adjusted to the narrower European gauge at the border.)

Negotiations finally began on November 12. Molotov, who had a faculty to irritate far more stable personalities than Hitler, exhibited his abrasive tactics with a vengeance before the Nazi leadership. His innate truculence was reinforced by his terror of Stalin, whom he feared much more than he did Hitler. Molotov's obsessive concern with his own domestic situation was typical of diplomats during the entire Soviet period, though it was particularly acute while Stalin was in power. Soviet negotiators always seemed much more aware of their domestic constraints than of those in the international arena.

Since foreign ministers were rarely members of the Politburo (Gromyko only became a member in 1973, after sixteen years as Foreign Minister), their domestic base was weak and they were always in danger of becoming scapegoats for negotiations gone wrong. Moreover, since the Soviets assumed that history was ultimately on their side, they were more inclined to stonewall than to seek broad solutions. Every negotiation with Soviet diplomats turned into a test of endurance; no concession would ever be forthcoming until the Soviet negotiator had convinced himself—and particularly those who read the cables in Moscow—that every last ounce of flexibility had been extracted from the other side. On the basis of this kind of diplomatic guerrilla warfare, they obtained whatever could be had through persistence and pressure, but they usually missed the opportunity for a real breakthrough. Soviet negotiators—with Gromyko as the master of the game—became extremely adept at wearing down opponents who were saddled with preconceived ideas and impatient for a settlement. On the other hand, they tended to miss the forest for the trees. Thus, in 1971, they lost the opportunity to hold a summit meeting with Nixon, which would have delayed his opening to Beijing, by spending months haggling over essentially meaningless preconditions —all of which the Soviets dropped as soon as Washington had acquired a Chinese option.

It is not possible to imagine two men less likely to communicate than Hitler and Molotov. Hitler was not in any event suited to negotiations, preferring to overwhelm his interlocutors with extended monologues while exhibiting no sign of listening to the response, if indeed he left time for a response. In dealing with foreign leaders, Hitler usually confined himself to passionate statements of general principle. On the few occasions he did participate in actual negotiations—as with the Austrian Chancellor Kurt von Schuschnigg or Neville Chamberlain—he adopted a bullying manner and put forward peremptory demands which he rarely modified. Molotov, on the other hand, was less interested in principles than in their application. And he had no scope for compromise.

In November 1940, Molotov found himself in a genuinely difficult position. Stalin was bound to be hard to please, torn as he was between his reluctance to contribute to a German victory and his worry that, should Germany defeat Great Britain without Soviet assistance, he might miss an opportunity to share in Hitler's conquests. Whatever did happen, Stalin was determined never to return to the Versailles arrangement, and attempted to protect his position by hedging every move. The secret protocol and subsequent events had made his conception of appropriate arrangements quite clear to the Germans—perhaps too clear. In this sense, Molotov's visit to Berlin was seen as an opportunity for elaboration. As for the democracies, Stalin had used the occasion of a visit in July 1940 by the new British Ambassador, Sir Stafford Cripps, to reject any possibility of a return to the Versailles order. When Cripps argued that the fall of France had made it necessary for the Soviet Union to take an interest in restoring the balance of power, Stalin replied icily:

> The so-called European balance of power had hitherto oppressed not only Germany but also the Soviet Union. Therefore the Soviet Union would take all measures to prevent the reestablishment of the old balance of power in Europe.[5]

In diplomatic language, "all measures" usually embraces the threat of war.

For Molotov, the stakes could hardly have been higher. Since Hitler's record left little doubt that he would not let 1941 go by without launching some kind of major campaign, it was probable that, if Stalin did not join him in attacking the British Empire, he might well attack the Soviet Union. Molotov therefore faced a *de facto* ultimatum masquerading as seduction—though Stalin underestimated how short the deadline actually was.

Ribbentrop opened the conversations by outlining why a German victory was inevitable. He urged Molotov to join the Tripartite Pact, undeterred by the fact that this treaty was an elaboration of what had originally been the Anti-Comintern Pact. On that basis, argued Ribbentrop, it would be possible to "establish spheres of influence between Russia, Germany, Italy, and Japan along very broad lines."[6] According to Ribbentrop, this should not lead to conflict, because each of the prospective partners was above all interested in expanding southward. Japan would move into

Southeast Asia, Italy into North Africa, and Germany would reclaim its former colonies in Africa. After many circumlocutions to emphasize his cleverness, Ribbentrop finally identified the prize which had been reserved for the Soviet Union: "... whether Russia in the long run would not also turn to the South for the natural outlet to the open sea that was so important for Russia."[7]

Anyone even vaguely familiar with Hitler's public statements knew this was nonsense. Africa had always been a low Nazi priority. Not only had Hitler never shown any particular interest in it, but Molotov probably had read enough of *Mein Kampf* to realize that it was *Lebensraum* in Russia that Hitler was really after. Having silently sat through Ribbentrop's exposition, Molotov now inquired matter-of-factly, though somewhat insolently, to what sea the Soviet Union was supposed to be seeking this outlet. Answering with another ponderous circumlocution, Ribbentrop finally mentioned the Persian Gulf, as if it were already Germany's to give away:

> The question now was, whether they could not continue in the future also to do good business together ... whether in the long run the most advantageous access to the sea for Russia could not be found in the direction of the Persian Gulf and the Arabian Sea, and whether at the same time certain other aspirations of Russia in this part of Asia— in which Germany was completely disinterested—could not also be realized.[8]

Molotov had no interest in so bombastic a proposal. Germany did not yet possess what it purported to offer, and the Soviet Union did not need Germany to conquer these territories for itself. Expressing his willingness in principle to join the Tripartite Pact, Molotov immediately hedged the concession with the argument that "precision was necessary in a delineation of spheres of influence over a rather long period of time."[9] This, of course, could not be completed on just one visit to Berlin and would require extended consultations, including a return visit to Moscow by Ribbentrop.

That afternoon, Molotov met with Hitler in the newly completed marble Chancellery. Everything had been arranged to awe the proletarian minister from Moscow. Molotov was led along a vast corridor on both sides of which, every few yards, tall SS men in black uniforms came to attention and raised their arms in the Nazi salute. The doors to Hitler's office reached all the way to the high ceiling and were thrown open by two particularly tall SS men whose raised arms formed an arch beneath which Molotov was ushered into Hitler's presence. Seated at his desk along the far wall of the enormous room, Hitler silently observed his visitors for a few moments, then sprang up and, still without saying a word, shook hands with each member of the Soviet delegation. As he invited them to sit down in the lounge area, some curtains were parted and Ribbentrop and a few advisers joined the group.[10]

Having inflicted the Nazi version of majesty on his guests, Hitler laid out his idea of the purpose of their meeting. He proposed agreeing on a joint long-term strategy because both Germany and the Soviet Union "had at their helm men who possessed sufficient authority to commit their countries to a development in a definite direction."[11] What Hitler had in mind was setting up a kind of joint Monroe Doctrine with the Soviets for the whole of Europe and Africa, and dividing the colonial territories between themselves.

Demonstrating that he had not been in the least intimidated by his reception, seemingly drawn from some Viennese operetta's vision of grandeur, Molotov confined himself to a series of precise questions: What was the ultimate purpose of the Tripartite Pact? Of Hitler's definition of his self-proclaimed New Order? Of the Greater Asian Sphere? Of German intentions in the Balkans? Was the understanding placing Finland in the Soviet sphere of influence still valid?

No one had ever taken over a conversation with Hitler in this manner, or subjected him to a cross-examination. In any event, Hitler was not interested in limiting German freedom of action in any area his armies were capable of reaching—certainly not in Europe.

The next day's meeting with Hitler was prefaced by a spartan lunch and did not make any better progress. Characteristically, Hitler started out with an extended monologue, during which he explained how he proposed to divide the world with Stalin:

After the conquest of England the British Empire would be apportioned as a gigantic worldwide estate in bankruptcy. . . . In this bankrupt estate there would be access for Russia to the ice-free and really open ocean. Thus far, a minority of 45 million Englishmen had ruled the 600 million inhabitants of the British Empire. He was about to crush this minority. . . .

In these circumstances there arose worldwide perspectives. . . . Russia's participation in the solution of these problems would have to be arranged. All the countries that could possibly be interested in the bankrupt estate would have to stop all controversies and concern themselves exclusively with apportioning the British Empire.[12]

Replying sardonically that he agreed with what he had understood, Molotov promised to report the remainder to Moscow. Concurring in principle with Hitler's statement that the Soviet Union and Germany had no conflicting interests, he immediately put the proposition to a practical test by inquiring what Germany's reaction would be if the Soviet Union extended a guarantee to Bulgaria similar to the one Germany had given to Romania (which would in effect block further extension of German influence in the Balkans). And what about the Soviet Union's annexing Finland? Clearly, self-determination was not a principle of Soviet foreign policy, and Stalin would not hesitate to annex non-Russian populations if he could do so without German interference. Not only the territorial settlement but the moral principles of the Versailles settlement were dead.

The tense atmosphere at the meeting did not ease any when Hitler pointed out rather testily that Bulgaria did not seem to have asked for a Soviet alliance. And he rejected the annexation of Finland on the ground that it went beyond the secret protocol, sidestepping the fact that going beyond the protocol had been the whole point of Molotov's journey to Berlin. The meeting was ending on a sour note. As Hitler rose, mumbling something about the possibility of a British air raid, Molotov reiterated his basic message: "The Soviet Union, as a great power, cannot remain aloof from the great issues in Europe and Asia."[13] Without specifying how the Soviet Union would reciprocate if Hitler granted its wishes, Molotov merely promised that, after he had reported to Stalin, he would convey his chief's ideas about an appropriate sphere of influence to Hitler.

Hitler was so annoyed that he did not attend a dinner hosted by Molotov at the Soviet Embassy—though most of the other Nazi leaders were present. The dinner was interrupted by a British air raid and, since the Soviet Embassy had no air-raid shelter, the guests scattered in all directions. The Nazi leaders shuttled off in limousines, the Soviet delegation to the Bellevue Castle (which currently houses the German president when he is in Berlin), while Ribbentrop took Molotov to his private air-raid shelter nearby. There, he brandished a German draft of Soviet adherence to the Tripartite Pact without seeming to understand that Molotov had neither the inclination nor the authority to go beyond what he had told Hitler. Molotov, on his part, ignored the draft and went on to raise the very issues Hitler had avoided, reiterating that the Soviet Union could not be excluded from any European question. He then specifically listed Yugoslavia, Poland, Greece, Sweden, and Turkey, conspicuously avoiding the grand vistas along the Indian Ocean which Ribbentrop and Hitler had earlier put before him.[14]

Behind Molotov's insolent and intransigent style was an attempt to gain time for Stalin to resolve a nearly insoluble quandary. Hitler was offering him a partnership in the defeat of Great Britain. But it did not take much imagination to realize that, afterward, the Soviet Union would stand naked before its would-be partners in the Tripartite Pact, all of them former associates in the Anti-Comintern Pact. On the other hand, if Great Britain were to collapse without Soviet assistance, it might be desirable for the Soviet Union to improve its strategic position for the inevitable show-down with Hitler.

In the end, Stalin never did decide which course to pursue. On November 25, Molotov sent Stalin's conditions for joining the Tripartite Pact to Ribbentrop: Germany would have to withdraw its troops from Finland and give the Soviet Union a free hand in that country; Bulgaria would need to join a military alliance with the Soviet Union and permit Soviet bases on its territory; Turkey would be required to accept Soviet bases on its territory, including the Dardanelles. Germany would stand aside if the Soviet Union pursued its strategic objectives in the Balkans and the Dardanelles by force. As an elaboration of Hitler's own offer that the area south of Batum and Baku be recognized as a Soviet sphere of interest, Stalin now defined the sphere to include Iran and the Persian Gulf. As for Japan, it would have to abandon any claim to mineral rights on Sakhalin Island.[15] Stalin had to know that these conditions would never be accepted since they blocked any further German expansion toward the east, and since he had offered no commensurable Soviet reciprocal act.

Stalin's reply to Hitler therefore primarily served to signal what he considered to be the Soviet sphere of interest, and as a warning that he would resist its impairment, at least diplomatically. Over the course of the next decade, employing the tactics of the tsars, Stalin proceeded to establish that sphere by agreement whenever possible, by force when necessary. He pursued the objectives outlined in the November 25 memorandum, first in concert with Hitler, next on the side of the democracies against Hitler, and finally through confrontation with the democracies. Then, toward the very end of his life, Stalin seemed on the verge of exploring a grand bargain with the democracies to safeguard what he never ceased to treat as the Soviet sphere of influence (see chapter 20).

For Hitler, the die was already cast. As early as the day of Molotov's arrival in Berlin, Hitler had ordered all preparations for an attack on the Soviet Union to continue, with the final decision to be delayed until an operational plan had been approved.[16] In Hitler's mind, the only decision had always been whether to attack the Soviet Union before or after he had defeated Great Britain. And Molotov's visit settled that issue. On November 14, the day Molotov left Berlin, Hitler ordered the staff plans of the summer to be turned into an operational concept for an attack on the Soviet Union by the summer of 1941. When he received Stalin's proposal of November 25, he ordered that no reply be returned. Nor did Stalin ever ask for one. German military preparations for a war on Russia now moved into high gear.

There has been considerable debate about whether Stalin ever grasped the impact of his tactics on a personality like Hitler. In all likelihood, he underestimated the deadly impatience of his adversary. For he seems to have assumed that Hitler was, like himself, a cool and careful calculator who would not willingly launch his armies into the vast spaces of Russia before he had concluded the war in the west. In this assumption, Stalin was wrong. Hitler believed that willpower could overcome all obstacles. His typical response to resistance was to turn it into a personal confrontation. Hitler could never wait for conditions to mature fully, if only because the act of waiting implied that circumstances might transcend his will.

Stalin not only was more patient but, as a communist, had more respect for historical forces. In his nearly thirty years of rule, he never staked everything on one throw of the dice and, mistakenly, believed that Hitler would not do so either. In the meantime, Stalin was morbidly concerned that rash Soviet deployments might trigger a German pre-emptive attack. And he misconstrued Hitler's eagerness to enlist him in the Tripartite Pact as proof that the Nazis were planning to devote 1941 to further attempts to bring down Great Britain. Apparently, Stalin believed that the following year, 1942, was to be the year of decision for a war with Germany. His biographer Dmitri Volkogonov told me that Stalin was keeping open the option of a pre-emptive war against Germany in that year, which may explain why Soviet armies were deployed so far forward in 1941. Expecting Hitler to state major demands before attacking, Stalin probably would have gone quite a distance to meet these demands—at least in 1941.

All such calculations failed because their basic assumption was that Hitler engaged in rational calculations; however, Hitler did not consider himself bound by a normal calculation of risks. Nary a year of Hitler's rule had gone by without his committing some action which his entourage had warned him was too dangerous: rearmament in 1934–35; reoccupying the Rhineland in 1936; occupying Austria and Czechoslovakia in 1938; attacking Poland in 1939; and the campaign against France in 1940. Nor was it Hitler's intention to let 1941 turn into an exception. Given his personality, he could only have been bought off if the Soviet Union had decided to join the Tripartite Pact with minimum conditions and had participated in a military operation against Great Britain in the Middle

East. Then, with Great Britain defeated and the Soviet Union isolated, Hitler would surely have gone on to fulfill his lifelong obsession for conquests in the east.

No amount of clever maneuvering on the part of Stalin could, in the end, prevent his country's ending up in much the same position as Poland had the year before. The Polish government could only have avoided a German attack in 1939 by agreeing to yield the Polish Corridor and Danzig, and then by joining a Nazi crusade against the Soviet Union—at the end of all of which Poland would still have been at Hitler's mercy. Now, a year later, it seemed that the Soviet Union could only buy a respite from German aggression by submitting to Nazi proposals (at the price of total isolation and by entering a risky war against Great Britain). In the end, however, it would still face an attack from Germany.

Steely-nerved, Stalin maintained his two-track policy of cooperating with Germany by supplying war materials while opposing it geopolitically, as if no danger existed at all. Though he was not willing to join the Tripartite Pact, he did grant Japan the sole benefit which Soviet adherence to the Pact would have brought it by freeing Japan's rear for adventures in Asia.

Though obviously unaware of Hitler's briefing to his generals that an attack on the Soviet Union would enable Japan to challenge the United States overtly, Stalin reached the same conclusion independently and set out to remove that incentive. On April 13, 1941, he concluded a nonaggression treaty with Japan in Moscow, following essentially the same tactics in the face of mounting Asian tensions that he had adopted toward the Polish crisis eighteen months earlier. In each case, he removed the aggressor's risk of a two-front war, and he managed to deflect war from Soviet territory by encouraging what he considered a capitalist civil war elsewhere. The Hitler-Stalin Pact had gained him a two-year respite, and the nonaggression treaty with Japan enabled him six months later to throw his Far Eastern army into the battle for Moscow, which decided the outcome of the war in his favor.

After concluding the nonaggression treaty, Stalin, in an unprecedented gesture, saw the Japanese Foreign Minister, Yosuke Matsuoka, off at the train station. Symbolic of the importance Stalin attached to the treaty, it also provided him with the occasion—in the presence of the entire diplomatic corps—to invite negotiations with Germany while flaunting his increased bargaining power. "The European problem can be solved in a natural way if Japan and the Soviets cooperate," said Stalin to the Foreign Minister loudly enough for everyone to hear—probably to imply that, with his eastern border secure, his bargaining position in Europe had improved, but perhaps also that Germany did not need to go to war with the Soviet Union to free Japan's rear for war with the United States.

"Not only the European problem," replied the Japanese Foreign Minister. "The whole world can be settled!" affirmed Stalin—as long as others do the fighting, he must have thought, and the Soviet Union receives compensation for their successes.

As a way of conveying his message to Berlin, Stalin then walked over to German Ambassador von der Schulenburg, put his arm around him, and announced, "We must remain friends and you must now do everything to that end." To make sure he had used every channel, including the military, to convey his message, Stalin next walked over to the acting German military attaché and said loudly, "We will stay friends with you, whatever happens."[17]

Stalin had every reason to be concerned about German attitudes. As Molotov had hinted in Berlin, he had been pressing Bulgaria to accept a Soviet guarantee. Stalin had also negotiated a friendship and nonaggression treaty with Yugoslavia in April 1941, at the precise moment Germany was seeking transit rights through Yugoslavia to attack Greece—a course of conduct certain to encourage Yugoslav resistance to German pressures. As it turned out, the Soviet treaty with Yugoslavia was signed only hours before the German army crossed the Yugoslav frontier.

Stalin's principal weakness as a statesman was his tendency to ascribe to his adversaries the same capacity for cold calculation of which he was so proud in himself. This caused Stalin to underestimate the impact of his own intransigence and to overestimate the scope available in his, however rare, efforts at conciliation. This attitude was to blight his relations with the democracies after the war. In 1941, he was clearly convinced up until the time the Germans crossed the Soviet border that he might at the last minute stave off the assault by generating a negotiation—during which all the indications are that he was prepared to make vast concessions.

Stalin certainly did not fail to deflect an attack from Germany for lack of trying. On May 6, 1941, the Soviet people were informed that Stalin had taken over the position of Prime Minister from Molotov, who remained as Deputy Prime Minister and Minister of Foreign Affairs. It was the first time that Stalin emerged from the recesses of the Communist Party to assume visible responsibility for the day-to-day conduct of affairs.

Only circumstances of extreme peril could have propelled Stalin to abandon the aura of mysterious menace that was his preferred method of government. Andrei Vyshinsky, then Deputy Foreign Minister, told the Ambassador of Vichy France that Stalin's emergence in public office marked "the greatest historical event in the Soviet Union since its inception."[18] Von der Schulenburg thought he had divined Stalin's purpose. "In my opinion," he told Ribbentrop, "it may be assumed with certainty that Stalin has set himself a foreign policy goal of overwhelming importance for the Soviet Union, which he hopes to attain by his personal efforts. I firmly believe that, in an international situation which he considers serious, Stalin has set himself the goal of preserving the Soviet Union from a conflict with Germany."[19]

The next few weeks demonstrated the accuracy of the German Ambassador's prediction. As a way of sending a signal of reassurance to Germany, TASS, on May 8, denied that there were any unusual Soviet troop concentrations along the western borders. Over the following weeks, Stalin broke diplomatic relations with every European government in exile located in London—with the wounding explanation that their affairs should henceforth be dealt with by the German Embassy. Stalin simultaneously recognized the puppet governments Germany had set up in some of the occupied territories. In sum, Stalin went out of his way to assure Germany that he recognized all its existing conquests.

To remove any possible pretext for aggression, Stalin would not permit forward Soviet military units to be placed on heightened alert. And he ignored British and American warnings of an imminent German attack— in part because he suspected the Anglo-Saxons of trying to embroil him in a fight with Germany. Though Stalin forbade firing on the ever-mounting German reconnaissance overflights, well back from the front he did permit civil-defense exercises and the calling up of reserves. Obviously, Stalin had decided that his best chance for any last-minute deal was to reassure the Germans of his intentions, especially since, of the countermeasures available, none was really likely to make a decisive difference.

On June 13, nine days before the Germans attacked, TASS published another official statement denying widespread rumors of imminent war. The Soviet Union, the statement read, planned to observe all its existing agreements with Germany. The release also hinted broadly at the possibility of new negotiations leading to improved arrangements on all disputed issues. That Stalin had indeed been prepared to make major concessions could be seen from Molotov's reaction when, on June 22, von der Schulenburg brought him the German declaration of war. The Soviet Union, Molotov remonstrated plaintively, had been prepared to remove all its troops from the frontier as a reassurance to Germany. All other demands were negotiable. Molotov said, being uncharacteristically defensive, "Surely we have not deserved that."[20]

Apparently Stalin was so shocked by Germany's declaration of war that he fell into something of a depression for a period of about ten days. On July 3, however, he resumed command, delivering a major radio address. Unlike Hitler, Stalin was not a born orator. He rarely spoke in public, and when he did, he was extremely pedantic. In this address too he relied on a dry recitation of the monumental task that lay before the Russian peoples. Yet his very matter-of-factness conveyed a certain resolution and the sense that the job, however huge, was manageable.

"History shows," said Stalin, "that there are no invincible armies, and never have been." Issuing orders for the destruction of all machinery and rolling stock, and for the formation of guerrilla forces behind German lines, Stalin read off a sheaf of figures as if he were an accountant. His sole bow to rhetoric had been at the beginning of the speech. Never before had Stalin appealed to his people on a personal level—nor would he ever again: "Comrades, citizens, brothers and sisters, fighting men of our army and navy. I am speaking to you, my friends!"[21]

Hitler finally had the war he had always wanted. And he had sealed his doom, which, it is possible, he had also always wanted. German leaders, now fighting on two fronts, had overreached for the second time in a generation. Some 70 million Germans were engaged in combat against some 700 million adversaries once Hitler had brought America into the war in December 1941. Apparently even Hitler was awestruck at the task he had set before himself. Just hours before the attack, he told his staff: "I feel as if I am pushing open the door to a dark room, never seen before, without knowing what lies behind the door."[22]

Stalin had gambled on Hitler's rationality, and he had lost; Hitler had gambled that Stalin would quickly collapse, and he too had lost. But whereas Stalin's error was retrievable, Hitler's was not.

CHAPTER FIFTEEN

America Re-enters the Arena: Franklin Delano Roosevelt

For contemporary political leaders governing by public opinion polls, Roosevelt's role in moving his isolationist people toward participation in the war serves as an object lesson on the scope of leadership in a democracy. Sooner or later, the threat to the European balance of power would have forced the United States to intervene in order to stop Germany's

369

drive for world domination. The sheer, and growing, strength of America was bound to propel it eventually into the center of the international arena. That this happened with such speed and so decisively was the achievement of Franklin Delano Roosevelt.

All great leaders walk alone. Their singularity springs from their ability to discern challenges that are not yet apparent to their contemporaries. Roosevelt took an isolationist people into a war between countries whose conflicts had only a few years earlier been widely considered inconsistent with American values and irrelevant to American security. After 1940, Roosevelt convinced the Congress, which had overwhelmingly passed a series of Neutrality Acts just a few years before, to authorize ever-increasing American assistance to Great Britain, stopping just short of outright belligerency and occasionally even crossing that line. Finally, Japan's attack on Pearl Harbor removed America's last hesitations. Roosevelt was able to persuade a society which had for two centuries treasured its invulnerability of the dire perils of an Axis victory. And he saw to it that, this time, America's involvement would mark a first step toward permanent international engagement. During the war, his leadership held the alliance together and shaped the multilateral institutions which continue to serve the international community to this day.

No president, with the possible exception of Abraham Lincoln, has made a more decisive difference in American history. Roosevelt took the oath of office at a time of national uncertainty, when America's faith in the New World's infinite capacity for progress had been severely shaken by the Great Depression. All around him, democracies seemed to be faltering and antidemocratic governments on both the Left and the Right were gaining ground.

After Roosevelt had restored hope at home, destiny imposed on him the obligation of defending democracy around the world. No one has described this aspect of Roosevelt's contribution better than Isaiah Berlin:

> [Roosevelt] looked upon the future with a calm eye, as if to say 'Let it come, whatever it may be, it will all be grist to our great mill. We shall turn it all to benefit.' . . . In a despondent world which appeared divided between wicked and fatally efficient fanatics marching to destroy, and bewildered populations on the run, unenthusiastic martyrs in a cause they could not define, he believed in his own ability, so long as he was at the controls, to stem this terrible tide. He had all the character and energy and skill of the dictators, and he was on our side.[1]

Roosevelt had already served as Assistant Secretary of the Navy in Wilson's Administration, and had been the Democrats' vice-presidential candidate in the1920 election. Many leaders, among them de Gaulle, Churchill, and Adenauer, have been impelled to come to terms with the loneliness inherent in the journey toward greatness by a period of withdrawal from public life. Roosevelt's was imposed on him when he was struck down by polio in 1921. In an extraordinary demonstration of willpower, he overcame his disability and learned to stand with the aid of braces and even to walk a few steps, which enabled him to appear before the public as if he were not paralyzed at all. Until his report to the Congress on Yalta in 1945, Roosevelt stood whenever he delivered a major speech. Because the media cooperated with Roosevelt's attempt to play his role with dignity, the vast majority of Americans never realized the extent of Roosevelt's handicap or had its perceptions of him tinged by pity.

Roosevelt, an ebullient leader who used charm to maintain his aloofness, was an ambiguous combination of political manipulator and visionary. He governed more often by instinct than by analysis, and evoked strongly contrasting emotions.[2] As has been summarized by Isaiah Berlin, Roosevelt had serious shortcomings of character, which included unscrupulousness, ruthlessness, and cynicism. Yet Berlin concluded that, in the end, these were more than dramatically outweighed by Roosevelt's positive traits:

> What attracted his followers were countervailing qualities of a rare and inspiring order: he was large-hearted and possessed wide political horizons, imaginative sweep, understanding of the time in which he lived and of the direction of the great new forces at work in the twentieth century. . . .[3]

This was the president who propelled America into a leadership role internationally, an environment where questions of war or peace, progress or stagnation all around the world came to depend on his vision and commitment.

America's journey from involvement in the First World War to active participation in the Second proved to be a long one—interrupted as it was by the nation's about-face to isolationism. The depth of America's revulsion toward international affairs illustrates the magnitude of Roosevelt's achievement. A brief sketch of the historical backdrop against which Roosevelt conducted his policies is therefore necessary.

In the 1920s, America's mood was ambivalent, oscillating between a willingness to assert principles of universal applicability and a need to justify them on behalf of an isolationist foreign policy. Americans took to reciting the traditional themes of their foreign policy with even greater emphasis: the uniqueness of America's mission as the exemplar of liberty, the moral superiority of democratic foreign policy, the seamless relationship between personal and international morality, the importance of open diplomacy, and the replacement of the balance of power by international consensus as expressed in the League of Nations.

All of these presumably universal principles were enlisted on behalf of American isolationism. Americans were still incapable of believing that anything outside the Western Hemisphere could possibly affect their security. The America of the 1920s and 1930s rejected even its own doctrine of collective security lest it lead to involvement in the quarrels of distant, bellicose societies. The provisions of the Treaty of Versailles were interpreted as vindictive, and reparations as self-defeating. When the French occupied the Ruhr, America used the occasion to withdraw its remaining occupying forces from the Rhineland. That Wilsonian exceptionalism had established criteria no international order could fulfill, made disillusionment a part of its very essence.

Disillusionment with the results of the war erased to a considerable extent the distinctions between the internationalists and the isolationists. Not even the most liberal internationalists any longer discerned an American interest in sustaining a flawed postwar settlement. No significant group had a good word to say about the balance of power. What passed for internationalism was being identified with membership in the League of Nations rather than with day-to-day participation in international diplomacy. And even the most dedicated internationalists insisted that the Monroe Doctrine superseded the League of Nations, and recoiled before the idea of America's joining League enforcement measures, even economic ones.

The isolationists carried these attitudes toward their ultimate conclusion. They attacked the League of Nations in principle, on the ground that it jeopardized the twin pillars of historic American foreign policy—the Monroe Doctrine and isolationism. The League was believed to be incompatible with the Monroe Doctrine because collective security entitled, indeed required, the League to involve itself in disputes *within* the Western Hemisphere. And was inconsistent with isolationism because the League obliged America to involve itself in disputes *outside* the Western Hemisphere.

The isolationists had a point. If the entire Western Hemisphere were somehow excluded from the operation of collective security, what was to keep the other nations of the world from organizing regional groupings of their own and excluding them from the operations of the League? In that case, the League of Nations would have led to a restoration of a balance-of-power system, albeit on a regional basis. In practice, the internationalists and the isolationists converged on a bipartisan foreign policy. Both rejected foreign intervention within the Western Hemisphere and any participation in League enforcement machinery outside of it. They supported disarmament conferences because there was a clear consensus that arms caused war and that the reduction of arms contributed to peace. They favored internationally endorsed general principles of peaceful settlement, such as the Kellogg-Briand Pact, as long as these agreements did not imply enforcement. Finally, the United States was always helpful on technical, usually financial, issues with no immediate political consequence, such as working out agreed reparations schedules.

The gap in American thinking between approving a principle and participating in its enforcement became dramatically apparent after the 1921–22 Washington Naval Conference. The Conference was important in two respects. It provided for ceilings in naval armaments for the United States, Great Britain, and Japan, granting to the United States a navy equal in size to that of Great Britain, and to Japan a navy three-fifths the size of the United States. This provision reaffirmed America's new role as the dominant power in the Pacific alongside Japan. Great Britain's role in that theater was henceforth secondary. Most important, a second, so-called Four-Power Treaty among Japan, the United States, Great Britain, and France providing for the peaceful settlement of disputes was to replace the old Anglo-Japanese Alliance of 1902, and to usher in an era of cooperation in the Pacific. But if one of the signatories of the Four-Power Treaty disregarded its provisions, would the others take action against it? "The four-power treaty contains no war commitment. . . . There is no commitment to armed force, no alliance, no written or moral obligation to join in defense . . . ," President Harding explained to a skeptical American Senate.[4]

Secretary of State Charles Evans Hughes reinforced the President's words by putting all of the signatories to the pact on notice that America would under no circumstances participate in enforcement measures. But the Senate was still not satisfied. In ratifying the Four-Power Treaty, the Senate added reservations stipulating that this would not commit the United States to using armed force in repelling aggression.[5] In other words, the agreement stood on its own merit; failure to observe it would involve no consequence. America would decide each case as it arose, just as if there were no agreement.

In terms of the way diplomacy had been routinely practiced for centuries, it was indeed an extraordinary proposition that a solemn treaty conferred no right of enforcement, and that enforcement had to be separately negotiated with the Congress on a case-by-case basis. It was a foretaste of the debates between the Nixon Administration and the Congress after the Vietnam Peace agreement of January 1973, wherein the Congress argued that an agreement for which America had fought through three administrations of both parties did not confer any right of enforcement. According to that theory, agreements with America would reflect Washington's mood of the moment; whatever consequences grew out of them would likewise depend on Washington's mood at some other moment—an attitude not very likely to engender confidence in America's commitments.

The Senate's reserve had not inhibited President Harding's enthusiasm for the Four-Power Treaty. At the signing ceremony, he praised it because it protected the Philippines and marked "the beginning of a new and better epoch in human progress." How was it possible for a treaty without enforcement provisions to protect a prize as rich as the Philippines? Despite his position on the opposite end of the political spectrum, Harding invoked the standard Wilsonian liturgy. The world, he said, would punish violators by proclaiming "the odiousness of perfidy or infamy."[6] Harding, however, failed to explain how world public opinion was to be determined, let alone marshaled, and for what cause, so long as America refused to join the League of Nations.

The Kellogg-Briand Pact, the impact of which on Europe was discussed in chapter 11, turned into another example of America's tendency to treat principles as self-implementing. Although American leaders enthusiastically proclaimed the historic nature of the treaty because sixty-two nations had renounced war as an instrument of national policy, they adamantly refused to endorse any machinery for applying it, much less for enforcing it. President Calvin Coolidge, waxing effusive before the Congress in December 1928, asserted: "Observance of this Covenant . . . promises more for the peace of the world than any other agreement ever negotiated among the nations."[7]

Yet how was this utopia to be achieved? Coolidge's passionate defense of the Kellogg-Briand Pact spurred internationalists and supporters of the League to argue, quite reasonably, that, war having been outlawed, the concept of neutrality had lost all meaning. In their view, since the League had been designed to identify aggressors, the international community was obliged to punish them appropriately. "Does anyone believe," asked one of the proponents of this view, "that the aggressive designs of Mussolini could be checked merely by the good faith of the Italian people and the power of public opinion?"[8]

The prescience of this question did not enhance its acceptability. Even

while the treaty bearing his name was still in the process of being debated, Secretary of State Kellogg, in an address before the Council on
Foreign Relations, stressed that force would never be used to elicit compliance. Reliance on force, he argued, would turn what had been intended
as a long stride toward peace into precisely the sort of military alliance
that was so in need of being abolished. Nor should the Pact include a
definition of aggression, since any definition would omit something and
thereby weaken the nobility of the Pact's wording.[9] For Kellogg, the word
was not only the beginning, it was the end:

> A nation claiming to act in self-defense must justify itself before the bar
> of world opinion as well as before the signatories of the treaty. For that
> reason I declined to place in the treaty a definition of aggressor or of
> self-defense because I believed that no comprehensive legalistic defini-
> tion could be framed in advance. . . . This would make it more difficult
> rather than less difficult for an aggressor nation to prove its inno-
> cence.[10]

The Senate was no more impressed by Kellogg's explanations than it had
been six years earlier by Harding's exegesis of why the Four-Power Treaty
did not mean what it said. Now it added three "understandings" of its
own: in the Senate's view, the treaty did not limit either the right of self-
defense or of the Monroe Doctrine, nor did it create any obligation to
assist victims of aggression—which meant that every foreseeable contingency had been exempted from its provisions. The Senate endorsed the
Kellogg-Briand Pact as a statement of principle while insisting that the
treaty had no practical implications, raising the question whether involving America even in an enunciation of principle was worth the reservations it would inevitably elicit.

If the United States rejected alliances and was casting doubts on the
efficacy of the League, how was the Versailles system to be safeguarded?
Kellogg's answer proved far less original than his critique, being that old
standby, the force of public opinion:

> . . . if by this treaty all the nations solemnly pronounce against war as an
> institution for settling international disputes, the world will have taken
> a forward step, created a public opinion, marshaled the great moral
> forces of the world for its observance, and entered into a sacred obliga-
> tion which will make it far more difficult to plunge the world into
> another great conflict.[11]

Four years later, Kellogg's successor, Henry Stimson, as distinguished and
sophisticated a public servant as America had produced in the entire

interwar period, was not able to advance a better remedy against aggression than the Kellogg-Briand Pact—backed, of course, by the strength of public opinion:

> The Kellogg-Briand Pact provides for no sanctions of force. . . . Instead it rests upon the sanction of public opinion which can be made one of the most potent sanctions of the world. . . . Those critics who scoff at it have not accurately appraised the evolution in world opinion since the Great War.[12]

To a distant island power—as the United States stood vis-à-vis Europe and Asia—the disputes of Europe necessarily appeared abstruse and often irrelevant. Since America possessed a wide margin of safety to insulate it from challenges which threatened European countries without affecting American security, the European countries were in effect functioning as America's safety valves. A similar line of reasoning had led to Great Britain's aloofness from day-to-day European politics during the period of its "splendid isolation."

There was, however, a fundamental difference between Great Britain's "splendid isolation" of the nineteenth century and America's isolationism of the twentieth century. Great Britain, too, had sought to steer clear of Europe's daily squabbles. It recognized, however, that its own safety depended on the balance of power, and it was quite prepared to defend that balance by using the traditional methods of European diplomacy. In contrast, America never accepted the importance of either the balance of power or of the European style of diplomacy. Believing itself blessed by a unique and ultimately superior dispensation, America simply did not engage itself, and if it did, then only for general causes and in accordance with its own particular style of diplomacy—which was vastly more public, more juridical, and ideological than Europe's.

The interaction of the European and American styles of diplomacy during the interwar period therefore tended to combine the worst of both approaches. Feeling threatened, the European countries, especially France and the new nations of Eastern Europe, did not accept America's legacy of collective security and international arbitration, or its juridical definitions of war and peace. The nations which had become converts to the American agenda, principally Great Britain, had no experience in conducting policy on that basis. Yet all of these countries were very well aware that Germany could never have been defeated without America's help. Since the end of the war, the balance of power had become even less favorable toward the wartime Allies. In any new war with Germany, American help would be needed more urgently, and probably sooner than it had been the last time, especially since the Soviet Union was no longer a player.

The practical result of this mixture of fear and hope was that European diplomacy continued to drift further away from its traditional moorings and toward greater emotional dependence on America, producing a double veto: France would not act without Great Britain, and Great Britain would not act contrary to views strongly held in Washington, never mind that American leaders never tired of volubly insisting that they would in no circumstance risk war on behalf of European issues.

America's consistent refusal throughout the 1920s to commit itself to safeguarding the Versailles system proved to be terrible psychological preparation for the 1930s, when international tensions began to erupt. A foretaste of what lay ahead came in 1931, when Japan invaded Manchuria, separated it from China, and turned it into a satellite state. The United States condemned Japan's actions but refused to participate in collective enforcement. In censuring Japan, America introduced a sanction of its own, which at the time seemed like an evasion but which, a decade later, would, in Roosevelt's hands, turn into a weapon for forcing a showdown with Japan. This sanction was the policy of refusing to recognize territorial changes brought about by force. Originated by Stimson in 1932, it was invoked by Roosevelt in the fall of 1941 to demand that Japan withdraw from Manchuria and all of its other conquests.

On January 30, 1933, the world crisis began in earnest with Hitler's accession to the position of German Chancellor. Destiny had decreed that Franklin Delano Roosevelt, who did as much as any other individual to lay Hitler low, would take his oath of office a little more than four weeks later. Still, nothing in Roosevelt's first term foreshadowed such an outcome. Roosevelt rarely deviated from the standard rhetoric of the interwar period and repeated the isolationist themes handed down by his predecessors. In a speech before the Woodrow Wilson Foundation on December 28, 1933, Roosevelt addressed the imminent end of the agreed term of the Naval Treaties of the 1920s. He proposed to extend these accords by calling for the abolition of all offensive weapons and—harkening back to Kellogg—by a commitment that no nation permit its military forces to enter the territory of another.

The subject was as familiar as Roosevelt's solution to possible violations of what he was proposing. Once again, the censure of public opinion was invoked as the only available remedy:

> ... no such general agreement for the elimination of aggression or the elimination of the weapons of offensive warfare would be of any value

in this world unless every Nation, without exception, would enter into such an agreement by solemn obligation.... [T]hen, my friends, it would be a comparatively easy matter to separate the sheep from the goats.... It is but an extension of the challenge of Woodrow Wilson for us to propose in this newer generation that from now on war by governments shall be changed to peace by peoples.[13]

There was no provision for what might happen to the goats once they were separated from the sheep.

Roosevelt's proposal was moot by the time it was put forward, since Germany had left the Disarmament Conference two months earlier and refused to return. In any event, banning offensive weapons was not on Hitler's agenda. Nor, as it turned out, did Hitler suffer global opprobrium for having opted for rearmament.

Roosevelt's first term coincided with the heyday of revisionism about the First World War. In 1935, a special Senate Committee under North Dakota's Senator Gerald Nye published a 1400-page report blaming America's entry into the war on armaments manufacturers. Soon thereafter, Walter Millis' best-selling book, *The Road to War,* popularized the thesis for a mass audience.[14] Under the impact of this school of thought, America's participation in the war came to be explained by malfeasance, conspiracy, and betrayal rather than by fundamental or permanent interests.

To prevent America from once again being lured into war, the Congress passed three so-called Neutrality Acts between 1935 and 1937. Prompted by the Nye Report, these laws prohibited loans and any other financial assistance to belligerents (whatever the cause of war) and imposed an arms embargo on all parties (regardless of who the victim was). Purchases of nonmilitary goods for cash were allowed only if they were transported in non-American ships.[15] The Congress was not abjuring profits so much as it was rejecting risks. As the aggressors bestrode Europe, America abolished the distinction between aggressor and victim by legislating a single set of restrictions on both.

The national interest came to be defined in legal rather than gcostrategic terms. In March 1936, Secretary of State Hull advised Roosevelt in exclusively legal terms about the significance of the remilitarization of the Rhineland, which had toppled the military balance of Europe and left the countries of Eastern Europe defenseless: "It would appear from this brief analysis that the action of the German Government has constituted both a violation of the Versailles and Locarno pacts, but as far as the United States is concerned it does not appear to constitute a violation of our treaty[16] of August 25, 1921 with Germany...."[17]

After his landslide electoral victory of 1936, Roosevelt went far beyond the existing framework. In fact, he demonstrated that, though preoccupied with the Depression, he had grasped the essence of the dictators' challenge better than any European leader except Churchill. At first, he sought merely to enunciate America's moral commitment to the cause of the democracies. Roosevelt began this educational process with the so-called Quarantine Speech, which he delivered in Chicago on October 5, 1937. It was his first warning to America of the approaching peril, and his first public statement that America might have to assume some responsibilities with respect to it. Japan's renewed military aggression in China, coupled with the previous year's announcement of the Berlin-Rome Axis, provided the backdrop, giving Roosevelt's concerns a global dimension:

> The peace, the freedom and the security of ninety percent of the population of the world is being jeopardized by the remaining ten percent who are threatening a breakdown of all international order and law.... It seems to be unfortunately true that the epidemic of world lawlessness is spreading. When an epidemic of physical disease starts to spread, the community approves and joins in a quarantine of the patients in order to protect the health of the community against the spread of the disease.[18]

Roosevelt was careful not to spell out what he meant by "quarantine" and what, if any, specific measures he might have in mind. Had the speech implied any kind of action, it would have been inconsistent with the Neutrality Acts, which the Congress had overwhelmingly approved and the President had recently signed.

Not surprisingly, the Quarantine Speech was attacked by isolationists, who demanded clarification of the President's intentions. They argued passionately that the distinction between "peace-loving" and "warlike" nations implied an American value judgment which, in turn, would lead to the abandonment of the policy of nonintervention, to which both Roosevelt and the Congress had pledged themselves. Two years later, Roosevelt described the uproar that resulted from the speech as follows: "Unfortunately, this suggestion fell upon deaf ears—even hostile and resentful ears.... It was hailed as war mongering; it was condemned as attempted intervention in foreign affairs; it was even ridiculed as a nervous search 'under the bed' for dangers of war which did not exist."[19]

Roosevelt could have ended the controversy by simply denying the intentions being ascribed to him. Yet, despite the critical onslaught, Roosevelt spoke ambiguously enough at a news conference to keep open the option of collective defense of some kind. According to the journalistic practice of the day, the President always met with the press off-the-record, which meant that he could neither be quoted nor identified, and these rules were respected.

Years later, the historian Charles Beard published a transcript showing Roosevelt dodging and weaving but never denying that the Quarantine Speech represented a new approach, while refusing to say just what the new approach was.[20] Roosevelt insisted that his speech implied actions that went beyond moral condemnation of aggression: "There are a lot of methods in the world that have never been tried yet."[21] Asked whether this meant that he had a plan, Roosevelt replied, "I can't give you any clue to it. You will have to invent one. *I have got one.*"[22] He never explained what that plan was.

Roosevelt the statesman might warn against the impending danger; Roosevelt the political leader had to navigate among three currents of American opinion: a small group advocating unambiguous support for all "peace-loving" nations; a somewhat more significant group that went along with such support as long as it stopped well short of war; and a vast majority supporting the letter and the spirit of the neutrality legislation. A skillful political leader will always try to keep open as many options as possible. He will want to present his ultimate course as his own optimum choice rather than as having been imposed by events. And no modern American president was better at this kind of tactical management than Roosevelt.

In a Fireside Chat devoted mostly to domestic issues on October 12, 1937—a week after the Quarantine Speech—Roosevelt tried to satisfy all three groups. Underlining his commitment to peace, he spoke approvingly of a forthcoming conference of the signatories of the Washington Naval Treaty of 1922 and described American participation in it as a demonstration of "our purpose to cooperate with the other signatories to this Treaty, including China and Japan."[23] The conciliatory language suggested a desire for peace, even with Japan; at the same time, it would serve as a demonstration of good faith if cooperation with Japan should prove impossible. Roosevelt was equally ambiguous about America's international role. He reminded his audience of his own wartime experience as Assistant Secretary of the Navy: ". . . remember[ing] that from 1913 to 1921, I personally was fairly close to world events, and in that period, while I learned much of what to do, I also learned much of what not to do."[24]

Roosevelt surely would not have objected if his audience had interpreted this ambiguous statement to mean that his wartime experiences had taught him the importance of nonentanglement. On the other hand, if that was in fact what Roosevelt meant, he would have gained far more popularity had he simply said so. In the light of his later actions, it is more likely that Roosevelt meant to suggest that he would pursue the Wilsonian tradition by means of more realistic methods.

Despite the hostile reaction to his pronouncements, Roosevelt told Colonel Edward House, Wilson's erstwhile confidant, in October 1937, that it would take time to "make people realize that war will be a greater danger to us if we close all doors and windows than if we go out in the street and use our influence to curb the riot."[25] It was another way of saying that the United States would need to participate in international affairs in an as yet unspecified way to help quell the pattern of aggression.

Roosevelt's immediate problem was an outburst of pro-isolationist sentiment. In January 1938, the House of Representatives nearly passed a constitutional amendment requiring a national referendum for declarations of war except in the event of an invasion of the United States. Roosevelt had to make a personal appeal to prevent its passage. In these circumstances, Roosevelt viewed discretion as the better part of valor. In March 1938, the United States government did not react to Austria's *Anschluss* to Germany, following the pattern of the European democracies, which had confined themselves to perfunctory protests. During the crisis leading to the Munich Conference, Roosevelt felt obliged to emphasize repeatedly that America would not join a united front against Hitler. And he disavowed subordinates and even close friends who so much as hinted at that possibility.

In early September 1938, at a dinner celebrating Franco-American relations, the American Ambassador to France, William C. Bullitt, repeated a standard platitude—that France and the United States were "united in war and peace."[26] This was enough to trigger an isolationist uproar. Roosevelt, who could not have known of Bullitt's comments in advance since they were the sort of boilerplate rhetoric left to the discretion of ambassadors, nevertheless took pains to reject the insinuation that the United States was aligning itself with the democracies as being "100 percent wrong."[27] Later that month, when war seemed imminent and after Chamberlain had already met with Hitler twice, Roosevelt sent Chamberlain two messages, on September 26 and 28, urging a conference of the interested powers that, in the existing circumstances, could only magnify pressures for major Czech concessions.

Munich seems to have been the turning point which impelled Roosevelt to align America with the European democracies, at first politically but gradually materially as well. From then on, his commitment to thwarting the dictators was inexorable, culminating three years later in America's entry into a second world war. The interplay between leaders and their publics in a democracy is always complex. A leader who confines himself to the experience of his people in a period of upheaval purchases temporary popularity at the price of condemnation by posterity, whose claims he is neglecting. A leader who gets too far ahead of his society will become irrelevant. A great leader must be an educator, bridging the gap between his visions and the familiar. But he must also be willing to walk alone to enable his society to follow the path he has selected.

There is inevitably in every great leader an element of guile which simplifies, sometimes the objectives, sometimes the magnitude, of the task. But his ultimate test is whether he incarnates the truth of his society's values and the essence of its challenges. These qualities Roosevelt possessed to an unusual degree. He deeply believed in America; he was convinced that Nazism was both evil and a threat to American security, and he was extraordinarily guileful. And he was prepared to shoulder the burden of lonely decisions. Like a tightrope walker, he had to move, step by careful, anguishing step, across the chasm between his goal and his society's reality in demonstrating to it that the far shore was in fact safer than the familiar promontory.

On October 26, 1938, less than four weeks after the Munich Pact, Roosevelt returned to the theme of his Quarantine Speech. In a radio address to the Herald-Tribune Forum, he warned against unnamed but easily identifiable aggressors whose "national policy adopts as a deliberate instrument the threat of war."[28] Next, while upholding disarmament in principle, Roosevelt also called for strengthening America's defenses:

> ... we have consistently pointed out that neither we, nor any nation, will accept disarmament while neighbor nations arm to the teeth. If there is not general disarmament, we ourselves must continue to arm. It is a step we do not like to take, and do not wish to take. But, until there is general abandonment of weapons capable of aggression, ordinary rules of national prudence and common sense require that we be prepared.[29]

In secret, Roosevelt went much further. At the end of October 1938, in separate conversations with the British air minister and also with a personal friend of Prime Minister Neville Chamberlain, he put forward a project designed to circumvent the Neutrality Acts. Proposing an outright evasion of legislation he had only recently signed, Roosevelt suggested setting up British and French airplane-assembly plants in Canada, near the American border. The United States would supply all the components, leaving only the final assembly to Great Britain and France. This arrangement would technically permit the project to stay within the letter of the Neutrality Acts, presumably on the ground that the component parts were civilian goods. Roosevelt told Chamberlain's emissary that, "in the event of war with the dictators, he had the industrial resources of the American nation behind him."[30]

Roosevelt's scheme for helping the democracies restore their air power collapsed, as it was bound to, if only because of the sheer logistical impossibility of undertaking an effort on such a scale in secret. But from then on, Roosevelt's support for Britain and France was limited only when the Congress and public opinion could neither be circumvented nor overcome.

In early 1939, in his State of the Union message, Roosevelt identified the aggressor nations as being Italy, Germany, and Japan. Alluding to the theme of his Quarantine Speech, he pointed out that "there are many methods short of war, but stronger and more effective than mere words, of bringing home to aggressor governments the aggregate sentiments of our own people."[31]

In April 1939, within a month of the Nazi occupation of Prague, Roosevelt for the first time designated aggression against smaller countries as constituting a general threat to American security. At a press conference on April 8, 1939, Roosevelt told reporters that "the continued political, economic and social independence of every small nation in the world does have an effect on our national safety and prosperity. Each one that disappears weakens our national safety and prosperity."[32] In a speech before the Pan American Union on April 14, he went a step further by arguing that the United States' security interests could no longer be limited to the Monroe Doctrine:

> Beyond question, within a scant few years air fleets will cross the ocean as easily as today they cross the closed European seas. Economic functioning of the world becomes therefore necessarily a unit; no interruption of it anywhere can fail, in the future, to disrupt economic life everywhere.
>
> The past generation in Pan American matters was concerned with constructing the principles and the mechanisms through which this hemisphere would work together. But the next generation will be concerned with the methods by which the New World can live together in peace with the Old.[33]

In April 1939, Roosevelt addressed Hitler and Mussolini directly in a message which, though ridiculed by the dictators, had been cleverly designed to demonstrate to the American people that the Axis countries indeed had aggressive designs. Surely one of America's subtlest and most devious presidents, Roosevelt asked the dictators—but not Great Britain or France—for assurances that they would not attack some thirty-one specific European and Asian nations for a period of ten years.[34] Roosevelt then undertook to obtain similar assurances from those thirty-one nations with respect to Germany and Italy. Finally, he offered America's participation in any disarmament conference resulting from a relaxation of tensions.

Roosevelt's note will not go down in diplomatic history for meticulous staff work. For instance, Syria and Palestine, French and British mandates respectively, were listed as independent states.[35] Hitler had a grand time using Roosevelt's message as a prop in one of his Reichstag speeches. To general hilarity, Hitler slowly read the long list of countries which Roosevelt was imploring him to leave alone. As the Führer pronounced the names of country after country in a bemused tone of voice, peals of laughter echoed through the Reichstag. Hitler proceeded to inquire of each of the countries listed in Roosevelt's note, many of which were already quaking before him, whether they indeed felt menaced. They, of course, strenuously denied any such concern.

Though Hitler scored the oratorical point, Roosevelt achieved his political objective. By asking only Hitler and Mussolini for assurances, he had stigmatized them as the aggressors before the only audience that, for the moment, mattered to Roosevelt—the American people. To enlist the American public in supporting the democracies, Roosevelt needed to frame the issues in terms that went beyond the balance of power and to portray them as a struggle in defense of innocent victims against an evil aggressor. Both his note and Hitler's reaction to it helped him to achieve that objective.

Roosevelt was quick to translate America's new psychological threshold into strategic coin. During the same month, April 1939, he inched the United States closer to *de facto* military cooperation with Great Britain. An agreement between the two countries freed the Royal Navy to concentrate all of its forces in the Atlantic while the United States moved the bulk of its fleet to the Pacific. This division of labor implied that the United States assumed responsibility for the defense of Great Britain's Asian possessions against Japan. Prior to World War I, an analogous arrangement between Great Britain and France (which had led to the concentration of the French fleet in the Mediterranean) had been used as an argument that Great Britain was morally obliged to enter World War I in defense of France's Atlantic coast.

Isolationists observing Roosevelt's actions were deeply disturbed. In February 1939, before the outbreak of the war, Senator Arthur Vandenberg had eloquently put forward the isolationist case:

> True, we do live in a foreshortened world in which, compared with Washington's day, time and space are relatively annihilated. But I still thank God for two insulating oceans; and even though they be foreshortened, they are still our supreme benediction if they be widely and prudently used. . . .
>
> We all have our sympathies and our natural emotions in behalf of the victims of national or international outrage all around the globe; but we are not, we cannot be, the world's protector or the world's policeman.[36]

When, in response to the German invasion of Poland, Great Britain declared war on September 3, 1939, Roosevelt had no choice but to invoke the Neutrality Acts. At the same time, he moved rapidly to modify the legislation to permit Great Britain and France to purchase American arms.

Roosevelt had avoided invoking the Neutrality Acts in the war between Japan and China, ostensibly because no war had been declared, in reality because he believed that an arms embargo would hurt China far more than it would Japan. But if war broke out in Europe, it would be formally declared and he would not be able to resort to subterfuge to circumvent the Neutrality Acts. Therefore, in early 1939, Roosevelt called for a revision of the Neutrality Acts on the ground that they "may operate unevenly and unfairly—and may actually give aid to the aggressor and deny it to the victim."[37] The Congress did not act until after the European war had actually started. Indicating the strength of the isolationist mood, Roosevelt's proposal had been defeated three times in the Congress earlier in the year.

The same day that Great Britain declared war, Roosevelt called a special session of the Congress for September 21. This time, he prevailed. The so-called Fourth Neutrality Act of November 4, 1939, permitted belligerents to purchase arms and ammunition from the United States, provided they paid in cash and transported their purchases in their own or neutral ships. Since, because of the British blockade, only Great Britain and France were in a position to do so, "neutrality" was becoming an increasingly technical term. The Neutrality Acts had lasted only as long as there had been nothing to be neutral about.

During the so-called phony war, America's leaders continued to believe that only material aid was required of them. Conventional wisdom had it that the French army, behind the Maginot Line, and backed by the Royal Navy, would strangle Germany through the combination of a defensive ground war and a naval blockade.

In February 1940, Roosevelt sent Undersecretary of State Sumner Welles on a mission to Europe to explore the possibilities of peace during the "phony war." French Prime Minister Daladier inferred that Welles was urging a compromise peace that left Germany in control of Central Europe, though the majority of Welles' interlocutors did not interpret his remarks that way and, for Daladier, the wish may have been father to the thought.[38] Roosevelt's purpose in sending Welles to Europe had been not to mediate so much as to demonstrate his commitment to peace to his isolationist people. He also wanted to establish America's claim to participation should the "phony war" culminate in a peace settlement. Germany's assault on Norway a few weeks later put an end to that particular mission.

On June 10, 1940, as France was falling to the Nazi invaders, Roosevelt abandoned formal neutrality and came down eloquently on the side of Great Britain. In a powerful speech in Charlottesville, Virginia, he combined a scathing denunciation of Mussolini, whose armies had attacked France that day, with America's commitment to extend all-out material aid to every country resisting German aggression. At the same time, he proclaimed that America would increase its own defenses:

> On this tenth day of June, 1940, in this University founded by the first great American teacher of democracy, we send forth our prayers and our hopes to those beyond the seas who are maintaining with magnificent valor their battle for freedom.
>
> In our American unity, we will pursue two obvious and simultaneous courses; we will extend to the opponents of force the material resources of this nation; and, at the same time, we will harness and speed up the use of those resources in order that we ourselves in the Americas may have equipment and training equal to the task of any emergency and every defense.[39]

Roosevelt's Charlottesville speech marked a watershed. Faced with Great Britain's imminent defeat, any American president might have discovered in the Royal Navy an essential component to the security of the Western Hemisphere. But it is difficult to imagine any contemporary of Roosevelt —of either political party—who, having had the courage and foresight to recognize the challenge, would have had the willpower to lead his isolationist people, step by step, toward the commitment to do whatever was necessary to defeat Nazi Germany.

The expectation thus raised that America would, sooner or later, become Great Britain's ally was surely one of the most decisive elements in sustaining Churchill's decision to continue to fight alone:

> We shall go on to the end. . . . And even if, which I do not for a moment believe, this island or a large part of it were subjugated and starving, then our Empire beyond the seas, armed and guarded by the British Fleet, would carry on the struggle, until, in God's good time, the New World, with all its power and might, steps forth to the rescue and the liberation of the Old.[40]

Roosevelt's methods were complex—elevated in their statement of objectives, devious in tactic, explicit in defining the issues, and less than frank in explaining the intricacies of particular events. Many of Roosevelt's actions were on the fringes of constitutionality. No contemporary president could resort to Roosevelt's methods and remain in office. Yet Roosevelt had clearly seen that America's margin of safety was shrinking and that a victory of the Axis Powers would eliminate it. Above all, he found Hitler to be anathema to all the values for which America had historically stood.

After the fall of France, Roosevelt increasingly stressed the imminent threat to American security. To Roosevelt, the Atlantic was possessed of the same meaning which the English Channel held for British statesmen. He saw it as a vital national interest that it not be dominated by Hitler. Thus, in his State of the Union Address of January 6, 1941, Roosevelt linked American security to the survival of the Royal Navy:

> I have recently pointed out how quickly the tempo of modern warfare could bring into our very midst the physical attack which we must eventually expect if the dictator nations win the war.
>
> There is much loose talk of our immunity from immediate and direct invasion from across the seas. Obviously, as long as the British Navy retains its powers, no such danger exists.[41]

Of course, if that were true, America was obliged to make every effort to prevent Great Britain's defeat—in the extreme case, even to enter the war itself.

Roosevelt had for many months been acting on the premise that America might have to enter the war. In September 1940, he had devised an ingenious arrangement to give Great Britain fifty allegedly over-age destroyers in exchange for the right to set up American bases on eight British possessions, from Newfoundland to the South American mainland. Winston Churchill later called it a "decidedly unneutral act," for the destroyers were far more important to Great Britain than the bases were to America. Most of them were quite remote from any conceivable theater of operations, and some even duplicated existing American bases. More than anything, the destroyer deal represented a pretext based on a legal opinion by Roosevelt's own appointee, Attorney General Francis Biddle —hardly an objective observer.

Roosevelt sought neither Congressional approval nor modification of the Neutrality Acts for his destroyer-for-bases deal. Nor was he challenged, as inconceivable as that seems in the light of contemporary practice. It was the measure of Roosevelt's concern about a possible Nazi victory and of his commitment to bolstering British morale, that he took this step as a presidential election campaign was just beginning. (It was fortunate for Great Britain and for the cause of American unity that the foreign policy views of his opponent, Wendell Willkie, were not significantly different from Roosevelt's.)

Concurrently, Roosevelt vastly increased the American defense budget and, in 1940, induced the Congress to introduce peacetime conscription. So strong was lingering isolationist sentiment that conscription was renewed by only one vote in the House of Representatives in the summer of 1941, less than four months before the outbreak of the war.

Immediately after the election, Roosevelt moved to eliminate the requirement of the Fourth Neutrality Act—that American war materials could only be purchased for cash. In a Fireside Chat, borrowing a term from Wilson, he challenged the United States to become the "arsenal of democracy."[42] The legal instrument for bringing this about was the Lend-Lease Act, which gave the President discretionary authority to lend, lease, sell, or barter under any terms he deemed proper any defense article to "the government of any country whose defense the President deems vital to the defense of the United States." Secretary of State Hull, normally a passionate Wilsonian and an advocate of collective security, rather uncharacteristically justified the Lend-Lease Act on strategic grounds. Without massive American help, he argued, Great Britain would fall and control of the Atlantic would pass into hostile hands, jeopardizing the security of the Western Hemisphere.[43]

Yet, if this were true, America could avoid participation in the war only if Great Britain were by itself able to overcome Hitler, which even Churchill did not believe was possible. Senator Taft stressed this point in his opposition to Lend-Lease. The isolationists organized themselves as the so-called America First Committee, headed by General Robert E. Wood, Chairman of the board of Sears, Roebuck and Company, and supported by prominent leaders in many fields, among them Kathleen Norris, Irvin S. Cobb, Charles A. Lindbergh, Henry Ford, General Hugh S. Johnson, Chester Bowles, and Theodore Roosevelt's daughter, Mrs. Nicholas Longworth.

The passion behind the isolationists' opposition to Lend-Lease was captured in a comment by Senator Arthur Vandenberg, one of their most thoughtful spokesmen, on March 11, 1941: "We have tossed Washington's Farewell Address into the discard. We have thrown ourselves squarely into the power politics and the power wars of Europe, Asia and Africa. We have taken the first step upon a course from which we can never hereafter retreat."[44] Vandenberg's analysis was correct, but it was the world that had imposed the necessity; and it was Roosevelt's merit to have recognized it.

After proposing Lend-Lease, Roosevelt made his determination to bring about the defeat of the Nazis more explicit with every passing month. Even before the Act was passed, the British and American chiefs of staff, anticipating its approval, met to organize the resources about to be made available. While together, they also began planning for the time when the United States would be an active participant in the war. For these planners, only the timing of America's entry into the war remained yet to be settled. Roosevelt did not initial the so-called ABC-1 Agreement, according to which, in case of war, top priority would be given to the struggle against Germany. But it was clear that this was due to domestic imperatives and constitutional restrictions, not to any ambiguity about his purposes.

Nazi atrocities increasingly eroded the distinction between fighting to promote American values and fighting to defend American security. Hitler had gone so far beyond any acceptable norm of morality that the battle against him assimilated the triumph of good over evil into the struggle for naked survival. Thus, in January 1941, Roosevelt summed up America's objectives in what he called the Four Freedoms: freedom of speech, freedom of worship, freedom from want, and freedom from fear. These goals went far beyond those of any previous European war. Not even Wilson had proclaimed a social issue like freedom from want as a war aim.

In April 1941, Roosevelt took another step toward war by authorizing an agreement with the Danish representative in Washington (whose rank was minister) to allow American forces to occupy Greenland. Since Denmark was under German occupation and since no Danish government-in-exile had been formed, the diplomat without a country took it upon himself to "authorize" American bases on Danish soil. At the same time, Roosevelt privately informed Churchill that, henceforth, American ships would patrol the North Atlantic west of Iceland—covering about two-thirds of the entire ocean—and "publish the position of possible aggressor ships or planes when located in the American patrol area."[45] Three months later, at the invitation of the local government, American troops landed in Iceland, another Danish possession, to replace British forces. Then, without Congressional approval, Roosevelt declared the whole area between these Danish possessions and North America a part of the Western Hemisphere Defense system.

In a lengthy radio address on May 27, 1941, Roosevelt announced a state of emergency and restated America's commitment to social and economic progress:

> We will not accept a Hitler-dominated world. And we will not accept a world, like the postwar world of the 1920s, in which the seeds of Hitlerism can again be planted and allowed to grow.
> We will accept only a world consecrated to freedom of speech and expression—freedom of every person to worship God in his own way—freedom from want—and freedom from terror.[46]

The phrase "will not accept" had to mean that Roosevelt was in effect committing America to go to war for the Four Freedoms if they could not be achieved in any other way.

Few American presidents have been as sensitive and perspicacious as Franklin Delano Roosevelt was in his grasp of the psychology of his people. Roosevelt understood that only a threat to their security could motivate them to support military preparedness. But to take them into a war, he knew he needed to appeal to their idealism in much the same way that Wilson had. In Roosevelt's view, America's security needs might well be met by control of the Atlantic, but its war aims required some vision of a new world order. Thus "balance of power" was not a term ever found in Roosevelt's pronouncements, except when he used it disparagingly. What he sought was to bring about a world community compatible with America's democratic and social ideals as the best guarantee of peace.

In this atmosphere, the president of a technically neutral United States and Great Britain's quintessential wartime leader, Winston Churchill, met in August 1941 on a cruiser off the coast of Newfoundland. Great Britain's position had improved somewhat when Hitler invaded the Soviet Union in June, but England was far from assured of victory. Nevertheless, the joint statement these two leaders issued reflected not a statement of traditional war aims but the design of a totally new world bearing America's imprimatur. The Atlantic Charter proclaimed a set of "common principles" on which the President and Prime Minister based "their hopes for a better future for the world."[47] These principles enlarged upon Roosevelt's original Four Freedoms by incorporating equal access to raw materials and cooperative efforts to improve social conditions around the world.

The Atlantic Charter cast the problem of postwar security entirely in Wilsonian terms and contained no geopolitical component at all. "After the final destruction of the Nazi tyranny," the free nations would renounce the use of force and impose permanent disarmament on the nations "which threaten . . . aggression." This would lead to the encouragement of "all other practicable measures which will lighten for peace-loving peoples the crushing burden of armaments."[48] Two categories of nations were being envisaged: aggressor nations (specifically Germany, Japan, and Italy), which would be permanently disarmed, and "peace-loving countries," which would be permitted to retain military forces, though, it was hoped, at greatly reduced levels. National self-determination would serve as the cornerstone of this new world order.

The difference between the Atlantic Charter and the Pitt Plan, by which Great Britain had proposed to end the Napoleonic Wars, showed the extent to which Great Britain had become the junior partner in the Anglo-American relationship. Not once did the Atlantic Charter refer to a new balance of power, whereas the Pitt Plan had purported to be about nothing else. It was not that Great Britain had become oblivious to the balance of power after just having fought the most desperate war in its long history; rather, Churchill had realized that America's entry into the war would of itself alter the balance of power in Great Britain's favor. In the meantime, he had to subordinate long-term British objectives to immediate necessities—something Great Britain had never felt obliged to do during the Napoleonic Wars.

When the Atlantic Charter was proclaimed, German armies were approaching Moscow and Japanese forces were preparing to move into Southeast Asia. Churchill was above all concerned with removing the obstacles to America's participation in the war. For he understood very well that, by itself, Great Britain would not be able to achieve a decisive victory, even with Soviet participation in the war and American material support. In addition, the Soviet Union might collapse and some compromise between Hitler and Stalin was always a possibility, threatening Great Britain with renewed isolation. Churchill saw no point in debating postwar structure before he could even be certain that there would be one.

In September 1941, the United States crossed the line into belligerency. Roosevelt's order that the position of German submarines be reported to the British Navy had made it inevitable that, sooner or later, some clash would occur. On September 4, 1941, the American destroyer *Greer* was torpedoed while signaling the location of a German submarine to British airplanes. On September 11, without describing the circumstances, Roosevelt denounced German "piracy." Comparing German submarines to a rattlesnake coiled to strike, he ordered the United States Navy to sink "on sight" any German or Italian submarines discovered in the previously established American defense area extending all the way to Iceland. To all practical purposes, America was at war on the sea with the Axis powers.[49]

Simultaneously, Roosevelt took up the challenge of Japan. In response to Japan's occupation of Indochina in July 1941, he abrogated America's commercial treaty with Japan, forbade the sale of scrap metal to it, and encouraged the Dutch government-in-exile to stop oil exports to Japan from the Dutch East Indies (present-day Indonesia). These pressures led to negotiations with Japan, which began in October 1941. Roosevelt instructed the American negotiators to demand that Japan relinquish all of its conquests, including Manchuria, by invoking America's previous refusal to "recognize" these acts.

Roosevelt must have known that there was no possibility that Japan would accept. On December 7, 1941, following the pattern of the Russo-Japanese War, Japan launched a surprise attack on Pearl Harbor and destroyed a significant part of America's Pacific fleet. On December 11, Hitler honored his treaty with Tokyo by declaring war on the United States. Why Hitler thus freed Roosevelt to concentrate America's war effort on the country Roosevelt had always considered to be the principal enemy has never been satisfactorily explained.

America's entry into the war marked the culmination of a great and daring leader's extraordinary diplomatic enterprise. In less than three years, Roosevelt had taken his staunchly isolationist people into a global war. As late as May 1940, 64 percent of Americans had considered the preservation of peace more important than the defeat of the Nazis. Eighteen months later, in December 1941, just before the attack on Pearl Harbor, the proportions had been reversed—only 32 percent favored peace over preventing triumph.[50]

Roosevelt had achieved his goal patiently and inexorably, educating his people one step at a time about the necessities before them. His audiences filtered his words through their own preconceptions and did not always understand that his ultimate destination was war, though they could not have doubted that it was confrontation. In fact, Roosevelt was not so much bent on war as on defeating the Nazis; it was simply that, as time passed, the Nazis could only be defeated if America entered the war.

That their entry into the war should have seemed so sudden to the American people was due to three factors: Americans had had no experience with going to war for security concerns outside the Western Hemisphere; many believed that the European democracies could prevail on their own, while few understood the nature of the diplomacy that had preceded Japan's attack on Pearl Harbor or Hitler's rash declaration of war on the United States. It was a measure of the United States' deep-seated isolationism that it had to be bombed at Pearl Harbor before it would enter the war in the Pacific; and that, in Europe, it was Hitler who would ultimately declare war on the United States rather than the other way around.

By initiating hostilities, the Axis powers had solved Roosevelt's lingering dilemma about how to move the American people into the war. Had Japan focused its attack on Southeast Asia and Hitler not declared war against the United States, Roosevelt's task of steering his people toward his views would have been much more complicated. In light of Roosevelt's proclaimed moral and strategic convictions, there can be little doubt that, in the end, he would have somehow managed to enlist America in the struggle he considered so decisive to both the future of freedom and to American security.

Subsequent generations of Americans have placed a greater premium on total candor by their chief executive. Yet, like Lincoln, Roosevelt sensed that the survival of his country and its values was at stake, and that history itself would hold him responsible for the results of his solitary initiatives. And, as was the case with Lincoln, it is a measure of the debt free peoples owe to Franklin Delano Roosevelt that the wisdom of his solitary passage is now, quite simply, taken for granted.

CHAPTER SIXTEEN

Three Approaches to Peace: Roosevelt, Stalin, and Churchill in World War II

When he attacked the Soviet Union, Hitler launched the most massive land war in the history of mankind. The horror of that war was unprecedented even in comparison to the barbarity attending previous European conflicts. It was a genocidal struggle to the finish. As German armies thrashed their way deep into Russia, Hitler declared war on the United States, turning what had been a European war into a global struggle. The German army ravaged Russia, but was unable to score a knockout blow. In the winter of 1941, it was stopped at the outskirts of Moscow. Then, in the winter of 1942–43, the German offensive, this time aimed at southern

394

Russia, ground to a halt. In a vicious battle in frozen Stalingrad, Hitler lost the entire Sixth Army. The back of the German war effort was broken. The Allied leaders—Churchill, Roosevelt, and Stalin—could now begin to think about victory, and the future shape of the world.

Each of the victors was speaking in terms of his own nation's historical experiences. Churchill wanted to reconstruct the traditional balance of power in Europe. This meant rebuilding Great Britain, France, and even defeated Germany so that, along with the United States, these countries could counterbalance the Soviet colossus to the east. Roosevelt envisioned a postwar order in which the three victors, along with China, would act as a board of directors of the world, enforcing the peace against any potential miscreant, which he thought would most likely be Germany —a vision that was to become known as the "Four Policemen." Stalin's approach reflected both his communist ideology and traditional Russian foreign policy. He strove to cash in on his country's victory by extending Russian influence into Central Europe. And he intended to turn the countries conquered by Soviet armies into buffer zones to protect Russia against any future German aggression.

Roosevelt had been far ahead of his people when he discerned that a Hitler victory would jeopardize American security. But he was at one with his people in rejecting the traditional world of European diplomacy. When he insisted that a Nazi victory would threaten America, he did not mean to enlist America on behalf of restoring the European balance of power. To Roosevelt, the purpose of the war was to remove Hitler as the obstacle to a cooperative international order based on harmony, not on equilibrium.

Roosevelt was therefore impatient with truisms claiming to embody the lessons of history. He rejected the idea that a total defeat of Germany might create a vacuum, which a victorious Soviet Union might then try to fill. He refused to countenance safeguards against possible postwar rivalry among the victors, because these implied the reestablishment of the balance of power, which he in fact wanted to destroy. Peace would be preserved by a system of collective security maintained by the wartime Allies acting in concert and sustained by mutual goodwill and vigilance.

Since there would be no equilibrium to maintain but a state of universal peace, Roosevelt determined that, after the defeat of Nazi Germany, the United States should call its military forces back home. Roosevelt had no intention of permanently stationing American forces in Europe, even less of doing so in order to counterbalance the Soviets, which, in his view, the American public would never countenance. On February 29, 1944, before American troops ever set foot in France, he wrote to Churchill:

Do please don't ask me to keep any American forces in France. I just cannot do it! I would have to bring them all back home. As I suggested before, I denounce and protest the paternity of Belgium, France and Italy. You really ought to bring up and discipline your own children. In view of the fact that they may be your bulwark in future days, you should at least pay for their schooling now![1]

In other words, Great Britain would have to defend Europe without any help from America.

In the same spirit, Roosevelt rejected any American responsibility for the economic reconstruction of Europe:

I do not want the United States to have the postwar burden of reconstituting France, Italy and the Balkans. This is not our natural task at a distance of 3,500 miles or more. It is definitely a British task in which the British are far more vitally interested than we are.[2]

Roosevelt vastly overestimated the postwar capacities of Great Britain by asking it to handle simultaneously the defense and the reconstruction of Europe. Great Britain's position in this scheme was all the more overblown because of Roosevelt's deep disdain for France. In February 1945 at Yalta, the most important conference among the victors, Roosevelt chided Churchill in Stalin's presence for "artificially" trying to build France into a strong power. As if the absurdity of such an endeavor required no elaboration, he mocked Churchill's motive, which he described as an effort to establish a defense line along France's eastern border, behind which Great Britain would then be able to assemble its army.[3] At that time, this happened to be the only conceivable means of opposing Soviet expansionism.

Without being prepared to undertake a permanent American role, Roosevelt wanted the victorious Allies to supervise the disarming and partitioning of Germany and to subject various other countries to their control (amazingly, Roosevelt included France in the category of countries to be controlled). As early as the spring of 1942, on the occasion of a visit by Soviet Foreign Minister Molotov to Washington, Roosevelt sketched his idea of the "Four Policemen" to enforce peace in the postwar world. Harry Hopkins reported the President's thinking in a letter to Churchill:

Roosevelt had spoken to Molotov of a system allowing only the great powers—Great Britain, the United States, the Soviet Union, and possibly China—to have arms. These "policemen" would work together to preserve the peace.[4]

Finally, Roosevelt was determined to put an end to the British and French colonial empires:

> When we've won the war, I will work with all my might and main to see to it that the United States is not wheedled into the position of accepting any plan that will further France's imperialistic ambitions, or that will aid or abet the British Empire in *its* imperial ambitions.[5]

Roosevelt's policy was a heady mixture of traditional American exceptionalism, Wilsonian idealism, and Roosevelt's own canny insight into the American psyche, which had always been more attuned to universal causes than to calculations of rewards and penalties. Churchill had succeeded too well in fostering the illusion that Great Britain was still a great power capable of resisting Soviet expansionism on its own. For only such a conviction can explain Roosevelt's advocacy of a world order based on American troop withdrawals from overseas, a disarmed Germany, a France reduced to second-class status, and a Soviet Union left with a huge vacuum opening up before it. The postwar period thus turned into an exercise for teaching America just how essential it was to the new balance of power.

Roosevelt's scheme of the Four Policemen to bring about and guarantee global peace represented a compromise between Churchill's traditional balance-of-power approach and the unconstrained Wilsonianism of Roosevelt's advisers as epitomized by Secretary of State Cordell Hull. Roosevelt was determined to avoid the failings of the League of Nations and the system which had been established in the wake of the First World War. He wanted some form of collective security, but knew from the experience of the 1920s that collective security required enforcers, and this was to be the role of the Four Policemen.

Roosevelt's concept of the Four Policemen was in fact structurally similar to Metternich's Holy Alliance, though American liberals would be horrified at such a thought. Each system represented an attempt to preserve the peace through a coalition of victors upholding shared values. Metternich's system had worked because it had protected a genuine balance of power, the key countries of which had in fact shared common values, and Russia, though at times disruptive, had more or less cooperated. Roosevelt's concept could not be implemented because no real balance of power emerged from the war, because there was a profound ideological gulf between the victors, and because Stalin, once free of the threat of Germany, had no inhibition about pursuing Soviet ideological and political interests even at the price of confrontation with his erstwhile Allies.

397

Roosevelt made no provision for what might happen if one of the proposed Policemen refused to play the role assigned to it—especially if that Policeman turned out to be the Soviet Union. For, in that case, the despised balance of power would have to be reconstructed after all. And the more thoroughly the elements of traditional equilibrium were jettisoned, the more herculean the task of creating a new balance of power would become.

Had he searched the world, Roosevelt could not have found an interlocutor more different from himself than Stalin. Whereas Roosevelt wanted to implement the Wilsonian concept of international harmony, Stalin's ideas about the conduct of foreign policy were strictly those of Old World *Realpolitik*. When an American general at the Potsdam Conference tried to flatter Stalin by observing how gratifying it had to be to see Russian armies in Berlin, Stalin replied tartly, "Tsar Alexander I reached Paris."

Stalin defined the requirements of peace in the same way that Russian statesmen had for centuries—as the widest possible security belt around the Soviet Union's vast periphery. He welcomed Roosevelt's emphasis on unconditional surrender because it would eliminate the Axis Powers as factors in a peace settlement and prevent the emergence of the German equivalent of Talleyrand at a peace conference.

Ideology reinforced tradition. As a communist, Stalin refused to make any distinction between democratic and fascist nations, though he no doubt considered the democracies less ruthless and perhaps less formidable as well. Stalin possessed no conceptual apparatus to enable him to forgo territory on behalf of goodwill, or "objective" reality for the mood of the moment. Therefore, he was bound to propose to his democratic Allies the same arrangements that he had asked of Hitler a year earlier. Cooperation with Hitler had made him no more sympathetic to Nazism than his subsequent alliance with the democracies impelled him to appreciate the virtues of free institutions. He would take from each temporary partner whatever was possible through diplomacy, and seize by force whatever had not been granted to him freely—as long as he could do so without risking war. His lodestar remained the Soviet national interest as refracted through the prism of communist ideology. To paraphrase Palmerston, he had no friends, only interests.

Stalin had proved most ready to negotiate postwar aims when his military position was the most difficult. With the knife literally at his throat, he attempted to do so in December 1941, when Foreign Secretary Anthony Eden visited Moscow, and again in May 1942, when he sent Molotov to London and then to Washington. These efforts were thwarted, however, because Roosevelt was passionately opposed to any detailed discussion of peace aims. After the battle of Stalingrad, Stalin became increasingly certain that the war would end with the Soviet Union in possession of most of the territories likely to be in dispute. Having less and less to gain from negotiations, Stalin entrusted the shape of the postwar world to the reach of his armies.

Churchill would have been quite prepared to enter a negotiation with Stalin about the postwar European order before Stalin was ever in a position to seize his prizes. After all, expansionist allies like Stalin had been encountered and overcome more than once in British history. Had Great Britain been more powerful, Churchill surely would have sought to extract practical settlements from Stalin while he was still in need of assistance—much as Castlereagh had obtained his allies' commitment to the freedom of the Low Countries well before the end of the Napoleonic Wars.

Churchill had been in the war longer than either of his partners. For nearly a year after the fall of France in June 1940, Great Britain had stood alone against Hitler and had been in no position to reflect on postwar aims. Sheer survival was absorbing all of its energy, and the outcome of the war was quite uncertain. Even with massive American material help, Great Britain could not have hoped to win. If America and the Soviet Union had not entered the war when they did, Great Britain would have eventually been driven to compromise or defeat.

Hitler's attack on the Soviet Union on June 22, 1941, Japan's attack on Pearl Harbor on December 7, 1941, and Hitler's bizarre declaration of war on the United States a few days later guaranteed that Great Britain would be on the winning side no matter how long and painful the war turned out to be. Only from that moment on could Churchill realistically begin to deal with war aims. He would have to do so in a context that was unprecedented for Great Britain. As the war went on, it became more and more apparent that Great Britain's traditional goal of maintaining a balance of power in Europe was moving out of reach and that, after unconditional surrender was imposed on Germany, the Soviet Union would emerge as the dominant nation on the Continent, especially if the United States withdrew its forces.

Churchill's wartime diplomacy therefore consisted of maneuvering between two behemoths—both of which threatened Great Britain's position, albeit from opposite directions. Roosevelt's advocacy of worldwide self-determination was a challenge to the British Empire; Stalin's attempt to project the Soviet Union into the center of Europe threatened to undermine British security.

Trapped between Wilsonian idealism and Russian expansionism, Churchill did his best, from a position of comparative weakness, to vindicate his country's ancient policy—that, if the world is not to be left to the strongest and the most ruthless, peace must be based on some kind of equilibrium. He also clearly understood that, at the end of the war, Great Britain was no longer able to defend its vital interests all by itself, much less to police the balance of power. However outwardly self-assured, Churchill knew—better than his American friends, who still believed that Great Britain would be able to maintain the European equilibrium by itself—that his nation's wartime role was to be its last as a truly independent global power. For Churchill, therefore, no aspect of Allied diplomacy was more important than creating bonds of friendship with America so solid that Great Britain would not need to face the postwar world alone. This was why, at the end of the day, he generally gave in to American preferences—although he often succeeded in convincing his American partner that Washington's strategic interests closely corresponded to those of London.

It proved to be a formidable task. For Roosevelt and his associates were profoundly suspicious of British motives, specifically of the possibility that Churchill might be concerned above all with advancing British national and imperial interests and enhancing the balance of power rather than their own approach to world order.

Most other societies would have treated the British pursuit of the national interest as a matter of course. To American leaders, however, it represented a flaw inherent in the British character. At a private dinner shortly after the attack on Pearl Harbor, Roosevelt had put it this way:

> Our popular idea of that role may not be entirely objective—may not be one hundred per cent true from the British point of view, but there it is; and I've been trying to tell him [Churchill] that he ought to consider it. It's in the American tradition, this distrust, this dislike and even hatred of Britain. . . .[6]

Since Roosevelt did not want to discuss war aims before Stalingrad, and since Stalin preferred to let the battle lines determine the political outcome afterward, most of the wartime ideas about a postwar order came from Churchill. The American reaction to them was aptly captured by Secretary of State Hull in November 1943, in terms highly disparaging to traditional British verities:

> . . . there will no longer be need for spheres of influence, for alliances, for balance of power, or any other of the special arrangements through

400

which, in the unhappy past, the nations strove to safeguard their security or to promote their interests.[7]

Throughout the war, Roosevelt was, on a human level, closer to Churchill than he was to almost any American. Yet, on specific issues, he could also be more acerbic toward the Prime Minister than he was toward Stalin. In Churchill, he found a wartime comrade-in-arms; in Stalin, he saw a partner in preserving postwar peace.

America's ambivalence toward Great Britain was focused on three issues: America's own anticolonial tradition; the nature of wartime strategy; and the shape of postwar Europe. To be sure, Russia was also a huge empire, but its colonies were contiguous to its territory and Russian imperialism had never impinged on the American consciousness in the same way that British colonialism had. Churchill might complain that Roosevelt's comparison of the Thirteen Colonies with British possessions in the twentieth century demonstrated "the difficulties of comparing situations in various centuries and scenes where almost every material fact is totally different. . . ."[8] Roosevelt, however, was less interested in refining historical analogies than in laying down fundamental American principles. At his very first meeting with Churchill, at which the two leaders proclaimed the Atlantic Charter, Roosevelt insisted that the Charter apply not just in Europe, but everywhere, including the colonial areas:

> I am firmly of the belief that if we are to arrive at a stable peace it must involve the development of backward countries. . . . I can't believe that we can fight a war against fascist slavery, and at the same time not work to free people all over the world from a backward colonial policy.[9]

The British War Cabinet utterly rejected such an interpretation:

> . . . the Atlantic Charter . . . was directed to the nations of Europe whom we hoped to free from Nazi tyranny, and was not intended to deal with the internal affairs of the British Empire, or with relations between the United States, and, for example, the Philippines.[10]

The reference to the Philippines was intended to restrain what London considered American overexuberance by bringing home to America's leaders what they stood to lose if they pressed their arguments too far. Yet it ended up missing its mark because America was in fact practicing what it preached, having already decided to grant independence to its only colony as soon as the war ended.

The Anglo-American debate over colonialism would not end. In a 1942 Memorial Day address, Roosevelt's friend and confidant Undersecretary of State Sumner Welles reiterated America's historic opposition to colonialism:

> If this war is in fact a war for the liberation of peoples it must assure the sovereign equality of peoples throughout the world, as well as in the world of the Americas. Our victory must bring in its train the liberation of all peoples. . . . The age of imperialism is ended.[11]

Roosevelt subsequently sent a note to Secretary of State Hull, informing him that Welles' statement was authoritative—the sort of gesture which does not exactly strengthen the bonds of affection between a secretary of state and his deputy because it implies that the deputy has the closer relationship with the president. Hull eventually succeeded in having Welles dismissed.

Roosevelt's views on colonialism were prescient.[12] He wanted America to take the lead in the inevitable liberation of colonial areas lest the quest for self-determination turn into a racial struggle—as Roosevelt confided to his adviser, Charles Taussig:

> The President said he was concerned about the brown people in the East. He said that there are 1,100,000,000 brown people. In many Eastern countries, they are ruled by a handful of whites and they resent it. Our goal must be to help them achieve independence—1,100,000,000 potential enemies are dangerous.[13]

The debate about colonialism could have no practical consequence until the end of the war, by which time Roosevelt would no longer be alive. But the controversy over strategy had immediate implications, reflecting widely differing national concepts of war and peace. Where American leaders tended to believe that military victory was an end in itself, their British counterparts sought to relate military operations to a precise diplomatic plan for the postwar world.

America's most significant military experiences had been its own Civil War, which had been fought to the finish, and the First World War. Both of which had ended in total victory. In American thinking foreign policy and strategy were compartmentalized into successive phases of national policy. In the ideal American universe, diplomats stayed out of strategy, and military personnel completed their task by the time diplomacy started —a view for which America was to pay dearly in the Korean and Vietnam wars.

By contrast, for Churchill, war strategy and foreign policy were closely linked. Since Great Britain's resources were far more limited than those of the United States, its strategists had always been obliged to focus on means as much as ends. And, having been nearly bled white by the First World War, British leaders were determined to avoid another similar carnage. Any strategy which held the promise of minimizing casualties appealed to them.

Almost as soon as America had entered the war, Churchill therefore proposed an attack on what he called the soft underbelly of the Axis in Southern Europe. At the end of the war, insistently though in vain, he urged Eisenhower to capture Berlin, Prague, and Vienna ahead of the Soviet armies. To Churchill, the attractiveness of these targets was neither the vulnerability of the Balkans (which are, in fact, extremely difficult terrain) nor the military potential of the Central European capitals, but their utility in limiting postwar Soviet influence.

America's military leaders reacted to Churchill's recommendations with impatience bordering on outrage. Viewing the soft-underbelly strategy as another example of the British proclivity to enlist America in national British pursuits, they dismissed it on the ground that they would not risk lives for such secondary objectives. From the onset of joint planning, the American commanders were eager to open a second front in France. Indifferent as to the location of the front lines as long as the war ended in total victory, they argued that only in this manner could the main force of the German army be brought to battle. By March 1942, General George Marshall, the United States Army Chief of Staff, infuriated at British resistance to his plans for a second front, threatened to reverse the so-called ABC-1 decision of a year earlier, which had given priority to the European theater, and to switch the main American effort to the Pacific.

Roosevelt now showed that he was as strong a leader in wartime as he had been in guiding his country into the war. Overriding Marshall, Roosevelt reminded the quarreling generals that the initial decision to give priority to the defeat of Germany had been made in the common interest, not as a favor to Great Britain:

> It is of the utmost importance that we appreciate that defeat of Japan does not defeat Germany and that American concentration against Japan this year or in 1943 increases the chance of complete German domina-

tion of Europe and Africa. . . . Defeat of Germany means the defeat of Japan, probably without firing a shot or losing a life.[14]

Roosevelt went along with much of Churchill's strategy but drew the line at a landing in the Balkans. Roosevelt supported the landing in North Africa in November 1942 and, after the conquest of the northern shore of the Mediterranean, a landing in Italy in the spring of 1943, which knocked Italy out of the war. The second front in Normandy did not come about until June 1944, by which time Germany was so weakened that Allied casualties were greatly reduced and a decisive victory was within reach.

Stalin was as passionate an advocate of the second front as were American military leaders, but his motives were geopolitical rather than military. In 1941, he was no doubt eager to draw German forces away from the Russian front. In fact, he was so desperate for military assistance that he invited Great Britain to send an expeditionary force to the Caucasus.[15] In 1942, during the German advance into southern Russia, he continued to press insistently for a second front, though he no longer mentioned an Allied expeditionary force.

Stalin's clamor for a second front continued even after the battle of Stalingrad, in late 1942, had signaled that the tide was turning against Germany. What Stalin found so attractive about a second front was, above all, its distance from Eastern and Central Europe and the Balkans, where Western and Soviet interests were most likely to clash. And it also guaranteed that the capitalists would not escape undamaged from the war. Characteristically, Stalin, even while he insisted on having a voice in Allied planning in the West, denied the democracies the slightest access to Soviet planning or any more than the barest minimum knowledge of Soviet military dispositions.

As it turned out, the Allies drew as many German divisions into Italy— some thirty-three—as Stalin had requested in his demands for a second front in France (he kept asking for between thirty and forty).[16] Still, Stalin accelerated his protests against the Southern strategy. From his point of view, its primary flaw was its geographic proximity to countries which were the object of Soviet ambitions. Stalin pressed for a second front in 1942 and 1943 for the same reason that Churchill sought to delay it: because it would draw the Allies away from the politically disputed areas.

In the debate about the origin of the Cold War, it came to be argued by some distinguished critics that the failure to open a second front earlier had caused Stalin's intransigence in Eastern Europe. According to this line of reasoning, the delay in opening a second front aroused Soviet anger and cynicism far more than any other factor.[17] It defies credulity, however, that the old Bolshevik, fresh from a pact with Hitler and a negotiation to divide the world with the Nazi leader, could be "disillusioned" by *Realpolitik*—if indeed that is what the Allied policy was. It is difficult to imagine the organizer of the purge trials and of the Katyn massacres driven to cynicism by a strategic decision to relate military to political objectives. He played the second front gambit as he did everything else—coldly, calculatingly, and realistically.

The Joint Chiefs of Staff were in any event merely reflecting the conviction of America's political leadership, which was to postpone any discussions of the postwar world until after victory had been achieved. This was the fateful decision that shaped the postwar world and made the Cold War inevitable.

As a general rule, countries striving for stability and equilibrium should do everything within their power to achieve their basic peace terms while still at war. As long as the enemy is in the field, his strength indirectly enhances that of the more peaceful side. If this principle is neglected and the key issues are left unresolved until the peace conference, the most determined power ends up in possession of the prizes and can be dislodged only by a major confrontation.

An Allied agreement on postwar aims, or at least a discussion of them, was especially necessary during World War II because of the policy of unconditional surrender promulgated by Roosevelt and Churchill at Casablanca in January 1943. Roosevelt had proposed the policy for a variety of reasons. He feared that a discussion of peace terms with Germany might prove divisive, and he wanted to focus all of the Allies' energy on winning the war. He was also eager to reassure Stalin, who was then in the throes of the battle of Stalingrad, that there would be no separate peace. But above all, Roosevelt wanted to prevent another round of German revisionist claims later on about how Germany had been tricked into ending the war by unfulfilled promises.

Yet Roosevelt's refusal to discuss the shape of the postwar world while the war was in progress threw America's vast influence behind an outcome which lacked such crucial elements as a balance of power or any criteria for political solutions. In all matters to which the Wilsonian assumptions of an underlying harmony were relevant, Roosevelt played the major role in shaping the postwar world. Under his aegis, a series of international conferences elaborated blueprints for the cooperative components of the postwar world order: for what became the United Nations (at Dumbarton Oaks), for world finance (at Bretton Woods), for food and agriculture (at Hot Springs), for relief and rehabilitation (in Washington), and for civil aviation (in Chicago).[18] But he was adamant in his refusal to discuss war aims, or to risk disagreement with the Soviets on that subject.

At first, Stalin treated Roosevelt's evasion of a discussion of the postwar settlement on the geopolitical level as a tactical maneuver designed to exploit his military difficulties. For him, the war had been about creating a new and more favorable balance of power out of the vacuum left by the imminent disintegration of the Axis. Far too traditional to expect the West to leave the final peace terms to the outcome of military operations, Stalin had tried to involve Eden in December 1941 in a postwar settlement even as German troops were advancing toward the suburbs of Moscow. Stalin's introductory remarks on that occasion made it clear that he was not talking about the Atlantic Charter. Declarations of principle, he said, were like algebra; he preferred practical arithmetic. Stalin did not want to waste time on abstractions, and preferred to trade reciprocal concessions, hopefully in the form of territory.

What Stalin had in mind was plain, old-fashioned *Realpolitik*. Germany should be dismembered, and Poland moved west. The Soviet Union would return to the borders of 1941, meaning specifically the Curzon Line with Poland and the retention of the Baltic states—a clear violation of the principle of self-determination as proclaimed in the Atlantic Charter. In return, the Soviet Union would support any demand Great Britain might choose to make for bases in France, Belgium, the Netherlands, Norway, and Denmark[19]—all of them British allies. Stalin viewed the situation as any eighteenth-century prince would have: to the victor belong the spoils.

On the other hand, Stalin was not yet making any demands about the political future of the Eastern European countries, and he indicated some unspecified flexibility about the frontier with Poland. Nevertheless, Great Britain could not totally violate the Atlantic Charter only three months after its proclamation. And America's leaders would not so much as consider what seemed to them a return to the secret arrangements that had blighted the diplomacy of the First World War. Even so, the terms offered by Stalin, however brutal, were better than what finally emerged from the war—and they probably could have been improved by negotiation. Eden avoided a deadlock by promising to report on his conversations with Stalin to Churchill and Roosevelt, and to continue the dialogue afterward.

Despite the extremity of his military situation—and perhaps because of it—Stalin returned to the subject in the spring of 1942. Churchill was quite prepared to explore a Soviet *quid pro quo* for recognition of the 1941 frontiers. But Roosevelt and his advisers, bent on avoiding any semblance of balance-of-power arrangements, rejected a discussion of postwar issues. Hull wrote to Churchill on behalf of Roosevelt:

> ... it would be a doubtful course to abandon our broad basic declarations of policy, principles, and practice. If these are departed from in one or two important instances, such as you propose, then neither of the two countries parties to such an act will have any precedent to stand on, or any stable rules by which to be governed and to insist that other Governments be governed.[20]

Stalin next tried to bring matters to a head by sending Molotov to London in May 1942. In the preparatory discussions for that visit in April 1942, the Soviet Ambassador, Ivan Maisky, raised Stalin's terms of four months earlier.[21] The Soviet Union now demanded pacts of mutual assistance with Romania and Finland for the postwar period. Considering that German armies were still deep inside the Soviet Union, this came as another extraordinary expression of Stalin's long-range goals—though, it must be noted, it still fell far short, both in terms of reach and of substance, of the satellite orbit which emerged at the end of the war in the absence of an agreement.

Churchill encountered violent opposition from Washington to pursuing these conversations. Hull described the Anglo-Soviet exchanges as contrary to the Atlantic Charter, as a defiance of America's historic opposition to territorial changes by force, and as a throwback to the power politics of a discredited past.[22] Roosevelt weighed in with Stalin along much the same lines. Stalin replied with a curt note acknowledging receipt of Roosevelt's message but without commenting on it, a clear signal that it had not been favorably received. In a note sent simultaneously to Churchill, Stalin urged him to ignore "American interference."[23]

Early in the war, Stalin was clearly eager for an arrangement on the 1941 frontiers; and he was much too cynical not to have expected a request for some kind of *quid pro quo*. Nothing is more futile than historical might-have-beens; the price Stalin was willing to pay will never be known because Roosevelt cut short the Anglo-Soviet dialogue by inviting Molotov to Washington.

On the occasion of Eden's visit to Moscow in December 1941, Stalin had indicated his flexibility on the issue of Poland's borders by calling it an "open question."[24] With 20/20 historical hindsight, Stalin might have been willing to trade the recognition of the 1941 borders for his acceptance of the Eastern European governments-in-exile (which he had not yet challenged) with a caveat for the Baltic States to return to their 1940 independent status and permit Soviet bases on their territory. This might then have led to an outcome for Eastern Europe on the Finnish model—respectful of Soviet security but also democratic and free to conduct a nonaligned foreign policy. It would surely have been better for the well-being of the peoples of Eastern Europe than what transpired and, in the end, even for the Soviet Union.

All such prospects vanished as soon as Molotov reached Washington at the end of May 1942 and learned that America was asking the Soviet Union not for a political arrangement but for an agreement to a new approach to world order. Roosevelt presented Molotov with the American alternative to Stalin's (and Churchill's) ideas on spheres of influence. Quite simply, the formula was a return to Wilson's concept of collective security as modified by the idea of the Four Policemen. Such an arrangement, argued Roosevelt, would provide the Soviet Union with better security than the traditional balance of power.[25]

Why Roosevelt believed that Stalin, who had made such Machiavellian proposals to Churchill, would find world government attractive is not clear. Perhaps he thought that, if worse came to worst and Stalin insisted on keeping the territory his armies had conquered, it would be easier domestically to acquiesce to a *fait accompli* than to agree to Stalin's demands while the military outcome was still uncertain.

Roosevelt was more specific regarding the colonial issue. He proposed an international trusteeship for all former colonies which "ought for our own safety to be taken away from weak nations" (a category in which he included France).[26] And he invited the Soviet Union to become a founding member of the Trusteeship Council.

Had Molotov been more of a philosopher, he might have reflected on the circularity of history by which, in the space of eighteen months, he had been offered membership in two different, opposing, alliances: by Hitler and Ribbentrop in a tripartite pact consisting of Germany, Italy, and Japan; and by Roosevelt in a coalition including the United States, Great Britain, and China. In each case, the suitor had tried to woo Molotov with the prospect of exotic lands to the south: Berlin had offered the Middle East; Washington, colonial trusteeships. In neither case would Molotov permit himself to be deflected from his single-minded pursuit of immediate Soviet objectives within the reach of Soviet armies.

Nor did Molotov see any need to adjust his tactics to the interlocutor at hand. In Washington, as he had done earlier in Berlin, Molotov agreed in principle to join the proposed arrangement. That the Four Policemen would have placed him in the company of the sworn enemies of the grouping whose offer he had likewise entertained eighteen months earlier did not seem to disturb him. Nor, as in Berlin, did Molotov's agreement in principle imply any cause for him to abandon Stalin's territorial ambitions in Europe. In Washington, as in Berlin, Molotov was adamant about the 1941 borders, about demanding a dominant Soviet influence in Bulgaria, Romania, and Finland, and special rights in the Straits. On both occasions, he deferred the colonial issue to a later date.

In all probability, Stalin could hardly believe his good fortune when Molotov informed him of Washington's refusal to discuss a political settlement while the war was in progress. For this meant that he needed to make no concessions as long as the German army was still in the field. Significantly, once Stalin understood that America was deferring a political settlement into the postwar period, he abandoned his usual persistent, hectoring style and never raised the subject again. With his bargaining position improving at each step closer to an Allied victory, Stalin stood to gain the most by delaying political discussions and by seizing as much booty as he could, if only to use these gains as bargaining chips at a peace conference. Nobody was more conscious than Stalin of the old adage that possession is nine-tenths of the law.

Roosevelt's reluctance to jeopardize postwar cooperation with the Soviet Union by prematurely discussing war aims may have had a strategic as well as a Wilsonian rationale. Roosevelt may have been aware of the possibility of Soviet postwar expansionism but may have felt trapped between his people's convictions and the looming strategic peril. To maintain the war effort, Roosevelt above all needed to appeal to American ideals, which deplored spheres of influence and the balance of power. It was, after all, only a few years since the Congress had enthusiastically passed the Neutrality Acts, and the ideas underlying them had not disappeared. Roosevelt may have concluded that, whatever the Soviet intentions, his optimum strategy was to give Stalin a reputation to uphold. For only against such a backdrop would he have a chance to mobilize America to resist Soviet expansionism if it really came to pass.

This is the view of Arthur Schlesinger, Jr., who has argued that Roosevelt had prepared a fall-back position in case Soviet-American relations went sour: "a great army, a network of overseas bases, plans for peacetime universal military training and the Anglo-American monopoly of the atomic bomb."[27]

True, Roosevelt had all of these means at his disposal. But his motivation in assembling them was to spruce up the war effort rather than as a hedge against Soviet expansionism. The bases had been acquired to make possible the transfer of destroyers to Great Britain; the atom bomb was aimed at the Nazis and Japan; and all indications are that Roosevelt would have demobilized the army rapidly and brought it home—indeed, he said so on many occasions. No doubt, once Roosevelt had become convinced of Stalin's bad faith he would have become a skillful and determined opponent of Soviet expansionism and would have had at his disposal the tools described. There is little evidence, however, that he had ever reached that judgment or viewed his military capabilities in terms of a possible confrontation with the Soviet Union.

As the war drew to a close, Roosevelt did express irritation with Stalin's tactics. Yet, throughout the war, Roosevelt had remained remarkably consistent, even eloquent, in his commitment to Soviet-American cooperation, and he considered no assignment more important than overcoming Stalin's distrust. Walter Lippmann may have been right when he said of Roosevelt, "He distrusted everybody. What he thought he could do was to outwit Stalin, which is quite a different thing."[28] If that was his intention, he did not succeed.

Roosevelt relied on personal relations with Stalin in a way that Churchill never would. When Hitler invaded the Soviet Union, Churchill explained Great Britain's decision to support Stalin with a phrase which involved neither personal nor moral endorsement: "If Hitler invaded Hell, he [Churchill] would at least make a favourable reference to the Devil!"[29] Roosevelt showed no such reserve. Shortly after America's entry into the war, he attempted to arrange a meeting with Stalin at the Bering Straits to the exclusion of Churchill. It was to be "an informal and completely simple visit for a few days between you and me" to achieve "a meeting of minds." Roosevelt would bring only Harry Hopkins, an interpreter, and a stenographer; the seals and the gulls would be their witnesses.[30]

The Bering Straits meeting never took place. But two summits did occur—at Teheran from November 28 to December 1, 1943, and at Yalta from February 4 to 11, 1945. On both occasions, Stalin went to great lengths to demonstrate to Roosevelt and Churchill that they needed the meeting much more than he did; even the settings were designed to reduce the Anglo-Americans' confidence in their ability to extract concessions from him. Teheran was only a few hundred miles from the Soviet border, and Yalta, of course, was on Soviet territory. In each case, the Western leaders had to travel thousands of miles, an especially arduous imposition on a man of Roosevelt's handicaps even at the time of the Teheran meeting. By the time of Yalta, the President was mortally ill.

Yalta has borne the opprobrium for the shape of the postwar world. Yet, when it occurred, Soviet armies had already crossed all their 1941 borders and were in a position to impose unilaterally Soviet political control over the rest of Eastern Europe. If a postwar settlement was ever to have been negotiated at any summit, the appropriate time would have been at Teheran, fifteen months earlier. Before then, the Soviet Union had been struggling to avert defeat; at the time of Teheran, the battle for Stalingrad had been won, victory was certain, and a separate Soviet-Nazi deal was highly improbable.

In Teheran, Roosevelt had initially planned to stay at the American legation, some distance from the Soviet and British embassies, which stood back to back. There was a constant worry that, en route to a meeting at the Soviet or British compound, Roosevelt might fall victim to a bomb-throwing Axis sympathizer. Therefore, at the first plenary session, which was held in the American legation, Roosevelt accepted Stalin's invitation to move to a villa in the Soviet compound. It was furnished according to the pretentious and gaudy style of Soviet interior design for high personages and, no doubt, was suitably bugged for the occasion.

Roosevelt could have offered no stronger signal of trust and goodwill than to accept Stalin's offer of Soviet lodgings. Yet the gesture left no significant impact on Stalin's strategy, which was to castigate Churchill and Roosevelt about the delay in opening the second front. Stalin liked to put interlocutors on the defensive. In this instance, it had the additional benefit of focusing attention on a region far from the areas that would soon be in contention. He elicited a formal promise to open a second front in France by the spring of 1944. The three Allies also agreed on the complete demilitarization of Germany and on their respective occupation zones. On one occasion, when Stalin urged the execution of 50,000 German officers, Churchill walked out and returned only after Stalin had followed him to give his assurances that he had been jesting—which, in light of what we now know of the Katyn massacre of Polish officers, was probably not true.[31] Then, at a private meeting, Roosevelt outlined his idea of the Four Policemen to a skeptical Stalin.

All of these issues delayed discussion of postwar arrangements, which was left until the last day of the Conference. Roosevelt agreed to Stalin's plan to move the frontiers of Poland westward and indicated that he would not press Stalin on the question of the Baltics. If Soviet armies occupied the Baltic States, he said, neither the United States nor Great Britain would "turn her out"—though he also recommended holding a plebiscite. The fact was, Roosevelt was as reluctant to undertake a full-scale discussion of the postwar world as he had been when Molotov visited Washington eighteen months earlier. He therefore put forward his comments on Stalin's postwar plans for Eastern Europe so tentatively as to sound almost apologetic. Roosevelt called Stalin's attention to the 6 million American voters of Polish extraction who were in a position to influence his re-election in the coming year. Though "personally he agreed with the views of Marshal Stalin as to the necessity of the restoration of a Polish state [he] would like to see the Eastern border moved farther to the west and the Western border moved even to the River Oder. He hoped, however, that the Marshal would understand that for political reasons outlined above, he could not participate in any decision here in Teheran or even next winter on this subject and that he could not publicly take part in any such arrangement *at the present time.*"[32] This could hardly have conveyed to Stalin that he was running a great risk by proceeding unilaterally; indeed, it implied that America's agreement after the election was largely a formality.

The reason Roosevelt was putting forward American political goals so halfheartedly was that he viewed his principal objective at Teheran as establishing the concept of the Four Policemen. One of the methods he used to attempt to gain Stalin's confidence was to dissociate himself ostentatiously from Churchill, as he reported to Frances Perkins, an old friend and his Secretary of Labor:

> Winston got red and scowled, and the more he did so, the more Stalin smiled. Finally, Stalin broke out into a deep, hearty guffaw, and for the first time in three days I saw light. I kept it up until Stalin was laughing with me, and it was then that I called him "Uncle Joe." He would have thought me fresh the day before, but that day he laughed and came over and shook my hand.
>
> From that time on our relations were personal. . . . The ice was broken and we talked like men and brothers.[33]

The reinvention of Stalin, organizer of purges and recent collaborator of Hitler, into "Uncle Joe," the paragon of moderation, was surely the ultimate triumph of hope over experience. Yet Roosevelt's emphasis on Stalin's goodwill was not a personal idiosyncrasy, but vented the attitude of a people with more faith in the inherent goodness of man than in geopolitical analysis. They preferred to see Stalin as an avuncular friend rather than as a totalitarian dictator. In May 1943, Stalin disbanded the Comintern, the Communist Party's formal instrument of world revolution. It came at a moment in time when world revolution could hardly have been either a top Soviet priority or a serious capability. Yet Senator Tom Connally of Texas, a key member of the Senate Foreign Relations Committee and soon to be its chairman, greeted Stalin's move as a fundamental turn toward Western values: "Russians for years have been changing their economy and approaching the abandonment of Communism, and the whole Western world will be gratified at the happy climax of their efforts."[34] Even *Fortune* magazine, a bastion of American capitalism, wrote in a similar vein.[35]

At the end of the Teheran Conference, therefore, the American people saw nothing unusual in their president's summing up its achievements through a personal evaluation of the Soviet dictator:

> I may say that I "got along fine" with Marshal Stalin. He is a man who combines a tremendous, relentless determination with a stalwart good humor. I believe he is truly representative of the heart and soul of Russia; and I believe that we are going to get along very well with him and the Russian people—very well indeed.[36]

When, in June 1944, the Allies landed in Normandy and advanced from the west, Germany's doom was sealed. As the military situation turned irrevocably in his favor, Stalin progressively raised his terms. In 1941, he had asked for acceptance of the 1941 borders (with a possibility of modifying them), and indicated a willingness to recognize the London-based free Poles. In 1942, he began to complain about the composition of the Polish government-in-exile. In 1943, he created an alternative to it in the so-called free Lublin Committee. By late 1944, he had recognized the Lublin group—dominated by communists—as the provisional government, and banned the London Poles. In 1941, Stalin's primary issue had been frontiers; by 1945, it had become political control of territories beyond those frontiers.

Churchill understood what was taking place. But Great Britain had become too dependent on the United States to sustain solitary initiatives. Nor was Great Britain strong enough to oppose by itself Stalin's increasingly bold creation of a Soviet sphere in Eastern Europe. In October 1944, Churchill undertook an almost quixotic enterprise to settle the future of Eastern Europe directly with Stalin. During a visit to Moscow which lasted eight days, Churchill jotted down a spheres-of-influence arrangement and handed it to Stalin. In it, he envisaged a delineation of spheres in terms of percentages, with Great Britain obtaining 90 percent in Greece, and the Soviet Union 90 percent in Romania and 75 percent in Bulgaria; Hungary and Yugoslavia were divided according to a 50-50 basis. Stalin accepted on the spot—though Molotov, in the best Soviet tradition of horse trading, sought in a dialogue with Eden to shave the British percentages, giving the Soviets a greater edge in every East European country except Hungary.[37]

The British effort had a certain pathos about it. Never before had spheres of influence been defined by percentages. No criteria to measure compliance existed, or any means of enforcement. Influence would be defined by the presence of the contending armies. In this manner, Greece fell into the British sphere, with or without the agreement, while all the other states—except Yugoslavia—became Soviet satellites regardless of the percentages assigned to them. Even Yugoslavia's freedom of action resulted not from the Churchill-Stalin agreement but from the fact that it had been under Soviet occupation for only a very brief period and had liberated itself from German military occupation through a major guerrilla effort of its own.

By the time of the Yalta Conference in February 1945, nothing remained of the Churchill-Stalin agreement. The Soviet army was already in possession of all the disputed territories, making the frontiers issue largely moot. Moreover, it was intervening massively in the internal arrangements of all the occupied countries.

Already in severely failing health, Roosevelt had to fly from Malta to a snowy airport in Saki, in the Crimea, and from there was driven the ninety miles to Yalta in some five hours over difficult, snow-covered roads. His quarters were a three-room suite in the Livadia Palace. (In the nineteenth century, Livadia had been a favorite winter resort of the tsars: in 1877, Alexander II had planned his Balkan invasion from there; in 1911, Tsar Nicholas II had built a white granite palace on the bluffs overlooking the Black Sea, which became the site of the Conference of the Big Three.)

The tactics of the participants did not change with the new surroundings. Churchill was anxious to discuss postwar political arrangements but was overruled by his two colleagues, each of whom pursued his own distinct agenda. Roosevelt sought an agreement on voting procedures for the United Nations, and to nail down Soviet participation in the war against Japan. Stalin was happy enough to discuss both subjects, because the time spent on them would not be available for a discussion of Eastern Europe, and because he was eager (not reluctant, as some Americans thought) to enter the war against Japan, which would make it possible for him to share in the spoils of that victory as well.

Churchill was above all concerned with the European balance of power. He wanted to restore France to Great Power status, to resist the dismemberment of Germany, and to reduce exorbitant Soviet demands for reparations. Though Churchill was successful with respect to all three issues, they were essentially sideshows to the settlement of Eastern Europe—which was even then being foreclosed daily by the behavior of the Red Army. By this time, Stalin had prepared a riposte to Roosevelt's ploy that the Soviet Union should make concessions in order to spare him the wrath of his domestic opposition: when Roosevelt asked that the city of Lvov remain with Poland in order to pacify his domestic Polish critics, Stalin replied that, much as he would like to oblige, his own Ukrainian population would create an insuperable domestic problem for him.[38]

In the end, Churchill and Roosevelt accepted Russia's 1941 borders, a painful step for Churchill, whose country had gone to war to preserve Poland's territorial integrity. They agreed as well that Poland's western frontier would be moved toward the Oder and Neisse rivers. Since there were two Neisse rivers, the final delineation was left unresolved. Churchill and Roosevelt accepted the Moscow-created Lublin government with the proviso that it be broadened to include some democratic political figures from the London-based Polish government-in-exile.

Stalin's concession to his allies was a Joint Declaration on Liberated Europe, which promised free elections and the establishment of democratic governments in Eastern Europe. Stalin obviously thought that he was promising the Soviet version of free elections, especially since the Red Army would have already occupied the countries in question. This is in fact what happened, though Stalin vastly underestimated the seriousness with which Americans have traditionally approached legal documents. Later, when it decided to organize resistance to Soviet expansionism, America did so on the basis of Stalin's failure to keep his word —as given at Yalta and as the American leaders and public had understood it.

Stalin's reaction to Roosevelt's appeal to join the war against Japan illustrated how different his rules of the coalition game were from Roosevelt's. In a discussion from which Churchill was excluded—even though Great Britain had been an early victim of Japanese aggression—nothing was heard of Allied unity as its own reward or of avoiding political issues so as to create favorable preconditions for the Four Policemen. Stalin felt not the least bit inhibited about insisting on special benefits while the war was still going on, and on being paid in strategic, not emotional, coin. The *quid pro quo* he demanded was unabashedly resurrected from the days of the tsars.

Stalin's claim to the southern part of Sakhalin Island and to the Kurile Islands did bear a certain, albeit vague, relationship to Soviet security and Russian history. But his demand for free ports in Darien and Port Arthur and the right to manage the Manchurian railways was straight out of tsarist imperialist textbooks from the turn of the century. In Roosevelt's least comprehensible decision at Yalta, he granted these demands in a secret agreement which amounted to returning to Moscow the predominant role in Manchuria that it had lost in the Russo-Japanese War—one it was not to lose until the Chinese communists took over Beijing in 1949.

After the Yalta Conference, all was jubilation. In reporting to the Congress, Roosevelt emphasized the agreement reached on the United Nations but not the decision regarding the political future of either Europe or Asia. For the second time in a generation, an American president was returning from Europe to proclaim the end of history. "The Yalta Conference," affirmed Roosevelt,

> ... ought to spell the end of the system of unilateral action, the exclusive alliances, the spheres of influence, the balances of power, and all the other expedients that have been tried for centuries—and have always failed. We propose to substitute for all these, a universal organization in which all peace-loving Nations will finally have a chance to join. I am confident that the Congress and the American people will accept the results of this Conference as the beginnings of a permanent structure of peace.[39]

In other words, Roosevelt had granted Stalin a sphere of influence in northern China to encourage him to participate in a world order that would make spheres of influence irrelevant.

When the Yalta Conference ended, only the unity of the wartime alliance was being celebrated; the fissures that would later undo it were not yet widely perceived. Hope still reigned supreme and "Uncle Joe" was viewed as an uncomplicated partner. Reflecting on Yalta, Harry Hopkins expressed his concern that Stalin, the presumed moderate, might buckle under pressure from hard-liners in the Kremlin:

> The Russians had proved that they could be reasonable and farseeing and there wasn't any doubt in the minds of the President or any of us that we could live with them and get along with them peacefully for as far into the future as any of us could imagine. But I have to make one amendment to that—I think we all had in our minds the reservation that we could not foretell what the results would be if anything should happen to Stalin. We felt sure that we could count on him to be reasonable and sensible and understanding—but we never could be sure who or what might be in back of him there in the Kremlin.[40]

The theme that the incumbent in the Kremlin was in his heart of hearts a peaceful moderate in need of help in overcoming his intransigent colleagues was to remain a constant of American discussions ever after, regardless of the Soviet leader. Indeed, these assessments survived even into the postcommunist period, when they were applied, first to Mikhail Gorbachev, and then to Boris Yeltsin.

The importance of personal relations among leaders and of the existence of an underlying harmony among nations continued to be affirmed by America as the war drew to a conclusion. On January 20, 1945, in his fourth inaugural address, Roosevelt described his approach by quoting from Emerson: ". . . the only way to have a friend is to be one."[41] Soon after Yalta, Roosevelt characterized Stalin to the Cabinet as "having something else in him besides this revolutionist Bolshevist thing." He ascribed that special quality to Stalin's early education for the priesthood: "I think that something entered into his nature of the way in which a Christian gentleman should behave."[42]

Stalin, however, was a master practitioner of *Realpolitik,* not a Christian gentleman. As the Soviet armies advanced, Stalin was implementing what he had privately told Milovan Djilas, then a Yugoslav communist leader:

> This war is not as in the past; whoever occupies a territory also imposes on it his own social system. Everyone imposes his own system as far as his army can reach. It cannot be otherwise.[43]

Stalin's rules of the game were demonstrated dramatically in the final stages of the war. In April 1945, Churchill pressed Eisenhower, as Commander-in-Chief of the Allied forces, to seize Berlin, Prague, and Vienna ahead of the advancing Soviet armies. The American chiefs of staff would not consider the request, using it as a final opportunity to teach their British ally the need for military planning unaffected by political considerations: "Such psychological and political advantages as would result from the possible capture of Berlin ahead of the Russians should not override the imperative military consideration, which in our opinion is the destruction and dismemberment of the German armed forces."[44]

Since there was no significant German armed forces left either to dismember or to destroy, rejecting Churchill's appeal was clearly a matter of principle for the American chiefs of staff. Indeed, the chiefs felt so strongly about their view that General Eisenhower took it upon himself to write directly to Stalin on March 28, 1945, to inform him that he would not advance on Berlin, and to propose that American and Soviet troops meet near Dresden.

No doubt astonished that a general would address a head of state on any subject, let alone a matter of such political importance, Stalin was also not in the habit of turning down free political gifts. On April 1, he replied to Eisenhower that he agreed with his assessment; he, too, considered Berlin of secondary strategic interest and would devote only minor Soviet forces to capture it. He also agreed to a link-up along the Elbe, in the general area of Dresden. Having been handed the prize, Stalin proceeded to show that he, at least, had his political priorities straight. Contravening his assurances to Eisenhower, he ordered the main thrust of the Soviet ground offensive to be aimed at Berlin, giving Marshals Zhukov and Koniev two weeks to launch an attack he had told Eisenhower would not take place until the second half of May.[45]

By April 1945, two months after Yalta, Stalin's violations of the Yalta Declaration on Liberated Europe had become flagrant, especially with respect to Poland. Churchill was reduced to sending a plaintive letter in which he appealed to "my friend Stalin." Accepting Stalin's proposition that no individuals hostile to the Soviet Union should serve in the new Polish government, Churchill pleaded for the inclusion of some of the members of the Polish government-in-exile in London who met his test. By this time, the mere lack of hostile sentiments was no longer enough for Stalin; only a *totally* friendly government would do. On May 5, 1945, Stalin replied:

> . . . we cannot be satisfied that persons should be associated with the formation of the future Polish Government who, as you express it, "are not fundamentally anti-Soviet," or that only those persons should be excluded from participation in this work who are in your opinion "extremely unfriendly towards Russia." Neither of these criteria can satisfy us. We insist, and shall insist, that there should be brought into consultation on the formation of the future Polish Government only those persons who have actively shown a friendly attitude towards the Soviet Union and who are honestly and sincerely prepared to co-operate with the Soviet State.[46]

The adjectives "active" and "friendly" were, of course, applicable only to members of the Polish Communist Party and, from among these, only to those Party members totally subservient to Moscow. Four years later, even lifelong communists suspected of national feelings would be purged.

But was an alternative strategy feasible? Or were the democracies doing the best they could, given the geographic and military realities that existed at the time? These are haunting questions, because, in retrospect, everything that happened seems inevitable. The longer the interval, the more difficult it becomes to imagine an alternative outcome or to prove its viability. And history refuses to be played back like a movie reel in which new endings are spliced in at will.

Restoration of the 1941 Soviet frontiers was nearly impossible to prevent. A more dynamic Western policy might have achieved certain modifications, even the return of some form of independence to the Baltic States, perhaps linked to the Soviet Union by treaties of mutual assistance and the presence of Soviet military bases. If this had ever been attainable, it would only have been so in 1941 or 1942, when the Soviet Union was teetering at the brink of catastrophe. And it was understandable that Roosevelt should have been loath to burden Soviet decision-makers with such distasteful choices at a moment when, America not yet having entered the war, the greatest fear was an imminent Soviet collapse.

After the battle of Stalingrad, however, the issue of Eastern Europe's future could have been raised without risking either a Soviet collapse or a separate peace with Hitler. An effort should have been made to settle the political structure of territories beyond the Soviet frontiers and to achieve for these countries a status similar to that of Finland.

Would Stalin have made a separate peace with Hitler if the democracies had been more insistent? Stalin never made such a threat, though he did manage to create the impression that it was always a possibility. Only two episodes have come to light indicating that Stalin might have considered a separate arrangement. The first dates to the early days of the war, when panic was rampant. Allegedly, Stalin, Molotov, and Kaganovich asked the Bulgarian Ambassador to explore with Hitler the possibility of settling for the Baltics, Bessarabia, and slices of Belorussia and the Ukraine—in essence, the 1938 Soviet frontiers—but the Ambassador supposedly refused to transmit the message.[47] And Hitler surely would have refused such a settlement while German armies were heading toward Moscow, Kiev, and Leningrad, and had already gone far beyond what the "peace offer"—if that is what it was—suggested. The Nazi plan was to depopulate the Soviet Union up to the line from Archangel to Astrakhan, which was far beyond Moscow, and to reduce that part of its population as had managed to avoid extermination into slavery.[48]

The second episode is even more ambiguous. It occurred in September 1943, eight months after Stalingrad and two months after the battle of Kursk, which wiped out most of the German offensive armor. Ribbentrop presented Hitler with a strange tale indeed. A Soviet deputy foreign minister who had at one time been Ambassador to Berlin was visiting Stockholm, and Ribbentrop interpreted this as an opportunity for exploratory talks of a separate peace along the 1941 borders. It was almost surely wishful thinking, because at that point Soviet armies were approaching the 1941 frontiers on their own.

Hitler rejected the alleged opportunity, telling his Foreign Minister,

"You know, Ribbentrop, if I came to an agreement with Russia today I'd attack her again tomorrow—I just can't help myself." He spoke in the same vein to Goebbels. The timing was "totally unsuitable"; negotiations would have to be preceded by a decisive military victory.[49] As late as 1944, Hitler still believed that, after repelling the second front, he would be able to conquer Russia.

Above all, a separate peace, even along the 1941 frontiers, would have solved nothing for either Stalin or Hitler. It would have left Stalin face to face with a powerful Germany and the prospect that, in another conflict, the democracies would abandon their treacherous partner. And it would have been interpreted by Hitler as advancing the Soviet armies toward Germany without any assurance that they would not resume the war at the earliest opportunity.

Roosevelt's concept of the Four Policemen foundered on the same obstacle as had Wilson's more general concept of collective security: the Four Policemen simply did not perceive their global goals in the same way. Stalin's lethal combination of paranoia, communist ideology, and Russian imperialism translated the notion of the Four Policemen impartially enforcing world peace on the basis of universally shared values into either a Soviet opportunity or a capitalist trap. Stalin knew that Great Britain by itself was no counterweight to the Soviet Union and that this would either create a huge vacuum in front of the Soviet Union or serve as the prelude to later confrontation with the United States (which, as a first-generation Bolshevik, Stalin was bound to consider the more likely result). On the basis of either hypothesis, Stalin's course of action was clear: he would push Soviet power as far westward as possible, either to collect his spoils or to put himself into the best bargaining position for a diplomatic showdown later.

For that matter, America was itself unprepared to accept the consequences of its President's Four Policemen. If the concept were to work, America had to be willing to intervene wherever peace was threatened. Yet Roosevelt never tired of telling his fellow Allies that neither American troops nor American resources would be available to restore Europe, and that preserving the peace had to be a British and Russian task. At Yalta, he told his colleagues that American troops would not stay longer than two years in occupation duty.[50]

If that was true, the Soviet Union was bound to dominate Central Europe, leaving Great Britain with an insuperable quandary. On the one hand, it was no longer strong enough to maintain the balance of power against the Soviet Union all by itself. On the other hand, to the extent that Great Britain would attempt some sort of solitary initiative, it was likely to encounter traditional American objections. For example, in January

1945, *The New York Times* reported a secret communication from Roosevelt to Churchill on the British attempt to maintain a noncommunist government in Greece. According to that report, Roosevelt had made it quite clear that the American public's favorable disposition toward postwar Anglo-American cooperation was fragile: ". . . the British have been told with force and authority that the mood can change as mercurially as the English weather if the American people once get the idea that this war . . . [is] just another struggle between rival imperialisms."[51]

But if America refused to defend Europe, and British attempts to act alone were labeled as imperialist, the doctrine of the Four Policemen would lead to the same vacuum that the concept of collective security had in the 1930s. Until American perceptions changed, resistance to Soviet expansionism would be impossible. By the time America came to grips with this danger and re-entered the fray, the result would be the very spheres of influence it had so strenuously avoided during the war, albeit with a much less propitious demarcation line. At the end of the day, geopolitics could not be denied. America was drawn back into Europe; Japan and Germany were restored in order to rebuild the equilibrium; and the Soviet Union embarked on forty-five years of tension and strategic overextension leading to its final collapse.

Asia presented another difficult problem. Roosevelt had included China in the Big Four partly as a courtesy and partly to have an Asian anchor to his global design. However, China was even less capable than Great Britain of carrying out the mission Roosevelt had assigned to it. At the end of the war, China was an underdeveloped country in the throes of civil war. How could it serve as a world policeman? When Roosevelt discussed his idea of the Four Policemen at Teheran, Stalin had raised the reasonable question of how Europeans would react if China were to try to settle their disputes. He added that, in his view, China would not be strong enough for such a global role, and suggested instead the creation of regional committees to maintain the peace.[52] Roosevelt rejected this suggestion as tending toward spheres of influence; peace had to be defended on a global basis or not at all.

And yet, when all these ambiguities surrounding Roosevelt have been catalogued, the question remains whether any other approach could have commanded the support of the American people. Americans, after all, have always been more prepared to believe that a system based on the explicit rejection of democratic principles might suddenly reverse course than that they might have anything to learn from previous peace settlements—none of which, in the real world, had prospered without equilibrium or lasted for any length of time without a moral consensus.

Churchill's geopolitical analysis proved far more accurate than Roosevelt's. Yet Roosevelt's reluctance to see the world in geopolitical terms was the reverse side of the same idealism which had propelled America into the war and enabled it to preserve the cause of freedom. Had Roosevelt followed Churchill's prescriptions, he would have improved America's bargaining position but might have sacrificed its ability to sustain the confrontations of the Cold War that were still ahead.

That Roosevelt went more than the proverbial extra mile during the war was the precondition for the great initiatives by which America would restore the global equilibrium—although the United States denied the entire time that this was what it was in fact doing. Roosevelt's conception of the postwar world may have been far too optimistic. But in light of American history, this position almost surely represented a necessary stage that America needed to traverse if it hoped to overcome the crisis ahead. In the end, Roosevelt led his society through two of the most tremendous crises of its history. He would surely not have been so successful in those endeavors had he been more imbued with a sense of historical relativity.

However inevitably, the war ended with a geopolitical vacuum. The balance of power had been destroyed, and a comprehensive peace treaty remained elusive. The world was now divided into ideological camps. The postwar period would turn into an extended and painful struggle to achieve the settlement which had eluded the leaders before the war ended.

CHAPTER SEVENTEEN

The Beginning of
the Cold War

Like Moses, Franklin Delano Roosevelt saw the Promised Land, but it was not given to him to reach it. When he died, Allied armies stood deep inside Germany, and the battle for Okinawa, the prelude to the planned Allied invasion of Japan's main islands, had just begun.

Roosevelt's death on April 12, 1945, was not unexpected. In January, Roosevelt's doctor, alarmed by the sharp fluctuations in his patient's blood pressure, had concluded that the President would survive only if he avoided any tension. Given the pressures of the presidency, that assessment was tantamount to a death sentence.[1] For one mad moment, Hitler and Goebbels, who were trapped in encircled Berlin, deluded themselves into believing that they were about to witness a replay of what German history books describe as the miracle of the House of Brandenburg—when, during the Seven Years' War, as Russian armies stood at the gates of Berlin, Frederick the Great was saved by the sudden death of the Russian ruler and the accession of a friendly tsar. History, however, did not repeat itself in 1945. Nazi crimes had welded at least one unshakable common Allied purpose: to eliminate the scourge of Nazism.

The collapse of Nazi Germany and the need to fill the resulting power vacuum led to the disintegration of the wartime partnership. The purposes of the Allies were simply too divergent. Churchill sought to prevent the Soviet Union from dominating Central Europe. Stalin wanted to be paid in territorial coin for Soviet military victories and the heroic suffering of the Russian people. The new President, Harry S. Truman, initially strove to continue Roosevelt's legacy of holding the alliance together. By the end of his first term, however, every vestige of wartime harmony had vanished. The United States and the Soviet Union, the two giants at the periphery, were now facing off against one another in the very heart of Europe.

Harry S. Truman's background was as different from that of his great predecessor as could be imagined. Roosevelt had been a member in good standing of the cosmopolitan Northeastern establishment; Truman came from the Midwestern rural middle class. Roosevelt had been educated at the best preparatory schools and universities; Truman had never gone beyond the secondary school level, though Dean Acheson was to say of him affectionately and admiringly that he was a Yale man in the best sense of the word. Roosevelt's entire life had been a preparation for the highest office; Truman was a product of the Kansas City political machine.

Selected as vice president only after Roosevelt's first choice, James Byrnes, was vetoed by the labor movement, Harry Truman gave little indication in his prior political career that he would turn out to be an extraordinary president. Without any real foreign policy experience and left equipped by Roosevelt with only the vaguest of road maps, Truman inherited the task of winding down the war and building a new international order even while the design established at Teheran and at Yalta was coming apart.

As it turned out, Truman presided over the beginning of the Cold War and the development of the policy of containment that would eventually win it. He took the United States into its first peacetime military alliance. Under his guidance, Roosevelt's concept of the Four Policemen was replaced by an unprecedented set of coalitions which were to remain at the core of American foreign policy for forty years. Espousing America's faith in the universality of its values, this plain man from the Midwest encouraged prostrate enemies to rejoin the society of democratic nations. He sponsored the Marshall Plan and the Point Four Program, through which America devoted resources and technology to the recovery and development of distant societies.

I met Truman only once, early in 1961, while I was a junior professor at Harvard. A speaking engagement in Kansas City provided me with an occasion to call on the ex-President at the Truman Presidential Library in nearby Independence, Missouri. The passage of the years had not diminished the former President's jauntiness. After taking me on a tour of the institution, Truman invited me to his office, which was a replica of the White House Oval Office during his presidency. Having heard that I was consulting part-time at the Kennedy White House, he asked me what I had learned. Drawing on standard Washington cocktail-party wisdom, I replied that the bureaucracy appeared to me to function as a fourth branch of government, severely constricting the president's freedom of action. Truman found this remark neither amusing nor instructive. Impatient at being subjected to what he labeled "professor talk," he responded with an expletive, then introduced his view of the role of the president: "If the president knows what he wants, no bureaucrat can stop him. A president has to know when to stop taking advice."

Quickly retreating to more familiar academic ground, I asked Truman for which foreign policy decision he most wanted to be remembered. He did not hesitate. "We completely defeated our enemies and made them surrender," he remarked. "And then we helped them to recover, to become democratic, and to rejoin the community of nations. Only America could have done that." Afterward, he walked with me through the streets of Independence to the simple house in which he lived so that I could meet his wife, Bess.

I recount this brief conversation because it captured so completely Truman's quintessentially American nature: his sense for the majesty of the presidency and the responsibilities of the president, his pride in America's strength, and, above all, his belief that America's ultimate calling was to serve as a fount of freedom and progress for all mankind.

Truman embarked on his own presidency from deep within the shadow of Roosevelt, who had by his death been elevated to near-mythic stature. Truman genuinely admired Roosevelt but, in the end, as every new president must, he shaped the office he had inherited from the perspective of his own experiences and values.

Upon becoming President, Truman had a far less emotional commitment to Allied unity than Roosevelt had had; to the son of the isolationist Midwest, Allied unity represented more of a practical preference than an emotional or moral necessity. Nor had Truman experienced the exaltation of wartime partnership with the Soviets, whom in any event he had always viewed warily. When Hitler attacked the Soviet Union, the then Senator Truman rated the two dictatorships as being morally equivalent, and recommended that America encourage them to fight to the death: "If we see that Germany is winning, we ought to help Russia, and if Russia is winning we ought to help Germany and that way let them kill as many as possible, although I don't want to see Hitler victorious under any circumstances. Neither of them think anything of their pledged word."[2]

Despite Roosevelt's deteriorating health, Truman had not been invited to participate in any of the key foreign policy decisions during his three-month tenure as Vice-President. Nor had he been briefed about the project to build the atom bomb.

Truman inherited an international environment whose dividing lines were inchoately based on the position of armies advancing from east and west. The political fate of the countries liberated by Allied armies had not yet been resolved. Most of the traditional Great Powers still had to adjust to their changed roles. France was prostrate; Great Britain, though victorious, was exhausted; Germany was being carved into four occupation zones—having haunted Europe with its strength since 1871, its impotence now threatened it with chaos. Stalin had advanced the Soviet frontier 600 miles west to the Elbe, while a vacuum was opening up in front of his armies due to the weakness of Western Europe and the planned withdrawal of American forces.

Truman's first instinct was to get along with Stalin, especially since the American chiefs of staff remained anxious for Soviet participation in the war against Japan. Although he had been put off by Molotov's intransigent behavior at his first encounter with the Soviet Foreign Minister in April 1945, he ascribed the difficulties to a difference in historical experience. "We have to get tough with Russians," Truman said. "They don't know how to behave. They are like bulls in a china shop. They are only twenty-five years old. We are over a hundred and the British are centuries older. We have got to teach them how to behave."[3]

It was a characteristically American statement. Starting out from an assumption of underlying harmony, Truman ascribed disagreements with the Soviets not to conflicting geopolitical interests but to "misbehavior" and "political immaturity." In other words, he believed in the possibility of propelling Stalin to "normal" conduct. Coming to grips with the reality, that the tensions between the Soviet Union and the United States had not been caused by some misunderstanding but were in fact generic, was the story of the beginning of the Cold War.

Truman inherited Roosevelt's top advisers, and he began his presidency intending to pursue his predecessor's conception of the Four Policemen. In an address on April 16, 1945, four days after taking office, Truman drew a bleak contrast between world community and chaos and saw no alternative to global collective security except anarchy. Truman rededicated himself to Roosevelt's faith in the special obligation of the wartime Allies to maintain their unity in order to establish and preserve a new peaceful international order, above all to defend the principle that international disputes should not be settled by force:

> Nothing is more essential to the future peace of the world than continued cooperation of the nations which had to muster the force necessary to defeat the conspiracy of the axis powers to dominate the world.
>
> While these great states have a special responsibility to enforce the peace, their responsibility is based upon the obligations resting upon all states, large and small, not to use force in international relations except in the defense of law.[4]

Apparently Truman's speech-writers did not feel that they owed him much variety, or perhaps they considered their standard text incapable of improvement, for they repeated the same point verbatim on April 25, in Truman's speech to the organizing conference of the United Nations in San Francisco.

Despite the high-flown rhetoric, hard geopolitical facts were shaping conditions on the ground. Stalin returned to his old ways of conducting foreign policy, and demanded payment for his victories in the only currency he took seriously—territorial control. He understood bargains and might have been willing to discuss some, but only so long as they involved precise *quid pro quos*—such as spheres of interest, or trading limits on communist influence in Eastern Europe for specific benefits like massive economic assistance. What was beyond the ken of one of the most unscrupulous leaders ever to have headed a major country, was the idea of basing foreign policy on collective goodwill or international law. In Stalin's view, face-to-face encounters between world leaders might register a correlation of forces or a calculation of the national interest, but they could not alter it. He therefore never responded to any of Roosevelt's or Churchill's appeals to return to their wartime camaraderie.

It is possible that the enormous prestige Roosevelt had garnered might have caused Stalin to moderate his approach for a little while longer. In the end, Stalin would make concessions only to "objective" reality; to him, diplomacy was but one aspect of a broader and unavoidable struggle to define the relationship of forces. Stalin's problem in dealing with American leaders was that he had great difficulty comprehending the importance of morality and legalism in their thinking on foreign policy. Stalin genuinely did not understand why American leaders should be making such a fuss over the domestic structures of the Eastern European states, where they had no ostensible strategic interest. The Americans' stand on principle, unrelated to any concrete interests as these had been conventionally understood, made Stalin look for ulterior motives. "I am afraid," reported Averell Harriman, while serving as Ambassador to Moscow, that

> ... Stalin does not, and never will, fully understand our interest in a free Poland as a matter of principle. He is a realist ... and it is hard for him to appreciate our faith in abstract principles. It is difficult for him to understand why we should want to interfere with Soviet policy in a country like Poland, which he considers so important to Russia's security, unless we have some ulterior motive. . . .[5]

Stalin, a master practitioner of *Realpolitik,* must have expected America to resist the new geopolitical balance established by the Red Army's presence in the center of the European Continent. A man of iron nerves, he was not given to making pre-emptive concessions; he must have reasoned that it was far better to consolidate the bargaining chips he already held while sitting warily in possession of his prizes, and to leave it to the Allies to make the next move. And the only moves Stalin would take seriously were those possessed of consequences which could be analyzed in terms of risk and reward. When the Allies failed to exercise any pressure, Stalin simply stayed put.

Stalin displayed toward the United States the same taunting manner he had adopted toward Hitler in 1940. In 1945, the Soviet Union, debilitated by tens of millions of casualties and the devastation of a third of its territory, faced an undamaged America possessing an atomic monopoly; in 1940, it had confronted a Germany in control of the rest of the Continent. In each case, rather than offer concessions, Stalin consolidated the Soviet position and tried to bluff his potential adversaries into believing that he was more likely to march farther west than to retreat. And in each case, he miscalculated the reaction of his opponents. In 1940, Molotov's visit to Berlin had strengthened Hitler's decision to invade; in 1945, the same Foreign Minister managed to transform American goodwill into the confrontation of the Cold War.

Churchill understood Stalin's diplomatic calculations and sought to counter them by making two moves of his own. He urged an early summit of the three wartime Allies to bring matters to a head before the Soviet sphere was consolidated. Pending that, he wanted the Allies to get into their hands as many bargaining chips as possible. He saw an opportunity for this in the fact that Allied and Soviet armies had met farther east than had been foreseen, and that, as a result, Allied forces were in control of nearly a third of the area assigned to the Soviet zone of occupation in Germany, including most of the industrialized portion. Churchill proposed using this territory as leverage in the forthcoming negotiations. On May 4, 1945, he cabled instructions to Foreign Secretary Eden, who was about to meet Truman in Washington:

> ... the Allies ought not to retreat from their present positions to the occupational line until we are satisfied about Poland, and also about the temporary character of the Russian occupation of Germany, and the conditions to be established in the Russianised or Russian-controlled countries in the Danube valley, particularly Austria and Czechoslovakia, and the Balkans.[6]

The new American administration, however, was no more hospitable to British *Realpolitik* than Roosevelt's had been. The patterns of wartime diplomacy were, therefore, repeated. American leaders were happy enough to agree to a summit scheduled at Potsdam, near Berlin, for the second half of July. But Truman was not yet willing to accept Churchill's suggestion that the way to deal with Stalin was to assemble rewards and penalties in order to produce the desired result. Indeed, the Truman Administration proved just as eager as its predecessor to teach Churchill that the days of balance-of-power diplomacy were irrevocably past.

At the end of June, less than a month before the planned summit, American forces withdrew to the agreed demarcation line, leaving Great Britain no other choice than to follow their example. Moreover, just as Roosevelt had vastly overestimated British capabilities, the Truman Administration envisaged itself in the role of mediator between Great Britain and the Soviet Union. Determined to avoid any impression of ganging up on Stalin, Truman, to Churchill's chagrin, rejected an invitation to stop in Great Britain on the way to Potsdam, to celebrate the Anglo-American victory.

Truman, however, had no inhibition about seeing Stalin without Churchill. Using the same pretext that Roosevelt had invoked when he tried to arrange the Bering Straits meeting—that, unlike Churchill, he had never met Stalin—he proposed a separate meeting with the Soviet ruler. But Churchill turned out to be just as sensitive about being excluded from a Soviet-American dialogue as Truman's advisers had been about giving the impression that Washington and London were acting in tandem. According to Truman's memoirs, Churchill testily notified Washington that he would not attend any summit which was a continuation of a conference between Truman and Stalin.[7] To carry out his role as self-appointed mediator and to establish direct contact with the leaders of the Allies, Truman decided to send emissaries to London and Moscow.

Harry Hopkins, Roosevelt's old confidant, was dispatched to Moscow; the envoy sent to see Churchill was, curiously enough, selected more on account of his ability to reassure Stalin than for his demonstrated skills at exploring what was on the British Prime Minister's mind. He was Joseph E. Davies, the prewar ambassador to Moscow who had written the best-selling book *Mission to Moscow.*

Though Davies was an investment banker, hence in communist eyes an arch-capitalist, he had developed the propensity of most American en-voys—especially of non–career diplomats—to turn into self-appointed spokesmen for the countries to which they are accredited. Davies' book about his ambassadorial adventures had parroted Soviet propaganda on every conceivable subject, including the guilt of the victims of the purge trials. Sent by Roosevelt on a wartime mission to Moscow, the egregiously miscast Davies had had the extraordinary insensitivity to show a movie based on his best-seller to a group of top Soviet leaders at the American embassy. The official report noted dryly that the Soviet guests had watched with "glum curiosity" as the guilt of their former colleagues was proclaimed from the screen.[8] (And well they might have. Not only did they know better, but they could not discount the possibility that the film might well be depicting their own futures.) Truman, therefore, could hardly have sent anyone to Downing Street less likely to appreciate Churchill's view of the postwar world.

Davies' visit to London in late May of 1945 proved nearly as surreal as his wartime mission to Moscow had been. Davies was far more interested in continuing America's partnership with the Soviet Union than in foster-ing Anglo-American relations. Churchill expounded to the American envoy his fear that Stalin intended to swallow up Central Europe, and stressed the necessity of a united Anglo-American front to resist him. Davies reacted to Churchill's analysis of the Soviet challenge by sardoni-cally asking the Old Lion whether perhaps "he and Britain had made a mistake in not supporting Hitler, for as I understood him, he was now expressing the doctrine which Hitler and Goebbels had been proclaiming and reiterating for the past four years in an effort to break up Allied unity and 'divide and conquer.' "[9] As far as Davies was concerned, East-West diplomacy would go nowhere unless it was based on the premise of Stalin's good faith.

Davies reported back to Truman in the same vein. Whatever Churchill's greatness, in Davies' view he was "first, last, and all the time" a great

Englishman, more interested in preserving England's position in Europe than in preserving the peace.[10] Admiral Leahy, initially Roosevelt's, now Truman's chief of staff, confirmed that Davies' view was widely held by endorsing Davies' report: "This was consistent with our staff estimate of Churchill's attitude throughout the war."[11]

Nothing better illustrates America's knee-jerk reaction to *Realpolitik*. Davies and Leahy were vocally displeased that the British Prime Minister should be primarily concerned with British national interests—something that the statesmen of any other country would have treated as the most natural thing in the world. Even though Churchill's pursuit of a balance of power on the Continent incarnated three centuries of British history, Americans viewed it as being somehow aberrant, and contrasted the quest for peace with the effort to maintain such a balance—as if means and ends were incompatible rather than complementary.

Hopkins, who had visited Moscow several times as a wartime emissary, found the atmosphere of his parallel mission extremely congenial. Even so, it is possible that his meetings with Stalin unintentionally deepened the deadlock over Eastern Europe and hastened the onset of the Cold War. For Hopkins followed his wartime pattern of emphasizing harmony over confrontation. He could not bring himself to impart to Stalin the extent to which his course was risking serious trouble with an aroused American public. Throughout his diplomatic career, Hopkins operated on the premise that all disagreements would dissolve in an atmosphere of understanding and goodwill—categories for which Stalin had very little comprehension to begin with.

Stalin saw Hopkins on six separate occasions in late May and early June. Applying his usual technique of placing his interlocutor on the defensive, Stalin complained about the termination of Lend-Lease and the general cooling off of Soviet-American relations. He warned that the Soviet Union would never yield to pressure—a standard diplomatic ploy that is used when the negotiator is searching for a face-saving means of determining what concessions are wanted without suggesting that he will accept them. Stalin purported not to understand America's concern about holding free elections in Poland. After all, the Soviet Union had not raised a comparable issue with respect to Italy and Belgium, where elections had also not yet been held. Why should the Western powers concern themselves with Poland and the countries of the Danube basin, which were located so close to the Soviet borders?

Hopkins and Stalin fenced inconclusively without Hopkins ever managing to convey to Stalin that Americans were deadly serious about the issue of Eastern European self-determination. Indeed, Hopkins exhibited the proclivity of most American negotiators to put forward even their most strongly held positions in a manner which avoids any suggestion of intransigence. Expecting compromise, they look for ways to give their interlocutors a graceful way out. The reverse side of this approach is that, once American negotiators lose faith in the other side's goodwill, they tend to turn intractable and at times excessively rigid.

The weaknesses of Hopkins' negotiating style were magnified by the extraordinary reservoir of goodwill toward Stalin and the Soviet Union that had been left over from the wartime alliance. By June 1945, Stalin had already unilaterally fixed Poland's eastern as well as western border, brutally promoted Soviet puppets in the government, and flagrantly violated his pledge at Yalta to organize free elections. Even so, Harry Hopkins found it possible to describe Soviet-American disagreements to Stalin as "a train of events, each unimportant in themselves[, that] had grown up around the Polish question."[12] Relying on Roosevelt's tactic from the days of Teheran and Yalta, he asked Stalin to modify his demands in Eastern Europe to help ease domestic pressures on the Truman Administration.

Stalin professed to be open to suggestions about how to make the new Polish government consistent with American principles. He invited Hopkins to recommend four or five individuals from the democratic side who might be added to the Warsaw government, which he claimed had been created by the Soviet Union due to the "compulsion" of military necessity.[13] Of course, token participation in a communist government was not the real issue; free elections were. And the communists had already demonstrated a remarkable skill at destroying coalition governments. In any event, Hopkins could not have impressed Stalin with America's grasp of the Polish situation when he admitted that he had no specific names to suggest for the new government.

In insisting on a free hand vis-à-vis his neighbors, Stalin was following traditional Russian practice. From the time Russia had emerged on the international scene two centuries earlier, its leaders had been attempting to settle disputes with their neighbors bilaterally rather than at international conferences. Neither Alexander I in the 1820s, Nicholas I thirty years later, nor Alexander II in 1878 understood why Great Britain insisted on interposing itself between Russia and Turkey. In these and subsequent instances, Russian leaders took the position that they were entitled to a free hand in dealing with their neighbors. If thwarted, they tended to resort to force. And once having resorted to force, they never withdrew unless they were threatened with war.

The visits of Truman's emissaries to London and Moscow proved, above all, that he was still trying to steer a course between Roosevelt's view of how to maintain the peace, in which America had no partners, and his growing resentment of Soviet conduct in Eastern Europe, for which he as yet had no policy. Truman was not ready to face the geopolitical realities victory had wrought, or to jettison Roosevelt's vision of a world order governed by the Four Policemen. Nor would America yet concede that the balance of power was a necessity of the international order and not an aberration of European diplomacy.

Roosevelt's dream of the Four Policemen came to an end at the Potsdam Conference, which lasted from July 17 to August 2, 1945. The three leaders met at the Cecilienhof, a cavernous, English-style country house set in a large park which had served as the residence of the last German crown prince. Potsdam was chosen as the site of the conference because it was in the Soviet zone of occupation, was accessible by rail (Stalin hated to fly), and could be protected by Soviet security forces.

When the American delegation arrived, it was still committed to the wartime view of a new world order. The State Department briefing paper, which served as the touchstone for the American delegation, asserted that the establishment of spheres of interest would be the greatest threat to world peace. Invoking Wilsonian orthodoxy, the paper argued that spheres of interest would "represent power politics pure and simple, with all the concomitant disadvantages.... Our primary objective should be to remove the *causes* which make nations feel that such spheres are necessary to build their security, rather than to assist one country to build up strength against another."[14] The State Department did not explain what, in the absence of power politics, might encourage Stalin to compromise, or what the cause of the conflict might be if it was not clashing interests. Nevertheless, the ubiquitous Joseph Davies, who came along as the President's adviser on the Soviet leaders, seemed pleased enough with his own recommendation—which amounted to indulging Stalin. At one point, after an intense exchange, Davies slipped a note to Truman which said: "I think Stalin's feelings are hurt, please be nice to him."[15]

Coddling people, especially communists, did not come naturally to Truman. Still, he gave it a heroic try. Initially he appreciated Stalin's curt style more than he did Churchill's eloquence. As he wrote to his mother: "Churchill talks all the time and Stalin just grunts but you know what he means."[16] At a private dinner on July 21, Truman pulled out all the stops, later confiding to Davies: ". . . I wanted to convince him that we are 'on the level' and interested in peace and a decent world, and had no purposes hostile to them; that we wanted nothing for ourselves, but security for our country, and peace with friendship and neighborliness, and that it was our joint job to do that. I 'spread it on thick,' and I think he believes me. I meant every word of it."[17] Unfortunately, Stalin had no frame of reference for interlocutors who proclaimed their disinterestedness in the issues before them.

The leaders at the Potsdam Conference sought to avoid the organizational problems that had plagued the Versailles Conference. Rather than getting bogged down in details and working under time constraints, Truman, Churchill, and Stalin would confine themselves to general principles. Their foreign ministers would then work out the details of the peace agreements with the defeated Axis Powers and their allies.

Even with that restriction, the conference had a vast agenda which included reparations, the future of Germany, and the status of such German allies as Italy, Bulgaria, Hungary, Romania, and Finland. Stalin extended this list by presenting the catalogue of demands that Molotov had submitted to Hitler in 1940 and had reiterated to Eden a year later. These demands included improved Russian transit through the Straits, a Soviet military base in the Bosporus, and a share of Italy's colonies. An agenda of such scope could not have possibly been fulfilled by the harassed heads of government in a two-week period.

The Potsdam Conference rapidly turned into a dialogue of the deaf. Stalin insisted on consolidating his sphere. Truman and, to a lesser extent, Churchill demanded the vindication of their principles. Stalin tried to trade Western recognition of Soviet-imposed governments in Bulgaria and Romania for Soviet recognition of Italy. In the meantime, Stalin persisted in stonewalling the democracies' demand for free elections in Eastern Europe.

In the end, each side exercised a veto wherever it had the power to do so. The United States and Great Britain refused to agree to Stalin's demand for $20 billion in reparations from Germany (half of which was to go to the Soviet Union), or to make the assets of their zones available for that purpose. On the other side, Stalin continued to strengthen the position of Communist Parties all over Eastern Europe.

Stalin also used the ambiguity in the Yalta agreement with respect to the Oder and Neisse rivers to extend Poland's borders farther west. At Yalta it had been decided that the rivers would serve as the demarcation between Poland and Germany, though, as already noted, no one seemed to have realized that there were in fact two rivers called "Neisse." Churchill had understood the eastern one to be the border. But, at Potsdam, Stalin revealed that he had assigned the area between the eastern and the western Neisse rivers to Poland. Stalin had clearly calculated that the enmity between Poland and Germany would become intractable if

Poland acquired historic German territories, including the ancient German city of Breslau, and evicted 5 million more Germans. The American and British leaders acquiesced in Stalin's *fait accompli* with the meaningless proviso that they would reserve their final position on the border question until the peace conference. This reservation, however, merely magnified Poland's dependence on the Soviet Union, and represented little more than empty posturing since it concerned territories from which the German populations were being expelled.

Churchill had come to Potsdam from a not particularly strong domestic position. Indeed, the rhythm of the conference, such as it was, was fatally interrupted on July 25, 1945, when the British delegation had to ask for a recess in order to return home to await the results of the first general election since 1935. Churchill never did come back to Potsdam, having suffered a crushing defeat. Clement Attlee took his place as the new Prime Minister, and Ernest Bevin arrived as Foreign Secretary.

Potsdam accomplished little. Many of Stalin's demands were rejected: the base on the Bosporus, his call for Soviet trusteeship of some of Italy's African territories, and his desire for four-power control of the Ruhr and Western recognition of the Moscow-installed governments in Romania and Bulgaria. Truman too was thwarted in some of his proposals—most notably with respect to the internationalization of the Danube. The three heads of state did manage to hammer out some agreements. A four-power mechanism for dealing with German questions was set up. Truman succeeded in getting Stalin to accept his approach to reparations: that each power would take reparations out of its zone of occupation in Germany. The crucial question of Poland's western border was ducked— the United States and Great Britain acquiesced in Stalin's Oder-Neisse Line, but reserved the right to consider revision at a later date. Finally, Stalin promised to help in the war effort against Japan. Much was left ambiguous and undone and, as often happens when heads of state cannot agree, the nettlesome issues were passed on to their foreign ministers for further discussion.

Perhaps the most significant incident at Potsdam concerned an item that was not on the formal agenda. At one point, Truman took Stalin aside to inform him of the existence of the atom bomb. Stalin, of course, already knew about it from his Soviet spies; as a matter of fact, he had known about it well before Truman did. Given his paranoia, he undoubtedly considered Truman's communication a transparent attempt at intimidation. He chose to act impervious to the new technology and to deprecate it by exhibiting no particular curiosity. "The Russian Premier," wrote Truman in his memoirs, "showed no special interest. All he said was that he was glad to hear it and that he hoped we would make 'good use of it against the Japanese.' "[18] This would remain the Soviet tactic with respect to nuclear weapons until it had developed its own.

Afterward, Churchill was to say that, had he been re-elected, he would have brought matters to a head at Potsdam and tried to force a settlement.[19] He never specified what he had in mind. The fact is that Stalin could have been induced to settle, if at all, only under extreme duress, and even then only at the last moment. Indeed, Churchill's yearning for a comprehensive solution defined America's dilemma: no American statesman was prepared to issue the kind of threat or pressure which Churchill envisioned and which Stalin's psychology would have required. American leaders had not yet come to grips with the reality that the more time Stalin was given to create one-party states in Eastern Europe, the more difficult it would become to get him to change course. At the end of the war, the American public was weary of war and confrontation, and wanted above all to bring the boys home. It was not ready to threaten further confrontation, much less a nuclear war, over political pluralism in Eastern Europe or its frontiers. Unanimity about resisting further communist advances was matched by unanimity about not running any military risks.

And confrontation with Stalin would not have been a tea party. The lengths to which Stalin was prepared to press his diplomacy were brought home to me in a conversation with Andrei Gromyko after he had left office in 1989. I asked him why the Soviet Union had risked the Berlin blockade so soon after a devastating war and in the face of America's nuclear monopoly. Much mellowed in retirement, Gromyko replied that several advisers had expressed the same concern to Stalin, who had dismissed it on the basis of three propositions: first, the United States, he had said, would never use nuclear weapons over Berlin; second, if the United States attempted to push a convoy through to Berlin on the Autobahn, the Red Army was to resist; finally, if the United States seemed about to attack along the whole front, Stalin reserved the final decision for himself alone. That was the point at which he would presumably have settled.

The practical result of Potsdam was the beginning of the process that divided Europe into two spheres of influence, the very scenario America's wartime leaders had been most determined to avoid. Not surprisingly, the foreign ministers' meeting was no more productive than their chiefs' summit had been. Possessing less authority, they also had less flexibility. Molotov's political as well as physical survival depended on the most rigid adherence to his instructions from Stalin.

The first meeting of the foreign ministers took place in London in

September and early October 1945. Its purpose was to draw up peace treaties for Finland, Hungary, Romania, and Bulgaria, all of which had fought on Germany's side. American and Soviet positions had not changed since Potsdam. Secretary of State James Byrnes demanded free elections; Molotov would not hear of it. Byrnes had hoped that the demonstration of the awesome power of the atom bomb in Japan would have strengthened the American bargaining position. Instead, Molotov behaved as obstreperously as ever. By the end of the conference, it was clear that the atom bomb had not made the Soviets more cooperative— at least not in the absence of a more threatening diplomacy. Byrnes told his predecessor, Edward R. Stettinius:

> ... we were facing a new Russia, totally different than the Russia we dealt with a year ago. As long as they needed us in the War and we were giving them supplies we had a satisfactory relationship but now that the War was over they were taking an aggressive attitude and stand on political territorial questions that was indefensible.[20]

The dream of the Four Policemen died hard. On October 27, 1945, a few weeks after the Foreign Ministers' Conference aborted, Truman, speaking at a Navy Day celebration, combined the historic themes of American foreign policy with an appeal for Soviet-American cooperation. The United States, he said, sought neither territory nor bases, "nothing which belongs to any other power." American foreign policy, as a reflection of the nation's moral values, was "based firmly on fundamental principles of righteousness and justice," and on refusing to "compromise with evil." Invoking America's traditional equation of private with public morality, Truman promised that "we shall not relent in our efforts to bring the Golden Rule into the international affairs of the world." The emphasis Truman placed on the moral aspect of foreign policy served as a prelude to another appeal for Soviet-American conciliation. There were no "hopeless or irreconcilable" differences among the wartime Allies, affirmed Truman. "There are no conflicts of interest among the victorious powers so deeply rooted that they cannot be resolved."[21]

It was not to be. The next Foreign Ministers' Conference, in December 1945, produced a Soviet "concession" of sorts. Stalin received Byrnes on December 23 and proposed that the three Western democracies send a commission to Romania and Bulgaria to advise these governments on how they might broaden their cabinets to include some democratic political figures. The cynicism of the offer, of course, demonstrated Stalin's confidence in the communists' grip on their satellites rather than his receptiveness to democratic verities. This was also the view of George Kennan, who derided Stalin's concessions as "fig leaves of democratic procedure to hide the nakedness of Stalinist dictatorship."[22]

Byrnes, however, interpreted Stalin's initiative as an acknowledgment that the Yalta agreement required some democratic gesture, and he proceeded to recognize Bulgaria and Romania prior to concluding peace treaties with these countries. Truman was outraged that Byrnes had accepted the compromise without consulting him. Although, after some hesitation, Truman did go along with Byrnes, it was the beginning of an estrangement between the President and his Secretary of State that would lead to Byrnes' resignation within the year.

In 1946, there were two more foreign ministers' meetings, which took place in Paris and New York. These completed the subsidiary treaties but witnessed an increase in tensions as Stalin turned Eastern Europe into a political and economic appendage of the Soviet Union.

The cultural gap between American and Soviet leaders contributed to the emerging Cold War. American negotiators acted as if the mere recitation of their legal and moral rights ought to produce the results they desired. But Stalin needed far more persuasive reasons to change his course. When Truman spoke of the Golden Rule, his American audiences took him literally, and genuinely believed in a world governed by legal norms. To Stalin, Truman's words were meaningless, if not tricky, verbiage. The new international order he had in mind was Pan-Slavism reinforced by communist ideology. The Yugoslav dissident communist Milovan Djilas recounted a conversation in which Stalin had said: " 'If the Slavs keep united and maintain solidarity, no one in the future will be able to move a finger. Not even a finger!' he [Stalin] repeated, emphasizing his thought by cleaving the air with his forefinger."[23]

Paradoxically, the drift toward the Cold War was accelerated by Stalin's knowledge of how weak his country really was. Soviet territory west of Moscow had been devastated, for the standard practice of retreating armies—first the Soviet, then the German—had been to blow up every chimney in order to deprive their pursuers of shelter against Russia's brutal climate. The number of Soviet war dead (including civilians) was over 20 million. In addition, the death toll in all of Stalin's purges, prison camps, forced collectivizations, and deliberately created famines has been estimated at another 20 million, with perhaps another 15 million that survived imprisonment in the gulag.[24] Now this worn-out country found itself suddenly faced with America's technological breakthrough of the atom bomb. Could it mean that the moment long dreaded by Stalin had finally arrived, and that the capitalist world would be able to impose its will? Had all the suffering and exertion, inhuman by even Russia's exorbitant tyrannical standards, brought them to nothing better than a one-sided capitalist advantage?

With almost reckless bravado, Stalin chose to pretend that the Soviet Union was acting from strength, not weakness. Volunteering concessions was, in Stalin's mind, a confession of vulnerability, and he viewed any such admission as likely to generate new demands and pressures. So he kept his army in the center of Europe, where he gradually imposed Soviet puppet governments. Going even further, he conveyed an image of such implacable ferocity that many thought him poised for a dash to the English Channel—a fear widely recognized by posterity as chimerical.

Stalin coupled his exaggeration of Soviet strength and bellicosity with a systematic effort to belittle American power, especially its most potent weapon, the atom bomb. Stalin had himself set the tone by his show of indifference when Truman informed him of the bomb's existence. Communist propaganda, supported by well-meaning academic followers around the world, elaborated on the theme that the advent of nuclear weapons had not changed the rules of military strategy and that strategic bombing would prove ineffective. In 1946, Stalin laid down the official doctrine: "Atomic bombs are intended to frighten people with weak nerves, but they cannot decide the outcome of a war...."[25] In Soviet public pronouncements, Stalin's statement was quickly expanded into a distinction between "transitory" and "permanent" factors of strategy, in which the atom bomb was classified as a transitory phenomenon. "The warmongers," wrote Marshal of Aviation Konstantin Vershinin in 1949, "exaggerate the role of the air force out of all proportion . . . [calculating] that the people of the USSR and the People's Democracies will be intimidated by the so-called 'atomic' or 'push button' war."[26]

An ordinary leader would have chosen respite for a society exhausted by war and the inhuman exactions that had preceded it. But the demonic Soviet General Secretary refused to grant his people any relief; indeed, he calculated—probably correctly—that if he ever gave his society a reprieve, it would begin to ask questions directed at the very foundations of communist rule. In an address to his victorious Red Army commanders shortly after the Armistice, in May 1945, Stalin used the emotional rhetoric of wartime for the last time. Addressing the group as "my friends, my countrymen," he described the retreats of 1941 and 1942:

Another nation might have said to the government: 'You have not justified our expectations, get out; we will set up a new government which will sign a peace with Germany and give us repose.' But the Russian people did not take that road because it had faith in the policy of its government. Thank you, great Russian people for your trust.[27]

It was Stalin's last admission of fallibility and the last time he addressed his people as the head of government. (Interestingly, in his address Stalin gave credit only to the Russian people, and not to any other nationality of the Soviet Empire.) Within months, Stalin again returned to his position as General Secretary of the Communist Party as the basis for his authority, his manner of addressing the Soviet people reverting to the standard communist appellation of "comrades," as he gave the Communist Party exclusive credit for the Soviet victory.

In another major speech, on February 9, 1946, Stalin established the marching orders for the postwar period:

> Now victory means, first of all, that our Soviet social system has won, that the Soviet social system has successfully stood the test in the fire of war and has proved its complete vitality. . . . [T]he Soviet social system has proved to be more capable of life and more stable than a non-Soviet social system, . . . the Soviet social system is a better form of organization of society than any non-Soviet social system.[28]

In describing the causes of the war, Stalin invoked the true communist faith; the war, he said, had been caused not by Hitler but by the workings of the capitalist system:

> Our Marxists declare that the capitalist system of world economy conceals elements of crisis and war, that the development of world capitalism does not follow a steady and even course forward, but proceeds through crises and catastrophes. The uneven development of the capitalist countries leads in time to sharp disturbances in their relations and the group of countries which consider themselves inadequately provided with raw materials and export markets try usually to change this situation and to change the position in their favor by means of armed force.[29]

If Stalin's analysis was correct, there was no essential difference between Hitler and the Soviet Union's allies in the war against Hitler. A new war was inevitable sooner or later, and what the Soviet Union was experiencing was armistice, not a true peace. The task Stalin set before the Soviet Union was the same as it had been before the war: to become strong enough to deflect the inevitable conflict into a capitalist civil war and away from an attack on the communist motherland. Gone was any lingering prospect that peace would ease the day-to-day lot of the Soviet peoples. Heavy industry would be emphasized, collectivization of agriculture continued, and internal opposition crushed.

Stalin's speech was delivered in the standard prewar format—as a catechism in which Stalin posed and then answered his own questions. To his chilled audience, the refrain was all too familiar: as yet unidentified enemies were being threatened with extinction for seeking to thwart the socialist blueprint. Based on the personal experience of nearly every Soviet citizen, no one could consider such statements to be empty threats. At the same time, Stalin was also setting ambitious new goals: a tenfold increase in the production of pig iron, a fifteen-fold increase in steel production, and a quadrupling of oil output. "Only under such conditions will our country be insured against any eventuality. Perhaps three new Five-Year Plans will be required to achieve this, if not more. But it can be done and we must do it."[30] Three Five-Year Plans meant that none of the survivors of the purges and of the Second World War would ever lead a normal life.

When Stalin delivered this speech, the foreign ministers of the victorious alliance were still meeting regularly, American troops were being rapidly withdrawn from Europe, and Churchill had not yet delivered his Iron Curtain speech. Stalin was re-establishing a policy of confrontation with the West because he understood that the Communist Party he had shaped could not sustain itself in an international or domestic environment dedicated to peaceful coexistence.

It is possible—indeed, I believe, likely—that Stalin did not so much set out to establish what came to be known as the satellite orbit as to strengthen his hand for an inevitable diplomatic showdown. In fact, Stalin's absolute control of Eastern Europe was challenged only rhetorically by the democracies and never in a manner which might have involved risks Stalin would have taken seriously. As a result, the Soviet Union was able to turn military occupation into a network of satellite regimes.

The West's reaction to its own nuclear monopoly deepened the stalemate. In an ironic twist, scientists dedicated to avoiding nuclear war began fostering the amazing proposition that nuclear weapons did not alter the alleged lesson of World War II—that strategic bombing could not be decisive.[31] At the same time, Kremlin propaganda about the unaltered state of the strategic environment was becoming widely accepted. The reason that American military doctrine of the late 1940s fell in with this view had to do with its own bureaucratic dynamics. By recoiling from identifying any one weapon as decisive, the chiefs of America's military services made their own organizations appear more indispensable. They thus developed a concept which treated nuclear weapons as a somewhat more effective high explosive in an overall strategy based on the experiences of the Second World War. In the period of the democracies' greatest relative strength, this concept led to the general misapprehension that the Soviet Union was militarily superior because its traditional armies were larger.

As in the 1930s, it was Churchill, now leader of the Opposition, who tried to recall the democracies to their necessities. On March 5, 1946, at Fulton, Missouri, he rang the tocsin about Soviet expansionism,[32] describing an "Iron Curtain" which had fallen "from Stettin in the Baltic to Trieste in the Adriatic." The Soviets had installed pro-communist governments in every country which had been occupied by the Red Army as well as in the Soviet zone of Germany—the most useful part of which, he could not restrain himself from pointing out, had been handed over to the Soviets by the United States. In the end, this would "give the defeated Germans the power of putting themselves up to auction between the Soviets and the Western Democracies."

Churchill concluded that an alliance of the United States and the British Commonwealth was needed to meet the immediate threat. The long-term solution, however, was European unity, "from which no nation should be permanently outcast." Churchill, the first and leading opponent of the Germany of the 1930s, thus became the first and leading advocate of reconciliation with the Germany of the 1940s. Churchill's central theme, however, was that time was not on the side of the democracies, and that an overall settlement should urgently be sought:

> I do not believe that Soviet Russia desires war. What they desire is the fruits of war and the indefinite expansion of their power and doctrines. But what we have to consider here today while time remains, is the permanent prevention of war and the establishment of conditions of freedom and democracy as rapidly as possible in all countries. Our difficulties and dangers will not be removed by closing our eyes to them. They will not be removed by mere waiting to see what happens; nor will they be removed by a policy of appeasement. What is needed is a settlement, and the longer this is delayed, the more difficult it will be and the greater our dangers will become.[33]

The reason prophets are so rarely honored in their own country is that their role is to transcend the limits of their contemporaries' experience and imagination. They achieve recognition only when their vision has been turned into experience—in short, when it is too late to benefit from their foresight. It was Churchill's fate to be rejected by his countrymen except for a brief time when their very survival was at stake. In the 1930s, he had urged his country to arm while his contemporaries were seeking to negotiate; in the 1940s and 1950s, he advocated a diplomatic show-down while his contemporaries, mesmerized by the self-induced illusion of their weakness, were more interested in building up their strength.

In the end, the Soviet satellite orbit emerged by degrees, and partly by default. Analyzing Stalin's speech calling for three new Five-Year Plans, George Kennan wrote in his famous "Long Telegram" how Stalin would view serious foreign pressure: "Intervention against USSR, while it would be disastrous to those who undertook it, would cause renewed delay in progress of Soviet socialism and must therefore be forestalled *at all costs* [emphasis added]."[34] Stalin could not have simultaneously reconstructed the Soviet Union and risked a confrontation with the United States. The much-advertised Soviet invasion of Western Europe was a fantasy; the likelier probability was that Stalin would have recoiled before a serious confrontation with the United States—though surely not without first carrying it quite a distance to test the seriousness of Western resolve.

Stalin had been able to impose Eastern Europe's frontiers without undertaking an inordinate risk because his armies already occupied those areas. But when it came to imposing Soviet-style regimes on those territories, he turned much more cautious. In the first two years after the war, only Yugoslavia and Albania established communist dictatorships. The other five countries which later became Soviet satellites—Bulgaria, Czechoslovakia, Hungary, Poland, and Romania—had coalition govern-ments in which the communists were the strongest but not yet the unchal-lenged party. Two of the countries—Czechoslovakia and Hungary—held elections in the first year after the war that produced genuine multiparty systems. To be sure, systematic harassment of noncommunist parties was taking place, especially in Poland, but there was still no outright Soviet suppression of them.

As late as September 1947, Andrei Zhdanov, who for a while was con-sidered Stalin's closest collaborator, was identifying two categories of states in what he termed "the anti-fascist front" in Eastern Europe. In the speech announcing the formation of the Cominform, the formal grouping of worldwide communist parties which succeeded the Comintern, he called Yugoslavia, Poland, Czechoslovakia, and Albania the "new democ-racies" (somewhat strangely in the case of Czechoslovakia, where the communist coup had not yet taken place). Bulgaria, Romania, Hungary, and Finland were placed in another category, without as yet being given a clear-cut label.[35]

Did this mean that Stalin's fallback position for Eastern Europe was in fact a status similar to that of Finland—democratic and national but respectful of Soviet interests and concerns? Until Soviet archives are opened, we are confined to conjecture. We do know, however, that, although Stalin told Hopkins in 1945 that he wanted a friendly but not necessarily communist government in Poland, his proconsuls were implementing the exact opposite arrangement. Two years later, after America had committed itself to the Greek-Turkish aid program and was forming the three Western occupation zones of Germany into what later came to be known as the Federal Republic (see chapter 18), Stalin had another conversation with an American secretary of state. In April 1947, after eighteen months of deadlocked and increasingly acrimonious four-power foreign ministers' meetings and a whole series of Soviet threats and unilateral moves, Stalin invited Secretary Marshall to a long meeting, in the course of which he stressed that he attached great importance to an overall agreement with the United States. The deadlocks and confrontations, argued Stalin, "were only the first skirmishes and brushes of reconnaissance forces."[36] Stalin claimed compromise was possible on *"all* [emphasis added] the main questions," insisting that "it was necessary to have patience and not become pessimistic."[37]

If Stalin was serious, the master calculator had miscalculated. For, once Americans' confidence in his good faith had been destroyed, there was to be no easy road back for him. Stalin had pressed his position too far because he never really understood the psychology of the democracies, especially America's. The result was the Marshall Plan, the Atlantic Alliance, and the Western military buildup, none of which could have been in his game plan.

Churchill had almost certainly been right—that the best time for a political settlement would have been immediately after the war. Whether Stalin would have made any meaningful concessions at that time would have depended to a great extent on the timing and the seriousness with which both the proposal and the consequences of its refusal had been presented to him. The sooner after the end of the war, the better the chances of success at minimal cost would have been. As America's retreat from Europe accelerated, so did the decline of the West's bargaining position—at least until the advent of the Marshall Plan and NATO.

By the time of Stalin's conversation with Marshall in 1947, the Soviet dictator had overplayed his hand. He was now distrusted in America to the same extent that he had previously basked in its goodwill. Even if America's leap from pure goodwill to indiscriminate suspiciousness had overshot the mark, it nevertheless reflected the new international realities. Theoretically, it might have been possible to consolidate a united front among the democracies while conducting negotiations with the Soviet Union about an overall settlement. But American leaders and their colleagues in Western Europe were convinced that the cohesion and the morale of the West were too fragile to withstand the ambiguities of a dual-track strategy. The communists represented the second-largest political parties in both France and Italy. The Federal Republic of Germany, which was then in the process of being formed, was split over whether it should seek national unity through neutralism. In Great Britain as well as in the United States, vocal peace movements were challenging the emerging policy of containment.

In a radio address on April 28, Secretary of State Marshall indicated that the West had passed the point of no return in its policy toward the Soviet Union. He rejected Stalin's hint of compromise on the ground that "we cannot ignore the factor of time involved here. The recovery of Europe has been far slower than had been expected. Disintegrating forces are becoming evident. The patient is sinking while the doctors deliberate. So I believe that action cannot await compromise through exhaustion. . . . Whatever action is possible to meet these pressing problems must be taken without delay."[38]

America had opted for Western unity over East-West negotiations. It had really had no other choice, because it dared not run the risk of following up on Stalin's hints only to find that he was using negotiations to undermine the new international order America was trying to build. Containment became the guiding principle of Western policy, and it remained so for the next forty years.

CHAPTER EIGHTEEN

The Success and the Pain
of Containment

In late 1945, American policymakers were at a loss. Potsdam and the ensuing foreign ministers' conferences had come to naught. Stalin seemed to be imposing his will on Eastern Europe without any regard for American pieties about democracy. In Poland, Bulgaria, and Romania, American diplomats were consistently being met with Soviet intransigence. In a defeated Germany and Italy, Moscow seemed to have forgotten the meaning of the word "partnership." What were American policymakers to make of all this?

In the spring of 1946, Truman began to resolve this question when he launched a "get-tough" policy by successfully demanding the Soviet evacuation of Azerbaijan. But he did so within the Wilsonian mold. Like Roosevelt, Truman rejected the balance of power, disdained justifying American actions in terms of security, and sought whenever possible to attach them to general principles applicable to all mankind and in keeping with the new United Nations Charter. Truman perceived the emerging struggle between the United States and the Soviet Union as a contest between good and evil, not as having to do with spheres of political influence.

Yet spheres of influence were in fact emerging, no matter what American statesmen called them, and they were to remain in place until the collapse of communism four decades later. Under United States leadership, the Western occupation zones of Germany were consolidated, while the Soviet Union turned the countries of Eastern Europe into its appendages. The erstwhile Axis Powers—Italy, Japan, and, after 1949, the Federal Republic of Germany—gradually moved toward alliance with the United States. Although the Soviet Union cemented its dominance over Eastern Europe by means of the Warsaw Pact, this nominal alliance was obviously being held together by coercion. At the same time, the Kremlin tried its utmost to interrupt the process of Western consolidation by fostering a guerrilla war in Greece and by encouraging mass demonstrations by West European Communist parties, especially in France and Italy.

American leaders knew that they had to resist further Soviet expansion. But their national tradition caused them to seek to justify this resistance on nearly any basis other than as an appeal to the traditional balance of power. In doing this, American leaders were not being hypocritical. When they finally came to recognize that Roosevelt's vision of the Four Policemen could not be implemented, they preferred to interpret this development as a temporary setback on the way to an essentially harmonious world order. Here they faced a philosophical challenge. Was Soviet intransigence merely a passing phase which Washington could wait out? Were the Americans, as former Vice-President Henry Wallace and his followers suggested, unwittingly causing the Soviets to feel paranoid by not adequately communicating their pacific intentions to Stalin? Did Stalin really reject postwar cooperation with the strongest nation in the world? Did he not want to be America's friend?

As the highest policymaking circles in Washington considered these questions, a document arrived from an expert on Russia, one George Kennan, a relatively junior diplomat at the American embassy in Moscow, that was to provide the philosophical and conceptual framework for interpreting Stalin's foreign policy. One of those rare embassy reports that would by itself reshape Washington's view of the world, it became known as the "Long Telegram."[1] Kennan maintained that the United States should stop blaming itself for Soviet intransigence; the sources of Soviet foreign policy lay deep within the Soviet system itself. In essence, he argued, Soviet foreign policy was an amalgam of communist ideological zeal and old-fashioned tsarist expansionism.

According to Kennan, communist ideology was at the heart of Stalin's approach to the world. Stalin regarded the Western capitalist powers as irrevocably hostile. The friction between the Soviet Union and America was therefore not the product of some misunderstanding or faulty communications between Washington and Moscow, but inherent in the Soviet Union's perception of the outside world:

> In this [communist] dogma, with its basic altruism of purpose, they found justification for their instinctive fear of outside world, for the dictatorship without which they did not know how to rule, for cruelties they did not dare not to inflict, for sacrifices they felt bound to demand. In the name of Marxism they sacrificed every single ethical value in their methods and tactics. Today they cannot dispense with it. It is fig leaf of their moral and intellectual respectability. Without it they would stand before history, at best, as only the last of that long succession of cruel and wasteful Russian rulers who have relentlessly forced [their] country on to ever new heights of military power in order to guarantee external security of their internally weak regimes. . . .[2]

From time immemorial, argued Kennan, the tsars had sought to expand their territory. They had sought to subjugate Poland, and to turn it into a dependent nation. They had regarded Bulgaria as being within Russia's sphere of influence. And they had sought a warm-water port on the Mediterranean, mandating control of the Black Sea Straits.

> At bottom of Kremlin's neurotic view of world affairs is traditional and instinctive Russian sense of insecurity. Originally, this was insecurity of a peaceful, agricultural people trying to live on vast exposed plain in neighborhood of fierce nomadic peoples. To this was added, as Russia came into contact with economically advanced West, fear of more competent, more powerful, more highly organized societies in that area. But this latter type of insecurity was one which afflicted rather Russian rulers than Russian people; for Russian rulers have invariably sensed that their rule was relatively archaic in form, fragile and artificial in its psychological foundation, unable to stand comparison or contact with political systems of Western countries. For this reason they have always feared foreign penetration, feared direct contact between Western world and their own, feared what would happen if Russians learned truth about world without or if foreigners learned truth about world within. And they have learned to seek security only in patient but deadly

struggle for total destruction of rival power, never in compacts and compromises with it.[3]

Such, argued Kennan, were Soviet purposes, and no amount of American cajoling was going to change them. America, Kennan argued, had to hunker down for a long struggle; the goals and philosophies of the United States and of the Soviet Union were irreconcilable.

The first systematic exposition of the new approach appeared in a State Department memorandum submitted to an interagency committee on April 1, 1946. Drafted by State Department official H. Freeman Matthews, it attempted to translate Kennan's essentially philosophical observations into operational foreign policy. For the first time, an American policy paper treated disputes with the Soviet Union as an endemic feature of the Soviet system. Moscow had to be convinced "in the first instance by diplomatic means and in the last analysis by military force if necessary that the present course of its foreign policy can only lead to disaster for the Soviet Union."[4]

Did these bold words, put forward less than a year after the end of the Second World War, imply that the United States would defend every threatened area around the vast Soviet periphery? Matthews recoiled before his own daring and added two qualifications. America, he argued, dominated the sea and the air; the Soviet Union was supreme on land. Calling attention to "our military ineffectiveness within the land mass of Eurasia," the Matthews memorandum limited the use of force to those areas where the power of "Soviet armies can be countered defensively by the naval, amphibious and air power of the U.S. and its potential allies."[5] The second qualification warned against unilateral action: "The Charter of the United Nations affords the best and most unassailable means through which the U.S. can implement its opposition to Soviet physical expansion."[6]

But where could these two conditions be fulfilled? The Matthews paper stipulated the following countries or territories as being at risk: "Finland, Scandinavia, Eastern, Central and South Eastern Europe, Iran, Iraq, Turkey, Afghanistan, Sinkiang, and Manchuria."[7] The trouble was that none of them was within range of relevant American power. Illustrating America's continued overestimation of Great Britain's capabilities, the memorandum appealed to it to perform the very role of balancer which American leaders had so strenuously opposed only a few years earlier (see chapter 16):

If Soviet Russia is to be denied the hegemony of Europe, the United Kingdom must continue in existence as the principal power in Western

Europe economically and militarily. The U.S. should, therefore . . . give all feasible political, economic, and if necessary military support within the framework of the United Nations, to the United Kingdom. . . .[8]

The Matthews memorandum did not explain in what way Great Britain's strategic reach exceeded that of the United States.

The second qualification was no easier to fulfill. In its short and futile lifespan, the League of Nations had shown the near-impossibility of organizing collective action against a major power. Yet the country designated by the Matthews paper as posing the principal security threat was a member of the United Nations and had a veto. If the United Nations would not act and the United States could not act, Great Britain's purported role was only a stopgap.

Clark Clifford, in one of his first assignments in a long and distinguished career as a presidential adviser, removed the ambiguities and limitations of the Matthews memorandum. In a Top Secret study dated September 24, 1946, Clifford fell in with the view that the Kremlin's policies could only be reversed if Soviet power was counterbalanced: "The main deterrent to Soviet attack on the United States, or to attack on areas of the world which are vital to our security, will be the military power of this country."[9]

By now, this had become conventional wisdom. But Clifford used it as a springboard from which to proclaim a global American security mission, embracing "*all* democratic countries which are *in any way menaced* or endangered by the U.S.S.R."[10] It was not clear what was meant by "democratic." Did this qualification limit America's defense to Western Europe, or was it a courtesy that extended to any threatened area and thus required the United States to defend simultaneously the jungles of Southeast Asia, the deserts of the Middle East, and densely populated Central Europe? In time, the latter interpretation became dominant.

Clifford rejected any similarity between the emerging policy of containment and traditional diplomacy. In his view, the Soviet-American conflict was not caused by clashing national interests—which by definition might be negotiated—but by the moral shortcomings of the Soviet leadership. Therefore, the goal of American policy was not so much to restore the balance of power as to transform Soviet society. Just as in 1917 Wilson had blamed the need for a declaration of war on the Kaiser rather than on the threat Germany posed to American security, so Clifford now ascribed Soviet-American tensions to "a small ruling clique and not the Soviet people."[11] A significant Soviet change of heart, and probably a new set of Soviet leaders, was required before an overall Soviet-American agreement would be possible. At some dramatic moment, these new leaders would "work out with us a fair and equitable settlement when they realize that we are too strong to be beaten and too determined to be frightened."[12]

Neither Clifford nor any subsequent American statesman involved in the discussion of the Cold War ever put forward specific terms to end the confrontation or to initiate a process that would bring about negotiations to do so. So long as the Soviet Union maintained its ideology, negotiations were treated as pointless. After a Soviet change of heart, a settlement would become nearly automatic. In either case, spelling out the terms of such a settlement in advance was deemed to inhibit America's freedom of action—the same argument that had been used during World War II to avoid discussion of the postwar world.

America now had the conceptual framework to justify practical resistance to Soviet expansionism. Since the end of the war, Soviet pressures had followed historic Russian patterns. The Soviet Union controlled the Balkans (except for Yugoslavia) and a guerrilla war was raging in Greece, supported from bases in communist Yugoslavia and the Bulgarian Soviet satellite. Territorial demands were being made against Turkey, along with a request for Soviet bases in the Straits—very much along the lines of the demands Stalin had made to Hitler on November 25, 1940 (see chapter 14).

Ever since the end of the war, Great Britain had supported both Greece and Turkey, economically as well as militarily. In the winter of 1946–47, the Attlee government informed Washington that it could no longer shoulder the burden. Truman was prepared to take over Great Britain's historic role of blocking a Russian advance toward the Mediterranean, but neither the American public nor the Congress could countenance the traditional British geopolitical rationale. Resistance to Soviet expansionism had to spring from principles based strictly on the American approach to foreign policy.

This imperative became apparent at a key meeting held on February 27, 1947, in the Oval Office. Truman, Secretary of State Marshall, and Assistant Secretary Dean Acheson sought to persuade a Congressional delegation led by Michigan Republican Senator Arthur Vandenberg of the importance of aid to Greece and Turkey—a formidable assignment, since the traditionally isolationist Republicans controlled both houses of the Congress.

Marshall led off with a dispassionate analysis setting forth the relationship between the proposed aid program and American interests. He elicited stereotypic grumblings about "pulling Britain's chestnuts out of the fire," the iniquities of the balance of power, and the burdens of foreign aid. Recognizing that the Administration was about to lose its case, Acheson asked Marshall in a whisper whether this was a private fight or whether anyone could join in. Given the floor, Acheson proceeded, in the words of one aide, "to pull out all the stops." Acheson boldly presented the group with visions of a bleak future in which the forces of communism stood to gain the upper hand:

> Only two great powers remained in the world. . . . United States and the Soviet Union. We had arrived at a situation unparalleled since ancient times. Not since Rome and Carthage had there been such a polarization of power on this earth. . . . For the United States to take steps to strengthen countries threatened with Soviet aggression or Communist subversion . . . was to protect the security of the United States—it was to protect freedom itself.[13]

When it became evident that Acheson had roused the delegation, the Administration stuck to his basic approach. From that point on, the Greek-Turkish aid program was portrayed as part of the global struggle between democracy and dictatorship. When, on March 12, 1947, Truman announced the doctrine that would later be named after him, he dropped the strategic aspect of Acheson's analysis and spoke in traditional Wilsonian terms of a struggle between two ways of life:

> One way of life is based upon the will of the majority, and is distinguished by free institutions, representative government, free elections, guarantees of individual liberty, freedom of speech and religion, and freedom from political oppression. The second way of life is based upon the will of a minority forcibly imposed upon the majority. It relies upon terror and oppression, a controlled press and radio, fixed elections, and the suppression of personal freedoms.[14]

Moreover, in defending independent countries, the United States was acting on behalf of democracy and the world community, even though a Soviet veto would prevent formal endorsement by the United Nations: "In helping free and independent nations to maintain their freedom, the United States will be giving effect to the principles of the Charter of the United Nations."[15]

Had Soviet leaders been more aware of American history, they would have understood the ominous nature of what the President was saying. The Truman Doctrine marked a watershed because, once America had thrown down the moral gauntlet, the kind of *Realpolitik* Stalin understood best would be forever at an end, and bargaining over reciprocal concessions would be out of the question. Henceforth, the conflict could only be settled by a change in Soviet purposes, by the collapse of the Soviet system, or both.

Truman had proclaimed his doctrine as "the policy of the United States to support free peoples who are resisting attempted subjugation by armed minorities or by outside pressures."[16] Inevitably, criticism of the objective of defending democracy appeared at both ends of the intellectual spectrum: some protested that America was defending countries which, however important, were morally unworthy; others objected that America was committing itself to the defense of societies which, whether free or not, were not vital to American security. It was an ambiguity which refused to go away, generating debates about American purposes in nearly every crisis that have not ended to this day. Ever since, American foreign policy has been obliged to navigate between those who assail it for being amoral and those who criticize it for going beyond the national interest through crusading moralism.

Once the challenge had been defined as the very future of democracy, America could not wait until a civil war actually occurred, as it had in Greece; it was in the national character to attempt the cure. On June 5, less than three months after the announcement of the Truman Doctrine, Secretary Marshall, in a commencement address at Harvard, did just that when he committed America to the task of eradicating the social and economic conditions that tempted aggression. America would aid European recovery, announced Marshall, to avoid "political disturbances" and "desperation," to restore the world economy, and to nurture free institutions. Therefore, "*any* government that is willing to assist in the task of recovery will find full cooperation, I am sure, on the part of the United States Government."[17] In other words, participation in the Marshall Plan was open even to governments in the Soviet orbit—a hint taken up in Warsaw and Prague and just as quickly squelched by Stalin.

Anchored to a platform of social and economic reform, the United States announced that it would oppose not only any government but any organization that impeded the process of European recovery. Marshall defined these as the Communist Party and its front organizations: ". . . governments, political parties, or groups which seek to perpetuate human misery in order to profit therefrom politically or otherwise will encounter the opposition of the United States."[18]

Only a country as idealistic, as pioneering, and as relatively inexperienced as the United States could have advanced a plan for *global* economic recovery based solely on its own resources. And yet the very sweep of that vision elicited a national commitment which would sustain the generation of the Cold War through its final victory. The program of economic recovery, said Secretary Marshall, would be "directed not against any country or doctrine, but against hunger, poverty, desperation and chaos."[19] Just as when the Atlantic Charter had been proclaimed, a global crusade against hunger and despair was found to be more persuasive to Americans than appeals to immediate self-interest or the balance of power.

At the end of all of these more or less random initiatives, there emerged a document which would, for over a generation, serve as the bible of the containment policy, indeed which supplied it with its very name. All the various strands of American postwar thought were brought together in an extraordinary article published in July 1947 in *Foreign Affairs*. Though it was anonymously signed by "X," the author was later identified as George F. Kennan, by then head of the Policy Planning Staff of the State Department. Of the thousands of articles written since the end of the Second World War, Kennan's "The Sources of Soviet Conduct" stands in a class by itself. In this lucidly written, passionately argued, and literary adaptation of his "Long Telegram," Kennan raised the Soviet challenge to the level of philosophy of history.

By the time Kennan's article appeared, Soviet intransigence had become the staple of policy documents. Kennan's distinctive contribution was to explain the ways in which hostility to the democracies was inherent in the Soviet domestic structure, and why that structure would prove impervious to conciliatory Western policies.

Tension with the outside world was inherent in the very nature of communist philosophy and, above all, in the way the Soviet system was being run domestically. Internally, the Party was the only organized group, with the rest of society fragmented into an inchoate mass. Thus the Soviet Union's implacable hostility to the outside world was an attempt to gear international affairs to its own internal rhythm. The main concern of Soviet policy was

> to make sure that it has filled every nook and cranny available to it in the basin of world power. But if it finds unassailable barriers in its path, it accepts these philosophically and accommodates itself to them. . . . There is no trace of any feeling in Soviet psychology that that goal must be reached at any given time.[20]

The way to defeat Soviet strategy was by "a policy of firm containment, designed to confront the Russians with unalterable counter-force at every point where they show signs of encroaching upon the interests of a peaceful and stable world."[21]

Like almost every other contemporary foreign policy document, Kennan's "X" article disdained the elaboration of a precise diplomatic goal. What he sketched was the age-old American dream of a peace achieved by the conversion of the adversary, albeit in language more elevated and far more trenchant in its perception than that of any contemporary. But where Kennan differed from other experts was that he described the mechanism by which, sooner or later, through one power struggle or another, the Soviet system would be fundamentally transformed. Since that system had never managed a "legitimate" transfer of power, Kennan thought it likely that, at some point, various contestants for authority might

> reach down into these politically immature and inexperienced masses in order to find support for their respective claims. If this were ever to happen, strange consequences could flow for the Communist Party: for the membership at large has been exercised only in the practices of iron discipline and obedience and not in the arts of compromise and accommodation. . . . If, consequently, anything were ever to occur to disrupt the unity and efficacy of the Party as a political instrument, Soviet Russia might be changed overnight from one of the strongest to one of the weakest and most pitiable of national societies.[22]

No other document forecast quite so accurately what would in fact take place after the advent of Mikhail Gorbachev. And in the aftermath of so total a collapse of the Soviet Union, it may seem carping to point out just how back-breaking an assignment Kennan had prescribed for his people. For he had charged America with combatting Soviet pressures for the indefinite future all around a vast periphery that embraced the cultures of Asia, the Middle East, and Europe. The Kremlin was, moreover, free to select its point of attack, presumably only where it calculated it would have the greatest advantage. Throughout subsequent crises, the American *political* objective was deemed to be the preservation of the *status quo*, with the overall effort producing communism's final collapse only after a protracted series of ostensibly inconclusive conflicts. It was surely the ultimate expression of America's national optimism and unimpaired sense of self-confidence that as sophisticated an observer as George Kennan could have assigned his society a role so global, so stern, and, at the same time, so reactive.

This stark, even heroic, doctrine of perpetual struggle committed the

American people to endless contests with rules which left the initiative to the adversary and confined America's role to strengthening the countries already on its side of the dividing line—a classic policy of spheres of interest. By abjuring negotiations, the containment policy wasted precious time during the period of America's greatest relative strength—while it still had the atomic monopoly. Indeed, given the premise of containment —that positions of strength had yet to be built—the Cold War became both militarized and imbued with an inaccurate impression of the West's relative weakness.

The redemption of the Soviet Union thus became the ultimate goal of policy; stability could emerge only after evil had been exorcised. It was no accident that Kennan's article concluded with a peroration instructing his impatient, peace-loving compatriots about the virtues of patience and interpreting their international role as a test of their country's worthiness:

> The issue of Soviet-American relations is in essence a test of the over-all worth of the United States as a nation among nations. . . . [T]he thoughtful observer of Russian-American relations will find no cause for complaint in the Kremlin's challenge to American society. He will rather experience a certain gratitude to a Providence which, by provid-ing the American people with this implacable challenge, has made their entire security as a nation dependent on their pulling themselves together and accepting the responsibilities of moral and political lead-ership that history plainly intended them to bear.[23]

One of the outstanding features of these noble sentiments was their peculiar ambivalence. They rallied America to a global mission but made the task so complex that America would nearly tear itself apart trying to fulfill it. Yet the very ambivalence of containment seemed to lend an extraordinary impetus to American policy. Though essentially passive with respect to diplomacy with the Soviet Union, containment evoked tenacious creativity when it came to building "positions of strength" in the military and economic realms. This was because merged in contain-ment were the lessons and beliefs derived from the two most important American experiences of the previous generation: from the New Deal came the belief that threats to political stability arise primarily from gaps between economic and social expectations and reality, hence the Marshall Plan; from the Second World War America learned that the best protec-tion against aggression is having overwhelming power and the willing-ness to use it, hence the Atlantic Alliance. The Marshall Plan was designed to get Europe on its feet economically. The North Atlantic Treaty Organi-zation (NATO) was to look after its security.

NATO was the first peacetime military alliance in American history. The immediate impetus for it was the communist coup in Czechoslovakia in February 1948. After the Marshall Plan was announced, Stalin accelerated communist control over Eastern Europe. He became rigid, if not paranoid, about the East European countries' fealty to Moscow. Lifelong communist leaders suspected of harboring the slightest national feelings were purged. In Czechoslovakia, the communists had emerged as the strongest party in free elections and controlled the government. Even that was not enough for Stalin. The elected government was overthrown and the noncommunist Foreign Minister, Jan Masaryk, the son of the founder of the Czechoslovak Republic, fell to his death from his office window after being almost certainly pushed by communist thugs. A communist dictatorship was established in Prague.

For the second time within a decade, Prague became the symbol around which resistance to totalitarianism was organized. Just as the Nazi occupation of Prague had been the final straw that caused Great Britain to draw the line in 1939, the communist coup nine years later led the United States and the democracies of Western Europe to unite in resisting the imposition of a similar fate on any other European country.

The brutality of the Czech coup reawakened fears that the Soviets might sponsor other, similar takeovers—for example, by fostering a communist *coup d'état* recognizing a new communist government and using military muscle to prop it up. Thus, in April 1948, several Western European countries formed the Pact of Brussels—a defensive pact designed to repel any forcible attempts to topple democratic governments. However, every analysis of the relative power positions indicated that Western Europe simply did not have sufficient strength to repel a Soviet attack. Thus, the North Atlantic Treaty Organization came into being as a way of tying America to the defense of Western Europe. NATO provided for an unprecedented departure in American foreign policy: American, along with Canadian, forces joined Western European armies under an international NATO command. The result was a confrontation between two military alliances, and two spheres of influence along the entire length of the dividing line in Central Europe.

This was not, however, the way the process was perceived in America. Wilsonianism was too powerful to permit America to call any arrangement protecting the territorial *status quo* in Europe an alliance. Every spokesman of the Truman Administration therefore went to great lengths to distinguish NATO from anything resembling a traditional coalition to protect the balance of power. Considering their oft-repeated goal of creating "positions of strength," this required a good deal of ingenuity. Administration spokesmen proved equal to the task. When Warren Austin, a former senator who became Ambassador to the United Nations, testified on behalf of NATO before the Senate Foreign Relations Committee in April 1949, he took care of the problem by pronouncing the balance of power dead:

> The old veteran, balance of power, was given a blue discharge when the United Nations was formed. The undertaking of the peoples of the United Nations to combine their efforts through the international organization to maintain international peace and security, and to that end, to take effective collective measures, introduced formally the element of preponderance of power for peace. And out went old man balance of power.[24]

The Senate Committee on Foreign Relations happily accepted this conceit. Most of the witnesses testifying on behalf of the Atlantic Alliance borrowed heavily from a State Department document entitled "Difference Between the North Atlantic Treaty and Traditional Military Alliances."[25] This extraordinary document purported to be a historical survey of seven alliances dating back to the early nineteenth century, from the Holy Alliance of 1815 to the 1939 Nazi-Soviet Pact. Its conclusion was that the North Atlantic Treaty differed from them all, "both in letter and in spirit." Whereas "most" traditional alliances "piously" denied "aggressive or expansionist intentions," they frequently had other than defensive ends.

Amazingly, the State Department document asserted that NATO was not designed to defend the *status quo* in Europe, which was surely news to America's allies. The Atlantic Alliance upheld principle, it was said, not territory; it did not resist change, only the use of force to bring about change. The State Department analysis concluded that the North Atlantic Treaty "is directed against no one; it is directed solely against aggression. It seeks not to influence any shifting 'balance of power' but to strengthen the 'balance of principle.' " The document hailed both the Atlantic Treaty and its contemporary, the Rio Pact for defense of the Western Hemisphere, as "developments in the concept of collective security" and endorsed the pronouncement of the chairman of the Senate Committee, Tom Connally, that the Treaty constituted not a military alliance but "an alliance against war itself."[26]

No history graduate student would have received a passing grade for such an analysis. Historically, alliances rarely named the countries against which they were aimed. Instead, they described the conditions which had to be met to bring the alliance into play—just as the North Atlantic Treaty Organization did. Since in 1949 the Soviet Union was the sole potential aggressor in Europe, it was even less necessary to name names than it had been in the past. The insistence that the United States was defending principle and not territory was quintessentially American, though hardly reassuring to countries whose greatest fear was Soviet territorial expansion. The argument that America was resisting change incurred by force and not change as such was equally boilerplate and equally disquieting; in all of Europe's long history, it was not possible to enumerate many, if any, territorial changes which had been the result of anything other than force.

Nevertheless, few State Department documents have ever been greeted with such unreserved approval by the normally wary Senate Committee on Foreign Relations as this one was. Senator Connally was relentless in his promotion of the Administration's theme that the intent of NATO was to resist the concept of aggression, not any specific nation. An excerpt from the testimony of Secretary of State Dean Acheson attests to Connally's unquenchable enthusiasm:

> THE CHAIRMAN [Senator Connally]: Now, Mr. Secretary, you brought out rather clearly—it won't hurt to reiterate it a little—that this treaty is not aimed at any nation particularly. It is aimed only at any nation or any country that contemplates or undertakes armed aggression against the members of the signatory powers. Is that true?
> SECRETARY ACHESON: That is correct, Senator Connally. It is not aimed at any country; it is aimed solely at armed aggression.
> THE CHAIRMAN: In other words, unless a nation other than the signatories contemplates, meditates or makes plans looking toward, aggression or armed attack on another nation, it has no cause to fear this treaty.
> SECRETARY ACHESON: That is correct, Senator Connally, and it seems to me that any nation which claims that this treaty is directed against it should be reminded of the Biblical admonition that "The guilty flee when no man pursueth."[27]

Once the Committee got into the spirit of the subject, it practically testified on behalf of all of the other witnesses—as, for example, during this exchange with Secretary of Defense Louis Johnson:

> THE CHAIRMAN: As a matter of fact, this treaty is not a general military alliance in any sense. It is limited to defense against armed attack.
> SECRETARY JOHNSON: That is right, sir.
> THE CHAIRMAN: It is the very opposite of the military alliance.

SENATOR TYDINGS: Defensive entirely.

THE CHAIRMAN: Defensive entirely. It is an alliance of peace, if you want to call it an alliance.

SECRETARY JOHNSON: I like your language.

THE CHAIRMAN: It is an alliance against armed attack, it is an alliance against war, and does not partake of the essentials of the primary obligations of a military alliance as we know military alliances at all; is that true?

SECRETARY JOHNSON: That is right, sir.[28]

In short, the Atlantic Alliance, not really being an alliance, possessed a claim to moral universality. It represented the majority of the world against the minority of troublemakers. In a sense, the role of the Atlantic Alliance was to act until such time as the United Nations Security Council "has taken the measures necessary to restore peace and security."[29]

Dean Acheson was a uniquely sophisticated Secretary of State who knew his history. One can imagine the sardonic gleam in his eye as he let the chairman of the Committee put him through his catechism. Acheson had a clear sense of the requirements of the balance of power, as evidenced by many subtle analyses of geostrategic issues.[30] But he was also sufficiently American in his approach to diplomacy to be convinced that, left to its own devices, Europe had made a mess of the balance of power, and that, for the concept of equilibrium to have meaning for Americans, it needed to be embedded in some loftier ideal. In a speech to the Harvard Alumni Association well after the ratification of the treaty, Acheson was still defending the Atlantic Alliance in characteristically American fashion—as a novel approach to international affairs:

> . . . it has advanced international cooperation to maintain the peace, to advance human rights, to raise standards of living, and to promote respect for the principle of equal rights and self-determination of peoples.[31]

In short, America would do anything for the Atlantic Alliance except call it an alliance. It would practice a historic policy of coalition so long as its actions could be justified by the doctrine of collective security, which Wilson had first put forward as the alternative to the alliance system. Thus the European balance of power was being resurrected in uniquely American rhetoric.

As important as the Atlantic Alliance, though less noticed by the American public, was the creation of the Federal Republic of Germany by merging the American, British, and French zones of occupation. On the one hand, this new state meant that the handiwork of Bismarck was being undone, because, for the indefinite future, Germany would remain divided. On the other hand, the existence of the Federal Republic implied a continuing challenge to the Soviet presence in Central Europe since the Federal Republic would never accept the communist East German Soviet state (which the Soviets had created out of their zone of occupation). For two decades, the Federal Republic refused to recognize what came to be called the German Democratic Republic and threatened to break diplomatic relations with any country that did recognize it. After 1970, the Federal Republic abandoned the so-called Hallstein Doctrine and established diplomatic relations with the East German satellite, though without ever giving up its claim to speak on behalf of the entire German population.

The decisiveness with which America threw itself into filling the power vacuum in Europe surprised even the most earnest supporters of the containment policy. "I little thought," Churchill later reflected, "at the end of 1944 that the State Department, supported by overwhelming American opinion, would in little more than two years not only adopt and carry on the course we had opened, but would make vehement and costly exertions, even of a military character, to bring it to fruition."[32]

Four years after the unconditional surrender of the Axis Powers, the international order contained many similarities to that of the period just before the First World War: two rigid alliances with very little diplomatic maneuvering room between them faced each other, this time all around the globe. There was, however, at least one crucial difference: the pre–World War I alliances had been held together by each side's fear that a switch in alliances by one of the partners could unravel the edifice with which they had identified their security. In effect, the most bellicose partner was permitted to pull the others toward the abyss. During the Cold War, each side was dominated by a superpower sufficiently indispensable and sufficiently reluctant to run risks to keep every ally from plunging the world into war. And the presence of nuclear weapons prevented the illusion of July 1914—that war could be short and painless.

American leadership of the Alliance guaranteed that the new international order would be justified in moral, and occasionally even messianic, terms. America's leaders made exertions and sacrifices unprecedented in peacetime coalitions on behalf of appeals to fundamental values and comprehensive solutions, instead of the calculations of national security and equilibrium that had characterized European diplomacy.

461

Later, critics would emphasize the alleged cynicism of that moral rhetoric. But no one acquainted with the authors of the containment policy could doubt their sincerity. Nor could America have sustained four decades of grueling exertion on behalf of a policy which did not reflect its deepest values and ideals. This is amply demonstrated by the degree to which moral values suffused even the most highly classified government documents, which were never intended for release to the general public.

A case in point is a National Security Council document (NSC-68) produced in April 1950, which was to serve as America's official statement on Cold War strategy. NSC-68 defined the national interest largely in terms of moral principle. In its view, moral setbacks were even more dangerous than material ones:

> ... a defeat of free institutions anywhere is a defeat everywhere. The shock we sustained in the destruction of Czechoslovakia was not in the measure of Czechoslovakia's material importance to us. In a material sense, her capabilities were already at Soviet disposal. But when the integrity of Czechoslovak institutions was destroyed, it was in the intangible scale of values that we registered a loss more damaging than the material loss we had already suffered.[33]

Once vital interests had been equated with moral principle, America's strategic objectives were cast in terms of worthiness rather than of power —to "make ourselves strong, both in the way we affirm our values in the conduct of our national life, and in the development of our political and economic strength."[34] The doctrine of America's Founding Fathers, that their nation was a beacon of liberty for all mankind, permeated American Cold War philosophy. Rejecting the strand of American thinking expressed in John Quincy Adams' warning against "going abroad in search of monsters to destroy," the drafters of NSC-68 opted for the alternative vision of America as crusader: "It is only by practical affirmation, abroad as well as at home, of our essential values, that we can preserve our own integrity, in which lies the real frustration of the Kremlin design."[35]

In these terms, the purpose of the Cold War was the conversion of the adversary: "to foster a fundamental change in the nature of the Soviet system," which was defined as "Soviet acceptance of the specific and limited conditions requisite to an international environment in which free institutions can flourish, and in which the Russian peoples will have a new chance to work out their own destiny."[36]

Though NSC-68 went on to describe various military and economic measures vital to building situations of strength, its central theme was neither the give-and-take of traditional diplomacy nor an apocalyptic final showdown. The reluctance to use or to threaten to use nuclear weapons during the period of America's atomic monopoly was rationalized in a uniquely American way: victory in any such war would produce a transitional, hence an unsatisfactory, outcome. As for a negotiated solution, ". . . the only conceivable basis for a general settlement would be spheres of influence and of no influence—a 'settlement' which the Kremlin could readily exploit to its great advantage."[37] In other words, America refused to consider winning a war or even a comprehensive solution which would leave the adversary unconverted.

For all of its ostensibly hardheaded realism, NSC-68 began with a peroration on democracy and concluded with the assertion that history would ultimately work in America's favor. What was unique about this document was its coupling of universal claims with the renunciation of force. Never before had a Great Power expressed objectives quite so demanding of its own resources without any expectation of reciprocity other than the dissemination of its national values. And these would be achieved through global reform, not global conquest, the usual path of crusaders. It so happened that for this endeavor American strength was, for a brief moment, unprecedentedly supreme, despite the fact that America had convinced itself that it was relatively weak militarily.

In those early stages of America's journey into containment, no one could have imagined the impending strain on the American psyche of conflicts whose principal goal was the internal transformation of the adversary, and which lacked any criteria that could be used to assess the success of each intermediate step. It would have seemed incredible to all those self-confident American leaders that their country would, within two decades, have to navigate a passage of searing self-doubt and domestic conflict before their prediction of the collapse of communism would be fulfilled. For the time being, they were fully occupied with committing America to its new international role while fending off criticisms of the revolutionary turn America's foreign policy was taking.

As containment slowly took shape, the criticism it encountered emerged from three different schools of thought. The first came from the "realists" exemplified by Walter Lippmann, who argued that the containment policy led to psychological and geopolitical overextension while draining American resources. The spokesman for the second school of thought was Winston Churchill, who objected to the postponement of negotiations until after positions of strength had been achieved.

Churchill's argument was that the West's position would never again be as strong as it was at the beginning of what came to be known as the Cold War, and that its relative bargaining position could therefore only deteriorate. Finally, there was Henry Wallace, who denied America the moral right to undertake the policy of containment in the first place. Postulating a fundamental moral equivalence between both sides, Wallace argued that the Soviet sphere of influence in Central Europe was legitimate and that America's resistance to it only intensified tension. He urged a return to what he viewed as Roosevelt's policy: to end the Cold War by a unilateral American decision.

As the most eloquent spokesman for the realists, Walter Lippmann rejected Kennan's proposition that Soviet society contained the seeds of its own decay. He considered the theory to be too speculative to serve as the foundation of American policy:

> In Mr. X's estimates there are no reserves for a rainy day. There is no margin of safety for bad luck, bad management, error and the unforeseen. He asks us to assume that the Soviet power is already decaying. He exhorts us to believe that our own highest hopes for ourselves will soon have been realized.[38]

Containment, argued Lippmann, would draw America into the hinterlands of the Soviet Empire's extended periphery, which included, in his view, many countries that were not states to begin with in the modern sense. Military entanglements that far from home could not enhance American security and would weaken American resolve. Containment, according to Lippmann, permitted the Soviet Union to choose the points of maximum discomfiture for the United States while retaining the diplomatic, and even the military, initiative.

Lippmann stressed the importance of establishing criteria to define areas in which countering Soviet expansion was a vital American interest. Without such criteria, the United States would be forced to organize a "heterogeneous array of satellites, clients, dependents, and puppets," which would permit America's newfound allies to exploit containment for their own purposes. The United States would be trapped into propping up nonviable regimes, leaving Washington with the sorry choice between "appeasement and defeat and the loss of face, or . . . support[ing] them [U.S. allies] at incalculable cost."[39]

It was indeed a prophetic analysis of what lay ahead for the United States, though the remedy Lippmann proposed was hardly congenial to the universalist American tradition, which was far closer to Kennan's expectation of an apocalyptic outcome. Lippmann asked that American foreign policy be guided by a case-by-case analysis of American interests rather than by general principles presumed to be universally applicable. In his view, American policy should have been aiming less at overthrowing the communist system than at restoring the balance of power in Europe, which had been destroyed by the war. Containment implied the indefinite division of Europe, whereas America's real interest should be to banish Soviet power from the center of the European Continent:

> For more than a hundred years all Russian governments have sought to expand over eastern Europe. But only since the Red Army reached the Elbe River have the rulers of Russia been able to realize the ambitions of the Russian Empire and the ideological purposes of communism. A genuine policy would, therefore, have as its paramount objective a settlement which brought about the evacuation of Europe. . . . American power must be available, not to "contain" the Russians at scattered points, but to hold the whole Russian military machine in check, and to exert a mounting pressure in support of a diplomatic policy which has as its concrete objective a settlement that means withdrawal.[40]

Destiny was surely profligate in the talent it bestowed on America in the immediate postwar period. American political leaders were distinguished and experienced men. And behind them stood a reservoir of such eminent personalities as John McCloy, Robert Lovett, David Bruce, Ellsworth Bunker, Averell Harriman, and John Foster Dulles, rotating in and out of government and always available to serve the president on a nonpartisan basis.

From among its intellectuals, America was able to draw on the thinking of both Lippmann and Kennan while they were at the height of their powers. Kennan correctly understood communism's underlying weakness; Lippmann accurately foretold the frustrations of an essentially reactive foreign policy based on containment. Kennan called for endurance to permit history to display its inevitable tendencies; Lippmann called for diplomatic initiative to produce a European settlement while America was still preponderant. Kennan had a better intuitive understanding of the mainsprings of American society; Lippmann, on the other hand, grasped the impending strain of enduring a seemingly endless stalemate and of the ambiguous causes which containment might lead America to support.

In the end, Lippmann's analysis found a substantial following, though mainly among the opponents of confrontation with the Soviet Union. And their approbation was based on only one aspect of Lippmann's argument, emphasizing as they did its critique while ignoring its prescriptions. They noted Lippmann's call for more limited objectives but overlooked his recommendation for a more offensive diplomacy. Thus it happened that in the 1940s the most compelling alternative strategy to the doctrine of containment came from none other than Winston Churchill, then the leader of the Opposition in Parliament.

Churchill had been widely credited with inaugurating the Cold War when he delivered his Iron Curtain speech at Fulton, Missouri. At every stage of the Second World War, Churchill had sought to limit Soviet expansionism in an effort to bolster the democracies' postwar bargaining position. Churchill supported containment, but for him it was never an end in itself. Unwilling to wait passively for the collapse of communism, he sought to shape history rather than to rely on it to do his work for him. What he was after was a negotiated settlement.

Churchill's Fulton speech had merely hinted at negotiations. On October 9, 1948, at Llandudno, Wales, Churchill returned to his argument that the West's bargaining position would never be better than it was at that moment. In a much-neglected speech, he said:

> The question is asked: What will happen when they get the atomic bomb themselves and have accumulated a large store? You can judge yourselves what will happen then by what is happening now. If these things are done in the green wood, what will be done in the dry? . . . No one in his senses can believe that we have a limitless period of time before us. We ought to bring matters to a head and make a final settlement. We ought not to go jogging along improvident, incompetent, waiting for something to turn up, by which I mean waiting for something bad for us to turn up. The Western Nations will be far more likely to reach a lasting settlement, without bloodshed, if they formulate their just demands while they have the atomic power and before the Russian Communists have got it too.[41]

Two years later, Churchill made the same plea in the House of Commons: the democracies were quite strong enough to negotiate, and would only weaken themselves by waiting. In a speech defending NATO rearmament on November 30, 1950, he warned that arming the West would not by itself change its bargaining position, which, in the end, depended on America's atomic monopoly:

> . . . while it is right to build up our forces as fast as we can, nothing in this process, in the period I have mentioned, will deprive Russia of

effective superiority in what are called now the conventional arms. All that it will do is to give us increasing unity in Europe and magnify the deterrents against aggression.... Therefore I am in favour of efforts to reach a settlement with Soviet Russia as soon as a suitable opportunity presents itself, and of making those efforts while the immense and measureless superiority of the United States atomic bomb organization offsets the Soviet predominance in every other military respect.[42]

For Churchill, a position of strength was already in place; for American leaders, it had yet to be created. Churchill thought of negotiations as a way of relating power to diplomacy. And though he was never specific, his public statements strongly suggest that he envisaged some kind of diplomatic ultimatum by the Western democracies. American leaders recoiled before employing their atomic monopoly, even as a threat. Churchill wanted to shrink the area of Soviet influence, but was prepared to coexist with Soviet power within reduced limits. The American leaders had a nearly visceral dislike of spheres of influence. They wanted to destroy and not to shrink their adversary's sphere. Their preference was to wait for total victory and for the collapse of communism, however far off, to bring about a Wilsonian solution to the problem of world order.

The disagreement came down to a difference between the historical experiences of Great Britain and America. Churchill's society was all too familiar with imperfect outcomes; Truman and his advisers came from a tradition in which, once a problem had been recognized, it was usually overcome by the deployment of vast resources. Hence America's preference for final resolutions and its distrust of the sort of compromise that had become a British specialty. Churchill had no conceptual difficulty combining the building of positions of strength with an active diplomacy pressing for a settlement. American leaders thought of these efforts as successive phases—just as they had in World War II and would again in Korea and Vietnam. The American view prevailed, because America was stronger than Great Britain, and because Churchill, as the leader of the British Opposition, was in no position to press his strategy.

In the end, the most vocal and persistent challenge to American policy came from neither the realist school of Lippmann nor Churchill's balance-of-power thinking, but from a tradition with roots deep within American radical thought. Whereas Lippmann and Churchill accepted the Truman Administration's premise that Soviet expansionism represented a serious challenge and only contested the strategy for resisting it, the radical critics rejected every aspect of containment. Henry Wallace, Vice-President during Roosevelt's third term, former Secretary of Agriculture, and Secretary of Commerce under Truman, was its principal spokesman.

A product of America's populist tradition, Wallace had an abiding Yankee distrust of Great Britain. Like most American liberals since Jefferson, he insisted that "the same moral principles which governed in private life also should govern in international affairs."[43] In Wallace's view, America had lost its moral compass and was practicing a foreign policy of "Machiavellian principles of deceit, force and distrust," as he told an audience in Madison Square Garden on September 12, 1946.[44] Since prejudice, hatred, and fear were the root causes of international conflict, the United States had no moral right to intervene abroad until it had banished these scourges from its own society.

The new radicalism reaffirmed the historic vision of America as a beacon of liberty, but, in the process, turned it against itself. Postulating the moral equivalence of American and Soviet actions became a characteristic of the radical critique throughout the Cold War. The very idea of America's having international responsibilities was, in Wallace's eyes, an example of the arrogance of power. The British, he argued, were duping the gullible Americans into doing their bidding: "British policy clearly is to provoke distrust between the United States and Russia and thus prepare the groundwork for World War III."[45]

To Wallace, Truman's presentation of the conflict as between democracy and dictatorship was pure fiction. In 1945, a time when Soviet postwar repression was becoming increasingly obvious and the brutality of collectivization was widely recognized, Wallace declared that "the Russians today have more of the political freedoms than they ever had." He also discovered "increasingly the signs of religious toleration" in the U.S.S.R. and claimed that there was a "basic lack of conflict between the United States and the Soviet Union."[46]

Wallace thought that Soviet policy was driven less by expansionism than by fear. In March 1946, while still the Commerce Secretary, Wallace wrote to Truman:

The events of the past few months have thrown the Soviets back to their pre-1939 fears of "capitalist encirclement" and to their erroneous belief that the Western World, including the U.S.A. is invariably and unanimously hostile.[47]

In his speech at Madison Square Garden six months later, Wallace laid down a direct challenge to Truman, which caused the President to demand his resignation:

We may not like what Russia does in Eastern Europe. Her type of land reform, industrial expropriation, and suppression of basic liberties offends the great majority of the people of the United States. But whether we like it or not the Russians will try to socialize their sphere of influence just as we try to democratize our sphere of influence. . . . Russian ideas of social-economic justice are going to govern nearly a third of the world. Our ideas of free enterprise democracy will govern much of the rest. The two ideas will endeavor to prove which can deliver the most satisfaction to the common man in their respective areas of political dominance.[48]

In a curious reversal of roles, the self-proclaimed defender of morality in foreign policy accepted a Soviet sphere of influence in Eastern Europe on practical grounds, while the Administration he was attacking for cynical power politics rejected the Soviet sphere on moral grounds.

According to Wallace, America had no right to intervene unilaterally around the globe. Defense was legitimate only with the approval of the United Nations (regardless that the Soviet Union had a veto there), and economic assistance should be distributed through international institutions. Since the Marshall Plan did not meet this test, Wallace predicted that it would ultimately earn America the enmity of mankind.[49]

Wallace's challenge collapsed after the communist coup in Czechoslovakia, the Berlin blockade, and the invasion of South Korea. As a presidential candidate in 1948, he gained only 1 million votes—most of them in New York—against more than 24 million for Truman, placing him fourth, behind the Dixiecrat candidate, Strom Thurmond.

Nevertheless, Wallace managed to develop themes which would remain staples of the American radical critique throughout the Cold War, and move to center stage during the Vietnam War. These emphasized America's moral inadequacies and those of the friends it was supporting; a basic moral equivalence between America and its communist challengers; the proposition that America had no obligation to defend any area of the world against largely imaginary threats; and the view that world opinion was a better guide to foreign policy than geopolitical concepts. When aid to Greece and Turkey was first being proposed, Wallace urged the Truman Administration to put the issue before the United Nations. If "the Russians exercised their veto, the moral burden would be on them. . . . [W]hen we act independently . . . the moral burden is on us."[50] Seizing the moral high ground meant more than whether America's geopolitical interests were being safeguarded.

Though Wallace's radical critique of American postwar foreign policy was defeated in the 1940s, its basic tenets reflected a deep strain of American idealism that continued to tug at the nation's soul. The same moral convictions which had conferred such energy on America's international commitments also had the potential to be turned inward by disillusionment with the outside world, or with America's own imperfections. In the 1920s, isolationism had caused America to withdraw on the ground that it was too good for the world; in the Wallace Movement, it revived itself in the proposition that America should withdraw because it was not good enough for the world.

Yet when America launched its first permanent peacetime international involvement, systematic self-doubt still lay far in the future. The generation which had built the New Deal and won the Second World War had enormous faith in itself and in the vastness of the American enterprise. And the nation's idealism was well suited to managing a two-power world, for which the subtle combinations of the traditional balance-of-power diplomacy were not nearly so appropriate. Only a society with enormous confidence in its achievements and in its future could have mustered the dedication and the resources to strive for a world order in which defeated enemies would be conciliated, stricken allies restored, and adversaries converted. Great enterprises are often driven by a touch of naïveté.

One result of the containment policy was that the United States relegated itself to an essentially passive diplomacy during the period of its greatest power. That is why containment was increasingly challenged by yet another constituency, of which John Foster Dulles became the most vocal spokesman. They were the conservatives who accepted the premises of containment but questioned the absence of urgency with which it was being pursued. Even if containment did in the end succeed in undermining Soviet society, these critics argued, it would take too long and cost too much. Whatever containment might accomplish, a strategy of liberation would surely accelerate. By the end of Truman's presidency, the containment policy was caught in a crossfire between those who considered it too bellicose (the followers of Wallace) and those who thought it too passive (the conservative Republicans).

This controversy accelerated because, as Lippmann had predicted, international crises increasingly moved to peripheral regions of the globe, where the moral issues were confused and direct threats to American security were difficult to demonstrate. America found itself drawn into wars in areas not protected by alliances and on behalf of ambiguous causes and inconclusive outcomes. From Korea to Vietnam, these enter-

470

prises kept alive the radical critique, which continued to question the moral validity of containment.

Thus surfaced a new variant of American exceptionalism. With all of its imperfections, the America of the nineteenth century had thought of itself as the beacon of liberty; in the 1960s and 1970s, the torch was said to be flickering and would need to be relit before America could return to its historic role as an inspiration to the cause of freedom. The debate over containment turned into a struggle for the very soul of America.

As early as 1957, even George Kennan had come to reinterpret containment in this light when he wrote:

> To my own countrymen who have often asked me where best to apply the hand to counter the Soviet threat, I have accordingly had to reply: to our American failings, to the things we are ashamed of in our own eyes, or that worry us; to the racial problem, to the conditions in our big cities, to the education and environment of our young people, to the growing gap between specialized knowledge and popular understanding.[51]

A decade earlier, before he had become disillusioned by what he considered the militarization of his invention, George Kennan would have recognized that no such choice existed. A country that demands moral perfection of itself as a test of its foreign policy will achieve neither perfection nor security. It was a measure of Kennan's achievement that, by 1957, all of the free world's parapets had been manned, his own views having made a decisive contribution to this effort. The parapets were in fact being manned so effectively that America permitted itself to indulge in a hefty dose of self-criticism.

Containment was an extraordinary theory—at once hardheaded and idealistic, profound in its assessment of Soviet motivations yet curiously abstract in its prescriptions. Thoroughly American in its utopianism, it assumed that the collapse of a totalitarian adversary could be achieved in an essentially benign way. Although this doctrine was formulated at the height of America's absolute power, it preached America's relative weakness. Postulating a grand diplomatic encounter at the moment of its culmination, containment allowed no role for diplomacy until the climactic final scene in which the men in the white hats accepted the conversion of the men in the black hats.

With all of these qualifications, containment was a doctrine that saw America through more than four decades of construction, struggle, and, ultimately, triumph. The victim of its ambiguities turned out to be not the peoples America had set out to defend—on the whole successfully—but the American conscience. Tormenting itself in its traditional quest for moral perfection, America would emerge, after more than a generation of struggle, lacerated by its exertions and controversies, yet having achieved almost everything it had set out to do.

CHAPTER NINETEEN

The Dilemma of Containment: The Korean War

The United States did not "bring its boys home" from Europe, as Roosevelt had envisioned. Instead, it remained deeply involved, setting up institutions and programs to guard against Soviet incursions and applying pressure on the Soviet sphere wherever possible.

For three years, the containment policy had worked as it had been conceived. The Atlantic Alliance served as a military bulwark against Soviet expansion, while the Marshall Plan strengthened Western Europe economically and socially. The Greek-Turkish aid program rebuffed the Soviet threat in the Eastern Mediterranean, and the Berlin airlift showed that the democracies were prepared to risk war to resist threats to their established rights. In each case, the Soviet Union recoiled rather than face a showdown with the United States.

But the containment theory had a major flaw, causing American leaders to act on the basis of two erroneous premises: that their challenges would continue to be of as unambiguous a variety as they had been during the Second World War; and, second, that the communists would wait passively for the disintegration of their own rule, as postulated by the containment theory. They failed to consider the possibility that the communists might seek to break out at some point, choosing as their target an area of maximum political or strategic complexity for the United States.

Containment had been sold to a reluctant Congress on behalf of Europe. The fear of a Soviet incursion into the Mediterranean had given rise to the Greek-Turkish aid program, and the danger of a Soviet attack on Western Europe had led to the formation of the North Atlantic Treaty Organization. The possibility of a Soviet thrust elsewhere had the character of an afterthought, if that.

Then, on June 25, 1950, America was suddenly forced to come to grips with the ambiguities of containment, when it was faced with military aggression by a communist surrogate against a country which Washington had declared to be outside America's defense perimeter and from which all American forces had been withdrawn the previous year. The aggressor was North Korea and the victim was South Korea—both located about as far from Europe, the focal point of American strategy, as it was possible to be. Yet, just days after the North Korean attack, Truman hastily assembled an expeditionary force from among the poorly trained occupation troops in Japan to implement a strategy of local defense which had never been envisaged in American planning or been proposed in Congressional testimony. America's postwar political and strategic doctrine had simply ignored the possibility of this kind of aggression.

American leaders had defined only two likely causes of war: a surprise Soviet attack on the United States or an invasion of Western Europe by the Red Army. "Plans for the national security," testified General Omar N. Bradley as Army Chief of Staff in 1948,

> must consider the possibility that the United States will be subject to air and air-borne attack at the outset. The likelihood and the practicability of this kind of attack increases daily. . . . We would [therefore] have to immediately secure bases from which an enemy might attack us by air. Next, we will have to launch an immediate counterattack . . . predominantly through the air. . . . To make our counterblows we will need bases which we do not have now. The seizing and holding of [these] bases . . . will require Army combat elements.[1]

Bradley failed to explain how or why the Soviet Union might pursue such a strategy three years after a devastating war, while the United States possessed the atomic monopoly, and the Soviet Union had no known capability for long-range air power.

Nothing in America's behavior would have led policymakers in Moscow or Pyongyang, North Korea's capital, to expect more than a diplomatic protest when North Korean troops crossed the 38th Parallel. They must have been as surprised as Saddam Hussein was when America shifted from the conciliation of the late 1980s to the massive deployment in the Persian Gulf in 1990. The communists in Moscow and Pyongyang had taken at face value the pronouncements of leading Americans that had placed Korea outside the American defense perimeter. They assumed that America would not resist a communist takeover of half of Korea after having acquiesced to a communist victory in China, which represented an incomparably more important prize. They had obviously failed to understand that repeated American declarations proclaiming resistance to communist aggression as a moral duty carried far more weight with American policymakers than strategic analysis.

Thus, the Korean War grew out of a double misunderstanding: the communists, analyzing the region in terms of American interests, did not find it plausible that America would resist at the tip of a peninsula when it had conceded most of the mainland of Asia to the communists; while America, perceiving the challenge in terms of principle, was less concerned with Korea's geopolitical significance—which American leaders had publicly discounted—than with the symbolism of permitting communist aggression to go unopposed.

Truman's courageous decision to take a stand on Korea was in flat contradiction to what American leaders had proclaimed only a year before. In March 1949, General Douglas MacArthur, Commander of America's Pacific forces, had placed Korea squarely outside the American defense perimeter in a newspaper interview:

> ... our line of defense runs through the chain of islands fringing the coast of Asia.
>
> It starts from the Philippines and continues through the Ryukyu Archipelago, which includes its main bastion, Okinawa. Then it bends back through Japan and the Aleutian Island chain to Alaska.[2]

In a speech before the National Press Club on January 12, 1950, Secretary of State Dean Acheson had gone even further. He not only consigned Korea to being outside the American defense perimeter, but specifically abjured any intentions of guaranteeing areas located on the mainland of Asia:

So far as the military security of other areas in the Pacific is concerned, it must be clear that no person can guarantee these areas against military attack. But it must also be clear that such a guarantee is hardly sensible or necessary within the realm of practical relationship.[3]

In 1949, President Truman, acting on the advice of the Joint Chiefs of Staff, had withdrawn all American military forces from Korea. The South Korean army was trained and equipped for little more than police functions, because Washington feared that South Korea would be tempted to unify the country by force if it were given the slightest capacity to do so.

Khrushchev's memoirs claim that the invasion of Korea was the brainchild of Kim Il Sung, the North Korean dictator. Stalin, initially wary, had allegedly gone along with the plan because he permitted himself to be convinced that the enterprise would succeed easily.[4] Both Moscow and Pyongyang had failed to understand the role of values in America's approach to international relations. When MacArthur and Acheson spoke about American strategy, they were thinking of general war with the Soviet Union, the only kind of war America's leaders had ever systematically contemplated. In such a war, Korea would indeed have been outside America's defense perimeter, and the decisive battles would have been fought elsewhere.

America's leaders had simply never thought about how they would react to an aggression confined to Korea, or to any comparable area. When they were obliged to confront such a situation so soon after the Berlin blockade, the Czech coup, and the communist victory in China, they interpreted it as proof that communism was on the march and had to be stopped on principle even more than on the basis of strategy.

Truman's decision to resist in Korea had a solid foundation in traditional concepts of national interest as well. Expansionist communism had been escalating its challenge with each postwar year. It had gained a foothold in Eastern Europe in 1945 as a byproduct of occupation by the Red Army. It had prevailed in Czechoslovakia by means of a domestic coup in 1948. It had taken over China in a civil war in 1949. If commmunist armies could now march across internationally recognized boundary lines, the world would have returned to the conditions of the prewar period. The generation which had lived through Munich was bound to react. A successful invasion of Korea would have had a disastrous impact on Japan, right across the narrow Sea of Japan. Japan had always considered Korea as the strategic key to Northeast Asia. Unopposed communist control would have introduced the specter of a looming Asian communist monolith and undermined Japan's pro-Western orientation.

Few foreign policy decisions are more difficult than to improvise military actions which have never been foreseen. Yet Truman rose to the occasion. On June 27, two days after North Korean troops crossed the 38th Parallel, he ordered American air and naval units into action. By June 30, he had committed ground troops from occupation duties in Japan.

Soviet rigidity eased Truman's task of leading his country into war. The Soviet Ambassador to the United Nations had been boycotting the Security Council and other United Nations institutions for months in protest against the world organization's refusal to turn China's seat over to Beijing. Had the Soviet Ambassador been less terrified of Stalin or been able to obtain instructions more rapidly, he would surely have vetoed the Security Council resolution proposed by the United States asking North Korea to cease hostilities and to return to the 38th Parallel. By failing to attend the session and to cast the veto, the Soviet Ambassador gave Truman the opportunity to organize resistance as a decision of the world community and to justify the American role in Korea in the familiar Wilsonian terms of freedom versus dictatorship, good versus evil. America, said Truman, was going to war to uphold the orders of the Security Council.[5] It was not, therefore, intervening in a faraway local conflict but opposing an assault against the entire free world:

> The attack upon Korea makes it plain beyond all doubt that Communism has passed beyond the use of subversion to conquer independent nations and will now use armed invasion and war. It has defied the orders of the Security Council of the United Nations issued to preserve international peace and security.[6]

Though Truman had powerful geopolitical arguments in favor of intervention in Korea, he appealed to the American people on the basis of their core values, and described intervention as a defense of universal principle rather than of the American national interest: "A return to the rule of force in international affairs would have far-reaching effects. The United States will continue to uphold the rule of law."[7] That America defends principle, not interests, law, and not power, has been a nearly sacrosanct tenet of America's rationale in committing its military forces, from the time of the two world wars through the escalation of its involvement in Vietnam in 1965 and the Gulf War in 1991.

Once the issue had been raised as being beyond power politics, it became extraordinarily difficult to define practical war aims. In a general war, which was what American strategic doctrine had contemplated, the quest was for total victory and for the unconditional surrender of the adversary, as it had been in World War II. But what was the political objective of a limited war? The simplest and most easily comprehensible war aim would have been a literal application of the Security Council resolutions—to push North Korean forces back to their starting point along the 38th Parallel. But if there was to be no penalty for aggression, how was future aggression to be discouraged? If potential aggressors came to understand that they would never do worse than the *status quo ante*, containment might turn into an endless progression of limited wars that would deplete America's strength—much as Lippmann had predicted.

On the other hand, what sort of penalty was compatible with commitment to a limited war? Inherent in the strategy of limited wars involving the superpowers—directly or indirectly—is the physical ability of either side to raise the stakes: this is what defines them as superpowers. A balance must therefore be struck. Whichever side convinces the other that it is willing to run the greater risk will have the advantage. In Europe, Stalin, contrary to any rational analysis of the relationship of forces, had managed to bluff the democracies into believing that his readiness to go to the brink (and beyond) exceeded theirs. In Asia, the communist side was reinforced by the looming menace of China, which had just been taken over by the communists and had the potential of raising the stakes without the direct involvement of the Soviet Union. The democracies were therefore more afraid of escalation than their adversaries—or at least so the democracies believed.

Another factor inhibiting American policy was the commitment to a multilateral approach via the United Nations. At the start of the Korean War, the United States enjoyed wide support from NATO countries like Great Britain and Turkey, which sent sizable troop contingents. Though indifferent to the fate of Korea, these countries supported the principle of collective action that they might later invoke in their own defense. Once this purpose was fulfilled, the majority of the General Assembly of the United Nations was far less eager to run the additional risks inherent in inflicting further penalties. America thus found itself in a limited war for which it had no doctrine and in defense of a distant country in which it had declared it had no strategic interest. Beset by ambivalence, America perceived no national strategic interest in the Korean peninsula; its principal aim was to demonstrate that there was a penalty for aggression. To make North Korea pay a price without triggering a wider war, America needed to convince those countries with a capacity to escalate, especially the Soviet Union and China, that American objectives were indeed limited.

Unfortunately, the containment theory, in the name of which America had engaged itself, produced precisely the opposite temptation: it induced Truman and his colleagues to expand the political battlefield. Without exception, the key members of the Truman Administration believed in a global communist design and treated Korean aggression as the first move in a coordinated Sino-Soviet strategy which might well be the prelude to a general assault. As American troops were deployed into Korea, they therefore looked for ways to convey America's determination to resist communist aggression throughout the Pacific area. They coupled the announcement of the dispatch of troops with an order to the Seventh Fleet to protect Taiwan against Communist China: "The occupation of Formosa by Communist forces would be a direct threat to the security of the Pacific area and to United States forces performing their lawful and necessary functions in that area."[8] Furthermore, Truman increased military aid to French forces opposing the communist-led independence struggle in Vietnam. (Governmental decisions usually have more than one motive; these actions had the added advantage from Truman's point of view of co-opting the so-called China Lobby in the United States Senate, which had been highly critical of his Administration's "abandonment" of mainland China.)

To Mao Tse-tung, fresh from his triumph in the Chinese civil war, Truman's announcements were bound to appear as the mirror image of America's fear of a communist conspiracy: he construed them as the opening move in an American attempt to reverse the communists' victory in the Chinese civil war. In protecting Taiwan, Truman was supporting what America still recognized as the legitimate Chinese government. The stepped-up aid program to Vietnam appeared to Beijing as capitalist encirclement. It all added up to giving Beijing the incentive to do the opposite of what America should have considered desirable: Mao had reason to conclude that, if he did not stop America in Korea, he might have to fight America on Chinese territory; at a minimum, he was given no reason to think otherwise. "The American imperialists fondly hope," wrote the *People's Daily,* "that their armed aggression against Taiwan will keep us from liberating it. Around China in particular their designs for blockades are taking shape in the pattern of a stretched-out snake. Starting from South Korea, it stretches to Japan, the Ryukyu Islands, Taiwan and the Philippines and then turns up at Vietnam."[9]

The American military strategy compounded China's misperception of America's intentions. As noted earlier, American leaders have traditionally viewed diplomacy and strategy as being separate activities. In the conventional view of the American military, they first achieve an outcome and then the diplomats take over; neither ever tells the other how to pursue its objectives. In a limited war, if military and political goals are not synchronized from the very beginning, there is always a danger of doing either too much or too little. Doing too much and allowing the military element to predominate erodes the dividing line to all-out war and tempts the adversary to raise the stakes. Doing too little and allowing the diplomatic side to dominate risks submerging the purpose of the war in negotiating tactics and a proclivity to settle for a stalemate.

In Korea, America fell into both of these traps. In the early stages of the war, the American expeditionary force was confined to a perimeter around the port city of Pusan at the southernmost tip of the Korean peninsula. Survival was the principal goal; the relationship between war and diplomacy was far from the minds of America's leaders. Douglas MacArthur, America's most talented general of this century, served as the Commander. Unlike most of his colleagues, MacArthur was not a devotee of the preferred American strategy of attrition. During the Second World War, despite the priority given to the European theater, MacArthur had developed the strategy of "island hopping," which bypassed the Japanese strong points and concentrated on weakly defended islands, bringing American forces from Australia to the Philippines in the space of two years.

MacArthur now applied the same strategy to Korea. Against the advice of his more orthodox superiors in Washington, he landed American forces at Inchon (the port of Seoul), well over 200 miles behind enemy lines, cutting North Korean supply lines with Pyongyang. The North Korean army collapsed and the road north lay open.

Victory led to perhaps the most fateful decision of the Korean War. If America was ever going to relate its military objectives to its political goals, this was the time. Truman had three choices. He could order a halt on the 38th Parallel and restore the *status quo ante*. He could authorize an advance farther north to exact a penalty for aggression. He could authorize MacArthur to unify Korea up to the Chinese border; in other words, to let the outcome of the war be dictated entirely by military considerations. The best decision would have been to advance to the narrow neck of the Korean peninsula, a hundred miles short of the Chinese frontier. This would have been a defensible line which would have included 90 percent of the population of the peninsula as well as the capital of North Korea, Pyongyang. And it would have achieved a major political success without challenging China.

Although MacArthur was a brilliant strategist, he was less perceptive as a political analyst. Ignoring China's historic memory of the Japanese inva-

480

sion of Manchuria, which had taken the same route through Korea, MacArthur pressed for an advance to the Chinese frontier at the Yalu River. Blinded by his commander's unexpected success at Inchon, Truman acquiesced. In abandoning any middle ground between the *status quo ante* and total victory, Truman gave up the geographic and demographic advantages of the narrow neck of the Korean peninsula. He traded a 100-mile-long defensive line located a considerable distance from the Chinese border for the necessity of protecting a 400-mile front right next to the main concentrations of Chinese communist power.

It could not have been an easy decision for China to challenge the world's greatest military power after the suffering, the devastation, and the casualties wrought by a Japanese invasion and a bitter civil war. Until Chinese archives are opened, it will not be known whether Mao would have intervened once American forces crossed the 38th Parallel, regardless of how limited their advance or how far north he would have allowed them to advance. But the art of policy is to create a calculation of the risks and rewards that affect the adversary's calculations. One way of influencing the Chinese decision to intervene would have been to stop the American advance at the narrow neck of the Korean peninsula, and to offer to demilitarize the rest of the country under some form of international control.

Washington was feeling its way in that direction when it ordered MacArthur not to approach the Yalu River with non-Korean forces. But the order was never translated into a political proposal to Beijing, nor was it ever made public. In any event, MacArthur disregarded the directive as being "impractical." And Washington, true to its tradition of not second-guessing a field commander, did not insist. MacArthur had been so unexpectedly successful at Inchon that America's political leaders were more than half convinced that he understood Asia better than they did.

When the Chinese People's Army struck, the shock of surprise induced a nearly panicky retreat of American forces from the Yalu to south of Seoul, which was abandoned for the second time in six months. Without a doctrine for limited war, the crisis caused the Truman Administration to lose control over the political aims. Depending on the fluctuations of combat, the political objectives were stated as stopping aggression, unifying Korea, maintaining the security of United Nations forces, guaranteeing a cease-fire along the 38th Parallel, and keeping the war from spreading.

When American ground troops entered combat in early July 1950, the objective was stated as "repelling aggression," though that term was never given a concrete meaning. After the landing at Inchon in September and the collapse of the North Korean army, the objective changed to "unification." Truman proclaimed it on October 17, 1950, but without putting forward a political framework for dealing with China. Truman's communications intended for Beijing never went beyond repeating sacramental protestations of good faith, which, to Mao, were precisely what was at issue: "Our sole purpose in Korea," said Truman in ordering the advance north,

> is to establish peace and independence. Our troops will stay there only so long as they are needed by the United Nations for that purpose. We seek no territory or special privilege in Korea or anywhere else. We have no aggressive designs in Korea or in any other place in the Far East or elsewhere.[10]

Mao was incapable of relying on such assurances from his principal capitalist adversary, who was at that moment protecting his mortal enemies in Taiwan. Nor did Truman concretely define the "aggressive designs" he was renouncing, or set a time limit on the removal of American troops from North Korea. The only way the United States could have kept Mao from intervening, if indeed that was possible, was by proposing the creation of some kind of buffer zone along the Chinese border. That was never attempted.

Over the next months, American forces would prove just how great a risk the Chinese leaders had run. Their early victories along the Yalu had been due to surprise and to the dispersal of American forces. It soon became apparent that the Chinese army did not have the firepower to overrun entrenched American positions and that, deprived of the element of surprise, it could not breach a well-established line—for example, along the narrow neck of the peninsula. Once American forces were reorganized, they proved that, at that stage of China's development, its forces were no match for American firepower.

No sooner had China entered the war than American objectives changed again, and literally within days. On November 26, 1950, the Chinese launched their counterattack; by November 30, Truman had issued a statement abandoning unification as a war aim and leaving it to "later negotiations." The vague concept of "halting aggression" again became America's principal goal:

> The forces of the United Nations are in Korea to put down an aggression that threatens not only the whole fabric of the United Nations, but all human hopes of peace and justice. If the United Nations yields to the forces of aggression, no nation will be safe or secure.[11]

By early January 1951, the front line was some fifty miles south of the 38th Parallel and Seoul was once again in communist hands. At that point, the Chinese repeated MacArthur's mistake of three months earlier. Had they offered to settle along the 38th Parallel, Washington would surely have accepted, and China would have gained the credit for defeating the United States Army a year after winning its own civil war. But, like Truman six months earlier, Mao was carried away by his unexpected successes and sought to expel American forces from the peninsula altogether. He too suffered a major setback. The Chinese incurred punishing casualties when they attacked fixed American positions south of Seoul.

By April 1951, the battle had turned once more, and American forces crossed the 38th Parallel for the second time. But the battle was not the only aspect of the war that had turned. For the Truman Administration was by now so traumatized by the shock of Chinese intervention that the avoidance of risk turned into its principal objective.

Washington's assessment of risks was based on a number of misconceptions, however. America assumed—as it would do a decade later in Vietnam—that it was facing a centrally controlled communist conspiracy to take over the world. And if Moscow called the shots, it followed that neither China nor Korea would have entered the war without being assured of Soviet backing. The Kremlin, Washington now believed, would not accept defeat; it would raise the ante after every setback for its clients. By aiming for limited victory, America might trigger a general war with the Soviet Union. America therefore could not afford to win even a limited victory because the communist bloc would pay any price in order not to lose.

The reality was quite different. Stalin had gone along with the North Korean attack only after Kim Il Sung had assured him that it would involve little risk of war. Insofar as Stalin encouraged the Chinese to intervene, it was probably to increase China's dependence on the Soviet Union. The real fanatics on the issue were in Beijing and Pyongyang; the Korean War was not a Kremlin plot to draw America into Asia so that it could then attack Europe. The deterrent to a Soviet attack on Europe was the Strategic Air Command, which was not used in Korea. The Soviet Union had little, if any, nuclear striking power. Given the disparity in nuclear strength, Stalin had far more to lose from general war than the United States. No matter how great the disparity in ground forces in Europe, it is highly improbable that Stalin would have run the risk of war with the United States over Korea. As it was, Stalin's aid to China was grudging, and he demanded cash payment for it, sowing the seeds of the Sino-Soviet rift.

America's leaders believed that they had learned the dangers of escalation, but they failed to consider the penalties of stalemate. "We are fighting to resist an outrageous aggression in Korea," said Truman in April 1951.

> We are trying to keep the Korean conflict from spreading to other areas. But at the same time, we must conduct our military activities so as to ensure the security of our forces. This is essential if they are to continue the fight until the enemy abandons its ruthless attempt to destroy the Republic of Korea.[12]

But fighting a war on behalf of the "security of our forces" is strategically vacuous. Since the war itself is what is risking their security, making "security of our forces" the objective must turn into a tautology. Since Truman offered no war aim other than inducing the enemy to abandon its efforts—in other words, at best a return to the *status quo ante*—the resulting frustrations generated pressures for victory. MacArthur did not consider stalemate a meaningful objective. He argued strenuously and eloquently that the danger of escalation had been inherent in the initial decision to intervene, and that it could not be mitigated by restraint in the conduct of military operations. If anything, they would increase these risks by prolonging the war. In testifying in 1951, MacArthur insisted: "You have got a war on your hands, and you can't just say, 'Let that war go on indefinitely while I prepare for some other war. . . .' "[13] Because he would not accept the Administration's view that the Korean War had to be conducted in a manner that avoided giving the Soviets a pretext for launching a full-scale attack, MacArthur advocated a strategy to defeat the Chinese armies, at least in Korea.

MacArthur's proposals included "an ultimatum that she [China] would either come and talk terms of a cease-fire within a reasonable period of time or her actions in Korea would be regarded as a declaration of war against the nations engaged there and that those nations would take such steps as they felt necessary to bring the thing to a conclusion."[14] At various times, MacArthur urged bombing Manchurian bases, blockading China, reinforcing American troops in Korea, and introducing Chinese Nationalist forces from Taiwan into Korea—based on what MacArthur considered "the normal way" to "bring about just and honorable peace at the soonest time possible with the least loss of life by utilizing all of your potential."[15]

Several of MacArthur's recommendations went far beyond the province of a theater commander. For example, introducing Chinese Nationalist forces into Korea would have amounted to a declaration of all-out war against the People's Republic of China. Once the Chinese civil war was transferred to Korean soil, neither Chinese side could end it before achieving total victory; and America would have enmeshed itself in an open-ended conflict.

Yet the fundamental issue was not so much the adequacy of MacArthur's specific recommendations as that he had posed the key question: was there any choice between stalemate and all-out war? By April 11, 1951, when Truman dismissed MacArthur, the debate broke out into the open. Characteristically courageous, Truman had no alternative except to dismiss a publicly insubordinate commander. But he also committed America to a strategy which left the initiative in the hands of the adversary. For in making the announcement, Truman modified American objectives once more. For the first time, "repelling aggression" was defined as reaching a settlement along the existing cease-fire line, wherever that might be—thereby creating another incentive for the Chinese to *increase* their military effort in order to obtain the best possible line:

> Real peace can be achieved through a settlement based on the following factors:
> One: The fighting must stop.
> Two: Concrete steps must be taken to insure that the fighting will not break out again.
> Three: There must be an end to the aggression.[16]

Unification of Korea, which the United States had sought six months earlier by force of arms, was relegated to the future: "A settlement founded upon these elements would open the way for the unification of Korea and the withdrawal of all foreign forces."[17]

MacArthur returned to a hero's welcome and a series of widely publicized Senate hearings. MacArthur based his case on what he described as the traditional relationship between foreign policy and military strategy:

> The general definition which for many decades has been accepted was that war was the ultimate process of politics; that when all other political means failed, you then go to force; and when you do that, the balance of control, the balance of concept, the main interest involved, the minute you reach the killing stage, is the control of the military. . . .
> I do unquestionably state that when men become locked in battle, that there should be no artifice under the name of politics, which should handicap your own men, decrease their chances for winning, and increase their losses.[18]

MacArthur had a point when he railed against stalemate as national policy. He had made political restrictions inevitable, however, by arguing against putting forward any political goals whatsoever, even those needed to support a local victory. If diplomacy were to be prevented from defining war aims, every conflict would automatically become an all-out war, regardless of the stakes and the risks, not a negligible consideration in the age of nuclear weapons.

The Truman Administration, however, went further. It not only rejected MacArthur's recommendations but argued that no alternative to its strategy of stalemate could possibly work. General Bradley, now chairman of the Joint Chiefs of Staff, defined three military options:

> Either to get out and forsake South Korea, try to fight it out in general where we are now without committing too great forces, or going to all-out war and committing sufficient forces to drive these people out of Korea. At the present time we are following the second course.[19]

In the American government, option papers nearly always urge the middle among three options. Because the foreign policy establishment tends to position its recommendations between the course of doing nothing and the course of general war, experienced bureaucrats know that the morale of their subordinates is enhanced if they pick the middle road. This was surely the case with Bradley's options, though the phrase "fight it out in general . . . without committing too great forces" simply restated the dilemma of a policy without clear-cut objectives.

Dean Acheson confirmed in the language of diplomacy that America's goal in Korea was indeed stalemate. American objectives in Korea were to "end the aggression, to safeguard against its renewal, and to restore peace."[20] Without defining any of these terms, Acheson went on to deprecate the effectiveness of the measures proposed by MacArthur: "Against the dubious advantages of spreading the war in an initially limited manner to the mainland of China," said the Secretary of State, "there must be measured the risk of a general war with China, the risk of Soviet intervention, and of world war III, as well as the probable effects upon the solidarity of the free world coalition"; it was "difficult to see how the Soviet Union could ignore a direct attack upon the Chinese mainland."[21]

If the United States dared not win but could not afford to lose, what were its options? When all the general phrases were reduced to specifics, it was stalemate on the battlefront and, therefore, at the negotiating table as well. In his memoirs, Truman summed up the views of all his subordinates, military and civilian alike:

> Every decision I made in connection with the Korean conflict had this one aim in mind: to prevent a third world war and the terrible destruction it would bring to the civilized world. This meant that we should not do anything that would provide the excuse to the Soviets and plunge the free nations into full-scale all-out war.[22]

The belief that the Soviet Union stood poised for general war revealed an extraordinary loss of touch with the real power relationships. Stalin was not looking for a pretext to start a general war; he was most eager to avoid it. Had he sought a confrontation, there were more than enough pretexts available in Europe or in the military actions already taking place in Korea. Not surprisingly, at no stage of the war did the Soviet Union threaten to intervene or to take any military action. Nothing in Stalin's cautious and suspicious character suggested a reckless adventurer; he always preferred stealth and indirection to actual confrontation, and had been especially careful not to run a risk of war with the United States— with good reason. Given the disparity in the nuclear capabilities of the two sides, it was the Soviet Union which had everything to lose in a general war.

Amazingly, all administration witnesses stressed the opposite point of view. Marshall claimed that it would take the United States another two to three years to prepare for a general war.[23] Bradley argued that "we are not in the best position to meet a global war."[24] Hence his famous quote that general war over Korea would "involve us in the wrong war, at the wrong place, at the wrong time, and with the wrong enemy."[25] Acheson too considered that more time was needed "to build an effective deterrent force."[26]

Why, in light of the emerging Soviet nuclear capability, America's leaders should have thought that the significance of their deterrent force would increase with the passage of time can only be explained as yet another manifestation of the strange premises of the containment theory —that America was weak when it in fact possessed an atomic monopoly, and that its position of strength could be improved while the Soviet Union was building up its own nuclear arsenal. Stalin was successful in deterring the United States from attempting a limited victory in Korea by capitalizing on this self-induced hypnosis and without having to do anything specifically threatening.

After the Chinese intervened, America never seriously explored the option of limited victory. The Truman Administration's basic postulate, that to try for more than stalemate was either impossible or risked all-out war, did not, in fact, exhaust the range of available options. An intermediate course such as the one I discussed earlier—a dividing line along the narrow neck of the peninsula, with the rest of the country demilitarized under international supervision—could have been pursued, or imposed unilaterally if it were rejected. China probably would not have had the means to prevent this—as General Matthew Ridgway, MacArthur's successor, also thought—without, however, recommending it.[27]

MacArthur was almost certainly right when he argued that "China is using the maximum of her force against us."[28] As for the Soviet Union, it would have had to decide whether, in light of the vast American nuclear superiority and Soviet economic weakness, an American advance over the relatively short distance between the 38th Parallel and the narrow neck of the peninsula justified the risk of general war. Of course, China might neither have acquiesced nor fought, but maintained a threatening stance wherever the line was established. But that situation would not have been very different from what finally emerged along the 38th Parallel. China would almost certainly have ceased to make any threats once its policy became dominated by the fear of Soviet aggression and had begun to move in the direction of the United States. Had the first communist military challenge against the United States suffered a demonstrable setback, greater caution might subsequently have been exercised by other militants in such areas as Indochina. And the Sino-Soviet split would almost certainly have been accelerated.

In the spring of 1951, a new American offensive under General Ridgway was grinding its way north, using traditional American tactics of attrition. It had liberated Seoul and crossed the 38th Parallel when, in June 1951, the communists proposed armistice negotiations. At that point, Washington ordered an end to offensive action; henceforth, all operations at battalion level and above had to be approved by the Supreme Commander—a gesture the Truman Administration believed would improve the atmosphere for negotiations by demonstrating to the Chinese that Washington was not aiming for victory.

It was a classically American gesture. Because of their conviction that peace is normal and goodwill natural, American leaders have generally sought to encourage negotiations by removing elements of coercion and by unilateral demonstrations of goodwill. In fact, in most negotiations, unilateral gestures remove a key negotiating asset. In general, diplomats rarely pay for services already rendered—especially in wartime. Typically, it is pressure on the battlefield that generates the negotiation. Relieving that pressure reduces the enemy's incentive to negotiate seriously, and it tempts him to drag out the negotiations in order to determine whether other unilateral gestures might be forthcoming.

This was exactly what happened in Korea. American restraint enabled China to end the process by which its army was being ground down by American technical and material superiority. Henceforth, and without significant risk, the Chinese could use military operations to inflict casualties and to magnify America's frustrations and domestic pressures to end the war. During the pause, the communists dug themselves into nearly impregnable positions across forbidding and mountainous terrain, gradually eliminating the American threat to resume hostilities.[29] This led to a drawn-out war of attrition, which was brought to a halt only because a painful equilibrium emerged between China's physical limitations and America's psychological inhibitions. Yet the price of stalemate was that the number of American casualties during the negotiations exceeded those of the preceding period of full-scale war.

The stalemate America sought descended on both the military and diplomatic fronts. The impact of military stalemate on the troops was well described by a British official observer, Brigadier A. K. Ferguson:

> It seems to me that the reputed objective of UN forces in Korea which is "to repel aggression and restore peace and security to the area" is much too vague under present circumstances to give the Supreme Commander in the field a military objective, the attainment of which would bring hostilities to a close.... Already many British and American officers and other ranks have asked such questions as "When will the war in Korea end?" "When do you think the UN forces can be withdrawn from Korea?" "What is our object in Korea?" Such questions tend to make me believe that, unless the British and American forces in Korea are given some definite goal at which to aim, the commander in the field will have the greatest difficulty in maintaining morale....[30]

In opting for stalemate, America incurred the first big postwar wrench in its foreign policy consensus. To MacArthur and his supporters, the Korean War was a frustration because its limits guaranteed military and political stalemate. To the Truman Administration, the Korean War was a nightmare because it was too big a war for its political objectives, and too small a war for its strategic doctrine. MacArthur sought a showdown over Korea even if it involved going to war against China, whereas the Administration sought to husband America's strength to resist the Soviet thrust against Europe postulated by the containment theory.

The Korean War thus revealed both the strengths and the limits of containment. In terms of traditional statecraft, Korea was the test case for determining the demarcation lines between the two competing spheres of influence, then in the process of being formed. But Americans perceived it quite differently, as a conflict between good and evil, and as a struggle on behalf of the free world. That interpretation endowed American actions with an enormous drive and dedication. It also caused containment to oscillate from the technical to the apocalyptic. Great acts of construction, such as the recovery of Europe and Japan, existed alongside a serious lack of appreciation for nuance and an extraordinary overestimation of Soviet capabilities. Issues capable of being encapsuled in moral or legal formulae were well and thoughtfully handled; but there was also a tendency to concentrate on the formula rather than on the purpose it was supposed to serve. In measuring America's success in Korea, Acheson was less concerned with the outcome on the battlefield than with establishing the concept of collective security: "The idea of collective security has been put to the test, and has been sustained. The nations who believe in collective security have shown that they can stick together and fight together."[31] Establishing the principle of collective action was more important than any specific outcome as long as defeat was avoided.

These aspects of the containment policy imposed a perhaps exorbitant burden on the American people, who were being asked to endure heavy casualties while their political leaders sought to navigate the narrowest of passages between resisting aggression and avoiding general war—without ever giving either term an operational meaning. The consequence of this approach was an outburst of frustration and a search for scapegoats. Marshall, and especially Acheson, were vilified. Alleged communist infiltration in Washington was systematically exploited by such demagogues as Senator Joseph McCarthy.

Nevertheless, the most significant aspect of the American public's reaction to the Korean War was not its restlessness with an inconclusive war but its endurance of it. In the face of all the frustrations, America persisted in bearing the burden of global responsibility in a seemingly endless struggle which imposed heavy casualties without leading to a definitive outcome. In the end, America achieved its goal, if at a higher price and over a longer period of time than was necessary. A decade and a half later, Americans would again experience an even deeper anguish over the conflict in Indochina.

A fundamental difference existed, however, between the Korean domestic challenge and the agony America later experienced over Indochina. The critics of the Korean War were urging victory, whereas the critics of the Vietnam War were advocating the acceptance and sometimes the importance of defeat. The controversy over the Korean War gave the Truman Administration a bargaining lever; Truman and his advisers could use the domestic opposition as a threat against North Korea and China, since its alternative was a more energetic prosecution of the war. The opposite was true of the war in Indochina. The opponents of the war who promoted unconditional withdrawal of American forces from Vietnam weakened the American bargaining position.

In the final analysis, all of the belligerents in the Korean War drew important lessons from it. The American statesmen of the period deserve to be remembered for the vision with which they committed forces to a distant country which, only a few months earlier, they had declared to be irrelevant to American security. When the challenge came, they had the courage to reverse themselves because they understood that acquiescence to the communist occupation of Korea would undermine the American position in Asia, especially America's crucial relationship with Japan.

At the beginning of a generation of world leadership, America passed its first test, albeit somewhat laboriously. Yet America's innocence was but the reverse side of an extraordinary capacity for dedication, which enabled Americans to endure the death and injury of nearly 150,000 of their own in a war without a conclusive outcome. The crisis in Korea led to an augmentation of strength in Europe and the creation of the North Atlantic Treaty Organization, which made it possible to sustain the long endurance contest that the Cold War was now sure to become. Where America paid a price was among the revolutionary leaders of Southeast Asia and elsewhere, who discovered a method of warfare that avoided large-scale ground combat yet had the ability to wear down the resolve of a superpower.

China's lessons were more mixed. Despite its substantial material inferiority, China had managed a stalemate with the American superpower through a combination of military and diplomatic maneuvers. But it also learned the price tag of confronting American military power frontally. There were to be no other Sino-American military clashes during the Cold War. And the Soviet Union's grudging and ungenerous support of Beijing planted the seeds for the Sino-Soviet rift.

The biggest loser in Korea turned out to be the Soviet Union, the country which American leaders thought had masterminded the whole enterprise. Within two years of the invasion of Korea, America had mobilized its side of the global dividing line. The United States tripled its defense expenditures and transformed the Atlantic Alliance from a political coalition into an integrated military organization headed by an American Supreme Commander. German rearmament was within view, and an attempt was being made to create a European army. The vacuum which had existed in front of Soviet armies in Central Europe was being filled.

Even if one assumes that America might have achieved more in Korea, the Soviets would henceforth be obliged to measure their successes in terms of mitigating losses and perhaps encouraging later communist adventurers, especially in Indochina. In return, they faced a massive tilt in the mobilized balance of power because of allied rearmament and the strengthening of allied cohesion.

This shift in what the Marxists call the correlation of forces was not lost on the leader who had specialized in basing his policy on such analysis. Within eighteen months of the invasion of South Korea, Stalin initiated a reassessment of Soviet policies that was to culminate in the most significant Soviet diplomatic overture of the immediate postwar period.

CHAPTER TWENTY

Negotiating with the Communists: Adenauer, Churchill, and Eisenhower

In March 1952, before the Korean War had ended, Stalin made a diplomatic overture to settle the Cold War for reasons quite contrary to the expectations of the fathers of containment. This initiative was not caused by the transformation of the Soviet system, as they had predicted. Instead, the arch-ideologue sought to protect the communist system from an arms race he must have known that it could not win. Indeed, given his combination of Marxism and paranoia, Stalin probably could not believe that America would mobilize so much power for primarily defensive purposes.

Stalin's offer said nothing about the establishment of a harmonious world order. Rather than do away with the conditions which had caused the Cold War, Stalin's proposal called for mutual recognition of that bugaboo of American thinking—two spheres of influence: one for America in Western Europe, the other for the Soviet Union in Eastern Europe with a unified, armed, neutral Germany between them.

Ever since, historians and political leaders have been debating whether Stalin's move represented a missed opportunity to settle the Cold War, or whether it had been a clever ploy to draw the democracies into a negotiation, the very opening of which would have blocked German rearmament. Was Stalin trying to tempt the West into actions that would have weakened its cohesion, or did he mean to reverse the ever-deepening East-West confrontation?

The answer is that Stalin himself had probably not decided how far he was prepared to go in order to ease tensions with the West. Though he made offers which the democracies would have eagerly accepted four years earlier, his conduct in the interim had made it nearly impossible to test his sincerity—indeed, it had rendered his sincerity almost irrelevant. For, whatever Stalin's ultimate intentions, testing them would have severely strained the cohesion of the Atlantic Alliance and therefore removed the incentive which had led to the offer in the first place.

In any event, the arch-calculator had neglected to consider one decisive factor: his own mortality. A year after Stalin had made the proposal, he lay dead. His successors did not have the tenacity to insist on a comprehensive negotiation, nor did they have the authority to make the sweeping concessions which would have been required to sustain it. In the end, the peace overture lingered as a tantalizing episode illustrating, above all, the vastly different premises that motivated the two sides in the Cold War.

Dedicated to the proposition that legal commitments create their own reality, America waited for Stalin to implement the Yalta and Potsdam agreements. Considering an agreement obligatory only if it reflected a balance of forces, Stalin waited for the democracies to insist on their rights in some manner that would enable him to analyze the risks and rewards of carrying out the agreement. Pending that, Stalin would bide his time, collecting as many bargaining chips as possible in preparation for some concrete move—or what Stalin considered a concrete move— by the democracies.

That moment seemed to have arrived in the early 1950s. The United States had launched the Marshall Plan in 1947 and the North Atlantic Treaty Organization in 1949. The Federal Republic of Germany had come into being under Western auspices. Stalin's initial reaction was characteristically truculent; hence the Berlin blockade, the Czech coup, and his approval of the invasion of South Korea. Nevertheless, the United States succeeded in creating, step by step, a sphere of influence containing all the advanced industrial countries of the world.

For his part, Stalin had managed to construct a security belt in Eastern Europe, an achievement which nevertheless amounted to an extension of weakness. A calculator of power, he had to understand, and probably better than the leaders of the democracies could have, that what he had gained was no real accretion of strength, and that, on balance, the satellite orbit would prove to be a drain on Soviet resources. By contrast, the NATO countries and Japan represented a vast potential industrial reservoir. The long-term trends, so beloved of Marxist analysts, favored the American sphere of influence. In terms of *Realpolitik*, Stalin's empire was in deep trouble.

The American-led grouping had cut its teeth militarily, so to speak, during the Korean War and had developed an extensive military potential. Stalin seems to have realized that his challenges to the cohesion of the democracies had backfired. His truculence and heavy-handed policies in Eastern Europe had fostered unity in the Western coalition and brought a rearmed Germany into view.

The harmonious world postulated by American wartime thinking had been transformed into two armed camps, each driven by fears that turned out to be unfounded. American leaders perceived in the Korean War a Soviet strategy for luring America into distant Asian conflicts to facilitate a Soviet assault on the allied position in Europe, a gross overestimation of both Soviet power and Stalin's methods. At no stage in his career had that meticulous and shrewd analyst staked everything on one throw of the dice. At the same time, Stalin construed the Western buildup not as the defensive move that it actually was but as a pretext for the showdown he had always anticipated and had so consistently sought to avoid. Both sides were in fact preparing for what neither side intended—a direct, all-out challenge.

Stalin was not willing to test whether his nightmare was real. Whenever confronted with the possibility of a military conflict with America, Stalin invariably recoiled. He had done so when Truman demanded that Soviet troops leave Iranian Azerbaijan in 1946, and he had ended the Berlin blockade of 1948–49 before it could turn into a shooting war. Now, he energetically set about defusing the confrontation which he had brought on, signaling an impending change in course with one of the elliptical pronouncements that were his trademark.

In this instance, Stalin's approach was particularly obtuse, because he wanted to avoid giving the slightest hint of weakness to an adversary that was in the process of basing its policy on positions of strength. His goal was to indicate that he wished to avoid a confrontation without appearing to shrink from it. Stalin's pretext was a view put forward in a highly theoretical book published several years earlier by the economist Yevgenii Varga.[1] The author had argued that capitalist systems were becoming more stable and that war among them was therefore no longer inevitable. If Varga was right, the strategy Stalin had pursued since the 1920s—of playing the capitalists off against each other—would no longer work. The capitalists, far from fighting each other, might go so far as to unite against the socialist motherland, a possibility foreshadowed by the creation of NATO and the Japanese-American alliance.

Stalin countered this argument with an elaborate essay of his own entitled "Economic Problems of Socialism in the U.S.S.R.," which was published in October 1952 as a guideline for the forthcoming Party Congress.[2] In his article, Stalin reconsecrated the true communist faith as he had promulgated it in 1934, 1939, and 1946, to the effect that, far from becoming more stable, capitalism was facing an ever-accelerating crisis:

> It is said that the contradictions between capitalism and socialism are stronger than the contradictions among the capitalist countries. Theoretically, of course, that is true. It is not only true now, today; it was true before the Second World War. And it was more or less realized by the leaders of the capitalist countries. Yet the Second World War began not as a war with the U.S.S.R., but as a war between capitalist countries.[3]

Whenever Stalin recycled his familiar litany of the inevitability of war among the capitalists, the faithful understood that he meant to reassure them. According to Stalin's convoluted reasoning, the prospect of conflict among the capitalists meant that war between them and the Soviet Union was not imminent. Stalin's article was therefore an instruction to Soviet diplomacy to delay a showdown until the capitalists' internal conflicts had sufficiently weakened them.

In 1939, a comparable pronouncement had signaled Stalin's readiness to seek accommodation with Hitler. That analysis, Stalin now argued in 1952, remained correct, because, given their propensity for war, the capitalists risked less in fighting each other than in making war on the Soviet Union: ". . . whereas war between capitalist countries puts in question only the supremacy of certain capitalist countries over others, war with the U.S.S.R. must certainly put in question the existence of capitalism itself."[4]

This heavy theoretical chaff was Stalin's way of conveying a calming message to the capitalists, especially the United States. In effect, he was saying that the capitalists had no need to engage in pre-emptive war because the Soviet Union had no intention of posing a military challenge:

> ... the capitalists, although they clamour, for "propaganda" purposes, about the aggressiveness of the Soviet Union, do not themselves believe that it is aggressive, because they are aware of the Soviet Union's peaceful policy and know that it will not itself attack capitalist countries.[5]

In other words, the capitalists should not misunderstand the rules of the game he was playing: Stalin wanted to enhance Soviet power and influence, but he would stop his pressures well short of war.

Whereas Stalin knew that his ideological pronouncements would suffice for his comrades, he was aware that his capitalist adversaries required more solid fare. If tensions were to be relaxed and there was to be any hope of returning to the old game of playing the capitalists off against each other, Moscow needed to ease at least some of the pressures that had led to what Stalin considered an artificial sense of unity within the capitalist world.

Stalin made such an effort on the diplomatic level, and in a language the democracies could understand, when, on March 10, 1952, he put forward his so-called Peace Note on Germany. After years of confrontation and stonewalling, the Soviet Union suddenly seemed interested in a settlement. Calling attention to the absence of a peace treaty with Germany, Stalin submitted a draft text to the other three occupying powers, urging that it be considered "by an appropriate international conference with the participation of all interested governments" and concluded "in the nearest future."[6] The Peace Note called for a unified, neutral Germany based on free elections, and one that would be allowed to maintain its own armed forces though all foreign troops would have to leave within a year.

Nevertheless, the Peace Note contained enough escape clauses to hold up an agreement indefinitely, even if the West accepted the principle of German neutrality. For example, the draft prohibited "organizations inimical to democracy and the maintenance of peace," which, in Soviet terminology, could have included all Western-style parties—as indeed it had already in Eastern Europe. Then, once the democracies agreed to come to the negotiating table, the Soviet negotiator, who would surely be the obdurate Molotov or an equivalent, would do his utmost to loosen Germany's ties with the West—a Soviet benefit implicit in the acceptance of the principle of neutrality—without paying the price of German unification.

Yet the tone and precision of Stalin's note suggested that his purpose transcended mere propaganda; rather, it seemed to be the opening move of a negotiation in which, for the first time in the postwar period, the Soviet Union might have been willing to pay a significant price for a relaxation of tensions. Rather uncharacteristically, Stalin's Peace Note included a paragraph which indicated some flexibility: "In proposing consideration of this draft the Soviet Government . . . expressed its readiness also to consider other possible proposals on this question."[7]

Had Stalin offered the so-called Peace Note four years earlier—before the Berlin blockade, the Czech coup, and the Korean War—it almost certainly would have stopped German membership in NATO in its tracks. Indeed, it is quite possible that German membership in the Atlantic Alliance would never have been considered. For the Note implied the sort of negotiation about the future of Europe that Churchill had been urging both during and after the war.

In the interval since 1948, however, the Atlantic Alliance *had* been formed and German rearmament launched. The European Defense Community (EDC), designed as a political framework for German rearmament, was being debated in European parliaments. In the Federal Republic, Adenauer had been elected Chancellor by only one vote (presumably his own) in a secret ballot of the Parliament, and the opposition Social Democrats, though thoroughly democratic, were urging the pursuit of unification instead of alliance with the West.

The Western leaders realized that all these initiatives would surely be stalled if they explored the Soviet proposal and that, once stalled, they might never regain momentum. In several European parliaments, most significantly in France and Italy, the Communist Parties represented nearly a third of the vote—the same proportion the communists had had in Czechoslovakia before the coup. And Western European Communist Parties were passionately opposed to all measures of Atlantic and European integration. Moreover, the treaty to determine the future of Austria was in its seventh year of negotiations, and the Korean armistice negotiations were already approaching their second year. For all the democracies knew, and for all we know at this writing, Stalin's purpose in seeking to open negotiations could well have been to undermine allied cohesion and to consolidate the satellite orbit.

This surely was Stalin's optimum goal. The weight of the evidence, however, is that he was also prepared to explore an overall settlement. One indication that he was keeping this option open was his reaction to Western responses to his Peace Note. On March 25, the three Western occupying powers—France, Great Britain, and the United States—returned identical replies, not with the goal of opening a negotiation but of bringing discussion of it to an end. They accepted the principle of German reunification but rejected the idea of neutrality. A unified Germany, they noted, should be free to enter "into associations compatible with the principles and purposes of the United Nations"—in other words, to remain in NATO. The Western reply accepted the principle of free elections but tied it to such conditions as an immediate right to free assembly and free speech, both of which were likely to undermine the Soviet hold on the East German communist regime well before elections could be held.[8] The Western Notes were designed to make a record, not to encourage a bargain.

Uncharacteristically, Stalin responded immediately and in a conciliatory tone. He reacted with the same speed, moreover, to every subsequent rebuff by the democracies. The Western Note of March 25 was answered on April 9; that of May 13 received a response on May 24; that of July 10 was answered on August 23. Each Soviet reply edged toward the Western position. Only the note of September 23 did not receive a reply.[9] By then, Stalin was preoccupied with the forthcoming Nineteenth Party Congress and, no doubt, was awaiting the outcome of the American presidential election.

Already in failing health, Stalin made a brief speech at the Party Congress which clothed a doctrine of peaceful coexistence in bellicose ideological language.[10] Immediately following the Party Congress, in December 1952, Stalin announced that he was prepared to meet with President-elect Dwight D. Eisenhower. The offer of such a summit was something he had never vouchsafed to Roosevelt, Truman, or Churchill, each of whom Stalin had maneuvered into the position of having to make the first move.

The simultaneous resumption of domestic purges inside the Soviet Union bore the grim and familiar imprint of an impending change in policy. Stalin had never felt comfortable implementing a new policy with personnel he had previously used to steer a different course, even if they had slavishly followed his own directives, and perhaps especially then. Stalin considered second thoughts to be the seeds of disloyalty and favored the definitive remedy of destroying those who had had the responsibility of carrying out the policy that was about to be modified. In 1952, something along these lines was obviously in preparation, with the loyalists of previous years as the apparent targets—the Foreign Minister, Vyacheslav Molotov; Lazar Kaganovich, an old Bolshevik member of the Politburo; and Lavrenti Beria, the head of the secret police. A new set of faces would appear to carry out Stalin's diplomatic design.

The intent of Stalin's diplomatic offensive was, at a minimum, to investigate what the Soviet Union might obtain for jettisoning the East German communist regime. Stalin had never recognized that regime as a full-fledged sovereign state, and had given it a status distinct from that of the other Eastern European satellites precisely to retain it as a bargaining chip should German unification ever be seriously negotiated.

As far as Stalin was concerned, that moment might well have arrived in 1952. By offering unification based on free elections, Stalin was signaling that the East German communist regime had become expendable. For, even if the communists dominated the East German elections, as the Western allies feared, the much larger population of the Federal Republic would have ensured a decisive victory for the pro-Western democratic parties. And, just as only Stalin himself could have had the willpower and ruthlessness to drive his exhausted people into confrontation with the democracies, he was also the sole communist leader with the authority to deal away a Soviet satellite.

Whenever Stalin miscalculated, as he did on this occasion, it was because he assumed that his counterparts were also conducting *Realpolitik,* and in the same cold-blooded fashion as he. In the immediate postwar period, he obviously thought that he could either intimidate them or, at the least, teach them that any attempt to exact concessions from the Soviet Union would be extremely painful and prolonged. But he also acted as if, when the time came to settle, the United States would do so on the basis of a calculation of existing conditions, unaffected by what had gone on before. Stalin seemed convinced that he would have to pay no price for having brutalized the democracies.

These assumptions turned out to be grievously wrong. The United States was not conducting *Realpolitik*—at least not as Stalin understood it. To American leaders, moral maxims were real, and legal obligations were meaningful. Stalin may have conceived of the Berlin blockade as a way of strengthening his bargaining position over Germany, or perhaps even of triggering a negotiation. And he may have viewed the Korean War as a way of testing the boundaries of containment. But America resisted these acts of aggression in the name of principle, not in defense of a sphere of interest; America had exerted itself in order to remedy an insult to a universal cause, not over a challenge to the local *status quo.*

Just as in 1945, when Stalin had treated America's goodwill as of no measurable account, he underestimated in 1952 the extent of disillusionment his actions had generated in the interim. In the period from 1945 to 1948, America's leaders had been eager for a settlement with the Soviet Union but were neither willing nor able to assemble the pressures which Stalin would have taken seriously. By 1952, Stalin was taking America's pressures seriously enough, but had succeeded too well in convincing American leaders of his bad faith. They therefore interpreted his overture as merely one more tactic in a Cold War struggle which could only end in victory or defeat. Compromise with Stalin was no longer on the agenda.

Stalin's timing could not have been less propitious. His Peace Note was put forward less than eight months before a presidential election in which President Truman, the incumbent, was not running. In the highly improbable event that Truman and Acheson were inclined to negotiate with Stalin, they would not have had enough time to complete the process.

To the Truman Administration, the Peace Note in any event offered far less than met the eye. The problem lay less in its terms, which might have been adjusted, than in the kind of world it envisaged. Germany was to be neutral though armed, with all foreign troops withdrawn from its territory within a year. Yet what was the precise meaning of these terms? How was "neutrality" to be defined, and who would supervise it? Would the Soviet Union thereby gain a permanent voice in German affairs and perhaps a veto over them in the name of supervising Germany's neutral status? And to what locations should the foreign troops be withdrawn? For the Western occupying forces, the answer was fairly clear—there was, in fact, no sustainable geographic base in Europe. In the 1950s, France might have been prepared to accept a major American force, but not for long and not without restrictions. Nor would the American Congress have approved such a redeployment when a neutral buffer zone had been created between Soviet and American forces. Whereas American forces would have had to return to America, Soviet troops would have only been obliged to withdraw to the Polish frontier, a hundred miles to the east. In short, a literal application of Stalin's proposal would have traded the dismantling of NATO, just as it was emerging, for a Soviet withdrawal of a mere one hundred miles.

Even if the withdrawal clause had been interpreted to mean that Soviet troops should retreat to Soviet territory, new complications would have arisen. For it was unlikely that any of the satellite regimes could have sustained themselves without a Soviet troop presence or the certainty of Soviet intervention in the event of an uprising. Would Stalin have agreed to prohibit Soviet armies from re-entering Eastern Europe even if a communist government were being dismantled? Given the conditions prevailing in 1952, that question answered itself. It was beyond the imaginations of the democratic leaders—and justifiably so—that Stalin, the old Bolshevik, would agree to such an upheaval.

But the most important reason Truman and Acheson cold-shouldered Stalin's overture had to do with Germany's long-term future as envisaged by the Peace Note. For, even if it had been possible to define German neutrality in such a way as to forestall permanent Soviet intervention and a level of German arms that would not have left Germany at the mercy of the Soviet Union, this would only have restored what had been Europe's dilemma since German unification in 1871. A strong, unified Germany in the center of the Continent pursuing a purely national policy had proved incompatible with the peace of Europe. Such a Germany would be stronger than any of the nations of Western Europe, and probably stronger than all of them combined. And in the 1950s, it would have been tempted by revisionist dreams in the East, spurred by 15 million recent refugees from territories which most Germans considered part of their country. It was tempting fate to turn loose a united, neutral Germany so soon after the war. Above all, such an outcome would have discredited the greatest German statesman since Bismarck, who bears the historic distinction of having guided Germany away from the legacy of Bismarck.

Konrad Adenauer was born in 1876 in the Catholic Rhineland, which had only been part of Prussia since the Congress of Vienna and had, historically, had misgivings about the centralized German Reich ruled from Berlin. Adenauer had served as Lord Mayor of Cologne from 1917 until he was removed by the Nazis in 1933. During the Hitler period, he withdrew from politics, spending some time in a monastery. Restored by the Allies as Lord Mayor of Cologne in March 1945, he was again dismissed in late 1945, this time by the British occupation authorities who frowned on his independent manner.

Possessed of the granitelike features of a Roman emperor, Adenauer also had the high cheekbones and slightly slanted eyes which suggested the hint of some Hun conqueror who might have trekked across the Rhineland in the previous millennium. Adenauer's courtly behavior, acquired in his pre–World War I youth, reflected a serenity which was startling in the leader of an occupied country few of whose adult citizens were able to recall a political past in which they could take pride.

In Adenauer's office in the Palais Schaumburg, an ornate, white construction of the Wilhelmine period, the curtains were always drawn, making anyone entering it feel as if he were in a cocoon where time stood still. Serenity was the quality most needed in a leader whose mission was to give his country, which had every reason to doubt its past, the courage to face an uncertain future. By the time Adenauer had become Chancellor at the age of seventy-three, it seemed as if his entire life had been a preparation for the responsibility of restoring self-respect to his occupied, demoralized, and divided society.

Adenauer's sense of inner security derived more from faith than from analysis. He was not a reader of books or a student of history like Churchill or de Gaulle. But he had spent his exile in reflection; he had gone through the school of his country's convulsions and possessed an extraordinary intuition for the trends of his period. He also had a penetrating understanding of the psychology of his contemporaries, especially their weaknesses. On one occasion, I recall Adenauer deploring the absence of strong leaders in the Germany of the 1950s. When I responded by mentioning one of his more dramatic contemporaries, Adenauer replied in his lapidary manner: "Never confuse energy with strength."

Adenauer strove to overcome Germany's turbulent passions by giving his country—with its history of extremism and its proclivity for the Romantic—a reputation for reliability. Adenauer was old enough to remember Bismarck as Chancellor. A devout Catholic son of the Rhineland, he had never cared for *Realpolitik,* not even when Germany was united, and he found the Kaiser's grandiloquent *Weltpolitik* offensive to his own sober and matter-of-fact style. He had no affinity for the Junker class, which had created imperial Germany. He believed that Bismarck's great error had been to base German security on the skill of maneuvering between East and West. In his view, a powerful, free-floating Germany in the center of Europe posed a threat to everybody at the expense of its own security.

Adenauer's response to the chaos of the immediate postwar world was that a divided, occupied country severed from its historic roots required a steady policy if it were to regain some control over its future. Adenauer refused to be diverted from this course by nostalgia for the past, or by the traditional German love-hate relationship with Russia. He opted unconditionally for the West, even at the price of postponing German unity.

Adenauer's domestic opponents, the Social Democrats, could point to an unblemished record of opposition to the Nazis. Their historic base of support was in the Soviet-occupied zone of Germany, which had been forced to become communist—a development the Social Democrats had courageously resisted. As suspicious of the containment policy as they were devoted to democracy, the Social Democrats assigned a higher priority to German unification than to Atlantic relationships. They fought Adenauer's pro-Western orientation and would have gladly paid for progress on Germany's national aims by making a commitment to neutrality. (In the mid-1960s, the Social Democrats reversed course: they endorsed the Atlantic Alliance and entered a "grand coalition" with the Christian Democrats in 1966, though reserving more tactical flexibility toward the East than Adenauer's Christian Democrats.)

Adenauer rejected the bargain on neutrality which the Social Democrats were willing to make, partly on philosophical grounds, but partly for cannily practical reasons. The aged Chancellor did not want to reawaken nationalist temptations, especially now that there were two German states, which, as Churchill had warned in his Iron Curtain speech, might put themselves up for auction. And he understood much better than his domestic opponents that, in the historical conditions of the time, a united, neutral Germany could only emerge from a peace settlement organized *against* Germany. Severe restrictions would be imposed on the new state, and international controls established. Powerful neighbors would have a permanent right of intervention. Adenauer considered this implicit subordination to be psychologically more dangerous for Germany than division. He opted for equality and integration with the West, and for respectability for his country.

Whether Stalin could have overcome the reservations of Adenauer and of the other democratic leaders and pushed matters toward a major diplomatic conference, or precisely what concessions, if any, he might have made there, will never be known. His proposal for a major conference would surely have been supported by Churchill. At any rate, Stalin's death made all such speculations moot. Sometime between the early hours of March 1, 1953, when he parted from colleagues with whom he had watched a movie, and 3:00 A.M. on March 2, when he was found lying on the floor of his dacha, Stalin suffered a major stroke. The time at which he was stricken is imprecise because his guards were too afraid to enter his room before the appointed time, so he may well have lain on the floor for hours before he was discovered. Stalin's associates—Malenkov and Beria, among others—kept vigil at his bedside until he died three and a half days later.[11] Doctors were summoned, although their ministrations could not have been free of ambivalence. They were, after all, the designated victims of Stalin's forthcoming purge of the "Kremlin doctors."

Stalin's successors felt a need for a respite from tensions with the West even more desperately than their former leader. However, they lacked his authority, his subtlety, his perseverance, and, most important, the political unity required to pursue so complicated a course. Stalin's successors were riven by the inevitable contest for power that followed. In the desperate war of all against all in which each tried to line up factions to support his own claim to authority, no one would accept responsibility for making concessions to the capitalists. This was evident from the way in which the purge of Beria was explained. In reality, his sin had been that he knew too much, and had threatened too many powerful colleagues.

Nonetheless, he was arrested at a Politburo meeting and executed shortly thereafter on the charge of having plotted to give up East Germany— even though the thrust of Stalin's Peace Note of the previous year and of all his subsequent exchanges with the West had been heading in precisely that direction.

According to Khrushchev's memoirs, Stalin's successors were deeply worried that the West might exploit Stalin's death for the long-awaited showdown with the communist world. Probably to discourage any thoughts of a coup, the tyrant had frequently warned his associates that the West would wring their necks like chickens after he was gone.[12] At the same time, Stalin's heirs' suspicions of the West were offset by the demands of their desperate struggle for power with each other. Even though the new leadership longed for a reprieve from the Cold War, every contestant for power knew that diplomatic flexibility could prove fatal until he had achieved absolute authority. But they were also uneasy about a continuation of tensions. In 1946, Churchill had remarked that Stalin wanted the fruits of war without war; in 1953, Stalin's successors sought the fruits of a relaxation of tensions without being willing or able to make concessions. In 1945, Stalin had produced a diplomatic deadlock to preserve his bargaining position vis-à-vis the West; in 1953, his heirs took refuge in a diplomatic deadlock to preserve their options vis-à-vis each other.

When statesmen want to gain time, they offer to talk. On March 16, a little more than a week after the dictator's death, Malenkov, who was now Prime Minister, invited negotiations without specifying their content:

> At present there is no litigious or unsolved question which could not be settled by peaceful means on the basis of mutual agreement of the countries concerned. This concerns our relations with all States, including the United States of America.[13]

But Malenkov made no concrete proposals. The new Soviet leaders were uncertain about how to achieve a relaxation of tensions and had much less authority than Stalin had had to forge new approaches. At the same time, the new Eisenhower Administration was as apprehensive about offering to negotiate with the Soviets as the Soviets were about offering concessions to the Americans.

The reason for the apprehension was the same on either side of the dividing line—both the Soviet Union and the United States dreaded uncharted territory. Each had trouble assimilating the changes which had occurred in the international environment since the end of the war. The

Kremlin was afraid that abandoning East Germany might unravel the satellite orbit—as it did a generation later. And, short of giving up East Germany, a genuine relaxation of tensions was not in the cards. The United States was concerned that opening up discussions on Germany might wreck NATO and, in effect, trade the Alliance for a conference.

To decide whether the West in fact lost any opportunity immediately after Stalin's death, three questions must be answered. Could the Atlantic Alliance have conducted a major negotiation with the Soviets without fragmenting? If pressed, would the Soviet Union have made meaningful offers? Would the Soviet leadership have exploited the negotiations as a way of stopping German rearmament and Western integration without in fact giving up its East German satellite or easing its hold on Eastern Europe?

American leaders were right in their assessment that the actual margin for negotiations was extremely narrow. A neutral Germany would have posed either a danger or an invitation to blackmail. There are some experiments in diplomacy which cannot be tried because failure invites irreversible risk. And the risk of a collapse of all that had been built in the Atlantic Alliance was significant.

It was in fact in everyone's interest—above all, in the Soviet Union's—that the Federal Republic remain part of the Western integrated system, though none of the insecure Soviet leaders were in a position to admit this. If Germany remained in the Atlantic Alliance, it was possible to agree to limitations of military deployment along the new lines of demarcation (thus, in effect, reducing the military potential of the unified Germany). But if the neutral territory embraced all of Germany, NATO would be emasculated and Central Europe would turn into either a vacuum or a potential threat.

Stalin's heirs could have been induced to accept a united Germany inside NATO (albeit with military restrictions) only if the democracies had been prepared to threaten military consequences or, at a minimum, an intensification of the Cold War. This was what Churchill, who had returned to office as Prime Minister in 1951, may have had in mind even while Stalin was still alive, as recorded by his private secretary, John Colville:

> W[inston] has several times revealed to me his hopes of a joint approach to Stalin, proceeding perhaps to a congress in Vienna where the Potsdam Conference would be reopened and concluded. If the Russians were unco-operative, the cold war would be intensified by us: "Our young men," W. said to me, "would as soon be killed carrying truth as death."[14]

But no other leader in the West was willing to run such risks, or to put forward proposals which could be easily attacked by critics of the Alliance for being too one-sided. America's leaders therefore stonewalled any major initiative, and, in the process, prevented a serious attempt to exploit the Soviets' confusion immediately after Stalin's death. On the other hand, they preserved the cohesion of the Atlantic Alliance.

The price of this stalemate was a shift of the debate away from the substance of negotiations to their desirability. And it was Churchill, now nearing the end of his career, who emerged as chief spokesman for a negotiation whose content he never described precisely. There was indeed a certain poignancy to the octogenarian Churchill, who had throughout his life been the exponent of the balance of power, pressing for a summit meeting as an end in itself.

American leaders unfairly ascribed Churchill's eagerness to negotiate to approaching senility. In fact, Churchill had been remarkably consistent, having advocated negotiations both during and immediately after the war as well as when the containment policy was first being formulated (see chapters 17 and 18). What had changed were the conditions under which these proposals were being made. In the 1950s, Churchill never spelled out the details of the global settlement he was urging. During the war, it seemed to have been based on the assumption that America would withdraw, or at any rate never station troops in Europe, as Roosevelt had insisted repeatedly. Then, and as the leader of the Opposition between 1945 and 1951, Churchill apparently envisaged the following components of an overall settlement with the Soviet Union: a neutral, unified Germany, a Western alliance system along the Franco-German frontier, the retreat of Soviet forces to the Polish-Soviet frontier, and the establishment of governments based on the Finnish model in the states bordering the Soviet Union—that is, neutral, democratic governments respectful of Soviet concerns but essentially free to pursue their own independent foreign policies.

A settlement along these lines before 1948 would have restored Europe to its historic dimensions. During the war and for several years afterward, Churchill was far ahead of his time. Had he not lost the 1945 election, he might well have given the emerging Cold War a different direction—provided that America and the other allies had been willing to risk the confrontation which seemed to underlie Churchill's preferred strategy.

Yet by 1952, the settlement which Churchill envisaged had become nearly impossible, short of a political earthquake. It is a measure of Adenauer's greatness that the kind of Federal Republic he had created would have been nearly unimaginable prior to 1949. Three years later, the world Churchill had envisaged after 1944 would have required ending the Federal Republic's integration with the West and obliging it to return to its former status as a freewheeling national state. In 1945, Finnish-type regimes in Eastern Europe would have been a return to normalcy. By 1952, they could no longer have been established by negotiation; they could only have come about through a Soviet collapse or a major confrontation. That confrontation, moreover, would have had to be conducted over the issue of German unification—and no Western European country was prepared to run such a risk on behalf of a defeated enemy so soon after the war.

Had the Atlantic Alliance been a single nation capable of conducting a unified policy, it might have adopted a diplomacy that sought an overall settlement along Churchill's lines. But in 1952, the Atlantic Alliance was far too fragile for such a gamble. Presidents from both of America's major political parties perceived no choice but to pursue their painful course of waiting for a Soviet change of heart behind positions of strength.

Eisenhower's new Secretary of State, John Foster Dulles, perceived the East-West conflict as a moral issue and sought to avoid negotiations on almost any subject until a basic transformation of the Soviet system had occurred—thereby challenging long-established British views. In its entire history, Great Britain had not often had the luxury of confining negotiations to friendly or ideologically compatible countries. Not having enjoyed anything like America's margin of safety even at the height of its power, Great Britain negotiated with ideological adversaries as a matter of course regarding practical arrangements relating to coexistence. Throughout, a clear working definition of the national interest had enabled the British public to judge the effectiveness of its statesmen. The British might experience occasional domestic disputes over the terms of a particular settlement, but almost never over the wisdom of negotiating.

True to British tradition, Churchill sought a more tolerable coexistence with the Soviet Union by way of near-permanent negotiations. American leaders, on the other hand, wanted to change the Soviet system rather than negotiate with it. Thus, the Anglo-American debate increasingly turned into a dialogue about the desirability rather than the substance of negotiations. During his 1950 electoral campaign, which ended in defeat, Churchill proposed a Four-Power summit—a revolutionary idea at that stage of the Cold War:

> Still I cannot help coming back to this idea of another talk with Soviet Russia upon the highest level. The idea appeals to me of a supreme effort to bridge the gulf between the two worlds, so that each can live their life, if not in friendship at least without the hatreds of the cold war.[15]

Dean Acheson, fresh from founding the Atlantic Alliance, thought such an enterprise premature:

> The only way to deal with the Soviet Union, we have found from hard experience, is to create situations of strength. . . . [W]hen we have eliminated all the areas of weakness that we can—we will be able to evolve working agreements with the Russians. . . . No good would come from our taking the initiative in calling for conversations at this point. . . .[16]

Churchill did not return as Prime Minister until October 1951, and chose not to press for a summit meeting for the remainder of Truman's term in office. He decided instead to await the new administration, to be led by his old wartime comrade Dwight D. Eisenhower. In the interval, he fell in with the prevailing tendency of justifying summits on the ground that, no matter who the Soviet leader was, he would prove receptive to a high-level agreement. In 1952, that leader was Stalin. In June of that year, Churchill told John Colville that, if Eisenhower were elected, he would "have another shot at making peace by means of a meeting of the Big Three. . . . He thought that while Stalin lived we were far safer from attack than if he died and his lieutenants started scrambling for the succession."[17]

When Stalin died shortly after Eisenhower became President, Churchill advocated negotiations with the new Soviet leader. Eisenhower, however, proved no more receptive to Churchill's idea of reopening talks with the Soviets than his predecessor had been. Reacting to Malenkov's overture of March 17, 1953, Churchill urged Eisenhower on April 5 not to miss any chance "of finding out how far the Malenkov regime are prepared to go in easing things up all around."[18] Eisenhower's response was to ask Churchill to await a policy statement he was planning to deliver before the American Society of Newspaper Editors on April 16 which, in effect, rejected Churchill's premise.[19] Eisenhower argued that the causes of tension were as familiar as the remedies: a Korean armistice, an Austrian State Treaty, and "an end to the direct and indirect attacks upon the security of Indochina and Malaya." He thereby lumped China and the Soviet Union together, which was a wrong assessment of Sino-Soviet relations, as later events would show, and produced clearly unfulfillable conditions since events in Malaysia and Indochina were largely outside Soviet control. No negotiations were necessary, Eisenhower said: it was a time for deeds, not words.

Viewing a draft of Eisenhower's speech in advance, Churchill worried that "a sudden frost nipped spring in the bud." Then, to show that he was unpersuaded by Eisenhower's arguments, he proposed a meeting of the

Potsdam powers—the United States, Great Britain, and the U.S.S.R.—to be preceded by a preparatory session between Churchill and Molotov, who had recently been reinstated as the Soviet Foreign Minister. Helpfully enclosing a draft of the invitation in his letter to Eisenhower, Churchill appealed to an improbable bond of friendship between himself and Molotov:

> ... we could renew our own war-time relation and ... I could meet Monsieur Malenkov and others of your leading men. Naturally I do not imagine that we could settle any of the grave issues which overhang the immediate future of the world. . . . I should of course make it clear I was not expecting any major decisions at this informal meeting but only to restore an easy and friendly basis between us. . . .[20]

To Eisenhower, however, a summit spelled a dangerous concession to the Soviets. Somewhat testily, he reiterated his demand that the Soviets meet some preconditions:

> In my note to you of April twenty-fifth I expressed the view that we should not rush things too much and should not permit feeling in our countries for a meeting between heads of states and government to press us into precipitate initiatives. . . .[21]

Though Churchill disagreed, he recognized that his country's dependence on the United States did not permit him the luxury of freewheeling initiatives on matters about which Washington felt so strongly. Without communicating directly with Malenkov, he did the next-best thing by telling the House of Commons much of what he might have conveyed to the Soviet Prime Minister in private. On May 11, 1953, he defined how his analysis differed from that of Eisenhower and Dulles: whereas the American leaders feared jeopardizing the cohesion of the Atlantic Alliance and the rearmament of Germany, Churchill was above all reluctant to jeopardize a more hopeful evolution within the Soviet Union:

> . . . it would be a pity if the natural desire to reach a general settlement of international policy were to impede any spontaneous and healthy evolution which may be taking place inside Russia. I have regarded some of the internal manifestations and the apparent change of mood as far more important and significant than what has happened outside. I am anxious that nothing in the presentation of foreign policy by the N.A.T.O. Powers should, as it were, supersede or take the emphasis out of what may be a profound movement of Russian feeling.[22]

Prior to Stalin's death, Churchill had urged negotiations because he had deemed Stalin to be the Soviet leader best able to guarantee the fulfillment of what he had promised. Now Churchill was urging a summit in order to preserve the hopeful prospects that had arisen after the dictator's death. In other words, negotiations were needed no matter what happened within the Soviet Union or who controlled the Soviet hierarchy. A conference at the highest level, Churchill urged, could settle the principles and direction of future negotiations:

> This conference should not be overhung by a ponderous or rigid agenda, or led into mazes and jungles of technical details, zealously contested by hordes of experts and officials drawn up in vast, cumbrous array. The conference should be confined to the smallest number of Powers and persons possible. . . . It might well be that no hard-faced agreements would be reached, but there might be a general feeling among those gathered together that they might do something better than tear the human race, including themselves, into bits.[23]

But what exactly did Churchill have in mind? How were the leaders to express their decision not to commit collective suicide? The only concrete proposal Churchill put forward was an agreement similar to the 1925 Locarno Pact, in which Germany and France had accepted each other's frontiers and Great Britain had guaranteed each side against aggression by the other (see chapter 11).

It was not a good example. Locarno had lasted a mere decade, and it had never resolved a single crisis. The notion that Great Britain, or any nation, could be so indifferent about the substance of potential controversies as to guarantee at one and the same time (and via the same instrument) the border of both an ally and a major adversary had been bizarre enough in 1925, and it had not improved any in the era of ideological conflict which prevailed three decades later. Who would guarantee which frontier against what danger? Were the Potsdam powers to guarantee all frontiers in Europe against all aggression? In that case, diplomacy would have returned full circle to Roosevelt's idea of the Four Policemen. Or did it mean that resistance was prohibited unless all the Potsdam powers concurred? In that case, the idea would serve as a *carte blanche* for Soviet aggression. Since the United States and the Soviet Union each regarded the other superpower as the chief security problem, how could a joint guarantee be a solution for both? Locarno had been designed as the alternative to a military alliance between France and Great Britain, and had been presented that way before Parliament and public. Would the new agreement modeled on Locarno dissolve existing alliances?

Churchill's case, however, did not depend on any particular negotiating position. On July 1, 1953, he rejected the theory that the Kremlin's policies were immutable and that the Soviet Union was somehow the first society to become immune to the erosion of history. According to Churchill, the West's dilemma resided in a combination of its refusal to recognize the Soviet satellite orbit and its unwillingness to risk war to undo it. The only way out was by launching a "reconnaissance in force" to determine the implications of the new Soviet reality. He wrote to Eisenhower:

> I have no more intention than I had at Fulton or in 1945 of being fooled by the Russians. I think however there is a change in the world balance, largely through American action and re-armament, but also through the ebb of Communist philosophy, which justifies a cold-blooded, factual study by the free nations while keeping united and strong.[24]

Churchill's hope was that "ten years of easement plus productive science might make a different world."[25] Churchill was no longer proposing a global settlement but a policy which later came to be called "detente." Churchill had recognized that the difficulty with containment in its original version was that, however powerful its analysis, its practical implementation amounted to endurance for its own sake until that distant day when the Soviet system somehow transformed itself. Containment might well imply an impressive destination, but it offered little in the way of sustenance along the journey. Its alternative was an immediate comprehensive settlement, which implied an easier journey to a less attractive destination but also risked the cohesion of the Atlantic Alliance and Germany's integration into the West—an exorbitant price for any foreseeable *quid pro quo* unless the German leaders themselves demanded it. What Churchill was now proposing was a middle ground—peaceful coexistence, to permit the erosion of time and to ease Soviet long-range policy.

The psychological strain of an era of confrontation without issue was evidenced by the changed attitude of George F. Kennan. Realizing that his original approach to the Soviet Union was turning into a rationale for endless military confrontation, he developed a concept for negotiating an overall settlement very similar to what Churchill had seemed to have had in mind in 1944–45.

The principal goal of Kennan's so-called disengagement scheme was the removal of Soviet troops from the center of Europe. For this, Kennan was prepared to pay with a comparable withdrawal of American forces from Germany. Arguing passionately that Germany would be able to defend itself with conventional weapons, as it had always done, especially if Soviet armies had to cross Eastern Europe before reaching Germany's borders, Kennan deplored excessive reliance on nuclear strategy. He supported a proposal by the Polish Foreign Minister, Adam Rapacki, for a nuclear-free zone in Central Europe comprising Germany, Poland, and Czechoslovakia.[26]

The difficulty with both the Kennan and the Rapacki schemes was the same as with Stalin's Peace Note: they would have traded German integration into the West for Soviet withdrawal from East Germany and parts of Eastern Europe, which, unless coupled with guarantees against Soviet intervention to protect communist regimes, would have led to a dual crisis: one in Eastern Europe, and another in finding a responsible national role for Germany, which had proved elusive since its unification in 1871.[27] In light of the conventional wisdom of the time, the Rapacki-Kennan concept of trading an American withdrawal of 3,000 miles for a Soviet withdrawal of a few hundred miles ran the additional risk of putting a premium on the weapons category, in which the Soviet Union was perceived to be preponderant, while stigmatizing nuclear weapons, which, at a minimum, made aggression incalculable. This was my own view at the time.[28]

Churchill, as so often before, had the right insight even if, for once, he did not have the appropriate remedy. The democratic publics would not be willing to sustain confrontation indefinitely unless their governments had first demonstrated beyond doubt that all the alternatives to conflict had been explored. If the democracies failed to develop a concrete program to ease tensions with the Soviets, both their publics and their governments ran the risk of being seduced by peace offensives in which the long-awaited transformation of Soviet society would be proclaimed on the basis of nothing more substantial than a change in Soviet tone. If the democracies were to avoid oscillating between extremes of intransigence and conciliation, they would have to conduct their diplomacy within a narrow margin: between an endless confrontation that was becoming increasingly oppressive as nuclear stockpiles grew on both sides, and a kind of diplomacy which tranquilized people's perceptions of the Cold War without really improving the actual situation.

The democracies were in fact in a strong position to operate within this narrow range, because their sphere of influence was far stronger than the Soviets', and because the economic and social gap between the superpowers was only likely to widen. History seemed to be on their side, provided they were able to combine imagination with discipline. This, at any rate, was the reasoning behind the later detente policy of

Nixon (see chapter 28). It was in fact the implication of Churchill's fall-back position in his letter to Eisenhower of July 1, 1953, when he spoke of "ten years of easement plus productive science" making for a better world.

Along with Adenauer, John Foster Dulles was the Western statesman who most firmly opposed risking the hard-won cohesion of the West in fluid negotiations. Dulles' assessment of the danger of what Stalin had proposed and which the disengagement theorists later put forward was essentially correct. Yet he also created a psychological vulnerability by arguing that the best way to preserve Western cohesion was to avoid negotiations altogether—as evidenced from this note of caution to a White House speech-writer in April 1953:

> ... there's some real danger of our just seeming to fall in with these Soviet overtures. It's obvious that what they are doing is because of outside pressures, and I don't know anything better we can do than keep up these pressures right now.[29]

With such pronouncements, Dulles reached the limits of the containment policy. Democratic societies needed some purpose beyond endurance in order to justify the Cold War. Though the political programs on the table were incompatible with the interests of the democracies, an alternative political conception of a peaceful evolution of Central Europe was needed—some program that emphasized keeping Germany inside Western institutions together with measures to ease tensions along the dividing line across Europe. Dulles avoided addressing this need, preferring to stalemate foreign ministers' talks with familiar positions in order to gain time for the consolidation of the Atlantic Alliance and the rearmament of Germany. For Dulles, such a policy avoided discord among the allies; for the confused post-Stalin leadership, it spared them the strain of having to make painful decisions.

Once Soviet leaders had realized that the democracies would not press Central European issues, they sought the much-needed respite with the West by concentrating on what Eisenhower and Dulles had defined as tests of good faith: Korea, Indochina, and the Austrian State Treaty. Instead of serving as the admission tickets to a negotiation on Europe, which Churchill had sought in 1953, these agreements came to substitute for them. In January 1954, a foreign ministers' meeting on the subject of Germany quickly deadlocked. Dulles and Molotov had in fact arrived at identical conclusions. Neither wished to engage in a fluid diplomacy; each preferred the consolidation of his own sphere of influence over a more adventurous foreign policy.

The positions of the two sides were not symmetrical, however. Stalemate served Moscow's immediate tactical and internal purposes, but it played into the hands of America's long-range strategy—even if all of the American leaders did not fully understand this. Since the United States and its allies were bound to win an arms race and their sphere of influence had the greater economic potential, properly conceived Soviet long-range purposes actually required a genuine easing of tensions and a realistic settlement of Central European issues. Molotov avoided making concessions which, however painful, might have saved the Soviet Union from strategic overextension and eventual collapse; Dulles avoided flexibility, for which he paid the price of needless domestic controversy and vulnerability to Soviet cosmetic peace offensives, but which also laid the basis for America's ultimate strategic victory.

Dulles used the respite to pursue his goal of integrating Germany into NATO. The problem of how to fit the Federal Republic into the Western military structure was nettlesome. The French were none too eager to see a fully rearmed Germany, nor did they want to sacrifice their national defense for an integrated Western defense which included Germany. For that would have meant partly putting the defense of their country in the hands of those who had ravaged France only a decade before, and it would have constricted France's ability to pursue its colonial wars. This was the reason why the plan for a European Defense Community foundered on French resistance. Dulles and Anthony Eden therefore turned to the alternative of simply integrating the Federal Republic of Germany into NATO. Under pressure, Paris went along while insisting that Great Britain commit itself to the permanent stationing of British troops on German soil. When Eden agreed to this proposal, France was given the concrete military assurances which the British had so consistently refused after the First World War. Henceforth, the British, French, and American troops were stationed in Germany as allies of the Federal Republic. What had started out as Stalin's initiative to end the division of Germany (for a time, vaguely endorsed by Churchill) ended up confirming the division of Europe. Ironically, Churchill, the apostle of spheres of influence, in the end sought to soften their impact and perhaps to eliminate them altogether; while Dulles, the Secretary of State of the country forever inveighing against spheres of influence, turned out to be the chief spokesman for the policy that froze them in place.

America, having become confident about the solidarity of its sphere, now felt it was safe to talk to the Russians. The fact was, however, that, with American and Soviet blocs in Europe consolidated, there was less and less to talk about. Both sides felt sufficiently at liberty to hold a summit, not in order to settle the Cold War, but precisely because they knew it would avoid all the fundamental issues. Churchill had retired, the Federal Republic was ensconced in NATO, and the Soviet Union had decided that preserving its sphere of influence in Eastern Europe was safer than trying to lure the Federal Republic away from its Western ties.

Thus the Geneva Summit of July 1955 proved to be a far cry from what Churchill had originally proposed. Instead of reviewing the causes of tension, the leaders attending the Summit barely mentioned the issues which had produced the Cold War. The agenda oscillated between attempting to score propaganda points and relegating the solution of East-West problems to amateur psychology. Eisenhower's "open-skies" proposal for aerial reconnaissance of each other's territories risked little; for it would have told the Soviets nothing they did not already know from their intelligence and public sources, while unveiling the enigma of the Soviet empire to American reconnaissance. I know from personal experience that the policy planners in the Eisenhower entourage who designed it—mostly under the auspices of Nelson Rockefeller, who was then a presidential adviser—would have been amazed had it been accepted. Nor did its rejection by Khrushchev entail any penalties for the Soviet Union. The issue of the future of Central Europe was passed on to the foreign ministers without guidelines.

The major result of the Summit was to demonstrate the democracies' psychological need for a respite from a decade of confrontation. Having held firm in the face of Stalin's earlier, specific proposals, the democracies now succumbed to a change in Soviet tone. They were like the marathon runner who, within sight of the finish line, sits down exhausted at the roadside and permits his competitors to catch up.

Eisenhower and Dulles had skillfully and tenaciously defused the residue of Stalin's Peace Note and of Churchill's eloquent calls for a summit by insisting on specific solutions to equally specific problems. Yet, in the end, they concluded that waiting for an internal Soviet change to occur conveyed too stern a message, and that devising alternative negotiating positions might prove too divisive. Containment could only be sustained by offering their people some hope for an end to the Cold War. But, instead of coming up with a political program of their own, they fell in with what they had heretofore feared: the growing tendency to interpret Khrushchev's and Bulganin's less challenging style as a sign of a basic change in Soviet attitudes. The mere fact that a nonconfrontational meeting had occurred—however skimpy on substance—fueled the democracies' hope that the long-predicted Soviet transformation was in train.

Even before the summit assembled, Eisenhower had set the tone for the meeting. Abandoning his Administration's former insistence on concrete and detailed progress, he cast the goals of East-West diplomacy in largely psychological terms:

> Our many postwar conferences have been characterized too much by attention to details, by an effort apparently to work on specific problems, rather than to establish a spirit and attitude in which to approach them.[30]

Media reaction was ecstatic and converged on the proposition that something fundamental had taken place at the summit, though exactly what that was remained obscure. "Mr. Eisenhower had done even better than defeat an enemy in battle as had been his assignment a decade ago," read an editorial in *The New York Times*. "He had done something to prevent battles from happening. . . . Other men might have played strength against strength. It was Mr. Eisenhower's gift to draw others into the circle of his good will and to modify the attitudes if not the policies of the little band of visitors from the other side of the Elbe."[31]

Even Dulles was carried away by the "spirit" of Geneva. "Up until the time of Geneva," he told British Foreign Secretary Harold Macmillan two months later, "Soviet policy was based on intolerance which was the keynote of Soviet doctrine. Soviet policy is now based on tolerance which includes good relations with everyone. . . ."[32] The summit and its surrounding atmosphere had become their own rewards.

Entering into the spirit of things, Harold Macmillan argued that the true significance of the Geneva Summit had resided not in any specific agreement but in the personal relations that it had helped to establish among the leaders. Even in the homeland of balance-of-power diplomacy, atmosphere was being elevated into the key element of foreign policy:

> Why did this meeting send a thrill of hope and expectation round the world? It wasn't that the discussions were specially remarkable. . . . What struck the imagination of the world was the fact of the friendly meeting between the Heads of the two great groups into which the world is divided. These men, carrying their immense burdens, met and talked and joked together like ordinary mortals. . . . I cannot help thinking that last summer's Geneva idyll was not a vague or sham affair.[33]

If only history were more forgiving. American leaders had been right in their earlier assessment that the Cold War was the result of Soviet actions and not of Soviet rhetoric or personal conduct. The refusal of leaders on both sides to address the causes of the tension was bound to perpetuate them and to make them fester. If a mere meeting could have such impact on Western opinion, what incentive remained for the Soviets to make substantive concessions? Indeed, none would appear on any political issue for the next decade and a half.

The spheres of influence on either side of the German dividing line congealed. Between the time of NATO's founding and the opening of negotiations between the democracies and the Soviet Union, which led to the Helsinki Accords of 1975, the only political negotiations were those triggered by Soviet ultimatums over Berlin. Diplomacy moved increasingly into the field of arms control, which was the reverse side of the "positions-of-strength" approach. Its advocates sought to turn the limitation or control of armaments into a substitute for political dialogue; or, in the language of containment, to limit positions of strength to the lowest level compatible with deterrence. But, just as positions of strength would not automatically translate into negotiations, arms control did not automatically translate into a relaxation of tensions.

Even as the Geneva Summit was being hailed in the West as the beginning of a thaw in the Cold War, it had been ushering in the Cold War's most dangerous phase. For Soviet leaders had drawn quite different conclusions from it than the leaders of the democracies. Stalin's heirs had come into their own in the midst of general confusion and uncertainty about whether the democracies might exploit the general disarray to reverse Soviet postwar conquests. Yet, by June 1953, a mere three months after the tyrant's death, they had managed to put down an uprising in East Berlin, which was technically a four-power city, without any reaction from the West. They had procrastinated over German unification without encountering resistance, and communist political control of Central and Eastern Europe was being challenged only rhetorically. Finally, at the Geneva Summit they had received a certificate of good conduct without engaging in a serious exploration of any of the issues which had led to the Cold War.

Dedicated Marxists, they drew the only conclusion compatible with their ideology: that the correlation of forces was moving in their favor. No doubt this belief was reinforced by the Soviets' growing, albeit still relatively small, stockpile of nuclear weapons and their development of the hydrogen bomb. In his memoirs, Khrushchev summarized the summit: "... our enemies now realized that we were able to resist their pressure and see through their tricks."[34] In February 1956, seven months after the summit, at the same Party Congress at which he castigated Stalin, Khrushchev sized up the international environment in a manner which deprecated the democracies:

> The general crisis of capitalism continues to deepen.... The interna-
> tional camp of socialism is exerting ever-growing influence on the
> course of world events.... The position of the imperialist forces is
> growing weaker....[35]

The basic cause of the misunderstanding between the leaders of the
democracies and their counterparts in the U.S.S.R. was the former's insistence on applying to the Soviet *nomenklatura* the criteria drawn from
their own domestic experience. It was a profound misconception. The
second generation of Soviet leaders had been shaped by a past that would
have been unimaginable in the democracies. Apprenticeship to Stalin
had guaranteed psychological malformation. Only the salve of boundless
ambition could have made tolerable the pervasive sense of terror generated by the penalty of death or life in the Gulag for the slightest misstep
— or even for a shift in policy by the dictator himself.

The generation which grew up under Stalin could reduce its risks only
by servility to the master's whims and by the systematic denunciation of
colleagues. They made their nightmarish existence more tolerable by a
passionate belief in the system to which they owed their careers. Not
until the next generation would Soviet leaders experience the shocks of
disillusionment.

As the material on Stalin in Gromyko's memoirs reveals, Stalin's subordinates were aware of the atrocities being committed in the name of
communism.[36] Yet they assuaged their consciences, which in any case
were not terribly highly developed, by ascribing Stalinism to the aberrations of an individual rather than to the failure of the communist system.
Besides, they had little opportunity for systematic reflection because Stalin had seen to it that his top leadership was in a state of constant flux.
And the loss of position in Stalin's regime did not signal the advent of a
normal life in the "private sector"; for the fortunate few who managed to
survive, it meant public disgrace and complete isolation from erstwhile
colleagues.

The morbid suspiciousness which had become a way of life in the
Soviet *nomenklatura* characterized their conduct in the immediate post-
Stalin phase as well. Stalin's successors spent nearly five years in their
struggle for succession: in 1953, Beria was executed; in 1955, Malenkov
was removed from office; in 1957, Khrushchev defeated the so-called anti-
party group of Molotov, Kaganovich, Shepilov, and Malenkov, and by 1958
he attained absolute power after the dismissal of Zhukov. This turmoil
made a relaxation of tensions with the West a necessity for the Kremlin
leadership, though it did not keep it from selling arms to Egypt or suppressing the Hungarian Revolution.

The change in tone of the Soviet leadership did not translate into acceptance of Western notions of peaceful coexistence. In 1954, when Malenkov spoke of the danger of nuclear war, he may well have exhibited the first stirrings of the Soviets' recognition of the realities of the Nuclear Age. It is equally possible that he was attempting to undermine the democracies' confidence in the weapon on which they were basing their security. Khrushchev's condemnation of Stalin may have signaled a softening of communism, but he clearly used it as well as a weapon against Stalin's former associates, who represented his principal opposition, and as a means of achieving control over the Communist Party.

It is true that Khrushchev had the courage to purge Beria, or at least that he recognized the need to do so for the sake of his own survival; and he fitfully experimented with both an intellectual thaw and de-Stalinization in Eastern Europe. He was a forerunner of Gorbachev in that he started a process of change, the implications of which he did not understand and the direction of which he would have deplored. From this standpoint, it can be said that the collapse of communism started with Khrushchev.

That collapse was so total that it tempts one to forget how recklessly Khrushchev challenged the international community. He had a peasant's instinct for spotting the neuralgic points of the countries his ideology had defined as imperialist. He fomented a Middle East crisis, issued a series of ultimatums over Berlin, encouraged wars of national liberation, and placed missiles in Cuba. But while he caused the West much discomfiture, he achieved no permanent gains for the Soviet Union because he was better at starting crises than at knowing how to finish them. And because, despite all of its confusion, the West did in the end resist, the upshot of Khrushchev's aggressive actions was a vast expenditure of Soviet resources for no permanent strategic gain and for a severe humiliation during the Cuban missile crisis.

The 1955 Geneva Summit was the point of departure for all these adventures. On the way home from Geneva, Khrushchev stopped in East Berlin to recognize the sovereignty of the East German communist regime. It was a move Stalin had avoided. For the remainder of the Cold War, the issue of German unification would disappear from the international agenda because Moscow had consigned it to negotiations between the two German states. Since the political values of these states were incompatible and neither state was prepared to commit suicide, unification could only have come about by the political collapse of one of them. Thus, the Berlin crisis of 1958–62 had its origins at Geneva.

By 1955, a decade after Roosevelt's death, the postwar settlement in

Europe was emerging at last, not by negotiation among the victors of the Second World War but as a result of their inability to negotiate a settlement. It was precisely what Roosevelt had tried to avoid: two armed camps facing off in the center of the Continent and a massive American military commitment to Europe—a spheres-of-influence arrangement in every sense of the word. Yet it was an arrangement that provided for a certain stability. The German question, if unresolved, had at least been put on hold. The Soviets had to accept, if not recognize, the Western German state, and the Americans would do the same for East Germany.

But Nikita Khrushchev was not about to let the American sphere prosper uncontested. He would challenge the West in arenas which Stalin had always deemed to be outside the Soviet sphere of interest, causing the hot points of Soviet-American competition to move beyond Europe. The first of these hot points was to erupt in what came to be known as the Suez Crisis of 1956.

CHAPTER TWENTY-ONE

Leapfrogging Containment: The Suez Crisis

All the talk of peaceful coexistence emanating from the 1955 Geneva Summit could not alter the fundamental reality: the United States and the Soviet Union, far and away the pre-eminent powers in the world, were locked in geopolitical competition. A gain for one side was widely perceived as being a loss for the other. By the mid-1950s, the American sphere of influence in Western Europe was thriving, and America's demonstrated willingness to protect that sphere with military force deterred Soviet adventurism. But stalemate in Europe did not mean stalemate around the world. In 1955, just two months after the Geneva Summit, the Soviet Union made a major arms sale to Egypt by bartering weapons for cotton, then in oversupply—a daring move to extend Soviet influence into the Middle East. In making his bid for influence in Egypt, Khrushchev had in effect "leapfrogged" the *cordon sanitaire* which the United States had constructed around the Soviet Union, confronting Washington with the task of having to counter the Soviets in areas heretofore considered to be safely within the Western sphere.

Stalin had never been willing to stake Soviet credibility on the developing world. He considered it too far from home and too unstable, its leaders too difficult to control, and the Soviet Union not yet powerful enough to engage in distant adventures—though, in time, the growth of Soviet military power might well have changed his attitude. As late as 1947, Andrei Zhdanov, who had appeared to be among Stalin's closest advisers at the time, was still describing the Middle East as an area dominated by American and British imperialists competing with each other.[1]

The Soviet leaders could not have failed to understand that their first sale of arms to a developing country would inflame Arab nationalism, make the Arab-Israeli conflict more intractable, and be perceived as a major challenge to Western dominance in the Middle East. By the time the smoke cleared, the Suez crisis had destroyed the Great Power status of both Great Britain and France. Outside of Europe, America would henceforth be obliged to man the ramparts of the Cold War essentially alone.

Khrushchev's opening gambit was cautious enough. The Soviet Union was not even involved in the initial arms sale, since the transaction was technically Czechoslovakian, although that subterfuge was soon abandoned. However camouflaged, the sale of Soviet arms to the Middle East pressed on a neuralgic point of Western Europe, especially of Great Britain. After India, Egypt represented the most important legacy of Great Britain's imperial past. In the twentieth century, the Suez Canal had become the principal artery for the supply of oil to Western Europe. Even in its weakened state immediately after the Second World War, Great Britain continued to regard itself as the pre-eminent power in the Middle East, its dominance resting on two pillars: Iran, which supplied oil through a joint Anglo-Iranian company; and Egypt, which served as the strategic base. The Arab League was promoted by Anthony Eden in 1945 as the political framework for resisting outside penetration of the Middle East. Significant British forces remained in Egypt, Iraq, and Iran. A British officer, General John Glubb (Glubb Pasha), commanded Jordan's Arab Legion.

In the 1950s, this world came unglued. To the applause of the first generation of newly independent countries, Iranian Prime Minister Mossadegh nationalized Iran's oil industry in 1951 and demanded the withdrawal of British troops protecting the oil complex at Abadan. Great Britain no longer felt strong enough to undertake military action so close to the Soviet border without American support, which was not forthcoming. Moreover, it thought it had a fall-back position in its major base along the Suez Canal.

The challenge posed by Mossadegh ended two years later when the United States encouraged a coup to overthrow him. (In those days, Washington still considered covert operations more legitimate than military intervention.) Great Britain's pre-eminence in Iran was never restored, however. By 1952, Great Britain's military position in Egypt was crumbling as well. A group of young officers expressing the nationalist and anticolonial mood that was sweeping the region deposed the corrupt King Farouk. Their dominant figure was Colonel Gamal Abdel Nasser.

A powerful personality possessed of considerable charm, Nasser grew into a charismatic figure by appealing to Arab nationalism. He had felt deeply humiliated by the Arab defeat in the 1948 war with Israel. He saw in the establishment of the Jewish state the culmination of a century of Western colonialism. He was determined to expel Great Britain and France from the region.

Nasser's emergence brought into the open the dormant conflict between the United States and its principal NATO allies over the issue of colonialism. As early as April 1951, Churchill, then still the leader of the Opposition, had called for joint action in the Middle East:

> We are no longer strong enough ourselves to bear the whole political burden we have hitherto borne in the Mediterranean, or even to take the leading part in the diplomatic control of that theatre. But the United States and Britain together, aided by France . . . we three together would be in a most powerful position to deal with, say, the Egyptian problem and the whole question of the defence of the Suez Canal.[2]

When it came to the Middle East, however, America rejected the role it had played in Greece and Turkey, and would neither assume the legacy of European political pre-eminence nor allow itself to be associated with the colonial tradition. Both Truman and Eisenhower adamantly opposed British military action in Iran or Egypt on the ostensible ground that disputes of this kind should be adjudicated by the United Nations. In reality, they did not want to be identified with Great Britain's colonial heritage, which they correctly considered to be untenable.

Yet America was prone to its own illusions, one of which was that the independence movements of the developing world paralleled the American experience, and that the new nations would therefore support American foreign policy once they realized that the U.S. attitude about colonialism sharply differed from that of the old European powers. But the leaders of the independence movements were of a different type than America's Founding Fathers. While using the rhetoric of democracy, they lacked the commitment to it of the drafters of the American Constitution, who genuinely believed in a system of checks and balances. The vast majority of them governed in an authoritarian manner. Many were Marxists. Almost all of them saw in the East-West conflict an opportunity to overturn what they identified as the old imperialist system. However much America might dissociate from European colonialism, American leaders, to their chagrin, found themselves perceived in developing countries as useful auxiliaries from the imperialist camp rather than as genuine partners.

In the end, America was drawn into the Middle East by the containment theory, which required opposition to Soviet expansion in every region, and by the doctrine of collective security, which encouraged the creation of NATO-like organizations to resist actual or potential military threats. Yet, for the most part, the nations of the Middle East did not share America's strategic views. They thought of Moscow primarily as a useful lever to extract concessions from the West rather than as a threat to their independence. Many of the new nations managed to convey the impression that their takeover by the communists would hold more danger for the United States than it did for them, so that there was no need for them to pay any price for American protection. Above all, populist rulers like Nasser saw no future in being identified with the West. They wanted their volatile publics to perceive them as having wrested not only independence but freedom of maneuver from the democracies. Nonalignment was for them as much a domestic necessity as a foreign policy choice.

At first, neither Great Britain nor America fully grasped what Nasser represented. Both nations proceeded from the premise that Nasser's resistance to their policies was due to some specific set of grievances that could be redressed. What little chance existed for testing this hypothesis was vitiated by the different premises of the democracies. Great Britain sought to induce Nasser to accept its historic dominance, whereas the United States tried to lure Nasser into its grand strategy of containment. The Soviet Union discerned an opportunity to outflank "capitalist encirclement" and to acquire new allies by supplying them with arms without (as in Eastern Europe) having to assume responsibility for their domestic governance. Nasser cleverly used the conjunction of all of these impulses to pit the various contenders against each other.

The infusion of Soviet arms into the volatile Middle East accelerated this process. Great Britain's and America's best riposte would have been to isolate Nasser until it had become obvious that Soviet arms had gained him nothing, and then, if Nasser abandoned his Soviet ties—or, better still, if he was replaced by a more moderate leader—to follow up with a generous diplomatic initiative. That was to be the American strategy toward Anwar Sadat twenty years later. In 1955, the democracies chose the opposite tactic: they tried hard to conciliate Nasser by meeting many of his demands.

Like mirages in the desert, the hopes of the outside powers evaporated as soon as any effort was made to implement them. Great Britain found that, no matter how it sugarcoated its military presence in the region, it could not make it palatable to the local governments. America's schizophrenic policy of dissociating from Great Britain on Middle Eastern issues in order to enlist Nasser into a partnership with Great Britain in a global anti-Soviet strategy never got off the ground. Nasser had no conceivable incentive to abandon his Soviet ties. His incentive turned out to be the precise opposite, and he sought to balance every benefit from the United States by some move toward either the Soviets or the radical neutrals, and preferably both. The more Washington tried to placate Nasser, the more the wily Egyptian gravitated toward the Soviets, thereby raising the ante and seeking to siphon more benefits out of the United States.

In due course, the Soviet Union too was to experience the frustrations of dealing with the Nonaligned group. In the early stages of Soviet penetration of the Middle East, all was net gain. At a negligible cost to Moscow, the democracies were thrown on the defensive. Their internal conflicts mounted while a Soviet presence was forged in areas heretofore consigned to the Western sphere of influence. As time passed, however, the Soviets' passionate Middle Eastern clients involved Moscow in risks which were out of proportion to any conceivable Soviet gain. And whenever the Soviet Union tried to relate these risks to its own national interest, it incurred the displeasure, if not the contempt, of its newfound clients. This enabled Western diplomacy to demonstrate the Soviets' inability to fulfill their clients' goals—culminating in Sadat's turn away from Moscow starting in 1972.

Great Britain was the first to be forced to abandon its illusions about the Middle East. Its military base along the Suez Canal was one of its last significant imperial outposts, garrisoned by some 80,000 troops. Yet Great Britain was in no position to maintain a large force in the Canal Zone in the face of Egyptian opposition and without American support. In 1954, pressed by the United States, Great Britain agreed to withdraw forces from its Suez base by 1956.

American leaders were striving to combine two incompatible policies:

to end Great Britain's imperial role exploiting the remnants of British influence to build a structure of containment in the Middle East. The Eisenhower Administration devised the concept of the Northern Tier of nations—to be composed of Turkey, Iraq, Syria, and Pakistan, with Iran as a possible participant later on. A Middle Eastern version of NATO, its purpose was to contain the Soviet Union along its southern borders.

This concept came to fruition in the British-sponsored Baghdad Pact, but it proved flawed on several counts. For an alliance to be effective, it must reflect some sense of common purpose, a perception of common danger, and the capacity to pool strengths. None of these elements applied to the Baghdad Pact. The divisions and animosities among the nations in the area were greater than their mutual fear of Soviet expansion. Syria refused to join the Pact; Iraq, even while serving as its headquarters for two years, was far more concerned about fending off Arab radicalism than about Soviet aggressiveness; Pakistan viewed threats to its security as coming from India, not the Soviet Union.

Nor were the military forces of the various members of the Baghdad Pact designed to assist neighbors in the event of aggression by a superpower; their basic purpose was domestic security. Above all, Nasser, as the most dynamic force in the area, was determined to wreck the Pact, which he viewed as a devious maneuver to refurbish colonial domination of the Middle East and to isolate him and his fellow radicals.

Too divided to design punitive measures to counter the Soviet influence in the region, Great Britain and the United States next tried to coax Egypt away from Moscow by demonstrating the advantages of adhering to the Western camp. They pursued two policies to this end—promoting peace between Egypt and Israel, and helping Nasser to construct the Aswan Dam.

The peace initiative was based on the belief that the establishment of the Jewish state by force of arms in 1948 was the principal source of Arab radicalism. An honorable peace, it was thought, would remove that humiliation. But at that point, Arab radicals and nationalists were not seeking peace with Israel, honorable or otherwise. To them, the Jewish state was an alien presence injected into traditionally Arab lands on the basis of a 2,000-year-old claim and to expiate the Jews' suffering, which the Arab peoples had not caused.

If Nasser had made a genuine peace with Israel—that is, had settled for coexistence—he would have forfeited his claim to leadership of the Arab world. Determined not to be embarrassed before his Arab constituency, Nasser proposed that Israel give up the entire Negev, the southern desert region which it had conquered in 1948 and which constituted well over half of Israel's territory, and that the hundreds of thousands of Palestinian refugees evicted in 1948 be given the right to return.[3]

Israel would never agree to give up half of its territory or permit a repatriation of all Arab refugees, which would have swamped what was left of the state. Israel's way out was to insist on a formal peace agreement with open borders—a harmless-sounding request, but also the one demand Arab leaders found the most difficult to meet because it implied their permanent acceptance of the new state. Between Israel's demand for peace without offering territory and the Arab countries' demand for territory without defining peace, deadlock was inevitable. The first negotiation gave rise to a script that would be adhered to until Sadat's advent in Egypt, and for another twenty years in the rest of the Arab world—until the agreement between the PLO and Israel in September 1993.

By now, the United States and Great Britain were at loggerheads over a variety of issues. Though Dulles favored the Northern Tier policy, he was annoyed that Great Britain should have assumed its leadership, and wanted the Baghdad Pact to be centered on Egypt; which, in turn, fought the Pact tooth and nail. Great Britain would have preferred to overthrow Nasser; America, however uncomfortable with the Soviet arms deal, thought it wiser to propitiate him.

Anxious to restore their tattered unity, the Anglo-American leaders next turned their attention to the vast construction project of the so-called Aswan High Dam: 365 feet high and three miles long, it was to be built on the Upper Nile, near Egypt's border with the Sudan. It would regulate the irrigation of the Nile Valley, on which the subsistence of the Egyptian population had depended since time immemorial, and would free it from its annual dependence on the flooding of the Nile.

Anthony Eden, Nasser's most implacable foe, had first raised the prospect of joint Anglo-American support for the High Dam, with America bearing the lion's share (about 90 percent) of the burden. Why Eden, who was eager to get rid of Nasser, turned into the Aswan Dam's principal advocate can only be explained by his desire to be perceived as bestriding Mideast diplomacy and forestalling any Soviet attempt to follow up military assistance with economic penetration. On December 14, 1955, Great Britain and the United States made a formal offer to build the dam in two stages: some limited funds were made immediately available for the preparatory stage, during which a determination would be made of the extent and nature of assistance for the second stage, which involved the actual construction of the dam.[4]

It was a strange decision. Two governments were committing themselves to a monumental engineering and financial undertaking even though both preferred to see Nasser replaced and were deeply concerned about his drift toward the Soviet orbit. The two discordant allies consoled themselves with the belief that, even if the original grant did not win Nasser over, the second stage would make Egypt financially dependent on them in much the same way that the building of the Suez Canal had given the West financial control over Egypt in the nineteenth century.

Far from moderating Nasser, the Aswan Dam project aroused in him a sense of his importance. In order to preserve his bargaining leverage, he moved rapidly to undertake a series of compensatory moves. Haggling tenaciously over financial terms, he rejected American entreaties to help facilitate Arab-Israeli negotiations. When Great Britain tried to persuade Jordan to join the Baghdad Pact, pro-Egyptian riots broke out, which obliged King Hussein to dismiss Glubb Pasha, the British commander of the Arab Legion, in March 1956.[5]

On May 16, Nasser withdrew recognition from the government of Chiang Kai-shek, and established diplomatic relations with the People's Republic of China. This was a direct rebuke to the United States but especially to Dulles, who was deeply committed to Taiwan. In June, the new Soviet Foreign Minister, Dmitri Shepilov, came to Egypt with a Soviet offer to both finance and build the Aswan Dam, enabling Nasser to engage in his favorite pastime of playing the superpowers off against each other.

On July 19, Dulles decided to put an end to the charade. The Egyptian leader's recognition of Communist China had been the final straw that convinced Dulles to teach him a lesson. When the Egyptian Ambassador returned from Cairo with instructions to accept all American technical proposals, Dulles replied that Washington had come to the conclusion that the dam was beyond Egypt's economic capabilities. No aid would be forthcoming.

Dulles had thought himself quite prepared for a strong Egyptian response. He told Henry Luce, publisher of *Time,* that the Aswan Dam decision was "as big a chess move as US diplomacy has made in a long time." Nasser, he argued, was "in a hell of a spot and no matter what he does, can be used to American advantage. If he turns to the Russians now and they say 'No,' this will undermine the whole fabric of recent Soviet economic carpet-bagging all over the world. . . . If the Soviets agree to give Nasser his dam, then we are working up plans to lay it on thick in the satellite countries as to why their living conditions are so miserable with the Soviets dishing out millions to Egypt."[6] What was conspicuously lacking in Dulles' observation was a willingness to back up a "big move" with a readiness to run big risks. It was but another example of Dulles' congenital tendency to overestimate the role of propaganda, especially behind the Iron Curtain.

However flimsy the political rationale for the dam had been in the first place, the manner in which the American offer of aid was withdrawn courted a major crisis. The French Ambassador to Washington, Maurice Couve de Murville (who would later become de Gaulle's Foreign Minister), accurately predicted what was about to happen: "They will do something about Suez. That's the only way they can touch the Western countries."[7]

Before a vast crowd in Alexandria on July 26, 1956, Nasser gave his answer to Dulles, couching his riposte in an appeal to Arab nationalism:

> This, O citizens, is the battle in which we are now involved. It is a battle against imperialism and the methods and tactics of imperialism, and a battle against Israel, the vanguard of imperialism. . . .
>
> Arab nationalism progresses. Arab nationalism triumphs. Arab nationalism marches forward; it knows its road and it knows its strength. Arab nationalism knows who are its enemies and who are its friends. . . .[8]

Deliberately challenging France, he told the crowd: "We can never say that the battle of Algeria is not our battle." In the middle of his speech, Nasser pronounced the name of Ferdinand de Lesseps, the Frenchman who had built the Suez Canal. It was the code word for Egyptian military forces to seize control of the Canal. This enabled Nasser, near the end of his delivery, to announce to the frenzied multitude: "At this moment as I talk to you some of your Egyptian brethren . . . have started to take over the canal company and its property and to control shipping in the canal —the canal which is situated in Egyptian territory, which . . . is part of Egypt and which is owned by Egypt."[9]

The differences in perspective among the democracies which had characterized the prelude to the Suez crisis now blighted their reaction to it. Eden, who had risen to the position of Prime Minister the year before, after too long a wait, was temperamentally unsuited to make decisions under pressure. Being Churchill's immediate successor would have proved enough of a burden, but it was compounded by Eden's having acquired a reputation for strength that was entirely at variance with his psychological and, indeed, physical frailties. Only a few months earlier, he had undergone a major operation, and was in constant need of medication. Most of all, Eden was the captive of his formative years. A fluent Arabist, he had grown up in the period of British domination of the Middle East, and was determined to stop Nasser, single-handedly if necessary.

France was even more hostile to Nasser. Its major interests in the Arab world were in Morocco and Algeria, the former a French protectorate, the latter a department of Metropolitan France containing a million Frenchmen. Both North African countries were in the process of seeking independence, for which Nasser's policies provided emotional and political support. The Soviet arms deal raised the prospect that Egypt would become a conduit for Soviet arms to the Algerian guerrillas as well. "All this [is] in the works of Nasser, just as Hitler's policy [was] written down in *Mein Kampf*," declared France's new Prime Minister, Guy Mollet. "Nasser [has] the ambition to recreate the conquests of Islam."[10]

The analogy to Hitler was not really on the mark. Implying that Nasser's Egypt was determined to conquer foreign nations, it ascribed a validity to Middle Eastern borders that the Arab nationalists did not recognize. The borders in Europe—except for those in the Balkans—reflected in the main a common history and culture. By contrast, the borders of the Middle East had been drawn by foreign, largely European, powers at the end of the First World War in order to facilitate their domination of the area. In the minds of Arab nationalists, these frontiers cut across the Arab nation and denied a common Arab culture. Erasing them was not a way for one country to dominate another; it was the way to create an Arab nation, much as Cavour had built Italy, and Bismarck had created Germany out of a plethora of sovereign states.

However inexact their analogy, once Eden and Mollet had nailed their flag to the anti-appeasement mast, it should have become clear that they would not retreat. They belonged to the generation, after all, that viewed appeasement as a cardinal sin, and Munich as a permanent reproach. Comparing a leader to Hitler or even to Mussolini meant that they had moved beyond the possibility of compromise. They would either have to prevail or lose all claim to governance—most of all in their own eyes.

The reaction of Eden and Mollet to the nationalization of the Suez Canal was violent. Eden cabled Eisenhower the day after Nasser's speech: "If we do not [take a firm stand], our influence and yours throughout the Middle East will, we are convinced, be finally destroyed."[11] Three days later, in the House of Commons, he cut off any possibility of retreat:

No arrangements for the future of this great international waterway could be acceptable to Her Majesty's Government which would leave it in the unfettered control of a single Power which could, as recent events have shown, exploit it purely for purposes of national policy.[12]

France was no less firm. On July 29, the French Ambassador to London informed the British Foreign Secretary that France was prepared to put its forces under British command and to pull troops out of Algeria for joint action against Egypt.[13]

When Dulles appeared in London on August 1 for consultations, he seemed to share these views. Proclaiming that it was not acceptable for any one nation to control the Canal, especially if that nation was Egypt, he insisted that:

> A way had to be found to make Nasser *disgorge* what he was attempting to swallow. . . . We must make a genuine effort to bring world opinion to favour the international operation of the canal. . . . It should be possible to create a world opinion so adverse to Nasser that he would be isolated. Then if a military operation had to be undertaken it would be more apt to succeed and have less grave repercussions than if it had been undertaken precipitately.[14]

He proposed that a Maritime Conference composed of twenty-four of the principal maritime nations meet in London in another fortnight to devise an international system of free navigation through the Canal.

Dulles' call for a conference was the beginning of a puzzling and, for Great Britain and France, maddening, and ultimately humiliating process. Even Dulles' opening shot was an effort to couple tough language with a time-wasting diplomacy. In no time at all, it became apparent that the allies were not of one mind about the crisis. Eden and Mollet saw the overthrow or humiliation of Nasser as an end in itself, whereas Eisenhower and Dulles looked at the crisis in terms of long-range relations with the Arab world. Both sides operated from flawed preconceptions: Eden and Mollet acted as if the end of Nasser would restore the situation which had existed prior to his accession to power; Eisenhower and Dulles seemed to believe that, if not Nasser, then some other nationalist leader in the region might yet be induced into a NATO-like Middle East security system. It was also their view that military action against Nasser would so inflame Arab nationalism that Western influence would be ruined for a generation—a far darker scenario than losing control over the Canal.

Neither assumption proved correct. Pre-Nasser Egypt was gone forever. The other nationalist leaders who had modeled themselves after Nasser were immune to the siren songs of containment. Their main bargaining chip was the Cold War itself, which they exploited to the same degree that they condemned it. And the real issue was what would inflame Arab nationalism more—Nasser's victory or his defeat.

From a strictly analytical point of view, America ought to have shared the British and French perception that Nasser's brand of militant nationalism represented an insuperable obstacle to a constructive Middle East policy. A demonstration that reliance on Soviet arms served no positive purpose might have obviated decades of upheaval in the developing world. From that point of view, it would have been desirable to face down Nasser. But, having accomplished his defeat, the United States could not participate in a restoration of British and French colonial dominance. Where America should have separated from its allies—if it were absolutely necessary—was not at the beginning of the Suez Crisis, but upon its successful conclusion. A demonstration that reliance on Soviet support was disastrous for Egypt should have been followed by support for the reasonable nationalistic aims of a moderate successor to Nasser—much as America reacted to Sadat in the 1970s.

The democracies, however, were not ready for so complicated a strategy. Great Britain and France did not accept that the precondition for overthrowing Nasser was their being prepared to grant many of his demands to a more moderate successor. America did not understand how important it was for its policy that two close NATO allies be permitted to adjust to the new circumstances without undermining their image of themselves as Great Powers. For once a nation's image of itself is destroyed, so is its willingness to play a major international role. This was why Harold Macmillan, then Chancellor of the Exchequer, told Ambassador Robert Murphy, a Dulles emissary, that, if Great Britain did not confront Nasser now, "Britain would become another Netherlands."[15] America's leaders, however, opted for a chance to win over the radical nationalists, first by dissociating themselves from Great Britain and France diplomatically, later by publicly opposing them and demonstrating the limits of their capacity to shape Middle East events—in other words, bringing home to them the end of their roles as Great Powers.

Treating the Canal regime as a legal issue, Dulles focused on the potential disruption of the sea-lanes and was fertile in coming up with legal formulae to get around possible obstacles to free transit through the Canal. Eden and Mollet, however, were determined not to accept nationalization of the Suez Canal; they tried to turn it into a pretext for bringing down Nasser or, at a minimum, for humiliating him. Nasser finally played for time, as revolutionaries often do after a *fait accompli*. The longer their action stands, the more difficult it becomes to reverse it—especially by using force.

Eisenhower was passionate in his opposition to the use of force, even for the purpose of upholding the principle of free passage through the

Suez Canal, which Dulles had publicly supported in London. Dulles had brought with him a letter from the President to Eden stressing the "unwisdom even of contemplating the use of military force at this moment. . . ." Eisenhower went so far as to imply that unilateral British action would risk America's willingness to sustain NATO and, by implication, might leave America's allies at the mercy of Moscow. If war broke out, the letter read, before Great Britain had clearly demonstrated that it had exhausted every peaceful means of settling the crisis, it "could very seriously affect our peoples' feelings towards our Western allies. I do not want to exaggerate, but I could assure you that this could grow to such an intensity as to have the most far-reaching consequences."[16]

On the face of it, no two countries seemed less likely to clash than Great Britain and the United States, led by men who shared so many wartime experiences. Eden could not believe that Eisenhower might transform his misgivings about unilateral British and French actions into open opposition. And Eisenhower was convinced that, at the end of the day, France and Great Britain would not dare to act without America's support. British and American leaders prized their "special relationship," which was reinforced by wartime partnership and personal friendship. But during the Suez Crisis, they were thwarted by a fundamental clash of personalities. The British leaders found Dulles a prickly interlocutor, and Eden came to regard him with distaste.

By family tradition and personal avocation, John Foster Dulles seemed exceptionally well-suited for the office of Secretary of State. His grandfather, John Foster, had served as Secretary of State under President Benjamin Harrison; his uncle, Robert Lansing, had been Wilson's Secretary of State at the Versailles Peace Conference. Although John Foster Dulles had been a corporate lawyer until well into his middle age, his enduring preoccupation was with foreign policy.

American secretaries of state have traditionally affirmed America's exceptionalism and the universal validity of its values. Dulles was no different except that his form of exceptionalism was religious rather than philosophical. His first experience with international affairs had been as head of a Protestant commission engaged in promoting world peace. He once stated proudly, "Nobody in the Department of State knows as much about the Bible as I do."[17] And he sought to apply the principles of his stern Presbyterian faith to the conduct of day-to-day American foreign policy. "I am convinced," he wrote in 1950, "that we here need to make our political thoughts and practices reflect more faithfully a religious faith that man has his origin and destiny in God."[18] Though Dulles represented a classic American phenomenon which Gladstone's generation of Englishmen would have easily recognized, the postwar generation of British leaders resented his righteousness and thought him duplicitous rather than spiritual.

Unfortunately, Dulles' tendency to deliver sermons to his interlocutors too often overshadowed his superb knowledge of foreign affairs and, in particular, his thoughtful analysis of the dynamics of the Soviet system. Churchill described Dulles as "a dour Puritan, a great white bespectacled face with a smudge of a mouth," and, in lighter moments, occasionally referred to him as "Dullith." Eden had little confidence in Dulles from the very beginning. In 1952, before Eisenhower had appointed Dulles as Secretary of State, Eden voiced his hope for some other counterpart: "I do not think I would be able to work with him."[19]

Dulles had many qualities which made him vastly influential. His work ethic and devotion to principle had impressed Eisenhower. Konrad Adenauer regarded Dulles as "the greatest man" he had ever known, and one who "kept his word."[20] Dulles' rigid conception of a bipolar world, his wariness of letting himself be cajoled or pressured into concessions to Moscow, and his dour resolve endeared him to Adenauer and other leaders who feared a separate Soviet-American bargain.

In London, however, Dulles' invocations of a higher morality accentuated the increasingly incompatible perspectives of London and Washington. Throughout, Dulles vociferously supported the stated objectives of Great Britain and France while just as consistently resisting the use of force to vindicate them. He was extraordinarily creative about coming up with ideas to overcome the crisis, but, on closer examination, these dissolved into a time-consuming stalling action to blunt the Anglo-French rush to war. Had Dulles been prepared to insist on his own proposals, they might well have served as a practical solution to the Suez crisis— perhaps not the preferred outcome for Great Britain and France, but one they could have lived with.

Yet Dulles had barely returned to the United States before he disavowed the use of force, even if his own proposals to the Maritime Conference were rejected by Nasser. On August 3, he said:

> We do not . . . want to meet violence with violence. We want, first of all, to find out the opinion of the many nations vitally interested because we believe that all the nations concerned, including Egypt, will respect the sober opinion of the nations which are parties to the internationalizing treaty of 1888, or by its terms, entitled to its benefits.[21]

Moralistic rhetoric would not alter the reality that Dulles' refusal to consider force was pointing allied diplomacy toward a dead end. The only way to induce Nasser to accept Dulles' proposed Canal regime was by threatening him with British and French military intervention if he refused. Yet Dulles balanced each of his schemes for international control of the Canal with some statement emphatically abjuring the use of force, which practically invited Nasser to reject them.

Dulles had joined Great Britain and France in calling for a conference of the twenty-four principal users of the Suez Canal, including the eight countries that had signed the Constantinople Convention of 1888 establishing the regime Nasser was attempting to abrogate. The United States voted with the majority of eighteen nations to propose a new Canal regime, which accepted Egyptian sovereignty and participation by Egyptian personnel, but also established the Conference participants as *de facto* administrators of the Canal. However fertile in coming up with expedients, Dulles proved unwilling to employ sanctions other than public opinion to implement them. Denying that there was any inconsistency between his proposals and what he seemed to be prepared to do about them, Dulles insisted that, in the end, moral persuasion would convince Nasser to yield. In his view, most people:

> . . . pay decent respect for the opinions of mankind. . . . And because I believe that, I am confident that out of this conference there will come a judgment of such moral force that we can be confident that the Suez Canal will go on, as it has for the last 100 years, for the years in the future to serve in peace the interests of mankind.[22]

As it happened, moral pressure proved insufficient in precisely the same proportion to which physical force had been ruled out. On September 10, Nasser rejected the proposals of the London Maritime Conference.

Three days later, Dulles came up with another ingenious proposal. This time he proposed a Users' Association to operate the Canal and to collect dues by a kind of picket line of ships off the ports of Port Said and Suez, at either end of the Canal just outside of Egypt's territorial waters. If Nasser did not yield, the Users' Association would go ahead without him; if he went along, he would abdicate control over Canal revenues to an international body. The intricate scheme might well have worked had not Dulles, as he did with the Maritime Conference, undercut his own proposal. At a press conference on October 2, Dulles once again disavowed the use of force. He used the occasion as well to lecture Eden on the inappropriateness of the proposition that NATO should deal with Suez-type crises:

> There is some difference in the approaches to the Suez Canal problem. That difference relates perhaps to some rather fundamental things. In

some areas the three nations are bound together by treaties, such as the Atlantic pact area.... In those the three ... stand together.

Other problems relate to other areas and touch the so-called problem of colonialism in some way or other. On these problems the United States plays a somewhat independent role.[23]

Dulles' legal interpretation was valid enough, though, in the future, the shoe would turn out to be on the other foot. For America's allies would invoke the same argument when America needed their support in Vietnam and in other so-called "out of area" scenarios. Thus during the 1973 Middle East War, the European allies refused to permit the American airlift to Israel to overfly their territories, reversing the Suez script. Henceforth, it would be America's allies which would refuse to apply NATO obligations outside the strictly defined treaty area. What infuriated Great Britain and France in 1956 was not so much the legal interpretation as Dulles' strong implication that, in the Middle East, the United States defined its vital interests substantially differently from the way its European allies did.

This proved especially galling to London, because, only the day before Dulles' press conference, Eden had cabled Eisenhower that the issue was no longer Nasser but the Soviet Union:

> There is no doubt in our minds that Nasser, whether he likes it or not, is now effectively in Russian hands, just as Mussolini was in Hitler's. It would be as ineffective to show weakness to Nasser now in order to placate him as it was to show weakness to Mussolini.[24]

To Eden, Dulles' statement meant that the United States did not accept his proposition that the ultimate threat to Egypt came from the Soviet Union. He had wanted to frame the Egyptian issue in terms of the containment policy, whereas Dulles seemed to be writing off the whole affair as a colonial imbroglio which the United States, determined to preserve its image of moral purity, would not touch.

It is difficult to believe that Dulles was unaware of how dangerous a game he was playing. Though he acted as if he believed that the American public would respond best to lofty, self-righteous, and moralistic pronouncements, Dulles also had vast practical experience. He has left no explanation for his actions during the Suez crisis. It is plausible, however, that he was torn by two contradictory impulses. Given his attitude toward communism, he in all likelihood concurred with Eden and Mollet's analysis of the dangers of Soviet penetration of the Middle East. This would explain why his interpretation of Nasser's motives was indistinguishable from Eden's, and why the abruptness of his rejection of the Aswan Dam took even the British Cabinet (which had had a general warning) by surprise.

At the same time, Dulles was Secretary of State to a President who was passionately opposed to war in the way only an experienced military man can be. Eisenhower was not interested in the nuances of the balance of power; even if a long-range danger to the global equilibrium did exist in the Middle East, he concluded that America was strong enough to resist later on, and well before its actual survival was at stake. To Eisenhower, the Suez crisis was not sufficiently threatening to merit the use of force. His friendly grin notwithstanding, he had a very strong personality and a not very pleasant one when crossed.

As Dean Acheson once said, the effectiveness of a secretary of state depends on knowing who the president is. Dulles certainly knew, but Eden and Mollet, who believed Eisenhower to be an amiable figurehead, did not. They chose to ignore the implications of a letter Eisenhower had written to Eden on September 2 about the Maritime Conference, in which he warned once more against the use of force:

> ... the peoples of the Near East and of North Africa and, to some extent, of all of Asia and all of Africa, would be consolidated against the West to a degree which, I fear, could not be overcome in a generation and, perhaps, not even in a century particularly having in mind the capacity of the Russians to make mischief.[25]

Dulles was caught between an adamant Eisenhower and an outraged group of European allies. Eden and Mollet were beyond the point of retreat, and were infuriated by the incongruity between the toughness of Dulles' stated objectives and his repeated disavowal of the practical means for achieving them. They never understood how strongly Eisenhower was opposed to the use of force, or how dominant his views were. For Dulles, the gap between his allies and Nasser was less of a problem than the one between his President and the President's personal friends in Europe. He gambled on closing that gap with his dexterity, hoping that time might alter either their position or Eisenhower's, or lead Nasser into making some mistake that would solve everyone's dilemma. Instead, Dulles caused France and Great Britain to risk everything in a desperate throw of the dice.

The dilemma of Dulles' tactics was summed up in a journalist's question at a press conference on September 13: "Mr. Secretary, with the

United States announcing in advance it will not use force, and with Soviet Russia backing Egypt with its propaganda, does that not leave all the trump cards in Mr. Nasser's hands?"[26] Though Dulles replied vaguely that moral force would prevail, the question was right on the mark.

The growing rift among the democracies encouraged the Kremlin to raise the stakes. Stunning Washington, it replaced Western aid to the Aswan Dam with its own, and stepped up arms shipments to the Middle East. A boisterous Khrushchev told the Yugoslav Ambassador: "Don't forget that, if a war starts, all our support will be with Egypt. If my son were to come to me to volunteer to fight for Egypt, I would encourage him to go."[27]

After Dulles' October 2 press conference abjuring the use of force a second time, a desperate Great Britain and France decided to go ahead on their own. British and French military intervention was now only a few tactical moves away. One of these was a final appeal to the United Nations, which had played a curious role throughout the whole affair. At first, Great Britain and France had sought, with American backing, to avoid the United Nations altogether, fearing the Nonaligned group's solidarity with Egypt. As they edged closer to the end of their diplomatic tether, however, France and Great Britain did appeal to the United Nations as a sort of last perfunctory gesture to demonstrate that, because of the world organization's futility, they had no other choice than to act alone. The United Nations was thus transformed from a vehicle for solving international disputes to a final hurdle to be cleared before resorting to force, and, in a sense, even as an excuse for it.

Unexpectedly and for a brief moment, the United Nations rose to the occasion. Private consultations among the Egyptian, British, and French foreign ministers produced agreement on six principles which were very close to the majority view of the Maritime Conference. An Egyptian operating board and a supervisory Board of Users were established. Disputes between the two boards were to be settled by arbitration. Eisenhower was elated as he spoke before a television audience on October 12:

> I have an announcement. I have got the best announcement that I think I could possibly make to America tonight.
>
> The progress made in the settlement of the Suez dispute this afternoon at the United Nations is most gratifying. Egypt, Britain and France have met, through their foreign ministers, and agreed on a set of principles on which to negotiate; and it looks like here is a very great crisis that is behind us.[28]

Though Eisenhower had not exactly said, "Peace is at hand," the celebrations his statement evoked turned out to be premature. The very next night, on October 13, the Security Council was asked to endorse the Six Principles and encountered an unpleasant surprise. In two separate votes, the Principles were unanimously approved but their implementing measures were vetoed by the Soviet Union.

The Six Principles had been the last chance to settle the crisis peacefully. American pressure on Egypt might have induced it to ask the Soviet Union to withdraw its veto—assuming that veto had not arisen from the collusion of these two countries in the first place. Then too, American pressure on the Soviet Union in the form of a warning that, in a showdown, the United States would stand with its allies, might have kept the Soviets from casting the veto. But the United States was determined to maintain the friendship of its allies *and* to keep open its option toward the Nonaligned group. America's attempt to straddle incompatible policies made war inevitable.

Eden and Mollet had gone along with every formula for avoiding war: the Maritime Conference, the Users' Association, and now the Six Principles. In each case, a promising beginning had run aground; in no case had America used its diplomatic influence on behalf of proposals Dulles had either devised or endorsed. But even though Great Britain and France had many understandable reasons to go to war, they imposed a fatal burden on themselves by using a ridiculously obvious stratagem as a pretext. Concocted by France, the ploy required that Israel invade Egypt and advance toward the Suez Canal, whereupon Great Britain and France would demand, in the name of freedom of navigation, that both Egypt and Israel withdraw to a distance of ten miles from the Canal. In the event of Egypt's refusal, which was fully expected, Great Britain and France would occupy the Canal Zone. What was to be done afterward remained vague. The plan would be triggered a week before the American presidential election.

Everybody lost by this convoluted scheme. For one thing, it was totally inconsistent with the diplomacy in train since Nasser's seizure of the Suez Canal, which had been geared to establishing some sort of international regimen over the operation of the Canal. Since the various internationally endorsed schemes to guarantee free navigation had aborted, the logical next step would have been for Great Britain and France to impose one of them by force. Though their unilateral action would no doubt have been widely opposed, it would at least have been comprehensible in light of the preceding diplomacy. By contrast, the actual French and British maneuver was too transparent and too cynical.

Each of the partners would have been better off pursuing its objectives independently. Great Britain and France undermined their claim to be major powers by seeming to need Israel's help to take on Egypt. Israel lost the moral advantage of its neighbor's refusal to discuss peace by allowing itself to appear as a tool of colonialism. Great Britain's position in Jordan and Iraq, its key Middle East bastions, was weakened. Eisenhower was deeply offended by a maneuver so seemingly geared to his presumed reluctance to antagonize Jewish voters in the last week of an election campaign.[29] It takes perseverance to find a policy which combines the disadvantages of every course of action, or to construct a coalition that weakens every partner simultaneously. Great Britain, France, and Israel managed just that feat.

Seemingly oblivious to the international outrage awaiting them, Great Britain and France compounded their political problems by adopting a military strategy so deliberate as to give the appearance of procrastination. On October 29, Israel invaded the Sinai. On October 30, Great Britain and France demanded that both sides withdraw from the Canal, which Israeli troops had not yet reached. On October 31, Great Britain and France announced that they would intervene on the ground. Yet British and French troops did not land in Egypt for another four days, and never fulfilled their mission to seize the Canal in the few days they were on the ground.

What no one had counted on was America's aroused sense of righteousness. On October 30, twenty-four hours after Israel's initial attack, the United States submitted a tough resolution in the Security Council ordering Israeli armed forces "immediately to withdraw . . . behind the established armistice lines."[30] No demand was made to condemn Egyptian-sponsored terrorism or the illegal Arab blockade of the Gulf of Aqaba. When Great Britain and France entered the conflict on October 31, Eisenhower turned on them as well in a television address on the same day:

> As it is the manifest right of any of these nations to take such decisions and actions, it is likewise our right—if our judgment so dictates—to dissent. We believe these actions to have been taken in error. For we do not accept the use of force as a wise and proper instrument for the settlement of international disputes.[31]

So absolute a renunciation of force was not a principle the Eisenhower Administration had ever applied to itself—for example, when it arranged the overthrow of the Guatemalan government two years earlier. Nor was it followed two years later, when Eisenhower ordered American troops into Lebanon. This was the first and only time that the United States was to vote with the Soviet Union against its closest allies. Eisenhower told the American people that, in view of the expected British and French veto in the Security Council, he would take his case to the General Assembly, where their veto would not apply.

On November 2, the General Assembly demanded an end to the hostilities by an overwhelming vote of sixty-four to five. At an overnight session on November 3–4, it passed an even stronger resolution and began to discuss a United Nations peacekeeping force for the Canal—a token move to facilitate British and French withdrawal, since United Nations forces are never kept on the soil of a sovereign country against its wishes, and Nasser was certain to demand their removal.

By November 5, a United Nations peacekeeping force was established. That same day, Great Britain and France announced that their troops would withdraw as soon as the United Nations force was in place—perhaps with the *arrière pensée* that their forces could be part of the United Nations contingent. Adding to the poignancy of America's collusion in the humiliation of its closest allies, Soviet forces crushed Hungarian freedom fighters that very day, in the face of what can only, and with excessive charity, be described as token United Nations opposition.

On the night of November 5, a week after the British and French ultimatum and twenty-four hours after Soviet tanks had begun to crush the Hungarian uprising, the Soviet Union was heard from. The obvious split between America and its allies enabled Moscow to pose as Egypt's protector at minimal risk, unleashing a veritable blizzard of communications. Foreign Minister Shepilov wrote to the President of the Security Council; Prime Minister Bulganin addressed himself to Eden, Mollet, Eisenhower, and David Ben-Gurion, the Israeli Prime Minister. The theme in all five messages was the same: "predatory" aggression against Egypt must cease; the United Nations needed to organize a joint effort to that end; the Soviet Union would cooperate by making its naval and air forces available.

As if all these pronouncements were not menacing enough, Bulganin's letter contained warnings that were tailored to each of the separate addressees. Eden, for instance, was vouchsafed the first explicit Soviet threat of rocket attacks against a Western ally, albeit in the guise of this rhetorical question:

In what situation would Britain find herself if she were attacked by stronger states, possessing all types of modern destructive weapons? And such countries could, at the present time, refrain from sending naval or air forces to the shores of Britain and use other means—for instance, rocket weapons.[32]

Lest the query be misunderstood, Bulganin inserted one more menacing sentence: "We are fully determined to crush the aggressors by the use of force and to restore peace in the East."[33] Similar warnings were issued to Mollet. Though less specific, the letter to Ben-Gurion was even more threatening, because it stressed that Israeli actions were putting "in jeopardy the very existence of Israel as a state."[34]

Finally, in his letter to Eisenhower, Bulganin proposed joint Soviet-American military action to put an end to the hostilities in the Middle East. He went so far as to hint at a third world war: "If this war is not curbed, it is fraught with the danger of, and can develop into, a third world war."[35] Coming from the only other country in a position to start such a war, this was ominous indeed.

The Soviet threats featured that extraordinary bravado which was to become the distinguishing feature of Khrushchev's diplomacy. At the precise moment that Soviet troops were brutally suppressing freedom fighters in Hungary, the Soviet Union had the temerity to bemoan the fate of alleged victims of Western imperialism. Only a reckless nature could have permitted Khrushchev to voice the threat of a third world war in 1956, when the Soviet Union was incomparably weaker than the United States, especially in the nuclear field. The Soviet Union was not only in no position for a showdown but, as it became imminent, Khrushchev would have been obliged to retreat as ignominiously as he in fact did six years later over the Cuban missile crisis.

Eisenhower indignantly rejected joint military action with the Soviet Union and warned that the United States would resist any unilateral Soviet military move. At the same time, the Soviet warning intensified Washington's pressure on Great Britain and France. On November 6, a run on the pound sterling took on alarming proportions. Contrary to previous practice, America stood at the sidelines and refused to step in and calm the market.

Battered in the House of Commons, finding little support in the Commonwealth, and utterly abandoned by the United States, Eden threw in the towel. On November 6, he agreed to a ceasefire starting the next day. British and French forces had been on the ground for less than forty-eight hours.

The British and French expedition had been ham-handedly conceived and amateurishly implemented; designed in frustration, and lacking a clear-cut political objective, it doomed itself to failure. The United States could never have supported so flawed an enterprise. Yet the gnawing question remains whether America's dissociation from its allies needed to be quite so brutal. Did the United States really have no other choice than either to support the French and British adventure or to oppose it outright? Legally, the United States had no obligations toward Great Britain and France beyond the clearly defined NATO area. But the issue was not strictly legal. Was the United States' national interest really served by bringing home in so ruthless a fashion to two of America's most indispensable allies that they had lost all capacity for autonomous action?

The United States was under no obligation to push United Nations deliberations at the extraordinarily rapid pace that it did, or to support resolutions which ignored the sources of the provocation and focused entirely on the immediate issues. The United States could have called attention to all the various international schemes to insulate the operation of the Canal, to the illegal Arab blockade of the Gulf of Aqaba, or to Nasser's encouragement of terrorist raids against Israel. Above all, it could, and should, have linked its condemnation of British and French actions with condemnation of Soviet actions in Hungary. By acting as if the Suez issue were entirely moral and legal, and as if it had no geopolitical basis, the United States evaded the reality that an unconditional victory for Nasser—an outcome in which Egypt gave no guarantees with respect to the operation of the Canal—was also a victory for a radical policy encouraged by Soviet arms and sustained by Soviet threats.

The heart of the problem was conceptual. America's leaders put forward three principles during the Suez crisis, each of which reflected long-standing verities: that America's obligations toward its allies were circumscribed by precise legal documents; that recourse to force by any nation was inadmissible except when narrowly defined as self-defense; and, most important, that the Suez crisis had provided America with an opportunity to pursue its true vocation, which was leadership of the developing world.

The first point was made in Eisenhower's address of October 31, in which he threw America's full diplomatic weight against Great Britain and France: "There can be no peace—without law. And there can be no law —if we were to invoke one code of international conduct for those who oppose us—and another for our friends."[36] The notion that international relations could be exhaustively defined by international law had roots deep within American history. The assumption that America should act as the impartial moral arbiter of the behavior of nations, unaffected by national interest or geopolitics or alliances, is part of that nostalgia. In the real world, however, diplomacy involves, at least in part, the ability to discriminate among cases and to distinguish friends from opponents.

The strict constructionist view that the sole legitimate cause for war is self-defense was put forward in December 1956 by John Foster Dulles, who interpreted Article 1 of the NATO treaty as creating that obligation:

> ...the point was that we considered that such an attack under the circumstances would violate the charter of the United Nations, and would violate article 1 of the North Atlantic Treaty itself, which requires all the parties to that treaty to renounce the use of force, and to settle their disputes by peaceful means. That is our complaint: that the treaty was violated; not that there was not consultation.[37]

Nobody had ever interpreted Article 1 of the North Atlantic Treaty in so pacifist a way; no one would do so again. The idea that the charter of a military alliance contained a binding obligation for the peaceful resolution of all disputes was surely mind-boggling. In any event, the real issue was not legal, but whether an alliance does not include the tacit obligation to show some understanding for an ally's definition of its vital interests even outside a strictly defined treaty area, and perhaps a little compassion for an occasional difference in judgments.

George Kennan and Walter Lippmann, the two great adversaries in America's earlier debate over containment, clearly thought so. George Kennan urged forbearance:

> We have fumbled on certain past occasions; and our friends have not turned against us. Moreover, we bear a heavy measure of responsibility for the desperation which has driven the French and British Governments to this ill-conceived and pathetic action.[38]

Walter Lippmann went further and argued that America had a stake in British and French success:

> The Franco-British action will be judged by the outcome. . . . The American interest, though we have dissented from the decision itself, is that France and Britain should now succeed. However much we may wish they had not started, we cannot now wish that they should fail.[39]

The third premise of America's policy, its secret dream of emerging as the leader of the developing world, proved impossible to fulfill. Richard Nixon, probably the most sophisticated student of the national interest among America's postwar leaders, placed America into the vanguard of the anticolonial struggle on November 2, four days before the election, when he proclaimed:

> For the first time in history we have shown independence of Anglo-French policies toward Asia and Africa which seemed to us to reflect the colonial tradition. That declaration of independence has had an electrifying effect throughout the world.[40]

In the light of Nixon's later pronouncements, it is hard to believe that he was doing anything other than following instructions.

Yet that was not at all what actually happened. Nasser did not moderate his policies toward either the West or its Arab allies. His radical constituency would not have permitted him to admit that he had been saved by American pressures even if he had been inclined to do so. On the contrary, to impress that very constituency, he accelerated his attacks on moderate, pro-Western governments in the Middle East. Within two years of the Suez crisis, the pro-Western government of Iraq was overthrown and replaced by one of the most radical regimes in the Arab world, eventually giving rise to Saddam Hussein. Syria too turned increasingly radical. Within five years, Egyptian troops entered Yemen in what turned into a futile effort to overthrow the existing regime. Since, in the end, the United States inherited the strategic positions abandoned by Great Britain, the full fury of Nasser's radicalism was unleashed against America, culminating in a break of diplomatic relations in 1967.

Nor did America improve its standing among the rest of the Nonaligned. Within a few months of the Suez crisis, America was no better off among the Nonaligned than Great Britain. It was not that the majority of the Nonaligned had suddenly become ill-disposed toward the United States, only that they had come to understand their leverage. What these nations remembered most about the Suez crisis was not America's support of Nasser but that Nasser had achieved major successes by his dexterity at playing the superpowers off against each other. The Suez crisis also served as the Nonaligned nations' first exposure to another seminal truth of the Cold War: that applying pressure on the United States generally elicited protestations of good faith and efforts to alleviate the stated grievance, whereas applying pressure on the Soviet Union could be risky, because the Soviets' invariable response was a tough dose of counterpressure.

In the decades following the Suez crisis, these tendencies became magnified. Castigation of American policies turned into the ritual of Nonaligned conferences. Condemnation of Soviet actions in declarations published at the end of periodic Nonaligned meetings was extremely rare and circumspect. Since it was statistically unlikely that the United States was always wrong, the Nonaligned's tilt had to reflect a calculation of interest, not a moral judgment.

The most profound consequence of the Suez crisis ran along both sides of the fault line through Central Europe. Anwar Sadat, then chief propagandist for Egypt, wrote on November 19:

> There are only two Great Powers in the world today, the United States and the Soviet Union. . . . The ultimatum put Britain and France in their right place, as Powers neither big nor strong.[41]

America's allies drew the same conclusion. The Suez crisis brought home to them that one of the premises of the Atlantic Alliance—the congruence of interests between Europe and the United States—was at best only partially valid. From this point on, the argument that Europe did not need nuclear weapons because it could always count on American support ran up against the memory of Suez. Great Britain, of course, had always had an independent deterrent. As for France, an article of November 9, 1956, in the French daily *Le Populaire* expressed what was to become a fixed French attitude: "The French government will without doubt take the decision shortly to manufacture nuclear weapons. . . . The Soviet threat to use rockets has dissipated all fictions and illusions."[42]

The Suez players were not alone in feeling the jolts of America's disavowal of its closest allies. Chancellor Adenauer, as good a friend of America as there was in postwar Europe, vastly admired Dulles. Yet even he viewed America's Suez diplomacy as a potential precursor of some kind of global arrangement between the United States and the Soviet Union for which Europe would end up paying the price.

Adenauer happened to be in Paris on November 6, the day Eden and Mollet decided they would have to yield to American pressures. According to French Foreign Minister Christian Pineau, Adenauer said:

> France and England will never be powers comparable to the United States and the Soviet Union. Nor Germany, either. There remains to them only one way of playing a decisive role in the world; that is to unite to make Europe. England is not ripe for it but the affair of Suez will help to prepare her spirits for it. We have no time to waste: Europe will be your revenge.[43]

This statement illuminates the reasoning behind later Franco-German policy, culminating in de Gaulle's 1963 treaty of friendship and consultation with Adenauer.

Great Britain, drawing many of the same analytical conclusions as France had about its own relative weakness, put them in the service of quite a different policy. Turning away from European unity, Great Britain opted for permanent subordination to American policy. Before Suez, Great Britain had already become well aware of its dependence on the United States, though it had continued to conduct itself as a Great Power. After Suez, it interpreted the "special relationship" with America as a means of gaining maximum influence over decisions which were essentially made in Washington.

The most pernicious impact of the Suez crisis was on the Soviet Union. Within a year of the "spirit of Geneva," the Soviet Union had managed to penetrate the Middle East, to put down a revolt in Hungary, and to threaten rocket attacks against Western Europe. Throughout, international opprobrium had focused on Great Britain and France, while much more brutal actions by the Soviet Union in Hungary had received at best perfunctory condemnation.

Khrushchev's ideology and personality caused him to ascribe American conduct to weakness rather than to high principle. What had begun as a tentative Czechoslovakian arms deal with Egypt had turned into a major Soviet strategic breakthrough which divided the Atlantic Alliance and caused developing nations to turn to Moscow as a way of increasing their bargaining power. Khrushchev was euphoric. His high spirits propelled him onto a roller-coaster ride through one confrontation after another, starting with his Berlin ultimatum of 1958 and ending with his humiliation during the Cuban missile crisis of 1962.

For all the pain it caused, the Suez crisis had marked America's ascension into world leadership. With a sigh of relief, America used the occasion of Suez to cut itself loose from allies it had always held accountable for the blight of *Realpolitik* and for their flawed devotion to the balance of power. But, life being what it is, America would not be permitted to remain pristine. Suez turned out to be America's initiation into the realities of global power, one of the lessons of which is that vacuums always get filled and that the principal issue is not whether, but by whom. Having evicted Great Britain and France from their historic roles in the Middle East, America found that responsibility for the balance of power in that region had fallen squarely on its own shoulders.

On November 29, 1956, the United States government, hailing the recent Baghdad Pact summit of the leaders of Pakistan, Iraq, Turkey, and Iran, declared: "A threat to the territorial integrity or political independence of the members would be viewed by the United States with the utmost gravity."[44] It was the diplomats' way of saying that the United

States would undertake the defense of the Baghdad Pact states, a role for which Great Britain was now too weak and too discredited.

On January 5, 1957, Eisenhower sent a message to the Congress asking for approval of what came to be known as the Eisenhower Doctrine—a threefold Middle East program of economic aid, military assistance, and protection against communist aggression.[45] In his State of the Union Address of January 10, 1957, Eisenhower went even further by proclaiming America's commitment to the defense of the entire free world:

> First, America's vital interests are worldwide, embracing both hemispheres and every continent.
> Second, we have community of interest with every nation in the free world.
> Third, interdependence of interests requires a decent respect for the rights and the peace of all peoples.[46]

America's attempt to dissociate from Europe had landed it in the position of having to assume by itself the burden of protecting every free (that is, noncommunist) nation in every region of the globe. Though during the Suez crisis America was still attempting to deal with the ambiguities of equilibrium in the developing world via the United Nations, within two years American forces would be landing in Lebanon in pursuit of the Eisenhower Doctrine. A decade later, America would be grappling with it all alone in Vietnam, most of its allies having dissociated from it by invoking many an argument from the days of Suez as scripted by America itself.

CHAPTER TWENTY-TWO

Hungary:
Upheaval in the Empire

In 1956, two concurrent events transformed the postwar pattern of international relations. The Suez crisis marked the end of innocence for the Western Alliance; henceforth, the Western allies would never again be able fully to believe in their own avowals of a perfect symmetry of interests. Simultaneously, the bloody suppression of the Hungarian uprising showed that the Soviet Union would maintain its sphere of interest, by force if necessary, and that talk of liberation was empty. There could no longer be any doubt that the Cold War would be both protracted and bitter, with hostile armies facing each other across the dividing line of Europe as far into the future as anyone could see.

The Hungarians' doomed struggle against Soviet domination grew out of an explosive mix of historic Russian imperialism, Soviet ideology, and fierce Hungarian nationalism. In one sense, Hungary was just another victim of the Russian expansionism which had been going on relentlessly since the time of Peter the Great. Historically the Russian state had sought to repress nations trying to conduct a truly independent policy on Russia's borders—a temptation which has persisted into the post–Cold War period. But that was usually only the beginning of Russia's problems. After quelling independence, the Russians were obliged to maintain a costly military presence in the neighboring state, draining Russia's treasury without enhancing Russia's security. As George Kennan wrote, ". . . the Czars' regime actually perished of indigestion (from) the Western minorities in Europe which it had been foolish enough to bite off."[1]

The same pattern was repeated under communist rule. Stalin recovered all the tsarist territory that had been lost at the end of the First World War, and added what came to be known as the satellite orbit in Eastern Europe, occupied by the Red Army and controlled by Soviet-style governments imposed from Moscow. Imperial rule, which was complicated enough under the tsars, grew even more problematic under the communists, who compounded their subject populations' hatred of foreign rule by imposing an untenable economic system.

Soviet-style central planning proved intolerable in the long run, even in the Soviet Union; in the satellite orbit, it was disastrous from the start. Before the Second World War, Czechoslovakia's standard of living had been comparable to that of Switzerland. Afterward, it was reduced to the gray and monotonous pattern which characterized the entire communist sphere. Poland had an industrial base as large as Italy's and greater resources, but was sentenced to subsist at the Eastern European level of institutionalized poverty. East Germans saw the communist system as the sole obstacle to sharing in the economic well-being of the Federal Republic. The population of every country in Eastern Europe was convinced that it was sacrificing its own well-being for the sake of communist ideology and Soviet hegemony.

Whereas in the Soviet Union communism could present itself as an indigenous phenomenon, in Eastern Europe there could be no question that it had been imposed under duress and that ancient national traditions were being suffocated. Even with full control over the police, the mass media, and the educational system, the communists in the satellite states were—and felt themselves to be—a beleaguered minority. Lenin had written that it would be folly for the Bolsheviks to follow the policies of Tsar Nicholas II by imposing their ways on their neighbors. But by the time of Stalin's death, the main distinction between communist rule and that of the autocratic tsar was that Stalin had in fact been far more brutal and heavy-handed. Ultimately, Soviet policy came up against the same problem that had confounded Russia earlier in its history: Eastern Europe, communized to enhance the security of the Soviet state, consumed resources and high-level attention to the point of becoming more of a burden than a strategic prize.

Stalin believed that the Eastern European satellites could only be held in place by total and intrusive control from Moscow. In 1948, Tito, the only communist ruler in Eastern Europe who had come to power largely by his own efforts, let it be known that Belgrade would pursue its own course independent of directives from Moscow. Stalin retaliated by expelling Yugoslavia from the Cominform. Belying Stalin's expectation that he would collapse quickly, Tito survived, with the aid of the Western democracies, which temporarily suspended their ideological objections to old-fashioned balance-of-power considerations.

Stalin reacted to Tito's show of independence by resorting to his tried-and-true method for restoring discipline—show trials throughout the satellite orbit, leading to the juridical murder of anybody capable of independent thought. As in the Moscow purges of the previous decade, few—if any—of the victims of this latest terror had engaged in opposition. They were, after all, lifelong communists who had served as the instruments of Soviet-imposed communist rule: Rudolf Slansky in Czechoslovakia, Laszlo Rajk in Hungary, Traicho Kostov in Bulgaria, and Wladyslaw Gomulka in Poland (the only one who survived). The purge of these men, all of whom their publics had regarded as tools of Moscow, brought home the moral bankruptcy of the communist system even to those few who still believed in its pronouncements.

Too insecure to pursue the tyrant's brand of repression, Stalin's successors were also too divided to permit heterodoxy within the Soviet bloc. They were caught up in two contradictory fears: that repression in Eastern Europe would thwart the much-needed relaxation of tensions with the West, and that liberalization in the satellite orbit might lead to the collapse of the whole communist edifice. (Fear of Western reaction had not, however, kept them from sending tanks to put down an East German uprising in June of 1953.) By 1955, they had decided to live with Eastern European nationalism as long as a country's leadership remained safely communist, and they chose reconciliation with Tito as the appropriate symbol of their new approach. In May 1955, Khrushchev and Bulganin visited Belgrade to patch things up. However, as was to be the case with every subsequent attempt at reform, the effort to liberalize served to open the floodgates.

After Khrushchev's speech to the Twentieth Party Congress in February 1956 detailing Stalin's crimes, communism was discredited even further. The exception was Yugoslavia, where it had grafted itself onto a nationalistic cause. It soon transpired that Stalin had correctly understood the Titoist threat to the Soviet Union. For the leaders of the satellite countries faced the paradox that, in order to achieve any kind of public approval, they needed to acquire some nationalistic credentials. They had to present themselves as Polish, Czech, or Hungarian communists rather than as puppets of the Kremlin. In the wake of Khrushchev's visit to Belgrade, the Kremlin's control over the satellite regimes of Eastern Europe came under increasing stress.

Throughout these events, the United States maintained an essentially passive attitude. A central premise of containment had been to leave the liberation of Eastern Europe to the erosion of time and not to challenge Soviet control frontally. During the 1952 presidential campaign, John Foster Dulles attacked this policy as being too passive in an article in *Life* magazine entitled "A Policy of Boldness." Dulles argued that the nations of Eastern Europe—for which he coined the term "captive nations"— were close to despair, "because the United States, the historic leader of the forces of freedom, seems dedicated to the negative policy of 'containment' and 'stalemate.' " He urged the United States to make "it publicly known that it wants and expects liberation to occur."[2]

Yet what did "liberation" mean operationally? Dulles was too serious a student of Soviet affairs to respond brutally to doubt that the Soviet Union would suppress any upheaval. After all, Stalin was still alive when Dulles wrote his article. Dulles therefore explicitly rejected the encouragement of "a series of bloody uprisings and reprisals." What he had in mind, Dulles said, was "peaceful separation from Moscow" on the Tito model, helped along by American propaganda and other nonmilitary measures.

Whereas Acheson had supported Tito after his break with Moscow based on *Realpolitik*, Dulles imbued essentially the same policy with a touch of universal idealism by calling it "liberation." In practice, Dulles' liberation theory was an attempt to increase the cost to Moscow of consolidating its conquests without increasing the risks for the United States. Dulles was encouraging Titoism, not democracy, and the difference between his ideas and those of Acheson turned out to be an oratorical nuance.

To be sure, Dulles' critics ascribed to him views on freeing Eastern

Europe which he had not actually expressed. But it was also the case that he refrained from correcting them. Dulles had been a principal patron of institutions such as Radio Free Europe and Radio Liberty, the major purpose of which was to keep the principles of freedom alive in Eastern Europe while encouraging sentiments capable of igniting revolt. There was nothing subtle about Radio Free Europe's approach. On the theory that its pronouncements were not official, it advocated "liberation" in the most literal and militant sense of the word. Unfortunately, the distinction between the "private" and "official" musings of government-financed American institutions proved too elusive for East European freedom fighters to comprehend.

It thus happened that, at almost precisely the same moment that the Western democracies were preoccupied with Suez, the Soviet Union found itself in severe straits in two of its key satellites, Poland and Hungary.

Poland was the first to ignite. In June, riots in the industrial city of Poznan were bloodily suppressed and resulted in dozens of deaths and hundreds more wounded. In October, those leaders on the Polish Communist Party's Central Committee who had survived Stalin's purges of the previous years decided to ally themselves with the cause of Polish nationalism. Gomulka, purged and disgraced in 1951, was asked to return as First Secretary of the Communist Party, attending his first Politburo meeting on October 13, 1956. Soviet Marshal Konstantin Rokossovsky, who had been installed as Defense Minister and had been imposed as a member of the Polish Politburo since 1949, was dismissed, ending one of the most humiliating symbols of Soviet tutelage. The Polish Communist Party issued a proclamation that Poland would henceforth pursue a "national road to socialism," a statement which, given Poland's passionate nationalist feelings and indifference to socialism, could hardly have sounded reassuring to Moscow.

For a moment, the Kremlin toyed with the idea of military intervention. Soviet tanks began to move toward the principal cities when, on October 19, Khrushchev, accompanied by his Politburo colleagues Kaganovich, Mikoyan, and Molotov, descended on Warsaw.

The Polish leaders did not blink. They informed the Soviet General Secretary that his visit was not being treated as a party-to-party meeting and that he would therefore not be received at the Communist Party Central Committee headquarters. Instead, the Soviet delegation was asked to repair to the Belvedere Palace, which was reserved for state guests.

At the last moment, Khrushchev recoiled. On October 20, Soviet troops were ordered to withdraw to their bases. On October 22, Khrushchev endorsed Gomulka's installation as General Secretary of the Communist Party in exchange for the promise that the new leaders would preserve the socialist system and maintain Poland's membership in the Warsaw Pact. Formally, the Soviet defense system had remained intact. Nevertheless, the reliability of the Polish troops in any war with the West could no longer be considered unqualified, to put it charitably.

The Soviet Union backed down and permitted national communism to carry the day in Poland, in part because repression would have meant coping with a population of over 30 million whose proven courage and willingness to resist foreigners was magnified by memories of historic Russian oppression and Soviet atrocities. But most important, at the same moment the Kremlin was being tested even more severely in Hungary.

A country of 9 million people, Hungary had undergone the same cycle of Soviet oppression as its neighbors. Since the 1940s, it had been governed by the ruthless Mátyás Rákosi, an orthodox Stalinist. In the 1930s Stalin had actually ransomed him from a Budapest prison in return for Hungarian flags captured by the tsar's army in 1849. Many Hungarians would have reason to regret that bargain when Rákosi returned with the Red Army and set up a system of repression that was considered severe even by Stalinist standards.

Shortly after the Berlin uprising of 1953, Rákosi's time finally ran out. Summoned to Moscow, he was told by Beria in the inimitably brutal Stalinist fashion that, although Hungary had been ruled by diverse nationalities, it had never had a Jewish king, and the Soviet leadership was not about to allow one now.[3] Rákosi was replaced by Imre Nagy, who had the reputation of being a reform communist and, as it happened, was a Jew as well—though he applied less tyrannical methods. Two years later, after the overthrow of Georgi Malenkov in Moscow, Nagy was dismissed and Rákosi returned as Prime Minister. Once again, strict communist orthodoxy was imposed. Artists and intellectuals were repressed, and Nagy was expelled from the Communist Party.

Stalin's successors lacked his deadly single-mindedness, however. Not only was Nagy permitted to survive, he published a treatise challenging the Soviet Union's right to intervene in the domestic affairs of fellow communist states. Meanwhile, Rákosi, now in his second tour of power, proved to be no more responsive to the aspirations of his people than he had been during his first. After Khrushchev's denunciation of Stalin at the Twentieth Party Congress, Rákosi was again replaced, this time by his close associate Erno Gero.

Though Gero proclaimed himself a nationalist, he was so closely identified with Rákosi that he was unable to stem the patriotic tide sweeping the country. On October 23, the day after Gomulka's formal return to power in Poland, public outrage boiled over in Budapest. Students distributed a list of demands that went considerably beyond the reforms that had been achieved in Poland; these included freedom of speech, a trial for Rákosi and his associates, the departure of Soviet troops, and Nagy's return to office. When Nagy appeared before a huge throng in Parliament Square, he was still a reform communist and his program consisted of introducing some democratic procedures into the communist system. He asked the disappointed crowd to have confidence that the Communist Party would implement the reforms needed.

But it was too late to ask the Hungarian people to entrust the hated Communist Party with rectifying its own transgressions. What happened next was straight out of a movie in which the main character is induced, reluctantly and perhaps even uncomprehendingly, to undertake a mission he did not choose that then turns into his destiny. A staunch, if reformist, communist his entire life, Nagy seemed determined in his initial appearances during the uprising to salvage the Communist Party, much as Gomulka had done in Poland. But as the days passed, he was transformed by the passions of his people into a living symbol of the truth laid down by de Tocqueville a century earlier:

> . . . experience suggests that the most dangerous moment for an evil government is usually when it begins to reform itself. Only great ingenuity can save a prince who undertakes to give relief to his subjects after long oppression. The sufferings that are endured patiently, as being inevitable, become intolerable the moment it appears that there might be an escape. Reform then only serves to reveal more clearly what still remains oppressive and now all the more unbearable.[4]

Nagy was to pay with his life for the vision of democracy that overtook him so belatedly. After the Soviets crushed the revolution, they offered Nagy the opportunity to recant. His refusal and subsequent execution assured him a place in the pantheon of those martyred to the cause of freedom in Eastern Europe.

On October 24, public demonstrations turned into a full-blown revolution. Soviet tanks, hastily entering the fray, were set on fire and government buildings were seized. On the same day, Nagy was appointed Prime Minister and two members of the Soviet Politburo, Mikoyan and Suslov, arrived in Hungary to assess the situation. By October 28, the Soviet visitors appeared to have reached a conclusion similar to the one Khrushchev had drawn in Warsaw—to settle for a Titoist Hungary. Soviet tanks began to withdraw from Budapest. But even that move could not calm matters as it had in Poland. The demonstrators were now demanding nothing less than the establishment of a multiparty system, the departure of Soviet troops from all of Hungary, and withdrawal from the Warsaw Pact.

As these events unfolded, American policy remained ostentatiously circumspect. Despite all its talk of "liberation," Washington had clearly not anticipated so elemental an outburst. It seemed torn between a desire to help the process along as much as possible and its fear that too forward a policy would give the Soviets a pretext for intervention. Above all, Washington demonstrated that it is rarely able to handle two major crises simultaneously. While Hungarian students and workers battled Soviet tanks in the streets, Washington stood silent. Moscow was never warned that the threat or the use of force would jeopardize its relations with Washington.

The United States did appeal to the Security Council on October 27, in light of "the situation created by the action of foreign military forces in Hungary."[5] But it was dealt with in so desultory a fashion that a vote on the resulting Security Council resolution did not come until November 4, after the Soviet intervention had already occurred.

The interval was filled by Radio Free Europe, which took it upon itself to interpret American attitudes, urging Hungarians to step up the pace of their revolution and to reject any compromise. For example, on October 29, Radio Free Europe greeted Imre Nagy's installation as the new Prime Minister with this hostile broadcast:

> Imre Nagy and his supporters want to revise and modernize the Trojan Horse episode. They need a cease-fire so that the present government in power in Budapest can maintain its position as long as possible. Those who are fighting for liberty must not lose sight even for a minute of the plans of the government opposing them.[6]

When, on October 30, Nagy abolished the one-party system and appointed a coalition government composed of representatives of all the democratic parties that had participated in the last free elections, in 1946, Radio Free Europe remained unconvinced:

> The Ministry of Defense and the Ministry of the Interior are still in Communist hands. Do not let this continue, Freedom Fighters. Do not hang your weapons on the wall.[7]

Although Radio Free Europe was funded by the American government, it was run by an independent board and by administrators who did not receive official instructions from the administration. However, it was too much to expect Hungary's freedom fighters to understand the distinction between the United States government and the pronouncements of a radio station which had been expressly created as a vehicle for promulgating the "liberation" policy which the Secretary of State had claimed to be his own invention.

On the few occasions the Eisenhower Administration did speak out, it seemed above all eager to reassure the Soviets. Unintentionally, its pronouncements proved nearly as inflammatory as the Radio Free Europe broadcasts. On October 27, as Soviet troops seemed to be pulling out of the Hungarian capital, Dulles delivered a speech in Dallas which made it seem as if the United States was hoping to lure Hungary out of the Soviet orbit without Moscow's noticing it. Any Eastern European country that broke with Moscow, said Dulles, could count on American aid. Nor would this aid be conditioned "upon the adoption by these countries of any particular form of society." In other words, to be eligible for American aid, an Eastern European country did not need to become democratic; it was enough for it to pursue the Titoist model, and to leave the Warsaw Pact. In an archetypal American statement, Dulles coupled this comment with an assertion of selflessness. According to its Secretary of State, the United States had "no ulterior purpose in desiring the independence of the satellite countries," nor did it look upon them as "potential military allies."[8]

Far from proving reassuring, that staple of American diplomatic rhetoric—the claim to an absence of any ulterior motive—has usually been interpreted as a sign of either unpredictability or arbitrariness, even among non-Marxist leaders. At any rate, at that point Moscow was far more anxious about American actions than about American motives. Eight years earlier, Moscow had vetoed Eastern European participation in the Marshall Plan because it had perceived American economic aid as a form of capitalist ensnarement. Dulles' offer of economic aid to defectors from the Warsaw Pact was bound to confirm that specter. The potential political earthquake was rendered all the more credible by Dulles' flamboyant implication that Hungary's reversal of its military alliances was being prevented, above all, by American self-restraint.

Paralleling Dulles' course of incendiary reassurance to the Soviets, Eisenhower delivered a speech on October 31 which was particularly notable for its omission of so much as a hint that the Soviet Union would incur penalties if it resorted to repression. Eisenhower was probably persuaded to adopt a conciliatory tone because, the day before, the Soviet Union had promulgated seemingly forthcoming, if ambiguous, criteria for the stationing of Soviet troops in Eastern Europe. At the same time, Eisenhower must have been aware of the massive movement of Soviet reinforcements into the rest of Hungary, which had begun simultaneously. Eisenhower's restraint toward the Soviet Union was all the more remarkable when compared to his castigation of Great Britain and France regarding Suez in the same broadcast.

With respect to Hungary, Eisenhower emphasized that, although the United States hoped for an end to Soviet domination of Eastern Europe, "we could not, *of course,* carry out this policy by resort to force."[9] For such a course would be "contrary both to the best interests of the Eastern European peoples and to the abiding principles of the United Nations,"[10] a truth which had clearly eluded both Radio Free Europe and the freedom fighters, who were at that moment pleading for American help. Meanwhile, Eisenhower continued, he had endeavored "to remove any false fears that we would look upon new governments in these Eastern European countries as potential military allies. We have no such ulterior purpose. We see these peoples as friends, and we wish simply that they be friends who are free."[11]

America's disavowal of ulterior motives sounded no more persuasive to the Kremlin coming from the President than it had been from the lips of his Secretary of State. The Soviets, who conducted foreign policy according to a mixture of Marxist ideology and Russian national interests, simply could not understand the American disavowal of having any selfish motives. But the renunciation of force was something the Politburo could comprehend, for this would eliminate its greatest fear should it decide to settle scores in Eastern Europe, as it was obviously preparing to do.

The irony of the Eisenhower Administration's two formal statements in the midst of the Hungarian Revolution was that both should have been so unintentionally provocative. The reassurance that America sought no allies in Eastern Europe disquieted the leaders in the Kremlin because it sounded as if Eastern Europe were acquiring the option to reverse alliances; America's renunciation of force inflamed the crisis by easing Soviet apprehensions about the American reaction if the Red Army crushed the uprising.

In the meantime, matters in Budapest had spun out of the control of even the reformist political leadership. On October 30, revolutionaries seized the Budapest office of the Communist Party and massacred its occupants, including, oddly enough, one of Nagy's closest associates. That afternoon, Nagy announced the formation of a new government on the basis existing in 1945, during the regime of the democratic parties' coalition. The end of communist one-party rule was symbolized by the presence in the Cabinet of Béla Kovacz as a representative of the bourgeois Small Holders' Party. A few years earlier, Kovacz had been indicted for treason. In addition, Cardinal Mindszenty, long a symbol of opposition to communism, was released from prison and spoke before enthusiastic crowds. Demanding the withdrawal of Soviet troops from all of Hungary, Nagy began negotiations with the two Politburo emissaries, Mikoyan and Suslov, to that effect. A host of political parties opened offices and began to publish newspapers or pamphlets.

After giving Nagy the impression that his proposal was negotiable, Mikoyan and Suslov left for Moscow, ostensibly to prepare for the next round of talks. That same evening of October 31, both *Pravda* and *Izvestia* published an official Kremlin statement, promulgated the day before, that the stationing of foreign troops in a fellow communist country required the approval of the host country and of the entire Warsaw Pact:

> . . . stationing the troops of one or another state which is a member of the Warsaw Treaty on the territory of another state which is a member of the treaty is done by agreement among all its members and only with the consent of the state on the territory of which and at the request of which these troops are stationed or it is planned to station them.[12]

On the basis of these words, Eisenhower included a highly optimistic interpretation of the Soviet Government declaration in his October 31 broadcast, noted above: ". . . if the Soviet Union indeed faithfully acts upon its announced intention, the world will witness the greatest forward stride toward justice, trust and understanding among nations in our generation."[13]

As forthcoming as the Soviet statement sounded on the question of general principle, Washington had ignored two crucial caveats: first, the implication that the withdrawal of troops required the same procedure as their stationing, which gave the Soviet Union a veto; second, the paragraphs specifically addressed to Hungary with the ominous warning that the Soviet Union would not "permit" what it defined as Hungary's "socialist achievements" to be abandoned, and would defend them together with the other socialist countries if necessary:

> To guard the socialist achievements of people's-democratic Hungary is the chief and sacred duty of the workers, peasants, intelligentsia, of all the Hungarian working people at the present moment.
> The Soviet government expresses confidence that the peoples of the socialist countries will not permit foreign and domestic reactionary

forces to shake the foundations of the people's democratic system. . . .
[T]hey will strengthen the fraternal unity and mutual aid of the socialist
countries to buttress the great cause of peace and socialism.[14]

What the statement referred to as the "people's democratic Hungary" had
ceased to call itself that and was, in fact, no longer in a position to
preserve either itself or its so-called socialist achievements. Nagy, a lifelong member of the communist cadre, could not have failed to understand the import of the Soviet warnings, or of the changes he was himself
fostering. Yet, by this time, Nagy, caught between the fury of his people
and the implacability of his communist allies, was riding a tide he could
neither control nor direct. Unlike the Polish people, the Hungarians were
demanding not the liberalization of the communist regime but its very
destruction; not equality with the Soviet Union, but a total break from it.

On November 1, having already created what was in effect a coalition
government, Nagy took the final, irrevocable step of declaring Hungary's
neutrality and its withdrawal from the Warsaw Pact. This too went far
beyond anything Gomulka had attempted in Poland. In a dignified statement that was to serve as his death sentence, Nagy announced on Hungarian radio:

> The Hungarian national Government, imbued with profound responsi-
> bility toward the Hungarian people and history, and giving expression
> to the undivided will of the Hungarian millions, declares the neutrality
> of the Hungarian People's Republic.
>
> The Hungarian people, on the basis of independence and equality
> and in accordance with the spirit of the U.N. Charter, wishes to live in
> true friendship with its neighbors, the Soviet Union, and all the peoples
> of the world. The Hungarian people desires the consolidation and
> further development of the achievements of its national revolution
> without joining any power blocs.[15]

At the same time, Nagy asked the United Nations to recognize Hungarian
neutrality. He never received a reply.

The pathos of Nagy's appeal was matched by the indifference with
which the so-called world community received it. Neither the United
States nor its European allies took steps to induce the United Nations to
deal with Nagy's message on an urgent basis. And the Soviets were beyond appeals to moderation. On the morning of November 4, the Soviet
forces which had been pouring into Hungary for days struck without
warning and savagely suppressed the Hungarian Revolution. János Kádár,

a former victim of Stalin's purges whom Nagy had elevated to General Secretary of the Communist Party and who had mysteriously disappeared a few days earlier, returned with the Soviet troops to establish a new communist government. Pal Maleter, the Commander of the Hungarian army, was arrested while negotiating Soviet troop withdrawals with the Commander of Soviet forces in Hungary. Nagy, who had taken refuge in the Yugoslav embassy, accepted a promise of safe passage to Yugoslavia but was arrested when he left the building. Cardinal Mindszenty took refuge in the American legation, where he was to remain until 1971. Nagy and Maleter were later executed. Stalin's spirit remained alive and well in the Kremlin.

Not until November 4 did the United Nations, which, throughout this entire critical period of Soviet troop buildup, had been exclusively occupied with denouncing Great Britain and France over Suez, finally turn to what was by then the Hungarian tragedy. A Security Council resolution asking the Soviet Union to withdraw was quickly vetoed by the Soviet Ambassador. A special session of the General Assembly voted on a similar resolution affirming Hungary's right to independence and demanding the dispatch of United Nations observers to Hungary. It was the second resolution of that fateful day, the General Assembly having meanwhile created a United Nations emergency force for the Middle East. The Middle East resolution passed unanimously, with even Great Britain and France joining the consensus. The Hungarian resolution passed by a vote of fifty to eight with fifteen abstentions. The Soviet bloc voted against it, while such leaders of the Nonaligned group as India and Yugoslavia abstained, as did every Arab country. The Middle East resolution was implemented; the Hungarian resolution was ignored.

In the aftermath of the brutally suppressed Hungarian uprising, the question arose whether a more forceful and imaginative Western diplomacy might have forestalled or eased the tragedy. Clearly, Soviet troops in Hungary had been massively reinforced over a period of many days. Was it within the power of the democracies to have kept them from striking? The American government had itself first raised the banner of liberation. Its propaganda via Radio Free Europe had produced a surge of hope exceeding even what Dulles had predicted in his 1952 *Life* article. When Hungary exploded, the American legation in Budapest must have conveyed to the State Department what every journalist knew: that the political structure of communist Hungary was dissolving. With the remarkable array of Kremlinologists such as Charles Bohlen, Llewellyn Thompson, Foy Kohler, and George Kennan available for advice, it is hard to believe that the State Department did not at least consider the possibility of Soviet military intervention. In any event, the Eisenhower Administration made no effort to raise the cost of Soviet intervention.

During the upheaval in Hungary, America fell far short of its rhetoric. The unwillingness to risk war to overturn communist control of Eastern Europe had been explicit American policy for a decade. But Washington's failure to explore seriously any option short of war in order to affect events opened up a huge gap between what Washington had proclaimed and what it was actually prepared to support. The United States never explained the limits of American support to the fledgling, inexperienced Hungarian government. Nor did it, through the many channels available to it, ever advise the Hungarians about how to consolidate their gains before taking further, irrevocable, steps. In its communications with the Soviet leadership, the United States relied largely on public statements which ended up creating incentives that were quite the opposite of what the Eisenhower Administration had intended.

A firmer, clearer American stance would have been essential to render the Soviet decision to intervene less calculable, or at least not quite so seemingly devoid of consequence. The Kremlin could have been warned that repression in Hungary would involve major political and economic costs, and put a freeze on East-West relations for the foreseeable future. The American and United Nations stance on Hungary could have been made more consistent with the reaction to Suez. Instead, America and its allies acted as if they were bystanders, with no direct stake in the outcome.

The democracies were in no position to go to war over Hungary, but they could have raised the specter of the political and economic costs of Soviet repression. As it was, the Kremlin paid next to no price for its actions, not even economically. A little over two years after the Hungarian tragedy, and despite a Soviet ultimatum over Berlin, British Prime Minister Harold Macmillan visited Moscow in what was the first visit there by a prime minister since the war; within three years, Eisenhower and Khrushchev were celebrating the spirit of Camp David.

Suez provided an occasion for the Arab nations, as well as for such leaders of the Nonaligned as India and Yugoslavia, to assail Great Britain and France. Yet, when it came to Hungary, this same group of nations refused to criticize Soviet actions, much less to condemn them in the United Nations. Some relationship between United Nations votes on Hungary and Suez would have been desirable. At the least, American measures against Great Britain and France should have been geared to reciprocal attitudes by the Nonaligned nations toward Soviet actions in Hungary. As it turned out, the Soviet Union's acts in Hungary cost it no influence among the Nonaligned, while the United States garnered no additional influence among that group as a result of its stand over Suez.

In the 1950s, the so-called Nonaligned group represented a novel approach to international relations. Neutral nations had, of course, always existed, but their distinguishing feature had been a passive foreign policy. By contrast, the Nonaligned of the Cold War period did not perceive their neutrality to require noninvolvement. They were active, occasionally shrill, players promoting agendas established in forums designed to pool their strengths and enhance their influence, in effect forming an alliance of the Nonaligned. Though they were highly vocal in their complaints about international tensions, they knew how to profit from them. They learned how to play the superpowers off against each other. And since they feared the Soviet Union more than they did the United States, they generally sided with the communists without feeling any reciprocal need to apply the same moral stringency to the Soviet Union as they did toward the United States.

On November 16, Prime Minister Jawaharlal Nehru presented to the Indian Parliament his own turgid rationale for why India had refused to approve the United Nations resolution condemning Soviet acts in Hungary.[16] The facts, he said, were "obscure"; the resolution was improperly worded; and the call for free elections supervised by the United Nations was a violation of Hungary's national sovereignty.

The facts had been anything but obscure, and India's reaction was entirely in keeping with the practices of *Realpolitik*. Quite simply, India did not want to give up Soviet support in international forums; it saw no point in incurring Soviet wrath and sacrificing potential arms supplies over some distant European country when China and Pakistan stood on its own borders, and the Soviet Union itself was not so very distant.

India did not conceive of foreign policy as a debate in the Oxford Union, however its diplomats might pretend that they were in the discriminating audience with the right to choose a winner purely on the basis of moral merit. India's leaders had attended schools in England and had read American classics. They combined the rhetoric of Wilson and Gladstone with the practices of Disraeli and Theodore Roosevelt. From the Indians' point of view, this made eminent sense as long as their interlocutors did not delude themselves into thinking that Indian rhetoric was a guide to Indian practice, or that Indian foreign policy was governed by abstract, superior morality.

On December 18, six weeks after the Hungarian tragedy, Dulles explained the reasoning behind America's response to the uprising at a press conference. Amazingly, he was still trying to reassure the Soviet Union of America's peaceful intentions:

> ... we have no desire to surround the Soviet Union with a band of hostile states and to revive what used to be called the *cordon sanitaire*, which was developed largely by the French after the First World War with a view to circling the Soviet Union with hostile forces. We have made clear our policy in that respect in the hope of facilitating in that way an evolution—a peaceful evolution—of the satellite states toward genuine independence.[17]

It was an astonishing statement. What, after all, was containment if not an attempt to surround the Soviet Union with forces capable of resisting its expansionism? Equally remarkable was Dulles' apologetic tone so soon after a demonstration of Soviet ruthlessness in Hungary and a simultaneous display of saber-rattling in the Middle East. At a press conference in Australia on March 13, 1957, Dulles bluntly summed up the American attitude. A lawyer at heart, he rested his case on the absence of any legal obligation:

> ... there was no basis for our giving military aid to Hungary. We had no commitment to do so, and we did not think that to do so would either assist the people of Hungary or the people of Europe or the rest of the world.[18]

Dulles continued missing the point. The issue was not a legal one; not whether America had fulfilled its commitments but whether it had lived up to the implications of its pronouncements.

Having proclaimed a universal mission, it was inevitable that America would encounter gaps between its principles and its national interest. The confluence of Suez and Hungary was one such occasion. America's great dream had always been a foreign policy which carries all before it by the compelling and universal nature of its maxims. Yet for a decade, American policymakers had been frustrated by the ambiguities of world leadership—by the concessions to imperfect causes that are grist for the mill of day-to-day diplomacy, and by the attention that must be paid to the views of allies with very different historical perspectives. Suez had seemed to provide an occasion for remedying this defect and for bringing policy into correspondence with principle. The very pain associated with the act of turning on its closest allies had the effect of penance in that it served to reconsecrate America's moral purity.

Hungary was a more complex case, for it would have required the application of power in some form. Yet America's leaders were not willing to risk American lives for a cause which, however offensive to their consciences, involved no direct American security interest. Principle permits no ambiguity and no gradations. In Suez, America could insist on the pure application of its maxims because the consequences involved no immediate risk. In Hungary, it acquiesced to *Realpolitik,* just as other nations do, because insistence on principle would have carried with it the unavoidable risk of war, perhaps even nuclear war. And when lives are at stake, the statesman owes it both to his people and to himself to explain the relationship between the risks and the interests, however broadly and generously these may be defined. The Soviet Union was clearly prepared to run bigger risks to preserve its position in Eastern Europe than the United States was willing to brave in order to liberate Hungary. Nothing could get around this equation. In terms of its rhetoric prior to the uprising, America's policy on Hungary was weak indeed; in terms of its interests, the refusal to run the risk of war was both inevitable and fitting—though it does not explain the reluctance to raise the cost of Soviet intervention by nonmilitary means.

The juxtaposition of Hungary and Suez established the coordinates of the next phase of the Cold War. The Soviet Union had managed to preserve its position in Eastern Europe; the democracies—including the United States—had suffered a relative decline in their position in the Middle East. The Soviet Union had found a way to bypass containment. The day after its troops had ravaged Budapest, and while the fighting was still going on, Khrushchev was threatening rocket attacks on Western Europe and inviting the United States to undertake joint military action in the Middle East against its closest allies. The United States had left Hungary adrift in the sea of historical evolution, and American allies with a sense of their impotence.

What was not clear at the time was the inherent weakness of the Soviet Union. Ironically, the communist proponents of the relationship of forces had launched themselves on an enterprise they would prove incapable of sustaining. The communist leaders might declaim about objective factors to their hearts' content, but the fact remained that the only revolutions taking place in developed countries were occurring inside the communist sphere. In the long run, the Soviet Union would have been safer and economically stronger if it had surrounded itself with Finnish-style governments in Eastern Europe because it would not have needed to assume responsibility for the internal stability and economic progress of those countries. Instead, imperialism in Eastern Europe drained Soviet resources and frightened the Western democracies, without enhancing Soviet strength. Communism could never translate its control of government and media into public acceptance. If the communist leaders of Eastern Europe did not want to sit entirely on Soviet bayonets, they were obliged to adapt to the programs of their nationalist opponents. Thus, after an initial period of bloody terror, Kádár gradually moved toward the goals charted by Nagy, though he stopped short of withdrawing from the Warsaw Pact. A generation later, latent Soviet weakness would cast the Hungarian uprising as a harbinger of the ultimate bankruptcy of the communist system. Despite all that had happened, within ten years Hungary was to be internally freer than Poland and its foreign policy more independent of the Soviet Union. And thirty-five years later, in the next phase of Moscow's attempt at liberalization, the Soviets would entirely lose control over events.

The outcome of 1956 contributed to another generation of suffering and oppression. However short the interval before the final collapse may seem to historians, it cannot begin to measure the anguish which the totalitarian nature of the system imposed on its countless victims. In the immediate aftermath, Moscow—misreading the balance of forces as much as the capitalists had—found every reason to be satisfied. Interpreting the year's events as a tilt in the balance of forces in its favor, the Politburo embarked on its gravest challenge yet of the Cold War—the ultimatums over Berlin.

CHAPTER TWENTY-THREE

Khrushchev's Ultimatum: The Berlin Crisis 1958–63

At the Potsdam Conference, the three victors had decided that Berlin would be governed by the four occupying powers—the United States, Great Britain, France, and the Soviet Union—which would jointly administer Germany as well. As it turned out, the four-power administration of Germany lasted little more than a year. By 1949, the Western zones were merged into the Federal Republic, and the Russian zone became the German Democratic Republic.

According to the four-power arrangement for Berlin, that city was not a part of Germany—East or West—but was officially under the rule of the four victorious Allies of World War II. The Soviets occupied a large sector in the eastern part of the city, the Americans had a sector in the south, and the British and French had theirs in the west and north. All of Berlin was now an island inside of what had become the German Democratic Republic. As the years wore on, the East Germans and the Soviets found the three western sectors of Berlin to be a thorn in their side, a showcase of prosperity in the midst of the dismal grayness of the communist bloc. Most important, West Berlin served as a conduit for those East Germans seeking to emigrate to the West: they would simply take the subway to one of the western sectors of the city, and then apply to emigrate.

Amazingly, despite Berlin's obvious four-power status, unambiguous arrangements for access to it had never been negotiated. Although the four powers had designated the various roads and air corridors to be used to reach Berlin, they had not explicitly agreed on the mechanisms of passage. In 1948, Stalin had tried to take advantage of this lacuna by instituting the Berlin blockade on the technical ground that the access routes were under repair. After one year of the Western airlift, access was restored, but the legal authority remained as vague as ever.

In the years immediately following the blockade, Berlin grew into a major industrial center with needs which, in an emergency, could no longer have been met by an airlift. Although Berlin was still technically a four-power city and the Soviet Union was responsible for access, the East German satellite actually controlled the routes from its capital, East Berlin. Berlin's position was therefore highly vulnerable. The road, rail, and air links were easy prey for interruptions so seemingly trivial that they were difficult to resist by force even though they might cumulatively threaten the freedom of the city. Theoretically, all military traffic was supposed to pass through a Soviet-controlled checkpoint, but this was a fiction; an East German guard controlled the gates, and Soviet officers lounged in a nearby shack in the event of disagreement.

Small wonder that Khrushchev, looking around for a spot in which to demonstrate a permanent shift in the correlation of forces, decided to exploit Berlin's vulnerability. In his memoirs, he noted: "To put it crudely, the American foot in Europe had a sore blister on it. That was West Berlin. Anytime we wanted to step on the Americans' foot and make them feel the pain, all we had to do was obstruct Western communications with the city across the territory of the German Democratic Republic."[1]

Khrushchev's challenge to the West's position in Berlin occurred at the precise moment when the democracies had convinced themselves once again that the incumbent General Secretary was their best hope for peace. Even so skeptical an observer of the Soviet scene as John Foster Dulles responded to Khrushchev's speech to the Twentieth Party Congress in February 1956 by professing to have discerned a "notable shift" in Soviet policy. The Soviet rulers, he said, had concluded that "the time had come to change basically their approach to the non-Communist world. . . . Now they pursue their foreign policy goals with less manifestation of intolerance and less emphasis on violence."[2] By the same token, in September 1957, less than one year after the crises in Suez and Hungary, Ambassador Llewellyn Thompson reported from Moscow that Khrushchev "really wants and is almost forced to a detente in relations with the West."[3]

Khrushchev's conduct did not support such optimism. When, in October 1957, the Soviets launched the Sputnik, an artificial satellite, into an earth orbit, Khrushchev interpreted this essentially one-shot accomplishment as proof that the Soviet Union was outstripping the democracies in the scientific as well as the military field. Even in the West, the contention that a planned system might ultimately prove superior to a market economy was beginning to gain credence.

President Eisenhower stood nearly alone in his refusal to panic. As a military man, he understood the difference between a prototype and an operational military weapon. Khrushchev, on the other hand, taking his own boasts seriously, embarked on a protracted diplomatic offensive to translate the supposed superiority of Soviet missiles into some kind of diplomatic breakthrough. In January 1958, Khrushchev told a Danish journalist:

> The launching of the Soviet sputniks first of all shows . . . that a serious change has occurred in the balance of forces between the countries of socialism and capitalism in favor of the socialist nations.[4]

In Khrushchev's fantasy, the Soviet Union, besides being scientifically and militarily ahead of the United States, would soon exceed it in industrial output as well. On June 4, 1958, he told the Seventh Congress of the Bulgarian Communist Party: "We are firmly convinced that the time is approaching when socialist countries will outstrip the most developed capitalist countries not only in tempo but also in volume of industrial production."[5]

As a devout communist, Khrushchev was practically required to seek to translate this presumed change in the balance of forces into diplomatic coin. Berlin was his first target. Khrushchev opened the challenge with three initiatives. On November 10, 1958, he delivered a speech demanding an end to Berlin's four-power status and warning that the Soviet Union intended to turn control of its access over to its East German satellite. From that day forward, Khrushchev vowed: "let the U.S.A., Britain and France build their own relations with the German Democratic Republic and come to agreement with it if they are interested in any questions concerning Berlin."[6] On November 27, Khrushchev transposed the essence of that speech into formal notes to the United States, Great Britain, and France declaring the Four-Power Agreement on Berlin null and void and insisting that West Berlin be transformed into a demilitarized "free city." If no agreement was reached within six months, the Soviet Union would sign a peace treaty with East Germany and turn over its occupation rights and access routes to the German Democratic Republic.[7] Khrushchev had delivered the equivalent of an ultimatum to the Western allies.

On January 10, 1959, Khrushchev submitted to the other three occupying powers a draft peace treaty which defined the new status of both Berlin and East Germany. Later that month, Khrushchev spelled out the rationale for his policy before the Twenty-first Communist Party Congress. Like a confidence man selling his wares, he had in the meantime escalated his assessment of Soviet power even further, suggesting that, together with the People's Republic of China, the Soviet Union was *already* producing half of the world's industrial output; therefore, "the international situation will change radically."[8]

Khrushchev had chosen the point of attack with great skill. The challenge inherent in East German control of the access routes to Berlin was indirect. It confronted the democracies with the choice of recognizing the East German satellite or threatening to go to war over the technical issue of who was to stamp transit documents. Nevertheless, Khrushchev's bluster, to which he was by nature inclined, masked a real weakness in the Soviets' position. East Germany was losing manpower by the hundreds of thousands as its citizens, often its most talented professionals, fled to West Germany via Berlin. Berlin was turning out to be a gigantic hole in the Iron Curtain. If the trend continued, East Germany, a self-proclaimed "worker's paradise," would not have any workers left.

The East German state was the most fragile link in the Soviet sphere of influence. Faced with the larger, more prosperous West Germany on its border, and recognized diplomatically only by its fellow Soviet satellite states, East Germany lacked legitimacy. The manpower drain through Berlin threatened its very survival. If something was not done, the leaders of East Berlin reasoned, the whole state could collapse in a matter of years. That would mean a devastating blow to the Soviet sphere of influence, which Khrushchev was attempting to consolidate. By cutting off the escape route, Khrushchev hoped to give his East German satellite a new lease on life. And by forcing a Western retreat, he sought to weaken the Federal Republic's Western ties.

Khrushchev's ultimatum went to the heart of Adenauer's policy. For nearly a decade, Adenauer had rejected all the proposals to advance unification by sacrificing his Western ties. The Soviet Union had dangled neutralism before the German public in Stalin's peace plan of 1952, and Adenauer's domestic opponents had supported it. Adenauer had staked his country's future on the proposition that American and German interests were identical. The tacit bargain was that the Federal Republic would join the Atlantic defense system and that the allies would make German unification an integral part of East-West diplomacy. Therefore, for Adenauer, the Berlin crisis was far more than a question of access procedures. It tested the very wisdom of the Federal Republic's Western orientation.

As far as Adenauer was concerned, there was simply no getting around the fact that every enhancement in the status of East Germany reinforced the Soviet claim that unification had to be left to negotiations directly between the two German states. At a time when the Social Democratic Party was still neutralist, such a *de facto* recognition by the allies of the German Democratic Republic would have revolutionized German domestic politics. According to de Gaulle, Adenauer told a Western summit in December 1959:

> If Berlin were to be lost, my political position would at once become untenable. The Socialists would take over power in Bonn. They would proceed to make a direct arrangement with Moscow, and that would be the end of Europe.[9]

In Adenauer's view, Khrushchev's ultimatum had above all been designed to isolate the Federal Republic. The Soviet agenda for negotiations placed Bonn in a no-win situation. In return for any concessions it might make, the West would at best receive what it already had: access to Berlin. At the same time, the East German satellite would be given a veto on German unification which would lead either to a stalemate or to an outcome Adenauer described in his memoirs as follows:

> ... we could not buy the reunification of Germany at the price of loosening Germany from the Western bloc and giving up the achievements of European integration. Because the result would be that a defenseless, unbound Germany in the middle of Europe would be created, that necessarily would be tempted to play off the East against the West.[10]

In short, Adenauer saw no benefit in *any* negotiation under the conditions outlined by Khrushchev. However, if negotiations proved unavoidable, he wanted them to serve as proof of the wisdom of his reliance on the West. He strongly objected to responding to Khrushchev's ultimatum with concessions, and he preferred that the West base its plans for unification on free elections.

Adenauer's views, however, were not shared by his Anglo-American allies, least of all by Great Britain. Prime Minister Harold Macmillan and the British people were reluctant to risk war over the capital of a defeated enemy that had, moreover, been largely responsible for destroying their nation's pre-eminence as a Great Power. Unlike France, Great Britain did not identify its long-term security with the future of Germany. Twice in a generation, Great Britain had just barely been saved by American intervention from German assaults that had conquered most of Europe. Though Great Britain would have preferred to preserve the Atlantic Alliance, if forced to make a choice, it would risk isolation from Europe rather than separation from America. Adenauer's domestic dilemmas concerned British leaders far less than Eisenhower's did; in an ultimate crisis, the latter's ability to command domestic support would have a far greater impact on Great Britain's own survival. For all these reasons, British leaders refused to place any large bets on German unity, and interpreted Adenauer's misgivings as nationalism masquerading behind legalistic pedantry.

Pragmatists at heart, British leaders thought it was bizarre to risk nuclear war over the transfer of authority from Soviet officials to their East German surrogates in the affixing of a transit stamp. In light of the horrendous consequences of a nuclear war, the slogan *"Pourquoi mourir pour Danzig?"* ("Why die for Danzig?"), which had contributed to France's demoralization in 1940, would surely have paled before the much more invidious slogan "Why die for a transit stamp?"

Macmillan thus became a passionate proponent of negotiations—any negotiations—which might "improve" access procedures and would, at a minimum, waste time: "If all the Heads of State were swanning around each other's territories, one could hardly believe that there would be a sudden and fatal explosion," he later recalled.[11]

Of all the heads of the allies, Eisenhower bore the gravest burden of responsibility, because the decision to risk nuclear war ultimately rested on his shoulders. For the United States, the Berlin crisis brought home the realization that nuclear weapons, which throughout the decade of America's nuclear monopoly and near-monopoly had seemed to provide a quick and relatively inexpensive path to security, would, in the age of approaching nuclear parity, increasingly circumscribe America's willingness to run risks and thereby constrain its freedom of diplomatic maneuver.

As long as America remained essentially immune from attack, nuclear weapons gave it an advantage never previously enjoyed by any nation. As often happens, the most elaborate formulation of this advantage occurred at the moment when it was on the verge of disappearing. Near the end of the period of American nuclear monopoly, or near-monopoly, Dulles developed the concept of "massive retaliation" to deter Soviet aggression and to avoid protracted stalemates such as Korea in the future. Rather than resist aggression where it occurred, the United States would retaliate against the source of the trouble at a time and with weapons of its own choosing. However, the Soviet Union began developing its own thermo-nuclear weapons and intercontinental strategic missiles just as massive retaliation was being promulgated. The credibility of that strategy there-fore began to evaporate rather rapidly—even more quickly in perception than in reality. General nuclear war was a remedy simply out of propor-tion with most foreseeable crises, including the Berlin crisis. To be sure, the leaders of the democracies took Khrushchev's wildly exaggerated claims of Soviet missile strength far too literally (with Eisenhower as the notable exception). But it was beyond dispute by 1958 that a general nuclear war would, in a matter of days, produce casualties that dwarfed the cumulative totals of both world wars.

This stark equation produced a fundamental incompatibility between the kind of diplomacy required to make the threat of nuclear war credible and what was needed to rally democratic public opinion to confront the apocalyptic nature of the risk. Credibility in the face of Armageddon implied a hair-trigger reaction to challenges and a demonstration of reck-lessness so beyond normal calculation that no aggressor would ever dare to test it. But what the democratic public wanted, and was entitled to receive, was a calm, rational, calculating, and flexible diplomacy which would also cause the adversary to question America's resolve to go to the extreme of general nuclear war.

Early in the Berlin crisis, Eisenhower decided that it was more im-portant to calm the American public than to shock the Soviet leaders. In press conferences on February 18 and March 11, 1959, he advanced a number of propositions to defuse the nuclear threat which underlay American strategy. "We are certainly not going to fight a ground war in Europe,"[12] he said, and specifically placed the defense of Berlin into that category. It was unlikely, he avowed, that the United States would "shoot our way into Berlin."[13] In order to leave no loophole, he excluded de-fending Berlin with nuclear weapons as well: "I don't know how you could free anything with nuclear weapons."[14] These statements surely conveyed the impression that America's willingness to risk war over Ber-lin was very limited.

574

The mildness of Eisenhower's reaction was due in part to his assessment of Khrushchev, whom he still considered, together with most other American leaders, the West's best hope for peace. Khrushchev's ultimatum over Berlin had not changed Ambassador Thompson's views of two years earlier. On March 9, 1959, Thompson reiterated his impression that Khrushchev's principal concerns were domestic. According to the Ambassador, brinkmanship was Khrushchev's way of developing a pattern of coexistence that would serve as the prerequisite to economic reform and domestic liberalization.[15] How the threat of war established a pattern of coexistence was not explained.

Such analyses made no impression on the other member of the international quartet—French President Charles de Gaulle, who had just returned to office after twelve years in the political wilderness. He did not agree with the Anglo-American analysis of Khrushchev's motivations and was determined that the Berlin crisis should demonstrate to Adenauer that France was the Federal Republic's indispensable partner. He was more afraid of the danger of reawakening German nationalism than of Khrushchev's threats. At a minimum, he wanted to provide Adenauer with an anchor in the West; if possible, he would seek to enlist a disillusioned Adenauer in a European structure less dominated by America.

Whereas Eisenhower and Macmillan tried to find some Soviet demand that might be satisfied with little or no long-term damage, de Gaulle was adamantly opposed to such a strategy. He rejected the "exploratory talks" being urged by his Anglo-American partners because he saw nothing of any benefit to the West available for exploration. He disdained the schemes for a change in procedures that were being elaborated in Washington and London with the argument that they might "improve" access. Khrushchev, after all, had not issued his ultimatum in order to improve the West's access. In de Gaulle's opinion, the challenge had its origin in the Soviet domestic structure, not in any specific Soviet grievance. Eisenhower understood that the Soviet Union was militarily inferior; de Gaulle went a step further and ascribed Khrushchev's ultimatum to an inherently flawed, fragile, and vastly inferior *political* system:

... there is in this uproar of imprecations and demands organized by the Soviets something so arbitrary and so artificial that one is led to attribute it either to the premeditated unleashing of frantic ambitions, or to the desire of drawing attention away from great difficulties: this second hypothesis seems all the more plausible to me since, despite the coercions, isolation and acts of force in which the Communist system encloses the countries which are under its yoke . . . actually its gaps, its shortages, its internal failures, and above that its character of inhuman oppression, are felt more and more by the elites and the masses, whom it is more and more difficult to deceive and to subjugate.[16]

Soviet military power was therefore a façade designed to obscure the endless internal struggles inherent in the Soviet system:

> . . . in their camps the struggle between political trends, the intrigues of clans, the rivalries of individuals periodically lead to implacable crises, whose sequels—or even whose premonitory symptoms—cannot help but unsettle them. . . .[17]

Yielding to Soviet pressure would merely encourage Khrushchev to step up his foreign adventures as a way of deflecting attention from the fundamental internal crisis of his system, and it might make Germany ". . . seek in the East a future which she despairs of being guaranteed in the West."[18]

De Gaulle could well afford such clear-sighted intransigence because, unlike the American President, he did not bear the ultimate responsibility for initiating a nuclear war. When push came to shove, it is extremely doubtful that de Gaulle would have been more prepared to risk nuclear war than Eisenhower and, given the vulnerability of his country, he probably would have been less so. Yet, precisely because he was convinced that the principal danger of war was Western irresolution and that America was the only nation capable of deterring the Soviets, de Gaulle felt free to maneuver in ways that would oblige America to stand firm or to assume responsibility for whatever concessions might have to be made. It was not a pretty game, but *raison d'état* teaches hard lessons. And it was on the basis of *raison d'état* that de Gaulle reversed the Richelieu tradition of attempting to keep Germany weak and fragmented, which had been the essence of French Central European policy for 300 years.

De Gaulle had not arrived at his devotion to Franco-German friendship in a sudden fit of sentimentality. Since the time of Richelieu, French policy had been aimed at keeping the ominous German neighbor either divided or weak, preferably both. In the nineteenth century, France learned that it lacked the power to contain Germany by itself; alliances with Great Britain, Russia, and a host of smaller countries were the consequence. In the aftermath of the Second World War, even those options were disappearing. Great Britain and France combined had not been strong enough to defeat Germany in the two world wars. And with Soviet armies along the Elbe and East Germany a Soviet satellite, alliance with Moscow was more likely to result in Soviet domination of Europe than in the containment of Germany. This was why de Gaulle abandoned the traditional adversarial relationship with Germany and entrusted France's future to friendship with the hereditary enemy.

The Berlin crisis provided de Gaulle with an opportunity to advance his strategy. He carefully positioned France in the role of defender of the European identity and used the Berlin crisis to demonstrate France's understanding of European realities and its sensitivity to German national concerns. De Gaulle's was a complex approach that required the subtlest of balancing acts between showing support for German national goals and not encouraging the Germans to pursue them on their own or in collusion with the Soviet Union. De Gaulle had come to fear that Moscow's stranglehold on East Germany might enable Soviet leaders to emerge as the champions of German unity or to establish a free-floating Germany along the French frontier. France's age-old German nightmare had turned into the nightmare of a possible German-Soviet deal.

De Gaulle responded with characteristic boldness. France would concede German military and economic power, even its pre-eminence in these fields, and would support German unification in exchange for Bonn's recognition of France as the *political* leader of Europe. It was a cold calculation, not a great passion; de Gaulle surely did not die unfulfilled because Germany was not reunited in his lifetime.

Seeking to strike a balance between de Gaulle's flamboyant intransigence and Macmillan's quest for demonstrative negotiations, Dulles resorted to his familiar tactic of confusing the issue by submerging it in legalistic detail, which, to his way of thinking, had served him so well during the Suez crisis. On November 24, 1958, two weeks after Khrushchev's menacing speech, Dulles began exploring options on changing access procedures without actually yielding on substance. He wrote to Adenauer that he would try to "hold the Soviet Union to its obligations" while simultaneously dealing "on a *de facto* basis with minor [GDR] functionaries, so long as they merely carried out perfunctorily the present arrangements."[19] At a press conference on November 26, Dulles put forward the notion that East German officials might act as "agents" for the Soviet Union—a ploy reminiscent of his Users' Association from the days of the Suez crisis (see chapter 21).[20]

At a press conference on January 13, 1959, Dulles went a step further and signaled a change in America's historic position on German unification. After arguing that free elections were the "natural method" for unifying Germany, he added, "I wouldn't say that it is the only method by which reunification could be accomplished."[21] He even hinted that some sort of confederation of the two German states might prove acceptable: "There are all kinds of methods whereby countries and peoples draw together...."[22] He strongly implied that responsibility for unification might be transferred from the allies to the Germans themselves, under-cutting the essence of Adenauer's policy.

The German reaction was predictable, though no one had predicted it. Willy Brandt, then Lord Mayor of Berlin, expressed his "shock and dis-may." Dulles' agent theory, Brandt said, would encourage the Soviets to adopt an even more "uncompromising" stance.[23]

Truculence was not Adenauer's normal style. He also greatly admired Dulles. Nevertheless, he reacted to Dulles' musings much as Eden had during Suez. In a conversation with Ambassador David Bruce, Adenauer argued emotionally that Dulles' statements were undermining his govern-ment's policy, which had sought unification *through* the West and on the basis of free elections. "...[C]onfederation in any form," he insisted, would be "totally unacceptable."[24]

The difference in perspectives became painfully apparent in mid-Janu-ary 1959, when Adenauer sent the permanent Undersecretary for Political Affairs of the Foreign Ministry, Herbert Dittmann, to Washington to ex-press "shock" at the Soviets' proposal for a German peace treaty, and to urge a negotiating position based on the West's established policy. Dittmann's counterpart, United States Undersecretary of State Livingston Merchant, made it clear that, in this crisis, Adenauer could not count on Dulles' customary all-out support. Dulles, he argued, wanted to avoid *any* "extreme position," and "to get the Russians to the conference table." The Germans could best contribute by "provid[ing] us with new ideas."[25] As the crisis developed, whenever America and Great Britain asked for "new ideas," they were putting forth a euphemism for enhancing the status of the East German regime or for finding a formula to meet some Soviet demand.

It was ironic that Great Britain and the United States should be urging Germany onto a course that would almost certainly lead to greater Ger-man nationalism, while Adenauer, having far less confidence in his own countrymen, remained determined not to expose them to that tempta-tion. Eisenhower and Macmillan were placing their faith in the Germans' conversion; Adenauer could not forget their original sin.

Macmillan was the first to break ranks. On February 21, 1959, he jour-neyed on his own to Moscow for "exploratory talks." Since Adenauer disapproved of the whole enterprise and no allied consensus existed,

Macmillan's "exploration" of what concessions might be offered must have included the already familiar catalogue of "improvements" in access procedures, along with his customary appeal for peace based on personal relations among world leaders.

Khrushchev interpreted Macmillan's visit as another confirmation of a favorable tilt in the balance of forces and the augury of even better things to come. During Macmillan's visit, Khrushchev delivered a boisterous speech reaffirming his demands in an uncompromising fashion. In another speech after the Prime Minister's departure, he dismissed Macmillan's proposition that good personal relations among world leaders would ease the road to peace: "History teaches that it is not conferences that change borders of states. The decisions of conferences can only reflect the new alignment of forces. And this is the result of victory or surrender at the end of a war, or of other circumstances."[26] It was a bald-faced profession of *Realpolitik* that might well have come from the mouth of Richelieu or Bismarck.

After Adenauer's blow-up, Dulles pulled back. On January 29, he abandoned the "agent theory" and stopped hinting at confederation as the route to German unity. Dulles' retreat, however, was largely tactical. Convictions had not altered, nor had personalities. As during the Suez crisis two years earlier, American policy depended on reconciling the subtle nuances of difference between the approaches of Eisenhower and Dulles. Given his own analysis of the Soviet system, Dulles in all likelihood understood Adenauer's point of view and must have shared much of it. But, as before, Dulles had to figure out how to relate his strategy to the much more elemental approach of Eisenhower.

For, after all was said and done, most of the issues that concerned Adenauer struck Eisenhower as theoretical, if not irrelevant. It was indeed fortunate that Khrushchev was not privy to Eisenhower's personal ruminations. As early as November 27, 1958—the day of Khrushchev's formal ultimatum—Eisenhower indicated in a telephone conversation with Dulles that he was receptive to the idea of a free city without American troops, provided that both Berlin and its access routes were under United Nations jurisdiction.

When presidential advisers or cabinet members disagree with their chief, they have to decide whether to make their case while the disagreement is still largely theoretical or to wait for the moment of actual decision. The answer determines future influence because presidents are generally personalities of strong will that can be crossed only so often. If advisers choose to challenge hypothetical cases, they may generate unnecessary acrimony since the president may change his mind on his own. On the other hand, if they wait on events, they run the risk of being stampeded. Dulles opted for a middle ground. Warning Eisenhower against "paper agreements," he cautioned that keeping Berlin free required the presence of American troops.[27] As it turned out, the occasion for an actual decision never arose. By this time, Dulles was terminally ill, and six months later, on May 24, 1959, he died.

On July 1, Eisenhower returned to his theme of accommodation. In a meeting with Soviet Deputy Prime Minister Frol Kozlov, he responded to the Soviet complaint that America's position with respect to Berlin was illogical. "We admit it is illogical, but we will not abandon our rights and responsibilities—unless there is a way made for us to do so."[28] Maintaining one's rights until a way can be arranged to abandon them is hardly a stirring battle cry.

At Camp David in September 1959, Eisenhower told Khrushchev that America had no intention of staying in Berlin forever. "Clearly," he said, "we did not contemplate 50 years in occupation there."[29] Purporting to risk nuclear war on behalf of a city one is looking forward to vacating is not a great battle cry either.

On September 28, Eisenhower went even further, in essence conceding the basic premise of the Soviet challenge—that the situation in Berlin was indeed "abnormal":

It was brought about by a truce, a military truce, after the end of the war, an armistice, and it put strangely a few—or a number of free people in a very awkward position.[30]

What might have happened had Khrushchev either pressed the Soviet challenge or formulated some "compromise" based on the numerous hints he was receiving is painful to contemplate. Fortunately, Khrushchev's limited attention span, his misassessment of his own relative strength, and perhaps divisions within the Soviet leadership all conspired to impart an oddly inconclusive quality to Soviet conduct. Khrushchev's ultimatums alternated with lulls during which deadlines came and went without the Soviet leader ever insisting on the fulfillment of his demands or on a negotiation. The former would have revealed how determined the allies really were; the latter would have tested the obvious willingness of at least Great Britain and the United States to modify access to Berlin and the city's status. Khrushchev's failure to stick to his objective spared the Atlantic Alliance what might have turned into its greatest crisis.

Khrushchev pursued neither confrontation nor negotiation consistently. That alone should have raised a doubt in Western minds about the coherence of the Soviet system. To threaten nuclear war and challenge the European *status quo* without developing a strategy leading to at least a diplomatic showdown proved to be a foretaste of the paralysis that would grip the Soviet system some twenty years later. Khrushchev was apparently trapped between the "hawks" in his Politburo, who, believing his boasts about a tilt in the balance of power, thought that the West was not offering enough, and the "doves," who, aware of the actual military realities, were unwilling to run even the slightest risk of war with the United States.

In the midst of this strange process, Khrushchev permitted his first ultimatum to lapse without having anything more to show for it than a foreign ministers' conference two weeks before the expiration of the deadline. That meeting failed to make progress because Andrei Gromyko, who had recently been appointed as Foreign Minister, used the occasion to burnish his formidable skill at stonewalling, with which he was to torment the democracies' foreign ministers for a whole generation. In fact, deadlock was not what the Soviets needed as the ultimatum was expiring. It did, however, enable Eisenhower to gain some more time, by inviting Khrushchev to visit the United States.

The Soviet ruler toured the United States from September 15 to September 27, 1959, eliciting the same sort of euphoric public reaction that had been evoked by the Geneva Summit four years earlier. Once again, the meeting of the two heads of government emphasized atmosphere over substance, as symbolized by the slogan "the spirit of Camp David." *Newsweek* magazine published a scorecard which indicated that the visit's purported achievements by far outnumbered its failures. And whatever failures there were, it was said, concerned primarily the leaders' inability to make progress on the issue of Berlin—as if that were a minor matter. The list of achievements included cultural exchanges, increased trade, and greater scientific cooperation, none of which required a meeting of the heads of government. The most frequently cited benefit was what the Soviet leader was presumed to be learning about his hosts, which reflected the standard American belief that conflicts among nations are caused by misunderstanding rather than by clashing interests, and that no one could ever come, see, and leave America and still be hostile to its ways.

According to a *Newsweek* poll, Americans believed that Khrushchev had finally understood "that Americans from the President on down genuinely want peace."[31] If that was Khrushchev's actual judgment, the effect was surely double-edged. In any event, he kept that particular insight a state secret. Speaking a few weeks later, in early December, Khrushchev boasted that "the capitalist world is shaking under the blows of the Social-ist camp. . . . We have the will to win."[32]

Eisenhower too emerged from the summit with much the same convic-tion with which he had entered it: he remained willing, if not eager, to change the status of Berlin. At the end of the Summit, on October 1, Eisenhower described his idea of an appropriate way out of the crisis to his National Security Adviser, Gordon Gray:

> We must remember that Berlin is an abnormal situation; that we had found it necessary to live with it, and that it had come about through some mistakes of our leaders—Churchill and Roosevelt. However, he [Eisenhower] felt that there must be some way to develop some kind of a free city which might be somehow a part of West Germany, which might require that the U.N. would become a party to guaranteeing the freedom, safety and security of the city which would have an unarmed status except for police forces. He reiterated that the time was coming and perhaps soon when we would simply have to get our forces out.[33]

With Khrushchev fortunately unwilling to explore these or any other ideas, the Western allies achieved by default their principal objective of gaining time. In 1955, the Geneva Summit had permitted Khrushchev to achieve a relaxation of tensions without making substantive concessions; in 1959, Eisenhower achieved the same result by invoking the so-called spirit of Camp David.

The principal result of Camp David was another delay. Eisenhower and Khrushchev agreed to convene a meeting of the four powers occupying Berlin. But Eisenhower wanted first to consult his allies. De Gaulle re-fused the summit invitation unless Khrushchev first paid a state visit to Paris. Given all these preconditions, the earliest date for a summit turned out to be May 1960, to be held in Paris. Finally, two weeks before the meeting, an American U-2 spy plane was shot down over the Soviet Union. That flight gave Khrushchev the pretext to wreck the entire conference, which by then had already been over a year in gestation. It turned out to be just as well, since the American fallback position on Berlin had been a plan for a "guaranteed city," which incorporated many of Eisenhower's ruminations to Gordon Gray. In practice, the scheme differed from Khrushchev's free-city proposal primarily in the label accorded to the city's new status.

Although for several days the Western allies were concerned that Khrushchev might finally have his pretext for a showdown, it very quickly became apparent that the Soviet leader was seeking just the opposite—a pretext for avoiding a showdown. Verbal truculence became a substitute for the confrontation Khrushchev had threatened just as consistently as he had recoiled from it. Contrary to all expectations, when Khrushchev stopped in Berlin on his way back from the aborted Paris summit, he announced yet another postponement of his deadline, this time until after the American presidential elections.

By the time John F. Kennedy entered office, nearly three years had passed since Khrushchev had issued his first ultimatum. The passage of time had progressively reduced the credibility of his threat and the over-all sense of danger. Just when the Berlin issue seemed to be calming down, the Kennedy Administration's failed attempt to overthrow Castro at the Bay of Pigs and its indecisiveness over Laos apparently convinced Khrushchev that Kennedy was a soft touch. At a summit with Kennedy in Vienna in early June 1961, Khrushchev reinstated another six-month deadline, inaugurating one of the most intense periods of confrontation of the entire Cold War.

Reporting on the summit on June 15, Khrushchev told the world that the conclusion of a German peace treaty could no longer be delayed: "A peace settlement in Europe must be attained this year." For one of his speeches, Khrushchev appeared in the uniform of a lieutenant general, a courtesy rank Stalin had bestowed on him during the war. On another occasion, Khrushchev told the British Ambassador that it would take only six atomic bombs to destroy England and nine to obliterate France.[34] In September 1960, Khrushchev ended the informal nuclear test ban which both sides had observed for three years. As part of its test program, the Soviet Union set off a monstrous explosion of fifty megatons.

Khrushchev's demands for a postwar settlement were not new. Churchill had urged a postwar settlement as early as 1943; Stalin had proposed one in his 1952 Peace Note; George Kennan had advocated a settlement on Germany in the mid-1950s. But unlike other wars, there was to be no postwar settlement following the Second World War. The American and Soviet spheres of influence would be established step by step and by acquiescence to *faits accomplis* rather than by formal agreements.

The final act in defining the European spheres of influence began in the early hours of August 13, 1961. West Berliners awoke to find themselves virtually imprisoned. The East Germans had erected barbed-wire barricades between the Soviet sector of Berlin and the sectors occupied by the three Western powers, and had built a fence around the entire city of Berlin. Families on opposite sides of that wall were rent asunder. As the days went by, the wall was reinforced; concrete, land mines, and guard dogs became the symbols of the divided city and of communist inhumanity. The bankruptcy of a communist regime unable to induce its own citizens to remain within their country was revealed to all the world. Nevertheless, the communist leaders had plugged the hole in the dike of the Soviet bloc—at least temporarily.

The erection of the wall brought home to the democracies their Berlin dilemma. They were prepared to defend the freedom of Berlin against overt aggression, but they had not decided on their response below that threshold or, indeed, on how to define aggression. Almost immediately, Kennedy determined that the construction of the wall did not fit America's definition of aggression and decided not to challenge it militarily. The American attempt to play down the building of the wall was shown by the fact that, on the day it was first erected, Kennedy went sailing and Secretary of State Rusk attended a baseball game. There was no crisis atmosphere in Washington.

In truth, Kennedy's military options were quite limited. If American troops removed the barrier at the sector border, they might face a rebuilt wall a few hundred yards farther back. Would they then enter East Berlin to tear it down? Would the Western public support a war for the cause of free movement *inside* Berlin—when in practice East Berlin had been conceded long before as the capital of the East German communist satellite?

As it became clear that America would not resist the building of the wall by force, West Berlin and the Federal Republic experienced the kind of shock that comes from being confronted with a reality of which one was subconsciously aware but afraid to acknowledge. At the latest after the Hungarian Revolution, it should have been clear that the West would not challenge the existing spheres of influence militarily. Brandt was to claim later that his policy of *Ostpolitik,* which led to the recognition of the East German regime, resulted from his disillusionment with America's reaction to the building of the wall. In all likelihood, however, the Germans' shock would have been even greater had a war resulted from the effort to tear it down. Even Adenauer told Acheson that he did not want Berlin defended by a nuclear war, knowing full well that there was no other means by which it could be defended.

Both superpowers continued to jockey in an effort to define both their commitment and its limits. In July, Kennedy substantially increased the American defense budget, called up reserves, and sent additional forces to Europe. In August 1961, after the wall was built, Kennedy dispatched 1,500 troops on the Autobahn through the Soviet zone, daring the Soviets to stop them. Arriving without challenge, the troops were met with a rousing speech by Vice-President Johnson, who had flown ahead to greet them. Soon thereafter, General Lucius Clay, the hero of the Berlin blockade of 1948, was appointed as the President's personal representative in Berlin. Kennedy was staking American credibility on the freedom of Berlin.

Khrushchev had again maneuvered himself into the same sort of dead end as during the Eisenhower Administration. His bluster had evoked an American reaction he proved unwilling to challenge. And reports from Colonel Oleg Penkovsky, the extraordinary American mole in Soviet military intelligence, revealed that high-level Soviet officers were quite well aware of their lack of preparedness and frequently grumbled amongst themselves about Khrushchev's recklessness.[35] As early as 1960, Eisenhower had seen through Khrushchev's bluff, telling a visitor that, in the event of war, he would be far more worried about nuclear fallout from America's own weapons than about Soviet retaliation. Once he became President, Kennedy also quickly realized that the Soviet Union was inferior in overall strategic power.

This state of affairs favored the side wanting to preserve the *status quo*. At the same time, Kennedy was even more explicit than Eisenhower had been about his reluctance to run even a slight risk of nuclear war over Berlin. On the way back from his summit with Khrushchev at Vienna, he ruminated:

> ... it seems particularly stupid to risk killing a million Americans over an argument about access rights on an Autobahn ... or because the Germans want Germany reunified. If I'm going to threaten Russia with a nuclear war, it will have to be for much bigger and more important reasons than that.[36]

Eisenhower's strategy had been drawn from the original containment script. He strove to block the Soviets wherever they challenged the West. Kennedy's goals were more ambitious. He hoped to end the Soviet-American conflict once and for all through direct superpower negotiations— and to use the Berlin crisis as the turning point. The Kennedy White House therefore pressed for a more flexible diplomacy on Berlin and, if necessary, a unilateral one. To Eisenhower, Berlin had been a challenge to be endured and outlasted; to Kennedy, it was a way station on the road to his design of a new world order. Eisenhower or Dulles would come up with formulae to defuse a specific threat; Kennedy wanted to eliminate a permanent obstacle to peace.

The two presidents' attitudes toward NATO differed as well. Whereas

Eisenhower had commanded the wartime alliance in Europe, Kennedy had been involved with the war in the Pacific, where the American effort had been much more national and unilateral. Kennedy was not prepared to grant allies a veto over negotiations and, in truth, preferred to deal directly with the Soviet Union, as can be seen from this presidential directive to Secretary of State Dean Rusk, dated August 21, 1961, a week after the Berlin Wall went up:

> Both the calendar of negotiation and the substance of the Western position remain unsettled, and I no longer believe that satisfactory progress can be made by Four-Power discussion alone. I think we should promptly work toward a strong U.S. position in both areas and should make it clear that we cannot accept a veto from any other power. ... We should this week make it plain to our three Allies that this is what we mean to do and that they must come along or stay behind.[37]

In pursuit of this directive, Dean Rusk abandoned four-power negotiations in favor of a direct dialogue with Moscow. Rusk and Gromyko met a few times that fall at the United Nations. Other conversations took place between Ambassador Thompson and Gromyko in Moscow. Yet the Soviets would not so much as agree to an agenda for negotiations on the Berlin issue.

The trouble was that each side found itself trapped in a dilemma peculiar to the Nuclear Age. They could use their nuclear forces to protect their survival, but these weapons did not lend themselves to bringing about positive transformations. Whatever theoretical level of superiority might be calculated, the risk of nuclear war was out of proportion to any objective to be gained. Even a 5 percent risk of war is intolerable when the penalty involves the utter destruction of one's society—indeed, of civilization. At the end of the day, therefore, each side recoiled before the risk of war.

At the same time, neither side was in a position to substitute diplomacy for power. Despite the mounting tension, the arguments in favor of the *status quo* always seemed to outweigh the impulse to modify it. On the side of the democracies, an allied consensus proved impossible to achieve; on the communist side, Khrushchev's boasting may have raised the expectations of his colleagues to such an extent that even the major concessions the West was prepared to make seemed inadequate to the Kremlin hard-liners. In the end, Khrushchev tried to break the deadlock by his disastrous adventure of placing missiles into Cuba, which showed just how high the stakes had to be raised before military power could affect diplomacy.

These tendencies toward stagnation doomed the efforts of the Kennedy Administration to break the deadlock with diplomatic initiatives. Any concession conceivably acceptable to Khrushchev would weaken the Atlantic Alliance, and any settlement tolerable to the democracies would weaken Khrushchev.

The Kennedy Administration's effort to discover in the Soviet catalogue of demands any that could be met without risk was doomed to failure. On August 28, 1961, McGeorge Bundy, Kennedy's National Security Adviser, summed up White House thinking in a memorandum to the President: "The main line of thought among those who are now at work on the substance of our negotiating position is that we can and should shift substantially toward acceptance of the GDR, the Oder-Neisse line, a non-aggression pact, and even the idea of two peace treaties."[38] The memorandum did not state what the United States expected to receive in return.

Such attitudes made it inevitable that Washington would gradually separate itself from Adenauer. On September 22, an Administration leak had stated pointedly:

An authoritative United States source called on West Germany today to accept, in its own interests, the "reality" of the existence of two German states.

The source said West Germany would have better chances of achieving German reunification "by talking to the East Germans" instead of ignoring them.[39]

In December 1961, Bundy tried to reassure Bonn by referring to the "fundamental" American purpose of ensuring that the German people "shall not have any legitimate cause to regret their trust in us." At the same time, he warned against misinterpreting that reassurance to be a blank check: "We cannot grant—and no German statesmen have asked— a German veto on the policy of the West. A partnership of free men can never move at the call of one member only."[40]

In effect, these conciliatory phrases canceled each other out. Since the stated American and German positions were irreconcilable, and since Germany was totally dependent on the United States for the defense of Berlin, denying Bonn a veto could produce only one of two outcomes: risking war for a cause in which the Kennedy Administration had said it did not believe, or imposing views on Bonn that had been rejected by the German leaders. The former course could not have been sustained in the American Congress or in public opinion; the latter would have wrecked Germany's commitment to the West and the cohesion of the Atlantic Alliance.

Relations between Washington and Bonn grew progressively more testy. Fearing deadlock and a break with Adenauer, the State Department dragged its feet for several months and did not implement Kennedy's directive to push direct negotiations with Moscow—or rather it held meetings without providing many new ideas. Had Khrushchev possessed a sense of proportion, he might have realized that this was the moment to determine which of all the various Western hints might be translated into hard political coin. Instead, he kept raising the stakes and avoided negotiations.

During this period of suspended diplomacy and inter-allied tension, I was peripherally involved in White House policymaking as a consultant to the National Security Council. Although I was aware of the issues being debated and the various crosscurrents swirling around the President, I did not personally participate in the final decisions. NATO traditionalists —in particular Acheson, who functioned as an outside consultant during those intervals in which his acerbic tongue had not caused him to fall out of favor—were loath to negotiate at all. Like de Gaulle and Adenauer, they could see no conceivable improvement in any new access procedures, and expected only acrimony from attempts to negotiate on the issue of German unification.

As much as I admired Acheson, I did not believe that a strategy of stonewalling could be sustained. Whenever Khrushchev chose, he could force a negotiation; no Western leader, not even de Gaulle, could confront his public with the need for a showdown unless he had first demonstrated that he had explored every means to avoid one. Considering it dangerous to negotiate on the basis of a Soviet agenda, I thought it was vital to pre-empt this by coming up with an American plan for the future of Germany. I feared for the cohesion of the allies if decisions were relegated to a conference or left at the mercy of deadlines. On procedure, I favored negotiation; on substance, I was close to the traditional positions of Adenauer and Acheson.

My brief White House stint during the Kennedy years produced a number of encounters with Adenauer. These painfully served to bring home to me the extent of the distrust which the Berlin crisis had engendered between heretofore close allies. In 1958, shortly after the publication of my book *Nuclear Weapons and Foreign Policy*,[41] Adenauer had invited me to call on him, though I was then a relatively unknown junior professor. During that conversation, Adenauer told me emphatically not to be deceived by the appearance of a monolithic communist bloc extending from the Baltic to Southeast Asia: as far as he was concerned, a break between China and the Soviet Union was inevitable. He hoped, he said, that when it occurred the democracies would be ready to take advantage of it.

I had never heard that proposition before, nor did I believe it. Adenauer must have interpreted my amazed silence as acquiescence, for when he met Kennedy three years later, he concluded a peroration on the inevitability of a Sino-Soviet split by mentioning that I concurred with him. A little later, I received a message from Kennedy to the effect that he would be grateful if, henceforth, I would share my geopolitical insights not just with the German Chancellor but with him as well.

Assuming—perhaps as a result of this exchange between Adenauer and Kennedy—that I was closer to Adenauer than was probably the case, the White House asked me early in 1962 to attempt to ease the Chancellor's increasingly vocal concerns about the Kennedy Administration's Berlin policy. I was to brief Adenauer on the American approach to negotiations, military-contingency planning for Berlin, and, as a special consideration, America's nuclear capability, which, I was told, had never been shared with any ally except Great Britain.

It proved to be a formidable task. I had barely begun my presentation when Adenauer interrupted: "They have already told me this in Washington. It did not impress me there; why do they think it would impress me here?" I replied sharply that I was not a government employee, that I had been asked to call on him in order to ease his concerns, and that he should hear me out before drawing conclusions.

Adenauer was nonplussed. He asked how much of my time was spent working as a White House consultant. When I told him about 25 percent, he replied calmly: "In that case, I shall assume you are telling me 75 percent of the truth." This was uttered in the presence of the American Ambassador, Walter C. Dowling, who, according to Adenauer's formula, would have to have been lying all the time.

But even at that low point in German-American relations, Adenauer demonstrated that, for him, reliability was a moral imperative. Though nuclear strategy was not his consuming field of interest, he deeply appreciated the sign of confidence implicit in the nuclear briefing Washington had conveyed to him through me. Having emigrated from Germany at the age of fifteen some twenty-five years earlier, I did not feel my German vocabulary was equal to a discussion of nuclear weapons, and conducted my part of the conversation in English. Our interpreter was a member of the Chancellor's staff. Twenty-five years later, that official, who by then was quite elderly and in retirement, wrote to me to say that, like any interpreter worth his salt, he had made a record of the nuclear briefing and had presented it to Adenauer. The Chancellor's response was that he had given his word that the briefing would be kept confidential; therefore, retaining even a single file copy would be incompatible with that promise. And he ordered that all records relating to that part of our conversation be destroyed.

Nevertheless, by April 1962, German-American relations had spun out of control. On April 21, an American plan was leaked calling for the creation of an International Access Authority to control traffic in and out of Berlin. It was to consist of five Western parties (the three Western occupying powers plus the Federal Republic and West Berlin), five communist participants (the Soviet Union, Poland, Czechoslovakia, the German Democratic Republic, and East Berlin), and three neutrals (Sweden, Switzerland, and Austria). Unification would be promoted by a number of committees composed in equal parts of West and East German officials.

Not surprisingly, Adenauer was adamantly opposed to creating an Access Authority especially if East and West Germany would have equal status in it. Moreover, participation of representatives from both East and West Berlin would weaken the city's already fragile four-power status and further enhance the role of East Germany. Since the number of communists on the Access Authority equaled the number of representatives of the democracies, three weak, neutral countries subject to Soviet blackmail would have the decisive voice. Adenauer considered all this a poor substitute for an American commitment.

Adenauer decided to lance the boil by taking what was for him the unprecedented step of publicly criticizing his principal ally. At a press conference on May 7, 1962, he emphatically rejected the International Access Authority.

> It seems to me that this whole plan cannot be implemented. You know that in the end three countries, namely, Sweden, Austria, and Switzerland, are to have the decisive voice since the votes of the people from the East and West will probably balance out. Well then, I should like to ask you whether these countries would answer in the affirmative if they were asked whether they liked this role? I don't think so![42]

To underline the extent of his displeasure, Adenauer added a bitter dig at the Kennedy Administration's attempt to assign a higher priority to the developing world:

> I am also against colonies and I am all for development aid. But I also demand that 16,000,000 Germans [in East Germany] be allowed to live their own lives. We shall tell that to our friends and our enemies.[43]

These differences were never resolved. On July 17, 1962, Kennedy was still telling Anatoly Dobrynin, the new Soviet Ambassador, that "there might well be other issues on which we would be willing to press the Germans quite hard, such as, for example, on the structure of an access authority."[44] Since Adenauer had already publicly explained in great detail his objection to both the composition and the function of such an authority, Khrushchev should have known that he held the key to unleashing a major crisis within the Atlantic Alliance.

Amazingly, just as Soviet success seemed imminent, Khrushchev veered off course. Trying to achieve in one stroke the breakthrough which had eluded him for the past three years, Khrushchev placed Soviet intermediate-range missiles into Cuba. Khrushchev had obviously calculated that, if he succeeded in that adventure, his bargaining position in an eventual Berlin negotiation would be overwhelming. For the same reason, Kennedy could not permit such an extension of Soviet strategic power into the Western Hemisphere. His bold and skillful handling of the crisis not only forced Khrushchev to withdraw the Soviet missiles but, in the process, stripped his Berlin diplomacy of whatever credibility still remained to it.

Recognizing that he had run out of expedients, Khrushchev announced in January 1963 that the "success" of the Berlin Wall had made a separate peace treaty with Berlin unnecessary. The Berlin crisis was finally over. It had lasted five years. Through it, the allies had preserved their position on all the most essential matters—albeit with many a vacillation. For his part, Khrushchev had achieved no more than to build a wall to keep East Germany's unwilling subjects from bolting the communist utopia.

It was fortuitous for the West that Khrushchev had overplayed his hand, for the Alliance had come perilously close to breaking. The American position during both the Eisenhower and Kennedy administrations was based on the traditional American maxim that America was resisting change through the threat of force, not change as such. As an academic statement, this was unexceptional, provided only that there was a general understanding that the outcome of the crisis would be judged by substance, not method.

And in terms of substance, the various schemes under consideration within both the Eisenhower and Kennedy administrations were extremely risky. All had the common drawback of altering the existing framework in the direction urged by the Soviets. Nor could it have been otherwise, for the Soviet Union had surely not started the crisis in order to worsen its position. Every proposed *quid pro quo* would have obliged the Soviet Union to trade a threat it never should have made for some objective improvement in the status of its East German satellite and the modification of existing access procedures. Adenauer's twin nightmare—that the East German communists might acquire the means to exploit Berlin's vulnerability, and that a gap might arise between Bonn's obligations to the Alliance and its aspiration for national unity—was inherent in any of the proposed negotiating schemes.

Dean Acheson, who had, in his words, been "present at the creation" of the postwar alliance system, saw this clearly. In a letter to Truman on September 21, 1961, he predicted a humiliating Western defeat over Berlin "dressed up as statesmanship of the new order."[45] If such a defeat became unavoidable, argued Acheson, the future of the Western Alliance would depend on who assumed responsibility for the debacle. "It is better," he wrote to General Lucius Clay in January 1962, "to have the followers desert the leader, than to have the leader follow the followers. Who then picks up the pieces? Who is trusted to lead in a new start?"[46] It was the de Gaulle strategy in reverse.

In the course of the Berlin crisis, German priorities shifted. Throughout the postwar period, Adenauer's principal reliance had been on the United States. A year after Khrushchev's ultimatum, that was no longer the case. A State Department intelligence report of August 26, 1959, noted Adenauer's distress at the lack of unanimity among the allies. According to the report, Adenauer still hoped for a restoration of allied unity. But if a "US-UK combination appears to be moving toward an understanding with Khrushchev, Adenauer will be forced to shift his main reliance to France."[47]

Throughout the crisis, Khrushchev behaved like a chess player who, having made a dazzling opening move, sits back in the expectation that the opponent will surrender upon contemplating his dilemma without playing the game to the finish. In reading the diplomatic record, it is difficult to comprehend why Khrushchev never explored any of the innumerable negotiating options that were offered, debated, and so often hinted at. Among these were the Access Authority, the two peace treaties, and the "guaranteed-city" concept. In the end, Khrushchev never did act on any of his deadlines, or on the many options he had had to engage the Western allies in a negotiation. After three years of ultimatums and blood-curdling threats, Khrushchev's only real "success" was the building of the Berlin Wall, which ultimately came to symbolize the failure of the Soviet Berlin policy.

Khrushchev had snared himself in a tangled web of his own creation. Trapped, he found that he could not hope to achieve his demands without war. For this he proved never quite ready, and yet he dared not take the

West up on its offers to negotiate lest he be accused by the "hawks" in the Kremlin and his Chinese cohorts of having settled for too little. Too weak to steer his "doves" toward a more confrontational course, too unsure of his standing to impose concessions on his "hawks," Khrushchev procrastinated as long as he could, then staked everything on a desperate roll of the dice by placing missiles in Cuba.

The Berlin crisis—together with its culmination in the Cuban missile crisis—marked a turning point in the Cold War, though it was not perceived as such at the time. Had the democracies not become so consumed by their internal disputes, they might have interpreted the Berlin crisis for what it was—a demonstration of latent Soviet weakness. In the end, Khrushchev was obliged to continue to live with a Western outpost deep within Soviet territory, having failed to achieve any of the goals he had trumpeted when he launched the crisis. Thus the division of Europe into two blocks was reaffirmed again, as it had been in the Hungarian Revolution of 1956. Both sides would complain about that state of affairs, but neither ever attempted to alter it by force.

The cumulative result of the failure of Khrushchev's Berlin and Cuban initiatives was that the Soviet Union did not again risk posing a direct challenge to the United States, except during a brief flare-up at the end of the 1973 Middle East War. Though the Soviets assembled a vast force of long-range missiles, the Kremlin never deemed these sufficient to mount a direct threat to established American rights. Instead, Soviet military pressure veered off in the direction of supporting so-called wars of national liberation in such areas of the developing world as Angola, Ethiopia, Afghanistan, and Nicaragua.

For a decade, the Soviets made no further attempts to impede access to Berlin, which was continued under established procedures. In that interval, recognition of the East German regime came about gradually and as a West German decision supported by all the major German parties, not as an initiative imposed by the United States. In time, the allies exploited the Soviets' eagerness for the recognition of East Germany by insisting on the precondition that the Soviet Union put in place ironclad access procedures to Berlin as well as confirm its four-power status. The Soviets formally accepted these conditions in the Quadripartite Agreement of 1971. There was no further challenge to Berlin or the access routes until the wall was pulled down in 1989, leading to German reunification. Containment had worked after all.

CHAPTER TWENTY-FOUR

Concepts of Western Unity: Macmillan, de Gaulle, Eisenhower, and Kennedy

The Berlin crisis marked the final consolidation of the two spheres of influence that had, for nearly two decades, been jostling each other along the dividing line partitioning the European Continent. In the first phase of this process, from 1945 to 1948, Stalin had established the Soviet sphere of influence, turning the countries of Eastern Europe into satellite states and, implicitly, threatening Western Europe. In the second phase, from 1949 to 1956, the democracies reacted by forming NATO, by consolidating their occupation zones into the Federal Republic, and by initiating the process of Western European integration.

During the period of consolidation, there were periodic attempts by each camp to break up the sphere of the other. All these schemes failed.

Stalin's peace note of 1952, which had been designed to lure the Federal Republic out of the Western camp, never got anywhere—in part due to Stalin's death. The emptiness of Dulles' strategy for the "liberation" of Eastern Europe was demonstrated during the abortive Hungarian uprising of 1956. Khrushchev's Berlin ultimatum of 1958 represented another attempt to separate the Federal Republic from the West. But in the end, the Soviets had to settle for tightening their hold over their East German satellite. After the Cuban missile crisis, the Soviets concentrated on penetrating the developing world. The result was a bipolar stability in Europe, the paradoxical nature of which was summed up in 1958 by the great French philosopher and political scientist Raymond Aron:

> The present situation of Europe is abnormal, or absurd. But it is a clearcut one and everybody knows where the demarcation line is and nobody is very much afraid of what could happen. If something happens on the other side of the Iron Curtain—and we have the experience of a year ago—nothing happens on this side. So a clear partition of Europe is considered, rightly or wrongly, to be less dangerous than any other arrangement.[1]

It was precisely this stability that made it possible for latent differences within the so-called Atlantic Community to rise to the surface. In the immediate aftermath of the Berlin crisis, Macmillan for Great Britain, de Gaulle for France, and Kennedy for the United States were obliged to reconcile their clashing perspectives on the nature of the Alliance, the role of nuclear weapons, and the future of Europe.

Macmillan was the first British prime minister to confront explicitly the painful reality that his country was no longer a world power. Churchill had dealt with America and the Soviet Union as an equal. Even though his stance had not reflected the true balance of forces, Churchill bridged the gap between wishful thinking and reality with his genius and by invoking Great Britain's heroic wartime effort. When Churchill urged negotiations with Moscow in the immediate aftermath of the war, while he was the leader of the Opposition, and again after Stalin's death in 1953, when he was Prime Minister, he did so as spokesman for a major power which, though no longer in the front rank, was nevertheless capable of affecting the calculations of all the others. Throughout the Suez crisis, Eden still conducted himself as the head of government of a substantially autonomous Great Power with the capacity for unilateral action. By the time Macmillan was faced with the Berlin crisis, the illusion that Great Britain by itself had the capacity to change the strategic calculations of the superpowers could no longer be sustained.

An urbane, elegant skeptic, Macmillan represented the last of the old-style Tories. He was a product of the Edwardian Era, when Great Britain was the world's pre-eminent power and the Union Jack flew in virtually every corner of the globe. Though he was possessed of a wicked sense of humor, there was about Macmillan a melancholy inseparable from his being obliged to participate in England's steady decline after the harrowing experience of the First World War from the zenith of power. Macmillan would recount movingly the reunion of the four survivors of his class at Christ Church in Oxford. During the coal miners' strike of 1984, Macmillan—who by then had been out of office for some twenty years—told me that, though he greatly respected Mrs. Thatcher and understood what she was trying to do, he would never have been able to bring himself to conduct a fight to the finish with the sons of the men he had had to send over the top in the First World War, and who had sacrificed themselves so selflessly.

Macmillan was propelled to 10 Downing Street by the Suez debacle, the watershed event in his country's declining global role. Macmillan played his hand with great panache but not without a certain reluctance. As a former Chancellor of the Exchequer, he knew all too well that Great Britain's economy was on the decline, and that its military role would never match the vast arsenals of the nuclear superpowers. Great Britain had rejected the Common Market when it had first been proposed. Chamberlain's reference in 1938 to Czechoslovakia as a small, faraway country of which Britons knew little was an accurate description of the detachment with which a country that had spent a century and a half fighting colonial wars on the other side of the world viewed crises in Europe several hundred miles away.

But by the late 1950s, Great Britain could no longer view Europe from a distance, as a place where British forces occasionally intervened to put down a would-be tyrant. Macmillan therefore reversed the policy of aloofness from Europe and applied for membership in the European Community. Yet, despite the Suez debacle, Macmillan's foremost concern remained the cultivation of Great Britain's "special relationship" with the United States.

Great Britain did not consider itself an exclusively European power. After all, its dangers had too often originated in Europe while its salvation had come from across the Atlantic Ocean. Macmillan did not accept the Gaullist proposition that European security would be enhanced by dissociation from the United States. When all was said and done, Great Britain was probably at least as ready to fight for Berlin as France, though its motive would have been not so much to vindicate the vague concept of allied occupation rights as to support America in its assessment that the global balance of power was being threatened.

After Suez, France and Great Britain drew diametrically opposite conclusions from their humiliation at the hands of America. France accelerated its independence; Great Britain opted for strengthening the partnership with America. Visions of Anglo-American partnership had in fact preceded the Second World War, and had been nurtured since. As early as 1935, Prime Minister Stanley Baldwin had sketched them in a speech at Albert Hall:

> I have always believed that the greatest security against war in any part of the world whatever, in Europe, in the East, anywhere, would be the close collaboration of the British Empire with the United States of America.... It may be a hundred years before that desirable end may be attained; it may never come to pass. But sometimes we may have our dreams. I look forward to the future, and I see that union of forces for peace and justice in the world, and I cannot but think, even if men cannot advocate it openly yet, that some day and some time those who follow us may see it. . . .[2]

It did not take a hundred years for that dream to come true. Starting with the Second World War, Great Britain and the United States were bound by mutual necessities, even if these necessities were filtered through very differing historical experiences.

One important factor in forging a strong connection between the two nations was Great Britain's extraordinary ability to adjust to changing circumstances. It may well have been true, as Dean Acheson pointed out, that Great Britain had clung too long to the illusion of empire and had failed to define a contemporary role for itself in Europe.[3] On the other hand, in its relations with Washington, Great Britain demonstrated on an almost daily basis that, old country that it was, it did not deceive itself on fundamental issues. Having shrewdly calculated that they could no longer hope to shape American policy by the traditional methods of balancing benefits and risks, British leaders chose—especially after Suez—to tread the road to greater influence. British leaders of both parties managed to make themselves so indispensable to the American decision-making process that presidents and their entourages came to regard consultations with London not as a special favor toward a weaker ally but as a vital component of their own governance.

It was hardly the case, however, that Great Britain agreed with the American philosophy of international relations. The British have never shared the American view of the perfectibility of man, and have not been given to proclaiming moral absolutes. In terms of their philosophy, British leaders have generally been Hobbesian. Expecting the worst from man, they rarely find themselves disappointed. In foreign policy, Great Britain has always tended to practice a convenient form of ethical egoism: what was good for Great Britain was considered good for the rest of the world as well.

Considerable self-confidence not to speak of a sense of innate superiority was needed to carry off such a conception. When, in the nineteenth century, a French diplomat told British Prime Minister Palmerston that France had grown accustomed to Palmerston's pulling a diplomatic card out of his sleeve at the last moment, the plucky Englishman had responded, "God put the cards there." Yet Great Britain put national egoism into practice with such an intuitive sense of moderation that its presumption to represent the general good was frequently justified.

It was under Macmillan that Great Britain completed the transition from power to influence. He decided to embed British policy in American policy and to expand the range of British options by skillfully handling relations with Washington. Macmillan never contested a philosophical or conceptual point, and rarely laid down an open challenge to key American policies. He readily conceded the center stage to Washington while seeking to shape the drama from behind the curtains. De Gaulle frequently behaved obstreperously in order to make ignoring him painful; Macmillan made it so easy for the United States to solicit Britain's views that ignoring him would have been embarrassing.

Macmillan's tactics during the Berlin crisis embodied that approach. Access to Berlin did not seem to him worth a nuclear holocaust. On the other hand, risking the loss of the American connection was even greater anathema. He would stand alongside the Americans even in the event of a nuclear showdown, which was more than most of the other allies could guarantee. However, before he had to face that ultimate choice, Macmillan was determined to explore the available alternatives. Making a virtue out of necessity, he set out to present himself as the West's prime advocate of peace, to restrain precipitate American actions, and to demonstrate to his British public that "their leaders have made every effort to reach understanding and agreement."[4]

Means quickly turned into ends. Macmillan had enough confidence in his own dexterity to try to draw the sting from the Soviet challenge by engaging in skillfully managed negotiations. To Macmillan's way of thinking, the diplomatic process itself might serve to defuse the threat of Khrushchev's ultimatums by using one inconclusive negotiation after another to extend whatever deadlines the impetuous Soviet leader might announce.

To the extreme displeasure of Adenauer, Macmillan undertook an eleven-day-long journey to the Soviet Union in February–March 1959, even though by then Khrushchev had reiterated his initial ultimatum several times. Macmillan achieved nothing of substance while Khrushchev took advantage of his presence to repeat his threats. Nevertheless, the Prime Minister relentlessly and unflappably pursued the goal of scheduling a series of conferences as the most practical means for getting around Khrushchev's deadlines. He reflected in his memoirs:

> I was anxious to promote the concept of a series of meetings moving steadily forward from point to point in which "peaceful co-existence" (to use the jargon of the day)—if not peace—could reign unchallenged in the world.[5]

However, when talks become their own objective, they are at the mercy of the party most prepared to break them off, or at least the party that is able to give that impression. Thus Khrushchev found himself able to define what in fact was "negotiable." Eager to keep a dialogue going, Macmillan expended enormous ingenuity on seeking to discover some item on the Soviet agenda that could be pursued with relative safety. The day after receiving Khrushchev's formal note on Berlin on November 27, 1958, Macmillan had written to Selwyn Lloyd, his Foreign Secretary: "We shall not be able to avoid negotiation. How is it to be carried out? Will it necessarily lead to discussion of the future of a united Germany and possible 'Disengagement Plans'?"[6]

The common feature of the various disengagement plans was the establishment of zones of limited armaments in Central Europe, which had been defined as Germany, Poland, and Czechoslovakia, and the withdrawal of nuclear weapons from these countries. For Macmillan and, to a lesser degree, the American leaders as well, the location of these weapons had primarily symbolic importance. Since nuclear strategy would have to rely on America's nuclear arsenal (the overwhelming portion of which was not located on the European Continent), discussing a disengagement scheme with the Soviets seemed to Macmillan like a relatively innocuous way of buying time.

Adenauer opposed all of these schemes because once American nuclear weapons were removed from Germany, they would have to be returned to America, thus breaking what Adenauer considered the crucial political link in nuclear defense between Europe and America. His reasoning—or at least that of his defense experts—was that, as long as nuclear weapons were stationed on German soil, the Soviet Union could not risk attacking Central Europe without destroying these weapons. And since this would require a nuclear attack, an American response would be nearly automatic.

If America's nuclear weapons were removed to America, however, a conventional attack on Germany would become feasible. Adenauer was uncertain whether, in light of the devastation it would wreak upon their country, the American leaders' response would then be to initiate nuclear war. The exploration of negotiating options with respect to Berlin thus became a surrogate for the continuing debate over the military strategy of the Atlantic Alliance.

Whenever either Macmillan or Eisenhower undertook any solitary diplomatic initiative, the reaction of the other served to illustrate that vanity is never absent from the relations among statesmen. Although they were good personal friends, in early 1959, Eisenhower was irritated by Macmillan's foray to Moscow; and in the fall of the same year, Macmillan turned churlish when he learned that Eisenhower had invited Khrushchev to Camp David:

> The President, having got himself embroiled in the doctrine of "no Summit without progress at the Foreign Ministers' meeting," is now trying to disengage. The only way that he has thought of is to substitute jollification for discussion. So he is asking Khrushchev to stay with him in America and promising a return visit to Russia. All this seems rather odd diplomacy.[7]

It was not as odd as it was inevitable. Once Khrushchev realized that Great Britain would not separate from America, he concentrated on Eisenhower. In Khrushchev's view, Macmillan had served his purpose by inducing Washington to negotiate. For, in the final analysis, the only interlocutor who could deliver what Khrushchev sought was the American president. Thus all the principal, substantive discussions were those between Khrushchev and Eisenhower at Camp David, and later between Khrushchev and Kennedy at Vienna. Yet, the more America and the Soviet Union monopolized the international dialogue, the more they created an incentive among some NATO allies to seek to achieve some freedom of maneuver for themselves. As the Soviet threat to Western Europe diminished together with the common fear of Moscow, disagreements within the Atlantic Alliance became less risky, and de Gaulle attempted to use this state of affairs to encourage a more independent European policy.

But the choice of whose lead Great Britain would follow proved to be no contest. Since Macmillan preferred subordination to America to subordination to Europe, he had no incentive to encourage de Gaulle's design, and he never went along with moves to split Europe from America no matter what the pretext. Nevertheless, in defending vital British interests, Macmillan was every bit as tenacious as de Gaulle. This became apparent during the so-called Skybolt affair.

To extend the life of its aging bomber fleet, Great Britain had decided to buy Skybolt, a long-range American air-launched cruise missile then in the process of being developed. In the fall of 1962, without advance warning, the Kennedy Administration canceled Skybolt, allegedly on technical grounds but in fact to reduce the reliance on airplanes, which were thought to be more vulnerable than missiles, and almost certainly to discourage an autonomous British nuclear capability. A unilateral American decision made without prior consultation with Great Britain doomed the British bomber forces to rapid obsolescence. French warnings against dependence on Washington seemed to be confirmed.

The next phase of the Skybolt affair, however, demonstrated the benefits of the "special relationship" with America. Macmillan called in some of the chits he had accumulated through his patient fostering of American ties, nor was he any too gentle about it:

> If the difficulties arising from the development of Skybolt were used, or seemed to be used, as a method of forcing Britain out of an independent nuclear capacity, the results would be very serious indeed. It would be deeply resented both by those of our people who favoured an independent nuclear capability and by those who opposed it. It would offend the sense of national pride and would be resisted by every means in our power.[8]

Kennedy and Macmillan met in Nassau, where, on December 21, they agreed to modernize the Anglo-American nuclear partnership. America would compensate Great Britain for the Skybolt by selling it five Polaris submarines and associated missiles, for which Great Britain would develop its own nuclear warheads. To meet America's concern about maintaining central control of nuclear strategy, Great Britain agreed to "assign" these submarines to NATO, except in cases in which "the supreme national interest was at stake."[9]

The integration of British forces into NATO turned out to be largely token. Since Great Britain was free to use the submarines whenever in its "supreme national interest," and since, by definition, the use of nuclear weapons would never be considered except when the supreme national interest *was* at stake, the Nassau Agreement effectively conceded to Great Britain by consultation the same freedom of action France was trying to extort by confrontation. The difference between the British and French attitudes toward their nuclear weapons was that Great Britain was prepared to sacrifice form to substance, whereas de Gaulle, in striving to reassert France's identity, equated form with substance.

France, of course, was in an altogether different situation, because it had no prospect of gaining the same influence over American decisions that Great Britain enjoyed. Therefore, under the leadership of de Gaulle, France raised the philosophical issue of the nature of Atlantic cooperation in a way which turned into a contest for the leadership of Europe and, for America, into a reacquaintance with the historic style of European diplomacy.

The United States had been presiding over world affairs since the end of the Second World War in a manner not previously available to any nation. With only a small portion of the world's population, it was producing nearly a third of all the world's goods and services. Reinforced by an enormous edge in nuclear technology, America basked in a vast margin of superiority over any conceivable rival or combination of rivals.

For several decades, this surfeit of blessings had caused American leaders to forget how unrepresentative the attitudes of a devastated, temporarily impotent, and therefore pliant Europe were compared to Europe's conduct when it was dominating world affairs for two centuries. They failed to recall the European dynamism which had launched the Industrial Revolution, the political philosophy which had spawned the concept of national sovereignty, or the European style of diplomacy which had operated a complex balance-of-power system for some three centuries. As Europe recovered, with America's indispensable help, some of the traditional patterns of its diplomacy were bound to recur, particularly in France, where modern statecraft had originated under Richelieu.

No one felt this need more strongly than Charles de Gaulle. In the 1960s, at the height of his running controversy with the United States, it became fashionable to accuse the French President of suffering from delusions of grandeur. His problem was in fact the precise opposite: how to restore identity to a country suffused with a sense of failure and vulnerability. Unlike America, France was not supremely powerful; unlike Great Britain, it did not view World War II as a unifying, or even an edifying, experience. Few countries have experienced the travails of France after it had lost much of its youth in World War I.[10] The survivors of that catastrophe realized that France could not withstand another such ordeal. In these terms, World War II became a nightmare come true, rendering France's collapse in 1940 a psychological as well as a military disaster. And while France technically had emerged from the war as one of the victors, French leaders knew all too well that it had been saved largely through the efforts of others.

Peace brought no respite. The Fourth Republic experienced the same governmental instability as the Third and, in addition, it had to traverse the searing course of decolonization. Humiliated in 1940, the French army had been barely reconstituted when it was obliged to engage in nearly two decades of frustrating colonial wars, first in Indochina and then in Algeria, each of which ended in defeat. Blessed with a stable government and with its self-assurance enhanced by total victory, the United States could throw itself single-mindedly into whatever task its values dictated. Governing a country racked by a generation of conflict and decades of humiliation, de Gaulle judged policies not so much according to pragmatic criteria as according to whether they could contribute to the restoration of French self-esteem.

The resulting conflict between France and the United States became all the more bitter because the two sides, profoundly misunderstanding each other, never seemed to be talking about the same subject. Although they were generally unpretentious personalities, American leaders tended to be cocksure about their practical prescriptions. De Gaulle, whose people had turned skeptical after too many enthusiasms shattered and too many dreams proved fragile, found it necessary to compensate for his society's deep-seated insecurities by a haughty, even overbearing, demeanor. The interaction of the American leadership's personal humility and historical arrogance, and de Gaulle's personal arrogance and historical humility, defined the psychological gulf between America and France.

Because Washington took the uniformity of interests among the members of the Western Alliance for granted, it treated consultation as the cure-all for every disagreement. In the American view, an alliance was like a publicly held corporation; influence within it was deemed to reflect each party's proportionate share of ownership, and should be calculated in direct proportion to a nation's material contribution to the common effort.

Nothing within France's centuries-long tradition of conducting diplomacy led it to such conclusions. Ever since Richelieu, France's initiatives had invariably grown out of a calculation of risks and rewards. As the product of that tradition, de Gaulle was less concerned with the nature of consultative machinery than with accumulating options for the contingency of disagreement. De Gaulle believed that these options would determine the relative bargaining positions. To de Gaulle, sound relations among nations depended on calculations of interest, not on formal procedures for settling disputes. He did not view harmony as a natural state, but as something that had to be wrested out of a conflict of interests:

> Man "limited by his nature" is "infinite in his desires." The world is thus full of opposing forces. Of course, human wisdom has often succeeded in preventing these rivalries from degenerating into murderous conflicts. But the competition of efforts is the condition of life. . . . In the last analysis and as always, it is only in equilibrium that the world will find peace.[11]

My own brief acquaintance with de Gaulle provided a stark introduction to his principles. Our first encounter took place during Nixon's visit to Paris in March 1969. At the Elysée Palace, where de Gaulle was hosting a large reception, an aide located me in the crowd to say that the French President wished to speak with me. Somewhat awestruck, I approached the towering figure. Upon seeing me, he dismissed the group around him and, without a word of greeting or other social courtesy, welcomed me with this query: "Why don't you get out of Vietnam?" I replied with some diffidence that a unilateral retreat would undermine American credibility. De Gaulle was not impressed, and asked where such a loss of credibility might occur. When I indicated the Middle East, his remoteness turned into melancholy and he remarked: "How very odd. I thought it was precisely in the Middle East that your enemies were having the credibility problem."

The next day, after a meeting with the French President, Nixon invited me to comment on de Gaulle's exposition of his vision of a Europe composed of nation-states—the famous *"Europe de patries."* Foolhardily, for de Gaulle did not relish debating with assistants—or, for that matter, being in the presence of assistants—I asked how France proposed to keep Germany from dominating the Europe he had just described. Obviously, de Gaulle did not consider this query to merit an extensive reply. *"Par la guerre* (through war),"* he replied curtly—a mere six years after hc had signed a treaty of permanent friendship with Adenauer.

Single-minded devotion to the French national interest shaped de Gaulle's aloof and uncompromising style of diplomacy. Whereas American leaders stressed partnership, de Gaulle emphasized the responsibility of states to look after their own security. Whereas Washington wanted to assign a portion of the overall task to each member of the Alliance, de Gaulle believed that such a division of labor would relegate France to a subordinate role and destroy the French sense of identity:

It is intolerable for a great State to leave its destiny up to the decisions and action of another State, however friendly it may be. . . . [T]he integrated country loses interest in its national defense, since it is not responsible for it.[12]

This explains de Gaulle's nearly stereotyped diplomatic procedure of submitting proposals with a minimum of explanation, and, if they were rejected, implementing them unilaterally. For de Gaulle, nothing mattered more than for the French to see themselves and to be perceived by others as acting of their own free will. De Gaulle treated the humiliation of 1940 as a temporary setback to be overcome by stern and uncompromising leadership. To his way of thinking, France could never accept the slightest appearance of being subordinate, even to its feared and respected American ally:

... with regard to the United States—rich, active and powerful—[France] found herself in a position of dependence. France constantly needed its assistance in order to avoid monetary collapse. It was from America that she received the weapons for her soldiers. France's security was dependent entirely on its protection. . . . [T]hese undertakings in the guise of integration were automatically taking American authority as a postulate. This was the case with regard to the project for a so-called supranational Europe, in which France as such would have disappeared . . . a Europe without political reality, without economic drive, without a capacity for defense, and therefore doomed, in the face of the Soviet bloc, to being nothing more than a dependent of that great Western power, which itself had a policy, an economy and a defense—the United States of America.[13]

De Gaulle was not anti-American in principle. He was willing to cooperate whenever, in his view, French and American interests genuinely converged. Thus, during the Cuban missile crisis, American officials were astonished by de Gaulle's all-out support—the most unconditional backing extended to them by any allied leader. And he opposed the various schemes of disengagement in Central Europe, above all because it would leave American military forces too far away and the Soviet army too near:

... this "extrication" or "disengagement" in itself has no meaning for us which is of any value. For if disarmament did not cover a zone which is as near to the Urals as it is to the Atlantic, how would France be protected? What then, in case of conflict, would prevent an aggressor from crossing by a leap or a flight the undefended German no man's land?[14]

De Gaulle's insistence on independence would have remained theoretical had he not linked it with a number of propositions whose practical consequence was to weaken America's role in Europe. The first of these was the assertion that America could not be relied on to remain in Europe indefinitely. Europe had to prepare itself—under French leadership—to face its future alone. De Gaulle did not claim that he preferred such an outcome, and he seemed oblivious to the proposition that his assertions might turn into self-fulfilling prophesies.

During a visit to Paris in 1959, President Eisenhower tackled the issue head-on when he asked the French leader: "Why do you doubt that America would identify its fate with Europe?"[15] In light of Eisenhower's conduct during the Suez crisis, it was an odd and somewhat self-righteous question. De Gaulle politely responded by reminding Eisenhower of more remote lessons of its history. America had not come to France's rescue in the First World War until after three years of mortal peril, and America had entered the Second World War only after France was already occupied. In the Nuclear Age, both interventions would have come too late.

De Gaulle missed no opportunity to attempt to demonstrate that, on specific issues, America's judgment was less European than that of France, and he ruthlessly exploited Khrushchev's Berlin ultimatum. De Gaulle wanted France to be perceived in Bonn as a more reliable ally than America, and gradually to substitute French for American leadership. And when unilateral American initiatives placed several heretofore inviolate tenets of Western postwar Berlin policy on the diplomatic agenda, Adenauer's growing restlessness posed both a danger and an opportunity for France. Danger, because "if the German people were to change sides, the European balance would be upset, and this could be the signal for war"; opportunity, because German fears might enhance French influence in Europe.[16]

What de Gaulle had in mind was a Europe organized along the lines of Bismarck's Germany—that is, unified on the basis of states, one of which (France) would play the dominant role, with the same function that Prussia had had inside imperial Germany. Everybody would have had some role in de Gaulle's redefinition of the old dream of Richelieu's pre-eminent France: the Soviet Union would have seen to the division of Germany; the United States to Western Europe's defense against the Soviet Union; France to diverting German national aspirations into European unity. But, unlike Prussia, France was not the strongest state in Western Europe; it did not have the economic muscle to dominate the others and, finally, it was in no position to dominate an equilibrium containing the two superpowers.

These disagreements might have been left to the passage of time, especially since Adenauer was desperately eager to stay close to the United States. Moreover, all German leaders were so well aware of the disparity in power between France and the United States that they were not likely to trade American nuclear protection for France's greater vigilance on political issues.

There was one issue, however, over which national disagreement between France and America was built into the very essence of the problem and which brooked no delay: the control of military strategy in the Nuclear Age. Here, America's insistence on integration and France's call for autonomy were irreconcilable, and no buffers existed to soften the dispute. Since the power of nuclear weapons was without precedent, history could offer no reliable guide in formulating a military strategy. Every statesman was flying blind when trying to assess the impact of the new technology on both policy and strategy; conclusions about them emerged from academic theories for which there existed no empirical experience or data.

In the first decade of the postwar era, it seemed as if nuclear monopoly had fulfilled America's visions of omnipotence. But by the end of the 1950s it was becoming obvious that each of the nuclear superpowers would soon be able to inflict on the other a level of devastation no previous society could have imagined, threatening the survival of civilization itself.

This realization was at the heart of a revolution that was about to change the very nature of international relations. Though weapons had been progressively growing more sophisticated, their destructiveness had remained relatively limited up until the end of the Second World War. Wars required a vast mobilization of resources and manpower, which took time to accumulate and to assemble. Casualties mounted relatively gradually. Theoretically, a war could be stopped before it got out of hand.

Since power could only be increased in relatively small increments, the proposition that a state might possess too much power for rational political purposes would have appeared preposterous. Yet this was precisely what happened in the Nuclear Age. The superpowers' central strategic dilemma became not how to accumulate additional power, but how to circumscribe the vast arsenals at their disposal. Neither side ever managed to resolve that challenge. Political tensions which would formerly almost surely have led to war were contained by the fear of nuclear conflagration, creating a threshold of risk that would preserve the peace for half a century. But this state of affairs also brought about a sense of political frustration and made non-nuclear challenges more plausible and more frequent. Never had the military gap between a superpower

607

and a non-nuclear state been greater; never was it less likely to be invoked. Neither North Korea nor North Vietnam was deterred by America's nuclear arsenal from pursuing its objectives, even against American military forces; nor were the Afghan guerrillas deterred by the nuclear capacity of the Soviet Union.

For the first time in history, the Nuclear Age had made it possible to alter the balance of power by means of developments taking place entirely within the territory of a sovereign state. A single country's acquisition of an atomic bomb altered the balance more significantly than any territorial acquisition of the past. Yet, with the sole exception of an Israeli strike against an Iraqi nuclear reactor in 1981, no country during the entire Cold War ever resorted to force in order to prevent such an increase in the power of an adversary.

The Nuclear Age turned strategy into deterrence, and deterrence into an esoteric intellectual exercise. Since deterrence can only be tested negatively, by events that do *not* take place, and since it is never possible to demonstrate why something has not occurred, it became especially difficult to assess whether the existing policy was the best possible policy or a just barely effective one. Perhaps deterrence was even unnecessary because it was impossible to prove whether the adversary ever intended to attack in the first place. Such imponderables caused domestic and international debates on nuclear matters to run the gamut from pacifism to intransigence, from paralyzing doubt to an exorbitant sense of power, and from unprovable theories of defense to undemonstrable theories of arms control.

The potential strain in any alliance—the possibility of divergent interests—was exacerbated by these uncertainties. Historically, nations have in general, though certainly not always, adhered to alliances because the consequences of abandoning an ally were deemed to be more risky than fulfilling one's obligations. In the Nuclear Age, this rule no longer necessarily held true; abandoning an ally risked *eventual* disaster, but resorting to nuclear war at the side of an ally guaranteed *immediate* catastrophe.

To enhance nuclear deterrence, America and its allies had an incentive to emphasize both the certainty and the ferocity of their reaction to challenge. To increase the credibility of the threat, but also to reduce the scale of the disaster should deterrence fail, America had an even greater incentive to find ways to make nuclear war more calculable and less catastrophic. Discriminating targeting, central command and control, and a strategy of flexible response became increasingly fashionable among America's defense intellectuals. Yet all of America's allies resisted these measures because they feared that, to the extent that nuclear war could be made more calculable and more tolerable, aggression might become more likely as well. Then too, at the final moment, America might well recoil before permitting its nuclear arsenal to be unleashed, however limited the option so that Europe might wind up with the worst of both worlds: reduced deterrence and unfulfilled strategy.

These fears were far from trivial. At the same time, the American leaders' concern about the problem of multiple triggers posed by autonomous French and British nuclear forces was hardly trivial either. If European forces were used to strike at the Soviet Union, they might embroil America in a nuclear war. For it was entirely possible that the Soviet Union would retaliate against America in order to prevent it from profiting from damage inflicted on the Soviet Union. The more likely scenario, however, was one in which the Soviet Union's response against America's allies was so violent as to bring into question whether America could passively stand by while its closest allies were being devastated—whatever the provocation.

American leaders therefore were determined to avoid being forced into a nuclear war against their will. The decision to risk the destruction of their society was already sufficiently ominous without their having to worry about its being imposed on them by allies. On the other hand, America's "solution" to this dilemma—to deprive its allies of the capacity for independent action—ran up against the historical nightmares of European history. Europe's leaders were all too familiar with having to abandon or being abandoned by allies, and for reasons far less pressing than nuclear devastation. In their view, their survival depended on depriving America, to the greatest extent possible, of the option of separating itself from Europe in the event of an imminent nuclear war—or, if that failed, of having at their disposal national nuclear forces as a form of reinsurance.

The differences between the American and the European approaches to nuclear strategy presented an insoluble dilemma. Great Britain's and France's desire to retain some control over decisions affecting their destinies was both understandable and in keeping with their histories. America's concern about not compounding the perils of the Nuclear Age by the solitary initiatives of allies was equally valid. From the point of view of deterrence, there was indeed some merit to the British and French determination to create additional decision-making centers; the aggressor's calculations would be made more complicated by having to take into account the existence of independent nuclear forces. From the point of view of having a tolerable strategy for conducting a war, America's insistence on unified control made equal sense. The conflicting concerns were irreconcilable, representing the attempt of nations to determine their own fate under unprecedented circumstances and in the face of unimaginable dangers. America's reaction to the dilemma was to try to "solve" it; de Gaulle, considering it insoluble, sought to enhance French independence.

American policy was promulgated in two distinct stages, each of which reflected the personality of the president who was in office. Eisenhower's approach was to persuade the implacable de Gaulle that an independent French nuclear force was not necessary, and to treat attempts to create one as a sign of mistrust. With a characteristically American mix of legalism and idealism, Eisenhower searched for a technical solution to the American nightmare of a nuclear war unleashed by its allies. In 1959, on the occasion of a visit to Paris, he asked de Gaulle how the various national nuclear forces within the Alliance might be integrated into a single military plan. At that point, France had announced a nuclear program but had not yet tested a weapon.

With that question, Eisenhower elicited an answer he was not prepared to accept. For de Gaulle, the integration of nuclear forces was a political, not a technical, problem. It was symptomatic of the gulf between these two conceptions that Eisenhower seemed unaware that de Gaulle had answered his own question a year earlier in his proposal for a Directorate. Eisenhower strove for strategic options; de Gaulle sought political ones. Eisenhower was primarily concerned with an efficient command structure for wartime. De Gaulle was less interested in plans for conducting a general war (by which time he considered all to be lost anyway) than with augmenting his diplomatic options by maintaining France's freedom of action *prior* to any war.

On September 17, 1958, de Gaulle had submitted a memorandum to Eisenhower and Macmillan which conveyed his ideas about an appropriate NATO structure. He proposed a political Directorate within the Atlantic Alliance composed of the heads of government of the United States, Great Britain, and France. The Directorate would meet periodically, establish a joint staff, and design joint strategy, especially in relation to crises outside the NATO area:

> . . . political and strategic questions of world importance should be entrusted to a new body, consisting of the United States of America, Great Britain and France. This body should have the responsibility of taking joint decisions on all political matters affecting world security, and of drawing up, and if necessary putting into action, strategic plans, especially those involving the use of nuclear weapons. It should also be

responsible for the organisation of the defence, where appropriate, of individual operational regions, such as the Arctic, the Atlantic, the Pacific and the Indian Ocean. These regions could in turn be subdivided if necessary.

To show how serious de Gaulle was about his proposals, he conjoined them with the threat of French withdrawal from NATO. "The French government," he noted, "regards such an organisation for security as indispensable. Henceforth the whole development of its present participation in NATO is predicated on this."[17]

On one level, de Gaulle was demanding for France a status equal to America's special relationship with Great Britain. On a deeper level, he was suggesting a security arrangement similar to Roosevelt's idea of the Four Policemen, with France replacing the Soviet Union as one of the players—a sweeping concept of global collective security based on nuclear weapons, although, to be sure, the French nuclear capacity at that point was still incipient.

De Gaulle had penetrated to the heart of the nuclear problem: in the Nuclear Age, there could be no technical expedients to ensure coordination. The potential risk of using *any* nuclear weapons was so exorbitant that its avoidance tended to drive the various players to assume highly national and self-serving postures. The only hope for common action was to forge political relationships so intimate that the various participants in the consultative process would view themselves as a single unit. Yet such a relationship is the most difficult to attain among sovereign nations, and was, in any case, made nearly impossible by de Gaulle's diplomatic style.

Did de Gaulle envisage the Directorate as a stopgap until the French nuclear forces were strong enough to threaten autonomous action? Or was he aiming at a new and unprecedented cooperation that would anoint France with a special leadership role on the Continent? The answer will never be known because the Directorate idea received a very frigid reception from both Eisenhower and Macmillan. Great Britain was not ready to water down its "special relationship" with the United States; America had no wish to provide an incentive for the spread of nuclear weapons by creating a Directorate confined to nuclear powers, even less to incipient ones. The other NATO members rejected the implication that there were two categories of NATO membership—one for the nuclear powers, and another for the rest. And American leaders preferred to deal with the Atlantic Alliance as if it were a single unit—though how this could be reconciled with recent disagreements over Suez and Berlin was not self-evident.

The official reactions of Eisenhower and Macmillan were evasive. Having become accustomed to the relatively pliable and extremely transient prime ministers of the Fourth Republic, they responded to de Gaulle by putting forward essentially bureaucratic schemes in the expectation that, with the passage of time, de Gaulle's proposition would fade away. They accepted the principle of regular consultations but sought to limit them to a level below that of the heads of government, and indicated their preference that the agenda be confined to military issues.

The tactics of Eisenhower and Macmillan—of seeking to submerge substance in procedure—only made sense if one assumed that de Gaulle was being grandiloquently frivolous and had no place to go, two assumptions that turned out to be dead wrong. When thwarted, de Gaulle resorted to his signature tactic of bringing home to his interlocutors that, in fact, he had other options. He ordered the removal of American nuclear weapons from French soil, withdrew the French fleet from the integrated NATO command, and, in 1966, withdrew France from the NATO command altogether. But before he took that last fateful step, de Gaulle would clash with the dynamic young American President, John F. Kennedy.

Kennedy represented a new generation of American leaders. They had fought in the Second World War but had not directed it; they had supported the construction of the postwar order but had not been among its creators. Kennedy's predecessors, who had been "present at the creation," concentrated on preserving what they had built. The Kennedy Administration strove for a new architecture. For Truman and Eisenhower, the purpose of the Atlantic Alliance had been to resist Soviet aggression; Kennedy wanted to bring about an Atlantic Community that would lead the way into what later came to be called a new world order.

In pursuit of that objective, the Kennedy Administration developed a two-pronged approach of trying to find a rational application for nuclear weapons while evolving a political definition of what it understood by the Atlantic Community. Kennedy was appalled by the cataclysmic consequences of the still-dominant military doctrine of massive retaliation. Under the leadership of his brilliant Secretary of Defense, Robert McNamara, he strove to develop a strategy that created military options other than Armageddon and capitulation. The Kennedy Administration increased the emphasis on conventional forces, and sought to find a discriminating use for nuclear weapons. America's mounting vulnerability to nuclear attack by the Soviet Union led to the so-called strategy of flexible response, whose command system and multiple options were designed to enable the United States to determine, to the extent that the adversary cooperated, how and with which weapons a war would be fought, and on what terms it would be concluded.

Yet, for such a strategy to work, nuclear weapons would have to be kept under central—that is, American—control. Kennedy referred to the French nuclear program as being "inimical" to NATO, and his Secretary of Defense castigated the notion of European nuclear forces, including Great Britain's, with a variety of pointed adjectives, among them "dangerous," "expensive," "prone to obsolescence," and "lacking in credibility." Undersecretary of State George Ball weighed in with the argument that "the road toward nuclear proliferation has no logical ending."[18]

The Kennedy Administration therefore urged "integration" of all NATO nuclear forces and came up with a project to achieve this objective—the NATO Multilateral Force (MLF). A few hundred intermediate-range missiles with a range of 1,500–2,000 miles were to be placed on ships under NATO command. To underline the Alliance nature of this force, the ships would be composed of crews drawn from the participating nationalities.[19] But since the United States retained a veto, the MLF did not solve NATO's basic nuclear dilemma; it would be either redundant or useless.

On July 4, 1962, Kennedy proclaimed his lofty Declaration of Interdependence between the United States and a United Europe. The politically and economically integrated Europe would become an equal partner of the United States, sharing in the burdens and obligations of world leadership.[20] Elaborating on this symbolism in a later speech at the Paulskirche in Frankfurt, where the liberal German National Assembly of 1848 had met, Kennedy linked prospects for the Atlantic partnership with European integration:

> It is only a fully cohesive Europe that can protect us all against fragmentation of the alliance. Only such a Europe will permit full reciprocity of treatment across the ocean, in facing the Atlantic agenda. With only such a Europe can we have a full give-and-take between equals, an equal sharing of responsibilities, and an equal level of sacrifice.[21]

Kennedy's eloquent challenge ran aground on the morass of European ambivalence composed of growing economic strength and a sense of military impotence, especially in the nuclear field. The same qualities which rendered flexible response so attractive and so necessary for the United States raised doubts among its NATO allies. The practical consequence of the strategy of flexible response was that it would permit Washington to achieve greater freedom of political choice about the decision to go to war—an objective de Gaulle sought to constrict with the *force de frappe,* as he called the French nuclear force when it finally came into being in the 1960s. The very quality of deliberation and flexibility so desirable to America reinforced French arguments in favor of nuclear autonomy as a hedge against America's having second thoughts in a moment of crisis. Though America's goal had been to strengthen deterrence by making the nuclear threat more credible, most allies preferred to base deterrence on the opposite course—increasing the magnitude of the adversary's risk by sticking to a strategy of massive retaliation, no matter how nihilistic the consequences. What to do if the bluff did not work was never discussed, though the option of surrender cannot be excluded.

The debate about military integration had a certain theological quality about it. In peacetime, the NATO command is primarily a planning staff: operationally, the military forces of each ally remain under national command, and the right to withdraw forces is so implicit that it has never been challenged. This was demonstrated by the withdrawal of French forces for use in Algeria, and of American forces during a series of Middle East crises—in Lebanon in 1958, in the 1973 Arab-Israeli War, and during the 1991 Gulf War. While debating the theology and merits of "integration," neither the United States nor France ever defined what common action might be possible under the label of "integration" that would be prevented by the looser French concept of cooperation. No command arrangement could solve the essentially political problem thus analyzed by de Gaulle:

> The Americans, our allies and our friends, have for a long time, alone, possessed a nuclear arsenal. So long as they alone had such an arsenal and so long as they showed their will to use it immediately if Europe were attacked . . . the Americans acted in such a way that for France the question of an invasion hardly arose, since an attack was beyond all probability. . . . Since then the Soviets have also acquired a nuclear arsenal, and that arsenal is powerful enough to endanger the very life of America. Naturally, I am not making an evaluation—if indeed it is possible to find a relation between the degree of one death and the degree of another—but the new and gigantic fact is there.[22]

The Skybolt controversy brought all these latent conflicts to a head. Throughout his political life, de Gaulle had resisted the "special relationship" between America and Great Britain precisely because, in his view, it symbolized Great Britain's status as a Great Power equal to that of the United States while reducing France to a secondary position. To be sure, Kennedy had offered the same assistance to France's missile program as he had to Great Britain's. But, to de Gaulle, the nuance of difference between integration and coordination defined the essence of a truly independent policy. In any event, the fact that the Nassau Agreement had been negotiated by the Anglo-American leaders and communicated to de Gaulle publicly via the media guaranteed his rejection of it. Nor would he tie his country's nuclear capability to a technology which, like Skybolt, might be canceled at any moment. At a press conference on January 14, 1963, de Gaulle therefore rejected Kennedy's offer as publicly as he had received it, observing acidly: "Of course, I am only speaking of this proposal and agreement because they have been published and because their content is known."[23]

While drawing the line, de Gaulle also used the occasion to veto Great Britain's entry into the Common Market and, in the process, rejected Kennedy's view that the European end of the twin pillars needed to be organized along supranational lines:

> Any system that would consist of handing over our sovereignty to august international assemblies would be incompatible with the rights and the duties of the French Republic. But also, such a system would undoubtedly find itself powerless to sweep along and lead the peoples and, to begin with, our own people, in the domains where their souls and their flesh are in question.[24]

The high point of de Gaulle's challenge to American leadership came a few days later. De Gaulle and Adenauer signed a treaty of mutual friendship which provided for permanent consultation on all major issues:

> The two Governments will consult each other, prior to any decision, on all important questions of foreign policy, and in the first place on questions of common interest, with a view to arriving, insofar as possible, at a similar position.[25]

The substance of the treaty was not remarkable. Indeed, it was an empty vessel which could be filled with whatever French and the German leaders might put in it in the years ahead. Symbolically, however, it had considerable importance. Since the time of Bismarck's departure in 1890, France and Great Britain had opposed Germany in all international crises. Yet, when de Gaulle excluded Great Britain from the Common Market, despite strong American pressure, it was a German chancellor who helped to prevent France's isolation. France might not be strong enough to impose its own solutions on outstanding issues but, backed by Germany, it would be strong enough to block those of others.

Ultimately, the issue came down to the question of why nations cooperate. In the American view, all reasonable peoples in the end come to the same conclusion; hence, common objectives are taken more or less for granted, and emphasis is placed on the machinery with which to implement the underlying harmony. The European approach springs from a long history of conflicting national interests; reconciling these interests has been the essence of European diplomacy. European leaders perceive harmony as something which needs to be eked out of the environment from case to case, through deliberate acts of statesmanship. That belief was precisely what was at issue with respect to nuclear control in the 1960s; it was at the heart of de Gaulle's rejection of a supranational Europe, and would recur in the debate over the Maastricht Treaty in the 1990s. No doubt, de Gaulle was driven as well by less philosophical motives. A disciple of Richelieu, he perceived France's dominant role in the European Community as being threatened by British entry, both because of the weight which Great Britain represented and due to its affinity with the United States.

Still, however selfish his answers, de Gaulle's questions went to the heart of America's international role, especially in the post–Cold War era. For one of the most difficult lessons America has yet to learn is that nations cooperate for long periods only when they share common political goals, and that American policy must focus on these goals rather than on the mechanisms used to reach them. A functioning international order must leave enough room for differing national interests. And though it should attempt to reconcile them, it must never simply assume them away.

Kennedy's soaring vision of an Atlantic partnership based on the twin pillars of Europe and America supporting a common roof was resisted relentlessly by de Gaulle, who put forward his own concept of a far more intricate, if less elevated, set of relationships. Both concepts reflected their countries' histories and values. Kennedy's was an updating of the legacies of Wilson and Franklin Delano Roosevelt; de Gaulle's was an intricate version of classical European equilibrium based on a divided Germany, West German economic preponderance, French political dominance of the European Community, and America's nuclear protection as a form of insurance.

Yet, when all was said and done, de Gaulle was defeated by the very emphasis on old-fashioned national interest that he had so powerfully evoked. Wise statesmanship does not overreach. De Gaulle's brilliant analysis was vitiated by his failure to take into account that the French national interest was not compatible with driving disagreements with the United States to a point where America might dissociate from Europe— at least while the Soviet Union was still intact. France had the capacity to thwart American designs here and there, but it was at no point strong enough to impose its own.

Whether de Gaulle disregarded this truth or was too proud to acknowledge it, he frequently transposed essentially philosophical propositions into an assault on American intentions, as if sowing systematic distrust within the Alliance were the essence of French policy. In the process, de Gaulle frustrated his own design. His proposition that the decision on war and peace is, in the deepest sense, political was true enough. And his Directorate idea correctly called attention to the imperative to concert political purposes, especially outside the area covered by the Atlantic Alliance.

Yet de Gaulle tended to carry valid arguments to self-defeating extremes. It was one thing for him to reject structures which rendered agreement obligatory and sought to prevent autonomous action by procedural means, and quite another to conduct Atlantic relations in the form of permanent confrontation between Europe and America. His high-handed tactics ran too counter to the way Americans conceive of international relations, especially alliances, and was incompatible with the attitudes of the other members of NATO that, driven to choose between Washington and Paris, would always opt for the former.

This was particularly true with respect to France's relations with Germany. De Gaulle had made Franco-German cooperation the linchpin of his foreign policy. But although he had Germany's support for his Berlin policies and considerable sympathy for his views on nuclear control, there was a limit beyond which no German statesman would or could go in dissociating from the United States. Whatever their misgivings about individual American policies, German leaders had no desire to be left facing the Soviet Union with the sole backing of France. Regardless of how German leaders assessed the relative merits of the Anglo-American positions on the issues of nuclear control and European integration, none of them could possibly prefer reliance on the small French forces over America's vast nuclear arsenal, or on France's political backing over that of the United States. There was, therefore, an inherent limit to what de Gaulle was able to accomplish by taking an anti-American course; his efforts to prevent the emergence of a nationalistic Germany ran the risk of tempting German nationalism to maneuver among its various options.

It was a peculiarity of the crises of the 1960s that they always ran into the sand. After the Berlin crisis of 1958–63, there were no more frontal Soviet challenges to Western interests in Europe. After the Atlantic crises of 1960–66, NATO issues subsided to a peaceful coexistence between the American and French conceptions. During the 1970s, the Nixon Administration, in its "Year of Europe," sought to revive some of the spirit of Kennedy's approach on the basis of more modest proposals. It foundered on the old rock of Gaullist opposition, and for much the same reasons. From time to time, France tried to create a truly independent European military capability, but American reserve and German ambivalence kept these plans from becoming significant. As the decades passed, both the American and the French approaches were overtaken by events.

Ironically, in the post–Cold War world, the two adversaries now find themselves in an environment in which their ultimate cooperation has become the key to a creative Atlantic and European relationship. The Wilsonian vision of a community of democratic states operating on the basis of a common purpose and a division of labor was appropriate to the international order of the 1950s and 1960s, characterized as it was by the overriding external threat of a totalitarian ideology and of America's nuclear near-monopoly and economic superiority. But the disappearance of a single, unifying threat and the ideological collapse of communism, together with a more even distribution of economic strength, impose on the international order the need for a more subtle balancing of national and regional interests. Communism did collapse, as Kennan, Acheson, and Dulles had predicted. Yet, waiting at the end of that road was not a world of Wilsonian idealism but a virulent form of the very nationalism Wilson and his disciples had labeled as "old-fashioned." De Gaulle would not have been astonished by this new world. No doubt he would hardly have considered it "new" at all. He would have argued that it had been there all along, only thinly veiled by the transitory phenomenon of two-power hegemony.

At the same time, the collapse of communism and the unification of Germany have also overthrown most of de Gaulle's assumptions. Skeptical about everything except his own country's international role, de Gaulle overestimated France's capacity to manage the historical processes all by itself. The "new world order" has proved no more hospitable to de Gaulle's dream of French political predominance in Europe than it has to America's unchallenged global leadership. A unified Germany no longer needs its allies' certification of superior legitimacy vis-à-vis the East German rival. With the Soviet Union's erstwhile Eastern European satellites now also players in the game, France finds itself lacking the strength to organize a new European equilibrium all by itself. France's traditional option of containing Germany by seeking rapprochement with Russia is precluded by both of the foreseeable outcomes to the evolution of the former Soviet Union: if it ends in chaos and disarray, Russia will be too weak to act as a counterweight to Germany; if Russian nationalism prevails and recentralization occurs, the new state, still possessing thousands of nuclear weapons, might be too strong to serve as a French partner. Nor is it a foregone conclusion that such a state would opt for France. It would surely find an American or a German option at least as tempting. Above all, any attempt to encircle Germany would reawaken the very nationalism its leaders have so far managed to lay to rest, and which has been France's continuing nightmare. America thus remains France's most reliable, if conceptually most difficult, partner, as well as the only reinsurance available for its necessary policy of friendship with Germany.

So, at the end of the road which de Gaulle had originally designed to make America dispensable, and which America had hoped would integrate France more fully into NATO, cooperation between these two long-time friendly adversaries—something like America's special relationship with Great Britain—has emerged as a key to the equilibrium, just as it should have when, two generations earlier, Wilson had appeared in France to liberate the Old World from its follies and to raise its sights beyond the nation-state.

CHAPTER TWENTY-FIVE

Vietnam:
Entry into the Morass;
Truman and Eisenhower

It all began with the best of intentions. For two decades after the end of the Second World War, America had taken the lead in building a new international order out of the fragments of a shattered world. It had rehabilitated Europe and restored Japan, faced down Communist expansionism in Greece, Turkey, Berlin, and Korea, entered into its first peacetime alliances, and launched a program of technical assistance to the developing world. The countries under the American umbrella were enjoying peace, prosperity, and stability.

In Indochina, however, all the previous patterns of America's involvement abroad were shattered. For the first time in America's twentieth-century international experience, the direct, almost causal, relationship the nation had always enjoyed between its values and its achievements began to fray. The too universal application of their values caused Americans to begin questioning those values and why they should have brought them into Vietnam in the first place. A chasm opened between the Americans' belief in the exceptional nature of their national experience and the compromises and ambiguities inherent in the geopolitics of containing communism. In the crucible of Vietnam, American exceptionalism turned on itself. American society did not debate, as others might have, the practical shortcomings of its policies but America's worthiness to pursue *any* international role. It was this aspect of the Vietnam debate that produced wounds which have proved so painful and so difficult to heal.

Rarely have the consequences of a nation's actions turned out to be so at variance with their original intent. In Vietnam, America lost track of the basic principle of foreign policy that Richelieu had put forward three centuries earlier: ". . . the thing that is to be supported and the force that is to support it should stand in geometrical proportion to each other" (see chapter 3). A geopolitical approach geared to an analysis of national interest would have differentiated between what was strategically significant and what was peripheral. It would have asked why America had thought it safe to stand by in 1948, when the communists conquered the huge prize of China, yet identified its national security with a much smaller Asian country that had not been independent for 150 years and had never been independent in its current borders.

When, in the nineteenth century, Bismarck, the arch-practitioner of *Realpolitik*, found his two closest allies, Austria and Russia, at loggerheads over the turmoil in the Balkans, which lay a few hundred miles from Germany's frontiers, he made it clear that Germany would not go to war over Balkan issues; to Bismarck, the Balkans were, in his own words, not worth the bones of a single Pomeranian grenadier. The United States did not base its calculations on a similar algebra. In the nineteenth century, President John Quincy Adams, a shrewd foreign policy practitioner, had warned his countrymen against venturing abroad in pursuit of "distant monsters." Yet the Wilsonian approach to foreign policy permitted no distinction to be made among the monsters to be slain. Universalist in its approach to world order, Wilsonianism did not lend itself to an analysis of the relative importance of various countries. America was obliged to fight for what was right, regardless of local circumstances, and independent of geopolitics.

During the course of the twentieth century, one president after another proclaimed that America had no "selfish" interests; that its principal, if not its only, international goal was universal peace and progress. In this spirit, Truman, in his inaugural address of January 20, 1949, had grandly committed his country to the objective of a world in which "all nations and all peoples are free to govern themselves as they see fit...." No purely national interest would be pursued: "We have sought no territory. We have imposed our will on none. We have asked for no privileges we would not extend to others." The United States would "strengthen freedom-loving nations against the dangers of aggression" by providing "military advice and equipment to free nations which will cooperate with us in the maintenance of peace and security."[1] The freedom of every single independent nation had become the national objective, irrespective of those nations' strategic importance to the United States.

In his two inaugural addresses, Eisenhower took up the same theme in even more exalted language. He described a world in which thrones had been toppled, vast empires had been swept away, and new nations had emerged. Amidst all this turmoil, destiny had entrusted America with the charge to defend freedom unconstrained by geographic considerations or calculations of the national interest. Indeed, Eisenhower implied that such calculations ran counter to the American value system, in which all nations and peoples are treated equally: "Conceiving the defense of freedom, like freedom itself, to be one and indivisible, we hold all continents and peoples in equal regard and honor. We reject any insinuation that one race or another, one people or another, is in any sense inferior or expendable."[2]

Eisenhower described America's foreign policy as not being like that of any other nation; it was an extension of America's moral responsibilities rather than an outgrowth of a balancing of risks and rewards. The test of America's policies was not so much feasibility—which was taken for granted—as worthiness: "For history does not long entrust the care of freedom to the weak or the timid."[3] Leadership was its own reward; America's benefit was defined as the privilege of helping others to help themselves. Altruism so conceived could have no political or geographic bounds.

In his only inaugural address, Kennedy carried the theme of America's selflessness and duty to the world even further. Proclaiming his generation to be the linear descendant of the world's first democratic revolution, he pledged his Administration, in soaring language, not to "permit the slow undoing of those human rights to which this nation has always been committed, and to which we are committed today at home and around the world. Let every nation know, whether it wishes us well or ill, that we shall pay any price, bear any burden, meet any hardship, support any friend, oppose any foe to assure the survival and the success of liberty."[4]

The sweeping American global commitment was not related to any specific national-security interest and exempted no country or region of the world. Kennedy's eloquent peroration was the reverse of Palmerston's dictum, that Great Britain had no friends, only interests; America, in the pursuit of liberty, had no interests, only friends.

By the time of Lyndon B. Johnson's inaugural on January 20, 1965, conventional wisdom had culminated in the proposition that America's foreign commitments, springing organically from its democratic system of government, had erased altogether the distinction between domestic and international responsibilities. For America, Johnson asserted, no stranger was beyond hope: "Terrific dangers and troubles that we once called 'foreign' now constantly live among us. If American lives must end, and American treasure be spilled, in countries that we barely know, then that is the price that change has demanded of conviction and of our enduring covenant."[5]

Much later, it became fashionable to cite such statements as examples of the arrogance of power, or as the hypocritical pretexts for America's quest for domination. Such facile cynicism misreads the essence of America's political faith, which is at once "naïve" and draws from that naïveté the impetus for extraordinary endeavors. Most countries go to war to resist concrete, definable threats to their security. In this century, America has gone to war—from World War I to the Persian Gulf War of 1991—largely on behalf of what it perceived as moral obligations to resist aggression or injustice as the trustee of collective security.

This commitment was especially pronounced among the generation of American leaders who had in their youth witnessed the tragedy of Munich. Burned into their psyches was the lesson that failure to resist aggression—wherever and however it occurred—guarantees that it will have to be resisted under much worse circumstances later on. From Cordell Hull onward, every American secretary of state echoed this theme. It was the one point on which Dean Acheson and John Foster Dulles agreed.[6] Geopolitical analysis of the specific dangers posed by the communist conquest of a distant country was deemed subordinate to the twin slogans of resisting aggression in the abstract and preventing the further spread of communism. The communist victory in China had reinforced the conviction of American policymakers that no further communist expansion could be tolerated.

Policy documents and official statements of the period show that this conviction went largely unchallenged. In February 1950, four months before the start of the Korean conflict, NSC document 64 had concluded that Indochina was "a key area of South East Asia and is under immediate threat."[7] The memorandum marked the debut of the so-called Domino Theory, which predicted that, if Indochina fell, Burma and Thailand would soon follow, and that "the balance of Southeast Asia would then be in grave hazard."[8]

In January 1951, Dean Rusk declared that "to neglect to pursue our present course to the utmost of our ability would be disastrous to our interests in Indochina and, consequently, in the rest of Southeast Asia."[9] In April of the year before, NSC document 68 had concluded that the global equilibrium was at stake in Indochina: ". . . any substantial further extension of the area under the domination of the Kremlin would raise the possibility that no coalition adequate to confront the Kremlin with greater strength could be assembled."[10]

But was it really true, as the document implied, that every communist gain extended the area controlled by the Kremlin—especially given the experience of Titoism? And was it conceivable that the addition of Indochina to the communist camp could, by itself, overthrow the global balance of power? Since these questions were not raised, America never came to grips with the geopolitical reality that, in Southeast Asia, it was reaching the point where global commitment was turning into overextension—precisely as Walter Lippmann had cautioned earlier (see chapter 18).

There were in fact vast differences in the nature of the threat. In Europe, the principal threat emanated from the Soviet superpower. In Asia, the threat to American interests came from secondary powers which were at best surrogates of the Soviet Union and over which Soviet control was —or should have been understood to be—questionable. In reality, as the Vietnam War evolved, America came to fight the surrogate of a surrogate, each of which deeply distrusted the respective senior partner. In the American analysis, the global equilibrium was under assault by North Vietnam, assumed to be controlled from Beijing, which, in turn, was conceived to be controlled by Moscow. In Europe, America was defending historic states; in Indochina, America was dealing with societies that, in their present dimensions, were building states for the first time. The European nations had long-established traditions of how to cooperate in the defense of the balance of power. In Southeast Asia, statehood was just emerging, the concept of the balance of power was foreign, and there was no precedent of cooperation among the existing states.

These fundamental differences between the geopolitics of Europe and Asia, together with America's interests in each, were submerged in the universalist, ideological American approach to foreign policy. The Czech coup, the Berlin blockade, the testing of a Soviet atomic bomb, the communist victory in China, and the communist attack on South Korea were all lumped together by America's leaders into a single global threat—indeed, a centrally controlled global conspiracy. *Realpolitik* would have sought to limit the Korean War to the narrowest possible dimension; America's Manichean view of the conflict worked in the opposite direction. Endowing Korea with a global significance, Truman had coupled his dispatch of American troops with an announcement of a significant increase in military aid to France in its own war against the communist guerrillas in Indochina (then called the Vietminh), and had moved the Seventh Fleet to protect Taiwan. American policymakers drew an analogy between Germany's and Japan's simultaneous assaults in Europe and Asia in the Second World War, and Moscow's and Beijing's maneuvers in the 1950s, the Soviet Union replacing Germany, and China standing in for Japan. By 1952, a third of the French expenditures in Indochina were being subsidized by the United States.

America's entry into Indochina introduced a whole new moral issue. NATO defended democracies; the American occupation of Japan had imported democratic institutions to that nation; the Korean War had been fought to turn back an assault on the independence of small nations. In Indochina, however, the case for containment was initially cast in almost exclusively geopolitical terms, making it all the more difficult to incorporate into the prevailing American ideology. For one thing, the defense of Indochina ran head-on against America's tradition of anticolonialism. Technically still French colonies, the states of Indochina were neither democracies nor even independent. Although, in 1950, France had transformed its three colonies of Vietnam, Laos, and Cambodia into the "Associated States of the French Union," this new designation stopped well short of independence because France feared that, if it granted full sovereignty, it could do no less for its three North African possessions—Tunisia, Algeria, and Morocco.

American anticolonial sentiment during World War II had focused on Indochina with particular intensity. Roosevelt had disliked de Gaulle and, for that matter, was no great admirer of France, especially after its collapse in 1940. Throughout the war, Roosevelt had toyed with the idea of turning Indochina into a United Nations trusteeship,[11] though he began muting this scheme at Yalta. And it was abandoned by the Truman Administration, which was eager for French support in the formation of the Atlantic Alliance.

By 1950, the Truman Administration had decided that the security of the free world required Indochina to be kept out of communist hands—which, in practice, meant bending America's anticolonial principles by supporting the French struggle in Indochina. Truman and Acheson saw no other choice because the Joint Chiefs of Staff had concluded that the American armed forces were stretched to the limit by simultaneous commitments to NATO and Korea and that none could be spared for the defense of Indochina—even if it were invaded by China.[12] Hence they saw no choice except to rely on the French army, which would have to resist the Indochinese communists with American financial and logistical support. After victory in that struggle, America intended to reconcile its strategic and anticolonial convictions by pressing for independence.

As it turned out, America's initial commitment to Indochina in 1950 established the pattern for its future involvement: large enough to get America entangled, not significant enough to prove decisive. In the early stages of the quagmire, this was largely the result of ignorance about the actual conditions and the near-impossibility of conducting operations through two layers of French colonial authorities, as well as whatever local authorities the so-called Associated States of Vietnam, Laos, and Cambodia were permitted to establish.

Not wanting to be tarred as a party to colonialism, both the Joint Chiefs of Staff and the State Department sought to protect their country's moral flank by pressing France to pledge eventual independence.[13] This delicate balancing act finally landed in the lap of the State Department, which expressed its awareness of the complexities by naming its Indochinese program "Operation Eggshell." The label, unfortunately, conveyed a far greater understanding of the predicament than did the content of its program advance the solution. The idea was to prod France in the direction of granting independence to Indochina while urging it to continue waging the anticommunist war.[14] No one explained why France should risk lives in a war designed to make its presence in the region dispensable.

Dean Acheson described the dilemma with characteristic pungency. On the one hand, he said, the United States might "lose out" if it continued to support France's "old fashioned colonial attitudes"; on the other, if pressed too far, France might simply abdicate altogether with the argument: "All right, take over the whole country. We don't want it."[15] Acheson's "solution" turned out to be a restatement of the contradictions of America's policy: increasing American aid to Indochina while urging France and its chosen local ruler, Bao Dai, to "get the nationalists on his side."[16] He put forward no plan for resolving this dilemma.

By the time the Truman Administration prepared to leave office, evasion had matured into official policy. In 1952, a National Security Council document formalized the Domino Theory and gave it a sweeping character. Describing a military attack on Indochina as a danger "inherent in the existence of a hostile and aggressive Communist China,"[17] it argued that the loss of even a single Southeast Asian country would lead "to relatively swift submission to or an alignment with communism by the remainder. Furthermore, an alignment with communism of the rest of Southeast Asia and India, and in the longer term, of the Middle East (with the possible exceptions of at least Pakistan and Turkey) would in all probability progressively follow."[18]

Obviously, if that estimate was realistic, such wholesale collapse was bound to endanger the security and stability of Europe as well, and to "make it extremely difficult to prevent Japan's eventual accommodation to Communism."[19] The NSC memorandum offered no analysis of why the collapse had to be so automatic or so global. Above all, it failed to explore the possibility of establishing a firebreak at the borders of Malaya and Thailand, which had far greater stability than Indochina—as favored by the British leaders. Nor was the perception of the long-range danger to Europe shared by America's European allies, which, in the years to come, consistently refused to participate in the defense of Indochina.

The analysis that a potential disaster was brewing in Indochina was followed by a remedy that was not even remotely equal to the problem —indeed, in this case, it was no remedy at all. For stalemate in Korea had destroyed—at least for a time—America's willingness to fight another land war in Asia. "We could not have another Korea, we could not put ground forces into Indochina," argued Acheson. It would be "futile and a mistake to defend Indochina in Indochina."[20] This cryptic remark seemed to mean that, if Indochina had indeed become the hinge of the global equilibrium, and if China was indeed the source of the trouble, America would have to attack China itself, at least with air and naval power— precisely what Acheson had resolutely resisted with respect to Korea. It also left open the question of how America should respond if the French and their Indochinese allies were defeated by indigenous communist forces rather than by the entry of the Chinese into the war. If Hanoi was a Beijing surrogate, and Beijing a proxy of Moscow, as both the Executive Branch and the Congress believed, the United States would be forced to choose in earnest between its geopolitical and its anticolonial convictions.

We know today that, soon after winning its civil war, Communist China came to consider the Soviet Union as the most serious threat to its independence, and that, historically, Vietnam has had the same fear of China. Therefore, a communist victory in Indochina in the 1950s would, in all likelihood, have accelerated all these rivalries. That too would have presented a challenge to the West, but not that of a centrally managed global conspiracy.

On the other hand, the arguments of the NSC memorandum were not as shallow as they later appeared. Even in the absence of a central conspiracy, and for all the West knew at the time, the Domino Theory might *nevertheless* have been valid. Singapore's savvy and thoughtful Prime Minister, Lee Kuan Yew, clearly thought so, and he has usually been proven right. In the immediate postwar era, communism still possessed substantial ideological dynamism. A demonstration of the bankruptcy of its economic management was another generation away. Many in the democracies, and especially in the newly independent countries, considered the communist world to be poised to surpass the capitalist world in industrial capacity. The governments of many of the newly independent countries were fragile and threatened by domestic insurrection. At the very moment the NSC memorandum was prepared, a communist guerrilla war was being waged in Malaya.

Washington policymakers had good reason to be concerned about the conquest of Indochina by a movement which had already engulfed Eastern Europe and taken over China. Regardless of whether communist expansion was centrally organized, it seemed to possess enough momentum to sweep the fragile new nations of Southeast Asia into the anti-Western camp. The real question was not whether some dominoes might fall in Southeast Asia, which was likely, but whether there might not be better places in the region to draw the line—for instance, around countries where the political and security elements were more in harness, such as in Malaya and Thailand. And surely the conclusion of the NSC policy statement—that, if Indochina were to fall, even Europe and Japan might come to believe in the irreversibility of the communist tide and adjust accordingly—went much too far.

Truman's legacy to his successor, Dwight D. Eisenhower, was an annual military-assistance program to Indochina of some $200 million (somewhat over $1 billion in 1993 dollars) and a strategic theory in search of a policy. The Truman Administration had not been obliged to face the potential gap between its strategic doctrine and its moral convictions, or to confront the necessity of making a choice between the geopolitical rationale and American capabilities: Eisenhower was left with the responsibility of dealing with the first challenge; Kennedy, Johnson, and Nixon with the second.

The Eisenhower Administration did not question America's commitment to the security of Indochina, which it had inherited. It sought to reconcile its strategic doctrine and its moral convictions by stepping up pressures for reform in Indochina. In May 1953—four months after taking the oath of office—Eisenhower urged the American Ambassador to France, Douglas Dillon, to press the French to appoint new leaders with authority to "win victory" in Indochina, and at the same time to make "clear and unequivocal public announcements, repeated as often as may be desirable," that independence would be granted "as soon as victory against the Communists had been won."[21] In July, Eisenhower complained to Senator Ralph Flanders that the French government's commitment to independence was made "in an obscure and roundabout fashion —instead of boldly, forthrightly and repeatedly."[22]

For France, the issue had already gone far beyond political reform. Its forces in Indochina were enmeshed in a frustrating guerrilla war, with which they had no experience whatsoever. In a conventional war with established front lines, superior firepower usually carries the day. By contrast, a guerrilla war is generally not fought from fixed positions, and the guerrilla army hides among the population. A conventional war is about control of territory; a guerrilla war is about the security of the population. Since the guerrilla army is not tied to the defense of any particular territory, it is in a position to determine the field of battle to a considerable extent and to regulate the casualties of *both* sides.

In a conventional war, a success rate in battle of 75 percent would guarantee victory. In a guerrilla war, protecting the population only 75 percent of the time ensures defeat. One hundred percent security in 75 percent of the country is far better than 75 percent security in 100 percent of the country. If the defending forces cannot bring about nearly perfect security for the population—at least in the area they consider essential— the guerrilla is bound to win sooner or later.

The basic equation of guerrilla war is as simple as it is difficult to execute: the guerrilla army wins as long as it can keep from losing; the conventional army is bound to lose unless it wins decisively. Stalemate almost never occurs. Any country engaging itself in a guerrilla war must be prepared for a long struggle. The guerrilla army can continue hit-and-run tactics for a long time even with greatly diminished forces. A clear-cut victory is very rare; successful guerrilla wars typically peter out over a long period of time. The most notable examples of victory over guerrilla forces took place in Malaya and Greece, where the defending forces succeeded because the guerrillas were cut off from outside supply sources (in Malaya by geography, in Greece due to Tito's break with Moscow).

Neither the French nor the American army, which followed in its footsteps a decade later, ever solved the riddle of guerrilla war. Both fought the only kind of war they understood and for which they had been trained and equipped—classical, conventional warfare based on clearly demarcated front lines. Both armies, relying on superior firepower, strove for a war of attrition. Both saw that strategy turned against them by an enemy who, fighting in his own country, could exhaust them with his patience and generate domestic pressures to end the conflict. Casualties kept mounting while criteria to define progress remained elusive.

France conceded defeat more rapidly than America, because its armed forces were spread more thinly in their effort to hold all of Vietnam with a third of the forces America would eventually commit to defending half of the country. France was being whipsawed as America would be a decade later: whenever it concentrated its forces around population centers, the communists would dominate most of the countryside; when it attempted to move out to protect the countryside, the communists would attack the towns and the forts, one by one.

Something about Vietnam consistently blighted the reasoning power of foreigners who ventured into it. Bizarrely, the French Vietnam War came to a climax at a road junction called Dien Bien Phu, which was located in the remote northwestern corner of Vietnam, near the Laotian border. France had placed an elite force there in the hope of luring the communists into a pitched battle of attrition, and, in the process, maneuvered itself into a no-win situation. If the communists chose to ignore the French deployment, these forces would be wasted in a position far from areas of any strategic consequence. If the communists took the bait, their sole motive had to be the belief that they were within sight of decisive victory. France had reduced its options to irrelevance or defeat.

The French vastly underestimated the toughness and the ingenuity of their opponents—as the Americans would do a decade later. On March 13, 1954, the North Vietnamese launched an all-out attack on Dien Bien Phu which, already in its initial assault, overran two outlying forts that were supposed to dominate the high ground. They did so by using artillery which they were not even thought to possess, and which had been supplied by China in the aftermath of the Korean War. From then on, it was only a matter of time before the remainder of the French force would be ground down. Exhausted by what had become a war of attrition, and seeing little purpose in fighting only to have to withdraw from Indochina under American pressure, a new French government accepted a Soviet proposal to hold a conference on Indochina to begin that April in Geneva.

The imminence of this conference caused the communists to step up their military pressures and forced the Eisenhower Administration to choose between its theories and its possibilities. The fall of Dien Bien Phu would oblige France to yield a substantial portion, if not all, of Vietnam to the communists. Yet Dien Bien Phu could only be saved by a major military escalation for which France had neither the resources nor the will. The United States would have to decide whether to back the Domino Theory with direct military action.

When the French Chief of Staff, General Paul Ely, visited Washington on March 23, Admiral Arthur Radford, Chairman of the Joint Chiefs of Staff, left him with the impression that he would recommend a massive air strike against communist positions around Dien Bien Phu—possibly including the use of nuclear weapons. Dulles, however, was far too committed to collective security to contemplate such a step without laying some diplomatic groundwork for it. In a major speech on March 29, 1954, he in effect urged collective military action to save Indochina from the communists, using the traditional argument of the anti-appeasement school—that failure to act immediately would require much more costly actions down the road:

> . . . the imposition on South East Asia of the political system of communist Russia and its Chinese communist ally by whatever means would be a grave threat to the whole free community. The United States feels that that possibility should not be passively accepted but should be met by united action. This might involve serious risks but these risks are far less than those that will face us a few years from now if we dare not be resolute today. . . .[23]

Under the banner of "United Action," Dulles proposed that a coalition composed of the United States, Great Britain, France, New Zealand, Australia, and the Associated States of Indochina be formed to stop the communist drive in Indochina. Eisenhower joined him in urging collective action, though almost certainly to thwart intervention rather than to promote it. Sherman Adams, Eisenhower's Chief of Staff, described the President's attitude this way: "Having avoided one total war with Red China the year before in Korea, when he had United Nations support, he [Eisenhower] was in no mood to provoke another one in Indochina . . . without the British and other Western allies."[24]

Eisenhower embodied that strange phenomenon of American politics by which presidents who appear to be the most guileless often turn out to be the most complex. In this sense, Eisenhower was a precursor of Ronald Reagan, for he managed to obscure extraordinary manipulative skills behind a veneer of warm affability. As he would over Suez two years later, and again over Berlin, Dulles' words implied a hard line—in this case, the Radford plan of aerial intervention or some variation of it. Eisenhower's preference was almost certainly to avoid military action altogether. He knew too much about military affairs to believe that a single air strike could be decisive, and was reluctant to resort to massive retaliation (the official strategy) against China. And he had no stomach for a prolonged land war in Southeast Asia. Moreover, Eisenhower had had enough experience with coalition diplomacy to be aware of the extreme unlikelihood of United Action's being concluded in a time frame relevant to the fate of Dien Bien Phu. For Eisenhower, this no doubt provided a convenient way out, since he preferred the loss of Indochina to tainting America with the charge of being procolonial. As he wrote in an unpublished passage of his memoirs:

> ...the standing of the United States as the most powerful of the anticolonial powers is an asset of incalculable value to the Free World.... Thus it is that the moral position of the United States was more to be guarded than the Tonkin Delta, indeed than all of Indochina.[25]

Whatever their private reservations, Dulles and Eisenhower made a major effort to bring about United Action. On April 4, 1954, in a long letter, Eisenhower appealed to Churchill, who was then in his last year as Prime Minister:

> If they [France] do not see it through, and Indochina passes into the hands of the Communists, the ultimate effect on our and your global strategic position with the consequent shift in the power ratio throughout Asia and the Pacific could be disastrous and, I know, unacceptable to you and me. It is difficult to see how Thailand, Burma and Indonesia could be kept out of Communist hands. This we cannot afford. The threat to Malaya, Australia and New Zealand would be direct. The offshore island chain would be broken. The economic pressure on Japan which would be deprived of non-Communist markets and sources of food and raw material would be such, over a period of time, that it is difficult to see how Japan could be prevented from reaching an accommodation with the Communist world which would combine the manpower and natural resources of Asia with the industrial potential of Japan.[26]

Churchill, however, was not persuaded, and Eisenhower made no further effort to win him over. Devoted as he was to the "special relationship" with America, Churchill was an Englishman first and perceived more dangers in Indochina than benefits to be gained. He did not accept the proposition that the dominoes would fall quite so inexorably, or that one colonial setback would automatically lead to global catastrophe.

Churchill and Anthony Eden believed that the best place to defend Southeast Asia was at the borders of Malaya; Churchill therefore returned the noncommittal response that Eden would convey the Cabinet's decision to Dulles, who was about to leave for London. Churchill's avoidance of substance left little doubt that Great Britain was groping for ways to cushion its rejection of United Action. Had the news been favorable, Churchill would no doubt have conveyed it himself. Moreover, Eden's dislike of Dulles was proverbial. Even prior to the Secretary of State's arrival, Eden "thought it unrealistic to expect that a victor's terms could be imposed upon an undefeated enemy."[27]

On April 26, Churchill expressed his reservations personally to Admiral Radford, who was visiting London. According to the official record, Churchill warned of "war on the fringes, where the Russians were strong and could mobilize the enthusiasm of nationalist and oppressed peoples."[28] Indeed, there was no political rationale for Great Britain to become involved in a cause which Churchill described this way:

> The British people would not be easily influenced by what happened in the distant jungles of SE Asia; but they did know that there was a powerful American base in East Anglia and that war with China, who would invoke the Sino-Russian pact, might mean an assault by Hydrogen bombs on these islands.[29]

Above all, such a war would have thwarted the old warrior's great dream of his final year in office—to arrange a summit with the post-Stalin leadership "calculated to bring home to the Russians the full implications of Western strength and to impress upon them the folly of war"[30] (see chapter 20).

By now, enough time had passed that, regardless of Great Britain's decision, United Action could no longer save Dien Bien Phu, which fell on May 7 even as the diplomats were discussing Indochina in Geneva. As is often the case when collective security is invoked, United Action had turned into an alibi for doing nothing.

The debate over intervention at Dien Bien Phu showed, above all, the confusion which was beginning to descend on Vietnam policy and the growing difficulty of reconciling geopolitical analysis, strategic doctrine, and moral conviction. If it were true that a communist victory in Indochina would cause the dominoes to fall from Japan to Indonesia, as Eisenhower predicted in his letter to Churchill and in a press conference on April 7, America would have to draw the line regardless of the reaction of other countries, especially since the military contribution of the potential participants in United Action would have been largely symbolic. Though collective action was preferable, it was surely not a precondition to the defense of the global balance, if that was indeed what was at stake. On the other hand, at about the same time that the Administration was attempting to organize collective action, it had changed its military doctrine to "massive retaliation." Proposing to strike at the source of aggression, in practice, meant that a war over Indochina would be directed against China. Yet there was no moral or political basis for air attacks against a country that was only indirectly participating in the Vietnam War and for a cause which Churchill had characterized to Radford as too peripheral and too dangerous to be sustainable for very long in Western public opinion.

Without doubt, the post-Stalinist leaders in the Kremlin would have been extremely loath in their first year of power to confront America for China's sake. However, since America's military leaders were incapable of describing either the targets or the likely outcome of massive retaliation against China (or within Indochina, for that matter), and since Indochina's independence was still only a plan, no realistic basis for intervention existed. Eisenhower wisely deferred a showdown until the various strands of the American approach could be harmonized. Unfortunately, they were still not in harmony a decade later, when America, oblivious to the vastness of the enterprise, confidently took up the task at which France had failed ignominiously.

Since both the Soviet Union and China feared American intervention, the Eisenhower/Dulles diplomacy of making implicit threats helped to bring about an outcome to the Geneva Conference that on the surface was far better than the military situation on the ground warranted. The Geneva Accords of July 1954 provided for the partitioning of Vietnam along the 17th Parallel. To leave the way open for unification, the partition was described not as a "political boundary" but as an administrative arrangement for facilitating the regrouping of military forces prior to internationally supervised elections. These were to be held within two years. All outside forces were to be withdrawn from the three Indochinese states within 300 days; foreign bases and alliances with other countries were proscribed.

Cataloguing the various provisions, however, gives a misleading impression of the formality and stringency of the Geneva Accords. There were many signatories to different parts of the agreement but no contracting parties, therefore no "collective obligations."[31] Richard Nixon later summed up the hodgepodge as follows: "Nine countries gathered at the conference and produced six unilateral declarations, three bilateral cease-fire agreements, and one unsigned declaration."[32]

634

What it all amounted to was a way of ending the hostilities, partitioning Vietnam, and leaving the political outcome to the future. Amateur analysts often invoke the ambiguity of such agreements as a demonstration of the confusion or the duplicity of the negotiators—a charge later leveled against the 1973 Paris Peace Accords. Yet, most of the time, ambiguous documents such as the Geneva Accords reflect reality; they settle what it is possible to settle, in the full knowledge that further refinement must await new developments. Sometimes the interlude permits a new political constellation to emerge without conflict; sometimes the conflict breaks out again, forcing each party to review its bidding.

In 1954, an uneasy stalemate developed which none of the parties was as yet in a position to break. The Soviet Union was not prepared for confrontation so soon after Stalin's death and had only marginal national interests in Southeast Asia; China feared another war with America less than a year after the end of the Korean conflict (especially in light of the new American doctrine of massive retaliation); France was in the process of withdrawing from the region; the United States lacked both a strategy and the public support for intervention; and the Vietnamese communists were not yet strong enough to continue the war without outside sources of supply.

At the same time, nothing that was achieved at the Geneva Conference changed the basic views of the protagonists. The Eisenhower Administration had not altered its conviction that Indochina was the key to the Asian —and perhaps the global—balance of power; nor had it permanently abjured military intervention, only intervention at the side of colonial France. North Vietnam had not abandoned its objective of unifying all of Indochina under communist rule, for which its leaders had been fighting for two decades. The new Soviet leadership continued to avow its commitment to the international class struggle. In terms of doctrine, China was the most radical of the communist countries, though, as was learned decades later, it generally filtered its ideological convictions through the prism of its own national interest. And China's perception of its national interest caused it to be deeply ambivalent about having a major power, even a communist one, on its southern border—the inevitable result of Indochina's unification under communist rule.

Dulles maneuvered skillfully through this thicket. Almost certainly he preferred military intervention and the destruction of communism, even in the North. For example, on April 13, 1954, he stated that the only "satisfactory" outcome would be a complete withdrawal of the communists from Indochina.[33] Instead, he found himself at a conference whose only possible outcome would be to give communist rule in North Vietnam an air of legitimacy which, in turn, would expand communist influence throughout Indochina. With all the bearing of "a puritan in a house of ill repute,"[34] Dulles tried to construct a settlement which, though "something we would have to gag about," would also be "free of the taint of French colonialism."[35] For the first time in the course of America's involvement in Vietnam, strategic analysis and moral conviction coincided. Dulles defined the American goal as assisting in "arriving at decisions which will help the nations of that area peacefully to enjoy territorial integrity and political independence under stable and free governments with the opportunity to expand their economies."[36]

The immediate difficulty, of course, was that the United States had refused to participate officially at the Geneva Conference. It tried to be both present and absent—sufficiently on the scene to uphold its principles, yet far enough to the side to avoid domestic obloquy for having to abandon some of them. America's ambiguity was best expressed in a concluding statement which declared that the United States "takes note" of the final declarations and would "refrain from the threat or the use of force to disturb them." At the same time, the statement warned that "it would view any renewal of the aggression in violation of the aforesaid arrangements with grave concern and as seriously threatening international peace and security."[37] I know of no other instance in diplomatic history of a nation guaranteeing a settlement it has refused to sign, and about which it has expressed such strong reservations.

Dulles had not been able to prevent the communist consolidation of North Vietnam, but he hoped to prevent the dominoes from falling in the rest of Indochina. Faced by what he and Eisenhower perceived as the twin evils of colonialism and communism, he had jettisoned French colonialism and would henceforth be free to concentrate on containing communism. He viewed the virtue of Geneva to be its creation of a political framework which brought America's political and military objectives into harmony and provided the legal basis for resisting further communist moves.

For their part, the communists were preoccupied with establishing their system of government north of the 17th Parallel, a task they pursued with characteristic savagery, killing at least 50,000 people and putting another 100,000 into concentration camps. Some 80,000–100,000 communist guerrillas moved north, while 1 million North Vietnamese fled to South Vietnam, where the United States discovered in Ngo Dinh Diem a leader it thought it could support. He had an unblemished record as a nationalist; unfortunately, devotion to democracy proved not to be his forte.

Eisenhower's wise decision not to become involved in Vietnam in 1954 proved to be tactical, not strategic. After Geneva, he and Dulles remained convinced of Indochina's decisive strategic importance. While Indochina sorted itself out, Dulles put the finishing touches on the collective security framework that had misfired earlier in the year. The Southeast Asian Treaty Organization (SEATO), which came into being in September 1954, was composed, in addition to the United States, of Pakistan, the Philippines, Thailand, Australia, New Zealand, the United Kingdom, and France. What it lacked was a common political objective or a means for mutual support. Indeed, the countries refusing to participate in SEATO were more significant than its members. India, Indonesia, Malaya, and Burma preferred to seek safety in neutrality, and the Geneva Accords prohibited the three Indochinese states from joining. As for America's European allies, France and Great Britain were not likely to run risks on behalf of an area from which they had so recently been ejected. Indeed, France— and to a lesser degree Great Britain—almost certainly joined SEATO in order to gain a veto over what they considered the potential for rash American actions.

The formal obligations contained in SEATO were rather nebulous. Requiring the signatories to meet a "common danger" by their "constitutional processes," the Treaty neither established criteria for defining the common danger nor assembled the machinery for common action—as NATO did. Nevertheless, SEATO served Dulles' purpose by providing a legal framework for the defense of Indochina. This is why, strangely enough, SEATO was more specific about communist aggression against the three nations of Indochina—barred from membership by the Geneva Accords—than with respect to a communist attack on the signatories. A separate protocol designated threats to Laos, Cambodia, and South Vietnam as being inimical to the peace and security of the signatories, in effect providing a unilateral guarantee.[38]

Everything now depended on whether the new states of Indochina, especially South Vietnam, could be turned into fully functioning nations. None of them had ever been governed as a political entity within its existing borders. Hue was the old imperial capital. The French had divided Vietnam into three regions—Tonkin, Annam, and Cochinchina— governed by Hanoi, Hue, and Saigon respectively. The area around Saigon and in the Mekong Delta had only been colonized by the Vietnamese relatively recently, during the nineteenth century, at about the same time that the French arrived. The existing authorities consisted of a combination of French-trained civil servants and a maze of secret societies—the so-called sects—some of which had religious affiliations, but all of which supported themselves and maintained their autonomous status by shaking down the population.

Diem, the new ruler, was the son of an official at the imperial court of

Hue. Educated in Catholic schools, he had for a few years served as an official in the colonial administration in Hanoi but resigned when the French refused to implement some of his proposed reforms. He spent the next two decades as a scholar-recluse in his own country or in exile abroad—mostly in America—refusing offers from the Japanese, the communists, and the French-supported Vietnamese leaders to participate in their various governments.

Leaders of so-called freedom movements are typically not democratic personalities; they sustain themselves through years of exile and prison with visions of the transformation they will bring about once they seize power. Humility is rarely one of their attributes; if it were, they would not be revolutionaries. Installing a government that makes its leader dispensable—the essence of democracy—strikes most of them as a contradiction in terms. Leaders of independence struggles tend to be heroes, and heroes do not generally make comfortable companions.

Diem's personality traits were compounded by the Confucian political tradition of Vietnam. Unlike democratic theory, which views truth as emerging from a clash of ideas, Confucianism maintains that truth is objective and can only be discerned by assiduous study and education of which only a rare few are thought to be capable. Its quest for truth does not treat conflicting ideas as having equal merit, the way democratic theory does. Since there is only one truth, that which is not true can have no standing or be enhanced through competition. Confucianism is essentially hierarchical and elitist, emphasizing loyalty to family, institutions, and authority. None of the societies it has influenced has yet produced a functioning pluralistic system (with Taiwan in the 1990s coming the closest).

In 1954, there was little foundation in South Vietnam for nationhood, and even less for democracy. Yet neither America's strategic assessment nor its belief that South Vietnam had to be saved by democratic reform took account of these realities. With the enthusiasm of the innocent, the Eisenhower Administration hurled itself headlong into the defense of South Vietnam against communist aggression and the task of nation-building in the name of enabling a society whose culture was vastly different from America's to maintain its newfound independence and to practice freedom in the American sense.

Dulles had urged backing Diem all along, on the ground that he was "the only horse available." In October 1954, Eisenhower made a virtue out of necessity by writing to Diem with a promise of aid contingent on standards of "performance . . . in undertaking needed reforms." American assistance would be "combined with" an independent Vietnam that was "endowed with a strong Government . . . so responsive to the nationalist aspirations of its people" as to command both domestic and international respect.[39]

For a few years, everything seemed to fall into place. By the end of the Eisenhower Administration, the United States had given South Vietnam over $1 billion in aid; 1,500 American personnel were in South Vietnam; the United States embassy in Saigon became one of the largest missions in the world. The United States Military Advisory Group, containing 692 members, had ignored the limits on foreign military personnel established by the Geneva Accords.[40]

Against all expectations and with massive American intelligence support, Diem suppressed the secret societies, stabilized the economy, and managed to establish central control—astonishing achievements which were well received in the United States. After a visit to Vietnam in 1955, Senator Mike Mansfield reported that Diem represented "genuine nationalism" and had taken "what was a lost cause of freedom and breathed new life into it."[41] Senator John F. Kennedy endorsed the twin pillars of America's Vietnam policy, security and democracy, describing Vietnam not just as the "keystone of the arch" of security in Southeast Asia but as "a proving ground for democracy in Asia."[42]

Events soon revealed that America had been celebrating a lull in communist pressure, not a permanent achievement. America's assumption that its own unique brand of democracy was readily exportable turned out to be flawed. In the West, political pluralism had thrived among cohesive societies where a strong social consensus had been in place long enough to permit tolerance for the opposition without threatening the survival of the state. But where a nation has yet to be created, opposition may appear as a threat to national existence, especially when there is no civil society to provide a safety net. In these conditions, the temptation is strong, often overwhelming, to equate opposition with treason.

All of these tendencies become magnified in a guerrilla war. For the guerrillas' strategy is to undermine systematically whatever cohesion the governing institutions have managed to achieve. In Vietnam, guerrilla activity had never ceased, and in 1959 it moved into high gear. The guerrillas' initial goal is to prevent the consolidation of stable, legitimate institutions. Their favorite targets are the worst and the best government officials. They attack the worst in order to win popular sympathies by "punishing" corrupt or oppressive officials; and they attack the best because it is the most effective way of preventing the government from achieving legitimacy and of discouraging an effective national service.

By 1960, some 2,500 South Vietnamese officials were being assassinated every year.[43] Only a small number of the most highly motivated, and a much larger percentage of the most corrupt, would run such risks. In the contest between nation-building and chaos, between democracy and repression, the guerrilla enjoyed a huge advantage. Even if Diem had been a reformer on the American model, it is questionable whether he could have won the unequal race between the time scale needed for reform and the time scale sufficient for bringing about chaos. To be sure, even if his country had not been enmeshed in a guerrilla war, Diem would not have proven to be a significantly more democratic leader. A mandarin, he held as a model the Confucian ruler governing by virtue, not consensus, and who achieved legitimacy, the so-called mandate of heaven, by success. Diem recoiled instinctively from the concept of a legitimate opposition, as have all Chinese-style leaders from Beijing to Singapore and nearly all of the leaders of Southeast Asia facing much less severe domestic difficulties. For a while, Diem's achievements in nation-building obscured the lagging pace of democratic reform. However, as security within South Vietnam deteriorated, the latent conflicts between American values and South Vietnamese traditions were bound to deepen.

Despite the American-sponsored buildup of the South Vietnamese army, the security situation steadily worsened. The American military was motivated by the same self-assurance which characterized the American political reformers. Both were convinced that they had somehow discovered the infallible remedy for success in a strife-ridden country geographically and culturally remote from the United States. They went about the business of creating a Vietnamese army as a replica of their own. The American armed forces were geared to combat in Europe; their only experience in the developing world had been in Korea, where their task had been to fight a conventional army crossing an internationally recognized demarcation line amidst a generally supportive population, a situation very similar to what military planners had anticipated would happen in Europe. But in Vietnam, the war lacked well-defined front lines; the enemy, supplied from Hanoi, defended nothing and attacked indiscriminately; he was at once everywhere and nowhere.

From the moment the American military establishment arrived in Vietnam, it began applying its familiar method of warfare: attrition relying on firepower, mechanization, and mobility. All these methods were inapplicable to Vietnam. The American-trained South Vietnamese army soon found itself in the same trap as France's expeditionary force a decade earlier. Attrition works best against an adversary who has no choice except to defend a vital prize. But guerrillas rarely have a prize they must defend. Mechanization and organization into divisions caused the Vietnamese army to become nearly irrelevant to the struggle for its own country.

In those early days of America's involvement in Vietnam, the guerrilla war was still in its infancy, and the military problem was not yet dominant. It therefore seemed as if genuine progress were being made. Not until the very end of the Eisenhower Administration did Hanoi throw the guerrilla war into high gear, and it would still be some time before the North Vietnamese were able to set up a logistics system for supplying a major guerrilla war. In order to accomplish this, they invaded Laos, a small, peaceful, and neutral nation, through which they constructed what later became known as the Ho Chi Minh Trail.

As Eisenhower prepared to leave office, Laos was in fact his main concern. In *Waging Peace,* he described that country as the linchpin of the "Domino Theory":

> ... the fall of Laos to Communism could mean the subsequent fall— like a tumbling row of dominoes—of its still-free neighbors, Cambodia and South Vietnam and, in all probability, Thailand and Burma. Such a chain of events would open the way to Communist seizure of all Southeast Asia.[44]

Eisenhower considered the independence of Laos so crucial that he was prepared to "fight ... with our allies or without them."[45] Defending Laos was to be the most specific recommendation he made to President-elect Kennedy during the transition period prior to January 1961.

As the administrations were changing, the level and the nature of America's involvement in Indochina were not yet of a scale that staked America's global credibility beyond the point of repair. The American effort still bore some relation to regional security objectives; and it was not yet of a magnitude that the act of vindicating it would provide its own justification.

The Domino Theory had become conventional wisdom and was rarely challenged. But like Wilsonianism itself, the Domino Theory was not so much wrong as it was undifferentiated. The real issues posed by Vietnam were not whether communism should be resisted in Asia, but whether the 17th Parallel was the right place to draw the line; not what would happen in Indochina if the South Vietnamese domino fell, but whether another defense line could be drawn, say, at the borders of Malaya.

That issue was never carefully examined in terms of geopolitics. Munich having been the seminal lesson of that generation of American leaders, retreat was considered as compounding the difficulties and, above all, as being morally wrong. This, in fact, was how Eisenhower defended the American involvement in 1959:

> ... our own national interests demand some help from us in sustaining in Viet-Nam the morale, the economic progress, and the military strength necessary to its continued existence in freedom. . . . [T]he costs of continuous neglect of these problems would be far more than we must now bear—indeed more than we could afford.[46]

America's universalist tradition simply would not permit it to differentiate among the potential victims on the basis of strategic expediency. When American leaders invoked their nation's selflessness, it was because they genuinely believed in it; they were more likely to defend a country to vindicate principle than on grounds of the American national interest.

By choosing Vietnam as the place to draw the line against communist expansionism, America ensured that grave dilemmas would lie ahead. If political reform was the way to defeat the guerrillas, did their growing power mean that American recommendations were not being correctly applied, or that these recommendations were simply not relevant, at least at that stage of the struggle? And if Vietnam was indeed as important to the global balance as nearly all of America's leaders were asserting, did it not mean that geopolitical necessities would, in the end, override all others and oblige America to take over a war 12,000 miles from home? The answers to these questions were left to Eisenhower's successors, John F. Kennedy and Lyndon B. Johnson.

CHAPTER TWENTY-SIX

Vietnam:
On the Road to Despair;
Kennedy and Johnson

As the third consecutive president obliged to deal with Indochina, John F. Kennedy inherited a set of well-established policy premises. Like his predecessors, Kennedy considered Vietnam a crucial link in America's overall geopolitical position. He believed, as had Truman and Eisenhower, that preventing a communist victory in Vietnam was a vital American interest. And, like his predecessors, he viewed the communist leadership in Hanoi as a surrogate of the Kremlin. In short, Kennedy agreed with the two previous administrations that defending South Vietnam was essential to the overall strategy of global containment.

Although Kennedy's Vietnam policy was in many ways a continuation of Eisenhower's, there were important differences. Eisenhower had viewed the conflict the way a soldier would—as a war between two distinct entities, North and South Vietnam. To the Kennedy team, the Vietcong attacks on South Vietnam did not represent a traditional war so much as a quasi-civil conflict characterized by the relatively new phenomenon of guerrilla warfare. The Kennedy team's preferred solution was for the United States to build South Vietnam into a nation—socially, politically, economically, and militarily—so that it could defeat the guerrillas without risking American lives.

At the same time, the Kennedy team interpreted the military aspect of the conflict in even more apocalyptic terms than had its predecessors. Whereas Eisenhower had seen the military threat to Vietnam through the prism of conventional warfare, the Kennedy team believed—prematurely as it turned out—that a nuclear stalemate already existed between the United States and the Soviet Union which made general war, in the words of Secretary of Defense Robert McNamara, unthinkable. The Administration was convinced that its military buildup would remove the communists' opportunity to wage Korean-type limited wars. By a process of exclusion, it came to consider guerrilla warfare as the wave of the future and resistance to it the ultimate test of America's ability to contain communism.

On January 6, 1961, two weeks before Kennedy's inauguration, Khrushchev described "wars of national liberation" as "sacred" and pledged Soviet support for them. Kennedy's young New Frontier treated this pledge as a declaration of war against its hope of giving new emphasis to America's relations with the developing world. Today Khrushchev's speech is widely perceived as having been aimed primarily at his ideological tormentors in Beijing, who were accusing him of lapsed Leninism because he had just extended the Berlin ultimatum a third time, and because of his oft-expressed reservations about nuclear war. At the time, however, Kennedy, in his first State of the Union Address on January 31, 1961, treated Khrushchev's speech as proof of the Soviet Union's and China's "ambitions for world domination—ambitions which they forcefully restated only a short time ago."[1]

In September 1965, the same misunderstanding would occur during the Johnson Administration with respect to China, when Chinese Defense Minister Lin Piao's manifesto on "People's War" spoke grandly of "encircling" the world's industrial powers by revolutions throughout the Third

World.[2] The Johnson Administration interpreted this as a warning that China might intervene in Hanoi, ignoring Lin's subtext, which stressed the need for self-reliance among revolutionaries. Reinforced by Mao's comment that Chinese armies did not go abroad, it was meant as well to provide a strong hint that China did not intend to become involved again in communist wars of liberation. Apparently both sides in the Korean War had learned the same lesson; they were determined not to repeat it.

The Kennedy and Johnson administrations' interpretations of communist pronouncements caused Indochina to be no longer perceived as one battle among many in the Cold War. To the New Frontier, Indochina represented *the* decisive battle that would determine whether guerrilla war could be stopped and the Cold War won. Kennedy's interpretation of the conflict as a coordinated global conspiracy caused him to conclude that Southeast Asia was the place to restore his credibility after he had been browbeaten by Khrushchev at the Vienna Summit of June 1961: "[N]ow we have a problem," he told James Reston, who was then the leading columnist of *The New York Times,* "in trying to make our power credible, and Vietnam looks like the place."[3]

As in a classical tragedy in which the hero is led step by imperceptible step to his destiny by seemingly random events, the Kennedy Administration's entry into Vietnam was by way of a crisis from which its predecessors had been spared—the future of Laos. Few peoples have less deserved the suffering that befell them than the gentle, peace-loving Laotians. Wedged between forbidding mountain ranges that face Vietnam and the broad Mekong River, which marks the border with Thailand, the peoples of Laos asked nothing of their bellicose neighbor except to be left alone. That was one wish, however, that North Vietnam never granted them. Once Hanoi had launched its guerrilla war in South Vietnam in 1959, pressures on Laos inevitably increased. Had Hanoi tried to supply the guerrilla forces in the South through Vietnamese territory, it would have had to infiltrate across the so-called Demilitarized Zone, the demarcation line dividing Vietnam which extended for about forty miles along the 17th Parallel. That distance could have been sealed off by the South Vietnamese army with American support. Or else the North Vietnamese would have had to launch an attack by organized military units across the 17th Parallel, which would almost certainly have triggered American and perhaps SEATO intervention—something Hanoi appeared unwilling to risk until 1972, quite late in the Vietnam War.

By the cold-blooded logic that marked communist strategy during the entire war, Hanoi concluded that infiltration into South Vietnam via neutral Laos and Cambodia would involve fewer international penalties than an overt thrust across the 17th Parallel. Even though the neutrality of Laos and Cambodia had been guaranteed by the Geneva Accords of 1954 and reaffirmed by the SEATO Treaty, Hanoi made its judgment stick. In effect, it annexed the panhandle of sovereign Laos and established base areas both there and in Cambodia without significant opposition from the world community. Indeed what passed for world opinion fell in with Hanoi's bizarre reasoning: it was American and South Vietnamese efforts to interrupt the vast infiltration network on neutral soil that became castigated as "expansions" of the war.

The panhandle of Laos provided the North Vietnamese with access routes under a jungle canopy of some 650 miles along the entire border of South Vietnam with Laos and Cambodia. Over 6,000 North Vietnamese troops moved into Laos in 1959 with the ostensible mission of supporting the communist Pathet Lao, who, since the Geneva Accords of 1954, had been imposed by Hanoi in the northeastern provinces along the Vietnamese border.

As a military man, Eisenhower understood that the defense of South Vietnam had to begin in Laos. He apparently told Kennedy during the transition that he was prepared to intervene in Laos, if necessary unilaterally. Kennedy's first statements on Laos were consistent with Eisenhower's recommendations. At a press conference on March 23, 1961, he warned: "The security of all Southeast Asia will be endangered if Laos loses its neutral independence. Its own safety runs with the safety of us all—in a real neutrality observed by all."[4] Yet, when presenting his new defense policy only five days later, Kennedy insisted that "the basic problems facing the world today are not susceptible to a military solution."[5] Though not entirely inconsistent with a decision to defend Laos, this statement was not exactly a clarion call to military action. Hanoi never had any illusions that it was at war, and it would use all the means at its disposal to win it. Kennedy was more ambiguous. He hoped to prevail to contain the communists through political means and by compromise if at all possible.

In April 1961, shaken by the Bay of Pigs, Kennedy decided against intervention, choosing instead to rely on negotiations to buttress Laotian neutrality. Once the threat of American intervention was removed, negotiations on neutrality were certain to confirm Hanoi's stranglehold. As a matter of fact, it was the second time that Hanoi was selling Laotian neutrality, having already undertaken to respect it at the Geneva Conference in 1954.

While developing the logistics network which was later dubbed the Ho Chi Minh Trail, the North Vietnamese stalled the negotiations for a year.

Finally, in May 1962, Kennedy sent Marines to neighboring Thailand. This brought a rapid conclusion to the negotiations. All foreign troops and advisers were required to be withdrawn from Laos through international checkpoints. Every Thai and American adviser left as scheduled; of the over 6,000 North Vietnamese military personnel who had moved into Laos, exactly forty (yes, forty) departed through international checkpoints. As for the remainder, Hanoi brazenly denied that they were even there. The road to South Vietnam now lay wide open.

Eisenhower turned out to have been right. If Indochina were indeed the keystone of American security in the Pacific, as the leaders in Washington had claimed for over a decade, Laos was a better place to defend it than Vietnam; indeed, it was perhaps the only place to defend Indochina. Even though Laos was a remote and landlocked country, the North Vietnamese, as feared and hated foreigners, could not have waged a guerrilla war on its soil. America could have fought there the sort of conventional war for which its army had been trained, and Thai troops would almost certainly have supported American efforts. Faced with such prospects, Hanoi might well have pulled back to await a more propitious moment for full-scale war.

So cold-blooded a strategic analysis, however, was deemed inappropriate for a conflict still perceived largely in ideological terms. (Nor was it my own view at the time.) For a decade, American leaders had been making a case for defending Vietnam because it represented a key element in an Asian defense concept; to revise that strategy by suddenly designating a remote and backward mountain kingdom as the linchpin of the Domino Theory might have disrupted the domestic consensus.

For all these reasons, Kennedy and his advisers concluded that Indochina had to be defended in South Vietnam, where communist aggression had some meaning for Americans, regardless of the fact that they had just made a decision which made that task nearly impossible militarily. For not only did the supply routes through Laos lie open, but the crafty, mercurial ruler of Cambodia, Prince Sihanouk, decided that the game was up and acquiesced in the establishment of communist base areas all along Cambodia's border with South Vietnam. Thus was set up yet another Catch-22 situation: if the Cambodian base areas were left undisturbed, the North Vietnamese could attack the South and withdraw into safety for rest and refitting, making the defense of South Vietnam unmanageable; if the base areas were attacked, South Vietnam and its allies would be pilloried for committing "aggression" against a "neutral" country.

Faced with a crisis over Berlin, his reluctance to risk war in Laos, on the border of China, and in a country of which not 1 percent of the American public had ever heard, was understandable. The alternative, to abandon Indochina altogether, was never considered. Kennedy was loath to reverse a decade of bipartisan commitment, especially in the wake of the Bay of Pigs. Withdrawal would also have meant accepting defeat in what was viewed as a test case for overcoming the new communist strategy of guerrilla warfare. Above all, Kennedy believed the advice he was receiving, namely that American help would enable the South Vietnamese military forces to defeat the communist guerrillas. In those innocent days, no leading American of either party had the least suspicion that America was heading into a quagmire.

Kennedy had a record of public comment on Indochina that extended over a decade. As early as November 1951, he had struck the theme he would never abandon: force alone was not enough to stop communism; America's allies in that struggle had to build a political foundation for it.

> To check the southern drive of Communism makes sense but not only through reliance on the force of arms. The task is rather to build strong native non-Communist sentiment within these areas and rely on that as a spearhead of defense rather than upon the legions of General de Lattre [French commander in Indochina].[6]

In April 1954, during Dulles' United Action campaign to save Dien Bien Phu, Kennedy, in a Senate speech, opposed intervention so long as Indochina remained a French colony.[7] By 1956, after France had withdrawn and South Vietnamese independence had been achieved, Kennedy was ready to join the prevailing orthodoxy: "This is our offspring—we cannot abandon it." At the same time, he reiterated that the conflict was not so much a military as a political and moral challenge "in a country where concepts of free enterprise and capitalism are meaningless, where poverty and hunger are not enemies across the 17th parallel but enemies within their midst. . . . What we must offer them is a revolution—a political, economic and social revolution far superior to anything the Communists can offer." Nothing less than America's credibility was at stake: "And if it falls victim to any of the perils that threaten its existence—Communism, political anarchy, poverty and the rest—then the United States, with some justification, will be held responsible; and our prestige in Asia will sink to a new low."[8]

The trick, Kennedy seemed to be saying, was to make the victim less prone to aggression. That approach was to spawn a new concept not previously found in the diplomatic vocabulary, which is still with us today

—the notion of "nation-building." Kennedy's preferred strategy was to strengthen the South Vietnamese so that they could themselves resist the communists. Civic action and domestic reform were emphasized and the official rhetoric was modified to suggest that American prestige and credibility, not necessarily American security, were on the line in Vietnam.

Each new administration obliged to deal with Indochina seemed to become more deeply drawn into the morass. Truman and Eisenhower had established the military-assistance program; Kennedy's emphasis on reform led to growing American involvement in the internal politics of South Vietnam. The problem was that reform and nation-building in South Vietnam would take decades to bear fruit. In Europe in the 1940s and 1950s, America had bolstered established countries with strong political traditions by extending Marshall Plan aid and by means of the NATO military alliance. But Vietnam was a brand-new country and had no institutions to build upon. The central dilemma became that America's political goal of introducing a stable democracy in South Vietnam could not be attained in time to head off a guerrilla victory, which was America's strategic goal. America would have to modify either its military or its political objectives.

When Kennedy entered office, the guerrilla war in South Vietnam had reached a level of violence sufficient to prevent the consolidation of the Ngo Dinh Diem government without as yet raising doubts about its survival. This seeming plateau of guerrilla activity tempted the Kennedy Administration into the illusion that a relatively small additional effort could achieve complete victory. The temporary lull, however, was due primarily to Hanoi's preoccupation with Laos; it turned out to be the calm before the storm. Once the new supply routes through Laos were opened, the guerrilla war in the South began to accelerate again, and America's dilemmas grew progressively insoluble.

The Kennedy Administration embarked on its journey into the Vietnamese morass in May 1961 with a mission to Saigon by Vice President Johnson in order to "assess" the situation. Such missions almost invariably signal that a decision has already been reached. No vice president is in a position to make an independent judgment about a decade-old guerrilla war in a visit of two or three days. Though his access to intelligence and reporting cables is usually extensive (depending on the president), he does not have staffs adequate for extensive analysis, and none for follow-up. Vice presidential overseas missions are generally designed to stake American prestige, or to supply credibility for decisions that have already been made.

Johnson's trip to Vietnam was a textbook example of these rules. Before announcing the mission, Kennedy met with Senator J. William Fulbright, Chairman of the Senate Foreign Relations Committee, and warned him that American troops might have to be sent to Vietnam and Thailand. Senator Fulbright promised to be supportive, provided that the countries concerned had themselves requested assistance.[9] Fulbright's was a classically American reaction. A Richelieu, Palmerston, or Bismarck would have asked what national interest was being served. Fulbright was more concerned with America's legal and moral position.

Concurrent with Johnson's departure, a National Security Council directive dated May 11 established the prevention of communist domination of South Vietnam as an American national objective. The strategy was "to create in that country a viable and increasingly democratic society" through military, political, economic, psychological, and covert actions.[10] Containment was turning into nation-building.

Johnson reported that the greatest danger in Indochina was not the communist challenge—which, for unexplained reasons, he described as "momentary"—but hunger, ignorance, poverty, and disease. Johnson assessed Diem as admirable but "remote" from his people; America's only choice, he said, was between backing Diem and pulling out.[11] South Vietnam could be saved provided the United States moved quickly and decisively. Johnson did not explain how the United States could eradicate hunger, poverty, and disease in a time frame relevant to the pace of guerrilla warfare.

Having enunciated the principle, the Administration was next obliged to establish a policy. Yet, for the next three months, it was preoccupied with the Berlin crisis. By the time it could turn again to Vietnam, in the fall of 1961, the security situation had deteriorated to a point where it could only be alleviated by some kind of American military intervention.

General Maxwell Taylor, the President's military adviser, and Walt Rostow, Director of the State Department Policy Planning Staff, were sent to Vietnam to develop an appropriate policy. Unlike the Vice President, Taylor and Rostow were members of Kennedy's inner circle of advisers; like Johnson, they had well-established views on America's Victnam policy before they had even left Washington. The real purpose of their mission was to determine the scale and the manner in which America should increase its commitment.

As it turned out, Taylor and Rostow recommended a massive increase in the American advisory role at all levels of the Vietnamese administration. A so-called military logistics force of 8,000 men was to be dispatched, ostensibly to assist with flood control in the Mekong Delta but equipped with enough combat support to defend itself; a substantial increase in the number of civilian advisers was part of the recommendation.

The result was in fact a compromise between those in the Kennedy Administration who wanted to confine American participation in Vietnam to an advisory role and those who favored the immediate introduction of combat troops. The latter school was far from unanimous about what the mission of American combat troops ought to be; they were at one only in vastly underestimating the magnitude of the problem. Acting Assistant Secretary of Defense William Bundy estimated that the introduction of up to 40,000 combat troops, as recommended by the Joint Chiefs of Staff, had a 70 percent chance of *"arresting* things."[12] Since guerrilla war knows no halfway point between victory and defeat, "arresting things" would, of course, merely postpone the debacle while staking America's global credibility. Bundy presciently added that what he described as a 30 percent chance of failure would involve an outcome such as France had suffered in 1954. At the same time, Secretary of Defense Robert McNamara and the Joint Chiefs of Staff estimated that victory would require 205,000 Americans if Hanoi and Beijing intervened overtly.[13] As it turned out, this was less than half of the number of troops America ultimately committed to fight Hanoi alone.

Bureaucratic compromise often reflects the subconscious hope that something will happen in the interim to cause the problem to resolve itself. But in the case of Vietnam, there was no conceivable basis for such a hope. With the official estimates ranging between 40,000 men for stalemate and 205,000 men for victory, the Kennedy Administration had to view the commitment of 8,000 troops as either woefully inadequate or as a first installment in an ever greater American role. And while odds of 70 percent for "arresting things" might seem attractive, they needed to be weighed against the global impact of a disaster such as that France had suffered.

The momentum was clearly all in the direction of further increases, since Kennedy had not changed his assessment of what was at stake. On November 14, 1961, he told his staff that the United States' reaction to communist "aggression" would be "examined on both sides of the Iron Curtain . . . as a measure of the administration's intentions and determination." If America chose to negotiate rather than to send reinforcements, it might "in fact be judged weaker than in Laos."[14] He rejected a proposal from Chester Bowles and Averell Harriman for a "negotiation" to implement the Geneva Accords of 1954, a euphemism for abandoning the effort in South Vietnam.

But if negotiation was rejected and reinforcement was treated as inevitable, an open-ended American commitment could only be avoided if Hanoi backed off. That, however, would have required massive, not incremental, reinforcement, assuming it was achievable at all. America was not prepared to grasp the nettle that the real choice was total commitment or withdrawal, and that the most dangerous course was gradual escalation.

Unfortunately, graduated escalation was the fashion of the day. Designed to stop aggression without excessive application of force, it had the broader purpose of preventing military planning from running away with political decisions, as had happened on the eve of World War I. Graduated response was conceived originally as a strategy in nuclear war —incrementally escalating and thereby avoiding a total holocaust. When applied to guerrilla warfare, however, it ran the risk of inviting open-ended escalation. Each limited commitment involved the danger of being interpreted as inhibition rather than resolve, thereby encouraging the adversary to continue his climb along the ladder of escalation; time enough to settle, he might reason, when and if the risks in fact became intolerable.

Closer attention to the historical record would have indicated that the leaders in Hanoi were not about to be discouraged by esoteric American strategic theories, that they had a genius for overcoming Western technology, and that democracy was neither one of their objectives nor a system they admired. The joys of peaceful construction held no temptation for these hardened veterans of French solitary confinement and decades of guerrilla war. The American version of reform evoked their contempt. They had fought and suffered all their lives to establish a united, communist Vietnam and to expel foreign influence. Revolutionary war was their sole profession. If America had searched the world over, it could not have found a more intractable adversary.

The American objective, according to Roger Hilsman, who was then Director of the State Department's Bureau of Intelligence and Research, was to reduce the Vietcong to "hungry, marauding bands of outlaws devoting all their energies to staying alive."[15] But what guerrilla war in history offered a precedent for such an outcome? In Malaya, it had taken 80,000 British and twice that number of Malayan troops some thirteen years to defeat an opponent numbering no more than 10,000 who had no significant outside support or secure lines of communication, and few opportunities of adding to its numbers. In Vietnam, the guerrilla army numbered in the tens of thousands, and the North had organized itself as the rear area for the struggle, had built base areas along hundreds of miles of border, and retained the permanent option of intervening with an experienced North Vietnamese army whenever the guerrilla army came under too much pressure.

America had maneuvered itself into what could at best be a stalemate according to the Bundy estimate's requirement of 40,000 troops, of which it was still well short. When Kennedy took office, the number of American military personnel in Vietnam was close to 900. By the end of 1961, it had risen to 3,164; by the time Kennedy was assassinated in 1963, the figure was at 16,263, with more in the pipeline. In 1960, the number of Americans dead was 5; in 1961, 16; in 1963, 123; and in 1964, the last peacetime year before American combat units were committed, the number had risen to more than 200. The military situation, however, had not significantly improved.

The more America's military role in South Vietnam expanded, the more America emphasized political reform. And, the more insistent Washington became on domestic change, the more it Americanized the war. In his first defense review, on March 28, 1961, Kennedy restated his central theme: that, no matter how powerful America's strategic weapons were, it could nevertheless be nibbled away slowly at the peripheries "by forces of subversion, infiltration, intimidation, indirect or non-overt aggression, internal revolution, diplomatic blackmail, guerrilla warfare"[16]—dangers which could, in the end, only be overcome by political and social reform enabling the potential victims to help themselves.

The Kennedy Administration took for a truism what would turn out to be one of Indochina's many insoluble dilemmas; the insistence on simultaneous political reform and military victory set up a vicious circle. Within wide limits, the guerrillas were in a position to determine the intensity of warfare, and hence the level of security which was, in the short run, quite independent of the pace of reform. The greater the insecurity, the more heavy-handed the Saigon government was likely to become. And as long as Washington considered guerrilla successes the result, even in part, of lagging reform, Hanoi could maneuver in a way that would magnify American pressures on the Saigon government it was seeking to undermine. Trapped between fanatical ideologues in Hanoi and inexperienced idealists in Washington, Diem's government froze into rigidity and was eventually ground down.

Even a political leader less shaped by mandarin traditions than Diem would have found it daunting to build a pluralistic democracy amidst a guerrilla war and in a society fragmented by regions, sects, and clans. A credibility gap was inherent in America's entire enterprise, not so much because America's leaders deceived the public but because they deceived themselves about their capabilities, including the ease with which familiar institutions could be transferred to other cultures. Basically, the Kennedy Administration was implementing Wilsonian assumptions. Just as Wilson had believed that American notions about democracy and diplomacy could be grafted onto Europe in the form of the Fourteen Points, so the Kennedy Administration sought to give the Vietnamese essentially American rules by which to govern themselves. If despots in the South could be deposed and good democrats installed, the conflict raging in Indochina would surely subside.

Every new American administration sought to make increased aid to Vietnam conditional on reform. Eisenhower had done so in 1954; Kennedy was even more insistent in 1961, linking a massive increase of aid to the United States' being granted an advisory role on *all* levels of government. Predictably, Diem refused; leaders of independence struggles rarely see merit in tutelage. Senator Mansfield, visiting Vietnam at the end of 1962, reversed his own earlier judgment (see chapter 25) and agreed that the Diem government "appears more removed from, rather than closer to, the achievement of popularly responsible and responsive government."[17]

That judgment was correct. Yet the key question was to what extent these conditions were due to the inadequacies of the government, to a cultural gap between Vietnam and America, or to the depredations of the guerrillas. Relations between the Administration and Diem deteriorated throughout 1963. Media reporting from Saigon, which until then had been supportive of America's involvement, turned hostile. The criticisms did not question American objectives, as they would later, but the feasibility of bringing about a democratic, noncommunist South Vietnam in association with a repressive leader like Diem. Diem was even suspected of considering compromise with Hanoi—the very course which, a few years later, a subsequent South Vietnamese President, Nguyen Van Thieu, would be condemned for rejecting.

The final break with Saigon was provoked by a conflict between the South Vietnamese Buddhists and Diem, whose government had issued an edict prohibiting the flying of flags by sects, religious groups, or political parties. Implementing the order, troops fired at protesting Buddhist demonstrators, killing several of them in Hue on May 8, 1963. The protesters had real grievances which were soon taken up by the international media —though the lack of democracy was not one of them. The Buddhists, who were as authoritarian as Diem, refused to state any terms to which Diem might have responded, had he been so inclined. Ultimately, the issue was not democracy so much as power. Paralyzed by the guerrilla war and by its own inadequacies, the Diem government refused to make concessions. Washington multiplied its pressure on Diem to do so, and urged the removal of his brother, Ngo Dinh Nhu, who was in charge of the security forces, a *démarche* which Diem interpreted as a power play to leave him at the mercy of his enemies. The final breach occurred on August 21, when Nhu's agents raided a number of pagodas and arrested 1,400 monks.

On August 24, newly arrived Ambassador Henry Cabot Lodge was instructed to demand Nhu's removal and to warn Diem that, if he refused, the United States must "face the possibility that Diem himself cannot be preserved."[18] Saigon's military leaders were to be put on formal notice that future American aid depended on the removal of Nhu, something Lodge's Vietnamese interlocutors understood to mean that Diem had to be overthrown. Kennedy and McNamara subsequently repeated essentially the same demands publicly. Lest the generals failed to appreciate the hint, they were told that the United States would provide them with "direct support in any interim period of breakdown of central government mechanism."[19] It took the South Vietnamese generals nearly two months to gather their courage and to act on proddings by their insistent ally. Finally, on November 1, they overthrew Diem, killing him and Nhu in the process.

By encouraging Diem's overthrow, America cast its involvement in Vietnam in concrete. Ultimately, every revolutionary war is about governmental legitimacy; undermining it is the guerrillas' principal aim. Diem's overthrow handed that objective to Hanoi for free. As a consequence of Diem's feudal style of government, his removal affected every tier of civil administration down to the village level. Authority now had to be rebuilt from the ground up. And history teaches this iron law of revolutions: the more extensive the eradication of existing authority, the more its successors must rely on naked power to establish themselves. For, in the end, legitimacy involves an acceptance of authority without compulsion; its absence turns every contest into a test of strength. Prior to the coup, there had always existed, at least in theory, the possibility that America would refuse to become directly involved in military operations, much as Eisenhower had done when he pulled back from the brink over Dien Bien Phu nearly a decade earlier. Since the coup had been justified to facilitate a more effective prosecution of the war, withdrawal disappeared as a policy option.

Diem's removal did not unify the people behind the generals, as Washington had hoped. Though *The New York Times* hailed the coup as an opportunity "toward repulsing further Communist inroads throughout Southeast Asia,"[20] the opposite occurred. The underpinning of a pluralistic society is consensus on underlying values, which implicitly sets a limit to the claims of competing individuals or groups. In Vietnam, that consensus had been weak to begin with. The coup destroyed the structure that had been built up over a decade, leaving in its place a group of competing generals without political experience or political following.

During 1964 alone, seven more changes of government took place, none of which brought about a semblance of democracy, and all of which were the results of coups of one kind or another. Diem's successors, lacking his prestige as a nationalist and as a mandarin-style father figure, had little choice but to turn the war over to the Americans. In the wake of Diem's overthrow, it has been justly argued that "the question was not going to be how to encourage a regime in South Vietnam that America could support, but of finding one that would support her in keeping up the struggle against the jubilant Communists."[21]

The power brokers in Hanoi grasped their opportunity immediately. A Communist Party Central Committee meeting in December 1963 laid down the new strategy: guerrilla units would be strengthened, and infiltration into the South accelerated. Most important, North Vietnamese regular units would be introduced: "It is time for the North to increase aid to the South, the North must bring into further play its role as the revolutionary base for the whole nation."[22] Soon thereafter, the 325th North Vietnamese regular division began moving into the South. Before the coup, infiltration from the North had consisted largely of Southerners who had been regrouped in 1954; afterward, the percentage of Northerners rose steadily until, after the Tet Offensive of 1968, nearly all the infiltrators were North Vietnamese. With the introduction of regular North Vietnamese army units, both sides crossed their Rubicons.

Shortly after Diem's overthrow, Kennedy was assassinated. The new President, Lyndon Baines Johnson, interpreted intervention by regular North Vietnamese units as a classic case of overt aggression. The difference was that Hanoi was implementing a strategy while Washington merely had competing theories, none of which was pressed to its conclusions.

Suspended between its yearning for a nonmilitary victory and its foreboding of a military disaster, America faced a tragic quandary. On December 21, 1963, McNamara reported to the new President that the security situation within South Vietnam had become very disturbing. America could no longer avoid facing the choice which had been implicit all along: dramatic escalation of its military involvement or the collapse of South Vietnam. The Kennedy Administration had feared entering the war on the side of an undemocratic ally; the Johnson Administration feared abandoning the new, undemocratic Saigon government more than it did participation in the war.

In retrospect, the last moment at which America could have withdrawn from Vietnam at tolerable—though still heavy—cost would have been either just before or just after Diem was overthrown. The Kennedy Administration was correct in its assessment that it could not win with Diem. The Johnson Administration deluded itself into believing that it could win with his successors. In light of what followed the coup, it would have been easier for America to disengage by letting Diem collapse of his own inadequacies or, at a minimum, by not standing in the way of the negotiations he was suspected of planning with Hanoi. Kennedy had been analytically correct to reject any such scheme on the ground that it would inevitably lead to a communist takeover. The problem was that America was prepared neither to face the implications of the remedy nor to accept the probable outcome of letting matters run their course.

Some former members of the Kennedy Administration have argued that, after the 1964 presidential election, their President intended to withdraw the American forces, which were still being augmented. Others at least as well placed have denied this. All one can say at this remove about Kennedy's ultimate intention is that each successive reinforcement to Vietnam made his choices more stark, and the consequences of either commitment or withdrawal more painful and costly. And with each passing month, America's stakes were raised further, first only militarily but soon in terms of America's international standing as well.

Kennedy's assassination made America's extrication from Vietnam even more difficult. If indeed Kennedy had felt the sting of realization that America had embarked on an unsustainable course, he needed to reverse only his own decision; Johnson, on the other hand, would have had to jettison the apparent policy of a revered, fallen predecessor. This was especially the case as none of the advisers he inherited from Kennedy made the recommendation to disengage (with the notable exception of Undersecretary of State George Ball, who, however, was not in the inner circle). It would have taken a leader of truly extraordinary self-confidence and knowledge to undertake a retreat of such magnitude so soon after taking office. And when it came to foreign policy, Johnson was extremely unsure of himself.

In retrospect, the new President would have done well to undertake an analysis of whether the military and political objectives on behalf of which America had already invested so much were attainable, by what means, and over what period of time—indeed, of whether the premises which had generated these commitments were even correct. Aside from the fact that Johnson found the sophisticated aides whom he had inherited from Kennedy unanimously in favor of trying to win in Vietnam (again, with the exception of George Ball), it is doubtful that, if any such analysis had been made, the outcome would have been significantly different. McNamara's Defense Department and Bundy's White House staffs were gluttons for analysis. Both were men of extraordinary intelligence. What they lacked was criteria to assess a challenge so at variance with the American experience and American ideology.

America's initial motivation in involving itself had been that the loss of Vietnam would lead to the collapse of noncommunist Asia and to Japan's accommodation to communism. In terms of that analysis, in defending South Vietnam, America was fighting for itself, regardless of whether South Vietnam was democratic or could ever be made so. Such an analysis, however, was too geopolitical and power-oriented for Americans, and was soon overtaken by Wilsonian idealism. One administration after another had attempted a dual task, each part of which alone would have been difficult to achieve by itself: the defeat of a guerrilla army with secure bases all around an extended periphery, and the democratization of a society with no tradition of pluralism.

In the cauldron of Vietnam, America was to learn that there are limits to even the most sacrosanct beliefs, and was forced to come to terms with the gap which can arise between power and principle. Precisely because America was reluctant to accept lessons so contrary to its historical experience, it also found cutting its losses extraordinarily difficult. Thus the pain associated with both these frustrations was the result of its best not its worst qualities. America's rejection of national interest as the basis of foreign policy had cast the country adrift on a sea of undifferentiated moralism.

In August 1964, a presumed North Vietnamese attack on the cruiser *Maddox* led to an American retaliatory strike against North Vietnam that was endorsed nearly unanimously by the Senate via the so-called Gulf of Tonkin Resolution. This resolution was used in turn to justify retaliatory air raids a few months earlier. In February 1965, an attack on an American advisers' barracks in the Central Highland city of Pleiku triggered an American retaliatory raid on North Vietnam, which quickly turned into a systematic bombing campaign code-named "Rolling Thunder." By July 1965, American combat units were fully committed, and the American troop presence began to grow, reaching 543,000 by early 1969.

Subsequently, the issue of whether the Johnson Administration had been entirely candid with the American people about the attack on the *Maddox* became part of the increasingly acrimonious Vietnam debate. It was used to discredit both the Gulf of Tonkin Resolution and America's participation in combat. To be sure, the Tonkin Resolution was not based on a full presentation of the facts, even allowing for the confusion of combat. But neither was it a major factor in America's commitment to ground combat in Vietnam. Rather, it was a small step along a road which would have brought America to the same destination, given the convictions of all the leading personalities.

The methods used to achieve the Tonkin Resolution would not be possible today, and American democracy is the better for it. At the same time, neither Johnson's tactics nor his candor was significantly different from Franklin Delano Roosevelt's when he had edged America toward involvement in the Second World War—for example, Roosevelt's not altogether candid account of the torpedoing of the destroyer *Greer,* the pretext for engaging America in a naval war in the Atlantic in 1941. In each case, a president was defining unilaterally what America would not tolerate: German victory in the 1940s; the takeover of Indochina in the 1960s. Both presidents were prepared to put their country's military forces in harm's way and to respond should harm indeed befall them, as was likely. In each case, the ultimate decision to enter the war was based on considerations which went far beyond the immediate incidents.

The nightmare of Vietnam was not the way in which America entered the war, but why it did so without a more careful assessment of the likely costs and potential outcomes. A nation should not send half a million of its young to a distant continent or stake its international standing and domestic cohesion unless its leaders can describe their political goals and offer a realistic strategy for achieving them—as President Bush did later in the Gulf War. Washington should have asked itself two basic questions: Was it possible to establish democracy and achieve military victory more or less simultaneously? And even more crucial, will the benefits justify the costs? The presidents or presidential advisers who committed America to ground combat in Vietnam took an affirmative answer for granted.

The successful conduct of a guerrilla war requires the subtle blending of military and political strategies. American military leaders, however, have never been comfortable with gearing military to political objectives. Throughout the Vietnam War, the means were insufficient for the stated objectives, and objectives were only achievable—if at all—by risks which Washington was not prepared to run.

One of the principal lessons of the Korean War ought to have been that protracted, inconclusive wars shatter America's domestic consensus. Yet Washington seemed to have gleaned exactly the opposite lesson: that the source of frustration in Korea had been MacArthur's advance to the Yalu and his quest for all-out victory. In this light, the outcome of the Korean War was reinterpreted into the success of having prevented a Chinese victory. America's involvement in Vietnam became consciously confined to a similar goal: without triggering Chinese intervention, to demonstrate to North Vietnam that it would not be permitted to take over South Vietnam and that, therefore, its only choice was negotiation. But negotiation for what ends—especially in light of an enemy who equated compromise with defeat? America's leaders had surely forgotten that the last two years of the Korean War and the McCarthy period had nearly ripped apart an American society impatient with protracted stalemate.

Theoretically, only two strategies have any chance of prevailing in a guerrilla war. One is essentially defensive and seeks to deprive the adversary of control of the population. This strategy requires establishing nearly total security for enough of the population so that the guerrillas' gains among the remainder are not adequate for a coherent political base. General Maxwell Taylor seems to have had such a strategy in mind when he recommended establishing a series of enclaves protected by American forces while the South Vietnamese army sought to prevent consolidation of a clearly defined communist zone without trying to hold every last district day and night. The second possible strategy was to attack targets that the guerrillas had to defend, such as sanctuaries, supply depots, and home bases—for example, by interdicting the Ho Chi Minh Trail by ground forces and blockading both North Vietnam and the Cambodian ports servicing the sanctuaries. That strategy—at least conceptually—might have produced the relatively rapid war of attrition which the American military sought so desperately, and forced a negotiated outcome.

What could not work was the strategy which America in fact adopted: the mirage of establishing 100 percent security in 100 percent of the country, and seeking to wear down the guerrillas by search-and-destroy operations. No matter how large the expeditionary force, it could never prove sufficient against an enemy whose supply lines lay outside of Vietnam and who possessed extensive sanctuaries and a ferocious will. At the end of 1966, North Vietnamese Prime Minister Pham Van Dong told Harrison Salisbury of *The New York Times* that, though the United States was far stronger militarily, it would lose in the end because more Vietnamese than Americans were prepared to die for Vietnam, and to fight as long as it might take to outlast the Americans.[23] His assessment proved correct.

Johnson resolutely rejected any "expansion" of the war. Washington had convinced itself that the four Indochinese states were separate entities, even though the communists had been treating them as a single theater for two decades and were conducting a coordinated strategy with respect to all of them. Moreover, Washington's assessment of the overall international context had made it too preoccupied with Chinese intervention, ignoring Lin Piao's statement that Chinese armies would not go abroad, and which was reiterated by Mao to Edgar Snow, an American journalist sympathetic to the Chinese communists: Mao told Snow that China had no troops outside its own frontiers and had no intention of fighting anybody unless its own territory were attacked.[24] Thus it was that, in two separate wars a decade and a half apart, America paid a price for not taking Chinese statements seriously: in Korea, it had ignored Chinese warnings and marched to the Yalu, triggering Chinese intervention; in Vietnam, it disregarded assurances by the Chinese that they would not intervene, causing America to reject the only strategy which might have brought victory.

Concerned about Chinese intervention, determined to preserve the option of a relaxation of tensions with the Soviet Union, and eager to maintain a consensus behind his Great Society domestic program, Johnson opted for halfway measures which staked America's international position without achieving its stated goals. Trying to reconcile the objective of defeating a global conspiracy with the desire to avoid a global conflict, American policy managed only to stultify itself.

Attrition could not work so long as the guerrillas were able to choose when and where they would fight. Air operations against North Vietnam designed to cause steadily growing pain proved inconclusive because the North Vietnamese transportation system was too rudimentary to be crippled and too unessential to serve as a neuralgic target. Stalemate served Hanoi's purpose—especially a stalemate which could be confined to the territory of South Vietnam and caused heavy American casualties. All these frustrations gave rise to growing opposition to the war in America—an opposition whose initial rallying point became the cry to halt the very bombing campaign which was supposed to bring home to Hanoi that it could not win.

Washington was trying to prove that aggression does not pay and that guerrilla war was not going to be the wave of the future. What it failed to understand was how its adversary calculated the costs and benefits. Johnson thought the way out was to demonstrate moderation, to reassure Hanoi, and to offer compromise. Yet all of these were qualities much more likely to encourage Hanoi to persist and, in the process, to teach America that there are no awards for losing with moderation. Johnson explained America's goals this way:

> We are not trying to wipe out North Vietnam. We are not trying to change their government. We are not trying to establish permanent bases in South Vietnam. . . .

> ... we are there because we are trying to make the Communists of North Vietnam stop shooting at their neighbors ... to demonstrate that guerrilla warfare, inspired by one nation against another nation, can never succeed. ... [W]e must keep on until the Communists in North Vietnam realize the price of aggression is too high—and either agree to a peaceful settlement or to stop their fighting. ... [25]

He wanted the communist leaders in Hanoi to understand that

> ... the minute you realize that a military victory is out of the question and you turn from the use of force, you will find us ready and willing to reciprocate. ... We want an honorable peace in Vietnam. In your hands is the key to that peace. You only have to turn it. [26]

Johnson did not deserve the hatred and ridicule which such appeals evoked. He was, after all, restating traditional American verities. But neither he nor his society had any concepts for understanding an adversary who found such reassurances derisory; an adversary, moreover, to whom the American definition of compromise sounded like a call for surrender in the struggle of a lifetime.

To the tough, dedicated leaders in Hanoi, the concept of stability had no operational meaning. They had spent their adult lives fighting for victory, first against France, now against a superpower. In the name of communism they had brought incredible suffering to their people. "Leaving their neighbor alone" was the one thing Hanoi's leaders were inherently unable to do. Bismarck had once said that German unity would never come about through talk but by "blood and iron," which was precisely Hanoi's views on Vietnamese unity.

Americans of all persuasions kept appealing to Hanoi to participate in some democratic outcome, and racked their brains to devise workable election schemes. Yet none of the staples of American thought on international affairs held the slightest attraction for Hanoi except as tools by which to confuse Americans. Having established one of the world's most rigorous dictatorships, the Hanoi Politburo would never accept becoming simply one political party among many in the South. Hanoi had no conceivable incentive to stop using force; after all, it was bound to win as long as it did not lose, and it was certainly not losing—indeed, American strategy, which explicitly aimed at stalemate, abjured Hanoi's losing. Johnson's offer of a massive reconstruction program open to all, including North Vietnam, fell on deaf ears. [27] Hanoi wanted victory, not development aid, and, with characteristic arrogance, acted as if there was no need to choose between the two.

Once the tide of American public opinion turned against the war, Johnson's critics blamed him ever more stridently for the diplomatic stalemate. Insofar as these charges implied that Johnson was reluctant to negotiate, they missed the point. Johnson's eagerness to start negotiations was palpable to the point of being self-defeating. And it convinced Hanoi that procrastination was likely to elicit even more generous offers. Johnson ordered one bombing pause after another (he reports sixteen in his memoirs), leaving no doubt that the United States would pay an unreciprocated entrance price to get the negotiations started; Hanoi had every incentive to make that price as high as possible.

I was involved in one of the initiatives that illustrated both the Johnson Administration's eagerness to negotiate and Hanoi's skill at using that eagerness to serve its own ends. My own involvement with Vietnam evolved quite gradually. Throughout the 1950s, my thinking on foreign policy had been focused on Europe and on nuclear strategy. The Kennedy Administration included many individuals whom I admired, and I was favorably disposed toward its effort in Indochina without giving the issue much thought. I first began thinking seriously about Vietnam after three visits to that country, in 1965 and 1966, as a consultant on pacification to Ambassador Lodge. These occasions gave me an opportunity to travel to many of the provinces of South Vietnam and to hold discussions with the so-called provincial reporters of the American embassy—an extraordinarily able and devoted group of young foreign service officers in various districts around the country. These visits convinced me that the war could not be won by the prevailing strategy, and that America would need to extricate itself by negotiating with Hanoi, though I had no precise ideas about the content of such a negotiation.

In the summer of 1967, I attended one of the so-called Pugwash Conferences of scientists concerned with nuclear disarmament. Two participants who had heard of my visits to Indochina approached me with what seemed like an intriguing proposition. Raymond Aubrac, an official of the World Health Organization, had become acquainted with Ho Chi Minh in 1946, when the Vietnamese communist leader had stayed at his home in Paris during negotiations with France. Aubrac offered to visit Hanoi, accompanied by a fellow scientist from the peace movement, Herbert Marcovich, to appeal personally to Ho Chi Minh on the subject of negotiations. I informed Bundy, who had become Assistant Secretary of State, and Defense Secretary McNamara. They encouraged the visit, provided that the two scientists traveled in a private capacity and did not purport to represent official American views.

Aubrac and Marcovich journeyed to Hanoi, where they were received by Ho Chi Minh. After delivering a ritualized condemnation of American "aggression," Ho Chi Minh hinted that Hanoi would be willing to negotiate provided America stopped bombing North Vietnam. Mai Van Bo, Hanoi's diplomatic representative in Paris, was designated as the official contact.

Several exchanges followed by means of a complicated and decidedly undiplomatic procedure. Since Hanoi would not communicate directly with Washington prior to a bombing halt, I, a private citizen, served as intermediary. Even so, Hanoi, hoarding its every last negotiating chip, would not authorize its representative to deal with even an unofficial American. Thus, messages were passed to me from Washington, usually by Secretary McNamara, and then from me on to the two Frenchmen, who would deliver them to Mai Van Bo with whatever explanations I had been authorized to provide. McNamara was eager to end the war, and repeatedly implored me to extract from my invisible interlocutors any hint, however oblique, that would enable him to promote the cause of a negotiated outcome.

I attended part of the meeting between President Johnson and his advisers at which the final American offer was prepared. It was a melancholy experience. Clearly, Johnson's every instinct rebelled against a halt in bombing. Unsure as he was of his mastery of foreign policy, Johnson had had enough experience in politics to doubt the benefit of opening a negotiation with a unilateral concession. Yet he was desperate to end the war, battered as he was by domestic critics, and unwilling to overrule advisers who were eager to attempt diplomacy. In the end, Johnson yielded. The upshot was the so-called San Antonio Formula, devised after I had left the room, which Johnson presented in a speech in that city on September 29, 1967:

> The United States is willing to stop all aerial and naval bombardment of North Vietnam when this will lead promptly to productive discussions. We, of course, assume that while discussions proceed, North Vietnam would not take advantage of the bombing cessation or limitation.[28]

The San Antonio Formula was one of the decisive turning points of the war. America offered to stop military action against North Vietnam—a precise obligation—in return for "productive" talks, as long as Hanoi did not take advantage of the bombing halt. No criteria were put forward for defining either "productive" or "advantage." Yet, having demonstrated its capacity to manipulate the American domestic debate, Hanoi could have had few doubts that any American attempt to abrogate a bombing halt would be both controversial and time-consuming. Taking "no advantage" of the halt certainly did not seem to oblige Hanoi to stop guerrilla warfare or, for that matter, to abandon anything it was already doing; at most, the provision meant that Hanoi was not to escalate a winning strategy.

It was characteristic of Hanoi's negotiating tactics that even so one-sided an offer should have been refused. Indeed, Hanoi used the offer as a safety net to protect the all-out military effort it was about to unleash. Within days, my channel to Hanoi was broken off. The North Vietnamese, having grasped that the price of America's stopping the bombing was as modest as it was abstruse, sought to increase the pressures on Johnson before sitting down to talk and taking up the proposal. The Tet Offensive was only a few months away.

Hanoi had correctly sensed that the Americans' growing discontent would no more tolerate stalemate in Vietnam than it had in Korea. Yet there was a qualitative difference in the nature of the ensuing domestic controversies. The wisdom of America's involvement in Korea had never been challenged; the disagreement had concerned the measures required to make it succeed. With respect to Vietnam, the original widespread consensus behind United States policy suddenly evaporated. In Korea, Administration critics had wanted the United States to do more; their alternative to Truman's policy had been MacArthur's strategy of escalation. In Vietnam, the overwhelming majority of critics urged reducing the American effort—and, in time, abandoning it altogether; their views ranged from modification of America's strategy to unconditional withdrawal. In Korea, America's adversaries would have faced a much worse alternative had the opposition prevailed. In Vietnam, once the extent of the domestic rifts had become obvious, Hanoi quickly learned that a stalemated diplomacy combined with military pressures would work in its favor. Deadlocks would be blamed on lack of diplomatic initiatives by the Johnson Administration, and continuing American casualties would lead to calls for de-escalation, if not abandonment, of the war.

Criticism of America's Vietnam policy started out fairly conventionally, with reasonable questions being raised about whether the war could be won and about the relationship of means to ends. On March 11, 1968, Walter Lippmann applied his already well-established critique of containment to Vietnam. America, he argued, had overextended itself, and the policy of containment was destroying any rational balance between national goals and the resources by which they might be achieved:

The fact is that his [LBJ's] war aims are unlimited: they promise the pacification of all of Asia. For such unlimited ends it is not possible to win a war with limited means. Because our aims are limitless, we are sure to be "defeated."[29]

To symbolize the irrelevance of traditional categories of thought when applied to Vietnam, Lippmann placed the word "defeated" in quotation marks, signifying that Vietnam was irrelevant to American security. Withdrawal would, in that view, strengthen America's overall position.

The same point had already been made in 1966, when Senator Fulbright had criticized the United States for succumbing to the "arrogance of power" by confusing its "power with virtue and major responsibilities with a universal mission."[30] Less than two years earlier, Fulbright had chided de Gaulle for "confus[ing] the situation" by proposing that Vietnam be neutralized. At that time, Fulbright had warned that such a course might "set off an unforeseeable chain of events [for] she [France] is neither a major military force nor a major economic force in the Far East, and is therefore unlikely to be able to control or greatly influence the events which her initiative may precipitate." In 1964, Fulbright had only discerned two "realistic" options: "the expansion of the conflict in one way or another, or a renewed effort to bolster the capacity of the South Vietnamese to prosecute the war successfully on its present scale."[31]

What had happened in barely two years to persuade the Senator to downgrade Vietnam's status from vital to peripheral? And why did it reflect arrogance that the Johnson Administration had, in the meantime, carried out both of Fulbright's recommendations? America's leaders, true to their national traditions, had not been content with resting the case for American assistance to Vietnam on security grounds which might, sooner or later, permit a debate over the costs and benefits. Casting the issue in terms of bringing democracy to Southeast Asia, they abandoned any logical stopping point on the way in and—as it happened—on the way out as well.

The critics of the war traveled along the same road as the leaders who were conducting it, only in the opposite direction. They began by basing conclusions on eminently practical grounds: the war was unwinnable, the costs exceeded the benefits, and America was overextending itself. But the critics, who were the products of the same American idealism, rapidly extended their critique to the moral plane in two stages: first, on the ground that, morally, there was really little difference between Hanoi and Saigon, which neatly dispensed with the ideological reason for the war; second, that America's persistence in the war reflected not flawed practical judgment but a moral rot at the core of the American system. As a result, a policy which had enjoyed nearly universal support turned, in the course of two years, into an indictment of the morality of America's entire foreign policy and, a short while later, into a critique of American society itself.

In the post–World War II period, America had been fortunate to have never had to choose between its moral convictions and its strategic analysis. All of its key decisions had been readily justified as both promoting democracy and resisting aggression. South Vietnam, however, could by no stretch of the imagination be described as democratic. All of Diem's successor regimes felt beleaguered; South Vietnamese generals, who up to this time had been unknown to the public, were less than anxious to test their popularity at the polls. A convincing argument might have been made for the proposition that Saigon's new rulers were far less repressive than Hanoi's. That argument was, in fact, often made but never taken seriously. Moral relativism was unacceptable to a nation brought up on faith in the absolute distinction between good and evil.

Critics increasingly argued that, if Saigon failed to meet full democratic standards—which they knew in their hearts to be impossible—it deserved to be jettisoned altogether. As time went on, the Domino Theory, the central security premise on which the defense of Vietnam had been based for nearly two decades, was first abandoned and then ridiculed. In one of the most comprehensive articles, Yale Professor Richard Renfield combined Lippmann's criticism of strategic overextension with the charge that the two sides in the Vietnam conflict were morally equivalent; hence the war was senseless. In Vietnam, he argued, America was not so much resisting aggression as it was supporting the forces of conservatism against social change.[32]

Critics pointed to Saigon's many inadequacies to demonstrate the moral unacceptability of the American effort. In 1968, James Reston asked the question which had been tormenting so many Americans: "What is the end that justifies this slaughter? How will we save Vietnam if we destroy it in the battle?"[33] By 1972, Fulbright declared that Johnson had never understood that "the issue was not between a 'free people' and a 'totalitarian regime' but between rival totalitarian regimes; the fact that the war was not one of international aggression, 'direct' or otherwise, but an anticolonial war and then a civil war."[34]

Television was then just coming into its own. The regular evening newscasts were attracting audiences in the tens of millions, far more people than even the most popular print journalists could hope to reach in a lifetime. And they possessed the advantage of visual images to provide a running editorial commentary. The newscasts reflected a craving for drama and showmanship that, even with the best of intentions, could not always be balanced, if only because it was technically impossible to cover the atrocities the Vietcong were committing in the areas under their control. The news anchor turned into a political figure, in the sense that only a president could have reached as many people—and certainly not with such regularity.

Throughout the postwar era, Americans had responded to their leaders' appeals for sacrifice in order to assist distant societies. In the crucible of Vietnam, America's exceptionalism—the belief in the universal applicability of American values—which had conferred such momentum on postwar reconstruction, began turning on itself and adopting a kind of moral scorched-earth policy. As casualties mounted, the critique of American foreign policy shifted from challenging the effectiveness of the policy to questioning the necessity for it—from an assault on the worthiness of America's Vietnamese ally to challenging the worthiness of America, not just in Vietnam but globally as well.

What lent a special poignancy to the attacks on America's fitness to conduct a global policy was that they originated to a large extent in the universities and the intellectual community, which up to this time had contained the dedicated defenders of America's international idealism.[35] Involved in decision-making by Kennedy, many intellectual leaders were shattered when his assassination abruptly ended the New Frontier and further shaken by their students' antiwar protests. The modalities of extrication from Vietnam no longer held any interest for them; under pressure from their own students, many professors edged ever closer toward unilateral, unconditional withdrawal.

Challenging the assumptions of twenty years of bipartisan foreign policy, the radical wing of the Vietnam protest ridiculed anticommunism as being archaic: "[W]e refuse to be anti-Communist," said two pilgrims to Hanoi, Staughton Lynd and Tom Hayden. "We insist that the term has lost all specific content it once had. Instead it serves as the key category of abstract thought which Americans use to justify a foreign policy that is often no more sophisticated than rape."[36] Even Hans Morgenthau, the doyen of American philosophers of the national interest, was moved to a proclamation of America's immorality: "When we talk about the violation of the rules of war, we must keep in mind that the fundamental violation, from which all other specific violations follow, is the very waging of this kind of war."[37]

To the leaders of the generation that had been brought up on the essentially uncontested verities of the Cold War, these outbursts were truly shocking. Lyndon Johnson, himself a principal formulator of the postwar consensus, was at a loss as to how to deal with an assault waged by men and women from leading universities whose approbation he craved in direct proportion to his inability to find a common language with them. David Halberstam, who was by 1966 an acerbic critic of the war, had himself argued earlier "that Vietnam is a legitimate part of that (U.S.) global commitment . . . it is perhaps one of only five or six nations in the world that is truly vital to U.S. interests. If it *is* this important, it may be worth a larger commitment on our part."[38]

Johnson reacted by appealing to the orthodoxies of his predecessors, from Truman through Kennedy. But these had already begun to sound outdated, even irrelevant, to the critics. His offers for unconditional negotiations were rejected by Hanoi's leaders, who were far too subtle at their craft to provide a safety valve for America's domestic upheaval. To stem the tide, Johnson gradually modified his negotiating position, moving from demanding North Vietnamese withdrawal before America would stop hostilities to the San Antonio Formula for suspending bombing prior to negotiations; and from refusing to talk to Hanoi's front in the South, the National Liberation Front (or the NLF) to agreeing to talk to individual representatives of it, and, finally, to conceding NLF participation as a political entity in negotiations. He also tried to tempt Hanoi with an economic-aid program for all of Indochina. Each of these moves was dismissed by Hanoi as inadequate, and by the majority of U.S. domestic critics as insincere. The national debate became polarized between victory, for which there was no strategy, and withdrawal, for which there was no policy.

The Administration's more moderate critics—the group to which I belonged—urged a negotiated compromise. The real obstacle to that, however, was not Washington but Hanoi. The North Vietnamese communists had not spent a lifetime in mortal struggle to end it by sharing power or by de-escalating the guerrilla war, their most effective means of pressure. The Vietnamese communists were no more capable than Stalin had been a generation earlier of coming to grips with the equally unrealistic hope for a negotiation separate from some underlying balance of forces, or one simply left to the negotiating process itself. Johnson's frequent assurances that he would be flexible and open-minded seemed to Hanoi both naïve and irrelevant.

Ironically, America would have to pay the same price for compromise as it would for victory. Hanoi would accept compromise only if it felt too weak to win—that is, after it had been defeated. America would only be able to show moderation after the war, not during it. All the standard "solutions"—of both the Administration and the moderate critics—were rendered irrelevant by Hanoi's implacable determination. A cease-fire, which to Americans seemed a desirable way of ending the killing, would, in Hanoi's view, remove America's incentive to withdraw. A coalition government that was more than a fig leaf on the road to a communist takeover seemed to Hanoi's leaders to guarantee Saigon's survival.

The real choice before America was not between victory and compromise, but between victory and defeat. The difference between the North Vietnamese and the Americans was that Hanoi grasped that reality while neither Johnson nor his moderate critics would bring themselves to admit it. The practitioners of *Realpolitik* in Hanoi were convinced that the fate of Vietnam would be settled by the balance of forces on the ground—not at the conference table.

In retrospect, there can be little question that America did not need to pay any price for the opening of negotiations. Hanoi had decided to negotiate before the 1968 American presidential election, if only to commit both political parties to a negotiated outcome. But Hanoi's leaders would not enter negotiations without first making a major effort to tilt the military balance in their own direction. The instrument for improving their negotiating position became the Tet Offensive, which occurred during the lunar new year, or Tet. In each year, including 1968, a truce had been agreed on for that period. Nevertheless, on January 30, communist forces launched a large offensive against thirty South Vietnamese provincial capitals. Achieving total surprise, they seized key targets in Saigon, reaching even the grounds of the United States embassy and General Westmoreland's headquarters. The ancient capital of Hue fell to the communists and was held by them for twenty-five days.

Militarily, Tet is now recognized as a major communist defeat.[39] It was the first time that the guerrillas surfaced and engaged in open combat. The decision to launch a nationwide assault forced them to fight on battlefields they normally would not have chosen. Superior American firepower wiped out almost the entire guerrilla infrastructure, just as U.S. Army textbooks had predicted. Throughout the remainder of the war, the Vietcong guerrillas ceased being an effective force; almost all of the fighting was done by the North Vietnamese army's regular units.

In some respects, Tet vindicated America's military doctrine. By staking everything on one throw of the dice, the communists accepted the battle of attrition American strategy had longed for. Perhaps they had suffered greater casualties than official reports suggested; or perhaps they counted on America's eagerness to negotiate to provide them with a safety net.

Nevertheless, the Tet Offensive turned into a major psychological victory for Hanoi. One can reflect with some melancholy on the course of events had American leaders stepped up pressure on the North Vietnamese main-force units, which were now deprived of their guerrilla shield. Had America really gone for broke, it is probable that Johnson would have achieved the unconditional negotiations he was proposing, and maybe even an unconditional cease-fire. This is suggested by the rapidity —less than seventy-two hours—with which Hanoi accepted Johnson's renewed offer to negotiate, which was coupled with a partial bombing halt based on the San Antonio Formula.

American leaders, however, had had enough and not because public opinion had deserted them. Polls showed that 61 percent of the American people considered themselves hawks, 23 percent doves, while 70 percent favored continuation of the bombing.[40] The group that lost its nerve represented the very Establishment figures who had backed intervention all along. Johnson assembled a group of leaders from previous administrations, most of them hawks, including such stalwarts as Dean Acheson, John McCloy, McGeorge Bundy, and Douglas Dillon, among others. By a large majority, they advised that escalation be ended and the liquidation of the war begun. Given Hanoi's attitudes, which were not yet generally understood, this decision had to be the beginning of defeat. In fairness, I generally concurred with these "Wise Men," which proves that turning points are easier to recognize in retrospect than when they are taking place.

On February 27, 1968, television anchorman Walter Cronkite, then at the height of his influence, sent shock waves through the White House by predicting failure:

> It seems now more certain than ever that the bloody experience of Vietnam is to end in a stalemate. This summer's almost certain standoff will either end in real give-and-take negotiations or terrible escalation; and for every means we have to escalate, the enemy can match us. . . .[41]

The last proposition was open to considerable question; it simply could not have been true that North Vietnam was the only country in history to prove impervious to every conceivable calculation of risk and benefit. True, it had a higher threshold for suffering than almost any other country, but there was a threshold nonetheless. And the last thing Hanoi was interested in was the give-and-take of negotiations. Still, Cronkite's hyperbole contained a major element of truth: Hanoi's breaking point clearly exceeded America's.

The Wall Street Journal, which up to this point had been an Administration supporter, also jumped ship, asking rhetorically whether developments were "making hash of our original, commendable objectives? . . . If practically nothing is to be left of government or nation, what is there to be saved for what?" The *Journal* thought that "the American people should be getting ready to accept, if they haven't already, the prospect that the whole Vietnam effort may be doomed."[42] On March 10, NBC concluded a special program on Vietnam with what was fast turning into a common refrain: "Laying aside all other arguments, the time is at hand when we must decide whether it is futile to destroy Vietnam in order to save it."[43] *Time* magazine joined the chorus on March 15: "1968 has brought home the awareness that victory in Viet Nam—or even a favorable settlement—may simply be beyond the grasp of the world's greatest power."[44]

Leading senators entered the fray. Mansfield declared: "We are in the wrong place and we are fighting the wrong kind of war."[45] Fulbright raised the question of "the authority of the administration to expand the war without the consent of Congress and without any debate or consideration by Congress."[46]

Under the impact of such attacks, Johnson buckled. On March 31, 1968, he announced a unilateral partial bombing halt for the area north of the 20th Parallel, to be followed by a total bombing halt as soon as substantive negotiations began. He indicated that no further significant reinforcements would be sent to Vietnam, and again repeated the oft-invoked reassurance that "our objective in South Vietnam has never been the annihilation of the enemy."[47] Six weeks after Hanoi had violated a formal cease-fire by launching a devastating assault on American installations and killed thousands of civilians in Hue alone, Johnson invited Hanoi's leaders to participate in the economic development of Southeast Asia, a transparent hint at the prospect of economic aid. He also announced that he would not stand for re-election. The President who had sent 500,000 troops to Southeast Asia would leave their extrication to his successor.

It was one of the most fateful presidential decisions of the postwar period. Had Johnson not made this dramatic renunciation, he could have contested the election on the issue of Vietnam and secured a popular mandate one way or another. If his health did not permit him to risk a second term, Johnson should have kept up the pressure on Hanoi for the remainder of his term in order to leave his successor with the best possible options for whichever choice he and the Congress might agree on after the election. Given Hanoi's weakness in the wake of Tet, a policy of pressure in 1968 would almost certainly have produced a much better negotiating framework than the one that finally emerged.

By simultaneously de-escalating, renouncing his candidacy, and offering negotiations, Johnson combined every disadvantage. His potential successors vied with each other in making promises of peace, but without defining the term. Thus were created the conditions for public disillusionment once negotiations actually started. Hanoi had gained a bombing halt in exchange for essentially procedural talks, and was given the opportunity to restore its infrastructure in the South, albeit with North Vietnamese personnel. It had no incentive to settle with Johnson, and every temptation to repeat the same test of strength with his successor.

CHAPTER TWENTY-SEVEN

Vietnam: The Extrication; Nixon

It fell to the Nixon Administration to extricate the United States from its first experience with an unsuccessful war, and from the first foreign commitment in which America's moral convictions clashed with what was possible. Few foreign policy tasks have proved more wrenching; no country has managed such a transition without anguish.

Though France's withdrawal from Algeria was frequently cited as the model for America to follow, it in fact took de Gaulle somewhat longer than the four years required by the Nixon Administration to end America's involvement in Indochina. In extricating France from Algeria, de Gaulle had had to shoulder the burden of abandoning a million French settlers, some of whose families had been there for generations. In withdrawing American troops from Vietnam, Nixon had to liquidate a commitment which four American presidents over the course of two decades had proclaimed as being vital to the security of all free peoples.

Nixon took on this heartbreaking assignment under the most fractious

674

domestic circumstances since the Civil War. Even at a remove of twenty-five years, the abruptness of the collapse of America's national consensus on Vietnam comes as a shock. In 1965, America was dedicating itself—amidst general approval—to winning a guerrilla war against what was seen as a global communist conspiracy, and to building free institutions in Southeast Asia; two years later, in 1967, the same enterprise began to be perceived not only as having failed, but as the aberrant policy of war-crazed politicians. At one moment, the intellectual community was celebrating the advent of a progressive young president; at almost the next, it was accusing his successor of atrocities, systematic lying, and a lust for war, despite the fact that the new president's strategy—or at least his strategists—were essentially the same as those of his mourned predecessor. By the end of his presidency in 1968, Johnson could no longer appear in public except on military bases or at other locations from which violent protesters could be physically barred. Although he was an incumbent president, he did not even find it possible to appear at the 1968 national convention of his own party.

After a pause of only a few months, the violent opposition to the war resumed and even accelerated under Johnson's successor, Richard Nixon. What made the domestic debate so bitter and so nearly impossible to resolve was that the publicized disagreements were surrogates for a deeper underlying philosophical controversy. Nixon was eager to negotiate an honorable extrication, which he defined as almost anything except turning over to the North Vietnamese communists the millions of people who had been led by his predecessors to rely on America. He took credibility and honor seriously because they defined America's capacity to shape a peaceful international order.

On the other hand, the leaders of the Peace Movement considered the war so repugnant that an honorable extrication from Vietnam had come to sound like an absurdity. What the Nixon Administration perceived as potential national humiliation, the Vietnam protesters treated as a desirable national catharsis. The Administration sought an outcome that would enable America to continue its postwar international role as the protector and sustainer of free peoples—precisely the role that many in the Peace Movement wanted to end, viewing it as the arrogance and the presumption of a flawed society.

In the space of a single generation, America had traversed the Second World War, the Korean War, and a decade and a half of Cold War crises. Vietnam proved one exertion too many, the sacrifice that was too unbearable because it was so at odds with traditional American values and expectations. In the 1920s and 1930s, when the generation of Nixon and

Johnson had been in its adolescence, Americans had viewed themselves as being above the Machiavellian dealings of the Europeans. During the 1940s and 1950s, when that generation came of age, America believed it had been called on to undertake a righteous, global mission. Indeed, it emerged as the unchallenged leader of the free world. By the time these men were reaching the apex of their political careers in the 1960s, the Vietnam Peace Movement was questioning that global mission. By the 1970s, a new generation of Americans had arrived on the scene and viewed America as no longer pristine. To deserve to be involved world-wide, America required, in their view, a period of concentration on its own improvement.

Thus the generations were turning at the precise moment when America faced the most ambiguous moral challenge of the entire postwar period. The critics were repelled by graphic depictions on television of the war's brutality, and were increasingly uncertain about the moral stature of America's ally. Convinced that there simply had to exist *some* solution that permitted an instant end to the killing, their mood turned increasingly sour. American exceptionalism had sustained one of the great eras of American policy with its idealism, its innocence, and its dedication; now it turned relentless in demanding the same perfectionism of America's allies, and the absence of ambiguity in America's choices. Failing these, it envisaged only shame for America and doom for its ally.

America's moral righteousness inhibited a flexible diplomacy. Vietnam presented at best imperfect alternatives and heartbreaking choices. The intuitive impulse of the Peace Movement was to recoil from that world, seeking surcease in America's original vision of itself as the unsullied pillar of virtue. Perhaps a charismatic leader like Franklin Roosevelt, John Kennedy, or Ronald Reagan might have found a way to deal with this nostalgia. It proved beyond Richard Nixon's otherwise extraordinary talents. Unlike Johnson, Nixon was highly sophisticated in international affairs. He entered the presidency convinced, like many antiwar critics, that a clear-cut victory in Vietnam was no longer possible, if it ever had been. From the outset, Nixon understood that destiny had dealt him the thankless hand of having to arrange a retreat and some sort of exit from a demoralizing conflict. That he should have desired to implement this task with honor was natural for a president—it went with the job description. What he could not handle, either emotionally or intellectually, was the fact that the graduates of the best schools and the members of the Establishment whom he admired as much as he envied were urging a course of action which, in his view, amounted to a humiliating collapse for America and the betrayal of an ally.

Nixon chose to interpret the often violent protests on the part of those he considered privileged as the culmination of a personal attack upon him by the ideological enemies of a lifetime. In his eyes, this transformed the issue of Vietnam into a political battle. As sensitive and subtle as Nixon was in the conduct of diplomacy, he was also a street fighter when it came to domestic politics, relying on methods he never ceased to believe had been the stock-in-trade of many of his predecessors.

It will never be known whether an act of grace by the President might have assuaged the rage which had begun to swell long before Nixon took office. By the late 1960s, the violent protest of the students had grown into a global phenomenon, taking place as well in France, the Netherlands, and Germany—none of which was involved in a situation comparable to Vietnam or had racial problems in the American sense. Nixon was in any event too insecure and too vulnerable to start building bridges at that stage of his life.

In fairness, it must be noted that Nixon received little help from the Establishment, which, when all was said and done, had left him with the problem he was facing. Senior officials of the previous administrations that had involved America in the Vietnam War shared many of the convictions of the Nixon Administration. Men like Averell Harriman and former Secretary of Defense Clark Clifford had been among the principal practitioners of the postwar bipartisan consensus on foreign policy; normally they would have felt obliged to preserve some degree of national cohesion in a time of crisis, and would have closed ranks with a beleaguered administration on some agreed-upon minimum peace program.

This time, however, the shapers of the postwar foreign policy consensus could not bring themselves to support their President. In effect, they had been the first targets of the peace demonstrations—a fate they found particularly searing because in the vanguard of the Peace Movement were men and women whom they admired and had long considered as their core constituency. They had been the foot soldiers of the New Frontier and, metaphorically if not in fact, viewed the protesters as their progeny. Without approving of the Peace Movement's methods, key members of the Johnson Administration slid into *de facto* alliance with the more radical of the protesters. Their unending barrage of seemingly moderate objections to Administration policies kept their position one concession away from agreement with Nixon and compounded the President's resentment that they were thus keeping a national consensus just out of reach.

Nixon decided to soldier on in order to bring about an honorable peace. Because I was his principal associate in this effort, my account of it is inevitably affected by the role I played and by my concurrence with its basic premises.

In the interval between election and inauguration, Nixon had asked me to inform the North Vietnamese of his commitment to a negotiated outcome. Their reply was our introduction to what became Hanoi's standard demand: America's unconditional withdrawal coupled with the overthrow of Nguyen Van Thieu's government in Saigon.

Hanoi did not even bother to test the sincerity of Nixon's professions. Within three weeks of Nixon's inauguration, it launched a new offensive —the so-called Mini-Tet Offensive—during which an average of 1,000 Americans were killed each month over the next four months. Clearly, Nixon's offer to compromise had failed to stir any sense of reciprocity in those implacable leaders. Nor was Hanoi restrained in the slightest by its 1968 "understanding" with the Johnson Administration that it would not take advantage of the bombing halt.

The Nixon Administration had entered office hoping to develop a national consensus through reasonable compromise proposals, and thereby to confront Hanoi as a substantially unified nation. It soon became clear that, like his predecessors, Nixon had underestimated the tenacity and the determination of Hanoi. Ho Chi Minh had become increasingly certain that, given the inept Saigon leadership and faltering American commitment, Hanoi's forces could win an unconditional victory. A practitioner of *Realpolitik,* Ho was not about to concede at a negotiating table what he expected blood and bullets would win him on the battlefield.

There could have been no less promising addressees for a compromise peace than the dour heroes who constituted Hanoi's leadership. When the Nixon Administration entered office, the Democratic Party, which had launched the Vietnam adventure, had split sharply between an official platform and a "dove" minority position (backed by such leaders as Senators Ted Kennedy, George McGovern, and Eugene McCarthy) that had been rejected by the Democratic National Convention. Within nine months of entering office, the Republican Nixon Administration had exceeded the dove platform of the Democratic Party. Hanoi pocketed every American concession without a hint of reciprocity and unswervingly adhered to its demands for a fixed and unconditional deadline for American withdrawals and the replacement of the Saigon government by what was effectively a communist regime. Hanoi insisted that, unless both of these demands were met simultaneously, American prisoners would not be released. What Hanoi was demanding amounted to capitulation compounded by dishonor.

Presidents, however, cannot abandon a task because it proves more difficult than they had expected. Even before his inauguration, Nixon had ordered a systematic review of how to bring the war to a conclusion. Three options were analyzed: unilateral withdrawal; a showdown with Hanoi through a combination of military and political pressures; and a gradual shifting of the responsibility for the war to the Saigon government in order to permit the United States to withdraw gradually.

The first option, that of unilateral withdrawal, would later become the subject of much revisionist speculation. It has been argued that, upon coming into office, Nixon should have announced a date for withdrawal and ended the war by a unilateral American decision.[1]

Would that history were as simple as journalism. Though presidents have a large area of discretion, it is bounded by the political environment and constrained by practical reality. When Nixon came into office in 1969, neither political party had ever advocated unilateral withdrawal and no public-opinion poll showed any support for it. The "dove" platform rejected at the 1968 Democratic National Convention had called for a reduction of United States offensive operations, a mutual withdrawal of outside forces (including those of North Vietnam), and encouragement of a policy of reconciliation between the Saigon government and the National Liberation Front. Reciprocity was its rationale and no mention had been made of a unilateral pullout.

The Johnson Administration's peace program had been expressed in the Manila Formula, which proposed that American forces would begin withdrawing only six months after a North Vietnamese withdrawal, and only after the level of violence had been reduced. Even then, a substantial American residual force was slated to remain in Vietnam, on the model of Korea. The official Democratic platform had called for a free political contest in South Vietnam, but only after military operations had ended. Finally, the Republican platform had called for "de-Americanization" of the war, a change in military strategy, and negotiations based on neither "peace at any price" nor camouflaged surrender. When Nixon came into office, therefore, every wing of both major political parties had urged outcomes which, without exception, insisted on conditions that Hanoi would have to fulfill before the United States would withdraw. All had implied compromise, not surrender.

An immediate, unconditional, and unilateral American withdrawal would have posed insuperable practical problems as well. More than half a million Americans were fighting at the side of a South Vietnamese army of some 700,000 troops and were facing at least 250,000 regular North Vietnamese army troops and an equal number of guerrillas. In the early days of the Nixon Administration, an immediate commitment to unilateral withdrawal would have left a vast American expeditionary force trapped between the wrath of the South Vietnamese, America's betrayed allies, and the implacable assault of the North Vietnamese.

The Defense Department estimated that an orderly withdrawal could not be organized in less than fifteen months, during which time the position of American forces gradually would have weakened to a point where the residual forces could have turned into hostages of both Vietnamese parties. Even if one assumes that the South Vietnamese army simply would have collapsed rather than have turned on its American allies, the result would have been withdrawal amidst unspeakable chaos, especially since Hanoi would surely have sought to use its increasingly dominant position to impose even more stringent peace terms. Unilateral withdrawal had all the makings of an awesome and bloody fiasco.

Above all, the Nixon Administration was convinced that unilateral withdrawal would turn into a geopolitical disaster. Confidence in America's reliability had been painfully built over twenty years. It was the key component in the structure of the free world. A 180-degree reversal of a major American commitment extending over four administrations by a president heretofore identified with a conservative foreign policy would have produced profound disillusionment among America's allies, particularly among those most dependent on American support, regardless of whether they agreed with the details of America's Vietnam policy.

In these circumstances, the Nixon Administration concluded that it needed a strategy to affect Hanoi's calculation about the inevitability of its total victory and its ability to impose unilateral withdrawal. Therefore, the second option considered was to try to bring matters to a head rapidly through a combination of political and military measures. This was the strategy I personally preferred because I believed it would end the draining domestic struggle and enable the Administration to turn to more unifying tasks. This option had three components: (1) a Congressional endorsement to pursue the war; (2) a major effort at negotiations in which America would make every concession possible short of colluding in a communist takeover; and (3) an altered military strategy which, within South Vietnam, would concentrate on defending heavily populated areas while at the same time seeking to destroy Hanoi's supply routes by interdicting the Ho Chi Minh Trail in Laos, clearing out the base areas in Cambodia, and mining the harbors of North Vietnam. Over a period of four years, all of these measures were eventually adopted, and they did bring Hanoi to accept terms in 1972 that it had consistently rejected for a decade. Had they all been initiated simultaneously and while America still had a large ground combat force in Vietnam, the impact might have proved decisive.

Early in his term, Nixon might have gone to the Congress, outlined his idea for an honorable outcome of the Vietnam War, and asked for an endorsement, emphasizing that, in its absence, he would have no choice except to withdraw unilaterally, however appalling the consequences. Nixon rejected advice to that effect on two grounds. First, he viewed it as an abdication of presidential responsibility. Second, having served for six years in the Congress, he was convinced—almost certainly correctly— that the Congress would evade making a clear-cut choice and give him— at best—some ambiguous endorsement hedged by so many conditions as to magnify the problem.

At first, Nixon hesitated to attack the Vietnamese logistics system. Relations with the Soviet Union and China, which were still precarious, might have deteriorated further, and the triangular relationship which contributed so much to flexibility in later American foreign policy might have been delayed or thwarted. Frustrated public hopes for a relaxation of tensions in Vietnam might have inflamed the Peace Movement further. The military outcome seemed too uncertain and the domestic cost might prove unmanageable. The "forward strategy" would have encountered so much resistance among Nixon's closest advisers that it could only have been implemented by a shake-up of the Cabinet and such an expenditure of presidential energy that it might have blighted prospects for other vital, long-range initiatives.

The American people seemed to be asking their government to pursue two incompatible objectives simultaneously: they wanted the war to end and America not to capitulate. Nixon and his advisers shared this ambivalence. In seeking to navigate American policy through these contradictions, Nixon chose the third option—the so-called route of Vietnam-ization—not because he thought it was a brilliant *deus ex machina* but because, in his judgment, it kept in relatively safest balance the three key components of America's extrication from Vietnam: sustaining America's domestic morale, affording Saigon an honest chance to stand on its own, and giving Hanoi incentive to settle. Keeping these three dimensions of policy in some manageable relationship to each other became the ultimate test of America's extrication from Vietnam.

The American public was to be reassured by withdrawals of American forces and by serious negotiating efforts; South Vietnam would be provided a genuine opportunity to defend itself through massive American aid and training; Hanoi would be faced with both the carrot of peace initiatives and the stick of periodic retaliation to exhaust it and to serve as a warning that America's restraint had its limits. A complex strategy, Vietnamization nevertheless involved the huge risk that it simply might not prove possible to keep the three elements of the strategy synchronized; time might run out, and the policy might end up falling between two stools. It was a precarious undertaking at best, for every withdrawal would encourage Hanoi and every parting shot would inflame the Peace Movement.

In a memorandum I sent to Nixon dated September 10, 1969—much of which was drafted by Anthony Lake, who was then my executive assistant and is currently President Clinton's National Security Adviser—I addressed the risks of Vietnamization.[2] If Vietnamization took too long, the memorandum argued, public restlessness might increase rather than diminish. The Administration would then find itself in a no-man's-land between hawks and doves—too accommodating for the hawks, too bellicose for the doves. Government statements designed to placate both groups would "serve to confuse Hanoi but also to confirm it in its course of waiting us out":

> . . . "Vietnamization" will run into increasingly serious problems as we proceed down its path.
> —Withdrawal of U.S. troops will become like salted peanuts to the American public: the more U.S. troops come home, the more will be demanded. This could eventually result, in effect, in demands for unilateral withdrawal—perhaps within a year.
> —The more troops are withdrawn, the more Hanoi will be encouraged. . . .
> —Each U.S. soldier that is withdrawn will be relatively more important to the effort in the south, as he will represent a higher percentage of U.S. forces than did his predecessor. . . .
> —It will become harder and harder to maintain the morale of those who remain, not to speak of their mothers.
> —"Vietnamization" may not lead to reduction in U.S. casualties until its final stages, as our casualty rate may be unrelated to the total number of American troops in South Vietnam. To kill about 150 U.S. soldiers a week, the enemy needs to attack only a small portion of our forces. . . .[3]

If all this was true, the memorandum argued, Hanoi would focus on inflicting a psychological, not a military, defeat on the United States; it would prolong the war, stall negotiations, and wait for the American domestic situation to unravel—a prediction which substantially came true.

The memorandum foresaw many of our later difficulties; it was also doomed to irrelevance. For one thing, although it was submitted to the President, I did not follow it into the Oval Office. In Washington, ideas do not sell themselves. Authors of memoranda who are not willing to fight for them are more likely to find their words turn into *ex post facto* alibis than guides to action. Recoiling before the bitter opposition and domestic turmoil which the alternative of trying to force a showdown with Hanoi would have evoked, I never forced a systematic consideration of this option. Nor did the President investigate it, almost certainly for the same reason. Nixon had no incentive to overturn his decision in favor of the Vietnamization option so long as none of the government agencies concerned with Vietnam expressed any reservations. And none of them did, primarily because they were too shell-shocked by the demonstrations to want to get into the line of fire.

I have reviewed the anguish of that choice in order to show that, by the time Nixon took office, the only choices in Vietnam were among comparable evils. The fact that Vietnamization would prove excruciatingly difficult did not make the other options any more attractive. This central reality eluded the American critics of the Vietnam War, as it has indeed eluded much of the American public in other instances: foreign policy often involves deciding among imperfect choices. The choice Nixon faced in Vietnam was between almost equally unpalatable alternatives. After twenty years of containment, America was paying the price for overextension; there were no simple choices left.

Although Vietnamization was a risky course, on balance it was the best of the available options. It had the advantage of giving the American and South Vietnamese peoples a way of getting used to the inevitable American withdrawal. If, in the process of inexorably reducing the American forces, America succeeded in strengthening South Vietnam—and the Nixon Administration meant to do just that—America's objective would be achieved. If it failed and unilateral withdrawal became the only remaining choice, the final extrication could take place after American forces had shrunk to a level which reduced the risks of chaos and humiliation.

As this policy unfolded, Nixon was determined to make a major effort to negotiate, and asked me to implement this assignment. French President Georges Pompidou succinctly summed up what was ahead for me. Since his office arranged the logistics for my secret negotiations in Paris with the North Vietnamese, I briefed him after nearly every negotiating session. On one such occasion, when I was feeling especially dejected about the seemingly intractable stalemate, Pompidou remarked in his matter-of-fact, commonsense way: "You are condemned to succeed."

Public officials are not at liberty to pick the time of their service to their country or the tasks that await them. Had I been given any choice in the matter, I would certainly have selected a more accommodating negotiating partner than Le Duc Tho. Experience had reinforced what ideology had taught him and his colleagues on the Hanoi Politburo—that guerrilla wars are about winners and losers, not about compromise. In its early stages, Vietnamization did not impress them: "How can you expect to prevail with the South Vietnamese army alone when it could not win with the assistance of 500,000 Americans?" asked a supremely confident Le Duc Tho in 1970. It was a haunting question which tormented us as well. Over four years, a combination of strengthening Saigon and weakening Hanoi made a favorable answer appear within reach. Even at that, it would still take a blockade, a failed North Vietnamese offensive, and intense bombing to bring Hanoi to conclude an agreement.

The phenomenon of a totally implacable foe uninterested in compromise—indeed, seeking to turn deadlock into a weapon—was alien to the American experience. An ever-greater number of Americans yearned for compromise. But Hanoi's leaders had launched their war in order to win, not to cut a deal. Thus, the categories of the American debate—the many proposals for bombing halts, cease-fires, deadlines for American withdrawal, and coalition government—were never relevant to Hanoi's calculations. Hanoi bargained only when it was under severe pressure—in particular, whenever America resumed bombing, and most of all after the mining of North Vietnamese harbors. Yet recourse to pressure was precisely what most inflamed the critics at home.

Negotiations with the North Vietnamese took place on two levels. There were formal meetings of the four parties to the conflict at the Hotel Majestic in Paris, comprising the United States, the Thieu government, the NLF (Hanoi's South Vietnamese front organization), and the Hanoi government. Though months had been spent arguing about the shape of the table at which the NLF might be seated without implying its recognition by Saigon, the formal negotiations immediately ran into the ground. The forum was too large, the publicity too unrelenting, and Hanoi proved too unwilling to grant equal status to Saigon or, for that matter, even to its own surrogate, the NLF.

The Nixon Administration therefore continued the so-called private—that is, secret—talks, which were confined to the American and North Vietnamese delegations and had been started by Averell Harriman and Cyrus Vance, the negotiators during the last months of the Johnson Administration. Typically, Le Duc Tho's arrival in Paris would signal that Hanoi was ready for a round of talks. Although he held the fifth position in the Hanoi hierarchy, it was Le Duc Tho's conceit to call himself merely a special adviser to Xuan Thuy, a Foreign Ministry functionary who was technically the head of the North Vietnamese delegation at the Hotel Majestic.

The American bargaining position was to separate the military and the political issues and it did not change after 1971. This program called for a cease-fire followed by a total withdrawal of American forces and an end to resupply and reinforcement from the North. The political future of South Vietnam would be left to a free political contest. Hanoi's position until the breakthrough of October 1972 was to demand an unconditional deadline for total American withdrawal, and the dismantling of the Thieu government. The deadline was the admission price into negotiating on any other issue, and would hold regardless of success on the other topics. America was asking for compromise; Hanoi for capitulation. There was no middle road until a balance of forces on the ground made compromise possible—which lasted only as long as the balance of forces did.

The meetings were invariably requested by the American side, using General Vernon Walters, the military attaché at the United States embassy in Paris, as intermediary. (Walters later had a distinguished career as Deputy Director of Central Intelligence, Permanent Representative to the United Nations, and Ambassador to Germany, in addition to undertaking numerous sensitive presidential missions.) Maneuvering the United States into making the first move was one of Hanoi's relentless ploys to establish psychological dominance. The tactic showed how well Hanoi had grasped America's domestic crisis. If Le Duc Tho was in Paris for any length of time without being contacted by the United States government, he was certain to drop many hints to journalists or visiting members of the Congress about the Nixon Administration's failure to explore Hanoi's demonstrably peaceful intentions. Given the state of America's domestic controversy, such hints were sure to receive wide currency, and he was capable of dropping them even when talks were taking place.

During each of Le Duc Tho's visits to Paris between 1970 and 1972, five or six meetings would take place over a period of a few months. (There were also several meetings with Xuan Thuy alone. In the absence of Le Duc Tho, they proved a total waste of time.)

The negotiations followed a stereotyped procedure. As the formal head of the Vietnamese negotiating team, Xuan Thuy would begin with the same interminable recitation of the Vietnamese negotiating position that was familiar to us from the sessions at the Hotel Majestic. He would then "give the floor to Special Advisor Le Duc Tho." Immaculately dressed in a brown or black Mao suit, Le Duc Tho would then deliver an equally long speech focused on the philosophical issues as he saw them, interspersed with epic accounts of previous Vietnamese struggles for independence.

Until nearly the very end of the negotiations, Le Duc Tho's theme remained the same: the balance of forces was in Hanoi's favor and would be so increasingly; wars were fought for political objectives, hence the American proposal for a cease-fire and an exchange of prisoners was absurd and unacceptable; the political solution had to begin with the United States' overthrow of the South Vietnamese government. (At one point, Le Duc Tho even helpfully suggested a method for accomplishing this goal—the assassination of Thieu.)

All of this was presented with impeccable politeness, a frigid demeanor conveying moral superiority, and in a Marxist vocabulary impervious to interjections by the benighted imperialists. Le Duc Tho would give no quarter on even the most abstruse point that lent itself to ideological instruction. On one occasion, I sought a break in the talks, invoking what I considered a sufficiently tactful Marxist formulation—that "objective necessity" made an interruption necessary. This, however, merely caused Le Duc Tho to deliver another ten-minute lecture about the inappropriateness of an imperialist like myself using Marxist terminology.

The basic strategy behind Le Duc Tho's glacial way of proceeding was to convey that time was on his side because he was in a position to exploit America's divisions to his own benefit. In the course of the first set of meetings, between February and April 1970, he rejected a cease-fire, a fifteen-month withdrawal schedule,[4] de-escalation of fighting, and the neutralization of Cambodia. (Interestingly enough, in his catalogue of grievances, which spared us no detail, Le Duc Tho never mentioned the "secret" bombing of Cambodian sanctuaries.)

During the second set of negotiations, from May to July 1971, Le Duc Tho plumbed a new low of cynicism. At the public forum, the NLF had tabled a seven-point plan. Le Duc Tho proposed a somewhat different and far more specific nine-point scheme in the secret talks, specifically insisting that the latter serve as a basis for the real negotiations. In the meantime, communist spokesmen clamored for an answer to their public seven-point plan, and the Nixon Administration fell under attack for not responding to a proposal which the Vietnamese negotiators had made clear they did not want to negotiate. This charade went on until Nixon unveiled the maneuver publicly, whereupon Hanoi published a two-point "elaboration" of the seven-point plan, which soon elicited further public pressure on Nixon. After the final negotiations were over, I asked Le Duc Tho what exactly the two-point elaboration had elaborated. "Nothing," he replied with a smile.

During the third round of negotiations, which took place from August 1972 to January 1973, the breakthrough occurred. On October 8, Le Duc Tho abandoned his standard demand that America overthrow the Saigon government, and agreed to a cease-fire. From then on, matters moved rapidly to a conclusion. Le Duc Tho demonstrated that he was as ingenious at finding solutions as he had been obdurate during his period of stonewalling. He even changed his opening speech, which, though no shorter than before, turned into an exhortation to make progress. He did not, however, permit the onset of serious negotiations to limit his proclivity for making himself obnoxious. A sentence that he delivered unalterably each morning as part of his new litany was: "You make a big effort and we will make a big effort." One morning, he dropped the adjective, saying that America should make a big effort and that he would reciprocate with an effort. As a way of breaking the monotony, I called his attention to the omission. "I am so glad you noticed it," said my imperturbable interlocutor. "But yesterday we made a big effort and you only made an effort. So today we reverse the procedure: you have to make a big effort and we shall only make an effort."

Part of the trouble was that Le Duc Tho had only one objective, whereas, as a superpower, America had to have many. Le Duc Tho was determined to culminate his revolutionary career in victory; America had to balance domestic against international considerations, the future of Vietnam against maintaining America's global role. Le Duc Tho handled the American psyche as a skilled surgeon might operate on his patient; the Nixon Administration was obliged to fight on so many fronts that it only rarely had the opportunity to conduct an offensive diplomacy.

Indeed, from the outset and throughout the negotiations, the Nixon Administration had to devote an extraordinary amount of energy to fending off attacks upon its good faith. Despite the many unilateral, unreciprocated gestures Nixon had already made to Hanoi, the President incurred almost immediately upon taking office the criticism that he was not sufficiently dedicated to peace. By September 1969, the United States had offered the NLF participation in the political process and mixed electoral commissions, had withdrawn more than 10 percent of its forces, and had agreed to the total withdrawal of the remainder after a settlement— without having anything more to show for these concessions than endless repetitions of the communists' standard recitation of their demand for unilateral withdrawal and the overthrow of the Saigon government.

Nevertheless, on September 25, 1969, Republican Senator Charles Goodell of New York proclaimed that he would introduce a resolution requiring the withdrawal of all American forces from Vietnam by the end of 1970. On October 15, so-called Moratorium demonstrations took place all across the country. A crowd of 20,000 gathered at a noontime rally in New York's financial district to hear Bill Moyers, who had been President Johnson's assistant and Press Secretary, condemn the war. Thirty thousand gathered on the New Haven Green. Fifty thousand amassed on the Washington Monument grounds, within sight of the White House. In Boston, 100,000 people converged on the Common to listen to Senator McGovern while a skywriting plane drew a peace symbol in the sky overhead to suggest that the Administration was rejecting the desirability of peace.

As embodied in the Peace Movement, American exceptionalism did not permit any discussion of the practicalities of extrication, and treated attempts to do so as symptomatic of the Administration's surreptitious desire to continue the war. Having transmuted the war into a domestic conflict between good and evil at home, the Peace Movement preferred —for reasons it viewed as highly moral—America's collapse in Vietnam to an outcome which, precisely because it might be considered "honorable," might also whet its government's appetite for further foreign adventures.

This is why it proved impossible to find any common ground between the Peace Movement and the Administration. Nixon had reduced the American forces in Vietnam from nearly 550,000 to 20,000 in three years; casualties had dropped from some 16,000 or 28 percent of the total in 1968 to some 600 or some one percent of the total in 1972, the last wartime year. This did not ease the distrust or the pain. For the fundamental difference could not be bridged: Nixon wanted to leave Vietnam with honor and the Peace Movement believed that honor required America to leave Vietnam in effect unconditionally.

If ending the war was the only objective, the Saigon government became in the eyes of the critics an obstacle to peace rather than an ally. The original conviction that South Vietnam was a key element of American security had been discarded long ago. What remained was the sense that, in Vietnam, America was in bad company. The critics' new orthodoxy was that Thieu had to be replaced by a coalition government, if necessary by cutting off American funds to South Vietnam. The idea of a coalition government turned into the sovereign remedy of the domestic debate at the precise moment when the North Vietnamese negotiators were making it clear that, according to their definition, a coalition government was a euphemism for a communist takeover of the South.

The North Vietnamese had in fact devised a clever formula for confusing their American audience. They avowed that their goal was a tripartite "coalition" government composed of the NLF (their own pawns), a neutralist element, and members of the Saigon Administration who stood for "peace, freedom, and independence." As with so many of Hanoi's brazen maneuvers, one had to read the fine print to determine the real meaning of otherwise reasonable-sounding proposals. Only then did it become apparent that the three-part body would not govern Saigon but would negotiate *with the NLF* for a final settlement. In other words, a communist-dominated body would negotiate with an entirely communist group about the political future of South Vietnam. Hanoi was proposing to end the war through a dialogue with itself.

This, however, was not the way the issue appeared in American discussions. In his book *The Crippled Giant,* Senator J. William Fulbright asserted that the issue was between rival totalitarians.[5] Senator McGovern, who had in 1971 envisioned a "mixed government" in Saigon, in 1972, on the verge of being the Democratic presidential candidate, urged a withdrawal of U.S. forces, and a cutoff of military aid to South Vietnam.[6] The Nixon Administration was prepared to risk Thieu's government in internationally supervised free elections. What it refused to do was to overthrow an allied government installed by its predecessor in order to achieve America's extrication.

The Peace Movement's criterion for success was, simply, whether the war was in fact ending. And if the answer was negative, America's negotiating position was deemed to be flawed. The Peace Movement would not condemn Hanoi, either for its negotiating positions or for its method of conducting the war, thereby giving Hanoi every incentive to stonewall. By 1972, the United States had unilaterally withdrawn 500,000 troops. Saigon had formally offered to hold free elections and America to withdraw all its remaining forces within four months of an agreement. Thieu had agreed to resign one month before the elections. The United States had proposed the creation of a mixed commission to supervise the elections, all of this conditional on an internationally supervised cease-fire and the return of prisoners of war. None of these measures abated the assault on its motives or policies.

As the months went by, the domestic debate concentrated increasingly on Hanoi's precondition that the United States unilaterally set a fixed withdrawal date as the formula for ending the war. Proposals for fixed deadlines for withdrawal quickly became the staple of antiwar Congressional resolutions (there were some twenty-two in 1971, and thirty-five in 1972). Their nonbinding nature gave their sponsors the best of all worlds: dissociation from the Administration without responsibility for the consequences. Nothing seemed simpler than ending the war by just withdrawing from it—except that nothing in Vietnam was ever as simple as it appeared.

After meeting with North Vietnamese and NLF negotiators, members of the American Peace Movement kept reporting that they "knew" the release of prisoners and the settlement of other issues would follow rapidly once the United States had committed itself to a fixed, irrevocable deadline for withdrawal. In fact, Hanoi had never made such a promise, adhering to the same old script with the same tantalizing ambiguities that it had used over the 1968 bombing halt. Fixing a deadline would create "favorable conditions" for the solution of other problems, Le Duc Tho averred, but when it came to actual negotiations, he insisted that the withdrawal deadline, once established, would be binding regardless of what happened in other negotiations about a cease-fire or the release of prisoners. In the real world, Hanoi made the release of prisoners and a cease-fire dependent on the overthrow of the Saigon government. As Le Duc Tho kept explaining as if he were conducting a beginner's seminar in political science, that was why the war was being fought in the first place.

The greatest irony of the American domestic debate turned out to be that Hanoi was in fact totally uninterested in unilateral American withdrawal. This point is still misunderstood in much of the literature on the war. Until nearly the end, Hanoi never deviated from its standard formula: an irrevocable date for American withdrawal coupled with an American commitment to overthrow the South Vietnamese government on the way out. It was fundamentally uninterested in the nuances of the various withdrawal schedules which the well-meaning members of the Congress were willing to throw at its feet, except insofar as they fostered American divisions. Sweetening the pot by offering a slightly more conciliatory withdrawal schedule was not going to change the North Vietnamese position. The outcome of the conflict, to Hanoi's way of thinking, would be settled by force. It would gladly pocket whatever offers came its way without letting them affect its bargaining stance. The critics of the war thought that Hanoi would turn reasonable if America showed its willingness to go the extra mile. In this they were mistaken. Everything Washington heard from Hanoi amounted to a circular demand for surrender: unconditional withdrawal followed by the overthrow of the existing administration in South Vietnam, its replacement by Hanoi puppets, and then, when America was left with no cards to play, a negotiation about prisoners who could easily be held back in order to extract further concessions.

As things turned out, the withdrawal debate marked a turning point of the Vietnam War by demonstrating that many of the Administration's victories were indeed Pyrrhic. Nixon maintained his position on not agreeing to a fixed deadline for withdrawal except in return for other essential American objectives. But he had to pay the price of agreeing to total withdrawal *after* his conditions were met. South Vietnam was thus put into the position of having to defend itself alone against a more implacable enemy than any of America's other allies faced, and under conditions America had never asked any other ally to fulfill. American troops have been in Europe for two generations; the armistice in Korea has been protected by American forces for over forty years. Only in Vietnam did the United States, driven by internal dissent, agree to leave no residual forces; in the process, it deprived itself of any margin of safety when it came to protecting the agreement that was eventually reached.

Nixon had laid out the American terms for a settlement in two major speeches, on January 25, 1972, and on May 8, 1972. These terms were: an internationally supervised cease-fire; the return and accounting of prisoners; continuation of economic and military aid to Saigon; and leaving the political future of South Vietnam to be settled by the Vietnamese parties on the basis of free elections. On October 8, 1972, Le Duc Tho accepted Nixon's key proposals, and Hanoi finally gave up its demand that America collude with it in the installation of a communist government in Saigon. It agreed to a cease-fire, the return of all American prisoners, and an accounting of the missing-in-action. The Thieu government was left intact, and the United States was permitted to continue to furnish it with military and economic aid.

Le Duc Tho had heretofore refused even to discuss such terms. This was why he introduced the proposal that signified the breakthrough with the following statement:

> . . . this new proposal is exactly what President Nixon has himself proposed: ceasefire, end of the war, release of the prisoners, and troop withdrawal . . . and we propose a number of principles on political problems. You have also proposed this. And we shall leave to the South Vietnamese parties the settlement of these questions.[7]

None of the subsequent tragedies and controversies have been able to erase the elation those of us who had been shaping American policy felt when we realized that we were on the verge of achieving what we had sought through four anguishing years, and that America would not have to abandon the people who had relied on it. Nixon had declared on innumerable occasions that, once his terms were met, he would settle quickly. On August 14, 1972, I had told Thieu that, if Hanoi accepted President Nixon's proposals as they stood, America would rapidly conclude an agreement. We had an obligation to keep our pledge. And we had little choice but to keep it. Had we procrastinated, Hanoi would have published its proposal, forcing the Administration to explain why it had rejected its own terms and triggering a Congressional vote to cut off funds.

A combination of factors brought Hanoi to the point of accepting what it had consistently rejected: the cumulative depletion of its supplies as a result of the mining of North Vietnamese harbors, the attack on the Cambodian and Laotian sanctuaries in 1970 and 1971, the defeat of its spring offensive in 1972, the lack of political support from Moscow and Beijing when the Nixon Administration resumed the bombing of the North, and the fear that Nixon, once re-elected, would drive matters to a showdown.

The decisive factor was probably that in assessing the consequences of the 1972 presidential election, the careful calculators in Hanoi had for once made a major miscalculation. Hanoi seemed to believe that Nixon's all-but-certain overwhelming electoral victory would give him a free hand in the prosecution of the war. The Nixon Administration knew that the new Congress would be no more friendly to Nixon's Vietnam policy, and probably even more personally hostile toward him. One of the literally scores of Congressional resolutions for cutting off funding for the war was likely to pass—probably attached to a supplemental bill that would have to be introduced early in 1973 to pay for the expenses of defeating the communist spring offensive of 1972.

I greeted the prospect of peace with the hope that it would enable America to start the process of national healing and to reforge the bipartisan consensus that had shaped postwar American foreign policy. The Peace Movement, after all, would have achieved its goal of peace, while those who had strived for an honorable outcome could feel satisfied that their endurance had paid off. In my briefing, which outlined the terms of the final agreement, I reached out to adversaries of four years of domestic strife:

> . . . it should be clear by now that no one in this war has had a monopoly of anguish and that no one in these debates has had a monopoly of moral insight; and now that at last we have achieved an agreement in which the United States did not prescribe the political future to its allies, an agreement which should preserve the dignity and the self-respect of all the parties, that together with healing the wounds in Indochina we can begin to heal the wounds in America.[8]

The slim prospects for national unity had, however, collapsed irretrievably over the issue of Cambodia. Because Cambodia was the only theater of American combat in Indochina that Nixon had not inherited from his predecessors, it inflamed partisan debates, turning them into some of the most bitter controversies of the Vietnam era.

It is not my intention to reopen those controversies here. Their details have been dealt with elsewhere.[9] Essentially, the accusations of the Administration's critics boil down to two central charges: that Nixon gratuitously expanded the war into Cambodia, and that, in the process, American policy came to bear principal responsibility for the genocide carried out by the communist Khmer Rouge after their victory in 1975.

The idea that Nixon had frivolously expanded the war was a reincarnation of the strategic misconception of 1961–62 over Laos, namely that America's role in the war could be confined to South Vietnam even though Hanoi was fighting the war in all three countries of the Indochinese theater. The North Vietnamese army had built up a network of sanctuaries inside Cambodia, just across the border from South Vietnam, from which it launched division-size attacks on American and South Vietnamese forces. The sanctuaries were supplied either via the Ho Chi Minh Trail through Laos or via the Cambodian seaport of Sihanoukville—all in blatant violation of Cambodian neutrality. As American withdrawals accelerated, the military position of both South Vietnam and the American forces was bound to become untenable if that logistics network was left intact and ever-decreasing American forces were confronted by undiminished North Vietnamese troops with unlimited outside supplies. The Nixon Administration therefore made the tactical decision to attack the sanctuary areas by air in 1969, and on the ground in 1970. The air attacks were a riposte to a wave of North Vietnamese attacks in the South, which were killing 400 Americans a week and were in violation of Hanoi's "understanding" with President Johnson at the time of the 1968 bombing halt; the ground attacks were a strategy to protect American troop withdrawals, which were reaching 150,000 a year.

Without challenging the North Vietnamese logistics bases, no conceivable American withdrawal strategy could have worked. In each instance, the American offensive was welcomed by the Cambodian authorities, who saw them as a defense of their country's neutrality; after all, no one had invited the North Vietnamese into Cambodia.

Nonetheless, both American military steps became highly emotional issues in the United States, turning into a debate which has long since transcended military strategy. Cambodia quickly became assimilated into the basic Vietnam debate. The Administration policy reflected a strategy; the critique focused on the moral validity of the war itself. This attitude was magnified by the nation's inability to fathom the nature and the implacability of revolutionary ideology. All evidence shows that the Khmer Rouge had been fanatical ideologues as early as their student days in Paris in the 1950s. They were determined to uproot and destroy the existing Cambodian society and to impose a sort of mad utopia by exterminating everybody with the slightest "bourgeois" education.[10] To allege that they had been turned into killers by American actions has the same moral stature as would the argument that the Holocaust had been caused by American strategic bombing of Germany.

The purpose of these pages is not to seek a final judgment on matters about which passions have run so high that they have, in the interim, evolved their own cult literature. But America owes it to itself to recognize that, whatever the final judgment on the tactical wisdom of American decisions in Cambodia, it was, tragically, the Khmer Rouge who did the murdering, and the Cambodians who paid the penalty for America's domestic divisions. The critics, who made it impossible for America to continue assisting the Cambodian government in its efforts to resist the Khmer Rouge onslaught, did not realize that a bloodbath would follow the cutoff of American aid that they were advocating and finally brought about. They were surely horrified by it. Yet their misjudgment of the genocidal foe figured far less in their postmortems than did their condemnations of their own compatriots.

The test of a society is whether it can submerge its differences in the pursuit of common objectives, and whether it can keep in mind that societies thrive on their reconciliations, not on their conflicts. America failed that test in Indochina.

The wounds were so deep, however, that peace brought little joy. Whatever chance there had been for the agreement to become a vehicle for national healing was weakened by the three-month interval between the time when the initial agreement was reached and the time it was signed, and, above all, by the B-52 bombing of the Hanoi area in the second half of December 1972. Though civilian damage was minimal, the resulting outburst of antiwar demonstrations caused the signing of the agreement on January 27, 1973, to elicit, above all, a sense of exhausted and wary relief.

For their part, the protesters were not reconciled by Hanoi's acceptance of America's peace terms. They feared that, if Nixon's notion of peace with honor was permitted to stand, America might again be tempted into the same kind of international overcommitment for which, to them, Vietnam had become the despised symbol. Thus, they greeted the peace agreement with the same cynicism with which they had viewed the conduct of the war and diplomacy. Critics argued variously that the agreement was a political ploy, that the same terms had been available four years earlier, and that it was a betrayal of Thieu—notwithstanding that the demand that Thieu be overthrown had been a central theme of the Peace Movement's demands for years.

Nothing could have been further from the truth than the proposition that the agreement with Hanoi had been concluded to influence the national election. On balance, Nixon had considered concluding an agreement before the election a liability; his lead in the polls was unassailable and could only have been jeopardized by a debate about peace terms.[11] His motive for going ahead with the agreement was the precise opposite of what the critics alleged: he did not want electoral considerations to stand in the way of an agreement he had repeatedly promised the American people would be concluded as soon as the Administration's stated terms had been met.

One of the more persistent myths about the Nixon Administration's Vietnam policy has been the thesis that Nixon needlessly prolonged the war for four years since the same terms could have been obtained four years earlier. The problem with this thesis is its obliviousness to all the known facts. The historical record demonstrates overwhelmingly that America settled quickly as soon as its terms, consistently rejected by the North Vietnamese during the previous four years, were accepted.

In 1975, of course, the American effort in Indochina ended in a debacle which might have occurred at any earlier point had America's objective been capitulation. But neither the Administration nor the American people ever sought that objective; in the election campaign of 1968, *all* of the presidential candidates had advocated compromise, not capitulation. In 1972, the candidate urging capitulation was defeated in a landslide. Even so, the reader is free to draw the conclusion in retrospect that capitulation should have been the goal in 1969. Nothing in the political campaign of 1968 suggested that the American people or the political parties favored such an outcome.

The torment did not end with the Paris Agreement. No sooner had the war ended than the controversy moved to America's right to enforce the peace. There was not a single senior member of the Nixon Administration who did not have doubts about the precariousness of the agreement. We had gone to the outer limit of what could be conceded, as Nixon had always promised to do. And the domestic turmoil left the Administration with little maneuvering room.

Nevertheless, Nixon and I, along with many senior members of the Administration, believed that the military and economic provisions of the agreement would enable South Vietnam to resist foreseeable pressures from the North, provided the North Vietnamese adhered to the portion of the agreement that prohibited renewed infiltration. Nixon always recognized, however, that violations might occur, and of a magnitude that could be neither deterred nor resisted without American assistance. He was prepared to encourage North Vietnam to join the international community with a program of economic assistance. But if all else failed, the use of air power to enforce the agreement was never ruled out, either in the minds of members of the Nixon Administration or in its public pronouncements.

With the end of the war, the Administration gritted its teeth for the test of strength that experience had taught it was likely to occur over implementing the agreement. We took it for granted that we had the right —indeed, the responsibility—to defend an agreement in the pursuit of which 50,000 Americans had died. Were it otherwise, *any* peace agreement with the United States would be the legal equivalent of capitulation. Terms that will not be defended amount to surrender. If a nation is not permitted to enforce peace terms, it does better to abandon its cause simply and openly. Nixon and his key advisers announced their intention to defend the agreement on innumerable occasions[12]—for example, on May 3, 1973, in Nixon's annual Foreign Policy Report: "Such a course [massive violations] would endanger the hard won gains for peace in Indochina. It would risk revived confrontation with us.[13] . . . We have told Hanoi, privately and publicly, that we will not tolerate violations of the Agreement."[14]

The pattern of the previous five years repeated itself. Perhaps an undamaged, newly re-elected president could have insisted on the periodic sharp military measures which were required to enforce the agreement. But with Watergate already gnawing at the presidency, there was no chance of that. Even as thousands of North Vietnamese trucks were traversing the Ho Chi Minh Trail, nearly 50,000 North Vietnamese troops were entering Vietnam, and Hanoi stonewalled on giving an adequate accounting for America's missing-in-action—all of which were acts in flagrant violation of the agreement—opponents of the policy that had led to the agreement insisted that Nixon had no authority to enforce it, no matter how severe the violation. They treated the agreement as if it were the unilateral withdrawal they had always advocated. In June 1973, the Congress denied further funding "to support directly or indirectly combat activities in or over Cambodia, Laos, North Vietnam and South Vietnam by United States forces" after August 15, including aerial reconnaissance.[15] In July 1973, it became clear that there was no Congressional support for an economic-assistance program for North Vietnam.

The peace agreement was not self-enforcing; no such agreement could have been. North Vietnam still aimed for the union of Vietnam under its rule, and a piece of paper signed in Paris was not going to alter Hanoi's permanent goals. The Paris Accords had extricated the United States from the military conflict in Vietnam, but South Vietnam's lease on life depended on American support. The Congress had to decide whether to continue a containment-style policy in Indochina after American troops left. And it decided against it.

Even economic assistance to South Vietnam was being throttled. In 1972, the Congress had voted $2 billion in aid; in 1973, the amount was reduced to $1.4 billion, and in 1974, it was cut in half, even though oil prices had quadrupled. By 1975, the Congress was discussing a terminal grant of $600 million. Cambodia was cut off altogether, with the argument that it would help save lives—a euphemism for abandonment, and a grim joke in light of the genocide that followed. In 1975, Cambodia and South Vietnam were overrun by the communists within two weeks of each other, putting an end to America's emotional misery but not to Indochina's.

American idealism, the inspiration of so much of the postwar world order, had defeated itself with its own weapons. Four presidents had defined Vietnam as being vital to American security. Two presidents of different parties had identified America's honor with not abandoning those who had relied on America's pronouncements. Nixon had won the 1972 election in a landslide on the basis of just such propositions. In classic American fashion, both sides in the debate over Vietnam had perceived their goals in terms of moral absolutes and never found a means of bridging the gulf between them.

Even after twenty years, the American public debate has not attained an objective perspective and still seems more eager to assign blame than to draw lessons from the experience. The communist victory rapidly settled one of the perennial debates of the Vietnam War era—whether the specter of the expected bloodbath in the wake of a communist takeover was a figment of the policymakers' search for pretexts to continue the war.

In Cambodia, of course, genocide did occur. The new rulers killed at least 15 percent of their own population. In Vietnam, the suffering was less drastic. Still, hundreds of thousands of South Vietnamese were herded into "re-education camps," another name for concentration camps. In early 1977, communist authorities admitted to holding 50,000 political prisoners, though most independent observers believed the true figure to be closer to 200,000.[16] With respect to the so-called National Liberation Front of South Vietnam (the NLF), which had been advertised in the West for a decade as the putative centerpiece of a democratic coalition government, the conquering North Vietnamese made it clear that their actual plans were quite different. In 1969, the NLF had been transmogrified into the so-called Provisional Revolutionary Government of the Republic of South Vietnam, or the PRG. In June 1975, two months after the fall of Saigon, the PRG "Cabinet" met and decided upon a limited restoration of banking facilities in South Vietnam; advisory committees were set up to help manage the country, including some noncommunist politicians who had opposed Thieu; the PRG established diplomatic relations with eighty-two countries.

There was nothing Hanoi wanted less, however, than an independent South Vietnam, even a communist one; the temptations of Titoism would be nipped in the bud. The "Cabinet" decision was quickly rescinded, the advisory committees were given no role, and PRG ambassadors were never sent abroad. The government of South Vietnam remained in the hands of local military committees run by the North Vietnamese Communist Party and military officials. By June 1975, Hanoi's leaders and press began a publicity campaign calling for early reunification of the country —that is, formal annexation of the South—which was accomplished within a year.[17]

Although, in a strict sense, the only dominoes which fell were Cambodia and Laos, anti-Western revolutionaries in many other areas of the globe began to feel emboldened. It is doubtful that Castro would have intervened in Angola, or the Soviet Union in Ethiopia, had America not been perceived to have collapsed in Indochina, to have become demoralized by Watergate, and to have afterward retreated into a cocoon. At the same time, it has been argued with considerable plausibility that, had South Vietnam fallen in the early 1960s, the communists' attempted coup in Indonesia, which nearly succeeded in 1965, might have overthrown the government and produced another strategic disaster.

America, at any rate, paid a price for its adventure in Vietnam that was out of proportion to any conceivable gain. It was clearly a mistake to have staked so much on such ill-defined causes. America had become involved in the first place because it applied literally the maxims of its successful European policy to a region with radically different political, social, and economic conditions. Wilsonian idealism permitted no cultural differentiation, while the theory of collective security held that, security being indivisible, the fabric of the entire international order would unravel if even one strand were pulled out.

Too idealistic to base its policy on national interest, and too focused on the requirements of general war in its strategic doctrine, America was unable to master an unfamiliar strategic problem in which the political and military objectives were entwined. Imbued with the belief in the universal appeal of its values, America vastly underestimated the obstacles to democratization in a society shaped by Confucianism, and among a people who were struggling for political identity in the midst of an assault by outside forces.

Perhaps the most serious, and surely the most hurtful, domino which fell as a result of the Vietnam War was the cohesion of American society. American idealism had imbued both officials and critics with the misconception that Vietnamese society could be transformed relatively easily and quickly into an American-style democracy. When that optimistic proposition collapsed and it became apparent that Vietnam was far from being a democracy, disillusionment was inevitable. There was also a nearly incomprehensible misconception about the nature of the military problem. Lacking criteria for judgment, officials often misunderstood, and therefore often misstated, the issues. But when these officials claimed to be seeing a light at the end of the tunnel, that in fact was what most of them perceived. However misguided their assessments, they had above all deceived themselves.

It is always the case that issues which reach top policymakers are generally complex; simple, noncontroversial matters are settled at lower levels of the government by consensus. Yet, once a decision is made, however great his inner doubt about it, the policymaker becomes totally committed; hence the appearance of assurance with which it may be presented can be quite misleading. Moreover, this false impression is frequently compounded by the tendency of bureaucracies to embellish their own achievements.

Exposing intentional misrepresentation by the Executive Branch of our government is a crucial function of the media and of the Congress. There is no excuse for deliberate misrepresentation. But there is little basis for the claim that the basic issues of Vietnam were affected by the so-called credibility gaps. America had charged into Vietnam with all its flags flying; no one had sneaked it into Vietnam. The Congress was aware of the level of America's commitment, and it had voted the necessary appropriations year after year. To have wanted to prevent the communist takeover of a new nation may have been naïve, but it ought not to have led to the assault on America's core values which became such a central part of the national debate.

These bitter controversies continue to confuse the issue of what actually happened in Indochina, creating an intellectual vacuum about a period extending over two decades and four administrations of both political parties. America will only recover from Vietnam when it begins to draw some bipartisan lessons from that searing experience.

First, before the United States commits itself to combat, it should have a clear understanding of the nature of the threat it will be confronting and of the objectives it can realistically reach. It must have a clear military strategy and an unambiguous definition of what constitutes a successful political outcome.

Second, when America commits itself to military action, there can be no alternative to victory, as General Douglas MacArthur advised. Qualms cannot be stilled by hesitant execution; prolonged stalemate will sap the endurance and hence the will of the American public. This requires a careful elaboration of political goals and the military strategy to achieve them before the decision is made to go to war.

Third, a democracy cannot conduct a serious foreign policy if the contending factions within it do not exercise a minimum of restraint toward each other. Once victory over domestic opponents becomes the sole objective of a policy, cohesion evaporates. Nixon was convinced that it was the president's ultimate responsibility to defend the national interest, even if this went against his country's own passionate dissenters—perhaps especially then. Yet Vietnam showed that presidents cannot conduct war by executive fiat. Faced with violent demonstrations, Congressional resolutions progressively edging toward unilateral withdrawal, and the hostility of the media, Nixon should have gone to the Congress early in his term, outlined his strategy, and demanded a clear-cut endorsement of his policy. If he could not obtain that endorsement, he should have asked for a vote to liquidate the war and made the Congress assume responsibility.

As mentioned earlier, Nixon rejected such advice because he felt that history would never forgive the appalling consequences of what he considered an abdication of executive responsibility. It was an honorable—indeed, a highly moral and intellectually correct—decision. But in the American system of checks-and-balances, the burden which Nixon took upon himself was not meant to be borne by just one man.

In the Vietnam period, America was obliged to come to grips with its limits. For most of its history, America's exceptionalism had proclaimed a moral superiority which was backed by the nation's material abundance. But in Vietnam, America found itself involved in a war which became morally ambiguous, and in which America's material superiority was largely irrelevant. The picture-perfect families gracing the television screens of the 1950s had been the cultural support group for the moral high-mindedness of Dulles and the soaring idealism of Kennedy.

Thwarted in these aspirations, America searched its soul and turned on itself. Surely no other society would have had comparable confidence in its ultimate cohesiveness to thus rip itself apart, certain that it could put itself together again. No other people would have been so cavalier about risking breakdown in order to spark renewal.

In terms of immediate outcome, the domestic drama was a tragedy; however, in the long run, the anguish could turn into the price America had to pay in order to relate its moral perfectionism, which has inspired so many great American efforts, to the necessities of an international environment less hospitable and more complex than any in the past.

The experience of Vietnam remains deeply imprinted on the American psyche, while history has seemingly reserved for itself some of its most telling lessons. After its soul-searching, America recovered its self-confidence, and the Soviet Union, despite its monolithic appearance, paid a mortal penalty for moral, political, and economic overreaching. After a spurt of expansionism, the Soviet Union found itself mired in contradiction and finally collapsed.

These developments evoke some rather ironic reflections on the nature of history's lessons. The United States went into Vietnam in order to stop what it considered a centrally directed communist conspiracy, and it failed. From America's failure, Moscow drew the conclusion which the advocates of the Domino Theory had so feared—that the historical correlation of forces had shifted in its favor. As a result, it tried to expand into Yemen, Angola, Ethiopia, and ultimately Afghanistan. But in the process, it found that geopolitical realities applied just as much to communist societies as they did to the capitalist ones. In fact, being less resilient, Soviet overextension produced, not catharsis, as it did in America, but disintegration.[18]

The question remains whether events would have moved in the same direction had America simply remained passive and relied on the evolution of history to take care of the communist challenge. Or would such a renunciation have conferred an impetus and a conviction of inevitable victory on the communist world that would have been sufficient to delay, perhaps even to arrest, the Soviet collapse?

Whatever the academic answer, the statesman cannot adopt abdication as a principle of policy. He may learn to moderate his confidence in his assessments and to allow for the unforeseeable; but relying on the eventual collapse of a threatening adversary is a policy that offers no solace to the millions of immediate victims, and turns policymaking into a reckless gamble on intuition.

America's anguish over Vietnam was an extraordinary testament to its moral scruples, which is itself a good answer to all the questions about the ethical significance of the American experience. After a relatively brief interval, Americans recovered their bearing in the 1980s. By the 1990s, free peoples everywhere were again looking to America for guidance in constructing yet another new world order. And their greatest fear was not America's overweening involvement in the world but, once again, its withdrawal from it. This is why the sadness of the memories of Indochina should serve to remind us that American unity is both a duty and the hope of the world.

CHAPTER TWENTY-EIGHT

Foreign Policy as Geopolitics: Nixon's Triangular Diplomacy

For Nixon, the anguishing process of extricating America from Vietnam had, in the end, been about maintaining America's standing in the world. Even without that purgatory, a major reassessment of American foreign policy would have been in order, for the age of America's nearly total dominance of the world stage was drawing to a close. America's nuclear superiority was eroding, and its economic supremacy was being chal-

703

lenged by the dynamic growth of Europe and Japan, both of which had been restored by American resources and sheltered by American security guarantees. Vietnam finally signaled that it was high time to reassess America's role in the developing world, and to find some sustainable ground between abdication and overextension.

On the other side of the ledger, new opportunities for American diplomacy were presenting themselves as serious cracks opened up in what had been viewed throughout the Cold War as the communist monolith. Khrushchev's revelations in 1956 of the brutalities of Stalin's rule, and the Soviet invasion of Czechoslovakia in 1968, had weakened the ideological appeal of communism for the rest of the world. Even more important, the split between China and the Soviet Union undermined Moscow's pretense to be the leader of a united communist movement. All of these developments suggested that there was scope for a new diplomatic flexibility.

For twenty years, Wilsonian idealism had enabled American leaders to conduct their global role with missionary vigor. But the America of the late 1960s—stalemated in Indochina and torn by domestic conflict—required a more complex and nuanced definition of its international enterprise. Wilson had guided a country that was new to international affairs and confident in its ability to follow any problem through to its final resolution; Nixon inherited a society rent by frustration, whose future would depend on its ability to frame attainable long-term goals and to persevere in those goals even in the face of adversity without yielding to self-doubt.

Richard Milhous Nixon had inherited near–civil war conditions. Deeply suspicious of the Establishment, and in return mistrusted by many of its representatives, he nevertheless held fast to the conviction that the world's leading democracy could neither abdicate its responsibilities nor resign from its destiny. Few presidents have been as complex as Nixon: shy, yet determined; insecure, yet resolute; distrustful of intellectuals, yet privately deeply reflective; occasionally impetuous in his pronouncements, yet patient and farsighted in his strategic design, Nixon found himself in the position of having to guide America through the transition from dominance to leadership. Often ungenerous in his pronouncements and incapable of projecting personal warmth, Nixon nevertheless fulfilled, under the most difficult circumstances, the crucial test of leadership by moving his society from the familiar into a world it had never known.

No American president possessed a greater knowledge of international affairs. None except Theodore Roosevelt had traveled as much abroad, or attempted with such genuine interest to understand the views of other leaders. Nixon was not a student of history in the same way that Churchill or de Gaulle had been. He generally learned just enough about a country's past to absorb the rudiments of the facts pertaining to its circumstances—and often not even that much. Yet he had an uncanny ability to grasp the political dynamics of any country that had seized his attention. And his understanding of the geopolitical realities was truly remarkable. Nixon's handling of domestic politics could at times be distorted by ambition and personal insecurity. But when it came to foreign policy, his powerful analytical skills and extraordinary geopolitical intuition were always crisply focused on the American interest.

Nixon did not accept the Wilsonian verities about the essential goodness of man or the underlying harmony among nations to be maintained by collective security. Wilson had perceived a world progressing inexorably toward peace and democracy; America's mission in it was to help the inevitable along. For Nixon, the world was divided between friends and antagonists; between arenas for cooperation and those in which interests clashed. In Nixon's perception, peace and harmony were not the natural order of things but temporary oases in a perilous world where stability could only be preserved by vigilant effort.

Nixon sought to navigate according to a concept of America's national interest—repugnant as that idea was to many traditional idealists. If the major powers, including the United States, pursued their self-interests rationally and predictably, Nixon believed—in the spirit of the eighteenth-century Enlightenment—that an equilibrium would emerge from the clash of competing interests. Like Theodore Roosevelt—but unlike any other twentieth-century American president—Nixon counted on a balance of power to produce stability, and considered a strong America essential to the global equilibrium.

Both of these views were highly unfashionable at the time. Nixon stated the following in an interview with *Time* magazine on January 3, 1972:

> We must remember the only time in the history of the world that we have had any extended periods of peace is when there has been balance of power. It is when one nation becomes infinitely more powerful in relation to its potential competitor that the danger of war arises. So I believe in a world in which the United States is powerful. I think it will be a safer world and a better world if we have a strong, healthy United States, Europe, Soviet Union, China, Japan, each balancing the other, not playing one against the other, an even balance.[1]

At the same time, Nixon was reflecting the essential ambivalence of his society—so in need of being perceived as hardheaded, yet so dependent on drawing inner strength from its traditional idealism. Incongruously, the president most admired by Nixon—whose own maxims were anything but Wilsonian—was Woodrow Wilson himself. Every new president gets to choose the portraits of predecessors he wishes to hang in the Cabinet Room. Nixon chose those of Wilson and Eisenhower. When he ordered Wilson's old desk to be placed in the Oval Office, it was as if irony dogged Nixon: the desk which the White House custodian produced turned out to be, not Woodrow Wilson's, but that of Henry Wilson, Ulysses Grant's Vice President.

Nixon often invoked standard Wilsonian rhetoric. "We do have a destiny," he said, "to give something more to the world simply than an example which other nations in the past have been able to give . . . an example of spiritual leadership and idealism which no material strength or military power can provide."[2] Indeed, he shared the great American yearning for a foreign policy devoid of self-interest.

> Speaking for the United States, I can say this: We covet no one else's territory; we seek no dominion over any other people; we seek the right to live in peace, not only for ourselves but for all the peoples of this earth. Our power will only be used to keep the peace, never to break it, only to defend freedom, never to destroy it.[3]

The invocations of altruism by a president who in the same breath insisted that the future of the world should be decided by five great powers pursuing their own national interests represented a novel synthesis of the American experience. Nixon took American idealism seriously in the sense that he shared Wilson's passionate internationalism and belief in America's indispensability. But he felt equally obliged to relate America's mission to his own conclusions about the way the world actually worked. Even as Nixon wanted his country to stand for Wilson's values, he was also painfully aware that destiny had dealt him the thankless assignment of conducting America's retreat from crusading for those values by sending its armies around the world.

Nixon's point of departure was American exceptionalism, although his own extensive acquaintance with foreign leaders had taught him that the fewest of them were altruistic; given a truth serum, most of them would have opted for a certain amount of calculability in American foreign policy, and considered the American national interest more reliable than altruism. This was why Nixon preferred to operate on two tracks simultaneously: invoking Wilsonian rhetoric to explain his goals while appealing to national interest to sustain his tactics.

It was ironic that Nixon's commitment to an American role in the pursuit of world peace should have placed him in opposition to so many of his distinguished American contemporaries who had previously been identified with Wilsonianism but were now urging policies which, to Nixon, amounted to abdication from America's international role. Nixon, well aware that even his own view of America's global responsibility amounted to retrenchment when compared to that of his immediate predecessors, saw it as his task to define a *sustainable* role for an idealistic America in an unprecedentedly complex international environment—one in which, in Nixon's mind, Wilsonianism and *Realpolitik* would merge.

The containment strategy of the early postwar period had projected America into the front line of every international crisis; the soaring rhetoric of the Kennedy period had set goals that were beyond America's physical and emotional capacities. As a result, American righteousness was turning into self-hatred, and the criticism of overextension into abdication. In such an environment, Nixon perceived as his first task putting the Vietnam experience into some perspective. The United States remained essential to international stability, but it would not be able to sustain the freewheeling interventionism that had brought over 500,000 Americans into Indochina without a strategy for victory. The survival of mankind ultimately depended on the relationship of the two superpowers, but the peace of the world depended on whether America could distinguish between those responsibilities in which its role was merely helpful and those to which it was indispensable, and whether it could sustain the latter without tearing itself apart.

Nixon chose a rather unusual occasion to introduce his answer to these dilemmas. On July 25, 1969, he found himself in Guam at the beginning of a world trip that would take him from Southeast Asia to Romania. Earlier that day, he had witnessed the splashdown, near Johnston Island in the Pacific, of the first astronauts to land on the moon. Modern journalism, unwilling as it is to linger over even the most novel historical drama, requires a new event for every news cycle, especially during presidential trips. And Guam was on the other side of the international date line from the splashdown (which is why the splashdown is listed as having occurred on July 24) and therefore was part of another news cycle.

Realizing this, Nixon selected that occasion to put forward the principles that would guide his country's new approach to international relations. Though Nixon and his advisers had often discussed the new approach, there had been no plan to present it to the public on this particular occasion. Thus it was to everybody's amazement, including my own, that Nixon announced America's new criteria for involvement abroad.[4] Henceforth called the Nixon Doctrine, these were elaborated in a November 1969 speech and again in February 1970, in the President's first annual foreign policy report, an innovation of the period in which Nixon outlined the basic premises of his foreign policy.

The Nixon Doctrine dealt with the paradox that America's two postwar military engagements, Korea and Vietnam, had been on behalf of countries to which America had no formal commitment, and in regions which were technically not covered by alliances. With respect to these regions, the Nixon Doctrine sought to navigate between overextension and abdication by establishing three criteria for American involvement:

- The United States would keep its treaty commitments.
- The United States would "provide a shield if a nuclear power threatens the freedom of a nation allied with us or of a nation whose survival we consider vital to our security."
- In cases involving non-nuclear aggression, the United States would "look to the nation directly threatened to assume the primary responsibility of providing the manpower for defense."[5]

Reality, however, showed itself resistant to being thus encapsuled in formal criteria. The assurance that America would keep its commitments was boilerplate; like professions of chastity, it has limited plausibility since its abandonment is unlikely to be announced before the event. At any rate, the key issue in the Nuclear Age was not whether commitments would be kept, but how they would be defined and interpreted. The Nixon Doctrine offered no guide as to how to solve the allied disputes regarding nuclear strategy: whether nuclear weapons would be used and —to put it crudely—on whose territory; whether the allies would rely on general nuclear war, which primarily affected the superpowers, or on some version of "flexible response," which primarily threatened the territories of the victims of aggression.

The clause stating that the United States would provide a shield for countries "vital to our security" if they were threatened by a nuclear power contained two ambiguities: if the United States defended countries vital to its security only when they were threatened by a nuclear power, what would be the United States' attitude if a country important to its security was menaced by a non-nuclear power, or by a nuclear power choosing not to use nuclear weapons? And if support was more or less automatic in the face of a nuclear threat, was a formal alliance necessary?

The Nixon Doctrine also required threatened countries to assume a larger burden of their own conventional defense. But what would

America do if a threatened country gambled on American support regardless of its failure to share the burdens of defense—especially in the face of pressure by a nuclear power? Ironically, the Nixon Administration's emphasis on the national interest had the potential to supply an incentive for nations to ignore its injunction to make greater defense efforts. For, if the national interest was indeed the principal guide, America would be obliged to defend *any* area considered essential to its security without regard for the victim's merit or its contribution to the common defense. Herein lay all the dilemmas which later came into prominence under the rubric of allied burden-sharing.

The Nixon Doctrine was, therefore, primarily relevant to crises in peripheral areas not covered by formal alliances and threatened by Soviet surrogates, of which, as it turned out, there were very few. In its attempt to devise a "doctrine" for avoiding another conflict like Vietnam, the Nixon Administration developed a doctrine which applied primarily *to* situations like Vietnam which it was determined not to repeat.

Still, by the time Nixon came into office, East-West relations were themselves in obvious need of reassessment. The conflict with the Soviet Union had propelled America into global engagement, and it was the strategy of that conflict that needed to be reconsidered in light of the trauma of Vietnam. What made the reassessment so difficult was that, throughout the Cold War, much of the domestic debate over containment had been conducted in classically American categories that excluded geopolitics, with one group seeing foreign policy as a subdivision of theology and its opponents viewing foreign policy as a subdivision of psychiatry.

The fathers of containment—Acheson and Dulles and their colleagues—had, for all their sophistication on international affairs, conceived of their handiwork in essentially theological terms. Since they deemed the Soviet proclivity for world domination to be congenital, they did not consider Soviet leaders as suitable negotiating partners until the Kremlin had abandoned its ideology. And since the principal task of American foreign policy was seen as achieving the overthrow of the Soviets, comprehensive negotiations, or even a diplomatic blueprint for them, were pointless (if not immoral) until "positions of strength" had brought about a change in Soviet purposes.

A society devoid of experience with irreconcilable conflict and possessing an overwhelming faith in compromise as a solvent of disputes found it difficult to muster the patience for so stark a course. Many who believed in Acheson's and Dulles' moral premises tried to speed up the timetable for negotiations by claiming that the Soviet system had already transformed itself, or was about to do so. The American public's yearning for an end to confrontation made even the tough school of containment vulnerable to changes in atmospherics, as was reflected in the so-called spirits of Geneva and Camp David while Dulles was Secretary of State.

According to the "psychiatric school," the Soviet leaders were not so different from the American in their desire for peace. They acted intransigently partly because the United States had made them feel insecure. The "psychiatric school" urged patience in order to strengthen the peace-loving segment of the Soviet leadership, which was said to be divided between hawks and doves in much the same way that the American government was. The national debate turned increasingly to the magnitude of the supposed Soviet internal change without being able to resolve the original dilemma, which was that the containment policy, knowing no middle ground between confrontation and the *status quo,* had never answered the question of what to negotiate about.

By the early 1970s, both of these schools of thought were being challenged by a new radicalism. The Henry Wallace approach of the 1940s had been reincarnated and bore new labels, invoking a far more startling rhetoric which stood containment on its head. Not only did it argue, as its precursors had, that America had no moral right to oppose communism, but it asserted that opposition to communism actually strengthened communism. According to the new radicalism, communism did not need to be contained but survived. For, in the end, history itself would defeat it, if it merited defeat.

Describing a march on Washington, the novelist Norman Mailer summarized that point of view while advocating unconditional withdrawal from Vietnam:

> ... if the Communists prevailed in Asia ... divisions, schisms, and sects would appear. ... Therefore, to leave Asia would be precisely to gain the balance of power. ... [T]he more Communism expanded, the more monumental would become its problems, the more flaccid its preoccupations with world conquest. In the expansion of Communism, was its own containment.[6]

In maintaining that communism could best, and perhaps only, be defeated by its victories rather than by American opposition, the new radicalism preached the exact opposite of containment. Overextension being the root of communist weakness, the more communism advanced, the more surely it would collapse. The contention that in America's abstention from resistance to communism lay the seeds of victory over it was indeed a novelist's paradox.

Mailer's poetics were reinforced by far more sophisticated academic analysts who did not express themselves quite so idiosyncratically. The "convergence theory," espoused by such intellectual heavyweights as John Kenneth Galbraith,[7] in effect asserted that it was senseless for America to run huge risks in opposing communism when the two societies were destined to become more and more alike in the natural course of events.

East-West relations had reached a dead end. The traditional concept of containment had led to a diplomatic stalemate. Its principal alternative was a heresy that required the abandonment of all the premises of a generation of commitment. Yet no responsible American president could simply turn the fate of his country over to the presumed forces of history. It was, after all, no consolation to Carthage that a few hundred years after it was razed by Roman conquerors, Rome, too, disappeared.

Nixon rejected all three schools of thought and set about to establish the national interest as the basic criterion for long-range American foreign policy. The most important vehicle for this effort was the annual presidential foreign policy report. Four such annual reports on American foreign policy were issued starting in 1970. Drafted by my staff and me, these reports reflected the President's views and were issued in Nixon's name. As with all such statements, authorship is less significant than the president's assumption of responsibility for them. Although these reports put forward the conceptual approach of the new administration, they were not fully successful in this. The media, geared to events rather than to concepts, ignored them for the most part, except for the sections relating to Vietnam. And foreign leaders treated them as staff products with which they would deal when the circumstances to which the reports referred actually arose.

Nevertheless, for the student of the period they constitute the best road map for the foreign policy of the Nixon era, and would have done so for journalists and foreign leaders who, as it turned out, missed many an obvious hint by focusing on the day-to-day stuff of diplomatic exchanges. The basic theme of the reports was that American foreign policy would henceforth be geared to an analysis of the national interest, and that America would engage itself for political causes rather than the exegesis of legal principles. The President's first annual report on foreign policy, on February 18, 1970, expressed this view:

> Our objective, in the first instance, is to support our *interests* over the long run with a sound foreign policy. The more that policy is based on a realistic assessment of our and others' interests, the more effective

our role in the world can be. We are not involved in the world because we have commitments; we have commitments because we are involved. Our interests must shape our commitments, rather than the other way around.[8]

In a British or French state paper, such statements would have passed for truisms, and it would not have been deemed necessary to make a special point of them. In America, it was unprecedented for a president to stake his policy on the explicit affirmation of the national interest. None of Nixon's predecessors in this century—with the exception of Theodore Roosevelt—had treated American idealism as one factor among many, or the future in terms of permanent engagement as opposed to specific crusades with fixed terminal points.

In dealing with the Soviet Union, the report stated, American policy would be based on a precise understanding of the nature of the Soviet system that neither underestimated the depth of communist ideological commitment nor fell prey to the illusion that communist leaders "have already given up their beliefs or are just about to do so. . . ."[9] Nor would America permit itself to become emotionally dependent on relations with the Soviet Union. The criterion for progress would be substance expressed in precise agreements reflecting mutual interests and not atmospherics. Above all, relaxation of tensions had to proceed on a broad front:

> We will regard our Communist adversaries first and foremost as nations pursuing their own interests as *they* perceive these interests, just as we follow our own interests as we see them. We will judge them by their actions as we expect to be judged by our own. Specific agreements, and the structure of peace they help build, will come from a realistic accommodation of conflicting interests.[10]

The 1971 report repeated the same theme: "The internal order of the USSR, as such, is not an object of our policy, although we do not hide our rejection of many of its features. Our relations with the USSR, as with other countries, are determined by its international behavior."[11]

The emphasis on national interest was to come under intense conservative attack, especially after the Vietnam War ended and the urge for a release from international tensions had abated. The real issue was not, however, whether Nixon placed too much reliance on Soviet leaders, as the criticism had it at the time—which was absurd given Nixon's emphasis on concreteness and his pessimistic view of human nature—but on the strategy best suited to stopping Soviet expansionism. Nixon believed that, amidst the turmoil of Vietnam, the national interest provided the best criterion for resisting communist expansionism and retaining public support. His critics considered the emphasis on national interest as a form of moral disarmament.

In its determination to prevent further extension of the communist sphere, the Nixon Administration's views were indistinguishable from those of Acheson and Dulles preceding it, or from those of Reagan that followed. Even while the Vietnam War was raging, the Nixon Administration reacted neuralgically to any perceived geopolitical or strategic threat from the Soviet Union: in 1970, over the building of a Soviet naval base in Cuba, over the movement of Soviet surface-to-air missiles toward the Suez Canal, and in response to the Syrian invasion of Jordan; in 1971, over the Soviet role in the India-Pakistan War; and in 1973, against an implied threat by Brezhnev to intervene militarily in the Arab-Israeli War. The attitude continued into the Ford Administration in reaction to the dispatch of Cuban troops to Angola.

At the same time, the Nixon Administration's approach to containment differed from that of Acheson and Dulles in that it did not make the transformation of Soviet society a precondition to negotiations. Nixon parted company with the fathers of containment and chose a path reminiscent of Churchill, who in 1953 had called for talks with Moscow after Stalin's death. Nixon believed that the process of negotiations and a long period of peaceful competition would accelerate the transformation of the Soviet system and strengthen the democracies.

What Nixon defined as an era of negotiations served as a strategy for enabling America to regain the diplomatic initiative while the war in Vietnam was still in progress. Nixon's goal was to keep the Peace Movement confined to the issue of Vietnam and to prevent it from paralyzing every aspect of American foreign policy. Nor was Nixon's approach primarily tactical. He and his advisers believed that a quite possibly temporary confluence of interest in eased tensions existed between the two nuclear superpowers. The nuclear balance seemed to be approaching a kind of stability, or could be made to do so either unilaterally or by arms control negotiations. America needed breathing room in order to extricate itself from Vietnam and to construct a new policy for the post-Vietnam era, while the Soviet Union had perhaps even stronger reasons for seeking a respite. The buildup of Soviet divisions on the Chinese border implied that a Soviet Union faced with tensions on two fronts thousands of miles apart might well be ready to explore political solutions with America, especially if we succeeded in the opening to China—

which was a keystone of Nixon's strategy. Whatever its ideological convictions, the Soviet leadership might develop enough of a stake in Western relations to defer confrontation. In our view, the longer the Soviet confrontation with the West was delayed, the more unmanageable would become the task of holding together the Soviet Empire, especially since its political problems were compounded by economic stagnation. In other words, Nixon and his advisers believed that time was on the side of the United States, not of the communist world.

Nixon's view of Moscow was more nuanced than that of his predecessors. He did not see relations with the Soviet Union as an all-or-nothing proposition but as a mixed bag of issues with varying degrees of solubility. He endeavored to weave together all the many elements of the superpower relationship into an overall approach that was neither totally confrontational (like that of the "theologians") nor totally conciliatory (like that of the "psychiatrists"). The idea was to emphasize those areas in which cooperation was possible, and to use that cooperation as leverage to modify Soviet behavior in areas in which the two countries were at loggerheads. That, and not the caricatures which came to characterize the subsequent debate, was what the Nixon Administration understood by the word "detente."

There were many obstacles impeding this policy of "linkage," as it was dubbed—linking cooperation in one area to progress in another. The near-obsession with arms control among many influential Americans proved to be one such snag. The disarmament negotiations of the 1920s, which had been focused on reducing arms to nonthreatening levels, had failed disastrously. That goal had become even more complex in the Nuclear Age, because a "safe" level of nuclear weapons was almost a contradiction in terms. Nor could anyone imagine how to verify the required low levels in a territory as vast as the Soviet Union. Only as the Cold War was coming to an end did real reductions occur. But throughout the 1960s and 1970s, disarmament was subordinated to efforts to reduce specific, definable dangers, of which the most prominent was the effort to prevent a surprise attack—an enterprise that went under the name of arms control.

Policymakers had not expected that reducing the risk of surprise attack would emerge as a key issue in arms control negotiations. Common sense seemed to suggest that the vast destructive potential of the superpowers would cancel each other out and that each side would always be able to inflict unacceptable damage no matter what its adversary did. Then, in 1959, in one of the truly original articles of the Cold War period, the then Rand Corporation analyst Albert Wohlstetter showed that common sense was not an adequate guide to nuclear relationships. The fact that nuclear weapons were carried on airplanes concentrated on a relatively few bases might make it technically possible to destroy the adversary's strategic forces before they were launched.[12] In such circumstances, the attacking side might be able to reduce the counterblow to tolerable levels and emerge in a position to impose its will. By the same token, the fear of surprise attack might tempt preemption—that is, an attack for no other purpose than to forestall an anticipated surprise attack.

According to Wohlstetter, the nuclear balance was in fact highly unstable. The presumed gap between what came to be called first- and second-strike capabilities turned into the obsession of defense analysts and arms control experts. The idea developed that both sides might have an interest in negotiating arrangements to protect themselves against their ultimate danger. Academic seminars at Harvard, MIT, Stanford, and Cal Tech elaborated theories and practical proposals on arms control and strategic stability which were to sustain policymakers for the next two decades.

Wohlstetter's article did for strategic analysis what Kennan's "X" article had achieved for political analysis in 1947. Ever after, the diplomacy of arms control concentrated on limiting the composition and operating characteristics of strategic forces to reduce the incentive for surprise attack to a minimum.

But arms control introduced complexities of its own. The subject was so esoteric that it multiplied the anxieties of both policymakers and the public at large. For one thing, it oversimplified the nature of the problem. The decision to initiate nuclear war would not be made by scientists, who were familiar with these weapons, but by harassed political leaders, aware that the slightest miscalculation would destroy their societies, if not civilization itself. Neither side had any operational experience with the new technology and, in order to prevail in a nuclear war, thousands of nuclear warheads would have to be launched simultaneously. During the entire Cold War, however, the Soviet Union had never tested more than three missiles simultaneously, and the United States had never launched even one from an operational silo (because America's operational silos were located in the center of the country, and Washington was afraid of a forest fire if a test missile fell to Earth. So much for confidence).

Thus, the danger of surprise attack was in fact exaggerated by two groups with conflicting objectives: those who wanted substantial defense budgets to protect against the danger of surprise attack, and those who invoked the fear of surprise attack as a reason for shrinking the defense budgets. Since the issues were so complex, a premium was placed on skills in briefing. And emotions ran so deep that it was not easy to tell whether experts had been led to their conclusions by scientific study or whether they invoked science to support preconceived conclusions—too often the latter. Pity the policymaker who became hostage to the advice of scientists with widely divergent views, and who had devoted more years of study to nuclear issues than the statesman had hours available in which to consider them. Debates about such esoteric subjects as vulnerability, accuracy, and calculability attained the complexity of medieval disputes about theology while being, in fact, surrogates for long-standing philosophical disagreements dating back to the earliest days of containment.

During the most intense debate about arms control in the 1970s, conservative critics warned of the unreliability of Soviet leaders and the hostility of Soviet ideology. The advocates of arms control stressed the contribution of arms control agreements to a general atmosphere of eased relations, quite independently of the merit of the actual agreements. It was the old debate between the theologians and the psychiatrists refurbished in technological garb.

At first, arms control was simply grafted onto the containment theory. Reliance on positions of strength was espoused side by side with an arms control concept that purported to make containment less dangerous. As time went on, it became evident that arms control also made containment more permanent. There was less and less talk of a political settlement, and fewer attempts were made to negotiate one. Indeed, the safer the world appeared to arms controllers, the less reason statesmen found to leave familiar positions for the uncharted sea of political accommodation.

Crises came and went. Flare-ups occurred from Southeast Asia to the Caribbean and Central Europe, but both sides seemed to be waiting for the more or less automatic collapse of their adversary under the impact of historical evolution. In the interval until it would become apparent which side's view of historical evolution was prevailing, life would be made more tolerable by arms control negotiations. It seemed to be an environment consecrated to stalemate: the political doctrine (containment) had no answer to the arms race, and the strategic theory (arms control) offered no solution to the political conflict.

In this atmosphere, Nixon entered office and was being pressured by the Congress and the media to turn rapidly to arms control negotiations with the Soviets. He was reluctant to conduct diplomacy as if nothing had happened less than six months after Soviet troops had occupied Czechoslovakia. At a minimum, he wanted to prevent turning arms control into a safety valve for Soviet expansionism. The Nixon Administration set out to determine whether the Soviet eagerness to tranquilize an administration it perceived as being more forceful than its predecessor—and therefore more threatening to Soviet interests—could be used to elicit Soviet cooperation in removing the threat to Berlin, easing tensions in the Middle East, and, above all, ending the war in Vietnam. This approach was called "linkage," and it became wildly controversial.

One of the principal tasks of statesmanship is to understand which subjects are truly related and can be used to reinforce each other. For the most part, the policymaker has little choice in the matter; ultimately, it is reality, not policy, that links events. The statesman's role is to recognize the relationship when it does exist—in other words, to create a network of incentives and penalties to produce the most favorable outcome.

Nixon expressed these views in a letter to Cabinet members concerned with national security on February 4, 1969, two weeks after taking the oath of office:

> . . . I do believe that crisis or confrontation in one place and real cooperation in another cannot long be sustained simultaneously. I recognize that the previous Administration took the view that when we perceive a mutual interest on an issue with the USSR, we should pursue agreement and attempt to insulate it as much as possible from the ups and downs of conflicts elsewhere. This may well be sound on numerous bilateral and practical matters such as cultural or scientific exchanges. But, on the crucial issues of our day, I believe we must seek to advance on a front at least broad enough to make clear that we see some relationship between political and military issues.[13]

The debate about linkage lasted so long as to obscure just how simple the Nixon team's basic propositions were. The Cold War was an adversarial relationship between the two superpowers. Nixon said no more—but also no less—than that it was absurd to pick out one area of that relationship for improvement while confrontation continued in all the others. Selective relaxation of tensions seemed to Nixon and his advisers a strategy guaranteed to undermine the position of the democracies. It made no sense that a subject as complex and esoteric as arms control should be the test case for the prospects for peace while Soviet arms were encouraging conflict in the Middle East and killing Americans in Vietnam.

The concept of linkage encountered stormy weather in the foreign policy community. The American foreign policy bureaucracy is for the most part staffed by individuals who have dedicated themselves to what is, in American society, a rather unorthodox career so that they may promulgate and implement their views of a better world. Their opinions, moreover, are honed by a system in which policy emerges from bureaucratic struggles which, as Secretary of State George Shultz later pointed out, are never finally settled. Segmented into a series of individual, and at times isolated, initiatives geared to highly specific problems, American foreign policy is rarely approached from the point of view of an overall concept. *Ad hoc* departmental approaches have more—and more passionate—spokesmen than does an overall strategy, which often has no spokesman at all. It takes an unusually strong and determined president, skilled in the ways of Washington, to break this pattern.

Nixon's attempt to tie the opening of strategic arms negotiations to progress on political issues ran counter to the passionate conviction of both the arms controllers, who were eager to limit the arms race, and the Kremlinologists, who were convinced that American foreign policy should strengthen the Kremlin doves against the Kremlin hawks in their presumed policy disputes. The bureaucracy chipped away at the policy outlined in the President's letter by emphasizing arms control as an end in itself in leaks to the press. Though not "authorized," these leaks were also never disavowed. In *The New York Times* of April 18, 1969, "officials" described arms agreements with the Soviet Union as "an overriding goal of the Nixon foreign policy."[14] On April 22, the *Times* had "American diplomats" predicting Strategic Arms Limitation Talks (SALT) in June.[15] On May 13, *The Washington Post* quoted Administration sources to the effect that, by May 29, a date for the opening of talks would be set.[16] These cumulative pressures to progress on modifying Nixon's stated position of linking arms control to political issues were never posed as a head-on challenge; instead, a series of tactical, day-to-day comments were used to edge matters toward the position preferred by the bureaucracy.

Analysts outside the government were soon launching their own critique. On June 3, 1969, *The New York Times* called American trade restrictions linked to other issues "self-defeating." They were "cold-war policies" which were "inconsistent with the Nixon Administration's theory that it is time to move from an era of confrontation into one of negotiation and cooperation."[17] *The Washington Post* deployed the same argument. "Reality is too complex and sticky," it wrote on April 5, "to permit any President to believe he can line up so many different ducks in a row. Arms control has a value and urgency entirely apart from the status of political issues."[18] Nixon intended to broaden the dialogue with Moscow by delaying the SALT talks. Bureaucratic momentum and philosophical disagreement combined to expend assets Nixon would have preferred to husband.

It cannot be said that the Administration approach was immediately successful. In April 1969, an attempt to send future Secretary of State

Cyrus Vance to Moscow with authority to negotiate simultaneously on both strategic arms limitations and Vietnam failed.[19] The two issues were too incommensurable; the outcome of the strategic arms discussions was too uncertain, the Hanoi leadership was too intractable, and the time scale required for either negotiation too difficult to synchronize.

But, in the end, Nixon and his advisers did succeed in making the various strands of policy support each other. Linkage began working because the Nixon Administration managed to create a major incentive for Soviet moderation by achieving a dramatic opening to China. One elementary lesson for students of chess is that, in choosing among moves, one can do worse than to count the number of squares dominated by each choice. Generally, the more squares a player dominates, the greater his options and the more constrained become those of his opponent. Similarly, in diplomacy, the more options one side has, the fewer will be available to the other side and the more careful it will have to be in pursuing its objectives. Indeed, such a state of affairs may in time provide an incentive for the adversary to seek to end his adversarial role.

Once the Soviet Union could no longer count on permanent hostility between the world's most powerful and most populous nations—even more so if the two were actually perceived as having started to cooperate —the scope for Soviet intransigence would narrow and perhaps evaporate. Soviet leaders would have to hedge their bets because a threatening posture might intensify Sino-American cooperation. In the conditions of the late 1960s, improved Sino-American relations became a key to the Nixon Administration's Soviet strategy.

America's historic feeling of friendship for China collapsed when the communists won the civil war in 1949 and entered the Korean War in 1950. It was replaced by a policy of deliberately isolating the communist rulers in Beijing. A telling symbol of this state of mind was Dulles' refusal to shake hands with Zhou Enlai at the 1954 Geneva Conference on Indochina—which still rankled the Chinese Premier when he greeted me in Beijing seventeen years later and inquired whether I was one of those Americans who refused to shake hands with Chinese leaders. The sole remaining diplomatic contact between the two nations was through their respective ambassadors in Warsaw, who met at irregular intervals to exchange invectives. During the Chinese Cultural Revolution in the late 1960s and 1970s—whose cost in human lives and suffering was comparable to Stalin's purges—all Chinese ambassadors (except, for some inscrutable reason, the one in Egypt) were recalled to China, interrupting the Warsaw talks and leaving Washington and Beijing with no diplomatic or political contact whatsoever.

Interestingly enough, the leaders who had first perceived the opportunities inherent in a Sino-Soviet split were the two old men of European diplomacy, Adenauer and de Gaulle. Adenauer, relying on a book he had just read, started talking about it around 1957, though the Federal Republic was not yet in a position to conduct a global policy. De Gaulle felt no such restraints. He had correctly perceived in the early 1960s that the Soviets had a serious problem along their vast border with China, and that this would oblige them to seek a more cooperative relationship with the West. Being de Gaulle, he believed that this fact would accelerate a Franco-Soviet detente. Given Moscow's China problem, Moscow and Paris could conceivably negotiate away the Iron Curtain and pursue de Gaulle's vision of "Europe from the Atlantic to the Urals." But de Gaulle's France was not nearly strong enough to carry out such a diplomatic revolution. Moscow did not consider Paris an equal partner for detente. However, although de Gaulle's policy prescriptions were distorted by his perception of them through the French prism, his underlying analysis was prescient. For a long time, American policymakers, blinded by ideological preconceptions, failed to appreciate that the Sino-Soviet split represented a strategic opportunity for the West.

American opinion on China, such as it was, found itself divided along the familiar patterns of the Cold War. A small group of Sinologists treated the rift as psychological; they urged America to meet Chinese grievances by turning over the Chinese seat in the United Nations to Beijing and easing tensions through wide-ranging contacts. The vast majority of informed opinion, however, considered Communist China incurably expansionist, fanatically ideological, and intransigently committed to world revolution. America had involved itself in Indochina in large part to blunt what had been perceived as a Chinese-led communist conspiracy to take over Southeast Asia. Conventional wisdom had it that, even more than was the case with the Soviet Union, the Chinese communist system would need to be transformed before negotiations could be considered.

This view was reinforced from an unexpected quarter. Sovietologists, who for more than a decade had been urging permanent dialogue with Moscow, took a diametrically opposite stand with respect to China. Early in Nixon's first term, a group of former ambassadors to the Soviet Union, who were disquieted by Washington's first tentative feelers toward Beijing, called on the President with a solemn warning. The Soviet leaders, they argued, were so paranoid about Communist China that any attempt to improve American relations with Beijing would involve an unacceptable risk of confrontation with the Soviet Union.

The Nixon Administration did not share this view of international relations. Excluding a country of the magnitude of China from America's diplomatic options meant that America was operating internationally with one hand tied behind its back. We were convinced that increasing America's foreign policy options would soften, not harden, Moscow's stance. A policy statement I drafted for Nelson Rockefeller's bid for the 1968 Republican presidential nomination had stated: "... I would begin a dialogue with communist China. In a subtle triangle of relations between Washington, Peking, and Moscow, we improve the possibilities of accommodations with each as we increase our options toward both."[20] Nixon had put forward identical views even earlier, in language geared to traditional American notions of world community. In October 1967, he had written in *Foreign Affairs*:

> Taking the long view, we simply cannot afford to leave China forever outside the family of nations, there to nurture its fantasies, cherish its hates and threaten its neighbors. There is no place on this small planet for a billion of its potentially most able people to live in angry isolation.[21]

Shortly after receiving the presidential nomination, Nixon became more specific. In a magazine interview in September 1968, he stated: "We must not forget China. We must always seek opportunities to talk with her, as with the USSR.... We must not only watch for changes. We must seek to make changes."[22]

In the event, Nixon achieved his goal, though China was induced to rejoin the community of nations less by the prospect of dialogue with the United States than by fear of being attacked by its ostensible ally, the Soviet Union. The Nixon Administration, which did not immediately understand this dimension of the Sino-Soviet relationship, was alerted to it by the Soviet Union itself. It was not the first, or the last, time that clumsy Soviet foreign policy accelerated what the Kremlin feared the most.

In the spring of 1969, a series of clashes between Chinese and Soviet forces took place on a remote stretch of the Sino-Soviet border along the Ussuri River in Siberia. On the basis of the experience of two decades, Washington initially took it for granted that these skirmishes had been instigated by fanatical Chinese leaders. It was heavy-handed Soviet diplomacy that caused a reassessment. For Soviet diplomats were supplying detailed briefings of the Soviet version of events to Washington and inquiring as to what the American attitude would be if these clashes escalated.

The unprecedented Soviet eagerness to consult Washington on an issue with respect to which America had indicated no particular concern caused us to ask ourselves whether the briefings might not be designed to prepare the ground for a Soviet attack on China. This suspicion became reinforced when American intelligence studies triggered by Soviet briefings revealed that the skirmishes invariably took place near major Soviet supply bases and far from Chinese communications centers—a pattern one would expect only if the Soviet forces were in fact the aggressors. Further credence was given to this analysis by a relentless Soviet buildup along the entire 4,000-mile length of the Chinese border, which rapidly reached more than forty divisions.

If the Nixon Administration's analysis was correct, a major international crisis was brewing, even if most of the world was unaware of it. Soviet military intervention in China would signal the most serious threat to the global balance of power since the Cuban missile crisis. The application of the Brezhnev Doctrine to China would mean that Moscow would try to make the government in Beijing as submissive as Czechoslovakia's had been obliged to become the previous year. The world's most populous nation would then be subordinate to a nuclear superpower—an ominous combination which would restore the dreaded Sino-Soviet bloc, the monolithic nature of which had inspired such fear in the 1950s. Whether the Soviet Union was capable of realizing so vast a project remained far from clear. What was obvious, however—especially to an administration basing its foreign policy on a geopolitical conception—was that the risk could not be run. If the balance of power is taken seriously, then the very *prospect* of geopolitical upheaval must be resisted; by the time the change has occurred, it may well be too late to oppose it. At a minimum, the cost of resistance will go up exponentially.

Such considerations led Nixon to make two extraordinary decisions in the summer of 1969. The first was to put aside all the issues which constituted the existing Sino-American dialogue. The Warsaw talks had established an agenda that was as complex as it was time-consuming. Each side stressed its grievances: China's had to do with the future of Taiwan and Chinese assets sequestered in the United States; the United States sought the renunciation of force over Taiwan, China's participation in arms-control negotiations, and the settlement of American economic claims against China.

Instead, Nixon decided to concentrate on the broader issue of China's attitude toward a dialogue with the United States. Priority was given to determining the scope of the looming Sino-Soviet-American triangle. If we could determine what we suspected—that the Soviet Union and China were more afraid of each other than they were of the United States—an unprecedented opportunity for American diplomacy would come into being. If relations improved on that basis, the traditional agenda would take care of itself; if relations did not improve, the traditional agenda would remain insoluble. In other words, the practical issues would be resolved as a consequence of Sino-American rapprochement, not chart the path toward it.

In implementing the strategy of transforming the two-power world into a strategic triangle, the United States announced in July 1969 a series of unilateral initiatives to indicate the change in attitude. The prohibition against Americans' traveling to the People's Republic of China was eliminated; Americans were allowed to bring $100 worth of Chinese-made goods into the United States; and limited American grain shipments were permitted to China. These measures, though insignificant in themselves, were designed to convey America's new approach.

Secretary of State William P. Rogers made these hints explicit in a major speech approved by Nixon. He announced in Australia on August 8, 1969, that the United States would welcome a significant role by Communist China in Asian and Pacific affairs. If Chinese leaders abandoned their introspective "view of the world," America would "open up channels of communication." In the warmest comment about China by an American secretary of state in twenty years, Rogers called attention to the unilateral initiatives being taken by America in the economic field, steps designed "to help remind people on mainland China of our historic friendship for them."[23]

But if there was a real danger of a Soviet attack on China in the summer of 1969, there would not be enough time for these complex maneuvers to unfold gradually. Therefore, Nixon took perhaps the most daring step of his presidency by warning the Soviet Union that the United States would not remain indifferent if it were to attack China. Regardless of China's immediate attitude toward the United States, Nixon and his advisers considered China's independence indispensable to the global equilibrium, and deemed diplomatic contact with China essential to the flexibility of American diplomacy. Nixon's warning to the Soviets was also a tangible expression of his Administration's new emphasis on basing American policy on the careful analysis of the national interest.

Concerned about the Soviet military buildup along the Chinese border, Nixon authorized a strong, double-edged statement on September 5, 1969, to the effect that the United States was "deeply concerned" about a Sino-Soviet war. Under Secretary of State Elliot Richardson was charged with delivering the message; high enough in the hierarchy to leave no doubt that he was speaking on behalf of the President, Richardson was at the same time not so conspicuous as to challenge the Soviet Union head-on:

> We do not seek to exploit for our own advantage the hostility between the Soviet Union and the People's Republic. Ideological differences between the two Communist giants are not our affair. We could not fail to be deeply concerned, however, with an escalation of this quarrel into a massive breach of international peace and security.[24]

When a country abjures its intention of exploiting a conflict between two other parties, it is in fact signaling that it has the capacity to do so and that both parties would do well to work at preserving that neutrality. So too, when a nation expresses its "deep concern" over a military contingency, it is conveying that it will assist—in some as yet unspecified way—the victim of what it has defined as aggression. Nixon was unique among American presidents in this century by thus showing his preparedness to support a country with which the United States had had no diplomatic relations for twenty years, with which his own Administration had as yet had *no* contact whatsoever on any level, and whose diplomats and media were vilifying American "imperialism" at every turn. It marked America's return to the world of *Realpolitik*.

To emphasize the new approach, the importance of improved relations between China and the United States was stressed in each of the annual presidential reports on foreign policy. In February 1970—before there had been any direct contact between Washington and Beijing—the report called for practical negotiations with China and stressed that the United States would not collude with the Soviet Union against China. This was, of course, the reverse side of the warning to Moscow; it implied that Washington always had that option if driven to it. The February 1971 report repeated America's willingness to establish contact with China, and reassured China that America had no hostile intent:

> We are prepared to establish a dialogue with Peking. We cannot accept its ideological precepts, or the notion that Communist China must exercise hegemony over Asia. But neither do we wish to impose on China an international position that denies its legitimate national interests.[25]

Once again, the report reiterated America's neutrality in the conflict between the two major communist centers:

> We will do nothing to sharpen that conflict—nor to encourage it. It is absurd to believe that we could collude with one of the parties against the other....

> At the same time, we cannot permit either Communist China or the USSR to dictate our policies and conduct toward the other. . . . [W]e will have to judge China, as well as the USSR, not by its rhetoric but by its actions.[26]

The ostentatious renunciation of collusion with either of the communist giants served as an invitation to each to improve relations with Washington, and as a warning to each of the consequences of continued hostility. To the extent that both China and the Soviet Union calculated that they either needed American goodwill or feared an American move toward its adversary, both had an incentive to improve their relations with Washington. And both had been told as plainly as was possible—indeed, it was there for all to read—that the prerequisite for closer ties with Washington was to refrain from posing threats to vital American interests.

As things turned out, it proved easier to define a new architecture for relations with China than it was to implement it. The isolation between America and China had been so total that neither knew how to contact the other, or how to find a common vocabulary through which to assure the other that rapprochement was not intended as a trap.

China had the greater difficulty, partly because Beijing's diplomacy was so subtle and indirect that it largely went over our heads in Washington. On April 1, 1969—two months after Nixon took his oath of office—Lin Piao, China's Defense Minister, who was about to be named Mao's heir, in a report to the Ninth National Congress of the Communist Party dropped the heretofore standard designation of the United States as China's principal enemy. When Lin Piao described the Soviet Union as an equal threat, the fundamental precondition of triangular diplomacy had been fulfilled. Lin Piao also reaffirmed the statement Mao had made in 1965 to journalist Edgar Snow—that China had no troops outside its own frontiers and had no intention of fighting anybody unless its territory was attacked.

Among the reasons Mao's signals had been ignored was that the Chinese had vastly overrated the importance of Edgar Snow in America. Snow, an American journalist long sympathetic to the Chinese communists, was thought by the leaders in Beijing to possess a special credibility in the United States on Chinese matters. Washington, however, thought of him as a communist tool and was not prepared to entrust him with its secrets. Mao's gesture of placing Snow next to him on the reviewing stand at the Chinese Independence Day parade in October 1970 was lost on us. So was an interview Mao gave Snow in December 1970, during which he invited Nixon to visit China either as a tourist or as the American President. Though Mao had ordered his interpreter to turn over her notes to Snow (to establish his bona fides), Washington never learned of the invitation until the issue of Nixon's visit had already been settled through other channels many months later.

In the meantime, diplomatic contacts between the United States and China resumed in Warsaw in December 1969. These proved no more satisfactory than they had been in the past. Nixon had instructed Walter Stoessel, the extremely able and discreet American Ambassador in Warsaw, to approach the Chinese chargé at the first social function at which the two found themselves, and to invite him to resume ambassadorial talks. Stoessel's opportunity came on December 3, 1969, at an odd venue —a Yugoslav fashion show held in the Warsaw Palace of Culture. The Chinese chargé, entirely without instructions for the contingency of being approached by an American diplomat, at first ran away. Only when Stoessel finally cornered his interpreter could the message be delivered. By December 11, however, the chargé *had* received instructions on how to deal with the Americans, and invited Stoessel to the Chinese embassy for a resumption of the old Warsaw talks.

Deadlock developed almost immediately. Neither side's standard agenda lent itself to an exploration of the underlying geopolitical issues, which, in Nixon's view—and, as it turned out, in Mao's and Zhou's as well—would determine the future of Sino-American relations. Moreover, these issues were being filtered on the American side through a cumbersome process of consultation with the Congress and key allies, all of which guaranteed that progress, if there were to be any at all, would be tedious and subject to many vetoes.

The result was that the Warsaw talks produced more controversies inside the United States government than they did in the meetings between the parties. Nixon and I were therefore somewhat relieved when we learned that China was interrupting the ambassadorial talks to protest America's attack on the Cambodian sanctuaries in May 1970. From then on, both sides were probing for a more flexible channel. The Pakistani government eventually filled this need. The accelerated pace of the exchanges culminated in my secret trip to Beijing in July 1971.

I could not have encountered a group of interlocutors more receptive to Nixon's style of diplomacy than the Chinese leaders. Like Nixon, they considered the traditional agenda to be of secondary importance, and were above all concerned with exploring whether cooperation on the basis of congruent interests was possible. This was why, later on, one of Mao's first remarks to Nixon was: "The small issue is Taiwan; the big issue is the world."

What the Chinese leaders wanted was reassurance that America would not cooperate with the Kremlin in the implementation of the Brezhnev Doctrine; what Nixon needed to know was whether China might cooperate with America in thwarting the Soviet geopolitical offensive. Each side's goals were essentially conceptual although, sooner or later, these would have to be translated into practical diplomacy. A sense of common interest had to emerge from the persuasiveness of each side's presentation of its view of the world—a task for which Nixon was extremely well suited.

For these reasons, the early stages of the Sino-American dialogue focused primarily on the meshing of concepts and fundamental approaches. Mao, Zhou, and later Deng were all extraordinary personalities. Mao was the visionary, ruthless, pitiless, occasionally murderous revolutionary; Zhou, the elegant, charming, brilliant administrator; and Deng, the reformer of elemental convictions. The three men reflected a common tradition of painstaking analysis and the distillation of the experiences of an ancient country with an instinct for distinguishing between the permanent and the tactical.

Their negotiating style was as different from that of their Soviet counterparts as was possible. Soviet diplomats almost never discussed conceptual issues. Their tactic was to select a problem of immediate concern to Moscow and to batter away at its resolution with a dogged persistence designed to wear down their interlocutors rather than to persuade them. The insistence and the vehemence with which Soviet negotiators put forward the Politburo consensus reflected the brutal discipline and internal strains of Soviet politics, and transformed high policy into an exhausting retail trade. Gromyko symbolized the quintessence of this approach to foreign diplomacy.

Chinese leaders represented an emotionally far more secure society. They were less interested in fine drafting points than in building confidence. At Nixon's meeting with Mao, the Chinese leader wasted no time in assuring the President that China would not use force against Taiwan. "We can do without them [Taiwan] for the time being, and let it come after 100 years."[27] Mao asked for no reciprocity for the assurance America had been seeking for twenty years.

While drafting the Shanghai Communiqué with Zhou Enlai, I at one point offered to trade an offensive phrase in the Chinese draft for something in the American version to which Zhou might object. "We will never get anywhere this way," he replied. "If you can convince me why our phrase is offensive, I will give it to you."

Zhou's attitude was not the product of abstract goodwill but of a sure grasp of long-term priorities. At that point China needed to engender confidence; scoring debating points would have been against its interests. According to Mao, the principal security threat was the Soviet Union: "At the present time, the question of aggression from the United States or aggression from China is relatively small. . . . You want to withdraw some of your troops back on your soil; ours do not go abroad."[28] In other words, China did not fear the United States, not even in Indochina; it would not challenge vital American interests (regardless of what the United States might do in Vietnam), and was concerned primarily with threats from the Soviet Union (and, as it later transpired, from Japan). To underline his emphasis on the global equilibrium, Mao dismissed his own anti-imperialist pronouncements as "empty cannons."

The conceptual nature of the approach eased our early encounters. In February 1972, Nixon signed the Shanghai Communiqué, which was to provide a road map for Sino-American relations for the next decade. The Communiqué had an unprecedented feature: more than half of it was devoted to stating the conflicting views of the two sides on ideology, international affairs, Vietnam, and Taiwan. In a curious way, the catalogue of disagreements conferred greater significance on those subjects on which the two sides agreed. These affirmed that:

—progress toward the normalization of relations between China and the United States is in the interests of all countries;
—both wish to reduce the danger of international military conflict;
—neither should seek hegemony in the Asia-Pacific region, and each is opposed to efforts by any other country or group of countries to establish such hegemony; and
—neither is prepared to negotiate on behalf of any third party or to enter into agreements or understandings with the other directed at other states.[29]

Stripped of diplomatic jargon, these agreements meant, at a minimum, that China would do nothing to exacerbate the situation in Indochina or Korea, that neither China nor the United States would cooperate with the Soviet bloc, and that both would oppose any attempt by any country to achieve domination of Asia. Since the Soviet Union was the only country capable of dominating Asia, a tacit alliance to block Soviet expansionism in Asia was coming into being (not unlike the Entente Cordiale between Great Britain and France in 1904, and between Great Britain and Russia in 1907).

Within a year, that understanding between the United States and China was made both more explicit and more global: in a communiqué published in February 1973, China and the United States agreed to *resist* (upgraded from "oppose" in the Shanghai Communiqué) *jointly* (upgraded from what had been a "separate commitment") any country's attempt at *world* (upgraded from "Asian") domination. In the space of barely a year and a half, Sino-American relations had moved from strident hostility and isolation to *de facto* alliance against the pre-eminent threat.

The Shanghai Communiqué and the diplomacy leading up to it enabled the Nixon Administration to put in place what it called, perhaps somewhat grandiloquently, a new structure of peace. As soon as America's opening to China was announced, the pattern of international relations changed dramatically. Later on, relations with China were referred to in the West as the China "card," as if the policy of the tough leaders who ruled from the Forbidden City could be designed in Washington. In fact, the China "card" either played itself or it did not exist. The role of American policy was to establish a framework that reflected each nation's willingness to support the other where national interests coincided.

In the analysis of Nixon and his advisers, so long as China had more to fear from the Soviet Union than it did from the United States, China's self-interest would impel it to cooperate with the United States. By the same token, China did not pursue its opposition to Soviet expansionism as a favor to the United States, even though it served both American and Chinese purposes. Impressed as Nixon was by the clarity of thought of the Chinese leaders—especially of Premier Zhou Enlai—he had no conceivable interest in placing the United States unambiguously on either side of the conflict between China and the Soviet Union. America's bargaining position would be strongest when America was closer to *both* communist giants than either was to the other.

America's opening to China offers a good case study of the role of personalities in the conduct of foreign policy. What posterity comes to view as a new departure usually results from a series of more or less random acts which make it difficult to distinguish what had been a conscious choice from sheer momentum. Because Sino-American relations came into being after twenty years of near-total isolation, everything was entirely new and therefore significant in terms of what happened later. For both sides, necessity dictated that rapprochement occur, and the attempt would have had to be made no matter who governed in either country. But the smoothness and the speed with which it developed and the scope it assumed owed a great deal to the subtlety and single-mindedness of the leaders on both sides who brought it about and, on the American side in particular, to the unprecedented emphasis on the analysis of the national interest.

Mao, the dedicated communist, exuded the self-assurance of knowing that he was heir to a tradition of uninterrupted self-rule which had spanned three millennia. After submitting his vast country to the ideological binge and appalling bloodletting of the Cultural Revolution, Mao was just then in the process of infusing Chinese foreign policy with a certain practicality. For centuries, the Middle Kingdom had assured its security by playing off distant barbarians against immediate neighbors. Deeply worried about Soviet expansionism, Mao adopted the same strategy in his opening to the United States.

Nixon was not concerned with Mao's motives. His primary aim was to regain the American initiative in foreign policy. In seeking out what he termed an era of negotiations between the Soviet Union and the United States to overcome the trauma of Vietnam, Nixon relied neither on personal relations nor on the conversion of the Soviets but on a balancing of incentives as a way of making the Kremlin more malleable.

After America's opening to China, the Soviet Union faced challenges on two fronts—NATO in the West, and China in the East. In a period that was, in other respects, a high point of Soviet self-confidence and a low point of America's, the Nixon Administration managed to reshuffle the deck. It continued to see to it that general war proved too risky for the Soviets. After the opening to China, Soviet pressures below the level of general war became too risky as well, because they had the potential of accelerating the dreaded Sino-American rapprochement. Once America had opened to China, the Soviet Union's best option became seeking its own relaxation of tensions with the United States. On the theory that it might have more to offer to the United States than China, the Kremlin even imagined that it could succeed in maneuvering America into a quasi-alliance against China, which Brezhnev clumsily proposed to Nixon in both 1973 and 1974.[30]

In its new approach to foreign policy, America was not about to back the stronger against the weaker in any balance-of-power situation. As the country with the greatest physical capacity to disturb the peace, the Soviet Union would be given an incentive to moderate existing crises and to avoid stirring up new ones while faced with resistance on two fronts. And China, which had its own capacity to upset the Asian equilibrium, would be restrained by the need for American goodwill in setting limits to Soviet adventurism. Through all of this, the Nixon Administration would try to solve practical issues with the Soviet Union while maintaining a dialogue on global concepts with the Chinese.

Though most Soviet experts had warned Nixon that improved relations with China would sour Soviet-American relations, the opposite occurred. Prior to my secret trip to China, Moscow had been stalling for over a year on arrangements for a summit between Brezhnev and Nixon. By a sort of reverse linkage, it tried to make the high-level meeting dependent on a whole list of conditions. Then, within a month of my visit to Beijing, the Kremlin reversed itself and invited Nixon to Moscow. All Soviet-American negotiations began to accelerate once Soviet leaders had abandoned their attempts to extract unilateral American concessions.

Nixon was the first president since Theodore Roosevelt to conduct American foreign policy largely in the name of the national interest. The drawback of this approach was its dearth of emotional resonance among the American people. Though Nixon frequently spoke of a structure of peace, structures are instruments that do not of themselves evoke commitments in the hearts and minds of a society—especially one imbued with America's tradition of exceptionalism. Nor is the national interest quite so self-evident as the various presidential reports on foreign policy implied. In the absence of a well-established tradition, American leadership groups are not as comfortable with the concept of national interest as those of, say, Great Britain, France, or China. Even under the most optimal and tranquil circumstances, it would have taken the better part of a presidential term to establish a tradition of foreign policy based on Nixon's approach.

In his first term, Nixon had little opportunity for such an educational task because his society was rent by protest and the conviction that the United States government had become preoccupied with the threat of communism. From the very beginning, Nixon's second term was blighted by Watergate. A president facing impeachment was not likely to be accepted as the leader of an effort to reshape traditional thinking.

It was also the case that Nixon and his associates had put forward their approach in a manner that was too jarring to America's ideological traditions. Twenty years earlier, John Foster Dulles had clothed his realistic analyses in the rhetoric of exceptionalism; ten years later, Ronald Reagan would move the American public in support of a foreign policy which, in its operational details, did not significantly differ from Nixon's, by giving it an idealistic cast. Governing as he did during the Vietnam era, Nixon's dilemma was that the Dulles—or Reagan—style of rhetoric would have been like pouring oil on the fire. Then too, even in more tranquil times, Nixon was probably too cerebral to have adopted Dulles' or Reagan's style of rhetoric.

As the achievements of Nixon's foreign policy approach came to be taken for granted and the perils it had avoided receded, Nixon's (and my) approach turned increasingly controversial. Without Watergate, Nixon might have been able to rally the country to his style of diplomacy and

731

show that it was, in fact, the most realistic means of vindicating American idealism. But the combination of Vietnam and Watergate prevented the emergence of a new consensus. Even though Nixon had managed, despite the tragedy of Indochina, to maneuver his country into a dominant international position, his second term witnessed an extraordinarily intense debate about his nation's role in the world, and especially about its attitude toward communism.

CHAPTER TWENTY-NINE

Detente
and Its Discontents

By extricating the United States from the demoralizing bloodletting of Vietnam and refocusing the nation's attention on broader international questions, the Nixon Administration sought to forge what it called somewhat grandiloquently a "structure of peace." The triangular relationship among the United States, the U.S.S.R., and China unlocked the door to a series of major breakthroughs: the end of the Vietnam War; an agreement that guaranteed access to divided Berlin; a dramatic reduction of Soviet influence in the Middle East, and the beginning of the Arab-Israeli peace process; and the European Security Conference (completed during the Ford Administration). Each of these events contributed to the others. Linkage was operating with a vengeance.

Detente introduced a new fluidity to European diplomacy, a theatre that had been virtually petrified since the final consolidation of the East-

West spheres of influence in 1961. Until Willy Brandt was elected Chancellor in September 1969, successive West German governments had insisted that the sole legitimate German government resided in Bonn. The Federal Republic refused to recognize the East German regime and broke diplomatic relations with any government (other than Russia) that did grant recognition—the so-called Hallstein Doctrine.

After the Berlin Wall was built in 1961, the issue of German unification gradually disappeared from the agenda of East-West negotiations and the German quest for unity was temporarily put on ice. During these years, de Gaulle explored the possibility of negotiating with Moscow independently of the United States by proclaiming a policy of "detente, entente, and cooperation" with Eastern Europe. His hope was that, if Moscow perceived Europe as a free agent rather than as an American satellite, the Kremlin leaders, given their problems with China, might be induced to relax their hold on Eastern Europe. De Gaulle wanted West Germany to separate itself to some extent from Washington and to follow France's lead in its demarche to the Soviets.

De Gaulle had made the right analysis but overestimated France's capacity to exploit the more fluid international situation. The Federal Republic was not inclined to turn its back on a powerful America. Nevertheless, de Gaulle's concept was not lost on some German leaders, who came to believe that the Federal Republic might possess the bargaining chips which Paris lacked. Brandt, who served as the German Foreign Minister while the General was playing out his gambit, understood the implications of de Gaulle's vision. Those Germans who supported de Gaulle's initiative, he recalled,

> failed to grasp that the General would not pursue their dreams of a European nuclear deterrent (he firmly rejected German participation). They also overlooked the fact that he was engaged in devising a policy of detente which could never have been supported by the Union's [the German conservative party's] right wing and was really, in many respects, paving the way for our subsequent *Ostpolitik*.[1]

The Soviet invasion of Czechoslovakia in 1968 put an end to de Gaulle's initiative but, ironically, opened the door for Brandt when his turn as West German leader came in 1969.

Brandt put forward the then startling thesis that, since reliance on the West had produced stalemate, unification should be sought through German rapprochement with the communist world. He urged his country to recognize the East German satellite, to accept the border with Poland (the Oder-Neisse Line), and to improve relations with the Soviet Union. With East-West relations eased, the Soviet Union might prove less rigid on the issue of unification. At the least, the condition of the East German population might be ameliorated.

Initially, the Nixon Administration had grave reservations about what Brandt called *Ostpolitik*. With each German state seeking to seduce the other, they might finally come together on some nationalist, neutralist program, as Adenauer and de Gaulle had feared. The Federal Republic had the more attractive political and social system; the communists had the advantage that recognition of their state, once granted, was irreversible, and that it held the key to unification. Above all, the Nixon Administration feared for the unity of the West. De Gaulle had already broken the West's united front toward Moscow by pulling France out of NATO and by pursuing his own policy of detente with the Kremlin. Washington viewed the specter of West Germany breaking out on its own with trepidation.

Yet the more Brandt's initiative gained momentum, the more Nixon and his associates came to realize that, whatever the pitfalls of *Ostpolitik*, the alternative was riskier still. It had already become increasingly clear that the Hallstein Doctrine was unsustainable. By the mid-1960s, Bonn itself had modified it with respect to the Eastern European communist governments on the lame argument that they were not free to make their own decisions.

The problem went deeper, however. In the 1960s, it was inconceivable that Moscow would let its East German satellite collapse without a huge crisis. And any crisis that was the result of Germany's insistence on its national aspirations—or could plausibly be presented that way—contained a strong potential for splitting the Western Alliance. No ally wanted to run the risk of war on behalf of unifying a country which had been the cause of their suffering in wartime. There had been no rush to the barricades when Nikita Khrushchev threatened to turn over Berlin's access routes to the East German communists. Without exception, the Western allies had acquiesced in the building of the wall that divided Berlin and symbolized the partition of Germany. For years, the democracies had paid lip service to the idea of German unity while doing nothing to bring it about. That approach had come to the end of its possibilities. The Atlantic Alliance's German policy was collapsing.

Nixon and his advisers therefore came to accept *Ostpolitik* as necessary even while they believed that Brandt—unlike Adenauer—never had an emotional attachment to the Atlantic Alliance. There were only three powers capable of disrupting the postwar *status quo* in Europe—the two superpowers and Germany, if it decided to subordinate everything to unification. In the 1960s, de Gaulle's France had tried to undo the spheres of influence arrangement and it had failed. But if Germany, Europe's most powerful economy and the European country with the greatest territorial grievance, tried to unravel the postwar order, the consequences would be grave indeed. When Brandt showed himself intent on making his own overtures to the East, the Nixon Administration concluded that the United States should support him rather than obstruct his efforts and run the risk of cutting the Federal Republic loose from the bonds of NATO and the restraints of the European Community.

Moreover, support for *Ostpolitik* gave America the leverage needed to end the twenty-year-old crisis over Berlin. The Nixon Administration insisted on strict linkage between *Ostpolitik* and access to Berlin, and between both of these issues and overall Soviet restraint. Since *Ostpolitik* was based on concrete German concessions—recognition of the Oder-Neisse Line and of the East German regime in return for such intangibles as improved relations—Brandt would never obtain parliamentary approval unless concrete new guarantees for access to Berlin and its freedom were linked with it. Otherwise, Berlin would fall prey to communist harassment 110 miles inside the territory of an East German satellite, the sovereignty of which would now be recognized by the international community—exactly the situation which Stalin and Khrushchev had tried to bring about by blockades and ultimatums. At the same time, Bonn did not have enough leverage to pursue the Berlin issue by itself. Only America was sufficiently powerful to resist the potential pressures inherent in Berlin's isolation and with enough diplomatic leverage to bring about a change in access procedures.

Berlin's legal status as an enclave deep inside Soviet-controlled territory was grounded on the legal fiction that it was technically "occupied" by the four victors of World War II. Negotiations on Berlin therefore had, of necessity, to be conducted by the United States, France, Great Britain, and the Soviet Union. In due course, both the Soviet leadership and Brandt (through his extremely skillful confidant, Egon Bahr) approached Washington for help in breaking the deadlock. In an intricate negotiation, a new four-power agreement was reached in the summer of 1971 guaranteeing the freedom of West Berlin and Western access to the city. Henceforth, Berlin disappeared from the list of international crisis spots. The next time it appeared on the global agenda was when the wall came down and the German Democratic Republic collapsed.

In addition to the agreement on Berlin, Brandt's *Ostpolitik* produced friendship treaties between West Germany and Poland, West and East Germany, and West Germany and the Soviet Union. That the Soviets should place such emphasis on West Germany's recognition of the borders established by Stalin in fact indicated weakness and insecurity. The Federal Republic, a rump state, was on the face of it in no position to challenge a nuclear superpower. At the same time, these treaties gave the Soviets a big incentive for restrained conduct at least while they were being negotiated and ratified. While the treaties were before the West German parliament, the Soviets were reluctant to do anything that could jeopardize their approval; afterward, they were careful not to drive Germany back toward the Adenauer policy. Thus, when Nixon decided to mine North Vietnamese harbors and to resume the bombing of Hanoi, Moscow's response was muted. As long as Nixon was domestically in a strong position, detente successfully linked the whole range of issues between East and West all around the world. If the Soviets were to reap the benefits of the relaxation of tensions, they, too, were obliged to contribute to detente.

Whereas in Central Europe the Nixon Administration could relate several negotiations to each other, in the Middle East it used the detente policy as a safety net while it reduced the Soviet Union's political influence. During the 1960s, the Soviet Union had become the principal arms supplier to Syria and Egypt, and an organizational and technical supporter of radical Arab groups. In international forums, the Soviet Union acted as a spokesman for the Arab position and quite often for its most radical point of view.

So long as that pattern continued, diplomatic progress would be ascribed to Soviet support, while stalemate incurred the risk of repeated crises. The deadlock could only be broken if all the parties were obliged to face the fundamental geopolitical reality of the Middle East: that Israel was too strong (or could be made too strong) to be defeated even by all of its neighbors combined, and that the United States would hold the ring against Soviet intervention. The Nixon Administration therefore insisted that all the parties and not just America's allies indicate their willingness to make sacrifices before America engaged itself in the peace process. The Soviet Union had a high capacity for raising the level of tensions, but it had no means of bringing crises to a conclusion or of advancing its friends' causes diplomatically. It could threaten to intervene, as it had in 1956, but experience had amply demonstrated the Soviet tendency to recoil in the face of American opposition.

The key to Middle East peace, therefore, resided in Washington, not in Moscow. If the United States played its cards carefully, either the Soviet Union would be obliged to contribute to a genuine solution or one of its Arab clients would break ranks and begin moving toward the United States. In either case, Soviet influence among the radical Arab states would be reduced. This was why, early in Nixon's first term, I felt confident enough to tell a journalist that the new administration would seek to expel Soviet influence from the Middle East. Though that incautious remark created a furor, it accurately described the strategy the Nixon Administration was about to implement.

Not understanding their strategic dilemma, the Soviet leaders tried to lure Washington into supporting diplomatic outcomes that would strengthen the Soviet position in the Arab world. But as long as the Soviet Union kept supplying the radical Middle Eastern states with the bulk of their arms and their diplomatic programs were identical, the United States had no interest in cooperating with Moscow—though this was not always clear to those who considered cooperation with the Soviet Union an end in itself. In the view of Nixon and his advisers, the best strategy was to demonstrate that the Soviet Union's capacity to foment crises was not matched by its ability to resolve them. Arab moderation would be encouraged by rewarding responsible Arab leaders with American support when their grievances were legitimate. The Soviet Union would then either participate or be moved to the fringes of Middle East diplomacy.

In pursuit of this goal, the United States adopted two complementary policies: it blocked every Arab move that resulted from Soviet military support or involved a Soviet military threat; and it took charge of the peace process once frustration with the stalemate had brought some key Arab leaders to dissociate from the Soviet Union and turn to the United States. These conditions came about after the 1973 Middle East War.

Until then, the United States had had to traverse a rocky road. In 1969, Secretary Rogers presented a plan, subsequently named after him, which endorsed Israel's 1967 borders with "minor" rectifications in return for a comprehensive peace agreement. It suffered the usual fate of initiatives undertaken before the underlying reality had changed: Israel turned it down, refusing to accept the delineation of borders; the Arab countries rejected it because they were not ready to undertake a commitment to peace (however vague such an undertaking would turn out to be).

Serious military confrontations occurred in 1970. The first was along the Suez Canal, when Egypt started the so-called war of attrition against Israel. Israel retaliated with major air strikes deep inside Egypt, and the Soviet Union responded by installing a major air-defense system in Egypt, manned by some 15,000 Soviet military personnel.

The dangers were not confined to Egypt. Later that same year, the Palestine Liberation Organization (PLO), which had established almost a state within a state in Jordan, hijacked four aircraft and flew them to

Jordan. King Hussein thereupon ordered his army to attack the PLO and expelled its leaders from the country; Syria invaded Jordan; Israel mobilized. The Middle East seemed on the edge of war. The United States massively reinforced its naval forces in the Mediterranean and made clear that it would not tolerate any outside intervention. It soon became apparent that the Soviet Union would run no risk of confrontation with the United States. Syria withdrew and the crisis ended, though not without having first demonstrated to the Arab world which superpower was more relevant to shaping the future of the area.

The first sign that the Nixon strategy was having an impact came in 1972. Egyptian President Anwar Sadat dismissed all his Soviet military advisers and asked Soviet technicians to leave the country. At the same time, secret diplomatic contacts between Sadat and the White House began, though they were constrained, first by the American presidential election and then by Watergate.

In 1973, Egypt and Syria went to war against Israel. Both Israel and the United States were taken completely by surprise, demonstrating how preconceptions often shape intelligence assessments.[2] The American assessment was so dominated by the belief in vast Israeli superiority that all Arab warnings had been dismissed as bluff. There was no evidence that the Soviet Union actively encouraged Egypt and Syria to go to war, and Sadat told us later that Soviet leaders were pressing for a cease-fire from the beginning. Nor was the Soviet resupply of its Arab friends remotely comparable in scope and impact to America's airlift to Israel.

When the war ended, the Arab armies had fought more effectively than in any previous conflict. But Israel had crossed the Suez Canal to a point some twenty miles from Cairo and occupied Syrian territory to the very outskirts of Damascus. American support would be needed, first to restore the *status quo ante* and then to make progress toward peace.

The first Arab leader to recognize this was Sadat, who abandoned his previous all-or-nothing approach and turned from Moscow to Washington for assistance in a step-by-step process toward peace. Even Syrian President Hafez Asad, considered the more radical of the two leaders and the one more closely tied to the Soviet Union, appealed to American diplomacy about the Golan Heights. In 1974, there were interim agreements with Egypt and Syria which began a process of Israeli withdrawal in return for Arab security guarantees. In 1975, Israel and Egypt concluded a second disengagement agreement. In 1979, Egypt and Israel signed a formal peace agreement under the aegis of President Carter. Every American administration since then has made a major contribution to a peace process, including the first direct negotiations between Arabs and Israelis organized by Secretary of State James Baker in 1991, and an Israeli-Palestinian agreement under the aegis of Clinton in September 1993. The Kremlin played no significant role in any of these initiatives.

These pages cannot deal with the details of Middle East diplomacy, being principally concerned with how the United States used its relationship with Moscow to reduce Soviet influence in the Middle East without producing a major crisis. In the debates of the 1970s, Nixon's critics made much fun of his alleged desire to enmesh the Soviet Union in agreements for their own sake to achieve an illusory reduction of tensions. Yet Nixon's Middle East diplomacy was a good illustration of how Nixon and his advisers perceived the structure of peace, which the President so frequently invoked. It was not a starry-eyed quest for cooperation for its own sake but a method for conducting the geopolitical competition. American strategy was based on the proposition that the Soviet Union should be faced with the choice of either separating itself from its radical Arab clients or accepting a reduction of its influence. In the end, this strategy curtailed Soviet influence and placed the United States into the pivotal position in Middle East diplomacy.

The Nixon Administration pursued two courses to achieve this goal. During the Middle East War, it kept open an almost daily channel of communication with the Kremlin to avoid permitting decisions to be taken in the heat of the moment or on the basis of inadequate information. This could not prevent all the tensions inherent in clashing interests, but it reduced the danger of a crisis of misunderstanding. Simultaneously we conducted negotiations on a wide range of issues in order to give the Soviet leaders a stake they would be reluctant to jeopardize. The Berlin negotiations contributed to Soviet restraint in the Middle East until well into 1973. Afterward, the European Security Conference helped to moderate the Soviet reaction during the various diplomatic shuttles that moved the Soviet Union to the fringes of Mideast diplomacy. A delicate balance was needed between defining significant criteria for progress and making agreements ends in themselves, thereby incurring dependence on Soviet goodwill. Detente not only calmed the international situation, it created inhibitions which caused Soviet leaders to accept what amounted to a major geopolitical retreat.

Despite these successes, the Nixon Administration faced mounting controversy on the subject of its foreign policy. Any shift in foreign policy encounters resistance from adherents to the previous course; every successful negotiation must run the gauntlet of those who deny that an agreement generally reflects reciprocal concessions rather than unilateral satisfactions. Linkage ran counter to the legalistic traditions of the American foreign policy establishment. The opening to China offended the China lobby. The combination of adversarial and cooperative conduct implicit in detente with the Soviet Union grated on the traditional black-and-white assumption that every country was either friendly or hostile and not, as in the real world, a combination of both.

These disagreements were quite similar to what Wilson had faced in 1915–19, when he moved his isolationist country toward a world role; to what Roosevelt had encountered in 1939–41, when he committed America to the side of Great Britain; and to what Truman had had to contend with in 1946–49, when he developed the architecture of the Cold War.

The key difference was that these debates were now occurring in the midst of turmoil in Vietnam, followed immediately by Watergate. In the American system, the president is the only nationally elected figure; he is also the sole focus for defining national purposes. Other institutions can make pronouncements on foreign policy, but only the president is in a position to implement policy over an extended period of time. The Congress, as a legislative body, tends to segment issues into a series of individual decisions, which it then seeks to resolve through reciprocal compromises. The media can recommend a course, but they are in no position to deal with the nuances of day-to-day execution. But the essence of foreign policy is precisely the ability to accumulate nuances in pursuit of long-range goals. Thus, it falls to the president to chart the course. And although the other institutions are in a position to modify or even to thwart it, they are unable to bring about a coherent alternative.

All great departures in American foreign policy have resulted from strong presidents interacting with America's other institutions. The president serves as the educator whose moral vision provides the framework for the debate. But for Watergate, Nixon might have been able to translate the very tangible foreign policy successes of his first term into permanent operating principles—in the way Franklin Delano Roosevelt had created and then consolidated a new approach to American domestic policy, and Truman and Acheson had charted the course for the containment policy.

But Nixon's capacity to lead collapsed as the result of Watergate. This is not the occasion to delve into that tragedy: for present purposes, it is sufficient to stress that Watergate deprived Nixon of the moral authority essential for the educational task his policy required. On day-to-day matters he continued to the end to act decisively and with acumen. But on long-range or conceptual controversies, he remained capable of raising fundamental issues but was no longer sufficiently strong enough to shape their solutions. In the absence of the balance wheel of a strong president acting as moderator and integrator, each contending group could push its particular point of view to an extreme. A great part of the 1970s thus turned into an elaboration of the conflict over themes which had been part and parcel of previous great American initiatives—lacking, however, the synthesis which, in other formative periods, has conferred the necessary impetus on America's new departures.

Nixon's new approach to foreign policy challenged American exceptionalism and its imperative that policy be based on the affirmation of transcendent values. America's challenge, as Nixon and his advisers saw it, was to adapt these traditional verities to the new international environment. America's domestic experience had led it to interpret the international order as being essentially benign, and its diplomacy as an expression of goodwill and a willingness to compromise. In that scheme of things, hostility was seen as an aberration. Nixon's foreign policy, on the other hand, perceived the world as composed of ambiguous challenges, of nations impelled by interest rather than goodwill, and of incremental rather than final changes—a world, in short, that could be managed but could be neither dominated nor rejected. In such a world, no clear-cut terminal point beckoned, and the solution to one problem was more likely to turn into an admission ticket to the next one.

Such a world required a foreign policy geared to staying power as much as to salvation. Traditional American values remained as important as ever, but, unlike during Wilson's era, they could no longer be translated into an agenda of immediate, final outcomes. Instead, they would be needed to provide the inner strength for America to move through ambiguity to a world that was, everyone hoped, better than the one before, but never finally finished.

Nixon and his advisers saw no contradiction in treating the communist world as both adversary and collaborator: adversary in fundamental ideology and in the need to prevent communism from upsetting the global equilibrium; collaborator in keeping the ideological conflict from exploding into a nuclear war. Yet, having traversed the full emotional distance of America's disillusionment in Vietnam, many Americans began to look for reassurance through the reaffirmation of a moral commitment rather than a calculation of interest.

In the absence of a morally persuasive presidency, many of those reared on the traditional approach to American foreign policy—in both the liberal and the conservative camps—joined forces in opposing Nixon's new approach. Liberals did so because they considered the new emphasis on national interest amoral, conservatives because they were more committed to the ideological competition with Moscow than to the geopolitical one.

Because American thinking on foreign policy had been shaped by liberal ideas ever since Woodrow Wilson, there was no ready constituency for Nixon's style of diplomacy. Nixon did not embrace the pragmatic case-by-case approach preferred by the foreign policy specialists and the lawyers who shaped so much of liberal America's views on international relations. Nor did he endorse the Wilsonian concepts of collective security, judicial settlement of disputes, and emphasis on disarmament as the only, or even the principal, road to international order. As a result, liberals found themselves in an uncomfortable quandary: diplomatic results of which they approved in substance, such as the relaxation of tensions with the Soviet Union and the opening to China, were emerging from principles that were anathema to the Wilsonian tradition, such as emphasis on the national interest and the balance of power. Even when the Nixon Administration was successfully promoting policies which stemmed from Wilsonian ideals, such as increasing emigration from the Soviet Union, its tendency to pursue these goals through secret diplomacy compounded its estrangement from the representatives of the historic rhythm of American foreign policy.

To conservatives, Nixon's strategy of treating the Soviet Union as a geopolitical phenomenon was unfamiliar and uncongenial. The vast majority of them viewed the conflict with communism as being almost exclusively ideological. Convinced of America's imperviousness to geopolitical challenges, they treated issues at the front lines of containment as being of marginal concern and as too close for comfort to the traditional struggles of the European powers, which, on the whole, they held in low esteem. They had given up on Vietnam already during the Johnson Administration, seeing it as a diversion from the primary struggle—not, as Nixon did, as a crucial component of it. Being moral absolutists, they distrusted any negotiation with the Soviet Union, viewing compromise as retreat. The conservative wing of the Republican Party was prepared to swallow the opening to China through clenched teeth, as a contribution to the discomfiture of Moscow and as a tactical necessity for extricating America from Vietnam. But, having always been dubious about negotiating with Moscow and most at ease with the original Acheson-Dulles approach of waiting for the collapse of communism behind positions of strength, conservatives treated a wide-ranging negotiation on political and military issues as abandonment of the moral issue.

Traditional conservatives were gradually joined by recruits from an unexpected quarter—by liberal, strongly anticommunist Democrats who had been alienated from their party by the ascendancy of its radical wing. The McGovern candidacy in 1972 had completed the disillusionment of these self-styled neoconservatives, and the 1973 Middle East War gave them the first opportunity to state their foreign policy views coherently and on a national scale.

Dedicated anticommunists, the neoconservatives might have been expected to turn into moral supporters of an administration which had persisted in Vietnam in largest part to maintain America's claim to be manning the anticommunist ramparts. Like the conservatives, however, the neoconservatives were more concerned with ideology than with geopolitics. Several of their most influential figures had passionately opposed the Vietnam War. And they brought all their former reservations about Nixon into the new camp, giving him no credit for enduring the bitter struggle for an honorable peace. Because they neither liked nor trusted Nixon, they feared that he might abandon vital interests in an attempt to save his presidency.

The White House's cavalier treatment of the established government bureaucracy complicated matters further. During his first term, Nixon had shifted much of the conduct of diplomacy into the White House, as he had announced he would during his presidential campaign. Once the Soviet leaders had grasped that Nixon would never delegate the key foreign policy decisions, a back-channel of direct contact developed between Soviet Ambassador Anatoly Dobrynin and the White House. In this manner, the President and the top leadership in the Kremlin were able to deal directly with the most important issues.

Hell hath no fury like a bureaucrat scorned, and the Nixon White House compounded the problem by the insensitivity with which it overrode established procedure. By definition, a negotiation is about trading concessions. Yet those who are excluded from the ebb and flow of negotiations feel free to give expression to the fantasy of a negotiation in which all the concessions are made by the other side, and in which the American concessions could have been avoided had *their* advice been solicited. Deprived of the usual bureaucratic safety net and assailed by uneasy conservatives, frustrated liberals, and aggressive neoconservatives, the Nixon White House found itself in the strange position of being on the defensive with respect to a successful foreign policy.

In effect, the critics were urging the Administration to adopt a confrontational course at a time when America was reeling under the assaults of the Peace Movement, when the President was in the process of being impeached (and his successor, Gerald R. Ford, was appointed rather than elected), and when every Congressional session reduced the President's authority to threaten force and at the same time sought to cut the defense budget. The task at hand, as the Nixon Administration saw it, was to get beyond Vietnam without suffering geopolitical losses, and to establish a policy toward the communists that was geared to the relevant battlefields. Nixon saw detente as a tactic in a long-term geopolitical struggle; his liberal critics treated it as an end in itself while conservatives and neoconservatives rejected the geopolitical approach as so much historical pessimism, preferring a policy of unremitting ideological confrontation.

Ironically, by 1973, Nixon's policy had so tranquilized East-West relations that it became safe to challenge it at home. At the heart of the controversy was the deeper issue of whether it was either possible or desirable to wean American policy away from its faith in final outcomes and episodic involvements. Nixon argued that, in a multipolar world, change had to be sought through evolution. This required patience—not the traditional long suit of American diplomacy. Nixon's critics, reflecting the tradition of American exceptionalism, insisted that America commit itself to the goal of immediately reshaping Soviet society—a goal which had never been sought, not even during America's atomic monopoly. A major national debate was both inevitable and necessary between the proponents of foreign policy as strategy and of foreign policy as crusade; between those who believed that the wisest course was to discipline a rival superpower and those who insisted on chastising evil. What was not inevitable was the collapse of the presidency, which prevented a meaningful resolution of the debate.

In the absence of some overriding set of principles, each side in the controversy focused on different threats. Nixon's nightmare was geopolitical vulnerability to creeping Soviet expansionism. The conservatives' fear was moral disarmament or an apocalyptic nuclear showdown made possible by some Soviet technological breakthrough. The liberals' concern was American overemphasis on military security. The conservatives feared Soviet military dominance. The liberals wanted to avoid overextension. Nixon sought a sustainable long-term strategy.

The result was a maelstrom of conflicting and irresolvable pressures. Liberals watched closely for any sign of flagging commitment to arms control. Nixon vigilantly resisted geopolitical threats, from Cuba to the Middle East. Conservatives attacked what they perceived to be America's retreat from ideological confrontation and nuclear strategy. This led to the bizarre situation in which liberals were attacking the Nixon defense program for being too high, and conservatives were criticizing Nixon's arms control policy for being too conciliatory. The defense programs were put through the Congress by Nixon with conservative help over liberal opposition, and arms control measures were approved—where Congressional approval was needed—with liberal help against some conservative opposition.

The gravamen of most of these criticisms (in the end, even of the liberal ones) was a call to return to the original premises of containment and to wait behind strong defenses for the transformation of the Soviet system. Nixon agreed with the need for strong defenses, but he did not believe in a policy that would enable Moscow to shape the agenda of diplomacy and drive the American domestic crisis out of control. The critics thought that an active East-West diplomacy would dull the vigilance of the American people. Nixon believed that diplomatic flexibility was needed to buttress America's willingness to resist communism. He was determined to resist every Soviet expansionist move—which, in turn, some critics interpreted as injecting European-style geopolitics into what was primarily an ideological conflict.

In June 1974, Senator Henry Jackson circulated to his Subcommittee on Arms Control a critique of detente prepared by a group of eminent scholars that maintained:

> [i]n the present Soviet terminology, *détente* or "peaceful coexistence" denotes a strategic alternative to overtly militant antagonism against the so-called "capitalist countries." It does not imply the abandonment by the Soviet Union and its allies of conflict with the liberal Western countries. . . . Head-on conflict is to yield to indirect methods of combat, using non-military means, described as "ideological:" in Soviet practice this term covers subversion, propaganda, political blackmail and intelligence operations.[3]

George Meany, President of the AFL-CIO, expressed the same thoughts in layman's language before the Senate Foreign Relations Committee:

> Here's how the Soviet Union sees détente: Détente is based on U.S. weakness. Détente means intensification of ideological warfare. Détente means an undermining of NATO. Détente means ultimate Soviet military superiority over the West. Détente means recognition by the West of the Soviet Union's ownership of Eastern Europe. Détente means withdrawal of American forces from Europe.[4]

Such criticisms exasperated the Nixon Administration, which never had doubted that the Kremlin viewed detente as serving at least some Soviet purposes—otherwise Moscow would not have pursued it. The real issue was whether detente also served America's purposes. Nixon and his advisers thought that time was on the side of the democracies because a period of peace without expansion would strengthen the centrifugal forces within communism.

I stated the analysis underlying detente in March 1976 during the Ford Administration, which in effect pursued the same policy as the Nixon Administration and incurred the same adversaries:

> Soviet strength is uneven; the weaknesses and frustrations of the Soviet system are glaring and have been clearly documented. Despite the inevitable increase in its power, the Soviet Union remains far behind us and our allies in any overall assessment of military, economic, and technological strength; it would be reckless in the extreme for the Soviet Union to challenge the industrial democracies. And Soviet society is no longer insulated from the influences and attractions of the outside world or impervious to the need for external contacts.[5]

Left to the passage of time, the essentially theoretical debate over detente might have been overtaken by events. But the intellectual leader of the critics, the formidable Senator Henry Jackson, was far from ready to leave detente to the test of time, and mobilized support to stop it in its tracks. A Democrat from the state of Washington and one of America's most impressive public servants, Jackson was a serious student of international affairs, especially of the Soviet Union, and a world-class expert on defense. He combined erudition with a masterly grasp of how to manipulate the various branches of the government, bringing the Congress together with sympathetic elements in the Executive Branch. Jackson's staff, headed by the subtle Richard Perle, matched his erudition and exceeded even his finely honed manipulative skills.

Although he had been Nixon's first choice for Secretary of Defense, Jackson was to become the most implacable opponent of the Administration's Soviet policy. Throughout most of Nixon's first term, Jackson had stood reasonably steadfast on Vietnam, proving himself a staunch supporter of Nixon's efforts to preserve the sinews of American defense in the face of relentless Congressional pressure to cut the budget unilaterally. He had been indispensable in guiding Nixon's proposed Anti-Ballistic-Missile (ABM) defense system through the Senate. Nevertheless, at the end of Nixon's first term, the two parted company, even though their interpretations of Soviet purposes were nearly identical. Jackson did not agree with the ABM Treaty, which limited the number of missile defense sites for both sides to two, and he soon extended that opposition to the whole field of East-West relations.

Nixon's original program for missile defense (ABM) provided for a dozen defense sites around the perimeter of the United States. It would have been useful against smaller nuclear forces like China's and against less-than-all-out Soviet attacks, and could have provided a nucleus for an eventual full-scale defense against the Soviet Union.

But the Congress reduced the number of sites every year so that the Pentagon by 1971 had included only two sites for the next budget. Such a deployment served no conceivable strategic purpose; its sole utility was experimental. In addition, reflecting the antimilitary mentality of the period, the Congressional majority had cut the proposed defense budget in each Congressional session (not counting programs which the Nixon Administration never put forward because it knew they would be defeated).

These pressures converted the Defense Department into a sudden and uncharacteristic advocate of arms control. In early 1970, Deputy Secretary of Defense David Packard urged Nixon to undertake immediately a new SALT initiative "with which we can attempt to achieve an agreement at Vienna by mid-October or, at the latest, November." He considered a quick agreement essential, even if it was only partial, because the looming "squeeze on the national budget" was "likely" to cause "large reductions in defense programs, including strategic forces." Failing this, unilateral Congressional decisions would progressively "decrease our bargaining leverage."[6]

In this political setting, Nixon, in the summer of 1970, initiated a correspondence with Soviet Prime Minister Aleksei Kosygin which provided the framework for an agreement on the limitation of strategic arms (SALT) two years later. Until then, the Soviets had insisted that the arms control talks confine themselves to limiting defensive weapons in which the United States had a technological edge but to defer limits on offensive missiles, of which the Soviet Union was producing 200 annually of all types and the United States none. Nixon made it clear that he would never agree to so one-sided a bargain. The outcome of the Kosygin-Nixon correspondence was that the Soviets conceded that both offensive and defensive weapons be limited simultaneously.

The subsequent negotiations led to two agreements. The ABM Treaty of 1972 confined defenses to two sites and 200 missile launchers—too few to contain even a small-scale attack. Nixon agreed to the ceilings in order to preserve a nucleus of defense and because he feared that, otherwise, the Congress would eliminate even the experimental program. At the time, the defensive limitations were relatively free of controversy.

What drew fire was a five-year Interim Agreement which obliged both sides to freeze their strategic offensive-missile forces, whether land- or sea-based, at agreed levels. The United States had established its own levels five years earlier and deeming them sufficient had never had a program to increase them. The Soviet Union was producing 200 missiles a year. To reach the agreed ceiling, it had to dismantle 210 older long-range missiles. Bombers (in which the United States had the advantage) were not included in the ceilings. Both sides remained free to improve the technology of their forces.

It was difficult to compare the missile forces of the two sides. American missiles were smaller and more accurate; half of them were being equipped with multiple warheads (that is, each missile would carry several explosive devices). Soviet missiles were larger, cruder, and less flexible. They also exceeded America's by about 300. As long as each side made its own decisions, the disparity seemed to bother no one, no doubt because America had a large advantage in aircraft and, due to multiple warheads, a growing edge in warheads—which would only increase over the five years during which the agreement would be in effect.

Nevertheless, as soon as the SALT Agreement was signed at the May 1972 Moscow Summit, the disparity in agreed launchers suddenly became controversial. It was a strange state of affairs. Before SALT negotiations had even been conceived, the United States had established the existing ceilings. The Pentagon had made no effort to increase the level throughout Nixon's first term; no Pentagon request for larger strategic forces was received much less turned down. And even after higher and equal ceilings were agreed on in the follow-on accord at Vladivostok in 1974, the Defense Department never proposed increasing the number of launchers which had been established in 1967.

But a visitor from Mars observing America's domestic debate would have heard an amazing tale about how the United States government had "conceded" an inequality in missiles by agreeing to settle for its own unilateral program, which it had never planned to change in the absence of SALT, and which it never changed, even after the ceiling was removed two years later—not even in the Reagan Administration. A force level which the United States had adopted voluntarily because it provided America with more warheads than it did the Soviet Union, and which the United States was in no position to change for the duration of the agreement, was suddenly termed as dangerous when it was reaffirmed as part of that agreement.[7]

Unfortunately for Nixon and his advisers, "inequality" was one of those code words that create their own reality. By the time the Administration's rebuttal had compared launchers and warheads and planned and negotiated ceilings, eyes had glazed over, leaving only the uncomfortable feeling that what the Administration was defending was a "missile gap" disadvantageous to the United States.

The Nixon Administration saw in the SALT Agreement a means of protecting essential defense programs against Congressional assault in two ways: it insisted that the ceilings established by the agreement be treated as benchmarks by the Congress, and it coupled the agreement with a $4.5 billion increase in the defense budget for modernization. Even now, twenty years later, most key strategic programs (the B-1, the Stealth bombers, the MX missile, the strategic cruise missiles, the Trident missile and submarines) originated in the Nixon and Ford Administrations during the period that SALT I was in effect.

What looked like a debate regarding the missile forces of both sides was really a symbol of a deeper and very valid concern. Jackson and his supporters saw in the growing emphasis on arms control—indeed, the media's and the academic community's near-obsession with it—a potential threat to *any* serious defense policy. New military programs were increasingly being justified on the ground that they served as bargaining chips in future SALT negotiations. The Jackson forces feared that such a trend could erode any strategic rationale for defense. After all, what was the sense of allocating scarce resources to costly programs whose primary purpose was to be offered up for dismantling?

In this context, the debate about the provisions of the agreement was ultimately about how to come to grips with the end of America's strategic superiority. Theoretically, it had been understood for a decade that the destructiveness of nuclear weapons spelled stalemate, in that it precluded victory at any cost which a rational political leader could accept. That realization had caused the Kennedy Administration to develop the strategic doctrine of "assured destruction," which based deterrence on the capability of *each* side to devastate the other.

Far from solving the dilemma, this strategic doctrine had merely redefined it. A national strategy relying on the threat of suicide was bound to come to a dead end sooner or later. And SALT I brought home to the public what the experts had known for at least a decade. Suddenly, SALT was being blamed for a state of affairs which would have existed even more jarringly under conditions of unrestricted armaments. The dilemma was real enough, but SALT had not caused it. As long as deterrence was equated with mutual destruction, the psychological inhibitions against nuclear war would be overwhelming. America was building weapons useful only in discouraging the adversary's use of nuclear weapons, and not for their relevance to any foreseeable political crisis. Once that realization sank in, mutual assured destruction was bound to undermine morale and destroy existing alliances. This, and not SALT, was the real nuclear dilemma.

Thus, in its essence, the debate about SALT—and detente—reflected a rebellion against a world in which a deadly ideological conflict was being waged side by side an unavoidable strategic stalemate. The real clash over SALT invoked two very different assessments of the nuclear stalemate. Nixon and his advisers concluded that whichever side was capable of posing challenges short of nuclear war would, over time, acquire ever-greater blackmailing potential and be able to conduct a policy of creeping expansionism. This was why Nixon put his emphasis on resisting the geopolitical threat. In the absence of a counterforce capability—the ability to disarm the adversary in a first strike—American strategic power would become less and less suitable for the defense of overseas areas, including, in the end, even Europe (see chapter 24).

The groups associated with Jackson understood this and hankered after a restoration of America's strategic superiority. But they clothed their concern in the fear not only that America was losing its first-strike capability—which was true—but that, over time, the Soviet Union might acquire such a capability—which was not true, certainly not in a time frame relevant to the debate.

Jackson's nightmare was strategic vulnerability; Nixon's nightmare was geopolitical vulnerability. Jackson's concern was the balance of military forces; Nixon's principal concern was the global distribution of political power.[8] Jackson and his supporters tried to use SALT to force the Soviet Union to redesign its entire strategic force according to American preferences. Nixon and his advisers did not believe that America had the leverage for such a design in a period of Congressionally imposed reductions in the defense budget, though Reagan would later demonstrate the political utility of a determined American military buildup. Jackson and his supporters focused primarily on the strategic balance, the threat to which they treated as a largely technological problem. The Nixon Administration sought to prepare America for a role novel in its history but as old as the state system: preventing the accumulation by an adversary of seemingly marginal geopolitical gains which, over time, would overthrow the balance of power. The Jackson forces were relatively tolerant of geopolitical changes (Jackson voted against aid to the noncommunist side in Angola in 1975) but were zealous about the implications of the most esoteric weapons technology.

This deadlock drove the SALT debate into ever more abstruse realms until the controversy settled on the minutiae of weapons systems no layman could possibly understand, and over which the weapons experts themselves were deeply divided. In the perspective of a decade, the arguments about trade-offs between cruise missiles and Soviet Backfire bombers, equal total aggregates and unequal multiple warheads, read like medieval tracts recorded by the scribes of some secluded monastery.

The questions raised in the debate were fundamental and unavoidable. What caused the deadlock was the anguish of the presidency, which rendered a meeting of minds impossible. American idealism reigned supreme, unfettered by any incentives for political compromise. The President could exact no penalty and offer no rewards, the perquisites inherent in his office. The critics had no political incentive to adjust their view. The debate took on the aura of a faculty meeting between self-willed professors. Historians, however, will benefit from seeing the positions stated more clearly than is typically the case in a political process. America paid for its self-flagellation with a delay of nearly a decade in finally confronting its geopolitical necessities.

In the end, communism collapsed partly as a result of its own sclerosis, partly because of the pressures from a reinvigorated West. This is why the final judgment of history will undoubtedly be kinder to the opposing camps in America's domestic debate than they ever were to each other. It will perceive the approaches of Nixon and of his conservative critics as having been complementary rather than competitive, with one side of the debate stressing the geopolitical and the other the technological aspect of a struggle whose moral essence both viewed in a similar fashion.

Arms control turned out to be technically too ponderous to carry the weight of the philosophical controversy over the nature of American foreign policy. Gradually, the debate shifted to an issue more congenial to traditional American idealism, and one which had a greater resonance with the public at large—the proposition that human rights should rank among the principal goals of American foreign policy.

The human rights debate started out as an appeal for wielding American influence to improve the treatment of Soviet citizens but graduated into a strategy for forcing a Soviet domestic upheaval. As with arms control, the issue did not concern the objective, which was not in dispute, but the degree to which ideological confrontation should be the top priority of American foreign policy.

As a diplomatic subject, the issue of Jewish emigration from the Soviet Union had been the brainchild of the Nixon Administration. Prior to 1969, such emigration had never been on the agenda of the East-West dialogue; all previous administrations of both parties had treated it as falling within the domestic jurisdiction of the Soviet Union. None had been prepared to burden East-West relations, which were already sufficiently strained, with an additional controversy. In 1968, only 400 Jews had been permitted to emigrate from the Soviet Union, and no democratic country had raised the issue.

As American-Soviet relations improved, the Nixon Administration began discussing the subject in the presidential back-channel with the argument that Soviet actions would not pass unnoticed at the highest levels of the American government. The Kremlin began to respond to American "suggestions," especially after Soviet-American relations started improving. Each year, the number of Jewish emigrants rose, and by 1973 the annual figure reached 35,000. In addition, the White House regularly submitted to Soviet leaders a list of hardship cases—individuals who had been denied exit visas or whose families were separated, and some of whom were in prison. Most of these Soviet citizens were also permitted to emigrate.

All of this was taking place by what students of diplomacy would describe as "tacit bargaining." No formal requests were made, and no formal responses were given. Soviet actions were noted without being acknowledged. Indeed, the emigration practices of the Soviet Union were steadily improving, though no claim to that effect was ever made by Washington. The Nixon Administration stuck to these ground rules so meticulously that it never claimed any credit for improving Soviet emigration practices —even during election campaigns—until Henry Jackson turned the issue of Jewish emigration into a public confrontation.

What triggered Jackson was a curious decision by the Kremlin during the summer of 1972 to impose an "exit tax" on emigrants, allegedly to reimburse the Soviet state for the expense of having educated its departing citizens. No explanation was ever given; possibly it was an attempt to burnish the Soviet position in the Arab world, the precariousness of which had most recently been demonstrated by the expulsion of Soviet combat troops from Egypt. Or else the exit tax may have been designed to generate foreign exchange in the expectation that it would be paid for by American supporters of increased emigration. Fearful that the flow of emigration might dry up, Jewish groups appealed to both the Nixon Administration and their longtime supporter Henry Jackson.

While the Nixon Administration continued to work quietly to resolve the issue with Ambassador Dobrynin, Jackson devised an ingenious means of publicly pressuring the Soviet Union. As part of the 1972 summit, the United States had signed an agreement granting the Soviet Union "Most Favored Nation" (MFN) status in return for a settlement of the wartime Lend-Lease debt. In October 1972, Jackson introduced an amendment to bar MFN status to any country that restricted emigration. It was a tactically brilliant stroke. Most Favored Nation status sounds much more significant than it really is. What it denotes is nondiscriminatory status; it grants no special favors but simply extends to the recipient whatever privileges are available to all nations with which the United States maintains normal commercial relations (which then numbered over a hundred). MFN status facilitates *normal* trade on the basis of commercial reciprocity. Given the state of the Soviet economy, the level of such trade was not expected to be large. What the Jackson Amendment achieved was to make Soviet emigration practices a subject of not just public diplomacy but of legislative action by the American Congress.

There was no disagreement on substance between the Administration and Jackson. Indeed, the Administration had taken a stand on a number of other human rights issues. For example, I had made numerous and insistent appeals to Dobrynin on behalf of the dissident writer Aleksandr Solzhenitsyn which contributed to his leaving the Soviet Union. Jackson, however, did not favor quiet diplomacy in the pursuit of human rights and insisted that the American commitment to it be demonstrably affirmed—its successes vaunted, and its failures penalized.

In the beginning, the Congressional pressures served as useful reinforcements to the Administration's own efforts in the same direction. Soon, however, the difference went beyond method. Nixon, who had originated the concept of encouraging Jewish emigration, had done so as a humanitarian gesture (and perhaps as a marginally political one, although he never made use of it publicly). But he drew the line at subordinating all East-West relations to the issue of Jewish emigration because he did not believe that the American national interest was involved to that extent.

To Jackson and his supporters, the issue of Jewish emigration was a surrogate for the ideological confrontation with communism. Not surprisingly, they treated every Soviet concession as proof that their pressure tactics were working. The Soviet leaders did revoke the exit tax—whether due to remonstrations by the White House, the Jackson Amendment, or, more likely, both, though the final verdict must await the opening of Soviet archives. Emboldened, the Administration's critics asked for a doubling of the Jewish emigration figures and for the removal of restrictions on emigration for other nationalities according to a schedule to be approved by the United States. The Jackson forces also legislated restrictions on loans to the Soviet Union by the Export/Import Bank (the Stevenson Amendment) so that, on commercial matters, the Soviet Union ended up in a worse position after detente than before the relaxation of East-West tensions.

As the leader of a country that was just emerging from a debilitating war and heading into a crisis of the presidency, Nixon would run only those risks which his conception of the national interest required and which his country was prepared to back up. Yet his critics wanted American diplomacy to bring about the downfall of the Soviet system through unilateral demands in arms control, the withholding of trade, and a challenging advocacy of human rights. In the process, there occurred an extraordinary reversal in the positions of some of the key participants in the national debate. *The New York Times* had warned editorially in 1971 that "the tactic of withholding American trade as leverage for some later bargain over unrelated issues is far less likely to influence Soviet policy favorably than is the trade itself. ...."[9] Two years later, that editorial writer had reversed course. He condemned a trip by Treasury Secretary George Shultz to the Soviet Union as evidence that "the Administration is so intent on trade and détente that it is willing to shunt aside the equally important concern of the American people for human rights everywhere."[10]

Nixon had sought to encourage moderation in Soviet *international* conduct by making restraint in Soviet foreign policy the litmus test of increased trade with America. His opponents took linkage a step further by seeking to use trade as a means of producing *domestic* upheaval in the Soviet Union, and at a time when the Soviet Union was still strong and confident. Assaulted as a Cold Warrior four years earlier, Nixon was now castigated for being too soft and trusting toward the Soviet Union—surely the first time that this particular charge had been leveled against the man who had started his political career in the anticommunist investigations of the late 1940s.

Soon the very concept of improving Soviet-American relations was being challenged, as in this editorial from *The Washington Post:*

> The very difficult question of what is to be the substance of Soviet-American "detente" is passing from a debating phase to a political phase. A significant number of Americans now appear to believe it is neither desirable, possible, nor safe to improve relations with the Soviet Union unless the Kremlin liberalizes some of its domestic policies.[11]

America was veering back toward the true faith of Acheson and Dulles and of NSC document 68: the belief that a fundamental change in Soviet purposes and domestic practices had to precede serious negotiations between the United States and the Soviet Union. But whereas the early Cold Warriors had been content to rely on containment to bring this change about in the fullness of time, their successors were promising significant changes in the Soviet system as the result of direct American pressure and publicized American demands.

On several occasions during the Brezhnev era, Nixon and his associates confronted the Soviet leadership when the Soviet will to power had not yet eroded. And we found them to be formidable adversaries. A wholesale assault on the communist system under conditions of nuclear parity promised to be long and bitter. After Vietnam and in the midst of Watergate, we found ourselves in the position of a swimmer who, having just barely escaped drowning, is being urged to cross the English Channel and is then accused of pessimism when he displays a lack of enthusiasm at the prospect. Jackson had distinguished himself on the ramparts of the anticommunist geopolitical struggle, as he would do again; the same could not always be said of many of his recruits, whose sincerity we doubted far less than their staying power.

In an international crisis, the president is the indispensable focal point for the government. From this point of view alone, the Watergate period was hardly the ideal time for launching a deliberate policy of Soviet-American confrontation. The President was in the process of being impeached; the wounds of Vietnam were still open; and distrust of the Administration was so great that, after the Soviets had made an explicit threat to intervene in the war in the Middle East, a respected journalist found it possible to ask at a press conference in October 1973 whether United States forces had been put on alert to deflect attention from Watergate.

The controversy had returned to a debate dating as far back as John Quincy Adams about whether the United States should be content to affirm its moral values or whether it should crusade on their behalf. Nixon had sought to relate America's purposes to its capabilities. Within these limits he was prepared to enlist America's influence to promote its values, as his stand on Jewish emigration had shown. His critics insisted on the immediate applicability of universal principles, and impatiently dismissed questions of feasibility as proof of moral inadequacy or of historical pessimism. In urging that American idealism be discriminating, the Nixon Administration felt it was performing a vital educational function. How ironic that, at a moment when America was being told that it must learn its geopolitical limits in Vietnam, it should be urged by some national figures—several of whom had been in the vanguard of the Vietnam critique—to embark on an unlimited agenda of global interventionism on humanitarian issues.

As the Reagan years would demonstrate, a bolder policy toward the Soviet Union had much to recommend it, although these successes were not to come about until a later stage of evolution in Soviet-American relations. But while the detente debate was raging, America had yet to recover from Vietnam and to lay Watergate to rest. And the Soviet leaders first had to undergo a turnover in generations. The way the debate developed in the early 1970s, however, prevented an appropriate balance from being struck between the idealism which has sparked all the great American initiatives and the realism mandated by the changing global environment.

The critics of detente vastly oversimplified their case; the Nixon Administration contributed to the deadlock by responding too pedantically. Stung by the assault of former allies and friends, Nixon dismissed the criticism as having been politically motivated. However true that assessment might have been, it was hardly a profound insight to charge professional politicians with having political motives. What the Administration should have asked itself was why so many politicians were finding it expedient to join the Jackson chorus.

Trapped between undifferentiating moralism and overemphasis on geopolitics, American policy at the end of Nixon's term became stalemated. As the carrot of increased trade was withdrawn, the stick of increased defense spending, or even of a willingness to face geopolitical confrontations, was not forthcoming. SALT stalemated; Jewish emigration from the Soviet Union slowed to a trickle; and the communist geopolitical offensive resumed when a Cuban expeditionary force was sent to Angola, which established a communist government there while American *conservatives* opposed a strong American response. I pointed out the difficulties:

> If one group of critics undermines arms control negotiations and cuts off the prospect of more constructive ties with the Soviet Union, while another group cuts away at our defense budgets and intelligence services and thwarts American resistance to Soviet adventurism, both combined will—whether they have intended it or not—end by wrecking the nation's ability to conduct a strong, creative, moderate and prudent foreign policy.[12]

So it happened that even major diplomatic achievements of this period became controversial. The American diplomacy which has dominated the Middle East since 1973, and which had sharply reduced the Soviet influence in that strategic region, was presented for several years as a setback, until the momentum of the peace process dispelled even the skeptics' reservations.

A similar fate befell what posterity has judged to be a significant Western diplomatic achievement—the thirty-five-nation Conference on European Security and Cooperation, which produced the Helsinki Accords. This monster diplomatic process grew out of Moscow's deep-rooted sense of insecurity and unquenchable thirst for legitimacy. Even as it was building an enormous military establishment and holding down a score of nations, the Kremlin acted as if it were in constant need of reassurance. Its huge and growing nuclear arsenal notwithstanding, the Soviet Union demanded from the very countries it had been threatening for decades and which it had consigned to the dustbin of history some formula it could use to consecrate its acquisitions. In this sense, the European Security Conference became Brezhnev's substitute for the German peace treaty that Khrushchev had failed to extract with his Berlin ultimatum— and a grand confirmation of the postwar *status quo*.

The exact benefit envisaged by Moscow was not self-evident. The insistence with which the cradle of ideological revolution was seeking confirmation of its legitimacy from the proclaimed victims of historical inevitability was a symptom of extraordinary self-doubt. Probably the Soviet leaders were banking on the possibility that the Conference might leave behind some residual institutions to water down NATO, or even to make it irrelevant.

In this they deluded themselves. No NATO country was waiting to substitute the declaratory and bureaucratic paraphernalia of a European Security Conference for the military reality of NATO or the presence of American military forces on the Continent. Moscow, as it turned out, had much more to lose than the democracies from a conference which ended up giving all the participants, including the United States, a voice in the political arrangements of Eastern Europe.

After a period of ambivalence, the Nixon Administration went along with the proposed conference. Recognizing that the Soviet Union had its own, quite opposite, agenda, we nevertheless perceived a long-term opportunity. The borders of the countries of Eastern Europe had already been recognized by peace treaties concluded at the end of World War II between the wartime Allies and Germany's wartime satellites in Eastern Europe. They had been explicitly confirmed further in Willy Brandt's bilateral agreements between the Federal Republic and the countries of Eastern Europe as well as by other NATO democracies, especially France, with the countries of Eastern Europe (including Poland and the Soviet Union). Moreover, all NATO allies were pressing for a European Security Conference; at every meeting with their Soviet counterparts, Western European leaders moved closer to accepting the Soviet agenda.

Thus, in 1971 the Nixon Administration decided to add the European Security Conference to its list of incentives for encouraging Soviet moderation. We employed our strategy of linkage which was summed up by

State Department Counsellor Helmut Sonnenfeldt as boastfully as it was accurate: "We sold it for the German-Soviet treaty, we sold it for the Berlin agreement, and we sold it again for the opening of the MBFR [Mutual Balanced Force Reductions]."[13] The Nixon and then Ford Administrations shaped the outcome by making America's attendance dependent on restrained Soviet conduct on all other issues. They insisted on the satisfactory conclusion of the Berlin negotiations and the initiation of negotiations on mutual force reductions in Europe. When these were concluded, delegations from thirty-five nations came to Geneva, though their arduous negotiations were largely unreported in the Western press. Then, in 1975, the Conference emerged from obscurity when it was announced that agreements had been reached which would be signed at a summit-level meeting in Helsinki. American influence had helped to confine the recognition of borders to an obligation not to change them by force, which was a mere duplication of the UN Charter. Since no European country had the capacity to bring about a forcible change or a policy to that effect, the formal renunciation was hardly a Soviet gain. Even this limited recognition of legitimacy was vitiated by a statement of principle which preceded it—largely negotiated by the United States. It declared that the signatory states "consider that their frontiers can be changed, in accordance with international law, by peaceful means and by agreement."[14]

The most significant provision of the Helsinki Agreement turned out to be the so-called Basket III on human rights. (Baskets I and II dealt with political and economic issues, respectively.) Basket III was destined to play a major role in the disintegration of the Soviet satellite orbit, and became a testimonial to all human rights activists in NATO countries. The American delegation contributed to the final provisions of the Helsinki Accords. But it is the human rights activists who deserve tribute, because, without the pressures which they exerted, progress would have been slower, and there probably would have been less of it.

Basket III obliged all signatories to practice and foster certain enumerated basic human rights. Its Western drafters hoped that the provisions would create an international standard that would inhibit Soviet repression of dissidents and revolutionaries. As it turned out, heroic reformers in Eastern Europe used Basket III as a rallying point in their fights to free their countries from Soviet domination. Both Vaclav Havel in Czechoslovakia and Lech Walesa in Poland earned their place in the pantheon of freedom fighters by using these provisions, both domestically and internationally, to undermine not only Soviet domination but the communist regimes in their own countries.

The European Security Conference thus came to play an important dual role: in its planning stages, it moderated Soviet conduct in Europe and, afterward, it accelerated the collapse of the Soviet Empire.

The memory of contemporaries' attitudes toward the Helsinki Conference has mercifully faded. President Ford was accused of a historic sellout for attending the Conference and for signing the main document, the so-called Final Act, in 1975. *The New York Times* editorialized:

> The 35-nation Conference on Security and Cooperation in Europe, now nearing its climax after 32 months of semantic quibbling, should not have happened. Never have so many struggled for so long over so little. ... If it is too late to call off the Helsinki summit ... every effort must be made there, publicly as well as privately, to prevent euphoria in the West.[15]

I summed up the Ford Administration's attitude in a speech three weeks later:

> The United States pursues the process of easing tensions from a position of self-confidence and strength. It is not we who were on the defensive at Helsinki; it is not we who were being challenged by all the delegations to live up to the principles being signed. At Helsinki, for the first time in the postwar period, human rights and fundamental freedoms became recognized subjects of East-West discourse and negotiation. The conference put forward *our* standards of humane conduct, which have been—and still are—a beacon of hope to millions.[16]

It was a melancholy period, during which persuasion seemed futile. In a speech in March 1976, I challenged the challengers with some exasperation:

> No policy will soon, if ever, eliminate the competition and irreconcilable ideological differences between the United States and the Soviet Union. Nor will it make all interests compatible. We are engaged in a protracted process with inevitable ups and downs. But there is no alternative to the policy of penalties for adventurism and incentives for restraint. What do those who speak so glibly about "one-way streets" or "preemptive concessions" propose concretely that this country do? What precisely has been given up? What level of confrontation do they seek? What threats would they make? What risks would they run? What precise changes in our defense posture, what level of expenditure over what period of time, do they advocate? How concretely do they suggest managing the U.S.-Soviet relationship in an era of strategic equality?[17]

Nixon's "structure of peace" had responded to the nation's yearning for an end to distant adventures. Yet, for most of their history, Americans had taken peace for granted; defining peace as the absence of war was both too passive and too uninspiring to serve as a permanent theme of American policy. The Nixon Administration's concept of international relations was far more realistic than the one it had inherited and, in the long run, represented a necessary adjustment of American foreign policy. But it was not grounded on familiar principles—a lacuna which subsequent administrations filled in. In America, a geopolitical interpretation of international affairs had become as necessary as it was, by itself, insufficient. Nixon's critics, on the other hand, acted as if the international environment were somehow irrelevant, and as if American preferences could be imposed unilaterally and without requiring any more than an American proclamation.

In seeking to devise a viable approach to the revolutionary changes over which it presided, the Nixon Administration veered too far in the direction of stressing what it perceived as America's geopolitical necessities. Its critics and immediate successors tried to compensate by invoking absolute versions of American principles. The inevitable controversy was made unnecessarily painful by the disintegration of domestic unity under the dual impact of Vietnam and Watergate.

Yet, having held the world together during the Cold War, America did rediscover its bearing and managed to turn the tables on its Soviet opponent. And when the geopolitical threat vanished along with the ideological challenge, America was, ironically, forced without any choice in the 1990s into an altogether new consideration of where its national interest might lie.

CHAPTER THIRTY

The End of the Cold War: Reagan and Gorbachev

The Cold War had begun at a time when America was expecting an era of peace. And the Cold War ended at a moment when America was girding itself for a new era of protracted conflict. The Soviet empire collapsed even more suddenly than it had erupted beyond its borders; with equal speed, America reversed its attitude toward Russia, shifting in a matter of months from hostility to friendship.

This momentous change unfolded under the aegis of two rather improbable collaborators. Ronald Reagan had been elected in reaction to a period of America's seeming retreat to reaffirm the traditional verities of American exceptionalism. Gorbachev, who had risen to eminence through the brutal struggles of the communist hierarchy, was determined to reinvigorate what he considered a superior Soviet ideology. Reagan and Gorbachev each believed in the ultimate victory of his own side. There was, however, a crucial difference between these two unexpected collaborators: Reagan understood the mainsprings of his society, whereas Gorbachev had completely lost touch with his. Both leaders appealed to what they considered best in their systems. But where Reagan liberated his people's spirit by tapping reservoirs of initiative and self-confidence, Gorbachev precipitated the demise of the system he represented by demanding reform of which it proved incapable.

The collapse of Indochina in 1975 had been followed in America by a retreat from Angola and a deepening of domestic divisions, and by an extraordinary surge in expansionism on the part of the Soviet Union. Cuban military forces had spread from Angola to Ethiopia in tandem with thousands of Soviet combat advisers. In Cambodia, Vietnamese troops backed and supplied by the Soviet Union were subjugating that tormented country. Afghanistan was occupied by over 100,000 Soviet troops. The government of the pro-Western Shah of Iran collapsed and was replaced by a radically anti-American fundamentalist regime which seized fifty-two Americans, almost all of whom were officials, as hostages. Whatever the causes, the dominoes indeed appeared to be falling.

Yet, at this seeming nadir of America's international position, communism began to unravel. At one moment, at the beginning of the 1980s, it was as if communist momentum might sweep all before it; at the next, as history measures time, communism was self-destructing. Within a decade, the Eastern European satellite orbit dissolved and the Soviet empire fell apart, disgorging nearly all the Russian acquisitions since the time of Peter the Great. No world power had ever disintegrated so totally or so rapidly without losing a war.

The Soviet empire failed in part because its own history had tempted it inexorably toward overextension. The Soviet state was born against all odds, and then managed to survive civil war, isolation, and a succession of villainous rulers. In 1934–41, it skillfully deflected the looming Second World War into what it termed an imperialist civil war, and overcame the Nazi onslaught with the assistance of the Western Allies. Afterward, in the face of America's atomic monopoly, it managed to establish a satellite orbit in Eastern Europe and, in the post-Stalin period, to turn itself into a global superpower. At first, Soviet armies threatened contiguous areas but later extended their reach to distant continents. Soviet missile forces were growing at a rate which caused many American experts to fear that Soviet strategic superiority was imminent. Like the British leaders Palmerston and Disraeli in the nineteenth century, American statesmen perceived Russia to be on the march everywhere.

The fatal flaw in all this bloated imperialism was that the Soviet leaders lost their sense of proportion along the way, overestimating the Soviet system's ability to consolidate its gains, both militarily and economically, and forgetting that they were challenging literally all the other major powers from a very weak base. Nor could Soviet leaders ever admit to themselves that their system was mortally deficient in its capacity to generate initiative and creativity; that, indeed, the Soviet Union, despite its military power, was still a very backward country. They failed the unforgiving test of survival because the qualities by which the Soviet Politburo rose to eminence stifled the creativity needed to enable their society to grow, let alone to sustain the conflict which they had provoked.

Quite simply, the Soviet Union was neither strong enough nor dynamic enough for the role its leaders had assigned it. Stalin may have had a foreboding of the real balance of forces when he reacted to the American arms buildup during the Korean War with his Peace Note of 1952 (see chapter 20). In the desperate transition period following Stalin's death, his successors misinterpreted their ability to survive without being challenged by the West as proof of Western weakness. And they beguiled themselves by what they perceived to be dramatic Soviet breakthroughs in the developing world. Khrushchev and his successors drew the conclusion that they could do the tyrant one better. Rather than dividing the capitalist world, which had been Stalin's basic strategy, they would defeat it with ultimatums over Berlin, missiles in Cuba, and adventurism throughout the developing world. That effort, however, went so far beyond the Soviet capacity as to transform stagnation into collapse.

The communist disintegration became visible during Reagan's second term and turned irreversible by the time he left office. Considerable credit is due to the presidencies preceding Reagan's, as well as to that of his immediate successor, George Bush, who presided skillfully over the denouement. Nevertheless, it was Ronald Reagan's presidency which marked the turning point.

Reagan's was an astonishing performance—and, to academic observers, nearly incomprehensible. Reagan knew next to no history, and the little he did know he tailored to support his firmly held preconceptions. He treated biblical references to Armageddon as operational predictions. Many of the historical anecdotes he was so fond of recounting had no basis in fact, as facts are generally understood. In a private conversation, he once equated Gorbachev with Bismarck, arguing that both had over-come identical domestic obstacles by moving away from a centrally planned economy toward the free market. I advised a mutual friend that Reagan should be warned never to repeat this preposterous proposition to a German interlocutor. The friend, however, thought it unwise to pass on the warning, lest it drive the comparison all the more deeply into Reagan's mind.

The details of foreign policy bored Reagan. He had absorbed a few basic ideas about the dangers of appeasement, the evils of communism, and the greatness of his own country, but analysis of substantive issues was not his forte. All of this caused me to remark, during what I thought was an off-the-record talk before a conference of historians at the Library of Congress: "When you talk to Reagan, you sometimes wonder why it occurred to anyone that he should be president, or even governor. But what you historians have to explain is how so unintellectual a man could have dominated California for eight years, and Washington already for nearly seven."

The media avidly pounced on the first part of my statement. Yet, for the historian, the second part is by far the more interesting. When all was said and done, a president with the shallowest academic background was to develop a foreign policy of extraordinary consistency and relevance. Reagan might well have had only a few basic ideas, but these also hap-pened to be the core foreign policy issues of his period, which demon-strates that a sense of direction and having the strength of one's convictions are the key ingredients of leadership. The question of who drafted Reagan's pronouncements on foreign policy—and no president drafts his own—is almost irrelevant. Folklore has it that Reagan was the tool of his speech-writers, but that is an illusion fostered by many a speech-writer. After all, Reagan had himself selected the people who crafted his speeches, and he delivered them with extraordinary convic-tion and persuasiveness. Any acquaintance with Reagan leaves little doubt that they expressed his actual views and, on some issues, such as the Strategic Defense Initiative, he was far ahead of his entourage.

In the American system of government, in which the president is the only nationally elected official, coherence in foreign policy emerges—if at all—from presidential pronouncements. These serve as the most effec-tive directive to the sprawling and self-willed bureaucracy and supply the criteria for public or Congressional debates. Reagan put forward a foreign policy doctrine of great coherence and considerable intellectual power. He possessed an extraordinary intuitive rapport with the wellsprings of

American motivation. At the same time, he understood the essential brittleness of the Soviet system, a perception which ran contrary to most expert opinion, even in his own conservative camp.

Reagan had an uncanny talent for uniting the American people. And he had an unusually pleasant and genuinely affable personality. Even the victims of his rhetoric found it difficult to take it personally. Though he savaged me during his failed bid for the presidential nomination in 1976, I found it impossible to hold a lasting resentment, despite the fact that, as National Security Adviser, I had been briefing him for years without any protest on his part about the very policies he was now assaulting. When it was all over, I remembered not the campaign rhetoric but the combination of common sense and epigrammatic goodwill with which Reagan conducted himself during the briefing sessions. During the Middle East War of 1973, I told him that we would replace Israeli losses in aircraft but were uncertain as to how to limit the Arab reaction. "Why don't you say that you will replace all the aircraft the Arabs claim they have shot down?" Reagan suggested—a proposal which would turn the wildly inflated Arab propaganda against its originators.

Reagan's bland veneer hid an extraordinarily complex character. He was both congenial and remote, full of good cheer but, in the end, aloof. The bonhomie was his way of establishing distance between himself and others. If he treated everyone with equal friendliness—and regaled them all with the same stories—no one would have a special claim on him. The repository of jokes that were recycled from conversation to conversation served as protection against being blindsided. Like many actors, Reagan was the quintessential loner—as charming as he was self-centered. An individual widely perceived to have been an intimate of his said to me once that Reagan was both the friendliest and the most distant man he had ever known.

Reagan's 1976 campaign rhetoric notwithstanding, there was no significant conceptual difference among the various assessments of the international environment by the Nixon, Ford, and Reagan Administrations. All three were determined to resist the Soviet geopolitical offensive and considered history to be on the side of the democracies. There was, however, an enormous difference in their tactics and in the way in which each of these administrations explained its policies to the American people.

Shocked by the domestic divisions of the Vietnam War, Nixon had believed that a prior demonstration of serious efforts on behalf of peace was the precondition for sustaining whatever confrontations might be necessary to prevent further Soviet expansion. Leading a country that was tired of retreat, Reagan justified resistance to Soviet expansionism by an insistently confrontational style. Like Woodrow Wilson, Reagan understood that the American people, having marched throughout their history to the drumbeat of exceptionalism, would find their ultimate inspiration in historic ideals, not in geopolitical analysis. In this sense, Nixon was to Reagan as Theodore Roosevelt had been to Woodrow Wilson. Like Roosevelt, Nixon had had a far better understanding of the workings of international relations; like Wilson, Reagan had a much surer grasp of the workings of the American soul.

Reagan's rhetoric about America's unique moral standing mirrored what almost every other president has said at one time or another in this century. What rendered Reagan's particular variant of American exceptionalism unique was his literal interpretation of it as a guide to the everyday conduct of foreign policy. Whereas Reagan's predecessors had invoked American principles as the underpinning of a particular initiative —say, the League of Nations or the Marshall Plan—Reagan mobilized them as weapons in the day-to-day struggle against communism, as in this speech before the American Legion on February 22, 1983:

> By wedding the timeless truths and values Americans have always cherished to the realities of today's world, we have forged the beginnings of a fundamentally new direction in American foreign policy—a policy based on the unashamed, unapologetic explaining of our own priceless free institutions. . . .[1]

Reagan rejected the "guilt complex" which he identified with the Carter Administration, and proudly defended America's record as "the greatest force for peace anywhere in the world today."[2] In his very first press conference, he labeled the Soviet Union an outlaw empire prepared "to commit any crime, to lie, to cheat," in order to achieve its goals.[3] It would be the precursor of his 1983 description of the Soviet Union as the "evil empire," a direct moral challenge from which all his predecessors would have recoiled. Reagan overrode conventional diplomatic wisdom, and he oversimplified America's virtues in pursuit of a self-appointed mission to convince the American people that the East-West ideological conflict mattered and that some international struggles are about winners and losers, not about staying power or diplomacy.

The rhetoric of Reagan's first term marked the formal end of the period of detente. America's goal was no longer a relaxation of tensions but crusade and conversion. Reagan had been elected on the promise of militant anticommunism, and he was true to his word. In the fortunate position of dealing with a Soviet Union in precipitate decline, he rejected Nixon's emphasis on national interest as being too relativistic and disdained Carter's diffidence as being too defeatist. Instead, Reagan presented an apocalyptic vision of the conflict made more bearable by the historical inevitability of the outcome. In a speech at Westminster Hall in London in June 1982, he described his perception of the Soviet Union:

> In an ironic sense Karl Marx was right. We are witnessing today a great revolutionary crisis, a crisis where the demands of the economic order are conflicting directly with those of the political order. But the crisis is happening not in the free, non-Marxist West, but in the home of Marxism-Leninism, the Soviet Union. . . .
>
> Overcentralized, with little or no incentives, year after year the Soviet system pours its best resources into the making of instruments of destruction. The constant shrinkage of economic growth combined with the growth of military production is putting a heavy strain on the Soviet people.
>
> What we see here is a political structure that no longer corresponds to its economic base, a society where productive forces are hampered by political ones.[4]

When Nixon and I had said much the same thing ten years earlier, it had intensified the conservative critique of detente. Conservatives distrusted the invocation of historical evolution in the service of detente because they feared that negotiations with the communists might lead to moral disarmament. But they found the concept of inevitable victory appealing as a tool of confrontation.

Reagan believed that relations with the Soviet Union would improve if he could make it share his fear of nuclear Armageddon. He was determined to bring home to the Kremlin the risks of continuing expansionism. A decade earlier, his rhetoric would have driven domestic civil disobedience out of control and might have led to confrontation with a still confident Soviet Union; a decade later, it would have appeared antiquated. In the conditions of the 1980s, it laid the foundation for a period of unprecedented East-West dialogue.

Inevitably, Reagan's rhetoric came under sharp attack from believers in the established orthodoxies. "TRB," in *The New Republic* of April 11, 1983, was outraged at Reagan's description of the Soviet Union as an "evil empire," calling it "primitive prose and apocalyptic symbolism";[5] "primitive" was also the reaction of Anthony Lewis in *The New York Times* of March 10, 1983.[6] In 1981, the distinguished Harvard Professor Stanley Hoffmann denounced Reagan's militant style as "machismo," "neo-nationalism," and a form of "fundamentalist reaction" that had little to offer to a complex world in which American economic weaknesses were said to be no less serious than those of the Soviet Union.[7]

As it turned out, Reagan's rhetoric did not thwart major negotiations, as the critics had predicted. On the contrary, during Reagan's second term, an East-West dialogue of a scope and intensity not seen since the Nixon period of detente took place. This time, however, the negotiations enjoyed the support of public opinion and were applauded by the conservatives.

If Reagan's approach to the ideological conflict was a simplified version of Wilsonianism, his concept of the resolution of that struggle was equally rooted in American utopianism. Though framing the issue as a struggle between good and evil, Reagan was far from arguing that the conflict had to be fought to the finish. Rather—in typical American fashion—he was convinced that communist intransigence was based more on ignorance than on congenital ill will, more on misunderstanding than on purposeful hostility. Hence, in Reagan's view, the conflict was likely to end with the conversion of the adversary. In 1981, while recuperating from an attempt on his life, Reagan sent a handwritten letter to Leonid Brezhnev that tried to dispel Soviet suspicions of the United States—as if seventy-five years of communist ideology could be removed by a personal appeal. It was, almost verbatim, the same assurance which Truman had extended to Stalin at the end of World War II (see chapter 17).

> It is often implied . . . that we have imperialistic designs, and thus constitute a threat to your own security and that of the newly emerging nations. There not only is no evidence to support such a charge, there is solid evidence that the United States, when it could have dominated the world with no risk to itself, made no effort whatsoever to do so. . . .
> May I say, there is absolutely no substance to charges that the United States is guilty of imperialism or attempts to impose its will on other countries, by use of force. . . .
> Mr. President, should we not be concerned with eliminating the obstacles which prevent our people, those you and I represent, from achieving their most cherished goals?[8]

How was one to reconcile the conciliatory tone of Reagan's letter and the author's assumption that he possessed some special credibility with the recipient with Reagan's assertion, made only a few weeks earlier, that Soviet leaders were capable of any crime? Reagan felt no need to explain this apparent inconsistency, perhaps because he deeply believed in *both* propositions—the evil of Soviet conduct as well as the susceptibility of Soviet leaders to ideological conversion.

Thus, following Brezhnev's death in November 1982, Reagan sent a handwritten note—on July 11, 1983—to Brezhnev's successor, Yuri Andropov, once again disclaiming any aggressive designs.[9] When Andropov soon died as well and the infirm and aged Konstantin Chernenko became his successor (an obvious interim appointment), Reagan confided to his diary, which was clearly intended for publication:

> I have a gut feeling I'd like to talk to him about our problems man to man and see if I could convince him there would be a material benefit to the Soviets if they'd join the family of nations, etc.[10]

Six months later, on September 28, 1984, Gromyko paid his first visit to the White House during the Reagan Administration. Again, Reagan had recourse to his diary, to the effect that his principal goal was to remove the Soviet leaders' suspicions of the United States:

> I have a feeling we'll get nowhere with arms reductions while they are as suspicious of our motives as we are of theirs. I believe we need a meeting to see if we can't make them understand we have no designs on them but think they have designs on us.[11]

If Soviet conduct had been caused by suspicion of the United States for two generations, Reagan might well have assumed that the feeling was ingrained in the Soviet system and history. The fervent hope—especially in so vocal an anticommunist—that the Soviets' wariness could be removed in a single conversation with their Foreign Minister (who moreover represented the quintessence of communist rule) can only be explained by the irrepressible American conviction that understanding between peoples is normal, that tension is an aberration, and that trust can be generated by the strenuous demonstration of goodwill.

So it happened that Reagan, the scourge of communism, found nothing strange about describing the night before his first meeting with Gorbachev in 1985 and his feelings of nervous anticipation in terms of the hope that the meeting would settle the conflicts of two generations—an attitude closer to that of Jimmy Carter than of Richard Nixon:

> Starting with Brezhnev, I'd dreamed of personally going one-on-one with a Soviet leader because I thought we might be able to accomplish things our countries' diplomats couldn't do because they didn't have

the authority. Putting that another way, I felt that if you got the top people negotiating and talking at a summit and then the two of you came out arm in arm saying, "We've agreed to this," the bureaucrats wouldn't be able to louse up the agreement. Until Gorbachev, I never got an opportunity to try out my idea. Now I had my chance.[12]

Despite his rhetoric about ideological confrontation and the reality of conducting a geopolitical conflict, Reagan did not in his own heart believe in structural or geopolitical causes of tension. He and his associates considered concern with the balance of power too confining and too pessimistic. They strove not for gradualism, but for a final outcome. This faith gave the Reagan team an extraordinary tactical flexibility.

A biographer has written about one of Reagan's "dreams," which I too have heard him recount:

One of Ronald Reagan's fantasies as president was that he would take Mikhail Gorbachev on a tour of the United States so the Soviet leader could see how ordinary Americans lived. Reagan often talked about it. He imagined that he and Gorbachev would fly by helicopter over a working-class community, viewing a factory and its parking lot filled with cars and then circling over the pleasant neighborhood where the factory workers lived in homes "with lawns and backyards, perhaps with a second car or a boat in the driveway, not the concrete rabbit warrens I'd seen in Moscow." The helicopter would descend, and Reagan would invite Gorbachev to knock on doors and ask the residents "what they think of our system." The workers would tell him how wonderful it was to live in America.[13]

Reagan clearly believed that he had a duty to speed Gorbachev's, or any other Soviet leader's, inevitable recognition that communist philosophy was in error, and that once Soviet misconceptions about the true nature of America had been cleared up, an era of conciliation would rapidly follow. In this sense, and despite all of his ideological fervor, Reagan's views on the essence of international conflict remained strictly American-utopian. Since he did not believe in irreconcilable national interests, he could discern no insoluble conflicts between nations. Once Soviet leaders had changed their ideological views, the world would be spared the sorts of disputes which had characterized classical diplomacy. And he saw no intermediate stages between permanent conflict and lasting reconciliation.

Nevertheless, however optimistic, even "liberal," Reagan's views were of the ultimate outcome, he meant to reach his goal by means of relent-

771

less confrontation. According to his way of thinking, dedication to ending the Cold War did not require creating a "favorable" atmosphere or granting the unilateral gestures which were so beloved by the advocates of permanent negotiations. Sufficiently American to view confrontation and conciliation as successive stages of policy, Reagan was the first postwar president to take the offensive both ideologically and geostrategically.

The Soviet Union had not been obliged to deal with such a phenomenon since the tenure of John Foster Dulles—and Dulles had not been president, nor had he ever seriously attempted to implement his "liberation" policy. By contrast, Reagan and his associates took their professions literally. From the time of Reagan's inauguration, they pursued two objectives simultaneously: to combat Soviet geopolitical pressure until the process of expansionism had been first arrested and then reversed; and, second, to launch a rearmament program designed to stop dead in its tracks the Soviet quest for strategic superiority, and to turn it into a strategic liability.

The ideological vehicle for this reversal of roles was the issue of human rights, which Reagan and his advisers invoked to try to undermine the Soviet system. To be sure, his immediate predecessors had also affirmed the importance of human rights. Nixon had done so on the issue of emigration from the Soviet Union. Ford had taken the biggest step forward with Basket III of the Helsinki Accords (see chapter 29). Carter made human rights the centerpiece of his foreign policy and promoted it so intensely vis-à-vis America's allies that his call for righteousness occasionally threatened their domestic cohesion. Reagan and his advisers went a step further by treating human rights as a tool for overthrowing communism and democratizing the Soviet Union, hence as the key to a peaceful world—as Reagan pointed out in his State of the Union Address on January 25, 1984: "Governments which rest upon the consent of the governed do not wage war on their neighbors."[14] At Westminster in 1982, Reagan, hailing the tide of democracy around the world, called on the free nations

> . . . to foster the infrastructure of democracy, the system of a free press, unions, political parties, universities, which allows a people to choose their own way, to develop their own culture, to reconcile their own differences through peaceful means.[15]

The appeal to improve democracy at home was a prelude to a classically Wilsonian theme: "If the rest of this century is to witness the gradual growth of freedom and democratic ideals, we must take actions to assist the campaign for democracy."[16]

In fact, Reagan took Wilsonianism to its ultimate conclusion. America would not wait passively for free institutions to evolve, nor would it confine itself to resisting direct threats to its security. Instead, it would actively promote democracy, rewarding those countries which fulfilled its ideals and punishing those which fell short—even if they presented no other visible challenge or threat to America. The Reagan team thus turned the claims of the early Bolsheviks upside down: democratic values, not those of the Communist Manifesto, would be the wave of the future. And the Reagan team was consistent: it pressed both the conservative Pinochet regime in Chile and the authoritarian Marcos regime in the Philippines for reform; the former was induced to agree to a referendum and free elections, which replaced it; the latter was overthrown with American cooperation.

At the same time, the crusade for democracy begged fundamental questions which are of particular relevance to the post–Cold War period. How was one to reconcile this crusade with the long-held American doctrine of nonintervention in the domestic affairs of other states? To what extent should other objectives such as national security be subordinate to it? What price would America be willing to pay to promote its values? How was it to avoid both overextension and abdication? The post–Cold War world, which make the early Reagan years seem like distant history, will have to answer these questions.

Yet when Reagan took office, such ambiguities did not worry him as much as devising a strategy to interrupt the relentless Soviet advance of the previous years. The goal of Reagan's geostrategic offensive was to bring home to the Soviets that they had overreached. Rejecting the Brezhnev Doctrine on the irreversibility of communist gains, Reagan's strategy expressed the conviction that communism could be defeated, not merely contained. Reagan brought about the repeal of the Clark Amendment, which had prevented American aid to anticommunist forces in Angola, greatly stepped up support for the Afghan anti-Soviet guerrillas, developed a major program to resist communist guerrillas in Central America, and even extended humanitarian aid to Cambodia. It was a remarkable tribute to American cohesion that, a little more than five years after the debacle in Indochina, a determined president should again be contesting Soviet expansion around the world, this time successfully.

Most of the Soviet gains of the 1970s were reversed—though several of these retreats did not take place until the Bush Administration. The Vietnamese occupation of Cambodia was ended in 1990, elections were held in 1993, and refugees prepared to return home; Cuban troops withdrew from Angola by 1991; the communist-backed government in Ethiopia collapsed in 1991; in 1990, the Sandinistas in Nicaragua were brought to accept free elections, a risk no governing Communist Party had ever before been prepared to take; perhaps most important, Soviet armies withdrew from Afghanistan in 1989. All of these developments contributed to a decline in communist ideological élan and geopolitical conviction. Observing the collapse of Soviet influence in the so-called Third World, Soviet reformers were soon citing Brezhnev's costly and futile adventures as proof of the bankruptcy of the communist system, whose undemocratic style of decision-making they believed to be in urgent need of revision.[17]

The Reagan Administration achieved these successes by putting into practice what became known as the Reagan Doctrine: that the United States would help anticommunist counterinsurgencies wrest their respective countries out of the Soviet sphere of influence. This meant arming the Afghan mujahideen in their struggle with the Russians, supporting the contras in Nicaragua, and aiding anticommunist forces in Ethiopia and Angola. Through the 1960s and 1970s, the Soviets had abetted communist insurgencies against governments that were friendly toward the United States. Now, in the 1980s, America was giving the Soviets a taste of their own medicine. Secretary of State George Shultz explained the concept at a February 1985 speech in San Francisco:

> For many years we saw our adversaries act without restraint to back insurgencies around the world to spread communist dictatorships . . . any victory of communism was held to be irreversible. . . . Today, however, the Soviet empire is weakening under the strain of its own internal problems and external entanglements. . . . The forces of democracy around the world merit our standing with them. To abandon them would be a shameful betrayal—a betrayal not only of brave men and women but of our highest ideals.[18]

The high-flying Wilsonian language in support of freedom and democracy globally was leavened by an almost Machiavellian realism. America did not go "abroad in search of monsters to destroy," in John Quincy Adams' memorable phrase; rather, the Reagan Doctrine amounted to a strategy for helping the enemy of one's enemy—of which Richelieu would have heartily approved. The Reagan Administration dispensed aid not only to genuine democrats (as in Poland), but also to Islamic fundamentalists (in cahoots with the Iranians) in Afghanistan, to rightists in Central America, and to tribal warlords in Africa. The United States had no more in common with the mujahideen than Richelieu had had with the Sultan of the

Ottoman Empire. Yet they shared a common enemy, and in the world of national interest, that made them allies. The results helped to speed the collapse of communism but left America face-to-face with the tormenting question it has tried to avoid through most of its history, which happens to be the statesman's central dilemma: what ends justify which means?

Reagan's most fundamental challenge to the Soviet Union proved to be his military buildup. In all his electoral campaigns, Reagan had deplored the inadequacy of the American defense effort, and had warned of approaching Soviet superiority. Today we know that these fears reflected an oversimplification of the nature of military superiority in the Nuclear Age. But, whatever the accuracy of Reagan's perception of the Soviet military threat, it managed to rally his conservative constituency far more than Nixon's evocations of the geopolitical perils.

Prior to the Reagan Administration, a standard argument of the radical critique of American Cold War policy had been that arms buildups were pointless because the Soviets would always, and at every level, match the American effort. That turned out to be even more inaccurate than the perception of imminent Soviet superiority. The scale and pace of the American buildup under Reagan reinforced all the doubts already in the minds of the Soviet leadership as a result of debacles in Afghanistan and Africa, about whether they could afford the arms race economically and—even more important—whether they could sustain it technologically.

Reagan restored weapons systems which had been abandoned by the Carter Administration, such as the B-1 bomber, and began deployment of the MX missile, the first new American land-based intercontinental missile in a decade. The two strategic decisions which contributed most to ending the Cold War were NATO's deployment of American intermediate-range missiles in Europe and the American commitment to the Strategic Defense Initiative (SDI).

The NATO decision to deploy intermediate-range missiles (of 1,500-mile range) in Europe dated from the Carter Administration. Its purpose was to assuage West German Chancellor Helmut Schmidt's outrage at the unilateral American cancellation of the so-called neutron bomb—designed to make nuclear war less destructive—which Schmidt had supported over the opposition of his own Social Democratic Party. The intermediate-range weapons (partly ballistic missiles, partly ground-launched cruise missiles) were in fact designed for a different problem—to counter the large number of new Soviet missiles (the SS-20s) that were capable of reaching all European targets from deep within Soviet territory.

In its essence, the argument in favor of the intermediate-range weapons was political, not strategic, and it stemmed from the same concerns which twenty years earlier had generated allied debates about strategy; this time, however, America tried to allay Europe's fears. Bluntly put, once again the issue was whether Western Europe could count on the United States' using its nuclear weapons to repel a Soviet attack that was confined to Europe. Had America's European allies truly believed in America's willingness to resort to nuclear retaliation from the continental United States or from weapons based at sea, the new missiles on European soil would have been unnecessary. But America's resolve to do that was precisely what European leaders continued to doubt. For their part, American leaders had their own reasons for responding to European anxieties. It was part of the flexible response strategy to bring about options between all-out war focused on America and acceding to Soviet nuclear blackmail.

There was, of course, a more sophisticated explanation than a subliminal mutual distrust between the two sides of the Atlantic partnership. And that was that the new weapons organically linked the strategic defense of Europe with that of the United States. The argument went that the Soviet Union would not attack with conventional forces without first seeking to destroy the intermediate-range missiles in Europe which, because of their proximity and accuracy, could knock out Soviet command centers and ease the way for a devastating first strike by American strategic forces. On the other hand, attacking American intermediate-range missiles while leaving America's retaliatory force intact would be too risky as well. Enough intermediate-range missiles might survive to do serious damage, enabling the undamaged American retaliatory force to emerge as the arbiter of events. Thus the intermediate-range missiles closed a gap in the spectrum of deterrence. In the technical jargon of the times, the defenses of Europe and of the United States would be thereby "coupled": the Soviet Union would not be able to attack either area without incurring an unacceptable risk of a general nuclear war.

Technical "coupling" responded as well to a growing fear of German neutralism in the rest of Europe, especially in France. After the overthrow of Schmidt in 1982, the German Social Democratic Party seemed to be returning to nationalism and neutralism—to the point that, in the 1986 elections, one of its leaders, Oscar LaFontaine, urged that Germany leave the integrated NATO command. Massive demonstrations against missile deployment rocked the Federal Republic.

Sensing an opportunity to weaken Germany's ties to NATO, Brezhnev and his successor, Andropov, made opposition to the deployment of intermediate-range missiles the linchpin of Soviet foreign policy. In early

1983, Gromyko visited Bonn to warn that the Soviets would walk out of the Geneva arms control talks the day the Pershings arrived in West Germany, a threat certain to inflame the German protesters. When Kohl visited the Kremlin in July 1983, Andropov warned the German Chancellor that, if he accepted the Pershing IIs,

> [t]he military threat for West Germany will grow manifold. Relations between our two countries will be bound to suffer certain complications as well. As for the Germans in the Federal Republic of Germany and the German Democratic Republic, they would have, as someone [*Pravda*] recently put it, to look at one another through thick palisades of missiles.[19]

Moscow's propaganda machinery unleashed a major campaign in every European country. Mass demonstrations by various peace groups urged that disarmament rather than the new missile deployment be given priority and that a nuclear freeze be instituted immediately.

Whenever Germany seemed tempted by neutralism, which, in the French mind, spelled nationalism, French presidents attempted to provide Bonn with a European or Atlantic alternative. In the 1960s, de Gaulle had been a staunch defender of the German point of view on Berlin. In 1983, Mitterrand emerged unexpectedly as the chief European supporter of the American plan to deploy intermediate-range missiles. Mitterrand campaigned for the missiles in Germany. "Anyone gambling on uncoupling the European continent from the American would, in our view, jeopardize the balance of forces and therefore the maintenance of peace," Mitterrand told the German Bundestag.[20] Clearly, for the French President, France's national interest in seeing the intermediate-range missiles in Germany transcended any ideological affinity his French Socialists might feel for their German Social Democratic brethren.

Reagan came up with a ploy of his own to blunt the Soviet diplomatic offensive, offering to trade American intermediate-range missiles for the Soviet SS-20s.[21] Since the SS-20s were more of a pretext for the American deployment than its cause, the proposal raised grave questions about "decoupling" the defense of Europe from that of the United States. However, while the arguments for "coupling" were esoteric, the proposal to abolish an entire category of weapons was easy to understand. And since the Soviets overestimated their bargaining position and refused to discuss any part of Reagan's offer, the so-called zero option made it easier for European governments to go through with the missile deployment. It was a stunning victory for Reagan and for German Chancellor Helmut Kohl, who had staunchly stood by the American plan. And it showed that the infirm Soviet leadership was losing its capacity to intimidate Western Europe.

The deployment of intermediate-range missiles improved deterrent strategy; but when, on March 23, 1983, Reagan announced his intention to develop a strategic defense against Soviet missiles, he was threatening a strategic breakthrough:

> ... I call upon the scientific community in our country, those who gave us nuclear weapons, to turn their great talents now to the cause of mankind and world peace: to give us the means of rendering these nuclear weapons impotent and obsolete.[22]

Those last words, "impotent and obsolete," must have had a chilling ring in the Kremlin. The Soviet nuclear arsenal was the keystone of the Soviet Union's entire superpower status. For the twenty years of Brezhnev's tenure, achieving strategic parity with the United States had been the principal Soviet objective. Now, with a single technological stroke, Reagan was proposing to erase everything that the Soviet Union had propelled itself into bankruptcy trying to accomplish.

If Reagan's claim of a 100 percent effective defense came even close to realization, *American* strategic superiority would become a reality. An American first strike might then succeed because the defensive system might be able to contain the relatively small and disorganized Soviet missile force which had survived. At a minimum, Reagan's proclamation of SDI put the Soviet leadership on notice that the arms race they had started so recklessly in the 1960s would either consume their resources or lead to an American strategic breakthrough.

Reagan's SDI proposal touched a sore spot in the debate about American defense policy. Before the Nuclear Age, it would have been considered preposterous to base a country's defense on the vulnerability of its population. Afterward, the strategic debate assumed a novel character, in part because so much of it was conducted by an entirely new group of participants. Before the Nuclear Age, military strategy was thrashed out within general staffs or at military staff colleges with a few outside kibitzers, mostly military historians like B. H. Liddell Hart. The vast destructiveness of nuclear weapons made traditional military expertise less relevant; anybody who understood the new technology could play, and the players were, in the main, scientists, joined by a few other academicians.

Appalled by the destructiveness they had unleashed, the majority of technical experts convinced themselves that politicians were sufficiently irresponsible that, if they perceived even a minimal chance of making nuclear war tolerable, they might be tempted to unleash it. Therefore, it was the moral duty of scientists to advocate strategies so catastrophic as to scare even the most reckless policymaker. The paradox of that approach was that those who, quite rightly, considered themselves as most concerned about the future of civilization ended up advocating a nihilistic military strategy of civilian extermination.

Defense scientists had come to this view only gradually. During the first decade of the Nuclear Age, many of them had still been urging defense against an as yet largely nonexistent Soviet air threat. Deeply committed to preventing nuclear war, the scientists no doubt had in the back of their minds the utility of diverting resources from offensive weapons and thereby reducing the incentives for an American pre-emptive attack. After the emergence of an ever-growing Soviet nuclear capability with enough power to devastate the United States, the scientific community's prevailing advice paradoxically changed. Henceforth, the majority passionately advocated the doctrine of Mutual Assured Destruction, which based deterrence on the assumption that, given a high enough level of expected civilian casualties, neither side would start a nuclear war.

The theory of Mutual Assured Destruction marked a deliberate flight from rationality in strategic theory by basing defense on the threat of suicide. In practice, it conferred a vast advantage, certainly psychologically, on the side capable of posing challenges from which its adversary could only extricate itself by resorting to general nuclear war. In the 1960s and 1970s, this side had clearly been the Soviet Union, whose conventional military forces were generally assumed to be far superior to those of the West. At the same time, such a strategy guaranteed that nuclear war would destroy civilization itself. Thus, SDI found adherents especially among those who sought to avoid the intolerable choice between surrender and Armageddon.

The majority of the media and defense intellectuals, however, stuck to the generally accepted wisdom and opposed SDI. The best and fairest compendium of the various reservations was found in a book edited by Harold Brown, who had served as Secretary of Defense in the Carter Administration and as Secretary of the Air Force in the Johnson Administration.[23] Brown favored a research effort but argued that SDI was not yet practical.[24] One of his collaborators, Richard Betts, took the position that, at any level of deployment, the Soviets would find it possible to saturate the defense system, and at a lower cost than that of the American deployment.[25] Johns Hopkins Professor George Liska took the opposite tack. He assumed that SDI might work but that, once protected, America would

779

lack incentive to defend its European allies.[26] Robert Osgood combined all of the above criticism with a concern about undermining the 1972 ABM Treaty and complicating new arms control efforts.[27] Representing the view of many Western allies, British Foreign Secretary Geoffrey Howe warned against trying to create a "Maginot Line in space:"

> Many years of deployment may be involved. Many years of insecurity and instability cannot be our objective. All the Allies must continue at every stage to share the same sense that the security of NATO territory is indivisible. Otherwise the twin pillars of the Alliance might begin to fall apart.[28]

It was a novel and, in the long run, demoralizing concept that the price of maintaining an alliance should be keeping the civilian population of each ally totally vulnerable. It was also fallacious. For surely America's willingness to risk nuclear war on behalf of its European allies would increase in nearly direct proportion to America's capacity to protect its civilian population.

The experts had all the technical arguments on their side, but Reagan had got hold of an elemental political truth: in a world of nuclear weapons, leaders who make no effort to protect their peoples against accident, mad opponents, nuclear proliferation, and a whole host of other foreseeable dangers, invite the opprobrium of posterity if disaster ever does occur. That it was not possible at the beginning of a complicated research program to demonstrate SDI's maximum effectiveness was inherent in the complexity of the problem; no weapon would ever have been developed if it first had had to submit to so perfectionist a criterion.

The fashionable argument—that any defense could be defeated by being saturated—ignored the fact that saturation does not work in a straight line. Up to a certain level, SDI might work almost as Reagan described it; after that, it would progressively decline in effectiveness. But if the price of launching a nuclear attack were high enough, deterrence would increase, especially since the attacker could not know which warheads would get through or to what targets. Finally, a defense capable of intercepting a substantial number of Soviet missiles would be even more effective against the much smaller attacks of new nuclear countries.

Reagan was impervious to much of the technical criticism because he had not advocated SDI in strategic terms in the first place. Instead, he had presented it in terms of the "liberal" cause of bringing about the abolition of nuclear war. The postwar president most committed to building up America's military strength, including its nuclear capacity, stood at the same time for a pacifist vision of a world from which all nuclear weapons were banished. Reagan's overused epigram that "a nuclear war can never be won and must never be fought"[29] was indistinguishable from the stated objectives of his radical critics. Yet, just as in the duality of his approach to dealing with the Soviet Union, Reagan was deadly serious about both his arms buildup and his pacifism. Reagan described his attitude toward nuclear weapons in his memoirs:

> *No one* could "win" a nuclear war. Yet as long as nuclear weapons were in existence, there would always be risks they would be used, and once the first nuclear weapon was unleashed, who knew where it would end?
> My dream, then, became a world free of nuclear weapons. . . .[30]

Reagan's personal abhorrence of nuclear war was reinforced by a highly literal belief in the biblical prophecy of Armageddon. I heard him expound these views along lines nearly identical to what his biographer has described:

> Speaking as if he were describing a movie scene, he related a terrifying episode in the Armageddon story where an invading army from the Orient, 200-million strong, is destroyed by a plague. Reagan believes that the "plague" was a prophecy of nuclear war, where "the eyes are burned from the head and the hair falls from the body and so forth." He believes this passage specifically foretold Hiroshima.[31]

No member of the Peace Movement could have condemned the use of nuclear weapons more eloquently than Ronald Reagan. On May 16, 1983, he coupled an announcement that he was deploying the MX intercontinental missiles with the expression of his fervent hope that, somewhere along the line, the process would be reversed and that all nuclear weapons would be eliminated:

> I can't believe that this world can go on beyond our generation and on down to succeeding generations with this kind of weapon on both sides poised at each other without someday some fool or some maniac or some accident triggering the kind of war that is the end of the line for all of us.[32]

When Reagan put forward SDI, it was in language as passionate as it was unorthodox, even after it had been filtered through the bureaucratic "clearing process" to which all presidents are subject. In the event that negotiations on arms control went on too long, America would unilaterally end the nuclear peril by building SDI. American science, Reagan believed, would render nuclear weapons obsolete.[33]

Soviet leaders were not impressed by Reagan's moral appeals, but they were obliged to take seriously America's technological potential and the strategic impact of even an imperfect defense. As had happened with Nixon's ABM proposals fourteen years earlier, the Soviet reaction was the opposite of what the arms control advocates had predicted; SDI served to unlock the door to arms control. The Soviets returned to the arms control talks they had broken off over the intermediate-range-missile issue.

Critics alleged that Reagan was being cynical and that his sweeping vista of the elimination of all nuclear weapons was a cover for his efforts to spur the arms race. Reagan, however, was anything but cynical, giving expression to the optimistic faith of all Americans that that which is necessary is also attainable. Indeed, all his most eloquent statements on abolishing nuclear weapons were uttered extemporaneously.

Thus came about the paradox that the president who did so much to modernize America's strategic arsenal also contributed in a major way to delegitimizing it. Adversaries or allies who took literally what Reagan was saying publicly about nuclear weapons and privately about the imminence of Armageddon could only conclude that they were dealing with a president who was extremely unlikely to resort to the very weapons around which American defense had been built.

How often could a president repeat his standard line that "nuclear war must never be fought" before the credibility of the nuclear threat became eroded? How many reductions of nuclear weapons could be undertaken before the strategy of flexible response became technically unfeasible? Fortunately, the Soviets had by this time grown too weak to test this potential vulnerability, and America's worried allies were swept along by the accelerating decline of the Soviet Union.

That Reagan was anything but cynical became evident whenever he thought he saw an opportunity to implement his dream of a non-nuclear world. Convinced that the abolition of nuclear war was objectively of such overriding importance that all reasonable persons would agree with him, Reagan was quite prepared to proceed bilaterally with the Soviets on the most fundamental matters without consulting allies whose national interests might be equally involved. This happened most dramatically at Reagan's 1986 summit meeting with Gorbachev at Reykjavik. In a tumultuous and emotional roller-coaster ride lasting forty-eight hours, Reagan and Gorbachev agreed in principle to reduce all strategic forces by 50 percent within five years, and to destroy all ballistic missiles within ten years. At one point, Reagan came close to accepting a Soviet offer to abolish nuclear weapons altogether.

In this way, Reykjavik approached the Soviet-American condominium which allies and neutrals alike had feared for so long. If the other nuclear powers refused to go along with the Soviet-American agreement, they would suffer public opprobrium, superpower pressure, or isolation; if they agreed, Great Britain, France, and China would in effect have been obliged by the United States and the Soviet Union to abandon their independent nuclear deterrent, something the incumbent Thatcher and Mitterrand governments and China's leaders were not even remotely prepared to do.

The Reykjavik deal failed at the last moment for two reasons. At that still-early stage of his rule, Gorbachev simply overplayed his hand. He tried to link abolishing strategic missiles to a ban on SDI testing for a ten-year period but misjudged his interlocutor as well as his bargaining position. A wise tactic for Gorbachev would have been to propose publishing what had been agreed—namely the abolition of missile forces—and to refer the issue of SDI testing to the arms control negotiators in Geneva. This would have frozen what had already been agreed, and would have surely produced a major crisis, both in the Atlantic Alliance and in Sino-American relations. By pressing for more, Gorbachev came up against a promise Reagan had made before the summit—not to use SDI as a bargaining chip. When Gorbachev persisted, Reagan responded in a way no foreign policy professional would have advised: he simply got up and left the room. Years later, when I asked a senior Gorbachev adviser who had been present at Reykjavik why the Soviets had not settled for what the United States had already accepted, he replied: "We had thought of everything except that Reagan might leave the room."

Shortly afterward, George Shultz gave a thoughtful speech describing why Reagan's vision of eliminating nuclear weapons was actually to the West's advantage.[34] But the language of his speech, artfully phrased in support of a "less nuclear world," showed that the State Department—painfully conscious of allied concerns—had not yet signed on to Reagan's vision of the total abolition of nuclear weapons.

After Reykjavik, the Reagan Administration pursued that part of the Reykjavik agenda that was immediately realizable: the 50 percent reduction in strategic forces, which had been envisioned as the first stage of an overall agreement banning all missiles. Agreements were reached to destroy American and Soviet intermediate- and medium-range ballistic missiles in Europe. Because this agreement did not affect the nuclear forces of Great Britain and France, the interallied disputes of twenty-five years

earlier did not break out again. By the same token, the process of denuclearizing Germany was started, and, therefore, its potential decoupling
from the Atlantic Alliance. Germany would draw the full benefit from its
incipient denuclearization only by adopting a policy of no first use of
nuclear weapons—quite inconsistent with NATO strategy and American
deployments. Had the Cold War continued, a more national, less alliance-
oriented foreign policy in the Federal Republic might well have resulted,
which was why British Prime Minister Thatcher was so worried about the
emerging trend in arms control negotiations.

Reagan had transformed what had been a marathon race into a sprint.
His confrontational style linked to a risk-taking diplomacy would probably have worked at the beginning of the Cold War, before the two spheres
of interest had been consolidated, and immediately after the death of
Stalin. Such a diplomacy was essentially what Churchill had proposed
when he returned to office in 1951. Once the division of Europe was
frozen and so long as the Soviet Union still felt confident, the attempt to
force a settlement would have almost certainly produced a major clash
and strained the Atlantic Alliance, the majority of whose members wanted
no unnecessary tension. In the 1980s, Soviet stagnation made a forward
strategy appropriate again. Did Reagan recognize the degree of disintegration of Soviet willpower, or did self-will and opportunity coincide?

In the end, it made no difference whether Reagan was acting on instinct
or on analysis. The Cold War did not continue, at least in part because of
the pressures the Reagan Administration had exerted on the Soviet system. By the end of Reagan's presidency, the East-West agenda had returned to the pattern of the detente period. Once again, arms control was
the centerpiece of East-West negotiations, though with more emphasis on
arms reduction and a greater willingness to eliminate entire categories of
weapons. In the regional conflicts, the Soviet Union was now on the
defensive and had lost much of its ability to instigate trouble. With security concerns declining, nationalism grew on both sides of the Atlantic
even as allied unity continued to be proclaimed. America relied more
and more on weapons stationed on its own territory or at sea, while
Europe multiplied its political options toward the East. In the end, these
negative trends were superseded by the collapse of communism.

What had changed most radically was the way East-West policy was
being presented to the American public. Reagan had instinctively sand-
wiched tough Cold War geostrategic policies between an ideological crusade and a utopian evocation of peace that appealed simultaneously to
the two major strands of American thought on international affairs—the
missionary and the isolationist, the theological and the psychiatric.

In practice, Reagan was closer to classical patterns of American thinking than Nixon had been. Nixon would not have used the phrase "evil empire" to describe the Soviet Union, but he also would not have offered to give up all nuclear weapons, or expected to end the Cold War in one grand personal reconciliation with Soviet leaders at a single summit. Reagan's ideology shielded him whenever he made semi-pacifist pronouncements for which a liberal president would have been vilified. And his commitment to improving East-West relations, especially in his second term, together with his successes took the edge off his belligerent rhetoric. Whether Reagan could have sustained this tightrope act indefinitely had the Soviet Union remained a major competitor is doubtful. But Reagan's second term coincided with the beginning of the disintegration of the communist system—a process hastened by his Administration's policies.

Mikhail Gorbachev, the seventh in a direct line from Lenin, had been raised in a Soviet Union that enjoyed unprecedented power and prestige. Yet he was destined to preside over the demise of the empire built with so much blood and treasure. When Gorbachev assumed office in 1985, he was the leader of a nuclear superpower which was in a state of economic and social decay. When he was toppled from power in 1991, the Soviet army had thrown its support behind his rival, Boris Yeltsin, the Communist Party had been declared illegal, and the empire which had been so bloodily assembled by every Russian ruler since Peter the Great had disintegrated.

This collapse would have seemed fantastic in March 1985, when Gorbachev was anointed General Secretary. As had been the case with all of his predecessors, Gorbachev inspired both fear and hope. Fear, as the leader of a superpower all the more ominous for its enigmatic style of government; hope that the new General Secretary might usher in the long-awaited turn to peace. Gorbachev's every word was analyzed for a sign of an easing of the tension; emotionally, the democracies were amply ready to discover in Gorbachev the dawn of a new era, just as they had been with all of his predecessors after Stalin.

For once, the democracies' faith turned out not to be so much wishful thinking. Gorbachev was of a different generation than the Soviet leaders whose spirit had been broken by Stalin. He lacked the heavy-handedness of all previous products of the *nomenklatura*. Highly intelligent and suave, he was like the somewhat abstract figures from the nineteenth-century Russian novels—both cosmopolitan and provincial, intelligent yet somehow unfocused; perceptive while missing his central dilemma.

The outside world heaved a nearly audible sigh of relief. Here at last seemed to be the long-awaited and heretofore utterly elusive moment of the Soviets' ideological transformation. Until well into 1991, Gorbachev was considered in Washington to be an indispensable partner in the building of a new world order—to such an extent that President Bush chose the Ukrainian Parliament as the unlikely venue for a forum in which to extol the Soviet leader's qualities and the importance of keeping the Soviet Union together. Keeping Gorbachev in office turned into a principal objective of Western policymakers, who were convinced that any other figure would be far more difficult to deal with. During the strange, apparently anti-Gorbachev coup of August 1991, all the democratic leaders rallied to the side of "legality" in supporting the communist constitution which had put Gorbachev into office.

But high politics makes no allowances for weakness—even if the victim is not the principal cause of it. Gorbachev's mystique was at its height when he appeared in the guise of the conciliatory leader of an ideologically hostile, nuclear-armed Soviet Union. As his policy began to reflect confusion rather than purpose, Gorbachev's standing began to decline. Five months after the failed communist coup, he was induced to resign and replaced by Yeltsin through procedures every bit as "illegal" as those which had evoked Western wrath only five months earlier. This time, the democracies quickly rallied to Yeltsin with many of the same arguments they had invoked a short time earlier on behalf of Gorbachev. Ignored by an outside world which had so recently celebrated him, Gorbachev wandered into the limbo reserved for statesmen shipwrecked by striving for goals beyond their capabilities.

Gorbachev had in fact wrought one of the most significant revolutions of his time. He destroyed the Communist Party, which had been organized for the specific purpose of seizing and holding power, and which had in fact controlled every aspect of Soviet life. In its wake, Gorbachev left the shattered remnants of an empire which had been painstakingly assembled over centuries. Organized as independent states yet fearful of Russia's nostalgia for the old empire, these have turned into new elements of instability, threatened simultaneously by their former imperial masters and by the residue of various outside ethnic groups—often Russian—deposited on their soil by centuries of Russian domination. None of these results was even remotely what Gorbachev had intended. He had wanted to bring about modernization, not freedom; he had tried to make the Communist Party relevant to the outside world; instead, he ushered in the collapse of the system which had shaped him and to which he owed his eminence.

Blamed by his own people for the magnitude of the disaster which occurred during his incumbency, forgotten by the democracies, and embarrassed by his inability to sustain his power, Gorbachev has deserved neither the exaltation nor the ignominy which have alternatively been his lot. For he had inherited a truly difficult, perhaps insurmountable, set of problems. When Gorbachev assumed power, the scale of the Soviet debacle was just becoming apparent. Forty years of Cold War had forged a loose coalition of nearly all the industrial countries against the Soviet Union. Its erstwhile ally, China, had for all practical purposes joined the opposing camp. The Soviet Union's only remaining allies were the East European satellites, which were held together by the threat of Soviet force implicit in the Brezhnev Doctrine, and which represented a drain, not an augmentation, of Soviet resources. Soviet adventures in the Third World were turning out to be both expensive and inconclusive. In Afghanistan, the Soviet Union experienced many of the same trials America had undergone in Vietnam, the major difference being that these were occurring at the very borders of its own far-flung empire, not at some distant outpost. From Angola to Nicaragua, a resurgent America was turning Soviet expansionism into costly stalemates or discredited failures, while the American strategic buildup, especially SDI, posed a technological challenge which the stagnant and overburdened Soviet economy could not begin to meet. At a moment when the West was launching the supercomputer-microchip revolution, the new Soviet leader watched his country slip into technological underdevelopment.

Despite his ultimate debacle, Gorbachev deserves credit for being willing to face the Soviet Union's dilemmas. At first, he seems to have believed that he could revitalize his society by purging the Communist Party and by introducing some elements of market economics into central planning. Although Gorbachev had no idea of the magnitude of what he was taking on domestically, he understood quite clearly that he needed a period of international calm to pursue it. In this respect, Gorbachev's conclusions were not so different from those of all his post-Stalin predecessors. But whereas, in the 1950s, Khrushchev had still been convinced that the Soviet economy would soon overtake the capitalist system, Gorbachev, in the 1980s, had learned that it would take a long time for the Soviet Union to achieve any level of industrial output that could, even remotely, be considered competitive with the capitalist world.

To gain this breathing space, Gorbachev initiated a major reassessment of Soviet foreign policy. At the Twenty-seventh Party Congress in 1986, Marxist-Leninist ideology was nearly completely jettisoned. Previous periods of peaceful coexistence had been justified as temporary respites in which to rearrange the balance of forces while the class struggle continued. Gorbachev was the first Soviet leader to repudiate the class struggle altogether, and to proclaim coexistence as an end in itself. Though continuing to affirm the ideological differences between East and West, Gorbachev insisted that they were superseded by the need for international cooperation. Coexistence, moreover, was not conceived in the same way that it had been previously—as an interlude before an inevitable confrontation—but as a permanent component of the relationship between the communist and the capitalist worlds. It was justified not as a necessary stage on the road to an eventual communist victory, but as contributing to the well-being of all humanity.

In his book *Perestroika*—which means "reform"—Gorbachev described the new approach:

> To be sure, distinctions will remain. But should we duel because of them? Would it not be more correct to step over the things that divide us for the sake of the interests of all mankind, for the sake of life on Earth? We have made our choice, asserting a new political outlook both by binding statements and by specific actions and deeds. People are tired of tension and confrontation. They prefer a search for a more secure and reliable world, a world in which everyone would preserve their own philosophic, political and ideological views and their way of life.[35]

Gorbachev had already hinted at these views two years earlier, during a press conference at the end of his first summit meeting with Reagan in 1985:

> The international situation today is distinguished by a very important feature which we and the United States of America must take into account in our foreign policy. What I mean is this. In the present situation we are talking not only about confrontation between the two social systems, but about a choice between survival and mutual annihilation.[36]

Inevitably, veterans of the Cold War had difficulty recognizing just how much deeper Gorbachev's approach went than that of previous periods of coexistence. In early 1987, I had a meeting with Anatoly Dobrynin, who was then head of the International Department of the Central Committee (more or less the equivalent of the White House National Security Adviser) in the cavernous Central Committee building in Moscow. Dobrynin made so many disparaging comments about the Afghan government, which Moscow was supporting, that I asked him whether the

Brezhnev Doctrine was still in force. Dobrynin shot back: "What makes you think the Kabul government is communist?"

When I reported to Washington that this comment seemed to imply a Soviet readiness to jettison the Kremlin's Afghan puppets, the general reaction was that Dobrynin had been carried away by his desire to please an old friend—a quality I had failed to note in my nearly ten years of experience with the Soviet end of the "back channel." Nevertheless, the skepticism seemed justified because Gorbachev's doctrinal changes in foreign policy were not being immediately translated into recognizable policy changes. By rote, Soviet leaders described their new doctrine as a method by which to "deprive the West of an enemy image" and thereby to weaken Western cohesion. The self-proclaimed "new thinking," Gorbachev declared in November 1987, "has started to make its way in world affairs, destroying the stereotypes of anti-Sovietism and suspicion toward our initiatives and actions."[37] The Soviets' tactics in arms control talks seemed a replay of their tactics of the early Nixon years—of making an all-out attempt to undermine defensive systems while leaving the underlying offensive threat unchanged.

The government of a great power is like the supertankers that weigh hundreds of thousands of tons and have turning radiuses extending over dozens of miles. Its leaders must balance the impact they seek to make on the outside world against the morale of their bureaucracies. Heads of governments enjoy the formal prerogative of establishing the direction of policies; yet it falls to the governmental bureaucracies to interpret what their chiefs might have had in mind. And heads of government almost never have the time or the staff to supervise the daily implementation of their directives through every nuance of execution. Ironically, the larger and more complex the bureaucracy, the more this is the case. Even in governments less rigid than the Soviet system, policy changes frequently move at a glacial pace.

As time went on, Gorbachev's doctrinal change could no longer be evaded, not even by a bureaucracy shaped by the nearly thirty years of Gromyko's tenure as Foreign Minister. For Gorbachev's "new thinking" went far beyond adapting established Soviet policy to new realities; it altogether destroyed the intellectual underpinnings of historic Soviet foreign policy. When Gorbachev replaced the concept of the class struggle with the Wilsonian theme of global interdependence, he was defining a world of compatible interests and underlying harmony—a complete reversal of established Leninist orthodoxy and historical Marxism.

The collapse of ideology not only deprived Soviet foreign policy of its historic rationale and conviction, but compounded the inherent difficulty of the Soviets' situation. By the mid-1980s, Soviet policymakers faced an agenda on which any one item would have been difficult enough to overcome but which, in combination, proved insuperable. These were: relations with the Western democracies; relations with China; strains in the satellite orbit; the arms race; and the stagnation of the domestic economic and political system.

Gorbachev's initial moves did not vary from the standard Soviet pattern since the death of Stalin—to seek to relax tensions through atmospherics, or at least by what had in the past been largely atmospherics. On September 9, 1985, *Time* magazine published an interview with Gorbachev in which he put forward his notion of peaceful coexistence:

> You asked me what is the primary thing that defines Soviet-American relations. I think it is the immutable fact that whether we like one another or not, we can either survive or perish only together. The principal question that we must answer is whether we are at last ready to recognize that there is no other way to live at peace with each other and whether we are prepared to switch our mentality and our mode of acting from a warlike to a peaceful track.[38]

Gorbachev's dilemma was that, on the one hand, his statements were viewed in the context of what Malenkov and Khrushchev had said thirty years earlier, and that, on the other, they were too vague to encourage a precise response. In the absence of a proposal for a political settlement, Gorbachev found himself enmeshed in the orthodoxy of two decades during which East-West diplomacy had been identified with arms control.

Arms control had become an abstruse subject involving esoteric fine points that, even with the best intentions, would take years to resolve. But what the Soviet Union needed was immediate relief, not simply from tensions but from economic pressures, especially from the arms race. There was no hope of bringing this about through the laborious procedures of establishing agreed force levels, comparing incommensurable systems, negotiating elusive verification procedures, and then spending several years implementing them. In this manner, arms control negotiations were becoming a device for applying pressure on the rickety Soviet system—all the more effective because they had not been designed for that purpose.

Gorbachev's last opportunity to bring about a rapid end to the arms race, or at least to magnify the strains on the Alliance, passed at Reykjavik in 1986. But Gorbachev seems to have felt trapped, as Khrushchev was over Berlin a quarter of a century earlier, between his hawks and his doves. He may well have understood the vulnerability of the American negotiating position and he almost surely had by then grasped the imperatives of his own. But his military advisers probably told him that if he agreed to dismantle all missiles while SDI ran free, some future American administration might break the agreement and achieve a decisive advantage over a greatly reduced (or, in the extreme case, dismantled) Soviet missile force. This was technically true, but it was equally true that the Congress would almost certainly have refused to fund SDI if an arms control agreement based on the Reykjavik formula had brought about the elimination of all missiles. And it neglected the benefits to the Soviet Union of the nearly inevitable controversy which the Reykjavik plan would have generated between the United States and all the other nuclear powers.

Posterity is always more given to assigning the blame for failure to individuals than to circumstances. In fact, Gorbachev's foreign policy—especially on arms control—was a subtle updating of postwar Soviet strategy. And it was well on the way to denuclearizing Germany and establishing a premise for a more national German policy on two grounds: that America was less likely to risk nuclear war for a country which shrank from the risks of a nuclear strategy in its own defense, and that Germany might be increasingly tempted to buttress denuclearization with some kind of special status for itself.

Gorbachev offered a mechanism for the weakening of the Atlantic Alliance in a speech to the Council of Europe in 1989, when he put forward his idea of a Common European Home—a vague structure extending from Vancouver to Vladivostok in which everyone would be allied with everyone else, diluting the meaning of alliance to the point of irrelevance. What Gorbachev lacked, however, was time—the principal prerequisite in order for his policy to mature. Only some abrupt change would have enabled him to reallocate his priorities. But, after Reykjavik, he was forced to return to the time-consuming diplomatic process of 50 percent cuts in strategic forces and the zero option in intermediate-range missiles, which would take years to complete and were irrelevant to his basic problem—that the arms race was draining the Soviet Union of its substance.

By December 1988, Gorbachev had given up on the long-term gains almost within his grasp and retreated to making unilateral reductions in the Soviet armed forces. In a seminal speech at the United Nations on December 7, he announced unilateral cuts of 500,000 men and 10,000 tanks, including half of the tanks facing NATO. The rest of the forces stationed in Central Europe would be reorganized for purely defensive missions. Seeking to tranquilize China, Gorbachev also announced the withdrawal of the "major portion" of Soviet forces in Mongolia. The cuts were explicitly stated to be "unilateral," although Gorbachev added somewhat plaintively: "We do hope that the United States and the Europeans will also take some steps."[39]

Gorbachev's spokesman, Gennadi Gerasimov, explained the rationale: "We are finally doing away with that endlessly repeated myth of the Soviet threat, the Warsaw Pact threat, of an attack on Europe."[40] But unilateral cuts of such magnitude signal either extraordinary self-confidence or exceptional weakness. At that point of its evolution, self-confidence was hardly a Soviet attribute. Such a gesture, inconceivable at any time in the previous fifty years, was also the ultimate vindication of the original version of Kennan's containment theory; America had built positions of strength and the Soviet Union was crumbling from within.

Statesmen need luck as much as they need good judgment. And fortune simply would not smile on Mikhail Gorbachev. On the very day of his dramatic U.N. speech, he had to break off his American visit and return to the Soviet Union. A devastating earthquake had struck Armenia, stealing the headlines from his dramatic abandonment of the arms race.

On the Chinese front, no arms control negotiations took place, nor did Beijing have any interest in them. The Chinese conducted old-fashioned diplomacy and identified a relaxation of tensions with some kind of political settlement. Gorbachev began his overture to Beijing by offering negotiations about improving relations. "I would like to affirm," he said in a speech in Vladivostok in June 1986, "that the Soviet Union is prepared— any time, at any level—to discuss with China questions of additional measures for creating an atmosphere of good-neighborliness. We hope that the border dividing—I would prefer to say, linking—us will soon become a line of peace and friendship."[41]

But there was no "psychiatric" school of diplomacy in Beijing prepared to settle for a change in tone. The Chinese leaders put forward three conditions for an improvement in relations: an end to the Vietnamese occupation of Cambodia; Soviet withdrawal from Afghanistan; and the withdrawal of Soviet troops from the Sino-Soviet border. These demands could not be met quickly. They required first acceptance by the Soviet leadership and then a prolonged period of negotiations before they could be implemented. It took Gorbachev the better part of three years to make enough progress on each of the Chinese conditions to induce the tough bargainers in Beijing to invite him there to discuss an overall improvement of relations.

Once again, Gorbachev was dogged by bad fortune. When he arrived in Beijing in May 1989, the student demonstrations in Tiananmen Square were in full swing; his welcoming ceremony was interrupted by protests against his hosts. Protesters' shouts could be overheard later in the negotiating room of the Great Hall of the People. The world's attention was focused not on Beijing's relations with Moscow, but on the drama of the Chinese leadership struggling to hold on to power. The pace of events had once again outstripped Gorbachev's scope for accommodation.

Whatever problem he tackled, Gorbachev faced the same dilemma. He had come into office confronted by a restive Poland in which, since 1980, Solidarity had become an ever more potent factor. Suppressed by General Jaruzelski in 1981, Solidarity had re-emerged as a political force, which Jaruzelski could not ignore. In Czechoslovakia, Hungary, and East Germany, the Communist Parties' predominance was challenged by groups demanding more freedom and invoking Basket III of the Helsinki Accords on human rights. And periodic review meetings of the European Security Conference kept the issue alive.

The communist rulers of Eastern Europe found themselves in an ultimately insoluble quandary. To stanch their domestic pressures, they needed to pursue a more national policy, which in turn forced them to assert their independence from Moscow. But since they were perceived by their populations as tools of the Kremlin, a nationalist foreign policy was not enough to placate their publics. The communist leaders found themselves obliged to compensate for their lack of credibility by democratizing their internal structures. It quickly became obvious that the Communist Party—even where it still controlled the media—was not designed for democratic contests, being an instrument for seizing power and holding on to it on behalf of a minority. The communists knew how to rule with the help of the secret police, but not with the secret ballot. The communist rulers of Eastern Europe were thus caught in a vicious circle. The more nationalist their foreign policies, the greater became the demands for democratization; the more they democratized, the more intense would be the pressures to replace them.

The Soviet quandary was even more intractable. According to the Brezhnev Doctrine, the Kremlin should have quelled the incipient revolution that was gnawing at the satellite orbit. But Gorbachev was not only unsuited by temperament for such a role, it also would have undermined his entire foreign policy. For suppression of Eastern Europe would have solidified NATO and the Sino-American *de facto* coalition, and intensified the arms race. Gorbachev was increasingly facing a choice between political suicide and the slow erosion of his political power.

Gorbachev's remedy was to intensify liberalization. Ten years earlier, that might have worked; by the late 1980s, Gorbachev could not catch up with the power curve. His rule therefore marked a gradual retreat from the Brezhnev Doctrine. Liberal communists took power in Hungary; Jaruzelski was permitted to deal with Solidarity in Poland. In July 1989, in a speech to the Council of Europe, Gorbachev seemed to abandon not only the Brezhnev Doctrine, stipulating the right of Soviet intervention in Eastern Europe, but the satellite orbit itself, by renouncing "spheres of influence":

> Social and political orders in one country or another changed in the past and may change in the future. But this change is the exclusive affair of the people of that country and is their choice. . . . Any interference in domestic affairs and any attempts to restrict the sovereignty of states—friends, allies or any others—are inadmissible. . . . It is time to deposit in the archives the postulates of the cold war period, when Europe was regarded as an arena of confrontation, divided into "spheres of influence."[42]

The cost of maintaining the satellite orbit had become prohibitive. Even the Council of Europe speech sounded too oblique—though by historic Soviet standards it was clear enough. In October 1989, Gorbachev, on a visit to Finland, abandoned the Brezhnev Doctrine unambiguously. His spokesman, Gerasimov, joked to the press that Moscow had adopted the "Sinatra Doctrine" in Eastern Europe. "You know the Frank Sinatra song, 'I Did It My Way'? Hungary and Poland are doing it their way."[43]

It was too late to save the communists in Eastern Europe, or, for that matter, in the Soviet Union. Gorbachev's gamble on liberalization was bound to fail. To the degree that the Communist Party had lost its monolithic character, it became demoralized. Liberalization proved incompatible with communist rule—the communists could not turn themselves into democrats without ceasing to be communists, an equation Gorbachev never understood, although Yeltsin did.

Also in October of 1989, Gorbachev visited Berlin to celebrate the fortieth anniversary of the establishment of the German Democratic Republic and, in the process, to urge its Stalinist leader, Erich Honecker, to pursue a more reform-minded policy. Clearly, he would not have come to such a celebration had he suspected that there would never be another one, as was reflected in his speech on that occasion:

> We are constantly called on to liquidate this or that division. We often have to hear, "Let the U.S.S.R. get rid of the Berlin wall, then we'll believe in its peaceful intentions."

> We don't idealize the order that has settled on Europe. But the fact is that until now the recognition of the postwar reality has insured peace on the continent. Every time the West has tried to reshape the postwar map of Europe, it has meant a worsening of the international situation.[44]

Yet only four weeks later, the Berlin Wall came down, and within ten months Gorbachev had agreed to the unification of Germany as part of NATO. By then, every communist government in the former satellite orbit had been overthrown, and the Warsaw Pact had collapsed. Yalta had been reversed. History had exposed as nonsense Khrushchev's boasts that communism would bury capitalism. The Soviet Union, which had exhausted itself for forty years by seeking to undermine Western cohesion by threats and pressures, was reduced to soliciting Western goodwill because it needed Western aid more than it needed the satellite orbit. On July 14, 1989, Gorbachev appealed to the G-7 summit of the heads of government of the industrial democracies:

> Our perestroika is inseparable from a policy aiming at our full participation in the world economy. The world can only gain from the opening up of a market as big as the Soviet Union.[45]

Gorbachev had staked everything on two propositions: that liberalization would modernize the Soviet Union, and that the Soviet Union would then be able to hold its own internationally as a great power. Neither expectation was fulfilled and Gorbachev's domestic base collapsed as ignominiously as the satellite orbit had.

The Greek philosopher and mathematician Archimedes said: "Give me a place to stand and I will move the world." Revolutions consume their children because revolutionaries rarely understand that, after a certain point of social disintegration, there are no longer any fixed Archimedean points from which to exert leverage. Gorbachev started with the conviction that a reformed Communist Party could propel Soviet society into the modern world. But he could not bring himself to accept that communism was the problem, not the solution. For two generations, the Communist Party had suppressed independent thought and destroyed individual initiative. By 1990, central planning had ossified, and the various organizations designed to keep a check on every aspect of life were instead concluding nonaggression treaties with the very groups they were supposedly supervising. Discipline had turned into routine, and Gorbachev's attempt to liberate initiative unleashed chaos.

Gorbachev's difficulties began at the simplest level of attempting to

improve productivity and introducing some elements of market economics. Almost immediately, it became apparent that there is no accountability
in a planned system and therefore the most essential prerequisite for an
efficient economy is lacking. Stalinist theory postulated the dominance of
a central plan, but the reality was quite different. What was called "the
plan" was in fact such widespread collusion among the huge bureaucracies that it amounted to a massive confidence game to mislead the central
authorities. The managers responsible for production, the ministries
charged with distribution, and the planners supposedly issuing directives
were all flying blind, since they had no idea what the demand might be
and no way of adjusting their programs once these had been established.
As a result, each unit of the system selected only minimal targets, covering
up any shortfalls by making private deals with the other units behind
the back of the formal central machinery. All incentives worked against
innovation and this state of affairs could not be corrected because the
supposed leaders found it nearly impossible to discern the true state of
affairs in their society. The Soviet Union had reverted to the early history
of the Russian state; it had turned itself into a gigantic Potemkin village.

Attempts at reform collapsed beneath the weight of the entrenched
status quo, as had already happened to Khrushchev and later to Kosygin.
Since at least 25 percent of the national budget went to subsidizing prices,
no objective yardstick existed either for efficiency or for gauging economic demand. With goods allocated rather than purchased, corruption
became the only expression of the market.

Gorbachev recognized the pervasive stagnation but lacked the imagination or skill to break through its built-in rigidities. And the various supervisory bodies of the system had, with the passage of time, turned into part
of the problem. The Communist Party, once the instrument of revolution,
had no function in an elaborated communist system other than to supervise what it did not understand—a problem it solved by colluding with
what it was allegedly controlling. The communist elite had become a
mandarin class of the privileged; theoretically in charge of the national
orthodoxy, it concentrated on preserving its perquisites.

Gorbachev had based his reform program on two elements: *perestroika*
—restructuring—to gain the support of the new technocrats, and *glasnost*—political liberalization—in order to enlist the long-tormented in-
telligentsia. But since there were no institutions for channeling free
expression and generating genuine public debate, *glasnost* turned on
itself. And since there were no free resources except those reserved for
the military, living conditions did not improve. Thus Gorbachev gradually
cut himself off from his institutional support without gaining broader

public backing. *Glasnost* increasingly clashed with *perestroika*. Even the attacks on previous leaders had their downside. In 1989, a young member of Gorbachev's staff who had been detailed to accompany me to the Kremlin remarked to me: "What all this means is that every Soviet citizen older than twenty-five has wasted his life."

The only groups which understood the need for reform—without, however, being prepared to embrace the remedy—were the security services. The KGB knew from its intelligence apparatus just how far the Soviet Union had fallen behind in the technological competition with the West. The armed forces had a professional stake in determining the capabilities of their principal adversary. Understanding the problem did not, however, lead to solutions. The security services shared much of Gorbachev's ambivalence. The KGB would support *glasnost*—political liberalization—only as long as this did not undermine civil discipline; and the military establishment felt at ease with *perestroika*—economic restructuring—only as long as Gorbachev did not attempt to squeeze new resources for his modernization program out of a reduction of the armed forces.

Gorbachev's first instinct, to turn the Communist Party into an instrument of reform, foundered on the rock of vested interests; his next move —to weaken, but still preserve, the communist structure—destroyed the fundamental instrument of Soviet rule. Two steps were involved: to move the locus of Gorbachev's power out of the Party and into the parallel structure of government, and to encourage a move toward regional and local autonomy.

Gorbachev miscalculated on both counts. Since Lenin, the Communist Party had been the sole policymaking body. The government was the executive organ implementing, but not designing, policy. The key Soviet position was always that of the general secretary of the Communist Party; from Lenin through Brezhnev, the communist leader rarely held a governmental office. The result was that the ambitious and enterprising gravitated to the communist hierarchy while the governmental structure attracted administrators without policy flair or even interest in designing policy. By shifting his base from the Communist Party to the governmental side of the Soviet system, Gorbachev had entrusted his revolution to an army of clerks.

Gorbachev's encouragement of regional autonomy led to similar deadlock. He found it impossible to reconcile his desire to create a popular alternative to communism with his Leninist distrust of the popular will. He therefore devised a system of essentially local elections in which national parties—other than the Communist Party—were proscribed. But when, for the first time in Russian history, local and regional governments could be popularly elected, the sins of Russian history came home to roost. For 300 years, Russia had been incorporating nationalities in Europe, Asia, and in the Middle East but had failed to reconcile them to the ruling center. Not surprisingly, most of the newly elected non-Russian governments, which made up nearly half of the Soviet population, began to challenge their historical masters.

Gorbachev lacked reliable constituencies. He antagonized the vast network of vested interests characteristic of the Leninist state, but failed to attract new supporters because he could not bring himself to advance a viable alternative, either to communism or to the concept of the centralized state. Gorbachev had correctly identified the problems of his society, albeit through the blinkers of his inhuman system, thus keeping the solutions ever beyond his grasp. Like a man trapped in a room with perfectly translucent, unbreakable windows, Gorbachev could observe the outside world clearly enough, but was doomed by conditions within the room not to be able to comprehend exactly what he was seeing.

The longer *perestroika* and *glasnost* lasted, the more isolated and less confident Gorbachev became. The first time I met him, in early 1987, he was jaunty and exuded every confidence that the tinkering he was undertaking would make his country fit to resume its march toward supremacy. A year later, he had become less certain. "At any rate," he said, "the Soviet Union will never be the same again"—an oddly ambivalent statement about so Herculean an effort. When we met in early 1989, he told me how he and Shevardnadze had concluded sometime in the 1970s that the communist system needed to be changed from top to bottom. I asked how, as a communist, he had reached this conclusion. "Knowing what was wrong was easy," Gorbachev remarked. "Knowing what was right was the hard part."

Gorbachev never found the answer. During his last year in power, he was as a man caught in a nightmare, who sees a catastrophe bearing down on him but is unable to turn it or himself away from the encounter. Usually the purpose of concessions is to create a firebreak to preserve something that is considered essential. Gorbachev achieved the opposite. Each fitful new reform amounted to a half-measure and thereby accelerated the Soviet decline. Each concession created the threshold for the next. By 1990, the Baltic States seceded and the Soviet Union began to disintegrate. In what was surely the ultimate irony, Gorbachev's chief rival used the process by which the Russian Empire—acquired over three centuries—fell apart to overthrow Gorbachev himself. Acting in his capacity as the President of Russia, Yeltsin affirmed the independence of

Russia (and therefore, by implication, of the other Soviet republics), in effect abolishing the Soviet Union and, with it, Gorbachev's position as President of the Soviet Union. Gorbachev knew what his problems were but he acted both too fast and too slowly: too fast for the tolerance of his system, and too slowly to arrest the accelerating collapse.

In the 1980s, both superpowers needed time to restore themselves. Reagan's policies freed the energies of his society; Gorbachev's brought into the open the dysfunctions of his. America's problems were susceptible to changes of policy; in the Soviet Union, reform brought on an accelerating crisis of the system.

By 1991, the democracies had won the Cold War. But no sooner had they achieved far more than they had ever imagined possible than the original debate about the Cold War broke out all over again. Had the Soviet Union ever really been a threat? Would it not have gone into meltdown even without all the exertions of the Cold War? Had the Cold War been the invention of overwrought policymakers who were interrupting the underlying harmony of the international order?

In January 1990, *Time* magazine made Gorbachev "Man of the Decade," using the occasion to publish an article putting forth the essence of that thesis. "The doves in the Great Debate of the past 40 years were right all along," asserted the author.[46] The Soviet Empire had never been an actual threat. American policy either had been irrelevant or had delayed the Soviet upheaval. The democracies' policy over four decades deserved no significant credit, not even for changes in Soviet *foreign* policy. And if nothing had really been accomplished and events had just happened of their own accord, no lessons could be drawn from the collapse of the Soviet Empire—in particular, none that implied the need for American engagement in the creation of a new world order, which the end of the Cold War was making necessary. The American debate had come full circle. It was the old siren song of American isolationism—that America had not really won the Cold War but that the Soviet Union had lost it, and that four decades of effort had therefore been unnecessary because things would have worked out equally well—or perhaps better—had America left them alone.

Another version of the same reasoning held that there had indeed been a Cold War and that it had really been won, but the victory belonged to the *idea* of democracy, which would have prevailed regardless of the geostrategic measures surrounding the East-West conflict. That too was a version of escapism. Political democracy and the idea of liberty no doubt provided a rallying point for the disaffected—especially in Eastern Europe. Repression of the believers became increasingly difficult as the morale of the governing groups weakened. But the demoralization was in the first instance caused by the stagnation of the system and the growing realization on the part of the communist elite—the higher their rank, the more likely they were to know the facts—that their system was in fact losing the struggle which it had proclaimed as its ultimate purpose throughout a long and brutal history. It was at best a chicken-and-egg proposition. The democratic idea rallied opposition to communism but could not by itself have carried the day so quickly without the collapse of communist foreign policy and, in the end, of communist society.

That was certainly the view of Marxist interpreters of international affairs, who were used to analyzing the "correlation of forces" and found it much easier to discover the causes of the Soviet collapse than American observers. In 1989, Fred Halliday, a Marxist professor at the London School of Economics, concluded that the balance of power had shifted in America's favor.[47] Halliday considered this a tragedy but, unlike those self-tormenting Americans who were reluctant to credit their own country or its leaders, he acknowledged that a major shift in international politics had taken place during the Reagan years. America had succeeded in so raising the cost of Soviet involvement in the Third World that, in a chapter aptly titled "Socialism on the Defensive," Halliday interpreted Gorbachev's "new thinking" as an attempt to appease American pressures.

The strongest testimony to that effect came from Soviet sources. Starting in 1988, Soviet scholars began to acknowledge the Soviet responsibility for the breakdown of detente. Showing a greater understanding of the premises of detente than many American critics, the Soviet commentators pointed out that detente had been Washington's way of keeping Moscow from challenging the existing military and political *status quo*. By violating this tacit understanding and seeking unilateral gains, the Brezhnev leadership had evoked the reaction of the Reagan years that proved to be more than the Soviet Union could handle.

One of the earliest and most interesting of such Soviet "revisionist" commentaries came from Vyacheslav Dashichev, a professor at the Institute for the Economy of the World Socialist System. In an article in *Literaturnaya Gazeta* on May 18, 1988,[48] Dashichev pointed out that the historic "miscalculations and incompetent approach of the Brezhnev leadership" had united all of the world's other major powers into a coalition against the Soviet Union, and had provoked an arms race which the Soviet Union had not been able to afford. The traditional Soviet policy of standing apart from the world community while seeking to undermine it needed, therefore, to be abandoned. Dashichev wrote:

... as the West saw it, the Soviet leadership was actively exploiting detente to build up its own military forces, seeking military parity with the United States and in general with all the opposing powers—a fact without historical precedent. The United States, paralyzed by the Vietnam catastrophe, reacted sensitively to the expansion of Soviet influence in Africa, the Near East and other regions.

... The operation of the "feedback" effect placed the Soviet Union in an extremely difficult position in the foreign policy and economic respects. It was opposed by the major world powers—the United States, Britain, France, the FRG, Italy, Japan, Canada, and China. Opposition to their vastly superior potential was dangerously far beyond the USSR's abilities.[49]

The same point was made by Soviet Foreign Minister Eduard Shevardnadze in a speech on July 25, 1988, to a meeting at the Soviet Foreign Ministry.[50] He enumerated such Soviet mistakes as the Afghan debacle, the feud with China, the long-standing underestimation of the European Community, the costly arms race, the 1983–84 walkout from the Geneva arms control talks, the Soviet decision to deploy the SS-20s in the first place, and the Soviet defense doctrine according to which the U.S.S.R. had to be as strong as any potential coalition of states against it. In other words, Shevardnadze challenged almost everything the Soviet Union had done for twenty-five years. It was an implicit recognition that Western policies had had a major impact on the Soviet Union, for had the democracies imposed no penalty for adventurism, Soviet policy could have been described as successful and not in need of reassessment.

The ending of the Cold War, sought by American policy through eight administrations of both political parties, was much as George Kennan had foreseen in 1947. Regardless of how accommodating a policy the West might have conducted, the Soviet system had needed the specter of a permanent outside enemy to justify the suffering it was imposing on its people and to maintain the armed forces and security apparatus essential to its rule. When, under the pressure of the cumulative Western response that culminated in the Reagan years, the Twenty-seventh Party Congress changed the official doctrine from coexistence to interdependence, the moral basis for domestic repression disappeared. Then it became evident, as Kennan had predicted, that the Soviet Union, whose citizens had been reared on discipline and could not readily switch to compromise and accommodation, would turn overnight from one of the strongest to "one of the weakest and most pitiable of national societies."[51]

As noted earlier, Kennan eventually came to believe that his containment policy had been overmilitarized. A more accurate assessment would be that, as always, America had oscillated between overreliance on military strategy and emotional overdependence on the conversion of the adversary. I too had been critical of many of the individual policies which went under the name of containment. Yet the overall direction of American policy was remarkably farsighted and remained remarkably consistent throughout changes in administration and an astonishingly varied array of personalities.

Had America not organized resistance when a self-confident communist empire was acting as if it represented the wave of the future and was causing the peoples and leaders of the world to believe that this might be so, the Communist Parties, which were then already the largest single parties in postwar Europe, might well have prevailed. The series of crises over Berlin could not have been sustained, and there would have been more of them. Exploiting America's post-Vietnam trauma, the Kremlin sent proxy forces to Africa and its own troops into Afghanistan. It would have become far more assertive had America not protected the global balance of power and helped to rebuild democratic societies. That America did not perceive its role in terms of the balance of power compounded its pain and complicated the process, but it also served to bring about unprecedented dedication and creativity. Nor did it change the reality that it was America which had preserved the global equilibrium and therefore the peace of the world.

Victory in the Cold War was not, of course, the achievement of any single administration. It came about as a result of the confluence of forty years of American bipartisan effort and seventy years of communist ossification. The phenomenon of Reagan sprang from a fortuitous convergence of personality and opportunity: a decade earlier, he would have seemed too militant; a decade later, too one-track. The combination of ideological militancy to rally the American public and diplomatic flexibility, which conservatives would never have forgiven in another president, was exactly what was needed in the period of Soviet weakness and emerging self-doubt.

Yet the Reagan foreign policy was more in the nature of a brilliant sunset than of the dawn of a new era. The Cold War had been almost made to order to American preconceptions. There had been a dominant ideological challenge rendering universal maxims, however oversimplified, applicable to most of the world's problems. And there had been a clear and present military threat, and its source had been unambiguous. Even then, America's travails—from Suez to Vietnam—resulted from its application of universal principles to specific cases which proved inhospitable to them.

In the post–Cold War world, there is no overriding ideological challenge or, at this writing, single geostrategic confrontation. Almost every situation is a special case. Exceptionalism inspired America's foreign policy and gave the United States the fortitude to prevail in the Cold War. But it will require far more subtle applications in the multipolar world of the twenty-first century. America will finally have to face the challenge it has been able to avoid through most of its history: whether its traditional perception of itself as either strictly beacon or crusader still defines its choices or limits them; whether, in short, it must at last develop some definition of its national interest.

CHAPTER THIRTY-ONE

The New World Order
Reconsidered

By the beginning of the last decade of the twentieth century, Wilsonianism seemed triumphant. The communist ideological and the Soviet geopolitical challenges had been overcome simultaneously. The objective of moral opposition to communism had merged with the geopolitical task of resisting Soviet expansionism. No wonder that President Bush proclaimed his hope for a new world order in classically Wilsonian terms:

> We have a vision of a new partnership of nations that transcends the Cold War. A partnership based on consultation, cooperation, and collective action, especially through international and regional organizations. A partnership united by principle and the rule of law and supported by

an equitable sharing of both cost and commitment. A partnership whose goals are to increase democracy, increase prosperity, increase the peace, and reduce arms.[1]

Bush's Democratic successor, President Bill Clinton, expressed America's goals in very similar terms, expounding on the theme of "enlarging democracy":

> In a new era of peril and opportunity, our overriding purpose must be to expand and strengthen the world's community of market-based democracies. During the Cold War, we sought to contain a threat to survival of free institutions. Now we seek to enlarge the circle of nations that live under those free institutions, for our dream is of a day when the opinions and energies of every person in the world will be given full expression in a world of thriving democracies that cooperate with each other and live in peace.[2]

For the third time in this century, America thus proclaimed its intention to build a new world order by applying its domestic values to the world at large. And, for the third time, America seemed to tower over the international stage. In 1918, Wilson had overshadowed a Paris Peace Conference at which America's allies were too dependent on it to insist on voicing their misgivings. Toward the end of the Second World War, Franklin Delano Roosevelt and Truman seemed to be in a position to recast the entire globe on the American model.

The end of the Cold War produced an even greater temptation to recast the international environment in America's image. Wilson had been constrained by isolationism at home, and Truman had come up against Stalinist expansionism. In the post–Cold War world, the United States is the only remaining superpower with the capacity to intervene in every part of the globe. Yet power has become more diffuse and the issues to which military force is relevant have diminished. Victory in the Cold War has propelled America into a world which bears many similarities to the European state system of the eighteenth and nineteenth centuries, and to practices which American statesmen and thinkers have consistently questioned. The absence of both an overriding ideological or strategic threat frees nations to pursue foreign policies based increasingly on their immediate national interest. In an international system characterized by perhaps five or six major powers and a multiplicity of smaller states, order will have to emerge much as it did in past centuries from a reconciliation and balancing of competing national interests.

805

Both Bush and Clinton spoke of the new world order as if it were just around the corner. In fact, it is still in a period of gestation, and its final form will not be visible until well into the next century. Part extension of the past, part unprecedented, the new world order, like those which it succeeds, will emerge as an answer to three questions: What are the basic units of the international order? What are their means of interacting? What are the goals on behalf of which they interact?

International systems live precariously. Every "world order" expresses an aspiration to permanence; the very term has a ring of eternity about it. Yet the elements which comprise it are in constant flux; indeed, with each century, the duration of international systems has been shrinking. The order that grew out of the Peace of Westphalia lasted 150 years; the international system created by the Congress of Vienna maintained itself for a hundred years; the international order characterized by the Cold War ended after forty years. (The Versailles settlement never operated as a system adhered to by the major powers, and amounted to little more than an armistice between two world wars.) Never before have the components of world order, their capacity to interact, and their goals all changed quite so rapidly, so deeply, or so globally.

Whenever the entities constituting the international system change their character, a period of turmoil inevitably follows. The Thirty Years' War was in large part about the transition from feudal societies based on tradition and claims of universality to the modern state system based on *raison d'état*. The wars of the French Revolution marked the transition to the nation-state defined by common language and culture. The wars of the twentieth century were caused by the disintegration of the Habsburg and Ottoman Empires, the challenge to the dominance of Europe, and the end of colonialism. In each transition, what had been taken for granted suddenly became anachronistic: multinational states in the nineteenth century, colonialism in the twentieth.

Since the Congress of Vienna, foreign policy has related nations to each other—hence the term "international relations." In the nineteenth century, the appearance of even one new nation—such as the united Germany—produced decades of turmoil. Since the end of the Second World War, nearly a hundred new nations have come into being, many of them quite different from the historic European nation-state. The collapse of communism in the Soviet Union and the breakup of Yugoslavia have spawned another twenty nations, many of which have concentrated on re-enacting century-old bloodlusts.

The nineteenth-century European nation was based on common language and culture, and, given the technology of the times, provided the optimum framework for security, economic growth, and for influencing international events. In the post–Cold War world, the traditional European nation-states—the countries which formed the Concert of Europe until the First World War—lack the resources for a global role. The success of their effort to consolidate themselves into the European Union will determine their future influence. United, Europe will continue as a Great Power; divided into national states, it will slide into secondary status.

Part of the turmoil associated with the emergence of a new world order results from the fact that at least three types of states calling themselves "nations" are interacting while sharing few of the nation-states' historic attributes. On the one side are the ethnic splinters from disintegrating empires, such as the successor states of Yugoslavia or of the Soviet Union. Obsessed by historic grievances and age-old quests for identity, they strive primarily to prevail in ancient ethnic rivalries. The goal of international order is beyond their fields of interest and frequently beyond their imaginations. Like the smaller states embroiled in the Thirty Years' War, they seek to preserve their independence and to increase their power without regard for the more cosmopolitan considerations of an international political order.

Some of the postcolonial nations represent yet another distinct phenomenon. For many of them, the current borders represent the administrative convenience of the imperial powers. French Africa, possessing a large coastline, was segmented into seventeen administrative units, each of which has since become a state. Belgian Africa—then called the Congo, now Zaire—had only a very narrow outlet to the sea, and hence was governed as a single unit even though it constitutes an area as large as Western Europe. In such circumstances, the state too often came to mean the army, which was usually the only "national" institution. When that claim has collapsed, civil war has frequently been the consequence. If nineteenth-century standards of nationhood or Wilsonian principles of self-determination were applied to such nations, a radical and unpredictable realignment of frontiers would be inevitable. For them, the alternative to the territorial *status quo* lies in endless and brutal civil conflict.

Finally, there are the continental-type states—which will probably represent the basic units of the new world order. The Indian nation that emerged from British colonial rule unites a multiplicity of tongues, religions, and nationalities. Since it is more susceptible to religious and ideological currents within neighboring states than the European nations of the nineteenth century, the dividing line between its foreign and domestic policies is both different and far more tenuous. Similarly, China is a conglomerate of different languages held together by common writing, common culture, and common history. It is what Europe might have become had it not been for the religious wars of the seventeenth century, and what it might yet turn out to be if the European Union fulfills the hopes of its supporters. Similarly, the two superpowers of the Cold War period have never been nation-states in the European sense. America had succeeded in forming a distinct culture from a polyglot national composition; the Soviet Union was an empire containing many nationalities. Its successor states—especially the Russian Federation—are, at this writing, torn between disintegration and reimperialization, much as were the Habsburg and Ottoman Empires of the nineteenth century.

All this has radically changed the substance, the method, and, above all, the reach of international relations. Until the modern period, the various continents pursued their activities largely in isolation from each other. It would have been impossible to measure the power of, say, France against that of China because the two countries had no means of interacting. Once the reach of technology had broadened, the future of other continents was determined by the "Concert" of European powers. No previous international order has contained major centers of power distributed around the entire globe. Nor had statesmen ever been obliged to conduct diplomacy in an environment where events can be experienced instantaneously and simultaneously by leaders and their publics.

As the number of states multiplies and their capacity to interact increases, on what principles can a new world order be organized? Given the complexity of the new international system, can Wilsonian concepts like "enlarging democracy" serve as the principal guides to American foreign policy and as replacement for the Cold War strategy of containment? Clearly, these concepts have been neither an unqualified success nor an unqualified failure. Some of the finest acts of twentieth-century diplomacy had their roots in the idealism of Woodrow Wilson: the Marshall Plan, the brave commitment to containing communism, defense of the freedom of Western Europe, and even the ill-fated League of Nations and its later incarnation, the United Nations.

At the same time, Wilsonian idealism has produced a plethora of problems. As embodied in the Fourteen Points, the uncritical espousal of ethnic self-determination failed to take account of power relationships and the destabilizing effects of ethnic groups single-mindedly pursuing their accumulated rivalries and ancient hatreds. The failure to give the League of Nations a military enforcement mechanism underlined the problems inherent in Wilson's notion of collective security. The ineffectual Kellogg-Briand Pact of 1928, by which nations renounced war as a means of policy, showed the limits of exclusively legal restraints. As Hitler was to demonstrate, in the world of diplomacy, a loaded gun is often more potent than a legal brief. Wilson's appeal to America to go forth in the pursuit of democracy produced acts of great creativity. It also led it to such disastrous crusades as Vietnam.

The end of the Cold War has created what some observers have called a "unipolar" or "one-superpower" world. But the United States is actually in no better position to dictate the global agenda unilaterally than it was at the beginning of the Cold War. America is more preponderant than it was ten years ago, yet, ironically, power has also become more diffuse. Thus, America's ability to employ it to shape the rest of the world has actually decreased.

Victory in the Cold War has made it far more difficult to implement the Wilsonian dream of universal collective security. In the absence of a potentially dominating power, the principal nations do not view threats to the peace in the same way, nor are they willing to run the same risks in overcoming those threats they do recognize (see chapters 10, 11, 15, and 16). The world community is willing enough to cooperate in "peacekeeping"—that is, in policing an existing agreement not challenged by any of the parties—but it has been skittish about peacemaking —the suppression of actual challenges to world order. This is not surprising, since not even the United States has as yet developed a clear concept of what it will resist unilaterally in the post–Cold War world.

As an approach to foreign policy, Wilsonianism presumes that America is possessed of an exceptional nature expressed in unrivaled virtue and unrivaled power. The United States was so confident of its strength and the virtue of its aims that it could envision fighting for its values on a worldwide basis. American exceptionalism must be the point of departure for a Wilsonian foreign policy.

As the twenty-first century approaches, vast global forces are at work that, over the course of time, will render the United States less exceptional. American military power will remain unrivaled for the foreseeable future. Yet America's desire to project that power into the myriad small-scale conflicts which the world is likely to witness in the coming decades —Bosnia, Somalia, and Haiti—is a key conceptual challenge for American foreign policy. The United States will likely have the world's most powerful economy well into the next century. Yet wealth will become more widely spread, as will the technology for generating wealth. The United States will face economic competition of a kind it never experienced during the Cold War.

America will be the greatest and most powerful nation, but a nation with peers; the *primus inter pares* but nonetheless a nation like others. The American exceptionalism that is the indispensable basis for a Wilsonian foreign policy is therefore likely to be less relevant in the coming century.

Americans should not view this as a humbling of America or as a symptom of national decline. For most of its history, the United States was in fact a nation among others, not a preponderate superpower. The rise of other power centers—in Western Europe, Japan, and China—should not alarm Americans. After all, sharing the world's resources and the development of other societies and economies has been a peculiarly American objective ever since the Marshall Plan.

Yet if the premise of Wilsonianism is becoming less relevant and the dictates of Wilsonian foreign policy—collective security, the conversion of one's competitors to the American way, an international system that adjudicates disputes in a legal fashion, and unqualified support for ethnic self-determination—are becoming less practicable, on what principles ought America to base its foreign policy in the coming century? History provides no guidebook, nor even analogies that completely satisfy. Yet history teaches by example and, as America moves into uncharted waters, it would do well to consider the era before Woodrow Wilson and the "American century" for clues about the decades to come.

Richelieu's concept of *raison d'état*—that the interests of the state justify the means used to pursue them—has always been repugnant to Americans. That is not to say that Americans have never practiced *raison d'état*—there are many instances of it, from the time of the Founding Fathers' shrewd dealings with the European powers in the early decades of the republic to the single-minded pursuit of Western expansion, which was placed under the rubric of "manifest destiny." But Americans have never been comfortable acknowledging openly their own selfish interests. Whether fighting world wars or local conflicts, American leaders always claimed to be struggling in the name of principle, not interest.

For any student of European history, the concept of balance of power seems utterly obvious. But the balance of power, like *raison d'état,* is a development of the last couple of centuries, originally propagated by the English King, William III, who sought to rein in the expansionist drives of France. The concept that a coalition of weaker states would bind together to form a counterweight to the stronger was not in itself remarkable. Yet the balance of power requires constant tending. In the next century, American leaders will have to articulate for their public a concept of the national interest and explain how that interest is served—in Europe and in Asia—by the maintenance of the balance of power. America will need partners to preserve equilibrium in several regions of the world, and these partners can not always be chosen on the basis of moral considerations alone. A clear definition of the national interest needs to be an equally essential guide to American policy.

The international system which lasted the longest without a major war was the one following the Congress of Vienna. It combined legitimacy and equilibrium, shared values, and balance-of-power diplomacy. Common values restrained the scope of nations' demands while equilibrium limited the capacity to insist on them. In the twentieth century, America has tried twice to create a world order based almost exclusively on its values. It represents a heroic effort responsible for much of what is good in the contemporary world. But Wilsonianism cannot be the sole basis for the post–Cold War era.

The growth of democracy will continue as America's dominant aspiration, but it is necessary to recognize the obstacles it faces at the moment of its seeming philosophical triumph. Curbing the power of the central government has been a principal concern of Western political theorists, whereas, in most other societies, political theory has sought to buttress the authority of the state. Nowhere else has there been such an insistence on expanding personal freedom. Western democracy evolved in culturally homogeneous societies with a long common history (even America, with its polyglot population, developed a strong cultural identity). The society and, in a sense, the nation preceded the state without having to be created by it. In such a setting, political parties represent variants of an underlying consensus; today's minority is potentially tomorrow's majority.

In most other parts of the world, the state has preceded the nation; it was and often remains the principal element in forming it. Political parties, where they exist, reflect fixed, usually communal, identities; minorities and majorities tend to be permanent. In such societies, the political process is about domination, not alternation in office, which takes place, if at all, by coups rather than by constitutional procedures. The concept of a loyal opposition—the essence of modern democracy—rarely prevails. Much more frequently, opposition is viewed as a threat to national cohesion, equated with treason, and ruthlessly suppressed.

Western-style democracy presupposes a consensus on values that sets limits to partisanship. America would not be true to itself if it did not insist on the universal applicability of the idea of liberty. That America should give preference to democratic governments over repressive ones and be prepared to pay some price for its moral convictions is beyond dispute. That there is an area of discretion which should be exercised in favor of governments and institutions promoting democratic values and human rights is also clear. The difficulty arises in determining the precise price to be paid and its relationship to other essential American priorities, including national security and the overall geopolitical balance. If American exhortations are to go beyond patriotic rhetoric, they must reflect a realistic understanding of America's reach. America must be careful not to multiply moral commitments while the financial and military resources for the conduct of a global foreign policy are being curtailed. Sweeping pronouncements not matched by either the ability or the willingness to back them up diminish America's influence on all other matters as well.

The precise balance between the moral and the strategic elements of American foreign policy cannot be prescribed in the abstract. But the beginning of wisdom consists of recognizing that a balance needs to be struck. However powerful America is, no country has the capacity to impose all its preferences on the rest of mankind; priorities must be established. Even if the resources for it existed, undifferentiated Wilsonianism would not be supported once the American public clearly understood its corollary commitments and involvements. It runs the risk of being turned into a slogan to escape difficult geopolitical choices by means of pronouncements involving little apparent risk. A gap is threatening to open up in America's policy between its pretentions and its willingness to support them; the nearly inevitable disillusionment too easily turns into an excuse for withdrawing from world affairs altogether.

In the post–Cold War world, American idealism needs the leaven of geopolitical analysis to find its way through the maze of new complexities. That will not be easy. America refused to dominate even when it had the nuclear monopoly, and it disdained the balance of power even when conducting, as during the Cold War, what was in effect a spheres of interest diplomacy. In the twenty-first century, America, like other nations, must learn to navigate between necessity and choice, between the immutable constants of international relations and the elements subject to the discretion of statesmen.

Wherever the balance is established between values and necessity, foreign policy must begin with some definition of what constitutes a vital interest—a change in the international environment so likely to undermine the national security that it must be resisted no matter what form the threat takes or how ostensibly legitimate it appears. During its heyday, Great Britain would have gone to war to prevent the occupation of the Channel ports in the Low Countries even if they had been taken over by a major power governed by saints. For the greater part of American history, the Monroe Doctrine served as an operating definition of the

American national interest. Since Woodrow Wilson's entry into World War I, America has avoided defining a national interest with the argument that it was not opposed to change as such, but to the use of force to bring it about. Neither definition is adequate any longer; the Monroe Doctrine is too restrictive, Wilsonianism is both too vague and too legalistic. The controversy surrounding almost all American military actions in the post–Cold War period shows that a wider consensus on where America should draw the line does not yet exist. To bring it about is a major challenge to national leadership.

Geopolitically, America is an island off the shores of the large landmass of Eurasia, whose resources and population far exceed those of the United States. The domination by a single power of either of Eurasia's two principal spheres—Europe or Asia—remains a good definition of strategic danger for America, Cold War or no Cold War. For such a grouping would have the capacity to outstrip America economically and, in the end, militarily. That danger would have to be resisted even were the dominant power apparently benevolent, for if the intentions ever changed, America would find itself with a grossly diminished capacity for effective resistance and a growing inability to shape events.

America was projected into the Cold War by the threat of Soviet expansionism, and it has based much of its post–Cold War expectations on the disappearance of the communist menace. Just as attitudes toward Soviet hostility had shaped America's attitudes toward the global order—from the perspective of containment—so have Russia's reform efforts dominated America's thinking on the post–Cold War world order. American policy has been based on the premise that peace can be ensured by a Russia tempered by democracy and concentrating its energies on developing a market economy. In this light, America's principal task is conceived to be to strengthen Russian reform, with measures drawn from the experience of the Marshall Plan rather than from the traditional patterns of foreign policy.

With respect to no other country has American policy been geared as consistently to an assessment of its intentions rather than to its potential or even its policies. Franklin Roosevelt had staked his hopes for a peaceful postwar world to a considerable degree on Stalin's moderation. During the Cold War, the operative American strategy—containment—had as its declared aim changing Soviet purposes, and the debate concerning it was generally about whether the expected change in Soviet purposes had already occurred. Among postwar presidents, only Nixon consistently dealt with the Soviet Union as a geopolitical challenge. Even Reagan placed great stock in what amounted to the conversion of Soviet leaders.

Not surprisingly, in the aftermath of the communist collapse, it has been assumed that hostile intentions have disappeared, and, since the Wilsonian tradition rejects conflicting interests, American post–Cold War policy has been conducted as if traditional foreign policy considerations no longer apply.

Students of geopolitics and history are uneasy about the single-mindedness of this approach. They fear that, in overestimating America's ability to shape Russia's internal evolution, America may involve itself needlessly in internal Russian controversies, generate a nationalist backlash, and neglect the usual tasks of foreign policy. They would support a policy designed to modify Russia's traditional truculence and would for that reason favor economic aid and cooperative projects on global issues. They would argue, however, that Russia, regardless of who governs it, sits astride the territory Halford Mackinder called the geopolitical heartland, and is the heir to one of the most potent imperial traditions.[3] Even were the postulated moral transformation to occur, it would take time, and in that interlude America should hedge its bets.

Nor should America expect economic aid to achieve results in Russia comparable to those of the Marshall Plan. The Western Europe of the immediate postwar period had a functioning market system, well-established bureaucracies, and, in most countries, a democratic tradition. It was linked to America by the military and ideological threat from the Soviet Union. Behind the shield of the Atlantic Alliance, economic reform caused an underlying geopolitical reality to re-emerge; the Marshall Plan enabled Europe to re-establish its traditional pattern of domestic governance.

Comparable conditions do not exist anywhere in post–Cold War Russia. Alleviating suffering and encouraging economic reform are important tools of American foreign policy; they are not, however, substitutes for a serious effort to maintain the global balance of power vis-à-vis a country with a long history of expansionism.

At this writing, the vast Russian empire acquired over the course of two centuries is in a state of disintegration—much as it was in the period 1917–23, from which it recovered without interrupting its traditional expansionist rhythm. Managing the decline of a decaying empire is one of diplomacy's most formidable tasks. Nineteenth-century diplomacy slowed the unraveling of the Ottoman Empire and kept it from spilling over into a general war; twentieth-century diplomacy proved unable to contain the consequences of the disintegration of the Austro-Hungarian Empire. Collapsing empires generate two causes of tension: attempts by neighbors to take advantage of the weakness of the imperial center, and efforts by the declining empire to restore its authority at the periphery.

Both processes are going on simultaneously in the successor states of the former Soviet Union. Iran and Turkey are seeking to increase their roles in the Central Asian republics, where the population is largely Muslim. But the dominant geopolitical thrust has been Russia's attempt to restore its pre-eminence in all the territories formerly controlled from Moscow. In the name of peacekeeping, Russia seeks to re-establish some form of Russian tutelage, and the United States, focusing on the goodwill of a "reformist" government and reluctant to embrace a geopolitical agenda, has thus far acquiesced. It has done little to enable the successor republics—other than the Baltic states—to achieve international acceptance. Visits there by senior American officials are few and far between; aid is minimal. The activities of Russian troops on their territory, or even their presence, is rarely challenged. Moscow is treated *de facto* as the imperial center, which is also what it conceives itself to be.

This is in part because America has been dealing with the anticommunist and the anti-imperialist revolutions taking place on the soil of the former Soviet Empire as if they were a single phenomenon. In fact, they work in opposite directions. The anticommunist revolution has enjoyed substantial support throughout the territory of the former Soviet Union. The anti-imperialist revolution, directed against domination by Russia, is widely popular in the new non-Russian republics and extremely unpopular in the Russian Federation. For Russian leadership groups have historically perceived their state in terms of a "civilizing" mission (see chapters 7 and 8); the overwhelming majority of Russia's leading figures—whatever their political persuasion—refuse to accept the collapse of the Soviet Empire or the legitimacy of the successor states, especially of Ukraine, the cradle of Russian Orthodoxy. Even Aleksandr Solzhenitsyn, when writing about ridding Russia of the incubus of unwilling foreign subjects, urged the retention by Moscow of a core group of Ukraine, Belarus, and almost half of Kazakhstan,[4] nearly 90 percent of the former empire. On the territory of the former Soviet Union, not every anticommunist is a democrat, and not every democrat is opposed to Russian imperialism.

A realistic policy would recognize that even the reformist Russian government of Boris Yeltsin has maintained Russian armies on the territory of most of the former Soviet republics—all members of the United Nations—often against the express wish of the host government. These military forces have participated in the civil wars of several of the republics. The foreign minister of Russia has repeatedly put forward a concept of a Russian monopoly on peacekeeping in the "near abroad," indistinguishable from an attempt to re-establish Moscow's domination. Long-term prospects for peace will be influenced by Russian reform, but short-term prospects will depend on whether Russian armies can be induced to stay at home. If they reappear along the borders of the old empire in Europe and in the Middle East, the historic tension—compounded by fear and mutual suspicion—between Russia and its neighbors will surely re-emerge (see chapters 6 and 7).

Russia is bound to have a special security interest in what it calls the "near abroad"—the republics of the former Soviet Union—as distinguished from the lands beyond the old empire. But the peace of the world requires that this interest be satisfied without military pressure or unilateral military intervention. The key issue is whether to treat Russia's relationship to the new republics as an international problem subject to accepted rules of foreign policy, or as an outgrowth of Russia's unilateral decision-making which America will seek to influence, if at all, by appeals to the Russian leadership's goodwill. In certain areas—for example, the republics of Central Asia threatened by Islamic fundamentalism—the United States' national interest probably parallels Russia's, at least as it applies to resistance to Iranian fundamentalism. Cooperation there would be quite possible so long as it does not write a script for a return to traditional Russian imperialism.

At this writing, the prospects for democracy in Russia are as yet uncertain, nor is it clear that even a democratic Russia will conduct policies conducive to international stability. Throughout its dramatic history, Russia has marched to quite a different drummer from the rest of the Western world. It never had an autonomous church; it missed the Reformation, the Enlightenment, the Age of Discovery, and modern market economics. Leaders with democratic experience are in short supply. Almost all of Russia's leaders—as well as those in the new republics—held high office under communism; commitment to pluralism was not their first instinct, and it may not prove to be their last.

Moreover, the transition from a centrally planned to a market economy has proved painful wherever it has been attempted. Managers have no experience with markets and incentives; workers have lost their motivation; ministers have never had to concern themselves with fiscal policy. Stagnation, even decline, is nearly inevitable. No centrally planned economy has yet managed to avoid painful austerity on the road to market economics, and the problem has been compounded by the cold-turkey approach recommended by so many American expert advisers. Dissatisfaction with the social and economic costs of transition has enabled communists to gain significantly in postcommunist Poland, Slovakia, and Hungary. In the Russian parliamentary election of December 1993, the Communist and Nationalist Parties together achieved nearly 50 percent of the vote.

Even sincere reformers may see in traditional Russian nationalism a unifying force to achieve their objectives. And, in Russia, nationalism has historically been missionary and imperial. Psychologists can debate whether the reason was a deep-rooted sense of insecurity or congenital aggressiveness. For the victims of Russian expansion, the distinction has been academic. In Russia, democratization and a restrained foreign policy may not necessarily go hand in hand. This is why the argument that peace will be secured primarily by Russian domestic reform finds few adherents in Eastern Europe, Scandinavia, or China, and why Poland, the Czech Republic, Slovakia, and Hungary are so keen to join the Atlantic Alliance.

A course of action geared to foreign policy considerations would seek to create counterweights to foreseeable tendencies and not place all the chips on domestic reform. While supporting Russian free markets and Russian democracy, it would also seek to bolster the obstacles to Russian expansion. It could be argued, in fact, that Russian reform would be strengthened if Russia is encouraged to concentrate—for the first time in its history—on emphasizing the development of its national territory, which, extending over eleven time zones, from St. Petersburg to Vladivostok, gives no cause for claustrophobia.

For the post–Cold War period, American policy toward postcommunist Russia has staked everything on a kind of social engineering geared to individual leaders. In the Bush Administration, it was Mikhail Gorbachev and, under Clinton, it has been Boris Yeltsin, who, because of their perceived personal commitment to democracy, have been treated as the personal guarantors of a peaceful Russian foreign policy and of Russia's integration into the international community. Bush deplored the disintegration of Gorbachev's U.S.S.R., and Clinton has acquiesced in the efforts to restore Russia's old sphere of influence. America's leaders have been reluctant to invoke the traditional diplomatic brakes on Russian policy for fear of provoking Yeltsin's (and, before that, Gorbachev's) presumed nationalist opponents.

Russo-American relations desperately need a serious dialogue on foreign policy issues. It does Russia no favor to be treated as immune from normal considerations of foreign policy, for this will have the practical result of forcing it to pay a heavier price later on if it is lured into courses of action from which there is no retreat. American leaders should not fear frank discussions about where American and Russian interests converge and where they differ. The veterans of Russia's internal struggles are not blushing novices whose internal balances will be unhinged by realistic dialogue. They are quite capable of comprehending a policy based on mutual respect of each other's national interests. In fact, they are likely to understand such a calculus better than appeals to an abstract and distant utopianism.

Integrating Russia into the international system is a key task of the emerging international order. It has two components which must be kept in balance: influencing Russian attitudes and affecting Russian calculations. Generous economic assistance and technical advice is necessary to ease the pains of transition, and Russia should be made welcome in institutions which foster economic, cultural, and political cooperation— such as the European Security Conference. But Russian reform will be impeded, not helped, by turning a blind eye to the reappearance of historic Russian imperial pretensions. The independence of the new republics, recognized after all by the United Nations, must not be tacitly downgraded by acquiescence in Russian military moves on their soil.

American policy toward Russia should be geared to permanent interests, not to the fluctuations of Russian domestic politics. If American foreign policy makes Russian domestic politics its top priority, it will become the victim of forces essentially out of its control and lose all criteria for judgment. Should the foreign policy be calibrated toward every quiver of an essentially revolutionary process? Does America disengage from Russia whenever some domestic change occurs of which it does not approve? Can the United States afford to try to isolate Russia and China simultaneously and resurrect in the name of its domestic preferences the Sino-Soviet alliance? A less intrusive Russian policy at this stage would permit a steadier long-term course later on.

Advocates of what I have defined in chapter 28 as the "psychiatric" school of foreign policy tend to reject such arguments as "pessimistic." They say that, after all, Germany and Japan have changed their character, why not Russia? But it is also true that democratic Germany changed in the opposite direction in the 1930s, and that those who relied on its intentions suddenly found themselves face-to-face with its capabilities.

A statesman can always escape his dilemmas by making the most favorable assumptions about the future; one of his tests is his ability to protect against unfavorable and even unforeseen contingencies. The new Russian leadership is entitled to understanding for the anguishing process of trying to overcome two generations of communist misrule. It is not entitled to be handed the sphere of influence that tsars and commissars have coveted all around Russia's vast borders for 300 years. If Russia is to become a serious partner in building a new world order, it must be ready for the disciplines of stability as well as for its benefits.

The American policy that has come closest to the generally accepted definition of a vital interest has been toward its allies in the Atlantic area.

Although the North Atlantic Treaty Organization was usually justified in Wilsonian terms as an instrument of collective security and not as an alliance, it in fact represented the institution that most nearly harmonized America's moral and geopolitical objectives (see chapter 16). Since its purpose was to prevent Soviet domination of Europe, it served the geopolitical purpose of keeping the power centers of Europe and Asia from falling under the rule of a hostile country, whatever the justification given on its behalf.

The architects of the Atlantic Alliance would have been incredulous had they been told that victory in the Cold War would raise doubts about the future of their creation. They took it for granted that the prize for victory in the Cold War was a lasting Atlantic partnership. In the name of that goal, some of the decisive political battles of the Cold War were fought and won. In the process, America was tied to Europe by permanent consultative institutions and an integrated military command system—a structure of a scope and duration unique in the history of coalitions.

What came to be called the Atlantic Community—a nostalgic term far less in vogue since the end of the Cold War—has been marking time since the collapse of communism. Downgrading the relationship with Europe has become all too fashionable. The emphasis on the enlargement of democracy notwithstanding, America now seems to be giving less attention to societies that have similar institutions and with which it shares common attitudes on human rights and other basic values than to other regions of the world. The founders of the Atlantic ties—Truman, Acheson, Marshall, and Eisenhower—shared most Americans' reservations about the European style of diplomacy. But they understood that, without its Atlantic ties, America would find itself in a world of nations with which—except in the Western Hemisphere—it has few moral bonds or common traditions. In these circumstances, America would be obliged to conduct a pure *Realpolitik,* which is essentially incompatible with the American tradition.

Part of the reason for the decline of what was once the most vital American policy is that NATO has come to be taken for granted as part of a landscape that needs no further tending. Perhaps more important, the generation of American leaders which has reached prominence in the last decade and a half has been drawn mostly from the South and the West, where there are fewer emotional and personal ties to Europe than among the old Northeastern establishment. Moreover, American liberals—the standard-bearers of Wilsonianism—have frequently felt let down by democratic allies which practice a policy of national interest rather than of collective security and reliance on international law; they cite Bosnia and the Middle East as examples of a failure to agree in spite of common values. At the same time, the isolationist wing of American conservatism—the other form of exceptionalism—has been tempted to turn its back on what it disdains as Europe's Machiavellian relativism and selfishness.

Disagreements with Europe have the grating character of family squabbles. Yet, on nearly every key issue, there has been far more cooperation from Europe than from any other area. In fairness, it must be recalled that, in Bosnia, French and British troops were on the ground, and American troops were not, although the public rhetoric has created the opposite impression. And, in the Gulf War, the most important non-American contingents were, once again, British and French. Twice in a generation, shared values and interests brought American troops to Europe. In the post–Cold War world, Europe may not be able to rally itself to a new Atlantic policy, but America owes it to itself not to abandon the policies of three generations in the hour of victory. The task before the Alliance is to adapt the two basic institutions which shape the Atlantic relationship, the North Atlantic Treaty Organization (NATO) and the European Union (formerly the European Economic Community), to the realities of the post–Cold War world.

The North Atlantic Treaty Organization remains the principal institutional link between America and Europe. When NATO was formed, Soviet troops stood at the Elbe in a divided Germany. Generally believed capable of overrunning Western Europe with its conventional forces, the Soviet military establishment soon acquired a rapidly growing nuclear armory as well. Throughout the Cold War, Western Europe depended on the United States for its security, and post–Cold War NATO institutions still reflect this state of affairs. The United States controls the integrated command which is headed by an American general, and it has resisted French attempts to bring about a distinct European identity for defense.

The movement for European integration had its origin in two propositions: that, unless Europe learned to speak with one voice, it would gradually slide into irrelevance, and that a divided Germany must not be placed in a position where it would be tempted to float between the two blocs and play the two sides of the Cold War off against each other. At this writing, the European Union, originally composed of six nations, has grown to twelve and is in the process of expanding to include Scandinavia, Austria, and ultimately some of the former Soviet satellites.

The premises on which both of these institutions were founded have been shaken by the collapse of the Soviet Union and the unification of Germany. The Soviet army no longer exists, and the Russian army stands hundreds of miles to the east. For the immediate future, Russia's domestic turmoil renders an attack on Western Europe improbable. At the same time, Russian tendencies to re-establish the former empire have reawakened historic fears of Russian expansionism, especially in the former satellite states of Eastern Europe. No leader among Russia's immediate neighbors shares America's faith in Russian conversion as the key to his country's security. All prefer President Boris Yeltsin to his opponents, but only as the lesser of two potential threats, not as a figure who can banish their historic insecurity.

The emergence of a unified Germany compounds these fears. Aware that the two Continental giants have historically either carved up their neighbors or fought battles on their territory, the countries located between them dread the emerging security vacuum; hence their intense desire for American protection—as expressed in NATO membership.

If NATO is in need of adaptation to the collapse of Soviet power, the European Union faces the new reality of a reunified Germany, which threatens the tacit bargain that has been at the heart of European integration: the Federal Republic's acceptance of French political leadership in the European Community in return for a preponderant voice on economic matters. The Federal Republic was thus tied to the West through American leadership on strategic matters within NATO, and French leadership on political issues within the European Union.

In the years ahead, all the traditional Atlantic relationships will change. Europe will not feel the previous need for American protection and will pursue its economic self-interest much more aggressively; America will not be willing to sacrifice as much for European security and will be tempted by isolationism in various guises; in due course, Germany will insist on the political influence to which its military and economic power entitle it and will not be so emotionally dependent on American military and French political support.

These trends will not be fully apparent so long as Helmut Kohl, the heir of the Adenauer tradition (see chapter 20), is in office. Yet he represents the last of that type of leader. The emerging generation has no personal recollection of the war or of America's role in the rehabilitation of the devastated postwar Germany. It has no emotional reason to defer to supranational institutions or to subordinate its views either to America or to France.

The great achievement of the postwar generation of American and European leaders was their recognition that, unless America was organically involved in Europe, it would be obliged to involve itself later under circumstances far less favorable to both sides of the Atlantic. That is even more true today. Germany has become so strong that existing European institutions cannot by themselves strike a balance between Germany and its European partners. Nor can Europe, even with Germany, manage by itself either the resurgence or the disintegration of Russia, the two most threatening outcomes of post-Soviet upheavals.

It is in no country's interest that Germany and Russia should fixate on each other as either principal partner or principal adversary. If they become too close, they raise fears of condominium; if they quarrel, they involve Europe in escalating crises. America and Europe have a joint interest in avoiding unbridled national German and Russian policies competing over the center of the Continent. Without America, Great Britain and France cannot sustain the political balance in Western Europe; Germany would be tempted by nationalism; Russia would lack a global interlocutor. And without Europe, America could turn, psychologically as well as geographically and geopolitically, into an island off the shores of Eurasia.

The post–Cold War order confronts the North Atlantic Alliance with three sets of problems: internal relations within the traditional alliance structure; relations of the Atlantic nations to the former satellite states of the Soviet Union in Eastern Europe; and, finally, the relationship of the successor states of the Soviet Union, especially the Russian Federation, to the nations of the North Atlantic and to Eastern Europe.

The adjustment of the internal relationships within the North Atlantic Alliance has been dominated by the perennial tug-of-war between the American and French views of Atlantic relationships. America has dominated NATO under the banner of integration. France, extolling European independence, has shaped the European Union. The result of their disagreement is that America's role is too dominant in the military field to promote a European political identity, while France's role is too insistent on European political autonomy to promote the cohesion of NATO.

Intellectually, the dispute repeats the conflict between the concepts of Richelieu and the ideas of Wilson—between foreign policy as a balancing of interests and diplomacy as an affirmation of an underlying harmony. For America, the integrated NATO command has been the expression of allied unity; to France, it has been a red flag. American leaders have trouble understanding why a country would insist on the right to independent action if it did not wish to retain the option of leaving its ally in the lurch. France has seen in America's uneasiness about an independent European military role a hidden attempt at domination.

Each partner has, in fact, pursued a concept of international relations drawn from its history. France is heir of the European style of diplomacy, which indeed it originated over 300 years ago. Whereas Great Britain has had to abandon its role of guarding the balance of power, France, for better or worse, continues to stand for the policies of *raison d'état,* and for the precise calculation of interests rather than the pursuit of abstract harmony. Just as consistently, if for a shorter period, America has practiced Wilsonianism. Convinced of the existence of an underlying harmony, America has insisted that, since European and American objectives were identical, European autonomy was either unnecessary or dangerous.

The two great European challenges of the contemporary period—the integration of a united Germany into the West and the relationship of the Atlantic Alliance to the new Russia—cannot be dealt with by a literal application of the statecraft of either Richelieu or Wilson. The Richelieu approach fosters the nationalism of individual European countries and leads to a fragmented Europe. Undiluted Wilsonianism would weaken the European sense of identity. The attempt to build European institutions based on opposition to the United States will in the end wreck both European unity and Atlantic cohesion. On the other hand, the United States need not fear an enhanced European identity within NATO because it is difficult to imagine autonomous European military action on any scale and in any area without American political and logistics support. In the end, it is not the integrated command that generates unity but a sense of shared political and security interests.

The controversy between the United States and France, between the ideals of Wilson and Richelieu, has been overtaken by events. Both the Atlantic Alliance and the European Union are indispensable building blocks of a new and stable world order. NATO is the best protection against military blackmail from any quarter; the European Union is an essential mechanism for stability in Central and Eastern Europe. Both institutions are needed to relate the former satellites and successor states of the Soviet Union to a peaceful international order.

The future of Eastern Europe and of the successor states of the Soviet Union are not the same problem. Eastern Europe was occupied by the Red Army. It has identified itself, culturally and politically, with West European traditions. This is especially true of the Visegrad countries of Poland, the Czech Republic, Hungary, and Slovakia. Without ties to Western Europe and Atlantic institutions, these will become a no-man's-land between Germany and Russia. And for these ties to be meaningful, the Visegrad countries will have to belong to both the European Union and the Atlantic Alliance. To become economically and politically viable, they need the European Union; and, for security, they look to the Atlantic

Alliance. In truth, membership in one institution implies membership in the other. Since most members of the European Union are members of NATO, and since it is inconceivable that they would ignore attacks on one of their members after European integration has reached a certain point, membership in the European Union will, by one device or another, lead to at least *de facto* extension of the NATO guarantee.

So far, the issue has been evaded because East European membership in both institutions has been blocked. However, the reasoning behind the two exclusions has been as different as that between the European and the American political traditions. Europe has based its decision to expand the European Union eastward on *Realpolitik:* it has accepted the principle and offered associate membership pending the reform of the East European economies (and, in the process, to shelter the economies of Western Europe from competition for a while longer). This would make ultimate membership a technical issue to be taken care of by the passage of time.

The American objection to NATO membership for the Visigrad countries is one of principle. Going back to Wilson's historical objection to alliances—because they were based on the expectation of confrontation —President Clinton has used the occasion of a NATO summit in January 1994 to offer an alternative vision. Explaining why the United States did not favor the admission of Poland, Hungary, the Czech Republic, and Slovakia into NATO, he argued that the Atlantic Alliance could not afford to "draw a new line between East and West that could create a self-fulfilling prophecy of future confrontation. . . . I say to all those in Europe and the United States who would simply have us draw a new line in Europe further east that we should not foreclose the possibility of the best possible future for Europe, which is a democracy everywhere, a market economy everywhere, people cooperating everywhere for mutual security."[5]

In this spirit, President Clinton put forward a scheme which he called the Partnership for Peace. It invites *all* the successor states of the Soviet Union and *all* of Moscow's former East European satellites to join what amounts to a vague system of collective security. An amalgamation of Wilsonianism and the Wallace critique of containment described in chapter 16, it applies the principles of collective security; equating the victims of Soviet and Russian imperialism with its perpetrators, it gives the same status to Central Asian republics at the borders of Afghanistan as it does to Poland, the victim of four partitions in which Russia has participated. The Partnership for Peace is not a way station into NATO, as is often misleadingly asserted, but an alternative to it, just as the Locarno Treaty (see chapter 11) was an alternative to the British alliance which France sought in the 1920s.

Yet Locarno showed that there is no middle ground between an alliance based on common purpose and a multilateral institution that is based not on a common perception of the threat, but on the fulfillment of specified conditions of domestic governance. The Partnership for Peace runs the risk of creating two sets of borders in Europe: those that are protected by security guarantees, and others where such guarantees have been refused—a state of affairs bound to prove tempting to potential aggressors and demoralizing to potential victims. Care must be taken lest, in the name of avoiding confrontation, a strategic and conceptual no-man's-land is created in Eastern and Central Europe—the source of so many European conflicts.

It will prove impossible to solve the twin problems of security for Eastern Europe and of integrating Russia into the international community as part of the same program. If the Partnership for Peace is made an aspect of NATO, it may well undermine the Atlantic Alliance by diverting it into activities unrelated to any realistic security mission, magnify the sense of insecurity of Eastern Europe, and yet, being sufficiently ambiguous, fail to placate Russia. Indeed, the Partnership for Peace runs the risk of being treated as irrelevant, if not dangerous, by the potential victims of aggression while being treated in Asia as an ethnic club directed primarily against China and Japan.

At the same time, relating Russia to the Atlantic nations is important. There is a place for an institution that calls itself the Partnership for Peace provided it deals with missions that all of its members interpret in substantially the same manner. Such common tasks exist in the field of economic development, education, and culture. The Conference for Security and Cooperation in Europe (CSCE) could be given expanded functions for these purposes, and renamed the Partnership for Peace.

In such a design, the Atlantic Alliance would establish a common political framework and provide overall security; the European Union would accelerate membership for former Eastern European satellites; and the North Atlantic Cooperation Council (NACC) and the Conference for Security and Cooperation in Europe, perhaps renamed as the Partnership for Peace, would relate the republics of the former Soviet Union—and especially the Russian Federation—to the Atlantic structure. A security umbrella would be extended over the new democracies in Eastern Europe. If Russia remained within its borders, the focus on security would shift over time to the Partnership. The common political and economic projects would increasingly dominate the East-West relationship.

The future of the Atlantic relationship does not reside in East-West relations, but in its decisive role in helping America cope with the foreseeable evolution of the twenty-first century. At this writing, it is impossible to tell which of the conceivable surging forces will be most dominant or most threatening, or in what combination: whether it will be Russia, China, or fundamentalist Islam. But America's ability to deal with any of these evolutions will be enhanced by the cooperation of the nations of the North Atlantic. In this manner, what used to be called "out of area" issues will become the core of the North Atlantic relationship, which should be reorganized for that purpose.

There has been a surge of American interest in Asia as symbolized by the proposal for a Pacific Community made by Clinton at a meeting with the Asian heads of government in 1993. But the term "community" applies to Asia in only the most limited sense, for relationships in the Pacific are fundamentally different from those in the Atlantic area. Whereas the nations of Europe are grouped in common institutions, the nations of Asia view themselves as distinct and competitive. The relations of the principal Asian nations to each other bear most of the attributes of the European balance-of-power system of the nineteenth century. Any significant increase in strength by one of them is almost certain to evoke an offsetting maneuver by the others.

The wild card is the attitude of the United States, which has the capacity —though not necessarily the philosophy—to function in much the same way that Great Britain did in maintaining the European balance of power until the two world wars of the twentieth century. The stability of the Asia-Pacific region, the underpinning of its vaunted prosperity, is not a law of nature but the consequence of an equilibrium which will need increasingly careful and deliberate tending in the post–Cold War world.

Wilsonianism has few disciples in Asia. There is no pretense of collective security or that cooperation should be based on shared domestic values, even on the part of the few existing democracies. The emphasis is all on equilibrium and national interest. Military expenditures are already rising in all the major Asian countries. China is on the road to superpower status. At a growth rate of 8 percent, which is less than it has maintained over the 1980s, China's Gross National Product will approach that of the United States by the end of the second decade of the twenty-first century. Long before that, China's political and military shadow will fall over Asia and will affect the calculations of the other powers, however restrained actual Chinese policy may prove to be. The other Asian nations are likely to seek counterweights to an increasingly powerful China as they already

826

do to Japan. Though they will disavow it, the nations of Southeast Asia are including the heretofore feared Vietnam in their grouping (ASEAN) largely in order to balance China and Japan. And that too is why ASEAN is asking the United States to remain engaged in their region.

The role of Japan will inevitably be adapted to those changed circumstances, though, following their national style, Japanese leaders will make the adjustment by the accumulation of apparently imperceptible nuances. During the Cold War, Japan, abandoning its historic self-reliance, basked in the protection of the United States. A determined economic competitor, it paid for freedom of maneuver in the economic field by subordinating its foreign and security policies to Washington's. So long as the Soviet Union could be perceived as the principal security threat by both countries, it made sense to treat American and Japanese national interests as identical.

That pattern is not likely to continue. With Korea and China gaining in military strength, and with the least impaired portion of Soviet military power located in Siberia, Japanese long-range planners will not indefinitely take the absolute identity of American and Japanese interests for granted. When every incoming American administration begins its term by proclaiming a reassessment of existing policies (or at least implying that they are subject to change), and when confrontation over economic issues becomes the rule rather than the exception, it is difficult to argue that American and Japanese foreign policy interests can never diverge. In any event, Japan's perspective with respect to the Asian mainland differs from America's because of geographic proximity and historic experience. Therefore, the Japanese defense budget has been creeping upward until it has become the third largest in the world and, given Russia's internal problems, perhaps the second most effective.

When, in 1992, then Japanese Prime Minister Kiichi Miyazawa was asked whether Japan would accept a North Korean nuclear capability, he answered with very un-Japanese directness by the single word "no." Did this mean that Japan would develop its own nuclear capability? Or that it would seek to suppress North Korea's? The mere fact that these questions can be asked suggests the possibility of a Japan cut loose, to some extent, from American security and foreign policy moorings.

That even more pointed analyses would be possible with respect to the other major powers shows how shifting and perhaps even precarious the Asian equilibrium might become. To the extent that the United States attempts to preserve the equilibrium of Asia, it cannot wait until the balance is already in jeopardy. Its policy must be sufficiently flexible to be able to influence all available Asian forums. To some extent, this is already happening. An auxiliary role in ASEAN (for Southeast Asia) and a major participation in the Asia-Pacific Economic Cooperation (APEC) have been established.

But the limits of America's influence over such multilateral institutions have become evident as well. Clinton's proposal for a more institutionalized Pacific Community on the European model was received with polite aloofness, largely because the nations of Asia do not view themselves as a community. They do not want an institutional framework that might give potential Asian superpowers—or even the United States—a major voice in their affairs. The nations of Asia are open to American exchanges of ideas; they also favor keeping America sufficiently involved so that, in an emergency, it can help ward off threats to their independence. But they are too suspicious of powerful neighbors and to some extent of the United States to favor formal, Pacific-wide institutions.

America's capacity to shape events will therefore, in the end, depend primarily on its bilateral relations with the major countries of Asia. This is why America's policies toward both Japan and China—at this writing, much buffeted in controversy—assume such critical importance. For one thing, the American role is the key to helping Japan and China co-exist despite their suspicions of each other. In the immediate future, Japan, faced with an aging population and a stagnating economy, might decide to press its technological and strategic superiority before China emerges as a superpower and Russia recovers its strength. Afterward, it might have recourse to that great equalizer, nuclear technology.

With respect to either contingency, close Japanese-American relations will be a vital contribution to Japanese moderation and a significant reassurance to the other nations of Asia. Japanese military strength linked to America worries China and the other nations of Asia less than purely national Japanese military capabilities. And Japan will decide that it needs less military strength so long as an American safety net exists—even if it is less inclusive than previously. A substantial American military presence in Northeast Asia (Japan and Korea) will be needed. In its absence, America's commitment to a permanent role in Asia would lack credibility, and Japan and China would be increasingly tempted to pursue national courses of action which, in the end, could well be directed against each other and all the buffer states in between.

Revitalizing and clarifying Japanese-American relations on the basis of parallel geopolitical interests will face major obstacles. The economic disagreements are familiar; the cultural obstacles may prove even more insidious. These are most painfully—and sometimes maddeningly—evident in the different national approaches to decision-making. America decides on the basis of status; somebody in authority, usually the president, occasionally the secretary of state, selects his preferred course from the available options, more or less by dint of his position. Japan operates by consensus. No single person—not even the prime minister—has the authority to make a decision. Everyone who must carry out the decision participates in the formation of the consensus, which is not considered complete until all have agreed.

All of this practically guarantees that, at meetings between an American president and a Japanese prime minister, substantive differences are compounded by misunderstanding. When the American president expresses agreement, he is foreshadowing action; when the Japanese prime minister assents, he is conveying an attitude which implies not so much that he agrees with the American position as that he has understood it and will submit it to his consensus group. He presumes it is clear that his authority does not extend beyond that. For negotiations on Asia's future to thrive, America requires greater patience, and Japan must put itself in a position to discuss meaningfully long-range policies on which the future cooperation ultimately depends.

In a curious way, the firmness of Japanese-American relations will be the reverse side of the Sino-American relationship. Despite a considerable affinity for Chinese culture, Japan has been torn between admiration and fear, between the desire for friendship and the urge to dominate. Sino-American tension tempts Japan to dissociate from the United States in an effort, if not to enhance its influence in China, at least not to diminish it by following the American lead too closely. At the same time, a purely national Japanese approach runs the risk of being interpreted in Beijing as an expression of the Japanese appetite for domination. Good American relations with China are therefore the prerequisite for good long-term relations with Japan, as well as for good Sino-Japanese relations. It is a triangle which each of the parties can abandon only at great risk. It is also an ambiguity with which the United States is not totally comfortable, since it runs counter to the American tendency to label nations neatly as either friend or foe.

Of all the great, and potentially great, powers, China is the most ascendant. The United States already is the most powerful, Europe must work to forge greater unity, Russia is a staggering giant, and Japan is wealthy but, so far, timid. China, however, with economic growth rates approaching 10 percent annually, a strong sense of national cohesion, and an ever more muscular military, will show the greatest relative increase in stature among the major powers. In 1943, Roosevelt had envisioned China as one of the "Four Policemen," but China soon thereafter sank into the turmoil of civil war. The Maoist China which emerged was intent on being an independent great power, but was frustrated by its ideological blinkers. Having put the ideological convulsions behind them, China's reformist leaders have pursued Chinese national interest with skillful tenacity. A policy of confrontation with China risks America's isolation in Asia. No Asian country would want to be—or could afford to be—supportive of America in any political conflict with China which it considered to be the result of misguided United States policy. In such circumstances, the vast majority of Asian nations would dissociate from America to a greater or a lesser degree, however much they might inwardly dislike doing so. For nearly every country looks to America to create a stable, long-term framework which will integrate both China and Japan—an option which is forfeited vis-à-vis *both* countries by Sino-American confrontation.

As the nation with the longest history of independent foreign policy and a tradition of basing its foreign policy on national interest, China welcomes American involvement in Asia as a counterweight to its feared neighbors, Japan and Russia, and—to a lesser degree—India. Yet an American policy that seeks simultaneously friendship with Beijing as well as with countries that are perceived as potential threats to Chinese security in Beijing—which is the correct U.S. stance—requires a careful and regular dialogue between Washington and Beijing.

For four years after the events of Tiananmen Square in 1989, this dialogue was inhibited by the American refusal to engage in high-level contacts—a measure never employed against the Soviet Union even at the height of the Cold War. Human rights thus moved to the center of the Sino-American relationship.

The Clinton Administration wisely restored high-level contacts; the future of Sino-American relations henceforth depends essentially on the substance of these exchanges. Clearly, the United States cannot abandon its traditional concern with human rights and democratic values. The problem is not America's advocacy of its values but the degree to which all aspects of Sino-American relations are made conditional on them. China finds condescending the implication that Sino-American relations are based not on reciprocal interests but on American favors which can be pursued or shut off at Washington's discretion. Such an attitude makes America appear both unreliable and intrusive, and unreliability is the greater failing in Chinese eyes.

For China, a country historically pre-eminent in its region—indeed, in the world known to it—any attempt to prescribe its institutions and domestic practices would cause deep resentment. This general sensitivity is magnified by the Chinese view of the West's involvement in its history. Ever since the Opium Wars of the early nineteenth century forcibly opened up the country, the West has been viewed by the Chinese as the agent of an endless series of humiliations. Equality of status, a fierce insistence on not bowing to foreign prescription, is for Chinese leaders not a tactic but a moral imperative.

What China seeks from the United States is a strategic relationship to balance neighbors it considers to be both powerful and covetous. To achieve this level of foreign policy coordination, China might be prepared to make some human-rights concessions, provided they can be presented as emerging from its own free choice. But American insistence on publicly prescribing conditions is perceived in China both as an attempt to convert its society to American values—hence humiliating—and as a lack of American seriousness. For it suggests that America has no national interest in the Asian equilibrium as such. But if America cannot be counted on for that purpose, China will have no interest in making concessions to it. The key to Sino-American relations—paradoxically, even on human rights—is a tacit cooperation on global, and especially Asian, strategy.

With respect to Europe, America shares a community of values but has not yet been able to devise a common policy or adequate institutions for the post–Cold War period; with respect to Asia, it is possible for America to define a desirable overall strategy but not a community of values. However, quite unexpectedly, a confluence of moral and geopolitical aims, of Wilsonianism and *Realpolitik*, is emerging in the Western Hemisphere.

The United States' early foreign policy in the Western Hemisphere was essentially one of Great Power interventionism. Franklin Roosevelt's Good Neighbor policy, announced in 1933, marked the turn toward cooperation. The Rio Treaty of 1947 and the Pact of Bogotá of 1948 provided a security component that was institutionalized in the Organization of American States. President Kennedy's 1961 Alliance for Progress introduced foreign aid and economic cooperation, though the farsighted policy was doomed by the statist orientation of the recipients.

During the Cold War, most of the nations of Latin America were governed by authoritarian, largely military, governments committed to state control of their economies. Starting in the mid-1980s, Latin America shook off its economic paralysis and began to advance with remarkable unanimity toward democracy and market economics. Brazil, Argentina, and Chile abandoned military government in favor of democratic rule. Central America ended its civil wars. Bankrupted by mindless borrowing,

Latin America submitted itself to financial disciplines. Nearly everywhere, state-dominated economies were progressively opened to market forces.

The Enterprise for the Americas Initiative announced by Bush in 1990, and the battle for a North American Free Trade Agreement with Mexico and Canada successfully concluded by Clinton in 1993, represent the most innovative American policy toward Latin America in history. After a series of ups and downs, the Western Hemisphere seems on the verge of turning into a key element of a new and humane global order. A group of democratic nations has pledged itself to popular governments, market economies, and hemisphere-wide free trade. The sole Marxist dictatorship remaining in the Western Hemisphere is Cuba; everywhere else, nationalistic, protectionist methods of economic management are being replaced by free economies hospitable to foreign investment and supportive of open international trading systems. Emphasizing reciprocal obligations and cooperative action, the ultimate and dramatic goal is the creation of a free-trade area from Alaska to Cape Horn—a concept that, a short time ago, would have been considered hopelessly utopian.

A Western Hemisphere–wide free-trade system—with NAFTA as the initial step—would give the Americas a commanding role no matter what happens. If the principles of the Uruguay Round of the General Agreement on Trade and Tariffs (GATT) negotiated in 1993 in fact prevail, the Western Hemisphere will be a major participant in global economic growth. If discriminatory regional groupings dominate, the Western Hemisphere, with its vast market, will be able to compete effectively with other regional trading blocs; indeed, NAFTA is the most effective means to forestall such a contest or to prevail in it should it occur. By offering associate membership to nations outside the Western Hemisphere that are prepared to observe its principles, an expanded NAFTA could create incentives to abide by free trade, and penalize nations insisting on more restrictive rules. In a world where America is often obliged to strike a balance between its values and its necessities, it has discovered that its ideals and its geopolitical objectives mesh substantially in the Western Hemisphere, where its aspirations originated and its first major foreign policy initiatives were conducted.

In launching itself for the third time in this century on creating a new world order, America's dominant task is to strike a balance between the twin temptations inherent in its exceptionalism: the notion that America must remedy every wrong and stabilize every dislocation, and the latent instinct to withdraw into itself. Indiscriminate involvement in all the ethnic turmoil and civil wars of the post–Cold War world would drain a crusading America. Yet an America that confines itself to the refinement of its domestic virtues would, in the end, abdicate America's security and prosperity to decisions made by other societies in faraway places and over which America would progressively lose control.

When, in 1821, John Quincy Adams warned Americans against the penchant to slay "distant monsters," he could not have imagined the sheer number and magnitude of monsters that would exist in the post–Cold War world. Not every evil can be combated by America, even less by America alone. But some monsters need to be, if not slain, at least resisted. What is most needed are criteria for selectivity.

America's leaders have generally stressed motivation over structure. They have placed more emphasis on affecting the attitudes than the calculations of their counterparts. As a result, American society is peculiarly ambivalent about the lessons of history. American films often depict how some dramatic event transforms a villain into a paragon of virtue (sometimes cloyingly so)—a reflection of the pervasive national belief that the past has no final claim and that new departures are always possible. In the real world, such transformations are rarely observed in individuals, even less so among nations which are composites of many individual choices.

The rejection of history extols the image of a universal man living by universal maxims, regardless of the past, of geography, or of other immutable circumstance. Since the American tradition emphasizes universal truths rather than national characteristics, American policymakers have generally preferred multilateral approaches to national ones: the agendas of disarmament, nonproliferation, and human rights rather than essentially national, geopolitical, or strategic issues.

The American refusal to be bound by history and the insistence on the perpetual possibility for renewal confer a great dignity, even beauty, on the American way of life. The national fear that those who are obsessed with history produce self-fulfilling prophecies does embody a great folk wisdom. Still, Santayana's dictum that those who ignore history are condemned to repeat it can be supported by even more examples.

A country with America's idealistic tradition cannot base its policy on the balance of power as the sole criterion for a new world order. But it must learn that equilibrium is a fundamental precondition for the pursuit of its historic goals. And these higher goals cannot be achieved by rhetoric or posturing. The emerging international system is far more complex than any previously encountered by American diplomacy. Foreign policy has to be conducted by a political system that emphasizes the immediate and provides few incentives for the long range. Its leaders are obliged to deal with constituencies that tend to receive their information via visual images. All this puts a premium on emotion and on the mood of the moment at a time that demands rethinking of priorities and an analysis of capabilities.

History, however, will not excuse failure by the magnitude of the task. What America must master is the transition from an age when all choices seemed open to a period when it can still accomplish more than any other society if it can only learn its limits. Through most of its history, America knew no foreign threat to its survival. When such a threat finally emerged during the Cold War, it was utterly defeated. The American experience has thus encouraged the belief that America, alone among the nations of the world, is impervious and that it can prevail by the example of its virtues and good works.

In the post–Cold War world, such an attitude would turn innocence into self-indulgence. At a time when America is able neither to dominate the world nor to withdraw from it, when it finds itself both all-powerful and totally vulnerable, it must not abandon the ideals which have accounted for its greatness. But neither must it jeopardize that greatness by fostering illusions about the extent of its reach. World leadership is inherent in America's power and values, but it does not include the privilege of pretending that America is doing other nations a kindness by associating with them, or that it has a limitless capacity to impose its will by withholding its favors. For America, any association with *Realpolitik* must take into account the core values of the first society in history to have been explicitly created in the name of liberty. Yet America's survival and progress will depend as well on its ability to make choices which reflect contemporary reality. Otherwise, foreign policy will turn into self-righteous posturing. The relative weight to be given to each of these components and the price associated with every priority define both the challenge and the stature of political leaders. What no leader must ever do is to suggest that choice has no price, or that no balance needs to be struck.

In traveling along the road to world order for the third time in the modern era, American idealism remains as essential as ever, perhaps even more so. But in the new world order, its role will be to provide the faith to sustain America through all the ambiguities of choice in an imperfect world. Traditional American idealism must combine with a thoughtful assessment of contemporary realities to bring about a usable definition of American interests. In the past, American foreign policy efforts were inspired by utopian visions of some terminal point after which the under-lying harmony of the world would simply reassert itself.

Henceforth, few such final outcomes are in prospect; the fulfillment of America's ideals will have to be sought in the patient accumulation of partial successes. The certitudes of physical threat and hostile ideology characteristic of the Cold War are gone. The convictions needed to master the emerging world order are more abstract: a vision of a future that cannot be demonstrated when it is put forward and judgments about the relationship between hope and possibility that are, in their essence, conjectural. The Wilsonian goals of America's past—peace, stability, prog-ress, and freedom for mankind—will have to be sought in a journey that has no end. "Traveler," says a Spanish proverb, "there are no roads. Roads are made by walking."

Notes

CHAPTER TWO
The Hinge: Theodore Roosevelt or Woodrow Wilson

1. Robert W. Tucker and David C. Hendrickson, "Thomas Jefferson and American Foreign Policy," *Foreign Affairs,* vol. 69, no. 2 (Spring 1990), p. 148.
2. Thomas G. Paterson, J. Garry Clifford, and Kenneth J. Hagan, *American Foreign Policy: A History* (Lexington, Mass.: D. C. Heath, 1977), p. 60.
3. Tucker and Hendrickson, "Thomas Jefferson," p. 140, quoting from *Letters and Other Writings of James Madison* (Philadelphia: J. B. Lippincott, 1865), vol. IV, pp. 491–92.
4. James Monroe quoted in William A. Williams, ed., *The Shaping of American Diplomacy* (Chicago: Rand McNally, 1956), vol. I, p. 122.
5. George Washington's Farewell Address, September 17, 1796, reprinted as Senate Document no. 3, 102nd Cong., 1st sess. (Washington, D.C.: U.S. Government Printing Office, 1991), p. 24.
6. Jefferson letter to Mme. La Duchesse D'Auville, April 2, 1790, in Paul Leicester Ford, ed., *The Writings of Jefferson* (New York: G. P. Putnam's Sons, 1892–99), vol. V, p. 153, quoted in Tucker and Hendrickson, "Thomas Jefferson," p. 139.
7. Thomas Paine, *Rights of Man* (1791) (Secaucus, N.J.: Citadel Press, 1974), p. 147.
8. Alexander Hamilton, "The Federalist No. 6," in Edward Mead Earle, ed., *The Federalist* (New York: Modern Library, 1941), pp. 30–31.
9. Jefferson letter to John Dickinson, March 6, 1801, in Adrienne Koch and William Peden,

eds., *The Life and Selected Writings of Thomas Jefferson* (New York: Modern Library, 1944), p. 561.

10. Jefferson letter to Joseph Priestley, June 19, 1802, in Ford, ed., *Writings of Thomas Jefferson,* vol. VIII, pp. 158–59, quoted in Robert W. Tucker and David C. Hendrickson, *Empire of Liberty: The Statecraft of Thomas Jefferson* (New York/Oxford: Oxford University Press, 1990), p. 11.

11. Tucker and Hendrickson, "Thomas Jefferson," p. 141.

12. John Quincy Adams, Address of July 4, 1821, in Walter LaFeber, ed., *John Quincy Adams and American Continental Empire* (Chicago: Times Books, 1965), p. 45.

13. Message of President Monroe to Congress, December 2, 1823, in Ruhl J. Bartlett, ed., *The Record of American Diplomacy* (New York: Alfred A. Knopf, 1956), p. 182.

14. *Ibid.*

15. President James Polk, Inaugural Address, March 4, 1845, in *The Presidents Speak,* annot. by David Newton Lott (New York: Holt, Rinehart and Winston, 1969), p. 95.

16. Quoted in Williams, *Shaping of American Diplomacy,* vol. 1, p. 315.

17. See Paul Kennedy, *The Rise and Fall of the Great Powers* (New York: Random House, 1987), p. 201 and pp. 242ff; also, Fareed Zakaria, "The Rise of a Great Power, National Strength, State Structure, and American Foreign Policy 1865–1908" (unpublished doctoral thesis, Harvard University, 1992), chapter 3, pp. 4ff.

18. Zakaria, *ibid.,* pp. 7–8.

19. *Ibid.,* p. 71.

20. Paterson, Clifford, and Hagan, eds., *American Foreign Policy,* p. 189.

21. President Roosevelt's Annual Message to Congress, December 6, 1904, in Bartlett, ed., *Record of American Diplomacy,* p. 539.

22. Roosevelt's statement to Congress, 1902, quoted in John Morton Blum, *The Republican Roosevelt* (Cambridge, Mass.: Harvard University Press, 1967), p. 127.

23. *Ibid.,* p. 137.

24. Roosevelt letter to Hugo Munsterberg, October 3, 1914, in Elting E. Morison, ed., *The Letters of Theodore Roosevelt* (Cambridge, Mass.: Harvard University Press, 1954), vol. VIII, pp. 824–25.

25. Blum, *Republican Roosevelt,* p. 131.

26. *Selections from the Correspondence of Theodore Roosevelt and Henry Cabot Lodge 1884–1918,* ed. by Henry Cabot Lodge and Charles F. Redmond (New York/London: Charles Scribner's Sons, 1925), vol. II, p. 162.

27. Blum, *Republican Roosevelt,* p. 135.

28. *Ibid.,* p. 134.

29. Quoted in John Milton Cooper, Jr., *Pivotal Decades: The United States, 1900–1920* (New York/London: W. W. Norton, 1990), p. 103.

30. Blum, *Republican Roosevelt,* p. 134.

31. Roosevelt, in *Outlook,* vol. 107 (August 22, 1914), p. 1012.

32. Roosevelt to Munsterberg, October 3, 1914, in Morison, ed., *Letters of Theodore Roosevelt,* p. 823.

33. Roosevelt to Cecil Arthur Spring Rice, October 3, 1914, in *ibid.,* p. 821.

34. Roosevelt to Rudyard Kipling, November 4, 1914, in Robert Endicott Osgood, *Ideals and Self-Interest in America's Foreign Relations* (Chicago: University of Chicago Press, 1953), p. 137.

35. Woodrow Wilson, Annual Message to Congress on the State of the Union, December 2, 1913, in Arthur S. Link, ed., *The Papers of Woodrow Wilson* (Princeton, N.J.: Princeton University Press, 1966–) vol. 29, p. 4.

36. Roosevelt letter to a friend, December 1914, in Osgood, *Ideals and Self-Interest,* p. 144.

37. Woodrow Wilson, Annual Message to Congress, December 8, 1914, in Link, ed., *Papers of Woodrow Wilson,* vol. 31, p. 423.

38. *Ibid.,* p. 422.

39. Woodrow Wilson, Commencement Address at the U.S. Military Academy at West Point, June 13, 1916, in *ibid.,* vol. 37, pp. 212ff.

40. Woodrow Wilson, Remarks to Confederate Veterans in Washington, June 5, 1917, in *ibid.,* vol. 42, p. 453.

41. Woodrow Wilson, Annual Message to Congress on the State of the Union, December 7, 1915, in *ibid.,* vol. 35, p. 297.

42. Woodrow Wilson, An Address in the Princess Theater, Cheyenne, Wyoming, September 24, 1919, in *ibid.,* vol. 63, p. 474.

43. Woodrow Wilson, An Address to a Joint Session of Congress, April 2, 1917, in *ibid.,* vol. 41, pp. 526–27.

44. *Ibid.,* p. 523.

45. Woodrow Wilson, An Address to the Senate, January 22, 1917, in *ibid.,* vol. 40, p. 536.

46. Selig Adler, *The Isolationist Impulse: Its Twentieth-Century Reaction* (London/New York: Abelard Schuman, 1957), p. 36.

47. *Ibid.*

48. Woodrow Wilson, Address, April 2, 1917, in Link, ed., *Papers of Woodrow Wilson,* vol. 41, pp. 519ff.

49. Woodrow Wilson, An Address in Boston, February 24, 1919, in *ibid.,* vol. 55, pp. 242–43.

50. Woodrow Wilson, Address, January 22, 1917, in *ibid.,* vol. 40, pp. 536–37.

51. See Chapter 6.

52. Woodrow Wilson, Remarks at Suresnes Cemetery on Memorial Day, May 30, 1919, in *ibid.,* vol. 59, pp. 608–9.

53. Woodrow Wilson, An Address Before the League to Enforce Peace, May 27, 1916, in *ibid.,* vol. 37, pp. 113ff.

54. Woodrow Wilson, An Address at Mt. Vernon, July 4, 1918, in *ibid.,* vol. 48, p. 516.

55. Woodrow Wilson, An Address to the Third Plenary Session of the Peace Conference, February 14, 1919, in *ibid.,* vol. 55, p. 175.

56. Roosevelt letter to James Bryce, November 19, 1918, in Morison, ed., *Letters of Theodore Roosevelt,* vol. VIII, p. 1400.

57. Roosevelt to Senator Philander Chase Knox (R.-Pa.), December 6, 1918, in *ibid.,* pp. 1413–14.

CHAPTER THREE

From Universality to Equilibrium: Richelieu, William of Orange, and Pitt

1. Louis Auchincloss, *Richelieu* (New York: Viking Press, 1972), p. 256.

2. In *Quellenbuch zur Österreichische Geschichte,* vol. II, edited by Otto Frass (Vienna: Birken Verlag, 1959), p. 100.

3. *Ibid.*

4. *Ibid.*

5. *Ibid.*

6. Joseph Strayer, Hans Gatzke, and E. Harris Harbison, *The Mainstream of Civilization Since 1500* (New York: Harcourt Brace Jovanovich, 1971), p. 420.

7. Quoted in Carl J. Burckhardt, *Richelieu and His Age,* trans., from the German by Bernard Hoy (New York: Harcourt Brace Jovanovich, 1970), vol. III, "Power Politics and the Cardinal's Death," p. 61.

8. *Ibid.,* p. 122.

9. Jansenius, *Mars Gallicus,* in William F. Church, *Richelieu and Reason of State* (Princeton, N.J.: Princeton University Press, 1972), p. 388.

10. Daniel de Priezac, *Défence des Droits et Prérogatives des Roys de France,* in *ibid.,* p. 398.

11. Mathieu de Morgues, *Catholicon françois,* treatise of 1636, in *ibid.,* p. 376.

12. Albert Sorel, *Europe Under the Old Regime,* trans. by Francis H. Herrick (Los Angeles: Ward Ritchie Press, 1947), p. 10.

13. In F. H. Hinsley, *Power and the Pursuit of Peace* (Cambridge: Cambridge University Press, 1963), pp. 162–63.

14. *Ibid.,* p. 162.

15. *Ibid.,* p. 166.
16. Quoted in Gordon A. Craig and Alexander L. George, *Force and Statecraft* (New York/ Oxford: Oxford University Press, 1983), p. 20.
17. G. C. Gibbs, "The Revolution in Foreign Policy," in Geoffrey Holmes, ed., *Britain After the Glorious Revolution, 1689–1714* (London: Macmillan, 1969), p. 61.
18. Winston S. Churchill, *The Gathering Storm, The Second World War,* vol. 1 (Boston: Houghton Mifflin, 1948), p. 208.
19. Quoted in Gibbs, "Revolution," in Holmes, ed., *Britain After the Glorious Revolution,* p. 62.
20. Speech by Secretary of State, Lord John Carteret, Earl of Granville, in the House of Lords, January 27, 1744, in Joel H. Wiener, ed., *Great Britain: Foreign Policy and the Span of Empire, 1689–1971,* vol. 1 (New York/London: Chelsea House in association with McGraw-Hill, 1972), pp. 84–86.
21. Churchill, *Gathering Storm,* p. 208.
22. Pitt Plan in Sir Charles Webster, ed., *British Diplomacy 1813–1815* (London: G. Bell and Sons, 1921), pp. 389ff.

CHAPTER FOUR
The Concert of Europe: Great Britain, Austria, and Russia

1. Sir Thomas Overbury, "Observations on His Travels," in *Stuart Tracts 1603–1693,* edited by C. H. Firth (London: Constable, 1903), p. 227, quoted in Martin Wight, *Power Politics* (New York: Holmes and Meier, 1978), p. 173.
2. Memorandum of Lord Castlereagh, August 12, 1815, in C. K. Webster, ed., *British Diplomacy, 1813–1815* (London: G. Bell and Sons, 1921), pp. 361–62.
3. Talleyrand, in Harold Nicolson, *The Congress of Vienna* (New York/San Diego/London: Harcourt Brace Jovanovich, paper ed., 1974), p. 155.
4. Wilhelm Schwarz, *Die Heilige Allianz* (Stuttgart, 1935), pp. 52ff.
5. Quoted in Asa Briggs, *The Age of Improvement 1783–1867* (London: Longmans, 1959), p. 345.
6. Klemens Metternich, *Aus Metternich's Nachgelassenen Papieren* (8 vols.), edited by Alfons von Klinkowstroem (Vienna, 1880), vol. VIII, pp. 557ff.
7. The material in these pages draws on the author's *A World Restored: Metternich, Castlereagh and the Problems of Peace 1812–1822* (Boston: Houghton Mifflin, 1973 Sentry Edition).
8. Quoted in *ibid.,* p. 321.
9. Quoted in Wilhelm Oncken, *Österreich und Preussen im Befreiungskriege,* 2 vols. (Berlin, 1880), vol. II, pp. 630ff.
10. Metternich, *Nachgelassenen Papieren,* vol. VIII, p. 365.
11. Quoted in Oncken, *Österreich und Preussen,* vol. I, pp. 439ff.
12. Metternich, *Nachgelassenen Papieren,* vol. I, pp. 316ff.
13. Quoted in Nicholas Mikhailovitch, *Les Rapports Diplomatiques du Lebzeltern* (St. Petersburg, 1915), pp. 37ff.
14. Quoted in Schwarz, *Die Heilige Allianz,* p. 234.
15. Quoted in Alfred Stern, *Geschichte Europas seit den Verträgen von 1815 bis zum Frankfurter Frieden von 1871,* 10 vols. (Munich-Berlin, 1913–24), vol. I, p. 298.
16. Quoted in Hans Schmalz, *Versuche einer Gesamteuropäischen Organisation, 1815–20* (Bern, 1940), p. 66.
17. Lord Castlereagh's Confidential State Paper, May 5, 1820, in Sir A. W. Ward and G. P. Gooch, eds., *The Cambridge History of British Foreign Policy, 1783–1919* (New York: Macmillan, 1923), vol. II (1815–66), p. 632.
18. Viscount Castlereagh, *Correspondence, Dispatches and Other Papers,* 12 vols., edited by his brother, the Marquess of Londonderry (London, 1848–52), vol. XII, p. 394.
19. Quoted in Sir Charles Webster, *The Foreign Policy of Castlereagh,* 2 vols. (London, 1925 and 1931), vol. II, p. 366.
20. Quoted in Briggs, *Age of Improvement,* p. 346.
21. Quoted in Webster, *Foreign Policy of Castlereagh,* vol. II, pp. 303ff.

22. Castlereagh's Confidential State Paper of May 5, 1820, in Ward and Gooch, eds., *Cambridge History,* vol. II, pp. 626–27.

23. Quoted in Kissinger, *A World Restored,* p. 311.

24. Quoted in A. J. P. Taylor, *The Struggle for Mastery in Europe 1848–1918* (Oxford: Oxford University Press, 1965), p. 54.

25. Canning, quoted in R. W. Seton-Watson, *Britain in Europe, 1789–1914* (Cambridge: Cambridge University Press, 1955), p. 74.

26. *Ibid.*

27. Canning's Plymouth speech of October 28, 1823, in *ibid.,* p. 119.

28. Palmerston to Clarendon, July 20, 1856, quoted in Harold Temperley and Lillian M. Penson, *Foundations of British Foreign Policy from Pitt (1792) to Salisbury (1902)* (Cambridge: Cambridge University Press, 1938), p. 88.

29. Sir Edward Grey, in Seton-Watson, *Britain in Europe,* p. 1.

30. Palmerston, in Briggs, *Age of Improvement,* p. 352.

31. Palmerston's dispatch no. 6 to the Marquis of Clanricarde (Ambassador in St. Petersburg), January 11, 1841, in Temperley and Penson, *Foundations of Foreign Policy,* p. 136.

32. *Ibid.,* p. 137.

33. Gladstone letter to Queen Victoria, April 17, 1869, in Harold Nicolson, *Diplomacy* (London: Oxford University Press, 1963), p. 137.

34. Palmerston, in Briggs, *Age of Improvement,* p. 357.

35. Disraeli to the House of Commons, August 1, 1870, in *Parliamentary Debates* (Hansard), 3rd ser., vol. cciii (London: Cornelius Buck, 1870), col. 1289.

36. Palmerston to House of Commons, July 21, 1849, in Temperley and Penson, *Foundations of Foreign Policy,* p. 173.

37. Palmerston, in Briggs, *Age of Improvement,* p. 353.

38. Clarendon to the House of Lords, March 31, 1854, quoted in Seton-Watson, *Britain in Europe,* p. 327.

39. Palmerston to House of Commons, July 21, 1849, in Temperley and Penson, *Foundations of Foreign Policy,* p. 176.

40. Quoted in Joel H. Wiener, ed., *Great Britain: Foreign Policy and the Span of Empire 1689–1971* (New York/London: Chelsea House in association with McGraw-Hill, 1972), p. 404.

41. Metternich, June 30, 1841, in Seton-Watson, *Britain in Europe,* p. 221.

CHAPTER FIVE

Two Revolutionaries: Napoleon III and Bismarck

1. Joseph Alexander, Graf von Hübner, *Neun Jahre der Errinerungen eines österreichischen Botschafters in Paris unter dem zweiten Kaiserreich, 1851–1859* (Berlin, 1904) vol. I, p. 109.

2. *Ibid.,* p. 93.

3. Hübner to Franz Josef, September 23, 1857, in Hübner, *Neun Jahre,* vol. II, p. 31.

4. William E. Echard, *Napoleon III and the Concert of Europe* (Baton Rouge, La.: Louisiana State University Press, 1983), p. 72.

5. *Ibid.,* p. 2.

6. Napoleon III to Franz Josef, June 17, 1866, in Hermann Oncken, ed., *Die Rheinpolitik Napoleons III* (Berlin, 1926), vol. I, p. 280.

7. Franz Josef to Napoleon III, June 24, 1866, in *ibid.,* p. 284.

8. Quoted in A. J. P. Taylor, *The Struggle for Mastery in Europe 1848–1918* (Oxford: Oxford University Press, 1954), p. 102.

9. Hübner to Ferdinand Buol, April 9, 1858, in Hübner, *Neun Jahre,* vol. II, p. 82.

10. *Ibid.,* p. 93.

11. Drouyn de Lhuys to La Tour d'Auvergne, June 10, 1864, in *Origines Diplomatiques de la Guerre de 1870/71* (Paris: Ministry of Foreign Affairs, 1910–30), vol. III, p. 203.

12. Quoted in Wilfried Radewahn, "Französische Aussenpolitik vor dem Krieg von 1870," in Eberhard Kolb, ed., *Europa vor dem Krieg von 1870* (Munich, 1983), p. 38.

13. Quoted in Wilfried Radewahn, *Die Pariser Presse und die Deutsche Frage* (Frankfurt, 1977), p. 104.
14. Goltz to Bismarck, February 17, 1866, on conversation with Napoleon III, in Oncken, ed., *Rheinpolitik,* vol. I, p. 90.
15. Quoted in Radewahn, *Pariser Presse,* p. 110.
16. Goltz to Bismarck, April 25, 1866, in Oncken, ed., *Rheinpolitik,* vol. I, p. 140.
17. Quoted by Talleyrand to Drouyn, May 7, 1866, in *Origines Diplomatiques,* vol. IX, p. 47.
18. Thiers speech, May 3, 1866, in Oncken, ed., *Rheinpolitik,* vol. I, pp. 154ff.
19. *Ibid.*
20. Quoted in Taylor, *Struggle for Mastery,* p. 163.
21. *Ibid.,* pp. 205–6.
22. The analysis of Bismarck's political thought draws on the author's "The White Revolutionary: Reflections on Bismarck," in *Daedalus,* vol. 97, no. 3 (Summer 1968), pp. 888–924.
23. Horst Kohl, ed., *Die politischen Reden des Fursten Bismarck, Historische-Kritische Gesamtausgabe* (Stuttgart, 1892), vol. 1, pp. 267–68.
24. Otto von Bismarck, *Die gesammelten Werke* (Berlin, 1924), vol. 2, pp. 139ff.
25. *Briefwechsel des Generals von Gerlach mit dem Bundestags-Gesandten Otto von Bismarck* (Berlin, 1893), p. 315 (April 28, 1856).
26. Otto Kohl, ed., *Briefe des Generals Leopold von Gerlach an Otto von Bismarck* (Stuttgart and Berlin, 1912), pp. 192–93.
27. *Briefwechsel,* p. 315.
28. Kohl, ed., *Briefe,* p. 206.
29. *Ibid.,* p. 211 (May 6, 1857).
30. *Briefwechsel,* pp. 333–34.
31. *Ibid.*
32. *Ibid.,* p. 353.
33. *Ibid.*
34. Bismarck, *Werke,* vol. 1, p. 375 (September 1853).
35. *Ibid.,* vol. 2, p. 320 (March 1858).
36. *Briefwechsel,* p. 334.
37. *Ibid.,* p. 130 (February 20, 1854).
38. Bismarck, *Werke,* vol. 1, p. 62 (September 29, 1851).
39. *Briefwechsel,* p. 334 (May 2, 1857).
40. *Ibid.,* p. 128 (December 19, 1853).
41. *Ibid.,* p. 194 (October 13, 1854).
42. Bismarck, *Werke,* vol. 14 (3rd ed., Berlin, 1924), no. 1, p. 517.
43. *Briefwechsel,* p. 199 (October 19, 1854).
44. Bismarck, *Werke,* vol. 2, p. 516 (December 8–9, 1859).
45. *Ibid.,* p. 139 (April 26, 1856).
46. *Ibid.,* pp. 139ff.
47. *Ibid.*
48. *Ibid.*
49. Otto Pflanze, *Bismarck and the Development of Germany: The Period of Unification, 1815–1871* (Princeton, N.J.: Princeton University Press, 1990), p. 85.
50. Quoted in J. A. S. Grenville, *Europe Reshaped, 1848–1878* (Sussex: Harvester Press, 1976), p. 358.
51. Bismarck, *Werke,* vol. 14, no. 1, p. 61.
52. Emil Ludwig, *Bismarck: Geschichte eines Kämpfers* (Berlin, 1926), p. 494.

CHAPTER SIX
Realpolitik Turns on Itself

1. Report of Laurent Berenger from St. Petersburg, September 3, 1762, in George Vernadsky, ed., *A Source Book for Russian History: From Early Times to 1917,* 3 vols. (New Haven, Conn.: Yale University Press, 1972), vol. 2, p. 397.

2. Friedrich von Gentz, "Considerations on the Political System in Europe" (1818), in Mack Walker, ed., *Metternich's Europe* (New York: Walker and Co., 1968), p. 80.

3. V. O. Kliuchevsky, *A Course in Russian History: The Seventeenth Century,* trans. by Natalie Duddington (Chicago: Quadrangle Books, 1968), p. 97.

4. Potemkin memorandum, in Vernadsky, ed., *Source Book,* vol. 2, p. 411.

5. Gorchakov memorandum, in *ibid.,* vol. 3, p. 610.

6. Gentz, "Considerations," in Walker, ed., *Metternich's Europe,* p. 80.

7. M. N. Katkov, editorial of May 10, 1883, in Vernadsky, ed., *Source Book,* vol. 3, p. 676.

8. F. M. Dostoyevsky, in *ibid.,* vol. 3, p. 681.

9. Katkov, editorial of September 7, 1882, in *ibid.,* vol. 3, p. 676.

10. Quoted in B. H. Sumner, *Russia and the Balkans, 1870–1880* (Oxford: Clarendon Press, 1957), p. 72.

11. George F. Kennan, "The Sources of Soviet Conduct," *Foreign Affairs,* vol. 25, no. 4 (July 1947).

12. Otto von Bismarck, quoted in Gordon A. Craig, *Germany 1866–1945* (New York: Oxford University Press, 1978), p. 117.

13. Quoted in Robert Blake, *Disraeli* (New York: St. Martin's Press, 1966), p. 574.

14. George F. Kennan, *Decline of Bismarck's European Order* (Princeton: Princeton University Press, 1979), p. 11ff.

15. *Ibid.*

16. Bismarck, February 19, 1878, in Horst Kohl, ed., *Politische Reden,* vol. 7 (Aalen, West Germany: Scientia Verlag, 1970), p. 94.

17. A. J. P. Taylor, *The Struggle for Mastery in Europe 1848–1918* (Oxford: Oxford University Press, 1954), p. 236.

18. Quoted in Blake, *Disraeli,* p. 580.

19. Quoted in Taylor, *Struggle for Mastery,* p. 237.

20. Disraeli speech, June 24, 1872, in Joel H. Wiener, ed., *Great Britain: Foreign Policy and the Span of Empire, 1689–1971,* vol. 3 (New York/London: Chelsea House in association with McGraw-Hill, 1972), p. 2500.

21. Lord Augustus Loftus, *Diplomatic Reminiscences,* 2nd ser. (London, 1892), vol. 2, p. 46.

22. Quoted in Firuz Kazemzadeh, "Russia and the Middle East," in Ivo J. Lederer, ed., *Russian Foreign Policy* (New Haven and London: Yale University Press, 1962), p. 498.

23. *Ibid.,* p. 499.

24. *Ibid.,* p. 500.

25. Quoted in Alan Palmer, *The Chancelleries of Europe* (London: George, Allen and Unwin, 1983), p. 155.

26. *Ibid.,* p. 157.

27. Quoted in Blake, *Disraeli,* p. 646.

28. W. N. Medlicott, *The Congress of Berlin and After* (Hamden, Conn.: Archon Books, 1963), p. 37.

29. Bismarck, in Kohl, ed., *Politische Reden,* vol. 7, p. 102.

30. See Medlicott, *The Congress of Berlin.*

31. Quoted in Kennan, *Decline of European Order,* p. 70.

32. Quoted in *ibid.,* p. 141.

33. Speech by Gladstone, "Denouncing the Bulgarian Atrocities Committed by Turkey," September 9, 1876, in Wiener, ed., *Great Britain,* vol. III, p. 2448.

34. Quoted in A. N. Wilson, *Eminent Victorians* (New York: W. W. Norton, 1989), p. 122.

35. Gladstone, quoted in Carsten Holbraad, *The Concert of Europe: A Study in German and British International Theory, 1815–1914* (London: Longmans, 1970), p. 166.

36. *Ibid.,* p. 145.

37. Bismarck to Kaiser Wilhelm, October 22, 1883, in Otto von Bismarck, *Die gesammelten Werke,* vol. 6C (Berlin, 1935), pp. 282–83.

38. Gladstone to Lord Granville, August 22, 1873, in Agatha Ramm, ed., *The Political Correspondence of Mr. Gladstone and Lord Granville, 1868–1876,* vol. 2 (Oxford: Clarendon Press, 1952), p. 401.

40. Quoted in Kennan, *Decline of European Order,* p. 39.

41. Quoted in *ibid.,* p. 258.

CHAPTER SEVEN
A Political Doomsday Machine:
European Diplomacy Before the First World War

1. Franz Schnabel, "Das Problem Bismarck," in *Hochland,* vol. 42 (1949–50), pp. 1–27.
2. Winston S. Churchill, *Great Contemporaries* (Chicago and London: University of Chicago Press, 1973), pp. 37ff.
3. Frederick the Great, quoted in *Memoirs of Prince von Bülow: From Secretary of State to Imperial Chancellor* (Boston: Little, Brown and Co., 1931), p. 52.
4. Quoted in Maurice Bompard, *Mon Ambassade en Russie, 1903–1908* (Paris, 1937), p. 40.
5. B. H. Sumner, *Russia and the Balkans 1870–1880* (Hamden, Conn.: Shoe String Press, 1962), pp. 23ff.
6. Serge Witte, quoted in Hugh Seton-Watson, *The Russian Empire, 1801–1917* (Oxford: The Clarendon Press, 1967), pp. 581–82.
7. Quoted in Lord Augustus Loftis, *Diplomatic Reminiscences,* 2nd. ser., vol. 2 (London, 1892), p. 38.
8. Quoted in Raymond Sontag, *European Diplomatic History, 1871–1932* (New York: The Century Co., 1933), p. 59.
9. Nikolai de Giers, quoted in Ludwig Reiners, *In Europa gehen die Lichter aus: Der Untergang des Wilhelminischen Reiches* (Munich, 1981), p. 30.
10. Baron Staal, quoted in William L. Langer, *The Diplomacy of Imperialism,* 1st ed. (New York: Alfred A. Knopf, 1935), p. 7.
11. Quoted in George F. Kennan, *The Fateful Alliance: France, Russia and the Coming of the First World War* (New York: Pantheon, 1984), p. 147.
12. Kaiser Wilhelm, quoted in Norman Rich, *Friedrich von Holstein: Politics and Diplomacy in the Era of Bismarck and Wilhelm II* (Cambridge: Cambridge University Press, 1965), p. 465.
13. Lord Salisbury, quoted in Gordon A. Craig, *Germany: 1866–1945* (New York: Oxford University Press, 1978), p. 236.
14. Quoted in Fritz Stern, *The Failure of Illiberalism* (New York: Columbia University Press, 1992), p. 93.
15. Quoted in Malcolm Carroll, *Germany and the Great Powers 1866–1914* (New York: Prentice-Hall, Inc., 1938), p. 372.
16. Chamberlain Speech, November 30, 1899, in Joel H. Wiener, ed., *Great Britain: Foreign Policy and the Span of Empire, 1689–1971,* vol. 1 (New York/London: Chelsea House in association with McGraw-Hill, 1972), p. 510.
17. Quoted in Sontag, *European Diplomatic History,* p. 60.
18. Quoted in Valentin Chirol, *Fifty Years in a Changing World.* (London, 1927), p. 284.
19. Memorandum by the Marquess of Salisbury, May 29, 1901, in G. P. Gooch and Harold Temperley, eds., *British Documents on the Origins of the War,* vol. II (London, 1927), p. 68.
20. Quoted in Sontag, *European Diplomatic History,* p. 169.
21. *Ibid.,* p. 170.
22. Kaiser Wilhelm, quoted in Reiners, *In Europa,* p. 106.
23. Kaiser Wilhelm, quoted in Craig, *Germany,* p. 331.
24. The Marquess of Lansdowne to Sir E. Monson, July 2, 1903, in Sontag, *European Diplomatic History,* p. 293.
25. Sir Edward Grey to Sir F. Bertie, January 31, 1906, in Viscount Grey, *Twenty-Five Years 1892–1916* (New York: Frederick A. Stokes Co., 1925), p. 76.
26. Sir Edward Grey to M. Cambon, French Ambassador in London, November 22, 1912, in *ibid.,* pp. 94–95.
27. Quoted in A. J. P. Taylor, *The Struggle for Mastery in Europe, 1848–1918* (Oxford: Oxford University Press, 1954), p. 443.
28. See, for example, Paul Schroeder, "World War I as Galloping Gertie: A Reply to Joachim Remak," *Journal of Modern History,* vol. 44 (1972), p. 328.

29. Crowe Memorandum of January 1, 1907, in Kenneth Bourne and D. Cameron Watt, gen. eds., *British Documents on Foreign Affairs* (Frederick, Md.: University Publications of America, 1983), part I, vol. 19, pp. 367ff.
30. *Ibid.,* p. 384.
31. *Ibid.*
32. Quoted in Sontag, *European Diplomatic History,* p. 140.
33. Quoted in Carroll, *Germany and the Great Powers,* p. 657.
34. Quoted in Klaus Wernecke, *Der Wille zur Weltgeltung: Aussenpolitik und Öffentlichkeit am Vorabend des Ersten Weltkrieges* (Düsseldorf, 1970), p. 33.
35. Speech by the Chancellor of the Exchequer, David Lloyd George, July 12, 1911, in Wiener, *Great Britain,* vol. 1, p. 577.
36. Quoted in Carroll, *Germany and the Great Powers,* p. 643.
37. Quoted in D. C. B. Lieven, *Russia and the Origins of the First World War* (New York: St. Martin's Press, 1983), p. 46.
38. Quoted in Taylor, *Struggle for Mastery,* p. 507.
39. Quoted in Lieven, *Russia,* p. 69.
40. Quoted in Taylor, *Struggle for Mastery,* p. 510.
41. *Ibid.,* pp. 492–93.
42. Quoted in Lieven, *Russia,* p. 48.
43. Quoted in Sontag, *European Diplomatic History,* p. 185.
44. Quoted in Craig, *Germany,* p. 335.

CHAPTER EIGHT
Into the Vortex: The Military Doomsday Machine

1. Obruchev memorandum to Giers, May 7/19, 1892, in George F. Kennan, *The Fateful Alliance: France, Russia and the Coming of the First World War* (New York: Pantheon, 1984), Appendix II, p. 264.
2. *Ibid.,* p. 265.
3. *Ibid.*
4. *Ibid.,* p. 268.
5. Quoted in *ibid.,* p. 153.
6. See Gerhart Ritter, *The Schlieffen Plan* (New York: Frederick A. Praeger, 1958).
7. Quoted in Frank A. Golder, ed., *Documents of Russian History 1914–1917,* translated by Emanuel Aronsberg (New York: Century, 1927), pp. 9–10.
8. *Ibid.,* p. 13.
9. *Ibid.,* p. 18.
10. *Ibid.,* p. 19.
11. Bethmann-Hollweg, quoted in Fritz Stern, *The Failure of Illiberalism* (New York: Columbia University Press, 1992), p. 93.
12. Bethmann-Hollweg to Eisendecher, March 13, 1913, quoted in Konrad Jarausch, "The Illusion of Limited War: Chancellor Bethmann-Hollweg's Calculated Risk, July 1914," in *Central European History,* March 1969, pp. 48–77.
13. Quoted in A. J. P. Taylor, *The Struggle for Mastery in Europe, 1848–1918* (Oxford: Oxford University Press, 1954), pp. 521–22.
14. Serge Sazonov, *The Fateful Years, 1909–1916: The Reminiscences of Serge Sazonov* (New York: Frederick A. Stokes, 1928), p. 31.
15. *Ibid.,* p. 153.
16. N. V. Tcharykow, *Glimpses of High Politics* (London, 1931), p. 271.
17. Sazonov, *Fateful Years,* p. 40.
18. Statement by Sir Edward Grey in the House of Commons on Secret Military Negotiations with Other Powers, June 11, 1914, in Joel H. Wiener, ed., *Great Britain: Foreign Policy and the Span of Empire, 1689–1971,* vol. 1 (New York/London: Chelsea House in association with McGraw-Hill, 1972), p. 607.
19. Telegram from Sir Edward Grey to the British Ambassador at Berlin, Sir E. Goschen, Rejecting a Policy of Neutrality, July 30, 1914, in *ibid.,* p. 607.

20. Quoted in D. C. B. Lieven, *Russia and the Origins of the First World War* (New York: St. Martin's Press, 1983), p. 66.
21. Quoted in *ibid.,* p. 143.
22. Quoted in *ibid.,* p. 147.
23. Sazonov, *Fateful Years,* p. 188.
24. Quoted in L. C. F. Turner, "The Russian Mobilization in 1914," in *Journal of Contemporary History,* vol. 3 (1968), p. 70.

CHAPTER NINE

The New Face of Diplomacy: Wilson and the Treaty of Versailles

1. Quoted in A. J. P. Taylor, *British History 1914–1945* (Oxford: The Clarendon Press, 1965), p. 114.
2. Quoted in A. J. P. Taylor, *The Struggle for Mastery in Europe 1848–1918* (Oxford: Oxford University Press, 1954), p. 535.
3. Quoted in *ibid.,* p. 553.
4. Werner Maser, *Hindenburg, Eine politische Biographie* (Frankfurt/M-Berlin: Verlag Ullstein GmbH, 1992), p. 138.
5. Sir Edward Grey to Colonel E. M. House, September 22, 1915, quoted in Arthur S. Link, *Woodrow Wilson, Revolution, War, and Peace* (Arlington Heights, Illinois: Harlan Davidson, 1979), p. 74.
6. Woodrow Wilson, Remarks in Washington to the League to Enforce Peace, May 27, 1916, in Arthur S. Link, ed., *The Papers of Woodrow Wilson* (Princeton, N.J.: Princeton University Press, 1966–   ), vol. 37, p. 113.
7. Woodrow Wilson, An Address to the Senate, January 22, 1917, in *ibid.,* vol. 40, p. 539.
8. Arthur S. Link, *Wilson the Diplomatist* (Baltimore: Johns Hopkins Press, 1957), p. 100.
9. *Ibid.,* pp. 100ff.
10. Woodrow Wilson, An Address to a Joint Session of Congress, January 8, 1918, in Link, ed., *Papers of Woodrow Wilson,* vol. 45, p. 538.
11. Woodrow Wilson, An Address at Guildhall, December 28, 1918, in *ibid.,* vol. 53, p. 532.
12. Wilson, Address to Senate, January 22, 1917, in *ibid.,* vol. 40, p. 536.
13. Anthony Adamthwaite, *France and the Coming of the Second World War, 1936–1939* (London: Frank Cass, 1977), p. 4.
14. André Tardieu, *The Truth About the Treaty* (Indianapolis: Bobbs-Merrill, 1921), p. 165.
15. Wilson's adviser David Hunter Miller, March 19, 1919, in David Hunter Miller, *The Drafting of the Covenant* (New York/London: G. P. Putnam's Sons, 1928), vol. 1, p. 300.
16. Quoted in Tardieu, *Truth About the Treaty,* p. 173.
17. Tardieu, in *ibid.,* pp. 174–75.
18. Bowman memorandum, December 10, 1918, in Charles Seymour, ed., *The Intimate Papers of Colonel House* (Boston/New York: Houghton Mifflin, 1926–28), vol. 4, pp. 280–281.
19. Quoted in Seth P. Tillmann, *Anglo-American Relations at the Paris Peace Conference of 1919* (Princeton, N.J.: Princeton University Press, 1961), p. 133.
20. Woodrow Wilson, An Address to the Third Plenary Session of the Peace Conference, February 14, 1919, in Link, ed., *Papers of Woodrow Wilson,* vol. 55, p. 175.
21. Bowman memorandum, in Seymour, ed., *Intimate Papers,* p. 281.
22. Quoted in Tillmann, *Anglo-American Relations,* p. 126.
23. Wilson's adviser David Hunter Miller, in Miller, *Drafting of the Covenant,* vol. 1, p. 49.
24. Quoted in Paul Birdsall, *Versailles Twenty Years After* (New York: Reynal & Hitchcock, 1941), p. 128.
25. Quoted in Miller, *Drafting of the Covenant,* vol. 1, p. 216.
26. *Ibid.,* vol. 2, p. 727.
27. Quoted in Tardieu, *Truth About the Treaty,* p. 160.
28. *Ibid.,* p. 202.
29. *Ibid.,* p. 204.

30. House Diary, March 27, 1919, in Seymour, ed., *Intimate Papers,* vol. 4, p. 395.

31. Sir Charles Webster, *The Congress of Vienna* (London: Bell, 1937).

32. Lloyd George memorandum to Woodrow Wilson, March 25, 1919, in Ray Stannard Baker, *Woodrow Wilson and World Settlement* (New York: Doubleday, Page & Co., 1922), vol. III, p. 450.

33. Quoted in Louis L. Gerson, *Woodrow Wilson and the Rebirth of Poland, 1914–1920* (New Haven, Conn.: Yale University Press, 1953), pp. 27–28.

34. Harold Nicolson, *Peacemaking 1919* (London: Constable & Co., 1933), p. 187.

CHAPTER TEN
The Dilemmas of the Victors

1. Woodrow Wilson, An Address in the Metropolitan Opera House, September 27, 1918, in Arthur S. Link, ed., *The Papers of Woodrow Wilson* (Princeton, N.J.: Princeton University Press, 1966–   ), vol. 51, pp. 131–32.

2. Quoted in Edward Hallett Carr, *The Twenty Years' Crisis, 1919–1939* (2nd ed., 1946) (New York: Harper & Row, paper reprint, 1964), p. 34.

3. Quoted in *ibid.,* p. 35.

4. Quoted in Anthony Adamthwaite, *France and the Coming of the Second World War, 1936–1939* (London: Frank Cass, 1977), p. 17.

5. Quoted in Stephen A. Schuker, *The End of French Predominance in Europe* (Chapel Hill, N.C.: University of North Carolina Press, 1976), p. 254.

6. Quoted in *ibid.,* p. 251.

7. *Ibid.*

8. *Ibid.,* p. 254.

9. Quoted in F. L. Carsten, *Britain and the Weimar Republic* (New York: Schocken Books, 1984), p. 128.

10. *Papers Respecting Negotiations for an Anglo-French Pact* (London: His Majesty's Stationery Office, 1924), paper no. 33, pp. 112–13.

11. Minutes of Cabinet Meetings; Conferences of Ministers, Cabinet Conclusions: 1(22), 10 January 1922, Official Archives, Public Record Office, Cabinet Office, CAB 23/29.

12. Carr, *Twenty Years' Crisis,* pp. 200ff.

13. Quoted in Carsten, *Britain and the Weimar Republic,* p. 81.

14. Tardieu letter to House, March 22, 1919, in André Tardieu, *The Truth About the Treaty* (Indianapolis: Bobbs-Merrill, 1921), p. 136.

15. John Maynard Keynes, *Treatise on the Economic Consequences of the Peace* (London: Macmillan, 1919).

16. Edward Hallett Carr, *The Bolshevik Revolution, 1917–1923,* vol. 3 (New York/London: W. W. Norton, paper ed., 1985), p. 16.

17. *Ibid.,* p. 9.

18. V. I. Lenin, *Collected Works* (Moscow: Progress Press, 1964), vol. 26, p. 448.

19. Quoted in Carr, *Bolshevik Revolution,* p. 44.

20. Quoted in *ibid.,* p. 42.

21. Quoted in *ibid.,* p. 70.

22. Quoted in *ibid.,* p. 161.

23. Quoted in Edward Hallett Carr, *German-Soviet Relations Between the Two World Wars, 1919–1939* (Baltimore: Johns Hopkins Press, 1951), p. 40.

24. Quoted in F. L. Carsten, *The Reichswehr and Politics, 1918–1933* (Oxford: Oxford University Press, 1966), p. 69.

25. Quoted in George F. Kennan, *Russia and the West Under Lenin and Stalin* (Boston/Toronto: Little, Brown, 1960), p. 206.

26. Quoted in *ibid.,* p. 210.

27. *Ibid.,* p. 212.

CHAPTER ELEVEN
Stresemann and the Re-emergence of the Vanquished

1. Quoted in Hermann Graml, *Europa in der Zwischen der Kriegen* (Munich, 1969), p. 154.
2. Viscount d'Abernon, *The Ambassador of Peace: Lord d'Abernon's Diary,* vol. II (London: Hodder & Stoughton, 1929), p. 225.
3. Quoted in Graml, *Europa,* p. 130.
4. Quoted in Stephen A. Schuker, *The End of French Predominance in Europe* (Chapel Hill, N.C.: University of North Carolina Press, 1976), p. 255.
5. Quoted in Henry L. Bretton, *Stresemann and the Revision of Versailles* (Stanford, Calif.: Stanford University Press, 1953), p. 38.
6. Quoted in Marc Trachtenberg, *Reparations in World Politics* (New York: Columbia University Press, 1980), p. 48.
7. Quoted in *ibid.*
8. Quoted in Bretton, *Stresemann,* p. 21.
9. Quoted in F. L. Carsten, *Britain and the Weimar Republic* (New York: Schocken Books, 1984), p. 37.
10. Quoted in Hans W. Gatzke, *Stresemann and the Rearmament of Germany* (Baltimore: Johns Hopkins University Press, 1954), p. 12.
11. *Gustav Stresemann, His Diaries, Letters and Papers,* edited and translated by Eric Sutton (London, 1935), vol. 1, p. 225.
12. Quoted in David Dutton, *Austen Chamberlain, Gentleman in Politics* (Bolton: Ross Anderson, 1985), p. 250.
13. Quoted in *ibid.,* p. 5.
14. Quoted in Jon Jacobson, *Locarno Diplomacy* (Princeton, N.J.: Princeton University Press, 1972), p. 90.
15. Quoted in Raymond J. Sontag, *A Broken World, 1919–1939* (New York: Harper & Row, 1971), p. 133.
16. Selig Adler, *The Isolationist Impulse: Its Twentieth-Century Reaction* (New York: Free Press, 1957), p. 217.
17. D. W. Brogan, *The French Nation, 1814–1940* (London: Hamilton, 1957), p. 267.
18. Quoted in Dutton, *Austen Chamberlain,* p. 251.
19. F. L. Carsten, *The Reichswehr and Politics, 1918–1933* (Berkeley: University of California Press, 1973), p. 139.
20. Quoted in Bretton, *Stresemann,* p. 22.
21. Quoted in Anthony Adamthwaite, *France and the Coming of the Second World War, 1936–1939* (London: Frank Cass, 1977), p. 29.
22. Winston S. Churchill, *The Second World War,* vol. 1, *The Gathering Storm* (Boston: Houghton Mifflin, 1948), p. 74.
23. Quoted in *ibid.,* p. 73.
24. Quoted in A. J. P. Taylor, *The Origins of the Second World War* (New York: Atheneum, paper ed., 1983), p. 66.

CHAPTER TWELVE
The End of Illusion: Hitler and the Destruction of Versailles

1. Alan Bullock, *Hitler and Stalin: Parallel Lives* (New York: Alfred A. Knopf, 1992), p. 380.
2. Henry Picker, *Hitlers Tischgespräche in Fuhrerhauptequartier 1941–1942,* ed., Percy Ernst Schramm (Stuttgart, 1963).
3. Phipps to Simon, November 21, 1933, quoted in A. J. P. Taylor, *The Origins of the Second World War* (New York: Atheneum, 1983), pp. 73–74.
4. MacDonald conversation wtih Daladier, March 16, 1933, in *ibid.,* p. 74.
5. *Ibid.,* p. 75.
6. Anglo-French meeting, September 22, 1933, in *ibid.,* pp. 75–76.

7. Quoted in Martin Gilbert, *Churchill: A Life* (New York: Henry Holt, 1991), p. 523.

8. Quoted in *ibid.,* p. 524.

9. Quoted in *ibid.,* p. 523.

10. Quoted in Robert J. Young, *In Command of France: French Foreign Policy and Military Planning 1933–1940* (Cambridge, Mass.: Harvard University Press, 1978), p. 37.

11. Quoted in Anthony Adamthwaite, *France and the Coming of the Second World War, 1936–1939* (London: Frank Cass, 1977), p. 30.

12. Quoted in Paul Johnson, *Modern Times: The World from the Twenties to the Eighties* (New York: Harper & Row, 1983), p. 341.

13. Quoted in Gilbert, *Churchill,* p. 531.

14. Quoted in *ibid.,* pp. 531–32.

15. Quoted in *ibid.,* p. 537.

16. Quoted in Winston S. Churchill, *The Second World War,* vol. 1, *The Gathering Storm* (Boston: Houghton Mifflin, 1948), p. 119.

17. Quoted in Gilbert, *Churchill,* p. 538.

18. Quoted in Adamthwaite, *France, 1936–1939,* p. 75.

19. Haile Selassie, June 30, 1936, quoted in David Clay Large, *Between Two Fires: Europe's Path in the 1930s* (New York/London: W. W. Norton, 1990), pp. 177–78.

20. Quoted in Josef Henke, *England in Hitlers Politischem Kalkul* (German Bundesarchiv, Schriften, no. 20, 1973), p. 41.

21. Gerhard Weinberg, *The Foreign Policy of Hitler's Germany: Diplomatic Revolution in Europe* (Chicago: University of Chicago Press, 1970), p. 241.

22. Anthony Eden, Earl of Avon, *The Eden Memoirs,* vol. 1, *Facing the Dictators* (Boston: Houghton Mifflin, 1962), pp. 375–76.

23. Quoted in Weinberg, *Foreign Policy of Hitler's Germany,* p. 259.

24. Quoted in *ibid.,* p. 254.

25. Churchill, *Gathering Storm,* p. 196.

26. Quoted in Gilbert, *Churchill,* p. 553.

27. *Parliamentary Debates,* 5th ser., vol. 309 (London: His Majesty's Stationery Office, 1936), March 10, 1936, col. 1976.

28. Quoted in Adamthwaite, *France, 1936–1939,* p. 41.

29. *Ibid.,* pp. 53ff.

30. *Ibid.*

31. Memorandum, Foreign Ministry Circular, quoted in Taylor, *Origins of Second World War,* p. 137.

32. Quoted in Adamthwaite, *France, 1936–1939,* p. 68.

33. Quoted in *ibid.,* p. 69.

34. Quoted in Gordon A. Craig, *Germany 1866–1945* (New York/Oxford: Oxford University Press, 1978), p. 698.

35. Adolf Hitler, *Mein Kampf* (New York: Reynal & Hitchcock, 1940), p. 175.

36. Halifax to Phipps, March 22, 1938, quoted in Taylor, *Origins of Second World War,* p. 155.

37. *Ibid.,* p. 191.

38. *Ibid.*

39. Bullock, *Hitler and Stalin,* pp. 582ff.

40. Quoted in *ibid.,* p. 589.

41. Quoted in Taylor, *Origins of Second World War,* p. 191.

42. Prime Minister W. L. Mackenzie King, September 29, 1938, in John A. Munro, ed., *Documents on Canadian External Relations,* vol. 6 (Ottawa: Department of External Affairs, 1972), p. 1099.

43. Prime Minister J. A. Lyons, September 30, 1938, in R. G. Neale, ed., *Documents on Australian Foreign Policy 1937–49,* vol. I (Canberra: Australian Government Publishing Service), p. 476.

44. Chamberlain to the House of Commons, October 3, 1938, *Parliamentary Debates,* 5th ser., vol. 339 (1938), col. 48.

CHAPTER THIRTEEN
Stalin's Bazaar

1. Quoted in T. A. Taracouzio, *War and Peace in Soviet Diplomacy* (New York: Macmillan, 1940), pp. 139–40.

2. Stalin speech to 15th Party Congress, December 3, 1927, quoted in Nathan Leites, *A Study of Bolshevism* (Glencoe, Ill.: Free Press of Glencoe, 1953), p. 501.

3. Stalin report to 17th Party Congress, January 26, 1934, in Alvin Z. Rubinstein, ed., *The Foreign Policy of the Soviet Union* (New York: Random House, 1960), p. 108.

4. Report to the 7th Congress of the Communist International, August 1935, in *ibid.*, pp. 133–36.

5. Robert Legvold, *After the Soviet Union: From Empire to Nations* (New York: W. W. Norton, 1992), p. 7.

6. Quoted in Anthony Adamthwaite, *France and the Coming of the Second World War, 1936–1939* (London: Frank Cass, 1977), p. 264.

7. Quoted in Anthony Read and David Fisher, *The Deadly Embrace: Hitler, Stalin, and the Nazi-Soviet Pact 1939–1941* (New York/London: W. W. Norton, 1988), p. 57.

8. Donald Cameron Watt, *How War Came: The Immediate Origins of the Second World War, 1938–1939* (London: William Heinemann, 1989), p. 109.

9. Quoted in Read and Fisher, *Deadly Embrace*, p. 59.

10. *Ibid.*

11. Quoted in Keith Feiling, *The Life of Neville Chamberlain* (London: Macmillan, 1946), p. 403.

12. Quoted in Watt, *How War Came*, pp. 221–22.

13. Quoted in Read and Fisher, *Deadly Embrace*, p. 69.

14. Quoted in *ibid.*, p. 72.

15. Alan Bullock, *Hitler and Stalin: Parallel Lives* (New York: Alfred A. Knopf, 1992), p. 614.

16 Quoted in Gordon A. Craig, *Germany 1866–1945* (New York/Oxford: Oxford University Press, 1978), pp. 711–12.

17. Quoted in Bullock, *Hitler and Stalin*, p. 616.

18. Quoted in *ibid.*, p. 617.

19. Quoted in *ibid.*, p. 620.

20. A. J. P. Taylor, *The Origins of the Second World War* (New York: Atheneum, 1961), p. 231.

CHAPTER FOURTEEN
The Nazi-Soviet Pact

1. Alan Bullock, *Hitler and Stalin: Parallel Lives* (New York: Alfred A. Knopf, 1992), pp. 679–80.

2. Quoted in *ibid.*, p. 682.

3. Anthony Read and David Fisher, *The Deadly Embrace: Hitler, Stalin, and the Nazi-Soviet Pact 1939–1941* (New York/London: W. W. Norton, 1988), p. 508; and Bullock, *Hitler and Stalin*, p. 687.

4. Read and Fisher, *Deadly Embrace*, p. 509.

5. Quoted in Martin Wight, *Power Politics* (New York: Holmes and Meier, 1978), p. 176.

6. *Documents on German Foreign Policy, 1918–1945*, series D (1937–1945), vol. XI, "The War Years" (Washington, D.C.: U.S. Government Printing Office, 1960), p. 537.

7. *Ibid.*

8. *Ibid.*, pp. 537–38.

9. *Ibid.*, p. 539.

10. Read and Fisher, *Deadly Embrace*, p. 519.

11. Bullock, *Hitler and Stalin*, p. 688.

12. Quoted in *ibid.*, p. 689.

13. Quoted in Read and Fisher, *Deadly Embrace*, p. 530.

14. *Ibid.,* p. 532.
15. In our times, it was argued—wrongly, in my view—that this was not really a Soviet "proposal." See the argument put forth (versus the argument of Zbigniew Brzezinski) in Raymond L. Garthoff, *Détente and Confrontation: American-Soviet Relations from Nixon to Reagan* (Washington: Brookings Institution, 1985), pp. 941–42.
16. Bullock, *Hitler and Stalin,* p. 688.
17. Quoted in Read and Fisher, *Deadly Embrace,* p. 568. See also Bullock, *Hitler and Stalin,* p. 716.
18. Quoted in Read and Fisher, *Deadly Embrace,* p. 576.
19. Quoted in *ibid.*
20. Quoted in *ibid.,* p. 640.
21. Quoted in *ibid.,* pp. 647–48.
22. Quoted in *ibid.,* p. 629.

CHAPTER FIFTEEN

America Re-enters the Arena: Franklin Delano Roosevelt

1. Isaiah Berlin, *Personal Impressions,* edited by Henry Hardy (New York: Viking Press, 1981), p. 26.
2. See *ibid.,* pp. 23–31.
3. *Ibid.*
4. U.S. Senate, *Conference on the Limitation of Armament,* Senate Documents, vol. 10, 67th Cong., 2nd sess., 1921–1922 (Washington, D.C.: U.S. Government Printing Office, 1922), p. 11.
5. Selig Adler, *The Isolationist Impulse, Its Twentieth-Century Reaction* (New York: Free Press; London: Collier-Macmillan, 1957), p. 142.
6. U.S. Senate, *Conference on Limitation of Armament,* pp. 867–68.
7. Quoted in Adler, *Isolationist Impulse,* p. 214.
8. Quoted in *ibid.,* p. 216.
9. *Ibid.,* p. 214.
10. Frank B. Kellogg, "The Settlement of International Controversies by Pacific Means," address delivered before the World Alliance for International Friendship, November 11, 1928 (Washington, D.C.: U.S. Government Printing Office, 1928).
11. *Ibid.*
12. Henry L. Stimson and McGeorge Bundy, *On Active Service in Peace and War* (New York: Harper & Brothers, 1948), p. 259.
13. Roosevelt Address before the Woodrow Wilson Foundation, December 28, 1933, in *The Public Papers and Addresses of Franklin D. Roosevelt* (New York: Random House, 1938), vol. 2, 1933, pp. 548–49.
14. Adler, *Isolationist Impulse,* pp. 235–36.
15. Ruhl J. Bartlett, ed., *The Record of American Diplomacy* (New York: Alfred A. Knopf, 1956), pp. 572–77. The First Neutrality Act, signed by FDR on August 31, 1935: arms embargo; Americans not permitted to travel on ships of belligerents. The Second Neutrality Act, signed by FDR on February 29, 1936 (a week before the reoccupation of the Rhineland on March 7): extended the First Act through May 1, 1936, and added a prohibition against loans or credits to belligerents. The Third Neutrality Act, signed by FDR on May 1, 1937: extended previous acts due to expire at midnight plus "cash and carry" provisions for certain nonmilitary goods.
16. Treaty between the United States of America and Germany, to restore friendly relations and terminate the state of war between them, signed in Berlin August 25, 1921.
17. Hull memo to FDR, March 9, 1936, quoted in William Appleman Williams, ed., *The Shaping of American Diplomacy,* vol. II, *1914–1968,* 2nd ed. (Chicago: Rand McNally, 1973), p. 199.
18. Address in Chicago, October 5, 1937, in Roosevelt, *Public Papers* (New York: Macmillan Co., 1941), 1937 vol., p. 410.
19. *Ibid.,* 1939 vol., Introduction by FDR, p. xxviii.

20. Charles A. Beard, *American Foreign Policy in the Making, 1932–1940: A Study in Responsibilities* (New Haven, Conn.: Yale University Press, 1946), pp. 188ff.

21. Quoted in *ibid.,* p. 190.

22. *Ibid.* Italics added.

23. *Ibid.,* p. 193.

24. *Ibid.*

25. Quoted in Adler, *Isolationist Impulse,* pp. 244–45.

26. Quoted in Anthony Adamthwaite, *France and the Coming of the Second World War, 1936–1939* (London: Frank Cass, 1977), p. 209.

27. Roosevelt Press Conference, September 9, 1938, in *Complete Presidential Press Conferences of Franklin Delano Roosevelt,* vol. 12, 1938 (New York: Da Capo Press, 1972), by date.

28. Radio address to the Herald-Tribune Forum, October 26, 1938, in Roosevelt, *Public Papers,* 1938 vol., p. 564.

29. *Ibid.,* p. 565.

30. Donald Cameron Watt, *How War Came: The Immediate Origins of the Second World War, 1938–1939* (London: William Heinemann, 1989), p. 130.

31. Annual Message to the Congress, January 4, 1939, in Roosevelt, *Public Papers,* 1939 vol., p. 3.

32. Franklin D. Roosevelt, *Complete Presidential Press Conferences of Franklin Delano Roosevelt,* vol. 13, 1939, p. 262.

33. Roosevelt, *Public Papers,* 1939 vol., pp. 198–99.

34. Watt, *How War Came,* p. 261.

35. "The President Again Seeks a Way to Peace. A Message to Chancellor Adolf Hitler and Premier Benito Mussolini, April 14, 1939," in Roosevelt, *Public Papers,* 1939, pp. 201–5.

36. Vandenberg speech in the Senate, "It Is Not Cowardice to Think of America First," February 27, 1939, in *Vital Speeches of the Day,* vol. v, no. 12 (April 1, 1939), pp. 356–57.

37. Quoted in Adler, *Isolationist Impulse,* p. 248.

38. Ted Morgan, *FDR: A Biography* (New York: Simon & Schuster, 1985), p. 520.

39. Address at the University of Virginia, June 10, 1940, in Roosevelt, *Public Papers,* 1940 vol., pp. 263–64.

40. Churchill speech to the House of Commons, June 4, 1940, in Martin Gilbert, *Churchill: A Life* (New York: Henry Holt, 1991), p. 656.

41. Roosevelt's State of the Union address of January 6, 1941, *Vital Speeches,* vol. vii, no. 7 (January 15, 1941), p. 198.

42. Quoted in Adler, *Isolationist Impulse,* p. 282.

43. *Ibid.*

44. Quoted in *ibid.,* p. 284.

45. Winston S. Churchill, *The Second World War,* vol. 3, *The Grand Alliance* (Boston: Houghton Mifflin, 1950), p. 140.

46. Radio Address Announcing the Proclamation of an Unlimited National Emergency, May 27, 1941, in Roosevelt, *Public Papers* (New York: Harper & Brothers, 1950), 1941 vol., p. 192.

47. The Atlantic Charter: Official Statement on Meeting Between the President and Prime Minister Churchill, August 14, 1941, in *ibid.,* p. 314.

48. *Ibid.,* p. 315.

49. Fireside Chat to the Nation, September 11, 1941, in *ibid.,* pp. 384–92.

50. Adler, *Isolationist Impulse,* p. 257.

CHAPTER SIXTEEN

Three Approaches to Peace: Roosevelt, Stalin, and Churchill in World War II

1. *Churchill & Roosevelt, The Complete Correspondence,* 3 vols., edited by Warren F. Kimball, vol. II, *Alliance Forged, November 1942–February 1944* (Princeton, N.J.: Princeton University Press, 1984), p. 767.

2. Quoted in Herbert Feis, *Churchill, Roosevelt, Stalin: The War They Waged and the Peace They Sought* (Princeton, N.J.: Princeton University Press, 1957), p. 340.

3. James MacGregor Burns, *Roosevelt: The Soldier of Freedom* (New York: Harcourt Brace Jovanovich, 1970), p. 566.

4. Message to Churchill, June 1, 1942, in Kimball, ed. *Churchill & Roosevelt,* vol. I, *Alliance Emerging, October 1933–November 1942,* p. 502.

5. Quoted in Elliott Roosevelt, *As He Saw It* (New York: Duell, Sloan and Pearce, 1946), pp. 115–16.

6. Quoted in Robert Dallek, *Franklin D. Roosevelt and American Foreign Policy, 1932–1945* (New York: Oxford University Press, 1979), p. 324.

7. Cordell Hull, address before Congress regarding the Moscow Conference, November 18, 1943, in *U.S. Department of State Bulletin,* vol. ix, no. 230 (November 20, 1943), p. 343.

8. Winston S. Churchill, *The Second World War,* vol. 4, *The Hinge of Fate* (Boston: Houghton Mifflin, 1950), p. 214.

9. Quoted in William Roger Louis, *Imperialism at Bay: The United States and the Decolonization of the British Empire, 1941–1945* (New York: Oxford University Press, 1978), p. 121.

10. Quoted in *ibid.,* p. 129.

11. Quoted in *ibid.,* pp. 154–55.

12. I am indebted for much of this analysis to Peter Rodman's forthcoming book on the U.S. and Soviet approaches to the Third World, to be published by Charles Scribner's Sons.

13. Memorandum by Charles Taussig, March 15, 1944, quoted in Louis, *Imperialism at Bay,* p. 486.

14. Quoted in Robert E. Sherwood, *Roosevelt and Hopkins: An Intimate History* (New York: Harper & Brothers, 1948), p. 605.

15. Feis, *Churchill, Roosevelt, Stalin,* pp. 11–13.

16. See Eric Larrabee, *Commander in Chief: Franklin Delano Roosevelt, His Lieutenants, and Their War* (New York: Harper & Row, 1987), p. 503.

17. Burns, *Roosevelt,* p. 374.

18. I am indebted to an unpublished speech by Arthur Schlesinger, Jr., "Franklin D. Roosevelt and U.S. Foreign Policy," delivered before the Society for Historians of American Foreign Relations, Vassar College, June 18, 1992.

19. Sir John Wheeler-Bennett and Anthony Nicholls, *The Semblance of Peace* (London: Macmillan, 1972), pp. 46ff.

20. Quoted in *The Memoirs of Cordell Hull,* vol. II (New York: Macmillan, 1948), p. 1452.

21. Wheeler-Bennett and Nicholls, *Semblance of Peace,* p. 49.

22. Hull, *Memoirs,* vol. II, pp. 1168–70.

23. Quoted in Feis, *Churchill, Roosevelt, Stalin,* p. 59.

24. Quoted in William G. Hyland, *The Cold War Is Over* (New York: Random House, 1990), p. 32.

25. Quoted in Sherwood, *Roosevelt and Hopkins,* pp. 572–73.

26. Quoted in *ibid.,* p. 572.

27. Schlesinger speech, "Roosevelt and U.S. Foreign Policy," p. 18.

28. *Ibid.,* p. 17.

29. John Colville, *The Fringes of Power: 10 Downing Street Diaries, 1939–1955* (New York/London: W. W. Norton, 1985), p. 404.

30. Feis, *Churchill, Roosevelt, Stalin,* pp. 131–32.

31. Alan Bullock, *Hitler and Stalin: Parallel Lives* (New York: Alfred A. Knopf, 1992), p. 821.

32. Feis, *Churchill, Roosevelt, Stalin,* p. 285. (Emphasis added.)

33. Quoted in Frances Perkins, *The Roosevelt I Knew* (New York: Viking, 1946), pp. 84–85.

34. Quoted in Bertram D. Hulen, "Washington Hails Reds' Step as Great Gain for the Allies," *New York Times,* May 23, 1943, p. 30.

35. "The United States in a New World," *Fortune,* suppl., April 1943.

36. Roosevelt's Christmas Eve Fireside Chat on Teheran and Cairo Conferences, December 23, 1943, in *The Public Papers and Addresses of Franklin D. Roosevelt,* 1943 vol. (New York: Harper & Brothers), p. 558.

37. Winston S. Churchill, *The Second World War,* vol. 6, *Triumph and Tragedy* (Boston: Houghton Mifflin, 1953), p. 198. See also Kimball, ed., *Churchill & Roosevelt,* vol. III, *Alliance Declining, February 1944–April 1945,* p. 351; and Hyland, *Cold War,* pp. 35–36.

38. Feis, *Churchill, Roosevelt, Stalin,* pp. 522–23.

39. Quoted in Dallek, *Franklin D. Roosevelt,* p. 520.

40. Quoted in Sherwood, *Roosevelt and Hopkins,* p. 870.

41. Franklin Roosevelt's Inaugural Address, January 20, 1945, in *The Presidents Speak,* annotated by Davis Newton Lott (New York: Holt, Rinehart and Winston, 1969), p. 248.

42. Quoted in Dallek, *Franklin D. Roosevelt,* p. 521.

43. Quoted in Milovan Djilas, *Conversations with Stalin* (New York: Harcourt, Brace & World, 1962), p. 114.

44. Quoted in Feis, *Churchill, Roosevelt, Stalin,* pp. 607–8.

45. Bullock, *Hitler and Stalin,* pp. 883–84.

46. Churchill, *Triumph and Tragedy* (paper edition with introduction by John Keegan, Boston: Houghton Mifflin, 1986), p. 436.

47. Dmitri Volkogonov, *Stalin: Triumph and Tragedy,* edited and translated from Russian by Harold Shukman (Rocklin, Calif.: Prima Publishing, 1991–92; original ed. New York: Grove Weidenfeld, 1991), pp. 412ff.

48. See Bullock, *Hitler and Stalin,* pp. 697ff.

49. Quoted in Joachim C. Fest, *Hitler,* translated from German by Richard and Clara Winston (New York: Harcourt Brace Jovanovich, 1974), p. 694.

50. Churchill, *Triumph and Tragedy,* p. 308.

51. Quoted in Dallek, *Franklin D. Roosevelt,* p. 505.

52. Feis, *Churchill, Roosevelt, Stalin,* p. 270.

CHAPTER SEVENTEEN
The Beginning of the Cold War

1. James MacGregor Burns, *Roosevelt: The Soldier of Freedom* (New York: Harcourt Brace Jovanovich, 1970), pp. 448–49.

2. Quoted in Selig Adler, *The Isolationist Impulse: Its Twentieth-Century Reaction* (New York: Free Press; London: Collier-Macmillan, 1957), p. 285.

3. Truman, paraphrased at late May 1945 meeting with leaders of National Citizens Political Action Committee, quoted in Richard J. Walton, *Henry Wallace, Harry Truman, and the Cold War* (New York: Viking Press, 1976), p. 119.

4. Address Before a Joint Session of the Congress, April 16, 1945, *Public Papers of the Presidents of the United States, Harry S. Truman,* 1945 vol. (Washington, D.C.: U.S. Government Printing Office, 1961), p. 5 (hereinafter cited as *Truman Papers*); repeated p. 22, in Truman Address of April 25, 1945.

5. Quoted in W. Averell Harriman and Elie Abel, *Special Envoy to Churchill and Stalin, 1941–1946* (New York: Random House, 1975), p. 474.

6. Winston S. Churchill, *The Second World War,* vol. 6, *Triumph and Tragedy* (Boston: Houghton Mifflin, 1953), p. 503.

7. Harry S Truman, *Year of Decisions,* Memoirs, vol. one (New York: Doubleday, 1955), p. 260.

8. Herbert Feis, *Churchill, Roosevelt, Stalin: The War They Waged and the Peace They Sought* (Princeton, N.J.: Princeton University Press, 1957), p. 133.

9. Quoted in *ibid.,* p. 652.

10. Fleet Admiral William D. Leahy, *I Was There: The Personal History of the Chief of Staff to Presidents Roosevelt and Truman Based on His Notes and Diaries Made at the Time* (New York/London/Toronto: Whittlesey House/McGraw-Hill Book Company, 1950), pp. 379–80.

11. *Ibid.,* p. 380.

12. Quoted in Robert E. Sherwood, *Roosevelt and Hopkins: An Intimate History* (New York: Harper & Brothers, 1948), p. 890.

13. *Ibid.,* p. 908.
14. State Department briefing book paper, "British Plans for a Western European Bloc," July 4, 1945, in U.S. Department of State, *Foreign Relations of the United States: The Conference of Berlin (The Potsdam Conference) 1945* (Washington, D.C.: U.S. Government Printing Office), vol. I, pp. 262–63.
15. Quoted in Terry H. Anderson, *The United States, Great Britain, and the Cold War, 1944–1947* (Columbia, Mo.: University of Missouri Press, 1981), p. 69.
16. Quoted in Robert J. Donovan, *Conflict and Crisis: The Presidency of Harry S Truman 1945–1948* (New York: W. W. Norton, 1977), p. 81.
17. Quoted in *ibid.,* p. 84.
18. Truman, *Year of Decisions,* p. 416.
19. Churchill, *Triumph and Tragedy,* p. 582.
20. Quoted in John Lewis Gaddis, *The United States and the Origins of the Cold War* (New York: Columbia University Press, 1972), p. 266.
21. Truman Address on Foreign Policy at the Navy Day Celebration, New York City, October 27, 1945, in *Truman Papers,* 1945 vol., pp. 431–38.
22. Quoted in Gaddis, *Origins of Cold War,* p. 280.
23. Milovan Djilas, *Conversations with Stalin* (New York: Harcourt, Brace & World, 1962), p. 114.
24. Robert Conquest, "The Evil of This Time," *New York Review of Books,* vol. XL, no. 15 (September 23, 1993), p. 27.
25. Quoted in Henry A. Kissinger, *Nuclear Weapons and Foreign Policy* (New York: Harper & Brothers, published for the Council on Foreign Relations, 1957), p. 367.
26. *Ibid.,* p. 371.
27. Quoted in Alan Bullock, *Hitler and Stalin: Parallel Lives* (New York: Alfred A. Knopf, 1992), p. 907.
28. Joseph Stalin's Election Address, "New Five-Year Plan for Russia," delivered over Radio Moscow on February 9, 1946, reprinted in *The New York Times,* February 10, 1946.
29. *Ibid.*
30. *Ibid.*
31. See P. M. S. Blackett, *Atomic Weapons and East-West Relations* (New York: Cambridge University Press, 1956).
32. Winston S. Churchill speech, "The Sinews of Peace," March 5, 1946, at Westminster College, Fulton, Mo., in Robert Rhodes James, ed., *Winston S. Churchill: His Complete Speeches, 1897–1963* (New York/London: Chelsea House in association with R. R. Bowker, 1974), vol. VII, *1943–1949,* pp. 7285ff.
33. *Ibid.,* p. 7292.
34. George F. Kennan, "Long Telegram" from Moscow, February 22, 1946, in *Foreign Relations of the United States, 1946* (Washington, D.C.: U.S. Government Printing Office, 1969), vol. VI, p. 697.
35. Andrei Zhdanov, "The International Situation," delivered at the Founding Conference of the Cominform, September 1947, in U.S. House of Representatives, Committee on Foreign Affairs, *The Strategy and Tactics of World Communism,* suppl. I, "One Hundred Years of Communism, 1848–1948," 80th Cong., 2nd sess., doc. no. 619 (Washington, D.C.: U.S. Government Printing Office, 1948), pp. 211ff.
36. Bullock, *Hitler and Stalin,* p. 922.
37. *Ibid.,* p. 923.
38. Radio Address, April 28, 1947, *U.S. Department of State Bulletin,* vol. XVI, no. 410, p. 924.

CHAPTER EIGHTEEN
The Success and the Pain of Containment

1. George F. Kennan, "Long Telegram" from Moscow, February 22, 1946, in *Foreign Relations of the United States, 1946* (Washington, D.C.: U.S. Government Printing Office, 1969), vol. VI, pp. 666–709.
2. *Ibid.,* p. 700.

3. *Ibid.,* p. 699.

4. H. Freeman Matthews, Memorandum by the Acting Department of State Member (Matthews) to the State-War-Navy Coordinating Committee, "Political Estimate of Soviet Policy for Use in Connection with Military Studies," April 1, 1946, in *Foreign Relations, United States, 1946,* vol. I, p. 1169.

5. *Ibid.*

6. *Ibid.,* p. 1170.

7. *Ibid.,* p. 1168.

8. *Ibid.,* p. 1170.

9. Clark Clifford, "American Relations with the Soviet Union: A Report to the President by the Special Counsel to the President," September 24, 1946, in Thomas H. Etzold and John Lewis Gaddis, eds., *Containment: Documents on American Policy and Strategy, 1945–1950* (New York: Columbia University Press, 1978), p. 66.

10. *Ibid.,* p. 67. (Emphases added.)

11. *Ibid.,* p. 68.

12. *Ibid.,* p. 71.

13. Quoted in Joseph M. Jones, *The Fifteen Weeks (February 21–June 5, 1947)* (New York: Viking Press, 1955), p. 141.

14. *Public Papers of the Presidents of the United States, Harry S Truman,* 1947 vol. (Washington, D.C.: U.S. Government Printing Office, 1963), p. 178.

15. *Ibid.,* p. 179.

16. *Ibid.,* p. 178.

17. George Marshall, "European Initiative Essential to Economic Recovery," Address at Commencement Exercises at Harvard University, June 5, 1947, in *U.S. Department of State Bulletin,* vol. XVI, no. 415 (June 5, 1947), p. 1160. (Emphasis added.)

18. *Ibid.*

19. *Ibid.*

20. "X" (George F. Kennan), "The Sources of Soviet Conduct," *Foreign Affairs,* vol. 25, no. 4 (July 1947), p. 575.

21. *Ibid.,* p. 581.

22. *Ibid.,* pp. 579–80.

23. *Ibid.,* p. 582.

24. Testimony of Ambassador Warren Austin, April 28, 1949, in U.S. Senate, Committee on Foreign Relations, *The North Atlantic Treaty,* Hearings, 81st Cong., 1st sess. (Washington, D.C.: U.S. Government Printing Office, 1949), pt. I, p. 97.

25. *Ibid.,* pt. I, appendix, pp. 334–37.

26. *Ibid.,* p. 337.

27. *Ibid.,* pt. I, p. 17.

28. *Ibid.,* p. 150.

29. U.S. Senate, Committee on Foreign Relations, *Report on the North Atlantic Treaty,* 81st Cong., 1st sess., June 6, 1949 (Washington, D.C.: U.S. Government Printing Office, 1949), p. 23.

30. See, e.g., Acheson's testimony before the Senate Foreign Relations and Armed Services Committees, August 8, 1949, in *State Bulletin,* vol. XXI, no. 529 (August 22, 1949), pp. 265ff, and his address to the U.S. Chamber of Commerce, April 30, 1951, in *State Bulletin,* vol. XXIV, no. 619 (May 14, 1951), pp. 766–70.

31. Acheson address, "Achieving a Community Sense Among Free Nations—A Step Toward World Order," before the Harvard Alumni Association, Cambridge, Mass., June 22, 1950, in *State Bulletin,* vol. XXIII, no. 574 (July 3, 1950), p. 17.

32. Winston S. Churchill, *The Second World War,* vol. 6, *Triumph and Tragedy* (Boston: Houghton Mifflin, 1953; paperback ed., with introduction by John Keegan, 1985), p. 266.

33. NSC-68, "United States Objectives and Programs for National Security," April 14, 1950, in *Foreign Relations, United States, 1950,* vol. I, p. 240.

34. *Ibid.,* p. 241.

35. *Ibid.*

36. *Ibid,* pp. 241–42.

37. *Ibid.,* p. 279.

38. Walter Lippmann, *The Cold War: A Study in U.S. Foreign Policy* (New York/London: Harper & Brothers, 1947), p. 13.

39. *Ibid.,* p. 23.

40. *Ibid.,* pp. 61–62.

41. *Winston S. Churchill, His Complete Speeches, 1897–1963,* ed. by Robert Rhodes James, vol. VII, 1943–1949 (New York/London: Chelsea House in association with R. R. Bowker, 1974), p. 7710.

42. *Ibid.,* vol. VIII (1950–1963), p. 8132.

43. Henry A. Wallace, *Toward World Peace* (New York: Reynal & Hitchcock, 1948), p. 118.

44. Henry A. Wallace, Address at Madison Square Garden, September 12, 1946, in Walter LaFeber, ed., *The Dynamics of World Power: A Documentary History of United States Foreign Policy, 1945–1973,* vol. II, *Eastern Europe and the Soviet Union* (New York: Chelsea House Publishers, 1973), p. 260.

45. Quoted in J. Samuel Walker, *Henry A. Wallace and American Foreign Policy* (Westport, Conn.: Greenwood Press, 1976), p. 129.

46. Quoted in *ibid.,* p. 121.

47. Wallace, memorandum for Truman, March 14, 1946, in Harry S Truman, *Year of Decisions,* Memoirs, vol. one (New York: Doubleday, 1955), p. 555.

48. Wallace Address at Madison Square Garden, September 12, 1946, in LaFeber, ed., *Dynamics of World Power,* pp. 258–59.

49. Wallace speech announcing his candidacy for President, December 29, 1947, in Thomas G. Paterson, ed., *Cold War Critics: Alternatives to American Foreign Policy in the Truman Years* (Chicago: Quadrangle Books, 1971), pp. 98–103.

50. Wallace, quoted in Alonzo Hanby, "Henry A. Wallace, the Liberals, and Soviet-American Relations," *Review of Politics,* vol. XXX (April 1968), p. 164.

51. George F. Kennan, *Russia, the Atom and the West* (New York: Harper & Brothers, 1957), p. 13.

CHAPTER NINETEEN

The Dilemma of Containment: The Korean War

1. U.S. House of Representatives, Subcommittee of the Committee on Appropriations, *Military Functions: National Military Establishment Appropriation Bill for 1949,* Hearings, 80th Cong., 2nd sess. (Washington, D.C.: U.S. Government Printing Office, 1948), pt. 3, p. 3.

2. General MacArthur, interview with G. Ward Price, *New York Times,* March 2, 1949, p. 22.

3. Secretary of State Dean Acheson, "Crisis in Asia: An Examination of U.S. Policy," remarks before the National Press Club, Washington, January 12, 1950, in *U.S. Department of State Bulletin,* vol. XXII, no. 551 (January 23, 1950), p. 116.

4. Nikita S. Khrushchev, *Khrushchev Remembers,* with an Introduction, Commentary, and Notes by Edward Crankshaw, translated and edited by Strobe Talbott (Boston: Little, Brown, 1970), pp. 368–69. Recently disclosed Soviet material suggests that the Soviet role was much more significant. See Kathryn Weathersby, "New Findings on the Korean War," *Cold War International History Project Bulletin,* Fall 1993, Woodrow Wilson Center, Washington, D.C.

5. Statement by President Truman issued June 27, 1950, in Harry S Truman, *Years of Trial and Hope 1946–1952,* Memoirs, vol. two (New York: Doubleday, 1956), pp. 338–39.

6. *Ibid.,* p. 339.

7. *Ibid.*

8. *Ibid.*

9. Quoted in Max Hastings, *The Korean War* (New York: Simon & Schuster, 1987), p. 133.

10. *Public Papers of the Presidents of the United States, Harry S. Truman,* 1950 vol. (Washington, D.C.: U.S. Government Printing Office, 1965), pp. 674–75 (hereinafter cited as *Truman Papers*).

11. Truman statement of November 30, 1950, in *ibid.,* p. 724.

12. *Truman Papers,* 1951 vol., p. 227.
13. U.S. Senate, Committee on Armed Services and Committee on Foreign Relations, *Military Situation in the Far East,* Hearings, 82nd Cong., 1st sess. (Washington, D.C.: U.S. Government Printing Office, 1951), pt. 1, p. 75 (hereinafter cited as MacArthur Hearings).
14. *Ibid.,* p. 30.
15. *Ibid.*
16. *Truman Papers,* 1951 vol., pp. 226–27.
17. *Ibid.,* p. 227.
18. MacArthur Hearings, pt. 1, p. 45.
19. *Ibid.,* pt. 2, p. 938.
20. *Ibid.,* pt. 3, p. 1717.
21. *Ibid.,* pp. 1718–19.
22. Truman, *Trial and Hope,* p. 345.
23. MacArthur Hearings, pt. 1, p. 593.
24. *Ibid.,* pt. 2, p. 896.
25. *Ibid.,* p. 732.
26. *Ibid.,* pt. 3, p. 1720.
27. General Matthew B. Ridgway, U.S.A., Ret., *Soldier: The Memoirs of Matthew B. Ridgway* (Westport, Conn.: Greenwood Press, 1974 reprint), pp. 219–20.
28. MacArthur Hearings, pt. 1, p. 68.
29. Hastings, *Korean War,* pp. 186ff.
30. Quoted in *ibid.,* p. 197.
31. MacArthur Hearings, pt. 3, p. 1717.

CHAPTER TWENTY
Negotiating with the Communists:
Adenauer, Churchill, and Eisenhower

1. Yevgenii S. Varga, *Changes in the Economy of Capitalism as a Result of the Second World War* (Moscow: Politicheskaya Literatura, 1946), quoted in Allen Lynch, *The Soviet Study of International Relations* (Cambridge: Cambridge University Press, 1967), pp. 20–28.
2. William G. Hyland, *The Cold War Is Over* (New York: Random House, 1990), p. 63.
3. Joseph Stalin, "Economic Problems of Socialism in the U.S.S.R.," in Bruce Franklin, ed., *The Essential Stalin: Major Theoretical Writings 1905–1952* (New York: Anchor Books, 1972), p. 471.
4. *Ibid.*
5. *Ibid.*
6. "Note from the Soviet Union to the United States Transmitting a Soviet Draft of a Peace Treaty with Germany, March 10, 1952," in U.S. Department of State, *Documents on Germany 1944–1985* (Washington, D.C.: U.S. Government Printing Office, undated), Department of State Publication #9446, pp. 361–64.
7. *Ibid.*
8. "Note from the United States to the Soviet Union Proposing Creation of a Freely-Elected All-German Government Prior to Negotiation of a Peace Treaty, March 25, 1952," in *ibid.,* pp. 364–65.
9. "Note from the Soviet Union to the United States Proposing Four-Power Rather Than United Nations Investigation of Conditions for Free All-German Elections, April 9, 1952," in *ibid.,* pp. 365–67; "Note from the United States to the Soviet Union Reasserting the Authority of the United Nations to Investigate Conditions for Free All-German Elections, May 13, 1952," in *ibid.,* pp. 368–71; "Note from the Soviet Union to the United States Proposing Simultaneous Four-Power Discussion of a German Peace Treaty, German Reunification, and Formation of an All-German Government, May 24, 1952," in *ibid.,* pp. 374–78; "Note from the United States to the Soviet Union Reasserting the Need to Investigate

Conditions for Holding Free All-German Elections as a First Step Toward German Reunification, July 10, 1952," in *ibid.*, pp. 385–88; "Note from the Soviet Union to the United States Proposing a Four-Power Meeting to Discuss a German Peace Treaty, Formation of an All-German Government, and the Holding of All-German Elections, August 23, 1952," in *ibid.*, pp. 388–93; "Note from the United States to the Soviet Union Urging 'a Single-Minded Effort . . . to Come to Grips with the Problem of Free Elections in Germany, September 23, 1952," in *ibid.*, pp. 395–97.

10. Stalin's Remarks at the Closing Session of the Nineteenth Congress of the Communist Party of the Soviet Union, October 14, 1952, *Current Digest of the Soviet Press*, vol. IV, no. 38 (November 1, 1952), pp. 9–10.

11. Alan Bullock, *Hitler and Stalin: Parallel Lives* (New York: Alfred A. Knopf, 1992), p. 968.

12. Nikita Khrushchev, *Khrushchev Remembers*, with an Introduction, Commentary, and Notes by Edward Crankshaw, translated and edited by Strobe Talbott (Boston: Little, Brown, 1970), pp. 392–94.

13. Council on Foreign Relations, *The United States and World Affairs*, 1953, p. 116.

14. John Colville, *The Fringes of Power: 10 Downing Street Diaries, 1939–1955* (New York/London: W. W. Norton, 1985), p. 654.

15. Quoted in Martin Gilbert, *Winston S. Churchill: Never Despair, 1945–1965* (Boston: Houghton Mifflin, 1988), p. 510.

16. Remarks at the White House, February 16, 1950, in *U.S. Department of State Bulletin*, vol. XXII, no. 559 (March 20, 1950), pp. 427–29.

17. Colville, *Fringes of Power*, p. 650.

18. Peter G. Boyle, ed., *The Churchill-Eisenhower Correspondence, 1953–55* (Chapel Hill, N.C./London: University of North Carolina Press, 1990), p. 36.

19. Address "The Chance for Peace," delivered before the American Society of Newspaper Editors, Washington, D.C., April 16, 1953, in *Public Papers of the Presidents of the United States, Dwight D. Eisenhower*, 1953 vol. (Washington, D.C.: U.S. Government Printing Office, 1960), pp. 179–88 (hereinafter cited as *Eisenhower Papers*). The story of the drafting of the Eisenhower speech is told in W. W. Rostow, *Europe After Stalin: Eisenhower's Three Decisions of March 11, 1953* (Austin, Tex.: University of Texas Press, 1982).

20. Letter to Eisenhower, May 4, 1953, in Boyle, ed., *Churchill-Eisenhower Correspondence*, p. 48.

21. Letter to Churchill, May 5, 1953, in *ibid.*, p. 49.

22. Speech to the House of Commons, May 11, 1953, in Robert Rhodes James, ed., *Winston S. Churchill: His Complete Speeches, 1897–1963*, vol. VIII, *1950–1963* (New York/London: Chelsea House in association with R. R. Bowker, 1974), p. 8483.

23. *Ibid.*, p. 8484.

24. Boyle, ed., *Churchill-Eisenhower Correspondence*, p. 83.

25. *Ibid.*

26. George F. Kennan, "Disengagement Revisited," *Foreign Affairs*, vol. 37, no. 2 (January 1959), pp. 187–210. See also Acheson's view in Dean Acheson, "The Illusion of Disengagement," *Foreign Affairs*, vol. 36, no. 3 (April 1958), pp. 371–82.

27. *Ibid.*

28. Henry A. Kissinger, "Missiles and the Western Alliance," in *ibid.*, pp. 383–400.

29. Quoted in Emmet John Hughes, *The Ordeal of Power: A Political Memoir of the Eisenhower Years* (New York: Atheneum, 1963), p. 109.

30. Radio and Television Address to the American People Prior to Departure for the Big Four Conference at Geneva, July 15, 1955, in *Eisenhower Papers*, 1955 vol., p. 703.

31. Editorial, *New York Times*, July 25, 1955.

32. Memorandum of a Conversation, Department of State, Washington, October 3, 1955, 10:01 A.M., "Call of the British Foreign Secretary re: *Soviet-Egyptian Arms Agreement*," in "Arab-Israeli Dispute, 1955," *Foreign Relations of the United States*, vol. XIV, p. 545.

33. Closing statement at Geneva Foreign Ministers' Conference, November 16, 1955, in *Documents on International Affairs*, Noble Frankland, ed., 1955 vol. (London: Oxford University Press, 1958), pp. 73–77.

34. Khrushchev, *Khrushchev Remembers,* p. 400.
35. Khrushchev report to the 20th Party Congress, *Pravda,* February 15, 1956, in *Current Digest of the Soviet Press,* vol. VIII, no. 4 (March 7, 1956), pp. 4, 6, 7.
36. Andrei Gromyko, *Memories,* translated by Harold Shukman (London: Hutchinson, 1989).

CHAPTER TWENTY-ONE
Leapfrogging Containment: The Suez Crisis

1. Andrei Zhdanov, "The International Situation," delivered at the Founding Conference of the Cominform, September 1947, in U.S. House of Representatives, Committee on Foreign Affairs, *The Strategy and Tactics of World Communism,* Supplement I, "One Hundred Years of Communism, 1848–1948," 80th Cong., 2nd sess., doc. no. 619 (Washington, D.C.: U.S. Government Printing Office, 1948), pp. 213–14.
2. Churchill remarks in the House of Commons, April 19, 1951, in Robert Rhodes James, ed., *Winston S. Churchill: His Complete Speeches, 1897–1963* vol. VIII, *1950–1963* (New York/London: Chelsea House in association with R. R. Bowker, 1974), p. 8193.
3. See Keith Kyle, *Suez* (New York: St. Martin's Press, 1991), pp. 70ff.
4. *Ibid.,* p. 85.
5. See *ibid.,* pp. 89ff.
6. Quoted in *ibid.,* p. 130.
7. Quoted in *ibid.*
8. Nasser Speech, Alexandria, July 26, 1956, in Noble Frankland, ed., *Documents on International Affairs, 1956* (London/New York/Toronto: Oxford University Press, 1959, issued under the auspices of the Royal Institute of International Affairs), p. 80.
9. *Ibid.,* p. 113; see also Kyle, *Suez,* p. 134.
10. Quoted in Kyle, *Suez,* p. 115.
11. Anthony Eden, *Full Circle: The Memoirs of the Rt. Hon. Sir Anthony Eden* (London: Cassell, 1960), p. 427.
12. *Parliamentary Debates* (Hansard), 5th ser., vol. 557, House of Commons, Session 1955–56 (London: Her Majesty's Stationery Office, 1956), col. 919.
13. Kyle, *Suez,* p. 145.
14. Eden, *Full Circle,* p. 437.
15. Quoted in Alistair Horne, *Harold Macmillan, Volume I: 1894–1956* (New York: Penguin Books, 1991), p. 405.
16. Eisenhower letter to Eden, July 1, 1956, in Dwight D. Eisenhower, *Waging Peace: The White House Years 1956–1961* (Garden City, N.Y.: Doubleday, 1965), pp. 664–65; see also Kyle, *Suez,* p. 160.
17. Quoted in Louis L. Gerson, *John Foster Dulles,* The American Secretaries of State and Their Diplomacy, vol. XVII (New York: Cooper Square Publishers, 1967), p. xi.
18. Quoted in *ibid.,* p. 28.
19. Stephen E. Ambrose, *Eisenhower,* vol. two, *The President* (New York: Simon & Schuster, 1984), p. 21.
20. Gerson, *Dulles,* p. xii.
21. Dulles statement of August 3, 1956, in U.S. Department of State, *The Suez Canal Problem, July 26–September 22, 1956: A Documentary Publication* (Washington, D.C.: Department of State, 1956), p. 37 (hereinafter cited as *Suez Canal Problem*).
22. Dulles remarks in radio-TV address, August 3, 1956, in *ibid.,* p. 42.
23. Dulles remarks as reported in *New York Times,* October 3, 1956, p. 8.
24. Eden, *Full Circle,* p. 498.
25. Eisenhower, *Waging Peace,* p. 667.
26. Quoted in *Suez Canal Problem,* p. 344.
27. Quoted in Kyle, *Suez,* p. 185.
28. "The People Ask the President," television broadcast, October 12, 1956, in *Public Papers of the Presidents of the United States, Dwight D. Eisenhower,* 1956 vol. (Washington, D.C.: U.S. Government Printing Office), p. 903 (hereinafter cited as *Eisenhower Papers*).

29. See, e.g., Eisenhower, *Waging Peace,* pp. 676–77.

30. *U.S. Department of State Bulletin,* vol. XXXV, no. 907 (November 12, 1956), p. 750.

31. Dwight D. Eisenhower, "Radio and Television Report to the American People on the Developments in Eastern Europe and the Middle East," in *Eisenhower Papers,* 1956 vol., p. 1064.

32. Frankland, ed., *Documents on International Affairs,* p. 289.

33. *Ibid.*

34. *Ibid.,* p. 292.

35. *Ibid.,* p. 293.

36. *Eisenhower Papers,* 1956 vol., p. 1066.

37. Dulles press conference remarks, December 18, 1956, in *State Bulletin,* vol. XXXVI, no. 915 (January 7, 1956), p. 5.

38. Quoted in Kyle, *Suez,* p. 426.

39. Quoted in *ibid.*

40. Quoted in Herman Finer, *Dulles over Suez: The Theory and Practice of His Diplomacy* (Chicago: Quadrangle Books, 1964), p. 397.

41. Quoted in Kyle, *Suez,* p. 477.

42. Quoted in *ibid.,* p. 495.

43. Quoted in *ibid.,* p. 467.

44. "US Support for Baghdad Pact," Department of State press release 604, November 29, 1956, in *State Bulletin,* vol. XXXV, no. 911 (December 10, 1956), p. 918.

45. Special Message to the Congress on the Situation in the Middle East, January 5, 1957, in *Eisenhower Papers,* 1957 vol., pp. 6–16.

46. Annual Message to the Congress on the State of the Union, January 10, 1957, in *ibid.,* p. 29.

CHAPTER TWENTY-TWO

Hungary: Upheaval in the Empire

1. Quoted in John Lewis Gaddis, *The Long Peace* (New York/London: Oxford University Press, 1987), p. 157.

2. *Life,* May 19, 1952.

3. Tibor Meray, *Thirteen Days That Shook the Kremlin,* translated by Howard Katzander (New York: Frederick A. Praeger, 1959), p. 7.

4. Quoted in Melvin J. Lasky, ed., *The Hungarian Revolution* (New York: Frederick A. Praeger, 1957), p. 126.

5. Appeal to the President of the Security Council, October 27, 1956, in *U.S. Department of State Bulletin* (November 12, 1956), p. 757.

6. Quoted in Meray, *Thirteen Days,* p. 140.

7. *Ibid.,* p. 169.

8. John Foster Dulles, "The Task of Waging Peace," address before the Dallas Council on World Affairs, October 27, 1956, in *State Bulletin,* vol. XXXV, no. 906 (November 5, 1956), p. 697.

9. Dwight D. Eisenhower, "Radio and Television Report to the American People on the Developments in Eastern Europe and the Middle East," October 31, 1956, in *Public Papers of the Presidents of the United States, Dwight D. Eisenhower,* 1956 vol. (Washington, D.C.: U.S. Government Printing Office, 1958), p. 1061 (hereinafter cited as *Eisenhower Papers*). (Emphasis added.)

10. *Ibid.*

11. *Ibid.,* p. 1062.

12. Declaration of the Government of the U.S.S.R. of October 30, 1956, "On the Principles of Development and Further Strengthening of Friendship and Cooperation Between the Soviet Union and Other Socialist States," appearing in *Pravda* and *Izvestia,* October 31, 1956, in *Current Digest of the Soviet Press,* vol. VIII, no. 40 (November 14, 1956), p. 11.

13. *Eisenhower Papers,* 1956 vol., p. 1062.

14. Government of the U.S.S.R., "On the Principles," p. 11.

15. Quoted in Paul E. Zinner, ed., *National Communism and Popular Revolt in Eastern Europe* (New York: Columbia University Press, 1956), p. 463.
16. Full Nehru speech in *Lok Sabha Debates,* pt. II, vol. 9, no. 3, colls. 260–67, in *Royal Institute of International Affairs,* vol. IV, no. 7, pp. 328–30.
17. Secretary Dulles' News Conference of December 18, 1956, in *State Bulletin,* vol. XXXVI, no. 915 (January 7, 1957), pp. 3–4.
18. Secretary Dulles' News Conference, Canberra, March 13, 1957, in *State Bulletin,* vol. XXXVI, no. 927 (April 1, 1957), p. 533.

CHAPTER TWENTY-THREE
Khrushchev's Ultimatum: The Berlin Crisis 1958–63

1. Nikita S. Khrushchev, *Khrushchev Remembers: The Last Testament,* with an introduction by Edward Crankshaw and Jerrold Schecter, translated and edited by Strobe Talbott (Boston: Little, Brown, 1974), p. 501.
2. John Foster Dulles, "Freedom's New Task," address to Philadelphia *Bulletin* Forum, February 26, 1956, in *U.S. Department of State Bulletin,* vol. XXXIV, no. 871 (March 5, 1956), pp. 363–64.
3. Quoted in William G. Hyland, *The Cold War Is Over* (New York: Random House, 1990), p. 97.
4. U.S. Senate, *Khrushchev on the Shifting Balance of World Forces, A Special Study Presented by Senator Hubert H. Humphrey,* 86th Cong., 1st sess., Senate Doc. no. 57 (Washington, D.C.: U.S. Government Printing Office, 1959), excerpts from Khrushchev interview with W. Sinnbeck, editor of *Dansk Folkstyre,* January 1958, p. 8.
5. *Ibid.* (Khrushchev remarks to the Seventh Congress of the Bulgarian Communist Party, June 4, 1958), p. 7.
6. Nikita S. Khrushchev, "Our Strength Lies in Fraternal Unity," address to Friendship Meeting of Peoples of Soviet Union and Polish People's Republic, November 10, 1958, reprinted in *Pravda,* November 11, 1958, in *Current Digest of the Soviet Press,* vol. X, no. 45 (December 17, 1958), p. 9.
7. Soviet Note of November 27, 1958, in *Documents on American Foreign Relations,* ed. by Paul E. Zinner (New York: Published for the Council on Foreign Relations by Harper & Brothers, 1959), pp. 220–31.
8. Khrushchev, Speech to the 21st Party Congress published in *Pravda,* January 28, 1959, in *Current Digest,* vol. XI, no. 4 (March 4, 1959), p. 19.
9. As recounted by de Gaulle, in Charles de Gaulle, *Memoirs of Hope: Renewal and Endeavor,* translated by Terence Kilmartin (New York: Simon and Schuster, 1971), p. 223.
10. Konrad Adenauer, *Erinnerungen, 1955–1959* (Stuttgart, 1967), pp. 473–74.
11. Harold Macmillan, *Pointing the Way, 1959–1961* (New York: Harper & Row, 1972), p. 101.
12. Eisenhower News Conference of March 11, 1959, in *Public Papers of the Presidents of the United States, Dwight D. Eisenhower,* 1959 vol. (Washington, D.C.: U.S. Government Printing Office, 1960), p. 244.
13. Eisenhower News Conference of February 18, 1959, in *ibid.,* p. 196.
14. Eisenhower News Conference of March 11, 1959, in *ibid.,* p. 245.
15. *The Berlin Crises 1958–1961, Documentary Collection for Oral History Session* (Harvard University, 1990), 2 parts, compiled by William Burr, David Rosenberg, and Georg Schild; Burr, "Select Chronology," pt. 1, March 9, 1959, entry (hereinafter cited as *Berlin Crises* project).
16. De Gaulle press conference, September 5, 1961, in *Documents on International Affairs: 1961,* ed. by D. C. Watt, John Major, Richard Gott, and George Schopflin (London: Oxford University Press for the Royal Institute of International Affairs, 1965), p. 111.
17. Press Conference on September 5, 1960, in *ibid.,* pp. 84–85.
18. De Gaulle, *Memoirs of Hope,* p. 223.

19. *Berlin Crises* project, pt. 2, Burr entry for November 24, 1958, Dulles to Adenauer.

20. Dulles' News Conference, November 26, 1958, in *State Bulletin,* vol. XXXIX, no. 1016 (December 15, 1958), pp. 947ff.

21. Dulles' News Conference, January 13, 1959, in *State Bulletin,* vol. XL, no. 1023 (February 2, 1959), p. 161.

22. *Ibid.*

23. *Berlin Crises* project, pt. 1, Burr entry for November 27, 1958, reporting on Brandt's late November 26 reaction to Dulles' November 26, 1958, news conference.

24. Marc Trachtenberg, "The Berlin Crisis," in *ibid.,* p. 39, recounting Bruce to Dulles message of January 14, 1959.

25. Entry in *ibid.,* Burr, January 13, 1959, recounting Herbert Dittman talk with Livingston Merchant.

26. Khrushchev Speech at Leipzig, March 7, 1959, in *Current Digest,* vol. XI, no. 13 (April 29, 1959), p. 5.

27. *Berlin Crises* project, Trachtenberg essay, p. 46.

28. *Ibid.,* p. 47.

29. *Ibid.*

30. Quoted in Jean Edward Smith, *The Defense of Berlin* (Baltimore: Johns Hopkins University Press, 1963), pp. 212–13.

31. *Newsweek,* October 5, 1959, p. 19.

32. Khrushchev speech before 10,000 Hungarian workers in "Khrushchev Cites '56 Kremlin Split on Hungary Move," *New York Times,* December 3, 1959, p. 1.

33. Gordon Gray, "Memorandum of Meeting with the President," in *Berlin Crises* project, Trachtenberg essay, p. 47.

34. Hyland, *Cold War Is Over,* pp. 120–21.

35. *Ibid.,* p. 120.

36. Quoted in Michael R. Beschloss, *The Crisis Years: Kennedy and Khrushchev 1960–1963* (New York: HarperCollins, 1991), p. 225.

37. Kennedy to Rusk memo, August 21, 1961, quoted in *Berlin Crises* project, Trachtenberg essay, p. 78.

38. Bundy to Kennedy memo, August 28, 1961, quoted in *ibid.*

39. "U.S. Source Advises Bonn to Talk to East Germany," *New York Times,* September 23, 1961, p. 1.

40. McGeorge Bundy, "Policy for the Western Alliance—Berlin and After," address to the Economic Club of Chicago, December 6, 1961, in *State Bulletin,* vol. XLVI, no. 1185 (March 12, 1962), p. 424.

41. Henry A. Kissinger, *Nuclear Weapons and Foreign Policy* (New York: Published for the Council on Foreign Relations by Harper & Brothers, 1957).

42. Excerpts of Adenauer's May 7, 1962, press conference, reprinted thereafter in *New York Times,* May 13, 1962, sect. IV, p. 5.

43. *Ibid.,* May 8, 1962, p. 4.

44. Quoted in Beschloss, *Crisis Years,* p. 400.

45. Acheson letter to Truman, September 21, 1961, in *Berlin Crises* project, Trachtenberg essay, p. 82.

46. Acheson letter to General Lucius Clay, in *ibid.,* pp. 82–83.

47. *Berlin Crises* project, pt. 2, Burr, entry for August 26, 1959, regarding State Department intelligence report, "Germany and the Western Alliance."

CHAPTER TWENTY-FOUR

Concepts of Western Unity: Macmillan, de Gaulle, Eisenhower, and Kennedy

1. Quoted in George F. Kennan, *Memoirs, 1950–1963,* vol. II (Boston/Toronto: Little, Brown, 1972), p. 253.

2. Address by Prime Minister Stanley Baldwin at Albert Hall, May 27, 1935, reported in *London Times,* May 28, 1935, p. 18.

3. On the Acheson speech at West Point, December 5, 1962, see Douglas Brinkley, *Dean Acheson: The Cold War Years, 1953–71* (New Haven, Conn.: Yale University Press, 1992), pp. 175–82.

4. Harold Macmillan, *Riding the Storm, 1956–1959* (New York: Harper & Row, 1971), p. 586.

5. Harold Macmillan, *Pointing the Way, 1959–1961* (New York: Harper & Row, 1972), p. 101.

6. Macmillan, *Riding the Storm,* p. 577. This was also more or less Eisenhower's reaction as to substance.

7. Macmillan, *Pointing the Way,* p. 82.

8. Harold Macmillan, *At the End of the Day, 1961–1963* (New York: Harper & Row, 1974), p. 357.

9. Text, Joint Communiqué, and Attached Statement on Nuclear Defense Systems issued on December 21, 1962, by President Kennedy and Prime Minister Macmillan, *U.S. Department of State Bulletin,* vol. XLVIII, no. 1229 (January 14, 1963), p. 44.

10. Some of the material on France and de Gaulle is adapted from the author's *The Troubled Partnership: A Re-appraisal of the Atlantic Alliance* (New York: Published for the Council on Foreign Relations by McGraw-Hill, 1965), pp. 41ff; and author's *White House Years* (Boston: Little, Brown, 1979), pp. 104ff.

11. "Address by President Charles de Gaulle Outlining the Principles of French Foreign Policy Following the Failure of the Summit Conference," May 31, 1960, in *Major Addresses, Statements, and Press Conferences of General Charles de Gaulle, May 19, 1958–January 31, 1964* (New York: French Embassy, Press and Information Division, 1964), p. 75.

12. De Gaulle Press Conference on April 11, 1961, in *ibid.,* p. 124.

13. Press Conference on July 29, 1963, in *ibid.,* pp. 233–34.

14. Press Conference on March 25, 1959, in *ibid.,* p. 43.

15. Quoted in Brian Crozier, *De Gaulle* (New York: Charles Scribner's Sons, 1973), pp. 533f. See also Dwight D. Eisenhower, *Waging Peace: The White House Years, 1956–1961* (Garden City, N.Y.: Doubleday, 1965), pp. 424–31.

16. Charles de Gaulle, *Memoirs of Hope: Renewal and Endeavor,* trans. by Terence Kilmartin (New York: Simon and Schuster, 1971), pp. 229–30.

17. Quoted in Crozier, *De Gaulle,* p. 525.

18. George Ball, "NATO and World Responsibility," *The Atlantic Community Quarterly,* vol. 2, no. 2 (Summer 1964), p. 211.

19. For a detailed discussion of this idea, see Kissinger, *Troubled Partnership,* pp. 127ff.

20. Kennedy's Address at Independence Hall, Philadelphia, July 4, 1962, in *Public Papers of the Presidents of the United States, John F. Kennedy,* 1962 vol. (Washington, D.C.: U.S. Government Printing Office, 1963), pp. 537–39.

21. Kennedy Address in the Assembly Hall at the Paulskirche in Frankfurt, June 25, 1963, in *ibid.,* 1963 vol., p. 520.

22. De Gaulle Press Conference on January 14, 1963, in *Major Addresses,* pp. 216–17.

23. Press Conference on January 14, 1963, in *ibid.,* p. 218.

24. Press Conference on April 19, 1963, quoted in Harold van B. Cleveland, *The Atlantic Idea and Its European Rivals* (New York: Published for the Council on Foreign Relations by McGraw-Hill, 1966), p. 143.

25. "The Common Declaration and the Treaty Between the French Republic and the Federal Republic of Germany," January 22, 1963, quoted in Roy Macridis, *De Gaulle, Implacable Ally* (New York: Harper & Row, 1966), p. 188.

CHAPTER TWENTY-FIVE
Vietnam: Entry into the Morass; Truman and Eisenhower

1. Inaugural Address, January 20, 1949, in *Public Papers of the Presidents of the United States: Harry S Truman,* 1949 vol. (Washington, D.C.: U.S. Government Printing Office, 1964), pp. 112–14.

2. Inaugural Address, January 20, 1953, in *Public Papers of the Presidents of the United*

States: Dwight D. Eisenhower, 1953 vol. (Washington, D.C.: U.S. Government Printing Office, 1960), p. 6 (hereinafter cited as *Eisenhower Papers*).

3. *Ibid.,* p. 7.

4. Inaugural Address, January 20, 1961, in *Public Papers of the Presidents of the United States: John F. Kennedy,* 1961 vol. (Washington, D.C.: U.S. Government Printing Office, 1962), p. 1.

5. Inaugural Address, January 20, 1965, in *Public Papers of the Presidents of the United States: Lyndon B. Johnson,* 1965 vol. (Washington, D.C.: U.S. Government Printing Office, 1966), p. 72.

6. See Dean Acheson, "The Peace the World Wants," address to United Nations General Assembly, September 20, 1950, *U.S. Department of State Bulletin,* vol. XXIII, no. 587 (October 2, 1950), p. 524; and Dulles, quoted in Jeffrey P. Kimball, ed., *To Reason Why: The Debate About the Causes of U.S. Involvement in the Vietnam War* (New York: McGraw-Hill, 1990), p. 54.

7. Quoted in Kimball, *To Reason Why,* p. 73.

8. *Ibid.*

9. Quoted in Thomas J. Schoenbaum, *Waging Peace and War: Dean Rusk in the Truman, Kennedy and Johnson Years* (New York: Simon and Schuster, 1988), p. 234.

10. NSC 68, "United States Objectives and Programs for National Security," April 7, 1950, in U.S. Department of State, *Foreign Relations of the United States,* 1950, vol. I (Washington, D.C.: U.S. Government Printing Office, 1977), pp. 237–38.

11. See William Roger Louis, *Imperialism at Bay: The United States and the Decolonization of the British Empire, 1941–1945* (New York: Oxford University Press, 1978), chh. 1 and 2.

12. George C. Herring, *America's Longest War, The United States and Vietnam 1950–1975* (New York: Alfred A. Knopf, 2nd ed., 1986), p. 18.

13. *Ibid.*

14. Schoenbaum, *Waging Peace and War,* p. 230.

15. Herring, *America's Longest War,* pp. 18–19.

16. *Ibid.,* p. 19.

17. "United States Objectives and Courses of Action with Respect to Southeast Asia," Statement of Policy by the National Security Council, 1952, in Neil Sheehan, Hedrick Smith, W. W. Kenworthy, Fox Butterfield, *The Pentagon Papers, as Published by the New York Times* (New York: Quadrangle Books, 1971), p. 29.

18. *Ibid.,* p. 28.

19. *Ibid.,* p. 29.

20. Quoted in Herring, *America's Longest War,* p. 22.

21. Quoted in *ibid.,* p. 26.

22. *Ibid.,* p. 27.

23. Quoted in Sir Robert Thompson, *Revolutionary War in World Strategy 1945–1969* (New York: Taplinger, 1970), p. 120.

24. Quoted in Stanley Karnow, *Vietnam: A History* (New York: Penguin Books, 1984), pp. 197–98.

25. Quoted in William Bragg Ewald, Jr., *Eisenhower the President: Crucial Days, 1951–1960* (Englewood Cliffs, N.J.: Prentice-Hall, 1981), pp. 119–20.

26. Eisenhower to Churchill, April 4, 1954, in Peter G. Boyle, ed., *The Churchill-Eisenhower Correspondence, 1953–1955* (Chapel Hill and London: University of North Carolina Press, 1990), pp. 137–40.

27. Anthony Eden, *Full Circle: The Memoirs of the Rt. Hon. Anthony Eden* (Boston: Houghton Mifflin, 1960), p. 124.

28. Quoted in Martin Gilbert, *Winston S. Churchill,* vol. VIII, *"Never Despair," 1945–1965* (Boston: Houghton Mifflin, 1988), pp. 973–74.

29. Quoted in *ibid.,* p. 973.

30. Quoted in *ibid.*

31. Townsend Hoopes, *The Devil and John Foster Dulles* (Boston: Little, Brown, 1973), p. 239.

32. Richard M. Nixon, *No More Vietnams* (New York: Arbor House, 1985), p. 41.
33. Dulles at London press conference, April 13, 1954, quoted in Hoopes, *Devil and John Foster Dulles,* p. 209.
34. *Ibid.,* p. 222.
35. Quoted in Herring, *America's Longest War,* p. 39.
36. Dulles instructions to Undersecretary Walter Bedell Smith, May 12, 1954, in connection with the Geneva conference, in *The Pentagon Papers,* p. 44.
37. U.S. Declaration on Indochina, July 21, 1954, in *State Bulletin,* vol. XXXI, no. 788 (August 2, 1954), p. 162.
38. Herring, *America's Longest War,* p. 45.
39. Eisenhower letter to Diem, October 23, 1954, in Marvin E. Gettleman, ed., *Viet Nam: History, Documents, and Opinions on a Major World Crisis* (Greenwich, Conn.: Fawcett Publications, 1965), pp. 204–5.
40. Herring, *America's Longest War,* p. 56.
41. Senator Mike Mansfield, "Reprieve in Vietnam," *Harper's,* January 1956, p. 50.
42. Senator John F. Kennedy, "America's Stake in Vietnam, the Cornerstone of the Free World in Southeast Asia," address delivered before the American Friends of Vietnam, Washington, D.C., June 1, 1956, in *Vital Speeches of the Day,* August 1, 1956, pp. 617ff.
43. Herring, *America's Longest War,* p. 68.
44. Dwight D. Eisenhower, *Waging Peace: The White House Years, 1956–1961* (Garden City, N.Y.: Doubleday, 1965), p. 607.
45. *Ibid.,* p. 610.
46. "Address at the Gettysburg College Convocation: The Importance of Understanding," April 4, 1959, in *Eisenhower Papers,* 1959 vol. (1960), p. 313.

CHAPTER TWENTY-SIX
Vietnam: On the Road to Despair; Kennedy and Johnson

1. *Public Papers of the Presidents of the United States, John F. Kennedy,* 1961 vol. (Washington, D.C.: U.S. Government Printing Office, 1962), p. 23 (hereinafter cited as *Kennedy Papers*).
2. Lin Piao, "Long Live the Victory of People's War!," *Peking Review,* vol. VIII, no. 36 (September 3, 1965), pp. 9–30.
3. Quoted in David Halberstam, *The Best and the Brightest* (New York: Random House, 1972), p. 76.
4. From Kennedy's opening statement at a news conference of March 23, 1961, in *Kennedy Papers,* 1961 vol. (1962), p. 214.
5. Special Message to Congress on the Defense Budget, March 28, 1961, in *ibid.,* p. 230.
6. *"Let the Word Go Forth": The Speeches, Statements, and Writings of John F. Kennedy, 1947–1963,* selected and with an introduction by Theodore C. Sorensen (New York: Dell Publishing, 1988), p. 371.
7. *Ibid.,* pp. 370ff.
8. Senator John F. Kennedy, "America's Stake in Vietnam, the Cornerstone of the Free World in Southeast Asia," address delivered before the American Friends of Vietnam, Washington, D.C., June 1, 1956, in *Vital Speeches of the Day,* August 1, 1956, pp. 617–19.
9. Lyndon Baines Johnson, *The Vantage Point: Perspectives of the Presidency 1963–1969* (New York: Holt, Rinehart and Winston, 1971), p. 55.
10. National Security Memorandum 52, signed by McGeorge Bundy, Presidential Adviser on National Security, May 11, 1961, in Neil Sheehan, Hedrick Smith, W. W. Kenworthy, Fox Butterfield, *The Pentagon Papers as Published by the New York Times* (New York: Quadrangle Books, 1971), p. 131.
11. Johnson to Kennedy memo, "Mission to Southeast Asia, India and Pakistan," May 23, 1961, in *Pentagon Papers,* p. 134.
12. Bundy, quoted in *Pentagon Papers,* p. 103.
13. McNamara memo to Kennedy, November 8, 1961, in *Pentagon Papers,* p. 154.

14. Quoted in George C. Herring, *America's Longest War: The United States and Vietnam 1950–1975* (New York: Alfred A. Knopf, 2nd ed., 1985), p. 83.

15. Quoted in *ibid.,* p. 86.

16. Kennedy's Special Message to Congress on Defense Policies and Principles, March 28, 1961, in *Kennedy Papers,* 1961 vol. (1962), pp. 229ff.

17. Quoted in Guenter Lewy, *America in Vietnam* (New York: Oxford University Press, 1978), p. 26.

18. State Department telegram to Lodge in Saigon, August 24, 1963, in *Pentagon Papers,* p. 200.

19. *Ibid.*

20. "Opportunity in Vietnam," editorial, *The New York Times,* November 3, 1963, sect. 4, p. 8E.

21. Quoted in Lewy, *America in Vietnam,* p. 28.

22. Quoted in *ibid.,* p. 29.

23. Harrison Salisbury, *Behind the Lines—Hanoi* (New York: Harper & Row, 1967), pp. 194–97.

24. Edgar Snow, "Interview with Mao," *The New Republic,* February 27, 1965, p. 17.

25. Johnson Address to the American Alumni Council, July 12, 1966, in *Public Papers of the Presidents of the United States, Lyndon B. Johnson,* 1966 vol. II (Washington, D.C.: U.S. Government Printing Office, 1967) p. 720 (hereinafter cited as *Johnson Papers*).

26. *Ibid.*

27. Johnson Address at Johns Hopkins University, April 7, 1965, in *Johnson Papers,* 1965 vol. I (1966), pp. 396–97.

28. Johnson Address on Vietnam to the National Legislative Conference, San Antonio, Texas, September 29, 1967, in *Johnson Papers,* 1967 vol. II (1968), p. 879.

29. Walter Lippmann, "On Defeat," *Newsweek,* March 11, 1968, p. 25.

30. Fulbright address, "U.S. Is in Danger of Losing Its Perspective," to the School of Advanced International Studies, Johns Hopkins University, Washington, D.C., May 5, 1966, as reprinted in *U.S. News & World Report,* vol. LX, no. 21 (May 23, 1966), pp. 114–15.

31. J. William Fulbright speech, "Old Myths and New Realities," delivered in the United States Senate, March 25, 1964, reprinted in *Vital Speeches of the Day,* April 16, 1964, pp. 393–94.

32. Richard L. Renfield, "A Policy for Vietnam," *Yale Law Review,* vol. LVI, no. 4 (June 1967), pp. 481–505.

33. James Reston, "Washington: The Flies That Captured the Flypaper," *New York Times,* February 7, 1968, p. 46.

34. Senator J. William Fulbright, *The Crippled Giant: American Foreign Policy and Its Domestic Consequences* (New York: Random House, 1972), p. 62.

35. For a brilliant analysis of this group, see Norman Podhoretz, *Why We Were in Vietnam* (New York: Simon and Schuster, 1982), pp. 85ff.

36. Quoted in *ibid.,* p. 100.

37. Quoted in *ibid.,* p. 105.

38. David Halberstam, *The Making of a Quagmire* (New York: Random House, 1965), p. 319.

39. Lewy, *American in Vietnam,* p. 76; Don Oberdorfer, *Tet!* (Garden City, N.Y.: Doubleday, 1971), pp. 329ff.

40. Arthur M. Schlesinger, Jr., *Robert Kennedy and His Times* (Boston: Houghton Mifflin, 1978), p. 843.

41. "Report from Vietnam by Walter Cronkite," CBS News special, February 27, 1968, quoted in Oberdorfer, *Tet!,* p. 251.

42. "The Logic of the Battlefield," *Wall Street Journal,* February 23, 1968, p. 14.

43. "Frank Magee Sunday Report," NBC, March 10, 1968, quoted in Oberdorfer, *Tet!,* p. 273.

44. "The War," *Time,* vol. 91, no. 11 (March 15, 1968), p. 14.

45. Mansfield statement in the Senate, March 7, 1968, in *Congressional Record,* vol. 114, pt. 5 (Washington, D.C.: U.S. Government Printing Office, 1968), p. 5659.

46. Fulbright statement in the Senate, March 7, 1968, *ibid.,* p. 5645.

47. Johnson television broadcast to the American people, March 31, 1968, in *Johnson Papers,* 1968–69 vol. I (1970), pp. 469–96.

CHAPTER TWENTY-SEVEN

Vietnam: The Extrication; Nixon

1. Walter Isaacson, *Kissinger: A Biography* (New York: Simon & Schuster, 1992), p. 484.

2. The memorandum is printed in its entirety in the chapter notes to Henry Kissinger, *White House Years* (Boston: Little, Brown, 1979), pp. 1480–82.

3. Quoted in *ibid.,* p. 1481.

4. All American withdrawal schemes were made conditional on a cease-fire and the release of all prisoners.

5. Senator J. William Fulbright, *The Crippled Giant: American Foreign Policy and Its Domestic Consequences* (New York: Random House, 1972), p. 62.

6. McGovern remarks on "The Today Show," NBC TV, June 8, 1972.

7. Quoted in Kissinger, *White House Years,* p. 1345.

8. Kissinger News Conference, January 24, 1973, in *U.S. Department of State Bulletin,* vol. LXVIII, no. 1753 (February 12, 1973), p. 164.

9. See Kissinger, *White House Years,* chh. VIII and XII; Henry Kissinger, *Years of Upheaval* (Boston: Little, Brown, 1982), chh. II and VIII; and Peter W. Rodman's exchange with William Shawcross in *American Spectator,* March and July 1981.

10. See Karl D. Jackson, ed., *Cambodia 1975–1978: Rendezvous with Death* (Princeton, N.J.: Princeton University Press, 1989).

11. See Kissinger, *White House Years,* pp. 1362ff.

12. See summary of U.S. statements in Kissinger, *Years of Upheaval,* pp. 1236–40.

13. "Fourth Annual Report to the Congress on United States Foreign Policy," May 3, 1973, in *Public Papers of the Presidents of the United States, Richard Nixon,* 1973 vol. (Washington, D.C.: U.S. Government Printing Office, 1975), p. 392.

14. *Ibid.,* p. 395.

15. Second Supplemental Appropriations Bill for FY1973 (HR 9055-PL93-50). See *Congressional Quarterly, 1973 Almanac,* 93d Cong., 1st sess. (Washington, D.C.: Congressional Quarterly, 1974), pp. 95, 861–62.

16. Joseph Fitchett, "Saigon Residents Found Intimidated by 'Occupation Force,'" *Washington Post,* November 6, 1978; see also Christopher Dickey, "Former Vietnamese Captive Describes Life—and Death—in Saigon Prison," *Washington Post,* December 20, 1978; Theodore Jacqueney, "They Are Us, Were We Vietnamese," *Worldview,* April 1977; Carl Gershman, "A Voice from Vietnam," *New Leader,* January 29, 1979, pp. 8–9.

17. International Institute of Strategic Studies, *Strategic Survey, 1975* (London: IISS, 1975), p. 94.

18. See the forthcoming book by Peter W. Rodman on the Cold War in the Third World, to be published by Charles Scribner's Sons, for a fuller discussion of this evolution of Soviet policy.

CHAPTER TWENTY-EIGHT

Foreign Policy as Geopolitics: Nixon's Triangular Diplomacy

1. Richard Nixon, quoted in *Time,* January 3, 1972, p. 15. See also Nixon's remarks to Midwestern News Media Executives in Kansas City, Missouri, July 6, 1971, in *Public Papers of the Presidents of the United States, Richard Nixon,* 1971 vol. (Washington, D.C.: U.S. Government Printing Office, 1972), p. 806 (hereinafter cited as *Nixon Papers*).

2. Remarks at Presidential Prayer Breakfast, February 5, 1970, in *Nixon Papers,* 1970 vol., pp. 82–83.

3. Radio and Television Address to the People of the Soviet Union, May 28, 1972, in *Nixon Papers,* 1972 vol., p. 630.

4. Nixon's Informal Remarks in Guam with Newsmen, July 25, 1969, in *Nixon Papers,* 1969 vol., pp. 544–56.

5. Address to the Nation on the War in Vietnam, November 3, 1969, in *ibid.,* pp. 905–6. See also Nixon's First Annual Report to the Congress on United States Foreign Policy for the 1970's, February 18, 1970, in *Nixon Papers,* 1970 vol., pp. 116ff.

6. Norman Mailer, *The Armies of the Night: History as a Novel, the Novel as History* (New York: New American Library, 1968), p. 187.

7. John Kenneth Galbraith, *The New Industrial State* (Boston: Houghton Mifflin, 1967), ch. XXXV.

8. First Annual Report to the Congress on United States Foreign Policy for the 1970's, February 18, 1970, in *Nixon Papers,* 1970 vol., p. 119.

9. *Ibid.,* p. 178.

10. *Ibid.,* p. 179.

11. Second Annual Report to the Congress on United States Foreign Policy, February 25, 1971, in *Nixon Papers,* 1971 vol., p. 304.

12. Albert Wohlstetter, "The Delicate Balance of Terror," *Foreign Affairs,* vol. 37, no. 2 (January 1959), pp. 211–34.

13. Quoted in Henry Kissinger, *White House Years* (Boston: Little, Brown, 1979), p. 136.

14. Peter Grose, "U.S. Warns Soviet on Use of Force Against Czechs," *The New York Times,* April 18, 1969.

15. Peter Grose, "A Series of Limited Pacts on Missiles Now U.S. Aim," *The New York Times,* April 22, 1969.

16. Chalmers M. Roberts, "U.S. to Propose Summer Talks on Arms Curb," *The Washington Post,* May 13, 1969.

17. "Clear It with Everett," editorial, *The New York Times,* June 3, 1969.

18. "Start the Missile Talks," editorial, *The Washington Post,* April 5, 1969.

19. See Kissinger, *White House Years,* pp. 265ff.

20. Quoted in *ibid.,* p. 165.

21. Richard M. Nixon, "Asia After Viet Nam," *Foreign Affairs,* vol. 46, no. 1 (October 1967), p. 121.

22. "Nixon's View of the World—From Informal Talks," in *U.S. News & World Report,* vol. LXV, no. 12 (September 16, 1968), p. 48.

23. Rogers Address Before the National Press Club, Canberra, Australia, August 8, 1969, in *U.S. Department of State Bulletin,* vol. LXI, no. 1575 (September 1, 1969), pp. 179–80.

24. Richardson address, "The Foreign Policy of the Nixon Administration: Its Aims and Strategy," in *ibid.,* vol. LXI, no. 1578 (September 22, 1969), p. 260.

25. Second Annual Report, in *Nixon Papers,* 1971 vol., p. 277.

26. *Ibid.*

27. Quoted in Kissinger, *White House Years,* p. 1062.

28. Quoted in *ibid.*

29. Joint Communiqué Issued at Shanghai, February 27, 1972, in *State Bulletin,* vol. LXVI, no. 1708 (March 20, 1972), pp. 435–38.

30. See Henry Kissinger, *Years of Upheaval* (Boston: Little, Brown, 1982), pp. 233, 294–95, 1173–74.

CHAPTER TWENTY-NINE

Detente and Its Discontents

1. Willy Brandt, *People and Politics: The Years 1960–1975,* trans. by J. Maxwell Brownjohn (Boston: Little, Brown, 1976), pp. 123–24.

2. See Henry Kissinger, *Years of Upheaval* (Boston: Little, Brown, 1982), pp. 459ff.

3. *"Détente:* An Evaluation," statement by Robert Conquest, Brian Crozier, John Erickson, Joseph Godson, Gregory Grossman, Leopold Labedz, Bernard Lewis, Richard Pipes, Leonard Schapiro, Edward Shils, and P. J. Vatikiotis, reprinted for use of the Subcommittee on Arms Control, Committee on Armed Services, United States Senate, 93rd Cong., 2nd sess. (Washington, D.C.: U.S. Government Printing Office, June 20, 1974), p. 1.

4. Statement of George Meany, President, American Federation of Labor and Congress of Industrial Organizations, to the Senate Foreign Relations Committee, October 1, 1974, in United States Senate, Committee on Foreign Relations, *Détente: Hearings on United States Relations with Communist Countries,* 93rd Cong., 2nd sess. (Washington, D.C.: U.S. Government Printing Office, 1975), pp. 379–80.

5. Henry Kissinger, "America's Permanent Interests," address before the Boston World Affairs Council, March 11, 1976, in *U.S. Department of State Bulletin,* vol. LXXIV, no. 1919 (April 5, 1976), pp. 427–28.

6. Quoted in Henry Kissinger, *White House Years* (Boston: Little, Brown, 1979), p. 1486.

7. For details of the debate, see Kissinger, *Years of Upheaval,* pp. 256–74, 1006–28.

8. See Coral Bell, *The Diplomacy of Détente* (New York: St. Martin's Press, 1977), pp. 201–222.

9. "Improving U.S.-Soviet Relations," editorial, *The New York Times,* February 22, 1971, p. 5.

10. "Trade and Freedom," editorial, in *ibid.,* September 18, 1973, p. 42.

11. "The Requirements of Detente," editorial, *Washington Post,* September 12, 1973.

12. Kissinger, "America's Permanent Interests," pp. 431–32.

13. Quoted in Timothy Garton Ash, *In Europe's Name: Germany and the Divided Continent* (New York: Random House, 1993), p. 260.

14. *Ibid.,* p. 223.

15. "European 'Security' . . . and Real Détente," editorial, *The New York Times,* July 21, 1975, p. 20.

16. Henry Kissinger, "American Unity and the National Interest," address before the Southern Commodity Producers Conference in Birmingham, Alabama, August 14, 1975, in *State Bulletin,* vol. LXXIII, no. 1890 (September 15, 1975), p. 392.

17. Kissinger, "America's Permanent Interests," p. 428.

CHAPTER THIRTY

The End of the Cold War: Reagan and Gorbachev

1. Ronald Reagan, Remarks at the Annual Washington Conference of the American Legion, February 22, 1983, in *Public Papers of the Presidents of the United States, Ronald Reagan,* 1983 vol., bk. I (Washington, D.C.: U.S. Government Printing Office, 1982–90), p. 270 (hereinafter cited as *Reagan Papers*).

2. *Ibid.,* p. 271.

3. Ronald Reagan, News Conference, January 29, 1981, in *ibid.,* 1981 vol., p. 57.

4. Reagan Address to Members of the British Parliament, London, June 8, 1982, in *ibid.,* 1982 vol., bk. 1, p. 744.

5. "TRB" (Richard Strout), "Reagan's Holy War," *The New Republic,* April 11, 1983, p. 6.

6. Anthony Lewis, "Onward, Christian Soldiers," *The New York Times,* March 10, 1983, p. A27.

7. Stanley Hoffmann, "Foreign Policy: What's to Be Done?," *New York Review of Books,* April 30, 1981, pp. 33–37, 39.

8. Text of Reagan letter in Remarks to Members of the National Press Club on Arms Reduction and Nuclear Weapons, November 18, 1981, in *Reagan Papers,* 1981 vol., p. 1065.

9. Ronald Reagan, *An American Life* (New York: Simon & Schuster, 1990), p. 576.

10. *Ibid.,* p. 592.

11. *Ibid.,* p. 603.

12. *Ibid.,* p. 634.

13. Lou Cannon, *President Reagan: The Role of a Lifetime* (New York: Simon & Schuster, 1990), p. 792.

14. Ronald Reagan, Address Before a Joint Session of Congress on the State of the Union, January 25, 1984, in *Reagan Papers,* 1984 vol., bk. I, p. 92.

15. Reagan, Address to British Parliament, June 8, 1982, in *ibid.,* 1982 vol., bk. I, p. 746.

16. *Ibid.,* p. 745.

17. See Peter W. Rodman's forthcoming book on the Cold War in the Third World, to be published by Charles Scribner's Sons.

18. Shultz Address, "America and the Struggle for Freedom," February 22, 1985 (Washington, D.C.: U.S. Department of State, Bureau of Public Affairs, February 1985), Current Policy no. 659, pp. 1–5.

19. Quoted in Leon V. Sigal, *Nuclear Forces in Europe* (Washington, D.C.: Brookings Institution, 1984), p. 86.

20. Mitterrand speech before the Bundestag on the occasion of the Twentieth Anniversary of the Franco-German Treaty of Cooperation, January 20, 1983 (France: Foreign Affairs Ministry, The Press and Information Service).

21. Reagan, Remarks to National Press Club, November 18, 1981, in *Reagan Papers,* 1981 vol., p. 1065.

22. "Reagan Proposes U.S. Seek New Way to Block Missiles," *The New York Times,* March 24, 1983, p. A20.

23. Harold Brown, ed., *The Strategic Defense Initiative: Shield or Snare?* (Boulder, Col., and London: Westview Press for the Johns Hopkins Foreign Policy Institute, 1987).

24. Harold Brown, "Introduction" and "Is SDI Technically Feasible?," in *ibid.,* pp. 4–7, 131–32, 138.

25. Richard Betts, "Heavenly Gains or Earthly Losses? Toward a Balance Sheet for Strategic Defense," in *ibid.,* pp. 238–39.

26. George Liska, "The Challenge of SDI: Preemptive Diplomacy or Preventive War?," in *ibid.,* p. 107.

27. Robert Osgood, "Implications for US-European Relations," in *ibid.,* pp. 266–68, 276–78.

28. Quoted in Dan Smith, *Pressure: How America Runs NATO* (London: Bloomsbury, 1989), p. 184.

29. Reagan, Address Before the Japanese Diet in Tokyo, November 11, 1983, in *Reagan Papers,* 1983 vol., bk. II, p. 1575.

30. Reagan, *American Life,* p. 550.

31. Cannon, *President Reagan,* p. 289.

32. Reagan, Remarks at a White House Briefing for Chief Executive Officers of Trade Associations and Corporations on Deployment of the MX Missile, May 16, 1983, in *Reagan Papers,* 1983 vol., bk. I, p. 715.

33. Reagan, Address to the Nation on Defense and National Security, March 23, 1983, in *ibid.,* p. 443.

34. George P. Shultz, "Nuclear Weapons, Arms Control, and the Future of Deterrence," address before the International House of Chicago and *The Chicago Sun-Times* Forum at the University of Chicago, November 17, 1986, in *U.S. Department of State Bulletin,* vol. 87, no. 2118 (January 1987), pp. 31–35.

35. Mikhail Gorbachev, *Perestroika: New Thinking for Our Country and the World* (New York: Harper & Row, 1987), p. 139.

36. Mikhail Gorbachev, press conference following Geneva Summit, November 21, 1985, in *Geneva: The Soviet-US Summit, November 1985, Documents and Materials* (Moscow: Novosti Press Agency Publishing House, 1985), p. 18.

37. Mikhail Gorbachev, address on the 70th anniversary of the Great October Socialist Revolution, November 2, 1987, in *Foreign Broadcast Information Service* (SOV-87-212, November 3, 1987), p. 55.

38. "An Interview with Gorbachev," *Time,* September 9, 1985, p. 23.

39. "Gorbachev Pledges Major Troop Cutback Then Ends Trip, Citing Vast Soviet Quake," *The New York Times,* December 8, 1988, p. A1.

40. *Ibid.,* p. A19.

41. Excerpts of Gorbachev's speech in Vladivostok, June 28, 1986, in *The New York Times,* June 29, 1986, p. A6.

42. Excerpts of Gorbachev's speech to the Council of Europe in Strasbourg, France, July 6, 1989, in *The New York Times,* July 7, 1989, p. A6.

43. "Gorbachev, in Finland, Disavows Any Right of Regional Intervention," *The New York Times,* October 26, 1989, p. A1.

44. "Gorbachev Lends Honecker a Hand," *The New York Times,* October 7, 1989, p. 5.

45. "Gorbachev Urges Economic Accords," *The New York Times,* July 16, 1989, p. 17.

46. Strobe Talbott, "Rethinking the Red Menace," *Time,* January 1, 1990, p. 69.

47. Fred Halliday, *From Kabul to Managua: Soviet-American Relations in the 1980s* (New York: Pantheon Books, 1989), pp. 17, 108–9, 134–35.

48. Vyacheslav Dashichev, "East-West: Quest for New Relations: On the Priorities of the Soviet State's Foreign Policy," in *Foreign Broadcast Information Service* (SOV-88-098, May 20, 1988), pp. 4–8.

49. *Ibid.*

50. Eduard Shevardnadze, "The 19th All-Union CPSU Conference: Foreign Policy and Diplomacy," *International Affairs* (Moscow), October 1988.

51. "X" (George F. Kennan), "The Sources of Soviet Conduct," *Foreign Affairs,* vol. 25, no. 4 (July 1947), p. 580.

CHAPTER THIRTY-ONE
The New World Order Reconsidered

1. President George Bush, "The U.N.: World Parliament of Peace," address to the U.N. General Assembly, New York, October 1, 1990, in *Dispatch* (U.S. Department of State), vol. 1, no. 6 (October 8, 1990), p. 152.

2. President Bill Clinton, "Confronting the Challenges of a Broader World," address to the U.N. General Assembly, New York, September 27, 1993, in *ibid.,* vol. 4, no. 39 (September 27, 1993), p. 650.

3. Sir Halford John Mackinder, *Democratic Ideals and Reality* (Westport, Conn.: Greenwood Press, 1962).

4. Alexander Solzhenitsyn, "How Are We to Restructure Russia? A Modest Contribution," *Literaturnaya Gazeta,* Moscow, September 18, 1990, in *Foreign Broadcast Information Service* (SOV-90-187, September 26, 1990), esp. pp. 37–41.

5. Remarks by President Bill Clinton to the Multinational Audience of Future Leaders of Europe, Hotel De Ville, Brussels, Belgium, January 9, 1994 (Brussels, Belgium: The White House, Office of the Press Secretary, press release, January 9, 1994), p. 5.

Acknowledgments

No one made a greater contribution than Gina Goldhammer, who edited the entire manuscript through its every draft. She was the focal point of all our efforts, and saw to it with extraordinary ability, infinite tact, and patience that everything merged at the proper moment.

Jon Vanden Heuvel's historical research was indispensable; in addition, he made innumerable helpful comments on the entire book as it took shape.

My old friend and associate Peter Rodman did much research, especially on the American material, and read each chapter. I am grateful to him for his helpful and insightful suggestions.

Rosemary Neaher Niehuss has been a longtime, indefatigable aide. She did research, especially on Korea and Vietnam, checked everyone else's research, tracked down elusive facts, and allowed nothing to escape her scrutiny. Valuable assistance came from Maureen Minehan and Stephanie Tone.

Jody Iobst Williams typed the manuscript from my nearly illegible handwriting and straightened out many a turgid sentence structure. Suzanne McFarlane freed me to concentrate on this book by keeping track of all my other activities with her customary tact and care.

I benefited greatly from William G. Hyland's suggestions on the Soviet material and from Norman Podhoretz's reading of an early draft.

Michael Korda at Simon & Schuster proved a marvelous editor and became a good friend. He bore with me as the original, fairly simple idea changed its focus and grew into a much more complicated and prolonged undertaking. The measure of his contribution is that whenever one of his urbane comments particularly galled me, I found on reflection that he was right.

Lynn Amato coordinated all Simon & Schuster activities with unfailing good humor and efficiency. All Simon & Schuster personnel—the copy editors, designers, production and promotion personnel—worked with touching dedication and consummate ability.

My wife, Nancy, was, as always, a sound counselor and indispensable moral support. She read the entire manuscript and made extraordinarily wise suggestions.

The shortcomings of the book are my own.

Henry A. Kissinger

Picture Credits

Page 6   Drawing by A. Forestier for the *London Illustrated News.* Bibliothèque Nationale/Jean Loup Charmet.

Page 10   *Farewell Address:* Courtesy Historical Documents Co., Philadelphia, Pennsylvania. *Washington inset:* Culver Pictures.

Page 17   U.N. Photo.

Page 29   *Both:* The Bettmann Archive.

Page 56   *Left:* Hulton Deutsch Collection Limited. *Right:* Ullstein Bilderdienst.

Page 78   Hulton Deutsch Collection Limited.

Page 103   *Left:* Hulton Deutsch Collection Limited. *Right:* © ND-VIOLLET.

Page 137   Bettmann/Hulton.

Page 168   The Bettmann Archive.

Page 201   UPI/Bettmann.

Page 218   Brown Brothers.

Page 246   UPI/Bettmann Newsphotos.

Page 266   © HARLINGUE-VIOLLET.

Page 288   UPI/Bettmann.

Page 332   UPI/Bettmann.

Page 350   Archive Photos.

Page 369   UPI/Bettmann Newsphotos.

Page 394   The Bettmann Archive.

Page 423   *Both:* UPI/Bettmann Newsphotos.

Page 446   © Erich Lessing/MAGNUM Photos.

Page 473   ACME.

Page 493   © Bob Henriques/MAGNUM Photos.

Page 522   © Erich Lessing/MAGNUM Photos.

Page 550   © Erich Lessing/MAGNUM Photos.

Page 568   Archive Photos.

Page 594   *Left:* Agence France-Presse/Archive Photos. *Right:* Deutsche Presse-Agentur/Archive Photos.

Page 620   Ullstein Bilderdienst.

Page 643   UPI/Bettmann Newsphotos.

Page 674   Archive Photos France.

Page 703   J. P. Laffont/SYGMA.

Page 733   AP/Wide World Photos.

Page 762   Michel Philippot/SYGMA.

Page 804   *United States:* © Gallant/The Image Bank. *Great Britain:* Paul Trummer/The Image Bank. *France:* Romilly Lockyer/The Image Bank. *Germany:* © Patrick Doherty/Stockphotos. *China:* Marcel Isy-Schwart/The Image Bank. *Russia:* Benn Mitchell/The Image Bank. *Japan:* Hank de Lespinasse/The Image Bank.

Index

ABC-1 Agreement, 389, 403–4
Abernon, Lord d', 252, 267–68
ABM Treaty, 747–49, 780
Abyssinia, 53, 249, 298–300, 302
Access Authority, 590–91, 592
Acheson, Dean, 538, 584
  on collective security, 459–60, 490
  containment policy and, 451–52, 459,
    618, 623, 709, 713, 741, 755
  Pacific defense policy and, 475–76, 486–
    487, 490, 626
  U.S.-Soviet relations and, 501–2, 509, 553,
    755
Adams, John Quincy, 34–35, 462, 621, 756,
  774, 833
Adams, Sherman, 631
Adenauer, Konrad, 283, 371, 498, 502–3,
  507, 514, 535, 587, 588–92, 604, 606,
  607, 735
  Access Authority and, 590–91, 592
  Berlin crisis and, 571–73, 575, 577, 578,
    579, 584, 589
  Franco-German mutual friendship treaty
    and, 547, 615–17
  nuclear weapons and, 589–90, 599–600
  Sino-Soviet rift as seen by, 588–89, 720
  Stalin's Peace Note rejected by, 502, 504
Adrianople, Treaty of, 173
Afghanistan, 152, 161, 178, 192, 249, 449,
  593, 775, 788–89, 824
  Soviet invasion of, 141, 701, 763, 774, 787,
    792
Aix-la-Chapelle, Congress of, 89, 90
Albania, 199, 443
Alexander I, Tsar of Russia, 54, 85, 86, 87,
  140, 142, 156, 398, 432
  Congress of Vienna and, 79, 83
  Pitt and, 75–76
Alexander II, Tsar of Russia, 163, 414, 432
Alexander III, Tsar of Russia, 163–64, 175,
  204, 206–8
Algeciras Conference (1906), 190, 191, 196,
  197
Algeria, 531, 603, 614, 625, 674
Allgemeine Zeitung, 185
Alliance for Progress, 831
Alsace-Lorraine, 134, 138, 159, 160, 180, 194,
  204, 219, 225, 239, 269, 351
America First Committee, 389

American Legion, 767
American Society of Newspaper Editors,
  509
Andropov, Yuri, 770, 776, 777
Anglo-American relationship:
  colonialism and, 401–2
  France and, 376–77, 596–97, 611, 612,
    614
  isolationism and, 96–97, 101, 385
  nuclear weapons in, 601–2
  overestimation of Britain's capability in,
    449–50
  "special" nature of, 43, 353–55, 384–87,
    548, 596–98, 601, 611, 612, 632–33
  World War II prelude and, 370, 386, 387,
    391–92
Anglo-French Entente (1907), 192
Anglo-French Naval Treaty, 197–98, 212–13
Anglo-French relationship:
  annexation of Savoy and Nice in, 110, 112
  Belgium and, 71, 97, 99, 115, 118, 222,
    251–52
  Common Market issues in, 615, 616
  Egypt and, 145, 159, 162, 171, 178, 233–
    234
  League of Nations and, 253–55
  Naval Treaty in, 197–98, 212–13
  post-Versailles rift in, 246, 250–55, 258,
    265
  Suez crisis in, *see* Suez crisis
  Triple Entente and, 192
  U.S. and, 376–77, 596–97, 611, 612, 614
  Weimar Germany and, 250–55
Anglo-French-Russian Entente (1907), 191–
  192
Anglo-Japanese Alliance, 373
Angola, 593, 698, 701, 713, 751, 757, 763,
  773, 774, 787
Anschluss, 249, 283, 297, 310–11, 381
Anti-Comintern Pact, 359, 363
appeasement policy, 114, 309, 310, 311–
  312
  Britain and, 306–7, 310, 311–12, 340
  France and, 306–7
  Suez crisis and, 531
Arab-Israeli conflict, 523, 527–28
Arab-Israeli War of 1973 (Yom Kippur War),
  537, 593, 614, 713, 738, 739, 743–44,
  766

Arab League, 523
Arab Legion, 523, 529
Arab nationalism, 523, 524, 530, 539
    U.S. and, 532–33
Argentina, 38, 831
Armand, Count, 115
Armenia, 154, 792
arms control, 518, 714, 752, 784, 790
    complexity of, 715–16, 748, 752
    containment policy and, 715–16
    missile deployment issue and, 776–77
    SDI and, 782
    surprise attack and, 714–16
    see also ABM Treaty; nuclear weapons;
        Strategic Arms Limitation Talks
arms race, 493, 515, 716
    economic pressures and, 790
    Reagan's military buildup and, 775
    SDI and, 775, 778, 782, 790–91
Aron, Raymond, 595
Asad, Hafez, 739
ASEAN (Association of Southeast Asian
    Nations), 827–28
Asia-Pacific Economic Cooperation (APEC),
    828
Associated States of the French Union, 625,
    631
Aswan Dam project, 527–30, 538, 539
Atlantic Alliance, see North Atlantic Treaty
    Organization
Atlantic Charter, 390, 401, 454
    Anglo-Soviet exchanges and, 406–7
    Pitt Plan compared with, 391
Atlantic Community, 819
atomic bomb, 409
    Potsdam Conference and, 435–37
    Soviet propaganda and, 441–42
    U.S. military doctrine and, 441–42
    U.S. monopoly on, 435–36, 437, 439, 441,
        466, 487, 573–74, 607–8, 763
    see also nuclear weapons
Attlee, Clement, 435
Aubrac, Raymond, 663–64
Austin, Warren, 458
Australia, 315, 480, 631, 632, 637
Austria, 72, 74, 104, 109, 121, 128, 179, 203,
    300, 301, 307, 308, 338, 590, 820
    Balkans and, 91–94, 194, 222
    Bismarck's policy and, 122–24, 129, 130,
        131–33, 155–57, 162
    Bosnia-Herzegovina annexed by, 195–96,
        209, 214
    Britain and, 99–100
    in conflict over Schleswig-Holstein, 112–
        114
    Congress of Vienna and, 79, 81

domination of Central Europe and, 57,
    59, 60, 80, 112
France and Piedmont's war against, 103,
    110–11, 130
Franco-Russian Agreement and, 181
Germany and, 123, 158–59, 249, 283, 297,
    310–11, 381
in Holy Alliance, 35, 82, 83, 119, 130, 131
Mediterranean Agreement and, 159
Metternich system and, 85–88
Morocco crisis and, 197
Napoleon III and, 106, 118
in Pitt Plan, 76
Prussia's conflicts with, 69, 80, 85, 100,
    107, 113–17, 129, 156
in Quadruple Alliance, 82
Reinsurance Treaty and, 164, 180–81
Revolution of 1848 and, 99
Russia's Balkan conflict with, 138–39,
    144, 146–47, 159–60
Russia's rivalry with, 86, 87, 93–94, 99,
    146–47, 153, 173, 199
Serbian ultimatum of, 211, 214
in Three Emperors' League, 155–59
Triple Alliance and, 186
Triple Entente and, 200
Wars of Succession, 69
World War I outbreak and, 211–12, 214–
    215
Austrian State Treaty, 498, 509, 514
Austro-Hungarian Empire, 138, 145, 146,
    164, 178, 201, 203, 210, 310, 814
    demise of, 217, 221, 242–43
    Reinsurance Treaty and, 164
    successor states to, 240, 241
    Treaty of San Stefano rejected by, 153
Austro-Prussian War, 103, 107, 109, 114–19
Azerbaijan, 446, 495

Baghdad Pact, 527, 529, 548, 549
Bahr, Egon, 736
Baker, James, 740
balance-of-power policy, 17–21, 29–30, 59,
    67–68, 99, 165–67, 221, 266, 398
    Bismarck's model of, 135–36, 165–67,
        171–72
    Britain and, 17, 70–73, 90, 98, 145, 220,
        266, 823, 826
    Congress of Vienna and, 79
    Enlightenment roots of, 21–22
    France and, 68, 70
    legitimacy principle and, 82–83, 167
    Metternich system and, 166, 397
    NATO and, 458, 460
    in new world order, 20–22, 76–77, 810,
        813, 823, 827

Nixon on, 705
Palmerston/Disraeli approach to, 161,
    162, 165–67
policy in Cold War vs., 22, 141, 182, 608
Reagan and, 771
Truman's rejection of, 446–47
Wilson's condemnation of, 226
    see also Realpolitik
Baldwin, Stanley, 291–92, 293, 295–96, 299,
    308, 597
Balfour, Arthur James, Lord, 243, 262
Balkan League, 199
Balkans, 112, 122, 154, 162, 163, 363, 621
    Austria and, 91–94, 194, 222
    Austro-Russian rivalry and, 85, 138–39,
        144, 146, 158, 159–60, 179–80, 199–
        200
    in Churchill's World War II plans, 403,
        404
    Crimean War and, 93
    crisis of 1876 in, 148–49
    Ottomans in, 152–53
    see also "Eastern Question"
Balkan War (1875–78), 173
Balkan War (1885), 173
Balkan War (1912), 199
Ball, George, 612, 657
Baltic states, 347, 352, 355, 798
Bao Dai, 626
Bark, Peter, 214
Basket III, *see* Helsinki Accords
Bavaria, 69, 81, 117, 268
Bay of Pigs invasion, 583, 646, 647–48
Beard, Charles, 380
Belgian Congo, 220, 807
Belgium, 118, 255, 340
    Anglo-French rivalry and, 71, 97, 99, 115,
        118, 222, 251–52
    in Fourteen Points, 225
    German invasions of, 42, 48, 99, 351,
        352–53
    Maginot Line and, 303
    Versailles settlement and, 239, 274, 301
    World War I and, 205, 206, 213
Belorussia, 259, 419
Ben-Gurion, David, 542, 543
Beria, Lavrenti, 499, 504–5, 519, 555
Berlin, Congress of, 155–58, 173, 177, 195,
    196, 202–3
Berlin, Isaiah, 370, 371
Berlin Agreement (1971), 736–37
Berlin blockade (1948), 190, 469, 473–74,
    476, 495, 498, 500, 569, 584, 624
Berlin crisis (1958–63), 568–93, 594, 617,
    650
    Access Authority and, 590–91, 592

Berlin Wall and, 583–84, 591, 592, 593
Camp David Summit and, 580–82
Cuban missile crisis and, 586, 591, 593
Four-Power Agreement and, 570–71
Geneva Summit and, 520
German unification and, 571–73, 577–78,
    587
Khrushchev's ultimatum and, 570–72,
    575, 595
Macmillan and, 573, 575, 577, 578–79,
    598–600
nuclear threat and, 573–74, 585, 586
post–World War II settlement and, 583–
    584
Sputnik and, 570
U-2 affair and, 582
U.S.-German relations in, 587–89
Berlin Memorandum, 149, 152
Berlin uprising (1953), 555
Berlin Wall, 229, 583–84, 591, 592, 593, 734,
    794–95
Bessarabia, 108, 156, 261, 336, 347, 355, 419
Bethmann-Hollweg, Theobald von, 184,
    208, 209, 213
Betts, Richard, 779
Bevin, Ernest, 435
Biddle, Francis, 388
Bismarck, Otto von, 94, 100, 103–36, 150,
    180, 217, 222, 310, 502, 531, 621
    Alexander III and, 163
    alliance system of, 147, 158–59
    Austro-German Treaty and, 158–59
    Austro-Prussian War and, 115–18
    background and personality of, 104
    balance of power policy of, 135–36, 165
        167, 171–72
    Berlin Memorandum and, 149
    "blood and iron" remark of, 662
    Budapest proposal of, 138
    Bulgarian crisis and, 163–64
    in conflict over Schleswig-Holstein, 113–
        114
    Congress of Berlin and, 154, 155–56
    Crimean War and diplomacy of, 131–32
    Disraeli contrasted with, 155
    domestic policy and, 120–24, 135, 150
    France-Piedmont-Austria War (1859) and,
        126
    Franco-Prussian War and, 118
    on Franco-Russian alliance, 132
    Gerlach and, 124–27, 146
    German Confederation and, 117, 129
    German unification and, 65–66, 105, 119,
        121, 133–34, 145–46, 229, 239
    Gladstone and, 162
    Goltz and, 114–16

Bismarck, Otto von (*cont.*)
　Holy Alliance and diplomacy of, 121, 122, 124, 125
　legacy of, 105, 120–21, 136
　"Master Dispatch" of, 131–33, 134
　Mediterranean Agreement and, 159
　Metternich system and, 121–31, 146
　Napoleon III and, 105, 123–24
　nonalignment strategy of, 122–24, 128
　Prussia's primacy and, 128–30
　Realpolitik and, 121, 125–28, 130, 133, 146, 165, 211
　Reinsurance Treaty and, 164
　successors to, 165, 170, 171–72, 175, 183, 204, 205
　Three Emperors' League (first) and, 146–147, 148, 153
　Three Emperors' League (second) and, 158, 163–64
　Triple Alliance and, 159
　William II and, 170–71, 209
Blum, Léon, 307
Bohlen, Charles, 562
Bolsheviks, Bolshevism, 221, 258, 259, 271, 333–34, 552, 773
Bosnia-Herzegovina, 53, 149, 154, 156, 195, 216, 809, 820
　Austria's annexation of, 195–96, 209, 214
　1908 crisis in, 195, 199, 214
Bourgeois, Léon, 236–37
Bowles, Chester, 389, 651
Bowman, Isaiah, 234
Bradford, Lady, 149
Bradley, Omar N., 474–75, 486, 487
Brandt, Willy, 578, 584, 758
　Ostpolitik of, 734–37
Brazil, 38, 831
Brest-Litovsk, Treaty of, 220, 227, 241, 257, 258–60
Bretton Woods Conference (1944), 405
Brezhnev, Leonid, 713, 730, 731, 756, 758, 769–70, 774, 776, 797
Brezhnev Doctrine, 722, 727, 773, 787, 788–789
　Gorbachev's retreat from, 793–94
　U.S. opening to China and, 722, 727
Briand, Aristide, 228, 253, 274, 276, 277–82, 334
British Cabinet, 89, 214, 255, 308, 538
　Abyssinia crisis and, 299
　Anglo-German naval accord and, 297–98
　Anglo-Soviet diplomacy and, 347–48
　Czechoslovakia crisis and, 311–12
　disarmament issue and, 293
　Nazi threat and, 340, 341, 342
British Parliament, 72–73, 342

British Somalia, 299
British War Cabinet, 270, 401–2
Brockdorff-Rantzau, Ulrich von, 282
Brogan, D. W., 281
Brown, Harold, 779
Bruce, David, 465, 578
Brussels, Pact of, 457
Buchanan, Andrew, 151–52
Buddhists, 654–55
Bukharin, Nikolai, 259
Bukovina, 355
Bulganin, Nikolai, 516, 542–43, 553
Bulgaria, 37, 148, 153, 154, 156, 160, 161, 176, 195, 214, 219, 362, 363, 366, 409, 413, 434
　crisis of 1885 in, 163–64, 173
　in Soviet orbit, 435, 437, 443, 446, 448, 451
Bullitt, William C., 381
Bülow, Prince von, 172, 186–87
Bundy, McGeorge, 587, 671
Bundy, William, 651, 653, 663
Bunker, Ellsworth, 465
Buol-Schauenstein, Karl Ferdinand von, 93
Burma, 624, 632, 637
Bush, George, 46, 53, 177–78, 659, 764, 785, 806, 817, 832
　new world order proclaimed by, 804–5
Bush Administration, 773, 817
Byrnes, James, 424, 437, 438

Cambodia, 625, 692, 696, 763, 792
　communist bases in, 647, 680, 681, 693–694
　Khmer Rouge in, 694, 697
　neutrality of, 645–46, 686, 693–94
　Vietnamese invasion of, 637, 773
Cambon, Paul, 191
Camp David Summit, 600
　Berlin crisis and, 580–82
Canada, 31, 37, 178, 315, 383, 832
Canning, George, 35, 95, 101, 145, 148, 162, 249
Capet dynasty, 65
Caprivi, Georg Leo von, 179
Caprivi Strip, 180
Carter, Jimmy, 739, 768, 770, 772
Carter Administration, 767, 775
Carteret, John, 73–74, 99
Casablanca Conference (1943), 405
Castlereagh, Robert Stewart, Lord, 87, 91, 95, 399
　Congress of Vienna and, 79, 81–82, 155, 161
　Congress system and, 74, 88–90
　Holy Alliance and, 83, 149

Castro, Fidel, 583, 698
Catherine II (the Great), Empress of Russia, 140, 338, 350
Catholic Church, 56, 57–58, 59, 60, 64, 123
Cavour, Count Camillo Benso di, 94, 110–111, 121–22, 531
Cecil, Edgar Algernon Robert Gascoyne-, Lord, 236–37, 248
Central America, 38, 774, 831–32
Chamberlain, Austen, 270, 274, 276, 281, 334
  Locarno Pact and, 273–74
Chamberlain, Joseph, 185–86, 276–77
Chamberlain, Neville, 308, 344, 358, 382, 596
  Locarno Pact and, 277
  Munich Agreement and, see Munich Conference
  Soviets distrusted by, 341–42
Charles V, Holy Roman Emperor, 57, 116
Chautemps, Camille, 297
Chernenko, Konstantin, 770
Chiang Kai-shek, 529
Chicherin, Georgi, 260, 263, 264
Chile, 38, 773, 831
China, Imperial, 25, 27, 145, 174, 178, 187
China, People's Republic of:
  anti-interventionist policy of, 644–45, 661
  communist victory in, 620–27, 719
  Cultural Revolution of, 719, 730
  domestic unrest in, 250, 792–93, 830
  Egypt and, 529
  Four Policemen concept and, 395, 421
  growth of, 826, 829
  in Indian foreign policy, 564, 632
  Indochina conflict and, 630, 632, 634, 635, 644–45, 660–61, 681
  Japan and, 25–26, 249, 286–87, 298, 377, 379, 380, 385, 826–30
  Kissinger's trip to, 726, 730–31
  Korean intervention and, 475–85, 488, 625, 661, 719
  in new world order, 23–24, 25, 26, 807–808, 826–31
  Reykjavik Summit and, 783
  Soviet relations with, 509, 571, 627, 787; see also Sino-Soviet rift
  Tiananmen Square demonstrations in, 792–93, 830
China, Republic of, see Taiwan
China, U.S. opening to, 713–32
  Brezhnev Doctrine and, 722, 727
  Chinese diplomacy and, 725–27
  domestic debate and, 479, 720–21, 741
  Kissinger's trip and, 726, 730–31
  Mao and, 725–30

  Nixon and, 713–32
  Richardson's speech and, 723–24
  role of personality in, 727, 729
  Shanghai Communiqué and, 727–29
  Sino-Soviet rift and, 713–14, 719–25, 728, 730–31
  Warsaw talks and, 726
  Zhou and, 719, 727, 729
China lobby, 479, 741
Christian Democratic Party, German, 503
Churchill, Winston, 72, 74, 75, 255, 305, 371, 379, 389, 394–422, 427, 499, 503, 505, 515, 530, 583, 595, 634, 704–5, 713, 784
  Allied occupation of Berlin favored by, 417
  Atlantic Charter and, 390–91, 401
  Balkans operation proposed by, 403, 404
  colonial issue and, 409, 410
  on containment policy, 461, 463–64, 466–67
  Davies' view of, 430–31
  on destroyers-for-bases deal, 388
  detente and, 512–13, 514
  East-West negotiations urged by, 498, 506–12
  Eisenhower's correspondence with, 512, 514, 632–33
  FDR's wartime correspondence with, 395–96, 421
  Four-Power Summit idea of, 508–11, 516
  German rearmament opposed by, 295–296
  Indochina conflict as perceived by, 632–633
  Iron Curtain speech of, 441, 442–43, 466, 504
  on Middle East policy, 524
  postwar Polish government and, 418
  post–World War II order and, 395, 399–400, 406–7, 422, 428–30
  at Potsdam Conference, 433–34, 435, 436
  spheres-of-influence arrangement of, 413–14
  at Teheran Conference, 410, 411, 412
  unconditional surrender policy of, 405
  U.S.-British "special relationship" and, 353–55, 387, 632–33
  wartime diplomacy and strategy of, 394–422
  William II described by, 171
  at Yalta Conference, 396, 410, 414–15
Clarendon, George William Frederick Villiers, Lord, 100, 108
Clark Amendment, 773
Clay, Lucius, 584, 592
Clemenceau, Georges, 230–32

Clifford, Clark, 450–51, 677
Clinton, Bill, 682, 740, 806, 817, 832
  "enlarging democracy" theme of, 805
  Pacific Community proposal of, 826, 828
  Partnership for Peace concept of, 824–25
Cobb, Irvin S., 389
Cobden, Richard, 100
coexistence, see detente policy; peaceful
  coexistence
Cold War, 23, 53–54, 165, 173, 226, 298,
    330–31 (map), 422, 461, 491, 514, 645,
    741, 801–2
  Arab nationalism and, 532
  balance-of-power system and, 22, 141,
    182, 608
  beginning of, 423–45
  Berlin crisis and, 593
  Bush influenced by, 177
  cultural gap and, 438
  early Anglo-U.S.-Soviet relations and, 427,
    430
  Eastern Europe and, 431–32, 434–35,
    438, 550–51, 564, 566
  Geneva Summit and, 516–19
  Great Debate on, 799–800
  Hungarian uprising and, 550–51, 564,
    566
  Japanese foreign policy in, 26
  linkage debate and, 717
  missile deployment issue and, 775–77
  as moral crusade, 54, 462–63, 471, 709
  Nonaligned nations and, 546, 564
  NSC-68 and, 462–63
  nuclear testing during, 715
  Potsdam Conference and, 433–36
  pre–World War I era and, 168, 198–99
  second front strategy and, 404–5
  Soviet weakness and, 438–39
  spheres of influence in, 328–29 (map)
  Suez crisis and, 523, 525
  U.N. and, 249–50
  see also containment policy; detente
    policy; Peace Note
collective security, 51–53, 74, 91, 160, 221–
    223, 246–50, 292, 335, 372, 376, 408,
    421, 426–27
  Abyssinian crisis and, 298, 300
  Acheson on idea of, 459–60, 490
  aggression and, 249, 253–54, 255
  alliances concept and, 247–48
  Britain and, 88, 97, 266–67
  Geneva Protocol and, 254–55
  Gulf War and, 250
  League of Nations and, 30, 53, 222
  NATO and, 460
  Paris Peace Conference and, 235, 236

  Russo-German neutrality treaty and, 282
  Soviet foreign policy and, 336, 338–39,
    340
  Suez crisis and, 525
  Treaty of Versailles and, 221, 222, 227,
    232, 235, 253–54
  U.N. and, 249–50
  weakness of, 53, 90–91, 235, 246–50, 340
Colombia, 39
colonialism, 401–2, 408–10, 524–26, 545–
  546
Colville, John, 506, 509
Cominform (Communist Information
  Bureau), 443, 552
Comintern (Communist International), 143,
  335, 412, 443
Common European Home concept, 791
Common Market, 24, 120, 596, 606–8, 615–
  616, 806, 820–24
communism:
  collapse of, 18–19, 54, 520–21, 618, 704,
    752, 763, 773–75, 784, 800, 814–18; see
    also new world order
  in convergence theory, 711
  post–World War II expansion of, 476,
    496–97, 519, 551–52, 566–67
  see also Cold War; containment policy;
    detente policy; specific countries and
    parties
Communist Manifesto, 773
Communist Party, Bulgarian, 570
Communist Party, Chinese, 725
Communist Party, Hungarian, 555, 556
Communist Party, North Vietnamese, 656,
  698
Communist Party, Polish, 418, 554
Communist Party, Soviet, 441, 520, 793
  Central Committee of, 338–39
  Comintern disbanded by, 412
  Gorbachev's purge of, 785, 786, 787
  in Kennan's "X" article, 454–55
  liberalization and, 794, 795, 796, 797
  Politburo of, 358, 499
  Soviet victory and, 440
  in U.S. foreign policy, 453–55
Communist Party congresses, Soviet:
  Seventeenth, 335
  Eighteenth, 338, 340, 343
  Nineteenth, 499
  Twentieth, 553, 555, 569
  Twenty-first, 571
  Twenty-seventh, 787, 801
Conference for Security and Cooperation in
  Europe (CSCE), 733, 740, 757–60, 793,
  818, 825
Confucianism, 638, 699, 730

Congress, U.S., 39, 230, 236, 370, 371, 501, 589, 627, 672, 716, 726, 747, 754
  ABM Treaty and, 747–48
  containment policy and, 474
  destroyers-for-bases deal and, 388
  detente conflict in, 744–45
  FDR's Four Policemen report to, 416
  foreign policy and, 741
  Four-Power Treaty and, 373–74, 375
  Fourteen Points and, 225
  Greek-Turkish aid program and, 451
  Neutrality Acts of, 378, 379, 385–86, 409
  Nixon and, 745–51
  peacetime conscription passed by, 388
  SALT and, 749–51
  Vietnam extrication and, 681, 685, 689, 690, 692, 696–97, 699
Congress system, 82, 88–91
Connally, Senator Tom, 412–13, 458, 459
Conservative Party, British, 277, 291; *see also* Tory Party, British
Constantinople Convention (1888), 536
Constitution, U.S., 21–22, 525
containment policy, 47, 424, 445, 446–72, 565, 566, 625, 650, 707, 713, 743, 813
  ambiguities of, 455–56, 471–74, 514–15
  arms control and, 715–16
  Britain and, 449–50, 467–68
  Churchill's criticism of, 463–64, 466–67
  Clifford and, 450–51
  conservative critique of, 470–71
  convergence theory and, 711
  Czech coup and, 457
  Dulles and, 470, 514–15, 709
  European recovery and, 453–61
  Greek-Turkish aid issue and, 451–52, 469, 473, 474
  Kennan's Long Telegram and, 443, 447–449, 454
  Kennan's reinterpretation of, 471
  Kennan's "X" article and, 454–56
  Korean War and, 479, 487, 489–90
  Lippmann on, 463–66, 467, 665–66
  moral values and, 461–62
  New Deal and, 456–57
  post–World War II success of, 473–74
  "psychiatric school" and, 709–11
  Soviet unilateral force reductions and, 792
  spheres of influence and, 447, 456
  success of, 593, 801–2
  Suez crisis and, 525–26, 527, 537, 545
  Truman Doctrine and, 452–53
  Wallace on, 464, 467–70, 710, 824
Coolidge, Calvin, 374
cordon sanitaire, 243

Council of Europe, 791, 794
Council on Foreign Relations, 375
Counter-Reformation, 59, 60, 66
Couve de Murville, Maurice, 530
Cowley, Henry, 110
Craftsman, 72
Crimean War, 79, 92–94, 100, 102–3, 105, 108–9, 111, 119, 131–32, 166, 173, 250
Crippled Giant, The (Fulbright), 689
Cripps, Stafford, 295, 359
Croatia, 240
Cronkite, Walter, 671
Crowe, Eyre, 192–93, 268, 353
Crowe Memorandum, 192–93, 268, 353
Cuba, 37, 39, 520, 713, 745, 757, 763, 764, 773, 832
Cuban missile crisis, 249, 520, 543, 548, 586, 591, 593, 595, 722
Cultural Revolution, 719, 730
Curzon, George Nathaniel, Lord, 261, 268, 276
Curzon Line, 261, 265, 341, 351, 406
Czechoslovakia, 590, 596, 599, 722, 793
  communist coup in, 457, 469, 495, 498, 625
  France and, 120, 275, 276, 296, 303, 308–309, 311, 313, 314–15, 317
  German occupation of, 316–17, 318, 337, 339, 340, 364
  German population of, 240, 244, 309, 311
  Hitler-Chamberlain meetings and, 312–313
  Munich settlement and, 314–16
  Soviet-Egyptian arms sale and, 523, 548
  Soviet intervention in, 249, 443, 476, 551, 624, 704, 716, 734
  Soviet pact with, 336, 337
Czech Republic, 817, 823, 824

Daladier, Edouard, 293, 313, 386
Danzig, 307, 317, 365
Darwin, Charles, 40, 127
Dashichev, Vyacheslav, 800–801
Davies, Joseph E., 430–41
Dawes, Charles G., 272
Dawes Plan, 278, 282–83
Declaration of Interdependence (1962), 613
Decree on Peace (1917), 259
Defense Department, U.S., 658, 680, 748, 749
de Gaulle, Charles, 120, 371, 503, 530, 572, 595, 598, 601–19, 625, 666, 705, 777
  Anglo-American relationship opposed by, 614–15
  detente and, 734, 735

de Gaulle, Charles (*cont.*)
  diplomatic style of, 603–5, 611
  Directorate concept of, 610–11, 617
  Eisenhower and, 606
  France's self-esteem and, 602–3
  Franco-American conflict and, 603–6
  Franco-German cooperation and, 547,
    615–18
  on integrated forces concept, 614–15
  JFK's partnership policy rejected by, 616–
    617
  on Khrushchev's ultimatum, 575–76, 582
  Kissinger's encounters with, 604–5
  Nassau Agreement rejected by, 615
  NATO's structure and, 610–12
  nuclear strategy and, 610
  raison d'état and, 576–77
  Sino-Soviet rift as seen by, 720
  unified Europe concept of, 606–8, 615–
    616
  withdrawal from Algeria and, 674
Delbos, Yvon, 307, 308–9
Delcassé, Théophile, 190
democracy, 18, 30, 57, 135, 166, 221–22, 382
  Confucianism contrasted with, 638
  independence movements and, 525
  post–World War II expansion of, 620–23,
    773
  in Russia, 816
  in South Vietnam, 637, 639, 653–56
  Truman Doctrine and, 453
  Western-style, 525, 811–12
  World War I and, 219
Democratic National Convention (1968),
  678, 679
Democratic Party, U.S., 370–71, 678, 679,
  743–44
Deng Xiaoping, 727
Denmark, 59, 112–14, 175, 389–90, 407
Denmark-Prussia-Austria War (Danish War),
  103, 112–14, 119
Derby, Edward Henry Smith Stanley, Lord,
  147
destroyers-for-bases deal, 387–88
detente policy, 123, 733–61
  ABM Treaty and, 747–49
  Arab-Israeli War of 1973 and, 739
  Churchill and, 512–13, 514
  Congressional approval and, 744–45, 747
  critics of, 743–46, 747, 754–57, 761, 768
  de Gaulle and, 734, 735
  geopolitical vs. ideological debate and,
    743–45, 756–57
  Helsinki Accords and, 758–60
  human rights debate and, 752–54
  Jackson and, 746–47, 750, 751, 757

Middle East conflict and, 737–40
  Nixon's foreign policy and, 741–47, 754–
    756, 761
  Reagan's first term and, 767–68
  reciprocal concessions vs. unilateral
    satisfactions and, 740–41
  SALT and, 749–52
  Soviet Union and, 123, 737–38, 747
  trade and, 754–55
  Wilsonian ideals and, 743
deterrence strategy, 608–10, 614
  intermediate-range missile deployment
    and, 776, 778
  Mutual Assured Destruction and, 750, 779
Diem, Ngo Dinh, *see* Ngo Dinh Diem
Dien Bien Phu, battle of, 630–31, 632, 633,
  648, 655
"Difference Between the North Atlantic
  Treaty and Traditional Military
  Alliances," 458
Dillon, Douglas, 628–29, 671
diplomacy:
  alliances concept and, 247
  communist, 334
  Congress system and, 82, 88–91
  European approach to, 616
  negotiations and, 508
  nineteenth-century style of, 276
  personalized relations and, 276
  in post–Cold War world, 23–24; *see also*
    new world order
  tacit bargaining and, 753
  triangular, *see* China, U.S. opening to;
    linkage concept; Nixon, Richard M.;
    Sino-Soviet rift
  Wilsonian vs. European, 248
Directorate concept, 610–12, 617
disarmament, 244, 255–56, 267, 279–80,
  285–86, 292–94
  see also ABM Treaty; arms control;
    nuclear weapons; Strategic Arms
    Limitation Talks
Disarmament Conference (1932–37), 285–
  286, 292, 293, 378
disengagement plans, 512–13, 599–600
Disraeli, Benjamin, 37, 39, 100, 145–56, 162,
  167, 249, 763
  on balance-of-power diplomacy, 99
  Balkan crisis and, 152–54
  Berlin Memorandum and, 149
  Congress of Berlin and, 154–55, 156
  on Franco-Prussian War, 134–35
  Gladstone and, 101, 150, 160–61
  London Protocol and, 152
  Russian expansionism and, 151–52
  war scare of 1875 and, 147–48

Dittmann, Herbert, 578
Djilas, Milovan, 417, 438
Dobrynin, Anatoly, 591, 744, 753, 754, 788–789
Dominican Republic, 37, 39
Domino Theory, 647, 667, 701
    Indochina conflict and, 624, 626–28, 631, 633, 636, 641
    NSC memorandum on, 624, 626–27, 628
Dostoyevsky, Fyodor, 143
Dowling, Walter C., 589
Dreyfus, Alfred, 230
Drouyn de Lhuys, Edouard, 113
Dual Alliance, 159
Dual Monarchy, see Austro-Hungarian
    Empire
Dulles, John Foster, 465, 510, 595, 618, 623, 700, 713, 755
    agent theory of, 577–78, 579
    Aswan Dam project and, 529–30, 538
    background and personality of, 534–35
    Baghdad Pact and, 528
    Churchill contrasted with, 510
    containment policy and, 470, 514, 709
    death of, 580
    Geneva Summit and, 517
    German unification and, 577–78
    Hungarian uprising and, 553, 558, 562, 564–65
    Indochina conflict and, 631, 632, 633, 635–39
    liberation theory of, 553–54, 772
    Life article of, 553, 562
    Maritime Conference proposal of, 532, 535–36, 538, 539, 540
    Northern Tier policy and, 528
    propaganda and policy analysis of, 529–530
    SEATO and, 637
    Soviet sphere of influence and policy of, 508, 529–30, 535, 553–54, 558, 569–70
    Suez crisis and, 532, 533–39, 540
    United Action proposal of, 631–33, 648
    on use of force, 535, 545, 574
    Users' Association proposal of, 536–37, 540, 577
    U.S. exceptionalism and, 534, 731
    West Germany in NATO and, 515
    Zhou and, 719
Dumbarton Oaks Conference (1944), 405
Durnovo, Peter, 206–7
Dutch East Indies, 392

Eastern Europe, 173, 407, 438, 443–44, 446, 447, 495, 551–53, 566–67, 594–95, 763, 787, 823–25

Cold War and, 431–32, 434–35, 438
communism in, 551–52, 566–67
de Gaulle's detente and, 734
European Security Conference and, 758
European Union and, 823–24
France and, 296–97
Gorbachev and, 793–95
liberation theory and, 554, 793–95
in NATO, 823–24
Partnership for Peace and, 824–25
U.S. foreign policy and, 427–28, 558, 563
"Eastern Question," 91–93, 148
    Fadeyev's analysis of, 143–44
    see also Balkans
Eastern Rumelia, 154
Eden, Anthony, 299, 429, 434, 633
    Arab League promoted by, 523
    Aswan Dam project and, 528–29
    Bulganin's message to, 542–43
    Canal nationalization as viewed by, 531–532
    Eisenhower's correspondence with, 533–534, 537, 538
    Moscow visit of, 398, 406, 407, 413
    Suez crisis and, 528–44, 547, 595
    West Germany in NATO and, 515
Edward VII, King of England, 177
"Eggshell, Operation," 626
Egypt, 519, 541, 737
    Anglo-French rivalry and, 145, 159, 162, 171, 178, 233–34
    Anglo-Russian rivalry and, 89, 92, 148, 162, 172
    Aswan Dam project of, 527–30, 538, 539
    China and, 529
    Israel's rapprochement with, 284, 739
    Soviet arms sales to, 522–26
    Soviets expelled from, 738, 739, 753
    Suez crisis and, see Suez crisis
Eisenhower, Dwight D., 403, 499, 511, 515, 524, 532, 563, 573, 600, 622, 654, 655, 706
    Berlin crisis and, 570, 574, 575, 578–82, 585
    Bulganin and, 542, 543
    Camp David Accords and, 580–82, 600
    Churchill's correspondence with, 512, 514, 632–33
    Churchill's Summit idea rejected by, 509–10
    de Gaulle's anti-Americanism and, 606
    de Gaulle's NATO challenge and, 610–12
    Directorate and, 611, 612
    on Domino Theory, 641
    Geneva Summit and, 516–17
    Hungarian uprising and, 558–59

Eisenhower, Dwight D. (*cont.*)
Indochina conflict and, 621, 628–29,
631–33, 634, 636–39, 642, 644, 646,
647, 649
"open-skies" proposal of, 516
as Reagan precursor, 631–32
on Sino-Soviet relations, 509
Stalin's correspondence with, 417–18
Suez crisis and, 532–44, 549
United Action proposal and, 631–32, 633
Wilsonian theme in foreign policy of, 622
Eisenhower Administration, 591
Guatemala coup and, 541
Hungarian uprising and, 558, 559, 563
Indochina conflict and, 628–30, 634, 635,
638–39, 641
Northern Tier concept of, 527, 528
U.S.-Soviet negotiations and, 505–6
Eisenhower Doctrine, 549
elections, British:
of 1880, 101, 160–61
of 1945, 435, 507–8
of 1950, 508
elections, U.S.:
of 1916, 45
of 1920, 370–71
of 1940, 388
of 1948, 469
of 1952, 499, 501, 502, 553
of 1956, 540, 546
of 1964, 657
of 1968, 670, 672–73, 675, 695, 721
of 1972, 689, 692, 695, 697, 739, 743
of 1976, 766
Elizabeth I, Queen of England, 177
Elizabeth Petrovna, Empress of Russia, 140
Ely, Paul, 631
Enlightenment, 21–22, 67, 75, 86
Entente Cordiale, 181, 186, 188, 189, 190,
191, 253, 728
Enterprise for the Americas Initiative, 832
Ethiopia, 300–301, 593, 698, 701, 763, 773–
774
Eupen-et-Malmédy, territory of, 239, 283
Europe:
balance-of-power system and, 19–20
Congress of Vienna's effect on, 79, 324–
325 (map)
Congress system and, 82
Eastern, *see* Eastern Europe
on eve of World War I, 326–27 (map)
JFK's Declaration of Interdependence
and, 613–14
Monroe Doctrine and, 35–36
nuclear weapons strategy of, 609–10
in post–Cold War world, 23–24

post–World War II growth of, 703–4
prospects for unity, 24, 120, 596, 606–8,
806, 820–24
Realpolitik and geography of, 137–38
reunified Germany and, 820–22, 823
Suez crisis and unity of, 547–48
European Defense Community (EDC), 498,
515
European Security Conference, *see*
Conference on European Security and
Cooperation
exceptionalism, U.S.:
containment and, 471
disillusionment and, 372
Dulles' form of, 534, 731
isolationism and, 142
new world order and, 810
Nixon and, 706, 731, 742, 745
Peace Movement and, 688
Reagan and, 767, 769, 785
Russian exceptionalism vs., 142
Vietnam War and, 621, 668, 676, 688, 700
Wilsonianism and, 809–10
Export/Import Bank, 754

Fadeyev, Rostislav Andreievich, 143–44
Farouk I, King of Egypt, 524
fascism, 308, 335
Federalist Papers, The (Madison), 21
Ferdinand II, Holy Roman Emperor, 59, 60–
62, 65, 66, 83
Ferguson, A. K., 489
Finland, 176, 249, 261, 347, 356, 357, 362,
408, 409, 419, 434, 449
Soviet Union and, 352, 437, 443–44
Flanders, Ralph, 629
Flandin, Pierre, 305
flexible response strategy, 608, 612–14, 708,
776, 782
Foch, Ferdinand, 250
force de frappe, 613
Ford, Gerald R., 744, 760, 772
Ford, Henry, 389
Ford Administration, 713, 733, 747, 759,
760, 766
Foreign Affairs, 454, 721
Foreign Ministers' Conferences (1945–46),
437–38, 446
Foreign Office, British, 186, 251, 268, 291,
305, 311
foreign policy, U.S.:
anticolonial tradition and, 625–26
arms control and, 752
Asian conflicts and geopolitics in, 621–
625, 827–31
Austrian *Anschluss* and, 381

balance-of-power doctrine and, 17–21, 166–67, 221
bureaucracy and, 717–18
collective security and, *see* collective security
colonialism issue and, 524–26
compartmentalization of, 402–3
containment and, *see* containment policy
Eastern Europe and, 427–28, 563
European conflicts and geopolitics in, 30–33, 624–25
German unification and, 577–78
human rights and, 622–23, 752; *see also* Helsinki Accords
isolationists and, 371–73
Kellogg-Briand Pact and, 374–75
Kennan's Long Telegram and, 443, 447–449, 454
Kennan's "X" article and, 454–56, 715
linkage debate and, 715, 717–18
Metternich system and, 166–67
Monroe Doctrine and, *see* Monroe Doctrine
moral foundation of, 19–23, 29–30, 33–37, 437, 456, 462
new world order and, 809–10, 813–14, 832–35
Nixon Doctrine and, 707–9
NSC-68 and, 462–63
post–Cold War world and, 23–24, 166, 818–20
presidency and, 741–42; *see also specific presidents*
raison d'état and, 810
and reform in Russia, 814, 817–18
spread of democracy and, 620–23, 811–812
Suez crisis and, 544–45, 548–49; *see also* Suez crisis
territorial expansion and, 31, 36, 37
see also specific countries
Formosa, *see* Taiwan
Fortune, 413
Foster, John, 534
Founding Fathers, 30, 462, 525
Four Freedoms, 389, 390, 391
Four Policemen concept, 395–98, 408, 411–412, 424, 447, 433, 511, 611, 829
failure of, 420–22
Holy Alliance compared with, 397–98
Molotov and, 396–97
Truman and, 426–27
Four-Power Agreement, 570–71
Four-Power Treaty, 373–74, 375
Fourteen Points, 19, 50, 225, 229–31, 239, 240, 241, 653–54, 808

Fourth Neutrality Act (1939), 385–86, 388
France, 17, 30–31, 69, 80, 89, 90, 132, 145, 178, 179, 501, 758, 821, 822–23
Algeciras Conference and, 41, 191
Alsace-Lorraine issue and, 134, 138, 144, 159, 180–81, 194, 204, 219, 225, 239, 269, 351
Anglo-U.S. relationship and, 376–77, 596–97, 611, 612, 614
appeasement policy and, 306–7
Austria-Piedmont War and, 103, 110–12
Austro-Prussian War and, 115, 116–18, 126
autonomy in NATO and, 600–606, 610–612, 614–16, 618
balance of power and, 68, 70
Balkans conflict and, 199–200, 203
Belgian independence and, 97, 222
Berlin crisis and, 571, 573, 575–77
Bismarck and, 122–25, 146, 159, 171
Briand-Stresemann meetings and, 278–279
Britain and, *see* Anglo-French relationship
communists in, 445, 447, 498
Congress of Vienna and, 79, 81–82
Crimean War and, 92–93
Czechoslovakia and, 120, 275, 276, 296, 303, 308–9, 311, 313, 314–15, 317
detente and, 734
disarmament issue and, 256, 279–80, 285–86, 292–94
Eastern European allies of, 296–97
economic decline of, 228–29
Entente Cordiale and, 181, 186, 188, 189, 190, 728
expansion of, 320 (map)
force de frappe of, 613
Four-Power Treaty and, 373
in Franco-Soviet Agreement (1935), 296–297, 302, 336
German rearmament and, 292–94
Holy Roman Empire and, 56–57, 58, 60, 62, 64
Indochina conflict of, 625, 626, 627, 628–631, 634, 635, 648
Kellogg-Briand Pact and, 280–81
League of Nations and, 235–36
Locarno Pact and, 273–76, 302, 511
Maginot Line of, 280, 302, 303
missile deployment issue and, 776, 777
Munich settlement and, 314, 316–17
mutual friendship treaty between Germany and, 547, 615–17
North African interests of, 530–31, 625, 674

France (*cont.*)
  nuclear strategy and, 609, 610
  Paris Peace Conference and, 232–38
  Peace Movement in, 677
  in Pitt Plan, 76
  Poincaré-Briand conflict and, 277–78
  population decline of, 228–29
  in post-Locarno period, 278–79
  in post-Revolution era, 105–6
  in post–World War I order, 250–55, 258, 265
  in post–World War II order and, 395, 396, 406, 414
  Prussia's defeat of, 118–19, 148
  public opinion and foreign policy of, 160
  raison d'état doctrine and, 59, 64–67, 71–72, 74, 823
  Rapallo Conference and, 262, 263, 264–265
  reparations issue and, 256–58, 262
  Reykjavik Summit and, 783
  Rhineland demilitarization and, 229, 233, 237, 251, 268, 274, 278, 280, 300–304, 306, 364
  Romania and, 102, 296
  Ruhr occupation by, 267–69, 272, 372
  Russo-Finnish War and, 352
  in SEATO, 637
  second Moroccan crisis and, 196–97
  self-image in foreign policy of, 119–20
  Sino-Soviet rift and, 720
  Spanish Civil War and, 308
  Stalin's Peace Note and, 499
  Stresemann's fulfillment policy and, 269, 271–72, 273, 282
  Suez crisis and, 523, 530–32, 533, 536, 539–41, 543–44, 547, 548, 559, 562, 563, 597
  Treaty of Mutual Assistance and, 253–55
  Tunisia and, 159
  United Action proposal and, 631
  Versailles settlement and, 234, 239–40, 242–43
  West Germany in NATO and, 515–16
  West Germany's friendship treaty with, 547, 615–17
  in withdrawal from NATO, 611, 612, 735
  World War I aftermath and, 221, 228–29, 250–55, 258, 265
  World War I outbreak and, 205–6, 210, 212–13, 216, 384–85
  World War II's effect on, 352–55, 359, 386, 395, 396, 406, 414, 602–3
  see also Anglo-French relationship
Franche-Comté region, 59–60
Franco, Francisco, 307

François-Poncet, André, 303, 304
Franco-Prussian War, 103, 118–19, 120, 134–35, 138, 204, 229, 256–57
Franco-Russian Agreement (1891), 180–81, 182, 202, 203, 204
Franco-Soviet Agreement (1935), 296–97, 302, 336
Franz Ferdinand, Archduke of Austria, 209, 211
Frederick II (the Great), King of Prussia, 40, 80, 129, 130, 169, 172, 350, 423
  raison d'état doctrine and, 69
Frederick III, King of Germany, 170
Frederick William IV, King of Prussia, 130
French General Staff, 303, 343, 351
French Revolution, 22, 30, 62, 74, 85, 105, 120, 123, 134, 258, 806
Fulbright, J. William, 650, 666, 667, 672, 689
fulfillment policy, 269, 271–72, 273, 276, 282

G-7 Summit, 795
Galbraith, John Kenneth, 711
Gamelin, Maurice, 303–4
General Agreement on Trade and Tariffs (GATT), 832
General Assembly, U.N., 249, 478, 542, 562
Geneva Accords (1954), 633, 634–36, 637, 639, 651, 719
  Laotian neutrality and, 646
Geneva Protocol (1924), 254–55
Geneva Summit (1955), 516–19, 520, 522, 581, 582
Genoa Conference, *see* Rapallo Conference
Gentz, Friedrich von, 140, 142
Gerasimov, Gennadi, 792, 794
Gerlach, Leopold von, 124–27, 130, 134, 146
German Confederation, 81, 109, 229
  Austria's role in, 123
  Bismarck and, 117, 129
  and conflict over Schleswig-Holstein, 112–13
  German unification and, 134
  Prussia's role in, 104, 122
German states:
  Austro-Prussian War and, 117
  Congress of Vienna and, 80–81, 85
  Franco-Prussian War and, 118–19
  Holy Roman Empire and, 56, 57, 59–60
German unification, 76, 137–38, 144–46, 169, 518, 520, 618
  Berlin crisis and, 571–73, 577–78, 587
  Berlin Wall and, 734
  Bismarck and, 65–66, 105, 119, 121, 133–134, 229, 239

Brandt and, 734–36
Dulles and, 577–78
European Union and, 820–23
Gaullist policies and, 618–19
German Confederation and, 134
Gorbachev's agreement to, 795
Napoleon III and, 104–5, 116–17
NATO and, 506–7, 735–36
new world order and, 820–22
Ostpolitik and, 734–37
Social Democrats and, 498, 503–4
Stalin's Peace Note and, 499–502, 571–72
U.S. foreign policy and, 577–78
Germany, Democratic Republic of (East), 229, 499, 506, 551, 568, 793
Access Authority proposal and, 590–92
Berlin crisis and, 569, 571, 577, 583–84, 590, 591–92, 593
Gorbachev's visit to, 794
Hallstein Doctrine and, 461, 734, 735
Soviet recognition of, 520
Stalin's Peace Note and, 500
Germany, Federal Republic of (West), 445, 758, 821
Access Authority proposal and, 590–92
Berlin crisis and, 569, 572, 577–78, 583–584, 587–89, 590–91, 592
creation of, 460–61, 494–95, 568
election of 1982, 776
France's mutual friendship treaty with, 547, 615–17
Hallstein Doctrine of, 461, 734, 735
integration of with West, 447, 498, 500, 506, 507–8, 594, 820–23
Locarno Pact and, 273–76, 277, 511
missile deployment issue and, 775–78
NATO and, 474, 498, 499, 515–16, 736
nuclear weapons in, 599–600, 784, 791
Ostpolitik and, 735–37
Peace Movement and, 677
rise of Adenauer in, 498
Germany, Imperial, 74, 99–100, 103, 111, 139, 148, 176, 201, 268, 607
Algeciras Conference and, 190–91
Alsace-Lorraine issue and, 134, 138, 144, 159, 180, 219
Austria's secret treaty with, 158–59
Bismarck's legacy to, 105, 136, 157–59, 169–72, 178–80
Bosnia-Herzegovina crisis (1908) and, 195–96
Brest-Litovsk Treaty and, 220, 257, 258–259
Britain and, 182–88
Entente Cordiale and, 190
Franco-Russian Agreement and, 181

Krüger Telegram and, 184–85
Moroccan crisis and, 190–91, 196
national movements and, 183–84
Navy Bill of, 188
post-Bismarck foreign policy of, 169–72, 178–80
public opinion in, 162–63, 182–83
Reinsurance Treaty and, 164, 179–80, 181, 189
Triple Alliance, 159, 186
TR's view of, 41, 42–43
World War I aftermath and, 221, 289–90; *see also* Versailles, Treaty of
World War I outbreak and, 48–51, 204–5, 208–10, 215, 216, 349
Germany, Nazi, 76, 288, 300, 334, 349, 446, 818
Austria's *Anschluss* with, 249, 283, 297, 310, 381
British declaration of war on, 385
British Naval Accord with, 297–98
collapse of, 423–24
Czechoslovakia occupied by, 316–17, 318, 337, 339, 340, 364
declaration of war on U.S. by, 368, 392–393, 394, 399
Disarmament Conference and, 292, 293, 378
expansion of, 321 (map)
France's fall to, 352–55, 359, 386
Halifax's visit to, 307–8
Hitler-Molotov meetings and, 361–62, 364
identified as aggressor nation, 383, 384
Molotov's visit to, 357–59
Munich settlement and, 314–16
Poland invaded by, 351, 364, 385
Poland's nonaggression pact with, 296
rearmament of, 291–95
Rhineland reoccupied by, 301–5
Soviet Union invaded by, 391, 394, 399
Soviet Union in war plans of, 367–68, 419
Soviet Union's rapprochement with, 262, 263–65, 267, 270, 282, 355–56
Spanish Civil War and, 307–8
Tripartite Pact signed by, 356
see also Nazi-Soviet Nonaggression Pact
Germany, Weimar, 279, 314
Anglo-French split and, 250–55
British aid to, 271–72
fulfillment policy of, 269, 271–72, 273, 276, 282
Kellogg-Briand Pact and, 281
League of Nations and, 250, 274, 278, 292
parity-security dichotomy and, 285–86
Polish border issue and, 281–82

Germany, Weimar (*cont.*)
  post–World War I order and, 250–53
  Rapallo Conference and, 263–64
  reparations and, 257–58, 272, 284–85; *see
    also* Versailles, Treaty of
  Russo-Polish War and, 261–62
  Soviet rapprochement with, 261, 262,
    263–65, 267, 270, 282
  Treaty of Mutual Assistance and, 254
Gero, Erno, 555–56
Glubb, John, 523, 529
Giers, Nikolai de, 175, 179, 181, 202, 204
Gladstone, William E., 100, 177
  Bismarck and, 162
  collective security and, 51, 74, 97, 160
  Disraeli and, 101, 150, 152, 160–61
  Midlothian Campaign of, 160–61
  morality in foreign policy of, 152, 155,
    160–62
  on obligations arising from alliances, 97
  William II and, 182
  Wilson compared with, 160–61
glasnost, 796–97, 798
Glorious Revolution, 71
Goebbels, Joseph, 294–95, 420, 423, 430
Goltz, Count von der, 114–15, 116
Gomulka, Wladyslaw, 552, 554–56, 561
Goodell, Charles, 687
Good Neighbor policy, 831
Gorbachev, Mikhail, 229, 417, 455, 520, 763,
    765, 817
  arms race and, 790–92
  August coup and, 786
  Berlin Wall and, 794–95
  Brezhnev Doctrine abandoned by, 793–
    794
  character of, 785–86
  Common European Home idea of, 791
  domestic reforms of, 785–87, 793–98
  East European unrest and, 793–94
  German unification and, 795
  glasnost and, 796–97, 798
  Kissinger's first meeting with, 798
  named "Man of the Decade," 799
  peaceful coexistence and, 790
  perestroika and, 788, 791, 796–97, 798
  and Reagan's dream of reconciliation,
    770–71
  regional autonomy encouraged by, 797–
    798
  resignation of, 786
  at Reykjavik Summit, 782, 783, 790
  Soviet foreign policy shaped by, 787–91
  spheres of influence renounced by,
    794
  Time interview of, 790

U.N. speech of, 791, 792
  Wilsonian themes and, 789
  Yeltsin and, 786
Gorchakov, Aleksandr, 141, 147, 151, 153,
    154–55, 175, 176
Grace of Alais, 61–62
graduated response strategy, 652
Grand Alliance, 71, 142, 246, 322 (map)
Gray, Gordon, 582
Great Britain, 30, 37, 69, 76, 80, 113, 115,
    116, 184, 207, 209–10, 434, 508, 812,
    821
  Abyssinian crisis and, 298–300
  Algeciras Conference and, 190–91
  Anglo-Russian Entente and, 191–92
  Anglo-Soviet spheres-of-influence
    proposal of, 413–14
  appeasement policy of, 306–7, 310, 311–
    312, 340
  Aswan Dam project and, 528–29
  Atlantic Charter violations considered by,
    407
  Austria and, 99–100, 153
  Austro-German alliance and, 159
  balance-of-power diplomacy and, 17, 70–
    73, 90, 98, 145, 220, 266, 823, 826
  Balkan issue and, 148–49, 160, 196, 198
  Berlin crisis and, 571, 573, 578
  Bismarck and, 122, 145, 146, 159–60, 171
  Central America and, 38
  Churchill and post–World War II
    diplomacy of, 428–30, 432
  collective security and, 88, 97, 266–67
  Common Market and, 596, 615
  Congress of Berlin and, 153, 154, 155–
    156
  Congress of Vienna and, 79
  Congress system and, 88–90, 95
  containment policy and, 467–68
  Crimean War and, 93, 94
  Czechoslovakia crisis and, 309, 312–18
  declaration of war on Germany by, 385
  declining global role of, 177–78, 595–99
  destroyers-for-bases deal and, 387–88
  Directorate concept and, 611–12
  disarmament issue and, 256, 279, 609,
    610
  Eastern Mediterranean policy of, 99–100
  Four-Power Treaty and, 373
  France and, *see* Anglo-French
    relationship
  Franco-Russian Agreement and, 181
  German navy and, 185, 188, 297–98
  German-Polish border issue and, 281–82
  German rearmament and, 291–95
  Germany's colonial agreement with, 180

Germany's post-Bismarck diplomacy
with, 178–80, 182–87
Glorious Revolution of, 71
in Grand Alliance, 71–72
Greek independence and, 98
Greek-Turkish aid program and, 451–52
Hitler's strategy and, 309, 353, 355, 363,
364–65
Holy Roman Empire and, 56 57
India and, 26, 41, 142, 151, 172, 178,
233
Indochina conflict and, 632–33
Iran and, 523–24
isolationist sentiment in, 72–74, 96–97
Japan's alliance with, 42, 171, 187–88
Kellogg-Briand Pact and, 281
Korean War and, 478
Krüger Telegram and, 184–85
League of Nations concept and, 223
Lend-Lease and, 388
Locarno Pact and, 273–76, 277, 278–79,
305, 511
Mediterranean Agreement and, 159,
178
Monroe Doctrine and, 35–36
Munich Agreement and, see Munich
Conference
Nassau Agreement and, 601–2
national interest doctrine of, 95–96
Nazi-Soviet Pact and, 346–47, 348
Ottoman Empire and, 101, 148, 151, 152,
153, 156, 222
Paris Peace Conference and, 232, 233–34,
237–38
parity-security dichotomy and, 285
"Perfidious Albion" epithet of, 98
Poland unilaterally guaranteed by, 342–
344, 345, 348
post–World War I order and, 220–21,
227, 229, 230, 250–53
post–World War II order and, 395–96,
399, 406, 420–21
pragmatic diplomatic style of, 98
public opinion and foreign policy of,
100–101, 160–61, 213
in Quadruple Alliance, 82
Rapallo Conference and, 263, 264–65
Reykjavik Summit and, 783
Rhineland reoccupation and, 277, 301–5
and rise of Hitler, 291, 293–94
Ruhr crisis and, 267 68
Russia and, 89, 98, 100, 142, 151, 171, 188,
191–92
Russo-Finnish War and, 352
in SEATO, 637
second front strategy and, 403, 404

Skybolt affair and, 601–2
Spanish Civil War and, 308
"splendid isolation" doctrine of, 97, 139,
145, 157, 167, 176–77, 178, 183, 185–
186, 189, 376
Stalin's Peace Note response of, 499
Stresa Conference and, 297–98
Stresemann's fulfillment policy and, 269,
271–72, 273
Suez Canal nationalization reaction of,
531
Suez crisis and, 523, 525–27, 531, 532,
533, 536, 539–41, 543–44, 546, 547,
548, 559, 562, 563, 597
Treaty of Mutual Assistance and, 253–55
Triple Entente and, 182–83, 192–94
United Action proposal rejected by, 631,
632–33
U.S. and, see Anglo-American relationship
Versailles settlement and, 230, 239–40,
242, 243, 244, 256–58
war strategy and foreign policy of, 147–
148, 403
Washington Naval Conference and, 373
West Germany in NATO and, 516
Wilsonian ideals and, 248–49
World War I outbreak and, 205, 207, 209–
210, 212–13, 216, 384–85
Great Depression, 283, 286, 291, 370, 379
Great Society, 661
Greece, 92, 98, 340, 342, 362, 366, 413, 414,
421, 453, 524, 620, 629
Anglo-U.S. aid to, 451–52, 469
guerrilla war in, 447, 451
Greek Revolution (1821), 89, 156
Greek-Turkish aid program, 451–52, 469,
473, 474
Greenland, 389
Greenwood, Arthur, 305
Greer (U.S. destroyer), 392, 659
Grey, Edward, 95–96, 191, 193–94, 212,
213, 220, 223–24, 353
Gromyko, Andrei, 175, 358, 436, 519, 581,
586, 727, 770, 777
Guatemala, 541
guerrilla warfare:
conventional warfare vs., 629–30
in Greece, 447, 451
in Malaya, 652
U.S. military policy and, 644, 648, 652,
660–61
in Vietnam, 639–41, 645, 649
Gulf of Tonkin Resolution, 658–59
Gulf War, 53, 250, 257, 475, 477, 614, 623,
659, 820
Gustavus Adolphus, King of Sweden, 62

Habsburgs, 57, 58, 59–60, 64, 72, 80, 98, 122, 806
Haile Selassie, Emperor of Ethiopia, 299, 300
Haiti, 39, 809
Halberstam, David, 669
Haldane, Richard Burdon, Lord, 188
Halifax, Edward Frederick Lindley Wood, Lord, 307, 311, 342, 353
Halliday, Fred, 800
Hallstein Doctrine, 461, 734, 735
Hamilton, Alexander, 33
Hanover, Kingdom of, 69, 80, 117
Hardenberg, Karl August von, 78
Harding, Warren G., 373, 374
Harriman, Averell, 428, 465, 651, 677, 684
Harrison, Benjamin, 534
Hatzfeldt, Count, 187
Haussmann, Georges Eugene, 107
Havel, Vaclav, 759
Hayden, Tom, 668
Helsinki Accords, 518, 760
    Basket III of, 759, 772, 793
    detente and, 758–60
    Final Act of, 18, 760
    New York Times editorial on, 760
Hendrickson, David, 34
Henry V, King of England, 125
Herald-Tribune Forum, 382
Herriot, Edouard, 254, 285
Hesse-Cassel, 117
Hilsman, Roger, 652
Hindenburg, Paul von, 279
Hitler, Adolf, 141, 256, 288–318, 378, 408, 440
    appointed Chancellor, 291, 377
    Britain in strategy of, 353, 354, 363, 364–365
    Chamberlain's meetings with, see Munich Conference
    and declaration of war on U.S., 368, 392–393, 394, 399
    demagoguery and egomania of, 288–91, 332
    German generals and, 309–10
    long-term strategy of, 309–10
    Molotov's meetings with, 360–62, 363, 434
    Munich settlement and, 314–16, 317
    negotiating style of, 312, 345–47, 358–59
    reaction of western democracies to, 291–292, 294–95, 301–2, 305
    revised secret protocol and, 350–52
    Rhineland occupation and, 301–2, 306
    separate peace proposal and, 419–20
    Stalin's relationship with, 332–35, 336, 355, 357–58, 364, 368
    U.S. domestic policy and, 384, 423–24
    Wilsonianism and, 317
Hitler-Stalin Pact, see Nazi-Soviet Nonaggression Pact
Hoare, Samuel, 299
Ho Chi Minh, 663–64, 678
Ho Chi Minh Trail, 641, 646, 660, 680, 693, 696
Hoffmann, Max, 259–60
Hoffmann, Stanley, 768–69
Holstein, Friedrich von, 184
Holy Alliance, 36, 88, 146, 149, 242, 458
    Austria in, 35, 82, 83, 119, 130, 131
    Bismarck's diplomacy and, 121, 122, 124, 125
    Congress of Paris and, 108
    Congress of Vienna and, 82–84
    Four Policemen concept compared with, 397–98
    Napoleon III and, 93, 105
    operational significance of, 84
Holy Roman Empire:
    decline of, 65, 80
    dominance of, 56–58, 61
    France and, 56–57, 58, 60, 62, 64
    German states and, 56, 57, 59–60
Honecker, Erich, 794
Hoover, Herbert, 49
Hopkins, Harry, 410, 416, 430–32, 444
Hossbach, Friedrich, 309
House, Edward, 223, 224, 238, 256, 381
House of Commons, British, 212, 248, 275, 295–96, 466–67, 510, 531, 543
House of Representatives, U.S., 381, 388
Howe, Geoffrey, 780
Hübner, Joseph, Baron von, 106, 107, 110
Hull, Cordell, 378, 388, 400–401, 402, 406–407, 623
human rights:
    detente and, 752–54
    Jackson Amendment and, 754
    Jewish emigration issue and, 752–54
    Reagan's policy of, 772–73
    Sino-American relationship and, 830–31
    U.S. foreign policy and, 622–23, 752
    see also Helsinki Accords
Hungarian Revolution (1848), 98
Hungarian Revolution (1956), 519, 548, 550–67, 595
    aftermath of, 567
    Cold War and, 550–51, 564, 566
    Eisenhower and, 558–59
    India and, 562, 564
    liberation theory and, 553–54, 558

Nonaligned group and, 562, 563–64
onset of, 555–56
Polish uprising and, 554–56
Radio Free Europe and, 557–58, 562
roots of, 551
Soviet suppression of, 542, 543, 560–62
State Department and, 562–63
Suez crisis and, 565–66
Titoism and, 552–54
U.N. and, 557, 559, 561, 562, 563
U.S. and, 553, 557, 558–59, 563, 564–65
Hungary, 57, 176, 243, 249, 313, 356, 413,
434, 437, 443, 793, 816, 817, 823, 824
Hussein, King of Jordan, 529, 739
Hussein, Saddam, 475, 546

Iceland, 390, 392
Ignatyev, Nicholas, 153
imperialism, 150, 401–2, 525, 763
India, 523, 527, 627, 637, 807–8
Britain and, 26, 41, 142, 151, 172, 178, 233
Hungarian uprising and, 562, 564
post–Cold War world and, 23–24, 26
Russian expansionism and, 100, 140, 142,
145, 151, 172
India-Pakistan War, 713
Indochina conflict, 392, 488, 509, 514, 603,
620–42
Associated States designation and, 625
Cambodia invasion and, 641
China and, 630, 634, 635, 644–45, 660–
661, 681
Churchill's perception of, 632–33
communist rivalries and, 627
Dien Bien Phu battle in, 630–31, 632,
633
Domino Theory and, 624, 626–28, 631,
633, 636, 641
Eisenhower Administration and, 628–30,
634, 635, 638–39, 641
FDR's attitude toward, 625
Geneva Accords and, 630, 634–35
guerrilla warfare and, 629–30, 639–41
JFK and, 639, 641, 643–44, 645, 647–48,
650, 651, 653
NSC-64 and, 623–24, 626–28
"Operation Eggshell" and, 626
partition of Vietnam and, 634–35
SEATO and, 637
Soviet Union and, 624, 627, 634, 635,
720
surrogate nature of, 624–25
Truman Administration and, 625–27
Truman and, 625–26, 628, 649
United Action proposal and, 631, 632–
634, 648

U.S. entry into, 621–26
see also Vietnam War; specific countries
Indonesia, 392, 627, 628, 632, 633, 637
Industrial Revolution, 106, 602
integrated forces concept, 614–15
Inter-Allied Military Control Commission
(IMCC), 239, 256, 278, 279, 314
International Access Authority, 590–91, 592
internationalism, 372–73, 374
Iran, 363, 449, 523–24, 527, 548, 815
Iraq, 250, 257, 299, 449, 523, 527, 541, 546,
548, 608
Iron Curtain speech, 441, 442–43, 466, 504
isolationism, isolationists, 18, 29, 805, 820
Anglo-American relationship and, 96–97,
101, 385
British Parliament and, 72–74
British "splendid" practice of, 139, 145,
157, 167, 176–77, 178, 183, 185–86,
189, 376
Congressional legislation of, 378
conscription and, 388
Great Debate and, 799–800
Kellogg-Briand Pact and, 373
League of Nations opposed by, 372–73
Lend-Lease opposed by, 388–89
Quarantine Speech reaction of, 379
Treaty of Versailles and, 238, 241–42
U.S. exceptionalism and, 142
U.S. foreign policy and, 369–73, 378, 381,
470
Wilsonianism and, 44, 45–46
Israel, 228, 523, 537, 540, 544, 737, 738–40
Egypt's rapprochement with, 284, 739
Iraqi reactor strike by, 608
Nasser's policy on, 527–28
1948 War and, 524
Suez invasion ploy of, 540
see also Arab-Israeli War of 1973; Suez
crisis
Israeli-Palestinian Peace Agreement (1993),
528, 740
Italy, 79, 93, 94, 116, 118, 122, 178, 190, 224–
225, 274, 306, 360, 404, 434, 447
Abyssinia and, 53, 249, 298–300
Algeciras Conference and, 191
communists in, 445, 447, 498
France-Piedmont-Austria War and, 110–
112
German-Austrian union and, 297, 300
Habsburg rule in, 56, 57, 59, 98
Kellogg-Briand Pact and, 281
as Locarno guarantor, 275, 299, 300
Mediterranean Agreement and, 159
Munich crisis and, 313–14
Rhineland reoccupation and, 301

Italy (*cont.*)
　Spanish Civil War and, 307–8
　Stresa Conference and, 297–99, 300
　Triple Alliance and, 159, 186, 356
　in World War I, 219, 231
　in World War II, 300–301, 383–86
Izvestia, 560

Jackson, Henry, 746–47, 750, 751, 753–54, 757
Jackson Amendment, 754
James II, King of England, 71
Jameson, Leander S., 184
Jansenius (Cornelius Otto Jansen), 63–64, 65
Japan, 354, 359–60, 363, 379, 384, 447, 495, 620, 632, 633, 658, 728, 826
　Britain's alliance with, 42, 171, 187–88
　China and, 25–26, 249, 286–87, 298, 377, 379, 380, 385, 826–30
　Four-Power Treaty and, 373
　Kellogg-Briand Pact and, 281
　Korea and, 57, 187, 476, 491
　opening of, 25–26
　Pearl Harbor attack by, 370, 392, 393, 399
　in post–Cold War world, 23–24, 827, 828–29
　post–World War II growth of, 703–4
　Russian expansionism and, 174
　Soviet entry into World War II and, 414, 415–16, 435
　Soviet nonaggression pact with, 365–66
　Tripartite Pact signed by, 356
　U.S. negotiations with, 392
　U.S. occupation of, 625
　Versailles settlement and, 239
　in war with Russia, 173–76, 190, 192, 194, 195, 196, 214, 416
　Washington Naval Conference and, 373
　in withdrawal from League of Nations, 287
Jaruzelski, Wojciech, 793, 794
Jefferson, Thomas, 30, 32, 33, 34, 39, 468
Johnson, Andrew, 37
Johnson, Hugh S., 389
Johnson, Louis, 459–60
Johnson, Lyndon B., 584, 623, 628, 671–73, 743
　antiwar movement and, 669, 675
　bombing halted by, 672, 693
　critics of, 663, 665–70
　Diem assessed by, 650
　Fulbright's criticism of, 667
　1968 candidacy declined by, 672–73
　Saigon mission of, 649–50

San Antonio Formula of, 664–65, 669, 670
　Vietnam goals explained by, 661–62
　Vietnam situation inherited by, 656, 657–658
　Vietnam War expansion rejected by, 660
Johnson Administration, 656–57, 678
　China misread by, 644–45, 661
　peace program of, 679
　Tonkin Gulf Resolution and, 658–59
Joint Chiefs of Staff, U.S., 405, 476, 486, 626, 631, 651
Joint Declaration of Liberated Europe, 415, 418
Jordan, 523, 529, 541, 713, 738–39
Junkers, 183–84, 503

Kádár, János, 561–62, 567
Kaganovich, Lazar, 419, 499, 519, 554
Kant, Immanuel, 86
Kapital, Das (Marx), 289
Kars, territory of, 108
Katkov, Mikhail, 142–43
Katyn massacres, 405, 411
Kaufmann, Konstantin, 152, 175
Kellogg, Frank Billings, 374–75, 377
Kellogg-Briand Pact, 18, 808–9
　isolationism and, 373
　Monroe Doctrine and, 281
　public opinion and, 375–76
　signing of, 280–81
　Stalin's reaction to, 334
　U.S. foreign policy and, 374–75
Kennan, George, 147–48, 438, 562, 583, 618
　on containment policy, 144, 464, 471, 792, 801
　disengagement theory of, 512–13
　Lippmann compared with, 465–66
　Long Telegram of, 443, 447–49, 454
　on Russian Imperial rule, 551
　on Russo-German alliance, 181, 264
　on Suez crisis, 545
　"X" article of, 454–56, 715
Kennedy, Edward M. "Ted," 678
Kennedy, John F., 590, 595, 600, 628, 655, 658, 676, 700, 831
　Adenauer and, 589–91
　assassination of, 653, 656, 657, 668
　Atlantic partnership vision of, 616–17
　Bay of Pigs and, 583, 646, 647–48
　Berlin crisis and, 584, 585–86, 591
　Berlin Wall reaction of, 584
　Cuban missile crisis and, 591
　Declaration of Interdependence of, 613
　human rights in foreign policy of, 622–623
　inaugural speech of, 19, 622–23

Indochina conflict and, 639, 641, 643–44, 645, 647–48, 650, 651, 652
Laotian neutrality and, 646–47
nation-building concept and, 648–49
NATO attitude of, 585–86, 612
partnership policy of, 601, 616
Vienna Summit and, 645
Kennedy Administration, 583, 587, 591, 644, 645, 663
Diem's overthrow and, 654–55, 657
flexible response strategy and, 612–13
Mutual Assured Destruction doctrine of, 750
NATO policy of, 612–14
nuclear strategy and, 601–2, 612–13
Skybolt affair and, 601–2
Kerr, Philip, 233
Keynes, John Maynard, 257
Khiva, principality of, 152
Khmer Rouge, 694, 697
Khrushchev, Nikita, 476, 505, 516, 518–23, 539, 563, 566, 736, 764, 787, 790, 795, 796
Berlin crisis and, 190–91, 569–71, 574, 575, 580–82, 585–93, 599, 606, 735, 758
bravado diplomacy of, 543, 548
Camp David Accords and, 580, 581–82, 600
Dulles on, 569–70
on Geneva Summit, 518–19
Macmillan's visit to, 578–79, 598–99, 600
Polish uprising and, 554–55, 556
Stalin denounced by, 552, 555, 704
U-2 affair and, 582
Vienna Summit and, 645
"wars of national liberation" and, 644
Kim Il Sung, 476, 483
Kipling, Rudyard, 43
Kissinger, Henry A.:
Adenauer briefed by, 588–90
de Gaulle's encounters with, 604–5
detente position as stated by, 747, 757
Dobrynin's meeting with, 788–89
Gorbachev's first meeting with, 798
Korean stalemate recommendation of, 487–88
LBJ and, 670, 671
McNamara-Hanoi exchanges and, 663–64
Paris Peace Accords negotiations and, 683–84, 686–87
Reagan briefed by, 766
Rockefeller policy statement drafted by, 721
secret Beijing trip of, 726, 730–31
Shanghai Communiqué and, 727

Solzhenitsyn appeals by, 754
Tho and, 686–87
Truman's meeting with, 425
Vietnam extrication and, 663–64, 677–78, 680, 682–84, 686–87, 691–93, 695
Vietnamization memorandum of, 682–83
Zhou and, 719, 727
see also China, U.S. opening to
Kliuchevsky, Vasili, 140
Knox, Philander Chase, 54
Kohl, Helmut, 777–78, 821
Kohler, Foy, 562
Kokand, principality of, 152
Koniev, Ivan, 418
Korea, 41, 57, 176, 187
Korea, People's Republic of (North), 249, 474, 475, 476, 477, 478, 608, 827
Korea, Republic of (South), 469, 474, 475–476, 625
Korean War, 403, 473–92, 645, 708
China's intervention in, 476, 477, 478, 479, 481–85, 488, 625, 661, 719
China's perception of U.S. and, 479–82
containment policy and, 479, 487, 489–90
global threat and, 624–25, 626
Inchon landing in, 480
Japan and, 476, 491
MacArthur's strategy for, 480–81, 484–86, 665
NATO and, 491
negotiations in, 488–89
onset of, 474–76
Sino-Soviet rift and, 483, 488, 491
Soviet Union and, 249, 477, 478, 483, 487, 488, 491–92, 495, 498
stalemate policy and, 485–89
Stalin and, 476, 478, 483, 492, 495, 498, 500
U.N. and, 249, 477, 478
U.S. war aims in, 477–78, 480, 481–84, 486, 489, 490
Vietnam War contrasted with, 490, 659–660, 665
Kostov, Traicho, 552
Kosygin, Aleksei, 748
Kovacz, Béla, 560
Kozlov, Frol, 580
Krivoshein, Aleksandr, 214
Krüger, Paul, 184–85
Krüger Telegram, 184–85
Kuwait, 299

Labour Party, British, 150, 286, 295, 305
LaFontaine, Oscar, 776
Laibach, Congress of, 90, 91, 149, 155
Lake, Anthony, 682

Lamartine, Alphonse de, 106
Lamsdorff, Vladimir, 175, 181
Lansdowne, Henry Charles Keith Petty-
    Fitzmaurice, Lord, 186–89
Lansing, Robert, 534
Laos, 583, 625, 637, 651, 680–81, 696, 698
    violated neutrality of, 645–47, 693
Lattre de Tassigny, Jean-Marie-Gabriel de,
    648
Latvia, 347
Laval, Pierre, 298, 299
League of Nations, 18, 310
    Abyssinian crisis and, 298–99, 300
    Anglo-French split and, 253–55
    Austria annexation and, 311
    British impetus for, 223
    collective security concept and, 30, 53,
        222, 235–37, 268–69
    enforcement and, 249, 282, 286–87, 374,
        450, 808
    Geneva Protocol and, 254–55
    Germany in, 250, 274, 278, 292
    IMCC and, 279
    Japan's withdrawal from, 287
    Monroe Doctrine as model for, 224,
        372
    Preparatory Committee of, 279
    Rhineland reoccupation and, 302
    Soviet Union and, 249, 250, 335–36
    TR on, 53–54
    Treaty of Mutual Assistance, 253, 255
    U.S. nonratification of, 54, 90, 91, 241–42,
        250
    Versailles settlement and, 230, 232, 248
    Wilson's vision of, 30, 51, 223–24, 234–
        235
Leahy, William D., 431
Lebanon, 541–42, 549, 614
Lebensraum, 346, 360
Le Duc Tho, 684–87, 690, 691
Lee Kuan Yew, 628
legitimacy principle, 94, 107, 117, 127, 146,
    211, 811
    balance of power and, 82–83, 167
    Prussian patriotism and, 125–26
    revolutionary wars and, 655
    Russian pursuit of, 141–42, 144, 156
    Vietnam War and, 655
Legvold, Robert, 336
Lend-Lease Act, 388–89, 431, 753
Lenin, V. I., 231, 258–61, 334, 552, 785,
    797
Lesseps, Ferdinand de, 530
Lewis, Anthony, 768
liberalism, 82, 104, 122
    Bismarck and, 128

Liberal Party, British, 295
liberation theory, 553–54, 558, 772
Liddell Hart, B. H., 778
Life, 553, 562
Lincoln, Abraham, 370, 393
Lindbergh, Charles A., 389
linkage concept, 715–19, 733
    detente and, 740–41
    Nixon and, 715, 717–19
    Sonnenfeldt's summation of, 758–59
    Soviet Union and, 716–17
    trade and, 754–55
Lin Piao, 644–45, 661, 725
Lippmann, Walter, 410, 471, 478, 624, 667
    on containment policy, 463–66, 467,
        665–66
    Kennan compared with, 465–66
    on Suez crisis, 545
    on Vietnam War, 666
Liska, George, 779–80
Lithuania, 347, 351
Litvinov, Maxim, 335, 344
Lloyd, Selwyn, 599
Lloyd George, David, 197, 218, 252–53,
    270
    Paris Peace Conference and, 230, 231–32
    Rapallo Conference and, 258, 262, 263,
        264, 267
    Wilson memorandum of, 241
Locarno Pact, 273, 302, 311, 314, 337, 824–
    825
    Chamberlain's role in, 277
    Germany's re-emergence and, 283–84,
        285, 290, 301, 303, 304, 378
    NATO-Soviet relations and, 511
    Rhineland and, 298, 300, 301, 304
    Versailles system undermined by, 274–
        276, 278–79, 283–84, 306, 307
Lodge, Henry Cabot, 41, 655, 663
Loftus, Lord Augustus, 151
London, Treaty of (1915), 231
London Conference (1913), 199
London Protocol (1877), 152
Long Telegram (Kennan), 443, 447–49, 454
Longworth, Alice Roosevelt, 389
Lorraine, Duchy of, 60
Louis XIII, King of France, 62
Louis XIV, King of France, 66, 70, 71, 129,
    205
Louis XVI, King of France, 144
Louis XVIII, King of France, 78
Lovett, Robert, 465
Lublin Committee, 413, 415
Luce, Henry, 529
Lusitania, 48
Luxembourg, 42, 118

Lynd, Staughton, 668
Lytton Commission, 287

Maastricht Treaty, 616
MacArthur, Douglas, 475, 476, 480–86, 488, 659, 700
  Korean War strategy of, 480–81, 484–85, 665
  stalemate strategy opposed by, 485, 486, 489
  Truman's dismissal of, 484–85
McCarthy, Eugene, 678
McCarthy, Joseph, 490, 660
McCloy, John, 465
MacDonald, Ramsay, 254, 285, 286, 291, 292
McGovern, George, 678, 688, 743
Mackinder, Halford, 814
Macmillan, Harold, 277, 517, 533, 563
  Anglo-U.S. special relationship and, 596, 601–2
  background of, 596
  Berlin crisis and, 573, 575, 577, 578–79, 598–99, 600
  Britain's declining global role and, 595–599
  de Gaulle's NATO challenge and, 610–12
  Directorate concept and, 610, 612
  Khrushchev visited by, 578–79, 599, 600
McNamara, Robert, 612, 644, 651, 656, 658, 663
Maddox, 658
Madison, James, 21, 31
Maginot Line, 280, 302, 303, 336, 348, 351, 386
Mahan, Alfred Thayer, 38
Mailer, Norman, 710–11
Maisky, Ivan, 338, 407
Mai Van Bo, 664
Malaya, 509, 627, 628, 629, 632, 633, 637, 641, 652
Malenkov, Georgi, 504, 505, 509, 510, 519, 555, 790
Maleter, Pal, 562
Manchuria, 249, 286–87, 298, 377, 392, 415–416, 449
Mandate Principle, 239
manifest destiny, 34, 142, 810
Manila Formula, 679
Mansfield, Mike, 639, 654, 672
Manteuffel, Otto von, 132
Mao Tse-tung, 645
  Korean intervention and, 479, 482, 483
  personality of, 727
  Snow and, 661, 725
  U.S. opening to China and, 725, 726, 727, 728, 729–30

Marcos, Ferdinand, 773
Marcovich, Herbert, 663–64
Maria Theresa, Archduchess of Austria, 350
Maritime Conference (1952), 532, 535–36, 538–40
Marlborough, John Churchill, Duke of, 99
Marshall, George C., 262, 403, 444–45, 451–454, 487, 490
Marshall Plan, 258, 424, 444, 451–54, 456, 457, 469, 473, 494, 558, 649, 650, 809, 813
Marx, Karl, 289, 768
Mary II, Queen of England, 71
Masaryk, Jan, 457
"massive retaliation" concept, 574, 612, 614, 632, 634
"Master Dispatch," 131–32
Matsuoka, Yosuke, 365
Matthews, H. Freeman, 449–50
Meany, George, 746
Mediterranean Agreement, 159, 178
Mein Kampf (Hitler), 289, 295, 309, 310, 336, 350, 355, 360, 531
Merchant, Livingston, 578
Metternich, Klemens von, 78, 89, 140, 154–155, 343
  basic tenets of, 104
  concept of "rights" as seen by, 84–85
  diplomacy of, 82, 86, 87–88, 144
  Holy Alliance and, 83, 85
  international system and, 85
  on Palmerston's diplomatic style, 101–2
  Russia's Baltic ambitions and, 91–92
  Wilson compared with, 79, 84
Metternich system, 82, 85–88, 144
  Austria and, 85–88
  balance-of-power policy and, 166, 397
  Bismarck's foreign policy and, 121–31, 146
  collapse of, 102, 103, 105, 131
  U.S. foreign policy and, 166–67
Mexico, 36, 37, 122, 224, 832
Middle East:
  borders in, 531
  Churchill on policy for, 524
  detente policy and, 737–40
  Nixon's diplomacy in, 738, 740
  peace process in, 738–40
  Soviet Union and, 525–26, 737–39, 740
  see also Suez crisis
Midlothian Campaign, 160–61
Mikoyan, Anastas I., 554, 556, 560
Millerand, Alexandre, 253
Millis, Walter, 378
Mindszenty, József, 560, 562
Mini-Tet Offensive, 678

Mission to Moscow (Davies), 430
Mitterrand, François, 229, 777, 783
Miyazawa, Kiichi, 827
Mohammed Reza Shah Pahlavi, 763
Moldavia, principality of, 94
Mollet, Guy, 531, 532, 537, 538, 540, 542,
  543, 547
Molotov, Vyacheslav, 344–45, 356, 366, 419,
  437, 497, 499, 510, 514, 519, 554
  Anglo-Soviet spheres-of-influence
    proposal and, 413–14
  Berlin visit of, 357–63, 428
  Four Policemen concept and, 396–97
  on German declaration of war, 367
  Hitler's meetings with, 360–62, 363, 434
  Potsdam Conference and, 434, 436
  Washington visit of, 396–97, 398, 407–12
Moltke, Helmuth von, 204, 205, 216
Mongolia, 792
Monroe, James, 35–36
Monroe Doctrine, 35–39, 235, 812–13
  Europe and, 35–36
  FDR's invoking of, 383
  Kellogg-Briand Pact and, 281
  as model for League of Nations, 224,
    372
  TR's corollary to, 39
Montenegro, 149
Montesquieu, Charles-Louis de Secondat,
  Baron de, 21, 67–68
moratorium demonstrations, 687–88
Morgenthau, Hans, 668
Morgues, Mathieu de, 64–65
Morocco, 178, 190, 192, 196, 199, 210, 298,
  531, 625
Moscow Summit (1972), 749, 753
Mossadegh, Muhammad, 523–24
Most Favored Nation (MFN) status, 753–
  754
Moyers, Bill, 688
Multilateral force (MLF), 613
Münchener Neueste Nachrichten, 196
Munich Conference (1938), 277, 312, 314–
  317, 337, 381–82, 623, 641–42
Murat, Joachim, 132
Murphy, Robert, 533
Mussolini, Benito, 297, 298–99, 300, 313,
  374, 384, 531
Mutual Assistance, Treaty of, 253–55
Mutual Assured Destruction (MAD), 750,
  779
Mutual Balanced Forces Reductions
  (MBFR), 759

Nagy, Imre, 555, 556, 557, 559, 560, 561,
  562, 567

Napoleon I, Emperor of France, 31, 74, 75,
  76, 78, 79, 85, 86, 88, 94, 104, 106, 132,
  141, 187, 205, 229, 246, 308
Napoleon III, Emperor of France, 94, 103–
  136, 153, 230
  Austria and, 106, 114–15, 118
  Austro-Prussian War and, 114–15
  Bismarck and, 105, 123–24
  and conflict over Schleswig-Holstein,
    112–14
  domestic policy and, 106–7
  foreign policy of, 107–10, 113, 419–20
  Franco-Prussian War and, 118–19
  German unification and, 104–5, 116–17
  Holy Alliance and, 93, 105
  legacy of, 104–5, 136
  Ottoman Empire and, 92–93
  Piedmont-Austria War and, 110–12
  Polish Revolution and, 109, 110, 112, 113,
    118, 119
  on Prussian and German nationalism,
    114
Napoleonic Wars, 22, 30, 77, 78, 94, 166,
  169, 220, 221, 222, 237, 250, 251, 314,
  391, 399
Nassau Agreement, 601–2, 614–15
Nasser, Gamal Abdel, 524, 525, 532–33, 542,
  544
  Aswan Dam project and, 528–29
  Baghdad Pact opposed by, 527
  emergence of, 524
  Israel policy of, 527–28
  Maritime Conference proposal rejected
    by, 535–36
  Suez Canal nationalized by, *see* Suez
    crisis
national interest:
  Britain's doctrine of, 95–96
  collective security and, 249, 819–20
  goals vs. tactics and, 706–7, 754–55
  new world order and, 810–11
  realistic assessment of, 711–13, 742,
    768
  Treaty of Versailles and, 248
  U.S. exceptionalism and, 706–7, 731,
    742–43
nationalism, 19, 82, 87, 94, 104, 111, 128,
  135, 138, 144, 163, 552, 822
  Arab, 523, 524, 530, 532–33, 539
  collapse of communism and, 618
  growth of, 784
Nationalist China, *see* Taiwan
National Liberal Party, German, 271
National Liberation Front (NLF), 669, 679,
  684, 687, 688–89, 690, 697–98
National Press Club, 475

National Security Council, U.S., 588, 650
  Domino Theory memorandum of, 624,
    626–27, 628
  NSC-64 of, 623–24
  NSC-68 of, 462–63, 624, 755
nation-building concept, 648–50
Nazi Party, German, 283, 284, 291, 312, 313
Nazi-Soviet Nonaggression pact, 260, 344–
    347, 350–68, 458
  Anglo-Soviet diplomatic failure and, 347–
    348
  secret protocol of, 347, 351–52, 355, 356,
    359, 362
  Stalin's revision of, 351–52
NBC, 672
Nehru, Jawaharlal, 564
Nesselrode, Karl Robert, Count, 175
Netherlands, 37, 57, 69, 71, 97, 407, 677
neutrality, 30–31, 497–98
  Stalin's Peace Note and, 501, 571–72
Neutrality Acts, U.S., 370
  FDR's proposed circumvention of, 382–
    383
  passage of, 378, 379, 409
  revision of, 385–86, 388
New Frontier, 644, 645, 668, 677
New Republic, 768
News Chronicle (London), 338, 339
New Statesman, 286
Newsweek, 581
new world order, 17–28, 804–35
  Asia in, 25–26, 826–31
  balance of power in, 20–22, 76–77, 810,
    813, 823, 827
  China in, 23–24, 25, 26, 808, 826–31
  collapse of communism in, 18–19, 800,
    814–18
  contradictions and limitations of U.S.
    leadership in, 18–20, 548–49, 804–5,
    809–10, 832–35
  differing perceptions and traits of
    participants in, 26–28, 807–8
  Eastern Europe in, 823–25
  fragmentation vs. globalization in, 23–24
  imposition of U.S. domestic values in,
    17–19, 22–23, 805, 811–13, 832–33
  Japan in, 25–26, 826–30
  Latin America in, 831–32
  NATO in, 818–24
  raison d'état practitioners in, 24, 810–
    811
  reunified Germany in, 820–22
  Russian Federation in, 23–26, 808, 814–
    818, 822–26
  threats to U.S. leadership in, 813, 823,
    827, 829–30
  unipolarity in, 809
  Wilsonianism and, 804–5, 808–9, 810,
    812, 813–14
New York Times, 421, 517, 645, 655, 660,
    718, 755, 760, 768
New Zealand, 631, 632, 637
Ngo Dinh Diem, 636, 637, 639, 649, 667
  Dulles' support of, 638
  LBJ's assessment of, 650
  overthrow of, 654–66, 657
Ngo Dinh Nhu, 654–55
Nguyen Van Thieu, 654, 686, 688, 690, 691,
    695, 698
Nicaragua, 593, 774, 787
Nice, annexation of, 110, 112
Nicholas I, Tsar of Russia, 85, 94, 100, 106,
    132, 142, 156, 163, 432, 552
Nicholas II, Tsar of Russia, 174–76, 198, 214,
    215, 414
Nicholson, Arthur, 199–200
Nicolson, Harold, 245
Nixon, Richard M., 41, 54, 124, 358, 514, 604,
    628, 766, 770, 785, 813
  ABM Treaty and, 747–48
  arms control negotiations and, 716
  on balance of power, 705
  Cambodia incursions and, 692–93
  Congress and, 745–51
  conservative critics of, 712–13
  detente and foreign policy of, 741–47,
    754–56, 761
  Doctrine of, 707–9
  on Geneva Accords, 634
  Jewish emigration issue and, 753, 754,
    772
  linkage concept and, 715, 717–19
  Mao and, 726, 727
  Middle East diplomacy of, 738, 740
  national interest and foreign policy, 706–
    707, 711–13, 731, 742–43, 754–55,
    768
  opening to China and, see China, U.S.
    opening to
  Peace Movement as interpreted by, 677–
    678, 713
  personality of, 704
  Realpolitik and, 707, 724
  SALT and, 718–19, 748–52, 757
  trade issue and, 755
  on U.S. and anticolonial struggle, 545–46
  U.S. exceptionalism and, 706, 731, 742,
    745
  Vietnam extrication and, 674–75, 677–79,
    681–83, 687, 690–91, 693, 695, 696,
    699, 700
  Vietnamization strategy and, 681–83

Nixon, Richard M. (*cont.*)
  Watergate scandal and, 696, 731–32, 741–742
  Wilsonian ideals and, 704–6, 707, 743
Nixon Administration, 374, 709, 730, 760–761, 766
  detente critics and, 714, 746–47, 757
  European Security Conference and, 758–759
  Jewish emigration issue and, 752–53
  linkage approach and, 716–17, 719
  Middle East and, 737, 738
  Ostpolitik and, 735, 736
  Peace Movement and, 675, 688, 744
  SALT and, 718–19, 748–52, 757
  Sino-Soviet relationship as seen by, 721–722
  "structure of peace" and, 733, 761
  Vietnam extrication and, 674–76, 678, 680, 684, 685, 686–87, 689, 692, 695–696
  Watergate period and, 756
  "Year of Europe" of, 617–18
Nixon Doctrine, 707–9
Noel-Baker, Philip, 285
Nonaligned group, 526, 539, 540
  Cold War and, 525, 564
  Hungarian uprising and, 562, 563–64
nonalignment policy, 122–24
Norris, Kathleen, 389
North American Free Trade Agreement (NAFTA), 832
North Atlantic Cooperation Council (NACC), 825
North Atlantic Treaty Organization (NATO), 80, 247, 466, 473, 474, 494, 496, 594, 625, 626, 637, 649, 784, 818–21
  autonomy question and, 600–606, 610–612, 614–16, 618
  balance of power and, 458, 460
  collective security and, 460–61, 545
  colonialism and U.S. rift with, 525–26, 545–46
  containment policy and, 456–61
  coupling concept in, 513, 777, 784
  Czech coup and, 457
  Directorate concept and, 610–12
  Eastern Europe countries in, 823–24
  European Security Conference and, 758
  France's withdrawal from, 611, 612, 614, 735
  Franco-American controversy and, 822–823
  French autonomy and, 602–6, 610, 614–616, 617
  German unification and, 506–7, 735–36

  integration debate and, 612–14, 791
  JFK's attitude toward, 585–86, 612
  Korean War and, 491
  missile deployment issue and, 775, 776
  Multilateral Force (MLF) and, 613
  in new world order, 818–24
  Ostpolitik and, 735–36
  Partnership for Peace idea and, 824–25
  Senate hearings on, 458–60
  Skybolt affair and, 601–2
  Suez crisis and, 536–37, 544–45, 547, 548
  Truman Administration and, 457–58
  unified Germany and, 820–21
  U.S. leadership of, 461–62
  Visegrad countries in, 823–24
  West Germany in, 475, 498, 499, 515–16, 736
  Wilsonianism of, 457
Northern Tier concept, 527, 528
North German Confederation, 117
Norway, 294, 352, 356, 386, 407
NSC-64, 623–24
NSC-68, 462–63, 624, 755
nuclear weapons:
  Anglo-American partnership and, 601–2
  Berlin crisis and, 573–74, 585, 586
  Cold War and, 461
  decoupling concept and, 513
  deterrence strategy and, 608–9, 610, 614
  Directorate concept and, 610–11
  disengagement plans and, 599–600
  European deployment issue and, 775–777
  flexible response strategy and, 609, 612–614
  Franco-German cooperation and, 617–618
  graduated response strategy and, 652
  Kennedy Administration and, 612–13
  military strategy debate and, 607–8
  Nassau Agreement and, 601–2
  non-nuclear challenge and, 608
  Reagan's attitude toward, 781, 782
  Skybolt affair and, 601–2
  Suez crisis and, 547
  testing of, 715
  U.S. vs. European approach to, 609–610
  on West German soil, 599–600
  Wohlstetter's article and, 714–15
  see also atomic bomb; Strategic Arms Limitation Talks; Strategic Defense Initiative
Nuclear Weapons and Foreign Policy (Kissinger), 588

Nye, Gerald, 378
Nye Report, 378

Obruchev, Nikolai, 202–3, 206, 215
Oder-Neisse Line, 734–35, 736
Olney, Richard, 38
"open-skies" proposal, 516
"Opinion on the Eastern Question"
    (Fadeyev), 143–44
Organization of American States, 831
Orlando, Vittorio, 231–32
Osgood, Robert, 780
Ostpolitik, 514, 584, 734–37
    Berlin Agreement and, 736–37
Ottoman Empire, 37, 62, 98, 139, 173, 806,
    814
    Anglo-Austrian relationship and, 92, 222
    Balkan crisis (1876) and, 149
    Berlin Memorandum and, 149, 152
    Britain and, 101, 148, 151, 152, 153, 156,
        222
    Napoleon III and, 92–93
    Russia and, 85, 89, 92–93, 98, 108, 122,
        141, 151, 153, 156, 174, 198
    Treaty of San Stefano and, 153–54

Pacific Community, 826, 828
Packard, David, 748
Pact of Bogotá, 831
Paine, Thomas, 32–33
Pakistan, 527, 548, 564, 627, 637, 726
Palestine Liberation Organization (PLO):
    Israel's agreement (1993) with, 528, 740
    Jordan's expulsion of, 738–39
Palmerston, Henry John Temple, Lord, 93,
    99, 100, 108, 112, 172, 398, 597, 623,
    763
    balance-of-power approach of, 161, 162,
        167
    Metternich on diplomatic style of, 101–2
    on national interest, 95, 96–97
Panama, 39
Panama Canal, 39
Pan American Union, 383
Panther Leap, 196–97
Paris, Congress of, 108, 110, 111
Paris, Pact of, *see* Kellogg-Briand Pact
Paris Peace Accords (1973), 374, 635, 693–
    697
Paris Peace Conference (1919), 19, 52, 230–
    245, 355
    Bowman memorandum and, 234–35
    collective security doctrine and, 235,
        236
    councils and committees of, 232
    formal guarantees issue and, 237–38

French position in, 232–38
League of Nations security provisions
    and, 235–37
procedures of, 231–32
representatives to, 230–31
self-determination principle and, 231,
    232
U.S.-French negotiations in, 235–37
Wilson at, 231–32, 234, 235, 236, 805
Partnership for Peace, 824–25
Pascal, Blaise, 169
Pathet Lao, 646
Paul I, Tsar of Russia, 87
Paul-Boncour, Joseph, 286
peaceful coexistence, 260–61
    Churchill's idea of, 512
    Gorbachev's notion of, 790
    Rapallo Conference and, 263
Peace Movement, 675–76
    in France, 677
    as global phenomenon, 675–77
    Nixon Administration and, 675, 688,
        744
    Nixon's interpretation of, 677–78, 713
    peace negotiations and, 689–91
    U.S. exceptionalism and, 688
    U.S. global mission opposed by, 675–76
    Vietnam War and, 675–76, 677, 682, 688,
        689–91, 692, 695
Peace Note (Stalin), 493–502, 505, 583, 595,
    764
    Acheson and, 501–2
    Adenauer's rejection of, 502, 504
    communist ideology and, 496–97
    flexibility and, 497–98
    German unification and, 499–502, 571–
        572
    neutrality and, 501, 571–72
    Stalin's motivation for, 494–96
    Western response to, 498–501, 516
Pearl Harbor attack, 370, 392, 393, 399
Penkovsky, Oleg, 585
Pensées (Pascal), 169
People's Daily, 479
"People's War" manifesto, 644–45
perestroika, 788, 791, 796–97, 798
Perestroika (Gorbachev), 788
Perkins, Frances, 412
Perle, Richard, 747
Perry, Matthew, 25–26
Persian Gulf War, *see* Gulf War
Peter I (the Great), Tsar of Russia, 551,
    763, 785
Pham Van Dong, 660
Philippines, 374, 401, 480, 637, 773
Phipps, Eric Clare Edmund, 291

Piedmont, 99–100, 103, 110–12
Piedmont-France-Austria War (Italian War), 103, 110–12, 119
Pineau, Christian, 547
Pinochet Ugarte, Augusto, 773
Pitt, William (the Younger), 56–77, 83, 86, 99, 222, 249
  Alexander I and, 75–76
Pitt Plan, 79, 220, 232
  Atlantic Charter compared with, 391
Poincaré, Raymond, 199–200, 267, 268, 277–78
Point Four Program, 424
Poland, 68, 79, 275, 277, 303, 311, 567, 590, 599, 734, 736, 758, 774, 816, 817, 823, 824
  Britain's unilateral guarantee of, 342–44, 345, 348
  German invasion of, 351, 364, 385
  Germany's border with, 265, 274, 281–282, 296, 313
  Lublin Committee and, 413, 415
  Napoleon III and Revolution of 1863 in, 109, 110, 112, 113, 118, 119
  post–World War II order and, 406, 407, 411–15, 418
  Russia's partition of, 75, 143, 144, 207, 243, 338
  Solidarity's emergence in, 793, 794
  Soviet occupation of, 352
  in Soviet orbit, 173, 431, 432, 434–35, 443, 446, 448, 551
  Teheran Conference and, 411–12
  uprising (1956) in, 554–55, 557, 561
  Versailles settlement and, 220, 225, 239, 243
  at war with Russia, 261
  World War II outbreak and, 336, 337–38, 340–41, 347, 350, 362, 365
"Policy of Boldness, A" (Dulles), 553
Polish Corridor, 239, 261, 264, 273, 307, 317, 365
Political Testament (Richelieu), 63, 65
Polk, James K., 36
Pompidou, Georges, 683
Populaire, Le, 547
Popular Front, 307
post–Cold War world, 330–31 (map)
Potemkin, Grigory A., 141
Potemkin, Vladimir, 337
Potsdam Conference (1945), 398, 433–37, 446, 494, 506
  atom bomb and, 435–37
  Berlin administration and, 568
  Cold War and, 433–36
  results of, 435, 436

Prague, Treaty of, 117
Pravda, 338, 560, 777
Priezac, Daniel de, 64
Provisional Revolutionary Government of the Republic of South Vietnam (PRG), 698
Prussia, 74, 76, 79–82, 111, 121, 138, 139, 140, 155, 169, 188, 338, 607
  alliances of, 35, 82, 94
  Austria's conflicts with, 69, 80, 85, 100, 107, 113–17, 129, 156
  Bismarck's foreign policy and, 122–24, 130–33
  and conflict over Schleswig-Holstein, 112–14
  Congress of Vienna and, 79, 81, 104
  Crimean War and, 130–33
  France defeated by, 118–19, 148
  German Confederation and, 104, 122
  Junkers of, 183–84, 503
  nonalignment strategy and, 122–23
  Realpolitik and diplomacy of, 122, 125–128
public opinion:
  Balkan crisis and, 160
  British foreign policy and, 100–101, 160–161, 213
  in Imperial Germany, 162–63, 182–83
  Imperial Russian policies and, 163
  Kellogg-Briand Pact and, 375–76
  Korean War and, 490
  Napoleon III and, 107
  Vietnam War and, 661, 663, 665–70
Pugwash Conferences, 663

Quadripartite Agreement, 593
Quadruple Alliance, 82–83, 88, 91, 229, 243, 314
Quarantine Speech (1937), 379–81, 382, 383

Radford, Arthur, 631, 633, 634
Radio Free Europe, 554, 557–58
Radio Liberty, 554
raison d'état doctrine, 22, 24, 34, 63–67, 111, 113, 120, 123, 806
  de Gaulle's use of, 576–77
  Frederick II's use of, 69
  as French foreign policy, 59, 64–67, 71–72, 74, 823
  in new world order, 24, 810–11
  Realpolitik and, 103
  Richelieu and, 58–59, 60, 63–64, 67
  success of, 63, 65, 67
  in U.S. foreign policy, 810
  Wilsonianism and, 66

Rajk, Laszlo, 552
Rákosi, Mátyás, 555, 556
Rapacki, Adam, 513
Rapallo Conference (1967), 246, 258, 262, 263–65, 270, 334–35
Rathenau, Walther, 264, 279
Reagan, Ronald, 18, 676, 731, 751, 756, 762–802, 813
    Armageddon prophecy and, 781
    balance of power and, 771
    Brezhnev's correspondence with, 769–70
    character of, 766
    diplomatic style of, 766–67, 771–73
    Eisenhower as precursor of, 631–32
    "evil empire" remark of, 767, 785
    foreign policy doctrine of, 765–66
    human rights policy of, 772–73
    nuclear weapons attitude of, 775, 781, 782
    personality of, 766
    preconceptions of, 764–65
    qualifications of, 765
    at Reykjavik Summit, 782–83
    rhetoric of, 766, 768–69, 771
    SDI proposal of, 778–82
    Soviet Union as perceived by, 768
    U.S. exceptionalism and, 767, 769, 785
    Wilsonianism of, 769, 772–73
Reagan Administration, 749, 766, 773–74, 783, 784
Reagan Doctrine, 774–75
Realpolitik, 137–67, 294, 298, 348, 495, 564, 566, 579, 621, 641, 819
    Balkan crisis (1876) and, 148–49
    Bismarck's practice of, 121, 125–28, 130, 133, 146, 165, 211
    definition of, 137
    domestic policy and, 131
    geography of Europe and, 137–38
    "Master Dispatch" and, 131–32
    Nixon and, 707, 724
    Prussian diplomacy and, 122, 125–28
    raison d'état doctrine and, 103
    Soviet practice of, 261, 263
    Stalin and, 335, 405, 407, 417, 428, 452–453, 495, 500
    Stresemann and, 271, 273
    Three Emperors' League (second) and, 158
    Truman Doctrine and, 452–53
    U.S. rejection of, 221, 431
    war scare of 1875 and, 147–48
    Wilsonian idealism and, 247, 316, 317
Reformation, 57–58, 61
Reichstag, German, 135, 149, 155, 162–63, 165, 283

Reinsurance Treaty, 164, 175, 179–80, 181
Renfield, Richard, 667
reparations, 264, 268
    Britain and, 256–58, 434
    Dawes Plan and, 272, 282–83
    France and, 256–58, 262
    Potsdam Conference and, 434, 435
    Stresemann and, 272–73
    Treaty of Versailles and, 256–58, 262–63, 267
    Weimar Germany and, 257–58, 272, 284–285
Republican Party, U.S., 44, 679, 743
Restitution, Edict of (1629), 61
Reston, James, 645, 667
revanche, 138, 228
Revolution of 1848, 104, 105, 120, 144, 156
Reykjavik Summit (1986), 782–83
Rheinisch-Westfälische Zeitung, 196
Rhineland, 80, 267, 281, 285, 298, 313, 372, 378
    France and demilitarization of, 229, 233, 237, 251, 268, 274, 278, 280
    German reoccupation of, 300–304, 306, 364
Rhodes, Cecil, 184
Ribbentrop, Joachim von, 346, 347, 357, 359–60, 361, 362–63, 367, 408, 419–20
Richardson, Elliot, 723–24
Richelieu, Armand Jean du Plessis, duc de, 17, 22, 56–77, 108, 112, 117, 124, 126, 187, 199, 308
    on basic principles of foreign policy, 621
    Edict of Restitution issued by, 61
    Grace of Alais granted by, 61–62
    Habsburg threat and, 59–65, 70, 122, 123, 189–90
    legacy of, 80, 81, 85
    raison d'état principle grafted by, 58–59, 60, 63–64, 67
Ridgway, Matthew, 488
Rietzler, Kurt, 184
Rio Pact, 458, 831
Road to War, The (Millis), 378
Rockefeller, Nelson, 516, 721
Rogers, William P., 723, 738
Rokossovsky, Konstantin, 554
"Rolling Thunder" campaign, 658
Romania, 219, 311, 340–41, 342, 356, 362, 413, 567
    France and, 120, 296
    Soviet domination of, 408, 409, 434, 435, 437, 443, 446
    Soviet Union's Bessarabia dispute with, 336, 347, 355
Roon, Albrecht Theodor Emil von, 136

Roosevelt, Franklin D., 18, 76, 175, 315,
    369–93, 394–422, 473, 499, 676, 741,
    805, 813, 831
  ABC-1 Agreement and, 389, 403–4
  aggressor nations identified by, 373, 384
  Atlantic Charter and, 390–91, 401
  Bering Strait meeting proposed by, 410
  on British vs. U.S. interests, 395–96, 400–
    401, 421
  at Casablanca Conference, 405
  character of, 371
  Charlottesville speech of, 386–87
  colonialism issue and, 402, 408
  death of, 423
  destroyers-for-bases deal and, 387–88
  Four Freedoms proclaimed by, 389,
    390
  Four Policemen concept of, see Four
    Policemen concept
  on Germany-first strategy, 403–4
  Greer incident and, 392, 659
  Indochina attitude of, 625
  Lend-Lease Act and, 388
  Monroe Doctrine invoked by, 383
  Munich Agreement and, 314, 381–82
  post–World War II order and, 395–96,
    399, 400–401, 405–10, 422
  Quarantine Speech of, 379–81, 382, 383
  revision of Neutrality Acts and, 385
  Stalin as characterized by, 417
  at Teheran Conference, 410, 411
  in U.S.-Japanese negotiations, 392
  wartime diplomacy and strategy of, 394–
    422
  at Yalta Conference, 396, 410, 414–16,
    420
Roosevelt, Theodore, 45, 50, 72, 162, 389,
    704, 705, 712, 731, 767
  global view of, 38–41
  Imperial Germany as seen by, 41, 42–43
  on League of Nations, 53–54
  Monroe Doctrine "corollary" of, 39
  Nobel Peace Prize awarded to, 42
  Russo-Japanese relationship as seen by,
    41–42, 49
Rostow, Walt, 650–51
Royal Air Force, British, 295, 354
Royal Navy, British, 36, 38, 42, 93, 98, 148,
    149, 251, 384, 386
Ruhr crisis, 229, 267–69, 272, 372
Runciman, Walter, Lord, 311
Rusk, Dean, 584, 586, 624, 655
Russia, Imperial, 132, 138–46, 165, 169, 183,
    193, 197, 202–16, 221, 227
  Algeciras Conference and, 190–91
  Anglo-Russian Entente and, 191–92

Asiatic Department of, 174
Austria's Balkan conflict with, 138–39,
    144, 146–47, 159–60
Austria's rivalry with, 86, 87, 93–94, 99,
    146–47, 153, 173, 199
autocratic system and foreign policy of,
    75, 175
Balkans and, 85, 91–92, 93, 94, 148, 149,
    152–54, 162, 178, 199–200
Bosnia-Herzegovina crisis (1908) and,
    195, 196
Britain and, 89, 98, 100, 142, 151, 171,
    188, 191–92
Bulgarian crisis and, 163–64
Congress of Berlin and, 155–57, 158
Congress of Vienna and, 79
Crimean War and, 93, 108
demise of, 221
dual nature of, 173–74
eighteenth-century development of, 74–
    75
Entente Cordiale and, 181, 188, 728
exceptionalism of, 142–44
expansionism of, 24–25, 100, 139–47,
    151–52, 156, 159–60, 172–75, 176, 551
in Holy Alliance, 35, 82, 119, 121, 124
India and, 100, 140, 142, 145, 151, 172
Japan's rivalry with, 41–42
Japan's (1905) war with, 173–76, 190,
    192, 194, 195, 196, 214, 416
Ottoman Empire and, 85, 89, 92–93, 98,
    108, 122, 141, 151, 153, 156, 174, 198
Paris Peace Conference and, 231
Poland partitioned by, 75, 143, 144, 207,
    243, 338
Polish Revolution (1863) and, 110, 112,
    113, 118
post-Versailles position of, 242–43
public opinion and foreign policy of, 163
in Quadruple Alliance, 82
Reinsurance Treaty and, 164, 180, 189
Sweden and, 74–75
Treaty of Brest-Litovsk and, 220, 227, 241,
    257, 258–60
World War I outbreak and, 202–3, 206–8,
    210–11, 214, 215–16, 348–49
Russian Federation, 173, 814–18
  Atlantic nations and, 825–26
  former Soviet republics and, 815–16, 818
  independence of, 798–99
  nationalism in, 817
  "near abroad" and, 815–16
  new Europe and, 618–19
  new world order and, 23–26, 808, 814–
    818, 822–26
  U.S. policy toward, 271–72, 817–18

Russian Revolution, 227, 259, 336, 337
Russo-Finnish War, 352
Russo-Japanese War, 173–76, 190, 192, 194, 195, 196, 214, 416
Russo-Polish War, 261, 262

Saar, 229, 278
Sadat, Anwar, 284, 526, 528, 533, 547, 739
St. Germain, Treaty of, 310
Sakhalin Island, 363, 415
Salisbury, Harrison, 660
Salisbury, Robert Arthur Talbot Gascoyne-Cecil, Lord, 100, 153, 154, 158, 175, 177–78, 183, 184, 186–87
Samoa, 185
Samuel, Herbert, 295
San Antonio Formula, 664–65, 669, 670
San Stefano, Treaty of, 153–54
Sardinia, 119–20, 132
   see also Piedmont
Savoy, 71, 110, 112, 203
Saxony, 69, 71, 81, 268
Sazonov, Sergei, 198, 210, 212, 215
Schacht, Hjalmar, 307
Schlesinger, Arthur, Jr., 409
Schleswig-Holstein, 103, 112–14, 117, 163
Schlieffen, Alfred von, 204–5
Schlieffen Plan, 204–6, 216
Schmidt, Helmut, 775, 776
Schnurre, Karl, 345
Schulenburg, Friedrich von der, 345, 346, 366, 367
Schurman, Jacob, 49
Schuschnigg, Kurt von, 358
Schwarzenberg, Felix, Furst zu, 106
Scioppius, Caspar, 61
second front strategy, 403, 404–5
Security Council, U.N., 249, 460, 477, 478, 540, 541, 542, 557, 562
Seeckt, Hans von, 261–62, 272
self-determination principle, 240, 244, 317, 406
   Paris Peace Conference and, 231, 232
   Wilsonian design and, 221–22, 225, 229, 239
Senate, U.S., 37, 227, 236, 485, 648
   ABM Treaty and, 747
   China lobby of, 479, 741
   Four-Power Treaty and, 373–74
   Kellogg-Briand Pact endorsed by, 375
   NATO hearings of, 458–60
   Tonkin Gulf Resolution and, 658
   Treaty of Versailles and, 238, 251
Senate Foreign Relations Committee, 281, 412, 458–60, 650, 746
Senate Subcommittee on Arms Control, 746

Serbia, 194, 195, 196, 199, 203, 209, 210–16, 240, 348
Seven Years' War, 68, 69, 75, 140, 423
Seward, William Henry, 37
Shanghai Communiqué, 727–29
Shaw, George Bernard, 22
Shepilov, Dmitri T., 519, 529, 542
Shevardnadze, Eduard, 798, 801
Shultz, George, 718, 755, 774, 783
Shuvalov, Count Peter, 149, 152, 153, 154, 157
Sihanouk, Norodom, 647
Silesia, 69, 80, 112, 130
Simon, John, 291
Singapore, 285, 628, 637
Sino-Soviet rift:
   Adenauer's view of, 588–89, 720
   de Gaulle's view of, 720
   diplomatic flexibility and, 704
   Eisenhower's assessment of, 509
   France and, 720
   Gorbachev's overtures and, 791–93
   Korean War and, 483, 488, 491
   Nixon Administration's perception of, 721–22
   Taiwan and, 722
   U.S. opening to China and, 713–14, 719–725, 728, 730–31
Skybolt affair, 601–2, 614
Slansky, Rudolf, 552
Slovakia, 57, 316, 816, 817, 823, 824
Small Holders' Party, Hungarian, 560
Smith, Adam, 21
Snow, Edgar, 661, 725
Social Democratic Party, German, 183, 498, 503–4, 572, 775, 776
"Socialism on the Defensive" (Halliday), 800
Solferino, battle of, 111
Solidarity, 793, 794
Solzhenitsyn, Aleksandr, 754, 815
Somalia, 809
Sonnenfeldt, Helmut, 759
Sonnino, Sidney, 231
"Sources of Soviet Conduct, The" (Kennan), 454–55
Southeast Asian Treaty Organization (SEATO), 637, 645
Soviet Union, 22, 23, 86, 199, 308, 311, 336–337, 340, 398, 406, 407, 566–67, 618, 808
   ABM Treaty and, 749
   Acheson on U.S. relations with, 501–2, 509, 553, 755
   Afghanistan invaded by, 141, 701, 763, 773, 774, 787, 792

Soviet Union (*cont.*)
arms race and economic pressures in, 790
Aswan Dam project and, 529
Atlantic Charter violations proposed by, 406
atomic bomb propaganda of, 441–42
August coup in, 786
Baltic states and, 347, 352, 355, 798
British unilateral guarantees and, 344, 347–48
Bulgaria in orbit of, 435, 437, 443, 446, 448, 451
Chamberlain's distrust of, 341–42
China and, *see* Sino-Soviet rift
Churchill's spheres-of-influence arrangement and, 413–14
coexistence principle and, 260–61
collapse of, 18–19, 173, 176, 455, 701, 760, 774, 785–86, 791–99, 806, 820
collective security and foreign policy of, 336, 338–39, 340
Czechoslovakian intervention of, 249, 476, 624, 704, 716, 734
Decree on Peace of, 259
early foreign policy of, 258–61
Eastern European orbit of, *see* Eastern Europe
Egypt and, 525–26, 738, 739, 753
European Security Conference and, 758–759
as "evil empire," 767, 785
excluded from Versailles settlement, 259
exit tax levied by, 753, 754
expansionism of, 141, 144, 249, 352, 409, 449–51, 476, 542, 543, 554–55, 560–62, 620, 624, 701, 704, 716, 728, 734, 763–764, 773, 774, 787, 792
Finland invaded by, 352
Franco-Soviet Agreement (1935) and, 296–97, 302, 336
Geneva Summit and, 519
German invasion of, 391, 394, 399
Germany's declaration of war on, 367–68
Germany's rapprochement with, 262, 263–65, 267, 270, 282, 355–56
glasnost and, 796–97, 798
Gorbachev's liberalization policy and, 793–95
Hitler-Molotov meetings and, 360–62, 364
in Hitler's long-range plans, 309–10
Hungarian uprising suppressed by, 542, 543, 560–62
Indochina conflict and, 624, 627, 634, 635, 720

Japan's nonaggression pact with, 365–66
Japan's war with, *see* Russo-Japanese war
Jewish emigration from, 752–54, 757
Joint Declaration violated by, 418
Kennan's Long Telegram and, 443, 447–449, 454
in Kennan's "X" article, 454–55
Korean War and, 249, 477, 478, 483, 487, 488, 491–92, 495, 498
League of Nations and, 249, 250, 335–336
Lenin on foreign policy of, 261
linkage concept and, 716–17
Marshall Plan reaction of, 453, 457
in Matthews memorandum, 449–51
Middle East and, 525–26, 737–39, 740
missile deployment issue and, 776–77
Most Favored Nation status and, 753–54
Munich Agreement and, 333, 337–38
perestroika and, 788–90
Poland occupied by, 352
Poland's uprising (1956) and, 554–55
post–World War I order and, 229, 231, 252
• post–World War II order and, 395, 398–399, 406, 407–9, 420–21
Quadripartite Agreement and, 593
Rapallo Conference and, 262–65
Reagan's perception of, 768, 770–71
Realpolitik and, 261, 263
regional autonomy and, 797–98
Romania dominated by, 405, 409, 434, 435, 437, 443, 446
Romania's Bessarabia dispute with, 336, 340–41, 347, 355
Russo-Polish War and, 261
SDI and, 778, 779, 782, 787
separate peace proposal and, 419–20
Sino-American cooperation and, 719–21, 723–24, 713–14, 728, 730–31
Sputnik launched by, 570
Stalin and post–World War II diplomacy of, 427–30, 438–41
Stalin's death and, 494, 504, 506, 507, 509, 520
Stalin's Peace Note and, 497–98, 571–72
Stalin's purges and, 337, 338–39, 341
Suez crisis and, 522–23, 525, 526, 529, 537–38, 539, 542–43, 546–47, 548
Titoist threat and, 552–53
in Treaty of Brest-Litovsk negotiations, 258–59
Treaty of Mutual Assistance and, 254
Tripartite Pact and, 356–57, 364
unilateral force reductions by, 791–92
U.S. trade with, 753–55

Vietnam War and, 624, 627, 634, 635, 681, 698

wars of national liberation and, 593, 644

World War I outbreak and, 348–49

World War II casualties of, 438

Yalta's Joint Declaration violated by, 418

Yugoslavia's treaty with, 366

see also arms control; Berlin crisis; Cold War; containment policy; detente policy; Helsinki Accords; human rights; Hungarian Revolution; Russian Federation; Strategic Arms Limitation Talks

Spain, 31, 35, 57, 59, 60, 66, 68, 69, 71, 74, 92, 193, 308

Spanish Civil War, 307

Spanish Netherlands, 59, 71

Spanish Succession, Wars of, 251

spheres of influence, 40

Churchill's proposed arrangement of, 413–14

in Cold War, 328–29 (map)

containment policy and, 447, 456

Gorbachev's renunciation of, 794

"splendid isolation" doctrine, 97, 139, 145, 157, 167, 176–77, 178, 183, 185–86, 189, 376

SS-20 missiles, 775, 777, 801

Stalin, Joseph, 259, 296–97, 332–49, 354–355, 392, 394–422, 435–36, 477, 511, 515, 521, 523, 736, 737, 805, 813

balance of power defined by, 398

Berlin blockade and, 569

Berlin occupation and, 417–18

Churchill's spheres-of-influence arrangement and, 413–14

communism as reconsecrated by, 496–97

death of, 494, 504, 506, 509, 713

Eastern European security belt and, 173, 443–44, 446, 447, 495, 551, 552, 594–595

Eighteenth Party Congress Address of, 338–39, 340

Eisenhower's Berlin correspondence with, 417–18

FDR's characterization of, 417

Five-Year Plan speech of, 441, 443

Four Policemen concept and, 411

Germany's declaration of war and, 367–368

Harriman's assessment of, 428

Hitler and, 332–35, 336, 346–47, 355, 357–58, 364, 368

Hopkins' talks with, 431–32, 444

Japanese nonaggression treaty and, 365–366

on Kellogg-Briand Pact, 334

Khrushchev's denunciation of, 552, 555, 704

Korean War and, 476, 478, 483, 492, 495, 498, 500

Lublin Committee and, 413, 415

and Marshall Plan, 444–45, 453

misjudgment of, 336, 339–40, 343–44, 412

Munich Agreement and, 337–38

Nazi-Soviet Pact negotiations and, 344–47

Peace Note of, *see* Peace Note

post–World War II order and, 395, 398–400, 406–8, 409, 410

at Potsdam Conference, 433–36

purges by, 316, 337, 338–39, 341, 438, 499–500, 505, 552, 554

Realpolitik and, 335, 405, 406, 417, 428, 452–53, 495, 500

Ribbentrop and, 347, 357

Russo-Finnish War and, 352

second front strategy and, 404–5

secret protocol revised by, 350–52

separate peace proposal and, 419

Soviet-Japanese nonaggression pact and, 365–66

Soviet post–World War II diplomacy and, 427–30, 438–41

Soviet strategy described by, 334–35

successors to, 504–5, 519, 764

at Teheran Conference, 410, 411, 421

Tripartite Pact and, 356–57

unconditional surrender favored by, 398, 405

U.S. *Realpolitik* as viewed by, 500–501

wartime diplomacy and strategy of, 394–422

and war with Japan, 415–16

at Yalta Conference, 396, 410, 414–16

Stalingrad, Battle of, 394–95, 399, 403, 404, 405, 411, 419

State Department, U.S., 433, 454, 588, 592, 650, 652, 783

Hungarian uprising and, 562–63

Indochina program of, 626

Matthews memorandum and, 449–50

NATO concept defended by, 458–59

Stern-Rubarth, Edgar, 283

Stettinius, Edward R., 437

Stevenson Amendment, 754

Stimson, Henry L., 375–76, 377

Stoessel, Walter, 726

Stolypin, Peter, 176

Strategic Arms Limitation Talks (SALT), 748–52, 757

detente and, 749–52

Strategic Arms Limitation Talks (*cont.*)
Nixon and, 718–19
signing of, 749
U.S. domestic debate on, 749–52
Strategic Defense Initiative (SDI), 765, 775, 778, 782, 787
critics of, 779–81
Mutual Assured Destruction and, 779
Reykjavik Summit and, 783, 790–91
Stresa Conference, 297–98, 299, 301
Stresemann, Gustav, 266–87, 290, 310
background and personality of, 271
Briand's meetings with, 278–79
death of, 283
fulfillment policy of, 269, 271–72, 273, 276
German-Polish border issue and, 274
Locarno Pact and, 274, 277
Nobel Prize awarded to, 274
Realpolitik and, 271, 283
reparations issue and, 272–73
Soviet diplomacy of, 282
Sudan, 185, 528
Sudetenland, 311, 313, 317
Suez crisis, 521, 522–49, 559, 596, 606, 631
Adenauer on outcome of, 547
aftermath of, 546–49
Anglo-French expedition and, 540–44
Anglo-U.S.-French rift and, 524–25, 532–535, 537–39
appeasement and, 531
Arab nationalism and, 523, 524, 530, 532–533, 539
Aswan Dam project and, 528–30
colonization issue and, 524–25, 545–46
consequences of, 547–49
containment policy and, 525–26, 527, 537, 545
Dulles and, 532, 533–39, 540
Eden and, 528–44, 547, 595
European unity and, 547–48
Hungarian Revolution and, 565–66
Maritime Conference proposal and, 532, 535–36, 538–40
nationalization of canal and, 530
NATO and, 536–37, 544–45, 547, 548
Nonaligned group and, 526, 546
Northern Tier concept and, 527, 528
nuclear weapons and, 547
U.N. and, 539–42, 544, 549
Users' Association proposal and, 537
suffrage, universal, 120–21, 135, 150, 162
Supreme Military Council, Soviet, 339
Suslov, Mikhail, 556, 560
Sweden, 37, 59, 60, 68, 69, 71, 74–75, 352, 362, 590

Switzerland, 311, 551, 590
Syria, 147, 384, 527, 546, 713, 737, 739

Taft, Robert A., 388–89
Taft, William Howard, 44
Taiwan, 479, 529, 625, 638, 722
Talleyrand, Charles de, 78–79, 82, 86, 94
Tardieu, André, 233–34, 238, 256
Taussig, Charles, 402
Taylor, A. J. P., 347
Taylor, Maxwell, 650–51, 660
Teheran Conference (1943), 410–13, 424, 426
Tet Offensive, 656, 665, 670–71, 672
Thailand, 624, 628, 632, 637, 645, 647, 650
Thatcher, Margaret, 150, 596, 783, 784
Thiers, Adolphe, 116–17
Thieu, Nguyen Van, *see* Nguyen Van Thieu
Thirty Years' War, 21, 59, 62, 65, 68, 80, 169, 806, 807
Tho, Le Duc, *see* Le Duc Tho
Thompson, Llewellyn, 562, 570, 575, 586
Three Emperors' League (first), 146–49, 151, 153, 157
Balkan crisis (1876) and, 148–49
Berlin memorandum and, 149
Three Emperors' League (second), 158–59, 163–64, 165, 195
Thurmond, Strom, 469
Tiananmen Square demonstrations, 792–93
Time, 529, 672, 705, 790, 799
Times (London), 286
Tisza, Stephen, 211
Tito, Marshal (Josip Broz), 552, 629
Titulescu, Nicolae, 306
Tocqueville, Alexis de, 556
Tonkin Gulf Resolution, 658–59
Tory Party, British, 73, 100, 150, 177; *see also* Conservative Party, British
Tracy, Benjamin, 38
Treatise on the Economic Consequences of the Peace (Keynes), 257
triangular diplomacy, *see* China, U.S. opening to; linkage concept; Nixon, Richard M.; Sino-Soviet rift
Trianon, Treaty of, 310
Tripartite Pact, 356, 359, 360, 361, 362, 363, 364, 365
Triple Alliance, 159, 178, 180, 186, 203
Triple Entente, 42, 50, 148, 182, 191–93, 200, 201, 210, 212, 261–62, 341
Troppau, Congress of, 90, 91, 149
Trotsky, Leon, 258–60
Truman, Harry S., 429, 467, 495, 499, 501, 509, 524, 612, 622, 665, 741, 805
background and character of, 424–25

balance of power rejected by, 446–47
Byrnes' falling out with, 438
collective security commitment of, 426–427
Four Policemen concept and, 426–27
"get-tough" policy of, 446
Greek-Turkish aid and, 451
Indochina conflict and, 625–26, 628, 649
Kissinger's meeting with, 425
Korean conflict and, 474, 477, 479, 480–487, 490–91
MacArthur dismissed by, 484–85
at Potsdam Conference, 433–36
presidency as viewed by, 425
U.S.-Soviet relations and, 425–27
Wallace's conflict with, 468–69
Wilsonianism of, 447
Truman Administration, 469, 479, 481, 483, 487, 489, 490, 501
Indochina conflict and, 625–27
NATO and, 457–48
Truman Doctrine, 452–53
Trusteeship Council, U.N., 408
Tucker, Richard, 34
Tunisia, 159, 625
Turkey, 340, 362, 449, 524, 527, 548, 620, 627, 815
Anglo-U.S. aid to, 451–52, 469
Imperial, see Ottoman Empire
Korean War and, 478
see also Greek-Turkish aid program

U-2 spy plane incident, 582
Ukraine, 75, 207, 220, 259, 261, 419, 815
unconditional surrender policy, 398, 405
"unipolar" world, 809
United Action proposal, 631–34, 648
United Nations, 18, 53, 54, 154, 414, 416, 427, 447, 449, 452, 469, 499, 579, 586, 625, 631, 720, 759, 808, 815, 818
General Assembly of, 249, 478, 542, 562
Gorbachev's speech to, 791, 792
Hungarian uprising and, 557, 559, 561, 562, 563
Korean War onset and, 249, 477, 478
in post–Cold War era, 249–50
Security Council of, 249, 460, 477, 478, 540, 541, 542, 557, 562
Suez crisis and, 539–42, 544, 549
Trusteeship Council of, 408
United States:
alliances of, 247; see also collective security
anticolonial tradition of, 625–26

contradictions and limitations in leadership of, 18–20, 548–49, 804–5, 809–10, 832–35
exceptionalism of, see exceptionalism, U.S.
expansionism of, 30–31, 36–37; see also Monroe Doctrine
imposition of domestic values of, 17–19, 22–23, 805, 811–13, 832–33
moral precepts of, 33–34, 221–23
threats to global leadership of, 813, 823, 827, 829–30
universal suffrage, 120–21, 135, 150, 162
Unkiar Skelessi, Treaty of, 173
Upper Silesia, 239, 252, 261
Urban VIII, Pope, 58
Users' Association, 536–37, 540, 577

Vance, Cyrus, 684, 719
Vandenberg, Arthur, 385, 389, 451–52
Varga, Yevgenii, 496
Vattel, Emmerich de, 68
Venetia, 115
Verona, Congress of, 90, 149, 155
Versailles, Treaty of, 83, 218–45, 268, 307, 344, 806
Anglo-French split after, 246, 250–55, 258, 265
Anschluss and, 310
Article 116 of, 262–63
Article 231 of, 245, 257
Belgium and, 239, 274, 301
collective security doctrine and, 221, 222, 227, 232, 235, 253–54
disarmament provisions of, 244, 255–56, 285
economic penalties of, 239–40
Foch's comment on, 250
Fourteen Points and, 229–30
Franco-German relationship and, 242–43
German reoccupation of Rhineland and, 301, 305, 306
Locarno Pact's undermining of, 274–76, 278–79, 283–84, 306, 307
Mandate Principle and, 239
military restrictions of, 239
national interests and, 248
psychological blight of, 243–45
punitive terms of, 229–30, 239–40, 242–243, 245, 372
reparations issue and, 256–58, 262–63, 267
rise of Hitler and, 289, 290, 297
Russo-German rapprochement and, 246, 264–65
Soviets excluded from, 259

Versailles, Treaty of (*cont.*)
  states created by, 240–41
  Stresa Conference and, 297
  terms of, 239–40
  Treaty of Mutual Assistance and, 253–55
  U.S. nonratification of, 238, 241–42
  "war guilt clause" of, 245, 257
  weaknesses of, 81, 242–45
Vershinin, Konstantin, 439
Victor Emmanuel, King of Italy, 300
Victoria, Queen of England, 97, 149
Vienna, Congress of, 22, 77–85, 102, 128,
    140, 228, 237, 240, 246, 806, 811
  Alexander I and, 79, 83
  balance of power and, 79
  Congress system and, 82
  Europe after, 324–25 (map)
  German Confederation created by, 80–
    81, 85
  Holy Alliance and, 82–84
  Quadruple Alliance and, 82–83, 229
  world order created by, 242, 244
Vienna Summit (1961), 645
Vietcong, 644, 652, 668, 670
Vietminh, 625
Vietnam, 57, 479, 625, 827
  Cambodia invaded by, 637, 773
  China and, 627
  partition of, 634–35
Vietnam, Democratic Republic of (North),
    608, 624, 635, 644, 660
  American domestic debate exploited by,
    665
  China's support of, 630
  Laotian neutrality violated by, 645–47
  peace negotiations and, 678–79, 684–85,
    688–89, 697–98
  Politburo of, 656, 663, 684
  reunification and, 697–98
Vietnam, Republic of (South), 644, 660
  democracy in, 637, 639, 653–56
  guerrilla warfare and, 639–41
  nation-building concept and, 648–49
  peace negotiations and, 684, 688, 689,
    691, 695, 696–97
  PRG of, 698
  reunification and, 697–98
  U.S. Military Advisor Group in, 639
  Vietnamization strategy and, 681–83, 684
Vietnam War, 403, 469, 477, 549, 643–73,
    674–702, 708, 713, 743, 744, 763
  aftermath of, 699–702
  American values and, 620–21, 662, 667,
    675–76
  bombing halted in, 672–73, 693
  Buddhist protests and, 654–55

Cambodia and, 641, 645–46, 686, 692–93
China and, 630, 634, 635, 644–45, 660–
    661, 681
Diem overthrow and, 654–66
DMZ and, 645
Dong's assessment of, 660
escalation of, 651–52, 653, 656
"forward strategy" and, 681
guerrilla warfare in, 639–41, 645, 649,
    652, 660–61
Ho Chi Minh Trail and, 641, 646, 660, 680,
    693, 696
JFK's policies and, 643–44, 645, 649–54
Johnson Administration and, 656–57
Kissinger's role in U.S. extrication from,
    663–64, 677–78, 680, 682–84, 686–87,
    691–92, 695
Korean War contrasted with, 490, 659–60,
    665
Laotian neutrality violated in, 645–47
LBJ on U.S. goals in, 661–62
LBJ's Saigon mission and, 649–50
legitimacy principle and, 655
lessons of, 659–60, 699–701
Lippmann's criticism of, 665–66
Manila Formula and, 679
media and, 654, 667–68, 671–72, 699
military vs. political objectives in, 659–61
Mini-Tet Offensive in, 678
Moratorium demonstrations and, 687–88
nation-building concept and, 648–49, 650
Peace Movement and, 675–676, 677, 682,
    688, 689–91, 692, 695
peace negotiations in, 661–63, 665, 683–
    687; *see also* Paris Peace Accords
"Rolling Thunder" campaign in, 658
San Antonio Formula and, 664–65, 669,
    670
SEATO and, 645–46
Soviet Union and, 624, 627, 634, 635, 681,
    698
surrogate nature of, 624–25
Tet Offensive in, 656, 665, 670–71, 672
Tonkin Gulf Resolution and, 658–59
unilateral withdrawal issue and, 678–80,
    689–90
U.S. domestic debate and, 661, 663, 665–
    675, 678–79, 685, 689, 692, 695, 697
U.S. exceptionalism and, 621, 668, 676,
    688
U.S. global mission and, 675–76
U.S. military establishment in, 639, 640–
    641, 653
Vietnamization strategy and, 681–83,
    684
Wilsonian ideals and, 653–54, 658, 698

see also Domino Theory; Indochina conflict

Volkogonov, Dmitri, 364

Voltaire (François-Marie Arouet), 67, 86

Vyshinsky, Andrei, 366–67

Waging Peace (Eisenhower), 641

Walesa, Lech, 759

Walewski, Alexandre, 114

Wallace, Henry, 447, 464, 467–70, 824

Wallace Movement, 470, 710

Wallachia, principality of, 94

Wall Street Journal, 671–72

Walpole, Robert, 100

Walsh, Thomas J., 281

Walters, Vernon, 685

War of 1812, 35

War of 1859, 103, 110–12, 119

Warsaw Pact, 447, 555, 557, 558, 560, 561, 567, 792, 795

Washington, George, 32, 48–49, 389

Washington Naval Conference (1921–22), 373

Washington Naval Treaty (1922), 377, 380

Washington Post, 718, 755

Watergate scandal, 696, 698, 731–32, 739, 741–42, 756

Wealth of Nations, The (Smith), 21

Webster, Charles, 240

Weimar Republic, *see* Germany, Weimar

Welles, Sumner, 386, 402

Wellington, Arthur Wellesley, Duke of, 86

Weltpolitik, 171, 183, 193, 220, 503

Western Hemisphere Defense system, 390

Westmoreland, William C., 670

Westphalia, Peace of, 21, 27, 65, 68, 76, 139, 290, 806

Whig Party, British, 72–73, 100

William I, Emperor of Germany, 118, 170

William II, Emperor of Germany, 49, 188, 190, 196, 198
   Bismarck compared with, 210
   Bismarck dismissed by, 170–71
   Churchill's description of, 171
   Gladstone and, 182
   Krüger Telegram and, 184–85
   Reinsurance Treaty and, 179–80
   World War I outbreak and, 209–10, 211, 214–16

William III, King of England, 56–77, 99, 266, 810

Willkie, Wendell, 388

Wilson, Henry, 706

Wilson, Woodrow, 18, 22, 29–55, 74, 390, 704, 705, 741, 743, 767, 808–9
   balance of power condemned by, 226

collective security concept and, 51–53, 91, 221–23, 248, 408, 809
   declaration of war sought by, 48–50, 450
   Fourteen Points of, *see* Fourteen Points
   Gladstone compared with, 160–62
   global view of, 46–48
   idealistic view of, 225–27
   isolationism and, 44, 45–46
   League of Nations as envisioned by, 30, 51, 223–24, 234–35
   legacy of, 247
   Lloyd George's memorandum to, 241
   Mandate Principle and, 239
   Metternich compared with, 79, 84
   Nixon's admiration for, 706
   at Paris Peace Conference, 230, 231–32, 234, 235, 236, 805
   punitive provisions of Versailles Treaty and, 229, 245
   TR contrasted with, 44

Wilsonianism, 244, 704, 808–9, 823, 826
   Alexander I as precursor of, 75
   Atlantic Charter and, 391
   Britain and, 248–49
   detente policy and, 743
   Gorbachev's use of, 789
   Hitler and, 317
   isolationism and, 44, 45–46
   JFK's Declaration of Interdependence and, 613–14
   NATO and, 457
   new world order and, 804–5, 808–9, 810, 812, 813–14
   Nixon and, 704–6, 707, 743
   raison d'état doctrine and, 66
   Reagan and, 769, 772–73
   Realpolitik and, 247, 316, 317
   self-determination principle and, 221–22, 225, 229, 239
   Truman and, 447
   U.S. exceptionalism and, 809
   U.S. foreign policy and, 29–30, 52–55, 91, 658
   Vietnam War and, 653–54, 658, 698
   Wilson's outline of, 44–46

Wirth, Joseph, 282

"Wise Men," 671

Witte, Serge, 174, 176

Wohlstetter, Albert, 714–15

Wood, Robert E., 389

World Health Organization, 663

World War I, 22, 44, 48, 157, 168, 289, 296, 302, 336, 351, 353, 384, 402, 596, 603, 606
   aftermath of, 221
   armistice announced in, 218

World War I (*cont.*)
  Austro-Russian relations and, 94
  British goals in, 220
  character of, 220–21
  democracy and, 219
  Europe on eve of, 326–27 (map)
  isolationist revisionism and, 378
  moral slogans and, 219
  public opinion at onset of, 183, 186, 213,
    226, 244
  stalemate in, 219
  technology and, 200, 202
  U.S. disillusionment and, 372
  U.S. entry into, 219, 221, 227
World War I, outbreak of, 98–99, 201–17
  Austria and, 211–12, 214–15
  Belgian neutrality and, 205, 206, 213
  Britain and, 205, 212–13, 216
  France and, 205–6, 210, 212–13, 216,
    384–85
  Franco-Russian Alliance and, 202, 203,
    204
  Franz Ferdinand's assassination and, 209
  Germany and, 204–5, 208–10, 215, 216,
    349
  military planning and, 202, 211–12
  mobilization concept and, 202, 204, 206,
    211–214, 215
  Russia and, 202–3, 206–8, 211–12, 214,
    215–16, 348–49
  Schlieffen Plan and, 204–6, 216
  technology and, 202, 206
  time element and, 213–14
  William II and, 209–10, 211, 214–16
World War II, 34, 47, 54, 74, 76, 80, 81, 155,
    173, 176, 223, 229, 284, 318, 457, 597,
    625
  Anglo-French Naval Treaty and, 197–98
  British diplomacy in, 399–400
  Entente Cordiale and, 186
  Germany-first strategy in, 403–4
  occupation of Berlin in, 417–18
  onset of, 351
  "phony war" in, 351, 352, 385–86
  postwar settlement and, 583
  second front strategy and, 403, 404–5
  separate peace proposals in, 419–20
  Soviet Union and outbreak of, 348–49
  unconditional surrender policy and,
    398
Württemberg, 81, 117

"X" article (Kennan), 454–56, 715
Xuan Thuy, 685

Yalta Conference (1945), 371, 396, 410, 424,
    426, 432, 434, 438, 494, 625
  Joint Declaration of, 415, 418
  postwar arrangements and, 414–15
  Soviet-Japanese warfare and, 415–16
"Year of Europe," 617–18
Yeltsin, Boris, 271, 417, 785–86, 794, 798–
    799, 815, 817, 821
Yemen, 546, 701
Yom Kippur War, *see* Arab-Israeli War of
    1973
Young Plan, 282–83
Yugoslavia, 240–41, 340, 362, 366, 413, 414,
    443, 451, 552–53, 562, 806, 807

Zaire, 807
Zanzibar, 180
zero option, 777, 791
Zhdanov, Andrei, 443, 523
Zhou Enlai, 719, 726, 727, 728, 729
Zhukov, Georgi, 418, 519